AMERICAN LAW *of* REAL ESTATE

J. DAVID REITZEL

Professor of Business Law
California State University, Fresno

ROBERT B. BENNETT, JR.

Associate Professor of Business Law
Butler University

MICHAEL J. GARRISON

Professor of Business Law
North Dakota State University

SOUTH-WESTERN
™
THOMSON LEARNING

Australia · Canada · Mexico · Singapore · Spain · United Kingdom · United States

Executive Publisher: Dave Shaut
Senior Acquisitions Editor: Scott Person
Developmental Editor: Sara Froelicher
Marketing Manager: Mark Linton
Production Editor: Chris Hudson
Manufacturing Coordinator: Charlene Taylor
Compositor: Trejo Production
Printer: Phoenix Color
Design Project Manager: Jennifer Mayhall
Cover and Internal Designer: Rik Moore

Library of Congress Cataloging-in-Publication Data
Reitzel, J. David.
    American law of real estate / J. David Reitzel, Robert B. Bennett, Jr., Michael J. Garrison.—1st ed.
        p. cm.
    Includes biographical references and index.
    ISBN 0-324-14368-0
    1. Real property—United States.   2. Vendors and purchasers—United States.   3. Real estate development—Law and legislation—United States.   I. Bennett, Robert B., 1955–   II. Garrison, Michael J., 1954–   III. Title.

KF570.R45 2003
346.7304'3—dc21

                                                                    2001049795

To Mary, Meredith, and Josh Bennett with love and gratitude for their unflagging support.

To my wife Amy and sons Patrick and Samuel for their patience, support, and love.

To Rosa and Danny Reitzel who saw me through and to
Professor Emeritus Wayne A. Brooks who got me started.

Brief Contents

Contents

Part II   The Real Estate Sales Transaction

Part III   Leasing and Improving Real Estate; Condominiums and Real Estate Investments

Part IV   Taxation and Regulation of Real Estate; Natural Resources and Agricultural Law

Preface

In writing *American Law of Real Estate,* the authors had three major goals:

- To present real estate law as a *national* body of law.
- To make the book useful to a broad range of persons interested in real estate law and practice.
- To make the book highly effective as a learning device.

Many real estate law books reflect the local character of real estate law, omitting or only sketching the topics not prominent in the state or region for which the book was written. Thus, in the East and Midwest, the law of community property and much of the law of mining and water rights commonly receive little or no attention, while books written for the community property states of the West typically omit discussion of common law marital property rights and other topics thought irrelevant to local western law. The result is a proliferation of local books focused too narrowly to serve well the highly mobile American public, whose members, especially business graduates, often move to states with different legal traditions. Our aim is to provide a balanced real estate law text that minimizes the real estate law surprises its users may encounter in the next state.

Our second goal is to serve as broad a spectrum of the academic and professional community as possible. Students seeking a real estate license will find the book useful, of course, but it should appeal as well to property managers, to investors and developers, and to consumers of real estate such as homeowners and apartment dwellers—to anyone seeking to own or use land or some interest in it. And the book will be of value to those studying real estate law as an aspect of general business, urban planning, finance, and the like, since considerable attention is devoted to environmental, tax, conservation, zoning, and other policy concerns. Yet, the book is highly practical. Two examples: Chapter 16 thoroughly discusses the impact of taxation—local, state, and federal taxation of realty and the income from it—on business decisions, including discussion of underlying tax policy. And Chapter 10, on financing the purchase of real estate, is unusual not only for its cogent discussion of the risks that lenders must consider when setting interest rates, but also for its Note on Lending Practices, which provides consumers and commercial borrowers alike with insights into how lenders' concerns may affect the availability and structuring of loans.

Finally, we have given special attention to making the book effective as a learning device. One of the more rigorous studies in law school, real estate law frustrates undergraduates terribly when poorly presented. To make the law concepts accessible, we provide coherent organization, clear expression, and abundant illustration throughout the book. We do not skimp on theory, but neither do we bury students in it. The early chapters carefully lay out law and theory, with ample use of concrete illustrations; later chapters emphasize applications and real estate practice, though this is found in early chapters, too. In every chapter students will find applications and test-your-knowledge materials such as edited cases, You Be the Judge boxes, and end-of-chapter case problems. The extensive glossary defines the terms set in **bold type** throughout the book, while additional key words and phrases are *italicized*.

To help further this pedagogical theme, an Instructor's Manual and a Test Bank accompany *American Law of Real Estate.* Among other features, the Instructor's Manual provides an answer for every question asked of students in boxes and after the edited cases; briefs of the edited cases; and solutions for the end-of-chapter case problems.

About the Authors

J. David Reitzel is Professor of Business Law at California State University, Fresno. Before that, he was Professor and Chairman of the Department of Business Law at The American College, Bryn Mawr, Pennsylvania, and Professor of Business Law at St. Cloud State University in Minnesota. Professor Reitzel holds a J.D. degree from Indiana University and B.S. and M.S. degrees from Purdue University. Admitted to the Indiana and federal bars in 1969, Professor Reitzel has served as Editor-in-Chief of the *American Business Law Journal* and has written numerous articles and papers, many dealing with business law education, environmental law, and real estate law. In 1992, he received the Ralph C. Hoeber Award for "Critical Thinking and the Business Law Curriculum," an article appearing in the *Journal of Legal Studies Education*. He is the lead coauthor of *Contemporary Business Law and the Legal Environment*, 5th edition.

Robert Bennett, Jr. is Associate Professor of Business Law at Butler University, Indianapolis, Indiana, where he has received twelve awards for outstanding teaching and five awards for outstanding research, including the Ralph C. Hoeber Award from the *American Business Law Journal*. He recently served as Editor-in-Chief of the *Journal of Legal Studies Education*. Before coming to Butler, he spent eleven years as an attorney in the private practice of law, specializing in real estate related business transactions in Charlotte, North Carolina. He has written and spoken extensively on real estate topics, including real estate law and practice, condominium and multifamily development and documentation, loan documentation and lender liability, and title insurance. He is a 1977 cum laude graduate of Davidson College and a 1980 magna cum laude graduate of the University of Georgia School of Law, where he was elected to the Order of the Coif. He was admitted to the bar in North Carolina in 1980 and in Indiana in 1994.

Michael J. Garrison is Professor of Business Law in the College of Business Administration at North Dakota State University, where he has also served as Associate Dean and Coordinator of Accounting. He received his J.D. degree from the University of North Dakota School of Law, graduating first in his class. A member of the Order of the Coif, he has authored numerous journal articles and conference proceedings and is a coauthor of *Contemporary Business Law and the Legal Environment*, 5th edition. He has been a staff editor for the *American Business Law Journal* and the *Midwest Law Review* and serves as a reviewer for the *Journal of Public Policy & Marketing*. Professor Garrison has been honored for his teaching and his research. In 1988 and again in 1990, he received the Ralph C. Hoeber Award and the Articles Editor Award for the best major article in the *American Business Law Journal*. In 1992, he was named Teacher of the Year in the College of Business Administration at North Dakota State University. Before joining the faculty in the College, he was engaged for five years in the practice of law. He has extensive practical experience in commercial litigation, including real estate foreclosure actions. He continues to practice law as "Of Counsel" for a Fargo law firm.

Part I   Nature of Real Estate Law; Ownership of Real Estate

Chapter 1 Nature and Sources of American Land Law

Everyone has a relationship to land. Even astronauts who defy the pull of gravity need food, clothing, and shelter—not to mention propulsion, communications, and guidance systems—all of which, for now at least, must be derived from the earth. The rest of the world's 6 billion people use the land in additional obvious ways: for farming, mining, manufacturing, roads and highways, government buildings, schools, museums, hospitals, military facilities, parks, wildlife preserves, rail and air transport, water collection and delivery, sewage treatment, garbage dumps, docks, wharves, buoy anchorages, power generators, transmission lines. The list is endless.

In terms of legal relationships to land, one can be an owner, a guest, a business visitor, a trespasser; a user of someone else's land for profit or convenience; a trustee holding or managing land for others; a creditor holding a security interest in land until the debt is paid; an agent or broker in its sale; a repairperson, improver, or inspector. Families and businesses alike must decide whether to buy or to rent the land they need. Governments—local, state, national—must decide what private land to take for public purposes. Trustees managing land for others must put it to prudent use. Disputes arise over who owns the land, how it may be used, and by whom. Real estate law covers all these concerns, and more.

This book introduces the real estate law of the United States. This chapter briefly surveys the nature of real estate law, the roles of real estate professionals, the origins and elements of modern American real estate law, and the methods used for describing land.[1]

Real Estate Law, Real Estate Professionals, and the Concept of Property

Nature of Real Estate Law

The law of most states originated in the ancient English **common law**, which judges developed case by case over the centuries as the national law of England. Nonlegislative in character, the common law mostly concerned government and the security of persons and property. English common law, which came to include a few statutes, was brought to this country in colonial times and adapted to American needs and customs. The modern American law of real property grew largely from these English and colonial sources. However, a substantial number of western and southern states have, in addition to common law elements, a number of land law concepts derived from the **civil law** of France and Spain.[2] Spanish influences are found in the property law of Arizona, California, Idaho, Nevada, New Mexico, Texas, and Washington, for example, while Louisiana's law is predominantly French in origin.

This non-English law content affects the millions of real estate consumers and practitioners who live in or move to states with civil law elements, or buy or inherit land located there. Similarly, those who move from the South or West to other parts of the country are likely to encounter English-based (Anglo-American) land law different from what they have known. Because the differences can be of consequence to those encountering them, this book discusses non-English as well as Anglo-American elements of property law.

A state's real estate law often is called "local" even though it usually applies statewide, and even though many federal statutes such as the Real Estate Settlement Procedures Act (RESPA) and the Interstate Land Sales Full Disclosure Act (ILSFDA) apply to real estate transactions. American real estate law, then, is a mixture of state and federal law, with the law of many states having some combination of common law and civil law elements.

Real estate law is a broad field. It concerns the kinds of interests people can have in land, the mechanics of acquiring and transferring property, and the rights that husband and wife have in property acquired during their marriage. It also deals with transactions in real estate, such as buying, financing, appraising; the duties of professionals who assist in carrying out those transactions; taxation of real estate; governmental limits on its use; government's right to take private property for a public purpose; the extraction of gas, oil, and minerals; protection of the environment from contamination by toxic wastes; commercial leasing; and other topics as diverse as water rights, condominiums, real estate investments, and aspects of agricultural law. Subsequent chapters of this book discuss these and related topics.

Functions of Real Estate Professionals

Real estate sellers and buyers often need help in finding each other and in negotiating the sale. Because most purchasers cannot pay cash, or do not wish to do so, they seek financing from lending institutions, such as banks, savings and loans associations, and insurance companies. Though most lenders are corporate financiers, some persons provide financing as individual investors. Real estate brokers, with their familiarity with sources of funds, can often assist in arranging for financing.

Many others may be involved in the acquisition, development, and management of real estate. Among them are developers, architects, surveyors, engineers, contractors in the building trades, lawyers, and insurance experts. Many different professionals and business people are likely to be involved in any given transaction. For example, in the sale of a residence, a lender may require a credit report on the buyer, a title search to establish that the seller has ownership rights to convey, a title insurance policy to cover losses if the seller's title proves to be defective, a survey of the land to investigate disputed boundaries or detect encroachments, hazard insurance (compensating for loss from fire and wind), and a variety of inspections. Lenders routinely require termite inspections in residential sales, and many buyers hire a home inspection company to make a prepurchase evaluation of the premises.

Because of stringent environmental protection laws, lenders, buyers, and tenants seek environmental audits to detect problems relating to the disposal of hazardous materials. Common in transactions involving commercial and industrial properties, but used increasingly in residential transactions as well, these audits usually are performed by professionals with science or engineering backgrounds. Large projects such as housing developments, highways, shopping centers, skyscrapers, dams, pipelines, and factories may require the services of additional professionals. They include geologists, urban planners, experts in land acquisition, mortgage bankers, construction lenders, firms that provide construction (surety) bonds, specialists in taxation and corporate finance, and, upon discovery of fossils or cultural artifacts, sometimes even anthropologists and paleontologists.

Property as a Legal Concept

Key to the study of real estate law is the meaning of *property*. To say that a thing is property suggests that someone "owns" it. Ownership implies a legal right to control the use of the thing. So the concept of property has two aspects: a "thing" (a car, a piece of land, a bank account), and a legal right in a person to control its use.

The Bundle of Rights

When referring to property, people often speak in terms of the thing itself—"my car," "my house," "my bank account." In law, however, it is much more convenient and useful to think of property as a legally protected *interest* in a thing, or, more to the point, as a *collection* of interests or rights that, together, constitute "ownership." This **bundle of rights** is an accumulation of legally defined rights, powers, privileges, and immunities enabling the owner of the bundle to possess, use, enjoy, encumber, and dispose of the thing free from interference by others, but within limits imposed by law for the protection of others.

The bundle of rights can be held exclusively by one person or shared with others. So, if Ann owns a farm, the law of property gives her a right of exclusive use, enjoyment, and control, including the right to sell the farm, rent it to someone, or give it away. If Ann leases (rents) the farm to Bob for ten years, he, as **lessee** (tenant), acquires a right of exclusive use for the agreed rental period, and Ann keeps for herself the other rights of ownership. If Ann bought the farm on credit, chances are she gave the creditor (the seller or a lender) a **security interest** in the farm by means of a **mortgage**. Although Ann as owner retains rights of usage and control, the security interest empowers the creditor to **foreclose** the mortgage (force the sale of the farm with a court order) if Ann fails to make her payments on the loan as agreed. Depending on how the bundle of rights is shared, several people may hold interests simultaneously in one parcel of land. For example, Ann owns the farm, she gave her bank a security interest (mortgage) on the farm to secure repayment of a loan, and she rented the farm to Bob.

Bob, the tenant, may also properly be called an owner—not of the land itself, but of a **leasehold** interest in the land. His leasehold is an ownership interest because the lease confers on him a right of exclusive possession, use, and enjoyment, and (unless prohibited by the lease) a right to dispose of all or part of the ten-year term by subleasing the premises or assigning the lease to another.

Some Basic Terminology

The vocabulary of real estate law appears throughout this book and in its Glossary. Presented here are some basic Anglo-American terms and a few of their civil law counterparts.

Anglo-American law divides property into two great classes: **personal property (personalty)** such as a car, bank account, or promissory note, and **real property** (also called **realty** or **real estate**) such as land together with its fixtures. These classes are further divided into tangible and intangible property.

Tangible property, whether personal or real, has physical existence. It is solid, liquid, or gaseous and can be perceived by the senses. Tangible *personal* property includes, among other things, **goods** (e.g., computers, food, industrial gases held in containers) and money. Tangible *real* property includes land, the air above it, its buildings and other fixtures, and the subsurface.

Intangible property, whether personal or real, is an abstract right created by law; it has no physical being, so cannot be seen, felt, or otherwise perceived by the senses. Intangible *personal* property includes shares in a corporation, patents, accounts receivable, insurance contracts, and other contract rights. Since these rights have no physical being, they usually are evidenced by writings that represent them. So corporate shares, for example, usually are evidenced by stock certificates (though the shares of some corporations are evidenced by entries in the corporate books). Corporate shares are intangible; the certificates representing them are tangible. Intangible *real* property includes, for example, fee simple ownership, life estates, leases, and easements. These abstract interests and others are discussed in Chapter 3 and in subsequent chapters.

The civil law classifies things as either **movables** (similar to personal property) or immovables (similar to real property). Both movables and immovables may be either **corporeal** (having physical being) or **incorporeal** (existing only as an abstract right created by the law). Some predominately common law states, such as Texas and California, use both civil law and Anglo-American terms in their property statutes. For example, a California statute defining property equates real property with immovables, and personal property with movables.

Most real estate law terms have one commonly understood meaning. Some have multiple legal meanings. Others have legal meanings that may differ from their ordinary ones. The following terms appear frequently in this book and some are used in various senses. Several are defined more fully in subsequent chapters.

- **Conveyance.** The transfer of an interest in land from one person to another by means of a document called a deed.

- **Deed.** A document signed by a **grantor**, by means of which the grantor transfers an interest in land to another person (the **grantee**).

- **Title.** *Title* has at least two meanings in the law of property.

  1. Usually, *full ownership* of a thing—the right to use, possess, enjoy, encumber, and dispose of it.

  2. Sometimes, the *document* giving evidence of title (ownership), as in the statement, "Yesterday the seller sent me the title to the house."

- **Security interest.** An interest in a debtor's property that the debtor gives to the creditor to secure payment of the debt. The creditor's security interest is only one right out of the debtor's bundle of rights. The security interest gives the creditor the legal right to force the sale of the property (the "collateral") if the debtor does not pay the debt as agreed. In the meantime, the debtor keeps the rest of the ownership rights, i.e., the right to use, possess, enjoy, encumber, and dispose of the collateral.

- **Mortgage.** The transfer in writing of an interest in land as security for a debt (or for some other obligation), on the understanding that when the debt is repaid, the transfer becomes void. The person transferring the interest (usually a borrower) is the **mortgagor**; the person receiving the interest (usually a lender) is the **mortgagee**.

- **Deed of trust.** A document serving the same function as a mortgage. By means of deed of trust, a debtor (the trustor) conveys an interest called "legal title" to a third person (the trustee) to hold as security for the benefit of the creditor (the beneficiary). In some states the deed of trust is widely referred to as a "trust deed." Ordinarily, however, a *trust deed* is understood to be a document (deed) that creates a trust for the general management of property and not for the limited purpose of providing a security interest for a lender, as where George transfers ownership of his land "in trust" to Tom for the benefit of George's child.

- **Encumbrance.** A right, claim, or charge against real property—e.g., a mortgage, tax lien, lease, or easement (right to use another's realty).

- **Lien.** A charge against personal or real property, imposed by law or created by voluntary agreement to secure payment of a debt. Tax liens are imposed by law; mortgages are created by agreement.

- **Foreclosure.** The legal process by which a creditor with a security interest or other lien right can, upon the debtor's **default**, force the sale of the collateral. A debtor defaults by failing to pay the debt or to carry out some other obligation imposed by the security agreement. In Louisiana's civil law, a **hypothecary action** serves a function similar to that of foreclosure.

- **Fixtures.** Goods such as water heaters, doors, furnaces, or sprinkler systems that are so physically attached or otherwise related to realty that they are classified as real estate. Similar to "fixture" is the civil law's **component part**.

- **Enjoyment.** Having the benefit of a property right. A landlord enjoys realty by receiving rents, a tenant by having the exclusive use of the premises for the agreed term. Pleasure can be, but is not necessarily, an aspect of enjoyment. A commercial tenant experiencing business failure because of a bad location probably gets no pleasure from the lease, but "enjoys" it in the legal sense by having exclusive possession for the agreed term.

- **Lis pendens.** A Latin phrase meaning "a pending lawsuit." When a suit develops over the ownership of real estate, the plaintiff ordinarily files a **notice of lis pendens** in the public records to warn potential buyers, lenders, and others that title to the realty is being contested, and that they might be bound by a judgment adverse to their interests. The notice thus serves to protect the plaintiff's rights during litigation.

Origins of the Law Governing Real Estate

American land law has important civil law elements, but its great foundation in all states except Louisiana is the English common law brought to America in colonial times. Modern American land law differs dramatically from its precolonial English origins, and yet has important similarities as well as shared concepts and terminology. This section presents a brief overview of how English land law developed, what aspects of it American lawmakers have found useful, and what the civil law has contributed to American land law.

The English Way—Feudal Tenure

From the ninth century in Europe, and later in England, *feudalism* was a system of government and land ownership in which one person, the *lord*, granted substantial rights in land and protection to a weaker person called a *vassal* in exchange for the vassal's promise to render services to the lord. The vassal became the lord's "tenant" or "grantee." This system of *feudal tenure* between lord and vassal took centuries to develop and was prompted by the fall of the western Roman Empire to German invaders in the fifth century.

The Romans gave ancient Europe a well-developed system of civil law and stability of government. But after the decline of the Roman Empire, nomadic invaders made life in Europe dangerous. The resulting Dark Ages (from about A.D. 476 to A.D. 1000) saw a significant erosion of government in continental Europe. Lacking organized government, people had to fend for themselves as best they could. To protect themselves, their families, and their property from outlaws, foreign invaders, and greedy neighbors, weaker men turned to the strongest among them for help.

The result was an early form of feudalism. In a ceremony of *homage*, vassal and lord made mutual promises of support and protection. The vassal took an oath of *fealty* (faithful service) to the lord and received a right to use a certain parcel of land in exchange for the promised services, usually agricultural. If a man seeking to become a vassal owned land, he probably turned it over to the lord as part of the bargain and received back the same kind of possession and usage rights that other vassals had. So, instead of owning the land outright, a vassal would "hold" it "of" (derive his rights from) the lord for as long as the vassal rendered the services promised to the lord. The vassal's land-holding was called his *fief* or *feud*. It became the *fee* or **fee simple** of modern law, discussed in later chapters.

The relationship between lord and vassal was *tenurial*, meaning that the vassal held the land in subordination to his lord, who had a superior right of control that could be exercised if the vassal behaved badly. If, for example, a vassal-tenant committed *felony* by breaching his obligation of faithful service, the lord could declare a *forfeiture* of the fief and take back possession of the land.

If the vassal fulfilled the obligation of loyal service, he had the right to possess and use the land for life and to keep the profits.

A vassal could grant his fief, or some part of it, to another vassal, and thereby be, simultaneously, a vassal of the lord above him and a lord to the vassal below. The vassal below could do the same. This process, known as *subinfeudation*, resulted in (1) a subdividing of the land into smaller and smaller parcels involving several layers of tenurial ownership; (2) a flow of services upward; and, (3) at the bottom, possession of the land by a multitude of peasant-vassals (tenants-in-possession) who actually worked the soil and kept the profits, minus any services, money, or goods owed to their lords. For several centuries after the collapse of the Roman Empire, peasants depended on the local lords for protection and a basic administration of justice. Eventually, though, central government reappeared and strengthened, and the king became the highest lord.

In 1066 came the event generally viewed as the beginning of English land law—the Norman (French) Conquest of England by William the Conqueror. Upon defeating the Anglo-Saxons in the Battle of Hastings, William became King of England, and his Norman administrators imposed a universal system of feudal landholding on the English population. Under it, all land was held of King William, who had confiscated much of it from Saxon nobles (great landowners with their own private armies) and redistributed it to his followers—Norman barons called *tenants in chief*, eventually numbering about 1,500. However, most of the peasants continued to work the land as before. The major changes occurred at the top of the ownership pyramid, with the king's substituting a friendly Norman tenant in chief for a Saxon predecessor.

During the next several centuries, land was granted in exchange for the wide variety of services needed in the early nonmoney economy to maintain the country and the upper classes. The services were of four basic types: *security* (military service), *splendor* (personal, household, and ceremonial services rendered to the medieval aristocracy), *spirit* (meeting the religious needs of the lord), and *subsistence* (food, clothing, bridge repair, and other physical necessities). Tenures were defined in terms of the kind of service required of the tenant. For example, the tenure called *knight-service* was military; the tenure called *socage* encompassed a broad range of subsistence services, mainly agricultural.

To maintain their power, the lords needed to control ownership of the land. Feudal law provided the needed controls. In early feudal times, for example, the tenant's heir could not inherit the fief at the tenant's death. Instead, the land went back to the lord, who regranted it to another vassal in a new ceremony of homage. Eventually, fiefs became inheritable, but with inheritability came a related control. If a tenant died without an heir, the lord had a right of *escheat*—the right to regain possession of the land now vacant because the tenant's line of descent had died out.

Yet, as noted in the following section, many rules of law developed that strengthened the ownership rights of tenants and foreshadowed modern rules of land law.

The American Way—Allodial Ownership

Modern American land law, adapted from the English common law that existed during and before the American Revolution,[3] has rejected many feudal features, especially those associated with maintaining the English nobility. Even during feudal times, some land on the European continent, and in England before the Norman Conquest of 1066, was owned outright under Roman (civil law) principles by individuals who had no tenurial relationship with—and no obligation of service to—any lord. This **allodial** ownership was absolute ownership free of any oath or obligation to a lord. Allodial ownership quickly became the norm in America after the Revolutionary War and is the type of ownership that exists throughout the United States today.

English Concepts Abandoned by American Land Law

Because of the American emphasis on personal independence, individual freedoms, free enterprise, and elected governments, several feudal English concepts unsuited to American land law were abandoned. Among them are:

- *Tenure.* In the United States, landowners do not hold land "of" (subordinate to) a lord or king (nor, usually, even of the state) and therefore owe no duty of service as a condition to keeping the land. Instead, ownership is allodial.

- The feudal type of *escheat.* If an American landowner dies without a will and without an heir, the land "escheats" to the state in which it is located, and the state thus acquires title. But the American type of **escheat** is not tenurial because it does not give the land back to a lord to regrant in exchange for homage and services. Instead, American escheat is based on the need for land ownership to go somewhere when a person dies without an heir, and the state is the preferable recipient of last resort.

- *Primogeniture.* Primogeniture (a doctrine under which a tenant's heir was the tenant's eldest son) kept land in the hands of males because they provided military service to the king. Like the modern English, Americans recognize that favoring the eldest male is neither needed today nor fair to other family members. Within limits imposed for the protection of a surviving spouse, an owner of realty may will ("devise") it to whomever he or she chooses. If there is no will, state **statutes of descent and distribution** divide ownership among children equally—that is, without regard to gender or age.

English Concepts Surviving in American Land Law

Even with all the changes, our law of real property reflects many fundamental concepts of English land law. Its influence is seen, for example, in the following general features of American land law:

- A classification scheme that defines and recognizes a variety of interests in a piece of land and enables an owner to grant lesser interests to others.

- Simultaneous ownership of or rights in a single parcel of land. Hermina, owner of Greenacre, can carve out lesser interests and distribute them in various ways. Or she and her brother Herman might own Greenacre together ("co-own" it), each having the same kind of ownership interest as the other.

- Potentially infinite ownership by a family through the process of inheritance.

- Free **alienation** of property—the right to sell or give away one's interest in land, or to dispose of it by will at death, without the consent of others, including the state.

- Private land-use control by individuals, apart from or in addition to governmental controls such as zoning laws.

- Protection of one's interest in land from interference by others, under the law of negligence, trespass, and nuisance discussed in later chapters.

● Contributions of the Civil Law

Because English law has so markedly influenced American land law, we may tend to overlook the contributions of European civil law. In the United States, the great contribution of the civil law is allodial ownership, a natural choice in colonial America and in France when the populations there renounced feudal tenures and removed land ownership from aristocratic control. At the state level, only Louisiana bases its property law entirely on civil law. But regionally, many common law states have significant civil law components or are affected by civil law concepts of other states, as, for example, in the areas of water rights and marital property rights. Water rights are discussed in Chapter 19.

Under community property laws derived from Spanish and French civil law, and in effect in nine states, husband and wife are presumed to be equal owners of marital property regardless of who earned or accumulated it. This presumption contrasts with the common law presumption that every item of property is individually owned by one spouse or the other unless they explicitly choose common ownership. Community property laws also cover citizens' out-of-state marital property, thus affecting ownership rights to some property located in purely common law states. Community property is discussed in Chapter 5 in the section on marital interests.

Modern American Law of Real Estate: Sources

In the American legal system, law has state and federal sources: constitutions, legislation (e.g., statutes, municipal zoning ordinances), administrative regulation, and judicial decisions. American real estate law is addressed in all of them. Here we outline the major sources of law and illustrate aspects of real estate law typical of each.

Federal and State Lawmaking Powers

The U.S. Constitution divides lawmaking power between the federal and the state governments. The drafters of the Constitution made the division by explicitly enumerating those areas where the federal government is permitted to legislate, and leaving the remaining areas to the legislative powers of the states. Under the supremacy clause of the Constitution, federal law prevails over conflicting state law.

The federal government is one of limited (i.e., enumerated) powers. It has only those powers expressly conferred upon it by the Constitution, plus any implied powers that are necessary and proper for carrying out the express powers. The Constitution identifies many powers that the federal government may exercise in the national interest. Among them are the powers to levy and collect taxes, regulate interstate commerce, coin money, borrow money on the credit of the United States, establish post offices and post roads, raise and support armies and navies, and establish a uniform bankruptcy law. In exercising its powers, the U.S. government develops and manages real estate that it acquires for those purposes or already owns.

To be constitutional, a federal law must further some express or implied power that the Constitution has conferred on the federal government. But rather early in U.S. history, the Supreme Court made clear that Congress has a wide range of implied powers and great discretion in exercising them. In 1816, for example, Congress chartered (incorporated) the Second National Bank of the United States, which opened a branch in Baltimore, Maryland. The Maryland legislature, a vigorous foe of national banking, imposed a heavy tax on all banks within the state not chartered by the state itself. When the Second National Bank refused to comply with the tax statute, the state assessed penalties and later brought suit to collect them. In hearings before the Supreme Court, Maryland argued that the Constitution did not expressly authorize the United States to establish a bank or create a corporation. Agreeing that the Constitution provided no such express power, the Court nevertheless held that these acts were within the implied powers of Congress because they were appropriate means for carrying out its express powers

BOX 1–1 YOU BE THE JUDGE

To prevent huge national surpluses of wheat that depressed wheat prices, the federal government enacted a law limiting the number of acres that a farmer could plant in wheat each year. Olaf, a Minnesota farmer, planted a few more acres in wheat than the federal law allowed. He did not sell the wheat from those extra acres, but instead used some for bread making and fed the rest to farm animals. The federal government sued Olaf for violating the law. In defense, Olaf alleged that the law was unconstitutional because by enacting it, Congress had exceeded its authority under the commerce clause. Was the statute unconstitutional? Explain.

(e.g., to raise armies, build roads), the financial aspects of which clearly supported the creation of a national bank.[4]

Today, the Constitution's commerce clause, as broadly interpreted by the Supreme Court, provides a major basis for extensive federal regulation of business activities, including many involving real estate. Any activity that "substantially affects commerce" between the states can be regulated by federal law.[5] Federal regulation can extend even to private activities that occur solely within one state, because the courts consider the cumulative effect of individual actions when deciding whether the conduct affects interstate commerce. For example, the Environmental Protection Agency has powers under a variety of federal statutes to force the cleanup of land contaminated by hazardous substances. These powers reach isolated, purely *intra*state incidents of pollution because an accumulation of local spills could eventually affect interstate commerce by imperiling the nation's food supply and waterways. If the government must do the cleanup itself, it acquires a federal lien against the property to cover the costs of cleanup. Thus, despite the federal government's being one of limited powers, the totality of its express and implied powers enables it to wield substantial authority over local realty.

In contrast to the federal government, each state government has a general **police power** derived from the Tenth Amendment of the Constitution. That amendment gives to the states (or to the people) all powers that the Constitution has not delegated to the federal government or denied to the states. The police power enables a state to enact a wide range of laws promoting order, safety, health, morals, and the general welfare and prosperity of its population without having to justify those laws in terms of express or implied powers. That is, the states have broad discretion to make law and do not have to find specific constitutional authority to legislate on a given topic. State legislatures delegate some of their police power to local governments, which use the delegated power to enact zoning ordinances and many other laws affecting real estate. Most real estate law is state or local.

● Constitutions

In addition to allocating powers between the federal and the state governments, the Constitution distributes powers among the federal government's legislative, judicial, and executive branches. This distribution has two consequences: a separation and an overlap of powers that together provide checks and balances against abuse of power by any single branch. In addition, a number of constitutional provisions specifically limit what the government (state or federal) may do to people and their property.

State constitutions, modeled after the U.S. Constitution, share many of its features, such as division of government into legislative, judicial, and executive branches; separation and overlap of powers; checks and balances among branches of government; and protection of people and property against unreasonable government intrusion. The discussion that follows deals with the U.S. Constitution, but many of the principles involved apply also to state constitutions.

Checks and Balances Among Branches of Government

The Constitution gives each branch of government its own areas of primary authority. For example, by giving the legislative branch the power to "make . . . laws . . . ," the Constitution places the main lawmaking responsibility on Congress. The primary function of the federal judiciary is to decide cases and controversies by applying the law. A key duty of the president as head of the executive branch is to "take Care that the laws are faithfully executed." However, though Congress is the main lawmaker whose function is not to be usurped by other branches, the courts decide whether enacted statutes are constitutional, interpret unclear statutes, and thus place limits (checks and balances) on congressional lawmaking power. Moreover, if no statute exists for a given type of dispute, the courts must decide such cases by applying existing judge-made law or devising a new rule if necessary, thus exercising a judicial lawmaking power that overlaps that of Congress and fills in gaps. But the lawmaking power of federal courts is secondary to that of Congress because Congress may, within limits, substitute legislation for judge-made law, thus imposing a control or limit on the common law.

In terms of federal law and lawmaking, the executive branch's main function is one of enforcement. However, the executive branch has considerable discretion as to the kind and degree of enforcement, so can render a given statute or judicial decision more or less effective. For example, the administration might decide to enforce strictly a federal statute that, to protect endangered species, prohibits wetlands from being drained and cultivated. Or it might decide that the statute is too harsh and seek to moderate its effects by a less rigorous enforcement. And like the judiciary, the president has a type of lawmaking power—the power to issue **executive orders** interpreting or implementing federal statutes, treaties, and the president's own constitutional powers. Executive orders have the force of law as to persons within reach of executive authority. Executive Order 11246, for example, prohibits federal contractors and subcontractors from discriminating against their employees on the basis of race, color, sex, national origin, or religion. This order affects the thousands of private firms and state and local governments receiving federal contracts, including those for the improvement of realty.

Limits on Government's Power over Property

The Bill of Rights (the first ten amendments to the U.S. Constitution) places limits on the actions that the *federal* government can take against people and their property. The Fourteenth Amendment, through a series of U.S. Supreme Court decisions, makes most of the Bill of Rights effective against the states as well. These and other constitutional protections operate against the *government*, whether federal, state, or local. Intrusions and offenses by *private* persons against another's property are dealt with by the private law—e.g., the law of trespass, nuisance, and negligence—and, where appropriate, by federal or state criminal law.

Many constitutional provisions contribute to the protection of private property, but three are basic: (1) the requirement of due process of law, (2) the guarantee of equal protection of the laws, and (3) protection from unreasonable searches and seizures.

Due Process. The Fifth and Fourteenth Amendments guarantee that no person shall be deprived of life, liberty, or property without due process of law. Due process has two aspects: the substantive and the procedural.

Substantive due process requires that a law have some rational purpose, and that the legislature use a reasonable means for achieving that purpose. That is, with regard to the *content* of a law (the rights and duties created), the government is not allowed to act in an arbitrary, capricious, or unreasonable manner. A city ordinance requiring Sam to spray his lawn with purple paint each Tuesday would seem to lack a rational purpose, so likely would be void for lack of substantive due process, even if the ordinance applied to all homeowners in the city. In contrast, an ordinance requiring that grass and weeds in lawns and vacant lots not be allowed to exceed one foot in height may be supportable as a fire prevention or health protection measure.

Procedural due process requires that a person affected by government action receive reasonable notice of the pending action and a reasonable opportunity to object or otherwise be heard. The school board's taking Mary's 50-acre orchard for the construction of a school is an exercise of the government's power of eminent domain (discussed in Chapter 16). But to be legitimate, this taking (condemnation) of private property must be for a public purpose (here, a public school), and the government (the school district) must pay a "just compensation" (usually, the market value of the land taken). Moreover—for the *procedural* aspect of due process—Mary must receive *notice* of the taking and be granted a *hearing* to challenge the action.

But how much notice is required, and what kind of hearing? Government action varies greatly in its degree of intrusion, from, say, temporarily suspending a business license for a minor infraction to imprisonment for a felony or a permanent taking of realty. Because of this variation, the courts have no set formula for what constitutes a constitutionally acceptable notice or hearing. Rather, the criterion is essential fairness to the person affected by the government's action. What "essential fairness" means depends on the circumstances. In general, notice must be given early enough to afford the person affected a reasonable time to prepare for any hearing that may be required, and the hearing must be of a type suitable for resolving the dispute. For minor matters, the notice period can be short and the hearing brief and informal. For serious deprivations, the notice period may need to be considerably longer and the hearing more elaborate, perhaps involving lawyers and formal courtroom procedures. For condemnation proceedings such as Mary's in the preceding example, statutes commonly prescribe how and when notice is to be given and what form the hearing shall take. Such statutes are, of course, subject to judicial review as to whether they provide essential fairness. If they do not, they will be held unconstitutional for lack of procedural due process.

Equal Protection. The Fourteenth Amendment prohibits the states from denying any person the equal protection of the laws, while the Fifth Amendment, the Supreme Court has held, imposes a similar ban on the federal government. Yet, the government discriminates among people in countless ways by assigning them to classes and treating the classes differently. State law requires minors but not adults to go to school. It permits minors but not adults to rescind their contracts for luxuries. Federal law requires young men but not young women to register for the military draft. Many state laws impose annually recurring taxes on land but not on the personal property used on it, or they tax the personal property at a different rate.

Thus, the equal protection guarantee obviously does not forbid governmental classifications and unequal treatment of different classes. It *does* require, however, that each such classification have a rational purpose, and that all members of the class be treated with substantial equality. A law imposing a tax on real estate has the rational purpose of raising revenue needed to support schools and other local government functions. The law's exempting from the tax any realty used for charitable or nonprofit educational purposes has the rational purpose of encouraging those desirable activities. The law's basing the tax on a fairly assessed valuation at a uniformly applied rate treats landowners within the class with substantial equality. In contrast, a law taxing farm land owned by women at a higher rate than farm land owned by men would violate the equal protection clause. Such a classification would be considered arbitrary because the rates are higher for some owners of farmland than for others.

Searches and Seizures. To protect individual privacy from unjustified government intrusions, the Fourth Amendment forbids unreasonable searches and seizures. The prohibition extends to one's person, home, private papers, personal effects, the nonpublic part of one's business, and any other thing or place regarding which he or she has a reasonable expectation of privacy. Any evidence resulting from an unreasonable search or seizure will be suppressed in court; the prosecution may not use this "forbidden fruit" (the evidence) from the "poisoned tree" (the unreasonable search) against the accused.

For a search or a seizure to be reasonable, it usually must be authorized by a **warrant** issued by a judge who must first find that probable cause for a search exists. **Probable cause** is a reasonable factual basis for a government official to believe that a violation of law has occurred. The warrant and probable cause requirements apply to civil as well as to criminal matters.

They also apply, in modified form, to inspections carried out by state and federal administrative agencies such as the Occupational Safety and Health Administration (OSHA). Generally, a search warrant is required for routine safety inspections of factories and other businesses unless the owner consents. Similarly, a city building inspector ordinarily must have a warrant to inspect for building code violations over the owner's objections. However, the Supreme Court has relaxed the probable cause requirement for noncriminal administrative searches. Unlike the police seeking a warrant in a criminal matter, administrative agencies need not demonstrate the likelihood of specific wrongdoing. Instead, an agency usually needs only to show that (1) the law creating the agency requires it to inspect that type of business, and (2) the agency has a fair and reasonable plan for enforcing the law.

Some warrantless searches are legal, but they too must be based on probable cause. For example, police may search an automobile without a warrant if they have probable cause to believe that it carries illegal drugs; and they need no warrant to seize evidence that is in "plain view." For their own protection, police arresting a suspected criminal may search the suspect and the immediate area for weapons.

The requirement of a warrant for routine administrative inspections of businesses does not apply to "closely regulated" industries if the regulatory process conforms to Supreme Court standards. Closely regulated industries are by definition so carefully monitored for the safety of the public that businesses within them have no reasonable expectation of privacy. Examples include the liquor, firearms, and mining industries, and New York junkyards where automobiles are dismantled and parts sold. A warrantless search of such businesses is reasonable, the Supreme Court has held, under the following circumstances:

1. A substantial government interest is served by the inspection.
2. A warrantless (surprise) inspection is necessary to further the regulatory scheme.
3. The regulatory statute informs the owner that the law authorizes searches.
4. The statute limits the discretion of inspectors.
5. The search has a properly defined scope.

In the examples just given, the government has a strong interest in collecting alcohol taxes and in protecting people from a variety of problems surrounding alcohol consumption, illegal trafficking in firearms and stolen cars, and unsafe mining conditions. Moreover, for its monitoring programs to be effective, the government must make surprise inspections. And statutes like the one regulating the New York junkyards give ample notice that regular inspections will be made.

Box 1–2 You Be the Judge

Pauline owns and operates a restaurant in Metropolis. It occupies most of a one-story building. She lives and maintains her business office in the remaining space, an apartment consisting of four rooms at the back of the building. The kitchen and related storage areas lie between her apartment and the large public dining room out front. Earnest Upright, an inspector from the state Department of Health, makes a surprise inspection visit. He asks to inspect the dining room, the kitchen and storage areas, and the office in Pauline's apartment. Pauline objects to the inspection because Upright has no warrant. Does Upright need a warrant to inspect the premises?

Role of State Constitutions

Like the U.S. Constitution, state constitutions create governments with three branches, separation and overlap of powers, checks and balances, and protection of life, liberty, and property. State constitutions also grant lawmaking authority to the state legislature (often called the *general assembly*), and to local governments. Accordingly, within limits imposed by state statutes and constitutional provisions, cities and other political subdivisions such as counties and towns may enact local laws, called **ordinances**, on a variety of topics.

Unlike the U.S. Constitution, state constitutions address real property in considerable detail, reflecting the fact that real estate is a state and local concern. For example, state constitutions give careful attention to the taxation of property. Though property tax laws vary greatly among the states, virtually all state constitutions classify property for tax purposes, establish a method for assessing value, specify what percentage of each class is subject to the tax, and exempt certain classes of property from taxation. Constitutions also deal with the control and management of public lands and with many other topics relating to realty. South Carolina's constitution provides that land owned or controlled by the State "shall never be donated . . . to private corporations or individuals, or to railroad companies. Nor shall such land be sold to corporations, or associations, for a less price than that for which it can be sold to individuals." Indiana's constitution regulates in unusually fine detail, providing that "The following grounds owned by the State in Indianapolis, namely: the State House Square, the Governor's Circle, and so much of out-lot number one hundred and forty-seven, as lies north of the arm of the Central Canal, shall not be sold or leased."

State protection of individual liberties can differ in extent from that provided by the U.S. Constitution. For instance, people often attempt to use privately owned shopping malls for speaking publicly on topics unrelated to the business of the malls. The U.S. Supreme Court has held that federal freedom of speech rights do not extend that far, that owners of private property have the right to deny access. The supreme courts of many states agree. The Connecticut and Oregon courts, for example, have interpreted their constitutions as conferring only the federal measure of speech rights and thus have maintained the federal balance between speech and property rights. In contrast, California's supreme court (in a ruling later upheld by the U.S. Supreme Court) has held that the state constitution permits greater access to private property for speech activity than does the U.S. Constitution. So in California, as in a few other states, freedom to speak on private property exceeds the freedom conferred by federal law.

As might be expected, a state constitution tends to reflect characteristics of the state, whether physical, cultural, political, or economic. For example, by their constitutions:

- Hawaii, a state of great natural beauty, mandates that government "shall conserve and protect Hawaii's natural beauty . . . and shall [develop and use its natural] resources in a manner consistent with their conservation. . . ." The constitution also provides for "public land banking," by which the state may "acquire interests in real property to control future growth, development and land use within the state."

- New Mexico, a mountainous, semiarid land with substantial forests, raises fire protection to a constitutional level by providing that its police power "shall extend to such control of private forest lands as shall be necessary for the prevention and suppression of forest fires."

- Idaho, where ranching is a major industry, requires the legislature to "pass all laws necessary to provide for the protection of livestock" against infectious diseases, and permits it to establish "such . . . regulations as may be necessary for the protection of stock owners and most conducive to the stock interests within this state."

- California, in a 1978 reaction to high taxes on real estate, limited the tax on realty to 1 percent of its full cash value as of the 1975–1976 county assessor's valuation, and limited subsequent reassessment and annual increases of the tax.

- Kansas and Texas are typical in giving agricultural land special tax treatment. Kansas provides that agricultural land may be valued for taxation on the basis of factors such as its agricultural income or productivity. Texas provides that the land shall be assessed *only* on the basis of such factors. Thus, farmland near cities ordinarily bears a smaller tax burden per acre than does land used for more lucrative purposes. Nevada accords similar treatment to land used for mining.

Often, provisions like these find their way into state constitutions because constitutions are more difficult than statutes to amend. Usually, amending a constitution requires a "super majority" of, say, two-thirds of the votes cast, while a statute can be changed or repealed by a simple majority of the legislature or the people voting in a referendum.

Statutes

Statutes (laws enacted by legislatures) affect property rights and ownership at all levels of government, with the greatest impact probably occurring at the state and local levels. Because the topics covered by statutes are so numerous, we can give here only a few illustrations.

Federal Statutes

A surprising number of federal statutes apply to real estate transactions. As noted in Chapter 18, many federal statutes deal with protection of the environment. Others provide for the forfeiture of land and other property used in certain criminal activities, impose liens on property for unpaid income taxes, and specify how individuals may acquire federal land or grazing or mining rights. The Internal Revenue Code taxes various kinds of income derived from real estate, such as rentals; income from the sale of farm and forest products; royalties received for oil, gas, and minerals; and traders' profits from buying and selling realty. The Bankruptcy Code, a federal statute governing the rights and duties of debtors enmeshed in financial difficulty, affects millions of people in every state and any land interest a debtor might own.

State and Local Statutes

State statutes parallel most of the functions just described, imposing taxes, liens, disclosure requirements for real estate financing, environmental protection requirements, and the like. They also provide for licensing of real estate brokers, contractors, and other professionals whose work relates to realty. And they define the interests in realty that one can have or create, prescribe transfer formalities, establish public recording systems, and govern the disposition of property upon the owner's death.

Local ordinances typically deal with zoning, fire and police protection, building requirements, historical preservation, maintenance of parks and roads, and other topics of local interest. Zoning, the process of dividing land into districts and imposing limits on land use within them, is discussed in Chapter 17.

As shown in Figure 1–1, political subdivisions of the state and their corresponding local lawmakers go by a variety of names, depending on the state. In all states but four, the **county** is the largest political subdivision. In Louisiana, the equivalent of a county is the **parish**, and in Alaska and New York City, the **borough**. In Connecticut and Rhode Island, *cities* and *towns* are the main units of local government. These two states have counties, but their counties lack government powers and serve mainly as judicial districts.

In many states, counties are further subdivided into **townships**. Townships are of two types: "civil" and "survey." *Civil* townships are political subdivisions of varying area and often irregular shape; they are units of government with legal powers granted by the state. Originating in New England, the civil township is now found mainly in the northeastern and north-central states. In contrast, the *survey* township is essentially a measuring device, a square-shaped unit of land approximately six miles on a side and 36 square miles in area, adopted by the U.S. government's rectangular survey system as a basis for describing and locating parcels of land. However, many states that have civil townships—Indiana, for example—have conformed them in size and shape to that of the survey township. The rectangular survey system is discussed later in this chapter, in the section entitled *Land Description Methods*.

Within counties, parishes, boroughs, and townships lie municipalities—cities, towns, and villages—each with its own officials and lawmaking authority. In Connecticut, Minnesota, New Jersey, and Pennsylvania, certain incorporated villages are called *boroughs* (not to be confused with boroughs that are equivalent to counties). A few cities are so large that they occupy several counties. The five boroughs of New York City, for example, are coextensive with five counties of New York State.

In counties, government authority usually resides in an elected *county council*, *county commission*, or *county board of supervisors*. In Louisiana parishes, the **police jury** is the governing body, while Alaskan boroughs have *councils*. Where civil townships exist, they typically are governed by a board of *township trustees*. Generally, municipalities are governed by a *city council* or a *town council*, while **boards of selectmen** govern New England towns.

Until recent years, an elected legislative body and an elected mayor with some degree of veto power have shared power in municipal government. Today, however, many municipalities have adopted a council-manager form of government, relying on an appointed professional manager instead of an elected mayor to handle administrative affairs. And traditionally, counties have had a central governing body with both legislative and administrative powers but no chief executive. Today, many counties have adopted a council-manager form of government in which the council legislates and an elected executive with veto power, or a professional manager appointed by the council, handles day-to-day administrative affairs.

● Administrative Regulations

State and federal statutes called *enabling statutes* create **administrative agencies** and delegate regulatory power to them. Thus, legislatures assign responsibility for functions that the legislatures cannot or do not wish to handle themselves, and they provide the agencies with a general guide

FIGURE 1–1 **Political Subdivisions and Their Governing Bodies**

Political Subdivision	Governing Body
County	Commission Council Board of Supervisors
Parish (Louisiana)	Police Jury
Borough (Alaska)	Council
Township (Civil)	Trustee Board of Trustees
City	City Council
Town	Town Council Board of Selectmen (New England)

within which they are to supply regulatory details. The regulation of nuclear power, for example, is beyond the expertise of most legislators; hence the federal Nuclear Regulatory Commission (NRC). Within the scope of delegated authority, the NRC develops rules and regulations designed to protect nuclear materials and facilities from theft and sabotage, to control the processing and use of uranium, and to protect the public health and safety. Agencies enforce their regulations in hearings presided over by administrative law judges.

Federal and state agencies together number in the hundreds and inevitably regulate a multitude of activities involving real estate. For example, federal agencies impose overflight rules on air traffic, limit the amount of gas or oil that may be extracted from land, and oversee the interstate activities of the electric power and natural gas industries. But the regulation of real estate financing and land use may be the most familiar to the public. Dealing with these topics and affecting millions of landowners are the Federal Housing Administration (FHA) and state agencies regulating banks and lending; the Environmental Protection Agency (EPA) and its state counterparts; and the Occupational Safety and Health Administration (OSHA) and its state counterparts. Many other state agencies have a direct and continuing impact on the real estate business and the use of realty. Among them are state real estate boards that license agents and brokers, state water control boards, and state commissions controlling the development of coastal areas.

Judicial Decisions

Real estate law also comes from judicial decisions—more specifically from appellate court decisions which, when published, become precedents for the guidance of lower courts. Many judicial decisions interpret legislation, and many create or add to the common law affecting real estate.

In deciding a case, a judge must apply relevant legislation (a statute, ordinance, or administrative regulation) after resolving any questions raised about its constitutionality. If the legislation is held constitutional, the judge will then resolve any disputes about its meaning. For example, a state disclosure statute requires the seller of residential realty to answer this question: "Are you [Seller] aware of any significant defects/malfunctions in any of the following? . . . Interior Walls . . . Foundations . . . Electrical Systems. . . ." Suppose that a seller knows of a hairline crack in the foundation but fails to disclose it, and upon discovering the crack the buyer brings suit to rescind (cancel) the contract. Is the crack a "significant defect" so that seller's failure to disclose it violates the law, thus giving the buyer a right to rescind the contract?

To decide, the trial judge must interpret the words of the statute. Here, the meaning of "significant defect" is critical. For a condition to be a "defect," does it have to impair the functionality of the property involved? If the crack is held to be a defect, the judge will then consider whether it is serious enough to be "significant," and here the degree of impairment and difficulty of repair become relevant. Suppose the judge holds that the hairline crack *is* a substantial defect for which the buyer may rescind the contract, and the seller appeals. The appellate court's decision, upon being published, adds to the case law interpreting the statute, regardless of whether the appellate court affirmed or reversed the trial court's judgment.

If no legislation covers a dispute, the trial court must apply the common law. Loosely defined, common law is a body of judge-made law in which legal rules have been distilled from an accumulation of appellate decisions. If the common law does not address the question involved, the trial court must develop an appropriate rule which, if upheld and published on appeal, adds to the common law.

The law of contracts, torts, agency, and property—all of which are basic components of real estate law—originated in the common law. In varying degrees, state statutes have codified some of this law and in so doing have either accepted the common law meanings or replaced them. Much of the common law remains untouched by statutes, so judges still have a key role in creating and shaping the law of real estate.

The buyer of a lot in a residential subdivision is likely to find that the contract of sale contains a number of **CC&Rs**, a shorthand expression for "conditions, covenants, and restrictions" that limit the use of individual lots in ways thought beneficial to all in the subdivision. Disputes arise over the CC&Rs. Contract law helps determine whether a particular condition, covenant (agreement), or restriction is enforceable, while property law indicates whether it is binding on future owners. The **tort law** of trespass, nuisance, and negligence protects owners against interferences by outsiders, and outsiders from misuse of property by owners. Agency law comes into play in principal-agent relationships, such as those in which a real estate broker (the agent), acting on behalf of a seller (the principal), brings seller and buyer together in a contract for the purchase of realty. Later chapters discuss extensively the application of these bodies of common law to realty.

BOX 1–3 YOU BE THE JUDGE

If you were the appellate judge in the cracked foundation case just discussed, would you affirm or reverse the trial court's opinion? Why?

Land Description Methods

For purposes of real estate financing, transfer, and taxation, an accurate description of the land—its shape, area, and unique location on the land mass—is essential. Contracts for the sale of land, deeds, leases, and mortgages are among the documents for which a legally sufficient land description is required.

To be "legally sufficient," a **land description**, often called the **legal description**, must give enough information for the tract or parcel to be distinguished from all others and for a competent surveyor to locate it. Informal descriptions in contracts of sale, such as "my farm on Henderson Road," have been upheld in court as sufficient to identify the subject of the sale, but using them is risky. Formal methods of land description are greatly preferred for their accuracy and detail. In the United States, people use three formal land description methods—metes and bounds, the rectangular survey system, and plats—to establish the geographic location of land. The rectangular survey system has not been adopted in all states. Whatever methods are available, however, may be used alone or in combination with others; no state requires the use of any particular method of land description.

The term *land description* refers only to geographic location, not to what is on the land or the interest being conveyed. A deed that accurately identifies the boundaries of the tract (and meets other legal requirements for a deed) conveys all the things within the boundaries, including houses, fences, outbuildings, and other improvements not described in the deed. If the description is not legally sufficient, no land interest is conveyed.

A land description is legally sufficient if a *competent surveyor* can physically locate the tract with it. To be competent, a surveyor must possess the special knowledge and abilities of those in the surveying profession. All states require surveyors to be licensed or "registered." To receive a license, the candidate must pass an examination on the various aspects of surveying. In most states, the candidate must complete a prescribed course of study before being allowed to sit for the exam. In addition, several states have enacted "Technical Standards" laws that identify standards by which, after licensure, the surveyor's work will be judged. Passing the exam and being licensed does not necessarily assure competence, but a licensed surveyor will be presumed competent, with the burden being on a challenger to demonstrate lack of competence.

Sometimes a document contains a land description that, by itself, cannot be understood. To give effect to the intention of the parties to the document, a court may have to interpret the description. As an aid to interpretation, the court may admit **parol evidence**[6] into court proceedings. For example, in deciding whether to enforce a contract for the sale of "my farm on Henderson Road," the court will admit parol evidence showing that the seller owns only one farm on Henderson Road, and that the seller and buyer had that farm in mind. To be legally sufficient, the description must also identify the state and the county, city, or town where the land lies; and it must provide the information needed for identifying the boundaries of the tract. If boundary information for the Henderson Road farm is not stated in the description itself, many courts permit it to be supplied by parol evidence. But the court will not supply land description terms that are completely missing.

Metes and Bounds

Imported from England in colonial times, the metes-and-bounds method is used throughout the United States and is the basic method in the states that have no rectangular survey system. The metes-and-bounds method employs natural and artificial monuments or markers such as road intersections, streams, walls, and surveyor's stakes to trace out the perimeter of the tract being identified.

To describe a parcel of land in terms of metes and bounds, a surveyor specifies a geographic starting point and then proceeds around the perimeter of the land until arriving back at the starting point. The starting point (usually called the "point of beginning") can be a natural monument such as "White Horse Rock" or an artificial monument such as a road intersection, a surveyor's stake, or "the south end of Blue Castle Bridge." Boundaries can be straight or irregular. Key terms used in the description process are:

1. **Mete:** A distance (e.g., 147 feet, 40 rods, one-half mile). In ascending order, the basic Anglo-American units of distance are:
   - inch
   - link (7.92 inches)
   - foot (12 inches)
   - yard (3 feet)
   - rod (16.5 feet; 5.5 yards)
   - chain (792 inches; 100 links; 66 feet; 22 yards; 4 rods; 1/80 mile)
   - mile (5,280 feet; 1,760 yards; 320 rods; 80 chains)

2. **Bound:** A direction or course, usually in terms of points on the compass (e.g., north; northwest, usually expressed as "North 45 degrees West). But "along Crooked Creek" also shows direction or course, without use of a compass.

3. **Call:** A statement or description of a boundary line in terms of metes and bounds. For example, "beginning at the intersection of Avenue Ten and Oak Road, north one mile on Oak Road to the intersection of Oak Road and Easy Street" is a call. A complete land description consists of several calls—whatever number is needed to identify the perimeter of the tract being described. A tract of irregular shape might require four more calls: "Then east along the south edge of Easy Street for 40 rods; from that point, south to Crooked Creek; then southeasterly along Crooked Creek to the north end of Great Battle Rock; then westerly to the point of beginning."

4. **Close:** The completion of a metes-and-bounds description so that the end of the last call connects to the point of beginning, enclosing the tract of land. The call "then westerly to the point of beginning" in the preceding example completes (closes) the description. If the description does not close, it is defective, and a deed containing it conveys no land.

So, a complete metes-and-bounds land description consists of a sequence of calls from a specified geographic point of beginning (the starting point), proceeding around the perimeter of the land, and closing back at that point of beginning.

Box 1–4 Apply Your Knowledge

Make a sketch of the tract described by the five calls in paragraph 3 (the paragraph defining "call") that precedes this box. Avenue 10 runs east and west; Oak Road runs north and south. In making the sketch, consider the following questions:

1. For this description, what is the point of beginning?
2. In the second call, what fraction of a mile is the 40 rods?
3. In what general direction does Crooked Creek flow?

Though the metes-and-bounds method is useful for describing tracts of irregular shape, the chances for error and conflict among the descriptive elements are many. To resolve internal inconsistencies, the courts apply the following priorities:

1. Natural monuments (considered the most reliable).
2. Artificial monuments and marked or surveyed lines (usually indicated by surveyors' stakes).
3. Adjacent tracts or boundaries.
4. Courses or directions.
5. Distances.
6. Area or quantity (considered the least reliable).

Suppose seller delivers to buyer a deed describing a boundary as "north 110 feet to the south edge of the Keppler tract," but in fact the distance is 210 feet to the south edge. If the deed is the only evidence of intention, a court would hold that 210 feet is the correct distance, because a call to an adjacent tract prevails over a contradictory distance call.

U.S. Government Survey System

By the Land Ordinance of 1785, the Continental Congress adopted a rectangular survey system to establish reliable boundaries for transferring public lands to settlers and to the states. Under this statute and later laws, the federal government surveyed public lands it already owned and the vast new territories it later acquired. Because of the need for uniform land descriptions, the federal government's survey boundaries are conclusive; that is, they are presumed accurate and cannot be changed by any state or court. The federal survey system covers most of the United States, but it is not available in some areas.[7]

Under this system, the public lands are laid out and divided into **quadrangles** approximately 24 miles on a side. Each quadrangle is subdivided into 16 uniquely identified survey townships approximately six miles on a side. Each township is further subdivided into 36 numbered squares called **sections**, each one mile on a side and containing 640 acres. An **acre** is 43,560 square feet. The result is a huge grid established by the government, employing the section as the smallest officially numbered unit. Each section can be divided into yet smaller tracts suitable for individual use and identified by reference to the official numbering system.

Meridians and Parallels

The sides of quadrangles and townships run north and south in alignment with meridians of longitude, and east and west in alignment with parallels of latitude. A **meridian** is a great circle encompassing the earth and running through the North and South poles. A **parallel** of latitude circles the earth at right angles to meridians, forming an east-west line. The equator is the largest parallel, a great circle midway between the North and South poles; other parallels are spaced at equal intervals north and south from the equator.

Initial Point

A survey system must have a point of reference from which surveying begins. For each land area to be surveyed, the government geographers established one or more centrally located and uniquely named "initial points" of reference—37 in all. An **initial point** is the intersection of a true meridian (called the *principal meridian* of the survey area) and a true parallel of latitude (called the *base line*) passing through the spot chosen for the initial point. Alabama and Mississippi share the initial point formed by the intersection of the Huntsville Meridian and the Huntsville Base Line. Alaska has its Copper River, Fairbanks, Kateel River, Seward, and Umiat initial points. One of California's three initial points lies at the top of Mount Diablo, which gives its name to the intersecting Mt. Diablo Meridian and Mt. Diablo Base Line.

Standard Parallels and Guide Meridians

To help correct for the curvature of the earth, the survey system employs "standard parallels" and "guide meridians," which form the boundaries of the quadrangles. *Standard parallels* intersect the principal meridian and extend east and west. They are located at 24-mile intervals north and south of the base line. Similarly, *guide meridians* are spaced along the base line—and, for correction purposes discussed in the next paragraph, along every standard parallel—at 24-mile intervals east and west of the principal meridian. Figure 1–2 illustrates one of four quadrangles found at the Mt. Diablo Initial Point. The quadrangle lies between the Mt. Diablo Meridian and the First Guide Meridian West, and between the Mt. Diablo Base Line and the First Standard Parallel North.

FIGURE 1–2 **Quadrangle Containing 16 Townships**

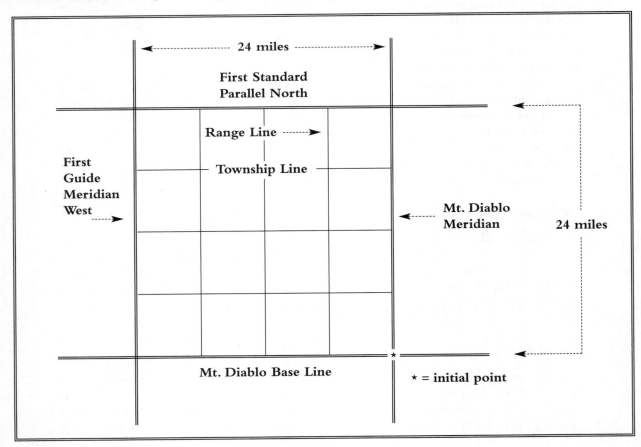

The earth's curvature causes a problem. As one travels north, meridians come closer together, converging at the North Pole. This convergence makes the quadrangles formed by guide meridians and standard parallels (and the townships contained within quadrangles) not truly square, but trapezoidal with the north edge being slightly shorter because the meridians angle nearer each other as they proceed north. If the convergence of meridians were not compensated for, northern quadrangles and townships would be smaller than southern ones. To keep quadrangles uniform in size, surveyors make corrections along each standard parallel (often called a *correction line*), beginning with the one farthest south.

A standard parallel forms, simultaneously, the north edge of a given quadrangle and the south edge of the next adjacent quadrangle to the north. Correction begins with the southernmost quadrangles lying on each side of the principal meridian, and proceeds east and west from it until the south edges of all quadrangles along each standard parallel are 24 miles long. Surveyors begin correction measurements at the principal meridian. They make the corrections by first marking the end of the southern quadrangle's shorter northern edge, and then moving the guide meridian a small distance east or west along that same standard parallel until the south edge of the northern quadrangle is 24 miles long. Thus, the east, south, and west edges of a quadrangle are always 24 miles long, with the northern edge always being shorter because of the convergence of meridians. Since 24-mile sections of guide meridians are moved east or west, guide meridians take a slightly zigzag path every 24 miles as they progress north—to the left (west) for guide meridians west of the principal meridian, and to the right for those east of it. The result is vertical rows or stacks of slightly trapezoidal "quadrangles" of uniform area from south to north.

Townships: Ranges and Tiers

The north-south lines separating the townships in Figure 1–2 are range lines, while the east-west lines are township lines. Range lines and township lines are six miles apart. Each square representing a township is formed by horizontal township lines at the north and south edges and vertical range lines at the east and west edges.

So that people can locate specific tracts of land, townships and sections within them are uniquely identified. As shown in Figure 1–3, the vertical rows of townships, called **ranges**, are numbered east and west from the principal meridian, with consecutive numbers extending across quadrangles to the outer limit of the large survey area served by the principal meridian. So, in Figure 1–3, Range 1 West (commonly called R1W) is the first vertical row of townships west of the Mt. Diablo Meridian, while R5W is in the next quadrangle to the west. Similarly, the horizontal rows, or **tiers**, of townships are numbered north and south from the base line to the outer

BOX 1–5 APPLY YOUR KNOWLEDGE

Figure 1–3 shows four quadrangles of townships, plus four other illustrative townships lying outside the four-quadrangle area. Some of the townships are identified with the two sets of letters and numbers required to describe its relative position within its quadrangle—Township T3S, R3E, for example. T3S is the number of the township line forming the south edge of the township; R3E is the number of the range line forming the east edge of the township.

For each of the six townships marked with **X**, give the two sets of letters and numbers needed for describing their positions within their quadrangles.

limits of the survey area. The tier called Township 1 North (T1N) is the first horizontal row north of the Mt. Diablo Base Line. The complete description for the individual township located immediately north and west of the Mt. Diablo initial point is: "Township 1 North [identifying the *tier* containing the township, not the township itself], Range 1 West, Mt. Diablo Base and Meridian," often abbreviated in land descriptions as "T 1 N, R 1 W, Mt. D. B. & M." In the other survey areas, townships are numbered in the same way, but of course have a different base and meridian name.

FIGURE 1–3 Range and Township Numbering

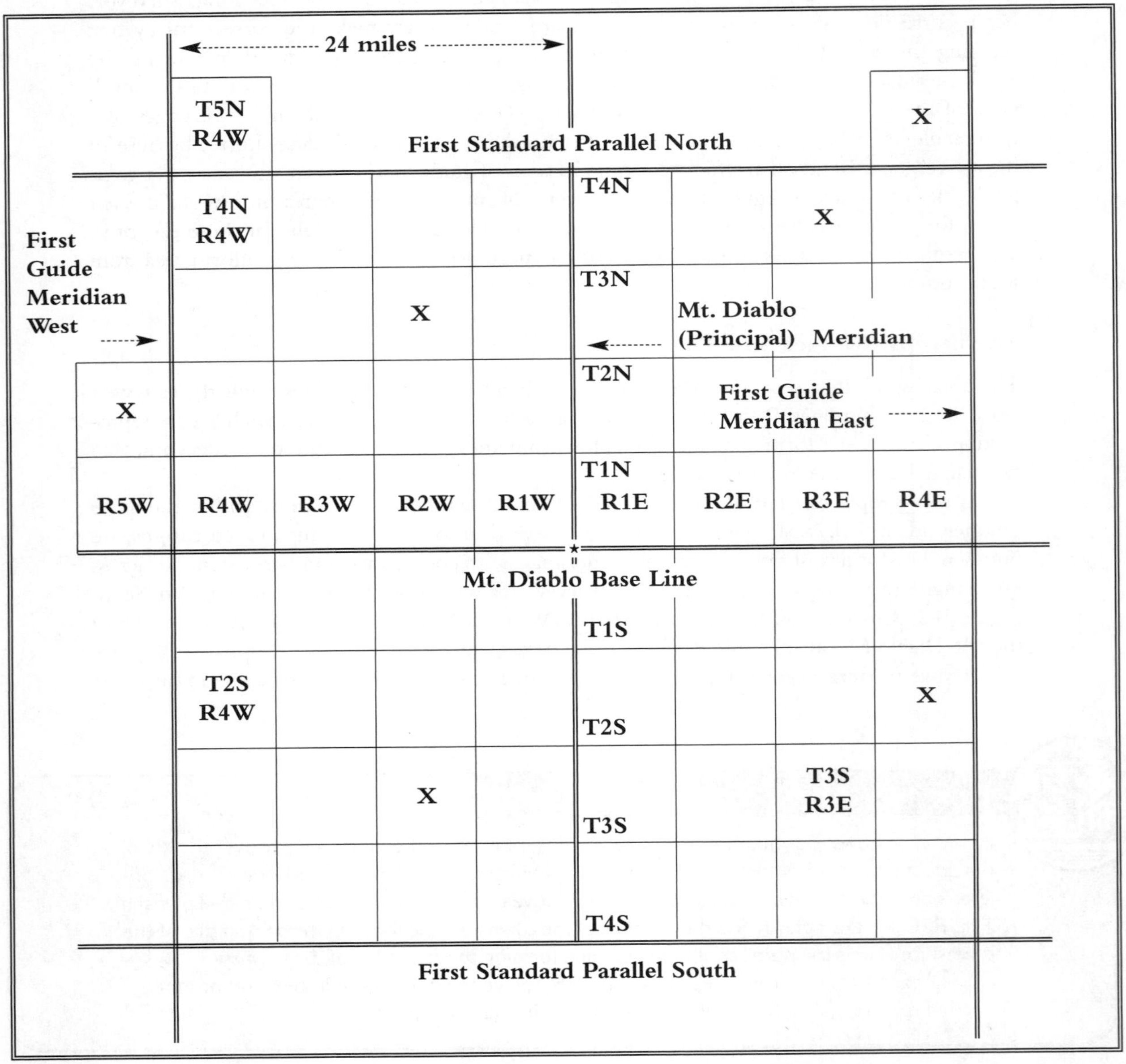

Townships: Sections

The 36 sections in each township are formed by parallel *section lines* a mile apart, running north and south and intersecting those running east and west. In every township, the resulting sections are numbered as shown in Figure 1–4.

Despite corrections made to keep townships uniform in size, the trapezoidal shape of townships remains because of the convergence of the range (north-south) lines. Because the northern side of a township is less than six miles long, its area is something less than 36 square miles.

To localize the effects of convergence, the survey system assigns deficiencies in area to each township as follows: Section lines are run from south to north, parallel to the east range line of the township for a distance of five miles. The intersecting east-west section lines create 25 sections of 640 acres each. The remaining 11 sections on the west and north edges of the township are adjusted in size to absorb deficiencies and excesses of area resulting from measurement errors and the convergence of meridians. A deficiency resulting from convergence is assigned to the six

FIGURE 1–4   **Numbering of Sections in a Township**

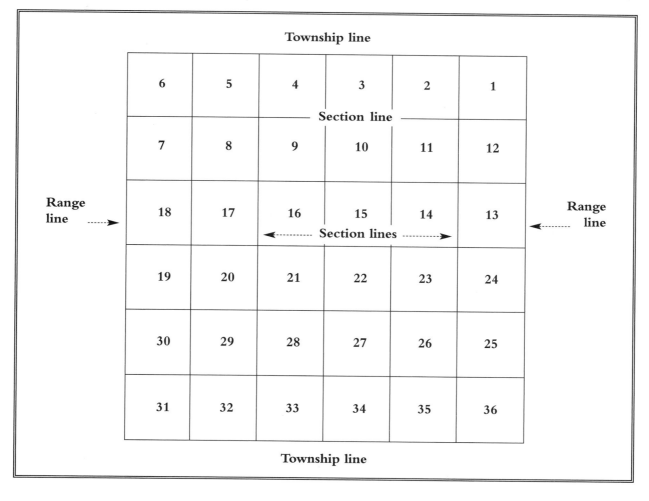

sections on the west side of the township, and by law is placed in the last half mile along the western boundary.

Although the section is the smallest officially numbered unit in the survey system, each section may be further subdivided into half sections (320 acres), quarter sections (160 acres), and so on, as illustrated in Figure 1–5.

A subdivision of a section gets its name from its position within the section. Figure 1–5 shows that section 21 is divided into five tracts: the "north half," the "southwest quarter," the "north half of the southeast quarter," the "southwest quarter of the southeast quarter," and the "southeast quarter of the southeast quarter." These descriptions are abbreviated as "N 1/2," "SW 1/4," and so on. If section 21 is located in township T3S, R3E in the Mt. Diablo survey area, the full unique description of the 40 acres at the far southeast corner is: "SE 1/4 of SE 1/4 of section 21, T 3 S, R 3 E, Mt. D. B. & M."

FIGURE 1–5 **Illustrative Subdivisions of Section 21**

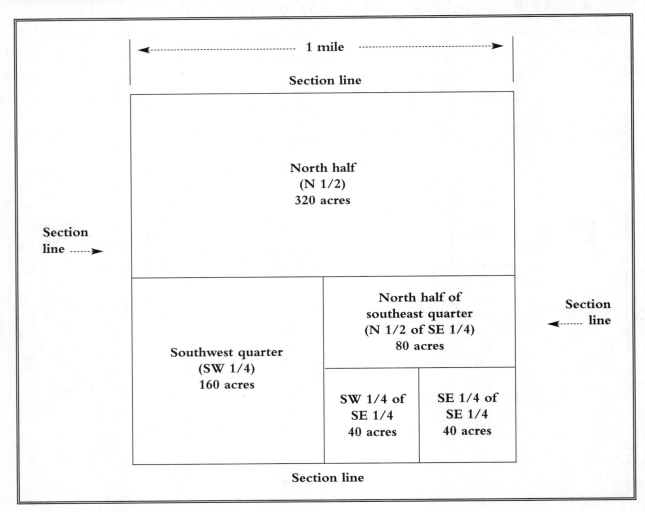

● Plats

The plat, found in all states, is the most easily used method of land description. A **plat** is a detailed map or drawing made by private parties, such as developers of residential areas, showing lots and their dimensions, blocks, streets, alleys, utility easements (rights of way), and other geographical features in a subdivision or tract of land.[8] Plats also state any conditions, covenants, and restrictions on land use that the developer has imposed. Lots shown in plats are numbered, and all other features are identified by name, letter, number, or some combination. So that it can serve as a land description device, a plat is linked to a known external monument such as a section corner in the rectangular survey system or the starting point in a metes-and-bounds description of the subdivision.

To be allowed to sell lots, a developer usually (1) must have the subdivision plat approved by an agency of local government such as the county planning commission, and (2) must record the plat in the public records, usually the county recorder's office. The planning commission imposes requirements as to lot sizes, open areas, sidewalks, street widths and curvatures, and other physical features. Recording the plat gives the public notice of its contents, including any limitations on land use included by the developer. In the recorder's office, plats are kept in books of maps or plats for easy reference.

The following is a legal description of a lot identified in a plat:

> *Lot 136 of Rolling Hills Subdivision No. 4, according to the map [plat] thereof recorded December 26, 1961, in Book 9 of Maps, pages 27 and 28, in the County of Madera, State of California, in the office of the County Recorder of said County.*

A deed to lot 136 need not restate the information found on the plat, because all information appearing on the plat, such as lot boundaries, restrictive covenants, and location of streets and parks, is "incorporated" into the deed "by reference." Thus, by referring to the recorded plat, as is done in the preceding example, the deed communicates the descriptive details the plat contains. Interested parties can easily find the plat itself by using the plat-locating information found in the description.

Self-Study Questions

1. In real estate law, what does the term *bundle of rights* mean, and what purpose does the concept serve?

2. Why is it inaccurate in most states to say that a lender keeps title to mortgaged property until all payments are made?

3. What is allodial ownership? How does it differ from ownership in a system of feudal tenure?

4. How does federal lawmaking power differ from that of the states?

5. How do the judicial, legislative, and executive branches of government participate in lawmaking and law enforcement?

6. Spike breaks into Gene's business and steals Gene's trade secrets. Gene sues Spike, alleging Spike violated Gene's constitutional right to freedom from unreasonable searches and seizures. Is this claim a valid basis for Gene's suit? Why?

7. How do the constitutional requirements for an administrative inspection of business premises differ from those for a police search of a person's home?

8. Explain how metes-and-bounds surveying works.

9. Using Figures 1–3 and 1–5 as guides, give a complete description of the southeastern 10 acres of section 21 in T5N, R4W of the Mt. Diablo survey area. Give the description for the corresponding section 21 in the Huntsville, Alabama, survey area.

10. When preparing a deed description of a lot by referring to a plat, why is it not necessary to give in the deed a detailed description of the lot boundaries?

Case Problems

1. The garbage collection ordinance of Morristown, New Jersey (Town), provided free collection service to all residential dwellings of three units or less, and to condominium developments where no more than 50% of the units are owned by one person or entity. Excluded from the ordinance, and therefore not receiving collection service, were all multifamily dwellings of four or more units, including a 140-unit garden apartment complex owned by WHS Realty Company (WHS). Alleging that the ordinance violated its right to due process and equal protection of the laws guaranteed by the federal and state constitutions, WHS filed a complaint demanding the same garbage collection service provided to other residents. The trial court concluded that the Town had no rational basis for excluding apartment complexes from the coverage of the ordinance. The appellate court affirmed the trial court's decision. The supreme court reversed the appellate decision, holding that a hearing was necessary to determine whether the Town's ordinance was rationally related to a legitimate state interest. After a four-day hearing, the trial court reaffirmed its prior determination that the ordinance violated the due process and equal protection clauses, and ordered the Town to collect garbage and recyclable materials from plaintiff's apartment complex on the same terms and conditions as those applying to condominium complexes. The Town appealed from the judgment invalidating the ordinance. Was the ordinance in violation of the due process and equal protection clauses? *WHS Realty Company v. Town of Morristown*, 733 A.2d 1206 (N.J. App. 1999).

2. Lon and Lora want to bring the plight of the nearly extinct albino miniature buffalo to the attention of the public and are seeking a shopping mall as the site for a "sit-in" they expect to be covered by TV and other national news media. They have found large shopping malls and enthusiastic news media in California and Connecticut. Both malls plan to bring suit to oppose the sit-in. Which state should Lon and Lora choose? Why?

3. Waldo, having flunked out of surveying school at the end of his first semester, purchased by mail order a cabin and lot located in the mountains of a distant state. Upon arriving there, he was unable to locate the lot using the description in the deed of conveyance. Does Waldo's inability to locate the lot make the description legally defective?

Endnotes

1. Sources for this chapter and others in the book include A. W. B. Simpson, *A History of the Land Law* (Oxford: Clarendon Press, 1986); Roger A. Cunningham, William B. Stoebuck, and Dale A. Whitman, *The Law of Property* (West Publishing Co., 1993); A. N. Yiannopoulos, Louisiana Civil Law Treatise—Property (West Publishing Co., 1991); Walter G. Robillard and Lane J. Bouman, *Clark on Surveying and Boundaries* (The Michie Company, 1992); and N. Stephan Kinsella, "A Civil Law to Common Law Dictionary," 54 La. L. Rev. 1265 (1994).

2. In contrast to the common law, civil law is legislative in origin and is worked out in considerable detail before being enacted. Civil law is found in a *code*, a systematic, comprehensive collection of laws drafted by committees or commissions and enacted by legislatures. The Roman Code of Justinian, published in A.D. 529 is an ancestor of the civil law found in many countries today, including that of France. Much of the Louisiana Civil Code—including its law of property—is derived from France's Code Napoleon, published in 1804.

In most of the United States, the expression *civil law* has a second meaning, namely, noncriminal law. Civil law in this Anglo–American sense refers to bodies of common law, for example, the law of contracts and the law of torts, permitting an individual to bring a private lawsuit against a defendant for damages and other remedies to compensate for a variety of injuries.

3. "Common law of England" has always been interpreted to mean English case law as modified by some basic English statutes and as supplemented by the law developed in the English courts of equity. The American Revolution began in 1775 and ended in 1783. Some states adopted the English common law as it existed in 1607, the year in which the first English colony was founded on this continent. Most states adopted it as it existed in 1776, the date of the Declaration of Independence.

4. *McCulloch v. Maryland*, 17 U.S. 316 (1819). In the same opinion, the Court held that Maryland's tax on the operations of the U.S. bank was unconstitutional, violating the principle that national law is supreme and cannot be interfered with by certain kinds of state tax law.

5. *United States v. Lopez*, 514 U.S. 549 (1995). Prior decisions interpreting the commerce clause used the expression "affects commerce." By adding "substantially," and refusing to uphold a federal statute banning guns in local schools as a proper exercise of the commerce power, the Lopez decision may have narrowed the application of the commerce clause a bit.

6. Evidence, usually oral, derived from sources outside the document.

7. The U.S. government surveys applied only to the *public* lands of the United States, not to land already privately owned or belonging to other nations. Lands never federally owned include the original thirteen states; Kentucky, Tennessee, and West Virginia; part of Florida; Hawaii; and, because of its early history as an independent nation, Texas. But Texas has its own rectangular survey system, similar to the U.S. government's, and some of the original thirteen states had devised their own rectangular systems.

8. The subdivision that a plat represents differs from a subdivision of a section in a survey township. A section subdivision simply identifies an area of land such as the "northwest quarter of section 21," while a plat shows the geographical features of a tract of any size or shape.

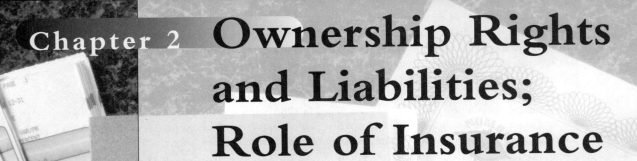

Chapter 2 Ownership Rights and Liabilities; Role of Insurance

George wants to sell his farm Blackacre, a tract of irregular shape covering approximately 1,800 acres. A crop of soybeans occupies 150 acres. About 250 acres is pasture land for cattle and horses. The rest is hilly, uncultivated woodland containing George's residence, several outbuildings, a rental house recently leased to a tenant for a term of three years, a large pheasant population and other wildlife, a small gravel pit, a vein of coal about 800 feet below the surface, and possibly some oil-bearing sandstone below the coal. To extract gravel, George has constructed a stationary dredge, lengthening it from time to time as the pit widens. Last week George's tenant installed three room-size air-conditioning units in the rental house without consulting George.

On the south end of Blackacre, a small dump containing tires and other debris from the farm smolders for much of the year, often releasing thick black smoke into a neighboring residential area. Some of the neighbors have complained, but others have not because they have been hunting for pheasant, rabbits, and deer on George's property despite the presence of "No Hunting" signs. A neighboring landowner recently opened a small nightclub near George's residence. The lights and loud music at late hours disturb George and his family.

Dora, a novice in the real estate business, wants to buy Blackacre for subdivision and resale to others. As a prospective developer, she has several concerns. She knows that George's interest in Blackacre is a fee simple estate, the most extensive interest that one can have in land. But upon buying Blackacre, what, exactly, will she own? May she later transfer some elements of Blackacre and keep the rest? Who is entitled to fixtures placed on the land by tenants and others? What are the possibilities of litigation with her neighbors?

A legally sufficient deed would convey to Dora an interest in all the land lying within the boundaries described in the deed, including, without the need to list them, all things that the law regards as part of the realty, such as fixtures. The first part of this chapter discusses the meaning of "the land"; an owner's rights in the land, its products, and any buildings or fixtures on it; and some private law that protects those rights from interference by outsiders. The second part deals with liabilities of owners for violating duties toward others. The last part addresses the role of insurance in land ownership.

A Landowner's Rights and Protections

People refer to real estate in various ways. They may give it a name such as "Blackacre," or simply call it the "condo," "property," "realty," "house," "farm," "ranch," "building," "mall," or "land," as in the statement, "I want to buy your warehouse" or "I'll sell you my ranch in Happy Valley." Whatever a piece of realty may be called, a person acquiring it receives specific ownership rights and accompanying protections.

Three Meanings of "Land"

In real estate transactions, *land* is used in at least three senses: (1) to describe the physical elements of the earth over which a landowner has control, such as soil, air, and minerals; (2) more broadly as a synonym for "real property," and (3) more narrowly to describe the subject of title insurance. Physically, land has three components—the surface, the airspace above it, and the subsurface. Upon and within these components may be, among other things, water; natural vegetation; crops; stands of timber; geothermal energy; solid minerals; "migratory" (flowing) minerals such as oil and gas; buildings, fences, irrigation systems, and other fixtures; and various forms of wildlife. In the statement, "Fires and earthquakes have ruined my land," the word land means the physical earth and the physical things on or in it.

But often *land* means *real property*. Real property (also called **realty** or real estate) consists of a tract of *earth* together with *things incidental and appurtenant to* (benefitting) it. "Things" includes legal rights. So, in addition to the earth and its physical components, real property includes any legal rights that "run with" the land when it is transferred. Betty owns Whiteacre but has no access to the main highway lying on the other side of neighbor Henry's land. Henry grants Betty a permanent access easement (a right of way) over his property. Thus Betty acquires a right (the easement) in someone else's (Henry's) property for the benefit of her own land. Then Betty sells Whiteacre to Melissa. The subject of the sale—the real property called Whiteacre—includes not only the physical land, but also the easement across Henry's land.

Upon buying Whiteacre, Melissa might purchase a policy (contract) of **title insurance** to indemnify her if the title that Betty intends to convey is defective. However, unless the policy states otherwise, the "land" covered by the title insurance policy includes only the physical land described in it, plus buildings, fixtures, and other physical elements the law treats as realty. For title insurance purposes, the "land" covered by the title policy does *not* include easements and other rights in *other people's* land unless the title policy expressly says so, and it probably will not say so unless Melissa pays an additional premium to cover the risk of defects in those rights. Title insurance is discussed more fully in Chapter 9.

Rights in the Land and Its Products

Dora buys Blackacre from George. What does she receive? Before the invention of the airplane, a landowner was thought to own the surface, the airspace above to the outer limits of the universe, and the subsurface to the center of the earth. The law of airspace ownership has changed considerably since then. Under modern law, a landowner is entitled to the surface, some airspace above it, the subsurface to the center of the earth, most things upon and within these components, and, of course, any easements or other rights appurtenant to the land.

Airspace

Soon after the beginnings of air traffic in the early 1900s, the courts began to retreat in varying degrees from the common law theory that surface owners also owned the airspace above without limit. Today, the question of airspace ownership is largely settled by federal law. In the leading case of *United States v. Causby*,[1] continuous low flights of military aircraft over the Causbys' North Carolina farm for takeoff and landing ruined their poultry business and otherwise deprived them of the enjoyment of their land. The Supreme Court held that the overflights so interfered with the Causbys' ownership rights as to constitute a "taking" of an air easement over their property, for which the government must pay.

In finding a taking, the Court laid out some key concepts relating to the ownership of airspace. First, applying federal statutes, the Court held that the air above the minimum safe altitude of flight prescribed by the Civil Aeronautics Authority (now the Federal Aviation Administration) is a public highway and part of the public domain:

> It is ancient doctrine that at common law ownership of the land extended to the periphery of the universe. . . . But that doctrine has no place in the modern world. The air is a public highway, as Congress has declared. Were that not true, every transcontinental flight would subject the operator to countless trespass suits. Common sense revolts at the idea. To recognize such private claims to the airspace would clog these highways, seriously interfere with their control and development in the public interest, and transfer into private ownership that to which only the public has a just claim.

Then the Court identified the scope of the surface owner's airspace rights:

[I]t is obvious that if the landowner is to have full enjoyment of the land, he must have exclusive control of the immediate reaches of the enveloping atmosphere. Otherwise buildings could not be erected, trees could not be planted, and even fences could not be run. . . . The landowner owns at least as much of the space above the ground as he can occupy or use in connection with the land. . . . The fact that he does not occupy it in a physical sense—by the erection of buildings and the like—is not material. As we have said, the flight of airplanes, which skim the surface but do not touch it, is as much an appropriation of the use of the land as a more conventional entry upon it.

So, in summary, the airspace above the federally prescribed minimum safe altitudes for flight is in the public domain and is not owned by the owner of the surface. However, the surface owner does own the airspace that is within the "immediate reaches" of the surface. "Immediate reaches" means the airspace actually occupied by trees, buildings, towers, and other things on the surface, plus whatever additional airspace is needed for the full and complete enjoyment of the surface and the things on it. As noted in the next section of this chapter, the owner of airspace can subdivide it and transfer some or all to others.

What are the minimum safe altitudes for flight that mark the lower boundaries of public airspace? The Federal Aviation Administration has established them as follows:[2]

Except when necessary for takeoff or landing, no person may operate an aircraft below the following altitudes . . .

   (b) *Over congested areas. Over any congested area of a city, town, or settlement, or over any open air assembly of persons, an altitude of 1,000 feet above the highest obstacle within a horizontal radius of 2,000 feet of the aircraft.*

   (c) *Over other than congested areas. An altitude of 500 feet above the surface, except over open water or sparsely populated areas. In those cases, the aircraft may not be operated closer than 500 feet to any person, vessel, vehicle, or structure. [Note that the federal altitude rules permit flying lower than 500 feet over open water and sparsely populated areas, although, except for helicopters, not within 500 feet laterally of people, vehicles, and structures.]*

   (d) *Helicopters. Helicopters may be operated at less than the minimums prescribed [in (b) or (c)] if the operation is conducted without hazard to persons or property on the surface.*

State law, too, puts limits on how low one may fly. Generally, state law prohibits flying so low as to imperil persons or property on the ground. The language of the North Carolina statute quoted in *Causby* is typical of flight regulation by the states: the flight of aircraft is lawful "unless at such a low altitude as to interfere with the then existing use to which the land or water, or the space over the land or water, is put by the owner, or unless so conducted as to be imminently dangerous to persons or property lawfully on the land or water beneath."

BOX 2–1 YOU BE THE JUDGE

Rachel owns a 10,000-acre cattle ranch in a dry, sparsely settled part of the country. The ranch supports only a few hundred cattle. Several times a month, Red Baron flies over the ranch in his biplane at altitudes as low as ten feet. Alleging that Baron has invaded her airspace, Rachel seeks an injunction prohibiting flights below 500 feet over her property. Assume that she will be entitled to the injunction if Baron has violated either the federal or the state overflight rules. Has he violated any of the FAA rules? Has he violated state overflight law?

When *Causby* was decided, the federal government's definition of navigable airspace did not include glide paths used for the takeoff and landing of aircraft. Later, Congress redefined navigable airspace to include glide paths. But the lower portions of glide paths near public airports sometimes intersect with and include airspace that is within the "immediate reaches" of neighboring land. Because navigable airspace is in the public domain, an aircraft's passing through privately owned "immediate reaches" included in a public airport's glide path is lawful and therefore not a trespass. What, then, is the consequence to landowners when their airspace conflicts with that of a glide path?

In *Griggs v. Allegheny County*,[3] the Supreme Court addressed that issue. In *Griggs*, flight rules for landings and takeoffs at the Greater Pittsburgh Airport required aircraft to fly at very low altitudes over plaintiff Griggs' residence. No flights violated regulations of the Civil Aeronautics Administration, but the intense noise of the planes during the many daily takeoffs and landings disrupted the residents' lives, impaired their health, and forced them to move from their home. The Court affirmed lower court rulings that defendant Allegheny County, as owner and designer of the airport, had taken an air easement over Griggs' property. The use of land by owners of the neighboring surface presupposes the use of some of the airspace above it. Although glide paths are a part of the navigable airspace, any use of a glide path that makes the surface owner's airspace unusable is a taking of private property for which the government must pay.

Surface and Subsurface

Ownership of the surface and the subsurface entitles Dora to the soil and most of its components, such as fixtures (except those that a tenant or someone else has a right to remove); natural vegetation; sand, gravel, and topsoil; and solid minerals such as metal ores and coal. If the land has water, oil, gas, or geothermal energy, she also has usage and extraction rights. And, as owner, she may sell, lease, or give away Blackacre or any part of it, including its airspace.

Subdivision. Dora plans to subdivide Blackacre and sell parts of it to others. She may do so by means of vertical or horizontal subdivision, or by a combination of the two. **Vertical subdivision** is the process of dividing a tract into smaller units, each of which consists of surface, subsurface, and airspace. A lot in a residential subdivision is an example. **Horizontal subdivision** is the division of earth or airspace into *layers*. For example, Dora could convey to a coal mining company "that portion of Blackacre lying below 500 feet beneath the surface." Thus, Dora would continue to own the first 500 feet of the subsurface, and the mining company would own the rest to the center of the earth, subject to a duty to support Dora's 500 feet of subsurface. Similarly, if Dora built a multistory condominium complex, she would be conveying layers of airspace to purchasers of units located above the ground floor.

Or, Dora might *vertically* subdivide a portion of Blackacre into, say, five lots for commercial use, and by *horizontal* subdivision of those lots reserve for herself all the subsurface below 100 feet beneath the surface, and all the airspace above 20 feet above the surface. Thus, a buyer of a commercial lot would receive the surface, the first 20 feet of airspace above it, and the first 100 feet of subsurface, while Dora would retain the mineral-bearing strata of the subsurface and an **air lot** beginning 20 feet above the surface.

But the air lot would be of no use to Dora unless she had access to it. If her remaining land surrounded the commercial lots, Dora could erect vertical beams on her land, fasten horizontal beams to them at, say, 21 feet above the surface, and use the resulting framework as a foundation or floor for a large structure above the buildings on the commercial lots.

Alternatively, to support the framework she could retain strategically located small spaces on the surface of the commercial lots, together with the airspace above each small space and the subsurface below it. This technique has long been used by industrial landowners for developing airspace they do not need for their own operations. In the early 1900s, for example, the Chicago and Northwestern Railroad created an air lot 23 feet above a portion of its tracks and sold it to Chicago's world-famous Merchandise Mart, together with (a) surface areas called **column lots** (each with its own airspace) for erecting vertical columns, and (b) cylindrical portions of the subsurface called **caisson lots** upon which the column lots and vertical columns would rest. Thus the Merchandise Mart came to be built over the C&N tracks, with the railroad continuing to own the land supporting its tracks. Other large structures have been built in air lots over Chicago's Illinois Central tracks, the Massachusetts Turnpike in Boston, and New York's Grand Central Station. Figure 2–1 illustrates an air lot supported by columns resting on column and caisson lots.

Water, Minerals, and Geothermal Energy. The states vary considerably in their treatment of rights to water, migratory minerals such as oil and gas, and geothermal energy. Chapter 19 discusses water and mineral rights. Here we are concerned mainly with questions of ownership.

FIGURE 2–1   **An Air Lot**

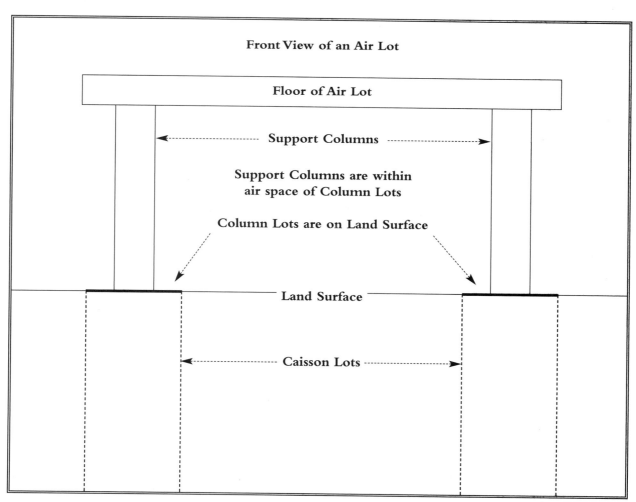

BOX 2–2 LAND ASSEMBLY, AIR RIGHTS, AND DONALD TRUMP

Developers of large-scale projects such as shopping malls and skyscrapers often must acquire the needed land from many different owners, in a process called land assembly. The land assembly for New York's Trump Tower—a 68-story complex containing condominium, office, and retail space—involved the acquisition of air rights and other interests in land. Wanting to build the Tower on 5th Avenue's Bonwit Teller site next door to Tiffany & Company, developer Donald Trump bought the old Bonwit Teller building from Genesco, Inc., for demolition. Genesco, however, did not own the land under the building but was only leasing it from the Equitable Life Assurance Society. So Mr. Trump had to acquire Equitable Life's interest. Moreover, to get a zoning change needed for the 664-foot height of the Tower, Mr. Trump had to acquire the air space above Tiffany's and a neighboring building. The land assembly therefore consisted of several different kinds of interests: Genesco's Bonwit Teller building, the remainder of its 29-year lease, the land upon which the building was constructed, and the air rights of Tiffany's and its neighbor.

Water: In all but a few states the owner of land does not own the water on or within it, having instead only a right to make reasonable use of the water.

Migratory minerals (oil and gas): In their natural condition, oil and gas are trapped under pressure within rock structures and are immovable until released by forces such as drilling or natural earth movements. But upon breach of a formation containing oil and gas, they flow to areas of lower pressure. So how should the law view oil and gas—as immovables that are part of the land and transferable with it, or as materials capable of moving underground and owned by no one until extracted?

In the so-called "ownership states," oil and gas in their natural state are viewed as immovables, as part of the realty. Consequently, the owner of the land also owns any oil it contains and can transfer ownership of the oil with *or apart from* the rest of the land. Other states—the "nonownership" jurisdictions—conclude that because oil is capable of migrating, no one owns it until it is extracted. In these states, a landowner has an exclusive right to drill for the oil and can transfer that right, but, having no ownership of migratory minerals until extraction, cannot transfer oil or gas that is still in the ground. In all states, oil and gas become personal property upon extraction.

The landowner's right to minerals, whether migratory or solid, constitutes an *interest in land* called the **mineral estate**, which can be conveyed like any other interest in land. In the ownership states, the grantee of the mineral estate receives ownership of any oil and gas; in the nonownership states, the grantee of the mineral estate receives only the exclusive right to drill.

Geothermal energy: Geothermal energy results from concentrations of hot water and steam lying deep within the earth, heated primarily by the decay of radioactive elements but also by magma (molten rock). Geothermal energy appears on the earth's surface in the form of the geysers, fumaroles, and hot springs of Yellowstone National Park; the hot springs in Arkansas; and similar natural phenomena in other parts of the country.

In addition, huge amounts of steam and hot water are trapped in rocks deep in the subsurface and are exploited commercially. Idaho, for example, a state with an abundance of geothermal resources, has drilled wells near its state offices in Boise to heat the buildings with hot water. In some parts of the country, mostly in the West, geothermal energy is tapped by drilling, transported in pipelines, and converted by steam turbines into electricity for distribution where needed. As of the early 1990s, The Geysers in northern California was the world's largest geothermal electrical power complex, supplying metropolitan San Francisco 105 miles to the south with most of its electrical needs.

Geothermal energy can also come from "artificial" sources. Within recent years, it has become feasible to drill deep into hot, dry rock and to inject surface water for the purpose of generating steam. Recognizing this process, a Louisiana statute, like those in other states, defines the term *geothermal resources* to include ". . . (b) steam and other gases, hot water, and hot brines resulting from water, gas, or other fluids artificially introduced into geothermal formations."[4]

Because of its ambiguous nature, geothermal energy is treated legally as water in some states and as a migratory mineral in others. In states treating it as water, geothermal energy therefore usually is not subject to ownership, but the owner of the land may use and transport the energy as permitted by state water law or, in a few states, by a special statute regulating geothermal energy. Where geothermal energy is viewed as a migratory mineral, the ability of a landowner to own it before extraction (and to sell it apart from the land) depends on whether the state is an ownership or a nonownership state.

Solid minerals: Solid minerals are part of the land and remain so until severed from the earth by quarrying or mining. Upon severance, solid minerals, gas and oil, and structures (e.g., buildings) lose their character as realty and become **goods**, an important category of *personal* property whose sale is governed by Article 2 of the Uniform Commercial Code (UCC).

As owner of Blackacre's mineral estate, George has the right to mine and sell the minerals. If George does not want to do the mining himself, he can sell the mineral estate apart from Blackacre to someone equipped for mining. Before selling Blackacre to Dora, George might have sold the mineral estate to Mining Co. in either of two ways:

1. By selling to Mining Co. the "mining rights" to Blackacre, that is the right to enter Blackacre and mine the coal.

2. By selling to Mining Co. the coal-bearing part of the subsurface and selling the rest of Blackacre to Dora.

As buyer of Blackacre, Dora has no claim to minerals that George previously severed and sold. Dora will, however, be entitled to the mineral estate as part of Blackacre if she qualifies as a "bona fide purchaser for value" of Blackacre. Dora has that status if she *in good faith* gave *value* for Blackacre (bought it) *without notice* of Mining Co.'s claim to the mineral estate. Unless the contract for the sale of the mineral estate or the deed of conveyance was recorded in the appropriate public records before Dora bought Blackacre, or unless she had prior notice of the transaction from some other source, she takes Blackacre free from Mining Co's claim, if, of course, she otherwise qualifies as a bona fide purchaser for value. The rights of bona fide purchasers are discussed further in Chapter 9.

Crops and Timber. Growing crops, timber, minerals, buildings, and other things attached to the land have a potentially confusing status in the law. Some are classified as goods, and some as either goods or land, depending on the circumstances. Sales of *goods* and secured transactions having goods as the collateral are governed by UCC Articles 2 and 9, respectively. Sales of *land* and security interests in land are governed by rules of the common law, many of which differ from their UCC counterparts.

The classification of a thing as either goods or land helps answer questions that landowners, purchasers, and creditors routinely encounter. For example, what contracting formalities are required for an enforceable sale of minerals or growing crops—those of the UCC or those of the common law? What must lenders do to protect their security interests in land or in crops? Is the buyer of the land entitled to previously sold crops that have not yet been removed?

The law governing contracts for the sale of goods (UCC Article 2) differs in many respects from the common law rules governing sales of interests in land. Article 2 rules of contract formation, for example, especially those involving acceptance of offers, differ dramatically from their common law counterparts. And the statute of frauds, which requires a contract for the sale of an interest in *land* to be evidenced by a writing to be enforceable, applies to all such contracts, however small the monetary value of the land. In contrast, in most states the statute of frauds applicable to *goods* (UCC § 2-201) requires a writing only for sales contracts involving goods worth $500 or more.

The public records for real estate and UCC transactions also differ, in what they contain and in terminology. All documents affecting title to *land*—including deeds of conveyance, tax liens, mortgages, and contracts for the sale of land—are or should be "recorded" in the county office provided for real estate records (usually called the recorder's office). After a document is recorded, every member of the public is considered to be on notice of its contents.

A similar public notice system exists in all states for UCC *credit* transactions, usually called "secured transactions in personal property." A document creating a security interest in goods, such as mined coal being sold on credit, is called a **security agreement**. To receive maximum protection from rival creditors who might claim an interest in the coal when it comes into the debtor-buyer's possession, the seller-creditor must give notice of its secured status by "perfecting" the security interest. To do so where the collateral is to be possessed by the debtor, the seller-creditor prepares a **financing statement** briefly describing the collateral and "files" it in a county office provided for UCC filings, but located apart from the *recorder's* office.

Financing statements covering goods that either are or are to become *fixtures* must be filed in the *recorder's* office as part of the land records. This filing is called a **fixture filing**.

So, for the purpose of complying with the appropriate body of law, which things attached to the land are "goods" and which are "land"? Under UCC § 2-107(1), a contract calling for the *seller* to sever (remove) solid minerals, oil, gas, or a "structure" or its materials from the seller's land is a contract for the sale of *goods* and is governed by the UCC. By implication from that same UCC section, if the *buyer* is to do the severing, the contract is for the sale of an interest in *land* and common law rules apply.[5] Another UCC provision states that a contract for the sale apart from the land of certain things "growing on or attached to" the land is a contract for the sale of *goods*, without regard to whether the subject matter is to be severed by the buyer or by the seller.[6] The things are:

1. Growing crops.

2. Timber to be cut.

3. Other things "attached to realty and capable of severance without material harm thereto [but not including minerals or structures]."

"Other things" encompasses (a) natural vegetation, including trees not classifiable as "timber to be cut," and (b) things attached to realty and commonly referred to as "fixtures" but which are not "structures." So, if the owner of Blackacre agrees to sell the wild strawberries growing there, the walnut tree on top of the hill, or the water heater in the guest house, the contract is for "goods" regardless of who is to sever them from the realty, and UCC rules apply to their sale. In contrast, if the owner agrees to sell the guest house itself (a "structure") for the *buyer* to remove, the contract is for the sale of an interest in land to which the common law rules of contracting apply.

Suppose George sold the still-growing soybean and hay crops to Feed Store before selling Blackacre to Dora. Is Dora entitled to the crops? She might be if she lacks notice of the crop buyer's rights. A number of states require a buyer of growing crops, standing timber, or other removable goods still attached to the land to file in the *recorder's* office a document notifying any subsequent purchaser of the land that the filer has a contract for the goods. Filing the notice protects a buyer of growing crops from the claim of a subsequent purchaser of the realty who, without notice to the contrary, might reasonably believe that the crop was included in the sale of the realty.

Wildlife. A landowner does not own the birds, animals, and other wildlife found on the land, but has an exclusive right of capture and so can become owner. The right of capture is limited by laws requiring licenses and establishing seasons and bag limits for hunting, fishing, and trapping. The landowner can allow others to exercise the right of capture by permitting them to hunt or fish on the property.

Rights in Fixtures

Fixtures are chattels (goods) that become so attached to or otherwise associated with realty as to be regarded by law as realty themselves. Doors and window screens affixed to a house are examples. When the house is sold, the doors and screens, being fixtures, are part of the realty conveyed to the buyer and automatically become the buyer's property without need for the contracting parties to say so. In contrast, the seller's tables, chairs, and other household items, being personalty, remain the property of the seller.

If the owner of a fixture—a furnace, water heater, bath tub, or central air-conditioning unit—severs it from the realty intending a permanent removal, the fixture becomes personalty once again. If removed only temporarily, say for repair, the fixture remains realty.

Fixture law provides a basis for classifying chattels associated with land as either realty or personalty, and thus helps resolve a variety of legal problems. Among them:

- What items a buyer of a house is to receive as part of the realty.
- What items a real estate tenant may remove when the lease expires.
- The tax status of chattels in states where real property is taxed but personal property is not, or where both are taxed but at different rates.
- In divorce settlements granting realty to one spouse, which chattels are a part of the realty and which are not.
- In mortgage foreclosures, what items are part of the real estate to be sold to satisfy the mortgage debt.
- Under insurance policies covering damage to realty, which damaged chattels are covered and which are not.

What Things Are Fixtures? Tests for Deciding

No absolute rule of law says that a particular thing is or is not a fixture. Rather, courts called upon to decide the question apply legal guidelines or "tests" on a case-by-case basis. The major tests used in most states today are:

- The intent of the annexor (or of the parties to a subsequent transaction involving the chattel).
- The degree of annexation to the realty.
- The degree to which the chattel is adapted to the use of the realty.

- The relationship of the parties who claim the chattel. Bearing on the relationship of the parties are the nature of the annexor's interest in the realty and who owned the chattel before it was attached.

Intent of the Annexor or the Parties. The key factor in determining whether a thing is a fixture is the annexor's intention in attaching the chattel to realty, or the intention of people dealing with it later. George's installing the stationary gravel dredge on Blackacre, intending it to stay there until the gravel is exhausted or until the dredge wears out, suggests a "permanent" improvement, and fixture status. But George and Dora can by agreement decide whether the dredge is personalty or realty and thus whether it passes to Dora as buyer of the land. If they agreed that the dredge was *not* included as part of the land, as between George and Dora the dredge would be considered George's personalty even if a court would otherwise have ruled it a fixture.

The same is true where neither party was the annexor of the chattel. If Dora received the dredge from George as a fixture, she might in later years wish to sell the gravel pit or the whole of Blackacre, but to keep the dredge. She can do so by stating in the contract for the sale of the realty that the dredge is her personalty and not a fixture. Thus, the key intent can be that of the *parties to the immediate transaction*, and not that of some long-ago annexor. Indeed, contract forms used in the sale of real estate commonly contain a printed list of things that usually are fixtures and provide space for the seller to make exceptions to the list by adding or subtracting items.

A chattel can be subject to different classifications simultaneously. George and Dora agree that the dredge, though affixed to the land, is personalty so that George can remove it upon sale of Blackacre. As long as the dredge remains attached to the land, however, tax authorities might classify it as a fixture and tax it as realty despite the parties' having characterized it as personalty.

In many disputes over chattels located on land, the parties involved have said nothing about fixture status. In the absence of an expression of intention, the courts must *infer* the annexor's or the parties' *probable* intent. To do so, the courts consider degree of annexation, degree of adaptation, and the relationship of the parties. In weighing these interrelated factors, the courts apply a sliding scale. For example, if a chattel is very highly adapted to the use of the realty, and thus probably was meant to be a permanent addition, a relatively low degree of attachment (or none) may suffice for the chattel to be a fixture. Conversely, a high degree of attachment might be required for fixture status where the use of the realty does not so clearly depend on the presence of the chattel.

Degree of Annexation to Realty. A number of older cases required that a chattel be physically attached ("annexed" or "affixed") to the land or a structure on the land to be considered a fixture. The great majority of states no longer make annexation an absolute requirement, though it remains an important consideration. In the absence of indicators to the contrary, the more firmly a chattel is attached to the realty, the more likely that fixture status was intended. Accordingly, fences, irrigation systems, and other things firmly imbedded in the soil, and things firmly attached to a preexisting fixture such as a large irrigation pump installed in a concrete well house, are likely to be held fixtures.

Annexation can be either actual or constructive. *Actual* annexation involves physical attachment by such processes as imbedding in concrete or soil, nailing, bolting, or integrating the thing into plumbing, heating, or electrical systems.

In rare instances, annexation is said to be *constructive*—presumed by law to exist without any physical attachment at all *if* the chattel is so highly adapted to the use of the realty that reasonable people would consider it part of the realty despite lack of physical attachment. Door keys, storm doors and windows temporarily detached and stored for the summer, remote control units for electric garage door openers, and garage doors temporarily removed for repair are examples.

Where a chattel is extremely heavy and highly adapted to the use of the land, a few courts have held that gravity alone is sufficient for annexation. A Delaware court, for example, held that a large water storage tank resting unannexed on a concrete foundation as part of the Wilmington water system was a fixture and thus was subject to a real estate tax. In a similar tax ruling, a California court held that two self-propelled cargo container cranes weighing 750 tons each were fixtures, even though they had wheels and rolled back and forth on marine terminal railbeds.

Constructive annexation plays a role in large-scale industrial and commercial financing. Developed in Pennsylvania and followed in other states, the **assembled industrial plant doctrine** confers fixture status on machinery and equipment without actual annexation if it is "placed in an industrial establishment for permanent use, and [is] indispensable in carrying on the specific business."[7] Originally applicable only to manufacturing firms, the doctrine was later extended to other businesses. By conferring fixture (realty) status on essential but unannexed equipment, the doctrine protects real estate mortgagees (creditors claiming the debtor's realty as collateral) from the claims of other creditors who would be entitled to the debtor's personality but not the realty.

Degree of Adaptation to Use of the Realty. The more that a chattel is adapted (suited) to the use being made of the realty, the more likely that the annexor intended it to be a fixture. But just what does "adaptation to use" mean?

In a 1939 case, the Ohio Supreme Court applied guidelines commonly used today.[8] The chattel was a new furnace purchased on credit from Holland Furnace Co., and only slightly attached to the buyer's house by means of metallic sleeves or sections of pipe slipped over the ends of air ducts. The homeowner agreed that the furnace would remain the seller's personal property until paid for. Then the homeowner defaulted in his payments on both the furnace and the house. The realty lender (Trumball Savings & Loan) brought action to foreclose its mortgage (force the sale of the house). Trumball had taken its mortgage before the old furnace was replaced, and bought the house at the foreclosure sale without notice of Holland's claim to the new furnace. After the sale, Holland demanded the furnace or its value from Trumball. Trumball refused the demand and claimed the furnace as part of the realty. Holland brought suit.

Affirming a lower court decision for Trumball, the Ohio Supreme Court held that although only slightly attached, the furnace was sufficiently adapted to the use of the realty to be a fixture to which Trumball was entitled as bona fide purchaser of the realty. The furnace was "indispensable for the comfortable enjoyment of a dwellinghouse in this climate," so was "an appropriate application," that is, it was necessary or helpful to the use of the realty. When installed, the furnace became "an integral and necessary part of the whole premises" that ordinarily "would not be taken out or dismantled until it was worn out by use." Thus, it probably was intended to be used in the house permanently or indefinitely. The contribution of the furnace to the permanent use and enjoyment of the house, the "lack of utility of the premises if it were severed, and the necessity of replacing it with another or similar kind if it were removed" all indicated to the court a high degree of adaptation to the use of the realty.

These guidelines can be applied to the stationary dredge on Blackacre. The dredge, which is lengthened as the gravel pit widens, is essential for extracting gravel in commercial quantities. Being custom-made for the pit, it is an integral and necessary part of the realty; removing it would reduce the utility of the gravel pit. And, because the dredge is not likely to be removed until worn out or until the gravel is exhausted, it has the permanence characteristic of fixture status. Given the dredge's bulk, weight, and high degree of adaptation, it is likely a fixture even if it rests on the land without actual attachment. In contrast, things not obviously necessary to the use of a particular piece of land, such as a mobile home in a forest area, would be considered personality unless so firmly affixed to the land that permanent installation as a fixture was likely intended.

Relationship of the Parties. To infer probable intent about fixture status, the courts give considerable weight to the relationship of the parties claiming the chattel. Relevant here are (1) the kind of interest in the realty held by the person who placed the item on it, and (2) who owned the chattel before it was attached. Two common relationships are illustrative.

Buyer and seller of realty: Lorna, owner of an apartment building, buys a bookcase and bolts it to a wall of an apartment that she later rents to Rita. As owner of both the realty and the chattel she attached, Lorna likely intended the bookcase as a permanent improvement—a fixture— that would enhance the value of her realty as rental property. If she sells the apartment building to Barbara, Barbara will be entitled to the bookcase (absent a contrary agreement), since it appeared to be a part of the realty and she likely included its value in the price she paid for the building. As between buyers and sellers of realty, then, the buyer ordinarily is entitled to chattels installed by the seller.

Landlord and tenant: In contrast, suppose that Rita, the tenant, bought the bookcase and installed it in her apartment without consulting Lorna. As tenant, Rita probably did not intend to enrich Lorna with property that Rita paid for, so the bookcase remains Rita's personal property. As between landlords and tenants, tenants generally may remove chattels they installed unless removal would cause material injury to the realty or the chattel.

Case 2.1 deals with how to tax the property of a cable TV distribution system.

Case 2.1

T-V Transmission, Inc. v. County Bd. of Equalization

338 N.W.2d 752 (Neb. 1983)

T-V Transmission, Inc., furnishes cable television service to subscribers in Pawnee County. An antenna, or headend, is installed outside the reception area of a community. Television signals are then sent through a channel processor, fed into a single cable, and brought into the community by attaching the cable to existing utility poles so that the cables run by every house in town. The television signal itself is then brought into each house by means of an aerial drop. An aerial drop is a cable with a support wire running from the utility pole to the house and attached to the house by means of a house hook. The cable then runs through a grounding block attached to a cold water pipe.

The cable inside the house runs from the grounding block, through the walls of the house, to a wall plate outlet inside and then is attached to the television set. These interior cables may be strung through an existing house or, upon request of the homeowner, may be built into the walls at the time of initial construction.

Defendant County Board of Equalization assessed the "station connects," or aerial housedrops, beginning at the utility pole and including the interior wiring, as personal property belonging to plaintiff T-V Transmission, Inc., rather than as fixtures attached to the real estate of each individual homeowner subscriber. The District Court affirmed the Board's assessment, and plaintiff appealed.

HASTINGS, J.

. . . Cable service to a particular house is installed and furnished only at the specific request of each individual subscriber. If the subscriber requests that the service be discontinued, a terminator is placed on the aerial drop at the utility pole end, but this lead-in drop and the interior cables are not removed. The former subscriber, if he so desires, may use the materials as a part of his own television antenna system.

The plaintiff has no agreement with its subscribers which would prevent the subscribers' use of these materials, and the plaintiff makes no claim on these cables nor seeks to recover or retrieve them when there has been a disconnection of the service. The plaintiff has no easement across the yards of subscribers to install or remove the cables, and . . . according to the plaintiff's witness, the . . . housedrops, have very little salvage value and are really abandoned by the company. The hope of the plaintiff is, of course, that when a different person occupies that house he will request a reconnection of the service.

. . .

The basic question involved in this appeal [is] Are the "station connects," or aerial drops, together with the [interior] cables, personal property which remain in the ownership of the plaintiff, or are they fixtures . . . which become a part of the real estate? . . . "'In determining this question, the following tests . . . have received general approval, viz.: 1st. Actual annexation to the realty . . . or something appurtenant thereto. 2d. Appropriation to the use or purpose of that part of the realty with which it is connected. 3d. The intention of the party making the annexation to make the article a permanent accession to the freehold. This intention [is] inferred from the nature of the articles affixed, the relation and situation of the party making the annexation, the structure and mode of annexation, and the purpose or use for which the annexation has been made. . . . The third test, namely that of "intention," appears by the clear weight of modern authority to be the controlling consideration.'" [Citation omitted.]

Research discloses but three reported decisions similar in nature to the instant case, all of which recognized the three-prong test of [fixture status]. [In the latter two decisions,] administrative agencies ruled that the entire system, from the utility pole to the television set, was a fixture. In the case decided by the California court, both parties stipulated that the cable from the utility pole to the house was to be treated as personal property belonging to the television company, but the court ruled that the remainder of the system, contrary to the contention of the taxing authority, became a fixture and was a part of the real estate.

We believe that there is little doubt that the entire system, from the utility pole inward, was annexed to the realty and was appropriated solely for the use of the occupants of that realty.

As to the . . . intention of the party making the annexation, we have both the testimony and the practice of the plaintiff that it had no right or intention of removing the property, and in fact had not done so, but had abandoned, in favor of the homeowner, all claim to the property that it might otherwise have had.

The judgment of the District Court is reversed and the cause remanded with directions to enter a judgment in conformity with this opinion.

QUESTIONS ABOUT CASE 2.1

1. What portion of the cable transmission system did the Nebraska court decide was a fixture? What is the tax consequence of this decision?

2. The California case cited in Case 2.1 held that the fixture portion of the cable system involved there was smaller than the fixture portion in Case 2.1. What accounts for the difference? In future Nebraska cases, could the fixture portion be smaller?

Who Is Entitled to a Fixture? More on Tenants' Rights

The fact that a chattel is annexed to realty does not necessarily mean that the owner of the land is entitled to it. By law, the chattels that tenants annex to rented realty in furtherance of their own purposes remain personalty unless otherwise agreed.

Traditional Common Law Rule and Trade Fixture Exception. Under the early common law of fixtures, a landowner was entitled to any chattels affixed to the realty by tenants, absent a contrary agreement. Unlike today's judges, the judges then looked almost exclusively to annexation and seldom tried to infer presumed intent. If the thing was annexed, in their view it was a fixture (realty).

But the equipment installed by a merchant-tenant for use in the tenant's business presented the courts with a problem. As the courts well knew, the probable intention of the tenant was to *remove* the equipment when the lease expired and not to leave it for the landlord. Yet, when annexed to the realty, these chattels met the common law test for fixture status. To resolve the problem, the courts did what courts often still do. They carved out an exception to the general rule. They gave the name **trade fixtures** to chattels that a tenant affixed to the realty for use in the tenant's trade, and classified them as the tenant's *personalty*, thus making them removable by the tenant upon termination of the lease unless otherwise agreed. The affixed chattels of residential tenants, however, continued to be viewed as ordinary fixtures (realty). Today, the courts of many states continue to recognize the common law concept of "trade fixture," and to hold that trade fixtures are personalty belonging to the commercial tenant. Moreover, many statutes use "trade fixture" in its original common law sense, especially in the area of taxation, to mean a commercial tenant's personalty.

Modern Common Law Rule and Statutes. In its treatment of residential tenants, the early common law of fixtures has seemed harsh and unreasonable. So under the modern common law, any tenant who attaches chattels to the real estate for *trade, agricultural, domestic, or ornamental* purposes is presumed not to intend permanent annexation, and can remove the personalty *if* removal can be effected without substantial injury to the realty or the fixture. In several states, statutes provide essentially the same thing. Thus, under modern law we can divide fixtures into two classes: *tenant's fixtures*, which remain the tenant's *personalty* because installed by the tenant for his or her trade, agricultural, domestic, or ornamental purposes; and *ordinary* fixtures, which are *realty* regardless of who installed them, because they generally benefit the realty and do not primarily serve a special purpose of the tenant's.

Time for Removal, Duty to Pay. Under the general rule, a tenant entitled to remove a fixture must do so before the lease expires, because entering the premises afterward without permission is a trespass. Where the tenant waits too long, the chattel by law becomes the property of the landlord. This rule applies especially to leases for a fixed term and is subject to numerous exceptions—so many, in fact, and in so many states, that the general rule seems in the process of being displaced by the more lenient minority rule. Under the minority rule, firmly in place in Ohio and recognized in varying degrees in several other states, the tenant has a reasonable time after the lease expires to remove the fixture.

Unless otherwise agreed, a landlord has no duty to pay for fixtures that the tenant annexed but is not entitled to remove. A tenant has no right to remove the following:

- An ordinary fixture installed by the tenant, such as a replacement electrical outlet. It belongs to the landowner.

BOX 2–3 YOU BE THE JUDGE

Timothy rents a house from Lorna, for a term of three years. Without asking Lorna's permission or otherwise consulting her, Timothy makes the following improvements. Upon expiration of the lease, both Timothy and Lorna claim the improvements. Who is entitled to them?

1. Timothy installs a floor-to-ceiling bookcase covering one wall in an extra bedroom used for an office. Made of intricately carved black walnut, the bookcase was installed in sections and is attached to the wall with screws and hooks.

2. In a major weight-bearing wall between the living room and the family room, Timothy installs floor-to-ceiling display shelves so that his collection of Tiffany art glass can be viewed from either room. The heavy vertical beams and the broad shelves are made of Honduras mahogany.

3. Timothy repairs the fireplace in the den by replacing bricks and mortar, and adds a built-in marble mantelpiece held in place by a special masonry cement so strong that the mantelpiece is virtually welded to the bricks under it.

- A tenant's fixture (e.g., trade fixture) whose removal would result in material, irreparable damage to the chattel or the realty.

- A tenant's fixture left on the premises beyond the time permitted by law for removal.

Tenants who damage the realty when removing their fixtures have a duty to make or to pay for repairs.

● Protection from Trespass

The law protects owners, tenants, and other occupiers of land from several types of interference by outsiders. Occurring most frequently are trespass, nuisance, and impairing the support of adjacent properties. Trespass can be committed by anyone and is discussed here. The wrongs of nuisance and impairment of support ordinarily are committed by neighboring landowners, so are discussed in the next section, entitled Landowners' Liabilities.

Nature of Trespass

In general, trespass is an unlawful physical interference with the property, person, or rights of another. The essence of trespass to *land* is a wrongful *entry*, forbidden because it interferes with the occupier's right of exclusive possession.

Under trespass law as widely enforced today,[9] trespass to land results from any of the following:

1. A person intentionally enters upon the surface, subsurface, or airspace of another's realty, or intentionally causes an object or a third person to enter, and does so without legal privilege or the owner's consent.

2. A person does the same things negligently, and therefore unintentionally. **Negligence** is the thoughtless or inadvertent failure to use reasonable care to avoid foreseeable harm to others to whom the person owes a duty of care.

3. A person engages in an ultrahazardous (abnormally hazardous) activity that causes something to harm the realty of another, even though the activity was done carefully and the resulting entry was unintentional. Ultrahazardous activity results in **strict** or **absolute liability** (liability "without fault"), imposed to hold persons engaging in abnormally dangerous activities responsible for losses despite the absence of negligence or intentional misconduct.

4. A person fails to remove from the land a thing he or she has a duty to remove.

5. A person fails to leave the land when permission or privilege to be there has ended.

An unconsented-to entry onto another's land is not a trespass if it is *privileged*. A person who has a *privilege* is exempted by law from liability for doing the otherwise forbidden act. In the law of trespass, many privileges exist. Some examples:

- Where a public highway is blocked, one is privileged to go onto private land to get around the blockage if there is no alternative route around it.

- Departing tenants may, within the time allowed by law, reenter the realty to retrieve their possessions.

- Public officials such as police officers, fire inspectors, and process servers may enter another's land to carry out their lawful duties.

- A landowner who is the victim of a private nuisance may, upon giving any required notice, enter the wrongdoing neighbor's land to abate (stop) the nuisance.

- In an emergency, a person whose life, safety, or property is seriously threatened may enter another's land to avoid the danger.

The emergency privilege may extend to an entry for safeguarding the lives and property of others. And in a number of situations, the owner of chattels may retrieve them from another's

BOX 2–4 APPLY YOUR KNOWLEDGE

Which of the following are trespasses?

1. You absent-mindedly walk into your neighbor's house, thinking it is your own.

2. You are cleaning leaves off your roof. Lightning strikes your house, causing you to fall into your neighbor's yard.

3. A neighbor two doors away shoots an arrow into your yard.

4. Your child accidentally kicks a soccer ball into your neighbor's yard.

5. You ask for and are granted permission to jog on El Largo Ranch. A week later the manager puts up "No Trespassing" signs. Despite the signs, you continue jogging on El Largo as usual.

6. You hire Drillers, Inc., to drill for oil on your property. Then, 300 feet below the surface, the drilling accidentally slants into your neighbor's land.

7. Waving a gun, but without entering your yard, Pinkerton chases Jones into your yard where Jones trips on a brick and breaks your birdbath.

8. Your neighbor's house is on fire. No one is at home. You break down the front door to rescue the cat and the classic antique highboy.

land—for example, where the chattels have been cast there by a tornado, flood, or other force of nature, or where the goods have come upon the land because of the landowner's wrongful conduct such as theft. If the chattel is on the land because of the chattel-owner's fault, however, he or she has no privilege of entry. Moreover, one who has such a privilege must exercise it only for the purpose giving rise to it. Exceeding the time or geographic limits of one's privilege is a trespass.

Remedies for Trespass

In law, a **remedy** is a means for compensating or otherwise giving redress to victims of wrongdoing. Remedies are civil or criminal. *Civil* remedies such as damages compensating a person for loss caused by another are available in civil courts. Newton drives negligently and injures Assad. Assad may sue Newton in civil court for damages compensating him for his injuries. *Criminal* remedies, such as fines or imprisonment, are available to the state (the plaintiff in criminal prosecutions) to redress injury to the rights of the public. Newton violates a state statute making reckless driving a crime. Upon conviction, Newton faces a fine, imprisonment, or other sanctions imposed by the state on behalf of the public.

Remedies for Criminal Trespass. Criminal trespass is limited to the types of willful or malicious trespasses defined in the criminal statutes as violations. Ordinarily, criminal trespass is a **misdemeanor**, a crime ranked lower than a felony and punishable by a fine or imprisonment for up to a year in a county jail or other place not constituting a penitentiary, which is reserved for convicted felons. If no statute makes a trespass criminal, it is a civil violation only.

The essence of criminal trespass is entering or remaining on another's property *knowing* that the act is unauthorized or unprivileged. Some state statutes list as many as 40 specific trespasses as criminal violations. Among the states, the more common forms of criminal trespass include:

- Willfully entering or remaining on another's land in defiance of an order by owner, the owner's agent, or the person in rightful possession (such as a tenant) not to do so.
- Willfully entering property that is posted "No trespassing."
- Willfully entering fenced or enclosed property of another.
- Without permission, remaining on another's property, knowing one's business there is finished.

BOX 2–5 APPLY YOUR KNOWLEDGE

Which of the following are criminal trespasses?

1. A hunter enters land posted "No trespassing" after trying but failing to find the owner at home.
2. A hunter enters land with permission, cuts fence to let his dog through, and continues to hunt after owner shouts to him, "Get off my property, you wretched lout!"
3. Because the residential lots in your neighborhood have no alleyways between them, school children climb your fence and cross your yard to get to the next street.
4. Disregarding your sign saying "No meter readers from hours of 6:00 A.M. to 6:00 P.M.," meter reader enters your property at 10:00 A.M. to read your meter.
5. Meter reader reads your meter and, seeing that no one is at home, takes a quick dip in your swimming pool.

Remedies for Civil Trespass. Much trespass is solely a civil violation, because no statute makes it a crime. However, a criminal trespass (one punishable by the state) is simultaneously a civil trespass entitling the offended owner, tenant, or other occupier to civil remedies in a private lawsuit separate from the criminal prosecution. The most common civil remedies for trespass are ordinary damages, restitution, and injunctive relief.

Ordinary **damages**, the remedy generally preferred by the courts, is an amount of money awarded to compensate the landowner for losses caused by the trespass. If necessary, a judgment for damages is enforced in a postjudgment process called **execution**, in which the clerk of court issues a writ (document) ordering the sheriff or other proper official to seize and sell the defendant's property in satisfaction of the judgment. The variety of losses or harms resulting from trespass is illustrated in the following numbered paragraphs.

The remedy of **restitution** requires the restoration of something wrongfully obtained, in such a way as to prevent the unjust enrichment of the wrongdoer. Tom, a trespasser, removes timber from Blackacre and at his sawmill converts it into lumber. Though the lumber is far more valuable than the unprocessed logs, Dora, the owner of Blackacre is entitled to the lumber or its value. Tom would be unjustly enriched by his trespass and theft if he were allowed simply to pay Dora for the logs while keeping the lumber or the profits from it.

An **injunction** is a court order requiring a defendant wrongdoer either to do something (remove debris from another's land) or to refrain from doing something (cease dumping debris on another's land). Unlike a judgment for damages, which is enforceable only against the defendant's *property*, an injunction is enforceable *personally* against the defendant. A defendant who willfully disobeys an injunction is in contempt of court and may be fined or jailed until he or she complies with the court's order. Whether to grant an injunction is discretionary with the court, which will grant or withhold it as fairness dictates. In deciding the matter, the courts are said to "balance the equities" or "balance the hardships" of the situation.

Like other equitable remedies (those granted by a *court of equity* to supplement or replace the remedy "at law"), the injunction ordinarily is available only when the remedy at law (money damages) is inadequate. Daily, Tina, a trespasser, rides her horse through Roberto's vineyard Montclair. Though she does only slight damage to the vines each day, her presence there worries Roberto and interferes with his right to exclusive possession and control of Montclair. Roberto's remedy at law is inadequate because no objective basis exists for determining the amount of money needed to compensate him for the concern and inconvenience that Tina's daily visits may cause. Moreover, for Roberto to collect the small amount of money damages that he can prove, he would have to file multiple lawsuits, and they might not deter Tina from trespassing. Because money damages would not be adequate to assure Roberto of the exclusive possession and control of Montclair, a court will enjoin Tina from further trespassing and in the same lawsuit will award damages to compensate Roberto for Tina's past trespasses.

The availability of civil remedies for trespass depends on the situation:

1. *Intentional trespass, no harm caused.* Where no harm results, an intentional trespasser nevertheless is liable for **nominal damages**, a token amount, usually $1. By awarding nominal damages to the landowner, a court recognizes officially that trespass has occurred, thus enabling the landowner to interrupt the continuous possession that a trespasser must show for acquiring ownership of the land by **adverse possession**. How and why a trespasser may acquire ownership by adverse possession is discussed in Chapter 6.

2. *Intentional trespass, harm caused.* An intentional trespasser who causes harm is liable to the landowner for compensatory damages, an amount sufficient to pay for actual harm caused. In addition, if the trespassory conduct is outrageous, the trespasser may be liable for punitive damages as well. **Punitive damages** are those imposed by a court to punish the wrongdoer for malicious, wanton, or wicked conduct, or to deter future misconduct by the wrongdoer and others.

Compensatory (ordinary) damages cover many harms or elements of damage caused by the trespass. Among them are:

- Physical damage to the land and to chattels on it.

- Loss of income if the rightful possessor's business is impaired or stopped by the trespass.

- Personal injuries to owners, family members, guests, invitees, and others with a right to be there.

- Mental distress. Usually courts will not award damages for mental or emotional distress resulting from destruction of property. But a trespasser who engages in malicious, wanton, or outrageous destruction may be liable for punitive damages. And courts tend to allow emotional distress damages for intentional injury to property of largely sentimental value, such as pets, family photographs, or the ancestral oak tree planted in the backyard by great-great-grandmother.

3. *Trespass resulting from negligence or ultrahazardous activity.* Where trespass results from negligence or from a carefully conducted ultrahazardous activity, the trespasser, being "innocent" in the sense of lacking evil intent, has no liability if the landowner suffered no harm—not even for nominal damages. But the innocent trespasser *is* liable for whatever harm the trespass caused.

4. *Continuing and permanent trespasses.* For a single instance of trespass, as where Edna drives through Felicia's melon field and damages the crop, the victim has only the amount of time specified in the state's **statute of limitations** within which to bring suit—usually two or three years from the time the trespass occurred. But suppose that Edgar builds an apartment complex and dumps the construction debris onto Alma's land. Edgar has committed a **continuing trespass**, so-called because the trespass continues and constitutes a new offense each day as long as the debris remains on the land. Each day that the trespass continues, the limitations period starts over, in effect giving the victim an unlimited amount of time to bring suit.

Alma has a choice of remedies:

- She can pay to have the debris removed and have damages covering the cost of removal and any harm caused by the debris, such as pollution of her well or loss of the use of the land affected by the debris.

- She can have an injunction requiring Edgar to remove the debris. In addition, she is entitled to damages for harm the debris caused.

- She can leave the debris there and sue for *present and prospective* damages compensating her for past and future harms. By doing so, she consents to the continuance of the trespass.

Another example of a continuing trespass is a building that overhangs a neighbor's land without touching the surface. But what if the building encroaches on the *surface* of the neighbor's land? The courts differ in their treatment of surface encroachments by buildings. Some courts

BOX 2–6 YOU BE THE JUDGE

Your neighbor, "Mean Johnnie," reaches through your fence and sets your cat Freddie afire as you watch. Frightened and injured, Freddie dashes wildly about the yard, scratching those he scrambles over, and setting fires in piles of recently raked dry leaves. Later you sue Johnnie for trespass. Will you win? If so, to what damages might you be entitled?

classify them as continuing trespasses so that the statute of limitations period begins anew each day. Most courts, however, treat them as permanent trespasses.

A **permanent trespass** is one in which the invader apparently intends to remain on the land, as where the trespasser builds a house, office building, or other permanent structure there. A permanent trespass is considered a single violation, so that the statute of limitations begins to run when the trespass occurs. The victim thus has only a fixed time within which to bring suit.

5. *Balancing of hardships test.* Trespasses, whether continuing or permanent, often take the form of relatively small encroachments. For example, on the outskirts of town, Josephus builds a five-story hotel that extends a few inches onto the surface of neighbor Ned's grazing land. Ned seeks an injunction ordering Josephus to remove the encroaching parts of the hotel from Ned's land. In deciding whether to grant the injunction, most courts would employ the "balancing of equities" or "balancing of hardships" test. Under this test, and in the exercise of its equitable discretion, a court may deny the injunction if the cost of removal or other hardship to Josephus greatly outweighs the harm to Ned. If the encroachment results from excusable mistake, as where Josephus had no reason to know that the boundaries shown on relevant maps are inaccurate, and if the value of the land occupied is low while the cost of removal or hardship to Josephus is great, the court will deny the injunction and leave Ned with his remedy at law, money damages. In contrast, if Josephus's trespass is *willful*, the court will grant the injunction, even if the hardship to Josephus is great and the harm to Ned is small. Josephus's trespass would be willful where, having tried but failed to purchase the strip of land from Ned, Josephus encroached anyway, hoping the court would accept his "hardship" allegation and force Ned to accept market-value damages for the strip of land.

If the balancing of equities favors granting Ned an injunction for the trespass, he is entitled also to any past damages that have accumulated. In lieu of the injunction, however, Ned might elect to sue for past and prospective damages. By doing so, he consents to the trespass. If the equities are against granting him an injunction, he is entitled only to past and prospective damages.

6. *Mistaken improvers.* Sometimes, though, the encroachment is far from minor. By mistake, Robroy builds his vacation cabin on Joan's mountain lot, which lies next door to his. Robroy is a **mistaken improver** and a trespasser. May he remove the cabin (or have payment for it), or is Joan entitled to keep it free of charge? Under the older common law rule, Joan would acquire ownership of the cabin and would have no duty to pay for it, regardless of Robroy's good faith, unless she "made the mistake of suing in equity, in which case [she would be] required to 'do equity' by paying . . . the value of the improvements."[10] Today the courts are more sympathetic to truly mistaken improvers acting in good faith, and, to prevent the unjust enrichment of landowners, are likely to require payment for the improvements or to grant the trespasser some other remedy.

Consistent with this newer judicial approach are the **betterment statutes** existing in many states. Such statutes, also called *occupying claimant, mistaken improver,* or *good faith improver statutes,* accommodate the interests of good faith improvers and burdened landowners in a variety of ways. Among them:

1. Where the landowner seeks damages, allowing the improver to set off against the landowner's damages any value added to the land by the improvement.

2. Or, where the landowner seeks only to stop the trespass, allowing the improver to remove the improvement but requiring repair of any damage caused by its installation or removal.

3. Or, if circumstances warrant, requiring the landowner to sell the occupied land to the improver at a price fair to both. This forced sale, or "private eminent domain" remedy,

might be appropriate where an improvement such as a ditch is not easily removable, is greatly beneficial to the improver, and does not seriously interfere with the landowner's uses.

Lack of good faith would, of course, disqualify the improver for a remedy. If Robroy knows he is building on the wrong land, he lacks good faith. An improver who does not actually know, but should know, is negligent and lacks good faith unless the degree of negligence is so slight as to be excusable.

Landowners' Liabilities

Thus far, the emphasis has been on a landowner's *rights*. But upon receiving rights in land, owners and occupiers acquire corresponding *duties* that the law imposes on them for the protection of passersby, neighbors, and persons entering the land. Violation of a duty results in *liability* for any harm caused by the violation.

Liability for Unreasonable Use of Property

Possessors of land can be liable to others on the basis of negligence or strict liability, or for intentional misconduct. Wilbert saws a large limb from a tree in his front yard, not noticing pedestrians approaching on the nearby sidewalk. If the limb strikes them, Wilbert likely is liable in negligence for their injuries, because he has a duty to foresee the danger and to exercise reasonable care in conducting activities on his land. Frances uses dynamite to break up a concrete wall on the perimeter of her shopping mall. Because she is engaging in an ultra-hazardous activity, she will be strictly liable to passersby and neighboring landowners for damage resulting from the blasting, despite her great care in using the dynamite. To break up a legal picket line outside the entrance to his bakery, Elvin throws rocks at the picketers, injuring several. Elvin has criminal and civil liability for the consequences of his intentional misconduct.

Two types of unreasonable land use are especially prominent in the law of real estate because they affect the rights of neighboring landowners: creating or maintaining a *nuisance* on one's land, and excavating in such a way as to *impair the support of adjacent or overlying properties.*

Nuisance

Nuisance is the use of one's land in such a way as to interfere unreasonably with someone else's use and enjoyment of his or her own land. Usually, the offensive action that constitutes a nuisance does not involve entry or invasion of the victim's land, though some nuisances such as smoke and dust *do* physically invade. Still, the invasion, if any, is somewhat different from the "entry" that is the essence of trespass.

Although a few courts have held that the entry of dust constitutes a trespass (and thus subjects the offending landowner to at least nominal damages for interference with the victim's right of exclusive possession), the great majority of courts hold that dust can constitute only a nuisance and not a trespass. For example, the court in *Adams v. Cleveland-Cliffs Iron Co.*, 602 N.W.2d 215 (Mich. App. 1999) commented as follows:

> *We agree with those authorities that have recognized, for practical purposes, that dust, along with other forms of airborne particulate, does not normally present itself as a significant physical*

intrusion. . . . Dust particles do not normally occupy the land on which they settle in any meaningful sense; instead they simply become a part of the ambient circumstances of that space. . . . We . . . hold that dust [though literally tangible] must generally be considered intangible and thus not actionable in trespass.

The court emphasized that where the possessor of land is menaced by noise, vibrations, or ambient dust, smoke, soot, or fumes, the possessory interest implicated is that of use and enjoyment, not exclusion, and the vehicle through which the possessor normally should seek a remedy is the doctrine of nuisance. Moreover, to prevail in nuisance, the possessor must prove significant harm resulting from the defendant's unreasonable interference with the possessor's use or enjoyment of the property. Thus, nominal damages will not be awarded in a nuisance suit.

Among the conditions likely to constitute nuisances are prolonged heavy smoke; offensive odors; excessive noise, light, or vibrations; the obstruction of rights-of-way; stored explosives; inflammable buildings or materials; keeping a vicious dog; and a host of other dangerous, annoying, indecent, or offensive acts or conditions—even repeated harassing telephone calls.[11] Such conditions deprive victims of comfort and convenience in the use of their land and are nuisances if the deprivation is unreasonable.

The law of nuisance protects anyone who has a *property right* that may be interfered with by the offender's unreasonable conduct. The plaintiff in a nuisance suit could be, for example, a fee simple owner, the owner of a life estate, a tenant, the holder of an easement, a mortgagor still in possession after foreclosure, or an adverse possessor without title (i.e., a trespasser in possession of someone else's land).[12]

Nature and Types of Nuisance. The legal test for a nuisance is whether the annoyance would offend a person of ordinary sensitivity. A minor annoyance such as a neighbor's occasionally barking dog is not a nuisance, but a dog that incessantly howls at night might be. To be a nuisance, the condition has to be truly annoying to normal people. Nuisance occurs, however, without regard to whether the wrongful condition or conduct was negligent or careful, intended or unintended, malicious or not malicious. A victim of nuisance may take action to **abate** (stop) it, but the specific abatement action that is available by law depends on whether the nuisance is *private*, *public*, or *mixed*.

A **private nuisance** is a tort committed against an individual (or a few persons), entitling the victim to bring a civil suit for abatement, or for damages, or for both. In addition to abatement provided by law, the victim may use self-help, including the use of reasonable force, to abate a nuisance. For example, Gloria may enter a neighbor's land to prop up, or even tear down, a dangerously leaning building that threatens to tumble onto her land if she can do so without a breach of the peace, has given the landowner any prior notice required by law, and is otherwise acting reasonably. She will not be liable for harming the offending property if the damage is necessary to abate the nuisance. She will, however, be liable for any excessive damage she causes and for any excessive force she uses.

A **public nuisance** is a condition that interferes with the comfort or convenience of the public by adversely affecting public safety, health, or morals. To be a public nuisance, the condition must affect a substantial number of people, and must affect all or most in approximately the same way. For example, Power Company builds a coal-burning generator that covers the town with thick black smoke, causing general discomfort for a substantial portion of the population, with individuals suffering various combinations of breathing difficulties, allergic reactions, and eye irritation. A public nuisance is both a civil and a criminal wrong, usually a misdemeanor.

Victims of a purely public nuisance cannot directly abate it. To have it abated, they must act through a county or city attorney or some other public official given the responsibility for abatement actions. This official has discretion to bring an abatement action or to withhold it, depending on whether action seems warranted. Thus, alleged offenders are protected against frivolous abatement suits. However, to protect against the official's unwarranted withholding of abatement action, the law usually permits citizens to seek a court order, called a "writ of mandate" or "writ of mandamus," directing the official to bring the action.

A *mixed nuisance* has characteristics of both a public and a private nuisance. An industrial plant may emit noxious fumes and smoke that adversely affect a substantial portion of a town's population in approximately the same way, by causing coughs, skin rashes, or eye inflammation. But a few individuals forced to park near the smokestack may suffer different or additional harm—loss caused by acid droplets falling on their cars and ruining the paint. The plant has created a public nuisance as to the general population and a private one as to the car owners. For the additional, special harm, the car owners are entitled to the remedies available for private nuisance.

Nuisance Per Se and Nuisance in Fact. A **nuisance per se** ("in itself") is a condition defined as a nuisance by a statute or an ordinance. Examples include a statute providing that a house of prostitution is a nuisance, and a statute declaring that a "spite fence" (one erected in a manner calculated merely to annoy a neighbor) is a nuisance. If neighbor Lenny proves that the forbidden act occurred, he is entitled to a remedy without proof that his use or enjoyment was unreasonably impaired. In nuisance per se, interference and its unreasonableness are conclusively presumed.

In contrast, a **nuisance in fact** is one not defined by statute. To prevail, plaintiff Marsha must prove not only the occurrence of the act, but also that it resulted in an unreasonable interference with her use or enjoyment of her land. Marsha's neighbor Ned regularly burns tires in his backyard, filling her house with smoke and the smell of burning rubber; Ned's dogs bark incessantly; a sorority and a fraternity across the street have frequent noisy parties. If no statute prohibits these activities, they are nuisances nevertheless if Marsha proves that the events occurred and that they unreasonably impaired the use and enjoyment of her property.

Continuing and Permanent Nuisance. A **continuing nuisance** is one in which the offensive use is uninterrupted or recurs with sufficient frequency to be considered a continuous offending use of the neighboring land. Each day that the nuisance continues, or each time that it recurs, a new wrong is committed, so that the statute of limitations period is renewed daily. The victim of a continuing nuisance has the usual remedies of abatement and damages. Orville's 15 olive trees hang over Rosita's fence and intrude 12 feet into her yard, dropping large quantities of messy fruit onto her land and inhibiting the growth of her flowers and shrubs. The trees constitute a nuisance for which Rosita can have an abatement action and damages. Or she may, in the exercise of self-help, trim the trees back to the boundary line and charge Orville with the cost of removal plus whatever other damage the trees have caused.

A **permanent nuisance** is one that cannot be physically abated, or one that the courts will decline to abate by injunction because the offending condition has great social utility. For example, a court would not grant an injunction shutting down a cement plant which, though carefully operated, still emits unavoidable amounts of dust, vibration, and noise that are unacceptable to reasonable neighbors. Shutting down the plant would deprive the public of a needed product, employment, and tax revenue. So the remedy for permanent nuisance is past and prospective damages, but no injunction. An injunction is available, however, if harm results from a plant's engaging in unnecessary and injurious methods of operation, or if its activities constitute a serious public nuisance.

Activities Authorized by Statute. All states have statutes authorizing activities with nuisance potential, such as the operation of airports and sewage treatment plants. To shield such activities from lawsuits aimed at shutting them down, many states provide further, as California does, that "[n]othing which is done or maintained under the express authority of a statute can be deemed a nuisance."[13] This seemingly blanket permission for the state to commit nuisance is, however, subject to limits.

One limit is the narrow interpretation commonly given to statutes authorizing activities with nuisance potential. For example, in *Varjabedian v. City of Madera*,[14] the California Supreme Court held that a statute authorizing the construction and operation of sewage treatment plants did not authorize the defendant city's plant to emit foul odors, because nowhere did the statute expressly authorize odor emission as a method of operation. Thus, the plaintiff was entitled to damages for losses caused by prolonged and intense foul odors produced by the plant.

Another limit is the due process clauses of the state and federal constitutions requiring the payment of a "just compensation" when the government takes private property for a public purpose such as a new school, hospital, or highway. Usually, the government agency seeking the property takes legal action, called **condemnation**, to acquire ownership of the land. But the government can "take" private property in other ways. One is by **inverse condemnation**: using its own property, perhaps unintentionally, in a way that deprives neighbors of the enjoyment of their property. A city's continuous production of foul odors in operating its sewage treatment plant, even if foul odors were authorized by statute, would impair the usefulness and value of neighboring residential properties and could result in takings for which the city must pay.

Zoning laws commonly permit industrial and commercial activity in specified geographic areas, without expressly authorizing a particular use. An industrial or commercial firm operating in an area zoned for its general type of business receives a measure of protection from nuisance suits. If its activities constitute a nuisance but are normal methods of operation, they will not be enjoined as a private nuisance. However, the victim may be entitled to damages, and if the activities are *unnecessary and injurious* methods of operation, the victim *can* have them halted by injunction. In addition, an activity such as the firm's poisoning the neighborhood's water supply could be enjoined as a *public* nuisance.

Effect of Coming to the Nuisance. Frequently, people move into an area knowing that a nuisance exists there. Under the old common law, a person knowingly "coming to the nuisance" was not entitled to relief. This rule has been greatly modified in most if not all states. Under the modern rule, anyone injured by a nuisance is entitled to a remedy even if the nuisance was there first, though the fact that the victim came to the nuisance is a factor to be considered in determining what remedy the victim should receive.

The modern rule has some exceptions. Harry owns a smoldering garbage dump. Hoping to profit from the law of nuisance, Susan searches the local real estate listings for a house next to the dump. She finds one, moves in, and immediately sues Harry for nuisance. To be entitled to a nuisance remedy, Susan must have bought the house in good faith and not for the sole purpose of filing a vexatious lawsuit. Because of her extortionate purpose, Susan is not entitled to either abatement or damages.

Case 2.2, a landmark "coming to the nuisance" decision, provides an innovative solution for a difficult problem.

Case 2.2

*Spur Industries, Inc.
v. Del Webb
Development Co.*

494 P.2d 700 (Ariz. 1972)

Since 1956, defendant Spur Industries, Inc., and its predecessor company had developed and operated a cattle feedlot in a farming area 14 to 15 miles west of Phoenix. In 1959, plaintiff Del Webb Development Co. began to plan the development of Sun City, a large retirement community, in the same general area, buying for that purpose about 20,000 acres of farmland for $750 per acre. Advertising extensively, Del Webb first offered homes in January 1960. The first unit completed was approximately 2½ miles north of Spur's feedlot. By May 1960, 450 to 500 houses were completed or under construction. At this time, Del Webb did not consider odors from the Spur feed pens a problem. By 1962, Spur had expanded the feedlot operation from approximately 35 acres to 114 acres. In the meantime, Del Webb continued to develop in Spur's direction, but as the development grew closer to Spur, Del Webb encountered great sales resistance because of flies and odor from Spur's feedlot.

By December 1967, Del Webb's property was within 500 feet of the feedlot. Del Webb filed a complaint alleging that more than 1,300 lots in the southwest portion of the Sun City development were unfit for sale as residential lots because of Spur's feedlot operation, which constituted a public nuisance because of the flies and odor drifting or being blown over the southern portion of Sun City. At the time of the suit, Spur was feeding between 20,000 and 30,000 head of cattle, which produced 35 to 40 pounds of wet manure per head each day, or more than a million pounds of wet manure daily for 30,000 head of cattle. From a judgment permanently enjoining Spur Industries from operating a cattle feedlot near Sun City, Spur appealed and Webb cross-appealed.

CAMERON, J.

. . . Although numerous issues are raised, we feel that it is necessary to answer only two questions. They are:

1. Where the operation of a business, such as a cattle feedlot, is lawful in the first instance, but becomes a nuisance by reason of a nearby residential area, may the feedlot operation be enjoined in an action brought by the developer of the residential area?

2. Assuming that the nuisance may be enjoined, may the developer of a completely new town or urban area in a previously agricultural area be required to indemnify the operator of the feedlot who must move or cease operation because of the presence of the residential area created by the developer?

. . .

The testimony indicated . . . that despite the admittedly good feedlot management and good housekeeping practices by Spur, the resulting odor and flies produced an annoying if not unhealthy situation as far as the senior citizens of southern Sun City were concerned. There is no doubt that some of the citizens of Sun City were unable to enjoy the outdoor living which Del Webb had advertised and that Del Webb was faced with sales resistance from prospective purchasers as well as strong and persistent complaints from the people who had purchased homes in that area.

. . .

May Spur Be Enjoined?

The difference between a private nuisance and a public nuisance is generally one of degree. A private nuisance is one affecting a single individual or a definite small number of persons in the enjoyment of private rights not common to the public, while a public nuisance is one affecting the rights enjoyed by citizens as a part of the public. To constitute a public nuisance, the nuisance must affect a considerable number of people or an entire community or neighborhood. . . .

Where the injury is slight, the remedy for minor inconveniences lies in an action for damages rather than in one for an injunction. . . . Moreover, some courts have held, in the "balancing of conveniences" cases, that damages may be the sole remedy. . . . We have no difficulty, however, in agreeing with the conclusion of the trial court that Spur's operation was an enjoinable public nuisance as far as the people in the southern portion of Del Webb's Sun City were concerned.

[An Arizona statute] reads as follows:

A. The following conditions are specifically declared public nuisances dangerous to the public health:
1. Any condition or place in populous areas which constitutes a breeding place for flies, rodents, mosquitoes and other insects which are capable of carrying and transmitting disease-causing organisms to any person or persons.

By this statute, before an otherwise lawful (and necessary) business may be declared a public nuisance, there must be a "populous" area in which people are injured. . . . It is clear that as to the citizens of Sun City, the operation of Spur's feedlot was both a public and a private nuisance. They could have successfully maintained an action to abate the nuisance. [Though the citizens of Sun City were not represented in this lawsuit,] Del Webb, having shown a special injury in the loss of sales, had a standing to bring suit to enjoin the nuisance. . . . The judgment of the trial court permanently enjoining the operation of the feedlot is affirmed.

Must Del Webb Indemnify Spur?

A suit to enjoin a nuisance sounds in equity. . . . In addition to protecting the public interest, however, courts of equity are concerned with protecting the operator of a [lawful], albeit [obnoxious], business from the result of a knowing and willful encroachment by others near his business. . . .

Were Webb the only party injured, we would feel justified in holding that the doctrine of "coming to the nuisance" would have been a bar to the relief asked by Webb, and, on the other hand, had Spur located the feedlot near the outskirts of a city . . . , Spur would have to suffer the cost of abating the nuisance as to those people locating within the growth pattern of the expanding city. . . .

There was no indication in the instant case at the time Spur and its predecessors located in western Maricopa County that a new city would spring up, full-blown, alongside the feeding operation and that the developer of that city would ask the court to order Spur to move because of the new city. Spur is required to move not because of any wrongdoing on the part of Spur, but because of a proper and legitimate regard of the courts for the rights and interests of the public.

Del Webb, on the other hand, is entitled to the relief prayed for (a permanent injunction), not because Webb is blameless, but because of the damage to the people who have been encouraged to purchase homes in Sun City. It does not equitably or legally follow, however, that Webb, being entitled to the injunction, is then free of any liability to Spur if Webb has in fact been the cause of the damage Spur has sustained. It does not seem harsh to require a developer, who has taken advantage of the lesser land values in a rural area as well as the availability of large tracts of land on which to build and develop a new town or city in the area, to indemnify those who are forced to leave as a result.

Having brought people to the nuisance to the foreseeable detriment of Spur, Webb must indemnify Spur for a reasonable amount of the cost of moving or shutting down. It should be noted that this relief to Spur is limited to a case wherein a developer has, with foreseeability, brought into a previously agricultural or industrial area the population which makes necessary the granting of an injunction against a lawful business and for which the business has no adequate relief.

It is therefore the decision of this court that the matter be remanded to the trial court for a hearing upon the damages sustained by the defendant Spur as a reasonable and direct result of the granting of the permanent injunction. . . .

Affirmed in part, reversed in part, and remanded for further proceedings. . . .

QUESTIONS ABOUT CASE 2.2

1. The Arizona Supreme Court stated, "Were Webb the only party injured, we would feel justified in holding that the doctrine of 'coming to the nuisance' would have been a bar to the relief asked by Webb." What "relief" did Webb receive? Who else benefitted from it?

2. Spur Industries' feedlot activity constituted the nuisance. Why did the court hold that Spur was entitled to damages from plaintiff Webb?

Impairing Lateral or Subjacent Support of Neighboring Property

Harold owns a tract of land surrounded by other tracts. Under the common law rules discussed in the next three paragraphs, he is entitled to lateral and subjacent support of his land by adjacent and underlying properties.

Lateral support results from the presence of land on each side of Harold's tract. If his neighbors excavate too deeply near his land, they risk removing his lateral support and causing his land to cave in or fall away. Harold's right is to have his land supported in its natural state, unburdened by artificial weights such as buildings. So, if excavation on neighboring land causes Harold's land in its natural state to subside, the excavating neighbor is strictly liable for the damage to Harold's land, no matter how carefully the excavation was done. To collect for damage to *burdened* land, however, Harold will have to prove negligence or intentional wrongdoing on the part of the excavator—will have to prove, that is, that the excavator should have foreseen that the excavation would harm Harold's burdened land, or did foresee the harm and proceeded anyway.

Subjacent support results from the presence of supporting land below the surface of Harold's land. If Harold horizontally subdivides his land by selling a coal-bearing substratum to a mining company, the mining company's removing too much coal from its subsurface level endangers the subjacent support of Harold's overlying land and may cause it to subside or to cave in completely.

A subjacent owner has a duty to support the overlying land in its natural, unburdened state. A minority of courts impose a greater duty, requiring the subjacent owner to support the land as burdened by any structures that were in place when the subjacent owner acquired the substratum.[15] Failure to maintain the required support results in the subjacent owner's strict liability for damage to the overlying land. In a few states, neighbors who remove underground water in such quantities that the plaintiff's land subsides are liable for impairing the subjacent support. In most states, however, the courts hold that impairment of subjacent support occurs only by the removal of solid materials.

Several states have statutes providing in some detail how excavations must be conducted. Generally the statutes require excavators to give adjoining landowners advance notice of an excavation and a right to enter the excavator's property to the extent necessary to shore up their own burdened land.

Liability to Persons on Property

A surprising variety of people, invited or uninvited, can enter one's property in the course of a year. Any entrant injured by conditions on the land, even a trespasser, may have a cause of action against the owner or other possessor for negligence or intentional misconduct that caused the injury.

Traditional Common Law Rule

Possessors of land may face liability to entrants under a long-standing common law rule still in effect in a majority of states. This rule classifies entrants as trespassers, licensees, or invitees, and imposes on the possessor a different standard of care toward each class of entrant. Trespassers receive the least protection; invitees receive the most.

Trespassers. Ordinarily, a possessor of land owes no duty of reasonable care to trespassers—no duty, that is, to inspect for hazards that trespassers might encounter, to make the land safe for them, or to conduct activities on the land in a way that does not endanger them. Because the presence of trespassers usually is unanticipated, a duty of inspection and warning imposed on possessors for the benefit of trespassers would be unduly burdensome. This rule protects a possessor's right of exclusive possession and control of the land, and emphasizes that a trespasser is a wrongdoer who must take the premises as he or she finds them.

In most states, however, the rule is subject to a variety of exceptions that reflect the law's concern for human safety, even that of trespassers. For example, where the possessor knows that a substantial number of people regularly trespass at a particular place, many courts hold that the possessor has at least a duty to warn of hidden dangers known to the possessor, and to exercise care in operating equipment there. So, a beaten path across a railroad track at an unauthorized crossing place creates a duty of care in the operation of trains at that location.[16] And possessors have a duty to avoid injuring trespassers whose presence has been discovered. The duty is at least to refrain from injuring them by willful or wanton conduct, but a number of courts go further, requiring possessors to use ordinary care to avoid inflicting injury. A possessor has, of course, a right to use reasonable force to restrain a trespasser engaging in destructive activity.

Trespassing children receive special protection because their immaturity may make them unable to perceive or appreciate dangers they encounter while trespassing. A possessor who has reason to know (1) that children are likely to trespass on the possessor's land, and (2) that an artificial condition unreasonably dangerous to them exists there must exercise reasonable care to eliminate the danger or otherwise protect the children.[17] So, an owner of an artificial irrigation or stock-watering pond, essential for farming but containing a dangerous entanglement of underwater weeds or wire, may have a duty to post conspicuous No Swimming signs warning older children of the danger, and perhaps to erect a fence that would keep younger children out.

Licensees. A **licensee** is a person permitted to enter another's property for the licensee's own purposes and not for the benefit of the possessor. Licensees include people whom possessors permit to take shortcuts across the possessor's land, or to enter to solicit charitable contributions, borrow tools, get in out of the weather, or take away discarded furniture for the licensee's own benefit. Like a trespasser, a licensee takes the premises as they are. The possessor has no duty to inspect the premises for dangers unknown to the possessor or to warn the licensee of obvious dangers. However the possessor must use reasonable care to warn the licensee of latent (not obvious) dangers of which the possessor has actual knowledge.

Odd as it may seem, *social guests* are in most states classified as licensees, the often-criticized reason being that a social guest has the same standing as the host's family, so takes the premises as they are. Thus, social guests, like other licensees, are entitled only to be warned of latent dangers known to the host. A few states (Connecticut, Florida, Indiana, Louisiana, and Maine) classify social guests as invitees. For reasons explained in the next section police officers, firefighters, and similar professionals traditionally are classified as licensees.

Invitees. Invitees, also called *business invitees*, enter the premises for the possessor's business benefit and at the possessor's express or implied invitation. Obvious examples are customers entering a store, restaurant, bank, or theater; drivers picking up or delivering mail or goods; and contractors and subcontractors working on the premises. To protect invitees, possessors of land must use reasonable care to inspect the premises and make them safe.

An invitee's business with the possessor supposedly must be of pecuniary benefit to the possessor, but *potential* pecuniary benefit usually is sufficient. So window shoppers and people strolling through a mall with no present intention to buy ordinarily qualify as invitees because they might buy in the future. Similarly, garbage collectors and meter readers are needed for the business to operate and thus usually have invitee status.

Professionals such as firefighters and police officers, however, are usually held to be mere licensees. Despite the fact that they often confer pecuniary benefits on possessors of property by protecting or rescuing it, they enter under a privilege conferred by law and are trained to detect and avoid the hazards of their professions. Given the dangerous or emergency situations they often encounter, it would be unrealistic to expect possessors to search out unknown dangers and make the premises safe for those who are trained to look out for themselves. Possessors therefore owe such professionals only the duties owed other licensees: reasonable care in warning of known dangers, and avoidance of willful or wanton conduct that could cause injury.

Modern Alternative Rule

The classification of entrants as trespassers, licensees, or invitees, with each class being owed a different duty of care, has been heavily criticized as arbitrary. Consequently, a substantial number of states have adopted or partially adopted an alternative rule announced in the leading case of *Rowland v. Christian.*[18] In that case the Supreme Court of California abolished, for California, the traditional classifications and substituted ordinary principles of negligence relating to foreseeability of harm. Under those principles, the duty owed by a possessor to an entrant is one of reasonable care in the circumstances, regardless of whether the entrant is a trespasser, licensee, or invitee. Within a few years after Rowland was decided, eight more jurisdictions abolished the traditional classifications and substituted the general negligence rule,[19] with another five dropping the distinctions between licensees and invitees but preserving the traditional limit on a possessor's duty to trespassing adults.[20]

Role of Insurance

Purchasers, owners, and possessors of realty face many risks that could result in devastating financial losses. To a purchaser, the greatest immediate concern may be the possibility that the seller lacks some or all of the ownership rights promised in the contract of sale. Title insurance, discussed in Chapter 9, is widely used to protect purchasers against defects in the seller's title. But possessors of the land also need protection against physical damage to the realty and against liability to others for injuries resulting from dangerous conditions on and dangerous uses of the land. **Property insurance** and **liability insurance** cover these latter risks and are the subject of the remainder of this chapter.

General Concepts

Insurance is a topic of vast complexity, but it boils down to the willingness of an insurance company contractually to assume a risk for its customer, the *insured*, in exchange for a payment of money called a *premium*. To make insurance feasible, and profitable, insurance companies draft their contracts, called *insurance policies*, very carefully. They precisely define the risk assumed and put limits on it, such as exclusions from coverage and deductible amounts that the insured must pay before the company may be called upon to pay. In addition, over the centuries numerous insurance doctrines and techniques aimed at controlling the company's exposure to risk have been incorporated into the law of insurance. Among them are the indemnity principle, the requirement of an insurable interest, and coinsurance clauses.

Indemnity Principle

The object of insurance is to *indemnify* (compensate) the insured for actual losses sustained when a covered risk materializes, not to provide the insured with a profit. Martina owns a house worth $100,000 and insures it for $100,000 with each of two fire insurance companies for a total coverage of $200,000. Then a forest fire completely destroys the house. Under the indemnity principle Martina will be entitled only to $100,000, the amount of her loss, and each insurance company will be liable for only $50,000.

Insurable Interest

To be able to enforce an insurance contract, the insured person must have an **insurable interest** in the thing insured. Susan has an insurable interest in property if, as a result of its destruction or damage to it, she will suffer monetary loss, or if she will be liable to others for damage it causes. Any interest in realty is an insurable interest to the extent of its value. A fee simple estate, a life estate, a leasehold for a term of three years, a fee simple remainder, a life remainder, even a mortgage on Blackacre held by a bank—all these and others are insurable property interests. And, because possessors of land can be liable to an entrant, neighbor, or passerby injured by conditions on the land or by the possessor's use of it, owners, tenants, and even adverse possessors have the insurable interest needed to qualify for liability insurance.

Coinsurance Clause

A variety of clauses used in insurance contracts are designed to provide an equitable rate structure for all insureds and to limit the amounts paid out by insurers. The **coinsurance clause** used in property insurance policies is an example.

The coinsurance clause addresses the problem of imbalance between partial and full losses. Most losses to buildings and other realty are partial, so the temptation to owners is to insure for only a fraction of a structure's value and thus pay a much smaller premium than would be charged for coverage at full value, in the hope, of course, that any partial losses within the policy limits will be fully reimbursed by the insurer. But the group of insureds paying for full-value coverage suffers about the same degree and types of loss that the partially covered group experiences. So, if both groups of insureds receive 100% reimbursement for their losses, those paying for full-value coverage receive less reimbursement for each dollar of premium paid than do those who insure for less than full value.

The coinsurance clause corrects for this problem by requiring a person to insure for a designated minimum percentage of the property's value in order to qualify for 100% reimbursement for partial losses. For commercial buildings, the required face amount of insurance usually is set at 80% of the building's *actual cash value*. In homeowners' policies, the requirement is 80% of the home's *replacement cost*, a term used because the courts have interpreted "actual cash value" in various ways. Eighty rather than 100% applies because concrete slabs, foundations, and other underground elements ordinarily are undamaged even by catastrophic occurrences such as fires and tornados. If a building is insured for less than the 80% (representing the actual cash or replacement value minus a credit for undestroyed elements), the owner is considered underinsured and receives only partial reimbursement for partial losses, as calculated under the following formula:

$$\text{Reimbursement} = \text{Actual loss} \times \frac{\text{Face amount of insurance}}{80\% \text{ of actual cash value of property}}$$

Henry's office building is valued at $100,000. Under an 80% coinsurance clause, he must take out a policy in the face amount of $80,000 to receive 100% reimbursement for partial losses. But Henry insures his building for only $40,000. Then lightning strikes it, causing a $10,000 loss. Because Henry insured the building for only 50% of the amount required by the coinsurance clause, he receives a 50% reimbursement for any loss—here, $5,000 for his partial loss of $10,000—and is considered a self-insurer as to the balance.

Types of Contracts and Standard Forms

Insurance can be purchased on a "specified perils" or an "all risks" basis. A **specified perils** contract insures against only the peril or perils named in the contract, such as "breakage of plate glass windows" or "all direct loss and damage by fire or lightning." In contrast, **all-risk** contracts do not enumerate the perils insured against, but instead insure against all perils except those that are specifically excluded from coverage, such as war, riot, or earthquake. Most commercial and residential insurance today is sold in all-risk or "package" policies, though specified-peril insurance remains available.

In the early days of insurance, each company had its own contract forms and a multitude of fine-print clauses that often contained unpleasant surprises for insureds. To provide uniformity and a greater degree of disclosure and consumer protection, Massachusetts, and later New York, developed a standard fire insurance contract form that all insurers in the state were required to use. The New York form was adopted by most states, with several making modifications. Today all states impose a standard form for fire insurance—usually the updated New York form. Standard forms are less common in other areas of insurance, though in most states certain standard provisions must be included. In all states, the state insurance commission must approve an insurer's forms before they can be used. The insurance commissions review the forms for misleading language, unreasonable exclusions, and deceptive provisions.

Property Insurance

In property insurance, three issues are key: the perils covered, the methods of providing the insurance, and the persons protected. Damage to the premises and their contents from fire, wind, flood, earthquake, explosion, runaway vehicles, falling airplanes, vandalism, and other perils can be insured against by combinations of specified perils contracts, or, much more commonly today, by various all-risk, package, or comprehensive policies, which are subject to policy limits, exclusions, deductible amounts, and a host of limiting doctrines and clauses.

Five methods of insuring property are commonly employed: specific coverage, blanket coverage, floaters, automatic coverage, and schedule coverage. *Specific coverage* protects a particular kind of property at a definite location, for example, "the Jones Hardware Store building on First Street, together with all fixtures, to a value of $200,000" or "the stock-in-trade of the Jones Hardware Store on First Street, to a maximum value of $25,000." *Blanket coverage* protects a particular kind of property at different locations or several kinds of property at one location. A *floating contract* (floater) covers goods in locations that are difficult or impossible to specify—for example, theatrical equipment located in various warehouses for short periods between concerts, or in transit to a concert location. Another type of floater is the homeowner's **personal property floater** used to cover personal effects, usually but not necessarily at a fixed location, on an all-risk basis. *Automatic coverage* is used where the insured cannot accurately state the value of covered property, as in a chain store operation involving different locations and fluctuating inventories. New inventory is automatically covered (within policy limits) when acquired. *Schedule coverage* is used for insuring the buildings and personal property of large organizations (e.g., utility companies, cities, states), the object being to minimize paperwork by listing many items on one form.

Among persons protected from loss are lenders who have financed the purchase of realty. Mortgagors (borrowers) and mortgagees (lenders) have insurable interests, as do both sellers and buyers of realty under a land contract. But insurance that protects a mortgagor does not always protect a mortgagee, so it is advisable for each to acquire insurance independently or to take care that an existing policy adequately covers losses to both.

Liability Insurance

Liability insurance protects possessors of land from losses resulting from their *negligence*, but not from their deliberate torts. Some policies of liability insurance protect possessors in situations involving strict liability, as where innocent bystanders are injured when Harmon has his obsolete office building razed by dynamiting. Liability insurance covers a wide range of hazards that may cause personal injury or property damage to third persons on or near the land. Liability insurance commonly is sold on an all-risk basis by means of a comprehensive liability policy. Exclusions from coverage, while present, tend to be minimal.

Homeowner's Insurance

Homeowner's insurance is a package combination of property and liability coverages. Standard form coverage is available throughout the United States in various combinations labeled HO-1, HO-2, and so on. *HO-1* covers basic perils such as fire, lightning, hail, windstorm, vandalism, theft, and breakage of glass. *HO-2* expands the coverage by adding the perils of falling objects, weight of ice and snow, freezing of plumbing, collapse of buildings, and the like. *HO-3* and *HO-5* are all-risk policies that cover all perils except those specifically excluded. Some HO policies are specifically designed for renters and condominium owners.

Self-Study Questions

1. The term *land* has three meanings. How could each be helpful to you as you consider buying Blackacre?

2. Dora buys Blackacre from George. What does she receive? How much airspace does a purchaser of land acquire?

3. How does vertical subdivision differ from horizontal subdivision? Which is associated with air lots? Why might column lots and caisson lots be needed?

4. Dora owns Blackacre. She wants to sell the oil and gas and the solid minerals apart from the land. May she do so?

5. The owner of Blackacre agrees to sell the wild strawberries growing there, the old walnut tree on top of the hill, and the water heater in the guest house, but the buyer must remove all three items. Is the contract for a sale of goods or a sale of realty? What difference does the classification make?

6. What are the tests for deciding whether a chattel is a fixture? Which test is the most significant? Illustrate the difference between actual and constructive annexation. What is the "assembled industrial plant doctrine"?

7. Under what circumstances may a tenant remove (and keep) a fixture he or she installed on the landlord's realty? Under what circumstances may a tenant not remove such a fixture?

8. How does trespass differ from nuisance? How does criminal trespass differ from civil trespass? For each of the following remedies for trespass, describe a situation in which the remedy would be appropriate: injunction, past and prospective damages, nominal damages, restitution.

9. Who may be a plaintiff in a nuisance suit?

10. Who has an insurable interest in realty?

Case Problems

1. On the south end of Blackacre, a small dump containing tires and other debris from the farm smolders for much of the year, often releasing thick black smoke into a neighboring residential area. Some of the neighbors have complained, but others have not because they have been hunting for pheasant, rabbits, and deer on George's property despite the presence of "No Hunting" signs. A neighboring landowner recently opened a small nightclub near George's residence. The lights and loud music at late hours disturb George and his family. Neighbor Ned brings an abatement action against George to stop the burning at the dump. George sues several hunters for trespass, and the state prosecutes them. George sues the nightclub owner to stop the lights and music. How is each lawsuit likely to be decided?

2. Mr. and Mrs. Cook owned a residence in the town of Scituate. Their cesspool lay partly under a neighbor's land. When the neighbor installed a swimming pool, the cesspool became unusable, and the Cooks were forced to find an alternative. The town required a septic system, but the only suitable site for it was a triangle of land ("the site") lying between the Cooks' lot and that of other neighbors, the Gouldings. Both the Cooks and the Gouldings claimed ownership of the site. The Cooks tried to negotiate with the Gouldings for the use of the site, but failed. The Gouldings sought a declaration that the Gouldings owned the site, and a preliminary injunction to prevent the Cooks from using it. The Land Court denied the injunction. The Cooks then entered the land and installed the system. Later, the court held that the Gouldings owned the land, but granted the Cooks an easement for the maintenance of the septic system "at a price to be negotiated by the parties." The Gouldings appealed from the grant of the easement. The Appeals Court affirmed the Land Court's decision. The Gouldings appealed to the Supreme Judicial Court of Massachusetts. Should the Land Court's granting the easement be upheld? In your answer, consider whether Cook was a good faith improver. *Goulding v. Cook*, 661 N.E.2d 1322 (Mass. 1996).

3. Underestimating the amount of noise and vibration, Greta buys and moves into a house near an automobile-body stamping plant that has been there for 30 years. Because of the plant's activity, Greta cannot sleep or otherwise enjoy her new home. She brings suit to shut down the plant and also seeks damages. How is the suit likely to be decided?

4. Samantha wants to demolish her one-story office building and replace it with a five-story building with three sub-basements extending 40 feet below the surface. For this construction, she must excavate a hole 50 feet deep within five feet of the property next door, which has a nine-story brick building on it. What potential liability to the next-door neighbor does she face? What might she do to avoid that liability?

5. Rascal trespasses onto your land late at night, falls into a deep open pit left unguarded by excavators working there the previous day, and suffers serious injuries. Rascal sues you for damages. Would Rascal prevail under the traditional rule governing a landowner's liability to entrants? Under the alternative rule stated in *Rowland v. Christian*?

6. Patricia owns a small hotel worth $2 million. She insures it for $300,000. A laundry fire causes $100,000 in damage. If her insurance policy contains an 80% coinsurance clause, to what reimbursement is she entitled?

Endnotes

1. 328 U.S. 256; 66 S.Ct. 1062 (1946).

2. 14 C.F.R. § 91.119 (1998).

3. 369 U.S. 84 (1962).

4. LA. R.S. 30:681.2 (1998).

5. John Edward Murray, Jr., *Murray on Contracts* (The Michie Co., 1990), §§ 12, 71D.

6. UCC § 2-107(2).

7. *Titus v. Poland Coal Co.*, 119 A. 540, 542 (Pa. 1923).

8. *Holland Furnace Co. v. Trumball Savings & Loan Co.*, 19 N.E.2d 273 (Ohio 1939).

9. See, e.g., *Restatement of Torts* (Second), § 166.

10. Dan B. Dobbs, *Law of Remedies* (West Publishing Co., 1993), p. 488.

11. Dan B. Dobbs, Robert E. Keeton, and David G. Owen, *Prosser and Keeton on Torts* (West Publishing Co., 1984), p. 620.

12. *Id.*, p. 621.

13. Cal. Civ. Code § 3482 (Deering, 2001).

14. 572 P.2d 43 (Cal. 1977).

15. Roger A. Cunningham, William B. Stoebuck, and Dale A. Whitman, *The Law of Property* (West Publishing Co., 1993), p. 423.

16. Dan B. Dobbs, Robert E. Keeton, and David G. Owen, *Prosser and Keeton on Torts* (West Publishing Co., 1984), p. 396.

17. *Id.*, p. 402 (discussing § 339 of the *Second Restatement of Torts* entitled "Artificial Conditions Highly Dangerous to Trespassing Children").

18. 443 P.2d 561 (Cal. 1968).

19. Alaska, Colorado, District of Columbia, Louisiana, Missouri, New Hampshire, New York, and Rhode Island.

20. Maine, Massachusetts, Minnesota, North Dakota, and Wisconsin.

Chapter 3

Interests in Real Property— An Overview; Freehold Estates

Gloria owns Blackacre, a large farm located next to the town of Hamlet. On the far northwest corner of the farm she recently opened a commercial gravel pit. Gloria wants to subdivide the east half of Blackacre into lots and sell them for new housing on the west edge of Hamlet. She expects to farm a part of the remaining half herself, rent part to her son Jack for use as a track for stock car races, and give the gravel pit and the surrounding 100 acres of gravel-bearing land to her niece Fran to use for the rest of Fran's life. Upon Fran's death, Gloria wants the Hamlet Environment Club to have the gravel pit area, but only for as long as the Club conducts nature studies there. Believing that Blackacre may have oil under it, Gloria intends to keep the mineral rights to all of Blackacre except the gravel pit area.

Because the law permits people to have and create a variety of interests in land, Gloria can carry out most or all of her plans. The first part of this chapter outlines the various interests—ownership and nonownership—that people may have in land. The second part discusses in more detail some of the *ownership* interests, called "estates."

Interests in Real Property—An Overview

Gloria's transactions will involve several of the land interests commonly held in this country, most notably some ownership interests discussed in this chapter and the chapter on leaseholds. Other interests mentioned here, such as easements and mineral rights, are discussed more fully in other chapters.

Ownership Interests

An ownership interest, called an **estate**, involves an exclusive right to possess, use, and enjoy the land, and to encumber (e.g., mortgage) and dispose of the interest. The key feature of an estate is the *right to exclusive possession* of the land, as opposed to a limited right of usage characteristic of lesser, nonownership interests. Ownership interests are classified as either freehold or nonfreehold estates.

Freehold Estates

A **freehold estate** is an ownership interest of indefinite, potentially infinite duration. "Potentially infinite duration" means that ownership could pass from parent to child to grandchild, and so on, forever. Or, if any family member in the chain chose to sell or give the land to a stranger, owner-ship could pass from the stranger to his or her child, and so on, forever. The main categories of freehold estates are:

- *Fee simple estates.* The **fee simple absolute** (usually called "fee simple" or "fee") is the greatest aggregate of ownership rights that a person can have in land. The owner of a fee simple estate has the exclusive right to possess, use, enjoy, encumber, and dispose of the land, subject only to certain government controls and interests. An inheritable estate, the fee simple descends to the owner's heirs unless the owner sold or gave it away before death, or devised it by will. (A person's **heirs** are those people designated by *law*—the state's statute of descent and distribution—to inherit property if the owner dies **intestate**, that is, with-out a will. In contrast, a person receiving real property under a *will* is a **devisee**.) As noted later in this chapter, other varieties of fee simple ownership are "defeasible," conferring somewhat lesser rights on the owners.

- *Life estates.* George owns Blackacre in fee simple and by deed transfers it "to Joan for her life." George has granted an ordinary **life estate** to Joan. As owner of the life estate, Joan has the exclusive right to possess, use, and enjoy the land during the rest of her life, a period of indefinite duration. She also may sell her life estate interest or give it as collateral for a loan. If George had granted Blackacre "to Joan for the life of Fred," Joan would have received a life estate **pur autre vie** (for the life of another). Life estates often are used in estate planning.

Nonfreehold (Leasehold) Estates

Nonfreehold estates, also known as *leasehold estates* or simply **leaseholds**, are those of a fixed or determinable duration. The transaction that creates a leasehold is called a **lease**. The person granting the leasehold is the **landlord** (also called the **lessor**); the person receiving it is the **tenant (lessee)**. A landlord creates a leasehold by "carving" it out of a greater estate—a fee simple, a life estate, or even a long-term lease such as one for 99 years. So, if Anne owns Blackacre in fee simple, she can lease all or a part of it to Ned for, say, a period of five years.

A leasehold is an ownership interest (an estate) because the tenant receives the exclusive right to possess, use, and enjoy the land for the time specified in the lease. Unless the lease states to the contrary, the tenant can also dispose of the leasehold interest by selling or giving it away, in whole or in part. So, unless the lease expressly forbids him to do so, Ned can **assign** his lease to Kay, or instead **sublease** part or all of Blackacre to her.

Though an estate in land, a leasehold is classified as personal property and is called a **chattel real**. The reason is found in the history of English land law. In the early years of leaseholds, if someone dispossessed Leonard of his leasehold estate (threw him off the land), there was no action available to him for recovering possession of the land. His only legal recourse was a personal action against the dispossessor for money damages. Actions granting *possession* of land were called *real actions*, and the property to which they applied (land) came to be known as "real property." Actions granting only a *money judgment* personally against the defendant were called *personal actions*, and the property to which they applied (e.g., movable property called *chattels*) became "personal property." Leonard's term of years, being enforceable only through a "personal" action, was regarded as personal property and was called a *chattel real*. Although feudal leasehold tenants eventually were given a real action (enabling them to regain possession), leasehold estates today are still called chattels real and are still considered personal property.

The status of a leasehold as personal property is significant today in only a few situations, for example, where the law imposes a tax on real property but not on personal property, and where a person wills "my real property to Jill and my personal property to Jack." Leases and the landlord-tenant relationship are discussed further in Chapter 12.

● Nonownership Interests and Privileges

People who do not own a particular parcel of land—who lack an *estate* and therefore the right of exclusive possession needed for ownership—might nevertheless have a right or privilege to use the land in some *limited* way, to prevent the owner from making certain uses, or to have the land serve as collateral for a debt. Nonownership rights, interests, and privileges include the following:

- *Easements and Profits.* An **easement** is an interest in another person's land entitling the easement owner to use the other person's land for a special purpose. Typical is an easement creating a right of way over a neighbor's land to reach Highway 47 or the beach, or the easement that a power company has to install and maintain a power line on the lands of customers and others. A **profit à prendre** (usually called a *profit*) is the right to remove something from the land of another, for example, to quarry limestone, extract oil, remove gravel. Easements and profits are discussed in Chapter 4.

- *Covenants and Equitable Servitudes.* **Covenants** are written promises or agreements to do or to refrain from doing something with one's own land. **Restrictive covenants** prohibit a person from using the land in a particular way—for example, a covenant not to keep pigs on the premises; or not to erect a building within twenty feet of boundary lines; or to use the property for residential purposes only. Found in deeds, subdivision maps, and other real estate documents, covenants create important rights and protections for landowners, especially for homeowners in housing developments. **Personal covenants** bind only the immediate parties to the agreement. **Real covenants** "run with the land" and bind not only the immediate parties but also their successors. An **equitable servitude**, also called an *equitable restriction*, is a land-use restriction enforceable in a court of equity against anyone who takes possession of the burdened land with notice of the restriction. Usually associated with housing subdivisions, equitable servitudes are intended to benefit the land that they "touch and concern." They bind a broader range of people than do real covenants. Covenants and equitable servitudes are discussed in Chapter 17.

- *Licenses.* A **license** is a permission or privilege to use another person's land for some purpose authorized by the other person. A license does not give the licensee an interest in the land itself—only a privilege of usage that the licensor ordinarily may revoke at any time. Agnes strolls through the shopping mall, entering various places of business. She is a business invitee making use of the license impliedly granted by the mall and the businesses to enter their premises as a potential customer. As noted in Chapter 4, some licenses are irrevocable.

- *Liens.* A **lien** is a charge against property to secure payment of a private debt, taxes, or some other obligation. A lien may be created by contract or imposed by law. If contractual, it is "voluntary." Voluntary liens against real estate are created by **mortgages**, **deeds of trust**, and **land contracts**, discussed in Chapter 10. Involuntary liens are imposed by operation of law without the consent of the owner. They include **mechanic's liens** and *tax liens*, discussed in Chapters 14 and 16.

Note on the Development of Servitudes Law

Easements, profits, equitable servitudes, real covenants, and irrevocable licenses are land-use devices that developed independently over the centuries. As a group they serve similar purposes. Called **servitudes**, they all create burdens on land that benefit, or serve, others than the owner of the burdened land. Indeed, some of these historically different devices, such as easements and irrevocable licenses creating rights of way, serve identical purposes. But because each device acquired its own peculiar legal characteristics as it developed, servitudes law as a whole has been confusing and contradictory in its application.

To simplify, modernize, and clarify the law of servitudes, the American Law Institute began in the 1980s to develop the *Restatement (Third) of Property (Servitudes)*, commonly referred to as the *Restatement of Servitudes*. A final draft of this reference volume was published in the early 2000s.

Though drafted by legal experts for use by lawyers, judges, and law school students, the *Restatement of Servitudes* is not itself law. Typically the principles and rules of a *Restatement* become law by being adopted by courts on a case-by-case basis, a process that could take years. Moreover, courts are free to ignore or reject *Restatement* principles, so some states might not ever adopt them. Because the movement to unify servitudes law is still in its infancy, this textbook presents the traditional law of land-use devices: easements, profits, and licenses in Chapter 4, and covenants and equitable servitudes in Chapter 17, with mention of the new *Restatement* rules where appropriate.

Co-ownership

Two or more people can own a parcel of land together, as co-owners. The co-owners have simultaneous, or concurrent, interests in each physical part of the land, but no individual right to a particular geographical portion. George gives (conveys) his residence to his daughters Alice and Benita as co-owners. Every physical part of the realty is owned simultaneously by both—the living room, garage, garden, tool shed, fruit trees, rocks, and doghouse. Neither co-owner can claim any physical part as exclusively hers. In the most common types of co-ownership, however, Alice and Benita each has an "undivided fractional interest" entitling her to the relevant portion of the realty's value. And each co-owner has other rights peculiar to the specific type of co-ownership. Chapter 5 discusses the various types of co-ownership, among them, the *tenancy in common*, *joint tenancy*, *tenancy by the entirety*, and *community property*.

Present Estates and Future Interests

Ruth owns Fairview Farm in fee simple and gives Lars a 25-year lease. Ruth has granted some of her bundle of rights to Lars and has kept the rest. Lars subleases Fairview Farm for five years to Edgar. Lars, too, has granted some of his rights to another and has kept the rest. When an owner such as Ruth or Lars "carves out" a lesser estate from a larger one, something new (the lesser estate) is created, and something is left over. What do we call these interests and who owns them? The lesser estate that Ruth carved out and gave to Lars (and which gives Lars the right of exclusive possession) is called a **present interest** or **present estate**. The leftover interest, which Ruth might either keep or transfer to someone else, is called a **future interest** or **future estate**.

Osgood owns Blackacre Farm and has retired from farming, but he wants to keep the farm in the family. He can do so, for a while at least, by creating present and future interests, a process that gives him a number of disposal options. For example, he can:

- Keep Blackacre (i.e., keep his fee simple ownership) and give his daughter Sara a lesser interest such as a life estate.

- Give Sara a life estate and give the rest of his ownership rights to his son Saul.

In the first disposition, Osgood retains his fee simple ownership but, by means of the life estate, gives Sara exclusive possession of Blackacre for her life. Sara's life estate is a present estate because it entitles her to immediate, exclusive possession of Blackacre. In the meantime, by keeping the rest of the bundle of rights, Osgood has created for himself a future interest called a **reversion** in fee simple. When Sara dies, her life estate ends and possession of the land goes back or reverts to Osgood (or to his heirs or devisees if Osgood dies before Sara).

Osgood's reversion is by definition a "future" interest because possession and enjoyment of the land are postponed to the future. His reversion is also "nonpossessory" because he does not regain possession until Sara's life estate ends.[1] Yet, despite the fact that the reversion is called a "future" interest, it is a presently existing interest that Osgood can sell or give away now. If he does so, Osgood's grantee will receive the reversion, but of course will not be entitled to possession until Sara dies.

In the second disposition, Osgood divides the bundle of rights into two parts, a life estate and a future interest called a **remainder**, and transfers them to Sara and Saul respectively, keeping nothing. Saul's remainder is in fee simple because Osgood owned Blackacre in fee simple and, by conferring the remainder on Saul, gave him the balance of Osgood's fee simple estate. Like a reversion, Saul's remainder is a presently existing interest that Saul can sell or give away now, though the grantee's possession is postponed until the life estate ends.

BOX 3–1 POINT TO CONSIDER

Saul has a remainder interest in Blackacre and wants to sell the remainder to you. Black-acre is worth $4 million. How much should you pay? What factors will you consider?

Would the price differ if, instead of Saul's having a remainder, Osgood had a reversion to sell?

Freehold Estates and Related Future Interests

We now take a closer look at the freehold estates, a category encompassing several varieties of fee simple and life estates. The discussion centers on several questions: What is the purpose or main use of each estate? How are the various estates created? Which ones involve future interests? What limits on usage do owners face? What limits can they impose on others? As the answers will reveal, the law of real property enables people to tailor their ownership interests to a variety of needs, key ones being business management, estate planning, and land-use control.

First, though, a preliminary question: In general, what are the mechanics for transferring an interest in land? For illustrative purposes, the focus here is on the transfer of a fee simple estate.

The owner of a fee simple can transfer (convey or devise) all or part of it during the owner's life or at death. If the transfer is made during life, the transfer (called a **conveyance**) is *inter vivos* (between living persons), and ordinarily is accomplished by delivery and acceptance of a **deed**, a document signed by the grantor, particularly describing the land, and usually stating what interest the grantee is to receive. To be enforceable, every conveyance of an interest in land except a short-term lease must be evidenced by a writing. Deeds are discussed in Chapter 9.

A transfer occurring at the owner's death is either *testamentary* (made by means of the decedent's **will**) or **nontestamentary** (made by operation of law to heirs named in the state's statute of descent and distribution). A transfer of land by will is called a **devise** and the transferee a devisee. A transfer of personal property by will is a **bequest** or a **legacy**; the recipient is a **legatee**. A person who leaves a will is called a **testator**. A person who dies without a will dies intestate and is called "the intestate." A will does not become effective until the death of the testator.

We also need to consider another preliminary topic: the nature of the language used to create or transfer an interest in land. To create or transfer an interest, the grantor uses "words of purchase" and "words of limitation." **Words of purchase** state who is to receive the interest.[2] **Words of limitation** indicate the quantum or amount of rights the grantee is to have, that is, what interest the grantor intends to transfer and its duration. When Osgood gave a life estate in Blackacre to his daughter Sara, the deed stated, in part, "to Sara for her life." "To Sara" are words of purchase because they reveal who is to receive the interest. "For her life" are words of limitation because they reveal the kind and duration of the interest, here, a life estate measured by Sara's life.

In the examples that follow, the grantor begins with a fee simple estate in Blackacre unless otherwise indicated.

Fee Simple Estates

A fee simple estate is either a fee simple absolute or a fee simple defeasible. Any fee simple is transferable and inheritable. Unlike a **fee simple absolute**, however, a fee simple defeasible has special words of limitation that allow it to be ended, perhaps unexpectedly, in ways explained later.

Fee Simple Absolute

Commonly known as the "fee simple" or the "fee," the fee simple absolute is the greatest aggregate of ownership rights that one can have in land. Ownership in fee simple absolute is "complete" ownership, subject only to certain restrictions and obligations imposed on the owner for the benefit of the public. These restrictions and obligations include the government's power of eminent domain (power to take private land for a public purpose), laws taxing real property, and zoning and other laws limiting the use of the land for the benefit or protection of others. Within these limits, the owner may use the land for any lawful purpose. For example, the owner may farm it, build on it, rent it out, use it as a dump or race track, open a mine or gravel pit, or subdivide and sell it. The owner of the fee (together with any co-owner) has, as owner of an *estate*, the exclusive right to possess, use, enjoy, encumber, and dispose of the land, and perhaps even lay waste to (damage or destroy) it. "Disposal" encompasses the right to sell the land during life and to give it away by deed or by will. If the owner dies intestate, the estate passes to the decedent's heirs, as determined by the statute of descent or distribution.

Waste is the act of destroying realty, or damaging or neglecting it to the extent that its value is substantially impaired. Within limits, the owner of the fee has a right to lay waste to the land. If Osgood in a fit of rage chooses to burn his barn, dynamite the apple orchard, and render the fields infertile with an acid spray, he may do so, in the absence of law protecting neighbors, wildlife, or the environment from his destructive acts. The law of nuisance, for example, forbids a property owner from engaging in acts of waste that would unreasonably disturb neighbors in the enjoyment of their own property.

Tired of farming, Osgood wants to give Blackacre to his daughter Sara. What language must he use in the deed? In earlier times, he could not convey a fee simple to Sara unless he used the words "to Sara and her heirs" in the deed of conveyance. This language was (and still is) understood to give Sara an inheritable estate—a fee simple. Under most state statutes today, however, the phrase "and her heirs" is *not* required. A grantor can use any language that reveals an intention to convey a fee simple: "to Sara in fee simple," "to Sara in fee," "to Sara forever" or "to Sara." Yet, to avoid doubts about the interest to be conveyed, many lawyers today use "and her [his] heirs" to denote a fee simple estate.

A will or a deed transfers the *whole estate owned* by the transferor unless the document clearly reveals an intent to convey a lesser estate. Osgood owns Blackacre in fee simple and gives Sara a deed stating, "I, Osgood, hereby give Blackacre to my daughter Sara." Sara gets a fee simple estate. If, however, Osgood actually had only a life estate in Blackacre, the same words would convey to Sara only the life estate, since Osgood cannot convey more than he owns.

Fee Simple Defeasible

Wills and deeds creating *defeasible* fee simple estates contain language that may end (defeat) the grantee's ownership, or that of a later owner, under circumstances specified by the limiting language. For example, a will or a deed may forbid the use of the land for the sale of alcoholic beverages. Because the creator of a defeasible fee has retained a right to regain ownership or to shift it to someone else if the forbidden act occurs, neither the grantee nor any of the grantee's successors receives the grantor's entire bundle of rights. Consequently, a defeasible fee is always accompanied by a future interest in favor of either the grantor or a third person.

The creator of a defeasible fee has broad discretion in restricting the use of the land. This fact makes defeasible fees a significant means of private land-use control. The grantor might give land to a church or a medical foundation on condition that intoxicating liquors will never be used or sold on the premises, or might require that the land be used only for a school or a cemetery, or might encourage a favorite area of scientific study by limiting the use of the land to the development of that scientific area. A number of restrictions, however, are void as against public policy and will not be enforced. Examples include the grantor's conditioning the retention of land on the grantee's obtaining a divorce or not marrying, avoiding an occupation that the grantor dislikes, excluding members of certain races from renting or buying the land, and in certain instances not contesting the grantor's will.

Defeasible fees are of three main types: (1) the fee simple determinable, (2) the fee simple on a condition subsequent, and (3) the fee simple subject to an executory limitation.

Fee Simple Determinable. Gloria wants to convey 50 acres of Blackacre to the Hamlet Environment Club as a nursery for seedling evergreen trees, but does not want the land used for any other purpose. To accomplish her objective, she conveys the land to the Hamlet Environment Club "so long as the property is used for growing seedling evergreen trees, the only use to which the land shall be put."[3] The Club has received a **fee simple determinable** entitling the Club and its successors to the land as long as they use it exclusively for growing evergreen seedlings. Gloria has retained a future interest called a **possibility of reverter**. If the Club or any successor quits growing evergreen seedlings, or puts the land to additional uses, the fee simple determinable expires by operation of law and possession reverts automatically to Gloria (or her heirs). Consequently, Gloria is entitled to the 50 acres as soon as a forbidden event occurs, without having to take legal action to regain ownership. However, if the Club or its successor refuses to vacate the premises, Gloria will have to undertake eviction proceedings to acquire possession. In most states, a possibility of reverter, like any other future interest, can be transferred by deed or by will.[4]

Fee Simple on a Condition Subsequent. To accomplish her goal, Gloria might have used different language, conveying the land to the Hamlet Environment Club "on condition that" or "provided that" the land be used for growing seedling evergreen trees, "but if that use ceases or if the land is used for any additional purpose, grantor shall have a right of entry and repossession." This language gives the Club a **fee simple on a condition subsequent**. Gloria has retained a future interest called a **right of entry for condition broken** (or a *right of reentry*), widely known today as a **power of termination**. If the Club or any successor ceases using the land exclusively for growing evergreen seedlings, Gloria (or her heirs) has an immediate right to enter and repossess the land. She does not, however, regain ownership automatically. All her future interest entitles her to is a power to terminate the defeasible estate for breach of the condition, with or without legal action. Until she exercises that power, the owner of the defeasible estate remains owner. In most states, a person who owns a power of termination (or a right of reentry) may transfer it by deed or by will.[5]

To exercise her power of termination, Gloria must take the steps required by law. Under the English common law, the owner of the right of entry had to make an actual entry onto the land, in the presence of witnesses. In the United States, actual entry is not required. In most jurisdictions, however, the person seeking to enforce the condition without an actual entry (but instead by taking legal action to acquire possession), must give to the owner of the defeasible fee a notice of intent to declare a forfeiture. In some states, notice of forfeiture is not required; the holder of the power can terminate the defeasible fee merely by filing (and winning) a lawsuit to recover possession of the land. This lawsuit is known in most states as an action in **ejectment**.

To be enforceable, a right of entry may have to be expressed in the deed or will. For reasons discussed later in this chapter, many courts view defeasible fees negatively and thus require the grantor to spell out clearly any right of termination, entry, or forfeiture. So, depending on the state, it may not be sufficient for grantor George to say simply, "Blackacre to Jane on condition that she use the land only for a school" and assume that a court will imply a right of entry for condition broken. For maximum assurance of that right, George should add the words, "and if Blackacre is ever used for any other purpose, grantor shall have a right of entry and repossession."

Fee Simple Subject to an Executory Limitation. Gloria wants to convey land in fee simple to Ann but wants the fee simple ownership to shift from Ann to Ben if certain circumstances occur. To carry out her purpose, Gloria grants Blackacre "to Ann and her heirs for as long as the land is used as a nursery for seedling evergreen trees, then to Ben and his heirs." Gloria has given Ann a fee simple (determinable) and, instead of keeping for herself a possibility of reverter, has given Ben an **executory interest**, here, a future interest similar to a possibility of reverter but owned by a third person, Ben, rather than by Gloria, the grantor. An executory interest is one that will not come into possession unless the prescribed circumstance occurs. If Ann or her successor ceases using Blackacre as an evergreen nursery, Ben or his heirs automatically receive fee simple ownership and a right of possession.

Executory interests can be either "shifting" or "springing." Gloria gave Ben a *shifting executory interest* (usually called a *shifting interest*) because ownership automatically moves or shifts from one line of grantees to another—from Ann or her successor to Ben or his heir—when Ann or a successor ceases using Blackacre as an evergreen nursery. Another example: Roger conveys land in fee simple "to Alfred, but if he dies without children surviving him, then to Beatrice." If Alfred never has children, or if his children predecease him, fee simple ownership shifts automatically to Beatrice or her heir upon Alfred's death.

Roger owns several farms and wants his unmarried son Arthur to have Blackacre, but only if Arthur marries Belle. So Roger conveys Blackacre "to Arthur and his heirs, from and after Arthur's marriage to Belle." By this wording, Roger keeps fee simple ownership of Blackacre and gives Arthur a *springing* executory *interest*. Arthur's interest is executory because he will not acquire the fee simple until he marries Belle. His interest is "springing" because upon his marriage to Belle, the fee simple, having remained in the grantor until the marriage, now automatically goes ("springs") from grantor Roger to grantee Arthur. Upon the marriage, the fee simple "vests" in Arthur. That is, Arthur receives a right of immediate possession.

The Problem of the Laughing Heir. Though useful in controlling the use of land, a defeasible fee can cause problems for an unsuspecting successor of the original grantee. The original grantee's recording the deed that created the defeasible fee gives everyone in the world notice not only of the grantee's rights but also of the language of defeasance stated in the original deed. Yet, years later, if the land has been transferred repeatedly with no restatement of the defeasible fee language in subsequent deeds or wills, a successor to the original grantee's title might not actually know that the fee is defeasible, despite having "record" notice of that fact. A successor who unwittingly makes a forbidden use of the property faces a nasty surprise—forfeiture of ownership at the hands of the defeasible fee's creator or that person's heir, sometimes called a "laughing heir" because of the delight that may attend a remote descendant's benefitting from a long-forgotten possibility of reverter or power of termination.

Suppose, for example, that 100 years ago the Reverend Rightly, retired and living in the home of his daughter Prudence, conveyed his residence Bountiful in fee simple to the Church of the Greater Light located next door, "on condition that alcoholic beverages will never be served on the premises, and if they are, grantor or his heirs shall have a right of entry and repossession." Needing money to remodel the sanctuary, the Church soon sold Bountiful. It was resold many times during the next 80 years, becoming first an office building and then a restaurant as the neighborhood changed from a quiet rural community to a bustling industrial center with an exuberant night life featuring a variety of nightclubs. Thirty years ago, the church was destroyed by fire. Finding that the greater community no longer supported alcoholic abstinence, the congregation sold the church site to a developer and rebuilt the sanctuary far away. Last year, Harold Hapless, the current owner of the restaurant Bountiful began selling fine wines as part of the evening meal service. Recalling the condition imposed by the Reverend Rightly long ago, Michael Monitor, a local historian and genealogist, located Reverend Rightly's only living descendant, liquor wholesaler Lawrence "Lucky" Fortune, and told him of his right of entry. Having never heard of the Reverend Rightly, but delighted to have the right of entry, Fortune promptly terminated Harold's ownership of the restaurant Bountiful, took over its management, and added a full-service bar.

This hypothetical situation illustrates a substantial problem with defeasible fees: people like Hapless can unwittingly forfeit their investments even though the reason for the use prohibition might long ago have disappeared, as where the character of a neighborhood changes. If, in addition, the land ends up in the hands of an heir who does not share the grantor's values, the grantor's intentions are doubly thwarted. Even where language of defeasance has not been violated, the presence of the future interest (a possibility of reverter, a right of reentry or power of termination, or an executory interest) is a problem for a developer who wants to use the land in a way that may violate a prohibition.

Hapless might have avoided losing Bountiful by having his attorney check the public records to determine whether there was a power of termination and who owned it, and then buying it. But this solution is feasible only if Fortune were willing to sell, and at a reasonable price. Or Hapless could simply have bought a policy of title insurance (discussed in Chapter 9), which would reimburse Hapless for losses resulting from any title problems that the title insurance company did not discover and report to Hapless before he completed the purchase of Bountiful. A recorded but undiscovered power of termination is such a title problem.

To reduce the impact of outdated use prohibitions and the incidence of harsh forfeitures, state courts and legislatures have taken a variety of remedial steps. However, the states are by no means uniform in the techniques they use in resolving the problem. The following list describes some of the more common controls on forfeitures.

- *Statutes of limitation.* Many legislatures have enacted statutes that impose a time limit for enforcing the future interest involved. The statutes vary in type. Some statutes impose a maximum time that the future interest itself will be effective—for example, forty years from the creation of the defeasible fee. When the forty years expires, the defeasible fee, if it has

BOX 3–2 POINT TO CONSIDER

Larry Fortune was happy to learn he had a right of reentry that would enable him to take ownership of the pleasant and profitable restaurant Bountiful. But what if the land had instead been an old landfill containing toxic pollutants now leaking into the city water supply? Under federal and state environmental protection laws, owners of contaminated land are held strictly liable for cleanup costs, simply because they are owners. These costs frequently add up to millions of dollars and for a variety of reasons often cannot be passed back to the persons who caused the pollution. Upon learning of the problem with the landfill, Larry decides to decline ownership. Can he do so, or is he automatically stuck with ownership of the landfill? Does it matter that he has a right of reentry instead of a possibility of reverter?

not yet been terminated, becomes in effect a fee simple absolute. Other statutes impose a time limit for bringing suit after a forbidden use or other terminating event has occurred— for example, seven or ten years for suing to evict a person who wrongfully continues in possession after violating the terms of a fee simple determinable. In a few states, the statute also applies to a violation of a fee simple on a condition subsequent, giving the owner of the power of termination only a limited time after breach of the condition to terminate the violator's estate.

- *Courts' interpreting ambiguous defeasible fees against grantor.* To protect the grantee from the automatic loss of ownership that results from violating the prohibition imposed by a fee simple determinable, many courts will interpret an *ambiguous* defeasible fee as creating a fee simple on a condition subsequent instead of a fee simple determinable. Gloria conveys Blackacre "to Ann and her heirs, on the assumption that Blackacre shall always be used as a school of dance, and if that use ceases, grantor wants the land back." When her dance business fails, Ann uses Blackacre as a collection center for the disposal of toxic wastes. Most courts would interpret the ambiguous conveyance as having created in Ann a fee simple on a condition subsequent, because under that interpretation Ann keeps ownership until Gloria (or an heir) takes the initiative to terminate it. In the meantime, Ann (or her successor) remains owner and is entitled to the land and its profits.

- *Courts' requiring clear proof that a terminating event has occurred.* Before allowing a forfeiture, the courts require clear proof that a forbidden use or other terminating event has occurred. Also, if the purpose of a defeasible fee is being substantially accomplished despite minor deviations from the required use by the grantee or a successor, or minor inadequacies of performance, the court is unlikely to find a violation that warrants termination or forfeiture.

BOX 3–3 APPLY YOUR KNOWLEDGE

Preceding paragraphs describe two types of statutes of limitation. Explain how each could work to prevent Gloria or her heir from taking Blackacre from Ann. Consider the time frames involved and what triggers the running of the statutory period.

Case 3.1 illustrates a court's reluctance to declare a forfeiture.

Case 3.1

Kinney v. State
710 P.2d 1290 (Kan. 1985)

In 1934, the Kinney Land and Cattle Company conveyed to the defendant State of Kansas approximately 790 acres of real estate located in Finney County, currently known as the Finney County State Park. Clauses five and six of the deed provided as follows:

> It is understood . . . that this conveyance constitutes a donation of the above property for state park purposes within the meaning of Chapter 124 and Chapter 127 of the Special Session Laws of 1933.

CLAUSE OF REVERSION

It is further agreed . . . that the premises herein described are to be used by the [state] as a public forestry, fish and game preserve and recreational state park, and in so using the said premises a lake of at least 150 acres is to be constructed thereon . . . and if the [state] fails to so use and maintain said premises, then . . . title to the said property . . . shall revert to the [Company], its successors or assigns.

In 1934, a dam was built on the land for the State. 2,200 feet long and 43 feet high, the dam had a capacity to create a lake of 325 acres. Over the years, the Kansas Fish and Game Commission improved the Finney County State Park by planting trees, building fences, and maintaining the dam and road. From time to time, the area behind the dam contained water, but the lake area never reached the 150-acre minimum specified in the deed. Alleging a breach of the reversion clause, heirs of the now-dissolved Kinney Company's stockholders claimed ownership of the land and brought suit to quiet title. The trial court granted partial summary judgment against plaintiff heirs, and they appealed.

PRAGER, J.

. . . The basic issue raised on the appeal is this: Does the fact that the Finney County State Lake . . . no longer contains a body of water of 150 acres [breach] the reversion clause so as to terminate the State's title to the real estate and cause title to revert to the plaintiffs? [To] determine this basic issue it would be helpful to consider certain general principles of law which are applicable in cases involving reversion clauses. In this case, the State, as grantee, owns a determinable or qualified fee in real estate which has all the attributes of a fee simple except it is subject to being defeated by the happening of a condition which is to terminate the estate. An estate in fee simple determinable is created by any limitation which: (1) creates an estate in fee simple and (2) [as here] provides that the estate shall automatically expire upon the occurrence of the stated event.

. . . In *Ritchie v. K.N.&D. Rwy.*, . . . it was held that an instrument containing a [defeasance clause], working a forfeiture of an estate, is to be strictly construed and its terms will never be extended by construction. This general rule is based upon the theory that, since a deed is the act of the grantor, it will be construed most strongly against him. . . .

The clause of reversion contained in . . . the warranty deed requires that the premises be used by the State . . . as a "public forestry, fish and game preserve and recreational state park." [The court then reviewed the statutes and court decisions that gave the fish and game commission broad discretion to use donated land for a public forestry, a fish and game preserve, or a recreational state park.]

These various statutes and authorities are cited to show the broad interpretation which has been given to the terms "forestry, fish and game preserve, and recreational state park." The trial court . . . granted partial summary judgment in favor of the defendants, holding that the terms of the deed do not support a forfeiture of the State's interest in the property simply because the lake . . . contained a body of water of less than 150 acres. . . .We agree with the trial court. The deed should be construed to require only that the State in good faith maintain the property as a public forestry, fish and game facility, and as a recreational state park. The grantor obviously had in mind an area dedicated to the protection and conservation of natural surroundings, game and fish, and a place where the people could enjoy such natural beauties. The lake is an important factor to be considered in determining whether the State in good faith has maintained the entire property for the intended uses. The maintenance of the lake, however, is not the controlling consideration but is only a part of the big picture. Under the circumstances, we hold that the trial court correctly held that the State of Kansas had not forfeited its title to the land simply because the quantity of water . . . has not been sufficient to completely fill an area of 150 acres. The quantity of water is bound to vary from year to year depending on the amount of rainfall and any other sources of water in the area.

. . . [H]owever, the trial court, instead of restricting its decision to a partial summary judgment on the single issue presented, found that all other issues in the case were moot and that judgment should be rendered in favor of the defendants. . . .We hold that, in entering that judgment, the trial court committed reversible error. The final summary judgment . . . was prematurely granted and denied to the parties the opportunity to complete their discovery and present evidence on the ultimate factual issue presented in the case: Whether the state has in good faith used and maintained the premises for the intended purposes. . . .

Although there was apparently some evidence presented to the trial court at the informal discovery conference that improvements had been made on the land and that the lake had contained water intermittently down through the years and that various sums of money have been spent on the property, such evidence has not been included in the record on appeal and the parties have not been furnished a full opportunity to complete their discovery and develop evidence to be presented [on the issues raised by the parties]. . . .[T]he case must be remanded to the trial court for further proceedings.

The judgment of the district court is affirmed in part and reversed in part and remanded for further proceedings in accordance with the views expressed in this opinion.

QUESTIONS ABOUT CASE 3.1

1. Since the plaintiffs proved that the state had not maintained a lake 150 acres in size as required by the deed, why was the court so reluctant to declare a forfeiture? Upon remand, what must the plaintiffs prove to win the case?

2. Recall the two types of statutes of limitation that protect owners of defeasible fees from the claims of the future interest holders. How could each type of statute have affected the outcome of this case?

Fee Tail

Suppose that Osgood owns Blackacre and wants it to stay in the family. In feudal times, Osgood's giving Blackacre to his child in fee simple would not necessarily accomplish his objective, since fee simple ownership enabled the child to transfer Blackacre to whomever he or she pleased. To overcome this problem, lawyers of the time developed the **fee tail**. To create it, Osgood would convey Blackacre "to my son Samuel and the heirs of his body." "Heirs of his body" meant his *lineal* heirs such as his children and grandchildren. The fee "tail" (from the French *tailler*, meaning "to cut") was "cut" or carved out of Osgood's fee simple. In effect, Osgood conveyed a succession of life interests to his lineal descendants and kept a future estate in fee simple. So, if the

BOX 3–4 YOU BE THE JUDGE

Melvin Berklund owned a cabin in Beehive, Montana. He transferred it to one of his sons. The deed read, in part, "In the event of the death of [the grantee son], above described property shall revert to [grantor Melvin]. Property cannot be sold by [son] during lifetime of [Melvin]." Within a few months, the son conveyed the property to a group of people consisting of himself, his wife, his siblings (two brothers and a sister), and their spouses. Angered by this transaction, Melvin threatened to burn the cabin. It soon caught fire, and Melvin was charged with arson. Tire tracks and other evidence resulted in his conviction. Melvin appealed, contending that he had not violated the arson statute because he had not burned "property of another" as the statute required for arson to have been committed. Melvin's reasoning? By conveying the property to himself and the rest of the group, the son had violated the clause stating that the "Property cannot be sold by [son] during lifetime of [Melvin]," and so had lost all ownership rights. Therefore, Melvin had burned only his own property and had not committed arson. Did Melvin burn "property of another"? In your answer, decide what kind of interest the son received, and whether he lost it automatically. From *State v. Berklund*, 704 P.2d 59 (Mont. 1985).

line of descent failed—for example because son Samuel had no children or Samuel's only child had no children—the fee tail would end and Osgood (or his collateral heir) would regain full fee simple ownership of Blackacre.

If the fee tail worked as planned, Osgood could restrict alienation and tie up ownership of Blackacre forever. For 187 years, from 1285 to 1472, the fee tail did work as planned. But many lineal descendants wanted to sell the land. Since a prospective purchaser would not buy it unless it was free of the entailment, lawyers invented ways to "disentail" the land so that it could be sold in fee simple. Eventually, an English statute permitted a tenant in tail to free the land from the entailment simply by transferring the land in fee simple by deed.

In the United States, only four states recognize the fee tail.[6] A substantial majority of the other states have statutes or decisional law abolishing the fee tail or limiting its effect. The statutes are of two major types. They either convert the purported fee tail into a fee simple in the first grantee named,[7] or give the first grantee a life estate, with that grantee's lineal descendants receiving a fee simple absolute.[8]

BOX 3–5 CALIFORNIA'S SOLUTION

California goes further than most states in preventing the forfeiture that can result from a defeasible fee. A 1982 California statute abolishes the fee simple determinable and its possibility of reverter. *Cal. Civ. Code*, § 885.020. Under the statute, language purporting to create a determinable fee creates instead a fee simple on a condition subsequent. So, in California, defeasance can no longer be automatic. California law also requires the owner of a right of entry (power of termination) to give notice of forfeiture to the owner of the defeasible fee before taking further action to terminate ownership, and to give that notice within a reasonable time after breach of the condition subsequent.

Life Estates

A **life estate** in real property is an ownership interest, the duration of which is measured by the life or lives of one or more persons. The person receiving the life estate is called the *life tenant.* Carved out of a larger estate such as a fee simple, a life estate is always accompanied by a future interest, usually a reversion or a remainder. Gloria owns Blackacre in fee simple and grants it "to my niece Fran for life." Fran has a life estate in Blackacre, and Gloria has a future interest—here, a reversion in fee simple. Gloria's granting Blackacre "to Fran for life, then to Paul" gives Fran a life estate and Paul a remainder in fee simple. The person who owns a reversion is a *reversioner;* the person owning a remainder is a *remainderman.*

Gloria's granting Blackacre "to Fran for life" could cause confusion over whose life was meant, Gloria's or Fran's. The courts uniformly hold the life estate is for Fran's life, not Gloria's. To avoid confusion, Gloria could have said, "to Fran for her life," but the use of "her" is not required.

Types of Life Estates

Life estates are either "conventional" or "legal." Created by a deed or a will, conventional life estates are commonly used for estate-planning purposes within families. Legal life estates are imposed by law, usually to protect surviving spouses from being disinherited.

Conventional Life Estates. Conventional life estates are either "ordinary" or "pur autre vie" (for the life of another). A life estate is "ordinary" where the measuring life is that of the life tenant. Gloria conveys Blackacre "to Fran for life." Fran receives an ordinary life estate which, like all life estates, is a saleable interest. However, an ordinary life estate is not inheritable, because it ends when the life tenant dies.

If Gloria had instead granted Blackacre "to Fran for the life of Paul," Fran would have received a life estate pur autre vie (for the life of Paul). In this conveyance, Paul has no interest in Blackacre; Gloria has simply used Paul's life instead of Fran's as the measuring life for Fran's life estate. Fran's life estate pur autre vie ends when Paul dies.

But what if Fran dies *before* Paul? Under the statutes of most states, her life estate does not end until Paul dies. In those states, Fran's heirs *do* inherit Fran's unexpired life estate pur autre vie.

Usually, conventional life estates are created by express language in a deed or a will. What language is required? In nearly all states, a deed or a will transfers the grantor's whole interest unless the grantor clearly reveals an intent to transfer a lesser interest. So, to create a life estate, the grantor will have to state clearly that a life estate is intended. However, no special wording is required to do this. Osgood owns Blackacre in fee simple. To give Sara a life estate, he could use the traditional words, "to Sara for life." Or he could use words of similar import, such as "to Sara until her death" or "for Sara, a life estate."

Osgood can create a life estate by grant or by reservation. Creating a life estate by *grant* means that Osgood carves it out of his fee simple and conveys (or devises) the life estate to someone else, either keeping a reversion for himself or transferring to a third person the remainder in fee simple. Creating a life estate by *reservation* means that Osgood conveys the fee simple to someone else and keeps (reserves) a life estate for himself.

A deed is effective to confer ownership only when it is delivered to the grantee (or to the grantee's agent, a person legally empowered to act on the grantee's behalf) and accepted by the grantee or the agent. On May 1, Osgood signs a deed granting to Sara a life estate in Blackacre. On May 5 he delivers the deed to her. Upon her acceptance of the deed, Sara acquires ownership of the life estate and a right immediately to possess Blackacre.

Some uses of life estates are illustrated in the following paragraphs. Each of the transactions begins with Osgood's owning Blackacre in fee simple. "Conveys" means that Osgood has signed and delivered a valid deed.

- Osgood conveys Blackacre "to Sara for life," saying nothing more. Sara has an ordinary life estate. Osgood, having disposed of no other interest, has a reversion in fee simple.

- Osgood conveys Blackacre "to Sara for life, then to Saul." Sara has an ordinary life estate. Saul has a remainder in fee simple. Osgood, having disposed of his total interest in Blackacre, has nothing left.

- Osgood conveys Blackacre "to Carla, reserving unto myself ownership of Blackacre for the rest of my life." Carla immediately owns Blackacre in fee simple, but because Osgood has retained a life estate, Carla's possession is postponed until Osgood dies.

- Osgood conveys Blackacre "to Anne for life, then to Bette for life, then to Clara for life." All three have ordinary life estates. Anne's is a *present* life estate entitling her to possession of Blackacre. Bette and Clara have *future* life estates, also known as "remainders for life." These remainders for life exist now and will become possessory if Bette and Clara live long enough. But if, for example, Bette dies before Anne and Clara, Bette's future life estate terminates, and Clara is immediately in line to take possession if she survives Anne. Osgood, having simply carved three successive life estates out of his fee simple, retained a reversion in fee simple.

- Osgood conveys Blackacre "to Anne for life, then to Bette for life, then to Clara for life, then to Donna and her heirs." Anne, Bette, and Clara have the present and future life estates described in the preceding paragraph, and Donna has a remainder in fee simple. Note that the words "then to Donna" would have been sufficient to give her the fee simple remainder, because the courts interpret the phrase as meaning "Donna and her heirs."

Osgood could have created the same interests by using a will instead of a deed. However, because a will does not become effective until the testator's death, a devisee under a will receives nothing until that time. In 1972, Osgood signs a valid will that devises Blackacre "to Sara for life, then to Saul." In 1999 Osgood dies. At Osgood's death, Sara acquires the life estate and a right to immediate possession of Blackacre. Simultaneously, Saul receives the remainder in fee simple.

Legal Life Estates. Legal life estates are imposed by law. Dower and curtesy, for example, are legal life estates developed at common law for the protection of surviving spouses. **Dower** was a widow's life estate in land acquired during the marriage but owned by the husband, who might have sold it or devised it to someone other than the widow. **Curtesy** was a similar interest that a surviving husband had in land owned by his wife. These interests are interests of *survivors*. A widow had no interest in the husband's land until the death of her husband; until then, she had only an "expectancy," also called an **inchoate** (incomplete) interest. Still existing in a few states, usually in a modified form, dower and curtesy are discussed further in Chapter 5.

BOX 3–6 APPLY YOUR KNOWLEDGE

Julia conveys Blackacre "to Andrew for the life of Sigfried, then to Imelda for life, then to Roger." What interests do Julia, Andrew, Sigfried, Imelda, and Roger have in Blackacre?

Rights of Life Tenant

As owner of a life estate, Fran has the exclusive right to possess, use, and enjoy the land for the rest of her life. She also may use her life estate as collateral for a loan or may dispose of the interest (but not the land itself) by selling it or giving it away. In other words, Fran has pretty much the same rights of usage during her life that a fee simple owner would have, with a notable exception: for the protection of owners of future interests, the owner of any kind of life estate has a duty not to commit waste on the property.

The monetary value of Fran's life estate depends on a host of variables. In negotiating a price, a prudent purchaser would consider not only the location of the land and any usage limits imposed by zoning laws, but also Fran's age, her health, the degree of risk in her lifestyle, and similar factors.

Duties of Life Tenant

A life tenant owes several duties to the owner of the future interest. Principal among these are the duty to keep the property in reasonable repair, the duty not to commit waste, and the duty to pay property taxes. In addition, the life tenant may have a duty to pay mortgage interest and to insure the property.

Duties to Repair and Not to Commit Waste. Linda has a life estate in Blackacre and Carl has the remainder in fee simple. When Carl's remainder becomes possessory, he has a right, within certain limits, to receive the real estate in reasonably good condition. Linda therefore has a duty to keep the property in a state of reasonable repair. In general, she must keep buildings structurally sound and cultivated land free from serious erosion, if, of course, she received structurally sound buildings and erosion-free land to begin with. If she received poor land and dilapidated buildings, she is not required to make substantial improvements. Nor is she usually required to repair flaws resulting from normal wear or use; she must correct such conditions only if they are likely to lead to serious deterioration. And she has no duty to replace property destroyed by forest fires, hurricanes, earthquakes, or other causes beyond her control. Basically, her duty is to preserve what she received, normal wear and tear (and casualties for which she is blameless) excepted.

The life tenant's duty of reasonable repair is related to the duty not to commit waste. A life tenant commits waste by damaging or neglecting the realty to the extent that the value of the future interest is substantially impaired. Intentional damage or destruction is called *voluntary waste*. Mere neglect, for example, failure to keep buildings in reasonable repair, is *permissive waste*. Waste does not include ordinary depreciation resulting from age and normal use, that is, from normal "wear and tear." Rather, to commit waste, a life tenant must intentionally or negligently cause injury beyond ordinary depreciation—an injury that substantially and permanently decreases the market value of a future interest.

What are some acts of waste? Linda's burning the house in a fit of rage, smoking negligently with the same result, failing to repair the roof so that rain ruins the interior, or selling much of the topsoil to suburban homeowners for landfill are clearly acts of waste. Other situations may or may not involve waste:

- Linda receives a life estate in a gravel pit and 100 acres of contiguous gravel-bearing land. She exhausts the gravel, leaving none for Carl. Has she committed waste? Probably not. The creator of the life estate likely intended the life tenant to have the income from the gravel pit, the clear purpose of which was extraction. Most courts hold that it is not waste for a life tenant to exhaust a mine that was open when the life estate was created. But a life tenant's opening a new mine, oil well, or gravel pit usually is considered an act of waste detrimental to the future interest, especially in the absence of such use when the life estate was created.

- Linda receives a life estate in a farm. May she cut and sell a large stand of timber to clear new ground for cultivation? The English considered this an act of waste. In the United States it is not waste if the land is chiefly valuable as farm land, and if removing the timber enhances the value of the land as a farm. But the cutting must be consistent with "good husbandry" and must actually improve the land as a farm. Where land is chiefly valuable for farming, a life tenant's removing a stand of timber from portions of the land *unfit* for cultivation probably would be waste.

- In 1975, Linda received a life estate in a beautiful Victorian house and lot in the city. Over the years, the house became surrounded by factories and railroad tracks. Though Linda has kept the house in good repair, by 2001 it could no longer be rented. Recently, Linda decided to demolish the house and to build a truck terminal there. Carl, the remainderman, objects, alleging waste. Is Linda free to carry out her plan? Probably yes, if the value of Carl's future interest is not diminished. Here, it would be increased, since the house cannot be rented and the land is more valuable for commercial use. This situation illustrates the "reasonable use" doctrine adopted in a number of states. It permits a life tenant to change the nature of the realty without liability for waste, if the change is warranted by substantial and permanent changes in the surrounding neighborhood, if the realty has little or no practical use or value unless changed, and if the change is a reasonable one.

Future Interest Owner's Remedies for Waste. To prevent the life tenant from committing waste, or to recoup losses resulting from it, the owner of a *vested* reversion or remainder in fee simple has a variety of remedies. A **vested interest** is one that has become possessory or is certain to do so. (In contrast, a *contingent interest*, discussed near the end of this chapter, receives considerably less protection from waste.)

First is a right of inspection to see if waste is occurring. If it is, the future interest owner is entitled to an injunction or to compensatory damages, or to both. Twenty or more states allow multiple damages for waste. Alaska, California, Iowa, and Maryland, for example, allow treble damages. In many states, including California, a life tenant who commits waste is subject to forfeiture of the life estate, especially if the waste is voluntary or "wanton."

Duties Regarding Real Estate Taxes, Mortgage Interest, and Insurance. For the duration of a life estate, the life tenant must pay the *general* real estate (property) taxes assessed against the land. Typically, these taxes are payable annually or semi-annually to the county or city where the land is located. In addition, the life tenant must pay his or her proportionate share of any *special* assessments imposed against the land for public improvements. Hendricks County builds a concrete road adjoining Blackacre, on which is imposed a special assessment of $60,000, payable immediately. The estimated life of the road is twenty years. Linda's life estate is expected to last for ten more years. Under a commonly used formula for apportioning the cost, Linda's share is $30,000 (which, ordinarily, she may pay in installments). Carl, the remainderman, must pay the rest. Formulas for apportionment of special assessments vary among the states.

When Linda received her life estate, Blackacre was encumbered by a mortgage in favor of First Bank. Linda must pay the interest on the mortgage debt. Remainderman Carl is responsible for retiring the debt itself, so he must repay the remaining principal amount.

Must Linda keep Blackacre insured against loss from fire, wind, or other disaster, for the benefit of the owner of the future interest? In most states, she has no such duty for property that was unencumbered (free of mortgage debt) when she received her life estate. However, if the deed or will that created the life estate requires Linda to insure the property, or if she received Blackacre encumbered by a mortgage or a deed of trust that required insurance, then she must make the insurance payments for the duration of her life estate.

Sometimes a life tenant or the owner of a future interest is forced to make a payment that the other was obliged, but failed, to make. For example, to avert a mortgagee's foreclosure action, a life tenant might pay a principal amount that the remainderman failed to pay. Or, for a similar reason, the remainderman might pay property taxes or a special assessment that the life tenant was supposed to pay. The person who paid the other's debt is entitled to reimbursement from the debtor.

The case that follows involves the grant of a fee simple with a reservation of a life estate. The question is, as between the deceased life tenant's probate estate and the remaindermen (now the owners of the fee), who gets the proceeds of homeowner's insurance paid for by the life tenant?

Case 3.2

Estate of Jackson
508 N.W.2d 374 (S.D. 1993)

In 1968, Mary Jackson conveyed a house to Iola Miller and Ileane Brosnan, and retained a life estate in the property. Jackson lived in the house until 1989 when she entered a nursing home. While in the nursing home, Jackson continued to pay the taxes and purchase insurance on the house.

In May 1991, a hailstorm seriously damaged the house. Jackson's insurance company assessed the damage and began processing her claim, but she died on June 1, 1991. As administrator of Jackson's estate, Iola Miller was advised by the estate's attorney to divide the insurance proceeds ($5,713.50) equally between herself and Brosnan. Miller and Brosnan then sold the house to Darrel Jackson for $7,000.

Later, deciding that the insurance proceeds belonged to the decedent's estate and should be distributed among the residuary beneficiaries of Jackson's will, and not to Miller and Brosnan, the estate's attorney claimed the insurance proceeds for the estate. Brosnan objected to the estate's final accounting. Holding that the insurance proceeds belonged to Jackson's estate, the probate court approved the final accounting. Brosnan appealed.

PER CURIAM.

Miller and Brosnan owned the house except for the life estate retained by Jackson. Jackson, as a life tenant, could use the property in any manner except that she could "do no act to the injury of the inheritance." . . . As a life tenant, Jackson also had the obligation to "keep the buildings and fences in repair from ordinary waste, and must pay the taxes and other annual charges, and a just proportion of the extraordinary assessments benefitting the whole inheritance." . . . In other words, Jackson was responsible to make necessary repairs to the house [to prevent waste]. . . . If she failed to make such repairs, the [owners of the fee (Brosnan and Miller) could have sued her for waste]. . . .

When Jackson died, the life estate ended. The probate court is specifically authorized to "fully and effectually adjudicate" the termination of a life estate. . . . However, the probate court focused only on the issue of who was entitled to receive the insurance proceeds. The probate court correctly concluded that since Jackson would have received those insurance proceeds if she had lived, her estate should receive them upon her death. [But] the probate court failed to consider Jackson's responsibility to repair the [damaged] life estate property. Since the house was damaged during her life estate, Jackson had an obligation to make necessary repairs [to avoid waste]. . . . After her death, her estate was responsible to fulfill that obligation. We reverse.

QUESTION ABOUT THE CASE 3.2

Was Mary required to insure the house during the period of her life estate?

_____

Termination of Life Estates

A life estate ends when the measuring life ends, but a life estate can terminate in other ways before the end of the measuring life. One way is by **merger** when, for example, the life tenant acquires the reversion or the remainder, or when the owner of a reversion or a remainder acquires the life estate. When all interests in the land end up in the hands of one person, the separate interests are said to "merge" into a fee simple in that person.

Like a fee simple, a life estate can be defeasible. So, if Lucky receives Blackacre "for his life, on condition that he will never grow tobacco on the premises," his doing so triggers the grantor's right of reentry (power of termination). And, as noted earlier, in a number of states a life estate can be terminated by court order for voluntary waste.

More About Remainders

The law of property gives estate planners great flexibility in the disposition of real estate. The remainder is a key element of most estate plans, given the variety of remainders it is possible to create.

Vested Remainders. Remainders are classified as "vested" or "contingent." A remainder is vested if two circumstances occur: (1) The natural expiration of the prior possessory estate is all that is required for the remainderman to receive possession, and (2) regardless of when the prior possessory estate ends, it is possible at that time to identify the person then entitled to possession. Hilda conveys Blackacre "to Lee for life, then to Sherri." Lee has a possessory life estate, and Sherri has a **vested remainder** in fee simple. Sherri's remainder is vested because (1) someone (Sherri) is entitled to possession immediately upon the natural expiration of Lee's life estate (i.e., upon his death) without the need for anything else to happen, and (2) it is possible at Lee's death to identify the specific person entitled to possession. That person is Sherri if she is still alive and still owns the remainder, or any person to whom she sold or gave the remainder, or her heirs or devisees if she still owned the remainder at her death.

Contingent Remainders. A remainder is contingent (i.e., is not yet "vested") if the remainderman's possession depends not only on the natural expiration of the prior possessory estate, but also on the happening (or nonhappening) of an additional event called a "condition precedent." A *condition precedent* is one that must be satisfied before the contingent remainder can vest. To say that a contingent remainder has "vested" means that because the specified event has occurred, the remainder is now certain to become possessory when the prior possessory estate naturally expires. Hilda conveys Blackacre "to Lester for life, then to Sherri if she reaches the age of 21 before Lester's death." Sherri is 12. Sherri has a **contingent remainder** in fee simple (and Hilda has a contingent reversion). Sherri's remainder is contingent because she is not entitled to possession upon the natural expiration of Lester's life estate unless she has satisfied the condition precedent of reaching the age of 21 before Lester's death. If she turns 21 before then, her contingent remainder vests on her birthday—becomes a vested remainder. If she dies before Lester, her contingent remainder ceases to exist and the reversioner (Hilda or her heirs or successor) gets possession of Blackacre.

BOX 3–7 APPLY YOUR KNOWLEDGE

Why does Hilda, in the preceding paragraph, have a reversion in fee simple?

The availability of contingent remainders increases estate planners' flexibility in serving their clients, by adding greatly to the number of options for disposing of realty. But contingent remainders carry with them certain problems. For example, as noted earlier, owners of contingent remainders receive little or no protection from a life tenant's committing waste. That protection is reserved largely for owners of *vested* remainders in fee simple. Contingent remainders can also violate the Rule Against Perpetuities.

Rule Against Perpetuities. The Rule Against Perpetuities prevents a person from controlling ownership of realty for an unreasonably long time after his or her death. Today's version of the original common law Rule is worded somewhat as follows: "No interest in real property is good unless it must vest, if at all, not later than 21 years after some life or lives in being at the time of the creation of the interest."

Under the Rule, a contingent interest that is not *certain* to vest within the prescribed time is *void when created*. By deed, George grants Blackacre "to Alice for life, then to Ben when Mt. St. Helens next erupts." Alice and Ben are alive when George grants them their interests. Alice's life is the measuring life, since the deed does not specify as the measuring life that of someone else living at the time of the grant. The 21-year period within which Ben's contingent remainder must vest begins to run at Alice's death.

For Ben's contingent remainder to be valid, it must be certain to vest no later than 21 years after Alice's death. Because Mt. St. Helens might not erupt for 1,000 years, or may never erupt, Ben's contingent remainder is not certain to vest within the required 21 years. Under the Rule, then, Ben's contingent remainder was void when George created it. Consequently, though Alice acquired a life estate, Ben acquired nothing and George has a reversion in fee simple. By imposing an outer time limit on George's ability to affect future property titles, the Rule prevents the uncertainty that future generations would experience if contingent interests were allowed to vest at the happening of unpredictable events.

However, the Rule can be violated in strange and unexpected ways, thus voiding contingent interests that seem deserving of enforcement. To alleviate such harshness, many states have modified the Rule Against Perpetuities by statute. Most commonly, a state statute imposes a wait-and-see requirement for vesting. Under some wait-and-see statutes, Ben's contingent remainder becomes vested if Mt. St. Helens actually does erupt before Alice's death or within the 21-year period afterward, but Ben's remainder becomes void at the end of the period if there is no eruption. If the remainder becomes void, possession of Blackacre reverts to George, the grantor.

Types of Vested Remainders

Further adding to conveyancing options are three kinds of *vested* remainders: (1) indefeasibly vested, (2) vested subject to open, and (3) vested subject to complete defeasance. Examples follow:

- Osgood conveys Blackacre "to Sara for life, then to Saul and his heirs." Saul is alive when the conveyance occurs. Saul has an indefeasibly vested remainder in fee simple—one that is certain to confer possession on him, his heir, or his transferee when Sara dies.

- Osgood conveys Blackacre "to Sara for life, remainder to the children of Saul." At the time of the conveyance, Saul had two children. Their remainder is vested, but because the remainder was granted to a class of people (Saul's children), the remainder is subject to open to accommodate any child of Saul's that may be born later but before Sara's death. If Saul has no more children, the two (or their heirs or successors) will share Blackacre equally upon Sara's death. If another child is born to Saul before Sara's death, the three children will share Blackacre equally.

- Osgood conveys Blackacre "to Sara for life, then to Saul and his heirs; but if the premises are ever used for the sale of alcohol, grantor shall have a right of entry and repossession." Saul has a vested remainder. But the "but if" language created a condition subsequent that cuts short, or defeats, Saul's remainder if the forbidden event occurs. So, at the time of the conveyance, Saul received a *vested* remainder that is *subject to complete defeasance* by the happening of the forbidden event. In fact, both the life estate and the remainder can be terminated, depending on when the alcohol is sold. The grantor has kept a power of termination (a right of reentry), just as the grantor of a fee simple on a condition subsequent keeps a power of termination. Another example: Osgood conveys Blackacre "to Sara for life, then to Saul for life." Sara has a present life estate, Saul has a vested remainder for life subject to complete defeasance should he die before Sara, and Osgood has a reversion in fee simple.

Self-Study Questions

1. What distinguishes estates from nonownership interests in land? How does a freehold estate differ from a nonfreehold estate?

2. In terms of purpose, how does a defeasible fee simple differ from a fee simple absolute?

3. You want to sell Blackacre to Paula Profit, but also want to prevent the construction of a basketball arena on the premises. (a) How can you convey fee simple ownership to Profit and still prevent the unwanted construction? (b) Of the two techniques for doing so, which should you use? Why?

4. (a) What is "the problem of the laughing heir"? (b) What ways does the law provide for resolving it?

5. How does a present estate differ from a future estate?

6. Give examples of two types of conventional life estates and a legal life estate.

7. In terms of usage rights of the owner, how does a life estate differ from a fee simple?

8. (a) What acts of a life tenant constitute waste? (b) What acts of a life tenant do not?

9. What are a life tenant's duties regarding real estate taxes, the payment of mortgage debt, and insurance coverage?

10. In the following disposition, who has what interests? Merlin conveys Blackacre "to Mary for life, then to Roger for life, then to Richard as long as alcoholic beverages are not sold on the premises."

Case Problems

1. In 1930, members of the Johnson family gave approximately 21 acres of land to the City of Hackensack, New Jersey, for use as a public park. The deed, which created a fee simple determinable, restricted the use of the land to park purposes and contained a clause stating that if the City "shall at any time cease to use said premises for park purposes, the title thereto shall revert to [the Johnsons]." Johnson Park contains tennis courts, basketball courts, baseball diamonds, an ice skating rink, a soccer field, swings, slides, and other playground equipment, park benches, and picnic tables. It also contains a pistol range, a greenhouse and nursery, and a maintenance garage. The Johnsons contended that the latter uses, together with the use of the northeast corner of the park as a dump site and the use of the park itself as a thoroughfare for dumping on adjacent property belonging to Fairleigh Dickinson University, were nonpark uses and automatically caused ownership of the land to vest in them. From a judgment for the City, the Johnsons appealed. Should the appellate court rule that the City had forfeited ownership to the Johnsons? From *Johnson v. City of Hackensack*, 491 A.2d 14 (N.J. Super. A.D. 1985).

2. You own Blackacre in fee simple and want your lawyer to draft a deed that will give possession to Annette for five years, a life estate to Jack after that if he completes his degree in engineering, and ownership back to you. (a) How might your lawyer word the deed to accomplish this result? (b) Under the deed, who would have what interests?

3. George Grantor decides to retire and give Blackacre Towers, his downtown office building, to his grandchildren, Jake and Jamie. Jake is 35 years old, and Jamie is two. Blackacre Towers has 30 suites, each renting for $1,000 per month for a total gross rental of $30,000 per month. Because Jake is a spendthrift and Jamie is a minor, George conveys Blackacre Towers to trustee Tom "for the life of Jake, then to Jamie." You are Tom's accountant. Because Tom has never done this kind of work before, he asks you the following questions: (a) What interests do George, Tom, Jake, and Jamie have in Blackacre Towers? (b) Who gets the $30,000 per month?

4. Gloria conveys Blackacre "to Fran for life, then to Jack." The northwest corner of Blackacre contains a commercial gravel pit. The rest is farm and orchard land. The house needs new paint but otherwise is in sound condition. During the next three years, Fran exhausts the gravel deposit in the northwest corner, opens a new pit to exploit another gravel deposit on the southeast corner, and cuts down 100 acres of apple trees to make room for a race track and parking area. Disturbed by this activity, Jack sues Fran, alleging four specific acts of waste:

   1. Failure to paint the house.
   2. Exhausting the gravel pit in the northwest corner.
   3. Opening the new gravel pit.
   4. Removing the apple trees.

In what ways, if any, has Fran committed waste? If there are some acts of waste, to what remedy is Jack entitled for each?

5. Throckmorton owns Big Ranch and wants to leave it to his only child, Sara, and ultimately in equal shares to Sara's children. Sara has two children now, is pregnant with twins, and hopes to have additional children within the next few years. What language of disposition should Throckmorton's will contain to accomplish his objective?

6. Rosita signs her will and leaves it with her lawyer. The will provides that her office building is to go "to Carl for life, then to Benita for life, then to Samuel." Rosita dies. (a) Which of the interests, if any, are vested? (b) What happens to Benita's interest if she dies before Carl?

Endnotes

1. Some writers on property law classify both present and future interests as "possessory" because possession of the land, either now or later, is characteristic of both kinds of interest. See, e.g., Thomas F. Bergin and Paul G. Haskell, *Preface to Estates in Land and Future Interests* (The Foundation Press, 1984). Other writers and the *Restatement of the Law of Property* (1936) characterize as "possessory" only those interests that give the owner present possession. So, under the Restatement, a life estate is a possessory interest, while the related future interest (remainder or reversion) is nonpossessory because its owner does not receive possession of the land until the life estate ends. This textbook adopts the Restatement terminology.

2. In the law of property, *purchase* has a special meaning that may seem odd. It means the acquisition of an interest in property by any means other than descent (i.e., other than intestate succession). So, a purchaser is a person who receives ownership in any kind of voluntary transaction, including a gift. Words *of purchase* indicate only *who* is to receive the interest, not whether the recipient paid anything for it.

3. Alternative wordings could be used, such as "*until* the premises cease being used for the purpose of growing evergreen seedling trees." The courts of some states may require additional language for enforcement of a fee simple determinable, such as "and if the land shall cease to be used for growing evergreen seedling trees, it shall revert to the grantor or his heirs." However, in most states, if the grantor used proper limitation language such as "until," "while," or "so long as," the fee simple determinable is effective *by operation of law* without the grantor's having to express the right of reverter. Roger A. Cunningham, William B. Stoebuck, and Dale A. Whitman, *The Law of Property* (West Publishing Co., 1993), § 2.4.

4. But some states, such as Illinois, prohibit the transfer of a possibility of reverter; and, as noted in Box 3–4 on page 80, California has abolished the fee simple determinable with its accompanying possibility of reverter.

5. But not in Illinois, whose statute says that possibilities of reverter and rights of reentry for breach of a condition subsequent are neither alienable nor devisable. *Ill. Rev. Stat.* ch 30, § 37b (1973). In contrast, California, though it has abolished the possibility of reverter, has a statute stating that a right of reentry *can* be transferred. *Cal. Civ. Code*, § 1046 (1872).

6. Delaware [Del. Code Ann. tit. 25, § 302 (2000)], Maine [Me. Rev. Stat. Ann. tit. 33, § 156 (2000)], Massachusetts [Mass. Ann. Laws, ch. 183, § 45 (2001)], and Rhode Island [R.I. Gen. Laws § 33-6-10 (2001)], but in modernized forms permitting easy disentailing. Cunningham, *supra* note 3, § 2.10.

7. Alabama, Arizona, California, Georgia, Indiana, Kentucky, Maryland, Michigan, Minnesota, Mississippi, Montana, Nebraska, New Jersey, New York, North Carolina, North Dakota, Oklahoma, Pennsylvania, South Dakota, Tennessee, Vermont, Virginia, West Virginia, Wisconsin, and Wyoming. In Texas, the fee tail is prohibited by the state constitution. *Id.* at n.3.

8. Arkansas, Colorado, Florida, Georgia, Illinois, Kansas, Missouri, New Mexico, and Vermont. *Id.* at n.5.

Chapter 4 Nonownership Interests: Easements, Profits, and Licenses

R uth owns Blackacre. As shown in Figure 4–1, Blackacre is a long, narrow ranch and forest area of irregular shape lying west of the scenic Rajun River, which flows through Happy Valley at the foot of the Purple Mountains. At Blackacre's western boundary, a state highway runs north and south, paralleling the river. Along the highway are several traffic turnouts from which travelers may view Happy Valley, the Rajun River, and the majestic Purple Mountains in the background.

FIGURE 4–1

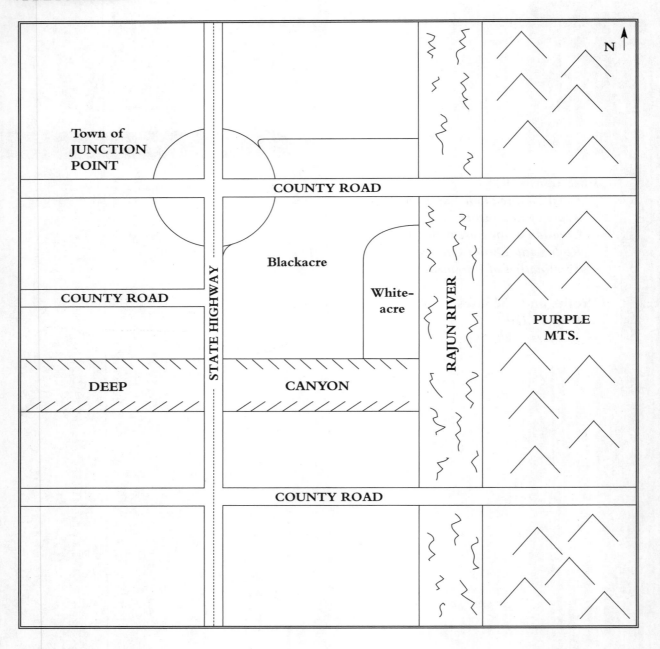

An east-west county road crosses Blackacre and intersects the state highway at Junction Point, a small town serving as headquarters for a mining company, a logging concern, and developers from nearby Metropolis interested in building retirement communities in Happy Valley. East of Blackacre lies Abner's Whiteacre, a tract of about 2,500 acres, which, like Blackacre, is rumored to have substantial coal deposits. Located on the west bank of Rajun River, and bounded on the north and west by Blackacre and on the south by a deep canyon owned by the United States, Whiteacre has no access to a public road.

In recent months, Ruth has received requests from people wanting to use her land in various ways. Abner wants a right of way across Blackacre to the state highway. A friend from Junction Point wants to hunt and fish on Blackacre. Mineco, Inc., wants the exclusive right to extract minerals there, while Timberco, Inc., seeks a similar right to harvest the timber. Hearing that Ruth might subdivide part of Blackacre for a housing development, Powerco, the local electric company, has inquired about rights of way for power lines. Concerned about the possibility of overdevelopment in Happy Valley, the Junction Point Conservation Club has asked Ruth to consider imposing strict limits on how residential lots may be developed on her land, or even to give up her development rights altogether by means of a conservation easement.

Each of these persons can acquire a right, called a *servitude*, to use Ruth's land without owning or leasing it. A **servitude** is a nonowner's interest in another's land that burdens (encumbers) the owner's estate for the benefit of the nonowner. A servitude gives its holder a right to use the other person's land in a particular way, or to prohibit a particular use. Common examples are an *easement* granting to a neighbor a right of way over the grantor's land for access to a public highway; a right, called a *"profit,"* to remove something (e.g., minerals, timber) from the land; and *restrictive covenants* (provisions in deeds) imposed on homeowners in a housing development to limit or prohibit land uses that may harm the neighborhood.

Individuals and business firms acquire servitude rights in a variety of ways: by *gift or purchase* from the landowner; by *transfer* (assignment) of existing servitude rights from the holder; by *acquiring land to which such rights have previously attached*; by a *court order*, as in the judicial declaration of an implied easement, discussed later in this chapter; by *prescription*, which results from a landowner's allowing trespassory use to ripen into rightful use; and by a *statute* allowing certain individuals to acquire an easement by exercising a "private right of eminent domain."

In addition, governments and government agencies commonly acquire easements and other interests in land by condemnation or by dedication. **Condemnation** is the government's exercising its power of eminent domain to force the sale of the interest to the government. **Dedication** is a private landowner's gift of an interest in land to the government.

Landowners often create servitudes by means of a writing called a *grant*. Unless the grant specifies a shorter time, the servitude has the duration of the estate held by the landowner. Ruth owns Blackacre in fee simple. Without imposing a time limit, she grants her neighbor Abner a driveway easement across Blackacre so he and others can get to the main highway. Like Ruth's fee simple estate, the easement she granted is of permanent or indefinite duration and creates a permanent burden on Ruth's land. But if Ruth owned only a life estate in Blackacre, she could not grant an easement that would exceed the duration of her life estate. Neither can a tenant grant an easement that exceeds the term of his or her tenancy.

This chapter discusses three kinds of servitudes—easements, profits, and licenses. Easements and profits are *interests* in the land of another. Being interests, they cannot be revoked by the grantor. In contrast, a license is not an interest in land, but is only a revocable personal *privilege*, usually created orally or implied by law, to go onto another's premises for a certain purpose. However, in rare instances discussed later in this chapter, some courts hold that a particular license is irrevocable. An irrevocable license is a servitude. Restrictive covenants are discussed in Chapter 17.

Easements

Easements provide great efficiency and flexibility in the use of land. To benefit most from easements, land users and planners need to understand their legal nature, the various types of easements, the methods of creating and terminating them, and the rights and duties of parties affected by them.

Legal Nature of an Easement

An easement differs markedly from an estate in land. One who has an *estate*—e.g., a fee simple estate, a life estate, or a leasehold estate—has a right of exclusive possession, occupancy, and control of the land. In contrast, an *easement* gives its holder only a right to *use* someone else's land for some special purpose not inconsistent with the general property rights of the landowner (i.e., owner of the estate). The familiar "right of way," a right to pass across another's land by means of a lane, path, road, or driveway, is one such usage right. Others include sewerage and drainage; the placement of utilities such as power lines, pipelines, communications towers, and fiber-optic cables; and recreational uses such as snowmobiling and skiing.

One aspect of an estate owner's exclusive possession and control is the right to "carve out" lesser interests such as easements and to grant them to others on a temporary or a permanent basis, while remaining in control of all that was not granted. Upon the granting of an easement, the estate owner and the easement holder have simultaneous interests in the same land, and both have rights of usage that may come into conflict. The easement that Ruth carved out from her fee simple conferred on Abner only a right to use the specified portion of Blackacre as a driveway. Ruth remains owner of the driveway area. As owner, she has the right to use it for all purposes consistent with Abner's driveway use. For example, she, too, may use the strip for access to the highway, may plant flowers on the untraveled portion of the driveway strip and harvest them for sale, and may use the strip in other ways, as long as she does not interfere with Abner's usage rights. Because Ruth's estate confers upon her the right of occupancy and control, she is said to have a *possessory* interest in Blackacre, including the part encumbered by the driveway easement. Because Abner's easement confers upon him only a usage right short of occupancy, he is said to have a *nonpossessory* interest in Blackacre.

An easement can be for a *fixed duration*, say of five years or for the life of its holder. If no fixed duration is specified or implied by law, the easement is "permanent" in the sense that a fee simple estate is permanent—binding on an indefinite number of successive owners until terminated in a way recognized by law. Termination of easements is discussed later in this chapter.

BOX 4–1 YOU BE THE JUDGE

In a lawsuit, Martin and Mary Harding were granted an easement for a roadway across land owned by Ella Pinello. The Hardings wanted to fence the roadway on both sides. Pinello objected because she wanted to graze cattle on both sides of the roadway. Furthermore, she wanted to install a locked gate where the Hardings would enter it. The trial court held that the Hardings could not fence the roadway, and that Pinello could install a locked gate, provided that the Hardings were given a key. Was the trial court correct (a) in refusing to allow the Hardings to fence the roadway? (b) in allowing Pinello to install a locked gate? *Harding v. Pinello*, 518 P.2d 846 (Colo. App. 1973).

Types of Easements

Easements are of many types. The major classifications focus on who is benefitted, the ways in which easements are created, and the kind of use or control the easement holder may exercise over the other person's land.

Easements Appurtenant and Easements in Gross

[handwritten: transferable — not transferable — when a type is not specified. easement]

An easement can be "appurtenant" or "in gross." Where doubt exists about which type it is, the law provides guidelines for classifying it as either appurtenant or in gross. The distinction matters because some easements in gross are not transferable, while all easements appurtenant are transferable as part of the land they serve.

Easements Appurtenant. An **easement appurtenant** is one benefitting a tract of land, called a **tenement**, without regard to who owns or possesses it. By definition an easement appurtenant involves a **dominant tenement** and a **servient tenement**. Ruth granted to Abner, owner of Whiteacre, "an easement of ingress and egress, thirty feet wide, along the south boundary of my ranch Blackacre." The benefitted land (Whiteacre) is the dominant tenement; the burdened land (Blackacre) is the servient tenement.

An easement appurtenant "runs with the land." That is, upon any change in the ownership or rightful possession of Whiteacre or Blackacre, the new owner or possessor automatically acquires the easement rights or burdens of the former owner or possessor. Abner sells Whiteacre to Harold. Harold automatically receives the easement across Blackacre (even if Blackacre has a new owner) without any special mention of it in the deed of conveyance. Thus, easements appurtenant are routinely transferred as part of the dominant tenement. However, they cannot be transferred apart from the land. For example, Abner could not keep Whiteacre and sell the easement to Development Co., nor sell Whiteacre and keep the easement.

An easement can be appurtenant to a tract of land even though the servient tenement does not adjoin it. Suppose that Abner's Whiteacre is separated from the state highway by several different tracts of land, with only Ruth's Blackacre adjoining Whiteacre. If Ruth and the other tract owners grant access easements to Abner, all the easements are appurtenant to Whiteacre, because they all benefit Whiteacre by providing access to the highway.

Easements in Gross. An **easement in gross** benefits a person rather than a tract of land. Some examples:

- Powerco (a corporate "person") acquires easements to construct and maintain power lines on the eastern twenty feet of a row of fifty adjacent lots in a residential neighborhood. Powerco owns no land in the area. The easements granted to Powerco by the residents are easements in gross because they benefit Powerco (a person) rather than a parcel of land. The lots are servient tenements, but there is no dominant tenement. Instead, Powerco has a dominant *interest*.

- Ruth's land has a lake on it. Her naturalist friend Martin lives in Junction Point in a rented apartment. Ruth grants in writing "to Martin a right of access across Blackacre along the old bridle path from the main highway to the lake for camping on the shore, fishing, and boating." Because Martin owns no land, Martin's easement is in gross.

- Maria owns a house next door to an office building owned by Russell, who is permanently confined to a wheelchair. Maria gives him a written "right of wheelchair access for as long as he needs it, from his building through the first-floor breezeway of my house to the bus stop on the other side of my house." Even though Russell owns the property next door to Maria's, his easement is in gross because it was granted to him for personal use and was not intended to run with the land for the benefit of future owners of Russell's land.

Easements in gross are most useful commercially if they can be transferred and if their usage rights can be shared with others without the consent of the grantor. For example, a regional power company buying a local utility obviously would prefer to receive existing construction and maintenance easements as part of the local utility's business rather than having to purchase them anew from the various landowners.

But the local utility has no dominant tenement whose transfer automatically carries the easements with it, only a dominant personal right of usage. Historically, the English courts held that easements in gross were not transferable. Such easements, the courts reasoned, were meant to confer only temporary, personal rights, and their holders should not be allowed to prolong the burden on servient tenements by granting those rights to strangers to the original easements.[1] American courts, however, have tended to favor transferability, often finding *commercial* easements in gross transferable, though usually denying transferability to purely personal, noncommercial ones unless the grantor has expressed a contrary intent. In the preceding examples, Powerco would be allowed in most or all states to transfer its construction and maintenance easements to a successor power company without the consent of the servient landowners. In contrast, the wheelchair-bound Russell probably would not be allowed to transfer his easement to a third person without the grantor's consent, because the easement was granted for a special, non-commercial reason personal to the individuals involved.

Whether a particular easement in gross is commercial or noncommercial may be unclear. To classify it, the courts usually consider the intent of the parties to the original easement transaction, as evidenced by the circumstances existing then. After a few months of boating and camping on Ruth's land, the naturalist Martin decides to sell his easement rights to the Junction Point Conservation Club so that its large membership can enjoy Ruth's lake and shore. Ruth objects to the transfer. If the language of the easement and other circumstances surrounding its creation show that Ruth intended it only for Martin's personal or family use, the easement will be held noncommercial and nontransferable. But if Ruth granted the easement knowing that Martin intended to share his access beyond family and friends, a court might declare the easement commercial and thus transferable over Ruth's objections.

Also aiding transferability is the judicial presumption favoring an easement appurtenant over an easement in gross where the easement could be interpreted as either. Ruth granted Abner a driveway easement across her Blackacre for access to his Whiteacre. Ruth's language "I hereby grant a driveway easement *to Abner*" could be interpreted as creating only a personal right—an easement in gross, possibly nontransferable, that expires at his death. More likely, in granting the easement, Ruth intended to give access to whoever might need it, such as Abner's family and friends, repair persons, meter readers, solicitors, delivery people, and even later owners of Whiteacre. A general right of access would make the land itself more useful and thus benefit Whiteacre, not just Abner. Where an easement can benefit land indefinitely, and in the absence of language clearly limiting usage rights to a particular person, the courts ordinarily interpret the easement as appurtenant so that it will run with the land.

Express, Implied, and Prescriptive Easements

The law also classifies easements according to the method of their creation, which dictates, in part, the formalities that easement holders must observe to acquire and protect their easement rights. An **express easement** is created by the use of language and conveyed to the grantee by a deed or a will. Therefore, it is subject to writing requirements discussed later in this chapter. An **implied easement** arises by judicial inference from circumstances surrounding the conveyance of an estate in land, and not from any agreement or expression of the parties. The prior use of the land and the facts surrounding its conveyance *imply* an easement right that the parties did not express. For an implied easement to exist, a court order must create it. A **prescriptive easement** arises from persistent, uninterrupted trespassing to which the offended landowner has not made a timely objection. The landowner's failure to take preventive measures within the time allowed by the statute of limitations results in the trespasser's acquiring a prescriptive easement and thus the right to continue the formerly trespassory use of the land. These types of easements—express, implied, and prescriptive—are discussed in more detail later in this chapter, in the section entitled "Creation of an Easement."

Affirmative and Negative Easements

An **affirmative easement** allows its holder to enter the servient tenement and use it in some way, for example by crossing it to get to the highway, or by installing and maintaining an underground drainage pipe to divert excess water from the dominant tenement to a stream located on the servient tenement.

The holder of a **negative easement** has no right to enter the servient tenement, but has a right to prohibit an otherwise lawful use of it or to require its owner to take action required by the easement. Ella acquires from her neighbor Mario an "easement of light, air, and view." The easement prohibits Mario from erecting structures or allowing the growth of vegetation that would impede Ella's light, air, or view. Moreover, if obstructions to light, air, or view exist when the easement is granted, Mario must remove them.

Private and Public Easements

A **private easement** is one whose enjoyment is restricted to one person, a few people, or a limited class of people. Ella's easement of light, air, and view is an example. So is Abner's easement across Ruth's Blackacre, since he can limit its use to those he wishes to visit his Whiteacre. Other examples of private easements include the following:

- A right of way granted to a railroad company for its tracks where the grantor retains fee simple ownership. Even though the public has a right to use the trains, it may do so only on terms dictated by the railroad and the government. Because the railroad's easement is

BOX 4–2 THE DOCTRINE OF ANCIENT LIGHTS

Under the English doctrine of ancient lights, a landowner acquired, by uninterrupted use for twenty years, a prescriptive easement over adjoining land for the unobstructed passage of light and air. This easement arose automatically from the fact of long-term, uninterrupted use, and not from any agreement between landowners. Because such easements limit building heights and consequently the development of neighboring properties, early American courts found the doctrine unsuited to conditions in this country, especially in the cities, and refused to adopt it. Today, American courts uniformly decline to grant an easement of light and air by implication or prescription; however, they will enforce express easements for light, air, and view.

private, the railroad has a right to exclude the public from the physical right of way, and often does so for safety and other reasons.

- Right of residents to use the streets in a private subdivision. Melanie subdivides her land into residential lots, sells them, and keeps ownership of the land identified on the plat as streets and alleys. Each person who acquires a lot in the subdivision automatically acquires a private easement to use the streets and alleys shown on the plat, even if the deed conveying the lot says nothing about street easements. Because the lot owners have private easements, they can prevent Melanie from closing a platted street or alley.

The enjoyment of a **public easement** is vested in the public generally, or in an entire community. Subject to government rules relating to safety and traffic control, every member of the public has an easement in gross to use public roads, streets, highways, navigable streams, and air space that is in the public domain. Even privately owned land can be subject to public easements. Melanie, owner of the platted streets in her subdivision, dedicates an easement of passage in them to the city or county. Having granted a public easement of passage, Melanie cannot exclude anyone from using the streets. However, if the streets had not been dedicated to public use (or taken by the government for that purpose), the easements involved would be private, and Melanie could restrict street use to lot owners and their invitees and licensees.

"Private Eminent Domain" Easements

Some states have statutes delegating the government's power of eminent domain to private landowners for the limited purpose of acquiring an easement appurtenant for utility services. California's statute, for example, provides: "Any owner of real property may acquire by eminent domain an appurtenant easement to provide utility service to the owner's property," if there is great necessity for the taking, and if the location of the easement provides the most reasonable service to the dominant tenement consistent with the least damage to the servient tenement.[2] "Utility service" means water, gas, electric, drainage, sewer, or telephone service. The person taking the utility service easement must, of course, pay the servient landowner a just compensation.

● Creation of an Easement

The method of creating an easement determines whether it must be evidenced by a writing, and also affects what the holder must do to make the easement binding against subsequent owners of the servient tenement.

Creation by Express Grant or Reservation

Express easements—those created by the use of language—result from either an express grant or an express reservation. In an express *grant*, the owner of the servient tenement conveys the easement to the owner of the dominant tenement, but remains owner of the servient tenement. Abner acquired his easement across the south end of Ruth's Blackacre by express grant from her; she remained owner of Blackacre. In an express *reservation*, a landowner conveys the land itself and keeps (reserves) an easement across it. Ruth lives on the south half of Blackacre. She sells the north half to Jason, reserving an access easement across the north half so that she can get to the creek at the north end of Jason's tract.

Writing and Other Formalities. Various state laws—the Statute of Frauds, the Statute of Deeds, and the Statute of Wills—impose writing and other requirements for creating and conveying express easements.

A grantor may sell an express easement to the grantee or make a gift of it. The sale of an easement involves two processes: making a contract (agreement) that creates the easement, and the grantor's conveying the easement to the grantee. Under the **Statute of Frauds**, a contract for the sale of an interest in land must be evidenced by a writing signed by the person, whether grantor or grantee, against whom it is to be enforced. The grantee may need to enforce the grantor's promise to convey the easement or to allow the usage rights promised; the grantor may need to enforce the grantee's promise to pay. The Statute of Frauds does not require that a contracting party's signature be witnessed.

Most states have, in addition to the Statute of Frauds, a separate Statute of Deeds imposing writing and other formal requirements for deeds of conveyance regardless of whether the underlying transaction is a contract or a gift. The **Statute of Deeds** requires that a deed name a grantee, be signed by the grantor, describe the land and the interest conveyed, be "acknowledged" in some manner (commonly by being notarized), and meet other requirements discussed in Chapter 11. To have a deed notarized, the grantor presents it to an official called a **notary public**, whose function, among others, is to certify the authenticity of the grantor's signature. Wills (and the easements they may create) take effect at the death of the grantor. To be valid, wills must conform to the writing and witnessing requirements of the state's **Statute of Wills**, discussed in Chapter 6.

Recording of Express Easements. An easement is not binding on a bona fide (good faith) purchaser of the servient tenement who lacks notice of the easement at the time of purchase. For maximum protection against later owners of the servient tenement and others who might wish to deny the existence of an express easement, the grantee of the easement (owner of the dominant tenement) should have the deed recorded in the county office provided for that purpose, usually called the *Recorder's Office* or the *Registry of Deeds*. **Recording** is the process of copying into the public records the contents of documents that the state recording act permits to be recorded—generally, any document affecting title to land. Recording a document puts the public on notice of its contents, even people who have not read it. Because the state recording acts prohibit the recording of an *unacknowledged* deed, the county recorder will not accept such a deed for recording. However, if it is otherwise complete and properly delivered to the grantee, an unacknowledged deed does convey the described interest to the grantee. Chapter 9 discusses the recording statutes and the process of recording.

Drafting Problems. Frequently, grantors create trouble for themselves by drafting easement documents (contracts, deeds, wills) without the aid of competent legal counsel. Courts try to give effect to vague, ambiguous, or otherwise poorly worded easement documents, but often must guess at the drafter's intentions and may adopt an interpretation that the drafter did not intend. To reduce the need for judicial interpretation, an easement drafter should (1) use legal language that unambiguously creates an easement—language that rules out other interests such as a fee simple estate, and (2) specify the purpose, location, width, and duration of the easement.

Ruth can give Abner access to the highway by granting him an easement across her land, by leasing the needed strip of land to him, or by making him the fee simple owner of the strip. The rights accompanying each of these interests—easement, leasehold estate, fee simple estate—vary greatly. If Abner's interest is an easement, Ruth remains owner of the strip and has a right to use it in ways that do not interfere with Abner's usage rights. If he has a lease, he is entitled to exclusive possession of the strip until the lease terminates, but his access to the highway ends then. If he has a fee simple estate, he owns the strip and has the right to exclude Ruth.

Abner and Ruth agree that he should have an easement. What legal language clearly creates it? Ordinarily, people seeking a right of passage across another's land ask for a "right of way."

Although "right of way" literally describes the *use* that Abner will make of Ruth's land, and not the *interest* that Abner will receive, the courts generally equate "right of way" with "easement" (of passage), as long as the document as a whole does not indicate that some other interest was intended. So, if Ruth states in a deed, "I hereby grant to Abner a right of way across my land," most courts would hold that "right of way" means "easement," since "across my land" makes clear that Ruth intends to remain owner of the land while granting Abner a right of usage.

Unfortunately, drafters intending to create an easement sometimes cause interpretive difficulties by using ambiguous phrases to describe the interest granted. Suppose, for example, that Ruth gives Abner a deed stating, "I hereby convey to Abner a strip of land for a right of way over and across Blackacre," and later a dispute develops over Ruth's use of the strip. To keep her from using it, Abner erects a fence. Whether he can legally exclude her depends on the interest she transferred to him. Was it the easement she intended, a fee simple estate, or some other interest? Ruth's deed does not clearly say. The most likely possibilities are an easement and fee simple ownership. The courts of many states have interpreted language similar to Ruth's as creating a fee simple estate, while in other states such language has been held to create an easement. Indeed, the courts within a given state have interpreted the same language differently. For example, an Oklahoma trial court held that an easement resulted from language like Ruth's, only to be reversed by the appellate court's ruling that a fee simple resulted.[3]

To avoid the interpretive difficulty, Ruth should describe the interest granted as an "easement" or a "right of use" instead of "a strip of land" or a "right of way." Under modern conveyancing law, a deed is presumed to transfer a fee simple estate unless the deed makes clear that a lesser interest such as an easement was intended. Unless adequately qualified, a transfer of a "strip of land" is generally understood to transfer full ownership of the land, not just a limited right to use it. Adding "right of way" does not dispel all doubt about the grantor's intention, because "right of way" can be understood to indicate the grantee's planned use of the land and not the *interest* that the grantor intended to part with. Indeed, many courts find "strip of land for a right of way" inadequate to rebut the presumption that a fee simple estate was intended. Other courts, however, have held that "right of way" *does* sufficiently qualify "strip of land" for them to hold that the document created an easement. The drafter who intends an easement should eliminate doubt by giving the interest its legally correct name, "easement."

To make clear that she intends an easement, Ruth should also use language of *transfer* historically associated with the creation of easements. It is appropriate to use either "convey" or "grant" for transferring an existing interest in land. *Grant*, however, is the word historically associated with the creation of easements and other nonpossessory interests, while "convey" traditionally indicates a freehold estate such as the fee simple. Because grantors commonly use "convey and warrant," "quitclaim and convey," and similar phrases to create or transfer an *estate,* a grantor intending to create an *easement* should avoid them and should use "grant" instead.

Confusion can result also from the incorrect use of "reserve" and "except." Wanda wants to convey Blackacre to Rosita and create an easement across it for the benefit of neighboring Greenacre, which Wanda also owns. To do so, Wanda *reserves* the easement across Blackacre: "I hereby convey Blackacre to Rosita and reserve an easement 30 feet wide along the south boundary of Blackacre for access between Greenacre and the highway." If instead she wanted to convey *part* of Blackacre to Rosita and to keep ownership of the rest, she would except from the conveyance the part that she will continue to own. "I hereby convey to Rosita all of Blackacre except the east 150 feet."

Sometimes, a grantor "excepts" an easement across granted land, even though *except* is properly used only for withholding ownership. In most situations, the misuse of except is inconsequential, since the courts can discover the grantor's true intent by evaluating other language in

BOX 4–3 APPLY YOUR KNOWLEDGE

Lorraine wants to give Kamali an express easement across the south end of her strip mall so that his customers can get to his neighboring retail store from the public street. Explain which of the following statements would be the best wording for the deed. Why are the other wordings less desirable? Rank these five wordings from "best" (most likely to be interpreted as an easement) to "worst" (least likely to be interpreted as an easement).

- "I hereby grant to Kamali a right of way thirty feet wide across the south end of my strip mall."
- "I hereby grant to Kamali an easement of access thirty feet wide across the south end of my strip mall."
- "I hereby convey to Kamali a strip of land thirty feet wide for a right of way across the south end of my strip mall."
- "I hereby grant to Kamali a strip of land thirty feet wide for a right of way across the south end of my strip mall."
- "I hereby convey to Kamali an easement of access thirty feet wide across the south end of my strip mall."

the deed. So, if the deed says "Grantor hereby excepts an easement 30 feet wide along the south boundary," the courts will hold that the intent to reserve an easement is sufficiently clear. The misuse of except *can* be a problem, however, where the grantor describes the reserved easement in a way that could cause a court to view it as a fee simple interest. If Wanda's intention is to reserve an easement 30 feet wide, she risks keeping a fee simple (and property tax liability) by saying "I except a right of way 30 feet wide" or, worse, "I except a strip of land 30 feet wide."

Making clear that the grantee is to receive an easement and not a greater interest is only part of the drafter's task. At least as important is the need, often neglected, to specify the *usage rights* the grantee is to have. Most easements burden the grantor's land indefinitely. If usage rights are left vague, the grantor or future owners of the servient tenement may find the burden increasing in unexpected and unpleasant ways, perhaps greatly reducing the value of the burdened land. The grantor therefore has a vital interest in controlling the usage rights conferred by the easement. To reduce the potential for litigation, the easement drafter should address the rights most likely to lead to dispute. They include:

- *Purpose of the easement.* Ruth might be willing to grant Abner an access easement for his one-family residence or for the traffic normal for his farm, but not for coal-mining operations or the 2,000-lot residential subdivision Abner plans to develop over the next five years. If the deed is vague about purpose and Abner uses the easement for purposes unacceptable to Ruth, she may have to bring suit to determine whether Abner has exceeded the scope of his easement.

- *Location.* Whether by accident or design, sometimes a landowner grants an **unlocated easement** (also called a "blanket" or a "floating" easement), that is, an easement whose location on the servient tract is not specified in the deed. A deed granting an unlocated easement, is valid; it merely leaves the exact location to be determined later by agreement of the parties or by use of the land. The grantor of an unlocated easement has first right to fix the location, but must act reasonably in doing so. If the grantor fails to fix a location

BOX 4–4 ABANDONED RAILROADS AND MODERN HIKING TRAILS

The abandonment of railroads is nothing new, nor is the competition for the newly freed roadbeds. In the early 1940s, when an Oregon logging railroad became unprofitable, the railway company removed the tracks and, over the objections of adjacent landowners, converted the roadbed into a road for use by logging trucks and other motor traffic. The adjacent landowners claimed fee simple ownership of the roadbed, alleging that the railroad's original deed of conveyance, being ambiguous, had conveyed only an easement to the railroad, which it had abandoned by removing the tracks. The court agreed with the landowners that the ambiguous deed had conveyed only an easement, but held that the railroad had not abandoned it. Moreover, the change in use from a railway roadbed to a road for motor transport was justified by changed circumstances.

In recent years, consolidation in the railroad industry has resulted in the abandonment of entire railroad lines, freeing thousands of miles of railroad right of way for other uses. Many communities want to convert the roadbed into nature, biking, and hiking trails and need to negotiate with whoever owns it. But who owns the roadbed? If the railroad company originally received from various landowners only easements for railroad use, abandonment of the easements extinguished them, and the granting landowners or their successors in interest have the fee simple free of the easements. If initially the railroad company received fee simple ownership of the roadbed, the company would remain owner of the land despite having ceased railroad operations. Unfortunately, many deeds were unclear about the rights conveyed, stating, in essence, "Landowner hereby conveys to Railroad Company a strip of land 300 feet wide for railroad use." Resolving the ambiguity has required, and continues to require, much litigation that more careful drafting might have prevented.

within a reasonable time, the grantee can do so, but also must act reasonably. Ruth grants Abner an unlocated roadway easement across Blackacre for an open-pit coal mine on Whiteacre. To avoid the noise, dust, and vibration caused by coal trucks, she later locates the easement at the extreme south end of Blackacre, far from her house. Contending that her choice of location will prove unreasonably costly for his coal-mining operation, Abner brings suit. If Ruth had negotiated a location and had stated it in the deed before granting the easement, she probably would have avoided litigation.

- *Width, duration.* Ruth should also specify the width of the easement to avoid the gradual widening over time that the law may otherwise permit to accommodate larger trucks or bulkier equipment. And if the easement is to be exclusively for coal removal and not for later uses such as subdivision development, Ruth may want to limit the duration of the easement as well as its purpose. She might, for example, limit the easement to a period of five years (perhaps giving Abner a right of renewal) or specify that the easement is to end when the coal is exhausted or when a maximum time expires, whichever occurs first.

Pipeline location can be a particular problem. Pipelines transporting oil, natural gas, geothermal energy, water, and even coal slurry can extend for long distances, and their locations usually must be planned years in advance of actual installation. Often not knowing what the final location will be, pipeline companies acquire and record unlocated easements across farms, ranches, and other large tracts. A deed granting an unlocated easement provides generally for "a pipeline easement" across the tract without specifying any fixed location, thus leaving the easement holder free to choose the precise location later by installing the pipeline. In the meantime, the tract or some portion of it may be subdivided for residential or commercial use. The subdivision developer will need to get the pipeline company to specify precisely the path it needs for the pipeline and to release its easement rights in the other areas of the tract. Otherwise the pipeline company will have a right to locate the pipeline anywhere on the tract that it wishes, potentially disrupting the subdivision development in progress, or even the completed subdivision.

The location of an originally unlocated pipeline or power line easement becomes fixed when the line is installed, and its location cannot be changed without the consent of the servient landowner. This widely accepted rule makes sense because of the great difficulties landowners would face if utility companies could relocate their lines at will. As the following case illustrates, however, the owner of land subject to an originally unlocated *driveway* easement may have a right to relocate the driveway without the consent of the easement holder. Why and under what circumstances?

Case 4.1

Lewis v. Young
705 N.E.2d 649 (N.Y. 1998)

Plaintiff Roger Lewis and defendant Neda Young own adjoining parcels of land, both formerly owned by the Browns. In 1956, the Browns divided their plot into three parcels. They retained a four-acre tract for themselves, and sold the smallest parcel to the Jaffes.

The deed to the Jaffes conveyed three easements across the Browns' lot. First, it provided for "the perpetual use, in common with others, of the [Browns'] main driveway, running in a generally southwesterly direction between South Ferry Road and the [Browns'] residence premises. . . ." Two additional easements, one for a 30-foot right of way and another for a 15-foot right of way, were also conveyed, each defined by exact distances, measured to the hundredth of a foot, and identified by reference to high water lines, monuments, neighboring properties, and other landmarks.

In 1990, the Youngs purchased the four-acre tract, intending to raze the then-existing small cottage, replace it with a large new residence, add an in-ground swimming pool, and build a tennis court. The Youngs' deed referenced all the foregoing easements. In 1992, the widow Jaffe died.

Construction of the Youngs' residence and tennis court started in 1993. Because the tennis court was partly situated in the path of the main driveway, the Youngs relocated it, placing it closer to the boundary line separating their lot from the other two parcels. The new main driveway, still running in a generally southwesterly direction between South Ferry Road and the Youngs' residence, overlapped the original driveway at some points. At its point of greatest separation, the relocated driveway was 50 feet from the original driveway.

In December 1993, plaintiff Lewis, Mrs. Jaffe's nephew, received the deed to the Jaffe property. A dispute arose over the condition of the relocated driveway. The Youngs agreed to improve the driveway upon completion of their home. Their home was completed in May 1994, about two months after Mr. Young's death.

In June 1994, plaintiff's attorney sent a letter giving Mrs. Young ten days to improve the relocated driveway as had been agreed. Unless that were done, the letter warned, his client, at defendant's expense, would "proceed in putting the driveway back where it was originally," despite the destruction of the tennis court, which stood in the way.

On February 1, 1995, plaintiff filed suit seeking a declaration of the parties' rights regarding the driveway easement and a permanent injunction compelling defendant to remove the tennis court and return the driveway to its original location. Defendant filed responsive pleadings. Plaintiff moved for partial summary judgment.

The supreme court (the name of the *trial* court in New York) granted plaintiff's motion for partial summary judgment, holding that plaintiff had a driveway easement which defendant had no right to move. The court found as a matter of law that "since the location of the subject easement [had] remained fixed for at least thirty-seven years . . . , it could not be relocated without plaintiff's consent." The court then granted plaintiff an order compelling defendant to restore the driveway to its original condition or to allow plaintiff to complete the restoration at defendant's expense. The Appellate Division affirmed the trial court's decision, and defendant Young appealed to New York's highest court, the Court of Appeals.

KAYE, C. J.

This battle between Southampton neighbors centers on an open question in New York law: can a landowner, without consent, relocate an easement holder's right of way over the burdened premises? We conclude that, under the particular circumstances presented [here], the landowner can move the right of way, so long as the easement holder's right of access and ingress is not impaired. We therefore reverse the Appellate Division order . . . directing restoration of the landowner's original driveway, and remit the matter to the trial court to determine remaining factual issues.

. . .

Analysis begins with a timeless first principle in the law of easements, articulated by this Court in 1865 and recently reasserted . . . : express easements are defined by the intent, or object, of the parties.

While we have not previously considered the particular question now before us, we have several times passed upon questions involving the type of easement at issue—a right of way. As a rule, where the intention in granting an easement is to afford only a right of ingress and egress, it is the right of passage, and not any right in a physical passageway itself, that is granted to the easement holder. As this Court observed more than a century ago,

> "A right of way along a private road belonging to another person does not give the [easement holder] a right that the road shall be in no respect altered or the width decreased, for his right . . . is merely a right to pass with the convenience to which he has been accustomed. . . .

Thus, in the absence of a demonstrated intent to provide otherwise, a landowner burdened by an express easement of ingress and egress may narrow it, cover it over, gate it or fence it off, so long as the easement holder's right of passage is not impaired. As a matter of policy, affording the [servient] landowner this unilateral, but limited, authority to alter a right of way strikes a balance between the landowner's right to use and enjoy the property and the easement holder's right of ingress and egress.

While enjoying a limited right to narrow, cover, gate and fence off such easements, can a landowner similarly relocate a right of way without the easement

holder's consent? Other jurisdictions have broadly required consent to the relocation of easements. That has not, however, been the unanimous view of lower
courts in New York.

[A number of] our prior relocation cases have not concerned rights of way.
Rather, the easement holder in those cases was given the right to build a
structure—a dock in one instance, a pipeline in the other—on the landowner's
property. Unlike the right of way now at issue, those easements could not be
enjoyed unless and until their locations were fixed on the landowner's property.
By contrast, enjoyment of an undefined right of ingress and egress over the land of
another does not require any fixed [location on] the landowner's premises.

The second category of cases to reach this Court involved relocation attempts
by the easement holder, not—as in the present case—by the [servient] landowner.
That, too, is a significant distinction. Traditionally, reasons given for denying
easement *holders* [emphasis added] the right to make changes in location are that
"treating the location as variable would depreciate the value of the servient estate,
discourage its improvement, and incite litigation" (Restatement [Third] of
Property [Servitudes] Tentative Draft No. 4, § 4.8(3), comment f). Those . . .
policy reasons, however, do not justify denying a [servient landowner a] limited
authority to move an unlocated right of way. Indeed, recognizing that authority
[is likely to increase] the value of the servient estate, and encourages the
landowner to make improvements. Moreover, because a landowner's authority to
relocate a right of way without consent is limited—in that relocation may not
impair the easement holder's rights—both parties have an incentive to resolve any
dispute prior to relocation. . . .

Thus, [on the basis of] our precedents and their underlying policy considerations, we conclude that . . . [i]n the absence of a demonstrated intent to provide
otherwise, a landowner, consonant with the beneficial use and development of its
property, can move [an unlocated] right of way, so long as the landowner bears the
expense of the relocation, and so long as the change does not frustrate the parties'
intent or object in creating the right of way, does not increase the burden on the
easement holder, and does not significantly lessen the utility of the right of way.

. . .

Applying these principles to the facts at hand, we must first determine whether,
in the 1956 Brown-Jaffe deed, it was the intention of the parties, in creating the
right of way that plaintiff now enjoys, to deny the [servient] landowner's right ever
to relocate his main driveway without the easement holder's consent. . . .

The search for the parties' intent begins with the words they used in creating
the easement. Here, the deed conveyed to the Jaffes a right to "the perpetual use,
in common with others, of [Mr. Brown's] main driveway, running in a generally
southwesterly direction between South Ferry Road and [Mr. Brown's] residence
premises. . . ." Under the terms of that grant, the Jaffes secured the right of convenient passage to and from their property, while the Browns retained the right to
use their property as they saw fit, so long as [that use] did not interfere with the
right of passage granted. . . .

The deed, however, does not reflect an intent to deny Mr. Brown the right . .
. to relocate the "main driveway" to his house. . . . Indeed, the indefinite description of the right of way suggests the opposite—namely, that the parties intended
to allow for relocation by the landowner. Notably, the parties themselves in the
same deed described two additional easements by explicit reference to metes and
bounds. Had they intended the [main driveway] to be forever fixed in its location,

presumably they would have delineated it in similar fashion. . . . The provision manifests an intention to grant a right of passage over the driveway—wherever located—so long as it meets the general directional sweep of the existing driveway. . . .

[T]he only remaining fact question is whether the relocation impairs or diminishes plaintiff's right of ingress and egress. [That question is for the trial court to decide.]

Accordingly, the order of the Appellate Division, insofar as appealed from, [is] reversed . . . , and [the] case [is] remitted to Supreme Court, Suffolk County, for further proceedings in accordance with the opinion herein.

QUESTIONS ABOUT CASE 4.1

1. From the servient tenant's viewpoint, what is the benefit of an unlocated driveway easement?

2. In this case, what limit is there on the right of the servient tenant to relocate the driveway?

3. Do courts in other states agree that easements of ingress and egress, originally unlocated but in place for many years, can be relocated by the current servient tenant?

Creation by Implication

The topic of implied easements can be confusing because it has been divided historically, and somewhat artificially, into "implied easements" and "easements by necessity." This book follows the traditional practice of discussing easements by necessity apart from other types of implied easements.

Implied easements, including those "by necessity," arise by judicial inference from circumstances surrounding the conveyance of an estate in land, and *not* from any agreement or expression of the parties. That is, the nature of the land and its use can suggest, or *imply*, an easement right that the parties did not express and may not consciously have considered. Because they result from court orders instead of a contract or agreement of the litigating parties, implied easements are not subject to the writing requirements of the Statute of Frauds. To protect the rights conferred by an implied easement, however, its recipient should record any creating document that resulted from the litigation, e.g., the judgment declaring the easement, or any deed the court requires the grantor to issue.

Easements Implied from Prior Use. An easement may be implied from the prior use of the land conveyed. Usually called simply an "implied easement," it arises where:

1. The grantor *conveys a part* of his or her land to another and keeps the rest.

2. Immediately before the conveyance there is a usage of the land *necessary* in some degree to the enjoyment of the conveyed or the retained part—a usage which the grantor or grantee wishes to continue after the conveyance.

3. The usage is *apparent* to grantor and grantee at the time of the conveyance.

For example, Alice sells the south 200 acres of her irrigated orchard to Dan for his use as an orchard, keeping for herself the north 200 acres and the five-acre pond at its northern edge that supplies the water necessary for irrigating both tracts. Water rights were not mentioned in the contract for the sale of the land, but Dan's need for the water was apparent to Alice and Dan during their negotiations and at the time of conveyance. If Alice withholds the irrigation water from Dan's tract, a court will infer from the prior use of the land that the conveyance contemplated a continuation of water rights necessary for Dan to continue using his land as an orchard. Thus Dan is entitled to an implied water easement (appurtenant to his land) across Alice's land. Dan's land is the dominant tenement, and Alice's the servient tenement.

The degree to which the usage must be "necessary" varies among the states. A few courts have said that the usage must be strictly necessary to the enjoyment of the tract. Under this test, Dan would not be entitled to an implied easement unless Alice's pond is the only source of water. The great majority of states, however, have adopted the test of "reasonable necessity," which is met if the person seeking the easement would encounter significant expense or inconvenience in acquiring an acceptable substitute. If Dan would have to drill a well on his 200 acres and install a pump to acquire irrigation water, or would have to pay for surface water from another source, he meets the "reasonable necessity" test and is entitled to an implied water easement across Alice's land.

Dan receives the water easement by *implied grant* because Alice granted the south 200 acres to him and, along with it, by implication, the easement across her land necessary for him to maintain the orchard use. Suppose instead that Alice had sold the north 200 acres and its irrigation pond to Dan and kept for herself the south 200 acres. Now Dan has control of the pond. If he denies irrigation water to Alice, she may be entitled to an easement by *implied reservation* over the land she sold to Dan, the theory being that she retained part of the land for herself and, with it, any easement rights across the sold part needed to maintain the use of the retained part.

Easement Implied from Subdivision Plat. Another type of implied easement arises where a person acquires a lot in a platted subdivision. A lot owner naturally assumes he or she will have a right to use the streets, alleys, and other common areas shown on the plat. In many states, a developer by law automatically dedicates such areas to public use simply by the act of subdividing, thus creating *public* easements. In states with no automatic public dedication (and even in states where public easements arise automatically), a lot owner has a *private* implied easement to use at least the subdivision streets necessary to get to a public road.

Easements Implied from Necessity. Sometimes land is divided into smaller parcels, with one or more being landlocked (surrounded by the land of others) and having no access to a public road. Land thus isolated is not likely to be very productive. Because public policy favors full productivity of land, a court will grant the owner of a landlocked parcel an easement by necessity across the land from which it was severed (separated), for access to a public road.

The requirements for an **easement by necessity** are:

1. Grantor's *conveyance of a part* of the grantor's land, with grantor keeping the rest, which usually adjoins the granted part.

2. The *necessity*, after the severance of the two parcels, to have access over one of them to reach a public street or highway from the other.

An easement by necessity differs from an easement implied from prior use. One difference is the range of possible uses that the dominant tenant will be permitted to make of the servient tenement. The use allowed under a prior-use easement depends on what the prior use was: such as continued use of a driveway or access to needed water. In contrast, an easement by necessity has only one purpose—to give its otherwise landlocked holder a right of way to a public road.

For example, near Junction Point, Rachel owns a quarter section (160 acres) located between tracts owned by Horace on the one side and by Harriet on the other. As shown in Figure 4–2, a steep cliff, part of the deep east-west canyon owned by the United States, forms the south boundary of all three properties. A county road runs along the north boundary of all three. Jerry buys the south 80 acres of Rachel's 160-acre tract, only to discover later that his land lacks access to the public road. Rachel refuses to grant him an express easement across her north 80 acres. Jerry is entitled to an easement by necessity—an implied easement appurtenant—across Rachel's land to the public road. Jerry's landlocked parcel is the dominant tenement; Rachel's land is the

FIGURE 4–2

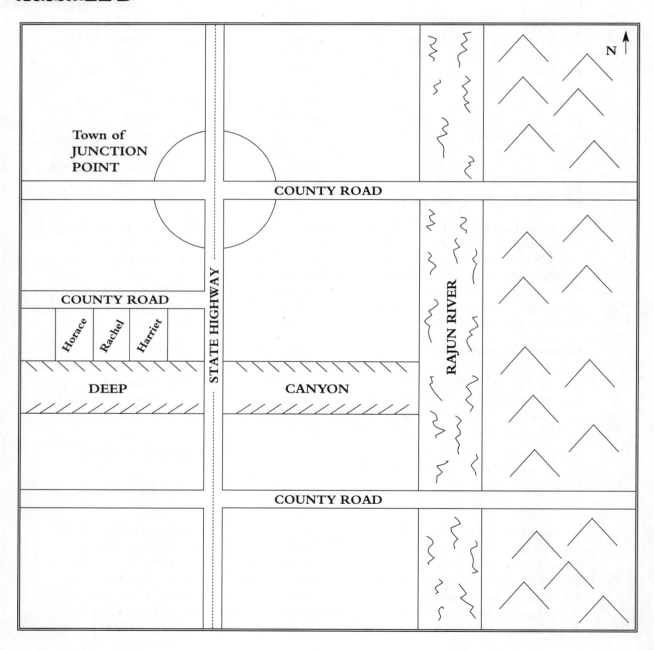

servient tenement. If Rachel had instead sold Jerry the 80 acres next to the county road and retained the landlocked parcel, *she* would be entitled to an easement by necessity upon Jerry's refusal to grant her an express easement.

A court will not grant an easement by necessity unless it is truly needed for access to the landlocked parcel. But, as with easements implied from prior use, the courts vary in their interpretations of "necessary." Under the test for necessity as traditionally stated and perhaps still applied in a few jurisdictions, a court will refuse to grant an easement by necessity if any other access exists, no matter how inconvenient its use may be. Suppose the cliff forming the south boundary of Rachel's land has a narrow public footpath leading down its face from her tract to another county road three miles to the south. Under the traditional test, Rachel would be denied an easement by necessity north across Jerry's land because she already has access to a public road, even though the access is totally inadequate for motor traffic.

Most courts today, however, have adopted a somewhat more relaxed test for necessity. They will grant the easement if, without it, the landowner could not make effective use of the isolated land. If, for example, Rachel's retained parcel were prime farmland or an area suitable for residential development, the narrow footpath to the south would be inadequate for the normal use of the land. So a court today probably would grant Rachel an easement by necessity to the north, sufficiently wide for her to use her land effectively.

A court will not grant an easement by necessity across land that was not involved in the original severance. Suppose that Rachel retains the parcel next to the cliff, no footpath exists, Jerry refuses to grant Rachel an express easement, and she seeks an easement by necessity across Horace's or Harriet's land. Rachel has no right to an easement by necessity across the land of strangers to the original severance—here Horace and Harriet—only across the parcel that was severed by the original grantor. Because the land of Horace and Harriet was not involved in the original severance, the only parcel subject to Rachel's easement claim is Jerry's.

But what happens if Rachel sells her landlocked parcel to Ned without seeking an easement by necessity, and Jerry sells his parcel to Carmen? Is Ned entitled to an easement by necessity across Carmen's parcel? Yes, because the two parcels were under *common ownership* when the original severance occurred, the *need for access existed then*, and the *need for access continues*. In fact, the right to an easement by necessity can lie dormant through many transfers of ownership and can be exercised many years after the original severance, as long as the need for access continues.

When the need ceases, however, so does the easement or any unexercised right to it. Ned (or some later owner of the landlocked parcel) buys Horace's adjoining land, which has access to the county road to the north. Because Ned's parcel merges with Horace's into one tract now owned by Ned, his formerly landlocked parcel is no longer landlocked and he no longer has a right to an easement by necessity across Carmen's land. If Ned had acquired an easement by necessity from Carmen *before* buying Horace's land, the purchase would eliminate Ned's need to cross Carmen's land, would extinguish the implied easement, and would permit Carmen to exclude Ned from her land. But the purchase of Horace's land would *not* extinguish any *express* access easement that Carmen may have granted to Ned, nor any access easement that Ned may have acquired by prescription.

Creation by Prescription

Strange as it may seem, a trespasser can acquire an easement in another person's land, or even acquire ownership of it, by trespassing long enough under the circumstances prescribed by law. A trespasser who claims *ownership* of the land may acquire *title* to it by completing the process of "adverse possession" discussed in Chapter 6. A trespasser who claims only a right to *use* the land may acquire a prescriptive easement by completing the process of "adverse *use*" discussed here.

The legal requirements for adverse use are similar to those for adverse possession, but the sets of requirements differ enough to warrant separate discussion. Uses commonly associated with prescriptive easements include roadways, driveways, walkways, and drainage areas across someone else's land.

The modern basis for a prescriptive easement (and for acquiring title by adverse possession) is that the victim of the trespass, knowing or having reason to know of it, has failed to take preventive action within the time allowed by law. Every state has a **statute of limitations**, which states the maximum time within which the victim of wrongdoing may bring suit. A person who fails to sue within the time permitted by the statute of limitations is said to have "slept on his rights," and thus loses them for failure to bring timely action. The maximum period for bringing a legal action affecting land varies greatly among the states. In most states, the period is 20 or 15 years, but in a substantial number the limitations period is much shorter: seven years or, as in Montana and California, five years. As applied in adverse use (and in adverse possession) cases, the statute of limitations provides a mechanism for resolving boundary and other ownership disputes, often long after the deaths of the people originally involved in the dispute-causing events.

A landowner can stop a trespasser's adverse use, thus preventing the trespasser from acquiring a prescriptive easement, by bringing a timely lawsuit in trespass (for an injunction and any damages) or in ejectment (to have a wrongful possessor removed from the premises). Or the landowner might use "self-help" instead of a lawsuit to stop the trespass, as where Lamar prevents unauthorized entry of his warehouse storage yard by locking the gates or hiring guards.

Unless stopped, a trespasser acquires a prescriptive easement by engaging in the conduct required by law, conduct likely to notify the landowner that the trespass is occurring. The trespasser's use must be (1) actual, (2) visible, open, and notorious, (3) hostile, (4) continuous and uninterrupted for the statutory period, and (5) exclusive. A brief description of these requirements follows:

- *Actual use.* The actual use that the trespasser makes of the victim's land during the statutory period, not some alleged or potential use, establishes the scope of any resulting prescriptive easement. Trespasser Martina rides her bicycle daily through Throckmorton's mountain ranch, creating a bike trail and eventually acquiring a prescriptive easement. Because her actual use was for biking, she cannot on the basis of that use later claim that she intended a roadway for her truck.

- *Visible, open and notorious use.* The adverse use must be "visible, open, and notorious," that is, observable by a passerby and known or knowable by the public. The requirement gives the landowner *notice* of the adverse use and the ability to detect it in the normal course of managing the property. Even if the owner fails to detect the trespass, the fact that it was visible, open, and notorious supports the trespasser's claim to a prescriptive easement.

- *Hostile (adverse) use.* To be "hostile" or "adverse," the trespasser's use must be contrary to the landowner's rights and must be done without the landowner's permission or consent. In essence, the trespasser must be asserting that he or she has a right to use the other person's land. No malice or threat of physical violence is required for this kind of hostility. If the use would give the landowner a cause of action in trespass or ejectment, it is sufficiently hostile. But if the landowner gives permission for use, it is not a trespass and cannot lead to a prescriptive easement.

- *Continuous and uninterrupted use.* To result in a prescriptive easement, the use must be continuous throughout the statutory period, but "continuous" does not necessarily mean "constant." Using another's land for a driveway only a few times per day or week probably is sufficiently continuous for a prescriptive easement to develop. So, likely, is frequent use of another's land throughout the winter for purely seasonal activities such as snowmobiling or skiing. But a substantial interruption of use will cause the statutory period to begin anew. For a year, Harmon rides his horse daily along the creek on Thelma's land, then sells his horse and quits riding for a few months before buying another horse and taking up daily riding again. Harmon's use is not continuous, and the statutory period starts over when Harmon resumes his daily riding.

- *Exclusive use.* To acquire a prescriptive easement, the trespasser must assert a right of usage that is peculiar, or "exclusive," to the trespasser. Maria gives all of the Jones family permission to cross her land to get to the public road, but denies such permission to Sam Smith. Over Maria's objections, Sam continuously crosses Maria's land on the path used by the Jones family. Sam, a trespasser, is asserting a usage right that is exclusive or peculiar to him. If Maria allows his use to continue, it can ripen into a prescriptive easement.

What happens if trespasser Sam crosses Maria's land for the first three years of the statutory period and then sells his land to Charles, who trespasses for the remainder of the statutory period? If the other requirements for a prescriptive easement have been met, Charles acquires a prescriptive easement because the law permits **tacking** of short periods of trespass together into one long enough to make up the statutory period, if there is a sufficient relationship between the successive trespassers. For example, Charles can tack his period of trespass onto Sam's because Charles is the buyer of Sam's land; similarly, a person who inherits land may tack onto the trespassory period of the decedent. Tacking fails, however, if a break occurs between the periods of trespass.

A prescriptive easement resulting from the trespassing of an adjoining landowner runs with the trespasser's land like any other easement appurtenant. Yet, because a prescriptive easement results from trespassory conduct and not from any oral or written agreement, it will not appear in the public records unless litigation confirms its existence and the judgment is recorded. Many prescriptive easements are never litigated, and for those that are, the litigation might not occur until decades after the creation of the easement.

The lack of record evidence poses a problem for the easement holder. A purchaser of the servient tenement who at the time of purchase lacks notice of the easement takes the land free from it. If the holder is to keep the easement in the absence of record notice, the purchaser of the servient tenement must have received timely notice in some other way, for example, by having been told of the easement, or by having observed physical evidence such as a trail or a roadway that would lead a reasonable person to inquire about the possibility of an easement.

The seller of the servient or the dominant tenement can run into another problem not uncommon with prescriptive (and implied) easements. A person who contracts to buy land is entitled to a **marketable title**—a title that is free from substantial defects or a significant possibility of a lawsuit over its quality. If title is not marketable, the buyer has a right to rescind the contract. Charles, owner of Fun Acres, does all the things necessary for acquiring a prescriptive easement across Maria's land to reach the public seashore on the other side. Ten years later, Charles contracts to sell Fun Acres to Gena, who wants the land especially because of its access to the seashore. She then learns that Maria claims that no prescriptive easement exists, has blocked Charles' trail, and intends to sue whoever tries to use it. Because of the potential for litigation, Charles' title is not marketable. He might make his title marketable by purchasing an express easement from Maria. If she refuses to sell, he can sue her to "quiet title"—that is, to have a court determine whether Charles has the ownership rights he claims. To establish his title as marketable, he will have to prove that he has the prescriptive easement. He can do so by proving that he did the trespassory things necessary to acquire it. Gena is not required to "buy a lawsuit" with Maria, so if Charles does not quiet his title before the time arrives for performing the contract (or within some additional time that the court might order), Gena will have a basis for rescinding the contract.

Creation by Dedication

Dedication is an owner's transferring an interest in land to the public for its use. Often, dedication produces substantial tax benefits for the donor of the interest, which can be a fee simple estate or a lesser interest such as an easement. Many dedications are purely voluntary gifts to the community. Other dedications are compelled by the government, for example those required of developers as a condition for receiving a building permit.

Types of Dedications. Dedication is governed by common law rules developed by the courts over the years, and also by statutes that set certain types of dedication apart and prescribe special procedures for them. Most states have both common law and statutory dedication.

A *common law dedication* must involve an offer and an acceptance. The landowner must *offer* the interest to a public body such as a city, town, or county, or to the public generally. An offer of dedication can be oral, since a dedication, being a gift of an interest in land and not a sale, is not covered by the Statute of Frauds. Then, because a gift of land often involves maintenance costs and other burdens, the governing officials must *accept* the offer to show their willingness to assume any burdens. The governing authority usually accepts the offer by adopting a resolution of acceptance that is placed in the public records, but it can accept in other ways such as by no longer taxing the property or by taking over its maintenance and control.

A common law dedication can be either express or implied. When accomplished by words, it is express. But it can be inferred from nonverbal conduct, as where a landowner knowingly permits public use of the land (thus impliedly making an offer) and the public impliedly accepts the offer by using the land for a length of time specified by law. Ernesto owns a farm adjacent to a public highway and opens three acres to travelers as a rest area, hoping to sell them farm produce on another part of the farm. Travelers use the rest area for more than the minimum time required by law for the public's acceptance. Because an implied dedication has occurred, Ernesto can no longer prevent public use of the rest area.

A *statutory dedication* results from compliance with a statute regulating dedications. For example, most states have special statutes governing dedications in residential subdivisions. Under many such statutes, a developer, simply by the act of subdividing, automatically dedicates to public use any streets, parks, and other public areas shown on the plat. Typically, the "automatic dedication" statutes provide that (1) the developer's submitting a subdivision plat to a local government for approval is an offer to dedicate the public areas, and (2) the local government's approving the plat is an acceptance of the offer. Thus, dedication of the public areas occurs even if dedication was not specifically mentioned.

Often, however, subdivisions of small size are exempted from the statutory coverage and thus from automatic dedication. If the developer of an exempted subdivision nevertheless chooses to dedicate, the requirements for a common law dedication apply. That is, the developer must particularly identify any areas offered for dedication, and for the dedication to be effective the local government must accept the developer's offer.

A *compelled dedication* occurs when a developer of a subdivision is required, as a condition to being granted permits needed for the project, to dedicate land for streets, parks, and other community uses. Generally, compelled dedications are upheld by the courts if a reasonable connection exists between the interest compelled to be dedicated and the burden the new population will place on public services.

Street Easements. Sometimes dedications for streets, roads, parks, and the like are vague about the interest granted. Did the donor dedicate an easement or a fee simple? In deciding, the courts give great weight to the use that the parties intended. If a common law dedication was for street or road purposes, the courts usually hold that the donor granted an easement and kept the fee.

(However, in *statutory* dedications involving subdivisions, the statutes commonly provide that the interest dedicated for streets is a fee simple estate.) If the common law dedication was for a park, cemetery, or school site, the courts are more likely to hold that the interest is a fee simple estate, an interest more in keeping with the permanent nature of the intended land use. Helen dedicates to Metropolis "a strip of land for use as a walkway and bicycle path between Commerce Mall and Parrot Park." Five years later, Metropolis demolishes Parrot Park and uses the land as a storage yard for road equipment, closing off and abandoning the walkway, which is now littered with rubbish and choked with weeds. Helen wants to reclaim the walkway as her property. Since Helen dedicated the interest for a walkway and bike path, a court likely would hold that she gave Metropolis an easement and kept for herself the fee simple ownership. Because abandonment of an easement extinguishes it, the fee simple that Helen kept would now be free of the easement and once again subject to her exclusive control.

Conservation Easements. The preservation of wildlife, natural resources, open spaces, and historic landmarks has become an important goal of government and of many in the private sector. Over time, many legal techniques for accomplishing that goal have been developed. Among them are *coastal zoning*, *wetlands control*, and *agricultural zoning*, all intended at least in part to preserve open space and wildlife without interfering unduly with normal commercial uses of the land. State and federal statutes are central to this type of regulation.

Also widely used in preservation efforts is the conservation easement. Broadly defined, a **conservation easement** is one given or acquired for the purpose of preserving open space, wildlife, natural resources, or other qualities that may be in danger of disappearing. One early type of conservation easement, still in use, is the *highway* or *scenic* easement purchased by the state or federal government in either a voluntary sale or a condemnation proceeding, and used for preserving open spaces, especially the natural scenic view along highways.[4] Felicia owns Fairwood Farm, which extends for several miles along the highway overlooking the Rajun River and the mountains to the east. Located near Metropolis, Fairwood Farm is an ideal site for a huge housing development or a commercial or industrial complex. But development would destroy the natural beauty of the area. To preserve it, the state can try to purchase a scenic easement from Felicia. If she refuses to sell, the state can use its power of eminent domain to condemn (take) the easement, but the state must pay her a just compensation. In its preservation efforts on behalf of the public, the state will prohibit or limit building and other development on the farm. Felicia, however, remains owner of the fee simple estate and will be allowed to continue normal farm operations.

Today "conservation easement," or an equivalent term, is used in special state statutes to mean a *gift*, an easement dedicated by a private landowner to the public for any of a wide range of conservation purposes. As of about 1997, forty-six states and the District of Columbia had some type of legislation for facilitating the creation and transfer of conservation easements.[5] The legislation was necessary because of common law doubts about their nature. Are they easements appurtenant or in gross? Most conservation easements truly are in gross but, being noncommercial, they might not be transferable under common law rules. Yet, to accomplish their intended purpose, they should run with the land and should be transferable to those who can best manage them. To remove doubt about their nature, most state statutes make clear that conservation easements are perpetual and run with the land. Some statutes provide that conservation easements are transferable.

Under most of the statutes, a landowner may grant a conservation easement only to a government unit (e.g., a city or a county) or to a private nonprofit organization, though six states permit individuals or business firms to hold such easements.[6] The donor creates the easement by making a contract of dedication with a government unit or a conservation organization and recording it in the appropriate land records. The contract typically limits the donor's ownership rights by restricting development of the property as needed to preserve the character of the realty involved. Upon recordation, the terms of the conservation easement are binding on present and future owners of the land.

Grantees hold conservation easements for a variety of purposes, among them to preserve scenic areas and open spaces for agricultural, forest, and recreational uses; to protect wildlife and natural resources; to preserve realty that has historic, architectural, or archaeological significance; and to maintain and enhance air and water quality.[7] In states permitting transfer of conservation easements, a city holding a preservation easement in a historic building but having no expertise in preserving historical landmarks could transfer the easement to the local Historical Preservation Society for better management. Similarly, a county or town could transfer its three-mile scenic river easement to the state conservation agency charged with protecting the whole river.

Conservation easements benefit not only the public, but also donors and grantees (the government). Unlike a scenic easement for which the government must pay, conservation easements, being gifts, involve no great government expenditures for land acquisition and none of the unpleasantness that may accompany a governmental taking. Among the benefits to easement *donors* are (1) their ability as owners of the fee simple to continue using the land, and (2) certain tax benefits. Of value to donors is a potential reduction in local real estate taxes. Granting the easement deprives the donor of development rights and should result in a lower property tax assessment that reflects the giving up of the easement interest. If the land has great value, as many large farms, ranches, plantations, and historical estates do, the donor can also reduce the federal income tax, the federal gift and estate tax, and state inheritance taxes by carefully structuring the gift to conform to the requirements of the Internal Revenue Code and state tax laws.

Rights and Duties Created by Easements

Disputes may arise between an easement holder and the owner of the servient tenement, since both have rights of usage in the same piece of land. Questions arise over the scope of the easement, the effect of changes in use by the dominant tenant, physical maintenance of the easement, and the rights of a bona fide purchaser of the servient tenement.

Scope of an Easement

The "scope" of an easement is the usage right that the easement holder received upon acquiring the easement. The scope of an *implied* or a *prescriptive* easement is defined by the conduct or events that produced it. For example, an easement implied from prior use for irrigation water is limited to irrigation usage and does not extend to nonirrigation purposes such as car washes or an artificial lake for a residential subdivision, or to an amount of irrigation water greatly exceeding that being used when the easement was created. Similarly, a prescriptive easement acquired by bicyclists for a mountain biking trail can be used for bicycle traffic but not automobile traffic.

Words of creation define the scope of an *express* easement. General language such as "for drainage" or "for a driveway," though often used, may lead to future disputes. How much water may flow over the servient tenement, and from what sources? For a driveway easement, how much traffic is permitted, and what kinds of vehicles? How wide is the driveway to be? More precise language in the creating document, including information about location, reduces the possibilities for conflict and tends to limit the duration and expense of any litigation that might arise. Pipeline easements, for example, usually are drafted in considerable detail. Typically, they give the pipeline company extensive rights to install and maintain one or more lines as the need for them arises, in exchange for a specified compensation for each line installed. Such easements, bind the parties to them and, when recorded, bind the subsequent owners of the servient tenements.

Changes in Use by the Dominant Tenant

Once the scope of an easement is established, fundamental changes in the usage rights it confers are not permitted without the consent of the parties bound by the easement. The easement holder may not suddenly and dramatically increase usage beyond that initially established; the owner of the servient tenement may not unilaterally restrict the easement holder's usage rights.

Yet, in all kinds of easements, flexibility of usage rights is necessary to accommodate changing circumstances. So if Morton grants Hilda a right of way across his land from her farm to the highway, he should anticipate increases in road traffic as Hilda's young children learn to drive or as she or her successor shifts to a more intensive type of farming. But what if she subdivides her farm into small lots for residential use? Can she convert the right of way into a main road serving the new community? Morton might have foreseen some subdivision and a limited increase in traffic. If so, the increase in usage may be permitted over his objections, as part of a normal, evolutionary expansion in the use of the dominant tenement. If, however, the increase in traffic is much greater than might reasonably have been anticipated, or if the right of way is used for unanticipated purposes such as a railroad spur line to serve a coal mine newly opened on Hilda's land, the *excess* use is a **surcharge** that will not be permitted. As to the excess use, the easement holder must get Morton's consent, or acquire by prescription the right to continue the excess use. If the subdivision becomes a government entity, it might acquire expanded easement rights from Morton by exercising its power of eminent domain.

Another example of surcharge is the use of an easement to serve land other than the dominant tenement. Humphrey owns Timber Acres and acquires an easement across Redding's land for transporting timber from Timber Acres to the railway on the other side of Redding's property. Humphrey then allows neighboring timber producers to use the easement for transporting their own timber to the railroad. Their use of the easement granted by Redding exceeds its scope and will not be permitted if Redding seeks to enjoin it.

Utility easements are a frequent subject of litigation today, because of the great economic value of space for TV antenna cables and fiber-optic cables for high-speed communications. Electric power companies, for example, may want to sell some of their easement rights to cable companies and to keep the rest for their own power systems. This process is called "division" or "apportionment" of an easement. Servient landowners object to apportionment, contending that cable installations require new easements which only the landowners may grant and for which only they should be compensated. Most easement documents drafted long ago did not address the subject of apportionment. Where easement documents are silent or unclear on apportionment, how are these disputes resolved?

State law on the transfer and apportionment of utility easements varies considerably, but some general principles exist. As noted earlier in this chapter, utility easements, being commercial easements in gross, generally are transferable in total to a successor company. So a regional power company buying a local electric utility acquires the local company's existing line easements without having to purchase them anew from individual landowners.

Apportionment, however, involves sharing an easement with one or more additional companies, which often use their newly acquired rights for purposes different from the purpose of the original easement. An electric power company might share its easement rights across Blackacre with a TV cable company for installing overhead cables, and with a fiber-optics company for installing cables underground. If permitted by law, this sharing provides considerable revenue to the power company and none to the landowner.

Whether the power company may apportion its easement depends on whether the easement is "exclusive" or "nonexclusive." The easement is *exclusive* if the grantee company received the right to make sole use of the easement. The holder of an exclusive easement may divide it among others without the consent of the landowner, as long as the total usage does not exceed the scope of the original easement. In contrast, the easement is *nonexclusive* if the landowner retained the right to grant additional easements to others. A landowner who grants a nonexclusive easement may grant easements in the same strip of land to others, as long as the additional easements do not interfere with the use of the original easement.

Whether an easement is exclusive or nonexclusive depends on the language of the creating documents. If they are silent or unclear on the topic, a court must decide. Most courts have held that in the absence of language expressly making utility easements nonexclusive, the companies have exclusive easements and thus can share them with others without the consent of the landowners. But recently a few courts have favored the landowners' position. For example, in Case 4.2, the court construes the language of easements granted to a power company and treats them as nonexclusive even though no easement language expressly says so.

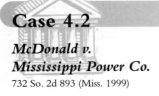

Case 4.2

*McDonald v.
Mississippi Power Co.*

732 So. 2d 893 (Miss. 1999)

Otis G. McDonald and other plaintiffs own in fee simple real property located in Mississippi. Thirty years before the filing of this action, Mississippi Power Company (MPC) obtained easements through the plaintiffs' property by eminent domain proceedings or by voluntary easements executed by the plaintiffs. Those easements gave MPC the right to

> construct, operate and maintain electric lines and all telegraph and telephone lines, towers, poles, wires, and appliances and equipment necessary or convenient in connection therewith from time to time and counterpoise wire and other counterpoise conductors, upon, over, under, and across a strip of land. . . .

MPC contracted with Southern Company for the installation of fiber-optic cables on plaintiffs' land, intending to lease them to others. The landowners objected to the installation of the cables. MPC and Southern brought suit for a declaratory judgment that under the existing easements they had the right to install and utilize fiber-optic cables. McDonald and the other landowners filed a counterclaim seeking injunctive relief and damages resulting from MPC's installation of the fiber-optic cable.

The Chancery Court granted summary judgment in favor of MPC, holding that "[l]aying of fiber optic cable is well within the express or implied language of the easements. Further, MPC has the right to enter the land for purposes of 'installing, operating, and maintaining the subject communication line.' MPC has 'an unfettered right . . . including . . . leasing or selling excess capacity on said lines, without further compensation to the landowners.'" The landowners (plaintiffs in the counterclaim) appealed.

WALLER, C. J.

It is clear that the [easement] gives MPC the right to maintain telephone lines which are "necessary or convenient" in providing electrical services. The first question here is whether a fiber optic cable is the equivalent to a telephone line.

[The court in *Ball v. American Telephone & Telegraph Co.*] held that an easement acquired for telephone and telegraph service could also be used to carry television signals. With this conclusion we wholly agree. Under the above easement, MPC has the right to maintain a telephone line for use in connection with providing electrical service. The clear intent of the easement was to grant MPC the right to install and maintain telephone lines to be used in connection with the providing of electrical services. A fiber-optic cable is nothing more than a technologically advanced or new type of telephone line. The chancellor was correct in holding that the granting clause of the above easement gives MPC the right to maintain a fiber-optic cable.

However, to say simply that MPC has the right, under the present easements, to utilize a fiber-optic cable does not fully answer the question. MPC wishes to sublet space on its fiber-optic cable to third parties for uses other than providing electricity. Unlike the easements before the *Ball* court, MPC's current easements contain limiting language which precludes them from utilizing the fiber optics cable for anything but services provided in connection with supplying electricity. . . . Although [the cable] would not constitute an additional servitude on the property, MPC without more definite easements simply does not have the authority [to use the cable for purposes other than those in connection with providing electricity]. Since MPC drafted . . . the easements in question, they are interpreted most favorably to the landowner. We find that the chancellor erred in holding that [its language] permitted MPC to sublease space on its fiber optics cables for [those other] purposes. . . .

Conclusion

MPC's rights, and those of its successors and assigns, are limited by the language of the easements in question, the plain language of which limits the use of telephone lines to be in connection with providing electrical services. . . . This action is reversed and remanded for proceedings not inconsistent with this opinion.

QUESTIONS ABOUT CASE 4.2

1. Would a fiber-optic cable installed by MPC surcharge, i.e., impose an excess burden on, the easements granted by the landowners? Why?

2. Are the landowners free to grant fiber-optic cable easements to a company other than MPC? If so, under what circumstances could the fiber-optic company use the strip of land covered by MPC's easement? (See text preceding Case 4.2 for information relating to this last question.)

Maintenance of Easements (Secondary Easements)

A **secondary easement** is one necessary to accomplish the purpose of a primary easement. Hortense grants Edmund an easement across her land for a drainage ditch to Mud Creek. The deed says nothing about a right of Edmund to enter her land to maintain the ditch. Edmund nevertheless automatically acquires a secondary easement for ditch maintenance and repair. To avert future disputes or litigation, the deed granting the primary easement should provide for secondary easements, at least in general terms such as "a right of maintenance and repair."

Absent a contrary agreement, an easement holder has the duty to maintain and repair the easement, but of course cannot expand its physical dimensions under the guise of repair. Richard acquires a driveway easement by prescription across Frank's residential lot and after a series of rainstorms demands that Frank fill and pave the rutted, washed-out driveway. Frank has no duty of improvement or repair. Richard then fills the driveway with crushed rock, rolling and grading the drive so that it is twice its original width. Richard has a right to improve the original drive, but is a trespasser as to the excess width. Frank may require Richard to restore the driveway to its original width, but cannot compel him to remove the rock from the original driveway.

Ordinarily, the easement holder, and not the owner of the servient tenement, is liable to users of the easement for injuries resulting from its inadequate maintenance. After the initial repair work, Richard allows the driveway to erode so that users risk sliding off the driveway into Castaway Creek. During a summer rainstorm, Hapless slips from the driveway into the creek and is seriously injured. Hapless sues easement holder Richard and landowner Frank for damages resulting from the poor condition of the driveway. Since only Richard had a duty of maintenance, only he is liable to Hapless for failure to maintain the driveway.

Rights of Bona Fide Purchasers

In the law generally, a **bona fide purchaser** of real or personal property is a person who *gives value* for (buys) it *in good faith* (honestly) and *without notice* of a rival claim to it. The term includes not only buyers but also lenders who have those qualifications. A bona fide purchaser (or lender) takes the property free of the claim. One reason for bona fide purchaser protection is to encourage buyers to pay full market value for the property. Without that protection, buyers might pay prices much lower than warranted by the actual probability of loss at the hands of an unknown claimant.

Real estate recording statutes, discussed in Chapter 9, enable people claiming an interest in realty to give notice of their interests to rival claimants by recording deeds and other relevant documents in the county office for real estate records. Because of the notice provided by recording, a subsequent purchaser or lender cannot qualify as a bona fide purchaser and thus cannot deprive the interest holder of ownership.

A bona fide purchaser of a servient tenement, by definition a person without notice of the easement, takes the realty free of it. If, however, the easement was recorded prior to purchase, the purchaser has **constructive notice** (also called "record notice") of it and takes the realty *subject to* the easement rights. Likewise, a purchaser with either actual or inquiry notice of an *un*recorded easement takes the servient estate subject to the easement. A purchaser who is aware of the easement's existence has *actual notice* of it. A purchaser who has knowledge of facts that, if investigated, would lead a reasonable person to conclude that an easement exists has *inquiry notice*, even though the purchaser is not in fact aware of the easement. Wheel ruts or a lane on land where none should be expected could give a purchaser or a lender inquiry notice of an implied or a prescriptive roadway easement. Seeing the wheel tracks, the purchaser is expected to investigate whether an easement exists. Failing to do so, the purchaser takes the servient estate subject to the easement that would have been revealed had the purchaser inquired.

To take realty free from rival claims, a grantee must meet all of the requirements for bona fide purchaser status. So, a grantee who fails to pay value for land burdened by an easement (e.g., receives the land as a gift) takes it subject to the easement, even if the easement was unrecorded and the grantee otherwise lacked notice of it.

Termination of Easements

Upon the termination of an easement, the owner of the servient tenement regains the exclusive possession and use of the realty. Easements can come to an end in several ways.

- *Express release.* The holder of any kind of easement may terminate it by delivering an express release to the owner of the servient tenement. Because releasing an easement transfers an interest in land, the release must comply with the statute of frauds and the statute of deeds. Ordinarily an easement is released by delivery of a quitclaim deed.

- *Lapse of time.* If an express easement has been limited to a fixed duration, the easement terminates when the specified time expires. Similarly, if the owner of a life estate or a leasehold has granted an easement, it expires when the estate of the grantor expires.

- *Fulfillment of purpose.* An easement granted for a particular purpose such as "the removal of gravel from Blackacre" terminates when the purpose has been accomplished. And an easement by necessity ends when the need for it no longer exists.

- *Merger.* An easement terminates by "merger" when the easement and the servient tenement are owned by the same person. Alfred has an easement across Betty's Greenacre. Later Alfred purchases Greenacre. At the time of purchase, Alfred's easement terminates by "merging" into his ownership of Greenacre.

- *Abandonment.* An easement terminates upon being abandoned by its holder. Abandonment is the *intentional* relinquishment of the easement by its owner. To prove abandonment, the owner of the servient tenement must show both an intent to abandon and a cessation of use. Mere nonuse of the easement by its owner does not constitute abandonment. [In California, however, nonuse of a *prescriptive* easement for a period of five years *does* terminate it. CAL. CIV. CODE § 811(4) (West 1995).]

- *Adverse possession or prescription.* The owner of the servient tenement can terminate an easement by adversely using or possessing the easement area continuously for the period required to acquire a prescriptive easement. Alma has a driveway easement across Betty's lot. Betty constructs an office building across the driveway and walls off the driveway entrance. These acts are hostile and adverse to Alma's easement rights and will terminate Alma's easement if permitted to continue for the applicable statute of limitations period.

- *Destruction of the servient tenement.* Sometimes an easement is in a structure and not in the land itself. Involuntary destruction of the structure terminates the easement. Raymond owns a commercial building. Jeanette owns a retail store next door. Beyond Jeanette's store is the parking lot serving both buildings. To provide Raymond's customers with easy access from the parking lot to Raymond's second-floor photography studio, Jeanette granted Raymond an easement in her stairway and second-floor hallway leading through an archway in the common wall between the buildings. An earthquake destroys Jeanette's building but not Raymond's. Raymond's easement is terminated.

BOX 4–5 APPLY YOUR KNOWLEDGE

An avid horseback rider, Jennings acquired an express easement from his neighbor Sara "for the use of the old lane on Sara's Fair Acres as a Jennings family bridlepath for the rest of my life." For twelve years, Jennings rode his horse Thunder almost daily on the four-mile lane. Then Thunder died, and Jennings never used the lane again. Sara died last month. Her heirs claim that Fair Acres is free of Jennings' easement because of (1) nonuse for the past 21 years, or (2) fulfillment of purpose, since Jennings is 87 years old and concedes that he is incapable of riding again. Has the easement been terminated?

Profits and Licenses

This chapter closes with a brief discussion of profits and licenses. Closely related to the easement, they both involve someone else's land.

Profits

A **profit à prendre**, usually called a *profit*, is the right to take or extract something from the land of another, such as timber, minerals, oil, gravel, or wild fruit. Landowners often grant profits in exchange for a payment per unit of material taken, called a **royalty**.

A profit differs from an easement in that an easement holder receives only a right to use the other person's land, while the holder of a profit has a right to remove something from the land. Yet, easements and profits are governed by the same legal principles. So, profits may be in gross or appurtenant, express or implied from prior use, acquired by prescription, and transferable and divisible in the same manner that easements are. Most profits are in gross and commercial, so are freely transferable. But a profit can be appurtenant, as where Sofia grants Tucker "a right to extract gravel from my Blackacre as needed to maintain the lanes and roadways on his Fairview Farm." And a noncommercial profit in gross is nontransferable, as where Thompson grants to Nettie, a city dweller, "the right, free of charge, to harvest seedless grapes from my Grapeland for her personal consumption and that of her immediate family."

Unless otherwise stated, a profit automatically includes an easement permitting the profit holder to enter the burdened land and to use the surface as necessary and convenient for the exercise of the profit. The grantor can, however, control the time and manner of entry and surface use, and the rate or amount of extraction, by expressing the limits in a granting document. The grantor can prevent surface entry entirely by including in the granting document a provision to that effect. Such provisions are not unusual where the profit holder can reach underground materials from neighboring land by means of tunnels or slant drilling. Where no such access is possible, a prohibition of surface entry likely is unenforceable because it is inconsistent with the interest granted.

Licenses

A **license** is a permission or privilege to use the land of another person (the **licensor**) for some purpose authorized by the licensor. A license does not give the licensee an interest in the land itself—only a privilege of usage that the licensor ordinarily may revoke at any time, and which terminates at the death of either the licensor or licensee. Agnes strolls through the shopping mall, entering various places of business. She is a business invitee making use of the license impliedly granted by the mall and the businesses to enter the premises as a potential customer. If she purchases a ticket to see a movie or a ballgame, she has received a license for that purpose. If she misbehaves at the mall, store, movie, or ballgame, the license, being revocable, may be canceled. The mall closes at 9:00 P.M.; the license ends then. The ballgame is over; the license has expired.

Frequently, landowners give oral permission to cross land or to use it in some other way. If put into writing, such a permission ordinarily would be an express easement. An oral permission, however, is only a license, revocable at the landowner's will. George has oral permission to drive across Cesar's land at any time to get to the highway. The resulting license is revocable.

However, if George spends a substantial sum improving his own property or that of the licensor in reasonable *reliance* on the continuation of the license, and with the *licensor's knowledge*, the license may have become irrevocable under estoppel principles recognized in many states. George crosses Cesar's land for two years without objection, creating a dirt lane across his and

Cesar's land. Then, as Cesar watches, George at his own expense paves the lane with asphalt. In many states, because of these circumstances Cesar would be estopped (prevented) from revoking the license. The resulting irrevocable license is a type of servitude, equivalent to an easement in the licensor's land.

Self-Study Questions

1. What is the relationship between "servitude" and "easement"?

2. How does an easement differ from an estate?

3. (a) Explain the difference between an easement appurtenant and an easement in gross. Illustrate each. (b) Are easements appurtenant and easements in gross transferable?

4. Explain how a state's Statute of Frauds, Statute of Deeds, and Statute of Wills might apply to the creation of an express easement.

5. (a) Aside from pipelines, where might an "unlocated" easement be used? (b) Describe one difficulty resulting from the use of an unlocated easement. Describe one benefit of using an unlocated easement.

6. (a) What do easements implied from prior use, easements by necessity, and prescriptive easements have in common? (b) How do they differ?

7. What is the difference between a scenic easement and the conservation easement provided for in state statutes?

8. Distinguish among a common law dedication of an easement, a statutory dedication, and a compelled dedication.

9. You own land in an area being subdivided for a new residential community. The local power company wants you to grant it an exclusive easement for the installation and maintenance of its power lines. Should you grant it an exclusive easement?

10. (a) How does a license differ from an easement or a profit? (b) Under what circumstances might a license become a servitude? (c) Give an example of a temporary irrevocable license.

Case Problems

1. Sam's house was located immediately north of Paul's house. Both houses were surrounded by walls on the west, north, and east sides. The only access from Sam's house to the street south of Paul's house was a footpath across Paul's lot, the easement for which had been reserved years earlier for the benefit of Sam's lot by the common grantor of both lots. Because of intruders from the neighborhood, Paul built a fence across the footpath and along the south boundary of his lot. The fence had a door that Paul kept locked. Because Sam's access to the street was now obstructed, he brought suit to have the fence removed. Paul argued that he needed to keep the door locked for the safety of his family. The trial court ordered Paul to remove the fence or to leave its door open at all times. Paul appealed. (a) In terms of the law of easements, what is the nature of the dispute between Sam and Paul? (b) Should the trial court's order be upheld, or should it be modified? If it should be modified, what change should the appellate court make? Adapted from *Messer v. Leveson*, 259 N.Y.S.2d 662 (App. Div. 1965).

2. Robert Drye purchased a lot in a subdivision of the Eagle Rock Ranch in Texas, expecting to have recreation privileges over the entire 1,000-acre Eagle Rock Ranch. Sales brochures and newspaper advertising featured recreational facilities and a club house located on a 19-acre tract

adjacent to the subdivision and owned by a separate corporation. These facilities and the whole ranch were advertised as for the use of members of the Eagle Rock Ranch Club, which included lot owners, but the membership application made clear that membership conferred no ownership rights of any kind in club property. The deeds to the lots referred to the recorded plat of the subdivision. However, the deeds contained no reference to easements or rights for pleasure and recreation in the general ranch area; and the major portion of the ranch outside the subdivision was not shown on the plat. When the Eagle Rock Ranch Club was closed for lack of profitability, Drye sued the seller of his lot, alleging that an implied easement, entitling Drye to the use of the whole ranch, arose at the time of purchase. Had Drye acquired an implied easement? *Drye v. Eagle Rock Ranch, Inc.*, 364 S.W.2d 196 (Tex. 1963).

3. Lancelot acquired a road easement across Georgette's 50-acre parcel for access to the state highway. Within a short time Lancelot divided his land into two parcels, gave one to his son for a home site, continued to live on the other, and paved the road with asphalt. As the son's family grew, the traffic on the road increased. Then Lancelot and his son acquired additional acreage from neighbors and subdivided it into 53 lots for residential purposes. The lots sold quickly. Soon all lot owners, Lancelot, and his son's family were using the road across Georgette's property. She brought suit to enjoin the use of the road by the lot owners and the family of Lancelot's son. Will she win the suit as to (a) the son's family? (b) the lot owners?

4. Baum acquired the Riverview Mobile Home Park in 1968. Earlier, in 1942, Standard Oil Company acquired and recorded an easement in the land for ingress, egress, and pipeline purposes. In 1971, Standard Oil required Baum to remove five mobile homes which encroached on the easement so that Standard Oil could enter to work on the pipeline. After Standard Oil completed its work, Baum installed concrete foundations for the mobile homes and put them back on their original sites. In 1980, Baum sold the park to the Stevensons, but did not inform them or his real estate agent about the pipeline easement or his temporary removal of the mobile homes to allow work on the pipeline. In 1993, Chevron Pipe Line Company, Standard Oil's successor in interest, informed the Stevensons that the five mobile homes encroached on the easement and would have to be removed to allow access to the pipeline. The title insurance policy that the Stevensons received at the time of purchase revealed Standard Oil's recorded easement for ingress and egress, but the policy did not disclose the existence of the pipeline, of which the Stevensons had no actual knowledge. Must the Stevensons remove the mobile homes? Adapted from *Stevenson v. Baum*, 75 Cal. Rptr. 2d 904 (Cal. Ct. App. 1998).

5. Virgil Howland purchased farmland through which ran a drainage ditch. The ditch was maintained by the local Drainage District under the terms of an easement received from a prior owner in 1967 and recorded in 1969. In 1980 Howland erected a pole barn seven feet from the bank of the ditch. The barn encroached on the district's easement, making a "clean out" (dredging) of the ditch impossible with equipment the district owned. The district sought an injunction compelling removal of the barn. At trial, Howland testified that he knew the district had an easement when he began construction, but did not know its true dimensions until later when he obtained a copy of the easement documents from the country recorder. He testified that he had earlier asked William Gard, the district's superintendent, about the easement's width. Gard's response was that getting the exact dimensions from district records would be time-consuming, but "I'd say [the easement is] approximately 75 feet," which Howland took to mean 75 feet wide. In fact, it measured 75 feet from the ditch's center line. Holding that Howland knew or should have known the correct dimensions of the easement, the trial court granted the injunction. Howland appealed. Should the trial court's decision be upheld? *Borrowman v. Howland*, 457 N.E.2d 103 (Ill. App. 1983).

6. Pauline had a life estate in Blackacre, and Roger had the remainder in fee simple. Soon after Pauline came into possession of the land, she granted her neighbor Fred an easement "across those parts of Blackacre necessary for removing the timber from it." Removing the timber would

require about ten years. Three years after granting the easement to Fred, Pauline died. Roger contends that the easement terminated then. Fred contends that the easement will not terminate until its purpose, removal of the timber, is accomplished. (a) Who is correct? (b) If Roger is correct, what is the legal basis for the termination?

Endnotes

1. Alan David Hegi, *The Easement in Gross Revisited: Transferability and Divisibility Since 1945*, 39 Vand. L. Rev. 109 (1986). American courts have disagreed on two questions: (1) whether easements in gross are transferable, and (2) whether the holder of an easement in gross may share it with others. The law of their transferability and divisibility varies considerably from state to state. In this section of the chapter, transferability is the focus. *Sharing* of easements in gross—their divisibility—is discussed in a later section, "Scope of Rights Created by an Easement."

2. Cal. Civ. Code § 1001 (Deering, 2001).

3. *Midland Valley R.R. Co. v. Arrow Indus. Mfg. Co.*, 297 P.2d 410 (Okla. 1956).

4. Note, *Conservation Easements and the Doctrine of Changed Conditions*, 40 Hastings L.J. 1187, 1190 (1989) (by Jeffrey A. Blackie).

5. Melissa Waller Baldwin, *Conservation Easements: A Viable Tool for Land Preservation*, 32 Land & Water L. Rev. 89, at n.159 (1997) (article not paginated in LEXIS-NEXIS Academic Universe version). The states without conservation easement statutes are Alabama, Oklahoma, Pennsylvania, and Wyoming, though Pennsylvania common law strongly favors the validity of conservation easements. *Id.* at n.160.

6. Hegi, *supra* note 1, at 125 n.95.

7. Unif. Conservation Easement Act § 1(1) (1981). As of 1997, adopted in seventeen states.

Chapter 5 Co-ownership of Real Estate; Marital Interests

Outline

George owns Blackacre in fee simple and conveys to Hilda a quarter-section (160 acres), which she names Whiteacre. He conveys the rest of Blackacre to "my daughter Jan for life, then to Ben." Hilda, Jan, and Ben hold their respective interests—the fee simple estate in Whiteacre, the life estate in the rest of Blackacre, and the remainder in fee simple—in **severalty**. That is, each person is the sole owner of the interest received from George.

In contrast, if George had conveyed an interest to two or more persons for them to own simultaneously, the result would have been some form of **co-ownership**, also called *concurrent ownership* or *cotenancy*. George conveys land in fee simple "to Hilda and Herman." Hilda and Herman are co-owners of the fee simple interest, and each co-owner, or **cotenant**, has the same rights in the interest that the other has. Any ownership interest (estate) in land can be co-owned. Thus Hilda and Herman can together own a fee simple estate, a life estate, a leasehold estate, or a future interest such as a remainder or a reversion. Both personal and real property can be co-owned. In this chapter, however, the focus is on co-ownership of real property.

Three main types of co-ownership exist in the United States: tenancy in common, joint tenancy, and tenancy by the entirety. **Tenancy in common** exists in all states. Most states have **joint tenancy**, but a few limit its availability to persons such as trustees and executors of decedents' estates.[1] In tenancy in common and in joint tenancy, land can be owned by any number of cotenants, who may or may not be related to each other. **Tenancy by the entirety**, however, always involves only two cotenants: husband and wife. It exists in about twenty states, but in some of these states it applies only to realty. Tenancy by the entirety is not available in the community property states.

Community property states are so-called because of the way the property of married persons is treated. Eight western and southern states—Arizona, California, Idaho, Louisiana, Nevada, New Mexico, Texas, and Washington—have community property systems derived from Spanish or French civil law. In those states, husband and wife are by law equal co-owners of any item of property acquired during the marriage, regardless of who earned or acquired it, unless the law defines it as (or the parties agree that it is to be) the "separate" property of one of them. Wisconsin has a similar system because its legislature adopted the Uniform Marital Property Act, which is based on community property principles. So, in those nine states, unless otherwise agreed, Wanda's $100,000 salary and the $40,000 she has saved out of it since her marriage are community property, owned in equal shares by her and her unemployed husband Harry. And, although Wanda holds title to their house and makes all the payments, it too is community property owned in equal shares by the spouses. In contrast, in a *non*community property state, any property acquired during marriage belongs in severalty to the spouse who earned or acquired it unless the spouses agree to the contrary by, for example, electing to hold it in some form of co-ownership.[2] If Wanda and Harry lived in a noncommunity property state, she would be the sole owner of her salary, her savings account, and the house, unless otherwise agreed. How these contrasting systems of marital property ownership work at the separation, divorce, or death of the spouses is a recurring topic of this chapter.

Co-owners who are entitled to the *present possession* of *land* are said to have **concurrent estates** in it. They hold their concurrent estates as tenants in common, joint tenants, or tenants by the entirety. The first part of this chapter discusses the three main concurrent estates and some specialized applications such as the co-ownership aspects of condominiums. The second part discusses the ownership rights of married persons, including the type of marital co-ownership found in the community property states.

Concurrent Estates

The legal rights and duties among cotenants, their creditors, and their heirs vary according to the type of cotenancy involved. For example, Carl, Shelley, and Gertrude own land as tenants in common. At Carl's death, his interest goes to his devisees or heirs, and does not pass to Carl's surviving cotenants (unless, of course, they happen to *be* Carl's devisees or heirs). In contrast, joint tenancy and tenancy by the entirety involve a "right of survivorship." So if Jane and Jill own Park Place as joint tenants and Jane dies, Jill becomes sole owner of Park Place "by right of survivorship." Similarly, in a tenancy by the entirety, the surviving spouse becomes sole owner at the death of the other spouse. The discussion that follows highlights the special features and uses of each kind of concurrent estate.

Tenancy in Common

Language of Creation; Presumption of Tenancy in Common

No particular wording is required for creating a tenancy in common. A conveyance by deed (or a devise by will) to two or more persons creates a tenancy in common unless the language used or the circumstances of the transfer meet the legal requirements for creating some other type of concurrent estate. For example, a conveyance of Rolling Acres "to Betty and Joan," "to Betty and Joan equally," "to Betty and Joan as tenants in common," or "one-fourth to Betty and three-fourths to Joan" creates a tenancy in common.

Sometimes, the language creating co-ownership is ambiguous, as where William conveys Rolling Acres "to Betty and Joan jointly." "Jointly" signifies co-ownership, but does not make clear which type of co-ownership William intended. Did he intend a joint tenancy or a tenancy in common? In all states, ambiguous wording such as this is presumed to create a tenancy in common. In a few states, however, a conveyance of realty to husband and wife automatically creates a tenancy by the entirety if the deed is silent about the type of co-ownership.

Nature of Ownership in Tenancy in Common

George's conveyance of Whiteacre "to Hilda and Herman as tenants in common," creates in each an **undivided fractional interest** in Whiteacre. Because their fractional interests are "undivided," neither Hilda nor Herman owns any particular rock, tree, building, or area of the land that George conveyed. Instead, they both have a right to share equally in the possession and enjoyment of the whole parcel and of each component part. If they sell the parcel, they share its monetary value in proportion to the size of their respective undivided fractional interests, which, in a tenancy in common, can be unequal.

If George had granted "four-fifths to Hilda and one-fifth to Herman," they would be entitled to four-fifths and one-fifth respectively. Despite the unequal shares, Herman would still share possession and use equally with Hilda. Thus, both would have the right to ride their horses over the whole parcel, fish the length of the stream, or hunt mushrooms throughout the woods free from interference by the other.

Where the grantor says nothing about share size, equal shares are presumed—halves for two tenants in common, thirds for three, and so on. In a purchase of land, the presumption of equal shares can be rebutted by one cotenant's proving that he or she paid a larger share of the purchase price, that no family relationship justifies equal shares, and that the person paying more had no intent to donate the excess value to the other cotenants.

Not only can tenants in common have shares that are unequal in *size*, but they can also hold different *kinds* of interests that may have been acquired at different *times*. Edna owns Forest Acres in fee simple. By deed, she conveys "to my brother Ned an undivided life estate interest in one-fourth of Forest Acres, remainder [of the one-fourth] in fee simple to our sisters Sylvia and Sara." Ned's life estate gives him a right of immediate possession, but he must share possession with Edna because she kept fee simple ownership of the remaining three-fourths without specifying a particular portion that would be subject to Ned's life estate. Because they have simultaneous rights to possess Forest Acres, Edna and Ned are tenants in common despite the fact that her interest is a fee simple estate while his is a life estate. Sylvia and Sara are *co-owners* of the fee simple remainder in one-fourth of Forest Acres, but are *not* tenants in common with the others (nor between themselves) because they have no present possessory interest, only a remainder conferring future possession on them or their successors.[3]

Rights of a Cotenant's Transferee

During life, a tenant in common can sell, lease, mortgage, or give away his or her undivided interest without the consent of the other cotenants, with the following legal consequences:

- A purchaser or a donee of the interest becomes a tenant in common with the other cotenants, receiving the same ownership rights that the granting cotenant had.

- A cotenant's lessee receives for the term of the lease the same possession rights that the lessor-cotenant had. If, however, the lessor-cotenant had less than a fee simple interest, the lessee cannot receive more than the lessor had. Hank has a life estate in High Towers Office Building, leases the building to Alice for a term of 15 years, and dies five years later. Alice's lease ends at Hank's death because her lease cannot exceed the period of Hank's life estate.

- A cotenant's mortgagee receives a security interest in the cotenant's share of the land, but not in the shares of the other cotenants.

Rights of Heirs and Devisees

If a tenant in common dies without having disposed of the undivided interest, it becomes a part of that cotenant's estate to be distributed to one or more *devisees* if the cotenant left a will, or to the cotenant's *heirs* if the cotenant died intestate. A devisee or an heir becomes a tenant in common with the decedent's surviving cotenants or their successors. Edna dies owning her three-fourths of Forest Acres. Her will devises one of those fourths to her son Gabriel and the other two to the local school for the blind. Thus, brother Ned (owner of the one-fourth life estate interest), Gabriel (devisee of one-fourth in fee simple), and the school (devisee of one-half in fee simple) are tenants in common. Upon Ned's death the following month, Sylvia and Sara's remainder in fee simple becomes possessory. Now Sylvia and Sara share an undivided one-fourth interest in Forest Acres (each sister having an undivided one-eighth interest) and are tenants in common with Gabriel (owner of one-fourth), and the school (owner of one-half).

Often, multiple heirs or devisees like Sylvia and Sara above receive an interest in realty as a group. Harry and Angus own a golf course as tenants in common. Harry, a widower, dies intestate, leaving his three children as his only heirs. Under the intestacy statute, the children take Harry's share as a group; as a group they hold the share as a tenant in common with Harry's surviving cotenant Angus. Moreover, as co-owners of the share, they are tenants in common among themselves, each owning an undivided one-third of Harry's share (i.e., a one-sixth interest in the golf course). If Harry had devised his interest "to my children Harriet, Helen, and Harry, Jr.," the result would be the same: Angus and the children would be tenants in common, with Angus owning one-half and the children owning one-sixth each.

Rights of Cotenant's Creditors

Each tenant in common and each joint tenant has an undivided fractional interest which is available to that cotenant's individual creditors. Leonardo and Myra own Blackacre as tenants in common (or as joint tenants). Myra defaults on a personal loan or fails to pay her taxes. The disappointed creditor may attach her interest and force its sale, but has no right against Leonardo's interest. Similarly, Leonardo's creditors have access to his fractional interest, but not to Myra's. If Leonardo and Myra have undertaken a *joint* debt, however, the creditor would have access to the fractional interests of both, as where Leonardo and Myra give First Bank a mortgage on Blackacre as security for a loan. In contrast, in most of the states recognizing tenancy by the entirety, the cotenants (husband and wife) have no fractional interests in the realty, so have nothing for their individual creditors to attach.

Rights and Duties Among Tenants in Common

Although each cotenant has a right to possess the entire parcel of land, simultaneous possession by all cotenants often is not possible, and conflicts are likely to arise over the use and control of the property. Albert devises Farview Farm to his children Richard and Betty. At Albert's death, Richard moves into the main house and takes over the management of the farm. Can Betty require that Farview Farm be physically divided into two smaller tracts so that she owns one while Richard owns the other? If the farm is not divided, several additional questions arise:

- May Richard exclude his sister from possession?
- Without his sister's permission, may Richard lease Farview Farm to a stranger or grant to a neighbor a right of way (easement) across it?
- How is the income from the farm to be divided?
- What are the cotenants' responsibilities for repairs, taxes, and other maintenance costs?

Cotenants' Right of Partition. For a variety of reasons, a cotenant may wish to put an end to a tenancy in common or a joint tenancy and to own his or her share in severalty. Cotenants might find management of the land difficult because they cannot get along with one another. Or a purchaser of a cotenant's interest might want to develop it independently, without the participation of the cotenants. Whatever the reason for separate ownership, a cotenant (including a purchaser at a defaulting cotenant's mortgage foreclosure sale) has a right of **partition**, that is, a right to have the land physically separated into smaller parcels that will be separately owned. Alice, Bernard, and Clarisa own Wildview as tenants in common. Alice sells her interest to Donald, a residential developer, who becomes a tenant in common with Bernard and Clarisa. Donald, like the other cotenants, has a right to have Wildview partitioned so that he owns his share in severalty.

The partitioning can be *voluntary*, that is, by agreement of the cotenants. If they cannot agree, the cotenant seeking partition may have a *court-ordered* (judicial) partition. In either type of partition, if Wildview has physical characteristics preventing it from being divided into parts of equal value, a party receiving a less valuable parcel is entitled to payment of a compensating amount called **owelty**. One-third of Wildview is a rocky highland, separated from the rest of Wildview by the Rajun River and accessible only by boat. Another third is low-lying marshland subject to a wildlife conservation easement that forbids development. The remaining third, located on a bluff overlooking the marshland, is an excellent site for a housing development and is far more valuable commercially than the other two-thirds. Unable to agree on the division of Wildview, the parties seek a judicial partition. As a condition to Donald's obtaining the more valuable land, the court may order Donald to pay Bernard and Clarisa an amount (owelty) sufficient to give each of them one-third of the total value of Wildview.

A physical division of co-owned land is called **partition in kind**, with each cotenant receiving one of the resulting parcels. Sometimes, however, a fair and equitable physical division is not possible, even with owelty. For such situations, all states have statutes providing for *partition by sale.* In a partition by sale, a court orders the sale of the realty as a single parcel and divides the proceeds among the cotenants. Eudora, Franklin, and Jerome inherit Riverview, their grandmother's large Victorian home situated in an exclusive neighborhood high on the banks of Dream River. The three-acre lot with its twelve-room house and extensive formal gardens is worth $1.5 million. If partitioned into three one-acre lots, the total value of the partitioned property would be reduced to $500,000. Unable to agree on who is to have the acre with the house and outbuildings, the grandchildren seek a judicial partition. To preserve the value of Riverview, the court will order its sale as a single parcel and an equal distribution of the proceeds to the grandchildren.

In the case that follows, the appellate court discusses whether the trial court is limited to choosing between partition in kind and partition by sale.

Case 5.1

Fernandes v. Rodriguez

735 A.2d 871 (Conn. App. 1999)

For investment purposes, Maria Fernandes and Eyvind Rodriguez purchased a house as joint tenants. Fernandes and Rodriguez intended to live together in one of its three apartments and to rent out the other two. The couple did not get along well in the management of the property. At one point, Fernandes was granted a restraining order against Rodriguez. After about three years of joint ownership, Fernandes brought suit to partition the property. Defendant Rodriguez counterclaimed, alleging that the plaintiff was living rent free in the apartment she occupied, and that she kept the net rental income of the remaining two apartments. He sought a money judgment for half of the net rental income and half of what should have been the rental of the apartment in which the plaintiff lived.

The trial court found that Rodriguez had paid $1,000 of the $14,892 down payment and closing costs, and that Fernandes managed the property and did extensive cleanup and repairs while defendant did little or nothing. Stating that it did not find the defendant's testimony credible and that it believed the testimony of Fernandes, the trial court ordered her to pay defendant $4,605, and ordered him to transfer his interest in the property to her. The $4,605 covered his share of the proceeds from the two rental apartments, reimbursement for the $1,000 he contributed to the down payment and closing costs, and payment for a 10% share of the equity in the house. The trial court, however, refused to award defendant anything for the rental value of plaintiff's apartment, on the assumption that defendant could have lived there. Finding that the defendant's interest in the real estate was minimal, the court held that defendant was not entitled to the remedy of a sale of the property. Defendant appealed.

DUPONT, J.

This is an appeal from a judgment of partition of real estate, in which the primary issue is whether the trial court could properly order . . . the defendant to execute and deliver to the plaintiff a quitclaim deed to [his share of the premises in exchange for a payment of money by the plaintiff]. The defendant claims that the trial court had no statutory authority to render such a judgment because [under the statute the defendant was entitled to] either partition in kind or a sale of the real estate. We hold that the trial court could properly [order the defendant to convey his interest to the plaintiff in exchange for a money payment from her].

. . .

This is the only . . . case in Connecticut of which we or the parties are aware in which the relief obtained in a partition action was solely the payment of money in exchange for a conveyance of title. In only one case was an issue raised similar to the issue here. In *Geib v. McKinney*, the defendants argued that because the plaintiff had only a minimal interest in the subject real estate, a partition by sale would be an improper remedy in a partition action. That argument was not addressed, however, because the Supreme Court upheld the trial court's reasonable finding that the plaintiff had more than a minimal interest. Because the plaintiff had more than a minimal interest, the court upheld the trial court's order of a partition by sale.

We look to [Connecticut statutes and related cases] for guidance. [Conflicting cases] provide clues as to whether a trial court has such power in an action for partition. Some cases contain language indicating that a court is limited in partition actions to rendering a judgment of either partition in kind or partition by sale of the real estate. [*Johnson v. Olmsted* is frequently quoted for the proposition] that there are only two modes of relief in statutory actions for partition. . . .

Another case recognizes that remedies other than sale or partition in kind were available in equity in partition actions. . . . An action for partition at common law was equitable in nature, requiring courts to examine all relevant circumstances. Those equitable considerations are whether partition should be in kind or by sale, [should be accomplished] by adjusting unequal shares through payments to an owner or [should be accomplished] by giving an accounting. Because the remedy to be chosen by a court relates, in part, to a determination of whether one of the owners has a minimal interest, a trial court may properly consider the percentage of ownership of each. . . .

It is not necessarily true that each tenant-in-common or joint tenant is entitled to an equal share in the real estate. . . . [In *Levay v. Levay*, the court noted that] "Equities must be considered and, if established, must be liquidated before distribution is ordered."

Here, the trial court found that . . . the defendant's interest was minimal and concluded that a sale would not be equitable. The defendant claims that the court could not end its inquiry with the conclusion that a sale was not an appropriate remedy, but had to determine also whether a partition in kind was warranted.

A partition in kind presents the same inequities as a sale when a co-owner has only a minimal interest. A partition in kind presents other problems in this case as well. The judgment of partition by a court must take into account the particular situation of the parties, which includes the physical attributes of the real estate and the interests of the owners. . . . In this case, the plaintiff had obtained an ex parte restraining order against the defendant, preventing him from entering the real estate. . . . It is unlikely that the parties could cooperate peacefully in managing the property, even if a partition in kind, giving him a 10 percent interest could be accomplished. Because of the minimal interest of the defendant, coupled with the other factors here, partition in kind was not appropriate.

. . .

The question remaining is whether the remedy ordered by the trial court was proper, given its conclusion that the defendant's interest was minimal. . . . In a situation where neither partition in kind [nor] a sale is equitable because a co-owner has only a minimal interest in the real estate, the trial court should be permitted to fashion an alternative equitable remedy because no owner can be compelled to continue ownership with another. "The determination of what equity requires in a particular case . . . is a matter for the discretion of the trial court."

. . .

The right to partition was established by the common law, and is fortified by the use of equitable principles and by the statutes. The statutes governing partition are remedial in nature and should be liberally construed. In essence, a complaint for partition seeks "no fault" relief. Once the cotenants or joint tenants determine they cannot coexist, the relief of severance of the ownership must be afforded, and the trial court must fashion an appropriate equitable remedy, if partition by sale or in kind would be inequitable. We do not disturb the black letter law that states that usually no remedy other than a partition by sale or in kind can be afforded in a partition action. We simply provide an exception for the limited situations such as the one of the present case, where one party's interest is very minimal and the other resides on the premises.

[A remaining claim of the defendant relates] to his counterclaim for one half of the rental value of the plaintiff's apartment. . . .

The finding of the trial court that the defendant could have lived in an apartment on the premises led to its conclusion that the defendant was not entitled to one half of the rental value of that apartment and it is that finding and conclusion that the defendant vigorously attacks as improper. We agree with the defendant. The plaintiff testified that in September, 1995, she obtained an ex parte restraining order to prevent the defendant from entering the premises. She testified that she called the police in September, 1995, because of an argument the two had about his placement of a dead bolt on the apartment door. . . . Given the plaintiff's testimony. . . we cannot conclude that the trial court's finding that the defendant could have lived in the apartment was based on the evidence. Accordingly, we must remand the case so that the trial court can establish the amount of money the plaintiff must pay the defendant for one half of the rental value of the apartment in which the plaintiff lived.

. . .

The judgment is reversed only as to the amount to be paid to the defendant by the plaintiff and the case is remanded for further proceedings to determine the amount . . . due the defendant . . . for one half of the fair rental value of the apartment in which the plaintiff resided. . . .

QUESTIONS ABOUT CASE 5.1

1. Under what circumstances will Connecticut courts order one of two co-tenants in a partition action to transfer his or her interest in the realty to the other in exchange for a money payment from the other?

2. Why would it be inequitable to Fernandes for a court to order sale of the property?

Cotenants' Right of Possession, Fiduciary Obligations, and Duty Not to Commit Waste. Richard's exclusive possession of Farview Farm is presumed rightful unless Betty objects. If she does object and he excludes her from the farm or any part of it, his action constitutes an ouster. **Ouster** is a wrongful dispossession that entitles the ousted cotenant to the remedy of **ejectment**, an action to restore possession to the person entitled to it.[4] In the ejectment action, the ousted cotenant may also collect any profits, called **mesne** (pronounced "mean") **profits**, to which he or she would have been entitled during the period of dispossession. Richard refuses Betty the use of the house, padlocks the barn so that she cannot stable her horse there, and locks the gates to the alfalfa field to keep her out. He has committed an ouster as to those parts of Farview Farm. Betty may bring an action in ejectment to regain possession and to collect mesne profits.

If Betty permits the ouster to continue for the statute of limitations period, Richard can acquire sole ownership of those parts by **adverse possession** (discussed in Chapter 6). If he excludes her totally, he can become the sole owner of the whole farm. To do so, he must claim absolute ownership of the farm and deny the existence of a cotenancy relationship. However, his sole possession as a cotenant is not enough, by itself, to constitute the *adverse* possession needed for him to become sole owner. Ordinarily an adverse possessor is an obvious trespasser and thus needs only to possess the land openly to communicate the wrongful act to the owner. But because Richard's sole possession as cotenant is presumed rightful, he must take additional action to make clear to Betty his intention to exclude (oust) her and have the property as his alone. When he does communicate that intention, his possession becomes wrongful, and the process of adverse possession commences. Richard becomes sole owner when all the requirements for adverse possession have been met, including Betty's failure to reverse the ouster within the time permitted by the statute of limitations.

A **fiduciary duty** arises where one person in a relationship, because of a relative lack of knowledge or sophistication, has a right to place trust and confidence in a more knowledgeable or experienced person (the fiduciary). A fiduciary may not take unfair advantage of the other party and is expected to act in that person's best interest. Cotenants have fiduciary duties among themselves when dealing with the realty. For example, a cotenant, being a fiduciary, may not secretly purchase the realty from a tax sale purchaser and later claim exclusive ownership, but instead must disclose the purchase to the other cotenants and give them an opportunity to contribute their share of the purchase price and remain co-owners. Similarly, a cotenant who buys a real estate mortgage from the bank holding it, and who thus becomes the creditor entitled to the mortgage payments, holds the mortgage for the benefit of all cotenants. So the creditor cotenant must allow the others to pay their share of the mortgage debt and thus preserve their ownership shares.

Because all cotenants have equal rights to possess and use the land, each cotenant has a duty to the others not to commit waste. As noted in Chapter 3, **waste** is the act of destroying realty, or damaging or neglecting it to the extent that its value is substantially impaired. If a cotenant commits waste, the other cotenants have appropriate remedies, usually an injunction or damages or both, depending on the circumstances.

Leasing or Selling the Land; Granting an Easement. One cotenant cannot lease or convey the whole property without the consent of all. Without consulting Betty, Richard attempts to lease Farview Farm to Roberta. His attempt to do so results only in his leasing his own undivided interest to Roberta, who for the term of the lease takes possession as a cotenant with Betty. The lease expires. Then, without consulting Betty, Richard purports to sell Farview Farm to Maria. His attempt to do so results only in a conveyance of his own undivided interest to Maria, who becomes Betty's cotenant.

Neither can Richard, without Betty's consent, grant an easement that will bind them both. An easement gives its holder a right of usage that conflicts with an unconsenting cotenant's right of possession. Consequently, the easement that Richard granted would be valid only as to his interest and, moreover, only when that interest is partitioned. Without consulting Betty, Richard grants Olga a right of way across the north part of Farview Farm. Olga cannot enforce the easement if Betty objects. But if Farview Farm is partitioned so that Richard later acquires the north part in severalty, Olga's easement becomes enforceable against Richard.

Possessing Cotenant's Duty to Account for Profits. At common law a cotenant in sole possession could keep all the rents and profits from the land without having to account to the other cotenants, unless the possessor had agreed to act as "bailiff" (manager) for the others, had leased the land from the cotenants, or was acting as guardian of or trustee for them. In 1704, an English statute, the Statute of Anne, made a rightfully possessing cotenant who was *not* a bailiff, lessee, guardian, or trustee liable to the other cotenants for certain rents and profits that exceeded the possessor's proportionate share.[5] This statute was interpreted to apply only to rents and profits that the possessor received from third persons such as a lessee of the land. If the profits arose instead from the possessor's own occupation and use of the land, sharing them with the other cotenants was not required. The courts reasoned that since the possessor's own efforts generated the profits, it would be unjust to allow absentee cotenants to share in them.

Most states today have a statute similar to the Statute of Anne, or have adopted it as part of their common law. In those states, a cotenant in possession must account for rents and profits received from third persons, but generally has no duty to account for the profits resulting from the possessor's rightful use of the land unless that use permanently reduces its value. Activities such as cutting timber and opening new mines, oil wells, and quarries ("extraction activities") all reduce the value of the land because valuable material is removed. A possessing cotenant who engages in extraction activities must account to the other cotenants for the profits.

In a minority of states, the sole possessor must account to the cotenants for *any* profits, whether from third persons or from the possessor's own efforts. In all states, a sole possessor who leases from the cotenants their shares of the land, or who acts as guardian of or trustee for them, must account to them for the rent or for their shares of the profits. But a cotenant in possession has no duty to share the income derived from improvements made by that cotenant alone. Without consulting Betty, Richard builds an auction house and parking lot on Farview Farm and conducts weekly auctions of livestock, farm equipment, and antiques. Betty is not entitled to a share of the auction profits.

Cotenants' Liability for Necessary Expenses and for Costs of Improvements. A cotenant who pays more than his or her share of necessary expenses is entitled to contribution from the other cotenants. Necessary expenses include repair costs, taxes, mortgage interest and principal, and insurance, but do *not* include the costs of maintaining improvements made by a cotenant without the consent of the others. Richard pays all the expenses incurred in his operation of Farview Farm and the new auction house. He may have contribution from Betty for the farm expenses, but not for those attributable to the auction house.

There is an exception to the right of contribution for tax and mortgage payments that exceed the possessor's pro rata share. As noted earlier, in most states, Richard would have no duty to account for the profits resulting from his own efforts in using the land as a farm. But if he pays more than his pro rata share of taxes and mortgage payments, *and the value of his use and occupation is greater than the excess payments*, he cannot have contribution for the excess. Otherwise, he would receive all the profits while Betty would be paying some of the costs of producing them. It makes sense, though, that Betty should contribute to such expenditures as repairs, because they preserve the value of the realty for her as well as for Richard.

If Richard gives Betty prior notice of needed farm repairs, the courts of most states would allow him to enforce his right of contribution in an independent lawsuit for the amount. The independent action normally is available also for repairs made necessary by an emergency such as a fire or flood, and for nonemergency repairs made when Betty is not reasonably available to approve them, as where she moves without leaving a forwarding address or fails to respond to communications. In contrast, if Richard fails to give prior notice of nonemergency repairs when Betty is available for consultation, Richard ordinarily may have contribution, but only in an action for an accounting or partition.

Betty also must contribute her share of the cost of any improvement to which she consented, for example, the construction of a drainage ditch or a farm machine shop. As to improvements to which she did not consent, such as the auction house and parking lot, Richard can have contribution from Betty, but only in an action for partition. In the partition action, the value of unconsented-to improvements would be included in the value of Farview Farm and shared by Richard and Betty, subject to Betty's duty to contribute her share of the costs.

Condominiums: Co-ownership of Common Areas

In this era of growing populations and limited availability of land for development, shared ownership arrangements have become popular for housing and other purposes. Shared ownership allows an individual to own or use a "unit" (part of a building or tract of land) and to have, with the owners of the other units, the ownership or use of certain common areas. "Common interest ownership" arrangements include *condominiums, planned unit developments, community apartment projects, stock cooperatives*, and *time-share arrangements*. Some are used primarily or exclusively for residential purposes. Others, such as the condominium and the planned unit development, are used for residential, business, or commercial purposes, or for some combination of them. Typically, a property owners' association collects a fee from the unit owners and, among other duties, manages and maintains the common areas. Created and regulated by the Uniform Common Interest Ownership Act or other legislation, these arrangements are discussed further in Chapter 15.

A person who acquires a **condominium** receives two basic property rights: (1) Ownership of a "unit," usually in fee simple, which is taxed separately to the unit owner as an interest in land. Often the unit is a cube of airspace in an upper story, the unit boundaries being marked by walls, floor, and ceiling. (2) An undivided fractional interest in the common areas, as a tenant in common with other unit owners. The common areas include the outside walls, roof, sidewalks, the land underlying the building or buildings, lawns that are not part of a unit, parking lot, swimming pool, tennis courts, and the like. Although the unit owner is a tenant in common as to the common areas, no unit owner has a right of partition, and no unit owner can separate his or her interest in the common areas from ownership of the unit. Transfer of the unit carries with it the right to use the common areas and the duty to contribute to their maintenance.

● Joint Tenancy

Nature of Joint Tenancy

Joint tenancy in land is a type of concurrent estate involving a "right of survivorship." A person creates a joint tenancy by conveying or devising an estate in land (e.g., a fee simple or a life estate) to a group of two or more people to own together as one entity, intending the last survivor to be the sole owner of the estate. From the time of the conveyance or devise to the group, each joint tenant is considered to own the whole estate simultaneously with all the others. Each joint tenant also receives an undivided fractional interest that he or she can dispose of during life. If the members of the group do not dispose of their undivided fractional interests and one member dies, ownership of the whole, being in the group from the time the joint tenancy was created, stays in the survivors.

It is sometimes said that the fractional interest of a deceased joint tenant "passes" to the surviving joint tenants "by right of survivorship." But the interest is not passed or transferred to anyone at the death of the joint tenant. Rather, by dying, the tenant simply loses all claim to the jointly held estate, and the fractional interest disappears. The surviving joint tenants stay on as co-owners, each now with a larger fractional share. The last survivor, being an owner of the whole estate from the time of the original grant, becomes sole owner of the property. In 1979 George conveyed Blackacre in fee simple to Alma, Ben, and Clara as joint tenants. Thus, in 1979, each co-tenant (1) became owner of the whole fee simple estate and (2) received an undivided one-third share in it. At Alma's death in 1989, her fractional interest terminated, and the size of Ben's and Clara's fractional interests increased to one-half each. When Ben died in 2000, Clara became sole owner of Blackacre.[6]

Because a joint tenant's fractional interest terminates at his or her death, the interest does not become a part of the deceased person's estate.[7] Consequently, the interest is not inheritable and cannot be disposed of by will. Delia and Ephraim own the Highland Hills Resort as joint tenants. Delia states in her will, "I leave my one-half interest in Highland Hills Resort to my son Duane." At her death, her interest in the resort ceases, her attempted devise of the interest to Duane fails, and Ephraim, as the surviving joint tenant, becomes sole owner of the resort. Moreover, because Delia and Ephraim owned the resort as joint tenants, Ephraim becomes sole owner without having to go through probate.

Probate is the often expensive and time-consuming process by which a court determines who is entitled to a decedent's property and oversees its transfer to the decedent's devisees or heirs. When a person dies owning realty in *severalty*, the land records (if the decedent's deed was recorded) or the decedent's unrecorded deed will continue to show the decedent as owner. At death, however, a decedent's will, or the intestacy statute if there is no will, automatically gives ownership of the realty to the decedent's devisee or heir. But because the decedent's deed or the land records still show the decedent as the owner, the probate court must provide the devisee or the heir with a deed showing that the land was transferred from the decedent's estate to the new owner. Otherwise the new owner will lack a marketable title. A land title is "marketable" if there is no serious doubt that a buyer will receive ownership. A missing link in a seller's "chain of title" creates such a doubt and gives a prospective buyer a basis for cancelling the contract of sale. Hence the need for a probate court to complete the chain of title by transferring title from the decedent's estate to the decedent's devisee or heir.

But property held in *joint* tenancy is *not* subject to the probate process, because the surviving joint tenant does not need a conveyance from a probate court to establish title. Ephraim has title to Blackacre under the deed that he and Delia received long ago. As surviving joint tenant, Ephraim avoids probate because he continues in the ownership he received under the deed creating the joint tenancy. To establish that he now is sole owner of Blackacre, Ephraim needs only to show that Delia died and thus lost her fractional interest in Blackacre. If recorded, the deed creating the joint tenancy reveals to the world the fact of joint tenancy and the identity of the joint tenants, thus enabling any interested stranger to determine who presently owns Blackacre.

Creation of Joint Tenancy

Creation of a joint tenancy and the right of survivorship that accompanies it requires observance of formalities derived from the common law. In many states, these formalities, called the "four unities," have been relaxed somewhat by statutes or by case law.

The Four Unities. At common law, a joint tenancy could not be created unless the four uni-ties of time, title, interest, and possession were present. Accordingly, for a transfer of land to result in a joint tenancy, the transfer had to meet the following four requirements:

1. Unity of *time*. The interests of all the cotenants must vest (take effect) at the same time.

2. Unity of *title*. The interests of all the cotenants must be created by the same deed, will, or other instrument of transfer and must come from the same transferor.

3. Unity of *interest*. The cotenants' individual fractional interests must be equal in *size*: e.g., halves for two cotenants, thirds for three. And the cotenants' interests must be of the same *type*. For example, all cotenants must receive a fee simple estate or all must receive a life estate. If one receives a fee simple while another receives a life estate, the resulting co-ownership is a tenancy in common, not a joint tenancy.

4. Unity of *possession*. All cotenants must have equal rights of possession and enjoyment of the whole parcel.

In most states, some of these requirements have been relaxed by legislation or by case law. The most common relaxations involve the unities of time and of title. At common law, Osgood, the owner of Blackacre in fee simple, could not create a joint tenancy merely by conveying Blackacre to himself and his brother Merlin as joint tenants, because under common law rules Osgood could not convey to himself land that he already owned. So if Osgood tried to transfer Blackacre to himself and Merlin, a court would rule that since Osgood already owned Blackacre, the at-tempted transfer was really only a transfer of one-half to Merlin. Because Osgood and Merlin re-ceived their interests at different times and under different instruments of conveyance, the transaction lacked unity of time and title, and a tenancy in common resulted. To create a *joint* ten-ancy with his brother, Osgood would have to convey Blackacre to a third-person **straw man** William, who in turn would convey Blackacre back to Osgood and Merlin as joint tenants. In most states today, a straw man is no longer needed for creating a joint tenancy.

Language Required; Presumption Against Joint Tenancy. A year before her death, Olivia conveys land "to Egbert and Justin as co-owners." Five years later, Egbert dies. Believing that Olivia intended a joint tenancy, survivor Justin claims sole ownership of the land. Egbert's heirs, however, claim a half interest in the land on the assumption that Olivia intended a tenancy in common. Because Olivia's words are ambiguous (capable of two or more equally plausible meanings), they do not reveal which kind of co-ownership she intended. To resolve the ambi-guity, a court interpreting the creating document (usually a deed or a will) must apply a pre-sumption. At common law, ambiguous language like Olivia's was presumed to create a joint tenancy, because keeping land in the hands of surviving co-owners was useful for purposes of feudal tenure. Since feudal tenure does not exist in the United States, interpreting an ambigu-ous deed as creating a joint tenancy serves no tenurial purpose and would result in disinherit-ing Egbert's heirs even though Olivia might not have intended such an outcome. To prevent unintended disinheritances (and, some authorities believe, to foster dispersal of land among heirs instead of consolidating it in the hands of often older, less productive survivors), U.S. courts interpreting ambiguous grants of co-ownership presume (or apply a statutory presump-tion) that a tenancy in common was intended.

To create a joint tenancy, then, a grantor must use language clearly revealing that intention. Some statutes require only that the language used show the intent to create a joint tenancy, with-out requiring any particular wording. Other statutes require that the intention be expressed by use of "joint tenants," "joint tenants and not tenants in common," "joint tenants with survivor-ship," or some equivalent phrase. Use of "joint tenants" or "joint tenancy" is sufficient in most

BOX 5–1 APPLY YOUR KNOWLEDGE

In 1985 Georgia conveyed her apartment complex Blackacre Arms to her children Alma and Ben as "joint tenants in common." Alma and Ben operated the complex together for several years, each receiving 50% of the net profits. When Alma died recently, Ben claimed sole ownership of Blackacre Arms. Alma's son Carlton, however, claimed one-half of Blackacre Arms as Alma's only heir. (a) As between Carlton and Ben, who owns Blackacre Arms? (b) Who would have owned it at Alma's death if in 1985 Georgia had conveyed it to Alma and Ben "as joint tenants in common with right of survivorship"?

states to create a joint tenancy, but to remove all doubt that a joint tenancy was intended, it would be better to use language such as "to Egbert and Justin as joint tenants with right of survivorship, and not as tenants in common." Ambiguous phrases such as "to Egbert and Justin jointly" have almost always been held to create a tenancy in common. A number of state statutes, however, establish the *opposite* presumption where two or more people are *coexecutors* of an estate or *cotrustees* of a trust. For efficiency in the administration of the estate or the trust, these statutes provide that *any* concurrent estate vested in coexecutors or cotrustees is a joint tenancy. Thus, at the death of a coexecutor or a cotrustee, survivors continue the administration.

Sometimes the language creating co-ownership is not truly ambiguous, but neither is it totally clear. In such instances, the courts will try to give the language a fair and reasonable interpretation as, for example, in the phrase "to A and B as co-owners in common, with right of survivorship." Used alone, "co-owners in common" suggests that a tenancy in common was intended. By adding "with right of survivorship," however, the grantor reveals an intention to create a joint tenancy, and most courts would so hold.

Rights of and Duties of Joint Tenants; Termination of Joint Tenancy

Like a tenant in common, a joint tenant has a variety of rights and duties. Among them are the right to possess the whole property, a right of partition, a right to contribution for necessary expenses, a duty not to commit waste, and a right during life to transfer (sell or give away) the undivided fractional interest.

A joint tenant's transferring the interest *severs* it from the joint tenancy by destroying the unity of title. Depending on the number of joint tenants, **severance** of the interest either totally or partially terminates the joint tenancy and converts it totally or partially into a *tenancy in common.* Alice and Benita own Blackacre as joint tenants. Alice sells her fractional interest to developer Donald, thus terminating the joint tenancy. Donald and Benita are now tenants in common. Upon receiving his interest from Alice, Donald probably will seek partition so that he can develop his share of the land independently. But if he remains a tenant in common with Benita until his death, his interest goes to his devisees or heirs, who as a group will now own the interest as a tenant in common with Benita.

If originally the property was held by three or more joint tenants—Alice, Benita, and Carl—Alice's selling her fractional interest to Donald would result in only a *partial* termination of the joint tenancy. Donald would become a tenant in common with Benita and Carl, but Benita and Carl would remain joint tenants as between themselves. So, if joint tenant Carl died after Alice sold her interest to Donald, Benita would own two-thirds as surviving joint tenant and would be a tenant in common with Donald, who owns the one-third he received from Alice.

BOX 5–2 APPLY YOUR KNOWLEDGE

Franklin, Gloriana, and Horatio own Southside Shopping Center as joint tenants. Gloriana sells her interest to Jackson. Then, in the following order, Franklin dies, Horatio dies, and Jackson dies. Who owns Southside Shopping center?

A voluntary transfer (sale, gift) or an involuntary transfer (e.g., mortgage foreclosure sale) of a joint tenant's whole interest results in severance and creates a tenancy in common. However, the transfer by a joint tenant of a *limited* interest in the joint tenant's fractional share does not necessarily result in a severance. Alan and Beatrice own Lee's Pizza Shop as joint tenants. Alan agrees that Beatrice shall have all the income from the co-owned property. Despite the agreement giving her all the income, Alan and Beatrice remain joint tenants. Similarly, if Alan and Beatrice own a condominium unit as joint tenants, Beatrice's agreeing that Alan shall have sole possession does not terminate the joint tenancy. In other situations, the legal effect of transferring a limited interest varies greatly from state to state, as the following examples reveal:

1. In states with a "title" theory of mortgages, a joint tenant's mortgaging his or her fractional interest results in a severance, because in those states the mortgage is viewed as an absolute conveyance of the fractional interest to the mortgagee-creditor. In "lien theory" states, a joint tenant's granting a mortgage to a lender is not viewed as an absolute transfer, but only as the granting of a security interest. In most lien theory states, a joint tenant's granting a mortgage does not result in a severance. In all states, however, *foreclosure* of a mortgage given by a joint tenant on his or her fractional interest *does* result in a severance, because a foreclosure sale transfers the encumbered interest to the buyer, thus destroying the unity of title. Mortgages are discussed in Chapter 10.

2. Usually, the recording of a judgment against a joint tenant does not, by itself, sever his or her interest from the joint tenancy, even though the recording creates a lien against the interest. But if the judgment creditor forces the sale of the interest, severance does occur.

3. Few cases deal with the question of whether a joint tenant's leasing his or her interest severs it. A California court held that a joint tenant's leasing his interest to a third person did not terminate the joint tenancy, and that the lessor's death terminated the lease, immediately giving the surviving joint tenant the right of sole possession. In contrast, a Maryland court held that a joint tenant's leasing the interest to another resulted in severance.[8]

Partition of realty held in joint tenancy results, totally or partially, in *several* ownership, not tenancy in common. Alma and Ben, who own Blackacre as joint tenants, agree to partition Blackacre, or one brings an action for partition in kind. Partition in kind terminates the joint tenancy and makes Alma and Ben owners in severalty of their respective tracts. If Alma, Ben, and Carol were joint tenants and Carol received partition in kind of her interest, Carol would own her share in severalty, while Alma and Ben would remain joint tenants as to the other two-thirds. Carol's merely commencing a partition action, however, does not terminate a joint tenancy, because she might choose to discontinue the suit.

Where one of two joint tenants or tenants in common transfers his or her interest to the other, the tenancy is terminated by "merger" of the two interests into one, and the transferee owns the property in severalty. Similarly, in a cotenancy of three or more, ownership in severalty results when one tenant receives the interests of all the others. In contrast, if all joint tenants keep their fractional interests but expressly agree that the right of survivorship shall be eliminated, the joint tenancy becomes a tenancy in common.

As noted earlier in this chapter, the law of most states no longer requires a person to use a straw man to convert sole ownership into a joint tenancy with another person. But is a straw man still required for *terminating* (severing) a joint tenancy? In most states the answer is "No."

In the leading case of *Riddle v. Harmon*, 162 Cal. Rptr. 530, 7 A.L.R.4th 1261 (Cal. App. 1980), Jack and Frances Riddle owned realty as joint tenants. Learning that at her death the property would be owned solely by her husband, Mrs. Riddle requested that the joint tenancy be terminated so that she could dispose of her interest by will. As advised by her attorney, Mrs. Riddle signed a deed as grantor, granting to herself an undivided one-half interest in the realty and expressing her intent to terminate the joint tenancy. She then signed a will leaving her interest in the property to a person other than Jack. After her death 20 days later, Jack sued Harmon, the executrix of Frances' estate, to quiet title to the property in himself. The trial court held the attempted severance invalid, and quieted title in Jack. Harmon appealed.

In reversing the trial court, the appellate court noted that the common law rule that a person cannot be both grantor and grantee simultaneously was obsolete. It was developed before deeds came into use, when "livery of seisin" (transfer of ownership) was accomplished in a public ceremony held on the land, with the grantor handing the grantee a lump of earth or a twig from a tree to symbolize the transfer. Since "[h]anding oneself a dirt clod is ungainly," both grantor and grantee were needed then. But livery of seisin has not been used since feudal times. In modern times, the courts have validated numerous ways of severing a joint tenancy, which is a clear right of a joint tenant. The straw man technique, based on the old assumption that the grantor and the grantee cannot be the same person, serves no useful purpose and is a barrier to efficient severance. The court held:

> *In view of the rituals that are available to unilaterally terminate a joint tenancy, there is little virtue in steadfastly adhering to cumbersome feudal law requirements. "It is revolting to have no better reason for a rule of law than that so it was laid down in the time of Henry IV. It is still more revolting if the grounds upon which it was laid down have vanished long since, and the rule simply persists from blind imitation of the past." (Holmes, Collected Legal Papers. . . .) Common sense as well as legal efficiency dictate that a joint tenant should be able to accomplish directly what he or she could otherwise achieve*

BOX 5–3   APPLY YOUR KNOWLEDGE

Sam and Diane own Magnificent Estates as joint tenants. How does each of the following affect their ownership rights?

- Lilith records a judgment against Sam.
- Diane mortgages her interest to raise money for a trip to Europe.
- Diane does not mortgage her interest. Instead, Sam sells his interest to Coach.
- Instead of selling to Coach, Sam sells his interest to Diane.
- Instead of selling, Sam files suit for partition and dies before partition is granted.
- Sam does not die, but instead receives a final judgment of partition and sells his share to Norm.

indirectly by use of elaborate legal fictions. . . . We reject [prior case law] because it rests on a common law notion whose reason for existence vanished about the time that grant deeds and title companies replaced colorful dirt clod ceremonies as the way to transfer title to real property. One joint tenant may unilaterally sever the joint tenancy without the use of an intermediary device.

Tenancy by the Entirety

In feudal England, husband and wife were considered legally to be one person. If Egbert conveyed Blackacre "to Bromley and Evelyn, husband and wife," the spouses received a single estate called an "entirety." Because the spouses were considered one person, neither spouse received a fractional interest in the resulting tenancy by the entirety, so neither had anything that could be granted to a third person without the consent of the other spouse. But the two, acting together, could dispose of the whole. If they failed to do so, the surviving spouse became sole owner at the death of the other. In the United States, nineteen states and the District of Columbia still permit tenancies by the entirety, sometimes in a modified form.[9] Divorce or annulment terminates the tenancy, which becomes a tenancy in common.

The marital property rights of spouses today differ greatly from those of spouses in feudal times. In feudal England, husbands acquired, at marriage, substantially full control over their wives' real property, including that held as tenants by the entirety. If Evelyn and Bromley held land as tenants by the entirety, Bromley was entitled to all the rents and profits. In the United States, the Married Women's Property Acts of the 1800s recognized husband and wife as two separate persons and conferred on married women the control of their property that they would have had if they had remained single—essentially, full control.

Nevertheless, where tenancy by the entirety exists today (the "entirety jurisdictions"), it retains many of its feudal characteristics. For example, neither spouse acting alone can sell, mortgage, or partition the land. Moreover, because neither spouse has a fractional interest, the land is free in many of the entirety jurisdictions from the claims of the creditors of either spouse. (By statute or court decision in a few entirety jurisdictions, however, a spouse *does* have an undivided fractional interest that is available to his or her creditors; and in most or all entirety jurisdictions creditors have access to entireties property for the *joint* debts of the spouses.) Today, the tenancy by the entirety serves mainly to give each spouse a right of survivorship; a veto power over the other's decision to sell or encumber the land; protection against an unwanted partition; and, in several states, protection from the claims of his or her creditors.

Determining Survivorship When Deaths Are Simultaneous

A cotenant with a right of survivorship obviously must survive the other cotenants to become sole owner of the property. Likewise, to inherit property under an intestacy statute or to receive property under a will, a prospective heir or a beneficiary of a will must survive the decedent. Sometimes, however, cotenants or a property owner and his or her prospective heir or beneficiary die together in an auto accident, plane crash, or explosion, or in other circumstances making it impossible to determine who survived.

To resolve the question of survivorship, the states have enacted laws establishing presumptions about survivorship and providing how property is to be distributed if the simultaneous deaths of interested parties cannot be ruled out. Two uniform laws—the Uniform Probate Code (UPC) and the Uniform Simultaneous Death Act (USDA)—deal with survivorship and have been adopted by a substantial number of states.[10] Both uniform laws cover (1) co-owners who have a right of survivorship, such as joint tenants, tenants by the entirety, and co-owners of POD ("payable on death") bank accounts, and (2) intestate succession, transfers by will, and other circumstances in which questions of survivorship must be resolved. The survivorship rules of the UPC differ from those found in earlier versions of the USDA, and many of the adopting states have made nonuniform amendments to the uniform acts. Consequently, the rules applying to survivorship questions vary considerably among the states.

Survivorship Provisions of Uniform Probate Code

Under the UPC, if none of two or more co-owners with a right of survivorship survives the others by 120 hours, the co-owners are considered to have died simultaneously. And, for purposes of intestate succession and transfer of property by a will, a person who fails to survive the decedent by 120 hours is considered to have died before the decedent. Illustrations follow:

1. *Cotenant with a right of survivorship.* Alice and Betty own Blackacre as joint tenants. While on a bus tour, their bus skids off the road. Alice dies immediately; Betty dies three days later. Under the UPC's 120-hour rule, since Betty did not survive Alice by 120 hours, they are considered to have died simultaneously. Where two joint tenants die simultaneously, one-half of the property passes as if one had survived by 120 hours, and the other half as if the other had survived by 120 hours. Thus, because Alice and Betty are considered to have died simultaneously, they are treated at death as if they had been tenants in common. Where three or more joint tenants die within 120 hours of the others, the same distribution principle applies. That is, the property is divided into equal portions and distributed as if the joint tenants had been tenants in common. Of course, if one of three joint tenants survives the others by 120 hours or more, he or she becomes sole owner. If two of three survive for that period, they remain joint tenants, each now owning half.

2. *Intestate succession.* Rudolph, a widower, dies in a plane crash in which his only child Eleanor is seriously injured. Eleanor dies three days later, survived only by her son Herbert. Rudolph had a substantial estate but no will. Under the intestate statute, Rudolph's heirs are, in the following order, (1) his surviving spouse and surviving children, (2) his surviving parents, and (3) his surviving grandchildren. Rudolph's wife died three years ago. His parents died twenty years earlier. Since daughter Eleanor failed to survive Rudolph for 120 hours, she is considered to have predeceased him too, so cannot inherit Rudolph's estate. Instead, grandson Herbert inherits directly from Rudolph and avoids an unnecessary round of estate administration expenses (Eleanor's) that would tend to deplete the estate. By limiting multiple administrations, the UPC survivorship rule conserves intestate estates and promotes efficiency in their administration.

3. *Transfer by will.* In her will, the widow Jennifer devises Blackacre to her son Ralph and leaves the rest of her estate to her daughter Pauline. Ralph and Pauline are Jennifer's only living relatives. On a vacation trip with Ralph, Jennifer dies in a ferryboat explosion that also seriously injures Ralph. Ralph dies two days later. Under the UPC's 120-hour rule, Ralph is considered to have predeceased Jennifer. The legal consequence is that the devise to Ralph "lapses" (fails), and that his sister Pauline receives Jennifer's entire estate, including Blackacre.

The UPC also provides, however, that survival by 120 hours is *not* required if a will or other "governing instrument" *expressly* indicates that no minimum period of survival is required, or that a longer period of survival is required. So, the 120-hour rule would not apply if Jennifer's will had provided that "Ralph shall receive Blackacre if he survives me, no matter how briefly," or that "Ralph shall receive Blackacre only if he survives me by a minimum of one hundred eighty (180) days after the day of my death."

Survivorship Provisions of Uniform Simultaneous Death Act

On questions of survivorship, the coverage of the USDA is similar to that of the UPC, encompassing such topics as intestate succession, transfers by will, and co-owners with a right of survivorship. In fact, in a number of states the two laws have been merged into one. For purposes of illustration, discussion of the USDA is limited here to the topic of joint tenancy.

An older version of the USDA provides two basic rules for determining who is entitled to property held in joint tenancy. (1) If there is "sufficient evidence" that a particular joint tenant survived the others, even by one second, he or she becomes the owner of the whole. (2) If the evidence is *not* sufficient to show that one joint tenant survived the others, all are considered to have died simultaneously. The property will then be divided into as many portions as there were joint tenants, and the share of each joint tenant will be distributed as if that joint tenant had survived the others. In essence, as under the UPC, simultaneous death of joint tenants results in their being treated as tenants in common for the distribution of the co-owned property.

The 1993 revision of the USDA and the 1990 revision of the UPC require that the evidence of survival be "clear and convincing." The 1993 revision of the USDA also adopts the UPC's 120-hour rule. However, the states differ in the degree to which they have conformed their survivorship provisions to the revised uniform laws. New Hampshire, for example, has adopted the 1993 version of the USDA, which requires not only that the evidence of a joint tenant's survival be "clear and convincing," but also that the survivor outlive the other joint tenants by 120 hours. In contrast, California, though it requires clear and convincing evidence of a joint tenant's survival, still accepts a mere instant of survival as sufficient for the survivor to become owner.[11]

Box 5–4 Apply Your Knowledge

New Hampshire residents Shirley and Roger own Blackacre, a fine piece of new Hampshire land, as joint tenants. They are injured in a car accident. Shirley dies instantly and Roger dies two days later. Shirley's heir is Charles; Roger's heir is Samantha.

1. As between the heirs, who is entitled to Blackacre?
2. If Shirley and Roger had been California residents owning California land as joint tenants at the time of the accident, who would be entitled to Blackacre?

Marital Interests

Sometimes a spouse disposes of marital property without the consent of the other spouse, or tries to disinherit the other by willing the property to a third person. During their childless marriage of 50 years, John and Martha acquired a house, a 50-unit apartment complex, stocks and bonds, numerous antiques, two luxury cars, and extensive household furnishings. For emergencies, they maintained a savings account of about $12,000. All the property, including the savings account, was held in John's name. John died. His will left the savings account to Martha and the rest of the property, worth about $4 million, to the Greater Metropolitan Social Club. What are Martha's rights in the property that John willed to the Social Club?

The states vary greatly in the degree to which they protect surviving spouses from disinheritance. In the community property states, each spouse owns one-half the community property. That half cannot be sold by the other spouse nor disposed of by the other spouse's will. Most common law states have statutes permitting a surviving spouse to take an "elective share" (also called a "forced share") of the decedent's estate in lieu of the property left by the decedent's will. In four states, surviving spouses have a marital interest, called dower or curtesy, in land and usually in personalty owned by other during the marriage or at death.

Only in Georgia may a decedent disinherit his or her spouse entirely.[12] So if Georgia law applies to John and Martha, she might not be entitled to any of the property that he left to the Social Club. Georgia law, however, may not be as harsh to surviving spouses as it may seem. First, the survivor is entitled to a year's support out of the decedent's estate. Second, although the Georgia statute provides that a testator "may bequeath his entire estate to strangers, to the exclusion of his spouse and children," it also provides that "[i]n such a case the will should be closely scrutinized; and, upon the slightest evidence of aberration of intellect, collusion, fraud, undue influence, or unfair dealing, probate should be refused."[13] A will that is refused probate is invalid, and the decedent who made it is considered to have died intestate. In that event, Georgia's intestacy statute confers the decedent's whole estate upon the surviving spouse if there are no children. In determining the validity of John's will, a Georgia court probably would invalidate it as unfair to Martha if she helped accumulate or manage the family wealth. Georgia courts have, in fact, denied probate to a number of wills attempting disinheritance.

Elective share statutes are discussed in Chapter 6. The remainder of this chapter deals with dower and curtesy, and with community property.

Dower and Curtesy

At common law, **dower** was the right of a widow to receive, at the death of her husband, a life estate in one-third of the lands owned by him at any time during their marriage, free from the claims of the husband's creditors. While the husband was alive, the wife's dower interest was **inchoate** (incomplete), ripening into a right of possession only upon the husband's death. In the meantime, he could not defeat his wife's inchoate dower interest by conveying the land unless she consented to the conveyance, nor could he deprive her of dower by will. Ordinarily, a wife released her dower interest by signing the deed of conveyance. **Curtesy** was a similar right of a widower to receive, at the death of his wife, a life estate in all the lands owned by her at any time during their marriage, *if* there were "issue" (a child or children) born of the marriage and capable of inheriting her estate.

In the United States, dower has been abolished in all but four states, and curtesy in all but two.[14] In these four states, dower and curtesy have been modified by statute to alleviate some of the problems historically associated with them. One such problem is that common law curtesy conferred greater rights on the husband than dower conferred on the wife, and some state statutes conferred greater rights on wives than on husbands. In the United States, such unequal treatment has been found unconstitutional as a denial of equal protection of the laws. As the statutes of the four remaining dower states indicate, many states avoided the constitutionality problem by making dower and curtesy equal in terms of the interest conferred on wife and husband, or by abolishing curtesy and giving both husband and wife a "dower" interest.

An economic problem has become apparent in modern times. Common law dower and curtesy gave the surviving spouse an interest only in realty, not in personal property. Because much of today's family wealth consists of personal property such as stocks, bonds, insurance, and pension rights, common law dower and curtesy are of limited usefulness as a protection against disinheritance. One solution has been to define dower and curtesy more broadly to include some or all personalty. Today, depending on the state, the dower interest ordinarily consists of a fee simple or a life estate in one-half or in one-third of the realty owned by the decedent during the marriage or at death, plus some fraction of the decedent's personalty.

Another problem arises when a person sells realty that may be subject to an unreleased dower interest. The seller's title may be unmarketable. In three states (Arkansas, Kentucky, and Ohio), dower attaches to land acquired by the husband *at any time* during the marriage. Terrance, a resident of such a state, bought Blackacre during the first year of his marriage to Bertha, sold the land to Hapless two years later without consulting Bertha, and died yesterday, ending 45 years of marriage. In the meantime, Hapless sold Blackacre to Alice, who sold it to Baxter, the present owner. The deed from Terrance's grantor and the deed from Terrance to Hapless identified Terrance as "a married man." All deeds were immediately recorded, thus putting Hapless, Alice, and Baxter on notice of Bertha's dower interest when they purchased Blackacre. Because Bertha's signature did not appear on the deed conveying Blackacre from Terrance to Hapless, Baxter presently owns Blackacre subject to Bertha's right of dower. Ordinarily, of course, a buyer's attorney (or a title insurance company) would search the land records, detect Bertha's outstanding dower interest, recognize it as a "cloud on title," and advise the buyer not to proceed with the purchase until the seller renders the title marketable, perhaps by purchasing the dower interest from Bertha.

The Massachusetts legislature addressed the marketability of title problem by (1) limiting dower to the lands owned by a person *at death*, thus allowing him or her to transfer good title during life without the spouse's participation, and (2) requiring a spouse claiming dower in lands owned at death to file in a timely manner a document electing dower instead of a statutory share. A spouse failing to do so loses the dower interest, and it can no longer be a cloud on title.

Community Property

The nine community property statutes[15] vary in detail, but are similar in basic principle: Wife and husband are equal co-owners of the community property regardless of who earned or acquired it. To illustrate the operation of the community property systems, we discuss primarily the law of California, the most populous community property state.

Requirement of Marriage

Marriage is a prerequisite to receiving the benefits of community property law. But marriage takes different forms, and not all community property states recognize all types of marriage.

All states recognize *ceremonial marriage*. A marriage is ceremonial if the parties meet the age and other personal requirements for marriage, acquire a marriage license, and declare in a ceremony that they take each other as husband and wife. The legal requirements for the ceremony are few: witnesses to the marriage must be present, the ceremony must be conducted by a person authorized to solemnize marriages, and the parties must make the marital declaration. A number of states, including the community property state of Texas, recognize *common law marriage*. A common law marriage, called in Texas an *informal marriage*, is one created by an agreement to marry, followed by cohabitation and representations to others that the parties are married, but without obtaining a marriage license and solemnizing the marriage.

A marriage (ceremonial or common law) that conforms to the legal requirements of the state in which it took place is *valid*. If the parties do not meet the legal requirements for a valid marriage, it is either *void* or *voidable*. A *void marriage*, for example, a marriage between close relatives or marriage to a person who is already married, is of no legal effect and is invalid from the beginning. In contrast, a *voidable marriage* is valid, but has an imperfection that entitles one party or the other to dissolve the marriage relationship. For example, in California a marriage undertaken by a party mistakenly believing that his or her spouse of an earlier, undissolved marriage is dead is voidable. The subsequent marriage is valid until either party obtains a court order of annulment. Similarly, a minor who marries without the parental consent required by law has a voidable marriage, as does a person who was of unsound mind when married, or whose consent was procured by fraud or force.

A *putative marriage* is a ceremonial or, where recognized, a common law marriage that is void, but which was entered into in good faith by one or both of the parties. Marta marries Gregory, not knowing that he is married to another woman. Marta's marriage is void, but she is Gregory's putative wife and in a number of states would have many of the benefits enjoyed by a wife in a valid marriage. In California, for example, at the termination of a putative marriage each putative spouse is entitled to half of the **quasi-marital property** acquired during the relationship. It is called "quasi-marital" because it consists of property that would have been community property if the marriage had been valid.

Except for Texas, the community property states do not recognize common law marriages contracted within their own states. So if California residents Tom and Rhonda hold themselves out as husband and wife, but lack a ceremonial marriage, neither has any interest in the other's property under the community property law. Most states, however, California included, have statutes recognizing valid marriages that were contracted in *other* states. Texas residents Roger and Olivia establish a common law marriage there, and then move to California. The Texas common law marriage, being valid in Texas, is valid in California as well, and both spouses have full rights under the California community property law. Other community property states (Arizona, Louisiana, New Mexico, and Washington) also have such statutes.

Moreover, even unmarried but cohabiting Californians have some protection under principles stated in the landmark case of *Marvin v. Marvin*.[16] That case held that actor Lee Marvin and his companion Michelle, unmarried but living together as man and wife, could make contractual arrangements for the ownership and pooling of their property, and the courts would enforce those arrangements. And, although the state of Washington rejects common law marriage, in the 1995 case of *Connell v. Francisco*,[17] the Washington Supreme Court applied that state's community property law to an unmarried couple living in a "meretricious" relationship, defined by Washington case law as "a stable, marital-like relationship where both parties cohabit with knowledge that a lawful marriage between them does not exist."[18] The court held, "For the purpose of dividing property at the end of a meretricious relationship, the definitions of 'separate' and 'community' property found in [the Washington statute] are useful and we apply them by analogy. Therefore . . . property acquired during the relationship would be presumed to be owned by both of the parties"[19] and is subject to a "just and equitable" distribution when the relationship terminates. Other community property states not recognizing common law marriages nevertheless allow an unmarried cohabitant to assert contract and property claims against the other party, on grounds such as quantum meruit (quasi contract) or breach of an express or an implied–in–fact contract.

Separate, Community, and Mixed Property

Separate property belongs to the spouse who brought it to or received it during the marriage. A spouse's separate property is subject to his or her exclusive control. What constitutes separate property varies somewhat among the states. The following list is based on California law, with some of the state variations being noted. A married person's separate property includes:

1. All property (real or personal) owned by that person before marriage.

2. All property acquired by that person *during* marriage by gift, bequest, devise, or descent.

3. In a majority of community property states, the "rents, issues, and profits" of (income from) separate property. This is the "California" ("American") rule. Idaho, Louisiana, and Texas, however, follow the "civil" ("Spanish") rule, which classifies income from separate property as *community* property.

4. Property exchanged for separate property or acquired with separate property funds.

5. Earnings and accumulations of a spouse after legal (court-ordered) separation.

6. Earnings and accumulations of a spouse while living "separate and apart" (no longer as husband and wife). California and Washington have statutes so providing, and a few other states have case law to that effect.

Community property consists of all property acquired during the marriage except separate property. (Wisconsin uses the terms *marital property* for community property and *individual property* for separate property.) The spouses own community property in equal shares without regard to who earned or took title to it, on the theory that its acquisition was a team effort by the marital unit. Paul and Paula marry and live in a community property state. Paul earns a handsome annual salary while Paula manages the household and cares for the children. Paul holds in his name all the property acquired during the marriage. Paul dies. His will leaves the property, now worth $1,000,000, to the Hamlet Jogging Society. Despite the will, Paula is entitled to her community property share, $500,000.

Historically, damages received by a spouse for personal injuries occurring during the marriage were classified as community property. Today, by statute or court decision, most community property states apportion the damages between separate and community property.[20] The portion awarded for lost earnings and community expenses are community property; the portion awarded for pain and suffering and loss of body parts is the separate property of the injured spouse. Taking a different approach, California distinguishes between injuries inflicted by a third person and injuries inflicted by the other spouse. If the injuries were inflicted by the victim's spouse, the damages are classified as the *separate* property of the victim.[21] If the injuries were inflicted by a third person, the damages are called "community estate personal injury damages," up to one-half of which may be assigned to the uninjured spouse if the court determines that justice requires sharing the damages.[22]

All property acquired during the marriage is *presumed* be community property. If a spouse contends that a particular item is his or her separate property, that spouse has the burden of proving separate property status. Often, the proof-making is straightforward, as where a deed conveying Blackacre to Matilda was recorded five years before her marriage to Michael. In other instances, the proof-making may be difficult or impossible because the spouses have commingled (mixed) their separate and community funds to such an extent that the separate funds can no longer be identified as separate.

Mixed property is a combination of separate and community property. Sara owns 160 acres of undeveloped land when she marries Bill. They both go to work for Acme Corporation and accumulate substantial savings. With these community funds and borrowed money they build a retail store and parking lot on ten acres of Sara's land. The land remains Sara's separate property, but the added value represented by the store and the parking lot is community property.

If Bill and Sara commingle their funds, separate property can lose its identity and become community property. Sara and Bill sell several items of separate property and deposit the proceeds in their joint bank account, together with their salaries and other community property earnings. Then they make withdrawals to pay for additional construction projects on Sara's land. Keeping track of the separate property and the community property elements can become quite difficult, especially if the land is mortgaged to finance its development and funds for repaying the debt come from community and separate sources such as the retail store income and the sale of stock that Bill inherited from his mother. To maintain the identity of their separate property, the spouses must keep careful records of bank deposits, property exchanges, and the like. As long as Bill, for example, can "trace" his land development contributions back to a separate property source such as his inherited stock, the value of his contribution remains his separate property. When tracing is not possible, the proceeds of the stock sale become community property.

Another mixed property problem arises when a spouse manages his or her separate property and it increases greatly in value. Living in a state where profits from separate property are also separate property, Sara inherits a block of AT&T stock, which pays an annual dividend. The dividend is a "profit" resulting from mere ownership of the stock and, like the stock itself, is Sara's separate property. Then Sara researches other securities, sells the AT&T stock, and reinvests the proceeds in other stocks that quickly quadruple in value because of her skill as an investor. What part of the gain may Sara claim as separate property, and what part is community property to be shared with her husband? The replacement stocks are her separate property, as is the portion of the gain that represents "issues and profits" from them. Dividends on stock and interest on bonds are issues and profits. But most of the increase resulted from Sara's devoting time and energy to investing. So, like wages and any other marital earnings requiring productive effort, the portion of the gain attributable Sara's efforts, beyond merely holding the securities as owner, is community property. If Sara's investing activity results in no gain or in a loss, there is, of course, no community property element, and Sara holds the stocks and dividends as separate property.

The case that follows indicates how the increased value of real estate held as separate property would be apportioned between separate and community property.

Case 5.2

Chance v. Kitchell
659 P.2d 895 (N.M. 1983)

Mr. Kitchell owned a lot with a single-family dwelling when he married Hazel D. Kitchell. The realty was subject to a mortgage and was Mr. Kitchell's separate property. In 1969, Mr. Kitchell died intestate. Under New Mexico's intestacy statute, Mrs. Kitchell received a one-fourth interest in the property, and Mr. Kitchell's two children (Mrs. Kitchell's stepchildren) shared the remaining three-fourths equally.

During the seven-year marriage, until Mr. Kitchell's death in 1969, community funds were used to pay the mortgage debt, taxes, and improvements on the property. After decedent's death, Mrs. Kitchell remained on the property until October 1, 1978, making all expenditures for the property from her separate funds. Between October 1, 1978, and March 2, 1982, she rented the property to others and continued to pay all the expenses related to the property.

On November 17, 1981, the stepchildren brought an action for partition of the property. Defendant Mrs. Kitchell counterclaimed, seeking an equitable lien on the property for the money she had expended on it. Plaintiffs answered the counterclaim and asked the trial court to award them the reasonable value of Defendant's occupancy and use of the premises and for an accounting of profits which Defendant realized from the premises as sole cotenant in possession. The trial court ordered partition of the property and found that "nothing [else] should be due by either party to the other." Defendant appealed.

RIORDAN, J.

Defendant asserts that during the time she was married to decedent, she should be awarded a community's lien for all community funds expended on behalf of decedent's property. Community funds expended on behalf of decedent's property consisted of principal, taxes, insurance, interest, improvement value or cost[,] and sewer and garbage paid on the property. However, [for] determining a community interest in community funds expended on behalf of property purchased by a spouse before marriage, the rule has commonly excluded payments for taxes, insurance and interest. Neither taxes, insurance nor interest increase[s] the equity value of property. The value of real property is generally represented by the owner's equity in it. The equity value does not include finance charges or other expenses incurred to maintain the investment. Therefore, taxes, insurance, interest[,] and garbage and sewer expenditures are not to be credited to Defendant. As for improvements made to the land, Defendant is entitled to the value of the improvements to the property, not the cost of the improvements.

Defendant next asserts that she is entitled to contribution for expenditures made after the decedent's death. She also asserts that Plaintiffs are not entitled to an offset for the reasonable rental value while she lived at the residence. Defendant correctly states the general rule that in the absence of an agreement to pay or ouster by the cotenant in possession, a tenant in common who occupies all or more than her proportionate share in the common premises is not liable, because of such occupancy alone, to her cotenant for the rent or the use of the premises. However, there is an exception to this general rule. When a cotenant in possession invokes the jurisdiction of a court of equity to obtain contributions from the cotenant out of possession for funds expended for the betterment of the common interest, the cotenant out of possession may defensively charge the cotenant in possession with a part of the reasonable value of the occupancy or use by the cotenant in possession and in some cases may hold the cotenant in possession accountable for profits realized from the premises.

In adding Defendant's expenditures in the light most favorable to Defendant and subtracting this amount from an agreed upon reasonable rental value, Defendant is monetarily indebted to Plaintiffs. However, Plaintiffs do not ask for this extra amount, only that the property be partitioned in accordance with intestate law, as the trial court did. Therefore, we affirm the trial court's decision on the matter.

QUESTIONS ABOUT CASE 5.2

1. The "community" (consisting of Mr. and Mrs. Kitchell) was entitled to a credit for payments of principal made out of community funds to retire the debt on Mr. Kitchell's house, but not for taxes and other costs. Why for principal but not for the other expenditures?

2. Suppose that during the marriage Mr. and Mrs. Kitchell spent $5,000 in community funds to remodel the bathroom and as a result the value of the house increased by $12,000. With what amount should the community be credited? What if the value of the house increased by only $3,000?

3. Was Mrs. Kitchell liable to the stepchildren for use and occupancy of the house? Why? Consider the court's discussion of the applicable general rule and its exception.

Transmutation, Premarital Agreements, and Quasi-Community Property

By a process called **transmutation** (in Wisconsin, called **reclassification**), husband and wife can convert (transmute) some or all of their separate property into community property, or community property into separate property, or the separate property of one into the separate property of the other. All community property states require a transmutation agreement to be in writing, and a transmutation of real property must be recorded to be effective as to third persons otherwise without notice of it.[23]

Transmutation can occur only during marriage, but parties planning to marry can accomplish the same result with a premarital (prenuptial) agreement. A **premarital agreement** is an agreement between prospective spouses made in contemplation of marriage and intended to be effective upon marriage. Often called a **"marriage settlement contract"** or an "antenuptial" agreement, it specifies how the property of the spouses is to be classified (e.g., as either separate or community) and distributed upon dissolution of the marriage, legal separation, or the death of a spouse. Premarital agreements can be especially useful where the prospective spouses are remarrying and want to provide for their previously established families.

Sometimes, of course, a wealthy person simply wants to limit the amount that the spouse-to-be will receive, and may hide assets or use other methods to accomplish that goal. If the prospective spouse did not execute the agreement voluntarily, or if it was unconscionable, it is not enforceable. An agreement is unconscionable if it is so one-sided as to oppress or unfairly surprise the disadvantaged party. Under the Uniform Premarital Agreement Act as adopted in California, a premarital agreement will not be enforced if it was unconscionable when executed, *and* before its execution the prospective spouse (1) was not provided a fair and reasonable disclosure of the other party's property or financial obligations, (2) did not waive his or her right to the disclosure, and (3) did not have adequate knowledge of the other party's financial circumstances.

In Wisconsin, transmutations and premarital property adjustments are treated together under one statutory provision. Under it, married couples and prospective spouses alike may adjust their property rights by means of a **marital property agreement**, which, for prospective spouses, does not become effective until the marriage. The Wisconsin law on property adjustments before and during marriage is similar to that of the other community property states.

Often, a married person individually acquires property in a common law state before the couple moves to a community property state, and continues to hold it in his or her name afterward. After the move, does the property remain individually owned, or does some or all of it become community property? Out of his earnings, Jim buys land in Indiana and holds it in his name alone. Then he and his wife Judy move to a community property state. If they move to Arizona, California, Idaho, New Mexico, Texas, or Washington, the Indiana land will be classified as **quasi-community property** (though Texas does not use that terminology), if it would have been community property in the state to which they moved. In the community property states, land acquired with the earnings of either spouse is community property unless otherwise agreed. So, in the absence of a contrary agreement, the Indiana land is quasi-community property in the states adopting that classification. Such property is distributed as if it were community property, though not for all purposes in all the states. Arizona, for example, recognizes quasi-community property only for the purposes of marriage dissolution and legal separation, while California recognizes it for all purposes: dissolution of the marriage, legal separation, and death of a spouse.

Management of Community Property

In all community property states, each spouse has the exclusive right to manage and dispose of his or her separate property. Within limits that vary from state to state, both wife and husband have the right to manage and control the community property. In California, for example, "either spouse" may manage, control, and (except by will) dispose of the community *personal* property, subject to the following restrictions that protect the nonmanaging spouse:

1. Without the written consent of the other spouse, a spouse may not give community personal property to a third person or sell it for less than a fair and reasonable value. The nonconsenting spouse may avoid the transaction and retrieve the property.

2. Without the written consent of the other spouse, a spouse may not "sell, convey, or encumber" community personal property used as the family dwelling (e.g., a mobile home), or any household furnishings or clothing of the other spouse or minor children if these items are community property.

Similarly, either spouse can manage and control the community *realty*, but to sell, convey, encumber, or lease it for more than one year, both spouses must join in executing the relevant documents.

In addition, a California spouse who is operating or managing a *business* that is community property has "the primary management and control" of the business. The managing spouse may act alone in all transactions for that business, but must give written notice to the other spouse before selling, leasing, exchanging, or encumbering all or substantially all of the personal property used in the business.

In transactions between themselves, and in the management of a community property business, each spouse has a fiduciary obligation to the other. "This confidential relationship imposes a duty of the highest good faith and fair dealing on each spouse, and neither shall take any unfair advantage of the other."[24] A spouse's fiduciary duties include providing the other spouse with (1) access at all times to any books kept regarding a transaction, (2) when requested, full information on any transaction that concerns community property, and (3) an accounting for any profit or benefit realized from dealing in community property without the consent of the other.

Wisconsin (and to a lesser extent, Texas) assigns the right to manage marital (community) property to the spouse in whose name it is held. Bill and Sara's office building is in *her* name although it is community property. In Wisconsin, she has the right to act alone in managing it.[25] If it were owned by "Bill *or* Sara," either could act alone in managing it. If it were owned by "Bill *and* Sara," they would have to act jointly in its management and control. Property that is not held in the name of either spouse—e.g., artwork, gold, antiques, bearer bonds—can be managed by either spouse.

Division of Separate and Community Property at Dissolution of Marriage

Dissolution of a marriage (divorce or annulment) also dissolves the marital community and makes necessary a division of the spouses' property. Statutes govern how the spouses' property is to be divided. As to *separate* property, in Arizona, California, Idaho, and Louisiana, the judge must award it to the spouse who owns it, though in California and Idaho the judge may award alimony or support allowances to one spouse out of the separate property of the other.[26] In Nevada, New Mexico, Texas, and Washington, the judge may divide the separate property on an "equitable" basis, with the identity of its owner during the marriage being only one of many factors in making the division at dissolution. In Wisconsin, *some* separate property remains the property of the spouse who acquired it, unless the judge's failure to divide it "will create a hardship on the other party or on the children of the marriage." The property consists of (1) gifts from third persons, and (2) property received "by reason of the death of another," e.g., life insurance proceeds; payments made under a deferred employment benefit plan or an individual retirement account; and property acquired by right of survivorship, by a trust distribution, by bequest or inheritance, or by a "payable on death" (POD) or a "transfer on death" (TOD) arrangement. If the court finds that failure to divide the property will cause hardship to the other spouse or the children, the court may "divest the [owning] party of the property in a fair and equitable manner."[27] In California, Louisiana, and New Mexico, the judge must divide *community* property equally, or at least "substantially equally." These states are called the "equal division" states. The other states, Wisconsin included, are "equitable division" states. In those states the judge can divide the community property unequally between the spouses as long as the division is made on a fair and equitable basis that reflects the particular circumstances of the parties. Factors ordinarily considered in equitable division states include:

1. The length of the marriage.

2. The property brought to the marriage by each party.

3. Whether one of the parties has substantial separate property not subject to division by the court.

4. The contribution of each party to the marriage, giving appropriate economic value to each party's contribution in homemaking and child care services.

5. The age and physical and emotional health of the parties.

6. The contribution by one party to the education, training, or increased earning power of the other.

7. The earning capacity of each party.

8. Which party has the greater need to occupy the family home.

9. The amount and duration of maintenance (alimony) and child or family support payments.

10. Other economic circumstances of each party, including pension benefits and future interests.

11. The tax consequences of the property division to each party.

Disposition of Separate and Community Property at Death of Spouse

At the death of a spouse, one-half of the community property belongs to the surviving spouse, and the other half belongs to the decedent's estate. In all community property states, a spouse may dispose of his or her separate property and one-half of the community property by will.

In all community property states except Louisiana, if a decedent dies intestate, the decedent's half of the *community* property goes to the surviving spouse, usually *without probate*, but children *of the marriage* do not receive any of the decedent's half of the community property. (In Nevada, the decedent's share of the community property *is* subject to probate administration unless it is "community property with right of survivorship.") Often, however, decedents have surviving children (or other descendants) from a former marriage. Arizona and Texas favor those children over the surviving spouse. In Arizona, the intestate decedent's half of the community property goes to the decedent's child or children and not to the surviving spouse. In Texas, the decedent's half goes to the decedent's "child or other descendant." So, in Texas, if the decedent's child does not survive the decedent but the decedent's grandchild does, the grandchild receives the decedent's half of the community property.

The *separate* property of an intestate decedent passes to heirs named in the state's intestacy statute. Intestacy statutes vary in many ways, but those of all the community property states except Louisiana are similar to those in the common law states. Ordinarily, if the spouse survives the decedent but no lineal descendants survive, the spouse receives all the separate property. If children or other descendants survive too, they and the spouse receive specified shares of the decedent's separate property. For example, if the spouse and one child survive, they usually share the separate property equally. If the spouse and two or more children survive, the spouse receives one-third and the children receive two-thirds. Like some common law states, Idaho gives the surviving spouse a fixed dollar amount (in Idaho, $50,000) plus a fractional share of the remaining property, and the descendants receive the other fractional share—usually one-half or two-thirds, depending on the number of descendants. Intestacy statutes are discussed further in Chapter 6.

Louisiana, the only civil law state, is unique in its treatment of separate and community property at the death of a spouse. As in the other states, the surviving spouse receives the decedent's share of the community property if the decedent died intestate and left no descendants. However, if an intestate decedent is survived by a child, the *child* inherits the decedent's share of the community property, and the surviving spouse receives only a "usufruct" over it.

A **usufruct** is the right of a usufructuary (the owner of the usufruct, here, the spouse) to use someone else's (the child's) property for a limited time. By law, the spouse's usufruct "terminates when the spouse dies or remarries, whichever occurs first."[28] In the meantime, the spouse has the right to use and profit from the property, whatever type of property it may be. If the property is land, the spouse is much like the owner of a life estate under the common law: The spouse may use the land and profit from it by, for example, renting it or selling its "natural fruits" such as crops, but must preserve the land substantially as it was when received. If the property subject to usufruct is corporate stock, the spouse is entitled to cash dividends as a "civil fruit" of the stock, but the child is entitled to anything representing principal, such as the stock itself and any stock dividends or shares resulting from stock splits. When the usufruct terminates, the child, who was the "naked owner" of the property during the term of the usufruct, becomes full owner.

As to the Louisiana decedent's *separate* property, the surviving spouse receives it only if the decedent has no surviving descendants, parents, brothers, sisters, or descendants of brothers and sisters. In Louisiana, then, a spouse's chances of receiving the decedent's separate property are far less than if the couple had lived in a common law or some other community property state, where the spouse would at least receive a share of the separate property.

● Homestead

A **homestead** is a person's residential dwelling plus the land it occupies, its outbuildings, and the like. Central to family life, the homestead receives special treatment for a variety of purposes: property tax relief, preserving the home for a surviving spouse and children at the homeowner's death, and, for financially distressed homeowners, protection of the home from claims of creditors.[29] Although discussed under the heading of "Marital Interests," many of the benefits attending a homestead are available to single as well as to married persons, and to "family units" not involving a husband and wife relationship, for example, a grandmother making a home for her orphaned grandchildren.

Property Tax Relief

As noted in Chapter 16, every state imposes an annual "ad valorem" (according to value) property tax on realty to pay for schools and other local needs. Many states have a "general homestead exemption" entitling homeowners in the state to a reduction in the assessed valuation of their residences and thus in the amount they must pay for property taxes. This *property tax* homestead exemption, discussed further in Chapter 16, is different from the debtor's homestead exemption, discussed here in a subsequent paragraph, granted to debtors to protect them from the claims of their creditors

Probate Homestead

A **probate homestead** is the real or personal property set aside out of a decedent's estate for the use of the surviving spouse and minor children as a home. In Kansas, for example, the survivors are entitled to 160 acres of land lying outside city limits, or to one acre lying within, or to a manufactured home or mobile home, as long as the property was and continues to be occupied by the decedent's family as a residence. The probate homestead includes all buildings and other improvements and is exempt from the decedent's debts.

Debtor Protection

All states protect financially distressed debtors by exempting certain types and amounts of property from the claims of their creditors. Typically eligible for exemption are the debtor's home; a motor vehicle; household furnishings and personal apparel; professional books and tools of the debtor's trade; professionally prescribed health aids; small amounts of family jewelry; alimony and support payments; unemployment and disability benefits; insurance, pension, and social security benefits; and other items that vary from state to state. Usually the amount a debtor can exempt from assets such as alimony, pensions, and insurance cannot exceed what is reasonably necessary for the support of the debtor and the debtor's dependents. In most states, the exemptions for the various categories of tangible personal property are quite modest, usually not exceeding a few hundred dollars. Exemptions for motor vehicles are somewhat higher, though they vary substantially among the states.

The *debtor's* **homestead exemption** was meant, originally, to protect the family from the forced sale of their home at the hands of creditors. Because of inflation and legislative inertia, or perhaps a change in exemption policy, however, the statutes of many states fall far short of that goal and for the great majority of debtors protect only a small fraction of home value. In contrast, the homestead exemptions of a few states have been criticized as overly generous and unfair to creditors.

A debtor's homestead exemption is available to any individual, married or single, who owns and occupies a home, which in a number of states includes personal property such as a mobile home or a boat used as a residence. Some states grant a larger homestead allowance to the head of a "household" or "family unit." Ordinarily, these terms include debtor and spouse, debtor and child or grandchild, debtor and parent or grandparent, debtor and deceased spouse's parent or grandparent, a debtor supporting a minor sibling, and a debtor supporting an adult relative incapable of providing his or her own support.

The debtor's homestead exemption is defined by dollar amount, by area, or by both. As of the year 2000, Georgia grants to debtors a homestead exemption of $5,000 and for disabled veterans a minimum of $32,500. New York has a $10,000 maximum. Illinois allows $7,500 per individual owner, with a maximum of $15,000 for two or more co-owners. Connecticut's homestead exemption is $75,000. California allows $50,000, $75,000, or $125,000, depending on the nature and age of the claimant. Mississippi allows the debtor to exempt up to 160 acres of land used as a residence (e.g., a family farm), but its value with improvements cannot exceed $75,000. Florida allows the debtor to exempt a 160-acre rural homestead or an urban homestead of one-half acre, together with all improvements, regardless of value. Kansas grants to debtors a homestead exemption for 160 acres of farming land, or one acre within the limits of an incorporated town, or a manufactured home or mobile home—each with improvements regardless of value. Texas is even more generous. It grants a homestead exemption not only for a residence but also for business property. The Texas amounts are (1) for an urban home *or* business, one acre plus improvements, regardless of value; (2) for an urban home or for a combination of home and business, ten acres plus the value of improvements; or (3) for a rural home for a family or a single adult person, 200 acres and 100 acres respectively, together with the value of improvements. In Florida, Kansas, and Texas, the occasional debtor with substantial assets has been able to exempt a multimillion dollar mansion (or, in Texas, business property) because the homestead exemptions there have no dollar limits.

In the 1970s, state exemption laws were so varied, and often so inadequate, that Congress built into the federal Bankruptcy Code of 1978 a set of exemptions that would be available to debtors seeking bankruptcy protection. The updated federal list includes, among many others, the following exemptions:

1. Up to $16,150 in real or personal property used as a residence.

2. Up to $2,575 for a motor vehicle.

3. $8,625 in total value for household furnishings and other things held primarily for personal, family, or household use, with maximum value of $425 for any particular item.

4. Up to $1,625 for implements, professional books, or tools of the debtor's trade.

5. Any unmatured life insurance contract owned by the debtor, other than a credit life insurance contract.

The states, however, were permitted to enact laws "opting out" of the federal exemption system, thus limiting their citizens to the state exemptions. Today, the great majority of states, at least 37, have opted out of the federal exemption system, but many "opt out" states have modernized and expanded their own systems. In the few states not opting out, a debtor may choose between the federal and the state exemptions.

Self-Study Questions

1. How do tenancy in common, joint tenancy, and tenancy by the entirety differ from one another?

2. Melissa deeds land "to Harland and Mary." What kind of co-ownership did Melissa create?

3. (a) How are *partition* and *owelty* related to each other? (b) How does *partition in kind* differ from *partition by sale*? Under what circumstances would partition by sale be used?

4. What is the relationship between *ouster*, *ejectment*, and *mesne profits*?

5. (a) Under what circumstance must a cotenant in possession of land share profits with those not in possession? (b) For what kinds of expenses is the possessing cotenant entitled to contribution from those not in possession?

6. Why does property held in joint tenancy pass to surviving joint tenants without probate?

7. Gloria and Rosa own Blackacre as joint tenants. Gloria sells her interest to Donald, thus severing the joint tenancy. What is the legal consequence of her severing the joint tenancy? What would have been the legal consequence if there had been three joint tenants?

8. Summarize the basic rules governing simultaneous death as they apply to (a) joint tenants, and (b) intestate succession.

9. Dower and community property are marital interests. How do they differ?

10. For what three purposes might homeowners want to declare a homestead?

Case Problems

1. Andrew Anderson owned a residence that he and his wife Christine occupied as their homestead. He died intestate. His only heirs were his wife and his daughter, Emma Anderson Newby. After Andrew's death, Christine occupied the residence for a number of years. During this time, her daughter Emma died intestate, leaving as her only heirs her husband Homer C. Newby and their three minor children. Alleging an ownership interest in the residence, Homer brought suit against Christine to have the residence partitioned. The trial court held that under the state's intestacy statute, Christine and Emma each had received from Andrew's estate an undivided one-half interest in the homestead, and that half of Emma's one-half interest (a one-fourth interest in the homestead) descended at her death to her husband and the other half to the children, so that each child owned a one-twelfth undivided interest. The court ordered partition and sale of the residence. Christine appealed, alleging that her son-in-law Homer, being outside the family and related only by marriage, was not entitled to have the property partitioned. The statute of "descents and distributions" provided that the husband is the heir of the wife, and the wife is the heir of the husband. Should the trial court's order of partition be upheld? Consider the kind of co-ownership, if any, that existed among Christine, Homer, and the three children, and what classes of owners are entitled to partition. *Newby v. Anderson*, 188 P. 438 (Kan. 1920).

2. While John and Althea were dating, they purchased some real property for about $650,000, intending to sell it quickly for a profit. At closing, they made a payment of about $268,500, which they paid in equal proportions. John took title in his name. A handwritten memorandum signed by John and Althea stated, "Any and all monies received from sale of said property to be divided equally prorated as to invested amounts paid at closing this day." Later, Althea paid off the balance of the mortgage debt and paid other expenses, and John deeded the property to himself and Althea as joint tenants. Soon after that, they signed and recorded a deed from themselves as joint tenants to themselves as tenants in common. Their personal relationship having deteriorated, Althea sued John to partition the property. The court ordered partition by sale, with distribution of the proceeds to reflect the amount that each party had actually paid out as they pursued their investment: 85% to Althea and 15% to John. John appealed, contending that the sale price of the property should be split 50–50 between the parties, with Althea receiving a credit from John's share of the proceeds for the amounts she had paid that exceeded her share of the total costs. This method of calculation would give him a few thousand dollars more than the trial court's method. Whose method of calculation was correct—the trial court's or John's? *HINT:* First decide what percentage of ownership each cotenant had. *Biondo v. Powers*, 743 So. 2d 161 (Fla. App. 1999).

3. In the early 1930s, Pink Cox and his siblings inherited 80 acres of land from Julius King. In 1932, the land was sold at a tax sale. In 1934, Pink redeemed the land by paying $40 to its purchaser, Robert Folmar. For the next 63 years, Pink had exclusive possession of the land, fenced it, paid the taxes on it, tore down an old house located there, cut and sold timber growing on it, and otherwise used it as his. Then he brought suit against his 30 relatives (the heirs of his deceased siblings) to quiet title to the property in his favor. He made two allegations: (1) His redemption of the property from the tax sale purchaser made him the owner because the relatives and their ancestors had failed to pay their pro rata shares of the $40 tax sale price. (2) His activities on the land constituted an ouster of his relatives, and his exclusive possession of the property afterward for more than the statute of limitations period made him the owner by adverse possession. The evidence at trial showed that his relatives lived out of state and that Pink had never told them about the tax sale redemption purchase, nor had he ever told them that he claimed the property as his own. (a) Was either of these allegations sufficient to make him sole owner? Why? (b) If not, what does Pink own today? Assume that Pink had a brother and a sister. *Cox v. Walker*, 739 So. 2d 3 (Ala. 1999).

4. In April 1955, during Ruth's engagement to Isadore, he showed her some business property that he owned in fee simple. She lent him $5,000, which he used to improve the property. A day before their marriage, Isadore conveyed the property to his children for a consideration of $10 (i.e., as a gift) and recorded the deed without disclosing the transactions to Ruth. In 1958, he signed a promissory note made out to Ruth for $5,000 and delivered it to his attorney to hold for her until after his death. Isadore died in 1964 without providing for her in his will. His estate had no funds with which to pay the amount of the note. She sued the estate, alleging a conspiracy between Isadore and his children to defraud her of her right of dower in the property he had conveyed to the children. Holding that there was no evidence of such a conspiracy, the trial court ruled in favor of the children. Ruth appealed. The Court of Appeals reversed the trial court's decision and granted Ruth a one-third interest in the realty. The children appealed to the Ohio Supreme Court. Was Ruth entitled to a dower interest in the property? *Perlberg v. Perlberg*, 247 N.E.2d 306 (Ohio 1969), *overruling Ward v. Ward*, 57 N.E.2d 1095 (Ohio 1900).

5. Sam and Diane lived together in Texas as man and wife but had no official marriage ceremony. They moved to California and saved $40,000 out of Diane's salary for a down payment on a house. Then, without buying a house, Sam and Diane separated permanently. Sam filed a lawsuit for dissolution of the marriage and for half the $40,000 as community property. Is he entitled to it under the California's community property law?

Endnotes

1. A Virginia statute [Va. Code Ann. § 55-20 (1999)] purports to abolish survivorship between joint tenants, but another statute (§ 55-21) preserves it for executors and trustees *and*, in addition, for all conveyances and devises "when it manifestly appears from the tenor of the instrument that it was intended the part of the one dying should then belong to the others." So, Virginia *does* permit joint tenancy with right of survivorship where the intent to create it is made clear. Moreover, in Virginia, merely designating husband and wife as "tenants by the entireties" or "tenants by the entirety" is sufficient to make clear that survivorship was intended.

2. In the noncommunity property states, marital property is governed by common law principles as modified by the Married Women's Property Acts of the 1800s, which conferred on married women the control of their property that they would have had if they had remained single.

3. Roger A. Cunningham, William B. Stoebuck, and Dale A. Whitman, *The Law of Property* (West Publishing Co., 1993), § 5.2 (citing Texas and Kentucky cases).

4. The common law action for ejectment has been modified by statute in most states. Other terms for the statutory version of ejectment include "action to recover possession of land," "action for summary process," "action for eviction," and "forcible entry and detainer action."

5. Cunningham, *supra* note 3, § 5.8.

6. One writer, however, contends that a deceased joint tenant's interest does pass to the surviving cotenants, and is not merely released at the joint tenant's death. Paul G. Haskell, *Preface to Wills, Trusts and Administration* 117 (The Foundation Press, Inc., 1987).

7. A decedent's estate consists of whatever property, real or personal, the deceased person owned at death, and is distributed according to the terms of the decedent's will or, if there is no valid will, according to the provisions of the state's intestacy statute.

8. Cunningham, *supra* note 3, § 5.4 at 201.

9. *Id.* § 5.5.

10. Most states have adopted the Uniform Simultaneous Death Act. Eighteen states have adopted the Uniform Probate Code or some portion of it.

11. Cal. Prob. Code § 223 (Deering 2001). A mere instant of survival is sufficient also for determining the rights of spouses under California's community property law. *Id.* § 103. California has, however, adopted the 120-hour rule for intestate successions occurring after December 31, 1989, and for California's "statutory will." *Id.* §§ 6211, 6403. The California statutory will is a simplified will form that California residents may elect to use.

12. Sidney Kwestel and Rena C. Seplowitz, *Testamentary Substitutes: Retained Interests, Custodial Accounts, and Contractual Transactions—A New Approach*, 38 Am. U.L. Rev. 1, 3 n.4 (1988).

13. Ga. Code Ann. § 53-2-9.

14. Arkansas (dower and curtesy), Kentucky (dower and curtesy), Massachusetts (dower for wife and husband; curtesy abolished), and Ohio (dower for wife and husband; curtesy abolished).

15. Arizona, California, Idaho, Louisiana, Nevada, New Mexico, Texas, Washington, and Wisconsin (which adopted the Uniform Marital Property Act).

16. 557 P.2d 106 (Cal. 1976).

17. 898 P.2d 831 (Wash. 1995).

18. *Id.* at 834. In contrast, in *Marvin v. Marvin*, "meretricious relationship" was defined as "prostitution." The California court held that the Marvins' relationship was not meretricious in the California sense of the word.

19. 898 P.2d at 837.

20. Cunningham, *supra* note 3, at 236.

21. Cal. Fam. Code § 781 (Deering, 2001).

22. *Id.* § 2603.

23. *See, e.g.*, Cal. Fam. Code § 852 (Deering, 2001).

24. *Id.* §§ 721, 1100(e).

25. Wis. Stat. § 766.51 (1999).

26. Cunningham, *supra* note 3, at 243.

27. Wis. Stat. § 767.255 (1999).

28. La. Civ. Code Art. 890 (2000).

29. This discussion of the homestead is *not* about the "homesteading" of earlier times, which was a method of acquiring federal land. Beginning in 1862, the federal government granted 160 acres of public land (later, 320 or 640 acres) to settlers who lived on and cultivated it for five years (later, three). Homesteading as a method of land acquisition ended in 1935.

Acquiring Ownership of Real Estate

Land, or an interest in it, can be acquired in a variety of ways. Some methods of acquisition, such as purchase and gift, are available to anyone competent to own land. Others, such as condemnation (the exercise of the power of eminent domain), are available only to governments or to those, such as utility companies, to whom the government has delegated the power. One method, adverse possession, surprises many who encounter it for the first time, because by that method a person can become owner of someone else's land by trespassing. This chapter surveys the principal ways of acquiring real estate.

Acquisition by Purchase

The most common way to acquire realty is to buy it from its owner. Less common is a purchase at a tax or a mortgage foreclosure sale, in which a creditor forces the sale of property securing the payment of taxes or repayment of a loan. Because they involve special problems and legal procedures, mortgage foreclosures and tax sales are discussed in Chapters 10 and 16. Leasing of realty, a topic of major commercial significance, is covered in Chapters 12 (residential leases) and 13 (commercial leases), while Chapter 19 deals with the sale of mineral rights. Here, we present an overview of the commercial sale of land as ordinarily transacted. Chapter 8 takes up in more detail the real estate contract discussed briefly here.

Parties and Documents Involved

It is possible to purchase land much as one would buy a loaf of bread—by an immediate exchange of money for a deed to the realty. However, because of the great risk to the buyer that the seller's title will be defective, and because most buyers prefer to finance the purchase, an immediate exchange seldom occurs. Instead, to give themselves time to investigate such matters as the soundness of the seller's title and the buyer's creditworthiness, seller and buyer commonly negotiate an executory (not yet performed) contract, the performance of which is to be completed at an agreed-to future time, usually four to six weeks after the contract is made. Depending on the region of the country, this contract goes by such names as "contract of purchase and sale," "contract to sell," "contract of sale," "real estate contract," "sales contract," "earnest money agreement," "offer and acceptance," or "deposit receipt." The final performance of the parties' contractual obligations—buyer's payment of the purchase price, seller's delivery of the deed—is called the **closing** of the transaction, which occurs on the scheduled **closing day**, often referred to as **law day**. During the time between the making of the contract and the arrival of law day, the parties to the contract prepare for their respective performances.

A typical real estate purchase involves a number of documents and individuals. Usually, the seller employs a real estate broker or agent to find a buyer and to act as an intermediary in the contract formation process between seller and buyer. Seller and broker create the agency relationship by means of a *listing agreement* in which the broker, for a commission usually expressed in terms of a percentage of the purchase price, agrees to find a buyer who is ready, willing, and able to purchase the realty for the price stated in the listing agreement. The agency relationship is discussed in Chapter 7.

As between seller and buyer, the two key documents are the *real estate contract*, which lays out in some detail the exchange agreed to by buyer and seller, and the *deed*, by which the seller conveys the ownership interest to the buyer. In addition, because most buyers want to finance the purchase price rather than pay cash, and usually do so by means of a loan from a third-party lender, the buyer ordinarily gives the lender a *mortgage* or a *deed of trust* on the property being purchased, as security for the loan. (If the *seller* does the financing, the parties likely would use an entirely different type of contract called an **installment land contract** or a **contract for deed**, discussed in Chapter 10.) Before making the loan, however, the third–party lender will require a *credit report* detailing the buyer's finances; an *appraisal* of the realty to determine how much it is worth and thus how large a loan the lender may safely make; a *termite inspection* to check the structural integrity of buildings; a *title search* or some alternative such as a *title insurance policy* to verify or otherwise assure the seller's ownership; a *wind and fire insurance policy* to cover physical damage to buildings while the loan is being repaid; and perhaps even a *survey* of the land to check the acreage or to detect encroaching structures or other problems that might undermine the value of the buyer's land as security for the loan. Hence the potential involvement of title lawyers, appraisers, insurers, surveyors, and others.

Finally, to ensure that the real estate transaction is properly completed, the seller (or the seller's broker) ordinarily sets up an **escrow agreement** or a less formal alternative with a neutral third party such as a title company, law firm, bank, or trust company. The neutral third party serves as the **closing agent**, sometimes referred to as the **escrow agent** or *escrowee*. The closing agent's function is to receive and hold the seller's deed and the buyer's payment until the obligations of each party have been performed, and then to deliver the payment to the seller and the deed to the buyer. As noted in Chapter 11, the closing agent attends to numerous related details such as paying the broker's commission out of the proceeds of sale, paying off any unpaid liens or prior mortgage debts still owed by the seller, and having the buyer's deed and any new mortgage or deed of trust recorded.

Earnest Money Deposit and Liquidated Damages

Ordinarily, a real estate contract requires the buyer to pay a portion of the purchase price at or near the time of contracting, the rest to be paid at closing. The amount paid at contracting is the *down payment*, also called an *earnest money deposit* because it indicates the buyer's intention to perform the contract.

If in negotiating the contract the buyer has a strong bargaining position, the contract might provide that the earnest money will be returned to the buyer if the sale does not close. If the seller is dominant, the contract may provide that the earnest money will be forfeited to the seller as "liquidated damages" upon the buyer's failure to perform the contract. **Liquidated damages** is an amount of money agreed to by the parties as a reasonable estimation of the damages likely to result from the buyer's breach of the contract. The risk of losing the earnest money discourages the buyer from simply walking away from a transaction that the buyer now finds unattractive. The seller's contractual right to keep the deposit as liquidated damages provides the seller with compensation for the buyer's breach and reduces the need for litigation. However, if the down payment greatly exceeds the actual damages likely to result from the buyer's breach, a court would not view the down payment clause as providing for liquidated damages, by definition a reasonable estimation of actual damages, but would instead hold it unenforceable as an attempt to impose an invalid *penalty*. In a number of states, liquidated damages and forfeiture provisions are regulated by statute, especially in sales of residential realty.

In a purely private real estate sale, the law does not require an earnest money deposit. Instead, custom or the economic concerns of sellers and lenders dictate a down payment and affect its amount, which can vary greatly according to market conditions. However, in at least one large area of real estate financing—government-insured home mortgages—the law *does* require a down payment. The Federal Housing Administration (FHA), for example, insures billions of dollars in home mortgage loans made by private lenders to low- and moderate-income borrowers. As a condition of insuring those loans and making them more saleable by the lenders, the FHA requires borrowers to make a down payment in an amount that is determined by an FHA formula.

Marketable Title Requirement

The seller (vendor) has a duty to deliver to the buyer (vendee) the type of ownership interest agreed to in the contract (e.g., a fee simple, a life estate, or a term of years). Moreover, that interest must be of the *quality*—must have the degree of freedom from defects—anticipated by the contract. The parties could specify that title must be perfect, but doing so would be unrealistic because most titles have some type of defect, however minor. For any given parcel of land, a title searcher is likely to find, say, an outstanding dower interest, an unpaid mortgage, or a long-forgotten deed granting an easement in gross to a neighbor long since dead. Because many such problems can be easily corrected, or because of their age or other circumstances they simply do not impair the seller's title, real estate contracts commonly specify that title be "marketable" ("merchantable") instead of "perfect." Indeed, if the parties are silent about the quality of title, the law requires only that it be marketable. A title is marketable if any defects in it are sufficiently minor that a reasonable buyer would be willing to accept it as sound.

"Time Is of the Essence" Clauses

Sometimes the buyer or the seller is not able to perform on law day. The seller might be unable to render the title marketable by then. The buyer might not yet have received a loan commitment from a lender. But what if performance can be made on the following day? Is it too late? The answer depends in part on whether "time is of the essence," that is, on whether exact conformity to the day and hour set for closing is required.

In the past, courts of law held that time was of the essence in all contracts for the sale of land, unless an express or implied agreement provided to the contrary. If seller John did not perform at the specified time, the nonbreaching buyer Betty was excused from performance, provided that she was ready, willing, and able to pay, and on law day offered to do so. Thus, John's being able to perform on law day was a "condition precedent" to his having further rights under the contract. A failure to perform on time not only deprived him of the right to proceed with the transaction, but also made him liable in damages to Betty.

The law courts' making time of the essence in all contracts resulted in needless hardship to the breaching party where the harm to the nonbreaching party was minor and the defect could be quickly corrected. To alleviate the hardship, the courts began to adopt an approach that enabled them to consider the "time is of the essence" question on a case-by-case basis. Today, in the exercise of their equitable jurisdiction, the courts routinely hold that failure to perform at the scheduled time is merely a breach of a contractual *promise*, a breach that does *not* excuse performance by the nonbreaching party unless special circumstances require strict observance of the law day schedule. Under this approach, unless performance on law day is of critical importance to Betty, John's inability to deliver marketable title on law day does not excuse Betty from her duty to pay, and John has an additional reasonable time to complete his performance. Time can be of the essence because of the nature of the property being sold, because of the personal circumstances of one of the parties, or because the parties so specified in their contract. Consider the following illustrations:

- Lance is selling a "spec" house (one that he built in speculation that he can profit by appropriately timing its sale in a wildly fluctuating market). The timing of the sale is critical to profitability and, to Lance, time is "of the essence" of his contract to sell the house to Bertha. Even though she is creditworthy, her bank delays making her a loan commitment. Given the possibility that the local housing market will shift suddenly downward, Bertha's failure to receive a loan commitment by law day excuses Lance from his performance obligation and entitles him to any damages resulting from her breach of the contract.

- Simon agrees to sell to Sara a house he recently inherited from his uncle. Knowing that Sara is moving from out-of-state and must have possession of the house on August 20 so that she can begin her new teaching job on August 21, Simon agrees to an August 20 closing. On that day he learns that his cousin Earl has challenged his claim of ownership. Simon cannot establish his chain of title unless the probate court rules in his favor, but the earliest date for a hearing on the matter is September 15. Because of her need for immediate accommodations, time is of the essence to Sara. She is excused from her performance obligation and is entitled to damages for Simon's breach of the contract.

- Concerned that Sylvia might delay taking possession of the office building Edmund has contracted to sell her, he insists that the contract of sale include a clause stating that "Time is of the essence of this contract." Sylvia does not appear at the closing, but e-mails a message stating that she needs another couple of days to locate an additional tenant. The clause is enforceable, Edmund's performance is excused, and he is entitled to damages resulting from Sylvia's breach.

Equitable Conversion

Because each parcel of land is considered unique, a contract for its sale is specifically enforceable in a court of equity. Sam agrees to sell his Victorian mansion to Martha, but gets "seller's remorse" and refuses to go through with the transaction. If the legal requirements for specific performance are met (among them, an honest and fair purchaser), Martha will be entitled to a court order requiring Sam to perform the contract by conveying the property to her. Thus, through the equitable remedy of specific performance, Martha gets the land itself and does not have to accept money damages (the "remedy at law") as a substitute.

In most states, the courts hold that as soon as the parties have entered into a specifically enforceable real estate contract, an **equitable conversion** occurs that changes the nature of their interests from what the parties had before the contract. Under the doctrine of equitable conversion, the purchaser immediately becomes the equitable owner of the realty, and consequently has, from the time of contracting, an interest in *real estate* ("equitable title") instead of personalty (a contract claim for the *value* of the realty). Correspondingly, the seller's interest, which before the contract was an interest in real estate, is converted by the contract into an interest in *personal* property, that is, the right to have the purchase price. True, the realty is still in the seller's name and will remain so until closing occurs, but the seller now has only a "legal" title, which the seller holds as trustee for the benefit of the purchaser during the time that the contract is executory.

BOX 6–1 APPLY YOUR KNOWLEDGE

Suppose that in the illustration on the following page, Martina had not specifically devised Blackacre to Tyrone, but had instead left "my realty to my son Tyrone and my personalty to my daughter Clara."

Who would be entitled to Blackacre? Why?

Who would be entitled to the proceeds of its sale? Why?

The doctrine of equitable conversion has been applied to resolve certain kinds of problems that may arise during the executory period, such as the death of the buyer or the seller, or the rights of judgment creditors of either. Martina owns Blackacre in fee simple and contracts to sell it to Luis. Before the date set for closing, Martina dies. Her will leaves Blackacre to her son Tyrone. Despite the provision in his mother's will, Tyrone is not entitled to Blackacre. Although Tyrone succeeds to his mother's title to Blackacre, he holds it as trustee for Luis, who became equitable owner of Blackacre before Martina died. So what does Tyrone receive? A number of courts would hold that since Martina made a specific devise of Blackacre to Tyrone, and then by selling it to Luis equitably converted the realty into personalty, the provision in her will is, in effect, a bequest to Tyrone of the purchase price.[1]

Risk of Loss

Sometimes, after contracting but before closing, real estate suffers damage from fire, flood, or other causes, without the fault of buyer or seller. As between the two, who must bear the loss? In a majority of states, unless the contract provides otherwise the buyer bears the risk and must pay the purchase price despite the damage, because under the doctrine of equitable conversion the buyer is considered the owner of the realty from the time of contracting.

This equitable conversion rule has been sharply criticized as arbitrary and unfair by virtually all experts writing on the topic of risk allocation in executory real estate contracts. They point out several problems with the majority rule. For example, although both vendor and vendee have an insurable interest in the realty while the contract is executory, most buyers do not have possession of the land during that period and usually do not think of themselves as owners until after closing when they can move in. Consequently, they are unlikely to insure against loss during the executory period. In contrast, sellers are likely to have casualty insurance before the sale and to keep it in effect until closing. Sellers, moreover, typically remain in possession until closing, or at least can monitor the condition of the premises, so are in a better position than buyers to prevent some types of destruction such as accidental fire or water damage.

Because of the great dissatisfaction with the equitable conversion rule, a large *minority* of states have rejected it and have adopted instead a rule that allocates loss on the basis of who has possession at the time of loss. One such rule is that of the Uniform Vendor and Purchaser Risk Act, which has been adopted in eleven states,[2] sometimes with modifications. Under this legislation, risk of loss remains with the seller until either possession or legal title is transferred to the buyer, whichever occurs first, unless the parties expressly provide for some other risk allocation formula. In other minority states, the courts have developed rules of similar effect. In the minority of states, then, if Michelle agrees to sell her condominium to Daniel, he will acquire the risk of physical damage to the premises when closing occurs, unless he moves in before then. If Michelle allows him to move in a week before closing, he receives the risk upon taking possession. A delay in closing *and* in his taking possession delays also the shifting of the risk.

A party is, of course, liable for loss caused by that party's fault, or which he or she has contracted to absorb. Contractual formulas can be useful in all states, but are especially needed in the equitable conversion states to overcome the arbitrariness of the equitable conversion rule. The following is one of many clauses that a real estate attorney might develop, depending on the circumstances of the parties:

> *(1) If the injury [to the property] is less than 10 percent of the purchase price, purchaser shall complete the contract; and (2) if the injury is greater than 10 percent purchaser has the option of completing or terminating the contract. If in either [(1) or (2) above] the contract is completed purchaser is entitled to an abatement [reduction of the purchase price] commensurate with the damage."*[3]

Options and Preemptive Rights (Right of First Refusal)

Often a person interested in a parcel of land does not want to buy it immediately, but wants instead to have it available for purchase later. Maxine has a ten-year lease on a commercial property and wants to buy it if her business thrives there. Tyler moves into town, rents a house for a year, and would like to buy it if his new employer makes him general manager of the factory within the year. In both instances, the owner of the realty might be willing to give the tenant an option to purchase it.

An **option**, also called an **option contract**, is an *offer* to sell or purchase property on stated terms (the "main offer"), coupled with a contract in which the offeror (optionor) promises to hold the main offer open for a fixed period in exchange for a small payment for doing so. If within the option period the offeree (optionee) accepts the offer, the optionor is bound to a contract. Richmond tells Betty, "I'll sell you my house for $90,000 [the main offer], and for $10 dollars I'll give you thirty days to decide." Betty pays the $10, thus creating an option contract. Richmond's main offer is now irrevocable for 30 days, and the option contract is binding on his estate if he dies before the option period expires.

Options can specify a much longer option period and involve more substantial consideration in exchange for the promise to hold the offer open. Maxine and her landlord Larry sign an agreement stating, "I, Larry, offer to sell Blackacre Plaza to Maxine for $400,000 plus 8.3% annual interest on the unpaid balance, principal to be paid in the form of a down payment of $40,000 plus equal annual installments of $40,000 per year until the purchase price is paid. For a consideration of $5,000, Maxine will have three years from the date of this document to accept this offer." Maxine pays the $5,000. Maxine has bought three years' time within which to decide whether to accept Larry's offer, which is irrevocable for the option period. If Maxine exercises the option during the three years by accepting Larry's offer, Larry is bound by the resulting contract.

Sometimes the parties to an option contract find themselves in a dispute over whether the option was exercised, especially where the value of the property has risen greatly and the optionor no longer wants to sell on the original terms. Early in the option period, Maxine rejects Larry's offer. A few months later, she changes her mind because the value of Blackacre Plaza has risen sharply, and attempts to accept Larry's offer. Upon his refusal to recognize a sale of the property, Maxine brings suit for specific performance. Is there a contract?

The answer depends on how the court views the rights of the optionee. Under an early view seldom if ever applied today, an optionee acquired only a right to make a single decision sometime during the option period, which ended when the decision was made. So the optionee's rejecting the main offer early in the option period exercised the option and terminated the main offer immediately. Today, however, the vast majority of states, perhaps all, have adopted the modern view that an optionee purchases an amount of time to map out a strategy in a potentially volatile business climate. For example, inability early in the option period to acquire a loan commitment might lead the optionee to reject the main offer, but success with another lender when the optionee's profits rise later in the option period might cause the optionee to reverse that decision and accept. The optionor should expect a degree of uncertainty and mind-changing on the part of optionee, and should not be allowed arbitrarily to cut the option period short. Under this view, if Maxine rejects the offer, she is allowed to accept later in the option period *unless* Larry relies on her rejection to his detriment by, for example, selling Blackacre Plaza to someone else. If she makes no decision within the option period, Larry's offer automatically expires and there is no contract.

In general, an optionee may assign (transfer) the option to a third person unless the option expressly forbids assignment or unless the circumstances surrounding the option give the optionor a valid reason to block its transfer. Henry owns Pleasant Acres, which consists of a small lake and 300 acres surrounding it. On the shore is a cabin that he and his best friend Wilfred have used for forty years during fishing season. No longer able to fish, Henry intends at his death to leave Pleasant Acres to the Wildlife Preservation Society for the protection of rare species of flora and fauna existing there. Knowing Henry's plan, Wilfred expresses interest in buying the cabin and five acres surrounding it so he can continue to fish at the lake. Assuming that the use of Pleasant Acres will remain unchanged, Henry grants him an option to purchase the cabin and the five acres, good for 90 days. Sixty days later, Wilfred becomes seriously ill and assigns the option to Fishing Tours, Inc., which intends to bulldoze the cabin, build a sound stage for concerts, and pave the five acres as a parking lot for large-group fishing outings at the lake. Because the assignment is incompatible with Henry's intentions for Pleasant Acres, Fishing Tours cannot enforce the option. In the absence of such personal factors or an enforceable nonassignability clause, however, options are routinely assignable.

A **preemptive right** gives its holder a **right of first refusal**, that is, a right to purchase property if the owner later decides to sell it to a third person. Like an option, a right of first refusal is enforceable if its holder gave consideration for it. Unlike an option, however, a right of first refusal does not give its holder an immediate right to compel an unwilling owner to sell the land, but merely requires the owner who eventually decides to sell to someone else to offer the property first to the preemptive right holder, on the terms stipulated in the document creating the preemptive right. Upon receiving the owner's offer to sell the property, the holder of the right of first refusal may elect whether to buy the property or not to buy it. If the holder chooses not to buy it, the owner is free to sell to the third person.

Acquisition by Inter Vivos Gift

A second way to acquire ownership of realty is to receive it as a gift. A **gift** is the voluntary transfer of an interest in real or personal property by its owner, the **donor**, to a **donee** for no consideration. Gifts can be *inter vivos* (a *present* transfer between living persons) or *testamentary* (taking effect at the death of the donor). Most testamentary gifts are made by the donor's will and are discussed in the section of this chapter on wills and trusts. Here, the focus is on inter vivos gifts.

Gifts Inter Vivos and Causa Mortis

A gift of property between living persons is classified as either a gift inter vivos or a gift causa mortis. Usually the gift being so classified is personal property.

Ordinarily, a **gift inter vivos** is irrevocable. Marita buys a new Corvette and delivers it to her son Rodolfo as a graduation present. Two weeks later, she reconsiders and wants the car back. She has no legal right to the car because the gift was irrevocable. However, she could have made the gift revocable by expressly conditioning it on the happening or nonhappening of some future event. If Marita had given the car to Rodolfo in his freshman year of college "on condition that you maintain a "B" average," the gift would be subject to an express "condition subsequent" (maintaining a "B" average). Rodolfo's failure to perform the condition defeats the gift.

In contrast, a **gift causa mortis** is automatically revocable by law, without the donor's having to state that it is revocable. A gift is "causa mortis" if the donor makes it in apprehension of his or her own imminent death from illness, injury, or peril. A gift causa mortis is automatically revoked if (1) the donor recovers from the illness or injury or escapes the peril, (2) the donor revokes the gift before death, or (3) the donee dies before the donor.

The terms *gift inter vivos* and *gift causa mortis* can be confusing, because both types of gift are made *between living persons*. In that respect both types are gifts *inter vivos*, the key distinction being that an ordinary gift inter vivos is not motivated by an apprehension of the donor's imminent death (and usually is irrevocable), while a gift causa mortis *is* so motivated and, for the protection of the distressed donor, is always revocable.

In rare instances *ordinary* inter vivos gifts, normally irrevocable unless a condition is expressed, are subject to *implied* conditions (those not expressed, but instead recognized or imposed by law). Contemplating marriage, Joseph gives Anita an engagement ring. Joseph is not likely to say to Anita as he places the ring on her finger, "Dear, I want this ring back if we don't marry." Yet, despite the obviously inter vivos character of this gift (Joseph and Anita probably are not contemplating death at this moment in their lives), most courts would not require Joseph to express the condition. Instead, they would hold that Anita's good faith continuance of the engagement is an implied condition to her right to keep the ring. In most jurisdictions, if she unjustifiably breaks the engagement, she must return the ring, while if *Joseph* unjustifiably breaks the engagement, Anita may keep the ring.

● Requirements for a Gift

The requirements for a valid gift are the grantor's *donative intent*; a *delivery* of the property interest to or for the donee; and, in theory, the donee's *acceptance* of the gift.

Donative Intent

If Simon silently hands Janet $100, an observer is not likely to know from that fact alone whether he intended a gift, a loan, a bailment for safekeeping, or some other transaction. Similarly, if Simon allows Janet to take possession of his farm Blackacre, that fact alone will not reveal whether he intended to lease Blackacre to Janet, give it to her, or simply hire her as manager. Janet alleges that Simon gave Blackacre to her. To prove that Simon intended a gift, Janet will have to produce evidence of his donative intent, such as Simon's written or oral statement to that effect. Other circumstances would have a bearing on the matter, such as a close family relationship between Simon and Janet together with his refusal to accept payment for or profits from Blackacre or his routinely referring to Blackacre as "hers." Even Simon's clear statement of donative intent would be negated, however, if it were induced by Janet's fraud, duress, or undue influence, or by Simon's lack of mental capacity or his excusable mistake.

Delivery

For a gift to occur, the donor must deliver the property to the donee or to a third party (agent or trustee) acting for the donee. Delivery of personal property is relatively straightforward. It can be an *actual delivery*, for example, the donor's handing the property to the donee. Or it can be a **constructive** (symbolic) **delivery** such as the donor's handing over all the keys to a safe deposit box containing the property, thus relinquishing all control over the property.

For a gift of realty, delivery is more complex than for a gift of personalty. Because land is incapable of physical delivery, the donor must use some form of symbolic delivery. But an oral description and transfer will not do, because under the statute of frauds any conveyance of an interest in land except a short-term lease must be in writing to be enforced.[4] Consequently, a *deed* is used for conveying real estate, whether as part of a sale transaction or as a gift. A deed is a document of transfer from the donor to the donee, identifying the property in terms of both its physical boundaries and the kind of interest to be conveyed (e.g., fee simple estate, life estate).

The physical acts for delivering the deed to the donee can vary greatly. For a gift inter vivos to be effective, the donor must have not only the donative intent required for a gift, but also an intention to make a *present transfer* of the interest to the donee. Jeremiah signs a deed naming Sharon as the donee of Blackacre and keeps the deed in his possession, intending to give it to her upon her daughter's graduation from medical school. There is no transfer of Blackacre, and no gift, until Jeremiah delivers the deed to Sharon or to someone acting on her behalf. In some cases, however, the donor physically delivered the deed to the donee, but made clear that no transfer of ownership was to take place until the happening of some future event. Courts have held in such cases that no gift occurred when the deed was physically delivered because the donor lacked the intent to make a present transfer. Conversely, courts have held that a gift occurred even though the donor kept possession of the deed for safekeeping, where the evidence revealed the donor's intent to make a present transfer of the interest. In short, when deciding whether a conveyance of the interest has occurred, the courts try to determine the donor's actual intent, and do not give conclusive weight to how the donor physically deals with the deed. The content and delivery requirements for a deed are discussed further in Chapter 10.

For a gift of realty, a recital of consideration in the deed ("for one dollar and other good and valuable consideration") usually is not needed. This lack of need for consideration would seem self-evident from the nature of a gift, which is a gratuitous transfer. But in the very few states still adhering to English common law concepts pertaining to "bargain and sale" deeds, a recital of consideration *may* be required for a deed of gift to be valid. It is not clear precisely which states are "bargain and sale" states. Consequently, if a state *might* be a "bargain and sale" state, lawyers who draft deeds of gift there routinely include a recital of consideration to avoid the unpleasant surprise of having the deed declared invalid for lack of the recital. In the great majority of states, however, no such recital is required for a deed of gift.

Acceptance

From the viewpoint of the donee, not all gifts are desirable. A dilapidated house, a rusted-out car, or land contaminated by hazardous wastes could involve far more expense to restore than the property might ever be worth. The third requirement for a gift, acceptance by the donee, gives the donee an opportunity to reject an unwanted gift. So if the donee is aware of the gift and refuses to accept it, there is no gift. Sometimes, however, a donee is unaware of the gift. The donee might be traveling, or might be in a coma from accident or illness, or the donor might have delivered the gift to a third party who did not inform the donee of the delivery. In such instances, acceptance is *presumed* if the gift is beneficial. Darla delivers a valuable antique to Henry's agent as a gift to Henry. Henry dies without learning of the delivery. If the gift is beneficial, the antique becomes a part of Henry's estate.

BOX 6–2 YOU BE THE JUDGE

Lee wins $10 million in the state lottery. To celebrate, he buys a newly built house for $400,000, has the deed made out to his friend Nora, and leaves it for her at her office in the custody of her secretary Bob. Nora is on a skiing vacation. Without learning of the gift, she dies in an avalanche. Upon hearing of Nora's death, Lee demands that Bob return the deed to him. Bob refuses, and Lee brings suit for the return of the deed. Who is entitled to the house?

Acquisition by Intestate Succession, Will, or Trust

When a person dies, the property left behind is the decedent's estate. The net estate—the property minus charges for taxes, the decedent's debts, and the expenses of estate administration—is distributed to those entitled to it under the decedent's will, subject, however, to limits imposed by law on the use of wills. Some of those limits are discussed later in this section of the chapter. If the decedent left no will, a state statute specifies who is to receive the property.

A decedent who leaves a valid will is said to have died **testate** and is called the **testator**. In the great majority of states, a gift of *real property* by will is a devise and the person receiving it is the devisee, while a gift of *personal property* by will is a bequest or legacy and the person receiving it is the legatee. In the states using this terminology, a testator "devises" real property and "bequeaths" personal property. At least one state, California, defines "devise" as a disposition of either real or personal property by will,[5] so in California a testator "devises" personal as well as real property. A will becomes effective at the moment of the testator's death. Before then, the will can be revoked, replaced, or modified.

If a decedent dies **intestate** (without a will), the state's intestacy statute, in some states called the statute of descent and distribution, says who is to receive the decedent's estate. A person receiving property under the intestacy statute is called an **heir**.[6] The decedent's surviving spouse and children, if any, are the heirs of first priority. If none survive the decedent, the decedent's more remote relatives inherit the estate. If no heirs exist, the decedent's estate escheats to the state.

Partial intestacy occurs when a decedent leaves a will that disposes of only part of the estate. For example, Kareem's will leaves his residence and his General Motors stock to his wife Alma, his lakeshore cottage to his friend Harold, and $50,000 to the Central City Youth Center. Harold dies before Kareem, who neglected to change his will. Because Harold must survive Kareem to be his devisee, the will does not dispose of the lakeshore cottage. Harold's dying first caused the gift of the cottage to "lapse." As to the cottage, therefore, Kareem died intestate and the cottage passed under the intestacy statute to Alma, Kareem's heir of first priority.

● Estate Administration

Estate administration is the process of winding up the affairs of the decedent and distributing the net estate in accordance with the will or the intestacy statute to the decedent's heirs, legatees, and devisees, often referred to as the decedent's successors. A court of appropriate jurisdiction, usually called the probate court, supervises the administration process, which is carried out by the decedent's personal representative. If the decedent died *intestate*, the personal representative is a person (or a bank or trust company) appointed by the court and called the administrator of the estate. A personal representative named in a *will* to administer the estate is called the **executor**, that is, the person who is to "execute" (carry out) the provisions of the will by collecting the testator's assets, paying the testator's debts and the expenses of administration, and distributing the remaining property to the appropriate persons. If the will does not name an executor, or if the named executor cannot or refuses to serve, the court appoints an **administrator**, known formally as the **administrator with will annexed**. Traditionally, a woman carrying out these functions was an executrix or administratrix, while a woman testator was a testatrix. Today the tendency is to refer to men and women alike as executors, administrators, and testators. The UPC uses the generic term **personal representative**.

Applicable Law

The law governing estate administration varies considerably among the states. Sixteen states (some commentators say 18) have adopted the Uniform Probate Code (UPC), but some have modified it substantially.[7] The UPC, a comprehensive statute covering all aspects of estate administration, spells out such things as:

- The priorities among heirs in intestate succession.
- The rules for resolving the problem of simultaneous death.
- The steps and procedures involved in the administration of intestate estates and the probate of wills.
- The rights of surviving spouses to take against an unfavorable will.
- The appointment and duties of the personal representative and others.

The other states have their own intestacy statutes, whose provisions often differ markedly from those of the UPC. For example, in a majority of states, title to the decedent's personal property passes to the personal representative pending administration, while title to the realty passes directly to the devisees or heirs. But under the UPC, title to both the personal and the real property passes directly to the decedent's successors, and *not* to the personal representative. In all states, however, the personal representative may sell the real and personal property to pay the debts and administrative expenses of the estate, and the personal representative has fiduciary obligations in carrying out the administration. Commonly, executors, administrators, and other fiduciaries must post a bond to compensate for losses resulting from improper administration, unless, for example, the will waives that requirement. Unlike the law of most states, the UPC gives the court discretion to dispense with the bond even if the decedent's will provides that a bond must be furnished.

Avoiding Probate

In estate administration the term **probate** has two meanings. Technically, probate is the judicial process of "proving" a will by (1) determining that the will is valid, and (2) making an official, conclusive declaration of its validity so that heirs, devisees, legatees, personal representatives, and others affected by the will can rely on it without fear that another court may later declare it invalid. To determine whether a will is valid, the probate court decides questions such as the following: Did the testator have sufficient mental capacity to make a will? Is the signature that of the decedent? Was the will executed in accordance with formalities required by law? Did the decedent intend this particular document as the will, or had it been revoked or replaced with another? Did the decedent make the will voluntarily, free from fraud, duress, and undue influence?

After certifying a will as valid, the court initiates the administration process by formally appointing an executor or administrator. Strictly speaking, *administration* is a separate process from the *probate* of (proving) the will. In its popular sense, however, "probate" means not just the process of proving a will, but also the process of administering estates, including intestate estates, as in the expression "probating the estate." Property held at death solely in the decedent's own name or as a tenant in common, is "subject to probate," so must pass through formal estate administration unless otherwise provided by law.[8]

Probate of an estate has distinct advantages, but also some disadvantages that make many people want to avoid it. Estate administration (probate of the estate) under court supervision is a systematic, orderly way of winding up the decedent's financial affairs. The process protects those who owe money to the estate by relieving them of liability when they make proper payment to the personal representative. If estate assets are sufficient, creditors of the estate receive payment. If any property remains, the decedent's successors get good title to it, free from the claims of others. And, if property such as stocks, bonds, or realty was in the decedent's name, the probate court officially transfers title to the successors in their own names. However, because of lawyers' fees, the fees of personal representatives, and other costs, estate administration can be expensive, and often it is time-consuming.

Will Substitutes. To avoid the expense and delay of estate administration, and sometimes to avoid having their gifts made a matter of public record, many property owners seek to "avoid probate" by using **will substitutes** that keep property owned by the decedent during life out of his or her estate and free from administration. The items of property that will substitutes keep out of the estate are called **nonprobate assets** because they are not subject to estate administration. The items of property that *are* administered are called **probate assets**. The totality of the probate assets is called the **probate estate**. The following are common examples of will substitutes used to keep property out of a decedent's estate:

- *Joint tenancy, tenancy by the entireties.* As noted in Chapter 5, these two types of co-ownership feature a "right of survivorship." Ronald owns Blackacre in joint tenancy with his sister Nora. Ronald's death releases any claim to Blackacre that Ronald had during life, and Nora remains owner of the whole parcel. Ronald's attempt to will his share of Blackacre to his daughter Rachel is ineffective because his interest terminated at his death and never became part of his estate.

- *Life insurance.* Sara purchases a policy (contract) of life insurance on her own life. The face amount of $50,000 is the "proceeds" of the policy, which the insurance company agrees to pay at her death to persons named in the policy as beneficiaries. She names her husband Al as beneficiary. If the policy is still in effect at Sara's death and she has not changed the beneficiary, Al receives the $50,000 free from probate because the insurance company is contractually obligated to pay him directly. If Al does not survive Sara, the proceeds go to her estate and now *are* subject to probate. Probate is also required if she never designated a beneficiary, or if she named her estate as beneficiary.

- *Joint bank accounts, payable on death (POD) accounts.* A joint bank account is one opened in the names of two persons, with the account agreement specifying that both have a right to withdraw money from the account and that the surviving account owner is entitled to any balance remaining at the death of the other. Carlton opens a joint bank account in the names of himself and his niece Ruth, and deposits $100,000 in it. During the next several years, both withdraw money from the account. At Carlton's death, $83,000 remains. Ruth receives it free from probate. The account would have been a "payable on death" (POD) account if Carlton had opened it in his name alone but had provided in the account agreement that at his death the remaining balance would be payable to Ruth. During his life, only Carlton could make withdrawals from the POD account. At his death, Ruth receives the balance free from probate.

- *Inter vivos trust.* An **inter vivos trust**, also called a **living trust** because inter vivos means "between living persons," is an arrangement for property management in which a person (the "settlor") during his or her life transfers property to another (the "trustee") to manage for the benefit of one or more third persons (the "beneficiaries"). Often, to retain control of the trust assets, the settlor retains a power to revoke the trust, but whether a living trust is revocable or irrevocable, upon creation it immediately confers a property interest on the beneficiaries. At the death of the settlor, the final disposition of the trust property is governed by the trust agreement, free from probate.

Disadvantages: Unexpected Heirs and Death Taxes. Although avoiding probate has certain advantages, it can also involve pitfalls for the unwary. For example, as noted in Chapter 5, if joint tenants die simultaneously, the law applying to simultaneous death provides in effect that the joint tenants shall be treated as tenants in common. In that event, at least part of the property might not go to the person or persons originally intended to have it. Moreover, it would now be subject to administration, and the time and cost savings of avoiding probate would be lost. Martha, age 79 and in ill health, owns an 18-story office building. She does not want to leave it to her son, whom she has not seen in 40 years. To avoid probate, Martha conveys the building to herself and her granddaughter Benita as joint tenants, assuming that Benita will survive her and receive the building without having to share ownership with Benita's husband, who is serving time in prison for fraud. Two years later, Martha and Benita die simultaneously in a car accident. Consequently, half of the property goes to Benita's estate and half goes to Martha's. Neither Martha nor Benita had a will, so their estates pass under the intestacy statute—Benita's half to her husband, her only heir, and Martha's half to her son, her only heir. Thus, the building unexpectedly ends up owned by a long-absent son and an in-law whom Martha did not like.

Avoiding probate and failing to make a will can also greatly increase "death taxes" and jeopardize the financial well-being of heirs. Without professional estate planning guidance, a person unfamiliar with state and federal death taxes might not understand that for the purpose of calculating them, many nonprobate assets are included in the decedent's "gross estate," which, as defined by the Internal Revenue Code for tax purposes and as understood by state tax authorities, is considerably broader than the decedent's "probate estate."

Death taxes are of two basic types: the **inheritance tax** imposed by a number of states, and the **estate tax** of the sort imposed by the federal government. A state's inheritance tax is imposed on heirs, devisees, and legatees for the privilege of receiving the property from the estate. An estate tax, whether state or federal, is imposed on the *decedent's* privilege of *transmitting* property at death and is called a **transfer tax**.

At least 14 states and Puerto Rico impose either an inheritance tax or their own estate tax.[9] Thirty-three states and the District of Columbia do not impose either an inheritance tax or an estate tax of their own. Instead, they levy a so-called "pick-up tax" on estates, equal in amount to a credit granted to estates by the Internal Revenue Code (IRC) for death taxes that the decedent paid to the state. In the 34 "pick-up" jurisdictions, therefore, federal law determines the total amount of a decedent's estate tax liability, and by means of the credit, the federal government shares that amount with the decedent's state so that the total tax burden on the decedent's estate does not exceed the federal amount. But most estates are too small to incur federal estate tax liability. Consequently, in the 34 "pick-up" jurisdictions, most estates escape both federal and state death taxes. (Beginning in 2002, the state *credit* will be gradually replaced with a *deduction*.)

In the inheritance tax jurisdictions, the tax is a percentage of the value of the property received by heirs, devisees, and legatees, and the tax rate and amount of exemptions vary according to the closeness of the relationship between the decedent and the individual successor. Closer relatives have larger exemptions and a lower tax rate. To ensure that decedents' successors pay the inheritance tax on property that they received outside probate, for example, as a surviving joint tenant, the states impose the tax on most nonprobate assets that successors receive. In most states, however, statutes exempt *insurance proceeds*, entirely or in part, from any kind of state death tax.

The federal estate tax applies to the decedent's "taxable estate," which is the decedent's "gross estate" as broadly defined for tax purposes by provisions of the Internal Revenue Code, and as reduced by certain deductions permitted by the Code. Most states have adopted or approximated the federal definition of gross estate. It includes not only the property actually owned by the decedent at death, but also the value of many nonprobate assets that the decedent owned or controlled during life and which now belong to others. Among them are the value of the following:

- The decedent's fractional share of property held in joint tenancy at death, or all of it if the decedent was the sole purchaser. However, a surviving *spouse's* share is not included in the decedent's gross estate.

- Proceeds of insurance on the decedent's life payable to others, if the decedent had at death any "incidents of ownership" of the policy such as a substantial (more than 5%) reversionary interest in the proceeds or a right to change the beneficiary.

- Property in trusts that the decedent could revoke during life.

- Property (including insurance proceeds) over which the decedent during life had a "power of appointment" (that is, a right to specify who would receive ownership of the property).

- Gifts made within three years of the decedent's death, that is, transfers in contemplation of death.

Once the gross estate is determined, it is reduced by a number of deductions. Key ones are the charitable deduction and, for married persons, the marital deduction. A competent estate planner can minimize the size of a person's gross and taxable estate (and the amount of the estate tax) by carefully structuring inter vivos gifts, using wills and trusts to take advantage of the deductions, and employing other estate planning techniques. The planning process can produce savings greatly exceeding the costs of probate, while assuring that the decedent's property will go to the decedent's intended beneficiaries. The federal estate tax is discussed further in Chapter 16.

Small Estates

Most states have a statute relieving small estates from the burden of administration. One type of statute frees an heir or a legatee from formal administration where the estate consists entirely of personal property not exceeding a modest amount, for example, $5,000.

A second type of statute involves administration, but permits a so-called "summary" procedure where the amount of the estate does not exceed the total amount that the successor by law takes free from the claims of creditors. For example, in all states a surviving spouse and children are entitled to receive from the decedent's estate, free from the claims of creditors, some combination of a "probate homestead" set apart by the probate court for the use of the spouse and minor children as a residence for a limited period, a family allowance for living expenses for a specified period, and an amount covering the reasonable expenses of the decedent's last illness and funeral expenses. Where the estate is equal to or less than the exempted amounts, the personal representative may immediately (1) distribute the estate to the successor without giving notice to creditors (since they have no claim to such assets), and (2) take the formal steps necessary for closing the estate.

⬤ Transfer of Property by Intestate Succession

Intestacy statutes designate who shall receive a decedent's estate in the absence of a will. They do so by establishing categories of heirs in terms of family relationships, the priority that a given category of heirs has in the scheme of distribution, and the amount of property to which various heirs are entitled. If no will exists, or if a will exists but is refused probate (i.e., is declared invalid), intestacy is total and the statute covers the entire estate. Where a will is valid but does not dispose of the whole estate, intestacy is partial, and the statute covers only the property not disposed of by the will.

Terminology

Some of the terminology used in intestacy statutes and in wills can be confusing. The following terms sometimes appear in statutes and wills.

1. *Lineal and collateral heirs.* **Lineal heirs** are those in a direct line from a common source (person) and include *descendants* (e.g., children, grandchildren, great-grandchildren) and

ascendants, or *ancestors* (e.g., parents, grandparents, great-grandparents). **Collateral heirs** are those "alongside" the lineal line: sisters, brothers, aunts, uncles, nieces, nephews, and cousins.

2. *Issue.* *Issue* is used in different senses. In its broadest sense, "issue" means all persons who have descended from a common ancestor, and is synonymous with "descendants," both lineal and collateral. Bertha has two children, Ross and Rita, each of whom has two children. Bertha's children and grandchildren are her "issue," or descendants. Especially in wills, however, the context often indicates that the testator used "issue" to mean, for example, only the testator's children, and not all of his or her descendants. If the language of the will clearly reveals that the testator used "issue" to mean such things as "my children" or "my descendants living at my death," the courts will give effect to the testator's intention.

3. *Per capita and per stirpes distribution.* In **per capita** distribution, each person receives an equal share. Nelson, a widower, dies intestate survived by his daughter Ramona, who has one child, and his son Justin, who has three children. Ramona and Justin, the children of Nelson, receive equal shares of Nelson's estate. If Justin had predeceased Nelson, however, Justin's share would have passed to his three children **per stirpes**. That is, the three children would receive as a group the share that their father would have received if he had survived Nelson. Thus, each child would be entitled to one-sixth of Nelson's estate. Persons who receive property per stirpes are often said to take it by *representation* because the group of per stirpes recipients (Justin's children) "represents" or takes the place of their immediate ancestor (Justin).

4. *Parcenary.* Sometimes an intestacy statute says that the real estate shall "pass in *parcenary*" (also called *co-parcenary*), which means that two or more heirs (co-parceners) in the first-priority category, such as Ramona and Justin in the preceding paragraph, share the real estate equally.

Identifying the Heirs

Although intestacy statutes differ considerably as to the details of distribution, some general similarities can be noted.

- To become an heir, a person must survive the decedent.

- As noted in Chapter 5, in the event of the simultaneous deaths of the decedent and a person who would have been heir, the potential heir is presumed to have predeceased the decedent so that the estate passes to the heir of next priority without having to pass through the estate of the predeceased person.

- The intestacy statutes set up categories of heirs, and most give first priority to the decedent's surviving spouse and children or their representatives. If no one in the first category survives, the heirs in the next category receive the estate.

The main provisions of the intestacy statutes of a common law state (Ohio) and a community property state (California) are given here as examples:

Ohio's Intestacy Statute

Section 2105.06. Statute of descent and distribution. When a person dies intestate having title or right to any personal property, or to any real estate or inheritance, in this state, the personal property shall be distributed, and the real estate or inheritance shall descend and pass in parcenary . . . in the following course:

(A) If there is no surviving spouse, to the children of the intestate or [if no children survived, to] their lineal descendants, per stirpes;

(B) *If there is a spouse and one child or its lineal descendants surviving, the first sixty thousand dollars if the spouse is the natural or adoptive parent of the child, or the first twenty thousand dollars if the spouse is not the natural or adoptive parent of the child, plus one-half of the balance of the intestate estate to the spouse and the remainder to the child or his lineal descendants, per stirpes;*

(C) *If there is a spouse and more than one child or their lineal descendants surviving, the first sixty thousand dollars if the spouse is the natural or adoptive parent of one of the children, or the first twenty thousand dollars if the spouse is the natural or adoptive parent of none of the children, plus one-third of the balance of the intestate estate to the spouse and the remainder to the children equally, or to the lineal descendants of any deceased child, per stirpes;*

(D) *If there are no children or their lineal descendants, then the whole to the surviving spouse;*

(E) *If there is no spouse and no children or their lineal descendants, to the parents of the intestate equally, or to the surviving parent;*

(F) *If there is no spouse, no children or their lineal descendants, and no parent surviving, to the brothers and sisters, whether of the whole or of the half blood of the intestate, or their lineal descendants, per stirpes;*

(G) *If there are no brothers or sisters or their lineal descendants, one-half to the paternal grandparents of the intestate equally, or to the survivor of them, and one-half to the maternal grandparents of the intestate equally, or to the survivor of them;*

(H) *If there is no paternal grandparent or no maternal grandparent, one-half to the lineal descendants of the deceased grandparents, per stirpes; if there are no such lineal descendants, then to the surviving grandparents or their lineal descendants, per stirpes; if there are no surviving grandparents or their lineal descendants, then to the next of kin of the intestate, provided there shall be no representation among such next of kin;*

(I) *If there are no next of kin, to stepchildren or their lineal descendants, per stirpes;*

(J) *If there are no stepchildren or their lineal descendants, escheat to the state.*

California's Intestacy Statute

Section 6401. Intestate share of surviving spouse.

(a) *As to community property, the intestate share of the surviving spouse is the one-half of the community property that belongs to the decedent. . . .*

(b) *As to quasi-community property, the intestate share of the surviving spouse is the one-half of the quasi-community property that belongs to the decedent. . . .*

(c) *As to separate property, the intestate share of the surviving spouse is as follows:*

(1) *The entire intestate estate if the decedent did not leave any surviving issue, parent, brother, sister, or issue of a deceased brother or sister.*

(2) *One-half of the intestate estate in the following cases:*

(A) *Where the decedent leaves only one child or the issue of one deceased child.*

(B) *Where the decedent leaves no issue but leaves a parent or parents or their issue or the issue of either of them.*

(3) *One-third of the intestate estate in the following cases:*

(A) *Where the decedent leaves more than one child.*

(B) *Where the decedent leaves one child and the issue of one or more deceased children.*

(C) *Where the decedent leaves issue of two or more deceased children.*

Section 6402. Intestate share of heirs other than surviving spouse. [T]he part of the intestate estate not passing to the surviving spouse under Section 6401, or the entire intestate estate if there is no surviving spouse, passes as follows:

(a) *To the issue of the decedent, the issue taking equally if they are all of the same degree of kinship to the decedent [e.g., all are the decedent's children], but if of unequal degree [e.g., one surviving child and the three children of another, predeceased child] those of more remote degree [i.e., the decedent's three grandchildren] take [by representation].*

(b) If there is no surviving issue, to the decedent's parent or parents equally.

(c) If there is no surviving issue or parent, to the issue of the parents or either of them, the issue taking equally if they are all of the same degree of kinship to the decedent, but if of unequal degree those of more remote degree take [by representation].

(d) If there is no surviving issue, parent or issue of a parent, but the decedent is survived by one or more grandparents or issue of grandparents, to the grandparent or grandparents equally, or to the issue of such grandparents if there is no surviving grandparent, the issue taking equally if they are all of the same degree of kinship to the decedent, but if of unequal degree those of more remote degree take [by representation].

(e) If there is no surviving issue, parent or issue of a parent, grandparent or issue of a grandparent, but the decedent is survived by the issue of a predeceased spouse, to such issue, the issue taking equally if they are all of the same degree of kinship to the predeceased spouse, but if of unequal degree those of more remote degree take [by representation].

(f) If there is no surviving issue, parent or issue of a parent, grandparent or issue of a grandparent, or issue of a predeceased spouse, but the decedent is survived by next of kin, to the next of kin in equal degree, but where there are two or more collateral kindred in equal degree who claim through different ancestors, those who claim through the nearest ancestor are preferred to those claiming through an ancestor more remote.

(g) If there is no surviving next of kin of the decedent and no surviving issue of a predeceased spouse of the decedent, but the decedent is survived by the parents of a predeceased spouse or the issue of such parents, to the parent or parents equally, or to the issue of such parents if both are deceased. . . .

Persons Disqualified from Inheriting

Most states have statutes placing limits on the right of inheritance. A child born out of wedlock, for example, ordinarily inherits only from its mother unless the natural parents married before or after the child was born, or paternity was established by adjudication before the father's death, or by clear and convincing proof afterward. In contrast, an adopted child inherits, and is inherited from, in essentially the same manner as a natural child.

Most states have statutes barring persons guilty of certain misconduct from inheriting from their victims. A Kansas statute prohibits a person convicted of murdering the decedent from receiving the decedent's estate, whether by inheritance, by will, as a surviving joint tenant, as beneficiary of a trust established by the decedent, or otherwise.[10] Texas limits the disqualification to a beneficiary of a life insurance policy convicted of "wilfully bringing about the death of the insured."[11] Indiana expands the disqualification to include a spouse living in adultery at the decedent's death and a spouse who has abandoned the decedent without just cause.[12]

● Transfer of Property by Using a Will

Within limits imposed by law, a testator may dispose of property at death by using a will. To protect the interests of testators and their successors, the making and enforcement of wills are closely regulated by statutes and case law.

Types of Wills; Revocation; Amendment

Various types of wills are recognized by some or all states. A **holographic will** is one entirely in the handwriting of the testator. It need not be witnessed, but it must be dated and signed by the testator. Some states recognize a holographic will that is partly printed if all the material provisions, the date, and the signature are written in the hand of the testator. A number of states do not recognize holographic wills. A **nuncupative will** is an oral will recognized in some states, but only under very limited circumstances. Typically, it may dispose of only a small amount of personal property, must be stated or dictated before witnesses by a testator in actual fear or peril of death or during the testator's final illness, and must be reduced to writing soon after it is made. A **statutory will** (available in California, Maine, Massachusetts, Michigan, New Mexico, and Wisconsin) is one whose provisions are spelled out in a state statute, which authorizes users to reduce the will to printed form. The testator then merely fills in blanks to indicate such things as who is to receive what property and who is to be the executor of the will and the guardian of minor children. The form must be signed by the testator and witnessed. The statutory will is a simple will, not suited for complex estates. A witnessed **formal will**, the most common type, is usually prepared by an attorney who customizes it to meet the needs of the particular testator, for example, a testator with a complex estate and a need to minimize death taxes. The formal will is the subject of this section of the chapter.

Whatever the type of will, it does not take effect until the testator's death. In the meantime, it may be revoked or amended. *Revocation* can be accomplished in a variety of ways, for example, by the testator's tearing up the will, burning it, or declaring in a subsequent will that "all previous wills are hereby revoked." Most states have a statute providing that the testator's divorce automatically revokes any provisions favoring the divorced spouse, unless the will provides otherwise. Under several state statutes, a will is revoked entirely if the testator marries after executing the will, unless the will indicates that it is to remain in effect after the marriage. In a few other states, entire automatic revocation occurs only if the testator marries and has children.

The most common way to *amend* a will is by use of a **codicil**, a written supplement that qualifies the will in some way. A codicil must be executed with the same formalities that are required for the will itself.

Requirements for a Will

Because a will disposes of property after the death of an owner who may have been aged, infirm, and subject to a variety of pressures when making the will, the law provides safeguards for the testator and successors as part of the will-making process. Two key ones are the requirements that the testator have testamentary capacity when making the will, and that the testator and witnesses observe certain formalities in the execution (signing and witnessing) of the will.

Testamentary Capacity. To make a valid will, a person must have **testamentary capacity**, that is, must be of sufficient age, usually 18, and of sound mind when the will is executed. Mary, age 78 and in ill health from a heart condition, made a will and died three months later. Mary's heart condition did not deprive her of testamentary capacity, nor would illiteracy, extreme old age, or physical weakness. To have testamentary capacity, Mary needed only to (1) understand generally the effect of making a will, the nature of her business, the general nature and extent of her property, and the identity of the "objects of her bounty" (the people or organizations to whom she wants to leave her property), and (2) be free of insane delusions that would cause her irrationally to dispose of her property in a way that a sane person would not. If Mary had testamentary capacity when she signed her will, it was effective at her death. If she lacked testamentary capacity when she signed the will, she died intestate.

Formalities for Creating a Will. The witnessing and other requirements for a valid will are strictly enforced to ensure that the testator freely chose to make the will, and to avoid the secrecy and fraud that otherwise might occur in the disposition of the estate. In all states the will must be in writing and signed by either the testator or someone signing on behalf of the testator at his or her request and in the testator's presence. A few states require "publication" of the will, that is, that the testator declare to the witnesses that the document they are signing is his or her will.

In all states except Vermont, the testator's signature must be witnessed by a minimum of two witnesses, who must sign the will as witnesses. Vermont requires three witnesses. Alternatively, if the witnesses cannot be present at the signing, they may witness the testator's later acknowledgment of the signature. The testator acknowledges the signature by declaring before a public official such as a notary public that the signature made earlier is the testator's. In some states, such as California and Virginia, the testator must sign or acknowledge in the presence of both witnesses at the same time. In most states, it is sufficient for the testator to sign or acknowledge in the presence of the witnesses separately.

Whether a will is valid to dispose of the testator's *personal* property is determined by the law of the state in which the testator is domiciled at death. A will meeting the requirements of that state disposes of all the testator's personalty, wherever located. To dispose of a testator's *real* property, however, a will ordinarily must comply with the requirements of the state in which the realty is located. This rule poses a problem where a testator is domiciled in one state and executes a will there, but owns real estate in another state with more stringent will formalities. For example, a will executed in Connecticut and meeting its requirements (two witnesses, "each of them subscribing in the testator's presence") would not comply with the more stringent requirements imposed by Louisiana (which requires the testator to sign "at the end of the testament and each other separate page" in the presence of a notary and two competent witnesses). Consequently, the Connecticut will would not be effective to dispose of real estate owned by the Connecticut testator but located in Louisiana. Indeed, nonconforming out-of-state wills frequently have been held ineffective to dispose of local realty. To alleviate this problem, many states, including Louisiana and Connecticut, have statutes providing that a will executed out-of-state but brought into the state for probate is valid if it complies with the formalities required by the state in which it was executed. Thus Louisiana *would* honor the nonconforming Connecticut will.

Some Limits on the Right to Dispose of Property by Will

Occasionally, a testator wishes to disinherit the surviving spouse or a relative by leaving him or her out of the testator's will, or to leave the unfavored person only a small amount. Sometimes a testator simply overlooks someone who normally would be included in the will, for example, a child that the testator erroneously thought had died, a spouse whom the testator married years after the will was executed, or a child born afterward. Whether intended or accidental, disinheritance can be devastating and unfair to members of the decedent's immediate family. Yet, testators in all states except Louisiana are free to disinherit their children and other relatives.[13]

Georgia permits a testator to disinherit his or her spouse as well.[14] In all other states, spouses receive substantial protection from disinheritance. A surviving spouse in the nine community property states owns one-half the community property and cannot be deprived of it by the decedent's will, while in four common law states a surviving spouse is entitled to dower or curtesy. In addition are the homestead and family allowances that state law provides for spouses and minor children, including those who have been disinherited. Here we discuss two additional protections against disinheritance: the "forced share" statutes, and statutes protecting "pretermitted" (omitted) children and overlooked spouses.

Protection of Spouses: Forced Share Statutes. All the common law states except Georgia have **forced share statutes**, sometimes called **elective share statutes**, to prevent intentional disinheritance. They are generally of two types. The "traditional" statute permits the spouse to choose between a specified portion of the decedent's estate (both real and personal property) and whatever property the decedent's will gave the spouse. The amount of the forced share varies among the states and, within a state, varies also according to the number of descendants who survived. Commonly, the spouse is entitled to one-half of the estate if no descendants survived, or to one-third if one or more descendants survived. In no event would the spouse receive more than the spouse's intestate share. Under the traditional statute, the spouse receives a fee interest in any land, not just a life estate; but because the decedent's creditors have first claim to the estate, it is possible the spouse would receive nothing. Moreover, the forced share applies only to the decedent's probate estate, and not to any nonprobate assets the decedent might have left to others.

Under a traditional statute, a decedent could defeat the spouse's forced share by using will substitutes to dispose of the estate. To prevent this from happening, a number of states have adopted a different type of forced share statute that gives the spouse a portion, e.g., one-third, of the decedent's "augmented estate." The augmented estate consists not only of the decedent's probate assets, but also many assets that the decedent transferred to others during the marriage by means of will substitutes. Thus, the spouse can retrieve much of the marital property that the decedent attempted to give away by means of joint tenancies, revocable trusts, and the like.

Statutes Protecting Pretermitted Children and Overlooked Spouses. Statutes in most states protect children whom the testator inadvertently failed to provide for in the will. The statutes vary considerably among the states. All give the omitted child what he or she would have received if the parent had died intestate, but some statutes apply only to children born after execution of the will, while others apply to all of the testator's children, whenever born. If the circumstances reveal that the testator's omission was intentional, the statute does not apply and the child receives nothing.

A similar problem arises when a person makes a will and later marries (or remarries) but dies without having changed the will to reflect the new marital status. A number of states have statutes providing that if there is no evidence that the omission of the spouse was intentional, the spouse receives the share provided for by the intestacy statute, which would be the whole estate in the absence of other survivors entitled to a share.

The case that follows involves an **antenuptial** (prenuptial) **agreement** in which a wife purportedly waives her elective share.

Case 6.1

Affiliated Banc Group, Ltd., v. Zehringer

527 N.W.2d 585 (Minn. App. 1995)

Prior to their 1986 marriage, Jack and Phyllis Zehringer entered into an antenuptial agreement, stating in part that

> Jack Zehringer agrees to establish, by subsequent will, a bequest to Phyllis J. Heairet, if she survives as surviving spouse . . . , which bequest is intended to be in lieu of spouse's share or election to take against the Will.

In a subsequent loan from Midwest Federal, Jack Zehringer granted mortgages on four nonhomestead parcels of land that he acquired before the 1986 marriage solely in his name. Midwest requested that Phyllis sign the mortgages but she refused. When these mortgages were executed, Midwest was unaware of the 1986 antenuptial agreement.

In 1990, Jack Zehringer defaulted on the Midwest loan. Affiliated Banc Group succeeded to the mortgagee interests of Midwest and is the foreclosing party in this action. The trial court granted Affiliated a summary judgment for the foreclosure, holding that Phyllis Zehringer had no interest in the land and that in the antenuptial agreement she had waived any inchoate interest she may have had. Phyllis appealed.

CRIPPEN, J.

Under current Minnesota law there is a question of what interest a spouse has in the separate, non-homestead property of the other spouse. Minn. Stat. § 507.02 (1994) provides that a spouse may execute a separate deed to convey non-homestead real estate owned by that spouse, "subject to the rights of the other spouse therein." This statute leaves unanswered the question of what the rights of the other spouse are.

At common law, a wife [had] an inchoate dower interest in her husband's real property prior to his death. The husband could use the land as he saw fit but he could not destroy his wife's inchoate interest. If the husband conveyed or mortgaged the land (excluding a purchase-money mortgage) the purchaser or mortgagee took the land subject to the wife's inchoate dower interest.

The Minnesota legislature abolished common law dower in 1875. Subsequently, the legislature enacted [Minn. Stat. § 525.16, which] allowed either spouse to elect against the will of the other and thereby take a one-third interest in any real property owned by the other spouse during the course of the marriage. Under this statute, said the Minnesota courts, both spouses retained an inchoate interest in any real property owned by the other spouse during the marriage. A spouse was free to convey his or her separate property but it was conveyed subject to the other spouse's inchoate interests.

Minn. Stat. § 525.16 was repealed in 1985 and replaced with the elective share provisions of the Uniform Probate Code [(UPC). The UPC] still allows one spouse to elect against the will of the other, but now the spouse receives one-third of the "augmented estate" as defined in [the UPC]. . . .

It is uncertain whether a spouse continues to retain an inchoate interest in the other spouse's non-homestead property under the Uniform Probate Code. But we need not resolve that question here. If appellant retained an inchoate interest in her husband's property, she waived that interest in her antenuptial agreement.

Whatever inchoate interest a spouse may have in the other spouse's property derives from the spouse's right to claim an elective share under the probate code. It follows, we conclude, that the waiver of the right to claim an elective share necessarily waives any inchoate interest in the other spouse's property.

A spouse may waive the right to claim an elective share, but a waiver of the elective share prior to marriage must be accomplished by an antenuptial agreement. . . . The antenuptial contract statute provides that the parties may employ an agreement . . . to bar a spouse from "all rights" in the other spouse's estate that are not secured by the agreement. Appellant does not argue that her antenuptial agreement violates [the statute]. The only question is whether the antenuptial agreement contains a waiver of appellant's right to claim an elective share. . . .

We agree with the trial court that appellant's antenuptial contract is unambiguous and waives appellant's right to claim an elective share. The antenuptial agreement states that appellant accepts a specific bequest from her husband's estate "in lieu of" her right to elect against her husband's will. Similar language has been held by other courts to be a waiver of the right to claim a statutory elective share.

Moreover, the stated purpose of the antenuptial agreement was to limit the claims that [Phyllis] may make against the estate . . . to preserve a portion of Jack Zehringer's estate for his children of a prior marriage and for the continuation of certain of his business enterprises. The only way to ensure those goals was for appellant to waive her right to elect against her husband's will.

Appellant . . . contends that the agreement cannot be enforced by a third-party mortgagee who was unaware of the agreement at the time of the mortgage. But appellant misstates the nature of the inquiry. Respondent is not seeking to enforce the antenuptial agreement as a third-party beneficiary; rather, it is seeking a determination of the parties' rights in the mortgaged property. The question is whether appellant's husband could mortgage the property free and clear of any claim by appellant. The antenuptial agreement is the instrument that determines the rights of appellant and her husband in the property at the time of the mortgage. The agreement must be considered in any determination of the parties' interest in the property.

Appellant also argues that any waiver in the antenuptial agreement was conditional, so that until she [receives] the promised bequest she did not waive her right to claim an elective share. We disagree. The language of the agreement does not suggest that the waiver is conditional. Moreover, if appellant's waiver was not effective until her husband's death, Jack Zehringer would be unable to reap the benefits of his bargain, namely the use of his property for the continuation of his business. If Jack Zehringer fails to leave the promised bequest, appellant may bring a cause of action against his estate to enforce the antenuptial agreement. If he makes the promised bequest but there are insufficient assets in the estate to satisfy it, this unfolds a risk appellant assumed by agreeing to accept a specific bequest in lieu of her elective share. . . .

The trial court correctly granted respondent's motion for summary judgment. Appellant waived her right to claim an elective share and thereby waived any inchoate interest she might have in the mortgaged property. Affirmed.

QUESTIONS ABOUT CASE 6.1

1. What was the purpose of the antenuptial agreement?

2. Why was Phyllis seeking to have the agreement set aside? Note that her husband Jack was alive at the time of this lawsuit.

● Transfer of Property by Using a Trust

Nature and Purpose of a Trust

A **trust** is an arrangement whereby a person (the **"settlor"**) transfers property called the "trust property" or the "res" to another (the "trustee") to manage for the benefit of one or more persons named as a "beneficiary" of the trust. The trustee, a fiduciary, owes a duty of strict loyalty to the beneficiaries. As a fiduciary, the trustee is required to manage the property solely in the interest of the beneficiaries, and to do so with the care and skill that a "man of ordinary prudence would use in dealing with his own property."[15] Ordinarily, the settlor and the trustee enter into a written "trust agreement" that states how the property is to be managed and when and to whom it is to be distributed. The trust agreement is made against the background of an extensive body of state law detailing the rights and duties of the parties, with special attention to the fiduciary duties of the trustee.

To facilitate management, the trustee takes title to the property in the trustee's own name. The trustee's title is called **legal title**. It is enforceable in a court of law for purposes of managing the trust property, but gives the trustee no beneficial interest in it. The trustee does, however, have a lien against the trust property for reasonable compensation in managing the property. The beneficiary has equitable title to the trust property. **Equitable title** is an ownership interest, enforceable in a court of equity, which confers upon the beneficiary a right to the profits and other benefits of ownership.

Assets initially placed in a trust, such as land, shares of stock, or money in a bank account, are *principal* (often called the "corpus" of the trust). Earnings such as rents from the land, dividends from the stock, and interest on the money in the bank account are *income*. The trust agreement entered into by the settlor and the trustee usually spells out in some detail how the income and principal are to be accumulated and distributed. For example, the trustee might be instructed to pay the income to one beneficiary for life and at the beneficiary's death to transfer the principal (the corpus) to another beneficiary. If the trust property is real estate, this disposition results in the familiar life estate to one beneficiary and the remainder in fee simple to the other. Because the remainderman is entitled to receive the realty in reasonably good condition, free of waste, the trustee must over the years allocate some reasonable portion of the gross income to the maintenance of the real estate. Thus, the "income beneficiary" is entitled only to net income, which is the gross income minus reasonable expenses, including the trustee's compensation.

Creation of a Trust

Trusts can be created in several ways.

1. A declaration by the owner of property (settlor) that he or she holds it in trust for another person. The settlor becomes the trustee and owes fiduciary obligations to the beneficiary. In most states, if the property is personalty, a trust established by declaration can be oral.

2. An inter vivos transfer of property by its owner to a trustee for the benefit of a third person. Transfer of the personalty to the trust requires an actual or constructive delivery to the trustee. Intangible property such as bank accounts and shares of stock must be registered in the name of the trustee. If the trust property is land, the settlor must execute an instrument stating that title to the land is being conveyed to the trustee, though physical delivery of a deed usually is not required.

3. A transfer of property by the owner's will to a trustee for the benefit of a third person.

The settlor can be the trustee. Where another person is trustee, the settlor can be a beneficiary of the trust, or even the sole beneficiary. And, while a sole trustee cannot be the sole beneficiary, the trustee can be one of several beneficiaries.

A trust created by will is "testamentary" because it takes effect only at the death of the settlor. Because the trust beneficiary receives equitable title only at the death of the settlor, the property involved is subject to probate as part of the settlor's estate. In contrast, if the trust is inter vivos, the beneficiary acquires equitable title while the settlor is alive and at the settlor's death takes the interest free from probate. Sam transfers Blackacre to Tom as trustee with instructions to pay Sam the income from Blackacre for Sam's life, and at Sam's death to convey the legal title to Sam's cousin Bertha. In effect, Sam has carved out a life estate for himself and has presently given Bertha an equitable remainder in fee simple. Sam's death will simply trigger her right of exclusive possession and the duty of Tom to convey his legal title to Bertha to complete her ownership. Even if Sam retains a power to revoke the trust, but dies without exercising the power, Bertha's remainder, having passed to her when Sam created the trust, is not subject to probate.

Acquisition by Adverse Possession

A trespasser may acquire ownership of another person's land by **adverse possession**, that is, by wrongfully occupying it for the period required by law while engaging in conduct likely to notify the landowner that the trespass is occurring. The trespasser acquires title if the victim of the trespass, knowing or having reason to know of it, fails to take preventive action within the time permitted by the state's statute of limitations. In most states, the period is 20 or 15 years, but in a few it is much shorter: seven years or, as in Montana and California, five years. A landowner can stop adverse possession by bringing a timely lawsuit in *trespass* (for damages or an injunction) or in *ejectment* (to have a wrongful possessor removed from the premises). Sometimes the landowner can use self-help instead of a lawsuit to stop the trespass, for example, by erecting a fence or a barrier to prevent the trespasser from occupying the land.

The doctrine of adverse possession provides a basis for resolving boundary and other ownership disputes, often long after the deaths of the people originally involved. Allowing a person to acquire title by adverse possession also rewards those who keep the land productive and protects those such as subsequent purchasers of the land who rely on the adverse possessor's apparent ownership. The successful adverse possessor does not merely take over the title of the former owner, but instead acquires an "original" title that begins a new chain of ownership.

Requirements for Adverse Possession

The requirements for acquiring title by adverse possession are similar to those discussed in Chapter 4 for establishing a prescriptive easement. The trespasser's possession must be (1) actual, (2) visible, open, and notorious, (3) hostile, (4) continuous and uninterrupted for the statutory period, and (5) exclusive. In a few states, the trespasser must also (6) pay the taxes on the property being adversely possessed. A brief description of these requirements follows:

Actual Possession; Constructive Possession Under Color of Title

Ordinarily, to acquire ownership by adverse possession, a trespasser must physically occupy the land in a way that an owner would, given the nature of the land and the uses commonly made of it. But the amount of land that the trespasser may eventually acquire is affected by whether the possession is *actual* or *constructive*. Tom, a trespasser, might simply tear down neighbor Ned's fence, brazenly claim Ned's farm as his own, and without any evidence of ownership begin farming a portion of it. Despite Tom's assertion that he owns all of Ned's farm, he actually possesses (and eventually can own) only the portion he cultivates, builds upon, encloses with a fence, or in some other way physically marks and uses as his own. If, however, Tom claims Ned's farm under "color of title" (sometimes referred to as a "claim of right," meaning a "claim of rightful occupation"), a court is likely to hold that he has *constructive* possession of the *whole* farm even though he is physically occupying only a part of it. Tom would have "color of title" if, for example, he had received a deed that is void because of a forged signature in the chain of title. The forged deed does not give Tom any ownership rights, but because he has a document that purports to make him owner, his claim of title is "colorable" (believable), and he is considered to possess all the land described in the deed even though he might not physically possess it all.

In a number of states, a person adversely possessing under "color of title" or who is paying the property taxes, is subject to a shorter statute of limitations period than other adverse possessors in the same state (e.g., seven years instead of the 20 required of other adverse possessors in the state).

Visible, Open, and Notorious Possession

Trespasser Tom's possession must be "visible, open, and notorious," that is, observable by a passerby and known or knowable by the public. Tom's open and notorious possession gives Ned notice of Tom's trespassing, regardless of whether Ned ever visits the land. If Ned is an absentee owner who fails to protect his interests by inspecting his land from time to time, he risks losing it to the person openly using it.

Hostile Possession

To be "hostile" or "adverse," Tom's possession must be contrary to Ned's ownership rights and must be done without his permission or consent. In essence, Tom must be asserting that he is the owner of Ned's land and that Ned is not the owner. No personal malice or threat of physical violence is required for this kind of hostility. If Tom's possession would give Ned a cause of action in trespass or ejectment, it is sufficiently hostile. But if Ned *permits* Tom to possess the land, for example, as a tenant, licensee, or easement holder, Tom's possession is permissive, not hostile. In such circumstances, Tom's possession is not a trespass and cannot result in ownership.

  Most courts find the required hostility if the trespasser merely occupies the land without permission, even if the occupation was by innocent mistake. But some courts, erroneously in the view of many legal experts,[16] deny the trespasser's claim of adverse possession if the trespass was by mistake, as where Tom intends to build a fence on the boundary between his land and Harrison's but locates it on Harrison's land fifteen feet beyond the true boundary. In those courts, if Tom testifies that he did not intend to take land that was not his, he will lose his claim of adverse possession for lack of the requisite hostility. He probably would win even in those courts, however, by testifying that he knew he was occupying Harrison's land and intended to take it as his own. As noted in Chapter 5, a cotenant's sole possession of land is presumed to be rightful, but the cotenant in possession can adversely possess the property by ousting the other cotenants.

Continuous Possession for the Statutory Period

The adverse possession must be continuous throughout the statutory period, but certain breaks in the trespasser's possession will not negate adverse possession. The trespasser could, for example, leave the land temporarily for normal purposes such as a trip to town or even a vacation without losing the continuity needed for adverse possession. The same is true where land is suitable only for seasonal use. Winter snowfalls on a mountain pasture closes it until the spring or summer. A trespasser who over the years uses the pasture in the same way that the owner would preserves the continuity needed for adverse possession. But a substantial interruption of use, for example, skipping a season of pasture usage, would cause the statutory period to begin anew.

  As with prescriptive easements, the law of adverse possession permits tacking of short periods of trespass together into one long enough to make up the statutory period, provided that a sufficient relationship exists between the successive trespassers. For example, two years after mistakenly locating his boundary fence on Harrison's land, Tom sells his land to Hortense. She can tack her period of trespass onto Tom's because she is the buyer of Tom's land.

Exclusive Possession

The trespasser's possession must be exclusive, that is, not shared with the owner. When Tom trespassed by building his boundary fence on Harrison's land, Tom was in exclusive possession of the strip of land between the fence and Tom's boundary. Trespassing cotenants, however, can share possession without negating its adverse quality. If Tom and his sister Marsha own the land next to Harrison's as cotenants, they are co-adverse possessors who will hold title to the strip as tenants in common if they meet the requirements for adverse possession.

Payment of Taxes

In a number of states, usually those having a short statute of limitations period, the trespasser must pay the annual property taxes assessed against the land to acquire it by adverse possession.[17] This requirement often prevents trespassers from acquiring title. In many instances, the trespasser's offer of payment will be refused by the tax assessor because title is held in a name other than that of the trespasser or because the taxes have already been paid by the owner. Payment by the owner is routine where the trespasser's claim is based on a mistakenly located boundary fence, because the owner's tax parcel description is not affected by the mistaken location. Failure to pay the taxes defeats the trespasser's claim of ownership, but in at least one state requiring payment of taxes, California, a trespasser who meets the other requirements for adverse possession can acquire a prescriptive easement. A cotenant in sole possession normally does pay the taxes, but to acquire title by adverse possession must oust the other cotenants.

Limitations on Adverse Possession; Marketable Title Problem

Some interests in land cannot be acquired by adverse possession. For example, only *possessory* interests can be taken by adverse possession. Ella has a life estate in Blackacre, and Jonas has the remainder in fee simple. Kurt, a trespasser, moves into Blackacre and meets all the requirements for adverse possession. He acquires the balance of Ella's life estate (and now has a life estate *pur autre vie*), but does not acquire Jonas's remainder in fee simple because it is not a possessory interest.

The state and federal governments own vast amounts of land, administered by great numbers of agencies. Often government employees do not know precisely what land the agency or the government owns, and the governments' vast holdings make adequate monitoring against adverse possession virtually impossible. For this and other reasons, most government land is protected by statute against adverse possession. A federal statute prohibits adverse possession of land owned by the United States. Many states have statutes exempting state lands from adverse possession. In a number of states without such statutes, the courts apply the common law rule that time does not run against the state.

Even so, considerable amounts of state and local land *can* be taken by adverse possession because a number of states have waived some of their immunity.[18] For example, although most or all states prohibit adverse possession of land held for public use such as a park, some permit adverse possession of land held by the state for a proprietary or commercial purpose. A few states, such as Kentucky and West Virginia, allow about the same degree of adverse possession of public lands as is allowed against private lands.

Like the prescriptive easement discussed in Chapter 4, title acquired by adverse possession results from trespassory conduct and is not evidenced by any deed or contract of sale. The lack of written evidence and related notice to prospective purchasers can make the adverse possessor's title unmarketable. By adverse possession, Tom acquires the strip of Harrison's land lying between the mistakenly located boundary fence and the true boundary. Tom then contracts to sell his land, including the strip, to Myrtle. Because of the potential for litigation with Harrison or his successors over the strip, Tom's title is not marketable and Myrtle may rescind the contract.

Case 6.2 involves cotenants and a claim of adverse possession.

Case 6.2

Wright v. Wright
512 S.E.2d 618 (Ga. 1999)

In 1940, H. L. Wright, Sr. ("Harve") and his eldest son H. L. Wright, Jr. ("Aitchey") acquired a 429.5-acre farm as tenants in common. The deed to the farm was in the names of Harve and Aitchey. Harve died two years later, survived by his wife, Leila, three adult sons (including Aitchey), and three minor children. The probate court awarded Harve's one-half interest in the farm to Leila and the minor children as their year's support.

Beginning in 1941, the farm was listed with the tax assessor exclusively in Aitchey's name, he received the benefit of the homestead exemption, and his wife Lorene paid the tax bills. By 1944, Aitchey and Lorene had paid off the entire mortgage. By 1950, the youngest of Aitchey's siblings had attained the age of majority; and Leila and all of her children had left the farm.

By deed recorded in 1962, Aitchey conveyed fee simple title to 8.623 acres of the farm to Jackson County, warranting that he had the right to sell and convey the land. At the same time, he conveyed a right-of-way easement for construction of a roadway. Later, Aitchey granted four flowage easements for dam and reservoir construction. He never sought permission from his siblings before making any of these conveyances.

Aitchey was overbearing and tyrannical, and there was ill will between himself and his siblings over ownership of the farm. One sibling testified that he knew from the time the property was purchased that Harve and his heirs had a half-interest in the farm, but he never discussed the issue of ownership with Aitchey. Others opined that Aitchey probably would have "killed them" or "run them off" if they had asserted a claim of ownership. In the early 1970s Aitchey's siblings heard rumors that "somebody was messing with the deeds," and as a result conducted their own title investigation, which confirmed that Harve and Aitchey jointly owned the property. But they were afraid to confront Aitchey with the information because of his tyrannical nature, believing that eventually (upon Aitchey's death) "everything would be settled."

Lorene testified that the siblings always referred to the property as "Aitchey's farm"; they knew Aitchey claimed sole ownership and they never asserted a contrary claim. The evidence showed that Aitchey worked the land day and night and made substantial improvements.

Sometime after Aitchey's death, Lorene and their children requsted that Harve's heirs execute quitclaim deeds conveying the property to Aitchey's estate. When they refused, Lorene and the children, as representatives of his estate, filed an action to quiet title on the theory that the estate had acquired title to the property by adverse possession.

At the close of plaintiffs' evidence, defendants (Harve's heirs) moved for directed verdict. The trial court denied the motion. The jury returned a verdict awarding the entire property to the plaintiffs (Lorene and the children) on the theory of adverse possession. Harve's heirs appealed, alleging that the verdict was not supported by the evidence.

THOMPSON, J.

There is no dispute that the parties jointly acquired the property as tenants in common. First, the 1940 warranty deed created a tenancy in common between father and son. And the . . . award of a year's support to Leila Wright and her . . . minor children vested them with a one-half undivided interest as tenants in common with Aitchey. When property is set apart for a widow and her minor children as an award of a year's support, they receive the title that the deceased held.

A party who asserts a claim of title by adverse possession against a cotenant has the burden of proving not only the usual elements of prescription, but also at least one of the elements of [a Georgia statute] which provides as follows: "There may be no adverse possession against a cotenant until the adverse possessor effects an actual ouster, retains exclusive possession after demand, or gives his cotenant express notice of adverse possession."

Although a presumption exists that a cotenant in exclusive possession is not holding adversely to his cotenants, but [instead] for the common benefit of the others, this presumption may be rebutted where the contrary appears. And while exclusive possession, payment of taxes, and the making of improvements alone do not necessarily establish an ouster, a conclusion of prescriptive title may be drawn where "'there have been unequivocal acts, such as . . . selling, [or] leasing . . . the premises, or a part of them.'" In addition, a cotenant in possession may satisfy the "express notice" criterion by showing either: (1) that actual notice of the adverse party was "brought home" to the nonpossessory cotenant; or (2) that there are "unequivocal acts, open and public, making the possession so visible, hostile, exclusive, and notorious that notice may fairly be presumed."

We conclude that the court properly denied the motion for directed verdict, and the evidence of record was sufficient to allow the jury to find that plaintiffs met their burden of establishing title by [adverse possession] against defendant cotenants. First, there was evidence that plaintiffs lawfully acquired the property in 1940, and exclusively and continuously occupied the farm since 1950, making valuable permanent improvements. Major dams and lakes were constructed after the flowage easements were granted. Express notice of adverse possession from one cotenant was "brought home" to the others in 1962, when by recorded deed, Aitchey purported to convey a "fee simple" interest in a portion of the land to a stranger, and by actual and notorious possession by the purchaser. A conveyance by one cotenant of a fee simple interest to a stranger in the commonly-held property is one of those exceptional state[s] of facts as may constitute an ouster. Moreover, plaintiffs offered direct evidence that the cotenant siblings knew of the hostile character of Aitchey's possession, but feared to confront him with their claim of one-half ownership. These statements are sufficient evidence for the jury to conclude that Aitchey's claim of ownership was brought home to his nonpossessory cotenants, or in the least, that notice to them may be fairly presumed.

The evidence of record . . . was sufficient to create issues of fact for determination by the jury. The jury resolved those issues in favor of the plaintiffs, and the evidence amply supports the verdict rendered.

Judgment affirmed.

QUESTIONS ABOUT CASE 6.2

1. In 1943, Harve's widow and children received his one-half interest in the 429.5-acre farm as the year's support to which they were entitled under Georgia law. Isn't that a large amount for a year's support? Is it significant that the 1940 purchase price was $2,000 and that they might have needed to sell the interest to maintain themselves?

2. One commentator believes that the court in this case erred in holding that Aitchey's sale of the 8.623-acre parcel was evidence of his adverse possession. Why would a sole possessor's sale or lease of jointly held property not be, in itself, evidence of adverse possession?

Acquisition by Government: Condemnation and Dedication

Federal, state, and local governments can acquire real estate in all the ways that a private person can, including adverse possession. They can acquire realty in two additional ways: by condemnation and by dedication.

The government's power of eminent domain enables it to take private property for a public use upon payment of a "just compensation." Condemnation is the exercise of that power by a government, by a government agency, or by a person or entity such as a utility company to whom the power has been delegated. Condemnation is discussed in Chapter 16. Dedication occurs when an owner transfers an interest in land to the public for its use. The dedicated interest can be a fee simple estate or a lesser interest such as an easement. Many dedications are purely voluntary gifts to the community. Other dedications are compelled by the government, for example, those required of developers as a condition for receiving a building permit. Dedication is discussed in Chapter 4 under the heading *Creation by Dedication*.

Self-Study Questions

1. What parties and documents are involved in the process of selling land? What is the purpose of escrows and similar arrangements?

2. Is a down payment required in a contract for the sale of land? If a buyer makes a down payment and breaches the contract before closing, is the seller entitled to keep the down payment?

3. (a) What is the "marketable title requirement?" (b) Are "time is of the essence" clauses enforceable?

4. (a) What kinds of problems are commonly resolved by applying the concept of equitable conversion? (b) If the real estate is destroyed or damaged before closing, who bears the loss?

5. (a) What is the difference between an option and a preemptive right? (b) How does a "gift inter vivos" differ from a "gift causa mortis"? (c) How could a deed be used as a will substitute? Is such a use advisable?

6. (a) What does "probate" mean? (b) How may probate be avoided? (c) Is avoiding probate a good idea? Why?

7. (a) Explain generally how a decedent's estate is distributed under an intestacy statute. (b) What is the difference between a "per capita" and a "per stirpes" distribution?

8. (a) For the purposes of making a will, what is testamentary capacity? (b) What formalities are required for a will? (c) Describe some limits on a person's right to dispose of property by a will.

9. (a) What is the main purpose of a trust? (b) What is the role of "legal" and "equitable" title?

10. What are the general requirements for acquiring ownership of real estate by adverse possession?

Case Problems

1. Krotz contracted to sell three adjoining parcels of land to Sattler. Title problems surrounding the smallest parcel, an abandoned railroad right-of-way, made swift closing on that piece impossible. But conveyance of the two other parcels by warranty deed took place on December 30, 1986, eighteen months after the parties entered into the contract of sale. Five years later Krotz learned that Sattler was installing a sanitary sewer line across the railroad property to connect with an adjoining real estate development. Alleging that Sattler did not own the railroad parcel, Krotz brought suit to quiet title. Sattler answered by claiming title. There having been no mutual intent to convey the railroad property in 1986, and given the years that had passed since the parties executed their agreement, the trial court held that Krotz was entitled to retain the property free of any claim by Sattler. Sattler appealed. The statute of limitations period for the real estate contract had not expired. Krotz would win the quiet title action only if Sattler had no interest in the parcel. Did Sattler have an interest in the railroad parcel? *Krotz v. Sattler*, 586 N.W.2d 336 (Iowa, 1998).

2. McDuck dies, survived by his friend Darlene and his son Donald. In McDuck's desk drawer is a deed signed by McDuck granting his ancestral home Blackacre to Donald. Typed on the envelope is the message, "For my son Donald upon my death." McDuck's valid will leaves Blackacre to his friend Darlene. Who is entitled to Blackacre?

3. Elizabeth, a resident of Ohio and a widow, has an estate worth $2 million. Her will leaves the entire estate to her friend Buckingham. Elizabeth dies, survived by a daughter Marlene, the three children of her son Norman who died five years earlier, and a first cousin Roger. Buckingham died three months before Elizabeth. Who is entitled to Elizabeth's estate?

4. Andrew, a resident of State A, owns two farms, one in State A and one in State B. He also owns two Rolls Royces. One is registered in State A and garaged on the farm there. The other is registered in State B and is garaged on the farm in State B. Andrew has only two relatives—brother Bill and son Sam. Andrew's will leaves both farms to Bill, and both Rolls Royces to Sam. The law of State A requires that two persons witness a testator's signature and sign in the presence of the testator and each other, but does not require that the witnesses' signatures be notarized. The law of State B has the same requirement for witnesses' signatures and, in addition, their signatures must be notarized. The witnesses to Andrew's will signed in the presence of the testator and each other, but the signatures were not notarized. Andrew dies, survived by Bill and Sam. Neither state has a statute accepting the will formalities of other states. (a) Who is entitled to the farms? (b) Who is entitled to the Rolls Royces?

5. To avoid probate, Warner, an unmarried man, made the following transfers of his property: Five years ago, 300 acres of land worth $1.5 million to himself in joint tenancy with his niece Alma; four years ago, $1.5 million to a revocable inter vivos trust for the benefit of his nephew Albert; and two years ago, $50,000 to an irrevocable inter vivos trust for the benefit of his business partner Harold. Warner died last week. What amounts, if any, should be included in Warner's gross estate for estate tax purposes?

6. Jennifer transfers her 100-unit apartment complex to Ralph in trust for the benefit of her older sister Alice and Jennifer's minor son Donald. Alice is to receive the income for life, and Donald the remainder in fee simple. Tenants pay $500 per month for their apartments which, with a vacancy rate of about 10%, produce a rental income averaging about $45,000 per month. Ralph pays Alice the amount of the rental receipts each month. Donald objects, alleging that Ralph has violated his fiduciary duty. Has Ralph acted improperly as trustee?

Endnotes

1. John E. Cribbet, *Law of Property* (The Foundation Press, Inc., 1975), at 152.

2. California, Hawaii, Illinois, Louisiana, Michigan, New York, North Carolina, Oklahoma, Oregon, South Dakota, and Wisconsin.

3. Cribbet, *supra* note 2, at 155 (quoting from an article by Milton R. Friedman of the New York Bar).

4. Probably better known are the statute of frauds provisions requiring that certain kinds of *contracts* be evidenced by a writing to be enforced, including a contract for the sale of an interest in land. However, the original Statute of Frauds enacted by Parliament in 1676 had provisions requiring other kinds of transactions to be evidenced by a writing, including any *conveyance* of an interest in land, whether as a part of a sale or as a gift. In the United States, the Statute of Frauds writing requirement for conveyances has usually been incorporated into the state's Statute of Deeds.

5. Cal. Prob. Code § 32 (Deering, 2000).

6. In the past, an intestate decedent's realty passed to certain survivors, while the personalty passed to others. The term *heir* was limited to those taking the realty, while those receiving personalty were called "next of kin" or "distributees." In most states today, both types of property pass in the same shares to the same person or persons. Today, therefore, the term *heir* commonly refers to takers of either personalty or realty. Paul G. Haskell, *Preface to Wills, Trusts and Administration* (The Foundation Press, Inc., 1987), p. 1.

7. The following states have adopted the UPC in its entirety, though sometimes with significant modifications: Alaska, Arizona, Colorado, Florida, Hawaii, Idaho, Maine, Michigan, Minnesota, Montana, Nebraska, New Mexico, North Dakota, South Carolina, South Dakota, and Utah. Several other states have adopted the UPC in an incomplete form. Uniform Probate Code Locator, available at www.law.cornell.edu/uniform/probate.html.

8. In California, for example, whether by intestacy or by will, a surviving spouse receives the decedent's share of the community property and some or all of the separate property, "and no administration is necessary," though the spouse may elect administration as a protection against claims of creditors. Cal. Prob. Code §§ 13500, 13502, 13553 (Deering, 2001).

9. The states are Connecticut, Indiana, Iowa, Kentucky, Louisiana, Maryland, Montana, Nebraska, New Hampshire, New Jersey, Ohio (estate tax), Oklahoma (estate tax), South Dakota, and Tennessee.

10. K.S.A. § 59-513 (1999).

11. Tex. Prob. Code § 41 (2000).

12. Burns Ind. Code Ann. §§ 29-1-2-14, -15 (2000).

13. Under the civil law of Louisiana, a decedent may not disinherit his or her child who is under the age of 24. The child, called a "forced heir," is entitled to one-fourth of the decedent's estate; two or more are entitled to one-half. There is no age limit if at the time of the decedent's death the child is permanently incapable because of mental incapacity or physical infirmity of taking care of his or her person or administering his or her estate. La. Civ. Code §§ 1493, 1495.

14. O.C.G.A § 53-4-1 (2000).

15. Austin Wakeman Scott, *Abridgement of the Law of Trusts* (Little, Brown and Company, 1960), § 174.

16. Roger A. Cunningham, William B. Stoebuck, & Dale A. Whitman, *The Law of Property* (West Publishing Co., 1993), p. 812.

17. E.g., California, Idaho, Minnesota, Montana, Nevada, and Utah.

18. Paula R. Latovick, *Adverse Possession Against the States: The Hornbooks Have It Wrong*, 29 U. Mich. J.L. Ref. 939, 946 (1996).

Part II — The Real Estate Sales Transaction

Chapter 7

Locating a Ready, Able, and Willing Buyer: Role of Real Estate Brokers

The purchase and sale of real estate is an expensive, time-consuming, and complicated legal transaction. For the seller, the first step in the sale process is to market the real estate to prospective purchasers and to locate a buyer who is willing and financially able to purchase on terms acceptable to the seller. Although owners can and sometimes do sell property on their own without the assistance of an agent, most employ the services of a **real estate broker** whose job it is to promote the sale of the property, find a willing buyer, negotiate the terms of the sale, and secure a written purchase agreement with the buyer. Brokers also provide assistance and guidance to the parties on other aspects of the transaction and ensure that the transaction is completed in a timely manner. Thus, brokers perform an important function in the real estate marketplace, and because of the professional nature of that role, brokers are subject to legal liabilities and regulatory controls to protect the public interest. This chapter will discuss real estate brokers, including the changing nature of the brokerage relationship, the duties brokers owe to sellers and buyers in a real estate transaction, and the regulation of the brokerage industry. Subsequent chapters in Part III will discuss other stages in real estate transactions and related legal issues.

The Changing Nature of the Brokerage Relationship

The relationship between brokers and the parties to a real estate transaction has changed significantly in recent years as the brokerage industry and the legal system have adapted to changes in the real estate marketplace. Traditionally, a real estate broker acted as an agent for the seller and represented only the seller's interests in the sales transaction. Today, sellers and buyers have a host of alternative brokerage relationships under which a broker can act in different capacities, including as the buyer's agent, as an intermediary with limited duties to either party, and as a dual agent for both parties.

The Traditional Brokerage Relationship

The traditional relationship between a seller of property and the broker with whom the seller listed the property for sale was based on **agency** law. An **agent** is a person who is authorized to act on behalf of an employer, called the **principal**, in negotiating and entering into transactions for the principal. Because the principal authorizes the agent to act on his or her behalf, the agent is a fiduciary who owes the principal strict duties of loyalty and good faith in the conduct of the relationship. This fiduciary duty requires the agent to place the principal's interests first, above the agent's own personal interests and above the interests of any third party. The fiduciary duty includes obligations to keep the principal informed of material information, to exercise due care in the agency work, and to account for any property and monies of the principal.

When an owner of property signs a **listing agreement** employing a real estate broker to handle the sale of his property, the seller is appointing the broker as his agent in the real estate sale. As the seller's agent, the **listing broker** has the authority to advertise the sale of the property, contact prospective purchasers, show the property to potential buyers, and employ other means to market the property. The broker's responsibility is to find a buyer who is financially able and willing to purchase on the seller's terms. A broker who finds such a buyer earns the compensation agreed to in the listing agreement, which is usually a commission based on a percentage of the purchase price.

Most listing agreements authorize the listing broker to work with other brokers, called **cooperating brokers**, to find a buyer for the property, frequently by listing the property with a local *multiple listing service (MLS).* A multiple listing service is an organization of local brokers who agree to pool their listings. MLS members are given the opportunity to find a buyer for any listed property and share in the commission on the sale. If a member broker other than the listing broker finds a buyer, this broker (called the **selling broker**) splits the commission with the listing broker (often on a 50/50 basis).

By listing the property with the MLS, the listing broker offers a *subagency* arrangement to MLS-member brokers. A subagent is appointed by an agent to assist the agent in the authorized transaction and to act on behalf of the principal. Under the MLS system, a selling broker is usually a subagent of the listing broker. The cooperating broker has strict agency duties to the seller even if the broker was first contacted by a buyer looking for property to purchase, which is often the case. Neither the listing broker nor the selling broker are agents of the buyer and neither owes agency duties to the buyer. Thus, the selling broker has no duty to inform the buyer of facts that might be important to the buyer's decision to purchase nor to give the buyer advice as to the terms of the contract, including price. In fact, a selling broker breaches his duty of loyalty to the seller if he conveys confidential information to the buyer, such as the price at which the seller is willing to sell. Moreover, the selling agent is under a duty to communicate all material information to the seller, which includes confidential information obtained from the buyer on the buyer's willingness to negotiate or the price at which the buyer is willing to purchase.

The selling broker's legal status as a subagent of the seller is inconsistent with the actual relationship that often develops between selling agent and buyer. It also runs counter to the expectations of the consuming public. A Federal Trade Commission study in 1983 found that 72% of home buyers believed that the selling brokers who helped them find their homes represented them in their purchase transactions, not the sellers. This misperception of the legal realities of the traditional brokerage relationship is understandable given the personal and professional relationships that develop between buyers and brokers. In the typical home sale, a person will contact a broker to locate an affordable home that fulfills the buyer's needs. The broker will frequently give the buyer advice about neighborhoods, types of properties, prices of properties that have recently sold, and other relevant market information. Brokers will identify suitable homes and then personally show them to the buyer. Throughout the process, the broker will work closely with the buyer and provide assistance and guidance. As a result, a relationship of trust and friendship develops, with the buyer relying on the broker's knowledge and expertise in making negotiating and purchasing decisions.

Not only do these actions create a situation that is potentially detrimental to buyers who don't understand the true relationship between the broker and the seller, but it also creates a "dual agency" trap for brokers. Dual agency, representing both sides in a real estate sale, is usually a breach of the broker's duty of loyalty. It creates an inherent conflict of interest because of the conflicting loyalties to seller and buyer. As an agent for the seller, a broker wants to secure the highest price with the fewest conditions to a sale. In contrast, an agent for a buyer wants the lowest price on the most favorable terms possible. Therefore, brokers can act as a dual agent only with the informed consent of both parties after full disclosure of the risks involved. The "dual agency" dilemma for the selling broker is twofold. First, Sam, a selling broker who acts in the best interests of the buyer in the transaction to the detriment of the seller's interests, may be acting as a dual agent (without consent) and breaching his fiduciary duty to the seller. If he breaches his fiduciary duty, he forfeits his commission on the sale and is liable for damages to the seller. Second, buyers have sometimes claimed that an implied agency was created by the actions of the selling broker toward the buyer. In contrast to an express agency that is created by words, written or spoken, an implied agency arises by nonverbal conduct. If an implied agency relationship exists between the selling broker and the buyer, actions of the broker that are consistent with the broker's traditional duty to the seller, such as providing information on the buyer's negotiating position, are a breach of any obligation the broker owes to the buyer. Such a breach can form the basis for a legal suit by the buyer against the broker and a complaint against the broker for unprofessional conduct.

Alternative Brokerage Arrangements

The conflicting roles of the selling agent under the traditional approach to the seller/broker relationship, and the problems for buyers and brokers created by it, were the impetus for changes in the brokerage industry. The profession, through its national organization, the NATIONAL ASSOCIATION OF REALTORS®,[1] supported a number of changes to improve the role of brokers in real estate transactions, and to provide alternatives to the traditional agency/subagency approach. In part, these changes were designed to protect the profession from legal liability, but they also were responsive to the needs of the consuming public in the real estate market. The two most important developments have been mandatory disclosure laws and brokerage relationship statutes. The disclosure laws that have been adopted in all states require brokers to disclose the nature of their relationship to their clients, usually through a standard disclosure form that is given to their clients. The disclosure form identifies for whom the broker acts as an agent and the duties the broker owes to the client. The second major change has been the development of brokerage relationship laws that define alternative types of brokerage contracts and the duties brokers owe to the parties under such relationships. These laws have helped facilitate the practice of brokers acting as buyer's agents, transaction brokers, and as designated agents.

Buyer's Agents

One obvious alternative model is for the selling broker to act not as a subagent of the seller but as the **buyer's agent**. This role matches the expectations of the buyer and the professional relationship that is often established between selling brokers and buyers. Increasingly, brokers are acting as buyer's agents in real estate transactions, and both buyers and brokers are finding this brokerage relationship to be beneficial. Brokers representing buyers have formed new professional associations, such as the Real Estate Buyers Agent Council (REBAC) of the NATIONAL ASSOCIATION OF REALTORS® and the National Association of Exclusive Buyer Agents, and these associations have developed ethical and professional standards for buyer's agents. Some brokers do not accept listings from sellers and work only for buyers, operating as so-called "exclusive buyer's agents." Part of the reason that buyer brokering has become so popular was a change in MLS rules. In 1993, the NATIONAL ASSOCIATION OF REALTORS® changed its MLS policy mandating subagency and allowed compensation to MLS members as subagents or as buyer's agents. This change allowed a buyer's broker to be paid from the commission on the sale, just as the traditional selling agent would be paid. A small number of states also have passed laws providing that in the absence of any agreement between a broker and the client, the broker is presumed to be acting as the buyer's agent in the transaction, a reversal of the traditional subagency presumption.[2]

Transaction Brokers

Transaction brokers (also called facilitators, intermediaries, limited agents, and independent contractors) are specifically authorized in 22 states and the District of Columbia[3] and may be permitted in other states. A transaction broker acts to facilitate the sale between a buyer and seller but does not represent either party as an agent. He or she functions as a mere intermediary to bring the parties together with limited legal duties to either one. The transaction broker is under statutory obligations, which usually include a duty to exercise due care in the conduct of the brokerage relationship and to deal openly and honestly with both parties. In some states that allow the transaction broker arrangement, disclosed and undisclosed dual agency are prohibited. As a transaction broker, the agent can handle the transaction for both parties without acting as a dual agent and hopefully without the problems associated with it.

Designated Agency

The transaction broker concept has not been embraced by the profession as well as buyer brokering, in part because a 1993 study commissioned by the NATIONAL ASSOCIATION OF REALTORS® recommended that the profession not promote the facilitator concept. The profession seems to be moving quickly, however, to adopt the most recent innovation in brokerage relationships, called **designated agency**. Traditionally, a brokerage firm and the licensed persons working for the firm were considered one and the same for purposes of dual agency. The firm could not, therefore, represent both the seller and buyer without potential dual agency problems even if different members of the firm represented the parties. Twenty states and the District of Columbia have now abandoned this position and allow dual representation of seller and buyer under designated agency.[4] Designated agency involves the manager of a brokerage firm, ordinarily the broker in charge, appointing one licensed member of the firm to represent the seller and another member to represent the buyer. The designated agents owe strict fiduciary duties to their respective clients. Many brokers consider designated agency superior to the transaction broker approach because the designated agents can act in a traditional agency role for their clients. However, it raises a host of thorny logistical and practical issues for firms who must at a minimum establish detailed policies and procedures governing the practice to ensure compliance with the law. Also, because it is a form of dual agency, legal issues relating to the agents' duties of loyalty will invariably occur in this setting. Nevertheless, designated agency may become a preferred form of brokerage relationship in the future.

Given the alternative brokerage relationships that can exist under modern real estate practice, it has become increasingly important for brokers to define the nature of their relationship with their clients at the beginning of that relationship. The following case demonstrates the need to clarify the relationship between the broker and the buyer and illustrates the heightened duties a broker owes to the buyer when acting as the buyer's agent in the transaction.

Case 7.1

Lewis v. Long and Foster Realty, Inc.
584 A.2d 1325 (Md. App. 1991)

In 1986, Lynne Lewis and James Lewis lived in a rented home in Howard County. Mrs. Lewis, a licensed family day care provider, operated a day care business in their residence. In April 1986, they sought assistance from Blaine Milner in locating a residence for sale in the Columbia, Maryland, area. Milner is an employee and licensed sales broker of Long and Foster. They informed Milner that Mrs. Lewis wished to continue operating her day care business and that they required a residence suitable for that purpose.

Milner showed them property in the Merion Station Townhouse complex of Harper's Choice Village in Columbia. Milner made inquiries concerning the operation of day care in the area, and relayed the information he obtained. Specifically, Milner told them Mrs. Lewis would need only to obtain a permit from the Harper's Choice Village for in-house business-related activities. The Lewises decided to purchase the property, with no indication made in the record or any claim by the broker that a contingency clause was placed in the contract.

The Lewises refurbished and remodeled their property to accommodate Mrs. Lewis' day care business. She obtained approval from the Village Board to operate her business and began caring for children on a daily basis in November 1986. On March 20, 1987, Mrs. Lewis received a letter from the Merion Station Homeowners' Association informing her that the Association considered the use of the residence for a day care business to be in violation of restrictions in the subdivision. The Restrictions and Declaration of record that affect the property include a Declaration that states "No dwelling or any part thereof shall be used for any purpose except as a private dwelling for one family, nor any business of any kind be conducted therein."

It is undisputed that Milner failed to tell the Lewises about this restriction at or prior to the settlement on their property. The Lewises brought suit against Milner, Long & Foster, and the case was dismissed before trial. The Lewises appealed the dismissal.

WEANT, J.

The [Lewises] first contend that a real estate broker owes a duty of care to the buyer whom he or she represents, and that, under a broker's duty, he is required to investigate restrictions on property which would affect a buyer's known use of that property. [They] maintain that the Maryland legislature has imposed a tort duty on real estate brokers through statute and regulation. They direct us to the Maryland Business and Professions Annotated Code which lists grounds for . . . the suspension or revocation of a real estate broker's license. A broker's license may be in jeopardy if the broker intentionally or negligently fails to disclose to any person with whom the applicant or licensee deals a material fact that the licensee knows or should know and that relates to the property with which the licensee or applicant deals. Numerous jurisdictions have looked to published ethical standards and licensing requirements to determine a standard of care for real estate brokers.

It is well-settled in Maryland law that a real estate broker's liability is founded on the law of agency. This court, however, recognizes that a real estate broker cannot serve two masters. During the term of agency, a real estate broker cannot act for both vendor and vendee in respect of the same transaction because of possible conflict between his interest and his duty in such case.

Typically, a seller is the broker's client because it is the seller who pays the broker's commission. This puts the broker in a fiduciary relationship with the seller, which requires a higher degree of loyalty and good faith. The broker owes no fiduciary duty to the buyer whose interests are adverse to the seller.

[The Lewises] make no allegations that they paid an initial fee to hire Milner and Long & Foster. The customary practice in the real estate trade, however, does not require a buyer to pay a fee to engage a real estate broker's services. When a real estate broker locates a buyer for listed property, the listing agent and the buyer's agent divide the commission. The commission is a percentage of the purchase price that is paid by the buyer. When a buyer enlists the services of a real estate broker, there is an implicit understanding by all parties that the broker will receive a fee, via a commission, at the culmination of the sale. Even though a buyer's purchase money passes through several hands before reaching his broker's pocket, a buyer's broker clearly receives a fee from his client.

The question of whether an agency relationship has been created is one for the jury. In their brief, [the Lewises] claim that they can produce evidence which could prove an agency relationship. An oral agreement is sufficient in Maryland law to support the establishment of an agency relationship with a real estate broker. In the past, Maryland law has held that no agency relationship exists between a buyer and a real estate broker. In these cases, however, only one real estate broker represented both the seller and the buyer of property. [The Lewises] situation is factually distinguishable. Milner and Long & Foster did not have a relationship with the seller of the home [they] purchased. That home was listed by another broker. The question of whether [the Lewises] and Milner and/or Long & Foster entered into an agency relationship is one for the fact-finder.

A real estate broker has no duty to investigate and report on defects which might exist in the property. That duty changes, however, when the parties are not conducting an arm's-length transaction. When a relationship of trust and confidence exists or when specific questions are asked concerning some aspect of a transaction, a duty of disclosure can arise. Milner undertook the task of locating and investigating property that was suitable for [the Lewis] day care business. In doing so, he assumed the duty to provide accurate information to [them]. Whether he used reasonable care in the performance of this duty, is a question which should be answered by a fact-finder.

Reversed and remanded [for trial on the merits].

QUESTIONS ABOUT CASE 7.1

1. What could Milner and/or Long & Foster have done to ensure that the broker would not be considered the agent for the Lewises in the transaction? What should the Lewises have done to make sure that Milner was acting as their agent in the sale?

2. What duty should a broker owe to a buyer he represents to investigate or uncover facts that are material to the buyer's intended use of the property? Should the buyer assume some burden to determine whether the intended use of the property is lawful?

The Listing Agreement

The **listing agreement** is the contract under which the owner employs the real estate broker to act on his behalf in the sale of the owner's property. It gives the broker a "listing" on the property for a defined period of time and the right to market the real estate and promote its sale. In exchange for the broker's services, the owner agrees to pay the broker some form of compensation, usually a commission based on a percentage of the sale price. Whether the broker is entitled to a commission is determined by the terms and conditions of the listing agreement. The listing agreement *is* a contract that defines the rights and obligations of the parties. Thus, in disputes between the broker and his or her client, the courts will look to the contract terms as well as the duties imposed by law to resolve such matters. A carefully drafted listing agreement is essential, therefore, to protect not only the rights of the broker but also the interests of the property owner.

Necessity of a Writing

In many states, a listing agreement must be in writing to be enforceable.[5] In those states, a broker acting under an oral employment contract is not entitled to a commission or other compensation even if the broker finds a purchaser and a sale of the property is completed. This provides a strong incentive for brokers to get their listings in writing. The precise requirements for the written listing agreement depends upon state law. Most states require that the listing agreement be signed by the owner or an authorized agent. The statutes further require that the listing agreement contain the essential terms of the contract, including a description of the property, the period of the listing, and the amount of the commission.

Types of Listing Arrangements

The three commonly used types of listing agreements differ in terms of the owner's obligation to pay the listing broker a commission if the purchaser is produced by another broker or by the owner. The three types are the **open listing**, the **exclusive agency**, and the **exclusive right to sell**.

Under an open listing, the owner hires a broker on a nonexclusive basis. Therefore, the owner can employ other brokers or sell the property on his own. The owner agrees to pay the listing broker only if the broker is the **procuring cause** of the sale, that is, the broker finds a purchaser who is ready, able, and willing to purchase on the terms set forth in the listing. Open listings are used more often in commercial real estate sales than in residential property listings. An open listing is advantageous to an owner of property because the seller can avoid payment of a commission by selling the property through his or her own efforts. The seller also has the freedom to employ other brokers if the seller believes that the listing broker's efforts have been unsatisfactory. On the other hand, the listing broker may be unwilling to put the time and money into marketing the property under an open listing because of the risk of losing the commission. This type of listing may actually reduce the broker's efforts on behalf of the owner and the probability of locating a purchaser for the property.

Brokers and multiple listing services prefer exclusive agency or right to sell listings. Under an exclusive agency, the owner employs the listing broker as his or her exclusive agent. As the exclusive agent, the listing broker is entitled to a commission if the broker finds a ready, able, and willing buyer or the property is sold through the efforts of another broker. The owner can hire other brokers, but will have to pay two commissions on the sale in the event the selling broker is the procuring cause of the sale. Ordinarily, therefore, the owner would not do so, and any other broker selling the property would be a cooperating broker sharing the commission with the listing broker. The owner does reserve the right to sell the property himself, and the broker is not entitled to a commission in the event the owner is the procuring cause of the sale.

The exclusive right to sell is the listing most protective of brokers and is the most common form of listing agreement, particularly in residential listings. Under an exclusive right to sell, the broker is entitled to a commission on any sale of the property, whether the sale was procured by the listing broker, another broker, or the seller. This type of listing is advantageous to brokers because the listing broker is assured of the commission and can, therefore, devote maximum efforts to finding a willing buyer. Sellers also benefit in the sense that brokers will be more inclined to put the resources into promoting the sale of the property under an exclusive right to sell than under an open listing or exclusive agency.

Terms of Listing Agreements

Standard form listing agreements are often used in the brokerage industry. Brokers and sellers often "fill in the blanks" of the contract with relevant information on the listing. It is important, however, that the listing agreement and any related documentation on the property be carefully prepared and reviewed. Drafting is important to protect the interests of the parties and to avoid disputes that may arise concerning the sale of the property. Serious attention should be given to clauses in the agreement concerning the duration of the listing (including any extension clauses), the type of listing and any exclusions, the amount and computation of the broker's commission, the terms and conditions of the sale, and the authority of the broker.

Duration of the Listing

In many states, the listing agreement must specify an expiration date. If it fails to do so, the agreement is unenforceable and the broker loses any right to a commission on the sale of the property. Residential listings typically run from 90 to 180 days, owners naturally preferring shorter terms and brokers preferring longer ones. The listing term is important to brokers for several reasons. First, the listing broker needs sufficient time to market the property. Second, most listings are exclusive and are marketed through an MLS service under which the listing broker will share in the commission even if another broker is the selling broker. Thus, the broker who secures the listing has acquired a valuable right that he would prefer to continue as long as possible. Finally, the broker is ordinarily entitled to a commission on the sale of the property only if a ready, able, and willing buyer is produced *during* the listing period. If the listing has expired and the owner or another broker finds a buyer, the original listing broker is not entitled to a commission on the sale.

What happens if the listing broker has negotiated with a purchaser during the listing period but the purchase agreement is not signed until after the listing has expired? Most listing agree-

BOX 7–1 YOU BE THE JUDGE

Norma R. Naff entered into a listing agreement with Betty Kennedy dba Coldwell Banker Top Lake Realtors on November 28, 1998. The contract provided that until May 28, 1999, the broker had the exclusive right to sell Naff's real estate and would receive a commission of 7 percent of the sales price. The contract also provided that a commission would be paid after the termination of the contract if the real estate was sold to a buyer procured by the broker. However, the broker left the time period for the extension blank when the contract was signed. It read, "Broker shall be entitled to the same brokerage fee if the property is sold within the _____ day period following the expiration of the Listing period to any person . . . with whom Broker has made contact relative to the sale before expiration of the Listing Period."

On January 12, 1999, an offer to purchase the real estate was made by Robert and Sheila Miller. A counteroffer was accepted on January 22, 1999, with the sales price being set at $174,500 and the broker agreeing to accept a reduced commission of $10,087.16 for the sale. The sale was contingent upon Buyers being able to sell their real estate. This contract expired on April 30, 1999 because the buyers had not sold their real estate. On May 28, 1999, the exclusive right to sell contract expired. On June 1, 1999, Naff and the buyers entered into a new contract to sell the real estate, and Naff sold the real estate to Buyers on June 29, 1999, for $174,500.

The broker claims a right to the commission on the sale under the extension clause of the listing agreement. She argues that the extension should run for a "reasonable time" which she contends is 90 days. Should the broker be entitled to a commission on the sale? How should the court interpret an extension clause that is silent as to duration?

ments contain an extension clause under which the broker is entitled to a commission if a sale is made within a set period of time (usually 90 to 180 days) after the expiration of the listing to a purchaser with whom the broker dealt during the listing period. This allowance is in part designed to prevent a property owner from delaying a sale to a purchaser until after the expiration of the listing in an attempt to avoid paying the broker a commission. Such extension clauses need to clearly specify what actions on the part of the broker in dealing with a purchaser will entitle the broker to the commission. These actions can range from contacting a purchaser, showing the property to the purchaser, introducing or referring the purchaser to the seller, or negotiating with the purchaser. To protect the broker, some listing agreements contain a clause allowing the broker to provide the owner with a list of "reserved prospects," the names of individuals who have dealt with the broker during the listing period. In the event one of the prospects enters into purchase agreement during the extension period, the broker is entitled to the commission.

Type of Listing and Exclusions

The listing should specify whether it is exclusive or nonexclusive, and if exclusive, whether it is an exclusive agency or exclusive right to sell. If the agreement is silent on the type of listing, or the language does not clearly indicate that the listing is exclusive, a court interpreting the listing agreement will presume that the parties opted for an open listing. Owners may insist upon exclusions from the listing, that is, prospective purchasers the owner has identified and for whom the broker is not entitled to a commission. Exclusions are commonly used in two situations. First, owners who have attempted to sell their property on their own may have developed prospects who might still be interested in the property. Because the owners developed the prospects without the aid of the broker, any sale to those prospective buyers is not a result of the broker's efforts. Second, owners may enter into a listing with a broker after a listing with another broker has not been successful. In that event, the first listing broker may have developed prospects and be entitled to a commission during the extension period under the first listing agreement. The owner will want those prospects excluded to avoid paying two commissions on the sale. Alternatively, some extension clauses provide that the listing broker is not entitled to a commission during the extension period "if the property has been relisted on an exclusive basis with another broker." Such a provision avoids the possibility of the owner having to pay two commissions in this situation. Thus, owners entering into a second listing agreement should review the terms of the first listing regarding the extension period and ensure that persons excluded from the second listing are specifically identified by name in the listing agreement.

Amount of the Commission

The amount of the commission, or a method of computing the commission, must be specified in the listing agreement. The traditional method of computing the commission is to base it on a percentage of the sale price, which is beneficial to both parties because it provides an incentive for the broker to get the highest price possible to maximize the commission. The agreed-upon percentage is subject to negotiation between the parties and varies from state to state and community to community. Presently, the typical commission is 5% to 7% on residential properties, 6% to 10% on agricultural properties and vacant land, and 1% to 5% on commercial properties. Although commission rates tend to be fairly uniform in many communities, arguably because of market competition, any attempt on the part of the brokerage industry to set a fixed commission or control commission rates is illegal under state and federal antitrust laws. In the landmark case of *McClain v. Real Estate Board of New Orleans*,[6] the U.S. Supreme Court held that a local brokerage organization was subject to the Sherman Act, the federal antitrust law that prohibits monopolies and price-fixing schemes.

Some listing agreements provide an alternative method of computing the broker's commission. One alternative arrangement is called a **net listing**. Under a net listing, the owner establishes a price based on the amount that he wants to "net" from the sale of the property after sales expenses and agrees to pay the broker the amount that the actual sales price exceeds this net price as the broker's commission. So, for example, if a home is net $60,000, and it sells for $70,000, the broker's commission is $10,000. In some states, net listings are illegal, and many real estate professionals consider net listings to be unethical and fraught with potential problems. For example, a broker who assists the buyer in setting the net price is subject to an obvious conflict of interest since the broker's commission will depend upon how low the net price is set. Similarly, even if the broker is not involved in establishing the net price, the possibility remains that the net price will be set at or close to the market value. If so, this price will act as a strong disincentive for the broker to use his or her best efforts to sell the property because the broker will realize a small commission on any sale close to market price. Because of these problems, many brokers avoid or refuse to enter into net listings in those states where they are permitted under the law.

Broker's Authority

The listing agreement should establish the broker's authority to act on behalf of the property owner. Standard form listing agreements will typically provide that the broker has the right to show the property and that the owner will assist the broker in making the property available for open houses and inspections by prospective purchasers. The broker will ordinarily be authorized to cooperate with other brokers and to offer cooperative arrangements with MLS-member brokers. Language in most listing agreements obligates the seller to provide the broker information on the property and authorizes the broker to share that information with cooperating brokers. Under the ordinary listing agreement, brokers have no express or implied authority to sign purchase agreements or enter into contracts for the property owner. Therefore, if the broker has such authority, it should be explicitly set forth in the listing agreement, and the extent of the authority should be specified in a "power of attorney" (written instrument setting forth the agency authority of the broker who is called an "attorney in fact") signed by the owner.

Terms and Conditions of the Sale

The listing agreement must specify the price for the property, any personal property that will be sold with the property (washers, dryers, machinery), and any fixtures that will not be sold with the property. Because many property owners (particularly residential ones) don't have the knowledge of market conditions or the background to do an accurate appraisal, brokers often conduct a market analysis to assist owners in setting the price for the property. Alternatively, owners can secure a professional appraisal of the property to determine its value. In either event, it is ultimately the owner's decision as to the price and other conditions for the sale, and the broker should not set the price for the sellers. This decision has important legal and practical implications for the seller. The broker will earn his or her commission by finding a financially able buyer who is willing to purchase on the terms set by the owner in the listing agreement. Thus, although an owner can reject an offer that meets the terms of the listing, the owner may be liable to pay a commission when such an offer is presented by a financially able purchaser.

The Broker's Right to Compensation

A broker who performs the obligations under the listing agreement is entitled to compensation. Ordinarily, the broker earns the commission when he or she either produces a **ready, able, and willing buyer** during the listing period or a sale is completed during the listing period. In an exclusive right to sell, a buyer must be produced or sale completed but the broker need not personally produce that buyer. In an open listing, however, the broker must establish that the broker produced the buyer and was the procuring cause of the sale.

Ready, Able, and Willing Buyer

The determination of whether a prospective purchaser is a ready, able, and willing buyer is critically important to the broker's right to the commission. A prospect is able to purchase if the individual is (1) legally competent to enter into a contract (not a minor or legally insane), and (2) financially able to make the initial down payment and any deferred payments under the terms of the sale. A purchaser who meets the financial ability standard has the necessary cash on hand to purchase the property or has sufficient personal assets and credit standing to secure the necessary financing for the purchase. "Ready and willing" means that the identity of the purchaser is revealed to the seller and the purchaser agrees to the terms of the sale established by the owner as set forth in the listing agreement. If the broker produces such a ready, able, and willing buyer, the broker has satisfied the obligations under the listing contract. The owner can still refuse to deal with the broker's prospect, and need not accept the buyer's offer. However, the broker is entitled to the commission whether the owner sells or does not sell the property to that buyer.

In contrast, if the broker presents a buyer who is not financially able to purchase or one who is unwilling to purchase on the seller's terms, the owner can reject the purchaser and has no liability to the broker. What happens if the purchaser agrees to terms different from the listing (e.g., a reduced price) or signs a purchase agreement with a buyer who defaults at the closing because of financial inability to complete the sale? If the owner agrees to a modification of the terms, the broker is entitled to the commission even if the sale is never completed due to the fault of the purchaser. Similarly, by accepting a buyer who is financially unable to purchase, the seller has waived any right to object to the buyer's financial soundness. The broker is entitled to the commission even when the buyer defaults on the sale due to financial inability to pay the purchase price. This common law rule places the burden on the owner, not the broker, to inquire as to the financial condition of any prospective purchaser and to make sure that the buyer presented by the broker has the necessary financial wherewithal to complete the sale.

This traditional rule has several exceptions. First, if the broker guarantees the financial ability of the buyer or misrepresents the buyer's financial condition to the seller, the broker is not entitled to the commission if the buyer defaults and the sale is not completed. Second, in some states, courts have reversed the common law rule and place the burden on the broker to ensure the financial ability of the buyer. The leading case for this modern view is the New Jersey Supreme Court's opinion in *Ellsworth Dobbs, Inc. v. Johnson*.[7] The court reasoned that the obligation to determine the financial ability of the buyer should logically and sensibly rest with the broker because it is the broker's obligation to present such a buyer and the owner should be able to assume financial ability when a broker presents a prospect. The court also believed that placing the burden on the broker is consistent with the parties' expectations in a real estate sale and the practical realities of the market. Sellers reasonably expect to pay the broker's commission from the sale proceeds only if the buyer performs at the closing. It should be understood, however, that if the seller prevents the completion of the sale, the broker is entitled to the commission even in states that require a completed sale. Finally, in a state that follows the common law rule, owners can insist upon a "no sale, no commission" clause that conditions the broker's right to the commission on a completed sale. Under such a provision in the listing agreement, the broker is not entitled to a commission if it is the buyer that causes the sale to fail.

Conditional Sales

To earn a commission, the broker must present a buyer who is willing to purchase unconditionally. What happens if the purchaser demands that the sale contract be conditional? For example, a residential purchaser who has not secured a bank commitment may insist that the purchase agreement be conditioned upon the purchaser securing financing for the sale. Because the broker has not presented a willing buyer, the broker has not earned the commission, and the owner can refuse to enter into the conditional contract. Owners who accept a conditional offer, do not obligate themselves to pay a commission if the sale is not completed because the condition is not met. So, in the preceding example, if the purchaser is unable to secure financing, the contract is canceled, and the broker is not entitled to the commission.

Procuring Cause

Under an exclusive right to sell, the broker earns the commission when a ready, able and willing buyer is presented, regardless of who produces the buyer, be it the listing broker, another broker,

Box 7–2 You Be the Judge

On February 26, 1985, Ron and Carol Lavielle entered into a one-year listing agreement with Arlin Heinrich, a real estate broker, concerning the sale of their property, the R. L. Oil & Gas Company, and two convenience stores, the Amoco Food Mart and Pop In Mart. Curt Larive became interested in the property and made an offer to purchase on September 24, 1985 at a total sales price of $780,000. The Lavielles made a counteroffer, which boosted the sales price to $850,000, that was accepted. The contract specified that it was contingent upon Larive obtaining a Small Business Administration loan.

A prerequisite to SBA consideration, however, was provision of either detailed financial statements, prepared by an accountant, of the business to be purchased or tax returns, covering, in either case, the previous three years. The Lavielles did not make the necessary financial records available, and Heinrich made numerous telephone calls to the sellers' business and home in November, and a trip to Hot Springs, in attempts to get the necessary financial records, to no avail. The only information the sellers made available was a projection of net profits for 1984 of $240,000. Heinrich gave up his attempts to get the financial records in December 1985, when it became clear that no sale could be concluded by the closing date.

Heinrich sued to collect the commission on the sale. The sellers defended arguing that the buyer was not financially able to complete the sale and that the sale was contingent upon the SBA loan. The broker countered that the sellers wrongfully refused to furnish the financial records the buyer needed to secure an SBA loan. The buyer testified that he had a net worth of approximately $300,000 at the time in question, and he would have to borrow to raise the major share of the $850,000 purchase price.

Should the broker be awarded the commission? Was the buyer financially able to purchase? Should the sellers be able to rely on the buyer's failure to secure an SBA loan in refusing to pay the commission?

or the owner. But under an open listing, the broker's right to the commission is dependent upon being the procuring cause of the sale. Also, under an exclusive agency, if the owner is the procuring cause of the sale, the broker receives no commission on the sale.

Procuring cause means that the actions of the broker were the primary and direct cause of the sale. Several courts use the following definition of procuring cause:

> The term "procuring cause" refers to a cause directly originating a series of events which without break in their continuity directly result in the accomplishment of the primary objective of the employment of the broker, namely, the producing of a purchaser who is ready, able, and willing to buy real estate on the owner's terms.

Under this procuring cause standard, the broker must establish that he or she brought the parties together and thereby effected the sale. Merely informing the ultimate purchaser of the property for sale or introducing the purchaser to the owner is insufficient to constitute the procuring cause. Also, the broker's efforts must result in the purchase agreement without any break in the chain of events. Often, one broker will initially handle the negotiations with a prospective purchaser but the negotiations will fail and be discontinued. A second broker who reinitiates contact with the same prospect and negotiates a purchase agreement will be considered the procuring cause of the sale.

The Broker's Duties and Liabilities as an Agent

Traditionally, the listing and selling broker acted as agent for the seller. Today, in addition to the traditional role of representing the seller, a broker may be acting as the buyer's agent or as a designated agent for either the seller or buyer. Therefore, a broker may have agency duties to the seller or the buyer depending upon the nature of the brokerage relationship. If an agency relationship exists with either party, the broker owes the principal strict duties of loyalty, information, due care, obedience, and accounting. A clear understanding of the duties imposed by agency law, and the liabilities should those duties be breached, is imperative.

Loyalty and Good Faith

As an agent, a broker is a fiduciary who owes any client the highest obligation of loyalty and good faith. The principal places trust and confidence in the integrity and fidelity of the broker and expects that as an agent, the broker will serve the principal's best interests. A broker breaches the duty of loyalty if the broker secretly profits from the a sale of the listed property, acquires an interest in the listed property without the seller's knowledge and consent, discloses or improperly uses confidential information obtained from the principal, or acts as an undisclosed dual agent.

The broker's loyalty is impaired by the receipt of any compensation for the sale of the property other than the agreed commission. Thus, a broker breaches the fiduciary duty by accepting any compensation from the buyer or other parties. A broker also cannot act as the purchaser of the listed property without the consent of the seller after full disclosure of all material facts. The reason is twofold. First, the broker as the purchaser enters a position adverse to the seller, a conflict of interest that must be fully disclosed and agreed to by the seller. Second, a broker may be tempted to take advantage of his or her superior position and knowledge to make a profit at the principal's expense by purchasing the listed property. A broker who has knowledge of an offer from a prospective purchaser could "pocket" the offer and not disclose it to the seller, purchase the property from the seller, and immediately resell it for a profit to that purchaser. Obviously, such conduct would be a breach of the broker's duty of loyalty. The law requires the principal's consent to any sale of the listed property to the broker and full disclosure of all facts to minimize the possibility of this type of self-dealing.

A broker is under a duty to maintain the confidentiality of information obtained from the principal. No broker can disclose that information or use it to disadvantage the principal. So, for example, a broker who is representing the seller breaches this fiduciary duty by disclosing to the buyer the "bottom line" price that the seller is willing to accept for the property. Similarly, disclosing the financial difficulties or insolvency of a seller is a breach of the broker's duty of loyalty. Revealing such information to the buyer affects the bargaining position of the seller and the price the seller will ultimately be able to realize on the sale.

Dual agency is generally not permitted. Because a broker acting as a dual agent enters into a position of trying to serve two principals whose interests are conflicting, a broker cannot act as a dual agent without the consent of both parties after full and fair disclosure of all material facts related to the dual representation. A broker who does not reveal a position of working as an agent for both parties acts as an undisclosed dual agent and breaches the duty of loyalty.

Information

The broker's duty of information is closely related to the duty of loyalty. Brokers are under a duty to disclose all *material* information so that their principals can make intelligent decisions. Information is material if the principal would want to consider it before making an offer or entering into a sales transaction. The information does not have to be so important that it would be the determinative factor on the principal's decision to buy or sell. Rather, the standard is whether the facts might reasonably be expected to influence the principal's decision. For example, the relationship of the principal to the broker is a material fact. If the buyer is a close relative of the broker (e.g., son or daughter), a business associate of the broker (e.g., a partner or officer of the brokerage firm), or there is a personal or professional relationship between the broker and the buyer (e.g., broker is officer of a corporate buyer), such relationship must be disclosed. Because of the potential conflict of interest when a buyer has a close relationship with the listing broker, failure to reveal the relationship is a breach of the broker's duty of information and loyalty.

The duty of information requires a listing broker to promptly forward all purchase offers to the seller for consideration. Even if the broker believes the offer will be unacceptable to the seller, the offer must be disclosed. Information about the buyer also must be disclosed, such as the buyer's financial condition and solvency. Buyer's agents owe similar duties of information to their clients. A buyer's agent is under a duty to disclose defects in the property that the agent is aware of since the condition of the property is of utmost importance to the buyer. Problems with the seller's title to the property and zoning limitations that would prevent the buyer from using the property for its intended purposes are also material facts. Brokers are not under a duty of information on matters that are collateral to the decision to buy or sell the property. For example, a broker is not ordinarily under a duty to inform the seller as to the tax consequences of the sale.

Due Care

A broker is expected to exercise reasonable care and skill in the conduct of the brokerage contract. Brokers are held to a professional standard of care, the level of expertise and judgment expected of a reasonably prudent real estate broker. This standard requires a detailed knowledge of real estate practices and procedures. Thus, a listing broker must exercise *due care* in advising the seller as to the market value of the property. Inflating the recommended listing price in an attempt to secure a listing on the property, which is not an uncommon practice, is unethical and a breach of the broker's duty of due care. Conversely, a broker who deflates the price of a house,

BOX 7–3 YOU BE THE JUDGE

Meta Jorgensen listed a residential property, close to her own home, with William Lavis and Robert Lossing, of Beach 'N' Bay Realty, Inc. The property was listed at $214,500. At the same time, Lavis and Lossing were working with the Albins, a wealthy Mexican family looking for investment property in southern California. Lavis and Lossing showed the Albins a number of commercial and residential investment properties in which the Albins expressed little interest. When the brokers showed them the Jorgensen property, the Albins decided to make an offer, and the brokers prepared an offer for $200,000. The brokers presented the offer to Jorgensen telling her that Beach 'N' Bay represented both Albins and Jorgensen in the transaction. She was also told that the Albins would make good neighbors, and the brokers discouraged her from making a counteroffer for $205,000. Jorgensen accepted the Albins offer.

Nine days later, and before closing, Lavis went to Mexico and secured an exclusive listing on the Jorgensen property at a price of $234,500. After closing, the brokers immediately listed the property for sale and it soon sold for $227,000. During and after this time, the agents handled other transactions for the Albins.

Jorgensen sued the brokers claiming a breach of fiduciary duty. She contended that the brokers should have disclosed that the Albins were purchasing the property as an investment rather than indicating that they were buying the property as a residence. She also asserted that the brokers should have disclosed the nature of their relationship with the Albins, that is, that the buyers were wealthy businesspersons whose future real estate dealings with the brokerage firm could prove very lucrative and much more profitable than the one-shot transaction with Jorgensen. The brokers argued that they disclosed the dual agency and secured Jorgensen's consent and that the information they failed to disclose was not material.

What arguments could be made in support of Jorgensen's position that the information about the Albins and their relationship to the brokerage firm was material? In your opinion, did the brokers breach their duties of loyalty and information?

---

in the hopes of securing the listing and making a commission on a quick below-market sale, breaches the due care standard.

In presenting and explaining offers on the property, the broker must exercise due care in advising the principal and in drafting any purchase agreement. A listing broker who drafts a purchase agreement must ensure that it accurately describes the property and the terms of the sale. Drafting documents can be extremely problematic for brokers because most courts will hold brokers to the same level of care expected of an attorney when a broker drafts legal instruments, such as purchase agreements and deeds. A broker who drafts an unenforceable purchase agreement or creates an unclear or ambiguous contract breaches the duty of due care. Due care also requires the broker to thoroughly explain the positive and negative aspects of an offer or transaction before a decision is made by the principal. A buyer's broker who failed to adequately explain the limitations imposed by restrictive covenants on the land was held to have breached the duty of due care. Likewise, a seller's broker who failed to fully explain the financial risks associated with an offer that included an unsecured note as part of the purchase price breached this duty.

Whether a broker is under a duty to make a reasonable investigation to discover relevant facts is an unsettled issue in the law. Brokers have a duty of inquiry in two situations. First, when a broker is put on notice of a problem with the property or the sale, the due care obligation requires further inquiry to protect a client's interests. A buyer's agent who became aware of a title problem but advised the buyer to proceed with the sale breached the duty of care by failing to investigate the title problem. Second, when a broker knows that certain conditions are essential to the sale or that the buyer needs property for a specific purpose, the broker may be under a duty of inquiry to ensure that those conditions have been satisfied. For example, in Case 7.1, the buyer claimed that the broker was under a duty of inquiry to ensure that the property was suitable for the buyer's intended use as an in-home day care business because the broker knew of the buyer's purpose for the property.

Accounting and Obedience

A broker is under a duty to account for any property or money of the principal. The most common problem area is the receipt and disbursement of earnest money deposits. Brokers are under a duty to place earnest monies in a separate escrow account pending the closing of the sale. A broker breaches the duty to account by converting the earnest money for personal use, commingling the money with personal funds, or wrongfully returning the earnest money to a buyer who, for example, unjustifiably refuses to complete the sale. A broker also breaches the duty of due care by failing to secure the earnest money required from the buyer under the purchase agreement.

The broker is under a duty to obey the lawful directives of the principal and act only within the scope of the broker's authority. A broker who exceeds that authority and makes an offer or enters into a transaction that is not authorized breaches the duty of obedience. Similarly, a broker who without the knowledge or participation of the seller misrepresents material facts relating to the property, thereby defrauding the purchaser, breaches the duties of obedience and due care.

Broker's Liabilities for Breach of Duties

Brokers are subject to several legal sanctions in the event they breach the duties owed to principals. First, brokers forfeit any commission if they breach their duty of loyalty or commit a serious breach of duties to principals. The forfeiture of compensation is considered a penalty designed to encourage brokers to comply with their strict fiduciary obligations and to discourage brokers from acting to their principals' detriment. Therefore, the law imposes this sanction regardless whether the principal suffers any loss from the broker's actions or the broker secretly profits from the breach. Thus, a broker who personally purchases property from the seller at the highest price obtainable forfeits the commission if he or she fails to disclose his or her interest and secure the principal's consent to such a sale. Moreover, the broker's actions need not be fraudulent or malicious. A failure to disclose material information relative to the transaction that the broker believes will not affect the principal's decision is still a violation of the broker's fiduciary duty and results in a forfeiture of the commission. In some cases, courts will disregard minor deviations from the broker's duty that are not harmful to the principal, but these cases are the exception, not the rule.

A broker also is liable to the principal for any damages the principal suffers as a result of the broker's breach of duty. The amount of damages recoverable will be based on the injury attributable to the breach. In some cases, it will be based on the profits realized by the defaulting broker. Thus, where a broker secretly acquires the principal's property and immediately resells it for a profit, the principal is allowed to recover the profits from the resale of the property. The profits wrongfully received by the broker are said to be held in trust for the principal. They also represent the injury caused by the broker's breach of duty. Ordinarily, the principal is entitled to recover only compensatory damages for a broker's failure to perform his or her duties. However, in the event the broker commits fraud or engages in other bad faith conduct, the law allows the jury to impose punitive or exemplary damages, an amount of money necessary to punish the broker for the wrongdoing.

By failing to live up to his or her duties, a broker is in breach of the listing agreement, which gives the principal the right to terminate the listing agreement and the agent's entitlement to a commission on any sale of the property. Generally, a listing agreement cannot be terminated by the parties (except by mutual consent) prior to the end of the listing period. A principal who terminates the agent's authority before the end of the term is liable to the agent for damages. But if the agent breaches any duties, the principal can terminate the listing agreement without liability to the broker. Also, a broker may suffer collateral legal consequences as a result of a breach of those duties. If the breach of duty is a violation of rules and regulations under the state licensing law, the broker may face license suspension or revocation, a separate administrative sanction for breach of professional standards.

The Broker's Duties and Liabilities to Third Parties

Generally, a broker has no duty under agency law principles to third parties with whom that broker deals. A broker's duty is to the principal. Thus, a listing broker is under a duty to promptly inform the principal of an offer from a prospective purchaser. But if the broker fails to convey the offer, the broker has not breached any duty *to the prospective purchaser* and the prospect cannot hold the broker liable for any damages suffered by the broker's failure to communicate the offer. The agent owes a fiduciary duty to the principal, not to third parties.

Nevertheless, brokers are under both professional and legal duties to third parties. Under accepted professional standards, brokers are expected to act openly and honestly in their dealings with third parties. From a legal standpoint, brokers cannot engage in intentional deception of third parties. Third parties can hold brokers responsible for damages they suffer when brokers commit fraud, either by misrepresenting material facts or failing to disclose facts that they are under a duty to disclose (fraudulent nondisclosure). In some states, courts have expanded brokers' duties to third parties and hold them liable for negligent misrepresentations, that is, unintentional misrepresentations that are a result of the broker's failure to exercise due care and skill.

Fraudulent Misrepresentation and Nondisclosure

Fraud is the intentional misrepresentation or concealment of material facts that causes harm to another person relying on the misrepresentation or deceived by the concealment. To establish fraud, the injured must prove the following:

- A misrepresentation (or concealment) of material facts.
- The wrongdoer's knowledge that the facts are false.
- The wrongdoer's intent to induce others to rely on the misrepresentation.
- The innocent party's justifiable reliance on the misrepresentation.
- Damages to the innocent party caused by the reliance.

A person who commits fraud is liable to the innocent party for both compensatory and punitive damages. In the alternative, the defrauded party can sue to rescind (cancel) the sale and recover whatever was paid under the sales transaction.

Thus, a listing broker who knowingly falsifies information relating to the listed property in an attempt to convince the buyer to purchase commits fraud if the buyer reasonably relies on the false information in purchasing the property and suffers damages as a result. For example, in *Fennel Realty Co., Inc. v. Martin*,[8] a broker told the buyers of a house that the inspection of the heating and air conditioning system indicated that the system was in operable condition and working fine. In fact, the repair technician told the broker that the furnace had a cracked combustion engine, it was unsafe, and needed major repairs. The court upheld a jury verdict for the buyers on their fraud claim against the broker, holding that when a broker is questioned about conditions in the property, and assumes the obligation to inspect it for defects, "the law imposes on the agent the duty of truthful disclosure of all material facts revealed by the inspection."

Fraud also can consist of a knowing concealment of facts or a knowing failure to disclose facts that one is under a duty to reveal. In most contractual settings, one is not under a general duty of disclosure and silence standing alone is not fraud. A seller or broker is not under a duty to volunteer information even when the information is material to the contract or affects the value of the property. A party is under a duty not to conceal material facts, and fraud occurs if a party actively hides material information. A broker who advises a client to panel over a "sagging" foundation wall to cover up the structural defect has committed fraudulent concealment.

Fraud also occurs when a broker breaches a duty to disclose material facts. A seller or broker may have a duty to disclose facts under statutes or under common law rules. Most states by statute require sellers of residential property to disclose certain information about the condition of the property, including heating and cooling systems, appliances, electrical and plumbing systems, the roof and siding, and specific defects, such as water seeping and flooding. However, these laws place the duty on the seller, not the broker, to make the disclosure. Under the common law, most courts also require sellers and their brokers to disclose latent defects and other material conditions that impact the value of the property. This common law duty arises only when (1) the defect or material condition is not apparent upon a reasonable inspection of the property, and (2) the broker has knowledge of the defect or condition. In the *Martin* case, the court also found the broker liable for fraudulent nondisclosure. It held that if a broker has "knowledge of a material defect or condition that affects health or safety and the defect is not known or readily observable by the buyer," the broker is under a duty of full disclosure. The broker's failure to disclose the defective and dangerous condition of the heating unit constituted fraudulent nondisclosure.

Most fraudulent nondisclosure cases have involved physical defects or unlawful conditions on the property that are not readily apparent to the buyer, such as basement water problems, unstable soil conditions, faulty wiring, major structural defects, housing or building code violations, and improvements in violation of zoning laws and building permit regulations. In recent years, the courts have expanded the type of information considered material to the sales transaction that the broker and seller must disclose. In the famous case of *Reed v. King*,[9] a California appeals court held that a seller and his broker were under a duty to disclose the fact that the property was the site of a mass murder (a woman and her four children were murdered in the house 10 years prior to the sale) since the murder stigmatized the house and depressed its market value. Recently, in *Strawn v. Canuso*,[10] the New Jersey Supreme Court held that a broker is under a duty to disclose unsafe off-site conditions that may affect the value of the property. The case involved a hazardous-waste dump site near a residential development, the existence of which the broker failed to disclose to home buyers. Thus, under these recent decisions, a broker may have a duty to disclose nonphysical latent defects relating to the property and even dangerous conditions in surrounding areas.

● Negligent Misrepresentation

Fraud is difficult to prove because it requires the injured party to establish that the broker knowingly and intentionally falsified or concealed material information. Although recklessness on the part of the broker will be sufficient to prove **constructive fraud** in many states, if the broker was simply careless or innocently misstated facts believed to be true, the broker is not liable for fraud. Frequently, a broker will repeat information about the property that the seller has provided without confirming the accuracy of the information. In such situations, the broker is not liable for fraud even if the information is later determined to be false and the buyer suffers damages relying on the false information. Brokers are entitled to rely on the truthfulness of their principals, and they are not under a duty to investigate information from them before disseminating it to others.

To protect purchasers in these situations, some states allow recovery for **negligent misrepresentation**. The difference between negligent misrepresentation and fraud is that knowledge of falsity is not required for negligent misrepresentation. The injured party still needs to prove a misrepresentation of a material fact reasonably relied upon to the party's detriment, but the injured party only needs to show that the broker was negligent in acquiring or disseminating the information. This legal definition imposes a duty of due care that may require brokers to make reasonable inquiries or reasonable inspections of the property to verify the truth of information provided by sellers. Courts adopting negligent misrepresentation do so for three primary reasons. First, brokers are considered professionals who have superior knowledge of the real estate they sell. Second, prospective purchasers should be able to rely on the truth and accuracy of representations brokers make about the property, just as they are able to rely on information supplied directly from sellers. Finally, allowing brokers to use misleading statements to sell property without liability encourages brokers to repeat information that they have not verified and discourages them from making reasonable inquiries to determine the accuracy of information they convey to purchasers.

Some courts have taken this theory one step further and have imposed liability on brokers for innocent misrepresentations, although most courts reject broker liability on this basis. In the next case, the Washington Supreme Court discusses the conflict among the states on the issue of a broker's liability for unintentional misrepresentations.

Case 7.2

Hoffman v. Connall
736 P.2d 242 (Wash. 1987)

In January 1983, Bryan G. and Connie J. Connall signed a listing agreement with Cardinal Realty. The sellers wanted to sell 5 acres of land north of Spokane. A few days after signing the listing agreement, one of the sellers showed the property to the Cardinal broker. The seller pointed to a stake or piece of pipe as the southeast corner of the property, and the broker saw that the stake lined up with an old fence line to apparently form the east boundary. The sellers had built a new fence approximately 6" inside the old fence line and a corral and horse shed stood just inside the new fence. The seller insisted that his corral was inside the property line.

The seller then showed the broker a wooden stake, which he said marked the southwest corner of the property. The broker saw that the stake was in line with a row of poplar trees that evidently formed the west boundary. To the north of the trees was a pole that apparently was near the northwest corner. The seller could not find the stake marking the northwest corner of the property, and the two men felt they were close to but could not exactly locate the northeast boundary.

James and Verna Hoffman read about the property in the newspaper. The property's improvement—corral, cattle chute, barn and shed—were important to the buyers because they owned a horse and wanted to get involved with 4-H horse activities. They called the broker and visited the property with him. He pointed out the fence as the east boundary, and the pole as the northwest boundary. He gave an approximate indication of the northeast corner but could not find the marker for the southwest corner. The broker did not recommend that the buyers obtain a survey.

The buyers bought the property on February 28, 1983. In May 1983 a neighbor told them that a recent survey showed that their east fence encroached upon his property. The buyers had their own survey done and discovered that the east-side improvements encroached upon their neighbor's property by 18 to 21 feet. The encroachment consisted of the fence built by the sellers and part of the corral, cattle run and horse shed. The buyers discovered it would cost almost $6,000 to move the improvements onto their own property.

The buyers brought an action for damages against the sellers and the broker, alleging that they misrepresented the true boundary lines. Following a bench trial, the trial court found as a fact that there was nothing to give the broker or the sellers notice that anything was wrong with the property lines. The court concluded that the broker did not breach the standard of care of a reasonably prudent real estate broker. The Court of Appeals reversed, holding that an owner of realty who innocently misrepresents its boundaries is liable to the purchaser. The court then extended liability for innocent misrepresentation to an owner's real estate agent and, in the alternative, held that the broker breached his duty to take reasonable steps to avoid disseminating false information to buyers. The broker sought review of the Court of Appeals decision.

ANDERSEN, J.

Two principal issues are presented.

ISSUE ONE. Should a real estate broker be held liable for innocently misrepresenting a material fact to a buyer of real property?

ISSUE TWO. Was the broker negligent in failing to verify the sellers' statements concerning the property's boundaries?

DECISION

ISSUE ONE CONCLUSION. A real estate broker is held to a standard of reasonable care and is liable for making "negligent," though not "innocent," misrepresentations concerning boundaries to a buyer.

We recognize that some other jurisdictions have agreed with the viewpoint of the Court of Appeals in the case and have held real estate brokers liable for making innocent misrepresentations on which buyers justifiably rely. The courts justify placing the loss on the innocent broker on the basis that the broker is in a better position to determine the truth of his or her representations.

At the other end of the spectrum from liability for innocent misrepresentation is the view that a real estate broker is an agent of the seller, not the buyer, and is protected from liability under agency law. Thus, an agent would be permitted to repeat misinformation from his principal without fear or liability unless the agent knows or has reason to know of its falsity. This principle has been upheld by approximately half the jurisdictions that have addressed the issue of broker liability for innocent misrepresentations. The Supreme Court of Vermont recently reaffirmed this rule, holding that "[r]eal estate brokers and agents are marketing agents, not structural engineers or contractors. They have no duty to verify independently representations made by a seller unless they are aware of facts that 'tend to indicate that such representation[s are] false.'"

A recent decision of our Court of Appeals declared a middle ground that we find persuasive. At issue in *Tennant v. Lawton*, 28 Wash. App 701, 615 P.2d 1305 (1980), was a broker's liability for misrepresenting that a parcel of land could support a sewage system and thus was "buildable." The *Tennant* court echoed the Vermont court in holding that a broker is negligent if he or she repeats material representations made by the seller that the seller knows, or reasonably should know, of their falsity.

The underlying rationale of [a broker's] duty to a buyer who is not his client is that he is a professional who is in a unique position to verify critical information given him by the seller. His duty is to take reasonable steps to avoid disseminating to the buyer false information. The broker is required to employ a reasonable degree of effort and professional expertise to confirm or refute information from the seller which he knows, or should know, is pivotal to the transaction from the buyer's perspective. While a broker must be alert to potential misrepresentations made by a seller, we decline to hold that a broker must guarantee every statement made by the seller. A real estate broker must take reasonable steps to avoid disseminating false information to buyers. In short, a real estate broker must act as a professional, and will be held to a standard of reasonable care. If a broker willfully or negligently conveys false information about real estate to a buyer, the broker is liable therefor.

ISSUE TWO CONCLUSION. The broker did not breach the standard of care of a reasonably prudent broker.

The broker in this case had no notice that anything was wrong with the boundaries as represented by the sellers. While hindsight suggests that the broker would have done well to check on the alleged survey, there was no testimony that such a check was the prevailing practice in the real estate business. Moreover, natural and manmade boundaries reinforced the sellers' representations concerning the legal boundaries.

Reversed.

DORE, J. (dissenting)

Contrary to the majority, I believe that a broker should be liable for any material misrepresentation he or she makes which induces buyers to act to their detriment. Washington courts have long held that a seller of land is always liable for misrepresentations, regardless of whether they are innocently or negligently made. The basis for this rule is the belief that the owners are presumed to know the attributes and specifications of their property. I agree with this rule and I see no reason not to apply this logic to brokers. Brokers possess more knowledge than buyers about the attributes of the property to be sold, and innocent buyers should be able to rely on representations made by the broker.

I believe the majority ignores the equities of the broker-buyer relationship by allowing brokers to misrepresent material aspects of the property in question with impunity unless the buyer demonstrates that the broker knew or should have known of the statement's falsity. As between an innocent buyer and an innocent broker, I believe the buyer should prevail. Even following the majority's proposed standard of care, if a seller bases his belief of the location of the property line on a prior survey, I believe that a reasonably prudent broker would verify the purported survey does in fact exist. Failure to make this simple inquiry is negligence and actionable even under the majority's reasoning.

QUESTIONS ABOUT CASE 7.2

1. Which opinion do you find more persuasive? What are the costs and benefits of imposing liability on brokers for innocent or negligent misrepresentations?

2. Although the court did not require the broker to review the property survey, should it have required the broker to advise the buyers that they should consider having a survey of the land?

Regulation of the Brokerage Industry

Every state and the District of Columbia has a licensing law under which real estate brokers and their salespersons are licensed and their conduct regulated. The purpose of the licensing law is to protect the public interest by regulating the brokerage profession and its practices. This oversight is accomplished by ensuring that brokers meet standards of professional competency before they engage in brokerage activities and by regulating the conduct and practices of brokers to prevent harm to sellers and buyers of real estate. Any broker who violates the professional standards established in the licensing law and the rules and regulations under the law is subject to serious sanctions, including license suspension or revocation.

The Real Estate Commission

Under state licensing laws, an administrative agency, usually called the real estate commission, is created to oversee and administer the licensing law. The real estate commission is generally an appointed body made up of representatives from the brokerage industry and from the general public. Among the powers of the commission are the following:

- Issuing licenses and license renewals to applicants meeting the requirements of the law.
- Creating and implementing rules and regulations governing the conduct and practices of brokers and salespersons.
- Investigating complaints against licensees, resolving such complaints on an informal basis, and if necessary, bringing administrative actions against brokers alleged to have violated rules and regulations on broker conduct or practices.
- Holding administrative hearings to resolve such complaints and suspending or revoking the license of brokers found in violation of the law or commission rules and regulations.

With these broad powers, the commission administers and enforces the licensing laws.

Real Estate Brokers and Salespersons

The two types of licensees are real estate brokers and real estate salespersons. A real estate broker is a licensee who is authorized to operate independently in the brokerage business and to engage in a wide range of brokerage activities. A **real estate salesperson** is a licensee who is associated with a real estate broker and who can act only under the direction and control of the broker. The salesperson cannot engage in brokerage activities except under the supervision of a broker. Brokers can employ salespersons and other brokers to work for their brokerage firms. These associates are referred to in the profession as **sales associates**.

Licensing Requirements for Brokers

Although the precise requirements for a broker or salesperson license vary from state to state, every state requires applicants to demonstrate professional competency and provide evidence of good moral character. To secure a salesperson license, the applicant must have a high school diploma and successfully complete a minimum number of hours in approved real estate courses. A college degree is required only in a few states. To prove knowledge of the brokerage profession, the applicant also must pass a real estate examination that covers basic real estate topics, including real estate law and the fundamentals of brokerage practice. To satisfy the character requirement, the applicant must demonstrate personal fitness to be a member of the profession by showing evidence of honesty and trustworthiness, which is ordinarily accomplished by supplying letters of reference from "character witnesses." Having a criminal conviction may preclude an applicant from obtaining a license, although this preclusion depends upon the severity and nature of the offense and the length of time that has passed since the offense.

The requirements for a real estate broker license are more demanding than for a salesperson license. In addition to proving evidence of good moral character, the applicant must meet experience and professional competency standards. To meet the experience requirement, broker applicants must have practiced a minimum number of years (typically 2 to 3 years) in the real estate industry as a salesperson. The applicant also must successfully complete a minimum number of hours of course work and pass an examination. The examination covers basic and advanced real estate topics, including real estate law and transactions, business ethics, economics, real estate finance, appraisal, office management, and brokerage practice. This examination is more comprehensive than the salesperson exam.

Brokerage Activities and Practicing Without a License

A license is required to engage in brokerage activities as defined under state law. This requirement obviously includes acting as the seller's or buyer's agent in the sale or lease of real estate. However, the types of brokerage activities requiring a license are much broader than simply handling a typical sale of real estate for the seller or buyer. Brokerage activities may include finding prospects for the listing or purchase of real estate, handling auctions of real estate, performing property management services, and other activities related to the sale of real estate.

Engaging in a brokerage activity without a license is a violation of the law and will subject the violator to multiple legal sanctions. First, a broker who acts without a license cannot recover any compensation or commission even if the work is competently performed and the client is not harmed by the lack of a license. Second, the real estate commission may order the person to cease and desist from the brokerage activity and impose other sanctions if its order is violated. Third, a violation of the license law is a criminal offense (usually a misdemeanor) for which the violator can be prosecuted.

Every licensing law has some exceptions that permit persons to engage in what otherwise would be brokerage activities. For example, owners can sell property on their own without violating the licensing law. Attorneys who prepare documents or handle various aspects of a real estate transaction in connection with their practice of law are excepted from the licensing law.

Trustees of bankrupt entities and administrators of estates who sell property also are excepted from the law.

Violations of Professional Standards

The licensing law and the rules and regulations established by the real estate commission establish professional standards for brokers in the conduct of their brokerage practice. These professional standards often parallel the fiduciary duties owed by brokers to their clients and to third parties under the law. Thus, licensing laws prohibit brokers from engaging in dual agency without their clients' consent. Although the standards set by the licensing law are similar to the common law duties, they provide more specific guidance in particular areas of practice, and in some areas the standards are more demanding than the duties imposed by the common law. Among the typical violations of professional standards are the following:

- Engaging in false, misleading or discriminatory advertising, including misrepresenting the property, its value, or the terms of sale.

- Falsely claiming to represent a party in a real estate transaction, as for example by placing a "For Sale" on property without authorization or offering property for sale or lease without the owner's knowledge and consent.

- Interfering with the relationship between another broker and that broker's client, including negotiating directly with another broker's client, causing the client to breach the listing agreement, and obtaining a listing from another broker's client when a broker knows that the other broker has an exclusive listing with the client.

- Mishandling earnest monies or other property of third parties, including failing to establish an escrow/trust account, unlawfully refusing to remit such monies, and commingling earnest monies with the personal funds of the broker.

- Failing to provide a client with documents relating to a real estate transaction, including a copy of the listing agreement, purchase agreement, and a complete, detailed closing statement.

- Dishonesty in dealings with the client or third parties, such as falsifying or assisting in the falsification of documents, falsely claiming that an appraisal of the property exists, and making other substantial misrepresentations.

The standards established under the licensing law are important for two reasons. First, a broker can be disciplined by the real estate commission for violating these standards. The commission has the power to impose a range of sanctions on licensees depending on the nature and severity of the violation, the culpability and past conduct of the licensee, and the public interest involved. Reprimands and small civil fines are often imposed for minor infractions, suspensions and revocations for more serious wrongs, as with criminal acts or substantial violations of professional standards. Second, courts in civil lawsuits against brokers will often look to the professional standards under the licensing laws to determine the duties a broker owes to clients and third parties. Therefore, the professional standards may set the standard of care for brokers in their practice, and a violation of the professional standards may form the basis for a civil lawsuit against a broker. (See Case 7.1.)

Recovery Funds

Although brokers who violate professional standards may be disciplined, the administrative sanctions do not provide compensation to the persons who may have been harmed by the broker's wrongful conduct. Victims must bring civil lawsuits to recover for the damages they suffered.

What happens if the injured party wins a lawsuit and secures a judgment against the broker, but the broker is bankrupt or otherwise unable to pay the judgment amount? Does the injured party have any recourse under the law? Yes, most states have a recovery fund established to pay the claim of an injured party in the event a judgment is uncollectible. The recovery fund is funded with a portion of the annual licensing fees that brokers and salespersons pay the state.

Recovery funds provide only limited relief to injured parties. To secure a recovery, the injured party must secure a judgment against a broker for fraud, deceit, dishonest practices, or conversion of funds. The broker's actions or conduct also must be in connection with a transaction for which the broker was required to have a license. Not every wrongful act by a broker is covered by the law. For example, brokers may commit fraudulent practices in transactions that are not related to their brokerage practice, such as fraudulent investment schemes and sales of their own property. Finally, even if the claim comes within the scope of the recovery law, the amount of recovery is limited to a dollar amount (typically $20,000 to $50,000).

Self-Study Questions

1. Explain the legal status of the listing broker and the selling broker under the traditional brokerage relationship.

2. Explain the alternative relationships that exist in modern brokerage practice, including buyer's agents, transaction brokers, and designated agents.

3. What are the three types of listing agreements? How do they differ?

4. What does "procuring cause" mean? Why is it important to brokers and sellers of property?

5. What is a net listing? Why do you think this type of listing is illegal in some states?

6. When is a buyer ready, able, and willing to purchase? Why are these qualifications important?

7. What duties does a broker owe to a principal? Who is the broker's principal?

8. What is the difference between fraudulent misrepresentation and negligent misrepresentation? Should the law impose liability on brokers for negligent or innocent misrepresentations?

9. Why are the professional standards established under state licensing laws important to brokers?

10. What are the present requirements for a person to secure a broker or salesperson license in most states? Should states require a college degree for a broker's license?

Case Problems

1. John Bennett, a licensed Massachusetts real estate broker, entered into a brokerage agreement with James McCabe and John Zitaglio, owners of "Ye Old Whaler," a summer motel located in Provincetown. During 1984, Bennett located a ready, able, and willing purchaser for the motel, and the sellers accepted a $400,000 offer for the property on May 15, 1984. Closing was scheduled for June 1, 1984, but a defect in the sellers' title prevented the parties from completing the sale. Neither of the sellers had any knowledge of the title defect at the time they entered into the agreement to sell the property. Because the sale could not be completed, the sellers instructed Bennett to return the deposit from the buyers. Bennett returned the deposit and then sought to hold the sellers liable for the 6% commission.

Massachusetts follows the rule of *Ellsworth v. Dobbs* that a broker is not entitled to the commission if the buyer is unable to complete the contract because of financial inability. The sellers argued that they should not have to pay the commission because the sale was not prevented by any wrongful conduct on their part. The broker argued that the *Ellsworth* rule should not be extended to excuse a seller from paying the commission when the sale fails because of the seller's lack of marketable title. What policy considerations favor the positions of the broker and the sellers? In your opinion, should the broker be entitled to the commission when the sale is not completed due to a title defect? *Bennett v. McCabe*, 808 F.2d 178 (1st Cir. 1987).

2. Norman Fauteux was responsible for liquidating a divorcing couple's marital property. Fauteux hired James Gilmer to help him sell some of the properties, and between 1992 and 1995, Gilmer received commission payments for selling approximately fifteen parcels. In September 1992, Fauteux and Gilmer entered into a one-year open listing agreement concerning property known as the North Hartland Dry Kiln. Fauteux agreed to pay Gilmer a commission if Gilmer procured a buyer for the property, which was listed at $1 million. As soon as the agreement was signed, Gilmer contacted the Cersosimo Lumber Company regarding the property, but the company expressed no interest in purchasing it. In September 1993, Fauteux and Gilmer signed a renewal one-year listing agreement concerning the property. By September 1994, the property had not sold, and Gilmer asked Fauteux to renew the listing agreement once again. Fauteux told Gilmer that he was reluctant to sign a renewal agreement because he was not sure whether his authority as liquidating agent would extend beyond December 1994. Nevertheless, Fauteux asked Gilmer to continue to seek a buyer for the property, assuring him that he would be paid a commission. In January 1995, Gilmer notified Cersosimo that the asking price for the subject property had been reduced from $1 million to $750,000. Soon thereafter, Gilmer began negotiating a deal with one prospective buyer and then with another when the first one withdrew its offer, but neither prospect purchased the property. On May 22, 1995, Gilmer gave Fauteux a renewal listing agreement with the understanding that he would sign it. Fauteux never signed the agreement and, in September 1995, sold the subject property to Cersosimo. When Fauteux refused to pay Gilmer a commission, Gilmer sued Fauteux. Following a hearing, a trial court determined that Gilmer had procured the sale of the kiln, and thus was entitled to a commission in the amount of $58,750. The court acknowledged the general rule barring real estate commissions absent an executed written listing agreement, but concluded that an exception should apply in this case because the parties had expressed a mutual intent to abide by a written listing agreement that, though unsigned, contained the same terms as those contained in their prior agreements. On appeal to the Vermont Supreme Court, Fauteux argued that the superior court erred in allowing a commission without an executed written listing agreement and in concluding that Gilmer's actions were the procuring cause of the sale. How should the appellate court resolve the two issues in the case? *Gilmer v. Fauteux* 723 A.2d 1150 (Vt. 1998).

3. Lonnie and Kathy Bazal decided to sell their home in Bowman Woods in June of 1995. They listed their home with Dick Brown, a broker with Skogman Realty Company. In mid-July 1995, Paul and Karen Rhines asked their broker, Marilyn Palma, whether she knew of a home for sale in Bowman Woods that would meet their needs, including space for four dogs. Palma, also a broker at Skogman, informed the Rhineses that she believed the Bazals' home would meet their needs. The Bazals were never informed that the Rhineses required space for four dogs. On July 22, 1995, the Bazals and the Rhineses agreed upon a cash price of $211,000 with a closing date of September 30, 1995. The Rhineses and the Bazals each signed a Consensual Dual Agency Agreement prepared by Skogman acknowledging that one Skogman broker was representing the Rhineses as buyers and a second Skogman broker was representing the Bazals as sellers in the transaction. On September 10, 1995, the Rhineses' attorney, Michael Donohue, prepared a title opinion that disclosed a restrictive covenant on the property limiting dog ownership to one per dwelling unit. Donohue wrote to Palma noting the "dog clause" problem and suggested that waivers be obtained or other solutions be considered. Skogman took no action to try to resolve the

problem. As a result, the closing did not take place. The Bazals relisted their home with Skogman for $216,000. The property ultimately sold for $201,000 in 1996, the home proving difficult to sell due to the time of year and because it was empty. The Bazals had reduced the asking price on the home on Brown's advice and due to the financial pressure of owning two homes.

The Bazals sued Marilyn Palma and Skogman Realty Company alleging a breach of the broker's fiduciary duties of information and due care. Specifically, the Bazals contended that Palma and Skogman owed them a duty to inform them of the "dog clause" problem and to use their best efforts to resolve the problem so that the sale could close. Skogman and Palma contended that they had no duty to disclose the "dog clause" problem and neither the restrictive covenant nor the Rhineses' plan to bring four dogs to the property were material facts. It further argued that it had no duty to close the transaction. How should these issues be resolved? *Bazal v. Rhines*, 600 N.W.2d 327 (Iowa App. 1999).

4. David and Molly Davis owned a home in Brandon, Mississippi. In the summer of 1986, they listed their home for sale through Susan Burton Williams. Phillip Moss and his wife, Dana, contacted Lee Hawkins Realty and met with David Anderson, an associate real estate broker. The Mosses informed Anderson that they were only interested in purchasing a home that had a "2-10" homeowner's warranty policy in effect.

Anderson ran the Mosses' specifications through a computer listing service that retrieved a list of approximately eight homes, one of which was the Davis home. He showed the Mosses the Davis home, at which time Mr. Davis informed Phillip Moss that his home was in fact covered by a 2-10 warranty. A sign posted on a tree in the front of the house stated that the warranty was in effect. After some negotiation, the Mosses entered into contract with the Davises. The contract provided that the remainder of the 10 year warranty would be provided to the purchasers. On November 26, 1986, the parties and brokers met for closing. The sellers selected a local law firm to handle the closing, and Jackie Root, a paralegal at the firm, acted on its behalf. During the closing, Moss requested a copy of the 2-10 warranty. After inspecting an unsigned document provided by the paralegal, Moss became concerned. Root and Williams then left the room with the document in order to investigate. When they returned, Root informed Moss that they had verified that the warranty was in existence, and Williams nodded her head affirmatively. Relying on Root's representation, Moss proceeded with the closing. Several months later, he noticed structural damage to the home and attempted to recover under the warranty. However, he was informed that a warranty was never in existence for his home. In 1992, the Mosses filed suit against Lee Hawkins Realty, David Anderson, David and Molly Davis, and Susan Burton Williams. They contended that Anderson and Lee Hawkins Realty breached their fiduciary duties to the Mosses by allowing the sale and closing to proceed without verifying the accuracy of the warranty. They also contended that Williams and Berg Realty committed negligence at the closing by falsely confirming the existence of a warranty on the home. Williams claimed that she owed no duty to the Mosses due to the fact that she was the agent representing the sellers. Williams also testified that by nodding her head affirmatively when Root informed Moss that his home warranty was valid, she simply meant that Root had confirmed the warranty.

Did the buyer's agent breach its fiduciary duty to the Mosses? On what theories of liability can the Mosses seek to hold Williams and her agency liable for damages? Who should prevail on the issues raised in the lawsuit? *Lee Hawkins Realty, Inc. v. Moss*, 724 So.2d 1116 (Miss. App. 1998).

5. Mr. and Mrs. William Strassburger listed property with Valley of California, Inc., doing business as Valley Realty. The property consisted of a one-acre parcel of land located in the City of Diablo that was improved with a 3,000 square foot home, a swimming pool, and a large guest house. Leticia M. Easton purchased the property for $170,000 from the Strassburgers in July of 1976. Shortly after she purchased the property, there was a massive earth movement on the parcel. Subsequent slides destroyed a portion of the driveway in 1977 or 1978. Expert testimony indicated that the slides occurred because a portion of the property was fill that had not been properly

engineered and compacted. The slides caused the foundation of the house to settle which in turn caused cracks in the walls and warped doorways. After the 1976 slide, damage to the property was so severe that experts appraised the value of the damaged property to be as low as $20,000. Estimates of the cost to repair the damage caused by the slides and avoid recurrence ranged as high as $213,000. Valley Realty was represented in the sale of the property by its agents Simkin and Mourning. The agents conducted several inspections of the property prior to sale. Evidence showed that they were aware of certain "red flags" that should have indicated soil problems. Despite the indications, the agents did not request that the soil stability of the property be tested and did not inform Easton of the potential soil problems. During the time that the property was owned by the Strassburgers, a minor slide in 1973 involved about 10 to 12 feet of the filled slope, and a major slide in 1975 dropped the fill about 8 to 10 feet in a circular shape 50 to 60 feet across. However, the Strassburgers did not tell Simkin or Mourning anything about the slides or the corrective action they had taken. Easton purchased the property without being aware of the soil problems or the past history of slides.

In December of 1976 Easton filed suit against Valley Realty and the Strassburgers, alleging fraudulent concealment, intentional misrepresentation, and negligent misrepresentation. The jury returned a verdict for negligence and awarded damages to Easton. On appeal, Valley Realty objected to the way in which the jury was instructed regarding its duty to the purchasers. The jury was instructed as follows: "A real estate broker . . . is under a duty to disclose facts materially affecting the value or desirability of the property that are known to him or which through reasonable diligence should be known to him." Valley Realty contended that a broker is only obliged to disclose known facts and has no duty to disclose facts which "should" be known to him "through reasonable diligence." In effect, Valley Realty maintained that a broker has no legal duty to carry out a reasonable investigation of property he undertakes to sell in order to discover defects for the benefit of the buyer. Should the court set aside the verdict against the broker on appeal based on an improper instruction of law? *Easton v. Strassburger*, 152 Cal.App.3d 90, 199 Cal. Rptr. 383 (1984).

Endnotes

1. "Realtor" is a registered trademark of the NATIONAL ASSOCIATION OF REALTORS®.

2. Louisiana, Maryland, Nebraska, and Washington take this position.

3. Alabama, Colorado, Florida, Georgia, Idaho, Illinois, Kansas, Michigan, Minnesota, Missouri, Montana, New Hampshire, New Jersey, New Mexico, Ohio, Oklahoma, Pennsylvania, South Dakota, Tennessee, Texas, Washington, and Wyoming.

4. Delaware, Florida, Georgia, Illinois, Iowa, Kansas, Kentucky, Louisiana, Maine, Maryland, Missouri, Nebraska, Nevada, New Mexico, North Carolina, North Dakota, Pennsylvania, Rhode Island, Tennessee, and Washington.

5. By statute or administrative regulation, the following states require a listing agreement to be in writing: Alabama, Arizona, California, Connecticut, Hawaii, Idaho, Indiana, Iowa, Kentucky, Michigan, Minnesota, Montana, Nebraska, Nevada, New Jersey, New Mexico, Oregon, Rhode Island, South Carolina, Texas, Utah, Vermont, Virginia, Washington, and Wisconsin.

6. 441 U.S. 942 (1980).

7. 236 A.2d 843 (N.J. 1967).

8. 529 So.2d 1003 (Ala. 1988).

9. 145 Cal. App. 3d 261, 193 Cal. Rptr. 130 (1983).

10. 638 A.2d 141 (1994).

Chapter 8 Reaching Agreement: Elements of the Real Estate Sales Contract

Outline

Purchasing a home is the single most significant capital investment that most families will make. The $149,000 median price of a new family home in the United States means that most families must obtain a loan to purchase their dream house.[1] The purchase is more difficult than almost any other because of the complexity of real property interests, the significant capital investment, and the timing required for family relocation. Buyers want assurance that the dream house will be theirs after they have gone to the trouble and expense of obtaining loan financing, selling their old house, and hiring movers. Their lenders must verify that the sellers actually own the property, and, of course, the sellers need presale assurance that they will be paid. Businesses seeking to buy, sell, or develop real estate face the same concerns.

The *real estate contract* protects the parties to it by assuring each party that the other will perform its part of the bargain or be legally responsible for the economic damages caused by failure to perform. This chapter reviews the requirements for a binding contract, the concerns addressed by a typical real estate contract, and the legal remedies available for its breach.

Requirements for a Valid Real Estate Contract

Law That Applies to Real Estate Contracts

Sales of real estate are governed primarily by the common law of contracts, that massive body of contract law developed over the centuries by the courts. The common law of contracts applies to most types of contracts, including those involving land, personal services, insurance, and loans of money. In contrast, specialized bodies of contract law adopted by state legislatures apply to transactions, such as the sale of goods, and supplement the common law. Much of the specialized law is found in the Uniform Commercial Code (UCC). The UCC is state legislation specifically designed to streamline and facilitate a variety of commercial transactions, occasionally by replacing common law rules, that would produce inefficient or unfair results if applied, to commercial transactions.

Often, the parties to real estate contracts need to consider whether some things on the land are subject to the common law contract rules or to the law governing sales of goods. As noted in Chapter 2, *goods* is a category of personal property that by UCC definition includes growing crops, timber, minerals severed from the realty by the seller, and other items on or in the land that are to be sold *apart* from it.[2] For example, Sara contracts in June to sell her growing corn crop to Grainco for fall delivery. The contract is for the sale of goods and is subject to the contract rules of UCC Article 2. But if Sara instead agreed to sell Blackacre and included the growing crops, timber, minerals, and fixtures *as part of the land*, they retain their character as realty and the common law contract rules apply. The common law rules of contracting differ in many ways from those governing the sale of goods under Article 2 of the UCC.

In the financing of real estate purchases, another specialized body of contract law, UCC Article 3, is significant. It governs the content, issuance, and transfer of *negotiable instruments*. Also called *commercial paper*, negotiable instruments include the promissory notes that most real estate purchasers issue to lenders for advancing the funds needed to pay for the realty. Lenders can hold these notes and collect the principal and interest payments as they come due, but more commonly the lenders sell the notes in the commercial paper market.

The problem of disputes among creditors over security for repayment of loans must also be addressed. To secure repayment, real estate lenders routinely require borrowers to give them a security interest in the realty, usually by means of a mortgage or a deed of trust entitling the lender to have the realty sold if the loan is not repaid. But *fixtures*, which are goods that are treated as part of the realty, may be subject to security interests held by unpaid vendors (fixture sellers) or other fixture financiers. Thus a conflict can arise between the financier of the land, who may claim a fixture as part of the land, and the financer of the fixture. Article 9 of the UCC governs security interests in fixtures—how they are acquired, how they are made good against rival creditors, and who has priority in a fixture if the land is not valuable enough to satisfy all creditors.

Aspects of these specialized bodies of law appear elsewhere in this book. The focus of this chapter, however, is the common law of contracts as applied to real estate transactions.

The Basic Requirements

The courts do not enforce merely social promises such as those to visit a friend or take a date to the prom. But they do enforce promises that are more commercial in nature, including those that are a part of a *contract*, such as a promise to buy a house or repay a loan. The real estate contract discussed in this book is a bargained-for exchange between willing parties, each seeking a benefit from the transaction, which is enforceable because of the mutual expectations of performance. Several elements are needed for this type of contract to exist: (1) *an agreement*, typically resulting from an offer and an acceptance of the offer; (2) an exchange of *consideration*, that is, each party's giving the thing or value ("consideration") sought by the other; (3) a *legal purpose* for the transaction; and (4) parties who have contractual *capacity*, that is, the mental and legal ability to make a contract. In addition, to be enforceable, certain types of contracts, including a contract for the sale of an interest in land, must be evidenced by a *writing* signed by the party against whom enforcement is sought.

Agreement: Offer and Acceptance

To have a valid contract, the parties must, through offer and acceptance, agree on the significant terms of the sale. Otherwise a court would have no basis for compelling the parties to perform their agreement or for providing a remedy to an aggrieved party for the other's breach. In a real estate contract the required terms include, at a minimum, an *identification of the parties*, a *sufficient description of the real estate*, the *price or other consideration*, and the *time set for conveyance*. If any of these terms is missing and cannot be inferred from the conduct of the parties, a court will not have a sufficient basis to enforce the agreement.

A contract results when an *offer* made by one party, the *offeror*, is accepted by the other party, the *offeree*. An *offer* is a statement or other communication by which the offeror gives the offeree a *power of acceptance* which, when exercised by the offeree, results in a contract. An offer normally does three things.

1. Indicates the exchange of consideration the offeror has in mind.

2. Identifies an offeree (the person or group that is to have the power of acceptance).

3. Reveals a commitment or promise by the offeror to deal with the offeree on the terms stated in the offer (i.e., to enter into an enforceable contract).

Some statements are not offers and cannot result in a contract. A mere statement of intention, such as "I would like to buy your house as soon as I can get the money" or "I would sell my warehouse for $300,000," is not an offer because it only suggests a consideration exchange without identifying an offeree or revealing a commitment to sell. Nor is a statement an offer if it merely solicits offers. Jerome writes to Tammy, "I would like to sell my house. I would consider $300,000 for it." Tammy replies, "I will buy your house for $300,000 cash." Jerome's statement was not an offer, since it did not specify Tammy as a person with whom Jerome was willing to deal and did not commit Jerome to dealing with her. Jerome's statement was only an invitation to Tammy to make an offer to him. Although Tammy's response was not an acceptance (because Jerome made no offer), Tammy's response was an offer to Jerome because it had (or incorporated from Jerome's statement) the qualities needed for an offer.

Likewise, advertisements normally are only invitations or solicitations for offers, because most advertisements merely announce a proposed consideration exchange without identifying an offeree or committing the advertiser to a sale. For example, "For sale, Blackacre for $80,000" falls short of being an offer because it does not identify anyone as an offeree and therefore does not create a power of acceptance in anyone. An advertisement *is* an offer, however, if it makes a commitment to sell to a specified person or group of persons (thus giving that person or group offeree status). For examples, Rodney's newspaper ad reading "For sale, the house at 417 High Street for $80,000 to the first financially responsible person who appears there at 9:00 A.M. on October 1 of this year" is an offer because it identifies not only the proposed exchange, but also a person with whom Rodney indicates a willingness to deal. Rodney's use of "first come, first served" would also sufficiently identify an offeree.

Sometimes an advertisement is worded in such a way that its recipient cannot tell whether it was meant as an offer. In such instances, courts interpret the ad as merely a solicitation of offers so that the prospective seller will be an offeree. Consequently, because people responding to the ad cannot claim offeree status themselves, the prospective seller avoids the possibility of being bound to multiple contracts for the same property and being subject to breach-of-contract lawsuits by disappointed contenders. Having offeree status permits the prospective seller to screen offerors for solvency.

Unless the duration of an offer is limited by its terms, it remains open for a reasonable time and can be accepted by the offeree until that time expires or until the offer is terminated by some act of the parties or by operation of law. What amount of time is reasonable depends on the circumstances, including the actions or statements of the parties, prior course of dealing between the parties, and industry customs. Termination by acts of the parties includes the offeror's revocation of the offer and the offeree's rejection of it. An offer terminates by operation of law in a number of ways: by lapse of time, destruction of the subject matter of the contract, death or incompetency of either of the parties, or by supervening illegality of the proposed contract.

Normally an offeror can *revoke* an offer at any time before the offeree accepts, even if the offeror has promised to hold the offer open for a fixed period. If, however, the parties entered into an **option contract** (discussed in Chapter 6), the offeror has a duty to hold the offer open for

BOX 8–1 YOU BE THE JUDGE

Compare the following situations:

- Tommy Hunter is showing Joe Ward his new house. Joe says admiringly, "Boy, Tommy, I'd give a million bucks to have a house like this." Tommy responds, "Deal."
- Joe faxes Tommy a note which says, "I will pay you $250,000 for your house at 353 Bleeker Street, Savannah, Georgia, with conveyance to be made by general warranty deed, subject to easements of record, on or before December 31." Tommy responds by return fax, "Deal."

Does either of these situations result in a contract between Tommy and Joe? Why?

the time promised. Ramona offers to sell her warehouse to Charles for $300,000, adding "and if you pay me $5 I'll give you a week to decide." Charles pays the $5. Under the resulting option contract, Ramona's offer is irrevocable for the week and Charles has that time within which to decide how to respond to the main offer. If Charles elects to accept to buy the warehouse for $300,000, he has "exercised his option."

The offeree's express or implied *rejection* of the offer terminates it. John offers to sell Tina his house for $100,000, adding "I will leave this offer open for a week." If the next day Tina says, "I don't want the house," the offer is expressly terminated. Similarly, a *counteroffer* terminates the original offer. John offers to sell Tina his house for $100,000, and Tina replies, "I will give you $50,000 for it." By making a counteroffer, Tina has impliedly rejected John's offer, thus permitting John to pursue more promising opportunities. Tina's counteroffer does, of course, give John the power to accept it and to form a contract at the $50,000 price.

If the subject matter of the offer is destroyed, the offer terminates automatically. Sam offers to sell Bonnie his house. That night the house burns down. The following day, before either of them learns of the fire, Bonnie accepts the offer. No contract is formed. The offer terminated automatically by destruction of the subject matter before acceptance of the offer.

Ordinarily, if either the offeror or the offeree dies or suffers incapacity before accepting an *offer*, it terminates immediately. But *contract rights*, once established, survive the contracting parties and become binding on their estates. Jane accepts Horace's offer to sell his house to her. The subsequent death or incapacity of either party has no effect on the contract. Jane's obligation to pay money and Horace's obligation to transfer the property will be performed by the personal representatives of their respective estates in the event of death, or their guardians in the event of incapacity. Suppose, however, that Horace sold Jane a 30-day option to buy his house, then died on the third day of the option period before Jane accepted the main offer. Can Jane accept on the 25th day? Like other contracts, an option contract, being a completed contract for the purchase of time to consider the main offer, survives Horace's death and remains open until the option period expires or until it is earlier exercised.

Acceptance is unequivocal assent to the terms of the offer, communicated to the offeror. Unless otherwise specified in the offer, it may be accepted in any manner and by any medium reasonable under the circumstances. Jacob sends Krista a letter containing an offer. At the end he writes, "This offer may be accepted only by signing on the space provided and returning this letter to me." Krista replies immediately by telegram: "I accept your offer." Although her purported acceptance is unequivocal and is communicated to the offeror, there is no contract because the method of acceptance does not meet the requirements of the offer.

Normally, an offer may be accepted only by the person (or persons) identified as offeree or, as discussed in Chapter 6, by an assignee of an option contract that is assignable. An offer may create the power of acceptance in a specified person, or in one or more of a group, or in anyone who conforms to such criteria as "the first financially responsible person to appear at this address on Tuesday, October 6."

Under the so-called "mailbox rule," a correctly addressed acceptance made by a medium expressly or impliedly authorized by the offer is effective when it is sent, e.g., dropped in the mailbox or otherwise put out of the offeree's control. If the offer explicitly requires a particular medium, that medium is authorized. Often, however, the offer does not specify the medium of acceptance. In that event, any medium that is reasonable under the circumstances is authorized.

Offers, rejections, and counteroffers are effective when received. An acceptance made by an authorized medium is effective when it is dispatched. An acceptance made by an unauthorized medium ordinarily is effective when received if the offer is still open. These timing rules create the possibility for troublesome fact situations. Consider the following:

BOX 8–2 YOU BE THE JUDGE

As an officer of your company, you have been given the responsibility of purchasing a new factory site. On October 6, the Bennett Real Estate Company sends you a letter offering to sell your company a described 10-acre industrial site for $300,000, marketable title to be delivered within 90 days. The letter states that the offer is to be held open until October 20. On October 10, you write Bennett a letter stating: "Your offer appears a little high; I will need board approval to exceed the current budget of $250,000, which I will try to get. However, I will pay $250,000 in cash and will close within thirty days." Bennett receives this letter on October 10. On October 12, the board of directors approves the $300,000 purchase price. On October 15, Bennett sends you a letter revoking the offer, which because of a postal strike does not arrive until October 21 at 9:00 A.M. On October 19, at 11:00 A.M., you send a response by Express Mail, which says, "I accept your offer to sell the 10-acre industrial site, described in your letter of October 6, for $300,000, marketable title to be delivered within 90 days." Because of a delay by the post office, this package is not delivered until October 21 at 10:00 A.M.

QUESTIONS:

- What is the legal effect of the promise to keep the offer open until October 20?
- What is the legal effect of your response letter sent on October 10?
- What is the legal effect of the revocation sent on October 12?
- Does your company have a contract to buy the site? If so, on what terms?

Consideration

Consideration is the promise or value that each party to a bargained–for exchange gives for the promise or value given by the other. The typical real estate contract is a *bilateral contract*. In a bilateral contract a party makes a promise for a return promise. For example, Bubba offers (promises) to pay Geraldine $250,000 in return for her promise to convey Blackacre to him. Each promise is consideration for the other.

Courts are reluctant to adjudicate the adequacy of consideration in contracts, unless there is some evidence of misconduct such as fraud. The courts have long accepted the economic theory that the parties themselves are the best judge of price. Consequently, the exchange agreed to by the parties ordinarily will be enforced, even if the judge thinks a different price is appropriate.

BOX 8–3 POINT TO CONSIDER

The offeror can easily avoid the uncertainty created by the application of the diabolical timing rules. Remember that the offeror has control over the terms of the offer. This principle means that the offeror can specify when the acceptance becomes effective. For example, when selling the industrial site described in the box above, Bennett Real Estate Company could have inserted the following provision in its offer to sell: "This offer shall become a contract if Buyer's written acceptance is received by Bennett Real Estate, at 25 North Main Street, Denver, Colorado, before 5:00 P.M. on October 20, 2000."

Legality

A court will not enforce an agreement if its subject matter is illegal, whether made so by statute or by a court decision holding that the agreement is contrary to public policy. The illegal agreement will be held *void*, and the court usually will refuse to aid either party to the agreement. In withholding contract enforcement for public policy reasons, courts normally consider (1) the strength of the public policy involved as evidenced by legislation or precedents within the jurisdiction, (2) whether refusal to enforce the contract will further the public policy, and (3) the relative culpability of the parties to the contract, particularly if a forfeiture of the consideration by one of the parties will be involved. Where only a portion or a clause of a contract is illegal, the court will read the rest of the contract as if the offending clause did not exist and will enforce the remainder of the contract if enough remains to enforce.

Although a real estate contract itself rarely presents legality problems, parties may encounter legality issues in two common areas related to the real estate transaction. First, financing real estate is subject to statutory limitations on usury. Second, real estate contractors and brokers are subject to state licensing requirements.

Most states have consumer protection statutes that establish a maximum rate of interest that lenders may charge in various types of loan transactions. Charging a greater rate of interest than the statutory maximum is referred to as **usury**. The consequences of usury can be severe: In some states, the lender loses all interest above the legal maximum. In other states, the lender loses all interest on the usurious loan. In a few states, courts view a usurious loan as an illegal contract, unenforceable as to both principal and interest.

All states require a license to carry on certain businesses, trades, or professions. In many cases the purpose of licensing requirements is simply to generate revenue. For example, annual business licenses or franchise fees are *revenue-raising* measures. However, all states impose some licensing requirements to protect the public from unqualified practitioners. These *regulatory* licensing statutes generally include some combination of educational requirements, the passing of qualification exams, or experience such as an apprenticeship or supervision in the subject area. Typically licensed under regulatory statutes are real estate brokers, attorneys, architects, and building contractors.

Licensing statutes of either type impose fines or penalties for noncompliance. Noncompliance with a *regulatory* licensing statute, however, may involve additional, more severe consequences, in particular, the loss of the right to collect payment for services rendered. Contracts in violation of regulatory statutes are against public policy, because the violation threatens the public safety. In most states, therefore, contracts entered into by unlicensed practitioners in violation of regulatory statutes are illegal and unenforceable. So Bob, an unlicensed real estate broker, may be unable to collect his commission, even though his efforts resulted in the sale of his client's realty. Likewise, unlicensed building contractor Brenda may be unable to collect her fee, even though she has already constructed the house.

Capacity

The law in every state attempts to protect people from their own improvidence when they are unable to protect themselves. Ordinarily, therefore, people who lack sufficient age or mental competence to appreciate the economic and legal consequences of contracting receive protection in the form of a right to *rescind* (cancel) certain contracts and thus avoid liability for payment. A party usually exercises the right to rescind by obtaining an equitable order of *rescission* (cancellation) from a court. An order of rescission terminates a contract and restores the parties to the extent possible to the positions they had prior to the contract.

Minority. In most states persons under the age of 18 (minors) either cannot contract or, much more commonly, *can* contract but have a right to disaffirm (cancel) their contracts because of their youth and lack of experience in business affairs. The right of disaffirmance extends for a reasonable period after the minor reaches the age of majority.

A number of states place specific limitations on the ability of a minor to enter into real estate transactions. California, for example, makes a minor's contract for the purchase or sale of realty *void*. California minors can *own* realty through, for example, purchase by the minor's legally appointed guardian or by receiving it as a gift, but they cannot purchase or convey it personally. In contrast, most other states permit minors to purchase or sell realty; but many states require minors who want to disaffirm their realty contracts to wait until they reach the age of majority.

Mental Incompetence. Like minors, individuals who are insane or otherwise mentally incompetent may be unable to understand the nature, subject matter, and consequences of their contracts. Depending on the circumstances, a transaction attempted by a mentally incompetent person will be either void or voidable. If a person has been declared mentally incompetent by a court, the incompetent's later attempt to contract is *void*, and the legal guardian appointed for the incompetent becomes the only one who can contract on behalf of the incompetent. Neither party to a void agreement can enforce it. Without adjudication of incompetence, the contract of a person who is actually incompetent is *voidable* by the incompetent, although the law limits the right of the incompetent to rescind the contract where the other party acted fairly and honestly and would be unreasonably disadvantaged by allowing the incompetent to rescind.

An adjudication of incompetence is not limited to cases involving the mentally ill. It may also be used to deal with problems of addiction, such as alcoholism, drug abuse, or habitual gambling, and any of these addictions may lead an individual to financial recklessness. Because of the frequency of such problems, an investigation by a title searcher for guardianship orders is a part of a routine examination of title.

In many types of mental impairment, the victim alternates between periods of incompetence and periods of lucidity. Most courts hold that a contract made during a lucid interval may be fully enforceable. Theoretically, temporary mental impairments resulting from alcohol or drug use should be treated similarly. If Alice is so intoxicated that she cannot comprehend the legal consequences of her agreement, most courts would be willing, in theory, to allow her to avoid the contractual obligations she undertook while intoxicated. Because of the potential for abuse, however, the courts have been less sympathetic to voluntary intoxication as a defense to an otherwise valid contract than they have been to other forms of mental impairment. As illustrated by Case 8.1, courts view claims of intoxication skeptically and will reserve the defense for extreme cases.

Case 8.1

Lucy v. Zehmer
84 S.E.2d 516 (Va. 1954)

This suit was instituted by W. O. Lucy and J. C. Lucy, against A. H. Zehmer and Ida S. Zehmer, his wife, seeking specific performance of a contract in which the Zehmers agreed to sell to W. O. Lucy a tract of land owned by A. H. Zehmer in Dinwiddie county containing 471.6 acres, more or less, known as the Ferguson farm, for $50,000. The contract was written by A. H. Zehmer on the back of a restaurant check after an evening of big talk and whisky drinking, in these words: "We hereby agree to sell to W. O. Lucy the Ferguson Farm complete for

$50,000.00, title satisfactory to buyer," and signed by the defendants, A. H. Zehmer and Ida S. Zehmer.

BUCHANAN, J.

In his testimony Zehmer claimed that he "was high as a Georgia pine," and that the transaction "was just a bunch of two doggoned drunks bluffing to see who could talk the biggest and say the most." That claim is inconsistent with his attempt to testify in great detail as to what was said and what was done. It is contradicted by other evidence as to the condition of both parties, and rendered of no weight by the testimony of his wife that when Lucy left the restaurant she suggested that Zehmer drive him home. The record is convincing that Zehmer was not intoxicated to the extent of being unable to comprehend the nature and consequences of the instrument he executed, and hence that instrument is not to be invalidated on that ground. . . .

The appearance of the contract, the fact that it was under discussion for forty minutes or more before it was signed; Lucy's objection to the first draft because it was written in the singular, and he wanted Mrs. Zehmer to sign it also; the rewriting to meet that objection and the signing by Mrs. Zehmer; the discussion of what was to be included in the sale, and the provision for the examination of the title, the completeness of the instrument that was executed, the taking possession of it by Lucy with no request or suggestion by either of the defendants that he give it back, are facts which furnish persuasive evidence that the execution of the contract was a serious business transaction rather than a casual, jesting matter as defendants now contend. . . .

The mental assent of the parties is not requisite for the formation of a contract. If the words or other acts of one of the parties have but one reasonable meaning, his undisclosed intention is immaterial except when an unreasonable meaning which he attaches to his manifestations is known to the other party. . . .

So a person cannot set up that he was merely jesting when his conduct and words would warrant a reasonable person in believing that he intended a real agreement. . . .

Whether the writing signed by the defendants and now sought to be enforced by the complainants was the result of a serious offer by Lucy and a serious acceptance by the defendants, or was a serious offer by Lucy and an acceptance in secret jest by the defendants, in either event it constituted a binding contract of sale between the parties. . . .

The complainants are entitled to have specific performance of the contracts sued on. The decree appealed from is therefore reversed and the cause is remanded for the entry of a proper decree requiring the defendants to perform the contract in accordance with the prayer of the bill.

Reversed and remanded.

QUESTIONS ABOUT CASE 8.1

1. Does it matter whether this whole scene was part of an elaborate joke by Zehmer?

2. How does the court give Lucy the "benefit of his bargain"?

Contractual Defenses: Enforceability of the Agreement

Although agreement, consideration, legality, and capacity result in the formation of a valid contract, it still may not be enforceable against the breaching party. The contract may have to be evidenced by a writing to be enforced, or the apparent agreement of the parties may be defective for some reason, as when the agreement has been obtained by fraud. These problems are normally raised as defenses to the attempted judicial enforcement of a contract.

Issues of Form

No particular form is required for real estate contracts. The parties are free to word their contracts as they wish, as long as agreement has been reached and the contract contains all of the significant terms. Many contracts, including some dealing with real estate, do not have to be in writing to be enforceable, although a writing is always helpful as an evidentiary matter. However, under the *statute of frauds*, many real estate contracts must be evidenced by a writing to be enforced, and where a written real estate contract is challenged as incomplete or erroneous, the *parol evidence rule* may be applied to determine whether the writing or evidence challenging it will prevail.

Statute of Frauds. In 1677, the English Parliament passed a statute entitled "An Act for the Prevention of Frauds and Perjuries," (commonly referred to as the **Statute of Frauds**), which required certain types of contracts to be evidenced by a writing to be enforceable. This act became a part of the common law of the United States. Therefore, the states have been surprisingly uniform as to which contracts must be evidenced by a writing. To be enforceable under the Statute of Frauds, a contract for the sale (or purchase) of an interest in land must usually be evidenced by a writing signed by the party against whom enforcement is sought. The interests in land for which such a writing is required include fee simple interests, life estates, future interests such as remainders and reversions, long-term leases (usually those for a year or more), express easements (but not prescriptive and implied easements), and mortgages and deeds of trust (because they represent a security interest in realty).

The writing need not be elaborate or formal, and only the party against whom enforcement is sought must sign it, but it must include all of the significant terms of the contract, including an identification of the parties, a sufficient description of the real estate, the price or other consideration, any credit terms, and the time of conveyance. Note that in Case 8.1, *Lucy v. Zehmer*, the memorandum that satisfied the Statute of Frauds was written on the back of a restaurant check and signed by the defendants, A. H. Zehmer and Ida S. Zehmer. The writing stated simply, "We hereby agree to sell to W. O. Lucy the Ferguson Farm complete for $50,000.00, title satisfactory to buyer," and sufficiently evidenced their probably considerably more elaborate contract.

Over the years, the courts have developed exceptions to the writing requirement, for two main reasons: (1) to prevent abuse of the writing requirement by, for example, a seller's entering an oral contract knowing a writing is required but intending later to rescind the contract for lack of the writing, and (2) to prevent hardship and injustice that can result from the unenforceability of oral contracts.

For real estate transactions, the most important exception is that for *part performance*. An oral contract for the sale of realty will be enforced if the parties actually perform the contract to such an extent that a court can see from their nonverbal conduct that a *sale*, as opposed to, say, a *rental*, was intended. Leroy orally agrees to buy Blackacre from Raymond, pays Raymond the purchase price, moves onto Blackacre, and begins fixing the place up. Impressed by the improvements,

Raymond decides to keep Blackacre and refuses to convey it to Leroy. Leroy sues. In considering whether to enforce oral contracts like Leroy's, courts focus on whether the buyer has paid all or a substantial part of the purchase price, taken possession of the property, and begun making improvements. A given state may not require all three actions, but usually the buyer's merely making payment, especially a partial payment, is insufficient, for two reasons. First, the payment at issue might be rental or might be for something other than the purchase of the land in question. Second, the parties can easily be returned to their precontract positions by requiring Raymond to return the money. In this case Leroy has performed his obligations under the oral contract to a degree sufficient for a court to see that the transaction was a sale. The courts of most states would hold that Raymond must convey the property to Leroy despite their failure to comply with the Statute of Frauds.

Parol Evidence Rule. A different set of policies is triggered when there is a written contract. It is common in business for a written contract to be the culmination of a series of oral and written communications between the parties over an extended period of time. The written contract is then generally assumed to be the final and complete agreement of the parties. This assumption is generally shared by courts through the application of the **parol evidence rule**, which prohibits the introduction *at trial* of evidence of prior or contemporaneous communications or negotiations (the "parol evidence") offered to vary the terms of a final, integrated written contract. Any side agreements or "gentlemen's agreements," which the parties have entered into, are likely to be unenforceable under the parol evidence rule. Therefore, the parties need to be sure that the written contract includes all of the promises between the parties.

Genuineness of Assent

Sometimes a party to a transaction alleges that the apparent agreement of the parties is not real because of some defect in the bargaining process that gives the wronged party a defense against enforcement of the contract. The most commonly asserted defense, and therefore the defense of the most concern, is fraud in the inducement.

Fraud and the Seller's Duty of Disclosure. Fraud in the inducement occurs when a person induces another into a contract by making an intentional misstatement of material fact. An innocent victim of fraud in the inducement can elect to rescind the contract or can enforce it instead and recover damages associated with the fraud, including punitive damages. Fraud in the inducement has four elements:

1. One party must have made a misrepresentation of a material fact.

2. The misrepresentation of fact must have been made with knowledge that it was false and with intent to deceive.

3. The innocent party must have reasonably relied on the misrepresentation.

4. The innocent party must suffer some harm or damage as a result of the reliance.

To be fraudulent, a misrepresentation normally must be of a material (significant) existing fact. A misrepresentation of law or legal status would not normally entitle the innocent party to any relief, because such statements should be recognized as the opinion of the other party and not be relied upon. Likewise "sales puffing" or "hype" is not grounds for relief, because it, too, is obviously opinion characteristic of persons interested in making a sale. Statements such as "This is a great house that is likely to appreciate quickly in value," "This house has the best location in the area," and "You'll have the world's finest neighbors" are statements of opinion that cannot be a basis for a fraud claim. In contrast, statements such as "The air conditioner was replaced just last year," "The roof does not leak," and "There is no underground storage tank on the property" are factual in nature and, if not true, provide the basis for a fraud claim. Occupying a middle ground are statements such as "This house is in A-1 condition" or "This house is in a residential zoning district." If made by a layperson, they probably are not sufficiently factual to be considered fraudulent, but if made by a professional such as a building inspector or a lawyer, they often are treated as factual by the courts and may be fraudulent if made with the intent to deceive.

Generally, an *innocent* misrepresentation of material fact, if reasonably relied upon, can be the basis for rescinding a contract. If the innocent misrepresentation was made negligently, the victim may also have damages (as in any cause of action for negligence). However, the courts will not award punitive damages if the defendant's misrepresentation was not intentional.

Currently considerable controversy surrounds the question of whether a party's failure to disclose an adverse fact of significance to the other party is fraudulent. Historically, courts have been reluctant to require parties to disclose adverse facts in real estate transactions, unless special circumstances are present. Among the special circumstances are the seller's knowledge of a dangerous latent (hidden) defect or the existence of a fiduciary relationship between the parties. The traditional legal principle has been characterized by the phrase *caveat emptor* ("let the buyer beware"). The law has assumed that a buyer of realty would conduct a thorough examination of the property. Consistent with the trend toward consumer protection, however, this principle of caveat emptor has been under legislative and judicial attack in recent years. Recently courts have been more likely to impose a duty on the seller to disclose any known material defects. This tension between the older principle of caveat emptor and the disclosure duty appears in an unusual guise in Case 8.2.

Case 8.2.

Stambovsky v. Ackley
572 N.Y.S.2d 672 (N.Y. 1991)

Plaintiff, to his horror, discovered that the house he had recently contracted to purchase was widely reputed to be possessed by poltergeists, reportedly seen by defendant seller and members of her family on numerous occasions over the last nine years. Plaintiff promptly commenced this action seeking rescission of the contract of sale. The trial court dismissed the complaint, holding that plaintiff has no remedy at law.

RUBIN, J.

The unusual facts of this case, as disclosed by the record, clearly warrant a grant of equitable relief to the buyer who, as a resident of New York City, cannot be expected to have any familiarity with the folklore of the Village of Nyack. Not being a "local," plaintiff could not readily learn that the home he had contracted to purchase is haunted. Whether the source of the spectral apparitions seen by defendants seller are parapsychic or psychogenic, having reported their presence in both a national publication ("Readers' Digest") and the local press (in 1977 and 1982, respectively), defendant is estopped to deny their existence and, as a matter of law, the house is haunted. More to the point, however, no divination is required to conclude that it is defendant's promotional efforts in publicizing her close encounters with these spirits which fostered the home's reputation in the community. In 1989, the house was included in a five-home walking tour of

Nyack and described in a November 27th newspaper article as "a riverfront Victorian (with ghost)." The impact of the reputation thus created goes to the very essence of the bargain between the parties, greatly impairing both the value of the property and its potential for resale. The extent of this impairment may be presumed for the purpose of reviewing the disposition of this motion to dismiss the cause of action for rescission.

While I agree with [the trial court] that the real estate broker, as agent for the seller, is under no duty to disclose to a potential buyer the phantasmal reputation of the premises and that, in his pursuit of a legal remedy for fraudulent misrepresentation against the seller, plaintiff hasn't a ghost of a chance, I am nevertheless moved by the spirit of equity to allow the buyer to seek rescission of the contract of sale and recovery of his down payment. New York law fails to recognize any remedy for damages incurred as a result of the seller's mere silence, applying instead the strict rule of caveat emptor. Therefore, the theoretical basis for granting relief, even under the extraordinary facts of this case, is elusive if not ephemeral.

"Pity me not but lend thy serious hearing to what I shall unfold" (William Shakespeare, *Hamlet*, Act I, Scene V [Ghost]).

From the perspective of a person in the position of plaintiff herein, a very practical problem arises with respect to the discovery of a paranormal phenomenon: "Who you gonna' call?" as the title song to the movie *Ghostbusters* asks. Applying the strict rule of caveat emptor to a contract involving a house possessed by poltergeist conjures up visions of a psychic or medium routinely accompanying the structural engineer and Terminex man on an inspection of every home subject to a contract of sale. It portends that the prudent attorney will establish an escrow account lest the subject of the transaction come back to haunt him and his client—or pray that his malpractice insurance coverage extends to supernatural disasters. In the interest of avoiding such untenable consequences, the notion that a haunting is a condition which can and should be ascertained upon reasonable inspection of the premises is a hobgoblin which should be exorcised from the body of legal precedent and laid quietly to rest.

It has been suggested by a leading authority that the ancient rule which holds that mere nondisclosure does not constitute actionable misrepresentation "finds proper application in cases where the fact undisclosed is patent, or the plaintiff has equal opportunities for obtaining information which he may be expected to utilize, or the defendant has no reason to think that he is acting under any misapprehension." However, with respect to transactions in real estate, New York adheres to the doctrine of caveat emptor and imposes no duty upon the vendor to disclose any information concerning the premises unless there is a confidential or fiduciary relationship between the parties or some conduct on the part of the seller which constitutes "active concealment" is required to impose upon the seller a duty to communicate undisclosed conditions affecting the premises.

Caveat emptor is not so all-encompassing a doctrine of common law as to render every act of nondisclosure immune from redress, whether legal or equitable. "In regard to the necessity of giving information which has not been asked, the rule differs somewhat at law and in equity, and while the law courts would permit no recovery of damages against a vendor, because mere concealment of facts under certain circumstances, yet if the vendee refused to complete the contract because of the concealment of a material fact on the part of the other, equity would refuse to compel him to do so, because equity only compels the specific performance of a contract which is fair and open, and in regard to which all material matters known to each have been communicated to the other.". . . Common law is not moribund. Ex facto jus oritur (law arises out of facts). Where fairness and common sense dictate that an exception should be created, the evolution of the law should not be stifled by rigid application of a legal maxim.

The doctrine of caveat emptor requires that a buyer act prudently to assess the fitness and value of his purchase and operates to bar the purchaser who fails to exercise due care from seeking the equitable remedy of rescission. For the purposes of the instant motion to dismiss the action pursuant to CPLR 3211(a)(7), plaintiff is entitled to every favorable inference which may reasonably be drawn from the pleadings specifically, in this instance, that he met his obligation to conduct an inspection of the premises and a search of available public records with respect to title. It should be apparent, however, that the most meticulous inspection and the search would not reveal the presence of poltergeists at the premises or unearth the property's ghoulish reputation in the community. Therefore, there is no sound policy reason to deny plaintiff relief for failing to discover a state of affairs which the most prudent purchaser would not be expected to even contemplate. . . .

Where a condition which has been created by the seller materially impairs the value of the contract and is peculiarly within the knowledge of the seller or unlikely to be discovered by a prudent purchaser exercising due care with respect to the subject transaction, nondisclosure constitutes a basis for rescission as a matter of equity. Any other outcome places upon the buyer not merely the obligation to exercise care in his purchase but rather to be omniscient with respect to any fact which may affect the bargain. No practical purpose is served by imposing such a burden upon a purchaser. To the contrary, it encourages predatory business practice and offends the principle that equity will suffer no wrong to be without a remedy. . . .

In this case at bar, defendant seller deliberately fostered the public belief that her home was possessed. Having undertaken to inform the public at large, to whom she has no legal relationship, about the supernatural occurrences on her property, she may be said to owe no less a duty to her contract vendee. It has been remarked that the occasional modern cases which permit a seller to take unfair advantage of a buyer's ignorance so long as he is not actively misled are "singularly unappetizing." Where, as here, the seller not only takes unfair advantage of the buyer's ignorance but has created and perpetuated a condition about which he is unlikely to even inquire, enforcement of the contract (in whole or in part) is offensive to the court's sense of equity. Application of the remedy of rescission within the bounds of the narrow exception to the doctrine of caveat emptor set forth herein, is entirely appropriate to relieve the unwitting purchaser from the consequences of a most unnatural bargain.

Accordingly, the judgment of [the trial court] . . . should be modified.

QUESTIONS ABOUT CASE 8.2

1. How do you explain the court's comment that the plaintiff here did not have "a ghost of a chance" at law, but went on to grant the equitable relief requested?

2. Does it matter that the particular defect at issue here probably cannot be empirically verified?

Should the result in Case 8.2 be the same for other cases of nondisclosure involving unreasonable fears that disclosure might produce? For example, assume that instead of a ghost, a gruesome murder had been committed in the house, or a resident of the house had died of a loathsome disease. Some states have attempted to resolve this issue by statute. For example, Missouri defines "psychologically impacted property" generally as property in which an inhabitant is or was infected with human immunodeficiency virus or diagnosed with AIDS or that the property was the site of a suicide, homicide, or other felony. The Missouri statutes then provide that the fact that a property is a "psychologically impacted property" is *not* a material or substantial fact which must be disclosed to a buyer in a real estate transaction. Indiana, Idaho, Louisiana, Massachusetts, Oklahoma, Rhode Island, Utah, California, and Colorado, among other states, have similar provisions.

BOX 8–4 POINT TO CONSIDER

A recent trend is for legislatures to require more disclosures on the part of sellers of real estate, particularly residential real estate. For example, Indiana requires sellers to deliver a residential real estate sales disclosure form that asks sellers to evaluate the condition of elements of the property in four categories based upon the seller's actual knowledge: "none/not included," "defective," "not defective," or "do not know." A "defect" is defined as "a condition that would have a significant adverse effect on the value of the property, or that if not repaired, removed, or replaced would significantly shorten or adversely affect the expected normal life of the premises." Sellers must detail specifics on the condition of the appliances, electrical system, water and sewer system, heating and cooling system, and roof. The seller must respond to other questions regarding the property: Are there any structural problems with the buildings, any encroachments? Is the property in a flood zone? Is there any litigation or administrative proceeding affecting the property? Although these disclosures are certainly no substitute for a detailed inspection of the property, they represent a step toward protecting consumers.

Other Grounds for Avoiding the Contract. Less common grounds for avoiding the obligations of a contract for lack of assent include *mistake* of one or both of the parties about a material contract term, *duress*, and *undue influence*.

Generally, mistake is not a sufficient basis for rescinding a contract, especially if the mistake relates to the value of the property or its suitability for the buyer's purposes. If the law were otherwise, contracting parties could avoid contracts for mere inconvenience. Some mistakes, however, are made under such circumstances that it is appropriate for courts to give relief. For example, where one party makes a serious mistake that the other party knew about or should have known about, the mistaken party may rescind. An unbelievably low bid in a construction project is an example; the offeree is not allowed to "snap up" an offer that is too good to be true. Also, in the rare event that both parties are mistaken regarding the same material fact (i.e., have made a mutual mistake of fact) the contract may be rescinded by either party. Joan seeks to buy "the Eagleton property on Fourth Street," but unknown to Joan there are two Eagleton properties and she is thinking of the one on East Fourth Street, while the seller is thinking of the one on West Fourth Street. Either Joan or the seller may rescind the contract.

Duress occurs when a party assents to a contract as a result of a wrongful threat made by the other party. In the words of the *Godfather* movies, duress is "an offer you can't refuse." "Assent" that is induced by duress is ineffective, and the contract is avoidable by the victim. To constitute duress, a wrongful threat must leave the victim of the threats with no reasonable alternative but to obey. Examples originally included threats of a physical nature, such as loss of life or bodily injury, or imprisonment. In recent years, courts have tended to take a more expansive view of what kinds of wrongful threats constitute duress. Section 176 of the Restatement (Second) of Contracts states that a threat is "improper" if "(a) what is threatened is a crime or a tort, or the threat itself would be a crime or a tort if it resulted in obtaining property, (b) what is threatened is a criminal prosecution, (c) what is threatened is the use of civil process and the threat is made in bad faith, or (d) the threat is a breach of the duty of good faith and fair dealing under a contract with the recipient." The Restatement would urge an even broader view of "improper" if the resulting contract is not on fair terms.

Undue influence is unfair persuasion resulting from the abuse of a dominant position or abuse of a close personal relationship or fiduciary relationship. For example, Hector's lawyer, Sarah, having gained Hector's trust over the years (and thus having become a fiduciary), manages Hector's property. Sarah has a duty to manage the property in the best interests of Hector, not for her own benefit. Or Fredrika, a sophisticated businessperson, persuades Frank, her younger, unsophisticated brother, to turn over his realty to her for her to manage. She then uses the property rent-free. In persuading him to hand the property over to her for her benefit, she has taken advantage of his trust arising out of their close personal relationship and has engaged in undue influence.

Performance, Discharge, and Breach

Previously, we have considered how parties form a contract. The next concern is how they satisfy their contractual obligations and what happens if they fail to do so.

Contracting parties usually do what they have agreed to do, and as a result their contractual obligations are extinguished, that is, are *discharged* by performance. But one or both parties may be discharged from the contract in ways other than by performance. First, one or both of the parties can be discharged by failure of a **condition** upon which the contract was based. A condition is an event or state of affairs that must occur before performance under a contract becomes due. For example, contracts for the sale of realty often are conditioned on the buyer's ability to obtain financing for the purchase within a time specified in the contract. If the buyer is unable to do so by the specified date, the obligations of both parties under the contract are discharged. If the buyer can obtain the funds within the specified time, the seller must convey the property and the buyer must pay.

Second, if the parties have not yet commenced performance of their (executory) contract, they may discharge their obligations by rescinding the contract and thus go back to their original positions. Mutual promises to rescind constitute the consideration necessary for a rescission agreement. Clark has a contract to sell Jose his house for $100,000. They change their minds and agree to terminate the contract. The agreement to rescind the contract is enforceable and both parties will be discharged. In this instance, each party would be giving up a legally enforceable contract right and providing the consideration necessary to support the other's agreement to terminate.

Third, in a variety of situations, a contract may be terminated and the parties discharged by operation of law. Bankruptcy of a party, a material alteration of the contract, impossibility of performing the contract, and an aggrieved party's failure to take legal action within the statute of limitations period all constitute such situations. For example, Barbara has a written contract to sell Blackacre to Vladimir for $100,000. Vladimir skillfully alters the contract to read $10,000. The material alteration discharges Barbara from her obligations under the contract. Another example: The Federal Bankruptcy Code gives the trustee in bankruptcy broad powers to discharge contractual obligations of the debtor, especially those under executory contracts.

Failure to perform one's contractual obligations is a breach of the contract, which leaves the nonbreaching party without the complete benefit of its bargain. Jerome contracts to sell Blackacre to Geraldine for $150,000 on or before October 20, 2001. On the scheduled closing date, Jerome conveys Blackacre to Geraldine but Geraldine pays only $140,000. Geraldine has breached the contract, and Jerome, the nonbreaching party, has not received the benefit of his bargain. Jerome may pursue any of the remedies (as outlined in the following examples) available for Geraldine's breach of contract.

A **material breach** of contract excuses the performance of the nonbreaching party. Whether a breach of contract is material depends on the circumstances surrounding the breach. Among the factors bearing on materiality are the economic significance of the breach, the extent to which the nonbreaching party can be compensated, the good faith of the respective parties, and the likelihood of a significant forfeiture by the breaching party. When Geraldine showed up with only $140,000 of the promised $150,000, Jerome could simply have refused to convey the property to her, since her breach, being material, excused his duty to perform.

If one party attempts to repudiate the contract before the time for its performance, this **anticipatory repudiation** of the contract is considered an immediate material breach. Consequently, the nonbreaching party is discharged from the obligation to perform and may pursue any remedies available for breach. In the previous example, assume that Geraldine writes Jerome on October 1, stating that "I just noticed that the shutters on that house are blue and I don't like blue, so I'm am not going to buy the house." Jerome can wait until October 20 in the hope that she will change her mind and perform then, but he is not required to wait. Geraldine's anticipatory repudiation of the contract discharged Jerome when it occurred, and freed him immediately to sell the house to another person and pursue any remedies that he has for breach.

Remedies for Breach of Contract

Contract law strives to protect the *expectations* of the parties to the contract, that is, to assure that the parties receive the "benefit of their bargain" and to put them in the economic position that they would have occupied if the contract had been fully performed. Usually courts accomplish this goal by awarding the nonbreaching party an amount of money damages sufficient to provide the value that he or she would have received if the breaching party had performed. In a typical real estate contract, a court can protect the seller's "expectation interest" by awarding as damages the difference between the agreed purchase price and the (presumably lower) market value of the property, plus any *incidental* or *consequential* damages. **Incidental damages** are costs incurred by the nonbreaching party in reasonable efforts to avoid postbreach loss, as by trying to obtain a substitute sale. **Consequential damages** are foreseeable losses incurred as a direct result of the breach.

Suppose that when Geraldine breached her promise to pay $150,000, Jerome relisted Blackacre, but the real estate market had turned soft so that Jerome needed six additional months to sell Blackacre to Moses for a disappointing $133,000. To resell the property, Jerome incurred additional listing and advertising expenses of $8,000. He also lost $5,000 in earnest money that he had put down on another house, which he could not purchase because he did not have the sales proceeds from Blackacre. To fully protect Jerome's expectation interest (i.e., to give him the benefit of his bargain), a court would award him $30,000. This amount represents the sum of (a) the $17,000 difference between the contract sales price ($150,000) and the lower market price ($133,000), (b) the $8,000 incidental damages incurred in reselling Blackacre, and (c) the $5,000 in consequential damages resulting from the loss of his earnest money deposit on the other house. For Jerome to recover the $5,000 in consequential damages, however, a court must conclude that Geraldine had reason to know when contracting for Blackacre that Jerome would suffer that particular loss if she breached the contract.

Often, seeking damages may be impractical for a seller. Pursuing remedies in court is time-consuming and expensive, and incidental and consequential damages may be difficult to prove. Establishing the market value of the property may also be difficult if the seller has not yet resold the property. To deal with the problems of establishing and proving damages, sellers often insist that a real estate contract include a liquidated damages clause.

A **liquidated damages** clause specifies an amount of money that the buyer or seller will pay in the event that either breaches the contract. The liquidated damages amount is an estimation by the parties of the amount of damages that one party (usually the seller) will incur in the event of breach by the other. For the clause to be enforceable, the amount of liquidated damages specified in it must be a reasonable estimate of the loss anticipated by the breach, given the difficulties of proving the loss. A clause fixing an unreasonably large amount as liquidated damages is interpreted by the courts as a *penalty* designed to compel performance and will not be enforced. Often a buyer is required to pay the liquidated damages as an earnest money deposit, which is payable to the seller in the event of breach by the buyer.

Upon a breach by the seller, a court can protect the *buyer*'s expectation interest by awarding the buyer, as damages, the difference between the price that the buyer agreed to pay and the (presumably higher) market value or market price of the property. However, the buyer may be dissatisfied with this remedy. First, the market price and the contract price may not differ significantly, or that difference may be difficult to for a jury to establish. Second, the buyer's true desire may have been to receive the land, not money damages.

A purchaser of land is not required to settle for money damages, but has instead a right to **specific performance** of the contract. A decree of specific performance is an order by a court of equity instructing an obligor to perform its obligations under a contract. Because a decree of specific performance is considered an extraordinary remedy, it is available only (1) where money damages are unsatisfactory or inadequate, and (2) where the person seeking it is acting reasonably and fairly. Because every parcel of real estate is considered unique, with values not compensable by money, a decree of specific performance is routinely available to deserving buyers for the seller's breach of the real estate contract.

In some circumstances, a court may conclude that it is not possible to protect the expectations of the nonbreaching party. However, the nonbreaching party may have relied on the contract and incurred expenses in preparing or tendering performance. In that event, the court will try to protect the *reliance* interest of the nonbreaching party, by attempting to return the nonbreaching party to its precontract position. The court normally achieves this result through an award of damages based on the extent of the nonbreaching party's reliance. Marv contracts to sell Blackacre to Felicia for $100,000. In reliance on the contract, Felicia makes a $3,000 earnest money down payment and incurs expenses of $300 for a survey of Blackacre, $100 for a termite inspection, $350 for a property inspection, $375 for an appraisal and credit report for an acquisition loan, $650 for a title examination, and $150 for a deposit on a moving van. In breach of the contract, Marv sells and conveys Blackacre to his brother-in-law Stewart for its market value of $100,000, and Felicia brings suit. In this instance, the court cannot order specific performance, because Marv no longer owns Blackacre and cannot convey it. Also, normal expectation-based damages would be unsatisfactory because there is no difference between the contract price and the market price (represented by the actual sales price). A court would, therefore, try to put Felicia back in the position she occupied before the contract was signed by awarding her $4,925, the total expenses she incurred in reliance on the contract.

Real Estate Purchase Agreement

Because of the variety of negotiable terms in any given real estate sales transaction, the contract of sale is likely to be "custom-made," tailored to fit the unique situation at hand. Yet, standard provisions have a place in real estate contracts to address many common problems that recur. In dealing with these common problems, real estate brokers and attorneys prefer the predictability that results from the use of contract clauses that have been tested and enforced by the courts. Also, to the extent that an attorney can use standard contract provisions, transaction costs for the parties can be reduced. Indeed, because of the need for cost savings in the highly competitive residential real estate market, the use of standard forms or standard provisions is nearly universal in residential contracts.

In many states, trade groups representing brokers and attorneys have jointly or separately developed approved form real estate contracts.[3] These forms attempt to anticipate and resolve issues that frequently arise in real estate transactions, and to resolve them in a manner fair to both buyer and seller. These form contracts are typically referred to as "earnest money agreements." The paragraphs that follow include a few sample provisions from forms jointly approved by the North Carolina Bar Association and the North Carolina Board of Realtors. Other states have forms of their own that reflect the peculiarities of their real estate law and practice.

Earnest Money Agreements

The earnest money agreement form usually is structured as an offer, to be submitted to the seller through a broker, together with the buyer's deposit of earnest money. **Earnest money** is a portion of the purchase price delivered to evidence the buyer's good faith and is typically tied to a liquidated damages provision to help assure the buyers' performance under the contract. If the seller accepts the offer, a contract is formed. The earnest money usually is held by the broker to be applied as agreed by the parties to the contract. The earnest money agreement frequently establishes some conditions on the parties' obligations, states the key promises of each party, and provides remedies for breach of the contract.

BOX 8–5 POINT TO CONSIDER

In most cases, it is presumed that the sellers will deliver possession of the property at the same time that title is delivered, i.e., at closing unless the parties agree otherwise. In some states, it is customary for the buyers to provide some time after closing for the sellers to actually move out. In addition to complicating some already thorny timing issues, deferring delivery of possession may create some serious practical and legal issues. First, the buyers will normally be paying on their acquisition loan and will still be paying for a residence. Second, the risk of loss is allocated by the laws of many states to the owner of the property if the parties do not agree otherwise. Many buyers would be surprised to discover that if the property burns down while the sellers are still in possession, the buyers bear the risk of loss. Third, the normal homeowners' insurance policy is designed to cover owner occupants. Finally, the contract should provide for a firm possession date, with the payment of rent (or liquidated damages) by the sellers following that date.

Promises of the Seller

The primary promise of the seller is to convey *marketable title* to the realty covered by the contract. Marketable title is discussed in Chapter 9. The seller normally promises to deliver possession of the property at a stated time, usually at the *closing* discussed in Chapter 11. The seller may also promise to allow appropriate inspections to be made in a timely manner, to maintain the property until closing, to pay all liens and taxes in connection with the property, and to pay the seller's negotiated share of the recording costs. Federal regulations require a seller to disclose the existence of any lead paint on the property.

Box 8–6 Point to Consider

The North Carolina Bar Association Contract provides:

Title must be delivered at closing by General Warranty Deed unless otherwise stated herein, and must be fee simple marketable title, free of all encumbrances except: ad valorem taxes for the current year (prorated through the date of closing); utility easements and unviolated restrictive covenants that do not materially affect the value of the property; and such other encumbrances as may be specifically approved by Buyer. The Property must have legal access to a public way. . . .

Seller agrees to use his best efforts to deliver to Buyer as soon as reasonably possible after the acceptance of this offer, copies of all title information in possession of or available to Seller, including but not limited to: title insurance policies, attorney's opinions on title, surveys, covenants, deeds, notes and deeds of trust and easements relating to the Property.

Promises of the Purchaser

The primary promises of the buyer are to accept the conveyance of the property and to pay the agreed-upon purchase price. However, the buyer will not want to do these things unless the property is in good physical condition and the seller can convey marketable title to the property. Usually, such concerns of the buyer are handled by "conditions precedent" to the buyer's obligation. A condition precedent is an event or state of affairs that must occur before performance under a contract becomes due.

Conditions Precedent to Closing

Conditions precedent are used routinely in an earnest money agreement to handle a variety of problems. For example, because the seller ordinarily has no liability for property defects discovered after the closing, the buyer must verify the physical condition of the property before closing. And the buyer and the buyer's lender need assurance that the seller owns the property. A diligent review of such matters normally requires the services of specialists such as title attorneys, home inspectors (or engineers), and surveyors. Because buyers do not want to go through with the purchase if the property does not meet their minimum standards, real estate purchase contracts typically condition the buyer's purchase obligation on the buyer's being satisfied with the specialists' reviews. If the conditions are not satisfied by a specified date, the parties' contractual obligations end.

Inspection of Title. A real estate sales contract usually requires the seller to deliver **marketable title** as a condition precedent to the buyer's duty to accept the conveyance and pay the purchase price. A marketable title is one that is free from significant defects such as liens or encumbrances that would affect the buyer's intended use of the property. To facilitate the examination of title (and to reduce the expense of the title search), the seller may be required to deliver to the buyer existing title evidence such as surveys and title policies.

Sale and Financing. The purchase of real estate is fraught with timing problems. A seller who sells and conveys a house without having another one to move into may have to find temporary accommodations. Conversely, sellers who agree to buy a house before selling their existing house risk having two houses and two mortgages, the expenses of which they may be unable or unwilling to bear.

A related problem is that buyers are seldom able to purchase real estate without the assistance of financial institutions. To obtain financing, a buyer must apply for a loan, satisfy the lender that the loan will be repaid as it comes due, and give the lender an interest in the realty as collateral to secure repayment of the loan. But lenders are reluctant to make final loan commitments until after the contract has been signed, and may be uneasy about the buyer's ability to make payments on the loan if the buyer's present home has not been sold. Moreover, to avoid problems resulting from fluctuating interest rates, a lender will commit for only limited time to making a loan at a stated rate of interest. A common solution to these problems is to make the buyer's obligations conditional upon the sale of the buyer's present home and conditional upon the availability of financing on acceptable terms.

Termite Inspection. In many parts of the country, termites, carpenter ants, and other wood-destroying insects are problems, especially where wooden parts of a structure touch the ground. In new construction, the soil usually is treated with an insecticide before construction to help prevent infestation. Once infestation has occurred, however, it may be difficult to rid a house of the insects, and they might already have caused damage. To detect and prevent infestations, a pre-closing termite inspection is routine in many parts of the country, and the purchase may be conditioned on a favorable inspection report. The sales contract should state who is to bear the expense of the inspection and, more importantly, who pays for any necessary repairs.

Engineering Report or Structural Inspection. The buyer of real estate is in a difficult position with respect to evaluating the condition of the property. The traditional rule of caveat emptor puts the burden on the buyer to perform a detailed inspection of the property. However, many defects would be unnoticed by the untrained observer. Therefore a structural inspection, or an engineering report in the case of commercial property, is a routine and recommended part of the preclosing process. An inspector examines the condition of the structure, roof, wiring, plumbing, appliances, and so on, and informs the buyer whether these elements meet building code requirements and are functioning as intended. Today, most structural inspections include a test for radiation from radon. Radon is a naturally occurring radioactive gas emitted by radioactive minerals found in rock strata. Some scientists contend that people breathing radon gas have an increased cancer risk. The gas may become concentrated in buildings, particularly in basements that are not well ventilated. If elevated radiation levels are found, remediation steps, such as installing additional ventilation, may be necessary.

As with a termite inspection, the parties will need to decide who bears the expense of the structural inspection and who bears the expense of any repairs. The allocation of the repair expense for structural or system defects may be a troublesome negotiating issue, because neither party will want to bear the expense of putting on a new roof or installing a new air conditioner. Box 8.7 presents an approach for resolving this issue.

BOX 8–7 POINT TO CONSIDER

Negotiating who bears repair expenses if an inspector discovers defects creates problems because of the potential magnitude of repairs. Disagreements on this issue often cause negotiations on potential real estate contracts to founder. Consequently, the North Carolina Bar Form attempts to defer the discussion until the extent of any problem is known by the parties. The form provides for detailed termite and structural inspections. If the inspections disclose the need for repairs the contract provides:

> Seller shall have the option of (i) completing them, (ii) providing for their completion, or (iii) refusing to complete them. If Seller elects not to complete or provide for the completion of the repairs, then Buyer shall have the option of (iv) accepting the Property in its present condition, or (v) terminating this contract, in which case all earnest monies shall be refunded.

One practical problem with this approach is that by the time the inspections are completed, both parties have often made emotional and financial commitments in reliance on the transaction. Literally, the moving van may be in the driveway. The structure of this provision does prevent potential contracts from falling apart because of insubstantial concerns, but this wording can and does lead to games of "chicken" between buyers and sellers, with the more committed party ultimately forced to absorb the bulk of the repair cost to keep the transaction intact.

Remedies for Breach of Contract

In addition to the remedies normally available for breach, the earnest money deposit provision often allows the nonbreaching seller to keep the earnest money as liquidated damages. In some states, if the seller elects to treat the earnest money as liquidated damages, that election eliminates the seller's right to pursue other remedies. Even in those states that do not require an election of remedies, pursuing the breaching party involves the expense and trouble of collection. Therefore, the seller should negotiate for an amount of earnest money sufficient to protect against the

BOX 8–8 POINT TO CONSIDER

The North Carolina Bar Form Contract provides for the delivery of earnest money as a portion of the purchase price and provides that the earnest money

> . . . is to be deposited and held in escrow by _____, as escrow agent, until the sale is closed, at which time it will be credited to Buyer, or until this contract is otherwise terminated. In the event: (1) this offer is not accepted; or (2) any of the conditions hereto are not satisfied, then all earnest monies shall be returned to Buyer. In the event of the breach of this contract by Seller, upon Buyer's request, all earnest monies shall be returned to Buyer, but such return shall not affect any other remedies available to Buyer for such breach. In the event this offer is accepted and Buyer breaches this contract, then all earnest monies shall be forfeited upon Seller's request, but receipt of such forfeited earnest monies shall not affect any other remedies available to Seller for such breach.

FIGURE 8–1   **Commercial Contract Drafting Checklist**[4]

1. Date
2. Identity of Parties
   a. Name
   b. Address
3. Legal Description
   a. Real Property
      (1) Metes and bounds
      (2) Area
      (3) Reference to recorded map or survey
      (4) Reference to Seller's deed
      (5) Description of appurtenant easements (if property is dominant tract)
      (6) Description of other appurtenant rights, e.g.:
         (a) Rights-of-way in adjoining streets/alleys
         (b) Riparian rights in adjacent waterways
         (c) Party wall rights
         (d) Railroad crossing or sidetrack agreements
      (7) Reference to rights under ground leases
   b. Improvements
   c. Fixtures
   d. Tangible personal property
      (1) Contract rights
         (a) Service contracts
         (b) Management contracts
         (c) License agreements (e.g., cablevision, satellite TV)
         (d) Franchise agreements
         (e) Leases
      (2) Warranties
      (3) Trade name
4. Purchase Price/Financing
   a. Gross purchase price
      (1) Medium of payment
      (2) Time of payment
   b. Method of payment
      (1) Earnest money deposit
         (a) Amount
         (b) When due
         (c) By whom held
         (d) Interest or noninterest bearing
         (e) Party entitled to interest
         (f) Whether interest applied to purchase price
         (g) Disposition in event of default
      (2) Purchase money financing (if any)
         (a) Note
            (i) Specify terms

FIGURE 8-1 **Commercial Contract Drafting Checklist (continued)**

    (ii) Check usury statutes
   (b) Security
    (i) Real property—Purchase Money Deed of Trust
    (ii) Rental income—Assignment of Rents
    (iii) Personal property—Security Agreement and UCCs
    (iv) Ownership interest in buyer—Pledge Agreement
  (3) Existing indebtedness
   (a) Description of existing loan
    (i) Type of document
    (ii) Date
    (iii) Parties
    (iv) Original principal balance
    (v) Approximate balance at closing
   (b) Whether being assumed or taken "subject to"
   (c) Prohibition against prepayment or modification?
  (4) Cash at closing
   (a) Method of payment
   (b) Adjustment for balance of existing mortgage (if purchase price previously stated)
5. Seller's Representations and Warranties
 a. Accuracy of information and documentation furnished to buyer
 b. Accuracy of rent roll:
  (1) Leases valid, effective, and unmodified
  (2) Summary of Leases accurate
  (3) Absence of liens or encumbrances
  (4) No amendments, cancellations, or evictions without buyer's consent
  (5) No future defaults
  (6) Fulfillment of all landlord's obligations
  (7) No leasing commissions due as of closing
  (8) No leasing, brokerage, or management agreements in effect as of closing (except as approved by buyer in writing)
  (9) No default or notice of default
  (10) No prepaid rentals, rent concessions, or setoffs
  (11) No tenant claims or counterclaims
  (12) No future prepaid rentals
  (13) No tenant defaults
  (14) Security deposits accurate and no tenant claims against same
  (15) Indemnity
 c. Termite letter prior to closing, and completion or repairs prior to closing (escrow or setoff if not completed)
 d. Status of existing loan(s):
  (1) Future compliance with requirements of loan documents
  (2) No restrictions on conveyances or secondary financing
  (3) No other loan documents
  (4) No unfulfilled lender requirements regarding maintenance and upkeep

FIGURE 8-1   **Commercial Contract Drafting Checklist (continued)**

         (5)   Maximum loan balance at closing

         (6)   Allocation of transfer/assumption fee or other costs

   e.   No postclosing employee obligations

   f.   No survival of service, maintenance, or management contracts

   g.   No threatened or pending litigation

   h.   No unpaid assessments

   i.   No new leases or agreements regarding property

   j.   Access to books and records

   k.   Furnishing of rental reports and monthly income and expense statements

   l.   Status of title

   m.   Condition of property

         (1)   Continued maintenance of property

         (2)   Operation of property

         (3)   Condition of mechanical systems at closing

         (4)   Condition of improvements at closing

         (5)   Leaseable space to be in rentable condition at closing

   n.   Assignment of warranties and guaranties

   o.   Compliance with applicable laws, ordinances, regulations; validity of certificate of occupancy; obligations to cure any violations

   p.   Absence of boundary disputes and encroachments

   q.   Access to public streets; vehicular access

   r.   Utilities:

         (1)   Continued availability

         (2)   No special fees or charges

         (3)   No special agreements

   s.   No changes required or recommended by insurance companies

   t.   Flood certification

   u.   Adequate drainage

   v.   Specific repair obligations (if any) (setoff or escrow if not completed)

   w.   Authority to sell

   x.   Zoning

         (1)   Proper zoning for present use

         (2)   To be zoned properly for intended use (if different from present use)

   y.   Obligation to remedy any noncompliance (setoff or escrow if not done)

   z.   Term—survival beyond closing (only as to preclosing violations)

6.   Buyer's Representations and Warranties

   a.   Compliance with assumed contracts and indemnity regarding same

   b.   No reliance on seller regarding:

         (1)   Financial matters

         (2)   Physical nature of property and improvements

         (3)   Any other matters except as expressly represented or warranted

   c.   Survival

7.   Conditions Precedent to Closing

   a.   Satisfactory title—title insurance commitment (ALTA Form) insuring:

FIGURE 8–1   **Commercial Contract Drafting Checklist (continued)**

    (1)   Title (subject only to "permitted exceptions")
    (2)   Access
    (3)   Zoning (if available)

  b.   Remedies for title defects—seller's right to cure

  c.   As-built survey approved by Buyer's attorney showing no exceptions or encroachments (except "permitted exceptions")

  d.   Receipt of satisfactory evidence regarding zoning (if title insurance not available) and compliance with existing building and fire regulations (unless "grandfathered")

  e.   Receipt of all required consents/estoppel certificates

  f.   Receipt of satisfactory evidence regarding proper authorization for sale

  g.   Performance of Seller's (Buyer's) agreements and covenants

  h.   Accuracy of Seller's (Buyer's) warranties and representations

  i.   Buyer's obtaining requisite financing (either from seller or third party). Specify basic terms, such as (1) amount, (2) interest rate, (3) term. Seller may require (1) good faith effort and (2) copy of loan commitment by certain date

  j.   Receipt of all governmental approvals required for Buyer's intended use (e.g., rezoning) if different from present use; Seller's agreement to cooperate in rezoning

  k.   Satisfactory resolution of any pending litigation

  l.   Receipt of all "closing documents" (listed in part 8h)

  m.   Absence of any tenancies (other than those shown on rent roll, all of which shall be in full force and effect)

  n.   Receipt of satisfactory inspection reports (including termite report)

8. Closing
  a.   Date, time
  b.   Buyer's option to extend (additional earnest money)
  c.   Seller's option to extend (to remedy title defects, correct violations)
  d.   Prorations (if any)
    (1)   Rents
      (a)   Seller entitled to delinquent rents
      (b)   Seller entitled to pro rata share of annual rents
    (2)   Utility charges
    (3)   Assessments for improvements
    (4)   Charges under contracts remain in effect
    (5)   Interest under existing mortgage
    (6)   Any escrow account under existing mortgage to be purchased by Buyer
    (7)   Other operating expenses
    (8)   Fuel
  e.   Assignment of tenant security deposits and other prepaid fees
  f.   Items to be paid for by Seller:
    (1)   Revenue Stamps
    (2)   Seller's attorneys fees
    (3)   Termite Report
    (4)   Brokerage commission (if any)
    (5)   Leasing commissions (if any)

FIGURE 8–1 **Commercial Contract Drafting Checklist (continued)**

        (6) Lender's attorneys fees

        (7) Servicing agent fee

        (8) Other costs incurred by seller in connection with performance

   g. Items to be paid by buyer:

        (1) Recording fees

        (2) Loan transfer fee

        (3) Title insurance premium

        (4) Survey

        (5) Buyer's attorneys fees

        (6) Inspections

        (7) Other costs incurred in connection with performance

   h. Seller's closing documents (attach as exhibits where possible)

        (1) General Warranty Deed (conveying good, marketable fee simple title subject only to "permitted exceptions")

        (2) Bill of Sale

        (3) Assignment of Leases

        (4) Owner's Affidavit

        (5) Any other documents required by title insurance company

        (6) Blanket Assignment

        (7) Assignment of Insurance Policies

        (8) As–Built Plans and Specifications

        (9) Reaffirmation of representations and warranties

     (10) Original leases, tenant files, keys, etc.

     (11) Original Certificate of Occupancy

     (12) Mortgagee Estoppel Certificate

     (13) Tenant Estoppel Certificates

     (14) Authorization of sale (and financing)

     (15) Any other consents/authorizations or documents required by title insurance company (or Buyer's counsel)

     (16) Notices to tenants (transfer of security deposits)

     (17) Seller's counsel's opinion regarding existence and power of Seller to convey

     (18) Notice to mortgagee regarding sale of property and transfer of escrows

     (19) Current bills

     (20) Contracts, licenses, permits

     (21) Title Insurance Binder

     (22) Any other documents deemed necessary by buyer's counsel

   i. Buyer's closing documents

        (1) All sums owed to Seller

        (2) Consents and authorizations regarding purchase and financing

        (3) Documents required by mortgage for transfer of loan

        (4) Counsel's opinion (if purchase money financing involved)

9. Brokerage Commissions

   a. Specify (1) amount, (2) to whom due, (3) when earned, and (4) by whom owed

FIGURE 8–1 Commercial Contract Drafting Checklist (continued)

    b.   Cross indemnification

10. Default

    a.   Buyer's remedies

        (1) Consummate and receive credit against sale price

        (2) Postpone and let Seller cure

        (3) Terminate, and

            (a) Receive back earnest money deposit if default beyond Seller's control, or

            (b) Receive back earnest money deposit and either liquidated damages or pursue remedies at law or in equity

    b.   Seller's remedies

        (1) Retain earnest money as liquidated damages

11. Condemnation or Destruction (risk of loss)

    a.   Destruction

        (1) Dollar limit on cost of repairs—option to terminate if greater

        (2) Seller to assign rights to any insurance proceeds

        (3) Credit against sale price if insurance proceeds insufficient

        (4) Buyer to participate in claim settlement proceedings

    b.   Condemnation (See Destruction)

    c.   Risk of loss (assumed by seller prior to closing)

12. Buyer taking property "as is" (except as expressly warranted)

13. Assignment

    a.   Purchaser's right to assign contract to related entity

    b.   Discharge from duties and liabilities

14. Notices

    a.   Addresses

    b.   When effective

    c.   Notice means "written notice"

15. Miscellaneous

    a.   Governing law

    b.   Cumulative rights to those at law and in equity

    c.   Nonwaiver

    d.   Merger clause

    e.   Binding upon successors

    f.   No oral amendments

    g.   Time of the essence

    h.   Possession delivered at closing

    i.   Execution in counterparts

    j.   Captions and headings not part of contract

    k.   Gender and number

    l.   Execution of additional documents

    m. Execution of Memorandum in recordable form

16. Signatures

    a.   Put "under seal"?

buyer's breach, but not so large that a court would rule it an unenforceable penalty. If the seller breaches the contract, the buyer is entitled to the return of the earnest money and, in addition, will normally be entitled to specific performance or damages.

The Option Contract

An option contract provides that an offer will be held open for a stated duration. As noted in Chapter 6, option contracts are especially useful in the sale of commercial realty. A buyer wanting to purchase property on given terms may be uncertain whether the necessary financing will be available. The seller may be reluctant to consent to an outright sale because if the buyer cannot obtain financing, the seller will have had the property off the market without any compensation. The option contract gives the buyer time to acquire financing, and the payment that the seller receives for granting the option compensates the seller for taking the property off the market. The option contract should cover all of the material terms of the sale. Upon the optionee-buyer's exercise of the option by a written notice of acceptance to the optionor-seller, the parties have a contract, with all of the associated obligations and remedies.

Commercial Real Estate Contracts

Sales contracts for commercial real estate resemble the residential earnest money agreement in structure and in the requirements for enforceability. The principal difference is in the size and scope of the project. Commercial real estate usually involves a larger financial commitment. And, by definition, commercial real estate represents an investment designed to produce a stream of income from the property. So, in addition to the normal concerns associated with purchasing real estate, prospective buyers of commercial realty will need to consider systematically all the factors that may affect the profitability of the endeavor, including the stream of income. To facilitate their assessments of particular commercial properties, real estate professionals use contract drafting checklists to make sure that all areas of concern have been discussed by the parties and are appropriately addressed in the contract of sale. Figure 8–1 provides a checklist that reveals the myriad considerations involved in purchasing income-producing property.

Self-Study Questions

1. What is the purpose of contract law?

2. What are the requirements for a valid contract?

3. What are the material terms in a contract for the purchase and sale of real estate? Why are these terms material?

4. How long is an offer to buy effective?

5. When is an acceptance of a contract effective to form a valid contract?

6. What are the requirements for *fraud*? Why is fraud a defense to an otherwise valid contract? How do courts distinguish fraud from permissible sale tactics?

7. What is the difference between *duress* and *undue influence*?

8. What is a *breach of contract*?

9. What remedies does an aggrieved buyer or seller of real estate have?

10. What is the significance of *earnest money* in an earnest money contract?

Case Problems

1. Joseph Cardi sued Alice Gump claiming that she fraudulently misrepresented the condition of the home that he bought from her. The defendant had signed a disclosure statement which indicated that the basement had no current water leakage, water accumulation, or excess dampness. In fact, the plaintiff claimed that the house had a basement with defects that led to water leakage and water accumulation. The evidence adduced at trial showed that the plaintiff had personally inspected the house five or six times and had two professional inspectors examine the house. Both inspectors noted some water marks or "efflorescence" on the basement walls, possibly as a result of water penetration through the basement walls, indicating drainage problems. What result? *Cardi v. Gump*, 698 N.E.2d 1018 (Ohio App. 1997).

2. Gerald Ashkouti signed a contract to purchase 66 acres of land for $3 million from a trust under the will of Marie Widener. The obligations of the buyer were conditioned upon a satisfactory inspection of the property, including zoning satisfactory for the buyer's purpose. During the inspection period, the parties executed an amendment to the contract prompting a rezoning request for 38 of the acres. The amendment provided that if the rezoning achieved a zoning of RM-13, the purchase price would remain $3 million and if the rezoning resulted in a zoning of RM-10, the purchase price would be $2.8 million. The rezoning attempt was denied. The Trust then sold and conveyed the property to another buyer for $3.2 million. Ashkouti sued claiming breach of contract. What result? *Ashkouti v. Widener*, 500 S.E.2d 337 (Ga. App. 1998).

3. A home seller completed a statutory disclosure form indicating that the basement walls had some cracks and crumbling and there was some water penetration in the northwestern corner. When the buyer inquired further, the seller indicated that the buyer could remove some of the basement paneling to check. The seller did not tell the buyer that the paneling had just been installed in anticipation of sale and that she had made pictures of the basement walls before, during, and after the installation. The buyer discovered after closing that the foundation was in fact badly cracked and disintegrating and sued. The applicable South Dakota disclosure statute provides that there is no liability for defects if the seller "truthfully completes" the disclosure statement. What result? *Engelhart v. Kramer*, 570 N.W.2d 550 (S.D. 1997).

4. A wife accuses her husband of sexual improprieties with their daughter and threatens to expose him to his employer, which would cost him his job. They execute a written agreement in which she agrees not to bring up their "past differences" in return for his conveyance to her of his interest in some property. Is this agreement enforceable? *Quiring v. Quiring*, 944 P.2d 695 (Idaho 1997).

5. Cain orally agreed to purchase an 806-acre farm from Cross for $1,000 per acre and paid a $10,000 down payment. Although Cain arranged for financing for the balance, Cross sold and conveyed the property to a third party. Cain sues for breach of contract. What result? *Cain v. Cross*, 687 N.E.2d 1141 (Ill. App. 1997).

6. The Mitchells contracted to sell a house to the Norrises. An inspection discovered that the septic system was not working properly. The sellers hired the inspector, Farmer, to make the necessary repairs. Farmer obtained a construction permit from the county containing the following provisions: "Recommendations: Summertime use, no laundry, aerated faucets, low flush toilets. Conserve water." After Farmer completed his work, the system was inspected and approved as meeting the conditions of the permit. The buyers were not given a copy of the permit, nor were they told of the conditions in the permit. Almost immediately after the closing, when the son began living in the house in January, he experienced problems with the septic tank. When the buyers then asked the sellers about the septic repairs, they were sent a copy of the construction permit containing the restrictions. When they then found out that it would be expensive to upgrade the system for year-round use, they sued for fraud. What result? *Norris v. Mitchell*, 495 S.E.2d 809 (Va. 1998).

Endnotes

1. Approximately 70 million families own homes in the United States, with roughly 890,000 new housing sales in 1998, and more than 4 million sales of existing single-family homes.

2. Uniform Commercial Code § 2-105 defines "goods" as "all things (including specially manufactured goods) which are moveable at the time of identification to the contract for sale other than the money in which the price is to be paid, investment securities (Article 8) and things in action. 'Goods' also includes the unborn young of animals and growing crops and other identified things attached to realty as described in the section on goods to be severed from realty (Section 2-107)."

3. In Minnesota, for example, the Minnesota State Bar Association and the Minnesota Association of Realtors have each created standard form contracts. These forms are compared and contrasted in Residential Real Estate Committee, Real Property Section, Minnesota Bar Association, *Minnesota Residential Purchase Agreements*-1998, available from http://www2.mnbar.org/realprop/mn98rpa.htm (1998).

4. A different form of this checklist was prepared by Woodard E. Farmer, Jr., Saxby M. Chaplin, Robert B. Bennett, Jr., and Timothy W. Gilbert for *Real Property Practice Handbook*, (1982), and revised by Woodard E. Farmer and published in Woodard E. Farmer, Jr., *Commercial Property Transactions* (1995).

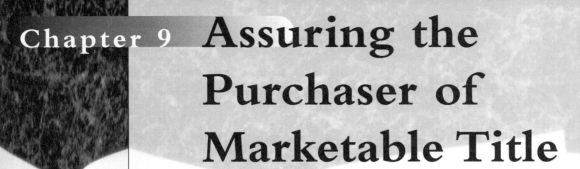

Chapter 9 Assuring the Purchaser of Marketable Title

In day-to-day purchase transactions, we tend not to think much about the quality of the seller's title. When we go into Wal-Mart for example, we do not ask to see the store manager's paid receipt for the goods before making our purchase. We simply assume that if we pay for the goods we will receive title. Our level of concern about title is higher, however, as our investment becomes more significant. Purchasers of real property make substantial investments. But most sales of real estate are isolated transactions, in that the buyers and sellers have no prior relationship and are unlikely to have a future relationship. Usually, buyers literally do not know with whom they are dealing. Even an honest seller may be ignorant about the state of the title, or the property may be subject to an encumbrance, such as an easement, that will adversely affect the buyers' intended use. And, most real estate being sold today is encumbered by debt still owed by the seller. This debt, like other matters affecting title, will be of obvious concern to the buyer.

Because lenders advance large sums for the purchase of realty, they too are concerned about the quality of the seller's title, as security for the buyer's new debt. To assure a lender that its loan will be repaid, the buyer must grant the lender a security interest in the realty. Then the lender, if not repaid, can force the sale of the property and have the proceeds applied to its debt.

For the protection of buyers and lenders, the law requires the seller to deliver "marketable title," unless the parties involved have agreed to a lesser quality of title. If the seller is obligated to deliver a marketable title but cannot do so, the buyer has no obligation to go through with the purchase and the lender is not obliged to make the loan. This chapter discusses the meaning of marketable title and surveys the techniques by which a seller may assure a buyer or lender that the seller's title is marketable.

The Requirement of Marketable Title

All real estate sales contracts contain an express or implied covenant requiring the seller to deliver marketable title, subject to any exceptions stated in the contract. Some title defects and other circumstances make a title unmarketable; others do not. This part of the chapter deals with the general nature of marketable title, and with what impairs and does not impair title marketability.

Nature of Marketable Title

Marketable title to land is one that is free from material defects, grave doubts, and the likelihood of litigation—a title, in other words, that would be acceptable to an objective, reasonably prudent purchaser. A marketable title usually is *not* a "perfect" or "complete" title. Indeed, few sellers of realty in America could deliver a perfect title, because few own the complete bundle of rights. The mineral rights to a parcel might have been sold to a mining or an oil company decades ago, or the use of the land may be restricted by covenants or zoning ordinances. Easements may burden the property. The seller may have mortgaged it or leased some or all of it to a third person. Title defects may even be remote enough in time or small enough that a reasonable buyer would not doubt the marketability of the seller's title.

What Impairs Marketability of Title

A seller's title is unmarketable if at least a reasonable possibility exists that the seller lacks all or part of the title that he or she purports to sell. For example, David agrees to sell Ursula a 30-acre parcel. Ursula's title search discloses that David inherited the land as tenant in common with his two sisters when his parents died. Because David owns only one-third of the 30-acre parcel, his title is unmarketable and the sales contract cannot be enforced against the buyer.

The seller's title may also be unmarketable if the title is subject to an encumbrance. An **encumbrance** is a right or interest of a third party in the property, which affects or impairs, but does not negate, the grantor's title. Examples are mortgages, judgment liens, liens for taxes or assessments, mechanics or materialmen's liens, easements, leases, and restrictive covenants. Ling agrees to buy Blackacre from Bill. Shortly before closing, during her final inspection of the property, she is ordered to leave by a surly individual who turns out to be Bill's tenant under an oral lease. Bill's title is unmarketable.

Or, Ling discovers before closing that Bill's neighbor, Scrugg, has for many years farmed a 100-foot-wide strip of Bill's land running the length of the parcel and claims the strip as his own. Regardless of whether Scrugg has established ownership by adverse possession, Ling faces a potential lawsuit if she buys the land, either by having to sue to establish her title or by having to defend her ownership against Scrugg's claim if he sues her. Bill's title is unmarketable.

The seller has no obligation to deliver marketable title until the closing. In fact, it is generally assumed that certain encumbrances, such as the seller's mortgage, will be satisfied by the proceeds of the sale and removed from record at or following the closing of the sale. By law or by custom, depending on the state, the buyer is expected to notify the seller of any title defects that are discovered so that the seller can eliminate or "cure" them before closing.

What Does Not Impair Marketability of Title

Conditions that may make the property undesirable do not necessarily affect the marketability of the title. The seller may have marketable title to property that proves to be in bad physical condition or infested by termites or subject to flooding. Some title defects may be so old or minor that a reasonable person would not fear loss. For example, a very old outstanding dower interest is a title defect, but if the interest is old enough that its owner probably has died, an actual claim is unlikely to arise.

Consider the court's struggle in the following case to determine whether a title defect renders a title unmarketable.

Case 9.1

P&D Enterprises v. Restifo

2000 Conn. Super. LEXIS 8 (Conn. Super. 2000)

[Reporter's Note: This decision is unreported and may be subject to further appellate review.]

On June 15, 1999, the plaintiff P&D Enterprises contracted in writing to sell the Restifos a residential property at 2 Newton Ponds in Woodbridge (the "property").

Just prior to the closing, a title search conducted by an attorney representing the defendants disclosed a Surface Water Agreement encumbering the property. This agreement was recorded on the land records on December 19, 1997, and was executed by the seller and the owners of an adjoining parcel, Alan and Winifred Elton. The Surface Water Agreement required the owner of the property to (1) ensure the free passage of surface water across the property; (2) reimburse the Eltons for any costs incurred by them to repair any damage to the driveway or other improvements on the Elton property caused by ponding on the Elton property; and (3) to maintain a landscape buffer between the two adjoining properties with fifteen trees planted seven feet apart along the eastern border of the property. The Surface Water Agreement also called for the payment of costs and attorneys fees incurred by the Eltons in any legal action to enforce the provisions of the agreement.

The Restifos refused to close, contending that the Surface Water Agreement rendered the title to the property unmarketable. The sales agreement explicitly stated that the title to be conveyed was to be marketable as determined by the Standards of Title of the Connecticut Bar Association.

DEMAYO, J.

Both sides cite as leading cases on the subject of "marketability" *Perkins v. August* and *Frank Towers Corp. v. Laviana.* Both cases are referred to in the Standards of Title, specifically comments 3 and 4 to Standard 1.1:

> "EXAMINING ATTORNEY'S ATTITUDE"
>
> The purpose of an examination of title is to secure for the attorney's client a title which is in fact marketable, even though marketability may not appear on the land records, subject to no other encumbrances than those expressly provided by the client's contract. Objections and requirements should be made only when their regularities or defects present a real and substantial probability of litigation or loss. . . .
>
> *Comment 3.* Neither the unwillingness of a vendee to accept a title nor the fact that the title is not satisfactory to his attorney renders a title unmarketable. A title defect will not render a title unmarketable unless it presents a real and substantial probability of litigation or loss which will prevent it from being sold at a fair price to a reasonable purchaser or mortgaged to a party of reasonable prudence as security for a loan. . . .
>
> *Comment 4.* When a vendee or lender refuses to accept a title because of a claimed defect, it is not the function of the trial court to try the title [but] rather to determine whether it is free from reasonable doubt in law or in fact.

In this case, the defendants consulted James Nugent, an attorney whose specialty is real estate law. He concluded that this title was unmarketable largely because of the serious uncertainties involved. Specifically, he noted, that the [Surface Water Agreement] had been in existence only since December 19, 1997, and hence no "history" could be ascertained to be relied on in evaluating its impact. He further stated that the [Surface Water Agreement] terms with no cap as to time, limit of liability, or frequency of suit rendered it a serious encumbrance.

Mr. Nugent's opinion and comments are particularly significant in light of the language, of the introduction to the Standards of Title. This language . . . is as follows:

> . . . Once the attorney has considered all the facts, he must then arrive at a conclusion of the ultimate issue: Is the title marketable? This is not a mere question of a good title or bad title. It is a question of the amount of the risk an attorney should assume for his client. It requires an attorney to consider what other title examiners are likely to do when they come to pass upon the title. Never mind the case law definition of marketability. Case law may decree that a mere suspicion cast upon a title is not sufficient to make it

unmarketable; or that a title is not unmarketable because the vendee is unwilling to accept it or because it is unsatisfactory to his attorney. Yet, attorneys know that out in the marketplace, the attitude of those attorneys who examine and approve titles for the purpose of passing upon their marketability is of even greater importance. Therefore, regardless of what case law may decree, every attorney knows that he owes a duty to his client to advise him not only whether, in his opinion, the particular title is good, but whether it is likely to be acceptable to a subsequent attorney acting for a potential purchaser or mortgage lender. From the attorney's point of view, a "marketable title" is not merely one which can be forced upon an unwilling purchaser. In actual practice, it is a title which will be accepted by another attorney who may be called to appraise the title at a later time. Therefore, although an attorney may himself be willing to waive a particular defect or irregularity as one which does not impair the title's validity or subject the owner to a conflicting claim, he must try to anticipate, whether there is a possibility that another attorney may subsequently reject the title, or, at least, demand that the defect be removed or the purchase price reduced as a condition of approving it.

The evidence before the court is that the title insurance company would have excepted the [Surface Water Agreement] from the title policy coverage. Further, Mr. Nugent testified that the attorney for the bank to which the defendants had applied for a mortgage was questioning the [Surface Water Agreement] and was demanding some protection from any judgment and ensuing consequences, or the complete removal of the [Surface Water Agreement].

On the basis of this evidence the court concludes that the title in question was unmarketable and that the defendants were justified in refusing to close title to the property. The court cannot find that this title was "free from reasonable doubt, in law or in fact." . . .

It is therefore the conclusion of the court that the application for a prejudgment remedy should be denied.

QUESTIONS ABOUT CASE 9.1

1. What burdens does the Surface Water Agreement place on the property?

2. Why were these burdens placed on the property?

3. Should these burdens be sufficient to render the title unmarketable?

Title Assurance Techniques

We turn now to the basic methods of assuring buyers and lenders that a seller's title is marketable. Title assurance methods include deed covenants, recording acts, examination of title, physical surveys, and title insurance.

Title Protection Under the Deed

A seller of *goods* (a type of personal property whose sale is governed by Article 2 of the Uniform Commercial Code) by law automatically warrants clear title to the goods unless the seller specifically disclaims the warranty. In sharp contrast, a seller of *real estate* does not automatically warrant clear title merely by executing a deed, the method normally used in the United States for transferring realty. In fact, one type of deed often is used precisely because the seller, by using it, avoids making warranties of title. Other types of deeds, however, do provide warranty protection, though they vary in the number and types of warranties made. The most common types of deeds are (1) the quitclaim deed, (2) the grant deed, and (3) the warranty deed. Before discussing the types of deeds and the title assurance associated with each type, it is necessary to provide some background on the nature and function of a deed and the requirements for its validity.

Nature and Function of a Deed

Transfers of title may be voluntary or involuntary. Sales and gifts of an interest in realty are *voluntary* transfers that, as noted in previous chapters, are accomplished by the grantor's delivering a written deed to the grantee. Delivery of the deed simultaneously extinguishes transferor's interest and establishes it in the transferee. *Involuntary* transfers include condemnation of property by government action (discussed in Chapter 16), transfers resulting from foreclosure of a mortgage (Chapter 10), and acquisition of title by adverse possession (Chapter 6). Deeds may be used to evidence involuntary transfers, but often they result from a court order. In adverse possession, ownership transfers automatically from the victim of the trespass to the successful adverse possessor (the trespasser) simply by virtue of the trespasser's having met the requirements for adverse possession. No deed is involved, although if a successful adverse possession is contested in court, the court will issue a ruling or order verifying that ownership is now in the adverse possessor.

Requirements for a Valid Deed

To be enforceable under the Statute of Frauds, a deed must be in writing and signed by the grantor. The grantee need not execute the deed. To be *valid*, however, a deed must also include the name or description of the grantee, words of grant indicating an intent to transfer title to the grantee, and a legally sufficient description of the land and the legal interest to be transferred.

For a deed to be recordable, statutes in all states require "proof of execution," that is, proof that the grantor's signature is genuine and that the deed was voluntarily made. Virtually all states require that the deed be "acknowledged" for this purpose. *Acknowledgment* is the grantor's declaration before a notary public, consul, officer in the armed forces, or some other official with certifying power that the deed and the grantor's signature are genuine. After verifying the grantor's identity, the official makes a written certification on the deed, adds his or her seal, and notes the acknowledgment in the official's record book. A few states require, in addition to acknowledgment, the signatures of one or two "subscribing witnesses." Some states accept subscribing witnesses or, in limited circumstances, the testimony of handwriting experts as alternatives to acknowledgment. However, neither acknowledgment nor recording is necessary for a deed to be valid as between the parties to it, though recording is of course advisable to provide maximum protection to the grantee against rivals claiming title to the property.

No consideration is required for a deed to be valid, because an owner who chooses to make a gift of the property normally has the right to do so. Governmental entities, however, are usually prohibited by law from making gifts, and individuals are prohibited by bankruptcy and creditor's rights laws from making a gift that would operate as a fraud on creditors. Transactions such as these are not valid unless the government and debtors receive payment.

A deed that meets all of the form requirements, including execution by the grantor, is still not effective to transfer title until the deed is *delivered* by the grantor and *accepted* by the grantee. Usually, acceptance is presumed if the conveyance would be beneficial to the grantee, often without evidence that the grantee even knew of the deed or its delivery. Delivery is required because it reveals an intention on the part of the grantor that the deed is to be operative. Although delivery may consist of a physical handing over of the deed to the grantee, delivery can take other forms. The key issue is the intent of the grantor. A deed is not delivered unless the grantor has the intent to presently transfer title, so the specific physical acts done to accomplish delivery are significant only to the extent that they reveal the grantor's intention. Consider the difference between the following two situations: (1) Alice executes a deed conveying Blackacre to Jethro and hands it to him, saying, "Take good care of my old home." (2) Alice executes a deed conveying Blackacre to Jethro and hands it to him, saying, "You have always been my favorite son, and I want you to have Blackacre when I die. Hang onto this deed and record it then." In the first situation, Alice has delivered the deed because her actions and words indicate an intent to make a present transfer of title. In the second situation, Alice made no delivery because her words indicate that she wanted the transfer to become operative at a future date.

If an otherwise valid deed is actually in the hands of the grantee, then the rebuttable presumption is that the deed has been properly delivered. If the deed remains in the possession of the grantor, the presumption is the opposite, that the grantor did *not* intend to deliver the deed. So unless the grantee can rebut the presumption by proving that the grantor *did* intend delivery, the deed transfers no title. Delivery is also presumed if the grantor records the deed.

Upon delivery of a deed, title to the property passes to the grantee immediately. Delivery is presumed to have occurred on the date, if any, stated in the deed, even though the deed might have been delivered before or after that date. What happens to the deed following delivery does not alter the ownership rights of the grantee. If the deed is lost or destroyed following delivery, the loss or destruction has no effect on the transfer of title, except, perhaps, to make proof of the transfer more difficult in the absence of recording.

Escrow

Escrow is the process by which a grantor delivers a deed to an independent third party (the escrow agent) to hold until stated conditions, such as payment of the purchase price and removal of liens, are satisfied. The agent is then to deliver the deed to the buyer. The delivery by the grantor and grantee of the deed, other documents, and the purchase money into escrow is only a conditional delivery that does not become binding on the parties until the escrow conditions are met. A grantor's merely setting up an escrow and delivering documents to the agent does not, in itself, complete the conveyance. No estate passes until the escrow conditions are satisfied.

Upon performance of the escrow conditions and the agent's recording the deed, courts treat the delivery of the deed as "relating back" to the time it was placed in escrow so that the grantee is considered to have received it then. Jacob executes a deed conveying Blackacre to purchaser Debbie, and delivers it to Acme Title Insurance Co., instructing Acme to record the deed and deliver it to Debbie after Acme updates the title, pays off the liens on Blackacre, and remits the balance of the purchase price to Jacob. Then Jacob walks out of the title company office and is killed by a speeding bus. Most courts would hold that upon Acme's satisfying the conditions delivery of the deed to grantee Debbie is effective as of (relates back to) the time that Jacob delivered it to Acme and gave the escrow instructions. Thus, delivery to Debbie would be effective prior to Jacob's death.

Void and Voidable Deeds

Certain defects in a deed, or in its execution and delivery, may give the grantor the right to avoid (rescind) a transaction. Depending on the type of defect, the deed will be *void* or *voidable*. A void deed has no legal effect. If a deed is void, no conveyance of ownership occurred, and the purported grantor is entitled to have the land back from whomever has possession of it. In contrast, a voidable deed *does* result in a conveyance, but the defect gives the grantor a basis for rescinding the deed against the grantor's immediate transferee and any subsequent transferee who does not qualify as a bona fide purchaser for value. A **bona fide purchaser for value** (usually called simply a **bona fide purchaser**, or a **BFP**) is a buyer, not a donee, who has given value in good faith, without notice of any problems affecting the deed. The law protects bona fide purchasers by allowing them to keep the land in most situations where the grantor's deed was merely voidable.

The distinction between a void and voidable deed is of little importance to a grantor who seeks to undo a transaction with the *immediate* grantee. A grantor will be able to avoid the transaction if the deed is either *void* or *voidable*. The distinction becomes important, however, if the grantee has further conveyed the property to a third party who is a bona fide purchaser. If a deed is *void*, the original grantor may undo the transaction against not only the immediate grantee but also any remote grantee, even a BFP. In contrast, if a deed is *voidable*, the original grantor may rescind the deed only as to the immediate grantee and any remote grantees who are not bona fide purchasers, but not as to a BFP.

A deed is generally considered to be *void* under any of the following circumstances:

- If someone forges the grantor's signature on the deed.

- In a few states, if the grantor is a minor (i.e., under the age of 18).

- If the grantor has been judicially declared incompetent or is entirely without understanding of the consequences of the transaction.

- If there is material alteration of the deed.

- If the deed is not delivered.

- If the deed is executed in blank and the grantee's name is filled in later.

For example, while Grandpa Jones is seriously ill, his son Jonathon forges Grandpa's name to a deed granting Grandpa's farm Blackacre to Beatrice, who in turn sells it to Jimenez, a good faith purchaser, for $100,000. Because the forged deed is *void*, Grandpa (or his guardian or estate) may rescind the transaction and retrieve Blackacre from Jimenez, even though Jimenez paid value in good faith.

A deed is generally held by courts to be *voidable* in the following circumstances:

- In most states, if the grantor is a minor and the time allowed for a minor to rescind against a BFP has expired.

- If fraud was used to induce the grantor to sign the deed, as where the grantee fraudulently misrepresents his or her ability to pay.

- If undue influence was exerted on the grantor.

- If the grantor was subjected to duress.

- If the grantor is of unsound mind, but does not suffer from the total lack of capacity, which would render the transaction void.

Assume, for example, that Larry wants to exchange Whiteacre for Marianne's Blackacre (a type of sale called "barter") and fraudulently induces her to execute a deed to Blackacre by misrepresenting the quality of the land in Whiteacre. Because Marianne's deed to Blackacre is *voidable*, she may rescind it and have Blackacre back from Larry. However, if in the meantime Larry sold Blackacre to Julio, a good faith purchaser, Julio is entitled to keep Blackacre and Marianne's only remedy is a lawsuit against Larry for fraud damages.

BOX 9-1 APPLY YOUR KNOWLEDGE

Fifteen years ago, you bought a house from Prudence. Unknown to you, Prudence had bought the house from Scurvy, who had forged his grandfather's name to a deed purportedly transferring the house from the grandfather to Scurvy. Scurvy died last year, survived by his sister Gloria, the grandfather's only living descendent. Who owns the house?

Types of Deeds

The types of deeds in general use in the United States include (1) quitclaim deeds, (2) grant deeds, and (3) warranty deeds, and various permutations of each. All are equally effective to transfer of title. They differ only in the level of protection afforded the buyer, and in the potential liability imposed on the seller if the seller's title proves defective and the buyer suffers a loss. Because of this variation in level of protection, the parties to a sales contract should agree upon the type of deed to be provided by the seller. Otherwise, the seller will normally provide the type of deed (the "default" deed) dictated by state law or customary practice in the particular state or locality. In California, for example, if the parties do not specify otherwise, the seller commonly delivers a grant deed, which provides a lower level of title assurance than does a warranty deed.

Quitclaim Deed. A **quitclaim deed**, also known as a "release deed," contains no warranties of title. It is used to convey, or release, whatever title that the grantor happens to have, even if that is no title whatsoever. Typical conveyance language found in a quitclaim deed is: "George Grantor hereby *remises, releases, and quitclaims* Blackacre unto Gloria Grantee." A quitclaim deed is appropriate in any situation where the transferor does not know what interest he or she owns. For example, a quitclaim deed is normally employed to correct title problems, such as a boundary dispute, where there is serious question as to who owns the property. It is also commonly used in property settlements accompanying a divorce, because the party ordered to transfer his or her interest to the other can do so without making any warranties to the transferee. A quitclaim deed is also used to release dower or curtesy interests or other encumbrances on property.

Grant Deed. In many western states, the default deed form is the **grant deed**, or **bargain and sale deed** as it is known in some states. The typical language creating a grant deed is "I, George Grantor, hereby *grant* [or bargain, sell, and convey] Blackacre to Gloria Grantee." The use of the word *grant* or the words *bargain, sell, and convey* transfers to the grantee any interest that the grantor has. In addition, statutes in several states impose two warranties, called *implied warranties*, on a grantor who uses a grant deed: (1) that the grantor has not transferred the property or any interest in it to anyone else, and (2) that the grantor has not encumbered the property nor permitted anyone else to do so.[1] Beyond these two statutory warranties, the grantor under a grant deed does not guarantee the absence of title defects.

Warranty Deeds. Although quitclaim deeds and grant deeds are effective to convey title, most buyers demand the protection afforded by deed warranties. Therefore, it is customary in most parts of the country for the grantor to include in the deed a number of assurances (called "warranties" or "covenants") regarding the title. Deeds with title covenants or warranties are referred to as **warranty deeds**, which, as noted later, are either *general* or *special*. The six types of title warranties in general use can be used in any combination. Three are classified as present covenants and three as future covenants.

Present Covenants. The three present covenants are the covenant of seisin, the covenant of right to convey, and the covenant against encumbrances. They are called present covenants because they are violated, if at all, at the time of the conveyance, and the applicable statute of limitations period begins to run then.

A **covenant of seisin** is an assurance that the grantor owns the estate or interest that the deed purports to convey. In the **covenant of right to convey**, the grantor guarantees that the grantor has the right to convey the interest that the deed purports to convey. The covenants of seisin and of right to convey overlap; it would be a rare circumstance for an owner to have ownership (seisin) but not the right to convey an interest in the real estate. In fact, breach of the covenant of seisin usually results in a simultaneous breach of the covenant of right to convey. Bubba executes a warranty deed conveying to Leroy a fee simple estate in Patricia's land, which Bubba neither owns nor has a right to convey. Bubba has breached both the covenant of seisin and the covenant of right to convey. But suppose Arnold, the owner of Blackacre, sells and conveys it to Sharon even though Arnold had given Baxter an option (discussed in Chapter 6) to purchase Blackacre. While the option is in effect, Arnold has no right to convey Blackacre, so has breached his covenant of right to convey. Because he owned Blackacre, however, he has not breached his covenant of seisin. If Sharon had notice of Baxter's option when she purchased Blackacre, Baxter may exercise it and require her to relinquish ownership of Blackacre. If he does so, Sharon has a cause of action against Arnold for breach of his covenant of right to convey.

The **covenant against encumbrances** assures the grantee that the realty is free of encumbrances at the time of the conveyance. If it is in fact subject to a mortgage, tax lien, lease, easement, or other encumbrance that has not been made an "exception" to the title warranted by the grantor, the grantee has a cause of action for breach of the covenant. In many states, an obvious or beneficial easement, such as an obvious roadway across land that Chuck wants to buy for subdividing into residential building lots, is not an encumbrance that would breach the covenant against encumbrances.

Future Covenants. The the covenant of warranty, the covenant of quiet enjoyment, and the covenant of further assurances are called future covenants because they oblige the grantor to defend the grantee or a subsequent owner against any claim adverse to the grantee's title or right of possession occurring after the conveyance to the grantee. The future covenants are breached only when a claimant eventually appears with superior title to the property and seeks to evict the grantee. These covenants "run with the land" and thus benefit the grantee's successors. Because applicable statutes of limitations begin to run only when the grantee or successor is evicted, the future covenants may have an indefinite duration.

For most purposes, the covenant of warranty and the covenant of quiet enjoyment are equivalent. The **covenant of quiet enjoyment** assures that the grantor's title is as purported in the deed and that neither the grantee nor a subsequent owner will face adverse claims that derive from the grantor or the grantor's predecessors in title. The **covenant of warranty** obligates the grantor to defend the title conveyed to the grantee against the title claims of all third parties. Jack conveys Blackacre to Tonya in fee simple under a warranty deed. Twenty years after closing, Sheila claims that she is entitled to a life estate in Blackacre because she was married to Jack at the time of the conveyance and has dower rights that she had never released. If Sheila's claim is valid, Jack must defend Tonya's title and pay damages to Tonya. If Tonya had conveyed Blackacre to Manfred before Sheila appeared, Jack would be obligated to defend Manfred against Sheila's claim.

The **covenant of further assurances** obligates the grantor to execute and deliver any additional instruments that may be necessary in the future to perfect the title that grantor purports to convey.

In a *general warranty deed*, the covenants of the grantor cover title defects occurring any time before the grantor's conveyance to the grantee, even defects existing *before* the grantor acquired ownership. Grantors concerned about the possibility of assuming the risk of title defects occurring before they owned the property can eliminate that risk by using a *special* warranty deed. In a *special warranty deed*, the covenants apply only to the time of the grantor's ownership. The grantee receives assurance that the grantor has done nothing to impair or encumber title *while the grantor owned the property*, but the grantor makes no warranty regarding the status of the title preceding the grantor's ownership.

The normal remedy for breach of either present or future covenants is money damages. If the breach involves an encumbrance such as a mortgage or a tax lien, the measure of damages is the amount necessary to satisfy the encumbrance. For nonmonetary encumbrances or defects, the measure of damages normally is the difference between (1) the value of the property without the encumbrance or defect, and (2) the value of the property with the defect. Natalie sells a 40-acre parcel to Jacqueline for $400,000 and gives her a warranty deed. Andy proves that he owns 10 acres of the parcel. In most jurisdictions, if the value of the remaining 30 acres is $300,000, Jacqueline is entitled to $100,000 plus attorneys' fees for breach of Natalie's covenant of seisin.

Reliance solely on title warranties is risky. For example, most jurisdictions limit the grantee's damages for breach of a deed warranty to the original purchase price plus attorneys' fees. This limitation is unsatisfactory to grantees whose realty has increased substantially in value since the purchase. Assume that Jacqueline in the preceding example had constructed a shopping center worth $2 million on the 10 acres that she lost in the title dispute. Recovery from Natalie of the original $400,000 purchase price (or in some states, only a pro rata share of the original $400,000 for the lost 10 acres, or $100,000) leaves Jacqueline with a large loss. Other practical problems arise out of reliance on warranties. If a breach of a covenant occurs, the grantee faces the problem of locating the grantor, filing a lawsuit, and winning and collecting a judgment. Deed warranties are only the personal guarantees of the grantor. By the time of the suit, the grantor may be insolvent or long dead and unable to make good on the warranty.

BOX 9–2 APPLY YOUR KNOWLEDGE

Sam Seller is negotiating an agreement to sell Blackacre to Bonnie Buyer. (a) If all other contract terms have been agreed upon, what kind of deed would Bonnie prefer to receive—quitclaim deed, grant deed, special warranty deed, or warranty deed? Why? (b) What type of deed might Sam prefer to deliver? Why?

After-Acquired Property

A grantor who purports to transfer a particular estate or interest in land by means of a grant or a warranty deed, but who actually owns only a lesser interest, transfers the lesser interest to the grantee *plus any interest in the property the grantor may acquire later.* This principle is often referred to as **estoppel by deed** or, more quaintly, as "feeding the estoppel." If the grantor purports to convey a certain estate that the grantor does not own, and later acquires the estate or some missing interest in it, the grantor will be estopped to deny (i.e., prevented from denying) later that the missing interest passed to the grantee. Maurice owns Blackacre, which is subject to an easement in gross in favor of Ruth Ann and her assignees, giving her a right to recreational use of the lake

BOX 9–3 POINT TO CONSIDER

In some situations, a party to a real estate transaction cannot be present to execute deeds and other transfer documents. That party (buyer or seller) can appoint someone else as an **attorney-in-fact** (agent) to execute the documents. To appoint an attorney-in-fact, the principal executes a written and acknowledged **power of attorney**, which must be recorded in the county where the land is located. The power of attorney may be a **general power of attorney** allowing the agent to transact all business on the principal's behalf, or it may be a **special power of attorney** allowing the agent to transact only one or a few items of business for the principal. All powers of attorney terminate automatically upon the death of the principal, and "nondurable" powers of attorney terminate automatically upon the incapacity of the principal.

A **durable power of attorney** survives the incapacity of the principal. Most powers of attorney involving real property are durable. To make a power of attorney durable, the principal must include language such as the following: "This power of attorney shall not be affected by the subsequent incapacity of the principal."

on Blackacre. By grant deed, Maurice conveys Blackacre to Ed in fee simple. A year later, Ruth Ann transfers her easement rights to Maurice and Maurice now wants to use the right of way. Ed objects. Because Maurice purported to convey a fee simple interest, he transferred the ownership interest that he then possessed plus the easement that he later acquired. Maurice will be estopped from asserting any rights in the easement.

Recording and Registration Systems

Before the enactment of the recording and registration acts, deed covenants were the primary means of title assurance, though for reasons already discussed, they are not highly effective as a means of title assurance. The advent of recording and registration systems has allowed grantees or their representatives to determine the status of title for themselves before purchase, instead of having to rely exclusively on deed covenants.

A primary purpose of government is to protect the property rights of individuals. Accordingly, each state has developed a system of land records, usually administered on a county-by-county basis, designed to enable interested parties to verify who owns real property. Although the state systems vary in detail, all take the form of either a recording or a registration system.

Registration and recording laws operate under fundamentally different premises. Under a registration system, the state issues a certificate of title as conclusive evidence of ownership. In contrast, a recording system is much like a public library of title-related documents,[2] and users of the library must review the records contained in the library and determine for themselves who owns the property.

Torrens Registration Systems

Named after its developer, Sir Robert Torrens, who introduced it in Australia in 1857, the Torrens system of title registration was later adopted in England, New Zealand, and parts of Canada, and in approximately 20 states. It is the basis of a number of modern registration systems in other countries today. In the United States, use of the Torrens system in the few states that have it is purely voluntary, because all states have a separate recording system that anyone may use.

The Torrens system is much like the auto registration system widely used in the United States. Autos are "titled" in the name of the owner, with all liens being recorded on the face of the certificate of title. The car owner or the lienholder has possession of the certificate, and the owner transfers title to the car by signing the certificate and delivering it to the buyer, who can use it to have a new certificate issued by the state. Torrens developed his system along similar lines, in fact basing it on the then-prevalent ship registration system.

In a Torrens system of land registration, title to a parcel of property is first registered by the owner's instituting a judicial proceeding similar to a suit to quiet title. In the proceeding, the owner presents proof of ownership and the court issues a decree certifying the owner's title and setting forth any exceptions to it. The official Torrens certificate is retained in a Torrens registry, and the landowner receives a copy of the certificate. As exceptions to title are added or removed, appropriate notations are made on the official certificate. To transfer title, the owner takes a deed and the owner's copy of the certificate to the registry, where the registrar issues a new certificate in the name of the new owner and cancels the transferor's old certificate. Under this system, the status of title to a parcel is easily verified. The buyer needs only to look at the official certificate in the Torrens registry to determine ownership and to see all title exceptions and encumbrances.

The local Torrens Act may provide that certain items such as local tax liens need not be shown on the certificate. In that event, a title examiner would need to check the tax lien files as well as the certificate to determine the status of title to a given parcel. The property may also be subject to zoning and building code requirements, to federal legislation creating federal flood zones and wetlands, and to federal environmental legislation, so a title examiner may need to check still other public records that are maintained separately from the real estate title records. However, some Torrens statutes protect against title claims arising from adverse possession, making the system especially attractive to owners of timber and mineral interests.

The Torrens system is arguably superior to the traditional recording system, for a number of reasons. Foremost is certainty and ease of the title determination, and in the absence of fraud, the Torrens certificate is conclusive evidence of ownership. State officials authenticate title, and the state bears losses resulting from its errors if the indemnity fund maintained for that purpose is adequate. Most encumbrances that are not noted on the Torrens certificate of title are ineffective. And when property transfers occur following registration, no expensive title search or title insurance is necessary because title is already authenticated.

Notwithstanding its apparent superiority, the Torrens system is not widely used in this country, primarily because of the time and expense involved in the initial registration. Commentators note that as long as the Torrens system is only a voluntary alternative to the traditional recording system, it is unlikely to be used much and simply creates confusion and administrative difficulties that outweigh its usefulness. Also, it is claimed, real estate lawyers, title companies (preparers of abstracts of title), and title insurance companies have a vested interest in the more cumbersome recording system that provides them revenue, and they therefore actively oppose the more efficient Torrens system. History seems to be on the side of the critics: New York and Illinois have recently eliminated their Torrens systems.

Recording Systems

In contrast to the Torrens system, a traditional recording system is maintained in every state. Each state has a public records office in each county, parish, or other local government unit, which serves as a repository of whatever documents the state statutes permit members of the public to "record," that is, have copied into the public records. The public records office is run by a government official whose functions are to receive original documents, review them for compliance with the form requirements established by the state recording statute, copy the documents that comply, index the copies, return the originals to their owners, and maintain the collection as a permanent record for public use. Although the public records office has different names among the states, such as Public Registry, Register of Deeds, or Recorder's Office, this text calls it the **recorder's office** and the official administering it the **recorder**.

Nature and Purpose of a Recording System; Effect of Recording. The main purpose of a recording system is to provide public information regarding land titles and, in the process, accomplish at least three goals: First, it gives prospective buyers and lenders a way to check the status of title and thus to determine whether it is safe to buy a parcel of land or to accept it as security for a loan. Second, it enables owners and lenders to notify the world that they claim an interest in a given parcel, and thus to protect their interests from rivals who might claim it. Third, it enables creditors and improvers of the realty to establish a lien against it to secure payment for improvements, taxes, water bills, and judgment debts against the property owner.

Users of the public land records would not be able to find what they want without some organizing principles, an index to the materials, and some guidance from the recorder or office employees. The "library" of the recorder's office consists of all documents that people have recorded to put the public on notice of their property interests. The recorder makes no judgments about the validity, enforceability, or legal effect of the recorded documents (any of which could be forged or subject to other defects), or about their effect on a particular land title. People seeking information at the recorder's office, such as prospective buyers and lenders, are expected to examine the available documents and to determine for themselves who owns a particular parcel of real property and what encumbrances affect it. Like a registration system, a recording system gives every member of the public notice of claims to a parcel of real estate. Unlike a registration system, however, a recording system does not assure its users that those claims are valid.

Who Is Protected: The Bona Fide Purchaser. A main goal of recording acts is to protect *bona fide purchasers for value (BFP)* from the claims of others alleging an interest in the property. To be a BFP of an interest in property, one (whether a buyer or a lender) must have given value for it, in good faith, without notice of any problems affecting the title. *Value* is the money, property, or services given in exchange for a real property transfer, but value is a concept different from "consideration." An *unperformed promise* to pay a sum of money or to perform some service would constitute consideration for the purpose of determining whether an executory contract of sale exists, but would not be the value required for the contracting party to have BFP status. To have that status, a buyer must have actually *performed*, for example, by paying the promised amount, or by having a lender deliver the promised amount to the buyer, or by rendering the promised service. For a *lender* to have BFP status, the lender must have made the loan as promised. However, consistent with the judicial position that the parties to a contract and not the courts should set the price, the courts give the parties to a contract of sale considerable discretion in determining the amount to be paid. Most courts hold that to constitute value, the amount paid must be *substantial in relation to the property's fair market value*, though it need not be the full fair market value. A nominal consideration of $10 for a valuable parcel would not constitute the value needed for BFP status.

To become a BFP, the grantee or mortgagee must also take the property interest without notice of any valid adverse claim or prior conveyance. Three types of notice may deprive a buyer of bona fide purchaser status: actual notice, constructive notice, and inquiry notice. A buyer has *actual notice* of any facts brought to the buyer's personal attention or discovered by him or her. For example, if the seller, or the seller's tenant or neighbor informs the buyer of an existing easement on the property, the buyer has actual notice of it. The buyer may also discover the easement, and acquire actual notice, by inspecting the property or by finding a notation of the easement in the public records.

Constructive notice is a type of notice imposed by law on the theory that prospective buyers *could have* discovered the conflicting claim if they had looked. A buyer normally has constructive notice of facts that would be apparent upon a visual inspection of the property and from questioning the person in possession of it, even if the buyer did not look or did not ask. A buyer also has constructive notice of information available in the public records even if the buyer did not examine the public records.

Inquiry notice is a form of constructive notice. Courts impose the duty on the buyer to *inquire* if the buyer acquires information from any source that *suggests* the existence of a prior conveyance or an adverse property interest and to make a reasonable investigation. If the buyer does not investigate, a court will treat the buyer as having any knowledge that an investigation would have revealed. Sam contracts to buy Blackacre from Cliff under a contract that provides for immediate occupancy. On his way to complete the transaction, Sam drives by Blackacre and notices smoke coming out of the chimney, cars in the driveway, and cattle grazing in the pasture behind the house. Sam has *inquiry notice* that Blackacre or some interest in it is being claimed by others. The occupants may be Cliff's tenants, Cliff may have previously sold the property to someone else, or the occupants may simply be trespassers. If Sam fails to investigate and buys the property while the occupants are rightfully there, he purchases Blackacre subject to their interest.

Documents Eligible for Recording and the Role of Acknowledgment. Although the recorder makes no judgment regarding the validity, enforceability, or effectiveness of any of the documents the parties present for recording, the documents must meet the often elaborate form requirements imposed by state statutes. Normally, only original documents with original signatures may be recorded.[3] Usually they must be acknowledged and, in some states, they must be sealed. Recall that an acknowledgment is the act of signing a document before a notary public or other public official to provide formal proof that the execution is the signor's free act and not done under compulsion. Acknowledgment provides some assurance that documents affecting title are genuine and not forged. Where a document is offered as evidence in court, an acknowledgment ordinarily eliminates the need to offer witnesses to establish the genuineness of the signature.

Because documents usually will be photographed, microfilmed, duplicated, or digitally scanned, other state or local requirements may also specify clarity of the textual materials, size of paper, and width of margins. Typically, surveys or maps may be recorded only if they meet explicit format requirements and bear the seal of a registered land surveyor.

Claims, Interests, and Problems Not Revealed by Recording Systems. Many potential title defects may escape the notice of title examiners, and thus cause loss to buyers and lenders, because evidence of the defects does not appear in the recorder's office. By their nature, some title interests are unlikely to appear in the public records because they arise through nonverbal conduct and not by agreement, producing nothing to record. Examples include prescriptive easements, interests acquired by adverse possession, and easements arising by implication or necessity. Also, if a property owner dies, title vests immediately in the devisees under a will, or in the decedent's heirs if there is no will. Information about devisees and heirs may be found, if at all, in the records of the probate court, not in the recorder's office. And spousal rights arising from common law or statutory dower or curtesy and community property statutes usually do not give rise to documents but still are valid against bona fide purchasers. And many interests and conveyances receive legal protection without recording. For example, oral short-term leases of realty are valid as against BFPs even though not recordable. Usually leases not exceeding one to three years are enforceable though oral or, if they must be in writing, they often are not required to be recorded.

Under a number of state lien statutes, a person who acquires a lien has a grace period within which to file public notice of it. During this grace period, the lien is effective even though it does not appear in the public records. The Uniform Commercial Code, for example, gives a seller or a lender extending credit for the purchase of a fixture 10 days after the fixture is annexed to the realty to file a notice of the creditor's purchase money security interest in the fixture.[4] Most states provide a longer grace period to persons seeking to acquire a mechanic's or a materialman's lien, which is a statutory lien on real property in favor of a person who performs or furnishes labor, professional design or surveying services, or materials for the improvement of real property. Depending on the state, these creditors have from 60 to 120 days following the completion of their part of the work or the furnishing of materials within which to file their "claim of lien" in the recorder's office. In the meantime, even though these liens are "off the record," they are still valid and enforceable against bona fide purchasers.

Conveyances by or to the federal government may not need to be recorded to defeat the rights of bona fide purchasers. Because of the Supremacy Clause of the U.S. Constitution, any federal laws relating to land transfer supersede state recording acts. Although federal agencies may not be required to record, they usually do so anyway to avoid future problems. Some federal agencies, however, *are* required by federal law to record their claims. For example, the Internal Revenue Services must record notice of tax liens it claims against a taxpayer's realty.

Another problem with the public records system is that the records themselves may be unreliable. For example, a recorded deed may never have been delivered, or it may be a forgery, or procured by fraud, or executed by a minor or a grantor who was incompetent at the time of execution. Such defects, which render a deed *void* or *voidable*, are nearly impossible for a title examiner to detect, yet they may have a devastating effect on the title.

Employee error in operating the recording system also contributes to unreliability of the records. For example, if a recorded document is incorrectly indexed, searchers may be unable to find it, so will lack notice of the interest it represents. The loss to a person who relies on erroneous records is likely to be great. If the error was caused by negligence of the recorder or an office employee, the recorder or employee is personally liable for any loss that results. Because the negligent person may not have the resources necessary to cover the loss, most states require recording officials to be bonded (insured), but insurance limits usually are low and courts are reluctant to hold public officials liable as individuals for large amounts. Under the law of agency, the local government as *employer* of the negligent official can in theory be held liable for the loss. In a number of states, however, the doctrine of *sovereign immunity* protects the local government; under that doctrine a person may not sue the government without its consent.

Priority Rules Under Recording Statutes. As the news media attest, sometimes a dishonest person sells the same piece of realty, or some interest in it, to several different purchasers. In one reported scam, a person purporting to be a landlord successively leased the same apartment to 11 college students, collected deposits from each, and left town. When school began, 10 students were surprised to learn that they had no place to stay. Other reports have involved successive sales of the same fee interest to as many as eight people. Conflicting claims to the same property can also arise by mistake. Whatever the reason for conflicting claims, only one grantee is entitled to the property interest, and the others will have to rely on a lawsuit for the grantor's fraud or breach of warranty in the often vain hope of collecting damages.

Which of the conflicting claims has priority? That is, which claimant is entitled to the interest? The rules of priority in the recording statutes resolve disputes over the interest and provide grantees with motivation to record their interests. However, the recording statutes differ in type among the states, and so do the rules of priority.

To understand the priority rules under the various recording acts, consider the following transactions: Oliver sells his farm, Blackacre, to Antonio for $1 million. After signing and delivering the deed and receiving payment, Oliver decides that it is the easiest money he has ever earned.

Accordingly, he sells Blackacre again to Beverly for another $1 million and delivers a deed to her as well. Antonio does not record his deed. When Beverly received her deed, she knew nothing of the earlier transaction between Oliver and Antonio. Thus we have two buyers of Blackacre, each of whom has an executed and delivered deed that appears to be valid on its face. Who owns Blackacre?

Before recording statutes came into use, as between the successive grantees the first taker won, on the theory that after the first transfer, the seller had nothing left to sell. Recording statutes in the United States have altered this result, but because the statutes vary in type from state to state, the outcome for competing claimants in one state often differs from that of another state. Yet, despite different results from state to state, most types of recording statutes are meant to protect subsequent (later) bona fide purchasers like Beverly, by encouraging potentially rival grantees such as Antonio to record their deeds and thus to give Beverly and the rest of the world notice of their ownership. In other words, the goal of the statutes is to protect innocent purchasers and lenders. The law does not require Antonio to record his deed. However, if Antonio fails to record, he may lose his priority over Beverly and, with it, his title to Blackacre. The practical effect of the recording acts is, of course, to give a grantee strong incentive to record the deed immediately. Indeed, it is almost the universal practice to record the deed immediately, often before funds are disbursed to the seller, to assure that no adverse claims will affect the buyer's title.

Among the 50 states, recording acts break down into three broad types: *notice statutes, race-notice statutes,* and *pure race statutes.* Each of these is discussed in turn.

Notice Statutes. Under a **notice statute**, a buyer who gives value for a property interest without notice of earlier claims takes the interest free of them. Because Beverly bought Blackacre with no notice of the earlier sale to Antonio, as between her and Antonio, her interest prevails and she immediately becomes owner of Blackacre. Note that under a notice statute, the act that makes Beverly the winner is her *buying* (or a lender's lending) without notice of Antonio's earlier deed. She immediately becomes owner, and his recording of his deed later does him no good. He has already lost title and cannot recapture it. However, the statute will not protect Beverly if at the time of purchase she had *any* notice of the earlier sale. If Antonio had recorded his deed before Beverly purchased Blackacre, she would have had "record" (constructive) notice even though she lacked actual knowledge, because she *could have* discovered his deed by searching the public records. In many states, even if Antonio had not recorded his deed, Beverly would be on *inquiry notice* of his interest if she knew or had reason to know that he was in possession of Blackacre when she purchased it. Beverly should, of course, promptly record her deed, because by doing so she preserves her priority over any innocent purchaser who might later have bought Blackacre from Oliver.

Race-Notice Statutes. Under a **race-notice statute**, a bona fide purchaser who is *first to record* prevails over rivals who claim the interest. In other words, to prevail under a race-notice statute,

Box 9–4 Point to Consider

Alabama Code: "No instrument affecting real estate is of any validity against subsequent purchasers for a valuable consideration, without notice, unless filed in the office of the recorder."

The following states have notice statutes: Alabama, Arizona, Arkansas (for documents other than mortgages), Connecticut, Florida, Illinois, Iowa, Kansas, Kentucky, Maine, Massachusetts, Missouri, New Mexico, Oklahoma, Rhode Island, South Carolina, Tennessee, Texas, Vermont, Virginia, West Virginia.

Beverly must not only receive her deed without notice of the prior sale to Antonio, she must also win a presumed "race" to the recorder's office between her and Antonio and record her deed before he records his. Under a race-notice statute, then, the act that makes Beverly (or Antonio) the winner is the act of *recording first*. If Antonio does so, he wins. Thus, under a race–notice statute Beverly has a dual motivation to record—to protect herself against future claimants, and to avoid losing out to a prior claimant like Antonio, who could still win by first recording his deed.

Pure Race Statutes. A pure **race statute** acquires its name from the hypothetical race between the title claimants. As between Antonio and Beverly, priority of title is awarded to the winner of the "race" to the courthouse. Under a pure race statute, the first grantee to record a deed (or mortgage) acquires the interest involved free from all rival claims, including earlier grantees of the same interest who have not recorded their deeds. To prevail over Antonio, Beverly need *not* be a bona fide purchaser. If she is the first to record, Blackacre becomes hers even if she has actual knowledge of Antonio's claim, though in at least one "pure race" state, North Carolina, she must have given value. The vast majority of the states are troubled by the possibility of this inequitable result. Therefore, pure race statutes are rare. North Carolina and Louisiana have pure

BOX 9–7 APPLY YOUR KNOWLEDGE

Obnoxious sold Greenacre to Alice, who expected to move in a month after closing. Three days later, Obnoxious sold Greenacre to Ben, who also expected to move in within a month after closing but knew nothing of Alice's transaction with Obnoxious. Obnoxious scheduled the closings in his office on different days, delivering a grant deed to Alice and a warranty deed to Ben. In each of the following situations, who is entitled to Greenacre?

- Alice recorded her grant deed a week after Ben received his warranty deed. Greenacre is located in a state with a notice type of recording statute.

- Alice recorded her grant deed a week after Ben received his warranty deed. Greenacre is located in a state with a race–notice type of recording statute.

- On his way to the closing, Ben saw a moving van unloading household furnishings at Greenacre. After closing, Ben recorded his deed before Alice recorded hers. Greenacre is located in a "notice" state.

- On his way to the closing, Ben saw a moving van unloading household furnishings at Greenacre. After closing, Ben recorded his deed before Alice recorded hers. Greenacre is located in a "race–notice" state.

race statutes for all property interests; and Arkansas, Delaware, Ohio, and Pennsylvania have pure race statutes for certain types of interests such as mortgages and oil and gas leases. The remaining states are nearly equally divided between notice statutes and race–notice statutes.

Recording Office Process, Deed Books, and Indices

Because of the incentive provided by the recording acts, most instruments affecting property are recorded. However, the work of discovering, examining, and evaluating these interests is left to the individual initiative of patrons using the facilities of the recorder's office. The government has no role in assuring the quality of any individual title. It simply makes the "library" of documents available to the public.

When documents are recorded, the recorder usually undertakes only a cursory review of the instrument to make sure that it complies with statutory formalities required for recording. For example, a state may require that signatures be originals and not copies, that signatures be notarized or otherwise acknowledged, that the proper corporate officers have signed on behalf of corporations, and that seals be affixed. Recording reflects no judgment regarding the legal sufficiency or validity of the document being recorded. If the instrument has the required statutory form, it will be recorded as presented to the recorder's office.

Most counties have a huge of number of recorded instruments accumulated over time. They must be carefully and painstakingly indexed if the recording acts are to accomplish their purpose of giving notice to interested parties. In fact, because of the large volume of land records, the modern trend has been to treat documents that are misindexed (erroneously indexed by the recorder' office) as if they were never recorded. In jurisdictions so treating misindexed documents, searchers lack constructive notice of them. If the error resulted from the negligence of a recorder's office employee, the employee is personally liable for any loss that results.

To make the public records usable, the typical recorder's office maintains two key types of records: (1) books containing the actual copies of recorded documents (e.g., "deed books" containing copies of deeds, leases, mortgages, releases of rights, and other documents affecting title to land; and "map books" or "plat books" containing copies of, for example, subdivision maps or plats; (2) "index books" (indices) listing alphabetically the names of the parties to a transaction, the date of recording, a brief description of the property involved, and the deed book or map book number and the page in the book where the copy of the document can be found.

Traditionally both types of records were kept in bound volumes. Today, bound volumes are giving way to more modern storage media such as microfilm canisters, microfiche, and computer disks. In deference to tradition, instruments are still referenced in many jurisdictions by "deed book" or "map book" and "page," even though books may be obsolete. In other jurisdictions, vocabulary has changed with the media, and instruments are referenced by a computerized record number or map number.

Although recorder's offices have always varied in how they index materials, and vary still more as computers and newer storage media are used, traditionally two basic types of indexing have been used in the United States, the *grantor-grantee index system* and the *tract index system*. In a **grantor-grantee index system**, instruments affecting real property are indexed in two separate index books (though the documents themselves are kept in deed books). The *grantor index* is an alphabetical listing of grantors by the grantor's surname (or entity name, in the case of a partnership or corporation). The *grantee index* lists alphabetically the names of grantees. Under a **tract index system**, documents relating to a particular tract are referenced chronologically and by reference to the tract, so that the complete history of the parcel can be found together on one page or in a few pages of the *tract index* book. Although easier to use than grantor-grantee indexing, tract indexing is used only in ten of the less populous states and in New York City, which has a "block index" system. In either system, to locate and examine the relevant documents, the examiner must use the appropriate index to find the correct deed book and page number (or computerized record number) for each document to be inspected.

The reason for maintaining indices is to enable a title searcher to establish a **chain of title** from the present owner as far back in time as is necessary for the searcher to be convinced that the present owner really does have ownership. For the greatest degree of certainty, the chain of title would need to be traced back to the first grant of the parcel by a sovereign (e.g., a state, the U.S. government, or, in the West, the Mexican government as to lands that later became states). As a practical matter, few chains of title need to be traced back more than, say, 60 years.

● Title Examination

A **title examination** is a thorough review of title information in the public records, a review upon which the examiner will base his or her opinion on the status of title. Of course, the ultimate issue under investigation is whether sellers (or borrowers) own the interests that they propose to sell or give over temporarily as a security interest. Key concerns are whether any of the sellers in the chain of title were incompetent and thus unable to convey the interest, whether it is subject to the lien of unpaid taxes and assessments, to easements or restrictive covenants on the property that might affect the buyers' intended use, and to mortgages or other encumbrances on the property. As previously discussed, many potential title problems will not be revealed solely by a visit to the recorder's office, but the part of the title examination conducted there will reveal a wealth of information.

Depending upon local practice, a title examination may be conducted by a lawyer, a paralegal, or a title insurance or abstracting company. Although legal training is helpful in performing a title examination, many title examiners do not have formal legal training. More important for an examiner is a careful, methodical approach and attention to detail.

Initial Considerations

To conduct a proper title examination, the examiner needs answers to some basic questions:

1. Where is the property located? This information provides a starting point under a *tract system* form of indexing, in which information is referenced by tracts and not owners' names. A street address often is useful in all systems, because many of the supplemental records that the examiner will review use the street address as a reference point. Also the property location will be a key in identifying relevant taxing, zoning, utility, and assessment districts.

2. Who is the purported owner of the property? This information provides the typical starting point for a title search under a *grantor-grantee indexing system*, which references information according to the names of grantors and grantees. If title is held by a corporation or partnership, the ownership entity can be verified by getting a copy of the corporate charter or partnership agreement from the seller or from the office in which such documents are filed.

3. Is the seller presently in possession of the property? If someone else is in possession, that person may have a leasehold or a life estate interest that detracts from the title the seller claims to have, or the person may even be an adverse possessor who potentially could entirely deprive the seller of title.

4. Are there loans secured by the property? If so, the secured loans probably will need to be satisfied as a part of the closing. Therefore, it will be helpful to obtain a list of the loans, together with any contact names or addresses that the seller possesses in order for the closing agent to obtain a current loan balance.

5. What does the seller know about the history of the title? Any information that the seller has about the previous owners helps save time in confirming the conclusions of the title examiner. The seller's existing documents such as title opinions, land surveys, or title insurance policies should be provided to the examiner.

With this preliminary information, the examiner begins the title search.

Method of Search

In a jurisdiction with a grantor-grantee index system, the search procedure usually begins with the grantee index. The examiner begins by looking for the name of the purported owner of the property (usually, a seller) in the grantee index, starting with the present date and working backward until the owner-grantee's name is found. The information for that person in the grantee index will enable the examiner to identify the owner's grantor. The examiner then looks up the owner's grantor in the grantee index. This process is repeated until the title examiner builds a chain of title back through the desired time period of search. In generating the chain of title from the grantee index, the examiner produces only a list of names. To find the recorded copies of the documents themselves, the examiner must use the book and page location information that accompanies each name in the grantee index.

Although it may be possible to search the records far enough back to find a grant of title from the sovereign in colonial times, such a search would be expensive and is rarely necessary. The period of the search usually is determined by practical considerations such as (a) the purpose of the search, (b) applicable **marketable title legislation**, which limits the enforceability of interests that are remote in time, (c) the length of adverse possession periods in the state, and (d) the practices of lenders or title insurers. A typical search period may be 60–75 years or less.

BOX 9–8 POINT TO CONSIDER

A recent Connecticut case, *Zagray v. Ostrager*, 1999 WL 711513 (Conn. Super, 1999), included the following discussion and chain of title in litigation over record title to real estate:

> In their effort to establish record title, the defendants offered the testimony of Richard Johnson. Mr. Johnson is a practicing attorney . . . specializing in title searching. Mr. Johnson indicated that to establish marketable record title, a root title must be found dating back forty years. Mr. Johnson's search went back to 1770 [to] the Colonial Commission grant. Attorney Johnson examined the land records in the town hall in Hebron. He testified as to the chain of title for the property in question and the adjacent property in order to determine title. . . . The court finds that the conclusion of Attorney Johnson as to marketable title to the disputed property to be credible and persuasive. . . . Exhibit 57 lists the following deeds [reproduced in part]: . . ."

Deed Type: Warranty Vol. 22 Pg. 897
Grantor: Henry A. Spafford
Grantee: 1/2 interest to Julia A. Clarke
Date of Execution: 3-23-1894 Recorded: 4-30-1894

Deed Type: Warranty Vol. 22 Pg. 909
Grantor: James C. Foote
Grantee: 1/2 interest to Mrs. Julia A. Clarke
Date of Execution: 4-4-1893 Recorded: 2-21-1895

Deed Type: Warranty Vol. 27 Pg. 268
Grantor: Julia A. Clarke
Grantee: Kolishman, Goldstein & Kolishman
Date of Execution: 6-5-09 Date Recorded: 6-14-09

Deed Type: Quit Claim Vol. 25 Pg. 652
Grantor: Goldstein
Grantee: I. & Z. Kolishman
Date of Execution: 12-13-09 Date Recorded: 12-2-11

Deed Type: Warranty Vol. 27 Pg. 345
Grantor: I. & Z. Kolishman
Grantee: Barnet Wallach
Date of Execution: 8-7-11 Date Recorded: 9-11-11

Deed Type: Warranty Vol. 27 Pg. 521
Grantor: Barnet Wallach
Grantee: Stephen & Agnes Zagray
Date of Execution: 11-2-16 Date Recorded: 1-24-19

The second part of the examination is to look up each of the owners in the chain of title in the *grantor* index to determine whether any of them made a conveyance or mortgage that detracts from the subject property interest. This process is referred to as **running the chain of title**. If, for example, a previous grantor mortgaged the land, the examiner would search for the mortgagee's later *release* or *satisfaction* of the mortgage which, if found in the records, cures what otherwise would be a title defect. Third, the examiner will find each of the referenced deed books and examine each document that the grantee and the grantor indexes have revealed, to confirm that it appears valid, that it transfers the land (or interest) that is the subject of the title search, and that no interest has been transferred outside the chain of title. A title examination in a jurisdiction using a tract index should have all of the instruments affecting a single parcel indexed together, making the search simpler.

Finally the examiner must check the other public records, such as tax and assessment rolls, judgment dockets, and "special proceedings dockets" where incompetency petitions or foreclosures might be recorded. Unpaid federal and state taxes are a lien on real property. Legal judgments are commonly a lien on all real property owned or later acquired by the judgment debtor in the county in which the lien is docketed. A judgment lien is effective for a number of years that varies from state to state, and the lien may be renewable. In addition to the searches previously described, the examiner may need to check building code and zoning records, the list of Superfund pollution sites maintained by the Environmental Protection Agency (discussed in Chapter 18), Uniform Commercial Code fixture filing indices, and bankruptcy court dockets to determine whether these sources reveal any defects in the title or diminish the value of the land as security for a loan.

Abstracts

At the conclusion of the search, the examiner will write a summary, or *abstract*, of the title. The abstract normally includes a condensed statement of the key facts of each transfer or instrument. Normally the abstracter simply reports the facts without expressing an opinion on their legal significance. In some jurisdictions private abstract companies provide abstracts, for a fee, for review by a real estate lawyer or title insurance company. Where the tract index system is used, some abstract companies even maintain duplicate sets of the public records.

Title Opinions

At the conclusion of the searcher's examination and preparation of the abstract, a title attorney may render a title opinion for the buyer, a lender, or a title insurance company. An opinion on title will commonly include the following elements:

1. A statement of who besides the client, if anyone, is entitled to rely on the opinion.
2. A description of the scope and time period of the examination.
3. A description of the property searched (including any easements or rights-of-way servicing the property).
4. A statement of who owns the property.
5. Any exceptions to the owner's fee simple title.

Customarily, the attorney renders a *preliminary opinion* on title to assure the buyer and the buyer's lender of the status of title before closing. The attorney will later provide a final opinion that traces title down to the date and time of closing and reflects the proper recording and indexing of the transfer documents. To avoid taking title subject to matters that may have been recorded between the time of the preliminary title opinion and closing, a prudent buyer or lender may wish to delay disbursing funds until this final opinion is completed.

Title Exceptions

Title exceptions are any *restrictions* on the owner's unfettered use or enjoyment of the property or *encumbrances* on the owner's fee simple interest, found during the examination. A title exception indicates that an owner has given away, or has had taken away, some of the bundle of rights represented by fee simple ownership. Title exceptions that could appear in a typical attorney's opinion letter include the following:

1. Easements affecting the subject property.
2. Restrictive covenants, which affect the use or enjoyment of the property.
3. Encumbrances such as mortgages and deeds of trust.
4. Actual or potential liens for property taxes.
5. Matters such as easements or setbacks revealed on recorded maps or surveys.
6. Judgments.
7. Actual or potential mechanics and materialmen's liens.
8. Pending lawsuits affecting the property.
9. Recorded leases and known unrecorded leases.
10. Standard exceptions for matters that would not be revealed by a search of the public records.

Physical Inspection and Survey of the Land

Many of the title defects that would not be revealed by an examination of the public records *would* be revealed by a survey and inspection of the property. For example, someone may be adversely possessing the property, the property may be located in a federally designated flood zone, the improvements may encroach on the neighbor's property, or the neighbor's improvements may encroach on the property whose title is being examined. Further, an examination of the public records may reveal restrictive covenants or zoning requirements that impose restrictions on property improvements, or easements may run across the property. From a seat in the recorder's office, the examiner cannot determine whether the improvements on the property are properly located, or where the easements are located. Therefore, it is customary for a registered land surveyor to survey and inspect the property. From this survey and inspection, the surveyor prepares a detailed map (plat) of the property.

The American Land Title Association (ALTA), the American Congress on Surveying and Mapping (ACSM), and the National Society of Professional Surveyors (NSPS) have jointly adopted "Minimum Standard Detail Requirements" for land title surveys.[5] The minimum standards require that the survey be performed on the ground and that the plat of the survey be at least 8½ × 11 inches and include the following:

- The surveyor's identifying information.
- The property boundary, drawn to a convenient scale, with the scale clearly indicated.
- A north arrow, with north oriented toward the top of the drawing.
- Identification of symbols and abbreviations.
- Supplementary or exaggerated (enlarged) diagrams, if necessary for clarity.
- Data necessary to indicate the dimensions and relations of the boundary from a located point of beginning.
- Record dimensions of the boundary, as well as measured dimensions, if different.
- Distances from parcel corners to the nearest street right-of-ways.
- Names and widths of streets abutting the property.

- Setback or building restriction lines.
- All monuments found during the survey.
- The character and evidence of possession.
- The location of buildings, fences, walls, and other improvements, including encroaching structural projections.
- All recorded easements.
- Driveways or alleys on the property.
- The location of cemeteries or burial grounds.
- The location of ponds, lakes, springs, or rivers on or adjoining the property.

On the basis of a survey performed to these exacting standards, a title examiner or a potential buyer or lender can elicit a wealth of information regarding potential encumbrances on title, without ever actually seeing the property.

Title Insurance

A title opinion with a supporting land survey provides a buyer or lender a reasonably high level of assurance about the status of title, because the title opinion is an informed legal judgment based on a diligent search of the appropriate records. For an even higher level of assurance, a buyer may purchase title insurance. **Title insurance** protects the policy holder against loss resulting from undisclosed encumbrances or defective title.[6]

A title insurance policy serves two basic functions. First, as in most other forms of casualty insurance, a title insurance company assumes and spreads risk by indemnifying the insured person for certain types of losses or damages and spreading its loss-payment obligation to policy holders by charging each an amount called a "premium." A title insurance company calculates its premiums by estimating its future losses and adding to that figure the administrative costs of running the company and a fair return on its investment as profit.

The second function of title insurance is risk avoidance and elimination. By carefully assessing the status of a title for which insurance is sought, title insurers play a key role in eliminating title defects that constitute potential claims. Only a small portion of the money that title insurance companies collect from insurance premiums is actually paid out in claims. The greater share of the premium goes to risk elimination, administrative costs, and profit.

Coverage of Title Defects

Purchasers of title insurance may be concerned that only a small fraction of premiums is ever paid out in claims. Title insurance, however, is chiefly valuable for other than indemnity reasons, including the following:

- *Increased marketability of property.* An *insurable title* is one that a reputable title insurance company will insure at its regular premium rates without material exceptions or exclusions from coverage. Accordingly, title insurance improves the marketability of a parcel of land by assuring buyers and lenders that it is subject to minimal defects and that the title insurance company will make compensation for any major defect that it overlooked in the process of deciding whether to insure. In addition, if the seller gives a warranty deed, title insurance coverage protects the seller from loss for breach of present and future warranties. In states using the grant deed, title insurance is even more significant, because grant deeds carry a lesser degree of warranty protection. For these reasons, the existence of a title policy will simplify and facilitate a sale or loan.

- *Lender requirement.* Lenders commonly require a lender's title insurance policy (one payable to the lender to protect its security interest) as a condition of their commitment to lend. One key rationale is that primary lenders sell loans on the secondary mortgage market, making marketability of the loan package a key consideration. Title insurance makes the loan more marketable.

- *Financial strength.* In the absence of title insurance, if an attorney has missed or failed to report a title defect in the attorney's opinion, the injured party must look to the resources of the law firm alone in a negligence action, together with any malpractice insurance the law firm may have. However, the acquisition and development costs of a real estate project, especially a commercial one, may exceed the limits of a law firm's malpractice coverage. Title insurance provides assurance that an injured lender or owner may look to a more solvent defendant.

- *Coverage of a known risk.* In some situations, a buyer may wish to purchase a parcel of property despite a known title defect that could render the property unsuitable for the intended use. Where the risk of loss is reasonably remote or the buyer is willing to pay an extra premium, a title insurer may be willing to provide affirmative insurance "coverage over" the known defect. For example, a title insurer might insure against a lease or a mortgage that is remote in time. Or, in the case of a proposed, unchallenged commercial development, the insurer may be willing to insure that residential restrictions are no longer enforceable because of changed circumstances within a residential subdivision. The covered risk is, of course, that the title insurer might be wrong and that the residential restrictions might in fact be enforced.

- *Protection against "hidden" or nonrecord defects in title.* As noted earlier, a large number of potential title defects are not detectable merely by examining the public records, for example a prescriptive easement or a title acquired by adverse possession. An attorney giving a title opinion properly excludes from it such "off-record" matters. Yet, title defects resulting from off-record circumstances can frustrate buyers and lenders and cause them loss. Title insurance protects against loss from nonrecord title defects.

- *Protection against title defects occurring before or after the search period.* Sometimes documents *do* appear in the records but were recorded before or after the period covered by the title search. The title opinion obviously would not reveal such documents. For example, unless the examiner takes the chain of title back to the original government grant, an undetected conflicting interest such as an unsatisfied mortgage granted before the beginning date of the search period may exist. Title insurance protects against such undiscovered interests. Likewise, if instruments or liens are recorded after the title opinion is rendered but before the deed to the buyer is recorded, the buyer's title would be subject to them. This risk is increased in many jurisdictions because of administrative delay, or **gap**, between the recording of a document and its actual appearance in the storage media and the indices. Discovering the document during the gap period may be difficult or impossible. Title insurance protects against losses caused by the gap period.

Consider the implications of the following case:

Case 9.2

Prochaska v. Midwest Title Guarantee Co.

932 P.2d 172 (Wash. App. 1997)

Helmuth and Beverley Prochaska, then residents of South Carolina, were vacationing in the Pacific Northwest when they found a lot in Whatcom County upon which they wanted to build their retirement home. The lot was owned by John Oldfin, a Florida resident. On August 11, 1988, the parties entered into a contract under which the Prochaskas agreed to pay $95,000 for the lot. The contract was sent to Select Escrow (Select) for closing.

On September 7, 1988, Select Escrow sent the closing documents to the parties. The next day, the Prochaskas signed them and returned them to Select with a cashier's check for $45,415.13. The remainder of the purchase price was paid through a loan from Community State Bank, the proceeds of which were deposited with Select on September 13, 1988. Oldfin signed the closing documents on September 9, 1988, and returned them to Select together with the statutory warranty deed and the excise tax affidavit. On September 13, 1988, Select forwarded the deed and a check for the excise tax to Ticor Title Insurance Company with instructions to record the deed. Ticor Title recorded the deed with the Whatcom County Auditor on September 14, 1988, at 10:14 A.M.

Meanwhile, on September 7, 1988, Midwest Title Guarantee Company of Florida had obtained a judgment for $122,210.50 against Oldfin in the Circuit Court of Collier County, Florida. A certified copy of the judgment was filed with the Whatcom County Clerk on September 14, 1988, at 10:05 A.M., nine minutes before the Prochaska's deed was recorded. Midwest Title's judgment was entered on the execution docket on September 16, 1988. Although Midwest Title was successful in collecting a portion of the judgment from Oldfin, by April of 1994 more than $100,000 remained unsatisfied. On April 26, 1994, Midwest Title caused a writ of execution to be issued against the Whatcom County property purchased by the Prochaskas from Oldfin. The Prochaskas assert that they first received notice of Midwest Title's judgment at this date, April 26, 1994.

In May, the Prochaskas brought a motion to determine the probable validity of their claim to the Whatcom County property levied upon by the sheriff. The Whatcom County Superior Court held that the Prochaskas had established the probable validity of their claim to the property against Midwest Title's judgment lien and the Whatcom County Sheriff's levy, and released the property from the levy. Two months later, in August 1994, the Prochaskas moved for summary judgment seeking to establish their superior claim to the Whatcom County property free and clear of Midwest Title's judgment lien. The court granted the Prochaskas' motion later entered judgment quieting title to the Whatcom County property in favor of the Prochaskas. Midwest Title appealed.

KENNEDY, C. J.

Midwest Title contends that the trial court erred in concluding as a matter of law that the Prochaskas took title to the Whatcom County property free and clear of its judgment lien. It argues that its judgment lien commenced upon the filing of the certified copy of the judgment with the Whatcom County clerk at 10:05 A.M. on September 14, 1988, and that because the deed conveying title to the Prochaskas was not recorded until nine minutes later, the Prochaskas took title to the property subject to the judgment lien. The Prochaskas argue that the judgment lien did not commence until the judgment was entered onto the execution docket on September 16, 1988, and that because the deed conveying title from Oldfin to them was recorded two days earlier, Midwest Title's judgment lien did not attach to the Whatcom County property while Oldfin owned it. . . .

A. Commencement of the Judgment Lien . . .

[W]hen Midwest Title transferred its Florida judgment to the clerk of the Whatcom County Superior Court, the clerk was required to treat the judgment "in the same manner as a judgment of the superior court of this state." . . .

. . . RCW 4.56.200(2) governs the commencement of the judgment lien in this case. That section applies, inter alia, to "judgments of the superior court for any county other than that in which the real estate of the judgment debtor to be affected is situated," and provides that the judgment lien commences upon filing with the county clerk. Thus, we conclude that Midwest Title's judgment lien commenced upon the filing of the certified copy of the judgment with the Whatcom County clerk at 10:05 A.M. on September 14, 1988, rather than two days later when the judgment was entered on the execution docket.

B. Judgment Debtor's Interest in Property

Under RCW 4.56.190, a judgment creates a lien against the judgment debtor's [Oldfin's] nonexempt real property. . . . A judgment creditor's lien attaches only to whatever interest the debtor has in property; the lien does not give the creditor a greater interest than that held by the debtor. Midwest Title contends that Oldfin was the owner of the Whatcom County property when its lien commenced at 10:05 A.M. on September 14, 1988, and that, accordingly, the Prochaskas took title to the property subject to the judgment lien. Noting that the statutory warranty deed was not recorded until nine minutes after its judgment was filed, and that other conditions of escrow were not fulfilled until several days after the recordation of the deed, Midwest Title argues that title to the Whatcom County property had not passed from Oldfin to the Prochaskas as of the time its lien commenced.

The Prochaskas respond that because the parties had deposited all documents and funds necessary to close the transaction with Select Escrow by September 13, 1988, and because Ticor Title was committed to issue the title insurance policy before the deed left its offices on the morning of September 14, the sale closed and Oldfin ceased to have an interest in the property before the filing of Midwest Title's judgment with the Whatcom County Clerk. Thus, according to the Prochaskas, Midwest Title's lien did not attach to the Whatcom County property because Oldfin had no interest in the property at the time the judgment was filed.

Midwest Title has the better argument. The deposit of a deed into escrow does not constitute a present conveyance if [it] is subject to conditions precedent yet to be satisfied. Here, several conditions precedent . . . remained unsatisfied at the time Midwest Title filed its judgment lien. In particular, the statutory warranty deed had not been recorded, the policy of title insurance had not been issued, existing encumbrances set forth in Schedule B of the preliminary commitment had not been removed, and taxes had not been prorated. Thus, title to the Whatcom County property had not passed from Oldfin to the Prochaskas at the time Midwest Title's judgment lien commenced. Accordingly the Prochaskas took title to the property subject to the lien.

C. Bona Fide Purchaser Doctrine

The Prochaskas assert that even if this court concludes that Midwest Title's judgment lien attached to the Whatcom County property prior to the passing of title from Oldfin to them, they deserve the protection of the bona fide purchaser doctrine. The bona fide purchaser doctrine provides that a good faith purchaser for value, who is without actual or constructive notice of another's interest in real property purchased, has a superior interest in the property.

We conclude that the Prochaskas are not entitled to the protection of the bona fide purchaser doctrine because the filing of Midwest Title's judgment provided constructive notice that the Whatcom County property was encumbered by its lien. Although the Prochaskas assert that notice is not provided until a judgment is entered on the execution docket, their assertion is supported by neither the law nor the record in this case. In [a prior case], this court held that the filing of a decree of dissolution in the King County Superior Court provided constructive notice to any subsequent purchaser or mortgagee that the debtor's King County property was encumbered by the judgment creditor's lien. . . . Thus . . . the record fails to indicate that entry of a judgment on the execution docket is necessary to provide notice to subsequent purchasers of the affected property.

D. Conclusion

Because Midwest Title's judgment lien commenced before title to Oldfin's property passed to the Prochaskas, and because the Prochaskas are not entitled to the protection of the bona fide purchaser doctrine, their remedies must lie against Oldfin, who issued the statutory warranty deed, or against Ticor Title, which issued the policy of title insurance, and not against Midwest Title.

Reversed and remanded for entry of judgment in favor of Midwest Title.

QUESTIONS ABOUT CASE 9.2

1. Should the fact that the Midwest Title's judgment had been filed but not yet indexed be significant?

2. Note that Ticor Title apparently maintained a "shadow title plant" for the purpose of doing its title searches without going to the deed registry. This approach is used by title companies in a number of jurisdictions to make title searches quicker and more efficient. How is that fact relevant in this case? Hint: Consider the "gap" problem.

Most title insurance policies are based on the forms developed by the American Land Title Association (ALTA). ALTA has developed several different suggested forms for use by individual title insurance companies. The two basic types of title insurance policies are those insuring the purchasers of property ("owner's policies") and those insuring lenders who receive a security interest in real property ("lender's policies").

Owner's Title Insurance

An **owner's policy** insures the owner's title to a parcel of real property, subject to exclusions, conditions, stipulations, and exceptions specified by the policy. Ordinarily, the owner insures the property for the amount of the purchase price. The title insurer indemnifies the owner for the amount of any loss up to policy limit. The owner's protection continues from the effective date of the policy until the owner (or a devisee, heir, or corporate successor) conveys the insured property, and remains in effect thereafter for breaches of a warranty deed executed by the insured upon sale of the property. The insured owner pays a single fixed premium and the policy of title insurance is not assignable.

Subject to the insurer's exclusions, exceptions, conditions, and stipulations, an owner's policy assures that title to the property described in the policy is vested in the insured, that there are no defects in or liens and encumbrances on such title, and that there is right of physical access to and from the property. Two types of ALTA owners' policies are in general use: a traditional title insurance policy, which is suitable for every type of real property development,[7] and an ALTA Homeowner's Policy of Title Insurance (the "Homeowner's Policy") designed for family residential housing of one to four units. The Homeowner's Policy is a simpler, more consumer-friendly policy form, written in plain language. Although different in approach from the ALTA owner's policy, the Homeowner's Policy provides essentially the same insurance coverage.[8]

Exclusions from Owner's Title Coverage. The form for the ALTA title insurance policy, like other types of insurance policies, contains a number of preprinted exclusions from coverage. The exclusion clauses eliminate the insurer's obligation to indemnify the insured for losses resulting from the excluded risks, unless the insurance company agrees by an endorsement to the policy to remove the exclusion. These exclusions address three categories of title defects: defects resulting from (1) government regulation, (2) government exercise of the powers of eminent domain, and (3) matters involving actions or omissions of the insured owner.

The ALTA policy normally does not insure against the exercise of the government's police power, including zoning matters and restrictions on subdivision, building, occupancy, or use. In some states, a zoning endorsement is available (sometimes requiring an additional premium) from the title insurance company. A zoning endorsement insures against loss if the zoning classification proves to be other than as stated in the endorsement. Otherwise, the buyer must independently verify that government regulations permit the intended use of the property. The ALTA policy likewise excludes liability for the government's exercise of its right of eminent domain, unless notice of the exercise of the right appears on record before the effective date of the policy.

The third, most contested general exclusion is actually a collection of matters that involve acts or omissions of the insured. The ALTA title insurance policy form excludes title defects, liens, encumbrances, adverse claims, and other matters that are "created, suffered, assumed or agreed to by the insured claimant." The intent of the exclusion is to protect the title company when the loss is the result of the insured's own conduct, such as when the insured knows of a defect and conceals that information from the title company. The ALTA policy also excludes coverage of property interests that are created in violation of creditors' rights law, including bankruptcy.

Conditions and Stipulations. The ALTA owner's policy form contains seventeen standard conditions and stipulations that spell out important rights and obligations of the parties to the insurance contract. These are discussed in the following five groupings.

First, the conditions and stipulations define the terms used in the contract. Only two need to be mentioned specifically. (1) The "insured" named in the contract includes anyone succeeding to the insured's interest by operation of law, such as heirs or devisees of the named insured. (2) The "land" insured by the policy does not include any property (or property interest such as an easement) beyond the physical boundaries identified in the legal description of the policy. Therefore, if improvements located on the property encroach onto adjoining premises, the encroachments are not insured against by the standard policy. Coverage for encroachments may be available through specific endorsement. Nor is the validity of easements over neighboring land assured by the policy.

Second, the ALTA policy provides that it remains in force for as long as the insured holds title to the premises or is the lender-beneficiary of a purchase money mortgage, or as long as the insured is liable on any covenants of title contained in a warranty deed associated with a sale of the property.

Third, the ALTA policy sets forth the obligation of the insurance company to defend any actions challenging title, with the insured having the responsibility of notifying the company when the title defect first becomes known. In addition to (or instead of) defending the title, the insurance company has the option of settling the claim with the claimant or terminating its liability under the policy by tendering the full policy limits to the insured. These options mean that the insurance policy is no guarantee that the insured will always be entitled to occupancy of the property. This factor should be considered in determining policy limits, which can exceed the purchase price to include damages for lost occupancy if the insurer agrees and the insured pays an additional premium. The insured may also want to purchase an inflation endorsement that increases the policy limits as the cost of living increases.

Fourth, the ALTA conditions and stipulations emphasize that the company will pay only the lesser of the amount of the actual loss suffered by the insured and the policy limits, together with the expenses of litigation. If an owner's policy and a lender's policy are issued insuring the same property, only one payment will be made. Payments may be made directly to the lender as a credit on the lender's mortgage. In most states, this one-payment provision allows substantial cost savings for simultaneously issued owner's and lender's policies.

Finally, the ALTA policy preserves the insurer's *subrogation rights* if it pays a claim under the policy. In insurance law, subrogation rights give the insurer the right to "step into the shoes" of its insured to assert any claim that the insured may have against others, in an effort to recover the amount that it has paid under the policy. For example, the insurance company might use its subrogation rights to sue a prior grantor for breach of the warranties contained in a warranty deed.

Exceptions to Coverage. In addition to the exclusions, conditions, and stipulations, the ALTA policy contains a schedule of *exceptions* to coverage, including both standard exceptions and special exceptions applicable to the insured property.

Standard Exceptions. The standard exceptions in the ALTA policy relate to matters not normally discoverable in a search of the recorder's office. The standard exceptions include (1) rights of parties in possession, (2) matters that would be revealed by a current, accurate survey, (3) easements, liens, encumbrances, or other claims not shown by the public record, and (4) mechanics' or materialmen's liens not shown by the public record.

Claims of parties in possession are excepted because possession under certain conditions can mature into a prescriptive easement or into title by adverse possession as described in Chapters 4 and 6. A title company is generally willing to delete this standard exception on the basis of either (1) the delivery of a surveyor's certificate identifying the parties in possession, or (2) an affidavit executed by the owner affirming that no parties are in possession other than the owner.

The standard exception for matters that would be revealed by a *survey* is normally removed upon the delivery of a survey meeting the ALTA minimum standards described earlier. Although the title insurance company will delete the standard exception upon delivery of the survey, the survey may disclose matters that the title company will want to list as special exceptions, such as encroachments. For example, the survey may reveal that a neighbor's garage encroaches on the subject property, or the owner's driveway encroaches on his neighbor's property or into a building setback, street right of way, or easement.

Mechanics' and materialmen's liens create significant title insurance problems in many states because in those states the liens are effective as of the date on which the work was started or the materials were delivered, even if the lien is not filed until later. This retroactive effect means that an innocent purchaser may well take title subject to lien liability without its being apparent on the public record. Luckily, liens of this type are uncommon except in connection with new development or construction. They normally arise where the owner has neglected to pay all bills for the new construction, or where the general contractor has not passed along payment to subcontractors. In most states, the title company will remove this standard exception upon receiving a lien waiver from the contractors or an affidavit from the owner that no improvements have been made to the property during the statutory lien period.

Special Exceptions. The title policy also includes special exceptions for other items affecting title to the insured premises. Special exceptions include those for taxes, liens, encumbrances, and restrictive covenants. To have them removed, the insured must confirm that these special exceptions do not affect the intended use of the property.

Lender's Title Insurance

The lender's title insurance policy is similar to the owner's policy, except that it insures the priority of the lender's mortgage or deed of trust rather than the fee simple ownership of the owner-mortgagor. The policy coverage is limited to the amount of the mortgage financing. The coverage increases (usually by endorsement to the policy) as the lender makes loan disbursements (e.g., as construction progresses), and coverage decreases as the debtor pays off the debt. The policy insures the lender against any liens or encumbrances having priority over the insured mortgage, and the lender is protected against any unrecorded mechanics' and materialmen's liens. It also insures against a finding of invalidity or unenforceability of the insured mortgage, except to the extent that the invalidity results from the lender's violation of usury, consumer credit protection, or truth in lending laws.

Title insurers usually issue owner's and lender's insurance policies simultaneously with little additional expense to the insureds because the policies insure overlapping risks. Any payment to the lender reduces the insurer's obligations under the owner's policy. Any payment to the lender also reduces the amount due on the owner's note, therefore the owner benefits.

Exclusions from Lender's Title Coverage. The standard ALTA lender's policy contains the same exclusions found in the owner's policy. It also excludes coverage of a loss resulting from unenforceability of the mortgage resulting from the failure of the insured lender to qualify to "do business" within the state where the land is situated. In many states, a lender's failure to qualify to do business when required by statute to do so may bar the lender from using the judicial system to exercise its remedies. Whether the lender is required to qualify or whether it has qualified may not be discernible from a search of the public records.

Conditions, Stipulations, and Exceptions to Lender's Coverage. In general, the conditions, stipulations, and exceptions in a lender's policy are similar to those in the owner's policy. One important aspect of the lender's coverage is that the lender's policy continues in effect if the lender becomes an owner by acquiring fee simple title through foreclosure of the property or by the debtor's giving the lender a deed in lieu of foreclosure.

Self-Study Questions

1. Given the choice, what type deed should the buyer of real estate prefer? Why?

2. What are the differences between a pure race recording statute, a notice recording statute, and a race-notice recording statute?

3. Why is an examination of title important?

4. What records will a buyer want to examine and why?

5. How is a title insurance policy superior to a warranty deed? To an attorney's opinion on title?

6. How does a Torrens System differ from a traditional recording system?

7. What is the difference between a grantor-grantee index and a tract index system? Which system would be easier to use? Why?

8. Why might it be a good idea for a buyer of real estate to get a survey?

9. Which title problems does an owner's title insurance policy exclude from coverage? Why?

Case Problems

1. The Stephensons conveyed a house to O'Neal by general warranty deed. Unknown to the buyer, the septic tank servicing the house was located on a neighbor's property. As a result of this encroachment, the buyer O'Neal filed a claim under the seller's title insurance policy. Commonwealth, the title insurer, paid the claim and then under its subrogation rights sued the Stephensons as grantor under the deed warranty against encumbrances. Should Commonwealth be permitted to recover against the Stephensons (the sellers) on their covenant against encumbrances? *Commonwealth Land Title Ins. Co. v. Stephenson*, 399 S.E.2d 380 (N.C. App. 1991).

2. Fifteen years ago you bought a Pennsylvania farm from George Smith, who acquired it a year after his marriage to Sara. You now want to sell the farm to Harmony Jones, but George sold the farm to you without getting the signature of his wife, Sara, on the deed. Consequently, Sara still has a dower interest, and thus a right to a life estate in the land. George has since died, and Sara is in a Pennsylvania nursing home. To avoid liability to Harmony if Sara asserts her dower interest, what kind of deed could you use for transferring the farm to her?

3. Sara agrees to sell and convey a parcel of land free and clear of all encumbrances to Buster. In his title search and physical inspection of the property, Buster discovers a number of problems. Which of the following matters are "encumbrances"? (a) Recorded easements running across the property. (b) Unrecorded public beach access rights that cross the subject property. (c) Unrecorded footpaths crossing the property. (d) An archeological site. *Create 21 Chuo v. Southwest Slopes*, 918 P.2d 1168 (Haw. App. 1996).

4. Oscar, a property owner, had been using an area adjacent to two lots that he owned as a convenient means of access to one of the lots. The area appeared on a recorded plat of the neighborhood marked as "not a public street." Equino, the owner of the area sued Oscar for trespass. Oscar notified his title insurer of the suit and demanded that the insurer defend him against Equino's claim. The title company refused to defend. Oscar sued the title company for the cost of defending his access across this area. Has the standard ALTA policy guaranteed him access across this area? *Haystad v. Fidelity National Title Ins. Co.*, 66 Cal. Rptr. 2d 487 (Cal. App. 1997).

5. Investguard, Ltd., the buyer of a parcel of real property, sued its title insurance company and the law firm that searched the title, claiming that because the insured property was located within a

flood plain, its title was unmarketable. What should be the result under a standard ALTA policy without endorsements? *Chicago Title Ins. Co. v. Investguard*, 449 S.E.2d 681 (Ga. App. 1994).

6. The Department of Transportation (DOT) instituted a condemnation action as a part of its project to widen North Carolina Highway 150. It based its valuation of the property to be condemned on its claim that it already owned an existing, unrecorded right-of-way easement that extended 75 feet from the centerline of the highway into the defendants' property. According to the defendants' property description in their chain of title, their property line was thirty feet from the centerline of the highway. If the DOT had an enforceable easement extending 45 feet into defendants' property, the amount DOT would have to pay defendants for their land would be decreased. In the valuation of the condemned property, should the DOT be given credit for the alleged 45-foot overlap into the defendants' property? *Department of Transportation v. Humphries*, 496 S.E.2d 563 (N.C. 1998).

7. Borum & Associates, Inc. ("Borum"), provided surveying and engineering services to the developer of a residential subdivision in Guilford County, North Carolina. When the developer failed to pay for the surveying services, Borum filed a lien and sued to enforce the lien. The Seelys bought one of the lots after the enforcement suit was filed but before judgment was entered, apparently with actual as well as constructive notice of the dispute. Borum ultimately sought sale of the plaintiffs' lot to satisfy its judgment against the developer for surveying services for the entire subdivision. The Seelys brought suit to set aside the judgment that Borum had obtained against the developer and to avoid foreclosure of the lien on their lot. The evidence showed that only approximately $600 of the $28,000 judgment was allocable to work that had been performed on the Seelys' lot. Should the Seelys be able to avoid foreclosure on the lien? Should the lien on the lot be $600 or $28,000? *Seely v. Borum*, 488 S.E.2d 282 (N.C. Ct. App. 1997), cert. denied, 494 S.E.2d 419 (N.C. 1997).

8. Benita buys Whiteacre for $500,000, paying $100,000 down and borrowing $400,000. The note that Benita signed provided for payments of interest for five years, with no reduction of principal during that time. Her lender receives a lender's title insurance policy. Benita receives an owner's title insurance policy with a policy limit of $500,000. Three years later, when the value of Whiteacre has risen to $700,000, Argus successfully claims ownership, proving that his name on a deed in Benita's chain of title was forged while he was in a coma. How much does the title insurer owe Benita's lender on this complete loss of title to Blackacre? How much does it owe Benita?

Endnotes

1. Among the states recognizing the grant deed and its implied statutory warranties are California, Idaho, Arizona, and Illinois. Among the states recognizing the bargain and sale deed with implied statutory warranties are Colorado, Nevada, Oregon, and Illinois.

2. This analogy is drawn from Roger A. Cunningham, et al., *The Law of Real Property* (1989) at 773, from which much of the information on recording and registration schemes is taken. *See also* Roger Bernhardt, *Real Property in a Nutshell,* 3rd ed. (1993); John E. Cribbet, *Principles of the Law of Property*, 2d ed. (1975); John E. Cribbet and Corwin W. Johnson, *Property: Cases and Materials* (1978); Roger A. Cunningham, et al., *The Law of Property* (1984); Woodard E. Farmer, Jr. et al., *North Carolina Real Property Practice Handbook* (1982); Patrick K. Hetrick and James B. McLaughlin, *Webster's Real Estate Law in North Carolina*, 3rd ed. (1988). Taylor Mattis, "Recording Acts: Anachronistic Reliance," *Real Property, Probate and Trust Journal* 25, no. 17 (1990); Ray E. Sweat, "Race, Race-Notice and Notice Statutes: The American Recording System," *Probate and Property* 27 (August 1989); and Carl Zollman, *A Treatise on the Modern Law of Real Property* (1940).

3. It is currently uncertain how the passage by Congress of the Electronic Signatures in Global and National Commerce Act, effective October 1, 2000, will affect state law requirements for original documents and original signatures.

4. Uniform Commercial Code, section 9–313(4)(a).

5. American Congress on Surveying and Mapping, "ALTA/ACSM Survey Requirements 1997: Minimum Detail Requirements for ALTA/ACSM Land Title Surveys," available at http://www.survmap.org.

6. See generally Roger A. Cunningham et al., *The Law of Property* (1984); Woodard E. Farmer, Jr. et al., *North Carolina Real Property Practice Handbook* (1982); Jeffrey S. Harlan, "Title Insurance," *Planning Your First Real Estate/Real Property Transactions* (1996); Patrick K. Hetrick and James B. McLaughlin, *Webster's Real Estate Law in North Carolina*, 3rd ed. (1988); and Herbert L. Toms, Jr., "A Basic Explanation of Title Insurance Coverage," *The Basics of Real Property Practice* (1984).

7. The most recent version of the form was adopted by ALTA in 1992. See generally, Bruce Castle and Steve Parsley, "New ALTA form expands coverage," *National Law Journal*, October 11, 1999, B1; and American Land Title Association available at http://www.alta.org.

8. A copy of the form is available at American Land Title Association, "ALTA Insurance Forms," available at http://www.alta.org/pub/membonly/forms.htm.

Chapter 10 Financing the Purchase of Real Estate: Mortgages, Deeds of Trust, and Other Security Arrangements

Most purchasers of realty borrow money from a lender to pay all or part of the purchase price. In return for the loan, called "debt financing," the borrower promises to repay the original sum borrowed, the **principal**, together with an investment return to the lender in the form of **interest**. Interest usually is stated as an annual percentage of the amount lent. Most who could afford to pay cash prefer to obtain debt financing, because it may produce tax advantages, it may be cheaper than alternative sources of capital, or it may allow purchasers employ their cash assets more productively elsewhere.

Because of the critical importance of debt financing in residential and commercial real estate transactions, this chapter begins with an overview of its theory, processes, and terminology. Then the chapter takes up the security devices commonly used in debt financing, and the rights and obligations of the parties to them. The security devices include mortgages, deeds of trust, the installment land contract, and Uniform Commercial Code security interests in fixtures, all designed to assure lenders that if the debt is not repaid, the lender will be able to force the sale of ("foreclose on") the realty or other collateral to cover the unpaid debt. Next is a discussion of the foreclosure process by which lenders convert their collateral into cash if the debtor does not repay the loan. The chapter concludes with a note on lending practices.

Financing the Purchase of Real Estate[1]

The *time value of money* is key to understanding debt financing. "Time value of money" expresses the principle that, given the choice, most of us would prefer to have and spend money today than to have and spend the same amount of money at a given date in the future. Therefore, if we have money now that someone else wants to borrow, we will lend it (and defer spending it ourselves) only if the borrower promises to pay back more in the future. And we want more back in "real" terms. In other words, we want borrowers to return to us more purchasing power than we had at the time of the loan. To accomplish this return, we as lenders take into account the existence of **inflation**, the economic phenomenon that makes a loaf of bread costing 49 cents in 1955 cost $2.29 today even though real costs of production and real profit margins have remained about the same in percentage terms throughout the years. *Borrowers* consider inflation a good thing because they will pay back the dollars they borrowed today with the same number of dollars in the future, but because of inflation, the value or purchasing power of those future dollars will be less at the time for repayment. *Lenders*, of course, are not happy with receiving dollars whose value has been eroded by inflation, so they take steps to compensate for the erosion.

The laws and practices of real estate lending are key in meeting society's need for capital. They are significant, also, to individual buyer-borrowers, but no less to lenders, whose prospective borrowers may not fully appreciate given the disdain historically accorded the moneylender. In real estate finance, a tension indeed exists among the interests of *lenders*, who expect repayment of their loans together with an appropriate return on their principal, the interests of *borrowers* who may need protection from overreaching by lenders, and the interests of *society at large* in assuring the availability of capital for investment. The health of the real estate finance industry depends on a fair balancing of all three interests, a balancing that must, among other considerations, take into account the types of risk that lenders face and their methods of compensating for those risks when setting interest rates.

Lenders' Risks Affecting Interest Rates

Interest rates usually include an increment designed to compensate lenders for the use of their capital (i.e., reflecting the time value of money), together with additional increments to compensate them for various kinds of risks that they assume in a loan transaction. The less risk that a transaction has for lenders, the more likely that lenders will make loans in the first instance, and at a lower interest rate. Thus, borrowers benefit indirectly from laws and procedures that reduce lenders' risks. Among the risks lenders must consider in setting interest rates are the *default risk* (also referred to as *credit risk* or *repayment risk*), the *liquidity risk*, and the *interest rate risk* (also referred to as *maturity risk* or *reinvestment risk*).

Default risk is the possibility that a borrower will not pay the mortgage indebtedness (principal and interest). To cover that risk, the lender adds to the basic interest rate an additional interest rate called the "default risk premium." This size of the **default risk premium** depends upon the creditworthiness of a particular borrower. For example, the so-called **prime rate** reflects the interest rate that commercial banks will charge their most creditworthy borrowers on short-term loans. Lenders charge a higher rate for less creditworthy borrowers to compensate for losses on loans that are not repaid in full. The most creditworthy borrower is generally considered to be the U.S. government. Most lenders base their default risk premiums on interest rates produced by government securities such as treasury bills and bonds. For example, in September, 2000, the interest rate on newly issued 10-year treasury bonds was approximately 5.9%, while rates on long-term, high-grade corporate debt were approximately 7.7%, the difference between the two representing, in part, a default risk premium charged to corporations.

Liquidity risk is the possibility that a lender who wants to sell the debt for cash might be unable to do so. The debt of borrowers who are not well known and debt that has other risk elements may be particularly hard to sell to others. This debt is said to be "illiquid." To make illiquid debt salable, a lender must reduce its price, likely incurring a loss in the process. As compensation for bearing the liquidity risk, lenders add a "liquidity risk premium" to the borrower's basic interest rate. A **liquidity risk premium** is the additional interest rate (beyond the basic rate) demanded by lenders as compensation for bearing the risk that they will not be able to sell the loan at its face value.

Interest rate risk, and the need for lenders to compensate for it, results from the fact that the market value of debt is inversely related to up or down movements in the prevailing interest rates. If market interest rates drop after a loan has been made, the right of the lender to receive the (higher) fixed rate of interest specified by the loan contract becomes more valuable. This increase in the loan's value occurs because prospective purchasers of the loan would pay a premium for it to collect the now higher-than-market interest that the loan carries. Conversely, if market interest rates *rise* after a loan has been made, the lender's right to receive the fixed interest rate specified by the loan contract is less valuable, since its prospective purchasers would prefer to buy loans made at the current (higher) market rate, or would prefer to make loans themselves at the now-higher market rate. The impact of interest rate fluctuations is illustrated in the box on the following page.

The value of a debt instrument is affected not only by market fluctuations in interest rates, but also by changes in the maturity date of the debt caused by those fluctuations. If interest rates drop, a borrower may attempt to "refinance," that is, get a new loan at a lower interest rate to repay the existing debt that has a higher interest rate. Thus, lenders are likely to receive their money back when they least desire it—when they cannot reinvest it at the original, higher interest rate. This risk of the borrower's prepaying at an inconvenient time and the lender's having to reinvest the proceeds at a lower interest rate is the **maturity risk** or the **reinvestment risk** and is an aspect of *interest rate risk*. Subject to limits discussed later, lenders often can compensate for early pay-offs by imposing a *prepayment penalty*. If interest rates *rise*, borrowers will, of course, postpone paying debts as long as possible to preserve the lower interest rate. To prevent a borrower from transferring a low-interest loan to a person who wants to buy the realty and assume the borrower's loan, the lender can employ a "due on sale" clause, also discussed later.

BOX 10–1 POINT TO CONSIDER

Assume that Marcus borrows $100,000 from Snively Savings and Loan Company and agrees to pay the prevailing rate of 8% per annum interest on the unpaid principal balance. He agrees to repay the loan over 30 years in amortized equal monthly payments of principal and interest of $733.76.

If the day after closing the prevailing interest rate jumps to 10%, this loan is much less attractive to Snively Savings and Loan, because it could now lend the same money ($100,000) at the higher rate. All other terms being equal, Marcus's loan now has a present value to Snively Savings and Loan of approximately $83,600, the amount of money that Snively would have to lend at the higher interest rate (10%) to get the same monthly payment ($733.76) on a 30-year loan.

If the day after closing the prevailing interest rate drops to 6%, the $100,000 loan at 8% is much more attractive to Snively Savings and Loan, because Snively could no longer lend the same money at the same rate. All other terms being equal, Marcus's loan now has a present value to Snively Savings and Loan of approximately $122,400, or the amount of money that Snively would have to lend at the lower prevailing rate (6%) to get the same monthly payment on a 30-year loan.

The actual values of these loans would not fluctuate quite as dramatically as these examples indicate, because the present values are affected by the likely actual maturity of the loan. Most real estate loans are paid back before their agreed maturity date. If interest rates drop, Marcus will probably pay the loan back in much less time than the 30 years originally agreed to.

In general, real estate lenders fall into two broad types: *portfolio lenders* and *secondary market lenders*. The two groups approach real estate lending and the various investment risks in fundamentally different ways. **Portfolio lenders** make loans for their own direct investment purposes. A portfolio lender attempts to make money on the difference between the interest return on its loan portfolio and its cost of the funds needed to make the loans. The lender's *cost of funds* includes (1) the interest paid on money the lender borrows to lend to its customers, the savings accounts that depositors have with the lender, and the certificates of deposit issued to nonaccount depositors, and (2) dividends paid to the lender's stockholders. In the past, the major portfolio lenders were banks, savings and loan associations (S&Ls), and insurance companies, though generally only insurance companies remain portfolio lenders today.

Portfolio lending came into some disrepute in the S&L crisis of the early 1980s. The principal cause of the crisis was a sudden and dramatic rise in S&Ls' cost of funds, caused by intense market competition for the deposits that S&Ls relied on to fund their loans. With the increase in cost of funds came a sharp rise in the interest rates the S&Ls had to charge their borrowers. In 1963, the average interest rate on conventional single-family mortgages nationally was 6%. It rose gradually to a 1977 level of 9.02%. Five years later, in 1982, the average rate nationally was a huge 15.31%, with a few individuals having to pay 22.5% for their home loans. Borrowers' interest rates rose so precipitously because the lenders' cost of funds was tied to short-term, market-sensitive instruments like savings deposits. To compete for depositors' funds in the 1980s, the S&Ls had to pay interest rates that had reached unprecedented highs. On the income side, however, their loan portfolios yielded low returns because the long-term loans in them carried low pre-1980s interest rates. Because the S&Ls' cost of obtaining funds now greatly exceeded the interest income they were receiving from loans made when prevailing interest rates were lower, the S&L industry became insolvent. S&L failures resulted in claims on the federal deposit insurance system of about $500 billion.

Secondary market lenders avoid portfolio risks by originating loans and promptly selling them to investors in the secondary mortgage market, instead of holding them in portfolio for the lender itself to collect. A secondary market lender makes money from origination fees collected from borrowers; from profits on the sale of its loans to investors; and from servicing fees for collecting loan payments, administering escrow accounts, and performing other services. Traditionally mortgage bankers were the dominant secondary market lenders, but in the past two decades the surviving S&Ls and commercial banks have also become secondary market lenders. Today, nearly all lenders are secondary market lenders, especially residential lenders.

Role of the Secondary Market

If portfolio lending is too risky for banks and S&Ls, who will buy their loans in the secondary market? A long-term mortgage loan portfolio is valuable to investors having long-term obligations that can be "matched" with long-term assets like mortgage loans. For example, life insurance companies use the income from long-term mortgage portfolios to fund the continuing payout obligations they have undertaken by insuring policyholders' lives. Also, investors with long-term horizons and a desire for secure, predictable returns, such as individuals and institutions seeking low-risk investments for their pension funds, often invest in mortgage loans.

However, these secondary market investors, being remote from the actual borrowers and properties involved, have little or no familiarity with local real estate conditions, or with local real estate documentation and practice, or with the details and risks of any particular secured loan that a local secondary market lender might offer for sale. Yet, for mortgage loans to be attractive to the secondary market investor, they must promise safety, certainty, and predictability. The role of the secondary market is to turn particular real estate financing investments, each of which may have risks peculiar to it, into a general investment that is *fungible* (i.e., interchangeable) for investors. This process, often referred to as **securitization**, is accomplished by "pooling" many individual mortgages together and issuing to investors "participation certificates" representing a fraction of the pool. Thus, an individual secondary market investor never buys a particular mortgage, but instead buys a share of a large (and safer) pool of mortgages.

To further its goals, the U.S. government has been actively involved in loan financing and securitization in the secondary market. For example, federal authorities want to make affordable housing widely available because, it is thought, affordable housing leads to increased prosperity and political stability. The government therefore intervenes in the marketplace in several ways. First, the Federal Home Administration (FHA) and the Veterans Administration (VA) provide government-guaranteed loans for veterans and for low-to-moderate income Americans who meet certain eligibility requirements. In these loan programs, if a borrower defaults on the loan, the applicable government agency covers any loss suffered by the lender. This guaranty runs in favor of portfolio lenders and secondary market investors and, obviously, eliminates the default risk in the transaction. Second, three quasi-governmental organizations are heavily involved in the secondary market: the Federal National Mortgage Association (FNMA, or Fannie Mae), the Federal Home Loan Mortgage Corporation (FHLMC, or Freddie Mac) and the Government National Mortgage Association (GNMA, or Ginnie Mae). Each of these entities buys from secondary market lenders loans that meet its eligibility requirements, either for the entity's own investment or for resale. Fannie Mae and Freddie Mac together bought 42% of the approximately $1.5 trillion in new mortgage loans made in 1998.

Resales of the loans usually take the form of mortgage participation (pass-through) certificates. An investor in a certificate acquires the right to a pro rata share of the principal and interest payable in connection with a pool of mortgages. These certificates are available for investments as small as $1,000 and give investors access to a diversified portfolio of debt instruments, reducing the default risk associated with individual loans. GNMA participation certificates are guaranteed by the federal government, virtually eliminating the default risk, and are available in denominations as small as $25,000. Readily marketable, GNMA, FNMA, and FHLMC certificates have little or none of the liquidity risk associated with individual loans. Because the investor receives a pass-through of principal repayments, including prepayments, the certificates diversify but do not eliminate reinvestment risk.

Although a 30-year FNMA certificate represents a pool of 30-year mortgages, the certificate itself is unlikely to be outstanding for 30 years, because many or most of the underlying mortgages will be paid off early through, for example, prepayments upon the sale of mortgaged real estate and early repayments of loans. In addition, the actual duration of the certificate and the stream of payments is inversely related to the prevailing market rate of interest, at least in part. If prevailing interest rates go up, then fewer prepayments will be made within the pool of mortgages and the duration of the certificate will be longer; if interest rates go down, the pool will experience more prepayments and the duration of the certificate will be shorter.

For example, Snively S&L makes a loan to Archer in the original principal amount of $100,000 for 30 years at 8% interest. It charges Archer a one-point (1%) origination fee for its services in originating the loan. If Snively makes the loan as a portfolio lender, it retains all of the risk and the reward associated with the loan. If Archer does not pay, Snively will have the unenviable task of trying to collect the loan. If instead Snively immediately sells the loan to Fannie Mae at par (face value), it receives back its $100,000 (which Snively can lend again), and may keep the origination fee and collect servicing fees for administering the loan, say 1/4% per year. Fannie Mae then puts the Archer loan in a pool with a number of other regionally diverse loans and sells them in the securities marketplace. If the pool containing Archer's loan has ten loans worth a total of $1 million, and Abigail buys a $10,000 participation certificate in that pool, Abigail will receive 1% of all of the principal and interest (minus fees and expenses) received on all of the loans in the pool. Fannie Mae guarantees the repayment of Archer's loan and undertakes the responsibility of collection if Archer does not pay. Abigail thus gets the benefit of a diversified pool of loans (ten rather than one) for a modest investment ($10,000 instead of $1 million). Of course, fees along the way include Snively, who collects a servicing fee, Fannie Mae, who collects a number of fees, and there may be securities underwriters who collect fees. The result is that Abigail's interest yield may be 7% per annum rather than the 8% that Archer agreed to pay. However, her return for a relatively secure investment will still be 1% to 1.5% higher than Treasury securities of comparable maturity.

These instruments have become a highly popular form of investment. The combined dollar value of various forms of pass-through certificates and mortgage-backed securities has grown from $25 billion outstanding in 1981 to more than $4 trillion outstanding in 1999.[2]

● Eligibility Requirements

As a condition for federal guarantees of FHA and VA loans, federal agencies impose loan eligibility requirements and uniform loan documentation and closing standards. Other types of loans have no governmental requirements. However, because FNMA and FHMLC have historically been the two largest secondary market investors, their own internal eligibility requirements have become the standard in the marketplace for residential mortgage financing and include standards for underwriting and loan documentation. For example, FNMA and FHLMC have produced a set of uniform loan documents for each state. These agencies also require that borrowers' credit-worthiness be verified through credit reports and confirmation of employment and income; that loans not exceed a stated percentage of the market value of the real estate security; and that the quality of the borrower's title be confirmed by a land survey, a title examination, and a lender's title insurance policy. Even portfolio lenders often comply with the eligibility requirements of FNMA and FHMLC in order to sell their loans in the secondary market and thereby reduce their liquidity risk.

Recently, investment banking firms have attempted to apply the residential secondary market practices to the market for commercial loans. That is, investment banks have tried to set uniform standards and documentation for commercial real estate loans and have sold participation certificates in pools of commercial real estate loans. These instruments go by various names, including **collateralized mortgage obligations** (CMOs). Although they lack federal government guarantees, they do offer investors the opportunity to participate at relatively modest levels of capital investment while receiving the benefits of standardization and diversification.

Despite a bewildering variety of terms relating to interest, duration, and other matters relating to the underlying mortgage loans in a pool, they commonly are "amortized" (paid in equal periodic payments, usually monthly, of principal and interest) over the term of the loan (e.g., 30 years). For the forty years preceding the S&L crisis, the 30-year, fixed-interest rate, level-monthly payment mortgage loan was the standard for residential financing. Since 1980, this loan type has continued to be widely used but has been supplemented by a number of innovative loan programs. Many of these loan programs employ a "variable interest rate" that permits the lender to adjust the interest rate up or down during the term of the loan, usually by reference to some external interest rate barometer. These programs relieve lenders from at least part of their interest rate risk. The box on the following page describes some common types of mortgage financing.

Nature of the Mortgage and the Deed of Trust

For debt financing to work, the borrower in each underlying loan transaction must provide the lender with a security interest in the real estate, thereby reducing the lender's default risk. The security interest is created by a mortgage or a deed of trust. If the borrower defaults on the debt, the lender can foreclose, that is, force the sale of the security (the real estate) and have the sale proceeds applied to the unpaid debt. This and the next two sections of the chapter discuss mortgages, deeds of trust, and the foreclosure process.

The Mortgage

A **mortgage** is the transfer of a real property interest from a borrower (**mortgagor**) to a lender (**mortgagee**) as security for an indebtedness usually evidenced by a promissory note. As is often the case in real property law, the current law and practice relating to mortgages have been heavily influenced by historical developments. At common law, the mortgage was created by a deed conveying a fee simple interest to the lender, subject to an express condition subsequent: if the borrower repaid the agreed sum by a certain date, the lender would reconvey the property to the borrower. The date set for paying the mortgage debt was called the *law day*, (a name also given in modern times to the closing date for a real estate contract). A borrower who failed to pay on law day lost ownership of the land to the mortgagee, even if the mortgagor had a valid reason for nonpayment and even if the amount of the debt was far less than the value of the property. Time

BOX 10–2 TYPES OF MORTGAGES

1. **Fixed Rate Mortgage:** The traditional mortgage financing, particularly in the residential context has been the fixed rate mortgage. The fixed rate mortgage has a fixed interest rate and a fixed duration, with an even—usually monthly—payment schedule. For example, a borrower of $100,000 at 10% annual interest rate on a 30-year fixed rate mortgage would pay $877.57 a month for 30 years. Because of the interest rate risk, a borrower might expect to pay a higher interest rate for this certainty, particularly in periods of interest rate volatility. A fixed rate loan often includes a due-on-sale clause. Because of the lender's reinvestment risk, the lender might demand a prepayment penalty if permitted by applicable law.

2. **Adjustable Rate Mortgage:** Adjustable rate mortgages have an interest rate that varies over time. The rate varies or adjusts at stated intervals as a function of the sum of an interest rate increment or **margin** above a stated **index**. In the context of mortgages, an index refers to an internal or external measure of market interest rates, usually a measure that has a direct or indirect relationship to a lender's cost of funds. Common indexes in use are the prime rate, LIBOR, Treasury bills or notes, certificates of deposits (CDs), or the 11th District Cost of Funds Index.

   a. A **prime rate** is the prevailing interest rate offered by lenders on short-term financing for their most creditworthy customers. Although theoretically, each lender may establish its own prime rate, they tend to move in lock-step because of competitive factors and the prevailing prime rate is published in the financial press.

   b. **LIBOR** is an acronym for the London Interbank Offering Rate Index. It is the prevailing interest rate that international banks charge each other to borrow dollars in the London money market. It tends to be a market sensitive, and therefore volatile, interest rate.

   c. **Treasury bills or notes** are debt instruments issued by the U.S. government. Treasury bills are short-term instruments and Treasury notes are long-term instruments. They are often chosen as an index for mortgage notes of similar terms because they represent an interest rate without default risk.

   d. **Certificates of deposit** are debt instruments issued by a bank and are one measure of a bank's cost of funds.

   e. **The 11th District Cost of Funds Index** tracks the weighted average of the cost of funds for Federal Home Loan Bank Board member banks located in California, Arizona, and Nevada, and is published monthly by the Federal Home Loan Bank Board. Because it is a moving average, it tends to be less volatile than some other interest rate options.

   Often an adjustable rate mortgage has payments that adjust at stated intervals.

3. **Balloon Mortgage:** A balloon mortgage contemplates a final, uneven payment of principal—a balloon payment—because the mortgage payments have been insufficient to fully amortize the mortgage debt. The parties often contemplate that the buyer will refinance the balloon payment when it becomes due. A common variation in the residential context is the 7/23 loan. In this type of loan, the payments are the same as a 30-year fixed rate loan, but the unpaid principal balance on the loan is due and payable at the end of seven years.

for payment was strictly "of the essence"; failure to pay on time resulted in a forfeiture of the mortgagor's land to the mortgagee.

This harsh result was modified by the English Courts of Chancery, which came to recognize the lender's interest as only a security interest, and not absolute ownership. Using its equitable powers, Chancery at first protected borrowers from the loss of their property only if (1) the borrower had a good reason for failing to pay on law day, and (2) although having defaulted, the borrower was now prepared to pay. For example, borrowers could get relief if they were victimized by the mortgagee's fraud, misrepresentation, or duress. Later, in recognition of the mortgagee's interest as a security interest only, Chancery routinely granted relief to tardy borrowers without their having to allege and prove an equitable ground for it. Essentially, borrowers now had the right to *redeem* their property, as long as they made the required payment within a reasonable time after law day. The right to redeem the property after default was referred to as the mortgagor's **equity of redemption** and eventually became recognized as a normal equitable interest in land.

A defaulting mortgagor's equity of redemption, however, made the mortgagee's title uncertain, because, despite the mortgagor's failure to pay on law day and probable inability to pay in the future, the mortgagor still had a right for a substantial time after default to bring a suit to redeem the property. In response to this problem, Chancery developed a procedure enabling the mortgagee to **foreclose** (terminate) the mortgagor's equity of redemption. To foreclose, the mortgagee would file a lawsuit for that purpose after the mortgagor's default, and Chancery would order the mortgagor to pay the entire loan balance by a given date. If payment was not made, the mortgagor's equity of redemption would be terminated and the mortgagee would receive the property free from it.

A modified version of these concepts has been generally adopted in the United States. A borrower who fails to comply with the terms of the mortgage loan is said to be in **default**. When a borrower defaults, the mortgage lender normally has the right to **accelerate** the indebtedness owed under the note, that is, to require immediate payment of the entire unpaid principal balance of the loan and accrued interest. Although the lender may then have the option of suing the borrower on the mortgage note for breach of the promise to pay and obtaining a judgment against the borrower's *general* assets, normally the lender will first foreclose the mortgage and thereby receive a first- (or a high-) priority claim to the *specific land* covered by the mortgage. The normal method involves a public sale of the property and the application of the foreclosure sale proceeds to the accelerated debt. In most states, if the proceeds are insufficient to pay the entire debt, the mortgage lender may be entitled to a *deficiency judgment* against the borrower for the difference. Mortgage law and practice vary significantly from state to state, and a lender's rights, duties, and remedies depend on the law of the state where the realty is located.

● The Deed of Trust

Thus far we have dwelt on the mortgage as a security instrument because of its historical significance and wide usage. An alternative security instrument, the *deed of trust*, exists in many states and in several is widely used. The **deed of trust** is a three-party instrument in which the borrower (**trustor** or **grantor**) conveys realty to a **trustee** to hold as security for the benefit of the lender (**beneficiary**). A deed of trust normally authorizes the trustee to sell the property upon the request of the lender after a default by the borrower. If the borrower repays the loan, the trustee must reconvey the realty to the trustor.

The deed of trust is purely a security device and should not be confused with an ordinary trust (discussed in Chapter 6), which confers general property management powers on the trustee. In a deed of trust arrangement, the trustee holds the realty on behalf of the beneficiary *for security purposes only*. The trustor is the functional equivalent of a mortgagor and the beneficiary is the functional equivalent of a mortgagee. Indeed, a deed of trust operates much like a mortgage with a power of sale and is treated that way by most jurisdictions for most purposes. Accordingly, unless otherwise noted in the following sections of this chapter, the term *mortgagor* includes *trustor*, and *mortgagee* includes *beneficiary*.

Title Theory Versus Lien Theory

The states differ substantially in how they view the legal nature of a mortgage. These views are generally characterized as the *title theory*, the *lien theory*, and the *intermediate theory*. **Title theory** states adopt the common law understanding of a mortgage as a transfer of a defeasible legal "title" from the borrower-mortgagor to the lender-mortgagee. The mortgagee's "title" is defeated when the note is paid in full, but in the meantime the mortgagee's title gives it the right to take possession of the property if the need arises (unless otherwise agreed in the mortgage). The majority of states have adopted the **lien theory**. In lien theory states, the mortgagee does not hold legal title to the realty but has merely a security interest in (lien on) the property; consequently, the mortgagor keeps the right of possession until valid foreclosure. Under the **intermediate theory**, the mortgagor has the right to possession until *default*, and the mortgagee has the right possession *after* default.

When the mortgagor defaults, who has the right of possession becomes significant. In any state, the mortgagor's default puts the mortgagee's security at risk, because a defaulting mortgagor may be on the verge of bankruptcy and might deliver rents and profits from the mortgaged property to other creditors rather than apply them to the mortgage debt. Or the defaulting mortgagor might simply abandon the premises, subjecting it to the risk of physical damage. In a title or an intermediate theory state, the mortgagee's right to take possession of the realty enables the mortgagee to protect the premises against waste, and to collect the rents and profits or to have a receiver appointed for that purpose. For the protection of the mortgagor, however, any rents collected by the mortgagee while it is in possession before foreclosure must be accounted for and applied to the outstanding mortgage debt.

Rights and Obligations of the Mortgagor and the Mortgagee

The mortgagor's primary obligation under the mortgage is to make the payments called for and secured by the mortgage. The mortgagee's primary obligation is to apply the mortgagor's payments to the debt. And each party normally has additional obligations imposed either by operation of law or by the mortgage instrument, together with related rights. This section of the chapter discusses a number of problem areas facing mortgagors and mortgagees, and the rights and obligations involved.

Most of the mortgagor's obligations are directed at protecting the mortgagee from events and interests that would undermine the mortgagee's security interest or adversely affect the value of the property as security for the debt. The mortgagor has, for example, a legal obligation to avoid *waste*. Waste is the abuse, destruction, or deterioration of the mortgaged property by one in possession beyond the normal wear and tear expected from occupancy. Unless otherwise agreed, the mortgagor can make the customary use of the property even if doing so reduces the value of the security. For example, the mortgagor may harvest crops on farmland, or timber on timberland; these uses are not waste. It is waste, however, for the mortgagee to tear down buildings on the property or to allow them to deteriorate from neglect. If waste has been made an event of default in the mortgage, an occurrence of waste would entitle the mortgagee to accelerate the loan. Even if waste is not defined in the mortgage as a default, the mortgagee normally has a cause of action if the mortgagor's activities constitute waste. The court may require the debtor to restore the collateral, or immediately to repay a sufficient amount of the unpaid principal to put the mortgagee back in a fully secured position.

Courts have recognized the right of both the mortgagor and the mortgagee to sue third parties that injure the mortgaged property. Normally, a mortgage instrument provides that the mortgagor may bring suit, but that any proceeds of the suit or any insurance proceeds related to the damage will be applied to restore the mortgaged property or to reduce the mortgage debt.

The mortgagor and mortgagee have insurable interests in the mortgaged realty entitling them to insure their respective interests against loss. An interest in realty is insurable if damage to the realty would cause pecuniary loss to the owner of the interest. The *mortgagor's* interest consists of possession and the other aspects of ownership included in the "bundle of rights" (e.g., a fee simple estate or some lesser interest such as a leasehold estate) minus the security interest granted by the mortgage; the *mortgagee's* interest is the title or the lien conferred by the mortgage as security for the debt. The interest of each can be protected by the purchase of title, casualty, or hazard insurance. The borrower's insurable interest extends to the full value of the borrower's interest in the property; the insurable interest of the mortgagee is limited to the amount of the secured debt.

Although borrower and lender each has a separate insurable interest, the normal practice is for the borrower to take out and pay for one policy that insures both parties as their interests may appear. The mortgage commonly has terms regarding how insurance proceeds are to be allocated between the borrower and the lender (i.e., applied to reduce the debt). For example, Carlton's $100,000 house is mortgaged to Snively S&L for $75,000. A fire at Carlton's house causes $25,000 in damage. Although Carlton's damages are obvious, Snively's are a little more subtle. After all, Carlton has not defaulted on the loan, and the damaged house is still worth the amount of Snively's loan. Nevertheless, Snively's security has been seriously impaired. Instead of a reasonably secure loan for 75% of the value of Carlton's house, Snively now has a much riskier 100% loan. Snively can be returned to its 75% loan position either by having at least $18,750 of the insurance proceeds applied to the loan (creating an outstanding loan balance of $56,250 on a house now worth $75,000) or by applying the insurance proceeds to restore the house to its original condition. In most circumstances, Snively would probably prefer to restore the property because doing so would make it more marketable. Before allowing the insurance company to pay the money to Carlton, Snively will likely put procedures in place to make sure that Carlton actually uses the insurance proceeds to repair the house.

When the government condemns mortgaged property by exercising its power of eminent domain, the mortgagee normally has the right to participate in the condemnation proceedings (for example, to contest the valuation of the property), and the mortgagee's security rights in the land attach to the condemnation award following the taking. Often, mortgages provide that if only part of the real estate is condemned (taken), the property is to be restored if restoration is feasible. If restoration is not feasible, the mortgagee usually shares in the award, at least to the extent that its security is impaired. Assume that, instead of fire damage to Carlton's house, the city condemned a substantial portion of Carlton's front yard to widen the street, thereby decreasing the market value of Carlton's property by $25,000. Carlton cannot restore the property because he cannot buy additional property to put in his front yard. Therefore, Snively will probably insist that at least $18,750 of the condemnation proceeds be applied to reduce the loan balance so that Snively will maintain its relative security position.

Normally the mortgage requires the mortgagor to pay any debts and avoid any land uses that might result in a lien on the property. The lender will naturally be concerned about indebtedness such as unpaid taxes, an unpaid assessment for sidewalks or street repairs, or the claims of unpaid contractors who may have statutory lien rights under the mechanic's lien law. These debts might create a lien superior to the mortgage lien, but even if such a debt is junior to the mortgage, the mortgagee may have to pay it if the mortgagor cannot, to protect against foreclosure by the rival lienholder. And the mortgage will likely prohibit the borrower from releasing any hazardous substances on the property, because a release could substantially reduce the value of the property and thereby reduce the lender's security. Under federal and state environmental protection laws, a toxic release could also trigger cleanup liability. Ordinarily, at least the polluter and the present owner (mortgagor) are the parties responsible for cleanup, but in rare instances even the *mortgagee* can be liable for cleanup costs.

Ad valorem property taxes and insurance premiums on the real estate normally are payable in annual or semiannual lump sums, which may be difficult for some borrowers to pay when due. Consequently, many lenders insist that borrowers make advance monthly payments into an **escrow account** to cover the tax and insurance bills when they come due. Lenders commonly require that borrowers deposit one-twelfth of the estimated annual payments for taxes and insurance monthly into a restricted escrow account with the lender, along with the normal monthly principal and interest payment. This requirement may be waived when the loan amount is less than 80% of the market value of the security.

Most mortgagees pay no interest on the amounts in mortgagors' escrow accounts, so any earnings accrue to the sole benefit of the mortgagee, providing it with an additional revenue source. To limit potential abuse of escrows, the Real Estate Settlement Procedures Act restricts the amount that lenders can require as escrow payments. Also, some states now require that the escrows be placed in interest-bearing accounts so that borrowers get some modest benefit from their escrowed funds.

A mortgagee who takes possession of the property before or after default, but without a foreclosure of the equity of redemption, becomes a **mortgagee-in-possession** with some significant responsibility and potential liability. Possession usually includes occupancy, but a more important aspect of possession is that the mortgagee, not the mortgagor, has control of the property and its rents and profits. The status of the lender as a mortgagee-in-possession is significant because it carries with it potential liability for failure to comply with governmental requirements imposed upon property owners, or for injury to third parties on the property. The mortgagee also assumes a duty to the borrower to manage the property in a reasonably prudent manner by maintaining the physical condition of the premises and avoiding waste. It must also account to the mortgagor—and perhaps to any junior lienholder—for the receipts and disbursements associated with its management and must apply the net proceeds to reduce the debt. If the property is not leased at the time the mortgagee takes possession, it may be required to use diligent efforts to lease the property. Upon failure to exercise the diligence of a reasonably prudent owner in re-leasing the premises, the mortgagee may become liable to the mortgagor for the reasonable rental value of the property. Because of this risk of liability, mortgagees often are reluctant to take possession without foreclosure, unless the borrower is "milking" the property (keeping rents and profits but not paying expenses), or the property is seriously deteriorating under the borrower's control.

A lender concerned about the mortgagor's creditworthiness or the physical condition of the collateral may not want to take possession, but may prefer instead to petition a court of equity to appoint a **receiver** to take possession of the mortgaged property, manage it, and collect the rents. Thus the lender avoids many accounting responsibilities of a mortgagee-in-possession, and much of the potential liability to third parties. The grounds for and difficulty of obtaining a receiver vary widely from state to state. Courts in lien theory states generally are more reluctant to deliver possession to a lender or to appoint a receiver than are the courts in a title theory state. In all states, courts may impose conditions for the appointment of a receiver, requiring some combination of the following for the appointment to be justified:

- An event of default under the loan documents.

- Waste committed by the borrower.

- A need to control rents to preserve the value of the security.

- Substantial delay between default and foreclosure and a consequent risk of loss to the lender.

- An insolvent mortgagor.

Typically, a clause in the mortgage provides that the mortgagee shall have the unrestricted right to the appointment of a receiver in the event of default. But the court's role is to determine on the basis of all the facts whether appointment of a receiver is warranted. The presence of such a clause in a mortgage is seldom a conclusive factor in a court's decision to grant or deny receivership. More persuasive factors center on whether a receiver is actually needed.

Transfer of the Mortgaged Property

The principle of free alienation (transfer) of property is fundamental in our legal system. Even in title theory states where "legal title" theoretically resides in the mortgagee, the mortgagor is recognized as the owner for the purpose of transferring the property to a buyer, and the mortgagee cannot impose unreasonable restraints on the mortgagor's right of alienation. For the protection of the mortgagee and others, however, the sale of mortgaged property is subject to *reasonable* limitations imposed by law or by the mortgage. For example, when the borrower transfers the mortgaged property, by law the property remains subject to the mortgage and the borrower remains liable for the original indebtedness and obligations under the mortgage. The mortgagor is relieved from liability only by payment of the indebtedness or by being released from the loan obligations by the lender.

For the protection of mortgagees whose mortgages remain unpaid at the time of sale, sellers usually transfer the mortgaged property in one of several basic ways:

- The buyer pays the closing agent the entire purchase price. The closing agent arranges for cancellation of the mortgage by paying the entire outstanding principal and accrued interest to the mortgagee and paying any remaining balance to the seller. This process is called *prepayment* because the mortgage debt is completely paid before the end of the loan term specified in the mortgage (e.g., 30 years).

- The buyer pays the seller only the value of the seller's equity interest, i.e., the difference between the agreed purchase price and the unpaid amount of the seller's indebtedness. Neither seller nor buyer pays off the loan at the time of sale. Instead, the buyer takes the property "subject to" the seller's mortgage, which continues to encumber the property.

- The buyer pays the seller only the value of the seller's equity interest. The seller does not pay off the mortgage debt. Instead, the buyer "assumes the mortgage" and agrees to perform the seller's obligations under the mortgage. Thus, the buyer replaces the seller as "principal debtor," and the seller becomes a surety "by operation of law" with liability to the lender if the buyer fails to pay.

The legal and practical effects of each of these possibilities will be considered in turn.

Prepayment

Prepaying the loan is the simplest and the most common way for the seller to discharge an existing mortgage. However, prepayment may be unavailable or unattractive to the seller.

Prepayment may not be an available option under the loan documents. At common law, unless otherwise agreed in the note or the mortgage, the borrower had no right to repay the loan before the agreed maturity date. The courts reasoned that the lender had made the loan expecting to receive the stated interest rate for the full term of the mortgage. If the borrower were allowed to pay the principal amount early when interest rates were declining, the lender would not receive the full benefit of its investment. In many states today, perhaps still a majority, the common law rule prevails: the lender may refuse early payment (absent a contrary agreement) and require the borrower to repay the loan over its full term. In a growing number of states, this common law principle has been modified by statute or judicial decision to *permit* prepayment if the loan documents are silent on the matter.

Although lenders in most states can forbid prepayment, most lenders permit it but require the borrower to pay a "prepayment penalty" for paying the loan off early. About ten states, however, flatly prohibit prepayment penalties in *residential* real estate loans, thus guaranteeing residential borrowers in those states the unrestricted right to prepay. Following the lead of FNMA and FHLMC (the main federally sponsored purchasers of mortgages in the secondary market), many home mortgage lenders have dropped prepayment clauses from their mortgage forms and no longer impose prepayment penalties. Other home lenders still impose prepayment penalties, which are routine in commercial loans.

Commercial lenders impose prepayment penalties for the economic reasons discussed earlier. To guarantee themselves a return on their investments, they frequently "match" assets and liabilities. If the mortgage rate of interest is higher than the prevailing market interest rates, the mortgagee may not want to be paid early. Therefore, it may prohibit prepayment entirely or may permit prepayment but demand a fee (prepayment penalty) to compensate it for the loss of the expected yield on the loan. Although often referred to as a prepayment penalty, the fee is actually treated as liquidated damages. Like liquidated damages in other contracts, the fee cannot be punitive and must be linked to the loss resulting from prepayment.

Often, prepayment is not attractive to the seller, as where interest rate on the existing mortgage is the same as or lower than the prevailing interest rates. For the seller, the existing below-market interest rate may increase the property's market value. If the mortgage remains in place (and contains no "due-on-sale" clause), the buyer not only receives a below-market interest rate, but may also avoid the transaction costs associated with a new loan. Where the buyer cannot obtain a new loan because of a poor credit rating, the parties may want to take advantage of the seller's credit by using one of the other methods to keep the existing loan in place.

Purchasing Subject to a Mortgage

Instead of prepayment, the seller might sell only the equity interest in the property without the buyer's taking any responsibility for the unpaid mortgage. The seller-mortgagor receives payment for the equity interest and remains liable for the debt and for all the terms of the mortgage, and the buyer receives property "subject to" the lender's rights under mortgage. Although not liable for payment of the seller's note or the lender's mortgage, the buyer does have a practical incentive to make the mortgage payments. If the payments are not made when due, the mortgagee will foreclose and the buyer will lose the equity interest in the property. For any deficiency following foreclosure, the lender has a cause of action against the seller, but not the buyer.

The "subject to" transaction is especially risky for the *seller* if:

- There is little or no equity in the property (because the seller remains liable for the whole mortgage debt).

- The real estate market is volatile (because, when real estate prices fall, equity is reduced and any deficiency is increased).

- The seller provides financing for part of the equity (thus accepting the buyer's debt in addition to the unpaid mortgage the seller is still responsible for).

- The buyer commits waste (thus reducing the value of the property in any foreclosure proceeding).

And because the *buyer* has no personal liability to the lender when buying "subject to" the mortgage, the lender faces a higher risk of default than is true of the mortgage assumption transaction discussed in the next section.

Assumption Agreements

Because of the risk factors involved in selling realty subject to the mortgage, the seller (or the seller's lender) may insist that the buyer "assume" (become personally liable to the lender for) the mortgage obligations. A buyer who assumes the mortgage replaces the seller as the "principal debtor" in the mortgage contract between the seller and the lender. As the new principal debtor, the buyer has the same liability that the seller had for performance of the obligations contained in the mortgage. However, the buyer's assuming the mortgage does not, by itself, free the seller from those obligations, since the seller has become a *surety by operation of law*. A **surety** is a person who is responsible for paying the debt of another person (here, the buyer if the buyer defaults on the mortgage). Suretyship "by operation of law" means that the seller's suretyship status is imposed by law, whether or not the seller is aware of that status, and not by agreement.

An assumption agreement places the lender in a more secure position than does a sale "subject to" the mortgage. Under the assumption agreement, the lender now has three sources of repayment of the mortgage debt: (1) the property subject to the mortgage, (2) the buyer's liability as new principal debtor, and (3) the seller's (the original borrower's) liability as surety on the debt. Sometimes a defaulting buyer is insolvent, so the mortgagee's suing the buyer would be futile. If an insolvent buyer defaults and the mortgagee declines to foreclose, but instead requires the seller-surety to pay, the surety is "subrogated" to the mortgagee's foreclosure rights (acquires them by substitution). Thus, the surety who must pay has a right to recoup the loss by bringing a foreclosure action against the buyer and forcing the sale of the mortgaged realty.

Lenders often release sellers (usually at the seller's request) from the suretyship liability, especially where the original mortgage agreement anticipated assumption and provided for lender approval of new principal debtor. However, especially in large commercial loans, a lender is unlikely to release the seller unless satisfied with the value of the security and convinced of the buyer's ability to pay. Some lenders charge an assumption fee for releasing the seller from liability.

Effect of a Due-on-Sale or a Due-on-Further-Encumbrance Clause

If the mortgage contains a "due-on-sale" clause, as most mortgages do, neither a sale subject to a mortgage nor a sale with an assumption of the mortgage is possible without the lender's consent. A **due-on-sale clause** accelerates the mortgage obligations (e.g., requires immediate payment of the debt) and permits the lender to foreclose if the mortgagor transfers the realty without the consent (usually *prior written* consent) of the mortgagee. Historically, mortgagees used the due-on-sale clause to guard against transfers that might increase the *default risk*, such as a transfer to a person of doubtful creditworthiness. At least since the S&L crisis, however, mortgagees have usually used due-on-sale clauses to control *interest rate risk*. So, if the prevailing market interest rates rise after a loan is made, and the borrower later decides to sell the mortgaged property, the lender can withhold consent to the transfer and use the due-on-sale clause to require immediate repayment of the debt. A lender could then use the proceeds to make a new loan at the higher prevailing market rate. More commonly, the lender, by threatening to invoke the due-on-sale clause, forces the buyer to agree to a higher interest rate.

Many lenders faced litigation and legislation intended to limit the use of due-on-sale clauses for this purpose. In response, a federal law, the Garn-St. Germain Depository Institutions Act of 1982,[3] now makes most due-on-sale clauses valid and enforceable, even if the lender's sole purpose is to increase the interest rate. The policy of the act is to enable investors to maintain the value of their investments by raising their interest rates as market rates rise. This policy applies to sales of residential as well as to sales of commercial properties.

Many transfers of residential properties, however, are not sales, but instead are transfers occurring in the normal course of family affairs, such as inheritance of the realty at the death of the borrower. An additional policy of the act, therefore, is to protect individuals from forced interest rate increases in family-related and other transfers that are not sales of the fee to strangers. Accordingly, the act *prohibits* the enforcement of due-on-sale clauses if (1) the mortgaged realty is *residential* property of one to four units, and (2) the transfer involved is any of those listed in the act or in the regulations of the Federal Home Loan Bank Board. Because the act preempts state law, due-on-sale acceleration in these transfers is prohibited even if state law permits it. Among the transfers for which the mortgage debt may *not* be accelerated are the following:

- Creation of a lien subordinate to the lender's mortgage, which does not relate to a transfer of rights of occupancy in the property (e.g., a second mortgage given on the property to provide college tuition for the borrower's child).

- Creation of a purchase money security interest for household appliances that become fixtures, such as a furnace.

- A transfer by devise, descent, or operation of law on the death of a joint tenant or a tenant by the entirety.

- The granting of a leasehold interest of three years or less not containing an option to purchase.

- A transfer to a relative resulting from the death of the borrower.

- A transfer where the spouse or child of the borrower becomes an owner of the property.

- A transfer resulting from a decree of dissolution of marriage, a legal separation agreement, or an incidental property settlement agreement, by which the spouse of the borrower becomes an owner of the property.

- A transfer into an inter vivos trust in which the borrower is and remains a beneficiary and which does not relate to a transfer of rights of occupancy in the property.

The economic effect of the act is profound. Because of the mobility of homeowners in American society, the average duration of a thirty-year residential mortgage loan is significantly less than thirty years, perhaps closer to five years. Thus, lenders have many opportunities to raise the interest rate in rising interest-rate markets by invoking the due-on-sale clause.

Commercial loan mortgages frequently contain not only a due-on-sale clause, but also a due-on-further-encumbrance clause, usually called a due-on-encumbrance clause. A **due-on-encumbrance**

clause accelerates the mortgage obligations if the mortgagor transfers an interest in the mortgaged property as security for a junior mortgage without the consent of the mortgagee. The purpose of this clause is to allow the mortgagee to evaluate whether its security is impaired by the second mortgage in order to ensure that the property generates sufficient income after operating expenses to satisfy both mortgages. The lender may condition its consent to a junior lien on the execution of an agreement with the junior mortgagee establishing their respective rights and obligations if the borrower defaults under either or both mortgages. Federal law prohibits due-on-encumbrance clauses in loans on family homes of one to four units.[4]

BOX 10–3 APPLY YOUR KNOWLEDGE

The Luechauers sold Blackacre to the McQuistons for $250,000. The Luechauers' 30-year loan with Snively S&L at 6.75% has a current principal balance of $150,000. The prevailing market interest rate on comparable loans is 8.25%.

- What options do the parties have in effecting the transfer given the existing mortgage?
- Which options do you think the buyers would prefer? The sellers?
- If the loan is secured by a first mortgage on a FNMA/FHLMC uniform instrument that contains a due-on-sale clause, does that affect your answer in the first question? How? Is Snively S&L likely to demand prepayment of the loan in the event of transfer? What happens if buyer and seller do not want to prepay?

Foreclosure of the Mortgage or Deed of Trust

Foreclosure of a mortgage involves terminating the mortgagor's equity of redemption and vesting fee simple title in the mortgagee. Because of the drastic impact on the mortgagor and others affected by foreclosure, it is not treated lightly by the courts. To foreclose, the mortgagee must follow all the steps prescribed by applicable law and by the loan documents themselves.

Default and Acceleration

Most installment notes and mortgages contain acceleration clauses that allow the holder of the note to require early payment of the loan upon the mortgagor's default. Events of default commonly specified in the mortgage documents include:

- The borrower's failure to make principal and interest payments when due.
- The borrower's failure to keep the property insured or to pay the taxes.
- Insolvency of the borrower.
- The borrower's commission of waste on the mortgaged premises.
- The filing of mechanics' or materialmen's liens.
- A release of hazardous substances on the mortgaged property.
- A transfer or further encumbrance of the mortgaged property.

The mortgagee accelerates by giving the borrower unequivocal written notice of the decision to accelerate, or, in some states, by performing some act clearly evidencing an intent to accelerate, such as commencing foreclosure proceedings.

Upon the mortgagor's default, the mortgagee can at its option declare the mortgage debt and related expenses immediately due and payable, unless, as is common, the mortgage gives the borrower the right to "cure" defaults or the right to "notice and cure." The right of **cure** is the borrower's right to rectify a default under the loan documents during a specified grace period. For example, if a note provides that monthly payments are due on the first day of each month, the borrower is in default if the payment is not made on or before the first. However, the mortgage may provide a grace period (e.g., 15 days) for the borrower to cure the default before the lender is entitled to accelerate or exercise other remedies. Alternatively, the mortgage or the promissory note (or state statutes) might provide that the applicable grace period begins to run only after *notice* of the default is sent to (or received by) the borrower. The notice gives the borrower the opportunity to cure the default quickly where, for example, it occurred simply by oversight.

Cure rights should be distinguished from *redemption* rights. If the borrower cures within the time permitted in the loan documents, the loan remains in effect and the payment process continues as if the default never took place. In most states, however, if the lender *accelerates* the loan (because the defaulting borrower failed to exercise a right of cure or had no such right), the borrower cannot reinstate the loan. But the borrower, having defaulted and triggered foreclosure proceedings, may *redeem* the property and avoid foreclosure by paying the entire indebtedness before the foreclosure sale and thus discharging the loan. The mortgagor's indebtedness includes principal, accrued interest, and allowable fees and expenses of collection. Redemption rights are discussed later in this chapter.

The exercise of the mortgagee's right to accelerate the loan (commence foreclosure proceedings) may be impaired by the Federal Bankruptcy Code, section 362 of which provides for an "automatic stay" of any proceedings intended to collect sums from the debtor. The moment a voluntary or involuntary bankruptcy petition is filed, it stays, or suspends, all litigation and other actions by creditors against the debtor or the debtor's property. Thus, once a bankruptcy petition has been filed, creditors cannot commence or continue most legal processes, such as acceleration, foreclosure, execution on judgments, or an action to repossess property in the hands of the debtor. If a creditor knowingly violates the automatic stay, any injured party, including the debtor, is entitled to recover actual damages, costs, and attorneys' fees and may be entitled to recover punitive damages as well. Under certain circumstances, however, a secured creditor may be entitled to relief from the automatic stay.

Methods and Process of Foreclosure

The purpose of a foreclosure proceeding is to give the purchaser at the foreclosure sale the same title to the land that the defaulting mortgagor had when the mortgage was created. For the purchaser to receive that title, the foreclosure proceeding must terminate the rights of the defaulting mortgagor and others who have an interest in the land. The defaulting mortgagor has, for example, a right to redeem the property by paying the mortgage indebtedness before the sale takes place. The redemption right of a mortgagor who fails to redeem is terminated by the sale.

Two main methods of foreclosure are used in this country, (1) *judicial foreclosure* and (2) the nonjudicial *power-of-sale foreclosure* in which the mortgagee or the trustee under a deed of trust conducts the proceedings without court supervision. Both methods culminate in a foreclosure sale of the mortgaged property, with the proceeds of the sale being distributed to the foreclosing mortgagee and, if sufficient funds remain, to appropriate others. Judicial foreclosure, the type most commonly used, is available in every state, and in some states is the only type permitted. Most states permit the mortgagee to use either type. In about half the states, the power-of-sale foreclosure is the prevailing method, though even in these states judicial foreclosure often is used, and in certain situations is required.

In two states, Connecticut and Vermont, *strict foreclosure* is the prevailing method. In *strict foreclosure*, there is no foreclosure sale. Instead, the court gives the defaulting mortgagor a specified time within which to pay the mortgage debt. If the mortgagor fails to pay by the deadline, title to the mortgaged property vests in the mortgagee without a sale. In both states, however, the courts have discretion to order a foreclosure by sale. Strict foreclosure is used in a few additional states, but only under limited circumstances, for example, where the mortgaged property is worth less than the mortgage debt and the mortgagor is insolvent. In the vast majority of jurisdictions, the mortgagor cannot be deprived of the equity of redemption without a valid foreclosure proceeding and foreclosure sale.

Judicial foreclosure involves a lawsuit against the mortgagor in which other parties having an interest in the property are made parties to the lawsuit. All judicial foreclosures involve numerous steps, usually the following:

- A preliminary title search to identify the parties who have interest in the property.
- Filing the foreclosure action.
- Service of process on all interested parties.
- A judicial hearing to determine whether the mortgagee is entitled to foreclose.
- A judgment.
- If the mortgagee prevails in the lawsuit, an opportunity for the mortgagor and others with an interest in the mortgaged property to exercise their respective redemption rights before sale.
- Notice of sale, actual sale of the mortgaged property, the court's issuance of a certificate of sale and a report of sale, and allocation of any surplus proceeds or determination of deficiency.
- In about half the states, a statutory redemption period following the sale, during which the mortgagor or others may exercise their statutory redemption rights.

Like any other lawsuit, judicial foreclosure can be expensive and time-consuming, and in a complicated, contested judicial foreclosure, resolution of the legal issues and the subsequent sale may take years. Because judicial foreclosure can also involve a substantial postsale redemption period, in states where judicial foreclosure is the only method of foreclosure, it may increase the lender's default risk and, with it, the cost of borrowing.

Identifying the parties with an interest in the mortgaged realty and making them defendants ("joining" them) in the impending foreclosure proceeding is a critical first step in foreclosure. Most interested parties are necessary (indispensable) to the foreclosure, but some are merely proper parties, whose joinder is helpful in but not required for a valid foreclosure. A party is necessary for foreclosure if his or her interest is needed to give the purchaser at the foreclosure sale the title that the defaulting mortgagor had when the mortgage was created. Necessary parties include the mortgagor as long as he or she has an interest in the mortgaged realty, the buyer of all or a part of the mortgagor's equity in the realty, the heir or devisee of a deceased mortgagor, and a number of persons acquiring an interest after the creation of the mortgage, such as lessees whose leases were created after the mortgage, junior mortgagees, holders of later-acquired mechanics' liens, and owners of later-created easements.

Unless *necessary* parties are *joined* in the lawsuit, the court has no power to order the sale of their interests at the foreclosure sale and those interests are not terminated by the sale. Nelson gives a first mortgage on Blackacre to First Bank (the "senior lienholder") and later gives a second mortgage on Blackacre to Second Bank (the "junior lienholder"). Then Nelson defaults on the first mortgage. To foreclose, First Bank must sue both mortgagor Nelson and junior lienholder Second Bank ("join" them as defendants) because the interests of both are needed for the foreclosure sale purchaser to receive the title that Nelson had when he entered into the first mortgage. If the mortgaged property sells for enough to cover both mortgage debts, Second Bank will be paid the amount it is owed out of the proceeds of the foreclosure sale. If the sale does not bring enough to pay anything to Second Bank, First Bank will receive whatever the sale produces, and Second Bank and First Bank may be entitled to a deficiency judgment against Nelson for any unpaid amounts. As noted later, however, a number of states have antideficiency statutes that prohibit deficiency judgments in certain types of loans.

Proper parties, in contrast, are those with an interest in the realty that is *not* needed to give the purchaser the defaulting mortgagor's title, but whose joining would be appropriate or helpful to the court in determining the ultimate rights of all. Among "proper" parties are mortgagees with mortgages senior to the one being foreclosed, and lessees whose leases were created before the foreclosing party's mortgage came into existence. Suppose that Nelson defaulted on *Second* Bank's mortgage instead of First Bank's, and that First Bank had recorded its mortgage before Second Bank's mortgage arose. Because of Second Bank's notice of First Bank's earlier mortgage, Second Bank's claim to the collateral is subordinate to First Bank's claim and cannot defeat First Bank's mortgage. Because First Bank's senior mortgage cannot be defeated by Second Bank's mortgage, Second Bank's suing First Bank in the foreclosure action would be futile. Therefore, First Bank is not a necessary party to Second Bank's foreclosure action. Only Nelson, the grantor of the second mortgage, is a necessary party, and the foreclosure sale purchaser will take the collateral subject to First Bank's mortgage. Yet, if the extent of First Bank's lien is not clear, Second Bank can join First Bank to acquire financial information that the foreclosure sale purchaser may need for an accurate valuation of the mortgaged property.

Incidentally, one justification for requiring joinder of necessary parties is that if interested parties have notice of the foreclosure sale, they will be motivated to bid at the foreclosure sale or to encourage others to bid. In practice, this bidding competition seldom occurs. Often the senior mortgagee is the only bidder at the judicial sale even after appropriate notice is given to all interested parties.

The method of conducting the sale itself is a matter of local law specifically regulated by state statute. The statutes typically provide for a public, auction-type sale, under the direction of the county sheriff or court personnel. The statute normally specifies the time and place of sale, together with the type of sale notice. The proceeds of sale, minus the expenses of the sale itself, are usually applied to mortgages or other liens in their order of priority. If the sale proceeds exceed the amount necessary to pay all liens, the excess is paid to the mortgagor.

For example, Debbie borrows $50,000 from Snively S&L, securing the loan with a first mortgage on Blackacre. She obtains a second mortgage loan of $25,000 from Bulldog Finance. Later, Debbie loses a lawsuit arising out of a traffic accident with Geraldine, who receives a judgment lien on the mortgaged property for $45,000. Debbie then defaults on all her obligations (totaling $120,000). Snively forecloses its $50,000 mortgage. Jackie buys Blackacre at the foreclosure sale. For the $65,000 net proceeds, Snively receives in full its $50,000, Bulldog receives $15,000 toward its mortgage obligation of $25,000, and Geraldine receives nothing. Jackie receives a conveyance of Blackacre in fee simple free and clear of all the liens. Debbie remains personally liable on the unpaid obligations unless protected by an antideficiency statute.

The successful bidder usually acquires no rights in the property until the bid is confirmed by the court. Once the bid is confirmed, the high bidder may be compelled to purchase the property or pay damages for failure to do so.

The other principal foreclosure method is the *power-of-sale foreclosure*, which is permitted in 29 states, the District of Columbia, and Guam. In a **power-of-sale foreclosure**, the property is sold, after default, at a public auction authorized in the mortgage or the deed of trust. In most states permitting power-of-sale foreclosures, there is no direct judicial involvement. Rather, depending on the state, the sale is conducted by the sheriff or other public official, by a designated third party, by the mortgagee, or by the trustee under a deed of trust. A mortgagee who conducts the sale usually cannot bid on the property.

Notice of foreclosure or notice of default must be given to interested parties. Otherwise, the power-of-sale foreclosure will be subject to attack for lack of procedural due process. But who is on the list of interested parties varies greatly among the states, as does the type of notice to be given. Some states require that notice be given to anyone having a recorded interest that is junior to the interest being foreclosed, while other states require only that notice be given to the mortgagor or the owner of the mortgaged property. In most states, notice by mail or by personal service is required. In a few states, however, notice can be given by publishing it in a newspaper.

The notice-giving and other formalities usually are much less rigorous in a power-of-sale foreclosure than in a judicial foreclosure. Partly for this reason, the power-of-sale foreclosure is more efficient and less costly. However, the speed and the absence of judicial supervision make the power-of-sale foreclosure more likely to be challenged in court. Consequently, the title conveyed to the buyer under a power-of-sale foreclosure may be less certain than a title acquired through judicial foreclosure.

Mortgagor's Rights of Redemption

The two types of redemption are the equity of redemption described earlier in this chapter and available in all states, and statutory redemption, available in about half the states.

Equity of Redemption and Clogging the Equity of Redemption

The **equity of redemption** (sometimes called the "equity of tardy redemption") is the mortgagor's right, *after* default and the commencement of foreclosure proceedings, to redeem by paying the total mortgage indebtedness *before* the foreclosure sale (or before an order of strict foreclosure) and thereby to become owner of the land free of the mortgage debt. Numerous additional persons—anyone with an interest in the mortgaged premises whose interest would be lost by the foreclosure—have a presale right to redeem whatever interests they may have. They include any successor to the mortgagor's interest such as (1) a contract purchaser of the land from the mortgagor, or (2) the mortgagor's devisee or heir; persons with a limited interest such as a life estate or an easement; co-owners such as a joint tenant; and junior lienholders such as a contractor with a mechanic's lien or a bank that has granted a second mortgage.

A second mortg*agee* redeems by paying to the first mortgagee the amount owed by the defaulting mortgagor. The second mortgagee thereby succeeds to the rights of and in effect becomes the first mortgagee. If the defaulting mortg*agor* does not redeem the property, the redeeming second mortgagee has a first-mortgage claim against the property now owned by the foreclosure sale purchaser. Other junior lienholders such as a third mortgagee, or even the holder of a mechanic's lien, have a similar right to "buy out" liens senior to theirs and thereby to improve their positions as creditors of the defaulting mortgagor or the foreclosure sale purchaser.

Since the emergence of the equity of redemption in the 1600s, lenders and their lawyers have struggled (unsuccessfully) to *clog the equity of redemption* (block or prevent its exercise), so that upon a mortgagor's default they could simply keep or sell the mortgaged property. They especially liked to do so where the value of the land greatly exceeded the unpaid debt, as it usually did. One early technique for clogging the equity of redemption was to structure the mortgage to look like a sale of the land. The borrower-seller would make an absolute conveyance of the land in exchange for the lender-buyer's oral or written promise to reconvey the property upon repayment of the debt. If the borrower defaulted on the loan, the lender, now apparently the owner of Blackacre, could deny that the transaction was a mortgage. If the lender's promise to reconvey was written, however, a court of equity probably would recognize the transaction as a mortgage and grant the borrower-mortgagor the equity of redemption. If the promise was oral, the borrower faced obvious difficulties of proof.

Today, because courts are reluctant to let the form of a transaction triumph over its substance, they carefully scrutinize any transaction that might frustrate, or clog, the borrower's equity of redemption. The key issue is whether the real property is in fact security for a debt. If it is, the transaction is in substance a mortgage, the borrower has an equity of redemption, and any agreement to the contrary is unenforceable. Evidence that a transaction is in substance a mortgage includes the following:

- An understanding that the "purchase price" is to be repaid to the "seller."

- The "seller's" continued possession of the property after the "conveyance."

- Admissions by the purported "buyer" that the transaction is one for security.

- The "seller's" continuing to pay the property taxes and to make improvements to the land.

- A low "purchase price" for land with a high market value. Normally, the amount of a loan is relatively low compared to the market value of the land, while in a true sale the purchase price approximates the market value.

Statutory Redemption

Statutory redemption, available in about half the states, is an additional right to redeem *after* a valid foreclosure sale. The statutes permit the mortgagor or the mortgagor's successor in interest to redeem the property by buying it back from the winning foreclosure sale bidder within a given period following the sale. A key purpose of statutory redemption is to give the mortgagor the opportunity to refinance the loan and thereby to avoid losing his or her "equity" (investment) in the realty. Until the redemption period expires, defaulting mortgagors in most statutory redemption states may keep possession of the property.

The redemption period varies among the states from a low of six months to a high of two years, with the majority of states specifying one year. In most of the statutory redemption states, if the mortgagor or the mortgagor's successor does not redeem the property, junior lienholders may do so, either at the end of the redemption period or within it, depending on the state. If the mortgagor or successor redeems within the time allowed, the redemption is final and defeats any redemption attempt by a junior lienholder.

The fact that the defaulting mortgagor has the right to possess the premises until the redemption period expires has a depressing effect on the amount that *outside* bidders (those other than the mortgagee) may be willing to pay. They are interested in investing, not just salvaging a bad loan. Until the redemption period has expired, they will lack the possession and use needed to profit from their investment, and will not even be certain that they may eventually keep the property. In the meantime, a mortgagor incapable of redeeming the property might "milk" it of rents and profits and might not properly maintain the premises.

In the states that have it, statutory redemption usually is available in both judicial and power-of-sale foreclosures. In several states, among them Arizona, California, Idaho, Utah, and Washington, statutory redemption is available to defaulting mortgagors only in *judicial* foreclosures. In those states, creditors using *power-of-sale* foreclosure avoid the lengthy, price-depressing redemption period. In California this benefit comes at a cost. There, anyone using power-of-sale foreclosure is denied a deficiency judgment against the defaulting debtor. When a person redeems within the statutory period, the effect is to cancel the foreclosure sale and to restore the redeeming party to the state of title that he or she had before the foreclosure sale.

Effect of the Foreclosure Sale

A valid foreclosure terminates the mortgagor's interest in the property, and it terminates any interest that was recorded after the mortgage was recorded, unless the mortgagee subordinated its interest to the later conveyance. This principle can lead to some unexpected results, as seen in the following case:

Case 10.1

Eagle Glen Unit Owners Ass'n v. Lee
514 S.E.2d 40 (Ga. App. 1999)

Ultima/R.B.M. Nesbitt Associates (Ultima) owned two adjacent parcels of real property and conveyed both parcels under a "deed to secure debt," Georgia's term for a mortgage, to secure a loan to Great Southern Federal Savings & Loan. Ultima, the borrower, built a condominium complex on one of the parcels and reserved the right to develop the other. As part of the declaration of condominium, the borrower created a road easement across both parcels. When the condominium project was sold, its parcel was released from the lien of the "deed to secure debt," but the undeveloped property was not released. The borrower defaulted and the lender foreclosed, selling the undeveloped property to the Lees. The condominium's unit owners association sued for a declaratory judgment, contending that the foreclosure extinguished the road easement on both parcels, thus depriving the Lees of a right-of-way across the condominium property to the public road. The trial court granted the Lees a summary judgment enforcing the easement across the condominium property. The unit owners appealed from the grant of summary judgment to the Lees.

JOHNSON, C. J. . . .

1. Easements may be terminated only by operation of law or by the express terms of the instrument granting the easement. For the following reasons, we find that the easement over the additional [undeveloped] property [purchased by the Lees] terminated by operation of law, while the [Lees'] easement over the association property continued in existence.

(a) Unit owners' easement over the additional property. A deed to secure debt conveys legal title in the real property to the grantee [mortgagee] with the grantor [mortgagor] retaining an equitable estate. Because legal title remains in the grantee until the terms of the security deed are satisfied, all subsequent conveyances of the real property after the deed to secure debt is executed remain subject to the security deed, unless the grantee releases the property by conveyance or contractually subordinates its rights. In this case, the security deed was executed before the [creation of the] condominium declaration which created the subject easement. Inasmuch as Great Southern did not release the additional property from the security deed or contractually subordinate its rights, the easement over that property remained subject to the security deed.

A valid foreclosure of a security deed not only vests legal title in the purchaser, but it also divests all of the grantor's rights in the property as well as the rights of those claiming through the grantor. Since the [unit owners'] easement over [the Lees'] property was subject to the security deed, the unit owners' easement [across the Lees' property] was extinguished by the foreclosure.

(b) Lees' easement over association property. While the easement over [the Lees'] property terminated by operation of law, namely, through the legal effect of the foreclosure of the security deed which predated the granting of the easement, the [Lees'] easement over the association property did not [terminate]. Therefore, this easement can be terminated only if the instrument granting it expressly so provides.

In interpreting an express easement, the cardinal rule is to ascertain the parties' intent. Arriving at this intention requires consideration of the whole instrument, the contract, the subject matter, the object, the purpose, the nature of restrictions or limitations, the attendant facts and circumstances at the time of making the instrument, and the consideration involved.

We also point out that the law does not favor the termination of easements. . . . [A]n easement acquired by grant is not extinguished by non-use without clear, unequivocal, and decisive evidence of an intent to abandon the easement. Nor is an easement extinguished by a tax sale. Our courts resolve doubtful cases in favor of that construction of the instrument which causes a right of ingress and egress to run with the land rather than merely with the original grantee of the easement.

The instrument in this case provides for a "perpetual easement" of indefinite duration and does not manifest any intention for the easement to be terminated. Although the [condominium] declaration provides that the easement over the association property is mutual, we cannot agree with the unit owners that "mutual" as used in this case means contingent or interdependent.

First, the declaration contains no language indicating that the continued existence of each easement depends upon the continued existence of the other. In fact, the declaration provides that the easements are to be perpetual unless and until all of the additional property is submitted to the declaration, a condition which no one claims occurred.

Second, it is clear from a review of the entire section on the ingress and egress easements that [its primary purpose] is to provide the owners of the additional property with an easement over the association property; indeed, the clause contains provisions regarding responsibilities for maintaining and paying to use the easement over the association property, but makes no such provisions as to the easement over the additional property. That the easement over the association property was the primary easement involved is supported in the record by a copy of the plat and by testimony from the Lees that the road provided their sole means of accessing their property. We do not see any indication in the record that Ultima intended "mutual" to mean that the continued existence of each easement would be contingent upon the continued existence of the other, particularly given the evidence that the primary objective of the grants was to provide the (subsequent) owners of the additional property with an easement over the association property, not to provide the unit owners with an easement over the additional property. We note that the easement over the association property was supported by consideration, namely the obligation to pay for maintaining the road.

In this case, it is not at all likely that Ultima, which owned both properties and granted both easements, intended that subsequent owners of the additional property would not be able to use the private road connecting their property to the public road if the owners of the association property lost their right to use the section of the road located on the additional property. The trial court did not err in granting summary judgment to the Lees. . . .

Judgment affirmed.

QUESTION ABOUT CASE 10.1

As indicated in a footnote in the opinion, Georgia uses a two-party mortgage instrument called a "deed to secure debt." Does Georgia appear to be a title theory state or a lien theory state? Does that make a difference in the outcome?

As discussed in Chapter 9, if a parcel is subject to two or more mortgages, they have the priority established by the state's recording act unless the parties agree otherwise. Similarly, a lease that was entered into before a mortgage has priority over the mortgage.

BOX 10–4 APPLY YOUR KNOWLEDGE

Blackstone Shopping Center, Ltd., borrows from Snively S&L the money to build Bedford Falls Shopping Center. To secure the loan, Blackstone executes a first mortgage to Snively. Upon completion of the shopping center, Blackstone leases 5,000 square feet of space to the Dogs B' Us Pet Shop at $15 per square foot per annum for a term of ten years. A year later, Blackstone defaults and Snively forecloses the mortgage, but fails to join Dogs B' Us. As the new owner of the Bedford Falls Shopping Center, Snively writes Dogs B' Us saying that if it wants to stay in the center, it must pay a higher rental rate of $17.50 per square foot per annum. Can Snively require the higher rental?

● Application of the Proceeds of Sale

The proceeds of the foreclosure sale normally are distributed as follows:

- First, expenses of the sale itself such as court costs, attorneys' fees, advertising, and trustee's fees.
- Second, amounts due to the mortgagee for the principal, interest, and fees associated with the mortgage loan.

- Third, amounts due to any junior mortgage or judgment lienors, in the order of their priority.
- Fourth, any remaining proceeds to the mortgagor.

This scheme of distribution means that the mortgagor, the mortgagee, and all junior lienors have an interest in seeing the sale produce as much money as possible. It is possible (though rare) for a junior lienor to bid at the first mortgagee's foreclosure sale to protect its junior position. Alternatively, the junior lienor may attempt to induce the senior mortgagee to forego its remedies temporarily, or "stand still," so that the junior lienor may protect its position by foreclosing first.

Mortgagor's Liability for Deficiencies

In most states, a mortgage lender may foreclose on the mortgaged property, sue the debtor personally on the note (and thus gain access to the debtor's *general* assets, i.e., unmortgaged property), or do both. If the lender chooses to foreclose but the mortgaged property is not sufficiently valuable to cover the debt, the lender may in most states also have a *deficiency judgment* against the debtor, regardless of the method of foreclosure used, for the amount of the mortgage indebtedness remaining unpaid. The deficiency judgment is a *personal* liability of the debtor for the unpaid amount, and enables the mortgagee to seek out and seize the debtor's other assets. In a *judicial* foreclosure, a deficiency determination is a part of the foreclosure action itself. In a *power-of-sale* foreclosure (in states permitting deficiency judgments), the mortgagee must bring a separate action at law to establish the deficiency.

Limits on the Deficiency Amount

Before granting a deficiency judgment, the court will scrutinize the foreclosure sale carefully, particularly where the mortgagee is the high bidder at the foreclosure sale, to ensure that the deficiency amount has not been manipulated to the detriment of the debtor. The deficiency amount can be inflated in various ways, for example, by failing to advertise the sale widely, by setting an odd time or an unusual day for the sale, by an interested bidder's discouraging ("chilling") competing bids, or by selling the property to a relative or friend for an unrealistically low price.

At least 22 states have *fair value legislation* aimed at protecting defaulting mortgagors from an inflated deficiency. Fair value statutes require that the deficiency be calculated in terms of the mortgaged property's fair market value or some similar measure such as its "true value" or the "appraised value." Hapless defaults on his mortgage. The indebtedness is $90,000, the fair market value of the mortgaged property is $60,000, and the winning bid at the foreclosure sale is $40,000. The deficiency chargeable against Hapless is $30,000, not $50,000.

Five western states (California, Montana, Nevada, Utah, and Idaho) have a "one action rule" that affects how and when a foreclosing creditor may have a deficiency judgment. Under this rule, the creditor must proceed exclusively by foreclosure (instead of suing on the note) and seek any deficiency in the foreclosure proceeding. A key purpose of the rule is to require the creditor to exhaust the debtor's mortgaged property before seeking a deficiency or access to the debtor's unmortgaged property. New Jersey has a one action rule applying mainly to residential mortgages.

Antideficiency Statutes

During the depression of the 1930s, a number of states passed **antideficiency statutes** to prohibit the collection of a deficiency following foreclosure. Their purpose was to prevent a family from losing its homestead and suffering a deficiency judgment as well. This problem often occurred when, because of widespread unemployment and dramatically falling prices for farm products, farmers and others could not repay loans taken out in more prosperous times. When the debtor defaulted, the mortgagee could make a very low, usually uncontested bid at the foreclosure sale, resell the property later when land prices returned to normal, and in the meantime obtain against the debtor a large deficiency judgment based on the unrealistically low sale price. Because the mortgagee was purchasing at a distress sale for a small fraction of the property's normal value and getting a deficiency judgment as well, the mortgagee received what amounted to a double recovery, a windfall. To debtors, this result seemed particularly harsh because, burdened by the deficiency that took years to pay off, they lacked resources for more productive endeavors. The legislative solution was the antideficiency statute forbidding deficiency judgments in certain types of foreclosures, most notably those involving residential realty, thus limiting the mortgagee to taking the property back and keeping any installments already paid before default.

Antideficiency legislation was useful in alleviating the windfall problem of the depression era, a problem that continues to some extent today. But it can have harmful effects. If a lender cannot resell foreclosed property for a reasonable value, the lender receives no windfall by having a deficiency judgment. Indeed, depriving such a lender of a deficiency judgment means that the lender must absorb the loss or pass it on to others, perhaps in the form of reduced dividends to shareholders or increased interest rates to customers. Antideficiency legislation has been sharply criticized on these and other grounds.

Nevertheless, a modern justification for antideficiency legislation applies to the residential real estate market. As a matter of lending routine, residential mortgage lenders, especially those selling their loans in the secondary market, systematically evaluate the various risks involved in making a loan and take numerous protective measures, almost all at the borrower's expense. Lenders commonly require most or all of the following: a credit report on the borrower to assess the ability to repay the loan, an on-site appraisal of the property to be mortgaged, a title search, title insurance benefitting at least the lender, private mortgage insurance, casualty insurance on the property, a termite inspection, a physical survey of the property, and an inspection of electrical and other systems of buildings. On rare occasions, residential lenders may even require an audit and correction of potential environmental pollution problems. Such measures as these are in addition to due-on-sale clauses, due-on-encumbrance clauses, lists of default events, and other terms and conditions in the mortgage documents protective of the mortgagee.

The systematic control of mortgage risk by lenders has led numerous commentators to question the need for a deficiency judgment, given that many debtors in default are insolvent and probably judgment-proof. Many commentators believe that lenders, having full control of the valuation process, are in the best position to detect and prevent the overvaluation of property that leads to default, and to absorb the loss if it occurs. Other commentators argue vigorously to the contrary, maintaining that lending is an art, not a science, and that catastrophic economic downturns or personal financial disasters such as illness or unemployment, which make a lending decision a bad one in retrospect, cannot be reliably predicted. Moreover, they contend, residential loans often are made on the basis of the borrower's total assets and not just on the value of the collateral for the specific loan. Consequently, it is unfair to lenders to deprive them of deficiency judgments against solvent debtors who for whatever reason defaulted on their home loans.

Of the approximately 17 states having a body of antideficiency law, the California law is considered the most complex because of the bewildering mass of sometimes contradictory case law interpreting and implementing the California statutes. Indeed, the antideficiency law of California has been termed "bizarre." Yet, the statutes themselves are a fair representation of statutes in other states and for purposes of illustration are discussed in the following box.

BOX 10–5 POINT TO CONSIDER

California limits a mortgagee's foreclosure options with its anti-deficiency statutes, its one-form-of-action rule, and its "fair value" statute.

Under Cal. Civ. Proc. Code § 580b, deficiency judgments are prohibited in certain *purchase money mortgages*. In general, a **purchase money mortgage** is a mortgage or a deed of trust given to a seller or to a third-party lender to secure the purchase price of the property. In California, § 580b limits the meaning of "purchase money mortgage" to two categories of purchase money security transactions and bans deficiency judgments as to both.

- First, a deficiency judgment is prohibited in *any* sale financed by the *seller* (the vendor), whether secured by means of an installment land contract (discussed later in this chapter) or by a mortgage or a deed of trust taken back by the seller. Regardless of the type of realty used as collateral—residential, commercial, raw land, or some other—the deficiency ban applies.

- Second, a deficiency judgment is prohibited in certain sales of residential property financed by a *third-party lender* (e.g., bank, S&L) with a mortgage or a deed of trust. The deficiency ban applies if the collateral is a "dwelling for not more than four families" and the dwelling is "occupied, entirely or in part, by the purchaser." So, a purchaser-debtor who occupies all or a part of residential realty of no more than four units is immune to a deficiency judgment.

If the *third-party lender*'s collateral is purchaser-occupied residential realty of five or more units, or is four or fewer units but not purchaser-occupied, or is any type of nonresidential property such as an office building or raw land, the mortgage (though in reality a purchase-money mortgage) lies outside the § 580b meaning of that term, and a deficiency judgment may be allowed. Why "may"?

The answer lies in another California antideficiency statute, § 580d, which bars a deficiency judgment in any foreclosure by *power of sale*, whether in a mortgage or in the deed of trust widely used in California. With a loan from First Bank, Hapless purchases a 100-unit apartment complex and occupies one unit. He defaults on the deed of trust securing the debt. First Bank, the beneficiary, forecloses by having the trustee exercise the power of sale contained in the deed of trust. First Bank is the winning bidder at the foreclosure sale, which realizes $500,000, leaving a $1 million deficiency. Because the foreclosure was by *power of sale* and not by judicial process, First Bank is not entitled to the deficiency even though there was no seller financing here, and even though the property was commercial. So why did First Bank foreclose by power of sale when a *judicial* foreclosure would have entitled First Bank to a deficiency judgment for the $1 million?

One reason is that Hapless had no assets other than his business law textbook and his 1980 Champ car with which to pay a deficiency judgment, so judicial foreclosure would have been futile. Beyond that, under California law, a *judicial* foreclosure, but not a power-of-sale foreclosure, is subject to the debtor's *postsale right of redemption* for a year after the foreclosure sale if the sale proceeds are insufficient to cover the mortgage debt. (The period is only three months if they *are* sufficient.) Moreover, during the redemption period, Hapless would have a right to possess the apartment complex. First Bank knows that a potential purchaser would be reluctant to bid at a judicial sale (or to buy from First Bank if it won), wait a year to take possession, and risk having Hapless find the resources with which to redeem the property. Faced with an insolvent debtor and a need to cut off his redemption rights, First Bank waived its right to a deficiency judgment by electing to use the power-of-sale foreclosure, which, when completed, gives First Bank immediate possession and a far more saleable property.

Suppose that Hapless had been solvent so that judicial foreclosure and a deficiency judgment were feasible. To how large a judgment would First Bank have been entitled, given that the sale price was $500,000 for a property worth $800,000? Under § 726b, California's fair value statute, Hapless is liable for only $200,000, the difference between the unpaid $1,000,000 loan indebtedness and the $800,000 "fair value" of the property, and not for the $500,000 difference between the foreclosure sale price and the unpaid debt. As in a number of other states, the California fair value is determined by the court in a fair value hearing following the judicial sale of the property.

Finally, the one-action rule set forth in § 726a requires that there be only one lawsuit or judicial foreclosure to collect a debt. If several properties are collateral for the loan, the lender must foreclose on all of them *and* seek any deficiency in a single lawsuit. A lender who fails to do so waives its rights to any collateral that was omitted. Moreover, the lender must exhaust all the real property security before it seeks the debtor's unmortgaged assets for the deficiency. A lender who proceeds directly against the borrower on the debt without first foreclosing on the mortgaged property may lose its security interest entirely.

The Installment Land Contract

The seller or buyer of realty might want seller financing without using a mortgage or a deed of trust. In many states, they may use the installment land contract, in some states called an *installment sale contract*, a *land contract*, or a *contract for deed*.

Nature of the Contract

An **installment land contract** is a long-term contract in which the buyer receives immediate possession of the land and agrees to pay the purchase price plus interest in installments, usually monthly, during the term of the contract, usually five, ten, or fifteen years. Typically the monthly payment includes an amount for property taxes and insurance. In return, the seller agrees to provide a deed to the property after the buyer pays the final installment. A method of seller financing similar in substance to a purchase money mortgage, the land contract often is used where a purchaser does not have sufficient funds for a down payment on the property or cannot qualify for a mortgage from a third-party lender.

Cancellation of the Contract

Ordinarily, an installment land contract makes time of the essence for payments and provides that previous payments will be treated as "rent" or "liquidated damages" if the buyer defaults. Thus, the buyer suffers a forfeiture of all payments made toward the purchase price prior to default. Obviously, the nearer the buyer is to making the final payment, the larger is the buyer's potential forfeiture. If the buyer does not default, the seller must deliver the promised deed. Most states enforce land contracts in accordance with their terms, one of which is that upon the buyer's default, the seller shall have a right to immediate possession. Consequently, the seller has no need to bring foreclosure proceedings. However, if the buyer remains in possession at the time of default, the seller will have to sue to evict the buyer.

Because the seller retains legal title until the final payment is made, and usually has substantial protections in the event of the buyer's default, the installment land contract is generally viewed as a seller-oriented financing device. However, for the seller, the process of remedying the buyer's default is often more difficult and time-consuming than in a power-of-sale foreclosure because the seller must file a lawsuit to evict a recalcitrant buyer. Also, states are increasingly likely to intervene through statutes or case law to protect buyers from forfeiture. If the buyer defaults early in the life of the contract, treatment of payments as rent seems quite fair. But if the default occurs when the payments are nearly completed, the seller's keeping the payments and repossessing the land seems grossly unfair to the buyer. Some states, like Minnesota, provide the buyer with a notice and cure period and set forth procedures that must be followed before the seller can terminate the buyer's interest. Other states, like Michigan, by judicial decision declare the buyer's forfeiture of equity void as unreasonable or as a penalty. Some, like North Carolina, recharacterize the transaction as a mortgage subject to an equity of redemption. Still others, such as California, do both. Observe the tension between these principles in the following case:

Case 10.2

Lamberth v. McDaniel
506 S.E.2d 295 (N.C. App. 1998)

Plaintiff sellers sold land to defendant buyers, who financed the transaction with an installment sale contract. The contract, executed on June 14, 1990, provided that sellers would hold the deed until buyers paid the purchase price plus interest. The buyers were also required to pay the property taxes until the purchase price was paid. The forfeiture provision of the contract stated in relevant part:

> 5. It is agreed and understood that if the Buyers shall be in default in the payment of any monthly installment as hereinabove set out for a period of more than thirty (30) days, or if the Buyers default in the performance of any other term and condition of this contract and said default continues for more than thirty (30) days, *then the Sellers may, at their option, declare the contract forfeited, and all sums paid by the Buyers hereunder shall be considered as rent for the property.* If the Buyers' rights under this contract shall be forfeited, then the Sellers shall be at liberty to make such disposition of the property as they may see fit, free and clear of any rights of the Buyers hereunder, and the Buyers further agree that after forfeiture they will give peaceful possession to the premises (emphasis added).

In November 1995, the buyers notified the sellers that they would delay payments because of financial difficulties. The buyers promised to catch up on payments as soon as possible, and sellers consented to late payments. Buyers made the November payment in January 1996, and again the sellers consented to late payments in the future. The property taxes were not paid from 1993 to 1996, and sellers paid them on behalf of buyers to avoid a tax lien.

In March, 1996, the sellers filed suit, alleging that the buyers' failure to make the payments constituted a forfeiture of the installment sale contract. Sellers sought to recover possession of the property, past due monthly payments, and the amounts sellers had paid for the property taxes. The buyers claimed that they had tendered the entire balance due upon being served with the complaint, and sought judgment requiring the sellers to convey the property upon receipt of the buyers' payment of the full balance due plus the buyers' expenditures for taxes and costs. Both parties moved for summary judgment. The trial court determined that the buyers were entitled to exercise their equity of redemption and entered judgment ordering the sellers to convey the property to the buyers upon receipt of the amounts owed. The sellers appealed.

MARTIN, J.

[The sellers'] sole argument is that the provisions of the installment sale contract allowing past payments to be treated as rent upon default [are] enforceable, and not subject to the equity of redemption. We disagree and affirm the trial court's summary judgment in favor of [the buyers]. . . .

"It has been held repeatedly that 'the relation between vendor and vendee in an executory agreement for the sale and purchase of land is substantially that subsisting between mortgagee and mortgagor, and [is] governed by the same general rules.'" *Brannock v. Fletcher*, 155 S.E.2d 532, 539 (N.C. 1967). Upon default, the vendor-mortgagees may choose a variety of remedies, including forfeiture if the contract allows.

However, upon default, vendee-mortgagors have the right to redeem their interest under the contract to prevent forfeiture. The right to redeem cannot be waived by contract at the time of the agreement.

> If the transaction be a mortgage in substance, the most solemn engagement to the contrary, made at the time, cannot deprive the debtor of his right to redeem. . . . Nor can a mortgagor, by any agreement at the time of the execution of the mortgage that the right to redeem shall be lost if the money be not paid by a certain day, debar himself of such a right. *Wilson v. Fisher*, 62 S.E. 622, 624 (N.C. 1908).

In *Brannock*, the Court indicated that the right to redeem under the law of mortgages would also apply to installment land contracts, even if vendees have surrendered the property and are behind in mortgage payments:

Having surrendered possession, they were still entitled—even if they were in arrears—to tender to defendants the unpaid balance of the purchase price within a reasonable time and to have specific performance of their contract to convey. . . . But until a vendee has made full payment he is not in condition to demand conveyance of the land. . . .

In the present case, defendants sought, after default, to exercise their right of redemption by tendering the entire balance due, plus interest. We affirm the trial court's determination that "defendants are entitled to redeem the property by the payment to the plaintiffs of the balance due of the purchase price, plus interest and ad valorem taxes."

Affirmed.

QUESTIONS ABOUT CASE 10.2

1. As indicated, in protecting the buyers, North Carolina represents a minority view. A majority of states would enforce the installment sale contract and the

resulting forfeiture. Yet, a growing number of states are acting to protect the buyer in installment sale contracts, either by statute or judicial decision. This case illustrates the policies that lead a court to recognize the equity of redemption in an installment sale contract. Is it fair for the court essentially to rewrite the parties' agreement for them?

2. In this case, the installment sale contract ends up being a bad option for both parties. They engage in several years of litigation, only to have their arrangement treated like a mortgage. Had they used the normal purchase money deed of trust with power of sale, which is the typical financing arrangement in North Carolina, the seller-mortgagee could have completed a foreclosure within two months after default, with much lower transaction costs. In light of these factors, why do you think the parties used the installment sale contract?

Security Interests in Fixtures

As noted in Chapter 2, fixtures are goods (other than ordinary building materials) that become so physically attached to or otherwise associated with realty as to be regarded by law as realty themselves. Examples include air-conditioning systems, heating systems, built–in appliances, light fixtures, and similar equipment.

Fixtures present some difficult financing and priority problems. For example, sellers of fixtures on credit often find themselves in disputes with mortgagees of the realty who, upon the mortgagor's default, claim the fixtures as part of the mortgaged property. Because fixtures begin their lives as goods (a category of personal property), these disputes are resolved by application of Article 9 of the Uniform Commercial Code (UCC), which governs the creation and enforcement of security interests in a broad range of personal property *and* in fixtures. Even though fixtures are considered part of the realty with which they are associated, they were included in the Article 9 coverage because interstate sellers of fixtures would thus be subject to one national, relatively uniform body of personal property security law instead of the diversity of state law governing security interests in realty.

If a thing is a fixture, a mortgagee of the realty to which the fixture is attached may have a claim to it that is superior to the claim of its unpaid seller. The fixture seller, however, can protect itself from the claims of most rival creditors by taking the steps specified by Article 9 for acquiring and "perfecting" a security interest in the fixture.

● Article 9 Terminology

In general, to create a security interest in personal property, and to make the security interest enforceable against the maximum number of rival creditors, the *secured party* seeking it (either a credit seller of the personalty or a lender) must complete two processes: "attachment" of the security interest to the collateral, and "perfection" of the security interest. **Attachment** is the process of creating the security interest by means of a **security agreement** (a contract) between the creditor and the debtor. For the security agreement to be enforceable, the secured party must give value, which usually is in the form of a loan; the security agreement ordinarily must be in writing and signed by the debtor; and the debtor must have rights in the collateral. **Perfection** is the process of making the resulting security interest good against others, usually by the secured party's filing a "financing statement" in a public office maintained for that purpose. The UCC filing office is separate from the recorder's office.

A **financing statement** is a document filed in the public records to alert the world to the existence of the secured party's security interest in the personalty covered by the security agreement. Like a recorded mortgage, the financing statement provides the secured party's rivals (e.g., a bank seeking a lien on the debtor's personalty property) notice of the secured party's lien on the personalty. Unlike the typical mortgage form, a financing statement usually is designed only to give inquiry notice, since under Article 9, it need contain only the barest essential information. If the secured party's rivals want to know more about the status of the lien on the personalty or the financial transaction involving it, they must inquire of the secured party. A financing statement must contain the names and addresses of the debtor and creditor, a general description of the collateral, and the signature of the debtor.

If the collateral is or is to become a *fixture*, the financing statement must give potential mortgagees or purchasers of the real estate notice of the secured party's security interest in the fixture. Therefore, Article 9 requires a "fixture filing." A **fixture filing** differs from an ordinary UCC filing in two ways. First, in addition to the ordinary requirements for a financing statement, the financing statement must state that it applies to a fixture, it must be filed in the *real estate records* (the recorder's office), and it must contain a description of the real estate to which the fixture is to be annexed. In some states, the fixture financing statement must be filed in a central state filing office, such as the Secretary of States's office, in addition to the local filing in the real estate records.

Two Common Fixture Priority Problems

Disputes over fixtures between fixture financiers (secured parties) and real estate financiers (mortgagees) can be exceedingly complex and are largely beyond the scope of this book. Two commonly occurring fixture priority problems, however, need mention here.

The first involves a *purchase money security interest* (PMSI) held by the seller or a third-party financier of a fixture. If the purchase money secured party (i.e., the seller or a bank) has properly perfected the PMSI, it has *priority over earlier perfected* security interests in the same collateral. Hank gets a $500,000 loan from First Bank to set up Hank's Hardware. The security agreement contains an *after-acquired property clause* providing that First Bank shall have a security interest in "all inventory, cash receipts, fixtures, and other hardware business property that Hank now owns or may hereafter acquire." First Bank immediately files an appropriate financing statement. Months later, Hank purchases a new furnace on credit from Heartland Furnace Sales and signs a security agreement for the purchase price. Under UCC § 9-313(4)(a), Heartland's PMSI prevails over First Bank's earlier perfected security interest *if* Heartland makes a *fixture filing* within ten days (20 days or some other period in some states) after the furnace is annexed to the realty. Similarly, Hank's perfected PMSI would prevail over an earlier recorded mortgage on existing realty (as opposed to new construction) to which the furnace is annexed.

The second involves *construction mortgages*. For decades, fixture financiers and financiers of new construction have been in conflict over who should have priority as to unpaid-for fixtures installed in *new* construction when the construction loan came into default, that is, whether the fixture should "feed the mortgage." UCC § 9-313(6) gives the construction lender priority over the fixture financier if the following sequence of events occurs: (1) construction mortgage is recorded; (2) fixture is annexed to the realty; and (3) the construction is completed. By observing this sequence of events, construction mortgagees who have advanced money for major appliances as well as for the basic structure can protect themselves from a surprise PMSI held by a fixture seller.

● Mobile Homes as Fixtures

Mobile homes present unique characterization problems. People live in them, but are they personalty or realty?

When mobile homes are first sold, they are movable personal property, and as to title and financing, they are treated in most states as motor vehicles are—quite differently from real estate and fixtures. In most states, title to motor vehicles is evidenced by a certificate of title issued by the Department of Motor Vehicles or a similar state agency. The motor vehicle is given as security by putting the certificate of title in the lender's possession or by noting the security interest directly on the certificate of title. Article 9 provides that a security interest in collateral subject to a certificate-of-title registration process (e.g., cars, mobile homes) *cannot* be perfected by filing a financing statement.[5] Rather, the security interest in a mobile home must be perfected by compliance with the certificate of title statute.

But once mobile homes are installed on a site, they are often "permanently" affixed to the real estate by removal of the wheels, attachment to water and sewer lines, and construction of stairs and a skirt or permanent foundation. Once they are affixed to the land, for most purposes they are treated as fixtures, or real estate.

● Notes on Lending Practices

As the introduction to this chapter indicates, a borrower should consider real estate finance from the lenders' point of view, if only to understand how to tailor a loan proposal to their concerns and thus increase the chances of receiving the loan. The concerns of residential and commercial lenders overlap, but those of commercial lenders are more numerous because of the size and complexity of commercial real estate financing projects. Commercial banks consider the following key factors when evaluating commercial real estate loan requests:

1. *Cash flow.* As one veteran lender put it: "Collateral is nice, but what I do is make loans. I want to know how I am going to be repaid." The ability to repay usually depends far more on the borrower's stream of net income than on the value of the borrower's collateral. To evaluate the borrower's ability to repay, a bank makes a careful *cash flow analysis,* also known as *debt service coverage analysis.* A cash flow analysis indicates how much cash the borrower will have available to repay the mortgage debt. In conducting it, the bank attempts to formulate realistic projections of revenues and necessary expenses other than mortgage debt service. Ideally, the cash surplus will be sufficient to pay the amortized principal and interest on the mortgage debt and provide a comfortable margin for error.

2. *Collateral position.* In addition to a healthy cash flow, however, the lender likes to have collateral as a secondary source of repayment. In commercial real estate lending, a bank ordinarily will lend only 70% to 75% of the collateral's appraised value for several reasons. First, appraisals may be unreliable, partly because they are calculations based on assumptions or projections of future events. If the assumptions or projections prove inaccurate, the calculations are also. Second, real estate prices can fluctuate wildly because of external factors such as demand, zoning, utility availability, prevailing mortgage interest rates, and tax policy. Third, if the borrower defaults and the bank is forced to foreclose on the realty, delay is likely, during which the borrower is not making payments. Still, the lender's interest and expenses accrue, increasing the amount needed to repay the lender in accordance with the terms of the loan.

3. *Bank's evaluation of the proposed project.* The bank will perform an independent evaluation of the feasibility of the borrower's proposal. A bank that believes the project will be

difficult or risky will be reluctant to commit funds to the venture. In a project evaluation, the significant considerations include:

- *Location.* The success of any real estate venture will be influenced by the project's location, visibility, public access, access to utilities, and proximity to job centers and recreational amenities.

- *Borrower's investment.* Banks consider how much capital the borrower has at risk in the project. A borrower with significant equity in a project is more strongly tied to the project, which commands more of the borrower's attention. Early in the project when risks and uncertainties are greatest, the bank may demand a greater proportion of equity-to-loan amount than later when uncertainties have subsided.

- *Borrower's experience.* The lender wants to know whether the borrower has experience completing similar projects, and how long the borrower has been in business, how successful the business has been, and what its reputation is.

- *Speculation or contract?* Often, projects are classified by whether they are being developed on speculation or pursuant to an existing lease or contract of sale. A request by a borrower for money to build a shopping center that presently has no tenants or to build 25 homes for which still-potential buyers will be less appealing to a lender than a request for financing to build a warehouse that has already been leased for ten years to Wal-Mart.

- *Borrower's financial position.* A lender is concerned about the borrower's general financial position. It does not want the borrower "milking" the project (the lender's security) to finance other ventures, nor does it want its collateral to be tied up in a bankruptcy proceeding. Also, the borrower should have sufficient financial strength to maintain the project if it does not perform as well as projected, so that the lender does not have to invoke its remedies. To this end, the lender will carefully examine the balance sheet and income statements of the borrower, often requiring that they be audited by a certified public accountant.

- *Personal or corporate guaranty.* A lender may require credit enhancement in the form of loan guarantees by persons or companies related to the borrower.

- *Industry outlook.* The real estate industry tends to be cyclical. Consequently, to assess the potential for success of individual projects, lenders try to forecast short- and long-term prospects for each sector of the industry.

- *Borrower's integrity.* A lender that doubts the borrower's character or integrity is likely to deny the loan request.

- *Lending guidelines.* Institutional lenders have guidelines setting limits on the amount of an individual loan and on the aggregate amount of loans within a given business sector. These guidelines may be the product of government regulatory activities or of the secondary mortgage markets, or they may simply represent the internal decision of the lender regarding how to allocate resources and control risk.

- *Past uses or users of the property.* Because of potential liability, a lender is concerned about environmental pollution on or near the property site. If lender liability for cleanup is possible, the loan is not likely to be made. Or a lender might be skeptical about making a loan if similar projects, such as supermarkets, have failed on this site in the past.

4. *Lender's business concerns.* In deciding whether to make or refuse a particular loan, a lender considers factors affecting the business of lending, including the following:

- *Market share.* Lending is a competitive business. A lender intent on increasing its market share may be more likely to approve even marginal loans.

- *Lending portfolio.* A lender may have reached or exceeded its comfort level on the type of loan that the borrower seeks. For example, a lender may refuse a loan for acquisition of an apartment building if it has many loans of this type in its portfolio.

- *Risk and return.* A lender looks at risk versus return. If a lender concludes that a particular loan involves higher than normal risk, the lender may still be willing to make the loan, but at a higher than normal interest rate. The higher interest rate will compensate the lender for the increased default risk.

- *Cross-selling opportunities.* A lender's decision to lend may be influenced by the possibility that the borrower might use other services such as checking or savings accounts, certificates of deposit, cash management services, and insurance or trust services, to which the loan in fact might be expressly or impliedly linked.

- *Competition.* A lender's decision may be influenced by competitors. A competitor of the lender may be willing to make the loan at a lower interest rate than the lender finds attractive, thus causing the lender to refuse the loan. Or the lender may be the competitor and thus be willing to make the loan for a smaller return than others demand.

Self-Study Questions

1. Explain the significance of default risk. Of liquidity risk. Of interest rate risk.

2. What is the difference between a portfolio lender and a secondary market lender?

3. How does the secondary market influence mortgage financing?

4. What is the difference between a mortgage and a deed of trust?

5. Why might a mortgagee demand a prepayment premium as a condition for allowing a borrower to prepay a loan?

6. What are the differences between a mortgage assumption and a transfer subject to a mortgage as viewed from the perspective of each of these parties: mortgagee-lender, mortgagor-seller, and buyer?

7. Why may it be necessary for a lender to "foreclose" a mortgage?

8. What is the difference between a judicial foreclosure and a power-of-sale foreclosure? Which is preferable from a mortgagor's perspective? Why? Which is preferable from a mortgagee's perspective? Why?

9. What are the practical effects of a foreclosure sale?

Case Problems

1. Alan Attorney bought a house encumbered by a deed of trust after determining that the deed of trust might be unenforceable as a result of being time-barred or "stale." The warranty deed recited that the buyer assumed and agreed to pay the mortgage. Alan then brought suit against the lender seeking a declaratory judgment that the deed of trust was not a valid encumbrance on title. What result? *Joyner v. Vitale*, 926 P.2d 1154 (Alaska 1996).

2. The buyers of a mobile home and lot brought suit against the sellers for breach of the warranty against encumbrances contained in the general warranty deed delivered by the sellers. The mobile home was subject to a purchase money lien at the time of sale held by General Electric Credit Corporation, who foreclosed on the mobile home following closing and removed it from the lot. The certificate of title issued by the DMV correctly listed GECC as a lien holder, but was apparently not delivered at the real estate closing, and no UCC financing statement was filed. What result? *Hughes v. Young*, 444 S.E.2d 248 (N.C. App. 1994), *cert. denied*, 448 S.E.2d 525 (N.C. 1994).

3. A mortgagee sued a mortgagor under an assignment of rents clause contained in a mortgage, for rents the mortgagor collected but did not transmit to the mortgagee after default under the mortgage. The mortgage was filed in a lien theory state. What result? *Ganbaum v. Rockwood Realty Corp.*, 308 N.Y.S.2d 436 (N.Y. Sup. Ct. 1970).

4. J. W. Plummer borrowed $500 from George Ilse. As a part of the transaction, he placed a warranty deed to George Ilse in escrow with a friend, J. W. Graves, under an escrow agreement. The agreement provided that if he did not pay the note in accordance with its terms, the escrow agent could deliver the deed to Isle in satisfaction of the debt. Plummer did not pay on time, and Graves delivered the deed to Ilse, who recorded it. Plummer then sued to have the deed set aside, claiming that he showed up at Ilse's office with the money on the day on which the deed was recorded. What result? *Plummer v. Ilse*, 82 P. 1009 (Wash. 1905).

5. Trident Center was a partnership composed of an insurance company and two law firms. Connecticut General Life Insurance Company lent more than $56 million to Trident at 12¼% per annum for 15 years, secured by a mortgage. The promissory note permitted prepayment of the loan only between years 13 and 15 of the loan, with a sliding prepayment fee, but no prepayment was permitted during the first 12 years of the loan. In the event of default during the first 12 years, Connecticut General had the option to accelerate the loan and impose a 10% prepayment fee. When interest rates fell dramatically in 1987, Trident sought to prepay the loan within the first 12 years and offered to pay an extra 10% prepayment fee. Connecticut General insisted that prepayment was barred. Trident brought suit, seeking a declaratory judgment that it had the right to prepay with the 10% prepayment fee. What should the court do? *Trident Center v. Connecticut General Life Ins. Co.*, 847 F.2d 564 (4th Cir. 1988).

Endnotes

1. *See generally*, Roger A. Cunningham et al., *The Law of Property* (Hornbook Series, 1984); Patrick A. Hetrick and James B. McLaughlin, Jr., *Webster's Real Estate Law in North Carolina*, 3rd ed. (1988); William R. Lasher, *Practical Financial Management* (1997); Grant S. Nelson and Dale A. Whitman, *Real Estate Finance Law*, 2d ed. (1985); Wayne E. Etter et al., "Conduits: A Source of Funds for Commercial and Multifamily Borrowers," *Tierra Grande* (April 1999); Jerry M. Miller, Jr., "What the Loan Closing Attorney Needs to Do to Keep the Lender Happy," *The Basics of Real Property Practice* (1984); *and* E. Garrett Walker, "Understanding and Explaining Adjustable Rate Mortgages—A Practical Guide to ARMs," *The Basics of Real Property Practice* (1984).

2. *See generally*, Fannie Mae, "Mortgage-Backed Securities" available at http://www.fanniemae .com/markets/mbssecurities/product_info/mbs/mbs.html; Freddie Mac, "Freddie Mac," available at http://www.freddiemac.com.

3. 12 U.S.C.A. § 1701j-3.

4. 12 U.S.C.A. § 1701j-3(d)(1).

5. UCC § 9-302(3).

6. The contributions of Scott Hansing, formerly a commercial loan officer with NBD Bank, are gratefully acknowledged.

Closing the Real Estate Sales Transaction

Areal estate sale contract specifies a date on which the buyer is to pay the purchase price and the seller is to deliver the deed. This final performance of the contract is called the *closing* or **settlement** of the transaction. The date scheduled for settlement is the *closing day*, often referred to as *law day*. During the time between the making of the contract and the arrival of law day, usually four to eight weeks, the parties prepare for their respective performances. The buyer arranges for payment, usually by acquiring a loan, while the seller removes any encumbrances that would otherwise impair the marketability of the seller's title.

To ensure a proper closing of the real estate transaction, the parties normally engage a *closing agent* (also known as an *escrow agent*). The closing agent's main function is to receive and hold the seller's deed and the buyer's payment in escrow (i.e., as a neutral third party) until the obligations of each party have been performed, and then to deliver the payment to the seller and the deed to the buyer. The closing agent also attends to numerous related details such as paying the broker's commission out of the proceeds of sale, paying off any unpaid liens or prior mortgage debts still owed by the seller, and having the buyer's deed and any new mortgage or deed of trust recorded.

At their best, closings are carefully choreographed to meet the needs of the parties, and to comply with the requirements of state and federal law. At their worst, closings can become barely controlled chaos. One unifying factor in a modern real estate closing is an avalanche of paper. This chapter discusses the role of the closing agent in facilitating closing, the constraints of federal law, and typical closing procedures and documents.

The Closing Process

Closing occurs when the seller conveys title to the buyer and the buyer pays the promised consideration. In the simplest real estate transactions, the closing could consist of the seller's handing over the deed to the buyer in return for cash at the local feed store or bait and tackle shop. Most closings are considerably more complex and involve the participation of trained professionals. These complexities arise from the need to protect the interests of all parties to the transaction, most of whom are strangers to each other. Further complexities arise from the need to draft documents suitable for lenders if the buyer finances the purchase price, verifying and conveying good title, and recording the deed of conveyance and any mortgage or deed of trust.

The Role of the Closing Agent

The personnel and procedures involved in real estate closings vary widely, depending on local law and practice. In many states, the closing normally takes place at the office of a real estate lawyer who, in handling the closing, may represent the buyer alone or all parties to the transaction. In some states, like New York, buyers and sellers normally are represented by their own lawyers at closing. In others, like Indiana, closings can be conducted without lawyers, though lawyers may be involved behind the scenes. In many states, the buyer's title insurance company conducts the closing at its office.

Whatever the local approach to closings, one participating professional usually is designated as the closing agent and charged with performing the administrative activities necessary for consummating the sales transaction. The closing agent may be one of the lawyers (typically the buyer's lawyer or a lawyer representing both sides) or the title insurance company. The closing agent's duties include:

- Contracting for or performing the title examination.
- Determining the amounts of unpaid principal balances, accrued interest, and penalties for all mortgages and other liens on the property that are to be satisfied out of the closing proceeds. These amounts are commonly referred to as **payoffs**.

- Ordering a physical survey of the property if required.
- Preparing transfer and loan documents in accordance with the contract of sale and the loan closing instructions.
- Preparing a settlement statement accounting for disbursements relating to the transaction.
- Reviewing the closing documents with the parties.
- Supervising the execution of the documents.
- Notarizing the documents.
- Confirming that the buyer has obtained hazard insurance insuring both buyer and the buyer's lender.
- Collecting the purchase price from the buyer, including any loan proceeds from the lender.
- Recording the transfer and mortgage documents.
- Disbursing the purchase price, which involves paying the expenses of the closing, paying off existing liens, and paying the net proceeds to the seller.
- Issuing or obtaining title insurance policies.
- Filing required tax reporting forms.
- Distributing final documents to the parties.

Because of the central role of the closing agent, the agent must be acceptable to all parties. The buyer and seller may state in the sales contract who is to be the closing agent, or the contract may specify which party selects the closing agent. The contract should also assign the responsibility for paying the closing agent.

When lenders and title insurance companies participate in a closing, approval of the closing agent often involves a more formal process. They may require that the closing agent be an attorney. However, the fact that a lawyer has been admitted to the practice of law does not guarantee proficiency in handling real estate transactions. Consequently, lenders and title insurance companies are careful to demand evidence of the attorney's competence and professional and financial responsibility. For example, to become an approved attorney for a lender, a lawyer often must provide the lender with an *errors-and-omissions liability insurance policy* or some other evidence of financial responsibility such as a fiduciary bond, together with an *insured closing protection letter* from a title insurance company acceptable to the lender.

Errors-and-omissions liability insurance, commonly known as malpractice insurance, insures lawyers or other professionals against claims resulting from professional negligence. The premiums charged for the insurance are based on the number of claims made against the lawyer for malpractice, that is, on the lawyer's "claims experience." In terms of claims against lawyers, real estate closings constitute one of the riskiest areas of law practice.

An **insured closing protection letter** is issued by a title insurance company on behalf of a closing attorney. The letter protects the lender from the negligence or fraud of the attorney. A title insurance company will issue insured closing protection letters only on behalf of attorneys who have demonstrated both financial and professional responsibility. Therefore, in addition to financial protection, an insured closing letter impliedly provides the lender with evidence of the lawyer's professional competence.

A title insurance company normally issues an insured closing protection letter only for closings involving its own title insurance. Three consequences flow from this practice. First, a law firm will have to be separately approved by each title insurance company for which the law firm does closings. Second, a law firm may need to be approved by several title insurance companies because the law firm cannot be certain which title insurance company the parties to the real estate contract will choose to insure the transaction. Third, to obtain the benefits of an insured closing protection letter, the lender may specify a particular title insurance company in its loan instructions, even though this may appear to usurp the right of the parties under the Real Estate Settlement Procedures Act (discussed later) to select the title insurer.

To determine which law firms qualify for its approved attorneys list, a title insurance company uses qualification criteria similar to those used by lenders. Like lenders, a title insurer requires law firms to demonstrate financial responsibility with a malpractice insurance policy, and the title insurer judges a law firm's competence by considering such factors as the type of practice experience the lawyers have, professional references, and the demonstrated ability of the lawyers. In states where title insurance companies compete with law firms for work as closing agents, a law firm or a lawyer may have difficulty obtaining an insured closing protection letter, because the title insurers would be working against their economic interests in issuing letters to their competitors. Conversely, an attorney who has already been approved by at least one title insurance company in the state will find it easier to become approved by additional title insurers who do not want to lose title insurance business to the insurer who has already issued a letter to the attorney.

Box 11–1 Point to Consider

In choosing a real estate lawyer, the buyer and seller in a real estate transaction should consider the same kinds of factors that lenders and title insurance companies consider: professional competence and financial responsibility. For rating general professional competence, several resources are available:

- Martindale Hubbell Legal Directory has established a rating system for lawyers based on peer reviews, which rates them from A to C or "unrated" on their professional ability and V for those that meet the professional ethics standards established by the reviewers. An AV-rated lawyer meets the highest standards of the reviewers for ethics and professionalism. Martindale Hubbell also provides information on a firm's practice areas, representative clients, and the professional and educational qualifications of its members.

- All states have established grievance and investigation procedures for complaints regarding lawyers and their professional performance. The results of these investigations are normally public records and available to consumers.

- Many law firms are members of the local Better Business Bureau or Chamber of Commerce, which frequently will make available records of grievances.

These sources provide basic information regarding legal competence. But real estate practice is a distinct legal specialty. To help judge professional competence within the specialty, the following additional resources may be helpful:

- Many states have established legal specialization certification programs. Although the programs vary a great deal, to become a certified real estate specialist requires a minimum level of experience concentrated in real estate, continuing professional education following law school, and passage of a qualification exam.

- Referrals or references from real estate professionals in allied fields, such as real estate brokers, mortgage lenders, title insurance companies, or surveyors.

Federal Law and the Closing

Although real estate law is primarily state law, federal law regulates many aspects of the real estate closing transaction. Most of the federal laws that apply are designed to protect consumers, and thus are more likely to affect residential closings than commercial ones; lawmakers assume that participants in large commercial real estate transactions have the knowledge and experience to protect themselves. Many of the federal laws directly affect the duties of the closing agent and the various parties to the closing.

The Real Estate Settlement Procedures Act

The most important federal statute affecting the residential closing process is the Real Estate Settlement Procedures Act (RESPA).[1] RESPA, together with its implementing Regulation X,[2] strives to introduce uniformity into the residential closing process and to provide consumers with accurate and timely information about the settlement process. The act also attempts to reduce costs associated with residential real estate transactions, to eliminate kickbacks or referral fees, and to limit the amount of loan escrow deposits imposed to ensure the payment of taxes and insurance. RESPA applies to most residential mortgage loan closings,[3] requiring the following:

- Delivery of a "special information booklet" to each loan applicant within three business days after the application is received.[4] The special information booklet must describe and explain in clear and concise language:

  1. The nature and purpose of each cost involved in the closing.
  2. The standard real estate settlement form.
  3. The nature and purpose of loan escrow accounts.
  4. The choices available to borrowers in selecting parties to provide closing services.
  5. Unfair practices and unnecessary charges to be avoided with respect to a closing.

- Within the same three-day period after application, delivery to each loan applicant of a good faith estimate of expenses for each of the closing services.[5]

- Use of a uniform settlement statement form, the so-called "HUD-1 Settlement Statement" form. The form must clearly itemize all charges imposed upon the buyer-borrower and the seller in connection with the settlement.[6]

- At the request of the borrower, an opportunity on the business day preceding the closing for the borrower to examine the HUD-1 Settlement Statement with respect to the expenses that are then known.[7]

- At the time of application, notification to the borrower as to whether the servicing of the loan may be transferred to a firm other than the lender, together with a statement of the percentage of lender's servicing that has been transferred during the preceding three years.[8]

- An accounting for escrows of amounts required for insurance and taxes, and timely payment by the lender of the insurance premiums and taxes for which the account is maintained. The lender may require an escrow of only the amount anticipated to be necessary to pay taxes and insurance premiums when they become due and payable, plus a cushion of an additional one-sixth of the anticipated annual payments.[9]

RESPA also regulates certain settlement charges and fees. The act prohibits lenders from charging fees for the preparation of Truth-in-Lending statements, HUD-1 settlement statements, or the escrow account statements required by law.[10] If a lender requires that a particular firm be used for closing services paid for by the borrower, the good faith estimate must clearly set forth the requirement and any relationship between the lender and the service provider.[11] Kickbacks and unearned referral fees are prohibited.[12] Not prohibited, however, are payments actually earned, such as fees for legal services actually rendered and commissions earned by agents of title insurance companies.[13]

The Truth-in-Lending Act

Before the passage of the Truth-in-Lending Act[14] and its associated regulations, known as Regulation Z,[15] many in the lending industry had become notorious for the confusing and misleading methods they used for calculating the interest they charged for loans. Most borrowers expected a lender to charge "straight" or "true" interest calculated in terms of annual percentage rate (APR), as would be the result if a lender advertised an interest rate of 6%, lent Horace $100 for a year, and then required him to repay the $100 principal plus $6 in accrued interest at the end of the year. This loan, which would yield an actual 6% to the lender, was the type of loan expected by the general public.

To the detriment of borrowers, however, many lenders structured loans differently. Although advertising a 6% interest rate, some would require payment of the $6 interest in advance and remit to the borrower only $94. The result was that the actual rate of interest was higher than 6%—about 6.38%. Other lenders advertising a 6% interest wanted the debt paid in monthly installments. To calculate the monthly payment, the lender would add the $6 interest to the $100 principal and divide the total by 12. The monthly payments would be $8.83 (with an adjustment to one or more payments so that total payments would add up to $106), but over the course of the 12 months, the average principal amount actually used by the borrower was about $50, since part of the principal was being repaid each month. The true interest rate on this loan was actually around 10.9%. Experienced business people usually could understand the calculations, but people inexperienced in such matters often did not know that the apparently low interest rate quoted by a lender was in fact quite high.

Complicating matters for borrowers, lenders began to charge not only interest, which the public easily recognized as a charge for the use of borrowed principal, but also other amounts such as loan origination fees, loan fees, and discount points. Although some of these amounts were additional charges for the use of money, lenders did not characterize them as interest, and many borrowers did not recognize them as interest. Some such charges were a legitimate response to market conditions in the lending industry. Others were not. Yet, regardless of the lender's motives for imposing them, the actual cost of the loan was often hidden from the borrowers, who found it difficult to compare financing programs offered by competing lenders. The problem became so serious for the unsophisticated that Congress enacted reform legislation, the Truth-in-Lending Act.

The Truth-in-Lending Act applies to consumer loans made by commercial lenders. A consumer loan is one made to an individual for personal, family, or household purposes, including the purchase of a home. Designed to assure meaningful disclosure of credit terms to consumers, the act does not apply to credit transactions for business, commercial, or agricultural purposes,[16] nor does it apply to corporations or other borrowers that are not natural persons.[17]

The Truth-in-Lending Act requires that the lender disclose to the borrower certain information about the loan, generally when the borrower applies for it.[18] The types of disclosures vary depending upon whether the loan is a fixed rate loan, a variable rate loan, a closed-end credit, or an open-end credit. A closed-end credit is a loan for a specified term with fixed payments and a specified due date, like the typical 30-year mortgage loan. An open-end credit is one whose duration depends on the needs or wishes of the borrower and whose outstanding loan amount can vary as a result the borrower's additional borrowings and a flexible repayment schedule. Examples of open-end credit would be the typical credit card and the typical home equity loan. Whatever the type of loan, the lender is required to disclose all of the finance charges imposed on the borrower, regardless of the name given to them, and to express the total finance charge in terms of an annual percentage rate (the "true" rate of interest) so that the borrower will have a basis for comparing the loan with others that might be available.

The **annual percentage rate** is an interest rate computation which includes the face interest rate of the note as adjusted by the borrower's other finance charges. The Truth-in-Lending Act defines "finance charges" broadly as "the sum of all charges, payable directly or indirectly by the person to whom the credit is extended, and imposed directly or indirectly by the creditor as an incident to the extension of credit."[19] These charges include loan fees, discount points, service or carrying charges, assumption fees, mortgage insurance premiums, and any mortgage broker's fees.[20] **Discount points** are credit charges paid in advance for the extension of credit. One discount point equals 1% of the original principal balance of the loan. For example, if a lender

BOX 11–2 APPLY YOUR KNOWLEDGE

Your friend, Harvey, comes to you and says that he is trying to choose between two 30-year mortgage loans for $100,000. The first lender, Sunshine Savings and Loan, has offered him a 7.50% mortgage with only a one percent origination fee. The second lender, Snidely Mortgage Company, has offered him a mortgage at 6.25%, but will require a one-percent origination fee together with four discount points, and will require him to maintain mortgage insurance with a premium of $45 per month for the life of the loan. Which is the better deal?

To answer this question you will need to compute an annual percentage rate, which will require a financial calculator.

(A) The annual percentage rate on the loan from Sunshine Savings and Loan would be computed by considering the following information:

1. The present value of the loan (after deduction of the origination fee) would be $99,000.
2. The loan would require 360 monthly payments of $699.21.
3. The loan is fully amortized, so the future value is $0.

The annual percentage rate on the loan from Sunshine Savings and Loan is **7.60%**.

(B) The annual percentage rate on the loan from Snidely Mortgage Company would be computed by considering the following information:

1. The present value of loan (after deduction of the origination fee and discount points) would be $95,000.
2. The loan would require 360 monthly payments of $660.72 (including principal and interest payments of $615.72 and mortgage insurance premium of $45).
3. The loan is fully amortized, so the future value is $0.

The annual percentage rate on the loan from Snidely Mortgage Company is **7.45%**. Therefore, the loan from Snidely Mortgage Company would be the better deal (but just barely). By requiring disclosure of the annual percentage rate, the Truth-in-Lending Act enables borrowers to quickly decide which is the better deal without having to buy a financial calculator. All they have to do is compare the APRs.

quotes an interest rate on home loans of 8% with four discount points, the annual percentage rate is higher than the face rate of 8%. If the lender charges four discount points on a 10-year loan of $100,000 payable in equal monthly installments, the borrower has to pay $4,000 (the four discount points) in addition to the stated interest rate, and the borrower is really getting the use of only $96,000. Without the discount points, the annual percentage rate in this example would be 8%. With the inclusion of the discount points, the annual percentage rate jumps to 8.95%.

Finance charges do not include any fees that would be imposed on a comparable cash transaction, such as the fee for the services of the closing agent. Also excluded from the meaning of "finance charge" are the following fees involved in a loan secured by a mortgage: fees or premiums for title examination, title insurance, or similar purposes; fees for preparation of loan-related documents; escrows for future payments of taxes and insurance; fees for notarizing deeds and other documents; appraisal fees, including fees related to any pest infestation or flood hazard inspections conducted prior to closing; and fees for credit reports.[21]

The Truth-in-Lending Act also gives the borrower a right to rescind a home improvement or other consumer mortgage loan. The act, however, provides *no* right to rescind a mortgage loan for the initial acquisition or construction of a dwelling.[22] The rescission period begins with the *later* of (a) the date the closing occurs, or (b) the date that required disclosures are made, and the period runs until midnight of the third business day thereafter. For this purpose, the regulations count Saturdays as a business day; Sundays and specified legal holidays do not count. Moreover, the lender must specify in the notice of the customer's right to rescind the precise date upon which the three-day rescission period expires. If the disclosures are never properly made, the rescission period runs for three years from the consummation of the transaction.[23] Because of the borrower's right to cancel the loan, lenders ordinarily will not give the loan proceeds to their borrowers until the rescission period has expired.

The importance of making the required disclosures in the prescribed manner is underscored by the following case.

Case 11.1

Powers v. Sims and Levin Realtors
396 F.Supp. 12 (E.D. Va. 1975)

Eugene and Lila Powers brought this action under the Truth-in-Lending Act, seeking rescission of a home improvement loan contract made with defendant Sims and Levin Realtors, together with money damages, because of the defendant's alleged violations of the Act and Regulation Z. Defendant, a Richmond Virginia real estate business engaging in real estate transactions, mortgage loans, and home improvement loans, is subject to regulation by the Truth-in-Lending Act because it regularly extends consumer credit.

The Powerses, septuagenarian social security pensioners, live in a heavily mortgaged home alleged to be in a substantial state of disrepair. The plaintiffs borrowed $5,000 from defendant and gave defendant a security interest in their house as collateral for the loan. The Powerses borrowed the money for the purpose of refinancing a $3,300 loan with the defendant and making certain home improvements. The terms of this loan and the circumstances surrounding its making are the subject of this lawsuit.

Plaintiffs allege that they borrowed the $5,000 with the understanding that they would be able to pay it back in $50 monthly payments. The plaintiffs then contracted with a contractor named Williford to supply the requisite home improvements. After the work had begun, Williford and his wife came to the plaintiffs' house and asked them to sign some papers, among them, a deed of trust creating a security interest in the home. Eugene Powers admits signing a number of the papers and Lila, who is blind, admits making her mark on some of them. Plaintiffs contend, however, that they did not read the papers, were not aware of what they were signing, and were not given copies of what they signed. Plaintiffs apparently were given a disclosure statement containing some details of the loan, but the statement did not comply with the requirements of the Truth-in-Lending Act.

MERHIGE, J.

The Truth-in-Lending Act was passed in 1968 after eight years of increasing congressional concern with consumer ignorance about and sharp practice in the consumer credit industry. The purpose of the act was to create the conditions for full dissemination of credit information to consumers so that they would have the facts with which to make rational and informed credit judgments. . . . The Act and the regulations promulgated under the Act by the Federal Reserve Board embody the further principle that full disclosure could be facilitated by requiring industry-wide standardization of credit terms and by strictly enforcing industry adherence to the standardized terms. The standardization requirement thus enables the consumer "to compare more readily the various credit terms available to him and avoid the uninformed use of credit."

The Truth-in-Lending Act is remedial in nature. It represents in large part a vigorous congressional response to a history of sharp and fraudulent practice in the home improvement loan industry. Since the Act was designed to remedy congressionally perceived widespread abuses by home improvement lenders, its requirements must be strictly enforced in order to promote the twin goals of disclosure and standardization and, thus, to afford consumers of credit the expansive protection envisioned by Congress.

The plaintiffs allege that the defendant has violated the act or implementing regulations by [among other things]:

1. Failing to identify the method of computing any unearned portion of the finance charge in the event of prepayment of the obligation . . . ;
2. Failing to print the terms "finance charge" and "annual percentage rate" in print more conspicuous than that used for other disclosures . . . ;
3. Failing to clearly and conspicuously disclose the total number of payments scheduled for repayment of the indebtedness . . . ;
4. Failing to state the total amount of the finance charge using the term "finance charge". . . ;

The Court concludes that it can appropriately dispose of plaintiffs' . . . contentions under Rule 56, F.R.Civ.P., since only questions of law are involved. . . .

2. Failure to Print the Terms "Finance Charge" and "Annual Percentage Rate" in Print More Conspicuous Than That Used for Other Disclosures.

Where the act and regulations require creditors to use the terms "finance charge" and "annual percentage rate," those terms must be "printed more conspicuously than other terminology required by [Regulation Z]. The terms "finance charge" and "annual percentage rate" were clearly intended to be the most important disclosures required by the act and implementing regulations and their importance was to be signified by their being printed in print more conspicuous than that used for any other disclosure.

Defendant's *"Disclosure Statement of Loan"* fails to give these two terms the prominence and importance required by section 226.6(a) and, therefore, fails to comply on its face with the mandate of the regulation. Defendant has printed the terms "finance charge" and "annual percentage rate" in *all caps*. Defendant has, likewise, printed the term "total payments," a disclosure required by section 226.8(b), and the terms "interest," "brokerage," and "payments" in *all caps*.

Defendant contends that its having underlined the term "finance charge" underscores the word's prominence and brings it into substantial compliance with the regulation. The regulation does not, however, state that its requirement that the terms "finance charge" and "annual percentage rate" be given special prominence on the disclosure statement can be satisfied by underlining. . . .

4. Failure to State the Total Amount of the Finance Charge Using the Term "Finance Charge."

Section 226.8(d)(3) of 12 C.F.R. requires creditors to disclose "the total amount of the finance charge, with description of each amount included, using the term 'finance charge'." Defendant's disclosure statement reads:

FINANCE CHARGES:

INTEREST	$2,093.15
BROKERAGE	250.00
TOTAL FINANCE CHARGES	$2,343.15

Defendant's disclosure statement nowhere contains the term "finance charge" as required by the regulation. The components of the finance charge—interest and brokerage—are broken down as required by the act and the implementing regulation, but the "total amount of the finance charge" which is explicitly required to be labeled "finance charge" is, instead denoted as TOTAL FINANCE CHARGES.

The requirement is quite technical, but the Congress did not intend creditors to escape liability where only technical violations were involved. Indeed, the technical requirements of the act must be strictly enforced if the goal of standardization of terms, which is a requisite if consumers are to be able to make meaningful comparisons of available credit alternatives, is to be achieved. The Court concludes that, since the defendant has failed to state the total amount of the finance charge using the term "finance charge," it has violated section 226.8(d)(3) of 12 C.F.R. and summary judgment shall be entered for plaintiff. . . .

The Truth-in-Lending Act provides a range of remedies for the debtor when the creditor violates its disclosure requirements. The aggrieved debtor may recover civil penalties and attorney's fees, and in certain circumstances may rescind the consumer credit transaction. Additionally, the creditor who refuses to rescind or otherwise comply with the [rescission] mechanism established by the Act may forfeit any interest that it may have in the property or home improvements which have been financed with the proceeds of the transaction. . . .

Because defendant's disclosure statement, even if it were received by the plaintiffs, was violative of the Act in at least four respects, plaintiffs were entitled to rescind the transaction until midnight of the third business day following receipt of a correct disclosure statement. Section 1635(b) of the Act give debtors a "continuing" and "open-ended" power of [rescission] so long as the *required* disclosures have not been made. . . . Since defendant never furnished plaintiffs a correct disclosure statement, plaintiffs' [rescission] notice of September 20, 1974, was effective to rescind the transaction. . . .

Because plaintiffs have prevailed in this action, they are entitled to attorney's fees and costs. Counsel for parties will be directed by the Court to meet and confer and, hopefully, to agree on reasonable attorney's fees. If counsel cannot within 10 days of the date of the Court's order reach agreement, counsel for plaintiffs will be directed to submit a statement of time spent litigating this action and the Court will award reasonable attorney's fees and costs.

QUESTIONS ABOUT CASE 11.1

1. The court points out that the Truth-in-Lending Act is remedial in nature. How is that significant? (Hint: Review the first two paragraphs of the judge's opinion.)

2. The court admittedly takes a technical view of the act's requirements. Should it be a defense that the defendant did give the plaintiffs a disclosure statement? That is, should the defendant's providing this particular disclosure statement relieve defendant of liability?

● FHA/VA Restrictions on Fees

Recall from Chapter 10 that the Veterans Administration (VA) and the Federal Housing Administration (FHA) are major forces in residential lending. FHA and VA regulations prohibit the charging of certain fees to the borrower, notwithstanding any agreement among the parties, when the loan is to be insured by the FHA or VA. The FHA or VA will review the completed closing package to ensure compliance with these prohibitions. If the purchaser is charged any of the prohibited fees listed in the box on the following page, the loan will not be insurable by the federal government.

Foreign Investment in Real Property Tax Act

Congress enacted the Foreign Investment in Real Property Tax Act of 1980 (FIRPTA),[24] to tax the gain or loss from the transfer of real property interests in the United States by nonresident individuals or foreign corporations as if they were U.S. residents. To ensure that these foreign persons do not elude the payment of this tax, the Internal Revenue Code[25] places the burden on the *buyer* of U.S. realty from a foreign person to deduct and withhold the tax. The amount of the required deduction is to be the *lesser* of (a) 10% of the amount realized by the seller on the transfer, or (b) the amount of the seller's tax liability (determined by the Internal Revenue Service on request). A buyer who is required to withhold and fails to do so becomes secondarily liable for payment of the seller's tax, together with interest and tax penalties.[26]

Buyers bearing this burden might not know whether the seller is a foreign person and, consequently, whether to withhold the tax. Therefore, buyers must withhold the statutory amounts

Box 11–3 Point to Consider

On FHA insured transactions, the FHA borrower cannot pay the following fees (if applicable), though they may be assessed against other parties to the transaction:

Notary Fees
Review Fees
Underwriting Fees
Tax Service Fee
Recording Fees for Mortgage Assignment
Final Construction Inspection Fee

On VA insured transactions, the veteran borrower cannot pay the following fees (if applicable), though they may be assessed against other parties to the transaction:

Tax Service Fee
Document Preparation Fee
Documentary Stamps on the Deed
Recording of Satisfaction or Release of Mortgage
Recording of Assignment of Mortgage
Termite Report Fee
Roof Inspection Fee
Amortization Schedule Fee
Warehousing Fee
Photocopying Fee
Express Mail Fee
Costs of Any Repairs to Property
Photographs
Water Analysis
Underwriting Fee
Attorneys' Fee, Settlement Fees, Closing Fees
Sales Commissions
Escrow Fee
Plumbing or Electrical Inspection Report
Flood Hazard Determination

on *any and all* transfers of U.S. real property interests unless the transaction fits into one of the regulatory "safe harbor" exceptions. The most common exceptions exempting buyers from the withholding requirements are the following:

1. The seller provides the buyer a U.S. taxpayer identification number and an affidavit stating that the seller is not a foreign person.

2. The buyer is acquiring the U.S. real property interest as a personal residence and the amount realized by the seller does not exceed $300,000.

3. The transfer is of a stock regularly traded on an established securities market.

The result is that the so-called FIRPTA affidavit (given by the seller and stating that the seller is not a foreign person) is a routine part of real estate transfers.

BOX 11–4 APPLY YOUR KNOWLEDGE

Mohammed, a citizen of Egypt, recently sold a parcel of real estate that he owned in Palm Beach, California. He bought the parcel in 1980 for $1 million and sold it for $3 million to Aretha, a citizen of the United States. (a) Who is responsible for paying the U.S. income tax on Mohammed's capital gains on this sale? (b) Who would be responsible for the capital gains tax if Mohammed had sold the realty to Foster, a citizen of Australia?

1099 Reporting Requirements

The IRS also requires that an informational tax report, a form 1099-S, be filed by a "real estate reporting person" (the closing agent or some other person as noted) on any sale or exchange of real estate, unless the transaction fits into one of the exempted categories.[27] The purpose of this requirement is to enable the IRS to cross-check the form 1099-S against the seller's federal income tax return to determine whether the seller reported any capital gains resulting from the sale of the real estate and paid the applicable capital gains tax. The 1099-S form requires the following information: the name, address, and taxpayer identification number of the seller; a brief description of the real estate; the closing date; the gross proceeds of sale; whether the seller will receive contingent payments or anything other than cash; and the name, address, and taxpayer identification number of the real estate reporting person.

The IRS is serious about having 1099-S forms completed and filed. To that end, the regulations make a series of parties to the transaction successively liable as the real estate reporting persons required to file the form. The principal responsibility for filing it is on the closing agent. However, if the closing agent fails to file the form, the other parties to the transaction are responsible for filing it, and the responsibility for filing falls on them in the following order unless they have agreed to a different order of responsibility: (1) the person preparing the settlement statement, (2) the buyer's attorney, (3) the seller's attorney, (4) the disbursing agent, (5) the mortgage lender, (6) the seller's broker, (7) the buyer's broker, and (8) the buyer. The consequences of failure to file can be severe, particularly if the person responsible for reporting engages in a number of transactions. The basic penalty for failure to file is $50 per return, up to $250,000 per calendar year. If the failure to file is intentional, the penalty increases to the *greater* of $100 per return or 5% of the aggregate amount of the gross proceeds of sales that should have been reported.

Cash Transactions Reporting Requirements

Cash serves as a medium of exchange precisely because it is readily transferable and generally accepted without any collection risks. Transfers of cash, without more, create no "paper trail" or other evidence of transfer; the bearer of cash is presumed to be its true owner. This characteristic makes cash a particularly attractive vehicle for those who want to avoid the scrutiny of the Internal Revenue Service or other governmental agencies. To conceal the sources of funds that result from illegal activities, or to avoid reporting requirements for legal business activities, tax evaders and other criminals often seek to "launder" money by running it through legitimate businesses or by investing the cash in real property or other assets. The federal government has responded by attempting to create a "paper trail" where otherwise there would be none.

To detect and control money laundering, the Internal Revenue Code requires that cash transactions in excess of $10,000 received by any person engaged in trade or business be reported to the Internal Revenue Service. The report is to be filed on IRS form 8300 within 15 days of the transaction and must include a statement of the amount of cash received, a description of the transaction, and a verification of the payer's name and tax identification number.[28] For this purpose, "cash" includes U.S. currency, foreign currency, bank checks not drawn on the payer's account, traveler's checks, and money orders having a face amount of less than $10,000.

Federal money laundering statutes make it a crime to facilitate money laundering by *knowingly* conducting or attempting to conduct a financial transaction designed to "conceal or disguise the nature, the location, the source, the ownership, or the control of the proceeds of specified unlawful activity" or to "avoid a transaction reporting requirement under state or federal law."[29] The statutes specifically provide that a defendant can *know* that the property represents the proceeds of unlawful activity, and thus can be convicted of aiding a money launderer, without knowing which specific offense the launderer has committed. Therefore, as the following case reveals, a real estate broker or closing agent is not allowed to be "willfully blind" to the sources of funds. One precaution that parties to the closing should follow is either to avoid or to diligently report cash transactions.

Violations of the money laundering statutes carry severe sanctions, such as a fine of up to $500,000 or twice the value of the funds involved, whichever is greater, or imprisonment of up to twenty years, or both. Federal statutes also authorize the forfeiture of property (or its products) involved in certain types of illegal activity, such as drug-related violations, gambling, racketeering, money laundering, and tax evasion.

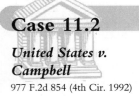

Case 11.2

United States v. Campbell

977 F.2d 854 (4th Cir. 1992)

Ellen Campbell, a licensed real estate agent, worked at Lake Norman Realty in Mooresville, North Carolina. Mark Lawing, a drug dealer in Kannapolis, North Carolina, decided to buy a house on Lake Norman. He obtained Campbell's business card from Lake Norman Realty's Mooresville office, called Campbell, and scheduled an appointment to look at houses.

Over the course of about five weeks, Lawing met with Campbell approximately once a week and looked at a total of ten to twelve houses. Lawing and Campbell also had numerous phone conversations. Lawing represented himself to Campbell as the owner of a legitimate business, L & N Autocraft, which purportedly performed automobile customizing services. When meeting with Campbell, Lawing would travel in either a red Porsche he owned or a gold Porsche owned by a fellow drug dealer, Randy Sweatt, who would usually accompany Lawing. During the trips to look at houses, which occurred during normal business hours, Lawing would bring his cellular phone and would often consume food and beer with Sweatt. At one point, Lawing brought a briefcase containing $20,000 in cash, showing the money to Campbell to demonstrate his ability to purchase a house.

Lawing eventually settled upon a house listed for $191,000 and owned by Edward and Nancy Guy Fortier. The listing with the Fortiers had been secured by Sara Fox, another real estate agent with Lake Norman Realty. After negotiations, Lawing and the Fortiers agreed on a price of $185,000, and entered into a written contract. Lawing was unable to secure a loan and decided to ask the Fortiers to accept $60,000 "under the table" in cash and to lower the contract price to $122,500. Lawing contacted Campbell and informed her of this proposal. Campbell relayed the proposal to Fox who forwarded it to the Fortiers. The Fortiers agreed, and Fox had the Fortiers execute a new listing agreement that lowered the sales price and increased the commission percentage (in order to protect the realtors' original commission on the sale).

Thereafter Lawing met the Fortiers, Fox, and Campbell in the Mooresville sales office with $60,000 in cash. The money was wrapped in small bundles and carried in a brown paper grocery bag. The money was counted, and the parties executed a new contract reflecting a sales price of $122,500. Lawing tipped both Fox and Campbell with "a couple of hundred dollars."

On the basis of the information provided by Campbell, William Austin, the closing attorney, prepared closing documents, including HUD-1 and 1099-S forms, reflecting a sales price of $122,500. Campbell, Fox, Austin, Lawing, Lawing's parents, and the Fortiers were all present at the closing. The closing documents were signed, all reflecting a sales price of $122,500.

ERVIN, C. J.

The money laundering statute under which Campbell was charged applies to any person who:

> . . . knowing that the property involved in a financial transaction represents proceeds from some form of unlawful activity, conducts or attempts to conduct such a financial transaction which in fact involves the proceeds of specified unlawful activity . . . knowing that the transaction is designed in whole or in part . . . to conceal or disguise the nature, the location, the source, the ownership, or the control of the proceeds of specified unlawful activity. . . .

The district court found, and Campbell does not dispute, that there was adequate evidence for the jury to find that Campbell conducted a financial transaction which in fact involved the proceeds of Lawing's illegal drug activities. The central issue in contention is whether there was sufficient evidence for the jury to find that Campbell possessed the knowledge that: (1) Lawing's funds were the proceeds of illegal activity, and (2) the transaction was designed to disguise the nature of those proceeds.

In assessing Campbell's culpability, it must be noted that the statute requires actual subjective knowledge. Campbell cannot be convicted on what she objectively should have known. However, this requirement is softened somewhat by the doctrine of willful blindness. . . .

The Government need not prove that the defendant had the purpose of concealing the proceeds of illegal activity. Instead, as the plain language of the statute suggests, the Government must only show that the defendant possessed the knowledge that the transaction was designed to conceal illegal proceeds. This distinction is critical in cases such as the present one, in which the defendant is a person other than the individual who is the source of the tainted money. It is clear from the record that Campbell herself did not act with purpose of concealing drug proceeds. Her motive, without question, was to close the real estate deal and collect the resulting commission, without regard to the source of the money or the effect of the transaction in concealing a portion of the purchase price. However, Campbell's motivations are irrelevant. Under the terms of the statute, the relevant question is not Campbell's purpose, but rather her knowledge of Lawing's purpose.

The sufficiency of evidence regarding Campbell's knowledge of Lawing's purpose depends on whether Campbell was aware of Lawing's status as a drug dealer. Assuming for the moment that Campbell knew that Lawing's funds were derived from illegal activity, then the under–the–table transfer of $60,000 in cash would have been sufficient, by itself, to allow the jury to find that Campbell knew, or was willfully blind to the fact, that the transaction was designed for an illicit purpose. Only if Campbell was oblivious to the illicit nature of Lawing's funds could she credibly argue that she believed Lawing's explanation of the under–the–table transfer of cash and was unaware of the money laundering potential of the transaction. In short, the fraudulent nature of the transaction itself provides a sufficient basis from which a jury could infer Campbell's knowledge of the transaction's purpose, if, as assumed above, Campbell also knew of the illegal source of Lawing's money. As a result, we find that, in this case, the knowledge components of the money laundering statute collapse into a single inquiry: Did Campbell know that Lawing's funds were derived from an illegal source? . . .

The evidence pointing to Campbell's knowledge of Lawing's illegal activities is not overwhelming. First, we find that the district court correctly excluded from consideration testimony by Sweatt that Lawing was a "known" drug dealer. Kannapolis, where Lawing's operations were located, is approximately fifteen miles from Mooresville, where Campbell lived and worked, and, as the district court pointed out, there was no indication that Lawing's reputation extended over such an extensive "community."

However, the district court also downplayed evidence that we find to be highly relevant. Sara Fox, the listing broker, testified at trial that Campbell had stated prior to the sale that the funds "may have been drug money.". . .

In addition, the Government presented extensive evidence regarding Lawing's lifestyle. This evidence showed that Lawing and his companion both drove new Porsches, and that Lawing carried a cellular phone, flashed vast amounts of cash, and was able to be away from his purportedly legitimate business for long stretches of time during normal working hours. The district court conceded that this evidence "is not [wholly] irrelevant" to Campbell's knowledge of Lawing's true occupation, but noted that Lawing's lifestyle was not inconsistent with that of many of the other inhabitants of the affluent Lake Norman area who were not drug dealers. . . .

We find that the evidence of Lawing's lifestyle, the testimony concerning Campbell's statement that the money "might have been drug money," and the fraudulent nature of the transaction in which Campbell was asked to participate were sufficient to create a question for the jury concerning whether Campbell "deliberately closed her eyes to what would otherwise have been obvious to her." As a result, we find that a reasonable jury could have found that Campbell was willfully blind to the fact that Lawing was a drug dealer and the fact that the purchase of the Lake Norman property was intended, at least in part, to conceal the proceeds of Lawing's drug selling operation. Accordingly, we reverse the judgment of acquittal on the money laundering charge.

QUESTION ABOUT CASE 11.2

The Court acknowledges: "It is clear from the record that Campbell herself did not act with purpose of concealing drug proceeds. Her motive, without question, was to close the real estate deal and collect the resulting commission, without regard to the source of the money or the effect of the transaction in concealing a portion of the purchase price." At what point did Campbell possibly cross the line from "good business" to criminality?

Box 11–5 Apply Your Knowledge

Algernon has contracted to buy a house in Shady Grove subdivision for $400,000. He shows up at the closing with a grocery sack full of currency, ready, willing, and able to close. (a) Given the large amount of cash, what is the closing agent, All-American Title Insurance Company, required to do? (b) What problem does All-American face if before the closing it discovers that some of the bills have a red dye on them and learns that the local newspaper yesterday reported a recent bank robbery in the neighboring county?

Closing Instruments and Procedures

Although the many state and federal compliance issues complicate the closing process, real estate professionals deal with most of them as a routine part of the closing process, thus assuring that they will be covered in every closing. The remainder of this chapter discusses typical closing instruments and procedures in light of state and federal legal requirements and the need to protect the parties to the transaction.

The Governing Documents

The instruments and procedures needed for a closing are dictated by federal and state compliance requirements and by two primary documents directly resulting from the real estate transaction itself: the contract of sale and the lender's loan commitment or loan instructions.

The Contract of Sale

As noted in Chapters 6 and 8, the Sales Contract (or Earnest Money Agreement) sets forth the promises of the respective parties and under the Statute of Frauds must be in writing to be enforceable. The contract should specify such critical matters as the time, date and place of closing, the purchase price, the type of deed required of the seller, allocation of closing expenses between seller and buyer, proration of taxes and rents, and any conditions that would excuse a party from the obligation to close. To the extent that the sales contract addresses such matters, it controls the closing; the closing agent (or the attorneys for the parties) must conform the closing documents to the specifications in the sales contract.

The Loan Closing Instructions

Because almost all real estate transactions have commercial financing, the lender is also likely to play an important role in structuring the closing. Ordinarily, a real estate lender will fund its loan only upon compliance by the buyer and seller with the lender's loan instructions or conditions, which can be quite complex. In commercial real estate closings, these instructions normally are found in a loan commitment letter; in residential transactions, the instructions normally appear in a document called loan instructions to the closing agent. These instructions have several purposes. First, the lender wants to assure that its funds are properly applied in accordance with its loan commitment to the borrower. Second, it wants a properly documented security interest in the real estate to secure repayment of the loan. Third, the lender may want to qualify the loan for federal insurance or for sale in the secondary mortgage market. Depending on the lender's future plans for the loan, the lender will stipulate that the loan meet the requirements of FHA, VA, FNMA, or FHLMC. Fourth, the instructions will explain the lender's requirements for surveys, inspection reports, hazard insurance, flood insurance (if the property is located in a federally identified flood hazard area), and title insurance. Fifth, the lender specifies what fees are to be collected by the closing agent and forwarded to the lender. Finally, the instructions will often specify to whom the closing documents, fees, and installment loan payments should be sent.

The Closing Documents

Real estate closings vary considerably in type and complexity. The array of closing documents needed for a particular closing depends not only upon the contract of sale and the lender's loan instructions, but upon other factors as well, such as the legal requisites for a conveyance in a particular jurisdiction (requirements vary among jurisdictions) and whether the property is residential or commercial. Commercial closings and their closing documents often differ from residential ones for a variety of reasons. Usually commercial closings involve considerably more money than residential closings, though in an age of extravagant residences, numerous exceptions exist. Many laws apply only to residential or only to commercial transactions, often on the assumption that residential closings involve relatively less sophisticated buyers who need protections that commercial buyers do not. Yet, because of a strong social and political bias in favor of home ownership, legislators are reluctant to impose requirements that would unduly increase residential transaction costs or otherwise inhibit home ownership. The following section discusses many of the common documents found in a real estate closing, with a notation in each subheading indicating whether they are more commonly found in residential or in commercial transactions, or in both.

Appraisal (Both Residential and Commercial Transactions)

The lender wants assurance that its collateral will have sufficient value to cover the unpaid portion of the loan if the borrower defaults in payment. Consequently, the lender ordinarily requires an appraisal of the property as a condition to making the loan. Ordinarily, the appraisal is ordered at the time of loan application and is completed and reviewed before closing. All lenders have limits on the amount of money they will lend on a given parcel of real estate. The limits are imposed either internally by the lender or by loan buyers or insurers in the secondary market. The limit is expressed as a percentage—the loan amount divided by the appraised value of the property. In VA-insured residential loans, a veteran of the armed forces usually can borrow 100% of the appraised value of the property up to a stated maximum dollar limit. In FHA-insured residential loans, the borrower can borrow 97% of the appraised value up to a stated limit. In "conventional" residential loans (i.e., loans that are not federally insured), most lenders will not lend more than 80% of the appraised value without additional security in the form of private mortgage insurance. *Private mortgage insurance* protects the lender against the risk of a deficiency following a default by the borrower. A deficiency results when the property being foreclosed upon is not sufficiently valuable to cover the unpaid debt (including the expenses of foreclosure). For this lender protection, the *borrower* pays a monthly premium for the mortgage insurance policy as a part of the mortgage payment. In commercial lending, where mortgage insurance is nonexistent and exercising remedies tends to be more difficult and time consuming, a loan-to-value limit of 80% or less is common.

Commitment for Title Insurance
(Both Residential and Commercial Transactions)

As discussed in Chapter 9, an examination of title is an indispensable part of any real estate transaction. If a loan finances part of the transaction, the lender usually will require a commitment for title insurance (also referred to as a "title insurance binder") as a condition to closing. The title insurance commitment represents the title insurance company's promise to issue a final title insurance policy in accordance with the terms of the commitment upon completion of the closing, recording of the deed and mortgage, update of title search through the date and time of recording, and payment of the applicable insurance premium. The title insurance commitment should be on an American Land Title Association (ALTA) approved form. Upon review of the title binder, the closing agent obtains payoffs of any mortgages, liens, judgments, assessments, and taxes. The closing agent satisfies any liens at closing; any unpaid liens will appear as exceptions on the title insurance policy when it is issued.

Survey (Both Residential and Commercial Transactions)

Like a title insurance policy, a physical survey of the property is advisable in any real estate transaction. A survey may be required if the acquisition of the real estate is financed, and one would be needed to obtain a title insurance policy free from exceptions for matters of survey. A survey provides considerable title information, including evidence of compliance with zoning and other restrictions, locations of improvements and easements, and the existence of or potential for boundary disputes.

Flood Certification (Both Residential and Commercial Transactions)

As a part of the survey work, the surveyor should locate the property with reference to area flood maps prepared by the U.S. Army Corps of Engineers. The Corps of Engineers is charged with locating areas of potential flood hazard as revealed by local elevations and topography. The Corps of Engineers prepares maps upon which it locates the likely areas of any potential worst case flooding, which are referred to as **special flood hazard areas**. The federal government requires that new construction within special flood hazard areas be subject to a permit system.[30] To obtain a permit, buildings must be elevated above or be made flood-proof up to the **base flood elevation**. The base flood elevation is the estimated height of the worst flooding to be expected in a century (the "one-hundred year flood line"). Owners must also carry flood insurance on improvements located within these designated flood hazard areas. A lender will require that the surveyor certify that no improvements on the property are located within a flood hazard area, or, if they are, the lender will require evidence that the borrower has obtained flood insurance on the affected improvements.

Surveyor's Report (Both Residential and Commercial Transactions)

If title insurance is to be obtained, the surveyor should provide an ALTA form surveyor's report. In the report, the surveyor discloses whether any conditions that might indicate title problems have been discovered, such as possession by someone other than the owner, violation of zoning or other restrictions, or unrecorded easements or driveways affecting the property.

Hazard Insurance Policy (Both Residential and Commercial Transactions)

Hazard insurance (also known in residential transactions as "homeowner's insurance") insures the owner and lender against loss or damage from stated casualties such as fire and wind damage, up to the policy limits. Although most reasonably prudent owners would voluntarily acquire hazard insurance to protect their investment, insurance is required, if the property is financed, to insure the lender "as its interest may appear." Premiums for hazard insurance usually are paid annually, in advance. The lender may require that the borrower deposit money with the lender in escrow to pay for the following year's premium when it becomes due and payable. Because hazard insurance policies are not assignable, upon a sale of the property the buyer must obtain a new policy.

Termite Report/Structural Inspection (Both Residential and Commercial Transactions)

Termites, carpenter ants, and other wood-destroying insects are a problem in many parts of the country. The problem they present is particularly acute where wooden parts of a structure come in contact with the ground. Therefore, a termite inspection prior to closing is routine if any of the structure is wood, as is more commonly the case in residential than in commercial construction.

Although termite inspections are required by lenders, buyers should procure a more thorough structural inspection of the property, including tests of all systems and an inspection of the foundation, roof, and structural integrity of the improvements. In commercial loan transactions, a structural inspection is often performed by a structural or civil engineer.

Tenant Leases (Commercial Transactions Only)

The market value of commercial property is determined by capitalizing the stream of net income that the property earns from tenant leases (or *could* earn from tenant leases upon full occupancy by tenants, should the building be vacant or owner-occupied). Therefore, the terms of any existing leases are of utmost importance to a prospective buyer of commercial realty or to a lender evaluating it as security. Lease terms of major concern include the rental rate, the duration of the lease, the description of the leased premises, maintenance and operating expense allocation, obligations of the landlord, the tenant's renewal rights, any options to purchase or rights of first refusal in the event of sale, restrictions on assignment, and events of default. Prospective buyers will carefully review copies of the leases prior to closing, with the original lease agreements being assigned and delivered by the seller to the buyer at closing.

Tenant Estoppel/Subordination Certificates (Commercial Transactions Only)

In addition to the lease agreements themselves, the prospective buyer (or lender) wants assurance that the leases are current, valid, and enforceable. The buyer also wants to know that the tenant does not have any claims or defenses against the selling landlord that the tenant might assert against the new landlord to avoid paying rent or as a reason to terminate the lease. Of course, it is customary to get assurances and warranties from the *seller* that the leases are valid and enforceable, without any defaults, claims, or defenses. However, it is much more comforting to get that assurance from the *tenant*. That assurance usually comes in the form of a document known as a tenant estoppel certificate.

A **tenant estoppel certificate** is a representation by the tenant that the lease is current and in good standing, with no defaults on the part of either the landlord or the tenant. The certificate is called an *estoppel certificate* because the tenant will be prevented by a court (i.e., estopped) from later asserting facts contrary to the facts contained in the certificate. For example, Teddy, owner of Teddy's Laundry, leases space in Central Shopping Center. In a tenant estoppel certificate, Teddy assures Justin, a prospective buyer of the shopping center, that Teddy and the landlord are in full compliance with the terms of their lease, thereby inducing Justin to purchase the property. A week later, Teddy's Laundry vacates the premises, and Justin sues Teddy for unpaid rent. As a defense to the lawsuit, Teddy claims that he was constructively evicted because the selling landlord had refused to fix the roof despite repeated demands over the course of two years. A court will refuse to listen to the default claims of Teddy, even if they are true, because hearing them would be unfair to Justin in light of his reliance on the tenant estoppel certificate.

Frequently, the buyer's lender will require the tenants to execute a subordination/nondisturbance agreement with the lender. The legal effect of a **subordination/nondisturbance**

agreement is that the tenant subordinates its leasehold interest to the lien of the lender's mortgage. Thus, the mortgagee's security interest has priority over the lease, notwithstanding the order of recording and the effect of the applicable recording act. But signing a subordination agreement creates a serious problem for the tenant. Under the agreement, if the mortgagee foreclosed its mortgage, the foreclosure would terminate the lease and the mortgagee could then evict the tenant. Such a drastic result gives the tenant little incentive to execute such an agreement. Therefore, a mortgagee seeking a subordination agreement usually includes a provision agreeing not to disturb the tenant in its possession after foreclosure if the tenant remains current on its lease obligations. The real concern of the lender, and the reason for the nondisturbance provision, is that the stream of rental payments continue after foreclosure without interruption.

Ordinarily, the subordination/nondisturbance agreement anticipates additional difficulties. The lender does not, for example, want the tenant to have a claim or defense under the lease as a result of some action of the landlord-borrower. Nor does the lender want the tenant to have the right to make lease payments for ten years in advance, thus enabling the defaulting landlord-borrower to skip off to Belize with the proceeds. To prevent such problems, the subordination/nondisturbance agreement usually requires the tenant to inform the mortgagee of any landlord defaults under the lease and to give the mortgagee the opportunity to cure them, and to refrain from paying rents to the landlord-borrower for more than one month in advance.

Seller's Authorization to Sell (Commercial Transactions Only)

If the seller is an entity such as a partnership or a corporation, as is likely in commercial transactions, the buyer will need to review documentation evidencing the seller's authority to sell the property, and the authorization for the seller's representative to sign on behalf of the seller.

Phase I Environmental Report (Commercial Transactions Only)

A Phase I Environmental Report (discussed in Chapter 18), or an environmental audit as it is sometimes called, has become a routine part of commercial real estate transactions. The audit was made necessary by the Comprehensive Environmental Response, Compensation, and Liability Act of 1980 (commonly referred to as CERCLA or the Superfund Act), as amended by the Superfund Amendments and Reauthorization Act of 1986 (SARA). CERCLA makes landowners, among many others, personally liable for the costs of cleaning up contaminated properties. CERCLA, however, exempts certain "innocent landowners" from personal liability for cleanup if they have diligently investigated for potential pollution problems, found none, and *had no reason to know* that any existed when they purchased the property. The environmental audit is the investigative tool that buyers and lenders use to avoid this personal liability. The audit seeks evidence of environmental contamination by a review of the historic and current uses of the property, and includes a physical inspection of the property by a trained professional such as an environmental engineer.

Deed (Both Residential and Commercial Transactions)

The deed is the fundamental document for transferring title to real property. The deed must be properly executed by the seller and delivered to and accepted by the buyer, and should be recorded. Recording in the county where the property is located is routinely required by a lender's loan instructions.

Lien Affidavit or Waivers (Both Residential and Commercial Transactions)

Because of the statutory lien (mechanic's lien) available in most jurisdictions to persons making improvements to real property, a *lien affidavit* or *lien waiver* is a common requirement. In a lien affidavit, the seller usually represents and warrants that no improvements have been made to the real property within the applicable lien period. If improvements have been made, the contractors and material suppliers will normally have to sign the affidavit, thus affirming that they have been paid in full for any work they have performed and that they claim no lien rights. Alternatively, unpaid contractors and suppliers must, by use of a lien waiver, relinquish any statutory lien rights against the property with respect to unpaid bills. Those waiving their lien rights do, of course, retain their contractual rights against the persons hiring them.

Note and Mortgage (Both Residential and Commercial Transactions)

A buyer who obtains a loan to purchase the property must sign (as the *maker*) a promissory note, usually one that is freely transferable (in negotiable form), promising to pay the amount of the indebtedness to the lender (as *payee*). In a residential loan transaction, the note is likely to be on a form approved by FHA, VA, FNMA, or FHMLC, a form designed to assure negotiability and thus to be more readily accepted by buyers in the secondary market.

The mortgage (or deed of trust, or deed to secure debt, depending on the jurisdiction) is the instrument conveying to the lender a security interest in the property to be purchased. If the borrower fails to pay the promissory note according to its terms, the lender may foreclose the mortgage. In a residential loan transaction, the mortgage is likely to be on a form approved by FHA, VA, FNMA, or FHMLC.

Borrower's Affidavit (Both Residential and Commercial Transactions)

A borrower's affidavit is a document used by a lender to verify certain factual information concerning the borrower and the property on which lender has based its loan decision. For example, many residential loan programs are restricted to buyers who will occupy the property themselves and not lease it out to others. The lender will require the borrower to sign an affidavit affirming that the borrower intends to occupy the property and not to rent it to others.

Nonforeign Affidavit (Both Residential and Commercial Transactions)

As noted earlier, the Foreign Investment in Real Property Tax Act of 1980 (FIRPTA) requires the seller to provide the buyer with a U.S. taxpayer identification number and an affidavit stating that the seller is not a foreign person—unless the transaction is exempt (e.g., the buyer is acquiring the property as a personal residence and the amount realized by the seller does not exceed $300,000).

IRS 1099 (Both Residential and Commercial Transactions)

Because the closing agent is required to file form 1099 (the informational form relating to capital gains) with the IRS and to deliver a copy to the seller at the end of the tax year, the closing agent normally prepares the form for review at closing by the parties. Alternatively, the closing agent may obtain a certification from the seller regarding its taxpayer identification number and forwarding address so that the closing agent can prepare and send the 1099 form after closing.

The Closing Statement (Both Residential and Commercial Transactions)

The closing agent prepares a closing statement, or settlement statement, accounting for all cash transactions with respect to the closing. It sets forth the money received by the closing agent—usually the loan proceeds from the lender and the net amount due from the buyer. The statement also describes and allocates between the parties all disbursements in connection with the closing.

The allocation of these expenses will be controlled by the sales contract as supplemented by the loan instructions and local law and practice. To the buyer's down payment normally will be added all of the buyer's closing expenses, which typically include expenses allocated to the buyer in the sales contract, expenses associated with the buyer's new loan, title search fees, title insurance premiums, recording costs, surveyor's fee, termite inspection, structural inspection, hazard insurance, and attorneys' fees. From the seller's sales proceeds will be deducted the expenses allocated to the seller in the sales contract, which typically include loan payoffs, expenses of mortgage releases or terminations, attorneys' fees, and commissions to real estate brokers.

Residential loans are subject to the RESPA, which requires that the settlement statement be provided on a form approved by the Department of Housing and Urban Development, the so-called HUD-1 form. Because of the availability of many user-friendly personal computer programs to produce the HUD-1 form without manual computations, this form often is encountered in commercial transactions as well.

Closing Procedures

Although closing procedures vary according to the policies or even the personal idiosyncracies of the closing agent, some aspects of closing are likely to be universal. First, if the closing agent does not know the parties involved in the closing, the agent may request some evidence of identity such as a driver's license. Second, the closing agent will explain the closing documents, and each of the parties will sign and deliver them into escrow with the closing agent. Third, the closing agent will record the deed and mortgages and update the title through the date and time of recording. Fourth, the closing agent will disburse all of the closing expenses listed in the closing statement, including the loan payoffs. Fifth, the closing agent will forward the note and the other loan documents to the lender. Sixth, the closing agent will record any mortgage satisfactions or releases evidencing payoff of the mortgages. Finally, the closing agent will cause the title insurance company to issue the final title insurance policies and will forward them with the recorded documents to the buyer and lender, respectively.

Two procedural difficulties crop up repeatedly in connection with closings. The first is the method of payment required of the parties. Normally, the closing agent will be disbursing all of the closing funds immediately after closing. Therefore, the closing agent usually will require immediately available funds from all parties as a condition of disbursement, even from trusted clients. Immediately available funds are those whose collection is assured because payment is to be made by a bank (instead of an individual), through, for example, a bank draft, a certified check, or an electronic funds transfer from a bank. Personal checks, being drawn on only an individual's bank account, are not immediately available funds and may not be acceptable. Cash would be immediately available, but because of the federal reporting requirements discussed earlier, most closing agents will discourage or prohibit cash transactions.

The second difficulty is that the parties, or their real estate agents, may pressure the closing agent to disburse funds prior to the title update and the recording of the closing documents. Although practices vary widely throughout the country, the safest practice is for the closing agent to disburse only *after* title update and recording. Otherwise, if the person doing title update discovers new liens or encumbrances that have appeared on the record since the date of the original title search, the closing agent will have to stop payment on the disbursements and may be liable for losses if unable to do so.

One or both of these difficulties are resolved by statute in some jurisdictions. North Carolina, for example, provides that the closing agent may not disburse any closing funds prior to the recording, and requires verification that the funds to be disbursed are deposited in the closing agent's trust or escrow account.[31]

● Disputes at Closing and the Use of Escrow Arrangements

A number of circumstances in real estate transactions cause disputes to arise. Real estate transactions are expensive and complicated, closing documents are complex, and a number of events, such as inspections, take place after the sales contract is signed, sometimes with unexpected and unwelcome results. The closing agent may guide the parties to an informal resolution of the dispute, such as a monetary credit on the closing statement to correct an error or ease a misunderstanding. If the dispute involves the performance of a third party such as a painter or a roofing contractor, the dispute may be resolved by the creation of an escrow and the execution of an escrow agreement. Suppose that the sale contract between the parties provides that the seller is to repaint the house prior to closing. The buyer comes to closing, but the painter contractor has not completed the work. Obviously, the seller has breached the contract. Does the buyer have to close? The answer is somewhat unclear when, as discussed in Chapter 8, the buyer is completely excused from the obligation to perform only if the breach by the seller is a *material breach* of the contract. A judicial resolution of whether this breach is material might take years. Instead of resorting to litigation, the parties might resolve this dispute by reducing the sale price in an amount sufficient to compensate for the unfinished painting. But what if the painters have already been paid? The seller will not want the sale proceeds to be reduced because the seller will end up paying for the paint job twice. The buyer will not want to pay the entire contract price for fear that the painters will not complete the job and the seller will have no incentive to force the painters to perform. One reasonable resolution is for the seller to escrow with the closing agent or some other neutral third party the amount of money necessary to complete the painting. The escrow agreement allows the parties to proceed with the closing in spite of the breach of contract.

An escrow should be established only with a *written* escrow agreement. The agreement should establish the conditions for the release of the escrow. A good escrow agreement should eliminate both the liability and discretion of the escrow agent. For example, the agreement should provide that the paint job must be inspected and approved by a named third party inspector, acceptable to both parties, by a given date. If the paint job is completed and approved by the inspector by the given date, the closing agent pays the money to the seller. If the approval is not received by the given date, the closing agent pays the escrowed money to the buyer.

Self-Study Questions

1. What is the purpose of a closing?

2. What does a closing agent do?

3. Why has the federal government elected to intervene in the real estate closing process?

4. Why are residential closings and commercial closings sometimes treated differently by federal law?

5. How does the Real Estate Settlement Procedures Act affect the loan closing?

6. How does the Truth-in-Lending Act affect the loan closing?

7. What effect does the IRS have on loan closings?

8. Why are so many documents necessary in a loan closing?

9. What are the likely sources of disputes in a closing?

10. Why are formal dispute resolution tools, like litigation, likely to be unsatisfactory to resolve disputes that arise in a closing?

Case Problems

1. The Mayfields had owned their home for many years. In financial difficulty, they sought and received a loan from Vanguard Savings & Loan Association, which paid off much of the existing debt on the Mayfields' home. Later, Vanguard agreed to refinance its loan with the Mayfields and to pay off the balance of their first mortgage. In setting up the new (replacement) loan, Vanguard took a mortgage on the Mayfields' realty, advanced $160 to pay a water and sewer bill, and charged an origination fee of $1,930 and $1,500 in closing costs. The total for the replacement loan was $24,686 with an interest rate of 20%. On December 2, 1986, the Mayfields received a disclosure statement and a notice of right to cancel. The loan was closed in January 1987. However, the notice did not state the precise date upon which the cancellation period would expire, and the disclosure statement stated that the loan was being secured by "the property being purchased," even though Vanguard's mortgage was not a purchase money mortgage. After making two payments, the Mayfields defaulted on the loan. In October 1987, citing the Truth-in-Lending Act, they wrote a letter to Vanguard rescinding the loan. Vanguard did nothing upon receipt of the letter; it did not remove the mortgage or return any of the money received from the Mayfields. The Mayfields sued to rescind the loan and to recover damages and attorney's fees. What is the likely result of the Mayfields' attempt to rescind the loan and recover damages? *Mayfield v. Vanguard Savings & Loan Association*, 710 F.Supp. 143 (E.D. Pa. 1989).

2. From February 1980 through October 1982, the Wilsons borrowed various sums from The Prudential Insurance Co. of America and from Agristore Credit Corporation and Collateral Financial Services, Inc., to finance their farming operation. The loans were secured by livestock, crops, equipment, and a real estate mortgage on the farming operation. The Wilsons defaulted on the loans. The Wilsons filed suit alleging that the defendants had failed to comply with the general disclosure requirements and the right-of-rescission disclosure requirements of the Truth-In-Lending Act. Assume that the Truth-in-Lending requirements were not met. How should the court rule? *Wilson v. The Prudential Insurance Co. of America*, 749 F.2d 502 (8th Cir. 1984).

3. Bornfield, a certified public accountant, prepared tax returns for the Terrells and Gonzagowski. During this period, the Terrells owned a variety of fledgling businesses and Gonzagowski was self-employed in the roofing business, but both testified that they earned most of their income during the applicable period from drug trafficking. To facilitate a closing on a parcel of property, Bornfield wrote a personal check on his account for $13,000 in return for $13,000 in cash from Gonzagowski. The closing agent refused to accept Bornfield's check. The evidence showed that Terrell and Gonzagowski had periodically provided Bornfield with cocaine and that income shown on the tax returns prepared by Bornfield was insufficient to cover the expenses shown on the returns. Charged with money laundering, Bornfield claims that he had no actual knowledge of the source of the cash. (a) Is his defense likely to be successful? (b) Aside from possibly suspecting a drug connection, why did the closing agent refuse to accept Bornfield's personal check? *United States v. Bornfield*, 145 F.3d 1123 (10th Cir. 1998).

4. Willis Hendley obtained a variable rate mortgage loan from Cameron-Brown Company. The interest rate was to be adjusted annually. Based on an index–plus–margin formula, the interest rate was to be calculated each year by adding to an external index a preset margin of 2.79%. At closing, Hendley received a Truth-in-Lending Disclosure Statement that identified the loan as a variable rate loan and provided that "the interest rate may increase during the term of this transaction if the index increases." Approximately 45 days before the end of the loan's first year, Cameron-Brown informed Hendley that the interest rate for the second year would increase from 9.875% to 11.875%, a period in which the external index actually declined from 10.53% to 9.61%. Hendley filed suit claiming that Cameron-Brown violated the Truth-in-Lending Act by failing to disclose that the initial interest rate on his loan was "discounted" (i.e., lower than the rate would

have been if it had been calculated by using the "index plus margin" formula). Cameron-Brown also failed to disclose that the interest rate could increase for reasons other than by an increase in the index. Is Hendley likely to be successful in his claim? *Hendley v. Cameron-Brown Company*, 840 F.2d 831 (11th Cir. 1988).

Endnotes

1. 12 U.S.C. § 2601 *et seq.*

2. 24 C.F.R. Part 3500.

3. 12 U.S.C. § 2602.

4. 12 U.S.C. § 2604.

5. 12 U.S.C. § 2604.

6. 12 U.S.C. § 2603.

7. 12 U.S.C. § 2603(b).

8. 12 U.S.C. § 2605.

9. 12 U.S.C. § 2609.

10. 12 U.S.C. § 2610.

11. 24 C.F.R. §§ 3500.7, 3500.15.

12. 12 U.S.C. § 2607(a).

13. 24 C.F.R. § 3500.14.

14. 15 U.S.C. § 1601 et seq.

15. 12 C.F.R. §§ 226 *et seq.*

16. 15 U.S.C. § 1603.

17. 15 U.S.C. § 16022(d).

18. The general disclosure requirements are contained in 12 C.F.R. § 226.17-18; required disclosures for closed-end home mortgages are contained in § 226.32; those for home equity plans are contained in 12 C.F.R. § 226.5b(d).

19. 15 U.S.C. § 1605(a).

20. 15 U.S.C. § 1605–1606.

21. 15 U.S.C. § 1605(e).

22. 15 U.S.C. § 1635; 12 C.F.R. §§ 226.15, 226.23.

23. 12 C.F.R. §§ 226.2(a)(6), 226.23(b)(5); 15 U.S.C. § 1635(f).

24. I.R.C. § 897 (26 U.S.C. § 897).

25. I.R.C. § 1445.

26. Including the 100% tax penalty provided by I.R.C. § 6672.

27. Treasury Regulations § 1.6045-4 (26 C.F.R. § 1.6045-4).

28. 26 U.S.C. § 6050I.

29. 18 U.S.C. §§ 1956-1957.

30. These requirements are contained in the National Flood Insurance Program, created by the National Flood Insurance Act of 1968, 42 U.S.C. §§ 4012, et seq., and the Flood Disaster Protection Act of 1973, as amended by the 1994 National Flood Insurance Reform Act, 42 U.S.C. §§ 4001, et seq.

31. N.C.G.S. § 42(A)-4.

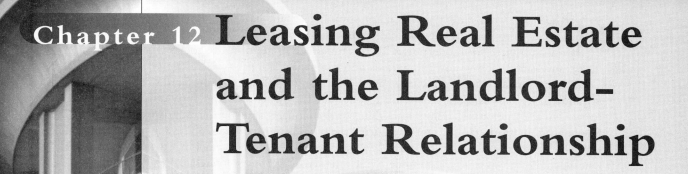

Chapter 12 Leasing Real Estate and the Landlord-Tenant Relationship

The lease arrangement between landlord and tenant has great economic significance today in its many residential and commercial applications. But the lease of olden times was unsuited for modern uses. To accommodate modern needs, courts and legislatures have transformed the law governing the landlord-tenant relationship.

At common law, a lease was viewed as a sale or transfer of land from landlord to tenant who acquired a *leasehold estate*. The tenant in effect became the owner of the property during the lease term, with the landlord retaining future rights to the property (called the **reversion**) but having few obligations relating to the premises during the time the tenant was in possession of the property. This approach to leases at common law was appropriate given the fact that the most prevalent type of lease was a farm lease under which the tenant's primary interest was in the land, not in the structures on the land. Tenants also had the tools and the skills to work the land and take care of the buildings on the property.

The Modern Development of Landlord–Tenant Law

With the industrial revolution, and the change from an agrarian to a manufacturing economy, and from a rural to an urban society, leases for residential and commercial purposes became more important to society than agricultural leases. Particularly in the multi-unit apartments that were created to house the urban workers of the nineteenth and twentieth centuries, the tenants' primary interest under the lease was not in the land but in the dwelling unit and the essential services (light, heat, water, etc.) provided as part of the lease arrangement. Similarly, rather than rely on their own skills to maintain the premises, tenants have become increasingly dependent on landlords for the upkeep and maintenance of the unit and the common areas of the premises.

The law of landlord-tenant has gradually evolved in response to the changing economic and social realities of modern leases. Today, landlord-tenant law is a unique combination of property and contract law principles. Rather than view a lease as a mere transfer of land, the modern approach stresses the contractual nature of the lease and the obligations imposed on the parties under that contract. The traditional common law rules governing the landlord-tenant relationship have therefore changed dramatically, particularly over the last thirty years. Two important developments have occurred. First, the courts have expanded the obligations of landlords under residential leases for the protection of tenants. For example, courts have imposed a duty on landlords to maintain residential premises in a habitable state, abandoning the common law rule that landlords had no obligation to maintain the leased property. Second, legislatures have subjected leases to greater regulatory control. Rent control laws and statutes restricting security deposits are just some of the examples of such legislative control.

Landlord-tenant law is not uniform, however. Substantial differences among the states exist in both the common law created by state courts and the rules developed by state legislatures. One attempt to harmonize this area of the law is the Uniform Residential Landlord and Tenant Act (URLTA), which has been adopted with modifications in 23 states.[1] Because of the importance of the URLTA as a model law, and its adoption in such a substantial minority of states, we will note its provisions in the chapter.

The Lease

The word **lease** is often used in two different ways in connection with the landlord-tenant relationship. From a legal perspective, a lease is the transfer by the landlord to the tenant of temporary possession and use of real property, called the **premises**, in exchange for a payment called rent. The landlord gives the tenant exclusive right to possess the property for a period of time (a property interest referred to as a **tenancy**) but retains ownership of the property, the tenant's rights reverting back to the landlord at the termination of the tenancy (the landlord's interest referred to as a reversion). Lease is also commonly used to refer to the document evidencing the tenancy, which sets forth the terms and conditions of the landlord-tenant contract. The term **rental agreement** is used under the URLTA to refer to the lease between landlord and tenant in a residential tenancy.

Creation of the Lease

The landlord-tenant relationship can be created in a number of ways. Like most contracts, a lease can be created by words or by conduct, orally or in writing. Although the parties ordinarily sign a written lease agreement in both residential and commercial settings, the law does not require all leases to be in writing. A writing is required only when the lease falls within the Statute of Frauds, the state law that specifies what contracts must be evidenced by a writing to be enforceable. The common law rule still followed in many states, including URLTA states, is that any lease for a period longer than one year must be in writing. State law differs on the matter, however, with some states mandating a writing only for longer-term leases. For example, Indiana[2] and Pennsylvania[3] require a writing only when the term of the lease is for more than three years.

If the law requires a writing, the writing must contain the essential terms of the lease contract, including an identification of the landlord and tenant, a description of the premises, the time period of the lease, and how the rent is to be computed. In some states, both parties must sign the lease, in others the common law rule is followed and only the "party to be charged" has to sign the lease. In these states, as with land sale agreements, only a party who signed the lease is bound to the contract, although taking possession and paying rent on property can substitute for a signature. To avoid any dispute on the matter, the better practice is for both the landlord and tenant to sign the lease.

Generally, the landlord and tenant are free to agree to whatever terms they want in a lease. However, state law may not permit certain provisions, and the courts have the power to declare terms of lease contracts illegal if they find that the lease violates public policy or the terms are unconscionable. For example, clauses in leases under which tenants agree to waive or forfeit their rights under protective landlord-tenant laws are usually not permitted because such provisions violate public policy. To prevent tenants from giving up their rights, and to encourage landlords to live up to their obligations under the law, most URLTA states prohibit waiver-of-rights provisions in rental agreements. Similarly, **exculpatory clauses**—clauses that release landlords from liability for their own negligence or other wrongdoing—have also been declared illegal by statute or by court decision. Some states, including many URLTA states, place restrictions on other types of provisions in leases that are onerous to tenants, including clauses calling on tenants to pay the landlord's attorney's fees in a lawsuit against the tenant. Attorney fee provisions in contracts are prohibited in some states while other jurisdictions enforce a clause calling for the payment of a reasonable attorney's fee when a landlord prevails in a lawsuit against a tenant.

Types of Tenancies

Traditionally, the law recognized four types of leasehold estates: the tenancy for years, the periodic tenancy, the tenancy at will, and the tenancy at sufferance. Although the common law categories are still important, modern law often treats the tenancy at will as a periodic tenancy.

BOX 12–1 TENANT SELECTION AND RETENTION

Tenant selection and retention is a major concern for landlords and property managers. It is estimated that one third of all apartment units turnover annually. Selecting trustworthy and stable tenants and adopting practices to retain good tenants can be one means of minimizing the costs and lost income associated with such turnover. Retention starts with careful selection of tenants. Landlords are advised to request detailed background information on prospective tenants in a comprehensive application form. This should be followed by a personal interview and background checks, particularly as to credit history and past tenancy experience. The goal of the selection process should be to identify reliable tenants who are financially sound and to eliminate those tenants who may cause problems. A number of retention strategies can also be employed to try to keep good tenants, including maintaining open lines of communication with tenants, being responsive to tenant complaints/problems, conducting periodic satisfaction surveys, establishing a sense of community in a residential complex, and economic incentives, such as rent concessions.

Selection and retention practices cannot violate federal, state, or local fair housing laws, and landlords need to be aware of the restrictions in such laws. The most important is the Fair Housing Act of 1968, a federal statute that prohibits housing discrimination on the basis of race, religion, ethnic background or national origin, gender, age, familial status, and disability. Familial status generally refers to whether the tenants have children under the age of 18 living with them, but also includes pregnant women. The disability protection requires landlords to make "reasonable accommodations" to enable disabled tenants to live in the premises. It includes allowing tenants to make changes in the dwelling unit (at the tenant's expense) that are necessary for the tenant to use the property. Some state and local laws also prohibit housing discrimination on other bases, such as marital status, sexual orientation, source of income, and military discharge status.

Policies and rules that might not appear to be discrimination can constitute illegal housing discrimination. Here are some examples:

- A "no pets" policy might be perfectly reasonable and legitimate for most tenants; however, a landlord may have to permit a blind tenant to keep a guide dog as a reasonable accommodation under the law.

- A landlord might have a legitimate concern that noise created by children of a prospective tenant would disturb elderly tenants in the building. Refusing to rent on that basis would be illegal; even steering the tenant to one particular unit in the building could constitute a fair housing violation.

- Rent concessions are a rational way to attract and keep good tenants, but discriminatory use of rent concessions would violate the law.

- Limiting the number of tenants in a dwelling unit appears to be nondiscriminatory, but applying such rules in a way that has a discriminatory impact on a family with children could violate the law. In one fair housing case, a single parent with one child successfully sued an apartment complex when she could not rent a one-bedroom apartment because of a "one person per bedroom" occupancy rule.

Proactive steps to retain good tenants makes sound business sense given the nature of the rental marketplace. Landlords need to be sensitive, however, to the implications their policies may have under the fair housing laws.

Tenancy for Years: Set-Term Leases

A lease for a fixed period of time, whether the period runs for several years or for six months, was called a **tenancy for years** at common law. Under such a set-term lease, the parties agree that the tenant will have possession of the premises for the period agreed upon in the lease. At the end of the term, the tenancy automatically ends without any further notice or action on the part of the landlord or tenant. If a tenancy is to continue at the end of the term, the parties will have to enter into a new lease.

Periodic Tenancies

A **periodic tenancy** is a lease arrangement under which the tenant leases the property for a period of time and the tenancy is automatically renewed at the end of the term for a like period of time unless either the landlord or the tenant take steps to terminate the tenancy. Week-to-week, month-to-month, and year-to-year leases are examples of common periodic tenancies. In contrast to a set-term lease, the landlord or the tenant must give advance notice in order to terminate a periodic tenancy. Thus, a month-to-month lease can usually be terminated only upon the giving one month's notice by one party or the other.

A periodic tenancy can be expressly created by a written lease or by oral agreement. It can also be created by the conduct of the parties. Sally leases an apartment to Bob, but the parties have no agreement as to the term of the lease. Bob takes possession of the premises and pays rent at the end of the month. A month-to-month tenancy has probably been created by the parties' actions. Similarly, the law often implies a periodic tenancy when the parties fail to enter into a binding lease but act as if there is a lease. If a tenant takes possession of property under an invalid lease and pays rent on a periodic basis, a periodic tenancy based on the period of the rent payment has probably been created. For example, Bob orally agrees to lease his farm to Sally for three years but no written lease is signed as required by the state Statute of Frauds. Nevertheless, Sally takes possession and pays rent on a yearly basis. Most courts would imply a year-to-year tenancy under the circumstances.

Short-term periodic tenancies (week-to-week and month-to-month leases) are most commonly used in residential leases. The flexibility of this form of lease, in terms of both ease of termination and ability to adjust the rent, make it attractive to some residential landlords. On the other hand, set-term leases are the norm in commercial tenancies as, for example, a lease of office space for three years. From the landlord's perspective, this type of lease has some distinct advantages. It locks the tenant into the lease of the premises for a time, thereby minimizing the costs relating to the turnover of units and finding new tenants. It also is one means of trying to retain good tenants, particularly in areas where the market for space is not tight. Set-term leases are also appealing to business tenants, the certainty and stability of the lease being essential for the tenant's business planning and operations.

Tenancy at Will

A **tenancy at will** exists if the landlord allows a tenant to take possession of the premises without any agreement as to the term of the lease. While Bob and Sally are negotiating for a long-term lease of a building, Bob allows Sally to move into the building and pay a nominal amount for rent. Sally would be considered a tenant at will until the set-term lease was executed. At common law, a tenancy at will could be terminated at the will of either party without any advance notice, as is required for periodic tenancies. Today, many states treat a tenancy at will as a periodic tenancy and require some advance notice to terminate it. Also, a tenancy at will may be transformed into a periodic tenancy by the actions of the parties. Accepting rent from a tenant at will on a weekly basis, for example, can be sufficient to create a week-to-week lease. From a practical standpoint, the tenancy at will has limited importance under modern landlord-tenant law.

Tenancy at Sufferance: Holdover Tenants

A tenant who is in possession of the premises under an enforceable lease but who remains in possession after the lawful termination of the lease creates a **tenancy at sufferance**. The landlord can consider the tenant a trespasser and evict the holdover tenant or enter into a new tenancy with him or her. If the landlord accepts rent from the holdover tenant, for example, a new tenancy is created by implication. At common law, no notice was required to terminate the tenancy at sufferance. A holdover tenant had usually received advance notice to terminate if the prior tenancy was a periodic one or was not entitled to notice if the prior tenancy was a set-term lease. Today, some states require notice to terminate a tenancy at sufferance.

As Case 12.1 demonstrates, the type of tenancy created has an effect on the rights and duties of the parties

Case 12.1

First Interstate Bank v. Tanktech,
864 P.2d 116 (Colo. 1993)

In May 1987, Tanktech, Inc., entered into a three-year lease with D & E Investment (D&E) under which Tanktech leased a building from D&E. The lease provided that the landlord, D&E, was responsible for the cost of repair and upkeep of the plumbing, electrical, and mechanical systems as well as the structural portions of the building. Prior to the lease, First Interstate obtained a mortgage on the building, which it foreclosed when D&E went into bankruptcy. After First Interstate acquired title to the property through the foreclosure, it did not enter into a new lease with Tanktech, but it allowed Tanktech to remain on the premises in exchange for monthly rental payments. In 1989, a ruptured water pipe caused a flood in the building and damage to Tanktech's property. Tanktech sued First Interstate for breach of the lease clause and for general negligence in the maintenance of the building. The trial court dismissed the contract claim, finding that the foreclosure extinguished the lease, and the jury concluded that First Interstate was not negligent. The Colorado Court of Appeals reversed. It applied the "holdover doctrine" and concluded that the terms of the preforeclosure lease governed because First Interstate accepted rent from Tanktech and allowed Tanktech to remain in possession of the premises, thereby creating an implied lease between the parties on the same terms as the prior lease.

ROVIRA, C. J.

Whether the landlord/tenant doctrine of holdover tenancy applies to a situation in which a subordinate lease has been extinguished through proper foreclosure proceedings is an issue of first impression for the court.

The operation of the holdover tenancy doctrine in Colorado is well established. A holdover tenant is one who continues in possession of the premises beyond the term of the lease. Once a lease expires and the tenant remains in possession of the premises, the landlord may elect to treat the tenant as a trespasser or may waive the wrong of holding over and continue the tenancy. In the later case, and in the absence of a new agreement, the law implies a new contract between the parties based upon the same terms and conditions as the expired lease.

In addition to being successive in time and occupying the same premises as the original lease, all of the Colorado holdover cases involve situations where the landlord and tenant were original parties to the lease. We have found no cases in which a third participant, not party to the original lease, was bound to the terms of the lease of which it might not be aware and which it had no power to negotiate. Here, there was no relationship between Tanktech and First Interstate which would justify binding First Interstate to the terms of the lease. . . . Common sense suggests that this is a correct result and that it would be inequitable to bind a party to the terms of a lease in which it had no ability to negotiate favorable or to reject unfavorable terms. . . .

Additionally . . . the court of appeals overlooks the distinction between a lease that is extinguished through foreclosure and one that simply expires at the end of the lease period. [T]he holdover doctrine applies when a tenant remains on the premises at the expiration of a lease term. In the holdover situation, both parties are aware of the terms of the lease. . . . Thus, if the landlord elects to treat the tenant as a holdover, a court will imply a contract based upon the terms of the original lease of which both parties are aware and to which they have previously consented. In contrast, once a lease is extinguished, there are no terms from which a court could imply a new contract. . . . Here, First Interstate took title to the property free and clear as if the preforeclosure D&E–Tanktech lease never existed; therefore, a court could not imply a contract based upon terms that were legally absent.

Finally, to complete our discussion we must determine what relationship existed between Tanktech and First Interstate subsequent to the foreclosure. . . . We find that by allowing Tanktech to remain on the premises and by accepting monthly payment, First Interstate entered into a month-to-month tenancy with Tanktech. . . . First Interstate owes the duty of care of a general landowner and was found not to have breached that duty by a jury.

Accordingly, the decision of the court of appeals is reversed and remanded with directions to reinstate the trial court's order . . . in favor of First Interstate.

QUESTIONS ABOUT CASE 12.1

1. Why is it assumed under the holdover doctrine that a landlord who accepts rent from a holdover tenant agrees to a tenancy under the same terms that existed under the lease between the parties?

2. Given the fact that First Interstate should have been aware of the terms of the lease when it allowed Tanktech to remain on the property without a new lease, do you agree with the court that it would be unfair to hold First Interstate to the terms of that lease?

Rights, Duties, and Liabilities of the Parties

The rights, responsibilities, and liabilities of the parties are determined by the terms of the lease and by the dictates of the law. The common law has always imposed certain duties on both the landlord and tenant that exist even in the absence of a specific provision in the lease. For example, a tenant's duty not to commit waste on the premises by damaging the property is an obligation imposed by law, which the landlord can enforce in an action for damages or other legal remedy. The terms of a lease can expand or limit the common law duties of the landlord and tenant. For example, a lease can require a tenant to maintain insurance on the property or give a security deposit to ensure against damage to the premises.

The most fundamental rights of the parties under a lease are the landlord's right to rent and the tenant's right to possession of the premises. These basic rights are discussed in the next two sections. Other important rights, liabilities, and remedies of the landlord and tenant are discussed in subsequent sections.

Landlord's Right to Rent

Rent represents the price paid to the landlord in exchange for the tenant's rights under the lease, including the right to possession of the premises. The lease should specify the amount of rent, when the rent is due, how it is to be paid, and any other charges the tenant must pay to the landlord (e.g., late fees, pet charges, parking fees) or third parties (e.g., for heat, electricity) incidental to the tenant's occupation of the leased premises. Some leases call for **prepaid rent**, that is, a payment of the last month's rent along with the first month's rent, although many state residential tenancy laws, including the URLTA, restrict the amount of prepaid rent that a landlord can collect. If the parties fail to agree as to the amount of rent, the law will require payment of an amount equal to the fair rental value of the property.

Rent can be computed in number of ways. Ordinarily, in a residential tenancy, rent will be a fixed dollar amount per month or period, often referred to as a **gross lease**. In leases for retail space, the landlord is usually entitled to a part of the tenant's profits under a **percentage lease**. Agricultural leases have historically called for payment of rent based on a share of the tenant's crops, a **crop-share lease**, although cash rent or a combination of cash and a share of the crops is often paid under modern farm leases.

Landlords may need the flexibility to change the rental payments in response to changing market conditions. Long-term commercial leases will often contain some form of **escalation clause** that allows the landlord to adjust the rent or that automatically increases the rent over time. We will discuss different types of commercial leases and escalation clauses in the next chapter. In a periodic tenancy, the landlord can increase the rent if he gives the tenant adequate notice of the change. Typically, landlords must provide the tenants one month's notice of a rent increase in a month-to-month tenancy, although in some states the notice time may be longer (e.g., 45 days in Hawaii[4]).

Rent control laws restricting the ability of landlords to increase the rent exist in some municipalities, including New York City and Washington, D.C. Such laws are a relic of the World War II era when the government imposed price controls to aid in the war effort and the nation experienced severe inflationary pressures. Under a rent control law, the amount of rent is initially fixed by the rent charged on a given date prior to the passage of the law. Adjustments to this base amount are permitted only according to the formula set forth in the law or with the approval of the rent control board. To ensure that landlords do not evict tenants in order to secure an increase in rent, evictions are permitted only for cause. In addition, some laws limit the ability of landlords to turn their properties into condominiums or other forms of residential housing to prevent any evasion of the law. Although designed to protect tenants from unreasonable rent increases, the laws have had a detrimental impact on the housing market, causing a loss of housing stock through abandonments and conversions, a lack of new investment in urban housing, and a shortage of housing in cities imposing such controls.

Tenant's Right to Possession of the Premises

A lease transfers the premises to the tenant for the term of the lease and gives the tenant the exclusive right to possess the leased property. This leasehold estate also gives the tenant the right to use the property for any lawful purpose not prohibited by the lease. It entitles the tenant to any rents or profits derived from the premises, although the lease may provide that the landlord has a right to a share of the profits. The tenant's possessory rights do not extend to the common areas of the property—apartment hallways, driveways, courtyards, and other areas open to all tenants—but the tenant does have a legal right to use the common areas for ordinary purposes as long as the tenant complies with any rules and regulations in the lease.

The tenant's right to possession allows the tenant to exclude all others from the premises, including the landlord. Leases contain an **implied covenant of quiet enjoyment**. Any action depriving the tenant of possession, by the landlord or by someone with superior rights to the property (e.g., a foreclosing mortgage holder), is a breach of the landlord's implied obligation of quiet enjoyment. Moreover, absent a right of entry in the lease, or one provided by law, the landlord has no right to enter the premises and interfere with the tenant's sole right of possession. As a result, standard form leases often give the landlord a limited right of entry to inspect the property and for other legitimate purposes. A right of entry is also provided by statute in most states. Entries to make repairs or improvements, to show the property to prospective tenants or purchasers, or in emergency situations, are often permitted under such laws. Usually, however, the landlord must give the tenant prior notice of the landlord's intent to enter the premises, and the landlord can enter only at a reasonable time.

Tenant's Right to Habitable Premises

Disputes between landlords and tenants over the condition of the leased premises have always been common. Landlords have sometimes allowed their properties to fall into disrepair, causing tenant complaints to landlords and code enforcement officials, rent withholding by tenants, and retaliatory eviction actions by landlords. In the residential market, landlords may not have an economic incentive to maintain their properties, and low-income tenants have never had the bargaining position necessary to force landlords to do necessary repairs. At common law, tenants had few rights when rental properties became dilapidated or when the landlord failed to make necessary repairs to the property or its systems. Because the lease was viewed as an effective transfer of the premises to the tenant, the tenant took the property with all of its defects, and the landlord had no continuing obligation to repair or maintain the premises other than the common areas of the premises.

This common law rule has given way to the realities of the rental market in a modern, urban society. Many courts have abandoned this rule and have adopted a **warranty of habitability** in residential leases (but not in commercial leases). Under this warranty of habitability, landlords have a duty to ensure that residential properties are habitable at the start of the lease and remain in a habitable state for the duration of the lease. The next case is an example of one court's approach to this issue.

Case 12.2

Wade v. Jobe
818 P.2d 1006 (Utah 1991)

In June 1988, Lyna Jobe and her three young children rented a house in Ogden, Utah, from Clyde Wade. After she took possession of the house, numerous problems arose, and within a few days, she had no hot water. The flame of the water heater had been extinguished by accumulated sewage and water in the basement, which also caused a foul odor in the house. The landlord pumped out the sewage and water and relighted the hot water heater, but the problems with the house continued. In November of 1988, Jobe notified Wade that she was withholding rent until the sewage problem was corrected. The Ogden City Inspector made several inspections of the house in December of 1988, finding numerous code violations and concluding that the sewage problem created a health and safety hazard to Jobe and her family. He issued a notice that the property would be condemned if the violations were not remedied. When Jobe moved out, Wade sued her for unpaid rent. She counterclaimed for breach of the implied warranty of habitability. The trial court rendered judgment for the landlord, following the common law rule that landlords are not under any obligation to maintain the leased premises. Jobe appealed to the Utah Supreme Court.

DURHAM, J.

The implied warranty of habitability has been adopted in other jurisdictions to protect the tenant as the party in the less advantageous bargaining position. The concept of a warranty of habitability is in harmony with the widespread enactment of housing and building codes, which reflect a legislative desire to ensure decent housing. It is based on the theory that the landlord warrants that the leased premises are habitable at the outset of the lease term and will remain so during the course of the tenancy.

In recent years, this court has conformed the common law in this state to contemporary conditions. . . . Consistent with prevailing trends in consumer law, products liability law, and the law of torts, we reject the rule of caveat emptor and recognize the common law implied warranty of habitability in residential leases.

The determination of whether a dwelling is habitable depends on the individual facts of each case. To guide the trial court . . . we describe some general standards that the landlord is required to satisfy. We note initially that the warranty of habitability does not require the landlord to maintain the premises in perfect condition, nor does it preclude minor housing code violations. Further, the landlord must have a reasonable time to repair. . . .

[T]he warranty of habitability requires that the landlord maintain "bare living requirements," and that the premises are fit for human occupation. Failure to supply heat or hot water, for example, breaches the warranty. . . .

Substantial compliance with building and housing code standards will generally [fulfill the] landlord's duty. . . . Evidence of violations involving health and safety, by contrast, will often sustain a tenant's claim. At the same time...a code violation is not necessary . . . so long as the claimed defect has an impact on the health or safety of the tenant.

Once the landlord has breached his duty to provide habitable conditions . . . the tenant may continue to pay rent . . . or withhold the rent. If the tenant continues to pay [rent], the tenant can bring an affirmative action to establish the breach and receive a reimbursement for excess rents paid. . . .

We remand this case to the trial court to determine whether the landlord breached the implied warranty of habitability. . . . If the trial court determines that he was not in breach, the landlord will be entitled to payment for all the past due rent. If the trial court determines that his breach of the warranty of habitability . . . rendered the premises virtually uninhabitable, the landlord's action to recover rent will fail. If the trial court determines that the landlord's breach partially excused the tenant's rent obligation, the tenant will be entitled to a percentage rent abatement.

QUESTIONS ABOUT CASE 12.2

1. Does the court's definition of habitability provide the clarity necessary for landlords to understand and comply with their obligations under the law?

2. If Jobe is successful in her counterclaim, what damages should be awarded for Wade's breach of the warranty of habitability?

The implied warranty of habitability has been adopted by many state courts, and a majority of state legislatures have passed statutes specifying the duties a landlord has with regard to the condition of residential properties. For example, Arizona's habitability statute, which was derived from the URLTA, requires a landlord to comply with all building codes; maintain in working order all appliances and systems (electrical, plumbing, etc.); supply running water and other services; and otherwise "put and keep the premises in a fit and habitable condition."

Can the lease between the parties eliminate or modify the warranty of habitability? To protect tenants from landlord attempts to escape their duties under habitability laws, many states have placed limits on agreements between landlords and tenants as to the repair and maintenance of the premises. For example, Delaware law requires that such an agreement be in a written contract separate from the lease, be supported by adequate consideration, involve work that is not necessary to bring the property up to the standards of the law, and not be an attempt on the part of the landlord to evade its duty of habitability.[5]

● Tenant's Remedies for Breach of the Warranty of Habitability

At common law, a tenant did not have any effective way to compel a landlord to make repairs or maintain the premises. Even when a landlord agreed in the lease to repair or maintain the premises, a tenant faced with a landlord who refused to make necessary repairs had only one possible remedy—sue the landlord for breach of the lease and recover damages. The tenant could not withhold rent because the common law viewed the tenant's duty to pay rent to be separate from any obligation on the landlord's part to maintain the premises. A tenant withholding rent could be lawfully evicted. Thus, tenants were not free to employ the most effective means to get landlords to comply with the lease terms.

Modern landlord-tenant law provides the tenant with several remedies in addition to the traditional common law suit for damages. In a majority of states, a tenant can withhold rent if a landlord breaches a warranty of habitability. Courts have treated the tenant's duty to pay rent as dependent upon the landlord's duties under the warranty of habitability. This rent-withholding remedy is not, however, universally accepted, and some states that recognize the warranty of habitability do not allow tenants to withhold rent or permit it only under certain circumstances. For example, North Carolina specifically prohibits a tenant from withholding rent without prior court approval.[6]

A second remedy, referred to as **repair and deduct**, is available in some states. This self-help remedy allows a tenant to repair the premises when the landlord fails to do so and then deduct the cost from the rent. In order to exercise this remedy, however, a tenant must ensure that the type of repair is covered under the self-help law and that the steps required under the repair-and-deduct statute are followed. Many states restrict the remedy to certain types of defects on the premises and place a dollar limitation on the repairs. So, for example, some states require the problem to be one that materially affects the tenant's safety or health or that involves necessary services, such as heat, light, water, or sanitation systems. In addition, the amount for the repairs is usually limited to the greater of a specific dollar figure (often $250 to $500) or all or part (usually one-half) of one month's rent. The tenant must also follow the procedures outlined in the law. First, the tenant must ordinarily notify the landlord of the condition that is in need of repair and of the tenant's intent to make repairs if the landlord fails to do so. Second, if the landlord fails to make the repairs in the time set by the law, the tenant can make the repairs and deduct the reasonable cost from the rent. States differ in terms of the time within which the landlord must repair as well as who can make the repairs. Some allow the tenant to make the repairs, but other laws require that the repairs be made by third-party contractors.

Box 12–2 You Be the Judge

In 1984, Anthony and Belinda Richie rented an apartment in Bethel, Ohio, from Dexter Miller at a rent of $200 per month. Throughout their occupancy, the apartment contained numerous defects, including dangerous wiring, holes in the floor, inadequate plumbing, and no heating. The Ritchies complained about these problems to Miller, but Miller disregarded most of their requests to repair the premises. In early 1987, the Clermont County Building Inspector declared the building a "serious hazard" under Ohio building codes. In February 1997, Miller sued to evict the Ritchies when they were delinquent in rent. The Ritchies counterclaimed for damages for breach of the statutory warranty of habitability. The tenants won at trial and were awarded damages of $3,000, apparently based on the cost to repair the property, with an offset to the landlord of $800 for unpaid rent. An Ohio appeals court reversed finding that the Ritchies had waived their rights by remaining on the premises without pursuing any other remedy under the law.

(a) Was there a breach of the warranty of habitability? (b) Should the tenant's occupancy of defective premises over an extended period of time constitute a waiver of the landlord's duty to maintain the property? (c) Should it constitute a waiver of the tenant's right to sue for damages for breach of the landlord's duty of habitability?

Tenant's Liability for Damages to the Premises

Tenants have a common law duty not to commit waste on the premises, which includes an obligation not to intentionally or carelessly damage the property. A tenant who negligently causes a fire on the premises, allows water to overflow from a bathtub or washing machine, breaks windows, doors, or locks, or otherwise causes or fails to prevent harm to the premises, has committed waste and is liable to the landlord for the resulting damages. At the end of the leasehold term, the tenant is under a duty to return the premises in the same condition it was in when the lease period began, reasonable wear and tear excepted. The lease between the parties may be more specific as to the tenant's duty regarding the condition of the premises, and many state laws set forth specific duties of a tenant in a residential lease.

To provide some protection from tenants damaging leased property, landlords usually require a **security deposit**. In the event of injury to the property, the landlord can withhold the deposit, or so much of it that is necessary to pay for the damages. In this way, the landlord avoids the expensive and time-consuming process of suing the tenant for the damages, which may result in a judgment that the landlord is unable to collect. On the other hand, security deposits can be abused by landlords. If a landlord without justification withholds a security deposit, the tenant will have to bring suit and bear the cost and expense of proceeding with an action. Practical and economic considerations may cause tenants not to pursue these remedies and simply give up the deposit even when the deposit is being withheld unlawfully.

Because of this potential for abuse, most states have passed security deposit legislation to protect tenants and to provide an appropriate balance between the rights of landlords and tenants. These laws vary from state to state but they have some common features. Limitations on the amount a landlord can retain as a security deposit are quite common. Usually a landlord is limited to one month's or two month's rent with accommodations in some states for additional amounts for tenants with pets. Many states require the monies to be deposited in a separate bank or trust account rather than commingled with the other funds of the landlord. The tenant is often entitled to interest at a set rate for the time that the money is on deposit. The landlord is given the right to withhold all or part of the security deposit to pay for damages to the property (including cleaning of the premises in many states), for unpaid rent, and for other damages relating to the tenant's breach of the lease, such as wrongful abandonment of the lease. In order to do so, however, the landlord must provide the tenant with an itemization or accounting of the damages (including supporting documentation in some states) within a set period of time (usually 14–30 days) after the termination of the lease. Failure to provide the written itemization often results in a forfeiture of the landlord's right to withhold the security deposit. In an attempt to minimize disputes as to whether a tenant caused specific damage to the property or whether a condition existed prior to the lease, landlords and tenants in some states must sign a checklist as to the condition of the premises, and any damages to the property, at the beginning and end of the tenancy. The tenant has a right to inspect the premises under such provisions. Security deposit laws also provide tenants with remedies in the event of a wrongful withholding of a security deposit. If withholding is willful or in bad faith, the tenant can often recover a punitive damage award (double or triple the amount of the security deposit), and/or attorney's fees and costs.

Landlord's Liability for Injuries to the Tenant and Others on the Premises

Liability for Dangerous Conditions on Premises

Consistent with the common law rule that the landlord was not under a duty to maintain the premises in a habitable state, the common law courts refused to hold landlords liable for physical injuries suffered by tenants or their guests that were caused by dangerous conditions on the premises. This general rule of nonliability was subject to at least four exceptions. First, a landlord could be held liable for injuries caused by undisclosed latent defects in the property of which the landlord was aware at the time of the lease. A "latent defect" is a defect that is hidden or one that would not be discoverable upon a reasonable inspection. Faulty wiring buried in the walls of a house would be an example of a latent defect. The landlord was liable for injuries to a tenant or guest caused by a latent defect only if he or she knew or should have known of it and failed to advise the tenant of the defect. Second, a "public use" exception held landlords liable for defects in the premises when the property was open to the public. Third, landlords could be held responsible for dangerous conditions in the common areas of the property. Landlords were under a duty to exercise reasonable care to protect tenants and guests from harm in common areas because they retained control over those areas. Lastly, when a landlord agreed to repair or voluntarily undertook repairs of the property, the common law imposed a duty to make the repairs in a reasonable fashion. Negligent repairs or failure to repair in violation of an express agreement in the lease could result in liability under this fourth exception. Despite these exceptions, the common law did not impose any broad duty to repair or maintain the premises in a safe condition and did not impose liability for most dangerous conditions that were open and obvious.

Today, some courts have abandoned the common law categories in favor of a general negligence standard in cases of landlord liability for injuries on the premises. This modern position imposes a duty on the part of landlords to exercise ordinary care in the maintenance of the premises and imposes liability for injuries to the tenant and others lawfully on the premises if the landlord was negligent. Circumstances such as the nature of the defect (latent or patent), the knowledge of the landlord, whether the dangerous condition was or was not in the common areas of the premises, are simply part of the overall analysis as to whether the landlord exercised reasonable care. Other courts have relied on the implied warranty of habitability to establish the requisite duty to impose liability for harm to tenant and guests. The court decisions are conflicting, however, with a number of state courts refusing to impose a duty on landlords based on the habitability warranty. Also, many courts continue to adhere to the common law rule and impose liability only under the four recognized exceptions.

Box 12–3 You Be the Judge

In 1988, Darline Newton moved from Idaho to Petersburg, Alaska, joining her husband Stan who had previously moved there. Stan and Darline rented a house in a trailer park owned by Enid and Fred Magill. Entry to the front door of the house was over a wooden walkway. The walkway was six feet long and five feet wide and was partly covered by an overhanging roof. The walkway would become slippery and hazardous when it was wet. It had no hand railing and no "antislip" material on its surface. On November 20, 1988, Darline slipped and fell on the walkway on her way to the house, breaking her ankle. She sued the Magills for negligence.

(a) Who will likely win the lawsuit? Consider what the outcome would be under the traditional common law rules as to landlord liability for dangerous conditions on the premises. (b) What is the tenant's best argument for the traditional rules? (c) Would the outcome be different if the court followed the modern approach and applied a general negligence standard to the claim? (d) What are the strongest arguments the landlord could make in defense of the suit? In your opinion, who should prevail?

Liability for Criminal Harm to Tenant

The traditional rule was that a landlord had no duty to protect tenants from the criminal acts of third parties and, therefore, had no liability for injuries to tenants from crimes committed on the premises. This rule was in line with the general common law position that no person is under a duty to protect another from criminal harm unless a special relationship exists between the parties or one party voluntarily assumes responsibility to protect another from criminal harm. Although the common law recognized such a special relationship in the innkeeper-guest context, the common law did not view the landlord-tenant relationship in this way. Thus, landlords had virtually no liability at common law for injuries to tenants caused by the criminal acts of third persons even when those crimes were committed on the premises and inadequate security measures were a contributing factor.

In recent years, many courts have abandoned the common law rule and have imposed a duty on landlords to protect tenants from criminal harm. The courts have created several theories of liability in this area. Some courts have found a duty to protect a tenant from criminal harm if the circumstances are such that a particular criminal act was foreseeable. Foreseeable means that the landlord could reasonably have expected a criminal act to occur either because of prior crimes of the same type on the premises or in the area. Some courts limit this duty to protect a tenant from foreseeable criminal acts to the common areas of the premises—stairways, elevators, garages and parking areas, and other open areas. The rationale for this rule is that the landlord is in control of the common areas and in a superior position to provide security in those areas. Unlike individual apartments or units, a tenant cannot provide safety measures in the common areas of the premises. This theory is actually an extension of the common law rule that a landlord is responsible for the maintenance of common areas. Finally, a landlord can assume a duty to protect the tenant from criminal harm. If the landlord agrees to provide security in the lease or voluntarily provides security measures on the premises, the landlord may be liable for a failure to employ reasonable security measures or to maintain existing security systems.

How we determine foreseeability is critically important in these cases because liability often depends upon whether the landlord could reasonably foresee the criminal act. The next case represents one court's approach to the question of foreseeability.

Case 12.3

Timberwalk Apartments v. Cain
972 S.W.2d 749 (Tex. 1998)

The plaintiff, Tammie Cain, was raped in her apartment by an intruder, Peter Saenz, about 3:00 A.M. on a Sunday morning. After the conviction of Saenz for sexual assault, the plaintiff sued Timberwalk Apartments, the owner of the 300-unit apartment complex in which she lived, and their management company, Sovereign Management. She contended that the defendants were negligent by failing to provide adequate security for their residents, specifically pin locks for sliding glass doors, alarm systems in the apartments, adequate lighting on the premises, routine surveillance, and guards. At trial, the facts surrounding the incident were undisputed except for the incidence of criminal activity at the apartment complex and in the surrounding area. The only serious crimes ever reported at the Timberwalk Apartments were the burglary of an automobile and the theft of another. No prior sexual assaults has been reported in the complex and the incidence of such crimes in the surrounding areas was low. The jury found for the defendants, but the Texas Court of Appeals reversed and remanded the case for a new trial. On appeal to the Texas Supreme Court, Timberwalk argued that it owed no duty to protect Cain from the assault because the attack on her was unforeseeable.

HECHT, J.

The foreseeability of an unreasonable risk of criminal conduct is a prerequisite to imposing a duty of care on a person who owns or controls premises to protect others on the property from the risk. . . . "Crime may be visited upon virtually anyone at any time or place," but criminal conduct of a specific nature at a particular location is never foreseeable merely because crime . . . may possibly occur almost anywhere. . . . In determining whether the occurrence of certain criminal conduct on a landowner's property should have been foreseen, courts should consider whether any criminal conduct previously occurred on or near the property, how recently it occurred, how often it occurred, how similar the conduct was to the conduct on the property, and what publicity was given the occurrence to indicate that the landowner knew or should have known about them.

For a landowner to foresee criminal conduct on property, there must be evidence that other crimes have occurred on the property or in its immediate vicinity. Criminal activity occurring farther from the landowner's property bears less relevance because crime rates may be expected to vary significantly within a large geographic area. . . .

Foreseeability also depends on how recently and how often criminal conduct has occurred in the past. The occurrence of a significant number of crimes within a short time period strengthens the claim that the particular crime at issue was foreseeable. . . .

The previous crimes must be sufficiently similar to the crime in question as to place the landowner on notice of the specific danger. . . . The prior crimes need not be identical. A string of assaults and robberies in an apartment complex make the risk of other violent crimes, like murder and rape, foreseeable. . . .

The publicity surrounding the crimes helps determine whether a landowner knew or should have known of a foreseeable danger. A landowner often has actual knowledge of previous crimes occurring on the premises through tenants' reports. . . . However, unreported criminal activity on the premises is no evidence of foreseeability. . . . [W]hen the occurrence of criminal activity is widely publicized, a landlord can be expected to have knowledge of such crimes. . . .

These factors—proximity, recency, frequency, similarity, and publicity—must be considered together in determining whether criminal conduct was foreseeable. . . .

The evidence in the present case is that no violent personal crimes occurred at the Timberwalk Apartments for ten years preceding Cain's sexual assault. . . . In the year preceding [the] assault, only one sexual assault occurred within a one-mile radius [of the complex]. That same year, six assault-type crimes occurred in neighboring apartment[s]. There is no evidence that any of these crimes was ever reported in the media, or that Timberwalk knew or had any way of knowing about them.

Applying the factors . . . we conclude that the risk that a tenant would be sexually assaulted was in no way foreseeable by Timberwalk.

Accordingly, we . . . reverse [the judgment of the court of appeals] as to Timberwalk, and render judgment that Cain take nothing against Timberwalk.

QUESTIONS ABOUT CASE 12.3

1. Had Timberwalk known of the six assault-type crimes in neighboring apartments, would that fact have changed the court's conclusion regarding foreseeability?

2. Should courts limit the landlord's duty to protect a tenant from foreseeable criminal harm to the common areas of the leased premises or should it apply to crimes like the rape of Cain that occur in a tenant's apartment unit?

Landlord's Remedies for Breach of the Lease

Landlords have a number of remedies in the event a tenant fails to pay rent, abandons the property, holds over at the end of the lease term, or otherwise breaches the terms of the lease. The two primary remedies are an eviction action to recover possession of the premises and a suit for damages for breach of the lease.

Eviction by Unlawful Detainer Action

Eviction of a tenant is accomplished in a speedy legal proceeding called a **forcible** or **unlawful detainer** action. It is most often employed when a tenant defaults on the payment of rent and the landlord opts to terminate the lease and recover possession of the premises. The suit is ordinarily commenced by serving the tenant with a three-day notice to quit—a demand that the tenant comply with the terms of the lease or vacate the property. If the tenant fails to comply within that time, the landlord can then proceed to file the suit and schedule a trial without the ordinary delays associated with the justice system. A hearing is scheduled within a short time of the filing, at which time the landlord must establish the case for eviction. At trial, the tenant has few defenses other than to show that he or she is not in default under the lease. If the landlord prevails, the landlord can then secure possession from the tenant, with the assistance of the sheriff if necessary.

In most states, a tenant can raise the defense of **retaliatory eviction** in an unlawful detainer action. Because a landlord can terminate a periodic tenancy *without cause* by simply giving notice to a tenant and thereafter securing an eviction in the summary forcible detainer process, the eviction process can be abused by landlords. For example, a landlord can retaliate against a tenant who complains to local code enforcement officers about unsafe or unhealthy conditions on the premises by terminating the lease and evicting the tenant. Given the potential for such bad faith evictions, many states have adopted laws preventing a landlord from evicting a tenant when that eviction is in retaliation for the tenant asserting tenant rights under the law. Some states also have adopted the defense of retaliatory eviction as a matter of common law through court decisions.

The facts surrounding a particular eviction may not derive from such a simple scenario. What if the tenant is in default in the payment of rent or has violated the terms of the lease or complained to the authorities only *after* receiving an eviction notice? Determining the motivation of the landlord is a difficult judgment to make, particularly when the facts are conflicting or in dispute. Also, a landlord can retaliate in a number of ways short of eviction (e.g., by increasing the rent). State statutes and court decisions have attempted to resolve these issues. The URLTA and many state residential tenancy laws prohibit any retaliatory action, including evictions and increasing rents, in response to a tenant reporting a violation to local housing authorities or complaining to the landlord about the uninhabitability of the premises. A presumption is often built into the law that any retaliatory action taken within a certain period of time (usually six months or a year) of a tenant's complaint is presumed to be unlawful unless the landlord presents evidence to the contrary. The defense is not available, however, when the tenant's complaint occurred only after a landlord gave notice of a change in the lease, or if the tenant is in default in rent, or the problem complained of is not a violation of the law or was caused by the tenant's actions. When the court finds that a retaliatory eviction occurred, it will usually enjoin the landlord from evicting the tenant. The landlord will be allowed to evict the tenant at some time in the future only if the landlord has a non-retaliatory reason for the termination.

Damages for Breach or for Holding Over

The landlord also has a right to recover damages from the tenant in the event of a breach of the lease by the tenant or a wrongful holding over. In cases where a tenant stays in possession after the termination of the lease, statutes often provide that the tenant is liable for double the amount of the rent for the period the tenant unlawfully held over. Otherwise, a landlord can recover the actual damages caused by the tenant's breach of the lease.

This remedy is most commonly used when a tenant abandons the premises prior to the end of the term. At common law, the landlord could accept a return of the property, that is, a **surrender** of the lease, and thereby terminate the tenancy by mutual agreement, or hold the vacating tenant liable for rent as it became due. The landlord was not under an obligation to retake possession of the premises or to find a substitute tenant. In fact, if the landlord retook possession, it could be interpreted as an *acceptance* of the tenant's surrender and offer to terminate the lease, releasing the tenant from any further obligation to pay rent.

To protect landlords from tenants who unlawfully abandon leased property, modern leases usually contain a **surrender clause** that permits, but does not require, a landlord to retake possession and relet the premises for the tenant's account for the remainder of the tenant's term. If the landlord, acting reasonably, receives a lower rental from the new tenant than the original tenant owed, the landlord has a cause of action against the original tenant for the difference.

● Landlord's Duty to Mitigate Damages

Whether a landlord is under a legal duty to retake possession and relet the premises upon an abandonment by the tenant is an issue that has divided the states. Under contract law, if a party to a contract breaches it, the nonbreaching party has a **duty to mitigate** his or her damages. That is, the nonbreaching party has a duty to minimize the losses that will result from the breach. For example, an employee who has been wrongfully fired must, by taking reasonable steps to find substitute employment in his or her field, minimize the damages caused by the employer's breach of contract. A nonbreaching party who fails to mitigate damages cannot recover the amount of damages or losses that could have been avoided. Thus, a fired employee who can find a comparable job at the same salary one month after wrongful termination can hold the employer liable only for one month's lost salary.

Under traditional leasing law, a landlord whose tenant abandoned the premises had no duty to mitigate damages, so had no obligation to find a substitute tenant. The landlord could leave the property vacant for the remaining term of the lease and hold the tenant liable for the unpaid rent. A minority of states still follow this rule. Courts in New York[7] and Pennsylvania,[8] for example, have recently refused to impose a duty to mitigate in the landlord-tenant context. These states have opted for the traditional position because it has the benefit of simplicity and avoids a number of difficult issues concerning the extent of the landlord's duty to mitigate. Indeed, imposing any duty to mitigate damages is considered unfair to landlords, because it allows a tenant who is acting wrongfully to force an innocent landowner to rerent the premises at his or her expense.

Most states, however, either by statute or court decision, impose a duty on a landlord to mitigate damages, at least under certain circumstances. Recent high court decisions in Texas,[9] Utah,[10] and Vermont[11] have adopted this modern approach. Requiring a landlord to retake possession of the premises abandoned by a tenant and to take reasonable steps to find a substitute tenant is consistent with contract law principles relating to mitigation. It also is considered sound from a public policy perspective, many courts reasoning that it is better to have a rule that encourages owners to put property to productive use, rather than leave property idle and unproductive.

Transfer of the Landlord's or Tenant's Interest

In the absence of some restriction in the lease, either party to a lease is free to transfer his property interest in the premises without the other party's consent. Frequently, however, modern leases restrict the right of the tenant to transfer his tenancy by requiring the landlord's consent for any assignment or sublease. In contrast, the landlord's right to transfer his interest is not limited by the typical lease; however, the new owner ordinarily takes the property subject to the tenant's leasehold interest.

Sale or Transfer of the Property by the Landlord

The owner-landlord is generally free to sell or transfer the property subject to the lease. The landlord's rights can be transferred in whole or in part. Sometimes the landlord will simply transfer his right to rental payments to a third-party creditor, called an assignment of rights under the leasehold contract, without any transfer of ownership rights or title to the property. At other times, a landlord will sell the property to a third-party purchaser, transferring the entire interest in the property to the buyer. The landlord has the right to sell his or her interest without the tenant's consent unless the lease restricts the landlord's right to do so. In some leases, for example, the tenant will have an option to purchase and/or a right of first refusal that limits the landlord's right to sell his or her interest in the property to another party. Ordinarily, however, the landlord's rights are not so encumbered. The tenant is protected by the law; the new owner of the property will take it subject to the existing lease; therefore, the tenant's right to continued possession of the premises must be respected by the new owner. In addition, the new owner will often be bound by the terms and conditions of the lease, either by express assumption of those duties in the contract of purchase or by implied obligation under law to comply with the lease terms.

Assignments and Subleases

A tenant can transfer the leasehold interest in one of two ways, by an **assignment** or a **sublease**. The difference between the two is in terms of the extent to which the tenant transfers his or her interest to the third party. In an assignment, the tenant's *entire interest* (or remaining interest) under the lease transfers to an *assignee*. The assignee tenant takes possession of the premises for the remaining term of the lease with all of the original tenant's rights under the lease. In a sublease, the tenant merely transfers some of his or her interest in the premises to a *subtenant* and retains all other rights under the lease. So, for example, Bob, a student tenant under a one-year lease, subleases his apartment to Sally during the three months of the summer while he is away from school. Sally will vacate the premises in the fall and Bob will move back into the apartment. This arrangement would be considered a sublease. Sally is the subtenant and Bob has essentially become her landlord under the sublease.

Liability of the Parties Under an Assignment or Sublease

The assignment of a lease involves two things: the *assignment* (to an assignee) of the tenant's remaining possessory interest under the lease, and the *delegation* (to the assignee) of the tenant's duties imposed on the tenant by the lease—for example the duty to pay rent. By agreeing to pay the rent, the assignee tenant assumes the original tenant's duty of payment and thus replaces the original tenant as the *principal debtor*. The landlord can, therefore, hold the assignee tenant liable for a failure to pay rent or breach of any other term of the lease. Note that the assignee tenant also acquires all rights under the lease, and thus can enforce the terms of the lease against the landlord.

The original tenant remains liable to the landlord if the assignee tenant breaches the lease because an assignment of a contract does not release a party from obligations under a contract without the other party's consent. The original tenant is considered a *surety* who guarantees that the assignee will perform the original tenant's obligations under the lease. Thus, if the assignee tenant does not pay the rent, the landlord can hold the original tenant responsible for it. The original tenant's recourse is to sue the assignee tenant for the rent paid to the landlord. To secure a release of the original tenant's obligations, the parties would have to enter into a *novation* agreement. A novation entails a substitution of parties and a release of the original party under a contract. To affect a novation, a landlord has to agree to release an existing tenant from any further liability and to look exclusively to a new substitute tenant for performance under a lease. Without a novation, the landlord can hold both the original tenant and the assignee tenant responsible for nonpayment of rent.

In contrast, a subtenant is not directly liable *to the landlord* under a sublease. The landlord is not a party to the sublease nor does the subtenant acquire any rights or assume any duties under the original lease. The subtenant's liability runs to the original tenant who is the only party liable to the landlord under the lease. Therefore, under a sublease, a landlord can hold only the original tenant liable for nonpayment of rent or performance of the lease terms, and only the tenant can hold the subtenant liable under their sublease.

BOX 12–4 APPLY YOUR KNOWLEDGE

In 1968, By-Pass Plaza, Inc., leased property to A&P for a grocery store. The written agreement provided that the lease would end on August 31, 1984, but the tenant had four options to renew the lease for five-year terms. Prior to the end of the original lease period, A&P assigned the lease to M&H. M&H then exercised the first option to renew and entered into a "sublease," transferring the premises to Burgess, Inc. The sublease provided that M&H was leasing the premises to Burgess for the remainder of the term of the lease between By-Pass and A&P and for the five-year extension of the lease. M&H later sold its business and transferred its interest in the lease to Fleming, Inc. When the first five-year extension period was about to end, Fleming notified Burgess that it would not be exercising the option to extend for another five-year period under the lease. Fleming began construction of a new grocery store at a nearby location. Burgess claimed that it had a right to exercise the option to renew under the lease and notified By-Pass that it was exercising its right to renew. Fleming objected and a lawsuit ensued.

Burgess made two arguments in the case. First, it claimed that its agreement with M&H was an assignment, not a sublease, because all of M&H's rights were transferred to it under the agreement. Second, it argued that even if it was a subtenant, it had a right to exercise the option to renew. How should these issues be resolved?

Restrictions on the Tenant's Right to Assign or Sublet

In the absence of a restriction in the lease or by statute, a tenant has the right to assign or sublet the premises without the consent of the landlord. Although statutes restricting tenants' rights to transfer exist in a few states, most states permit a tenant to transfer his or her interest in the property unless the lease restricts the tenant's rights. As a result, both residential and commercial leases usually restrict the right of the tenant to transfer the leasehold interest to a third party. Such restrictions can take many forms. The lease may prohibit any assignment or sublease or it may require the consent of the landlord for any transfer of the lease. Because the landlord has a legitimate interest in controlling the persons in possession of the landlord's property, the courts have traditionally enforced such restrictions.

On the other hand, restrictions on the tenant's right to transfer constitute a "restraint on alienation" (i.e., such terms restrict the ordinary right of the individual to transfer his or her property). Because restraints on alienation have been disfavored by the courts, the law takes a strict approach to any clause restricting a tenant's right to transfer. Thus, if a clause in a lease prohibits a tenant from assigning the property, but is silent as to the right to sublet the premises, the courts will interpret this clause as a restriction only on the tenant's right to assign the property. Under this strict interpretation, such a clause would not prevent the tenant from subletting the premises. As a result, leases are now carefully drafted to prevent any type of transfer by a tenant.

The most common form of restriction on the tenant's right to transfer is a clause requiring the consent (ordinarily in writing) of the landlord for an assignment or sublease. Standard form leases usually do not qualify or impose any conditions upon the landlord's discretion to decide whether to consent to a transfer. Under this type of consent provision, called a **silent consent clause**, a landlord can refuse to permit an assignment for any reason or for no reason at all. The prevailing judicial view is that a landlord can arbitrarily refuse to consent to a transfer under a silent consent clause. As a result, some tenants bargain for qualifying language that consent will not be "withheld unreasonably." In that event, the landlord must have some reasonable basis for withholding consent to an assignment or sublease. In addition, tenants have challenged the landlord's right to arbitrarily refuse consent under a silent consent clause and some courts now require the landlord to exercise discretion in good faith. In the next chapter, we will note the importance of this issue in the commercial lease context and the position adopted by a minority of state courts that consent cannot be withheld unreasonably, even under a silent consent clause.

Termination of the Lease

Expiration of the Lease and Notice to Terminate

The type of tenancy and the lease terms will determine when a lease will terminate, whether notice to the tenant is required to terminate it, and the amount of advance notice that must be provided to the tenant. In a periodic tenancy, notice is required to terminate. The advance notice required depends on the type of periodic tenancy and varies from state to state. In many states, the common law approach is followed. It requires notice be given at least one period in advance. So, a month-to-month tenancy requires thirty days' notice to terminate, a week-to-week requires at least seven days. In other states, a different period of time is set. Under the URLTA, ten days' notice is necessary to terminate a week-to-week tenancy and sixty days' notice for a month-to-month tenancy. For a year-to-year tenancy, the common law required six months' notice. Modern statutes often reduce that period down to 30–90 days. The parties can also change the notice required to terminate by specifying a different period of time in the lease, but the courts in many states will not permit the statutory time to be shortened by agreement—only lengthened.

With a set-term lease, no notice is required to end the tenancy; the lease automatically expires at the end of the lease term. However, the lease may require some advance notice to the landlord that the tenant will be vacating the premises or for the tenant to extend the lease term under an option to renew in the lease. For example, some residential leases require a tenant to notify the landlord sixty days in advance that the tenant will vacate the property. Also, in the event a tenant holds over, and the landlord elects to continue the tenancy as a periodic one, notice will be thereafter required to terminate the new lease, as in any periodic tenancy.

BOX 12–5 WHEN TO GIVE NOTICE TO TERMINATE?

Yvonne Morrison leased a lot to Linda Smith for $60 per month, payments to made on the first of the month. Morrison attempted to terminate the lease by giving Smith a notice to terminate dated June 15. The applicable Tennessee statute called for thirty days notice to terminate a month-to-month tenancy. Was the notice effective?

A Tennessee appeals court held that Morrison's notice was not effective to terminate the lease as of July 15. Applying the general rule followed in other jurisdictions, the court held that the notice must be thirty days before the commencement of the next month's term. Because the next month's term commenced on July 1, the notice was ineffective to terminate the tenancy in July. The court did hold, however, that the notice was effective to terminate the lease as of August 1 since the necessary thirty days notice before August 1 was provided to the tenant.

This interpretation of the notice requirements of the landlord-tenant law is well accepted by the courts in other states. One issue that is not as clear is whether notice can be given on the first of the month to terminate a tenancy at the end of the month. Some courts permit the notice to be given on the first. The Tennessee court suggested that Morrison could have given notice on June 1 to terminate the tenancy as of July 1, citing a prior Tennessee decision to that effect. In other states, the notice must precede the commencement of the tenancy period and, therefore, notice must be given one day before the first of the month. The lesson for landlords may be to provide tenants with a notice to terminate well in advance of the deadline, if possible, to reduce any "technical" problem with the termination notice.

Surrender and Acceptance

As in any contract, the parties can opt to cancel a lease by mutual agreement. The vehicle to accomplish a mutual rescission of the lease is a **surrender and acceptance**; the tenant must surrender the property to the landlord and the landlord must accept the return of the property. Surrender and acceptance can be express or implied. A deed signed by the tenant conveying the property to the landlord is an example of an express surrender and acceptance. An implied surrender and acceptance is based upon the conduct of the parties. At common law, if a tenant abandoned the property and the landlord took possession and relet the premises, the courts often considered this a termination of the lease, the tenant's abandonment being an offer to surrender, which was then accepted by the landlord's retaking possession of the premises.

The concept of an implied surrender and acceptance has always placed a landlord in a difficult position when a tenant abandons the property and fails to pay any further rent. At common law, the landlord could leave the property vacant and seek to hold the defaulting tenant liable for any unpaid rent. This strategy was risky, however, because the landlord was forced to look exclusively to the original tenant for the unpaid rent, and that party might be insolvent or the rent might be otherwise uncollectible. To avoid this risk, most modern leases contain a surrender clause that allows a landlord to reenter abandoned property and relet the property for the tenant's account. Under such clauses, the tenant continues to be liable for rent under the lease, but his or her liability is reduced by the amount of rent paid by any new tenant. Also, in states that impose a duty to mitigate damages when a tenant vacates the property, the courts will not necessarily follow the common law rule relating to an implied surrender and acceptance. If a landlord's conduct in reletting the property is consistent with (if not required by) the duty to mitigate, it will not usually be interpreted as an acceptance of the tenant's offer to cancel the lease.

Actual and Constructive Evictions

As we have noted in the prior section on the rights and duties of the parties, a tenant has a right of undisturbed possession of the premises. If a landlord evicts the tenant by physical force or by locking the tenant out of the premises, this **actual eviction** entitles the tenant to treat the lease at an end and cease paying rent. This wrongful termination is also a breach of the lease for which the landlord is liable to the tenant for damages.

A **constructive eviction**—a material breach of the landlord's implied covenant of quiet enjoyment that impairs the tenant's right to undisturbed possession—also results in a termination of the lease and releases the tenant from any further obligation to pay rent. A constructive eviction occurs when the landlord's actions render the premises unfit for occupancy or for the purposes for which the property was rented. In one case, a court found a constructive eviction when a frozen pipe in a residential apartment left the tenant without heat and water for two months.[12] A landlord's failure to provide adequate heating and air conditioning for a restaurant and bar was also considered a constructive eviction since these services were essential for the tenant's business.[13] To claim a constructive eviction, the tenant must treat the landlord's conduct as an eviction and abandon the property. A tenant who abandons the property can hold the landlord liable for any damages caused by the constructive eviction. On the other hand, a tenant who fails to vacate within a reasonable time of the detrimental actions of the landlord cannot rely on the doctrine of constructive eviction.

A constructive eviction also can be based on the landlord's failure to control the conduct of other tenants. Courts have found constructive evictions when the actions of other tenants constitute a nuisance such as with excessive noise, constant disturbances, or illegal activities on the premises. However, the landlord must have notice of the problem and be given an opportunity to correct it. If the landlord fails to act, and the tenant's use and enjoyment of the premises is substantially impaired, the tenant can claim a constructive eviction.

Destruction of the Premises

At common law, destruction of the premises did not result in a termination of the lease and thus a tenant had a continuing obligation to pay rent despite casualty to the building or to the part of the building being rented by the tenant. This rule was based upon the common law view of a lease as a transfer of property to the tenant and the notion that the tenant could continue to use and profit from the land, which was the primary purpose of early leases. The common law rule has been abrogated by statute in most states today, at least with respect to residential and commercial leases. Total destruction of the premises by fire or other casualty rendering the premises

BOX 12–6 YOU BE THE JUDGE

Echo Consulting Services Inc. leased the downstairs floor of a building for its business under a written lease that also gave Echo a "common right of access." The North Conway Bank purchased the building and became Echo's landlord when it assumed the lease. To make the main, street-level floor of the building fit for its banking operations, the bank undertook a series of renovations on the building. The renovations, occurring on and off during 1987, created noise, dirt, and sometimes caused interruptions in electrical service to the building. The remodeling work also blocked Echo's access to the parking lot and door in the rear of the building. Employees of Echo had to use the street-level parking lot in the front of the building for access, walking down to Echo's offices. The renovation work disrupted Echo's business operations, although the problems were intermittent and temporary.

Echo sued the bank claiming a constructive eviction. Should the court find a constructive eviction under the circumstances?

unfit for its intended use without the fault of either party results in a termination of the lease and discharges a tenant from any further obligation to pay rent. The URLTA rule provides that in the event of destruction of the premises, the tenant can terminate the tenancy by vacating and so notifying the landlord or vacate the damaged part of the premises and be entitled to a proportionate reduction in rent.

Modern leases often have clauses to resolve issues relating to the destruction of or damage to the premises. They typically provide for a termination of the lease (or at least for an option to terminate) in the event of a nonrepairable casualty to the premises or for an abatement in the rent when the damage is less extensive. The parties should carefully consider the language of such clauses to ensure a fair resolution of the matter, especially in the event of a partial destruction of the premises. This consideration is particularly important to tenants because some courts continue to follow the common law rule (and hold tenants liable for rent despite casualty to the premises) if the issue is not controlled by statute or governed by language in the parties' lease.

Self-Study Questions

1. (a) What is a lease? (b) What is a rental agreement? (c) What are the different ways the word *lease* is used in connection with the landlord-tenant relationship?

2. (a) How can the landlord-tenant relationship be created? (b) When does the law require a lease to be in writing? (c) What is the major advantage of having a written lease? (d) What terms should be included in any lease?

3. Explain the four types of tenancies that have traditionally been recognized by the law.

4. What is the implied covenant of quiet enjoyment and what protection does it provide the tenant?

5. (a) What is the common law rule relating to a landlord's obligation to repair or maintain the premises? (b) What are the exceptions to the rule?

6. Explain the importance to the residential tenant of the implied warranty of habitability.

7. How do security deposit laws balance the rights of landlords and tenants with respect to security monies deposited with landlords?

8. (a) What is a latent defect? (b) What liability does a landlord have to a tenant for injuries caused by latent defects on the premises? (c) How is the common law rule relating to latent defects differ-

ent from the modern approach to the land-lord's liability for dangerous conditions on the premises?

9. (a) Explain the differences between an assignment and a sublease. (b) Under what circumstances can a tenant assign or sublet the premises?

10. (a) What is a surrender and acceptance? (b) Explain how the issue of mitigation and the concept of an implied surrender and acceptance are related. (c) How should the courts resolve the issue of the duty to relet the premises upon an abandonment of a tenancy?

Case Problems

1. Michael Rogers leased a commercial building from Vernon and Alma Sage in Missoula, Montana. The parties had an oral lease with rent payable on the first of the month. Rogers agreed to put the utilities in his name and keep the premises clean. On July 24, 1989, the Sages sent Rogers a termination notice because of his failure to pay rent on time, failure to pay the utility bills, and his damage to the property. The parties reached an agreement to postpone the termination until October 1 if Rogers met certain conditions. He was to pay his rent on time, pay the utility bill, and pay $500 for cleaning the premises. He paid the utility bill but did not comply with the other conditions. The Sages expected him to move out but Rogers remained in the premises on October 1. The Sages gave him another termination notice on October 3 which gave him until November 1 to vacate. They later filed a lawsuit on December 1 claiming that they were entitled to possession. Rogers claimed that the notice to terminate dated October 3 was not sufficient since it did not give him 30 days before the November 1 deadline to vacate. The Sages argued that the notice was sufficient to terminate the tenancy as of December 1. (a) What type of tenancy did the parties create? (b) Should the October 3 notice be effective to terminate the tenancy as of December 1 or should the Sages be required to serve another notice to terminate? (c) What remedies do the Sages have if Rogers wrongfully refuses to vacate? *Sage v. Rogers*, 848 P.2d 1034 (Mont. 1993).

2. Shelley Morton leased an apartment in Baltimore, Maryland, that was owned by Amberwood Associates Limited Partnership and managed by Monocle Management. Despite a lease provision prohibiting pets, Morton kept her boyfriend's pit bull, named Rampage, on the premises. Various employees of the management company had encounters with Rampage, a vicious and threatening animal. While visiting Morton in her apartment, Shanita Matthews' 16-month-old son was attacked and killed by the dog. Matthews sued the owner and manager for negligence in the death of the child. Assume that the tenant's guest will be treated like the tenant. (a) What theories of liability could Matthews assert to recover damages from the defendants? (b) What are the owner's best arguments? Consider both the traditional common law rules and the modern approach to landlord liability for injuries on the premises. (c) Should the lease prohibition and the landlord's awareness of the dog's presence and vicious tendencies be factors in the resolution of the case? (d) Should the fact that the attack occurred inside the apartment be a factor? *Matthews v. Amberwood Associates*, 719 A.2d 119 (Md. 1998).

3. Ernest Winer leased the main floor of a house in Caspar, Wyoming, to Carla Wise. He allowed Carla to use the laundry facilities in the basement, but retained for himself the rest of the basement, including a bedroom, storage room, and living room and bar. Winer stored property in the basement and had a key to the house. The only access to the basement was through the main floor of the house. On June 6, 1992, Wise went to a local bar with some friends to drink and play pool. She returned to her house with the plaintiff, Larry Lyden, and other friends and continued socializing. An hour later Wise asked Lyden to go to the basement to check up on some of their friends who had gone to the basement to rest. Lyden slipped on an area rug on the landing of the

stairwell leading to the basement and was injured. The owner Winer had put the rug, which did not have a no-skid backing, on the stairs to protect the parquet wood floor. Lyden sued Winer for his injuries arguing that the landlord had a duty to maintain the basement in a safe condition because it was an area over which the landlord retained control. In Wyoming, the common law rules as to landlord liability are followed. (a) Under those rules, who should win if the case goes to court? (b) Are there any other theories of liability under the common law that Lyden could assert against Winer? *Lyden v. Winer*, 878 P.2d 516 (Wyo. 1994).

4. Alyson Marklein and Bettie Lewis leased an apartment from Horizon Investment Management for a one-year period in August of 1996 and paid a security deposit of $709. After moving in, they had a series of problems with the premises, including cracked and water-damaged walls, a defective stove, clogged drains and an inoperable toilet, and insect infestation, particularly roaches. The landlord corrected some of the defects and attempted but failed to exterminate the roaches. The tenants complained about the problems to employees of the landlord and learned that the building had been cited for building code violations, some of which had not been rectified. Unable to get the landlord to correct the defects, the tenants vacated the premises in December of 1996, claiming a constructive eviction. When the matter went to court, the landlord argued that the building inspection indicated that the structural problems with the walls did not render the premises uninhabitable. (a) The tenants claimed that the defects with the property and its systems coupled with the insect infestation constituted a constructive eviction. Who should prevail on that issue? (b) The landlord also retained the tenant's security deposit. If the tenants win on the constructive eviction, and if a typical security deposit law applies, should the court order monetary sanctions against the landlord under the circumstances? *Marklein v. Horizon Investments*, 583 N.W.2d 675 (Wis. App. 1998).

5. On March 1, 1974, Shawn Fitzgerald orally leased a house from Roger Parkin on a month-to-month basis. At that time, Parkin agreed to make certain repairs within a reasonable time. Repairs were not made and Fitzgerald notified the landlord by mail on July 1, 1974, that he was demanding repair of the defects and would withhold rent if the premises were not repaired. On July 18, at the request of the tenant, the premises were inspected by the Minneapolis Department of Inspections, and on July 22, the inspector cited Parkin with eight housing code violations. On July 29, Parkin served Fitzgerald with a timely termination notice, and he later brought an unlawful detainer action to evict him. Fitzgerald defended claiming a retaliatory eviction. At trial, Parkin argued that the eviction was not retaliatory, citing Fitzgerald's late payment of rent and his keeping a dog on the premises as the basis for the eviction. Nothing in the lease agreement prohibited the dog on the property, and the dog had not damaged the premises. Fitzgerald appealed. (a) The Minnesota retaliatory eviction law applied to the termination of any "tenancy." Should it apply to the termination of the oral lease? (b) If the retaliatory eviction law is applicable, was the landlord's eviction retaliatory? *Parkin v. Fitzgerald*, 240 N.W.2d 828 (Minn. 1976).

Endnotes

1. Alaska, Arizona, Connecticut, Delaware, Florida, Hawaii, Iowa, Kansas, Kentucky, Mississippi, Montana, Nebraska, Nevada, New Mexico, Ohio, Oklahoma, Oregon, Rhode Island, South Carolina, Tennessee, Vermont, Virginia, and Washington.

2. Burns Ind. Code Ann. § 32-2-1-1 (1998).

3. 33 P.S. § 1 (1998).

4. H.R.S. § 521-21 (1997).

5. 25 Del. C. § 5305 (1997).

6. N.C. Gen. Stat. § 42-44 (1997).

7. *Holy Properties L.P. v. Kenneth Cole Productions*, 661 N.E.2d 694 (N.Y. 1995).

8. *Stonehedge Square L.P. v. Movie Merchants Inc.*, 685 A.2d 1019 (Pa. 1998).

9. *Austin Hill Country Realty Inc. v. Palisades Plaza, Inc.*, 948 S.W.2d 293 (Tex. 1997).

10. *Reid v. Mutual of Omaha Ins. Co.*, 776 P.2d 896 (Utah 1989).

11. *O'Brien v. Black*, 648 A.2d 1374 (Vt. 1994).

12. *Johnson v. Cabrera*, 668 N.Y.S.2d 45 (1998).

13. *Las Vegas Oriental v. Sabella's of Nevada*, 630 P.2d 255 (1981).

Chapter 13

Commercial Leasing: The Landlord-Tenant Relationship in a Business Context

For a number of practical reasons, businesses of all kinds—retail, service, warehousing, manufacturing—often prefer to lease rather than purchase the realty they need for their operations. Yet, as in the purchase of real estate, leasing commercial space can involve considerable expense. Most commercial leases are for a much longer term than a typical residential lease, often ranging from five to forty years or more. Because of the long duration of a commercial lease, a business tenant commits substantial future revenues to the leasehold arrangement, and assumes significant legal liabilities. Thus, choosing the kind of realty to be leased—determining its suitability for the tenant's needs—is an extremely important business decision. Equally important is the degree of flexibility the tenant has under the lease terms should business conditions change requiring the tenant to alter its business operations accordingly.

Years ago, commercial leases were relatively short, simple documents. But as commercial leasing became more complex, landlords and their attorneys developed lease forms with detailed terms and conditions to deal with a multitude of contingencies and issues that may arise during a long-term commercial lease. These lease forms are generally favorable to the landlord. Similarly, attorneys for commercial tenants, especially tenants with a national presence, have developed lease language favorable to tenants. Today, many leases are the result of negotiations between landlord and tenant and reflect the relative bargaining power of the parties. Because lease language is central in determining the rights and duties of the parties, this chapter reviews major terms and clauses commonly found in commercial leases.

Nature of a Commercial Lease

Commercial leases are used in a variety of different business settings, and their terms vary accordingly. For example, commercial leases differ as to the extent of the interest that the tenant is to have in the landlord's property. A tenant may lease only the land, or may lease an entire building or structure on the land or only a unit or space in a building or center, such as an office in a multitenant building. Commercial leases also differ regarding the use of the premises, which the tenant may need for retail, wholesale, industrial, office, or other purposes. Commercial leases have certain basic terms and conditions in common. Other terms, however, vary from lease to lease, depending on the nature of the tenant's interest in the realty and the use that the tenant intends to make of the premises.

The **ground lease** is a long-term commercial arrangement, often for ninety years or more, under which the tenant leases only the land and then, at its own expense, constructs a building or other improvements on the property for use in its business. By leasing only the land and constructing its own improvements, the tenant minimizes land and building costs and can design the improvements to its exact needs.

Instead of seeking a ground lease, a commercial tenant may lease the land and an existing building from the landowner for such purposes as industrial operations, restaurant or theater uses, or retail or office purposes. Under such a lease, the tenant normally assumes responsibility for repairing and maintaining the building, for insuring the building, and for paying the property taxes. Often, the tenant has the right to make substantial alterations and improvements to accommodate its business needs. Or, instead of leasing an entire building, a tenant might lease only a unit or a space in an office building or retail center. In such situations, the landlord ordinarily assumes responsibility for most repairs and maintenance, particularly in the common areas of the building or center, although the tenant may have some responsibility for maintaining the premises and its systems.

Commercial leases also vary according to the tenant's specific use of the premises. In office leasing, for example, tenants use the space for administrative functions, for engaging in professional services, or for consulting and service businesses. The tenant's primary concern is with the condition and appearance of the premises, its fitness and functionality. Tenants expect the landlord to provide necessary services to the premises (water, heat, air conditioning) and to maintain the common areas of the building (stairways, elevators, parking lots) for the building's tenants, and the lease usually imposes primary responsibility for these obligations on the landlord.

Shopping center leases, too, have terms and conditions tailored to fit the business needs of retail landlords and tenants. In a shopping center, the landlord leases to numerous retail tenants, but operates the center as if it were a single enterprise. Restrictions on the tenants' use of the leased space and business operations are quite common. Fixed hours of operation and other controls may be imposed to maintain the center's overall appearance and image, and to ensure uniformity of operation within the center. In addition to a flat-rate monthly or yearly rental, shopping center leases usually contain percentage rent provisions, discussed later in this chapter, under which landlords receive a percentage of the tenant's gross sales as additional rent. Thus, shopping center landlords share in the commercial success of their tenants.

Shopping center landlords also attempt to assure a complementary mix of retail stores for the benefit of the center, including the attraction of "anchor tenants," discussed in the next paragraph. To achieve an appropriate mix, the landlord may grant some tenants the exclusive right to sell a particular product line or to engage in a particular type of business in the shopping center, while limiting other tenants to a certain type of business or precluding them from selling certain products.

Ordinarily, shopping centers have one or more **anchor tenants**. In larger shopping centers, the anchor tenant is a major department or discount store. In a small strip mall or neighborhood shopping center, the anchor tenant may be a grocery store, a drug store, or a convenience store. The anchor tenant is essential to the success of the shopping center because it draws customers to the center for the benefit of the other, smaller retail businesses.

The Premises

A commercial lease must identify or describe the premises. A ground lease or the lease of an entire building contains the legal description of the property, like that found in a deed of conveyance. For a lease of space within larger premises, the leased space is described by reference to a unit or space number within a building or project. To identify the space with sufficient certainty, the lease should incorporate the detailed floor plans for the building or project, usually as an exhibit attached to the lease, and identify the unit on those plans. The lease also should set forth the tenant's rights to use the common areas and other portions of the building or complex, such as storage areas or parking areas.

Measurement of the Premises

The lease contains a measurement of the space in the premises. This measurement is important for two reasons. First, the base rent is frequently stated in terms of the "rentable area" of the premises (e.g., $25 per rentable square foot per year). Second, the amount of additional rent that a commercial tenant pays to cover the operating costs of the landlord usually is based on the relation between the tenant's rentable area and the total rentable area in the building or project.

Although "rentable area" has no universally accepted definition, some customary methods are used in measuring commercial space. In retail and industrial leases, the rentable area is usually the total usable space within the premises. In office leases, the rentable area includes not only the "usable" area within the premises but also the tenant's share of common area space. Because of the importance of the calculation of the rentable area of the premises leased to the tenant, the lease should state the rentable area of the tenant's space, contain a standard for determining it, and include a mechanism for adjusting the rent if the actual area is larger or smaller than the rentable area specified in the lease. The parties are free to develop their own definition of rentable area, but drafting acceptable language for this purpose can be quite difficult. To avoid the drafting problem, many office leases incorporate the industry-wide *Standard Method for Measuring Floor Area in Office Buildings*, published by the International Building Owners and Managers Association (BOMA) and the American National Standards Institute (ANSI), also known as ANSI/BOMA Standard Z65.1-1996.

Tenant Improvements (Build Outs)

In many commercial leases, the space being rented is a mere "shell" that requires the installation of light fixtures, ceilings, partitions, doors, and electrical outlets. Often, the landlord agrees to make such improvements, called "tenant improvements" or "build outs," before the lease term and the tenant's possession commence, and to pay some or all of the cost. Ordinarily, the landlord agrees to provide at the landlord's expense a package of standard improvements that include, for example, a certain grade of carpeting and fixtures and specified partitions, doors, and outlets. The tenant pays for any upgrades. Thus, a tenant who wants better carpeting pays the extra cost for it. Under a **tenant allowance**, the landlord improves the space to the tenant's specifications, but pays only the cost up to the dollar amount of the allowance. Thus, the tenant controls the improvements but is liable for costs that exceed the amount of the tenant allowance.

Under either approach to tenant improvements, the landlord usually is responsible for construction of the "build outs," often hiring the same contractor who constructed the building. Landlords prefer this procedure because they can maintain control of the project. Tenants, too, may prefer it because they are relieved of having to arrange for and oversee their own leasehold improvements. Also, from a tax perspective, a tenant that installs its own improvements will have to depreciate their value and take the resulting income tax deductions over time, whereas all rental payments, including the portion of the rent attributable to landlord-provided improvements, are deductible business expenses in the year they were paid. To maintain "trade dress" uniformity and image quality, some retail chain store tenants insist upon controlling the construction of leasehold improvements. This "reverse build out" (so-called because the tenant improvements are overseen by the tenant rather than by the landlord) usually involves the landlord's contributing a set allowance toward the construction costs.

Regardless of whether the landlord or the tenant is responsible for the actual construction of build outs, the lease should provide time lines for the submission and approval of the plans and specifications for the improvements, or should incorporate the plans and specifications as an exhibit to the lease. The lease should also address the problem of delays in construction that prevent a tenant from taking possession or opening the business or office as planned. To provide an incentive for timely completion of the work, some leases include a **liquidated damages** provision under which the landlord pays a specified dollar amount for every day of delay beyond the agreed completion date.

Expansion and Relocation of the Premises

A provision in the lease may grant the tenant the right to expand the lease premises by renting additional space, usually space adjacent to the tenant's existing premises. An expansion clause adds flexibility to the lease arrangement, allowing the tenant to expand its space as its business grows.

Such clauses usually give the tenant either a "right of first refusal" or a "right of first offer" on the expansion space. Under a right of first offer, a landlord who wants to commence negotiations with a third party for the lease of the expansion space must first notify the tenant, who then has the first right to the expansion space on terms earlier agreed to by the tenant (often, at some "market rate" figure). The right exists for a limited time such as 14 days, after which the landlord is free to lease the space to others. Under a right of first refusal, a landlord who receives from a third party a good faith offer to lease the expansion space must notify the tenant of the offer and give the tenant an opportunity to lease the space on the terms offered by the third party. Under either type of expansion clause, the tenant who is in default under its lease loses the right to lease the expansion space.

Landlords may resist including expansion clauses in leases because of the delay and uncertainty they cause. In contrast, *relocation clauses* serve landlord interests. Landlords may need the flexibility to relocate tenants in a building or a shopping center because of changes in the center or in market conditions. For example, the expansion or renovation of a retail center may necessitate changing the location of existing shops. A relocation clause gives a landlord the right to move a tenant to a substitute premises. Generally, the landlord must give the tenant adequate notice of the relocation, say thirty to sixty days, and provide alternative space for the tenant. Tenants, particularly retail tenants, resist such clauses because of the disruption to the tenant's business caused by a relocation. Rather than eliminate the relocation option altogether, however, landlords may be willing to provide some protection to tenants who are forced to relocate. For example, the relocation clause might require the landlord to pay all expenses of the tenant's move and entitle the tenant to a space that is "comparable" in size, features, and leasehold improvements. Or the clause might provide that the tenant will not be relocated during certain times of the year.

BOX 13–1 YOU BE THE JUDGE

Gustave Kaplan, president of Gus Kaplan, Inc. (GKI), leased retail space to Timothy Kite in a building that had previously been used as a department store. The space was leased for the operation of a "fine jewelry store" under a renewable five-year lease with monthly rental of 14% of the store's gross sales. The premises, identified in the lease, with reference to a floor plan of the building, was a showcase complex facing the main entrance with 400 square feet. The complex had been designed for a jewelry department and had special features, including high-intensity lighting, locking jewelry showcases, and special security equipment. The lease contained a relocation clause that read as follows: "All of the mentioned store space, and reserve stock space is located in the store of the lessor, and may be changed from time to time by lessor at its option and expense." GKI became dissatisfied with Kite's operation of the store and its declining gross sales. Kite believed that GKI was interfering with its business by pressuring the store to carry cheap jewelry products from a firm owned by Kaplan's son-in-law. Eventually, GKI physically moved Kite's jewelry stock to a new location in the building when Kite was not present. The new space did not have the amenities, and was only half the size, of the jewelry department initially designated by the lease. When Kite discovered this, he abandoned the premises and later sued GKI for damages caused by the relocation. GKI contended that (1) under the relocation clause, it had a right to move the store contents to another location, and (2) the new space did not have to be comparable to the original space. Who should prevail on the two contentions made by GKI?

Rent

In residential tenancies, most leases provide for a fixed amount of rent per month. These **gross leases** are uncommon in commercial leasing, although a fixed amount of rent may be payable under some short-term leases and leases to the government. The overwhelming majority of commercial leases are **net leases**. Under a net lease, the tenant pays a fixed amount of base rent and agrees either to assume responsibility for the maintenance of the premises (and other expenses related to it) or to pay its share of the landlord's cost to operate and maintain the building or complex, including taxes, insurance, and maintenance of the common areas. In the lease of an entire building, a net lease is achieved by having the tenant agree to pay taxes, insurance, and the costs of maintaining the building. In a multi-unit building or shopping center, the landlord will be obligated to maintain and insure the building or center, and to pay the taxes on it, but the tenants will pay a proportionate share of those operating costs as additional rent. These customary arrangements are referred to as net leases because the base rent represents a return on the owner's investment in the property over and above (or "net of") the landlord's expenses. A net rental stream is important from a balance sheet perspective, but it also may be necessary for the landlord to secure financing from commercial real estate lenders.

● Base or Minimum Rent

Base rent is a fixed sum of money that a tenant agrees to pay on a monthly or annual basis. It is called *minimum rent* because the amount does not fluctuate with changes in the landlord's costs or the tenant's gross sales. In many net leases, the tenant also pays as additional rent an amount to cover the tenant's proportionate share of the landlord's operating expenses, so that the total rent is something more than the "base rent." The additional rent is adjusted in future lease periods to reflect increases (or decreases) in the landlord's operating costs. Under some commercial leases, base rent is defined differently, to *include* the tenant's share of the landlord's operating costs. As thus defined, base rent includes a minimum amount of rent plus a portion of the landlord's present operating costs (called the "expense stop"), with the operating cost component being adjusted in future lease periods to reflect increases or decreases in the "stop." To understand the true cost of renting the property, the tenant obviously needs to understand how base rent is calculated.

As a hedge against inflation, the lease may contain an escalation provision allowing the landlord to increase the base rent periodically. The lease may provide for increasing the base rent by fixed amounts over time, called "steps." The step approach has the benefit of simplicity and predictability, but it is arbitrary in the sense that increases are not tied to inflation in the retail leasing market or in the economy as a whole. To link rent increases to increases in inflation, some leases link rent adjustments to a recognized inflation index, such as the Consumer Price Index (CPI). However, the CPI is a measure of general inflation that usually does not accurately reflect inflation in the retail leasing sector. Moreover, the government publishes several different CPI indices, so the lease should specify which one is to be used. An alternative to a CPI adjustment is periodically to change the base rent to the prevailing market rate. For example, if the tenant elects to extend the term of the lease, or to renew it, the rent is usually adjusted then to the current market value. A market adjustment mechanism is more accurate than the CPI in tracking inflation in the industry, but it is more difficult to implement and may cause disputes between the parties. The process of defining "market rate" and establishing a neutral process for determining that rate (e.g., by using third-party appraisers) requires detailed provisions in the lease. Because of these drawbacks, a market rate adjustment is utilized only in large-scale commercial leases involving substantial amounts of rent.

Operating Expenses and Taxes

In a net lease, the tenant usually pays an amount in addition to base rent that represents the tenant's proportionate share of the landlord's **operating costs**. In shopping center leases, operating costs are sometimes referred to as **common area maintenance (CAM) charges**, the definition of which is a frequent area of negotiation in commercial leases. Operating costs usually include taxes, insurance, and expenses relating to the operation and maintenance of the landlord's building or complex, such as snow removal and holiday decorations generally benefitting the center. Under some commercial leases, however, taxes are treated separately from other operating costs. In addition to defining operating costs, the lease commonly provides for allocating the operating costs among the tenants, the method of payment, and reporting and auditing of operating costs to resolve disputes over the accuracy of the charges.

Definition of Operating Costs and Exclusions

Usually, operating costs are defined broadly as, for example, "all costs, charges, and expenses incurred by the landlord in connection with the ownership, operation, security, maintenance, repair, and replacement" of the building or complex. The clause thus broadly defining operating costs usually includes a list of the types of expenses that fall within it, such as the following:

- Real estate taxes, including installment payments of special assessments.

- Expenses for heating and cooling and other utility costs.

- Maintenance, repair, cleaning, janitorial, and landscaping expenses.

- Insurance and security expenses.

- Management fees and fees for other professional services paid in connection with the operation of the building.

Tenants often negotiate for exclusions of certain extraordinary expenses and costs not directly related to the operation or maintenance of the landlord's building. Agreed-to exclusions are specifically listed in the lease and usually include some of the following: leasing commissions and costs of marketing; payments of principal and interest on mortgages and other encumbrances; costs in connection with correcting defects in building design or construction; costs to remove hazardous materials from the building; costs caused by the landlord's negligence; costs related to the landlord's business entity, such as legal and accounting expenses to form that business organization; and costs for which the landlord is reimbursed, including insurance payments for damages to the landlord's property.

Tenants also may bargain for *ceilings* on certain expenses, especially those imposed by contracts with parties related to the landlord, that could be manipulated by the landlord. For example, a tenant might agree to pay for services or items supplied by a business affiliated with the landlord, but only "to the extent the same is not in excess of the fair market value" of the service or item. Management fees can be similarly "capped" to protect the tenant from unreasonable charges. For example, management fees can be limited to the prevailing rates in the market (e.g., no more than 10% of gross rent on an office building or 15% of operating costs of a retail center). Anchor tenants and others in strong bargaining positions may be able to negotiate for a "most favored nation" clause, which gives the tenant the benefit of the most favorable operating cost terms given to other tenants in the landlord's building or complex.

One problem area in defining operating costs is whether capital improvements should be included. Tenants argue that because capital improvements increase the value of the property, they should be treated as part of the landlord's investment for which the base rent is the compensation, and should not be charged to tenants as operating costs. Landlords contend that some capital expenditures actually reduce operating costs to the benefit of the tenants, so should be recaptured as part of the operating costs. Whether and to what extent capital expenditures will be included in operating costs depends on the bargaining strength of the parties.

Allocation of Operating Costs

Under a net lease, the operating costs must be allocated among the tenants according to some formula in the lease. Most often, a tenant's proportionate share of operating costs is based on the relation that the rentable area of the tenant's premises bears to the total rentable area of the building or complex. A typical provision reads as follows:

> *Tenant's proportionate share is a fraction, the numerator of which is the rentable area of the [tenant's] premises, and the denominator of which is the rentable area of all areas of the building designated by the landlord for lease.*

Under this formula, the denominator is the total *rentable* area and includes the areas actually rented as well as vacant offices or spaces. Landlords sometimes, however, attempt to increase the tenant's share of operating costs by defining it in terms of the actually *rented* areas of the building. If "rented area" instead of "rentable area" is used in the denominator of the allocation formula, the tenant's proportionate share of operating costs increases as vacancies increase. Tenants resist this method of allocation, arguing that the landlord should assume the costs of the unoccupied spaces and that the vacancy rate is not within the control of the tenant. But if tenants are unable to prevent the use of a "rented area" formula, they still may be able to negotiate a limit on the operating cost obligation, usually by specifying that the figure in the denominator for rented area cannot be lower than 90–95% of the total rentable area of the building or complex.

Reporting and Auditing of Expense Statements

Where a lease requires a tenant to pay a share of the landlord's operating costs, the lease must contain appropriate provisions governing the landlord's reporting and the tenant's payment of the expenses. Typically, the procedure under such provisions is as follows:

1. The tenant makes estimated payments during the year.
2. At the end of the year, the landlord provides the tenant with an expense statement detailing the actual operating costs and the tenant's proportionate share.
3. After the tenant receives the expense statement, the parties reconcile the estimated costs with the actual operating costs, and the tenant either pays more in the case of underpayment or receives a reimbursement for any overpayment.

To protect the tenant from an overstatement of actual operating costs and errors in the calculation of the total costs or the tenant's share, commercial leases provide for the auditing of expense statements to verify their accuracy. Under such audit procedures, the tenant has an opportunity to inspect the books and records of the landlord relating to the costs, and to dispute the accuracy of the statement and the legitimacy of particular charges or expenses. The audit provisions of the lease set a time limit, usually from thirty days to one year, for the tenant to conduct the audit and give notice of an inaccuracy in the expense statement. If the tenant alleges an inaccuracy and the matter is not resolved after the landlord is informed of the discrepancy, a dispute resolution procedure provided for in the lease, typically binding arbitration, can be invoked.

The lease may impose the costs of the audit on one of the parties. For example, the landlord may have to pay the tenant's audit costs if the actual operating costs are overstated by a given percentage, typically 2% to 5%, and the tenant may have to pay the landlord's costs if little or no discrepancy is substantiated in the audit. Because of the technical nature of the accounting issues involved, lease audits ordinarily are conducted by lease auditing specialists. A lease auditing industry has developed to conduct audits for both landlords and tenants. Note that landlords also employ lease auditors to audit tenants' gross sales reports under percentage leases.

● Percentage Rent

Percentage lease arrangements are common in retail and shopping center leases. Under a percentage lease, a tenant pays not only a base rent, but also, as additional rent, a percentage of its gross sales that exceed a certain base sales figure. The base figure can be set at any level the parties agree to, but it is often set at what is called the "natural breakpoint," or the gross sales level that would generate the base rent upon application of the rent percentage that was agreed to. For example, in a lease where the parties have agreed to a percentage rate of 10% and the base rent is $2,000 per month, the natural breakpoint is $200,000 (since 10% of $200,000 equals the $2,000 base rent figure). So, in addition to the $2,000 base rent, the tenant pays an additional rent of 10% of gross sales above the natural breakpoint of $200,000. If sales do not reach the breakpoint amount, the tenant still must pay the base rent. Thus, the landlord receives at least the base rent and also shares in the tenant's gross sales above the base level. Instead of using the "natural breakpoint" figure, the parties to the lease can set the base sales figure at some arbitrary or "artificial" level (e.g., $300,000 in the preceding example) for triggering the obligation to pay percentage rent. Also, the parties can agree to a pure percentage rent arrangement with no base rent and no threshold of gross sales before the tenant pays percentage rent.

The amount of percentage rent depends not only on the level of gross sales that triggers the percentage rent obligation, but also upon the percentage rate itself. This rate varies with the type of business the tenant is engaged in and the type of retail complex. High volume, low profit margin sellers (e.g., a grocery store) will generally pay a low percentage rate (e.g., 1%). In contrast, a low volume specialty retailer in a high profit-margin business (e.g., an upscale boutique) pays a much higher rate (e.g., 5% to 15%). A recent survey found the following ranges of percentage rates:

- Clothing stores, 3–6%
- Fast food restaurants, 4–7%
- Drug stores (chains), 2–4%
- Drug stores (independents), 5–8%
- Movie theaters, 6–10%
- Shoe stores, 6–8%[1]

The amount of percentage rent is also affected by the definition of gross sales in the lease. Landlords seek a definition of gross sales that is as broad as possible, usually all income derived from the business, including cash and credit sales; retail and wholesale sales; sales "at," "on," and "from" the premises; and incidental income from services. Tenants attempt to limit the scope of gross sales by incorporating in the lease exclusions from the definition. Typically excluded are the following: sales and excise taxes; refunds on merchandise returned by customers; sales made as an accommodation or at a discount to employees and others; sales of business property (e.g., equipment, machinery, fixtures) outside the regular course of business; finance charges on credit sales to customers; sales of money orders, travelers checks, postage stamps, and receipts from public telephones or vending machines on the premises; and fees paid to credit card companies.

Some percentage rent leases contain a recapture provision (sometimes called a "kick out" clause) allowing the landlord to cancel the lease if gross sales do not reach a specified minimum level. This minimum level of sales can be subject to a series of step increases over the course of the lease, the expectation being that the tenant's sales will increase over time. Although recapture provisions were originally inserted by landlords to allow them to terminate a tenant's lease, some recapture clauses also allow the tenant to terminate the lease if a minimum sales level is not obtained within a set time period.

The lease must address additional issues relating to percentage rent, for example, the timing of percentage rent. For cash flow reasons, tenants prefer to calculate and pay percentage rent on an annual basis. Landlords, however, prefer monthly or quarterly payments to prevent the averaging of sales over the entire year, thereby capturing as much percentage rent as possible during peak sales seasons. Regardless of the timing of the payments, the tenant files periodic reports of gross sales, and the lease includes audit terms similar to those for operating costs so that the landlord may check the accuracy of the tenant's reported gross sales.

Use of the Premises

Commercial leases invariably contain a "use" clause that describes the type of business or activities the tenant intends to conduct on the premises. The clauses can be **permissive**, allowing the tenant to use the property for a specific purpose but not limiting the tenant to that use, or **restrictive**, limiting the tenant to a specific use or uses. Use clauses also can be **exclusive**. An exclusive use clause gives the tenant the sole right to conduct a particular type of business or sell a particular product in a shopping center. "Exclusives" are most commonly used in retail leases.

Restrictive Uses and Covenants

A tenant can use the leased property for any lawful purpose, unless the lease expressly or impliedly restricts the tenant's use. A use is lawful if it is permitted under the zoning laws and is not prohibited by criminal statutes. A use clause that merely identifies a particular use for the premises does not necessarily limit the tenant to that described use. Unless the use clause contains restrictive language, a lease for a specific purpose will be interpreted as permissive. A clause that states that the property is being "leased for a law office" or that provides that the premises "may" be used for a restaurant are examples of permissive use clauses. Moreover, a use clause can be drafted to permit multiple uses (e.g., an office lease for "general office purposes") or to permit "any lawful use" on the premises.

Restrictive use clauses are common in commercial leases for a number of reasons. First, in shopping centers, landlords need an appropriate mix of different businesses to ensure the overall success and profitability of the center. Restrictive use clauses are used to maintain that mix. Moreover, where retail tenants have the exclusive right to conduct a particular business in the shopping center, restrictions must be placed on competitive uses by other tenants. Second, in other multi-unit developments, landlords may want to control the selection of tenants to maintain the compatibility of uses in the project. The owner of a professional building may prefer not to rent to or allow a business that might be objectionable to its tenants, for example, a "dating service" or a "fitness center." Third, under percentage leases, a change in the tenant's type of business can decrease the tenant's gross sales and, consequently, the amount of rent. To ensure maximum gross sales, the landlord may limit or prohibit changes in the tenant's business.

A restrictive use clause may read as follows: "The Premises shall be used by the Tenant for general office purposes, and *for no other purpose.*" In addition, leases commonly prohibit obnoxious or offensive uses of the property, especially excessive noises or other activity that would constitute a nuisance. In a shopping center lease, a tenant's use may also be subject to the "rules and regulations" of the landlord governing the safety and cleanliness of the shopping center.

Restrictive use clauses limit only the business activities the tenant conducts *on the premises*, but not the tenant's ability to conduct business at other locations. In shopping centers with percentage lease arrangements, however, landlords have a legitimate interest in restricting a tenant's business at other sites if that business would compete with the tenant's business at the landlord's center, thereby reducing the percentage rent. Therefore, **noncompetition agreements** (a type of **restrictive covenant**) are often a part of retail leases. The most common is a **radius clause** under which the tenant and its officers, directors, and shareholders agree not to engage in a competitive enterprise within a certain distance from the leased premises. The radius may be stated in terms of miles or city blocks. Ordinarily, landlords enforce such restrictions by seeking an injunction or a lawsuit for damages. In addition, the radius clause itself may contain a "recapture" remedy under which any income attributable to the competing business is treated as gross sales under the percentage rent provisions and "captured" for the benefit of the landlord, thereby discouraging the tenant from engaging in competition in breach of the restrictive covenant.

Exclusive Uses

Exclusive use clauses are common in retail and shopping center leases. If a tenant did not have the exclusive right to operate a particular type of business or sell a particular product within a center, the landlord could open a competing store or lease another space in the center to the tenant's competitor, and not be in breach of its lease with the tenant. To enhance the value of their businesses, tenants in retail settings frequently demand some type of "exclusive" as a protection against competition. Landlords resist granting exclusives because of the complications they cause in the landlords' dealings with other tenants and because of the landlords' diminished flexibility in conducting their own operations. Nevertheless, anchor tenants who are in powerful bargaining positions and specialty retailers in need of protection often can negotiate some type of exclusive use clause.

Types of Exclusives

Exclusives differ in terms of the scope of the protection afforded. A "limited exclusive" gives the tenant the exclusive right to conduct a specific type of business in the landlord's center. For example, a tenant with the exclusive right to engage in the business of a "grocery store" has a limited exclusive. It is characterized as "limited" because other tenants not operating as a grocery store are permitted, as an incidental part of their business, to sell food products customarily sold in a grocery store, and thus are not in violation of the exclusive. A "true exclusive" gives the tenant the exclusive right to sell a particular product or product line. A tenant with the exclusive right to sell "cosmetics, fragrances, and hair care products" has a true exclusive, because it precludes the sale of such products by any other business in the center. Often, an exclusive given to one store, for example a specialty shop, is subject to exceptions allowing anchor tenants or large department stores to sell the otherwise protected products. Exclusives subject to such exceptions are sometimes called "partial exclusives."

Scope of the Exclusive

Whatever form the exclusive takes, the grant of an exclusive presents a host of issues and drafting concerns that both landlords and tenants need to consider. Of primary concern to both parties is the scope of the exclusive. Landlords prefer exclusives that are limited in scope, while tenants prefer broad exclusive rights. The parties' wording of an exclusive also can present interpretive issues for the courts. For example, what types of restaurants are included in the phrase *fast-food restaurant*? Does *fast-food* encompass a cafeteria or a coffee shop? Because the courts are skeptical of restrictions on free trade, they give exclusives, restrictive use clauses, restrictive covenants, and other restrictions on competition a narrow application. Also, the courts interpret language in light of its common meaning and usage unless the lease defines the terms in another way. Thus, in interpreting the phrase *fast-food restaurant*, several courts have held that it does not include a cafeteria. Giving *fast-food* its ordinary and commonsense meaning, these courts reasoned that a cafeteria is different from a fast-food restaurant in that customers have a larger selection at a cafeteria than at a fast-food place, and they eat the food on the premises, using trays and silverware.

Another problem of interpretation arises where a product protected by an exclusive is sold, under an exception to the exclusive, by other businesses in the center who are not primarily engaged in such sales. The exclusive is commonly created by language providing that the landlord will not lease any portion of the shopping center to any business "primarily" or "substantially" engaged in the sale of the exclusive product. But to make it clear what businesses are not covered by the exclusive, the parties to the lease need to carefully define the meaning of terms such as "primarily engaged in the sale" of specified products. This clarification is ordinarily accomplished by specifying a level of sales that is considered "incidental" (e.g., 30% of the protected tenant's total sales), or by relating the excepted level of sales to a percentage of the competitor's floor space devoted to the sale of the exclusive products, or by doing both. Such an exception could read:

> The above exclusive shall not be deemed to prohibit the incidental sale of the exclusive items by other retailers in the Shopping Center. For purposes of this provision, a retailer's sales will be deemed incidental so long as (1) the sales do not exceed ten percent (10%) of the retailer's annual gross sales, and (2) no more than fifteen percent (15%) of the sales area in the premises of the retailer is devoted to the display of the exclusive items.

The exclusive use clause should also define the geographic scope of the restriction. If the tenant has an exclusive in a "shopping center," what specific area does "shopping center" cover? Does it extend to expansions and additions to the shopping center? Does it extend to satellite strip malls or other adjacent property owned by the landlord? The precise meaning of "shopping center" or similar language must be carefully expressed in the lease, because it will be given a restrictive interpretation by the courts. One alternative method of establishing the geographic scope of the exclusion is through a so-called "reverse radius" clause. A **reverse radius clause** extends the exclusive's reach to all properties owned by the landlord within a specific distance (e.g., 2 miles) from the premises. Although establishing a reverse radius avoids the necessity of carefully defining *center*, landlords rarely agree to such a clause because it limits the landlord's flexibility in developing the center and the landlord's other properties.

Remedies

A landlord granting an exclusive wants to ensure that the tenant actively engages in the sale of the protected product, especially if the lease is a percentage lease with minimal base rent. A "use it or lose it" clause is one way to encourage the tenant to stay in business and actually engage in sales of the protected product on an ongoing basis. Such a clause terminates the exclusive if the tenant goes out of business, abandons the premises, fails to make sales of or devote space to the protected product for a specified period of time, or otherwise changes its business in a way that substantially reduces sales of the protected product. The clause also can provide remedies to the landlord for the tenant's failure to "use" the exclusive. These remedies include termination of the lease and liquidated damages based on the past volume of sales of the protected product.

The tenant has a number of remedies if the landlord breaches the exclusive by (1) granting another tenant the right to sell the protected product (a "voluntary" breach), or (2) by passively permitting existing tenants to sell the protected product in violation of restrictions in their leases (a so-called "involuntary" breach). The tenant can sue the landlord for specific performance to compel the landlord to enforce the exclusive against tenants violating it. A suit for damages is available too, although proving the precise damages attributable to the landlord's breach may be difficult. As a last resort, the tenant may cancel the lease, but cancellation usually is not wise, because the tenant, who might have a substantial investment in the premises and a profitable customer base, would have to give up its business site and relocate.

It may be necessary, therefore, to supplement these remedies by providing for others in the lease. Some retail leases have an "abatement" provision that triggers a total or partial reduction of rent if the landlord breaches the exclusive. The abatement remedy provides a strong incentive for the landlord to halt violations of a tenant's exclusive rights and to avoid voluntary breaches of the exclusive. Abatement provisions generally require that the tenant give notice to the landlord of any violation of the exclusive. After the tenant gives the required notice, the landlord has an opportunity within a specified time (e.g., sixty days) to stop the violation ("cure" the breach). The abatement remedy is available only if the landlord fails to cure the problem, and abatement usually is limited to a partial reduction in rent during the period of the violation. Also, the amount of the rent reduction must be reasonable in light of the damages that would be expected from a violation of the exclusive. If a court determines that the amount is excessive or unreasonable, it will refuse to enforce the abatement provision, considering it an unlawful "penalty" clause.

In the case that follows, the tenant sought another common remedy for breach of the exclusive, an injunction against the competing tenant. The critical issue, however, was the interpretation of the exclusive use clause, and the scope of the tenant's exclusive right to operate a "drug store."

Case 13.1

Rite Aid of Ohio, Inc. v. Marc's Variety Store, Inc.

638 N.E.2d 1056 (Ohio App. 1994)

Rite Aid of Ohio, Inc., as lessee, operates a 9,600 square foot store with a pharmacy at the Brookgate Shopping Center in Brook Park, Ohio, under a 1981 lease with RMS Investment Corp. (RMS). The lease gave Marshall Drug, Rite Aid's predecessor, the right to operate a "retail drug and variety store" on the premises. Paragraph 8(a) of the lease, known as the "use clause," listed items that Rite Aid could sell:

> [P]roprietary and ethical drugs, health and beauty aids, sundries, tobacco products and smoking supplies, liquor, beer and wine . . . school supplies, housewares, small electrical appliances, toys, recreation equipment, cameras, photographic supplies and film processing, food for off-premise and on-premises consumption, books, newspapers, and magazines, and items kindred to the foregoing.

Paragraph 8(g) of the lease (the "exclusive-use clause") granted Rite Aid "the exclusive privilege for the operation of a Drug Store in the Shopping Center." When Rite Aid's predecessor entered into the lease, the anchor tenant at Brookgate was Zayre's, a general merchandise store selling every item listed in Paragraph 8(a) of the Lease, except prescription drugs.

In November, 1990, Ames, the anchor tenant, went out of business. The 45,000 square feet of anchor space remained unoccupied until October 1992, when the defendant opened a Marc's Variety Store. Before the opening, Rite Aid filed suit against Marc's, seeking injunctive relief which would prohibit it from operating a drug store at Brookgate. The trial court denied the request for an injunction and granted judgment for Marc's. Rite Aid appealed.

PORTER, J.

Rite Aid claims that the trial court erred in not enjoining Marc's operation [and not] giving effect to a prior lease restriction which provided that Rite Aid would have "the exclusive privilege for the operation of a Drug Store in the Shopping Center." Marc's carries health and beauty aids similar to those of Rite Aid but does not have a pharmacy for dispensing prescription drugs. The case therefore turns on whether or not Marc's operates a "Drug Store" in violation of Rite Aid's exclusive-use provision, although Marc's does not offer prescription drugs.

Total sales at Rite Aid's Brookgate drug store consisted of ninety percent pharmacy and health and beauty aid items and ten percent food and general merchandise items. Marc's principal product category breakdown chain-wide, by purchases, is food (41 percent), general merchandise, including tobacco (35 percent), and health and beauty aids (23 percent). The allocation of store space within Marc's Brookgate store is 45 percent devoted to general merchandise, 27 percent to food, and 14½ percent to health and beauty aids.

The Marc's store does not have a pharmacy or a pharmacist. Accordingly, Marc's does not call its store a "drug store," does not advertise itself as a "drug store," and does not sell prescription drugs at the store. One of the practical difficulties for Rite Aid at trial was to construct a definition of "drug store" which was broad enough to include Marc's while at the same time excluding other grocery and general merchandise stores similar to Marc's. Rite Aid's district supervisor defined "drug store" as "a store that has health and beauty aids, over-the-counter products and other product lines within the confine of the store . . . regardless of the relative percentages of each of those items."

Marc's pointedly argues that if "drug store" cannot be clearly defined and is given "a broad meaning," it would remove any limit on the scope of the lease's exclusive-use clause. That construction would enable Rite Aid to exclude from Brookgate any store which competes with it in the sale of *any* of its product categories, thereby threatening RMS's ability to lease the center's anchor space.

Contrary to Rite Aid's "broad meaning" approach, the trial court correctly found that Ohio law requires that the language of the exclusive-use clauses should be narrowly construed. The interpretation of a written contract is a matter of law for the court. The purpose of contract construction is to effectuate the intent of the parties. Common words appearing in the written instrument will be given their plain and ordinary meaning unless manifest absurdity results or some other meaning is clearly evidenced from the face or overall contents of the instrument.

The trial court relied in part on the statutory definition in Ohio law to support his conclusion that Marc's was not operating a drug store because it did not have a pharmacy. We believe such reasoning is sound. Drug stores have been regulated by statute in Ohio for many years. Under [Ohio statutes], a "drug store" must be "under the management or control of a legally registered pharmacist";

otherwise, it may not call itself a "drug store." It was entirely proper for the trial court to make use of statutory meanings which are in effect when a contract is made, if no other meaning is supplied by the contract itself. The trial court also found that Ohio's statutory definition of "drug store," as containing a pharmacy or offering prescription drugs, was consistent with the common meaning of "drug store" contained in 17 dictionary definitions introduced by defendants.

Rite Aid claims that the lease should be interpreted in light of the surrounding circumstances to give effect to the intent of the parties, to wit, to preserve Rite Aid from direct competition. The history of the relationship does not support this argument. When the original lease was entered in 1981, two other stores, Zayre's and Bi-Rite, already were selling all of the products which Rite Aid's predecessor was permitted to sell, *except* prescription drugs. It is also undisputed that when Rite Aid assumed the lease in 1988, Ames and Food Center (formerly Bi-Rite) were still selling all of those same products at Brookgate. Rite Aid's acquiescence in those stores' operation is evidence that it did not view the exclusive-drug-store-use provision as protection against competition in the sale of nonpharmacy items—that is, general merchandise, health and beauty aids, or the modest selection of food stuffs that Rite Aid carries.

The issue which the trial court properly addressed is whether Marc's is a "drug store" within the commonly understood meaning of the term. The exclusive-use provision guarantees Rite Aid freedom from competition by a drug store, not a discount merchandiser like Marc's.

Rite Aid asserts that Marc's is a "drug chain." Rite Aid cites the 1991 issue of a trade publication called *Chain Drug Review,* which placed Marc's on a list of drug chains. If Rite Aid's exclusive-use privilege was to prevent competition from other "drug store chains," then we presume appropriate language would have been inserted in the lease to effect that goal. Furthermore, an executive in the shopping center business gave competent testimony that Marc's is not even a drug store chain, but is rather a "merchandise discount" operation.

Summarizing, we find that the trial court's denial of an injunction is adequately supported by the evidence and the trial court did not abuse its discretion in making its ruling.

Judgment affirmed.

QUESTIONS ABOUT CASE 13.1

1. Would the court's decision have been different had the exclusive use clause given Rite Aid the exclusive privilege for the operation of a "Drug Store Chain"?

2. What lease terms should Rite Aid have insisted upon to protect itself from competition from discount merchandisers?

Antitrust Implications of Restrictions and Exclusives

The legality of restrictive use clauses, noncompetition agreements, and exclusives can be challenged under federal and state antitrust and unfair competition laws. These laws are designed to promote free trade and to prevent unreasonable restrictions on competition in the marketplace.

The most common federal basis for invalidating lease restrictions is the Sherman Antitrust Act. Section 1 of the Act prohibits any "contract, combination . . . or conspiracy in restraint of trade." Lease restrictions also can be challenged under the Federal Trade Commission Act that prohibits "unfair methods of competition." The states also have antitrust and unfair competition laws that provide an alternative basis to challenge lease restrictions.

Whatever the legal basis used to challenge lease restrictions, the validity of these terms is determined on a case-by-case basis that takes into consideration the nature of the restriction and its effects on competition. The courts have recognized that reasonable restrictions on trade incidental to retail leasing are a legitimate means of controlling the mix of uses in a shopping center. Such restrictions may also be essential to the success of the center as a whole and of the individual tenants. Thus, federal and state courts will not view these restrictions as "per se" violations of the antitrust laws. A per se violation (for example, a price fixing agreement among competing sellers) is one that the courts will invalidate regardless of its purpose or its effect on competition. Rather, the courts judge lease restrictions under what is called the "rule of reason" standard. The rule of reason approach examines the business purpose of a particular restraint, and its positive and negative effects on competition, to determine whether it is an unreasonable restraint on competition. In determining whether a particular lease restriction is an unreasonable restraint, the courts consider the product and the geographic market affected by the restriction; the availability of alternative sites for the business excluded from competing; the significance of the present and future competition eliminated by the restriction; the scope of the restrictive covenant, whether broad or limited in nature; and the business purpose or economic justification for the restriction in the lease.

Under this antitrust analysis, the courts have generally upheld exclusives and reasonable radius restrictions, including radius clauses restricting competition within 2–5 miles of a shopping center. In contrast, state and federal courts have invalidated lease restrictions considered to be unreasonable. Particularly suspect are restrictive agreements that anchor tenants have sometimes secured in shopping center leases, including provisions requiring the anchor tenant's consent to new tenants, and prohibitions on leases with "discount" stores. Unlike limited exclusives given to small retail merchants, these types of restrictions are more likely to be considered a product of

BOX 13–2 YOU BE THE JUDGE

Harmor Realty Corporation, the owner of Amity Shopping Center, leased one of its 25 retail spaces to Elida, Inc., a family-owned corporation doing business as Westville Home Bakery. Elida was given the "exclusive right to sell products normally sold by a bakery shop." The exclusive was subject to exceptions for the sale of bakery items by certain chain tenants in the center. The landlord agreed not to "rent any other space in the shopping center for the purpose of baking on the premises." During the term of the lease, Harmor leased another space in the shopping center to The Gourmet Shoppe, Inc., a business engaged in the sale of bakery items. Despite repeated demands by Elida, Harmor failed to take any action to stop the Gourmet Shoppe from selling bakery items. Elida sued both Harmor and the Gourmet Shoppe, seeking (1) an injunction preventing the violation of its exclusive, and (2) damages. In its defense, Harmor claimed that the exclusive constituted an unlawful restraint of trade in violation of the Connecticut antitrust law. (a) What additional facts would be necessary to resolve this contention? (b) Who is likely to prevail on this issue at trial?

overwhelming bargaining power and an attempt to stifle competition, rather than legitimate restrictions beneficial to both parties.

Continuous Operations

Under the typical lease, the tenant has two options: (1) to use the premises for the specified use, or (2) to refrain from using the premises. That is, a tenant ordinarily has no obligation to operate its business continuously over the term of the lease. Even when the tenant has the benefit of an exclusive-use clause and the rent is based on a percentage of gross sales, a tenant can cease business activities without being in violation of the lease. Ceasing business operations while the lease is in effect is sometimes referred to as the tenant's **going dark**.

A tenant's going dark causes obvious problems for the landlord. First, even though the tenant continues paying the base rent, the landlord loses any rental income that would have been payable under a percentage rent arrangement with the tenant. Second, the closing of one store, particularly that of an anchor tenant, can have a detrimental ripple effect on the financial viability of the shopping center by eroding the customer base of other tenants, who also may choose to go dark or vacate the premises, leading ultimately to the demise of the shopping center. Given the grave consequences to the landlord of a tenant's going dark, retail leases frequently contain an *express covenant of continuous operation* requiring the tenant to stay in business, and providing remedies for breach of the covenant. If a lease says nothing about the tenant's continuing its business, the courts are reluctant to imply a covenant of continuous operation. Nevertheless, in certain situations, the courts have found an *implied covenant of continuous operation* under a commercial lease, thus protecting the landlord from a tenant's going dark even in the absence of a continuous operation clause in the lease.

Express Covenant of Continuous Operation

A typical covenant of continuous operation reads as follows:

> *During the term of his lease, tenant shall continuously and uninterruptedly conduct its business in the entire premises, and shall remain open for business, fully fixtured, adequately staffed, and stocked with sufficient quantities of items offered for sale at competitive prices necessary to conduct its business in such a manner as to achieve the maximum volume of business in and at the premises.*

The language in this clause contrasts with other, less-extensive obligations that tenants often agree to under retail leases. For example, as part of an operating clause, retail tenants usually agree to operate during prescribed times and days, because landlords of malls and shopping complexes ordinarily require all the tenants to have the same hours of operation as part of the overall management of the center. However, neither a clause setting such hours, nor a lease provision requiring the tenant to *open* its store, fully stocked, at the start of the lease term, imposes an obligation on the tenant to operate continuously during the lease term.

Most express covenants of continuous operation contain exceptions and qualifications. The lease ordinarily excuses the tenant from continuous operation when the property is being renovated, repaired, or remodeled and when operations cease because of circumstances beyond the tenant's control, such as a strike or a fire or other casualty to the premises. A tenant may also be excused from the continuous operation clause by means of a so-called cotenancy clause in the lease. A **cotenancy clause** excuses the tenant from the continuous operation obligation if the retail center has significant unoccupied space. The clause typically allows the tenant to cease operations if (1) a specific anchor tenant or department store goes out of business or vacates the center, or (2) a substantial part of the center is unoccupied (e.g., 20% of the retail space). These circumstances are called cotenancy events. The cotenancy event must exist for a specified period (e.g., 12 months) before the tenant has a remedy under the cotenancy clause. If a cotenancy event exists for the required time, the tenant may have alternative remedies under the cotenancy clause, including a partial reduction in rent or termination of the lease.

Courts usually enforce a freely negotiated continuous operation clause. The landlord has several legal remedies for the tenant's breach of the clause, and may have additional remedies provided by the lease itself. Although landlords prefer that the tenant be compelled to live up to its operating agreement and stay in business, most courts have refused to grant specific performance because an order to stay open would require extensive court supervision, a day-to-day monitoring of business decisions and activities that those courts are unwilling to undertake. However, a growing number of courts today grant specific performance, and thereby force tenants to remain open, where other remedies would not provide adequate relief to the landlord. For example, courts have ordered anchor tenants to stay in business because of the devastating effects an anchor tenant's closing would have on the shopping center and its other tenants. Money damages, too, are available to the landlord for breach of the covenant of continuous operation. Although proving the losses attributable to the breach can be difficult, courts have allowed recovery for lost income and for the decrease in the value of the center. The lease can provide alternative remedies, including "recapture" of the lease. Recapture allows the landlord to retake possession of the premises when a tenant goes dark for a period of time set by the lease, and then relet (rent to a new tenant) or sublet the premises on behalf of the tenant and hold the tenant liable for any damages. Or the lease may allow the landlord to recover liquidated damages based on a formula in the continuous operation clause. For example, the clause can require a tenant that goes dark to pay an increased amount of base rent to offset the loss of percentage rent, or the tenant can be required to continue to pay percentage rent based on the tenant's prior gross sales (e.g., "highest gross sales during any 12 month period").

Implied Covenant of Continuous Operation

Generally, the courts will not imply a covenant of continuous operation in the absence of an express covenant in the lease. The parties to a commercial lease are usually sophisticated businesspersons who, being advised by experienced real estate attorneys, understand how to include an express covenant of continuous operation, but who may have been unable or have chosen not to do so. Many tenants are unwilling to obligate themselves to stay in business when their operations are unprofitable, so will not agree to operate continuously. Also, many landlords understand the nature of retail leasing and the inevitable change of tenants over the life of a shopping center, and are willing to assume the business risk that a tenant might close its doors.

Nevertheless, although implied covenants are disfavored by the courts, courts have imposed an implied covenant of continuous operation under circumstances where one is necessary to give effect to the express terms of the lease. In deciding whether such a covenant should be implied, the most important factor is the amount of the tenant's minimum or base rent in relation to the total rent. If the base rent is a nominal or minimal amount, or the total rent is based solely on percentage rent, the landlord will be expecting the percentage rent to provide it with adequate compensation under the lease. To generate that percentage rent, the tenant must stay in business. Consequently, an implied covenant of continuous operation may be essential to give full effect to the express terms of the lease relating to rent.

Other factors the courts consider are the following: economic interdependency of the tenants in a retail complex; whether the tenant has the benefit of an exclusive use clause; whether the tenant has a right to freely assign the lease or sublet the premises; and the relative sophistication and bargaining power of the parties. In the case that follows, the court examines these factors and others to determine whether to imply a covenant of continuous operation.

Case 13.2

Lagrew v. Hooks–SupeRx, Inc.

905 F.Supp. 401 (E.D. Ky. 1995)

Plaintiffs David C. Lagrew and his wife Betty own the Beaumont Plaza Shopping Center in Harrodsburg, Kentucky. Defendant Hooks-SupeRx, Inc., ("SupeRx") leased a 6,300-square-foot space in Beaumont Plaza under a long-term commercial lease that was originally executed on October 17, 1966. The initial term of the lease was fifteen years, with three five-year renewal options for a potential maximum term of thirty years. The lease provided for a base rent of $1.79 per square foot or $940.50 per month. In addition to base rent, the lessee paid 2% of sales exceeding $564,300, excluding the sale of cigarettes and other tobacco products.

At the time the lease was executed, the Kroger Company, Inc., was operating a full-service grocery store that served as the anchor tenant at Beaumont Plaza. Because Kroger was the parent company of SupeRx's predecessor, the leases executed between Beaumont Plaza and the two tenants were similar. SupeRx did have the right to sublet the space, with several significant limitations. It could not offer to sublease to food stores, department stores, variety stores, skating rinks, liquor stores, beer taverns, or any other business that might interfere with the exclusive rights granted by the landlord in leases to other tenants.

Because of declining profitability, SupeRx closed its doors in January 1991. In all likelihood, this decision was related to the closing of Kroger, the anchor tenant, in January of 1988. SupeRx opened a new drug store at Gateway Shopping Center located one mile from Beaumont Plaza, and it left the Beaumont Plaza site vacant. When SupeRx closed, nearly two years remained on the second of the three five-year renewal options. On July 1, 1992, despite its move, SupeRx exercised its third renewal option on the lease at Beaumont Plaza.

At that time, plaintiffs had begun preliminary negotiations with Rite-Aid Drug Company for the space at Beaumont Plaza. In the spring of 1992, plaintiffs attempted to ascertain SupeRx's intentions, but SupeRx refused to relinquish its rights to the final five-year option. Plaintiffs brought suit against SupeRx, requesting that the court determine whether the plaintiffs had the right to cancel the lease and recover damages for SupeRx's breach of its obligation to continuously operate its business at Beaumont Plaza. Before trial, the plaintiffs made a motion for a summary ruling on the issue of the existence of an implied covenant of continuous operation.

WILHOIT, J.

Plaintiffs' theory in this case is that the lease contains an implied covenant of continuous operation. SupeRx on the other hand, argues that no covenant of continuous operation existed in the lease and that the plain language of the lease precludes such a finding.

An implied covenant is one which may be reasonably inferred from the whole agreement and circumstances attending its execution. The courts have refused to prescribe a certain form for the construction of an implied covenant, instead looking to the true intentions of the parties.

To determine whether to imply a covenant of continuous operation, the courts look to the terms of the lease and the surrounding circumstances. Generally, the courts take several factors into account: (1) whether base rent is below market value, (2) whether percentage payments are substantial in relation to base rent, (3) whether the term of the lease is lengthy, (4) whether the tenant may sublet, (5) whether the tenant has rights to fixtures, and (6) whether the lease contains a noncompetition provision. Application of the relevant interpretive factors to the lease in the case at hand mitigate toward a finding of an implied covenant of continuous operation.

First, shopping centers are designed for going concerns, not empty store fronts. Thus, when an entity in the business of operating a retail drug store negotiates a lease with a shopping center, absent a showing of unusual circumstances, it is implicit that the lessor intends to operate a store and that the lessor is leasing the space for that purpose.

Second, the fixed base rent alone provides the lessor no hedge against inflation. No landlord using good sound business judgment would burden his 6,300-square-foot space in a shopping center for thirty years at base rent level without some hope of a satisfactory return on his commercial venture. Courts have found that where there is a showing of disparity between the fixed rent in the lease and the market value of the property, a covenant of continuous operation can be implied. Plaintiffs have tendered the affidavit of Edward Pease, who states that the $1.79 rate was below market in 1966. Mr. Pease's affidavit, supports a finding that the base rent was below market value at the time of execution.

The logical explanation is that percentage payments are intended as an integral part of the bargain to protect the lessor by creating a market-driven guarantee of a fair return. Percentage payments are the lessor's only hedge against inflation, and such payments are only possible when the lessee is operating on the premises. Thus, the lease's base-plus-percentage rent term is strong evidence in favor of a finding an implied covenant of continuous operation.

Third, once SupeRx began operating profitably, percentage payments quickly became substantial in relation to base rent. From 1976 until 1990 percentage payments exceeded 40% of base rent.

Fourth, while the limited sublease provision theoretically supports SupeRx's contention that the lease does not contemplate continuous operation by the lessee, the sublease term is so narrowly tailored that it implies that some suitable replacement business would occupy the leased space if not SupeRx.

Fifth, SupeRx argues that the lessee's right to retain fixtures negates any implication of a covenant of continuous operation. While a term requiring accession of fixtures would present stronger evidence that the parties intended the lessee to continuously operate on the premises, the absence of such a term does not necessarily prove the converse.

Sixth, the existence of a noncompetition provision is a factor to consider by this Court. SupeRx was given the exclusive right to operate from the shopping center a full-service drug store and the landlord committed not to lease space to a competitor within a radius of one and one-half miles of the Beaumont Plaza. This inures a benefit to SupeRx and in consideration for this agreement, the tenant impliedly agreed to continue to operate a particular type of business.

Finally, SupeRx's opening of a new store [near] Beaumont Plaza while simultaneously holding the Beaumont Plaza premises vacant smacks of bad faith. Even at substantially below market rates, the Beaumont Plaza lease is no bargain if not productively used unless SupeRx's motive is to deprive competitors of an auspicious, neighboring location. Such a design would be a restraint on trade. The Court will not permit an overly literal reading of the lease to allow SupeRx to achieve such an illegitimate end. Fairness in business dealing is of great importance. . . .

In sum, the implication of a covenant of continuous operation is necessary to a rational understanding of the lease in light of the surrounding circumstances. Accordingly, the Court must imply such a covenant. Since SupeRx ceased operations at the Center without subleasing to a suitable business as defined by the lease, as a matter of law, SupeRx is in breach of the lease. If SupeRx was unable to make a profit at the Beaumont Plaza, felt that a different location would improve their economic well-being, and could not find a sublessee meeting with the landlord's approval, SupeRx should have offered to surrender up their lease to plaintiffs. To hold the premises in order to keep out competition for their other location is completely unacceptable.

Judgment for the plaintiffs on their right to cancel the lease. Trial to be held on the issue of damages.

QUESTIONS ABOUT CASE 13.2

1. In its opinion, the court seems to suggest that the law should presume an implied covenant of continuous operation in shopping center leases, stating that "when an entity in the business of operating a retail drug store negotiates a lease with a shopping center, absent a showing of unusual circumstances, it is implicit that the lessor [landlord] intends [the lessee] to operate a store and that the lessor is leasing the space for that purpose." Is such a presumption appropriate for all shopping center leases?

2. The court gave considerable weight to the fact that SupeRx renewed its lease in an attempt to prevent competition from any business that would take over its space at the Beaumont Plaza, thus engaging in conduct that one commentator has called "going dark aggressively."[2] How important should this factor be in determining whether a tenant impliedly agreed to operate its business continuously?

Condition of the Premises

As noted in Chapter 12, under the common law a landlord had no obligation to repair or maintain the premises an agreement in the lease to do so, though the landlord did have a common law duty to maintain the common areas, and by an express provision in the lease could also assume a duty to make specific repairs or to maintain the property. However, under the common law doctrine of independent covenants, any obligation of the landlord to repair or maintain the premises was considered independent of the tenant's duty to pay rent. Therefore, if the landlord failed to comply with any duty under the lease to maintain the premises, the tenant could not refuse to pay rent. The tenant's only remedy was to sue the landlord for damages caused by the landlord's breach. The tenant's obligation to pay rent continued unless the landlord's breach was so serious that it deprived the tenant of the beneficial use of the premises and constituted a constructive eviction. In that event, the tenant had a right to refuse to pay rent, but the refusal had to be accompanied by the tenant's vacating the premises and terminating the lease.

Commercial Landlord's Duty to Maintain the Property

The combination of the two common law rules, the no-duty-to-repair rule and the doctrine of independent covenants, placed a tenant in a difficult position when a landlord refused to make necessary repairs or maintain the premises. In residential tenancies, the courts and legislatures have come to the aid of tenants by reversing the common law rules. Under the *warranty of habitability*, a residential landlord has a continuing obligation to maintain the property in a habitable state, and the tenant usually can withhold rent if the landlord breaches the warranty by failing to maintain the property. But in commercial leases, most courts have declined to impose any implied warranty of fitness on the landlord, and they continue to follow the doctrine of independent covenants. The rationale for the majority rule is that commercial tenants are in a stronger bargaining position than residential tenants to contract with the landlord for repairs, commercial tenants can protect themselves by carefully inspecting rented properties, and commercial landlords have a strong business incentive to maintain their rental property.

Despite these arguments, some courts have protected commercial tenants from defective property conditions, departing from the common law rules in one of two respects. First, a small number of state courts have imposed an implied warranty that the premises will be fit or suitable for the tenant's intended commercial use. The leading case is the Texas Supreme Court's decision in *Davidow v. Inwood North Professional Group*[3] in which a tenant under a medical office lease found numerous defects in the premises that the landlord failed to correct, including a leaky roof, a faulty air conditioning unit, rodents and pests in the office, and a lack of cleaning and normal maintenance.

Second, some courts have abandoned the doctrine of independent covenants and allow a commercial tenant to refuse to pay rent if the landlord refuses to maintain the premises or make necessary repairs. In a recent decision, *Richard Barton Enterprises, Inc. v. Tsern*,[4] the Utah Supreme Court held that a commercial tenant's duty to pay rent is dependent on the landlord's performance of obligations that were significant to the purpose for which the premises were rented. In *Tsern*, a tenant who rented the first and second floors of a building for an antiques dealership could not use the second floor to store its heavy goods because the freight elevator was inoperable and the roof leaked, defects that the landlord was specifically required to correct under the terms of the lease.

These cases do not appear to be a trend in the law. The courts in most states continue to follow the common law rules regarding the landlord's duty to maintain the property. Thus, the terms of the lease will continue to be critical in defining what repair and maintenance obligations the landlord and tenant have and what remedies are available for their breach.

Lease Terms Regarding Maintenance

In commercial leases, the maintenance duties specified in the lease will vary according to the nature of the lease and the bargaining strength of the parties. In shopping center and office leases requiring the tenant to pay its pro rata share of operating costs, the landlord assumes most of the repair and maintenance obligations, typically having the duty to "operate, maintain, repair, and replace the systems, facilities, and equipment" necessary for the operation of the premises. The landlord is responsible for not only the repair and maintenance of the structure, but also for common area maintenance (CAM), including cleaning, landscaping, security, and lighting. The landlord must also provide necessary services to tenants and the building, such as heating and air conditioning. Although many leases provide only that the landlord will maintain the facility in "good repair," some leases impose a higher standard on the landlord. For example, a retail lease might provide that the landlord will maintain the shopping center "in a manner typically provided in first class shopping centers."

Under a shopping center or office building lease, the tenant's maintenance obligations are fairly minimal. Ordinarily, the tenant will be responsible only for keeping the interior of the premises in good repair (e.g., keeping the walls and floors clean, repairing any broken windows and doors, and keeping the equipment and fixtures in good working order). Some retail and office leases impose additional duties on the tenant. For example, if a separate HVAC (heating, ventilation, and air conditioning) unit services each individual rental unit in a building, the lease commonly makes the tenant responsible for the repair and maintenance of the HVAC unit. Also, in some types of commercial leases, the tenant assumes primary repair and maintenance responsibilities. In a ground lease or a lease of a building to a single tenant for industrial or warehouse use, overall responsibility for repair and maintenance usually rests with the tenant.

Commercial leases can provide remedies for a breach of the landlord's or tenant's maintenance duties. Faced with the common law doctrine of independent covenants, commercial tenants often negotiate the inclusion of a "self-help" remedy, which gives the tenant the right to make necessary repairs when a landlord fails to do so. Before making the repairs, however, the tenant must give the landlord notice of the problem and time to correct it. If the landlord fails to do so, the tenant can make the repairs and set off the repair costs against the rent. Landlords resist such provisions because they disrupt the cash flow from the property. Even if agreeable to such a remedy, landlords often try to limit either the conditions under which tenants may make repairs or the dollar amount of the repairs. Landlords, too, may insist upon a self-help provision to correct breaches of the tenant's duty to repair, allowing the landlord to enter the premises and make necessary repairs if the tenant fails to do so after notice from the landlord.

In the next case, the court must decide who is responsible for the replacement of a heating and cooling unit serving the premises. The case is instructive because the lease included a common disclaimer that the premises were being leased on an "as is" basis.

Case 13.3

Capital City Mortgage Corp. v. Habana Village Art & Folklore, Inc.

747 A.2d 564 (D.C. 2000)

In December 22, 1995, Capital City Mortgage Corporation (landlord) leased commercial property at 1834 Columbia Road, N.W., to Habana Village Art & Folklore, Inc., for operation of a restaurant and night club. Among other things, the lease provided:

> That [the Tenant] will, at his risk, cost and expense, during the term of this agreement or any renewal or extension thereof, make all repairs or improvements to said premises as same become necessary or are required, except repairs to the roof not caused by the negligence of the Tenant, which Landlord will make when necessary and upon notice.

There was an additional, typed provision at the end:

The property is to be leased in "as is" condition except that the lessor is to repair the fire escape and roof. The lessee is to perform all minor and major maintenance.

A dispute arose between landlord and tenant regarding responsibility for replacement of the heating and cooling units, which had failed and, the parties agreed, could not be repaired. The tenant withheld rent because the landlord refused to replace the defective units. The landlord filed a complaint for possession of the premises. The trial court sustained the complaint and awarded the landlord $11,000 for unpaid rent. The court further ruled, however, that the landlord was responsible for replacing the heating and cooling units.

FERREN, J.

The tenant . . . argued at trial, and the court agreed, that the lease was ambiguous as to the parties' respective responsibilities for the premises. According to the trial judge, neither paragraph 18 of the lease (quoted above), a pre-printed clause in the standard lease agreement, nor the additional provision typed at the end of the lease (also quoted above), covered the replacement of heating and cooling units. Based on evidence of a conversation about the heating and cooling units that occurred before the lease was signed, the court construed the lease against the landlord, ruling that the tenant had asked for the typed provision specifically for the purpose of limiting its liability to "maintenance," not "replacement."

We examine, first, the applicable law. Leases of real property are to be construed as contracts. In this jurisdiction, we "adhere to the 'objective law' of contracts, whereby the written language embodying the terms of an agreement will govern the rights and liabilities of the parties, unless the written language is not susceptible of a clear and definite undertaking, or unless there is fraud, duress or mutual mistake." [To] determine whether a contract provision has more than one reasonable interpretation, it is necessary to look at the "face of the language itself, giving that language its plain meaning, without reference to any rules of construction." If the court finds that the contract has more than one reasonable interpretation and therefore is ambiguous, then the court—after admitting probative extrinsic evidence—must "determin[e] what a reasonable person in the position of the parties would have thought the disputed language meant."

Applying the foregoing principles, we conclude that the trial court erred in admitting extrinsic evidence, because none of the provisions at issue is ambiguous. The question is: whether the lease terms themselves are ambiguous and thus require interpretation by reference to extrinsic evidence. As we shall see, there is no ambiguity. First, according to paragraph 18 of the lease, the tenant will "make all *repairs* or *improvements*, except repairs to the roof not caused by the negligence of the Tenant" (emphasis added). Next, according to the typed addition, the property is to be leased "as is" except that (1) "the lessor is to repair the *fire escape and roof*" (emphasis added) and (2) "[t]he lessee is to perform all minor and major *maintenance*" (emphasis added). We conclude that replacement of—meaning a substitution for—the defective heating and cooling units does not amount to a "repair" or an "improvement" under paragraph 18. The parties agree that the existing units themselves could not be "restore[d] to a sound good state." New equipment was required. Such replacement, therefore, would not be a mere repair. Moreover, the leased premises already had received, at the lease inception, the "valuable addition," of heating and air conditioning. Replacement of an existing improvement, therefore, would not in itself be a further "improvement" (unless, perhaps the equipment was upgraded, an issue not presented here). Nor, finally, is replacement of the heating and cooling units a matter of "maintenance" under the typed addition.

If, therefore, these phrases were the only ones involved, we would agree with the trial court, even without regard to extrinsic evidence, that the tenant's specified responsibilities would not extend to replacement of the needed units. So what pertinent language is left? On whom does the lease impose this "replacement" responsibility during the term of the lease when the tenant insists on replacement? The word "replacement" is not used, but there is other, controlling language. Except for the specified obligations of the landlord, and more fundamentally, in addition to the responsibilities specified for the tenant, the tenant takes the property under the lease—in the words of the typed addition—"as is." Accordingly, if the heating and cooling units need replacement, not merely "repair" or "maintenance," during the lease term, such replacement plainly is up to the tenant holding the property "as is."

The tenant asks us to rule, nonetheless, that the tenant's affirmative obligation to provide "all minor and major maintenance," as well as to make "all repairs or improvements" (with exceptions), creates a negative implication that the tenant has no other, more burdensome obligation to keep the improved property in working order. But that cannot be true. That overall, "as is" provision binding the tenant, not the collection of narrower tenant obligations, specifies the tenant's responsibility—the tenant's minimum as well as its maximum burden—for keeping heating and cooling units in place and in working order during the term of the lease. Otherwise, the words "as is" would have no discernible meaning.

We conclude, to the contrary, that the lease agreement was not ambiguous. Its plain language allocates the contested responsibility to the tenant—contingent on the tenant's election to replace the units; no question of a mandatory duty to replace the units during the lease term, or at its end, is presented. The trial court accordingly erred in admitting the extrinsic evidence that suggested a different result.

Hence, we reverse the judgment and remand for further proceedings.

QUESTIONS ABOUT CASE 13.3

1. Why was the "as is" language so important to the court's ultimate decision?

2. How would you redraft the lease to protect the tenant from the problem that arose in this case?

● Compliance with Laws

Unless the lease provides otherwise, the landlord usually is responsible for complying with regulatory and statutory requirements relating to the property, including building and housing codes; safety, health, and environmental regulations; and zoning laws and other land-use controls. Shifting that responsibility to the tenant, or allocating it between landlord and tenant, usually requires a clause in the lease to that effect.

It is perfectly reasonable and customary, however, for the tenant to be responsible for complying with laws regulating the operation of its business or its use of the premises. Therefore, leases commonly provide that the tenant will comply with "all present and future laws, ordinances, rules, and regulations of governmental authorities governing the use, conditions, and occupancy of the premises." Nevertheless, because such compliance can be unexpectedly expensive, tenants may want to negotiate with the landlord regarding laws and regulations that impose substantial costs or require the making of substantial improvements to the premises.

Landlords and tenants need to be especially aware of the accessibility requirements of the Americans with Disabilities Act (ADA) and other fair housing laws. The ADA requires public accommodations to be accessible to disabled persons. "Public accommodations" is a broad term including many businesses whose buildings or space may be leased, including restaurants, bars, theaters, shopping centers, retail stores, and service-related businesses. Both landlord and tenant are potentially liable for violations of the Act, although federal regulations permit the lease to allocate responsibility for ADA compliance between the parties. To comply with the act, the landlord or the tenant may have to make structural changes (e.g., build ramps, make curb cuts, renovate bathrooms, install elevators and automatic doors) to ensure that disabled persons are not excluded from the premises. Tenants should bargain for lease provisions that require the landlord to undertake the construction and other activities needed for compliance with the law. As to the costs of making the changes, the landlord might agree to bear them, or they might be shifted to tenants and allocated among them as operating costs. If a tenant assumes any responsibility for ADA compliance, it should be limited to changes necessary to make the tenant's specific business premises comply with the law. To determine in advance the changes that may be required, tenants should consider an ADA audit prior to renting the property, and should also seek representations from the landlord that the building or center is in compliance with the accessibility standards.

Environmental clean up and removal costs can be a source of serious disputes between landlord and tenant. Tenants should bargain for provisions in the lease that specifically require the landlord to take any remedial action required by environmental pollution laws and to assume the costs of environmental remediation. Landlords need corresponding provisions imposing responsibility on the tenant for the removal of hazardous materials attributable to the tenant or its business activities.

Constructive Eviction

As noted earlier in this chapter, by law or under a lease provision, a landlord may have a duty to maintain the leased premises or common areas or to provide heating, lighting, and air conditioning, but a failure to do so will not necessarily permit the tenant to refuse to pay rent. Under the doctrine of independent covenants still in effect in most states, despite the landlord's breach of the lease, the tenant's obligation to pay rent continues unless the landlord's breach is so serious as to result in a breach of the landlord's *implied covenant of quiet enjoyment* and a constructive eviction. The **implied covenant of quiet enjoyment** is the common law obligation by which the landlord guarantees the tenant undisturbed possession of the premises. A **constructive eviction** occurs when the acts (or omissions) of the landlord deprive the tenant of the beneficial use of the premises. If the landlord makes the premises unfit for the tenant's intended use, for example, by failing to carry out its duty to maintain the common areas in a safe condition or to provide adequate lighting, heat, or cooling, the tenant has been constructively evicted (if the tenant actually departs the premises because of the unacceptable conditions).

Whether the landlord has breached the implied covenant of quiet enjoyment depends on several factors, among them the lease terms allocating responsibility for repairs, compliance with laws, and provision of services. A constructive eviction must be based on a breach of duties the *landlord* assumed under the lease, not simply on a problem with the condition of the premises. Under some leases, the landlord has no duty to remedy defects in the premises because by a provision in the lease the *tenant* assumed responsibility for them or took the premises in an "as is" condition. Whether a constructive eviction occurred also depends on the use the tenant was making of the property and the extent to which the landlord's wrongful acts actually interfered with that use. A breach by the landlord causing mere inconvenience or annoyance to the tenant does not constitute a constructive eviction. The landlord's breach must cause a more substantial problem such as rendering the premises unsafe or unusable for the tenant's business. Finally, whether a landlord's breach constitutes a constructive eviction depends on the nature of the landlord's actions or omissions. Courts require that the landlord's conduct be intentional, and that the eviction be a result of the acts or omissions of the landlord, not some third party.

A landlord's failure to maintain the premises or common areas in a safe or healthy condition as required by the terms of the lease can constitute a constructive eviction. For example, one court held that a badly leaking roof that the landlord failed to repair rendered the premises unfit for use as a restaurant. Similarly, a failure to provide necessary services that the landlord agreed under the lease to provide has been held to constitute a constructive eviction. A landlord who fails to provide an adequate water supply, to install a heating system, or provide electricity and air conditioning to the premises breaches the implied covenant of quiet enjoyment if the services are necessary for the tenant's business operations and the landlord has a duty to provide them. Courts have also found constructive evictions when landlords have disregarded government orders to bring their buildings in compliance with building, safety, and health codes.

The common law required a tenant who claims a constructive eviction to abandon the premises within a reasonable time after the landlord's wrongful conduct, and the abandonment requirement is still widely enforced. A tenant who fails to vacate waives any right to claim a constructive eviction and must continue to pay rent. Some courts, however, have modified the strict rule regarding abandonment of the premises and have recognized partial constructive evictions. In the case of a partial constructive eviction, the tenant is obligated to vacate only the part of the premises that has been rendered unfit for use by the landlord. For example, a tenant was allowed to vacate the second floor of a restaurant (and to reduce rental payments accordingly) when the landlord failed to comply with a government order directing the installation of fire sprinklers.

Alteration of the Premises

Commercial leases normally contain provisions addressing the tenant's right to alter the premises and the tenant's right to trade fixtures and signs on the premises.

● Alterations and Improvements

In general, a commercial tenant has no right to alter the premises even if the alterations improve the property or enhance its value. Although the tenant may have a right to make minor repairs, substantial changes to the property usually require either a provision in the lease authorizing the tenant to make such alterations or the informal consent of the landlord.

As in other landlord-tenant negotiations, the tenant's right to make alterations depends on the relative bargaining power of the landlord and the tenant, as well as on the nature of the lease. In some commercial leases, such as lease of an entire structure for industrial use, the tenant may by custom have wide latitude to make structural and nonstructural changes and improvements to the property. In other leases, the tenant may have to bargain for lease provisions allowing the tenant to make minor changes to the premises or alterations that cost no more than a certain dollar amount. Most commercial leases, however, severely restrict the tenant's right to make alterations, regardless of the nature of the changes.

To control alterations of the premises, landlords frequently insist on some form of veto over any changes by the tenant. Many commercial leases provide that the tenant cannot alter, improve, or make any additions to the premises without the landlord's prior consent. The landlord also may insist upon prior approval of the plans and specifications for the alteration, and may reserve the right to approve the contractor or materials used in the project, or both. Tenants sometimes can bargain for a limit on a landlord's veto power, requiring, for example, that the landlord's consent will not be "unreasonably withheld."

In addition to controlling the type of alterations made to the premises, landlords have a legitimate interest in making sure that the work is done at the tenant's sole cost and expense and that the contractors performing the work are paid. Otherwise, the owner may risk having mechanic's liens filed against the property. At a minimum, the lease will provide that the tenant will promptly pay all contractors for work performed and promptly secure the removal of all mechanic's liens that are placed on the property. Some leases require the tenant to have a performance bond sufficient to cover the costs of the project or to take other steps, such as a requirement that the tenant secure mechanic's lien waivers, to ensure that no mechanic's liens are recorded. In some states, to eliminate the possibility of a mechanic's lien, the landlord can post a notice on the property indicating that it is not responsible for work performed at the direction of the tenant on the premises. In those states, leases may incorporate an obligation on the part of the tenant not to interfere with or remove such notices posted by the landlord.

Ownership at the expiration of lease term of any alterations and improvements made by the tenant often is governed by the lease as well. Usually the lease provides that any alterations become part of the realty and belong to the landlord at the end of the term. Alternatively, the lease may provide that, at the option of the landlord, the leasehold improvements will be removed from the premises and the tenant will be responsible for any damage caused by the removal. Tenants resist any such obligation, because the removal of alterations often is costly.

Trade Fixtures and Signs

As noted in Chapter 2, under the modern common law of many states, a tenant who attaches personal property to the real estate for trade, agricultural, domestic, or ornamental purposes is presumed not to intend permanent annexation, and can remove the attached property if removal can be effected without substantial injury to the real estate. Other states accomplish the same result by adhering to the older common law rule of *trade fixtures*. That is, they recognize that a businessperson's equipment attached to the landlord's realty and highly adapted to its use as a business property is a fixture, but they classify it as a trade fixture that is removable by the tenant upon termination of the lease unless otherwise agreed.

A lease can, of course, provide that the landlord shall become owner of the tenant's trade fixtures when the lease expires. Far more commonly, however, lease provisions give tenants the rights they would have under the law in the absence of a lease provision favoring the landlord. Thus, commercial leases usually allow the tenant to remove trade fixtures when the lease expires, and tenants usually agree that any installation will not impair the structural integrity of the property or otherwise damage the plumbing, electrical, and other systems serving the premises. (Provisions allowing the landlord to retain *alterations* frequently exclude trade fixtures and other personal property of the tenant.) Also, the tenant is obligated to make any necessary repairs to the premises caused by the removal of its trade fixtures.

Landlords generally impose greater restrictions on the installation of signs and other advertising on the premises than on the installation of trade fixtures. Ordinarily, the tenant is required to secure the consent of the landlord for signs that are displayed in certain locations such as the outside of the building or areas visible from the common areas. Landlords may impose additional conditions, including restrictions on the number, size, color, and type of signs employed by the tenant. Some shopping malls and retail centers have uniform standards for signs as part of the overall design and image of the complex, and tenants will be required to adhere to those standards. As with trade fixtures, tenants ordinarily are allowed to remove signs at the expiration of the lease, subject to liability for damages caused by the removal.

Restrictions on Assignments and Subleases

As noted in Chapter 12, a tenant has the right to assign or sublet the premises unless the lease restricts the tenant's right to do so. For several reasons, however, commercial leases usually do restrict the assignment and subletting of the premises. First, to ensure an appropriate mix of tenants, especially in shopping center leases, the landlord needs to control who rents the property. Even in office leases, the landlord may be concerned about how the business of an assignee or a sublessee will fit with the businesses of other tenants. For example, the landlord of a professional office building rented to doctors, lawyers, or architects may find a "telemarketing" business with phone banks incompatible with the professionals' business activities. Second, a sublessee or assignee may not be as creditworthy as the original tenant, so might be more likely to default in the payment of rent, breach the lease, or go out of business. Or a substitute tenant may not have the original tenant's ability to attract customers, even if the substitute is engaged in the same line of business. If the lease is a percentage lease, a substitute's inability to generate the same level of gross sales as the original tenant poses a real problem for the landlord. The problem is compounded where an anchor tenant seeks to transfer its lease. The substituted anchor tenant may not be as good a fit for the center, so may seriously erode the customer base. In short, an uncontrolled change in tenants could undermine the value and profitability of the shopping center.

Yet, for sound business reasons, tenants often need the ability to transfer their leases. The tenant's business may have evolved to such an extent that a change in location or space requirements is necessary. Or a tenant may want to sell its business. To do so, the seller will need to transfer its lease to the buyer as part of the seller's business assets. And sometimes a shopping center or complex changes in character to such an extent that it no longer makes business sense for a tenant to remain there, as where an upscale jewelry or furniture store finds that other tenants are being replaced by discount houses, which the center's customer base now prefers. Rather than default on the lease obligations and incur liability for continuing rent, the tenant wants the right to assign or sublet the premises to another business. To protect their respective interests, landlords and tenants commonly negotiate lease provisions specifying the conditions under which a tenant can assign or sublet its lease.

Landlord's Consent to Assignments and Subleases

Commercial leases sometimes flatly prohibit any assignment or sublease of the premises, but the most common restriction by far is a clause that requires the landlord's prior consent to any transfer by the tenant. The clause may specify the circumstances under which the landlord will consent to a transfer. Or it may be silent as to the conditions under which the landlord will consent. A clause lacking standards for the granting of the landlord's consent is sometimes referred to as a "silent consent" clause. The important legal issue under a silent consent clause is whether the landlord can arbitrarily refuse to consent to a proposed assignment or sublease if a tenant presents a sublessee or assignee who is financially sound and an appropriate fit for the premises. The majority rule is that the landlord *can* arbitrarily withhold consent. That is, the landlord need not act in good faith, and its refusal to consent need not be based on reasonable concerns regarding the proposed subtenant or assignee tenant.

A growing number of courts have rejected this view and now require landlords to act reasonably even under a "silent consent" clause. A leading case is the California Supreme Court decision in *Kendall v. Ernest Pestana, Inc.*[5] *Kendall* involved a subtenant who wanted to assign his lease when he sold his business. The new owners had a stronger financial statement and greater net worth than the subtenant, but the landlord refused to consent to the assignment. The landlord demanded "increased rent" as a condition for his consent and claimed an absolute right to withhold consent to any transfer. The California Supreme Court rejected the landlord's argument, holding that a landlord must have a commercially reasonable objection before it can refuse to consent to an assignment of a lease. It should be noted, however, that the California legislature later modified the rule adopted in *Kendall*. Under the California statute, landlords are still required to act reasonably in considering a tenant's request to transfer a lease under a silent consent clause, but they can condition their consent on recovering any additional rent paid by the substitute tenant.

Reasonableness of Landlord's Refusal to Consent

In the jurisdictions that follow the majority rule, the tenant needs to bargain for a lease provision requiring the landlord to act reasonably in deciding whether to allow the tenant to transfer the lease. Typically, the provision states that consent "will not be unreasonably withheld or delayed by the landlord." This general requirement of reasonableness can be further defined by setting forth the circumstances in which the landlord can refuse to consent, such as the financial incapacity of the new tenant or the unsuitability of its business for the center.

Tenants also may negotiate for exceptions to the consent requirement so that certain types of transfers are not subject to the landlord's discretion, for example, a transfer to a company owned by or affiliated with the tenant. This exception allows the tenant to restructure its business organization (e.g., by merger or consolidation) and to transfer the lease to its new business entity without having to secure the landlord's consent. Also commonly excepted is a transfer of the lease as part of a sale of the business to a new owner. This exception often contains conditions that, if met by the new owner, make the transfer binding on the landlord. For example, the exception may provide that the transfer binds the landlord if the new owner meets certain financial responsibility standards and continues to operate the business in the manner that the original tenant did.

Where the law or a lease provision forbids a landlord from unreasonably withholding consent to the transfer of a lease, when does the landlord have a reasonable basis for refusing to consent? If a proposed tenant is financially unsound, or its proposed business is not viable, then a landlord acts reasonably in refusing consent. In contrast, a landlord who refuses to consent to a transfer of a lease to a well-established business with adequate financial resources to meet the lease obligations acts unreasonably unless other considerations justify its actions. The burden of proving that the landlord's refusal to consent was unreasonable rests with the tenant, who must show that a reasonably prudent person in the position of the landlord would not have refused to consent to the assignment or sublease.

In deciding whether to refuse consent, landlords may legitimately consider the suitability and fit of the assignee tenant's use for the premises. Especially in retail malls and centers, landlords can refuse to consent to a transfer if the proposed tenant's business will disrupt the tenant mix of the center. Retail landlords with percentage leases can refuse to consent if the proposed tenant's business will not generate the same level of gross sales as the tenant's business. Similarly, a landlord acts reasonably in refusing to consent when an assignee tenant's proposed use for the premises is prohibited by a restrictive use clause in the lease or conflicts with exclusives granted to other tenants. Another legitimate consideration is the extent of the alterations of the premises proposed by an assignee tenant. If the proposed tenant needs to make substantial alterations of the premises, the landlord's refusal to consent to the transfer probably is reasonable.

Tenant's Abandonment and Landlord's Duty to Relet

Given the long duration of the typical commercial lease and the landlord's interest in receiving continuous income from the premises, a landlord will be especially alert to its rights upon a tenant's abandonment of its premises. As noted in Chapter 12, the law provides the landlord with a number of remedies for the tenant's abandonment. First, the act of abandonment constitutes an implied offer to surrender the premises and terminate the lease. The landlord has the option of accepting the offer and releasing the tenant from any further obligations under the lease. Second, rather than accept the offer of surrender, the landlord usually can retake possession of the premises and attempt to relet the premises for the tenant's account. In addition, commercial leases generally contain a surrender clause giving the landlord the right to retake possession, relet the premises, and for the remainder of the lease term hold the tenant responsible for damages caused by the abandonment. In jurisdictions that recognize a duty of the landlord to mitigate its damages, the landlord has a *duty* to retake possession upon the tenant's abandonment and to make a reasonable effort to relet the premises. In jurisdictions not requiring mitigation of damages, the landlord has a third option, leaving the premises vacant and holding the tenant liable for the unpaid rent at the end of the term or as rent accrues.

Surrender and Acceptance

A tenant who abandons rented premises might affirmatively surrender them to the landlord, or might simply remain silent. Either way, the tenant is considered to have surrendered the premises to the landlord. The landlord may accept the surrender and thereby release the tenant from any further obligations under the lease. In that event, the lease is understood to be terminated by mutual consent of the parties.

Surrender of abandoned premises and its acceptance by the landlord can be either express or implied by operation of law. Express surrender and acceptance occurs when the parties agree to cancel the lease upon the tenant's abandonment. This agreement can be oral or written. To avoid a claim of an oral surrender and acceptance (often difficult to defend against), a commercial lease may require that any agreement to accept a surrender be in writing.

A surrender and acceptance by operation of law is based on the landlord's conduct in response to a tenant's abandonment of the premises. At common law, if a landlord took possession and relet the premises, these actions were deemed inconsistent with the tenant's continuing right to possession under the lease, and thus a surrender and acceptance occurred. Today, however, landlords ordinarily can retake possession and relet the premises *without* being considered to have participated in a surrender and acceptance. Indeed, most commercial leases contain a surrender clause that allows reentry and reletting for the tenant's account and specifically provides that those actions will not constitute a surrender and acceptance. Thus, the tenant's obligation to pay rent is not terminated. Moreover, in the states requiring the landlord to mitigate its damages, the landlord's reasonable efforts to relet the premises are not considered inconsistent with the tenant's rights, since those efforts are required by law to reduce the damages the tenant will have to pay for its breach.

Nevertheless, even when the lease contains a surrender clause, landlords need to be careful, upon a tenant's abandoning the premises, to ensure that any actions the landlord takes are not construed as an acceptance of the tenant's surrender of the premises. If the actions of the landlord constitute an acceptance, the lease is terminated and the tenant is discharged from any further obligation to pay rent under the lease. The landlord will not be considered to have accepted a surrender by simply taking the keys to the property, or by taking possession for the purpose of protecting the property from vandalism or other dangers, or by repairing or remodeling the premises to attract substitute tenants. If, however, the landlord takes possession of the premises for its own business or personal use or attempts to sell the property, these actions may be inconsistent with the tenant's continuing rights under the lease and contrary to the landlord's rights under a surrender clause. This type of conduct suggests that the landlord is not dealing with the premises for the tenant's account, but rather for the landlord's own account. If the significance of the landlord's taking possession is litigated, the tenant has the burden of establishing a surrender and acceptance by operation of law, and that burden will be heavy if the lease has a surrender clause.

BOX 13–3 YOU BE THE JUDGE

Crown Industries leased a space at the Mesilla Valley Mall from the Mesilla Valley Mall Company. When it was unable to renegotiate the terms of its long-term lease, it abandoned the premises and failed to pay any further rent. The Mall Company took possession of the premises and allowed Las Cruces Museum of Natural History to occupy the space rent free in the interest of promoting good community relations. The Mall Company made efforts to relet the premises by advertising the space in national publications and by showing the property to prospective tenants. The Museum understood that it would be required to move on one-day's notice if a paying tenant was located. No commercial tenant was located, and the Mall Company sued Crown Industries for approximately $35,000, the unpaid rent for the remaining term of the lease. Crown Industries defended by claiming that the Mall Company had accepted the surrender of the lease when it allowed the museum to take possession of the premises. The Mall Company conceded that the museum attracted tenants to the mall and, therefore, benefitted the shopping center and its tenants. It argued, however, that its actions were permissible under the surrender clause of the lease. The lease provided that reentry and reletting by the landlord "shall not be construed as an election to terminate this lease nor shall it cause a forfeiture of rents." Was there a surrender and acceptance of the lease in this case?

Landlord's Duty to Relet the Premises

The states are split on the issue of whether a commercial landlord must relet the premises upon a tenant's abandonment. In most states, by either statute or court decision, the landlord has a general duty to mitigate damages caused by a tenant's breach of the lease, and thus a duty to relet the premises upon abandonment. If the landlord fails to take reasonable steps to minimize the damages caused by the tenant's breach, the landlord cannot recover any damages that could have been prevented by the landlord's taking those steps. A number of states, however, follow the common law rule that a landlord need not take any active measures to minimize the damages caused by a tenant's abandonment. Rather, the landlord may leave the premises vacant and hold the tenant liable for the entire unpaid rent for the remaining term of the lease.

In the states requiring mitigation, the landlord's duty to relet is measured by a reasonableness standard. The landlord must use reasonable efforts to find a substitute tenant. Because this standard requires the landlord to seek out a substitute tenant, the landlord does not comply with the duty by simply waiting for prospective tenants to inquire about the property. However, the landlord is not required to take any extraordinary steps such as renting the premises to a financially unsound tenant, nor to incur unreasonable expenses such as those required for substantially altering the premises for a substitute tenant. And, if the issue of mitigation is raised in a lawsuit over unpaid rent, the burden of proving a failure to mitigate is on the tenant, who must establish that the landlord failed to act reasonably.

The courts examine the issue of reasonableness on a case-by-case basis. Some factors the courts consider important are whether the landlord placed "for rent" signs on the property, advertised the property for rent in customary outlets, or hired a real estate agent to locate prospects. In one case, a landlord who failed to use "for rent" signs, advertise the property for rent, or otherwise attempt to locate tenants was held to have breached the duty of mitigation. In another, a landlord who failed to respond to a prospective tenant who had expressed an interest in the property was held to have acted unreasonably. In contrast, a landlord who advertised the property for rent, contacted prospects, and showed the property to some of them, had satisfied his obligation even though no "for rent" signs were posted on the property and even though the premises remained vacant despite his efforts.

Self-Study Questions

1. (a) What is a ground lease? (b) Why would a tenant prefer a ground lease to a lease of a building?

2. Explain the importance of rentable area.

3. What is a net lease and how is it different from a gross lease?

4. What is generally included within and excluded from operating costs or common area maintenance charges?

5. (a) What is percentage rent? (b) What is the difference between the natural breakpoint and an artificial breakpoint under a percentage rent clause?

6. (a) Explain the difference among a restrictive use clause, an exclusive use clause, and a continuous use clause. (b) Why are such clauses frequently used in shopping center and retail leases?

7. (a) Why do some courts recognize an implied warranty that the commercial premises will be fit or suitable for the tenant's intended commercial use?

(b) Why do most courts refuse to recognize the implied warranty of suitability?

8. (a) What is a constructive eviction? (b) What factors do the courts consider in determining whether the landlord has breached its implied covenant of quiet enjoyment?

9. (a) What is a "silent consent" clause? (b) Should the courts impose a duty on commercial landlords to act reasonably when they consider a tenant's request to assign or sublet the premises under a lease with a silent consent clause?

10. (a) What policy reasons favor the imposition of a duty on the part of a landlord to take reasonable steps to relet the premises upon an abandonment by the tenant? (b) What policy reasons support the traditional rule that a landlord has no duty to mitigate damages?

Case Problems

1. Circle K Corporation leased property from Frank Collins agreeing to pay rent calculated at 2% of "gross sales" on the premises, with some exceptions. The lease, drafted by Circle K, defined gross sales as "gross receipts of every kind and nature originating from sales and services on the demised premises. . . ." Among other transactions, the definition excluded refundable deposits on beverage bottles, money order transactions, and sales taxes. The definition made no mention of lottery sales. After the lease was in effect, Arizona passed a state lottery and Circle K became one of its sales agents. Circle K advised Collins that it was going to sell lottery tickets, and it requested Collins to sign a statement agreeing that their sales would be excluded from the calculation of percentage rent. Collins did not sign the statement, but nevertheless Circle K began selling the tickets. In a subsequent lawsuit, Collins contended that Circle K owed percentage rent on the lottery sales. Circle K argued that it owed percentage rent only on the commissions it received from the state since the lottery proceeds were property of the state when it received them. Circle K also argued that it was selling its services to the state in exchange for the commission on the sale of lottery tickets and, therefore, the commission provided the appropriate percentage rent base. How should the court decide the issue raised in the lawsuit? *In re Circle K Corporation,* 98 F. 3d 484 (9th Cir. 1996).

2. In late spring 1991, John McNamara leased space at Long Leaf Mall for a retail jewelry store. The mall was owned by Wilmington Mall Realty Corp. and managed by Great Atlantic Real Estate-Property Management. Newby Toms, an agent for Great Atlantic, negotiated the five-year lease. McNamara renovated the store space at his own expense and commenced operations in August 1991. In January 1992, Toms told McNamara that an aerobics studio would be opened in a space adjacent to the jewelry store, but that under the terms of the studio's lease, it was required to do soundproofing and could be relocated if necessary. On February 17, 1992, the studio commenced operating. McNamara immediately began objecting to Toms that the music coming from the aerobics studio was too loud and could be heard in his store. By letter dated February 26, he notified Great Atlantic that he was dissatisfied with the lack of efforts to remedy the situation and demanded a resolution of the matter. Receiving no response, he contacted an attorney, who notified Great Atlantic by letter dated March 12, that McNamara would be depositing his current rental payment into an escrow account until the nuisance was abated. In response, Toms directed the studio to install insulation as required by the terms of the studio's lease. The insulation was installed, but the noise from the studio continued to disrupt McNamara's business. Great Atlantic informed him by letter dated March 31 that remedial action had been completed and it considered the matter closed. McNamara continued to complain about the noise. In late April or early May, Great Atlantic agreed to pump insulation into the wall space between McNamara's store and the aerobics studio. After this was done, Great Atlantic told him that it considered the matter closed and demanded that McNamara pay rent. McNamara paid no rent after April 1992, and continued to complain about the noise well into the fall. On December 24, he abandoned his space in the Mall and later sued Wilmington for breach of contract, alleging constructive eviction and breach of the covenant of quiet enjoyment. The jury returned a verdict for McNamara in the amount of $110,000 on the breach of contract claim. Wilmington argued on appeal that McNamara's abandonment of the premises was not within a reasonable time. (a) Was there a constructive eviction in this case? (b) Did McNamara abandon the premises within a reasonable time? *McNamara v. Wilmington Mall Realty Corp.,* 466 S.E.2d 324 (N.C. App. 1996).

3. The Calvin M. and Raquel H. Newman Trust (Newman) owned property at 59th and Adam Streets in Lincoln, Nebraska. In 1977, Newman leased it to a Texas-based supermarket operator, American Community Stores Corporation (ACS). Prior to the lease, Newman agreed to lend ACS $400,000 to expand the existing store. In exchange, ACS agreed to an annual fixed rent of approximately $28,000 and percentage rent of 1% of annual gross receipts up to $7.4 million, and 2% over $7.4 million. The percentage rent was intended as the return on Newman's loan for the new store. To protect Newman, the lease pro-

vided that ACS would operate the property as "a first-class supermarket and consistent with maximizing the gross receipts from operations." It also prohibited an assignment or sublease without Newman's consent. By 1984, Newman was being paid approximately $97,000 in rent annually, close to 70% of which was percentage rent. ACS ceased operations in 1985, and transferred the lease to Hinky Dinky Omaha-Lincoln Inc. (Hinky Dinky) without Newman's consent. During negotiations over the unauthorized sublease, Hinky Dinky provided Newman with information about its plans for the store, its managers, and its financial condition. At that time, ACS had a net worth of $100 million, Hinky Dinky had a net worth between $200,000 and $210,000. Newman objected to the transfer because it appeared that Hinky Dinky intended to maximize profits by cutting overhead and labor costs, even if it meant a reduction in gross receipts. Newman was willing to consent to the transfer if the percentage rent was abolished and the fixed annual rent was raised to $97,000, thus assuring that the income from the lease would not fall below the 1984 amount. Hinky Dinky rejected this offer, and Newman brought a forcible detainer action to evict it from the premises. Since Hinky Dinky remained in possession after 1985 (pending the outcome of the litigation), and Newman accepted rent during the period after 1985, there was evidence as to actual percentage rent generated by Hinky Dinky for the period 1986–1991. Although the evidence indicated a decline in percentage rent paid under the lease, the court refused to consider this evidence, holding that it was not relevant to whether Newman acted reasonably in 1985. (a) Do you agree about the relevance of the evidence? What would your answer be if the percentage rent had increased during that period? (b) Did Newman act reasonably in refusing to consent to the sublease? *Newman v. Hinky Dinky Omaha-Lincoln Inc.*, 512 N.W.2d 410 (Neb. App. 1994).

Endnotes

1. Elaine Roston, "The Current Evolution in Shopping Center Lease Clauses," National Lease Advisors, Inc. (2000).

2. Patrick A. Randolph, Jr., "Going Dark Aggressively," Real Prop. Prob. & Tr. J. (November/December 1996).

3. 747 S.W.2d 373 (Tex. 1988).

4. *Richard Barton Enterprises, Inc. v. Tsern*, 928 P.2d 368 (Utah 1996).

5. 40 Cal.3d 488 (1985).

Chapter 14 Improving Real Estate: Construction and Development; Mechanics' Liens

Improving real estate can be among the most exciting and creative of ventures. Developers buy "raw" land and shape it to meet their vision, whether the goal is a rolling, peaceful residential community or a bustling commercial enterprise like a shopping center, office building, or hotel. Real estate development can also be incredibly lucrative; some of the wealthiest individuals in the United States acquired their wealth through real estate development. However, as Mom used to say: "If it was easy, everyone would be doing it." For a while in the mid-1980s, it appeared that everyone was doing it. In the 1980s, Congress crafted a tax code that encouraged real estate development and ownership. The result was massive investment in real estate—and overbuilding. Then, in 1986, to slow the rate of real estate development, Congress dramatically revised the Internal Revenue Code, eliminating many of the tax advantages to real estate investment and ownership. The result was that only the most financially viable real estate projects—and developers—survived.

The rewards in real estate development are directly related to the risk. The risks are high because successful real estate development is expensive and extraordinarily difficult. Many of the difficulties are legal in nature. Successful development requires a detailed understanding of most, if not all, of the legal material discussed in this text. To cope with the great expense involved, developers normally must seek capital from third parties, either through capital investment sources (discussed in Chapter 15) or through loan financing (discussed in Chapter 10). Because interest accrues constantly, the profitability of development is directly related not only to the marketability of the product itself, but also to how quickly the developer can deliver the product to market. For example, if the developer builds a beautiful office building but cannot find a suitable tenant, the investment may be lost. Jerry Adler gives a detailed description of one such tragic failure in his book, *High Rise: How 1000 Men and Women Worked Around the Clock for Five Years and Lost $200 Million Building a Skyscraper.* Even if the developer has a tenant, if the office building is finished too late, the interest payments on the construction loan may make the project unprofitable.

This chapter provides an introductory overview to the common types of real estate development and reviews typical acquisition and development problems. It also discusses problems associated with contractors, including mechanic's liens and the peculiar issues associated with financing land acquisition, development, and construction.

Development of Real Estate[1]

Real estate developers create value by putting undeveloped, raw land to useful purposes. The goal of a developer may be to create a product that will go into the developer's inventory for sale, such as houses or condominium units, or to create an investment property such as an office building whose rental will produce a stream of income over time for the developer or a buyer. Thus, depending on the developer's goals, real estate development can be analogized to the production of goods on an assembly line or to the acquisition of an investment portfolio.

Types of Development

Although the types of real estate development are limited only by the creativity of developers and the vagaries of the marketplace, we will confine our attention to four typical types of real estate development that raise many of the fundamental legal and business issues associated with development: (1) single-family residential, (2) multifamily residential, (3) shopping centers, and (4) offices.

Residential Single-Family

In the typical single-family residential development, the developer purchases a tract of undeveloped ("raw") land and subdivides it into smaller lots for construction of housing (hence the common term *subdivision* to describe residential development). "Single-family housing" is so-called in real estate practice and in zoning ordinances because a house designed for one family is constructed on each lot. In the process of the development, the developer installs the roads and utilities such as water, sewer, telephone, electricity, and cable television necessary to service the houses that will be constructed on the lots. The developer profits by selling the lots for more than the acquisition cost of the raw land plus the costs of development (including any indirect costs such as administrative, legal, architectural, engineering, and financing costs). Figure 14–1 shows a parcel of raw land that has been subdivided into lots.

A subdivision developer faces a host of practical, legal, and marketing considerations, including the following:

- The undeveloped parcel must have access to utilities.

- The terrain must be suitable for the construction of the houses and the installation of roads and utilities.

- The subdivided lots must exceed the minimum size permitted by zoning laws, yet be attractive to the developer's intended market.

- The developer must provide for future maintenance of the roads and utilities.

To provide for future maintenance, developers in most jurisdictions **dedicate** (give) the completed roads and utilities to the public or the local government authority that will assume the maintenance obligations. Usually the government will accept the offer of dedication (and assume the obligations) only if the roads and utilities meet the appropriate specifications. A developer who does not dedicate the roads and utilities to the public must provide for their operation and maintenance in some other way, for example, by forming a community or homeowners association that has the authority to levy assessments. Similarly, a developer who provides recreational amenities for the subdivision usually delegates the duty of maintenance to the community association.

Once the subdivision is completed, the developer or a third-party builder constructs houses on the lots. The home builder profits by selling the house for a price greater than the cost of the lot plus the total house construction costs (including any indirect costs).

Residential Multifamily

In a residential multifamily development, the developer must still develop the raw land by installing roads and utilities, but ordinarily the developer does not subdivide the land into parcels for sale separately. Instead, the developer constructs buildings designed for multiple family use, with the buildings themselves being divided into apartments or condominium units. The developer profits from the sale of the condominium units, from the sale of the apartment complex, or from the rental of the apartment units. If the developer sells the property as an apartment complex, its price is typically a function of the actual or potential net rental income from the property.

Multifamily developments tend to have a much higher "density" than single-family developments. In real estate development, **density** refers to the number of units or families per acre. A high-rise apartment building in Manhattan may have hundreds of units per acre, while a typical single-family residential development may have a much lower density of one to four units per acre. Several effects result from higher density. The per-unit land acquisition and development costs for multifamily developments tend to be lower than for single-family developments, even

FIGURE 14-1   Recorded Subdivision Plat

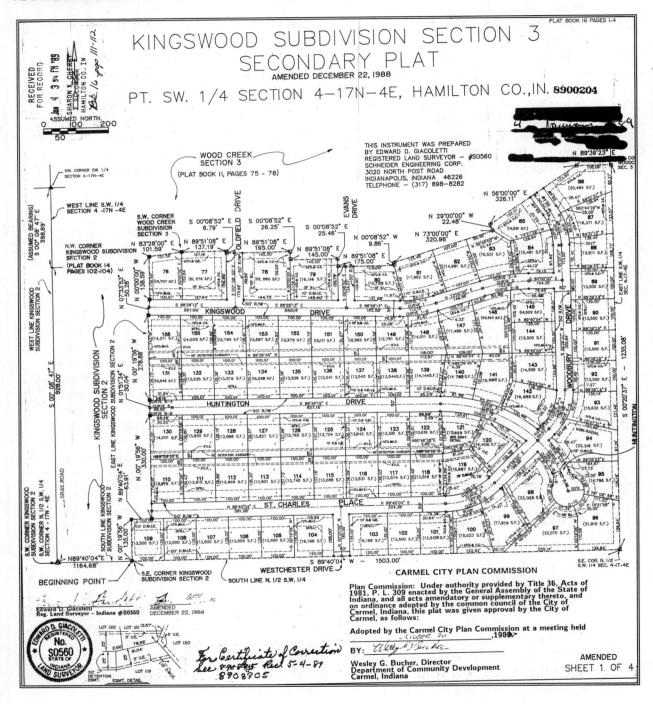

though land suitable for multifamily development tends to be more expensive per acre than land that is suitable for single-family development. On a square-footage basis, multifamily construction may be considerably more expensive than single-family construction because of more stringent building code requirements and the necessity for stronger materials. Increased density also means greater demand for government services such as schools, parks, water, sewers, and police and fire protection—and more noise and traffic. Because of the extra noise and traffic, many people do not want to live near a multifamily development. For all of these reasons, therefore, communities and zoning authorities tend to regulate and supervise multifamily developments more closely than single-family developments.

Shopping Centers

In many ways the development of a shopping center is similar to the development of an apartment complex. The developer must first develop raw land by installing roads and utilities. The developer does not normally subdivide the land into parcels for sale separately, at least not in the same way that the developer of a residential subdivision does. The developer then constructs buildings designed for use by retail tenants, with improvements such as canopies, malls, courts, landscaping, and parking lots designed for common use by the tenants and their customers. Like an apartment developer, the shopping center developer profits from the sale or rental of the shopping center. If the developer sells the shopping center, its price will be a function of the actual or potential net rental income from the property.

A significant difference, however, separates the development of apartments from the development of shopping centers. Apartments are more of a commodity product than are shopping centers. Apartment tenants lease for a relatively short term and are more or less interchangeable. In contrast, the success or failure of a shopping center depends upon the developer's acquiring and retaining a critical mass of long-term **anchor tenants** or **destination tenants** that will attract customers to the shopping center. Commonly, the anchor tenants are national or regional retail chains that spend large sums on promotion and advertising. Their presence will attract not only customers but also smaller, local retailers who hope to profit from the customer base drawn by the anchor tenants.

The profit for the developer hinges on the anchor tenants' having strong sales and on the center's attracting local retailers who will pay a comparatively high fixed rent. Because the development's success is based upon the anchor tenants, they must be "in place," that is, signed to long-term leases, before the developer can obtain financing and commence development. And because the success or failure of a shopping center development rests on the existence of anchor tenants, they are in a position to dictate the terms of their leases. Portions of the center rented to anchor tenants must be built to their specifications, and the rental rates must be attractive to them. Anchor tenants often pay a low fixed rental rate, together with a percentage of their sales. Because of their size and the low rental rate, anchor tenants have comparatively little risk if they fail to meet sales projections at a given shopping center.

In choosing shopping center sites, developers must consider their own needs as developers in addition to those of their tenants. Prospective retail tenants prefer sites in or near population centers that have retail zoning, very high traffic counts, and good accessibility for cars, while developers prefer sites that are reasonably flat, to minimize the site grading that will be necessary for store and parking lot construction. In some states, such as Colorado or West Virginia, sites that do not require considerable grading may be rare. Because a suitable site can be exceptionally expensive, the developer may have to invest large amounts of capital before it can commence development.

BOX 14–1 POINT TO CONSIDER

Because of the importance of anchor tenants in a successful shopping center, lease negotiations often focus on two critically important clauses in shopping center leases, so called "continuous operation" and "going dark" clauses. First, because the lease payments for anchor tenants are often composed of a low base rent together with a percentage of the tenant's sales at the location, the landlord wants assurance that the anchor tenant will be open for business and selling merchandise. Landlords often seek to extract an agreement that the anchor tenant "continuously operate" the business during the term of the lease. This provision would seem to be unnecessary under the logic that a tenant would not lease space it did not intend to use. However, shopping center leases tend to have long durations (20+ years) and business conditions change. An anchor tenant may be disappointed with the profitability of a particular location or may find a more desirable location. It may be willing to close the store and continue to pay the low base rent to avoid larger operating losses. Alternatively, it may be willing to pay the base rent simply to avoid having a competitor take the space.

Obviously, the desertion of an anchor tenant is a nightmare to the local tenants who signed leases in expectation of the customer traffic that anchor tenants generate. Therefore many smaller tenants request "going dark" clauses, which provide that if an anchor tenant departs and is not replaced by a comparable anchor tenant (in other words, the anchor space "goes dark"), the local tenant has the right to terminate its lease. Landlords are resistant to the inclusion of such clauses. The practical effect of the loss of anchor tenant may be the same whether or not the landlord allows "going dark" clauses. Most local tenant leases are short-term leases (three–five years) and the landlord will be unable to re-lease the space upon the expiration of the term. Also, many local tenants are not as well-capitalized as the anchor tenants. Therefore, the local tenants are likely to be unable to meet their lease obligations without the customer traffic provided by the anchor tenants.

Some state courts have been willing to intervene and *imply* a covenant to continuously operate upon the anchor tenants in shopping center leases in the absence of the agreement of the parties to the contrary.

Office

Office development is similar to apartment or shopping center development, in that the developer buys raw land, grades it, installs required roads and utilities, and constructs buildings and parking lots. The buildings are designed for office use rather than residential or retail use, and the developer profits directly or indirectly from the stream of rents generated from the office building. The developer may be responding to a general demand for office space in the community. However, the developer of a large office project (or the developer's lender) will want executed leases with anchor office tenants before development commences. In such a project, the developer typically tailors, or "up-fits," the internal layout of offices to the needs of individual tenants. **Up-fitting** is the installation of the internal walls, doors, painting, wallpaper, tile, carpeting, and other decorative features, a process that can be quite elaborate and expensive. Under the terms of the lease, the developer may pass along some of the up-fitting expense to the tenant.

Acquiring Land for Development

Acquiring land for development is no different in principle from acquiring any other type of real property, the methods of which are discussed in Chapters 6, 8, and 9. However, acquisition for development involves some special considerations.

First, obtaining acquisition and development financing is considerably more difficult, time-consuming, and uncertain than obtaining a home loan. To have a viable project and to obtain the necessary financing, the developer may need to find anchor tenants before acquisition and confirm that they are satisfied with the particular site and development plan. Because development financing usually takes much longer than the typical home loan, a developer is much more likely than a home buyer to need an *option contract* from the seller of the raw land instead of immediately executing a contract of purchase. In an option contract, the prospective seller of the land (offeror) sells the prospective buyer (the developer) a specified amount of time within which to decide whether to accept the seller's offer. The offeror agrees, for a consideration (the option price), not to revoke the offer to sell during the period of time specified in the option contract. The offeree (the developer) may decide whether to accept the offer to sell (i.e., may "exercise" the option) at any time during the option period. The developer uses the option period to confirm potential leases and financing before exercising the option and thereby creating the sales contract.

Second, because owners of land (and sometimes their lenders) are liable for environmental contamination caused by others, a Phase I environmental audit is necessary to inform the developer and its lender of any hazardous substances on the property and the extent of any cleanup that may be required. If the audit reveals a problem, the developer will have to decide whether to continue with the project at that site. The elements of the Phase I environmental audit and its importance are discussed in detail in Chapter 18.

Third, the developer should investigate the underground geology of the site. The soil has to bear the weight of buildings and other improvements without shifting or compacting. If the soil shifts or compacts after construction, the improvements may sink or crack, or even collapse. The Leaning Tower of Pisa is a famous example of a failure to evaluate soil conditions properly. However, though subsurface rock formations may be desirable to support improvements, they may create problems for the developer if grading or excavation of the site is necessary. Rock that cannot be removed ("ripped") using normal earthmoving equipment must be blasted with explosives, increasing the costs of development.

Complying with Subdivision Planning Regulations and Zoning Laws

A developer cannot assume that it will have the unrestricted right to develop its property. Most property desirable for development is subject to zoning or other governmental land use restrictions. For violating land use restrictions, the developer faces a variety of penalties, including being forced to remove any unapproved improvements.

If the zoning is not appropriate for the developer's intended use, the developer must explore the possibility of a zoning change, which may require the participation and cooperation of the current landowner. Even if the zoning is consistent with the developer's intended use, most zoning codes do not give blanket approval for development. Instead, to obtain the appropriate permits, the developer must have its specific development and building plans approved by the local zoning or planning authority. But the approval process may have become politicized. Communities do not always welcome a proposed development, even though it may create jobs and business and increase the community tax base. Neighboring property owners often oppose developments of particular types, particularly those that promise high density, noise, traffic, or pollution. Negative reaction to development is frequent enough to have earned an acronym in the development community: NIMBY, short for "Not In My Back Yard." Planning authorities are sensitive to these development issues. They also have legitimate concerns about the burdens on community services created by a proposed development.

Government involvement and permitting are prevalent at every step of the development process. The developer normally must obtain a **grading permit** prior to grading. Before granting it, the planning authorities must approve the developer's site-plan and erosion control plan. Grading removes ground cover. The authorities want assurance that the grading can be accomplished without the soil's washing into and clogging local storm sewers and streams. The developer also must obtain a **subdivision permit** before recording a subdivision plat or subdividing the property (see the approvals on the subdivision map in Figure 14–1). Normally the governing authority will condition its approval of the subdivision upon the developer's dedicating (offering) roads and utilities within the subdivision to the authority and its acceptance of the dedication. Then, before beginning any permanent improvements on the property, the developer must obtain a **building permit**. The governing authorities will review the architectural drawings for the proposed improvements and confirm that they meet the requirements of zoning and building codes. Finally, before the improvements can be occupied, the governing authority must issue a **certificate of occupancy** confirming that the improvements as constructed meet the applicable zoning and building codes.

● Assuring Utility Service

The developer must assure that the proposed development has appropriate utility service or be prepared to install it. The utilities that are necessary or desirable vary among developments, but normally include water, sewage disposal, telephone, electric power, and, often, natural gas and cable television. The burdens on particular utilities vary by type of development. For example, residential subdivisions demand greater water and sewer capacity than do shopping centers.

Water and Sewer

Water and sewage disposal are the most fundamental utility requirements for any type of development. In the simplest, low-density rural residential development, water may be obtained from wells that tap into naturally occurring aquifers. The developer must confirm that the water contained in the aquifer is sufficiently pure for drinking and is not contaminated by releases of wastes into the aquifer.

In a low-density development, sewage may be disposed of by means of a septic tank or drain field. Both of these devices depend on settling and filtration of solids out of sewage. The system then releases fluids into the soil where they are further filtered. The successful use of septic tanks or drain fields requires soil that is sufficiently porous to accept the fluids that are released (i.e., soil that percolates or "perks"). Therefore, the use of a septic tank or a drain field normally requires a permit from the local health department, which will test the soil characteristics before issuing the permit. Septic tanks and drain fields are common in rural areas. Though in common use, however, septic tanks and drain fields have disadvantages. First, they need to be located so that they will not be draining into the water supply if a well is the source of water. Second, rising water from rainfall can push sewage to the surface where it presents health hazards. Third, because septic tanks and drain fields depend on filtration, they will not eliminate chemical wastes or bacterial wastes.

Because of capacity limitations, developers use well-water and septic tank sewage disposal only in low-density development. For higher-density development, usually located in or near urban areas, a developer must find higher-capacity solutions and often can tap into municipal water and sewer systems. However, the developer usually must extend the subdivision's new water and sewer lines to the nearest existing water or sewer service, or directly or indirectly pay the expense of installation. Of course, the municipality must have sufficient additional capacity to support the proposed development. In areas of rapid development, municipal capacity may be insufficient, particularly sewage disposal capacity, which is stringently controlled by Clean Water Act permits issued by the Environmental Protection Agency.

Tying into existing water and sewer systems presents some planning challenges for the developer. Water usually is delivered under pressure so that the developer can install water lines on upgrades. To reduce expenses, developers prefer to install water lines where excavation has already been planned, such as within road rights-of-way. Sewage, however, is not under pressure and drains by force of gravity. Consequently, to avoid backups and blockage, a developer must install sewer lines so that the sewage will flow downhill, normally following natural downhill features like creekbeds. Otherwise, the developer must install pumps or lift-stations to move the sewage to outfalls.

If a high-density development does not have access to municipal water or sewer systems, the developer can provide its own water and sewage treatment facilities. But because of the great expense and engineering complexity involved, doing so is impractical for all but the largest developments.

Telephones

Although providing telephone service is not nearly as difficult a problem in most jurisdictions as providing water and sewer utilities, telephone service must nevertheless be negotiated with the local provider. Some localities have telephone capacity problems, particularly with the added demand created by dedicated fax and computer modem lines. Often, the principal development consideration is *how* telephone and electric power are to be delivered. For aesthetic reasons, the trend is to install both utilities underground, using underground conduits rather than aboveground poles. If underground power and phone lines are to be installed, the developer needs to plan the location and capacity of these lines carefully to avoid future excavation.

Electricity

Despite recent price and supply problems in California and other areas of the country, electric power is probably the most readily available of all utilities. Because the power companies have made electricity available throughout most of the country and are linked with each other to balance out capacity shortfalls and surpluses, the main development considerations continue to be the timing and location of service.

Gas

Especially for heating, natural gas usually is cheaper and more satisfying than electric power. Consequently, developers often gain a marketing advantage by providing buyers the option to tap into natural gas, particularly in residential developments. Like water, natural gas is delivered under pressure, and, like water lines, the gas lines normally are installed where excavation is already planned. And, as with water service, the developer often must install the gas lines or pay for their installation from the closest current service, a cost that may be prohibitively expensive in small developments.

● Access to Public Roads and Dedication

Because physical access to public roads is critical to the success of a development, most are located adjacent to major streets or highways. However, governing authorities usually limit access to specified street locations ("curb cuts") to assure the orderly movement of traffic and to facilitate community planning. And if automotive traffic flow is likely to be heavy, the developer may need to negotiate with governmental authorities for the installation of stop signs or traffic lights. Where access to the development is obtained by means of an easement over neighboring property, the developer must confirm that the easement will legally accommodate the additional or different burden contemplated by the development. Any roads installed by the developer must comply with governmental specifications designed to ensure safety, drainage, durability, and access for firetrucks and other emergency vehicles.

The developer normally must dedicate all roads and utilities to the relevant municipality, other governmental authority, or utility company. A completed dedication consists of the developer's *offer* of dedication and *acceptance* of the offer by the donee (government authority or utility). The acceptance can be express, or it may be implied from the donee's actually undertaking maintenance and repairs. Or the donee may reject the offer because the government or utility then becomes responsible for repairing and maintaining the improvements. Therefore, neither a governmental authority nor a utility will accept a dedication of improvements that do not meet its specifications or that pose serious maintenance or repair problems.

As governments face tax revolts at every level, one prominent issue in the last decade is the extent to which a governmental authority can condition the issuance of permits on the dedication of land or improvements for the benefit of the government. The following case imposes legal limits on the power of government to compel a dedication.

Case 14.1

Dolan v. City of Tigard
512 U.S. 374 (1994)

The City Planning Commission of Tigard conditioned approval of Dolan's application to expand her store and pave her parking lot upon her dedication of land for a public greenway along Fanno Creek to minimize flooding associated with her development and for a pedestrian/bicycle pathway intended to relieve traffic congestion in the city's Central Business District. She appealed to the Land Use Board of Appeals (LUBA), alleging that the land dedication requirements were not related to the proposed development and therefore constituted an uncompensated taking of her property in violation of the Fifth Amendment. LUBA found a reasonable relationship between the development and (1) the requirement to dedicate land for a greenway, since the larger building and paved lot would increase the runoff into the creek, and (2) the requirement to dedicate land for the pedestrian/bicycle path, which would alleviate the impact of increased traffic from the development by providing an alternative means of transportation. Both the Oregon Court of Appeals and the Oregon Supreme Court affirmed. Dolan appealed to the U.S. Supreme Court.

REHNQUIST, C. J.

The Takings Clause of the Fifth Amendment of the United States Constitution, made applicable to the States through the Fourteenth Amendment, provides:

"Nor shall private property be taken for public use, without just compensation." One of the principal purposes of the Takings Clause is "to bar Government from forcing some people alone to bear public burdens which, in all fairness and justice, should be borne by the public as a whole. . . ." Without question, had the city simply required petitioner to dedicate a strip of land along Fanno Creek for public use, rather than conditioning the grant of her permit to redevelop her property on such a dedication, a taking would have occurred. Such public access would deprive petitioner of the right to exclude others, "one of the most essential sticks in the bundle of rights that are commonly characterized as property. . . ."

On the other side of the ledger, the authority of state and local governments to engage in land use planning has been sustained against constitutional challenge as long ago as our decision in *Village of Euclid v. Ambler Realty Co.* "Government hardly could go on if to some extent values incident to property could not be diminished without paying for every such change in the general law." A land use regulation does not effect a taking if it "substantially advances legitimate state interests" and does not "deny an owner economically viable use of his land."

The sort of land use regulations discussed in the cases just cited, however, differ in two relevant particulars from the present case. First, they involved essentially legislative determinations classifying entire areas of the city, whereas here the city made an adjudicative decision to condition petitioner's application for a building permit on an individual parcel. Second, the conditions imposed were not simply a limitation on the use petitioner might make of her own parcel, but a requirement that she deed portions of the property to the city. . . .

Undoubtedly, the prevention of flooding along Fanno Creek and the reduction of traffic congestion in the Central Business District qualify as the type of legitimate public purposes we have upheld. It seems equally obvious that a nexus exists between preventing flooding along Fanno Creek and limiting development within the creek's 100-year floodplain. Petitioner proposes to double the size of her retail store and to pave her now-gravel parking lot, thereby expanding the impervious surface on the property and increasing the amount of storm water runoff into Fanno Creek.

The same may be said for the city's attempt to reduce traffic congestion by providing for alternative means of transportation. In theory, a pedestrian/bicycle pathway provides a useful alternative means of transportation for workers and shoppers: "Pedestrians and bicyclists occupying dedicated spaces for walking and/or bicycling . . . remove potential vehicles from streets, resulting in an overall improvement in total transportation system flow.". . .

We think a term such as "rough proportionality" best encapsulates what we hold to be the requirement of the Fifth Amendment. No precise mathematical calculation is required, but the city must make some sort of individualized determination that the required dedication is related both in nature and extent to the impact of the proposed development. . . .

If petitioner's proposed development had somehow encroached on existing greenway space in the city, it would have been reasonable to require petitioner to provide some alternative greenway space for the public either on her property or elsewhere. But that is not the case here. We conclude that the findings upon which the city relies do not show the required reasonable relationship between the floodplain easement and the petitioner's proposed new building.

With respect to the pedestrian/bicycle pathway, we have no doubt that the city was correct in finding that the larger retail sales facility proposed by petitioner will increase traffic on the streets of the Central Business District. . . . But on the record before us, the city has not met its burden of demonstrating that the additional number of vehicle and bicycle trips generated by petitioner's development reasonably relate to the city's requirement for a dedication of the pedestrian/bicycle pathway easement. The city simply found that the creation of the pathway "could offset some of the traffic demand . . . and lessen the increase in traffic congestion."

As Justice Peterson of the Supreme Court of Oregon explained in his dissenting opinion, however, "the findings of fact that the bicycle pathway system 'could offset some of the traffic demand' is a far cry from a finding that the bicycle pathway system will, or is likely to, offset some of the traffic demand." No precise mathematical calculation is required, but the city must make some effort to quantify its findings in support of the dedication for the pedestrian/bicycle pathway beyond the conclusory statement that it could offset some of the traffic demand generated.

Cities have long engaged in the commendable task of land use planning, made necessary by increasing urbanization, particularly in metropolitan areas such as Portland. The city's goals of reducing flooding hazards and traffic congestion, and providing for public greenways, are laudable, but there are outer limits to how this may be done. "A strong public desire to improve the public condition [will not] warrant achieving the desire by a shorter cut than the constitutional way of paying for the change."

The judgment of the Supreme Court of Oregon is reversed, and the case is remanded for further proceedings not inconsistent with this opinion.

QUESTIONS ABOUT CASE 14.1

1. What is the "rough proportionality" test imposed by the U.S. Supreme Court on the City of Tigard?

2. What factual showing would the City of Tigard have to make to avoid having the greenbelt and the pedestrian/bicycle path exactions held a taking for which the city must pay? How might the result in this case have been different if the city had required Dolan to construct a stoplight to handle additional traffic to the store?

Construction

Most developers do not have the expertise, specialized skill, or equipment necessary to design or build the improvements contemplated by the development, or they simply prefer to leave that work to others. To design the improvements and develop the plans and specifications, developers turn to architects. To grade the property and construct the improvements, developers employ contractors. These relationships are critical to the success of the development.

● Preconstruction Design Work; The Owner-Architect Relationship

Before closing on the property, the developer ordinarily will have to complete some design work to acquire financing for the development and to obtain development permits. Because of the cost of capital, the developer normally wants to be in a position to commence development or construction immediately after closing. Therefore, by closing most developers have already employed an architect.

An architect is a professional trained in the design and construction of real estate improvements, and in the characteristics of materials used in construction. Because of the danger attending faulty design and construction, architects must be licensed by the state. Most states require that architects meet prescribed educational requirements, including a practical apprenticeship, and pass a rigorous series of examinations to obtain a license. Although architects must have at least a general understanding of soil characteristics, grading, utilities, road construction, and other aspects of development, they may employ or subcontract parts of the development-related work to civil engineers, who have more specialized training in these areas.

Payment for the architect's services may be based on an hourly rate, a fixed fee, or a percentage of the proposed construction costs. Although the terms of contracts with architects are negotiable, the **American Institute of Architects**[2] **(AIA)** has developed a series of commonly used forms for architects' contracts and contractors' contracts. These contract forms have been developed by architects and, as might be expected, resolve many doubts in favor of the architect. However, the forms raise many of the common issues encountered in design, development, and construction and are, therefore, a good starting point for negotiation.

As the one responsible for transforming the developer's vision into the plans and specifications for the development and construction work, the architect needs to understand clearly the market for the product and the design characteristics that will be necessary to attract that market. For example, a developer, Julio, may want to construct a ten-story office building appealing to professional office tenants like lawyers and accountants. He tells Monica, the architect, the building must have certain features. For example, the floors must have a minimum of 15,000 usable square feet, the building must have a visual flair with lots of light, and the parking lot must contain a certain number of parking spaces for the tenants and their clients. The architect specifies the materials that will meet these needs. To provide an abundance of light, the architect may choose a glass exterior (a glass "curtain wall") for the structure. Because Monica knows that lawyers and accountants generate huge amounts of paperwork, which require massive storage units, she will specify structural materials that will support heavy loads. The architect will also adapt the developer's aesthetic requirements to the requirements of law. For example, Monica will design sprinkler systems and exit stairs to meet fire code requirements and will design ramps, elevators, and bathrooms that meet the requirements of the Americans with Disabilities Act. Considering the anticipated use and square footage, the architect will also suggest, among other things, what kinds of heating and cooling systems are necessary and how many restrooms will be necessary to serve the occupants. The end result of the communication between the architect and developer is a set of preliminary plans and specifications.

The preliminary plans and specifications enable the architect to give the developer a rough estimate of the development and construction costs. To get a more precise estimate, the developer can use the preliminary plans and specifications to obtain estimates, or even formal bids, from construction contractors. If the price estimates or bids exceed the developer's proposed budget, the developer and the architect may engage in a process referred to as "value engineering" to determine where in the design, construction, or materials selection they can achieve cost savings without undue sacrifice of quality and aesthetic appeal. For example, if the design can be altered to accommodate the use of prefabricated components rather than custom components constructed on-site, the architect can often realize significant cost savings.

● Construction Contracts

After the design, financing, and permitting phases of a development project, the developer undertakes the construction phase. In carrying it out, the developer has two main choices:

1. The developer could hire and supervise the firms and workers needed for the work, for example, a masonry firm to lay the foundation and do the brick and stone work, a framing crew to do the framing, and a plumbing contractor to do the plumbing.

2. The developer could hire a **general contractor** who will in turn hire and supervise firms in the various building trades who will serve as **subcontractors** for their part of the work. Because few developers have the necessary time and skills to supervise the actual building work themselves, most hire general contractors to oversee the construction phase of the project.

In theory, an oral construction contract is enforceable, because no provision of the Statute of Frauds requires a writing (ordinarily a construction contract is interpreted to be for the sale of services, not goods, and the contract can in theory be performed within one year). But the use of an oral contract would be foolhardy. Given the complexity and expense of most construction projects, construction contracts obviously should be articulated in writing.

General Contractors

General contractors are licensed by the states. To protect the consuming public from unqualified practitioners, licensing boards impose educational, experience, and testing requirements to assure that applicants for a contractor's license have the requisite knowledge of construction techniques. Although general contractors may employ skilled tradespeople full-time, a general contractor is more likely to subcontract with an outside firm, which provides skilled workers as needed on a particular job. By employing the general contractor, the developer has a single person or entity to look to for performance of the job.

Contract Pricing Methods

A contractor's pricing a building or other improvements on real property is more complex than a retail seller's pricing of a piece of personal property. Usually the seller of personalty knows with a fair degree of accuracy what the product cost to buy or produce, and therefore how much the seller should charge the buyer. Pricing the improvements on real property is much more difficult. Most buildings, for example, are constructed over a period of months or years, and much of the material and labor may not be procured until construction is nearly completed, long after the initial price quote. In quoting a price for the project, a general contractor must know not only the current prices for labor and materials necessary to comply with the plans and specifications, but also how those prices may fluctuate as construction progresses.

To manage pricing uncertainty, contractors use several common construction pricing methods that manage the uncertainty in different ways: (1) a fixed price or "lump sum" contract, (2) a "guaranteed maximum" contract, or (3) a "cost plus" contract. Sometimes these methods are used in combination.

In a "lump sum" contract, the general contractor quotes a fixed price for the improvements. If the contractor completes the project for less than the quoted price, the difference becomes additional profit to the contractor. If the general contractor's cost exceeds the quoted price, the contractor is still legally obligated to complete the job for that price and must absorb the loss. Although this technique has the appeal of simplicity, it may create some practical problems. A general contractor may inflate the quoted price as a hedge against error, or, upon learning that the quoted price is now inadequate, may try to cut corners in the construction process to increase profits. Alternatively, if it becomes clear to the contractor that the project is a money-loser, the contractor may divert time, attention, and resources to a more profitable project, or the contractor may simply refuse to complete the project. Naturally, the developer or the landowner can sue to enforce the contract or to collect damages, but either alternative is likely to be expensive, time consuming, and unsatisfactory.

A "guaranteed maximum" contract sets a maximum price for the project. The developer often gives the contractor incentive to seek cost savings under a guaranteed maximum contract by agreeing to split any cost savings from the guaranteed maximum with the contractor.

In a "cost plus" contract, the contractor charges the owner for the contractor's actual costs plus a fee for serving as contractor. The fee may be fixed at a certain sum or may be expressed as a percentage of the costs. Although the fee removes any incentive for the contractor to inflate the initial estimate and all cost savings accrue to the benefit of the landowner, the contractor also has no incentive to reduce costs, particularly if its fee is a percentage of the costs. Therefore, a cost-plus contract is often used in combination with a guaranteed maximum.

In addition to the architect's contract previously mentioned, the American Institute of Architects has produced contractors' contract forms designed to accommodate each of the pricing methods. The forms can be a helpful starting point for developers and others in their negotiations with contractors. The construction contract should incorporate the approved plans and specifications, and should specify in detail the services that the contractor is to provide and the method by which its fee is to be determined.

Regardless of the pricing method used, construction contracts often are subjected to a bidding process in which several general contractors compete for the job by offering a price they think will be lower than those of their rivals. The developer provides the architect's plans and specifications to the general contractors so that they may compile their "bids" (offers). A developer of a private project has no obligation to accept the lowest bid, but may instead accept a higher one for whatever reason the developer may have, or the developer may choose to accept none of the bids. Government entities, however, usually are required by law to accept the "lowest and best" bid to protect the taxpayers from the wasting of public funds, although the government, too, can reject all bids if none meets minimum requirements. The use of the bid process helps the developer identify and eliminate contractors who have obviously underestimated the time or cost necessary to construct the improvements and who, therefore, are likely to create problems. The bidding process also enables developers to eliminate contractors who have "padded" the project either to deal with pricing uncertainty or to produce unwarranted profits.

A general contractor may generate its bid in any way that it chooses, but to compute its bid for the project (the "prime contract"), usually it will seek bids from potential subcontractors and materials suppliers and will incorporate the "lowest and best" bids into the prime bid. This bidding procedure is used routinely on the bigger or more complicated projects.

Use of Subcontractors

Subcontractors contract with a general contractor and have no direct contractual relationship with the developer. Most subcontractors are skilled tradespeople—plumbers, masons, framers, electricians—who are separately licensed in their respective trades. Unless the prime contract provides otherwise, the selection and supervision of the subcontractors are entirely the responsibility of the general contractor. Because subcontractors have no direct contractual relationship with the developer, they expect to be paid by the general contractor, so are much concerned with the general contractor's solvency.

Changes in the Contract

Because construction may take place over an extended period, changes in the contract may be necessary as construction progresses. For example, the owner or architect may make design changes in response to the requests of prospective tenants. Many changes require adjustments to the agreed price. Regardless of whether the changes are price-related, however, they should be documented by written amendments known as "change orders," because oral modifications of the construction contract may be unenforceable under the parol evidence rule (discussed in Chapter 8).

Performance of the Contract

A general contractor must perform the construction contract according to its terms. If the plans and specifications have been incorporated into the contract, the contractor must deliver the improvements properly constructed in accordance with them. Otherwise, the general contractor will be liable for breach of contract. However, the contractor's breach must be material for the developer to be completely excused from its obligations under the contract. Because of the uncertainty associated with construction work, courts tend to give contractors considerable leeway before finding a material breach. The following landmark opinion by Justice Cardozo illustrates this judicial attitude and sets forth the appropriate measure of damages for a contractor's breach.

Case 14.2

Jacob & Young, Inc. v. Kent

129 N.E. 889 (N.Y. 1921)

Plaintiff Jacob & Young built a country residence for defendant Kent at a cost of approximately $77,000, and sued to recover a balance of $3,483.46 remaining unpaid. A specification for the plumbing work provided that "all wrought iron pipe must be well galvanized, lap welded pipe of the grade known as 'standard pipe' of Reading manufacture." Defendant learned in March 1915 that some of the pipe, instead of being made in Reading, was the product of other factories. Defendant complained to the architect, who ordered the plaintiff to do the work over. As the plumbing was encased within the walls except in a few places where it had to be exposed, obeying the order would require the demolition at great expense of substantial parts of the completed structure. The plaintiff left the work untouched, and asked the architect for a certificate that the final payment was due. Refusal of the certificate was followed by this suit.

The evidence shows that the omission of the prescribed brand of pipe was neither fraudulent nor willful. It was the result of the oversight and inattention of the plaintiff's subcontractor. Reading pipe is distinguished from Cohoes pipe and other brands only by the name of the manufacturer stamped upon it at intervals of between six and seven feet. Even the defendant's architect, though he inspected the pipe upon arrival, failed to notice the discrepancy. The plaintiff offered evidence that the brands installed, though made by other manufacturers, were the same in quality, appearance, market value, and cost as the brand stated in the contract—that they were, indeed, the same thing, though manufactured in another place. Defendant appealed.

CARDOZO, C. J.

We think the evidence, if admitted, would have supplied some basis for the inference that the defect was insignificant in its relation to the project. The courts never say that one who makes a contract [discharges] his duty by less than full performance. They do say, however, that an omission, both trivial and innocent, will sometimes be atoned for by allowance of [damages], and will not always be the breach of a condition to be followed by a forfeiture. . . .

In the circumstances of this case, we think the measure of the allowance is not the cost of [replacing all the pipe], but the difference in value [between the Reading and the non-Reading pipe], which would be either nominal or nothing. Some of the exposed sections might perhaps have been replaced at moderate expense. . . . The owner is entitled to the money which will permit him to complete [work poorly done or left undone], unless the cost of completion is grossly and unfairly out of proportion to the good to be attained. When [the cost of completion is excessive], the measure [of damages] is the difference in value [between the work or materials actually supplied and the work or materials required by the specifications]. Specifications call, let us say, for a foundation built of granite quarried in Vermont. On the completion of the building, the owner learns that through the blunder of a subcontractor part of the foundation has been built of granite of the same quality quarried in New Hampshire. The measure of allowance [for the contractor's imperfect performance] is not the cost of reconstruction [using Vermont granite]. "There may be omissions of that which could not afterwards be supplied exactly as called for by the contract without taking down the building to its foundations, and at the same time the omission may not affect the value of the building for use or otherwise, except so slightly as to be hardly appreciable." . . . The rule that gives [the contractor] a remedy in cases of [the contractor's] substantial performance, with compensation [to the contractor's employer] for defects of trivial or inappreciable importance, has been developed by the courts as an instrument of justice. The measure of the allowance [to the employer for the contractor's deficiencies] must be shaped to the same end.

[J]udgment . . . in favor of the plaintiff.

QUESTIONS ABOUT CASE 14.2

1. The buyer here bargained for Reading pipe. Why shouldn't the contractor be forced to tear out the walls and install Reading pipe?

2. How is the buyer getting the "benefit of his bargain" in this case?

Resolving Disputes Between the Contracting Parties

The parties to a construction contract can resolve their disputes using any means ordinarily available to resolve disputes. The traditional method is litigation, but litigation is an especially ineffective way to resolve disputes as construction progresses, because of the time and expense involved. Also, the typical state or federal judge, though usually expert in formal dispute resolution, knows little about construction and, like any jury that may be involved, must be educated by the parties and their lawyers regarding the source and nature of the dispute. Any misunderstanding of the construction process by the judge or jury may disadvantage one of the disputing parties. Therefore, dispute resolution techniques alternative to litigation may be preferable for resolving construction-related disputes. *Arbitration* and *mediation* are common alternatives for resolving disputes that arise in the construction industry.

Alternative Dispute Resolution. In **arbitration** the parties submit their dispute to an expert or a panel of experts acceptable to the parties, for a binding decision. If the parties use a panel, ordinarily the owner and the contractor each selects one member of the panel and these two panel members select a third. For construction disputes, a panel might consist of arbitrators drawn from construction or construction-related fields, such as other contractors, architects, engineers, or construction lawyers. One advantage of arbitration is that the parties need to spend little or no time educating the arbitrators about the nature of the dispute. Also, arbitration may involve fewer delays because, within limits, the panel can meet at the convenience of the parties. Because of these advantages, arbitration is included in all of the AIA form contracts as a dispute resolution tool.[3]

Yet, like litigation, arbitration can be a time-consuming, expensive, and adversarial process, with one or both of the parties being dissatisfied with the result. Another dispute resolution alternative, **mediation**, may avoid the disadvantages of arbitration. Like arbitration, mediation involves an expert, or a panel of experts, to whom the dispute is presented. Unlike arbitration, mediation is not binding on the parties. The role of the mediator is to present an unbiased point of view to assist the parties in resolving the dispute themselves through a process of negotiation. In choosing a mediator, the disputing parties might call upon a contractor or an architect (or some other construction professional) capable of expressing a considered opinion regarding whether the improvements were constructed in accordance with the plans and specifications and industry practice. If the improvements are not in conformance with these standards, the mediator is expected to suggest necessary modifications. Because the final outcome of mediation is a negotiated agreement of the parties, the process tends to be much less confrontational, time-consuming, and expensive than litigation or arbitration.

Construction Delays and Liquidated Damages. A recurring problem in construction is the contractor who delivers the improvements late. Each day of delay means that the developer incurs an additional day's interest on its construction loan and loses the opportunity to use the improvements to generate income. Construction delays have many causes. Some are the fault of the contractor, as where the contractor does not arrange for timely delivery of materials or equipment, has insufficient labor on the job, or pulls labor off the job to work on other projects. Some delays are beyond the contractor's control. For example, the weather may turn too cold to mix and pour concrete or to apply paint.

To compensate the developer for delay-related costs, construction contracts commonly include a deadline for the completion of construction, together with a **liquidated damages** clause requiring the contractor to pay a fixed sum ("liquidated damages") for each day of delay. The liquidated damages clause is an estimation of the amount of daily loss the developer or owner is likely to incur because of the contractor's delay. If the construction is not completed by the deadline, either the contractor must pay the amount of damages that have accumulated, or the contract price is reduced by that amount. To be enforceable, however, the liquidated damages clause must be a reasonable estimation of the actual damages resulting from the delay. A clause that imposes an unreasonably large amount will be ruled an unenforceable *penalty clause* meant to punish the contractor rather than fairly compensate the owner. Although the deadline for completion is commonly referred to as a "penalty date," and the delay-related damages are often called "penalties," the clause imposing them is nevertheless a liquidated damages clause if the amount is a reasonable estimation of the owner's loss. Normally, liquidated damages clauses are accompanied by a **force majeure clause**, which gives the contractor an extension of time if the reasons for the delay are beyond of the contractor's control. Such reasons include bad weather, other "acts of God," strikes, and shortages of materials.

Construction Bonds

Although the developer has a contract right to timely construction of the improvements in accordance with the plans and specifications, that right may be only theoretical if the contractor is or becomes financially unable to complete the project or to respond in damages for its failure to do so. To protect against the contractor's insolvency, the developer may demand an assurance that a financially solvent third party will step in to complete the project or pay damages if the contractor is unable or unwilling to do so. This service is performed in the construction industry by commercial *surety (bonding)* companies. For a payment called a premium, a surety company issues a surety bond ensuring that it will fund the completion of the project or pay the developer's damages up to a stated amount, or "penal sum." Like other insurers, the surety company evaluates the risk of nonperformance in deciding whether to provide the coverage and in establishing the premium. The inability of a contractor to obtain a surety bond may be a sign of its financial weakness and a warning to the developer to avoid that contractor.

Three types of bonds are used in the construction industry: the *bid bond*, the *performance bond*, and the *payment bond*.

Bid Bonds. A **bid bond** is used to pay damages to the developer if the contractor is awarded the contract but does not proceed with it. Instead of a bid bond, the developer may require a cash deposit from the contractor as a condition to participating in the bidding. The contractor forfeits the deposit if it receives the contract and does not proceed to perform it. The developer's requiring the cash deposit from the contractor serves the same purpose as requiring the contractor to purchase a bond, but because a surety company makes a risk assessment of contractors, a bid bond requirement, unlike a cash deposit requirement, may help weed out financially unqualified bidders.

Performance Bonds. In a **performance bond**, the surety agrees to pay for completing the project if the contractor begins the work but fails to complete it, up to the limit stated in the bond. Usually the surety has the option to (1) hire a substitute contractor to complete the work, or (2) allow the developer to hire the substitute. The surety "steps into the shoes" of the defaulting contractor. Thus, the surety will receive from the developer any of the contract price not previously paid to the defaulting contractor, and also acquires any rights or defenses that the defaulting contractor would have had against the developer.

In addition, the surety has so-called "special suretyship defenses" that release, or discharge, the surety from liability to the developer for acts by the developer and the defaulting contractor that *materially* increase the risk that the surety undertook under the performance bond. For example, if, after the surety agreed to the bond, the developer and the contractor made material modifications to the construction contract without the surety's consent, the surety would be discharged from liability on the bond. And, to aid the surety in recovering from the defaulting contractor amounts paid to the developer, the law gives the surety a right of *reimbursement* (repayment) against the contractor, and a right of **subrogation** (substitution), by which the surety acquires whatever legal rights the developer had against the contractor. For example, Alexander Construction Company agreed to build a small strip shopping center for Baker Development Company for $1 million. A large part of the work had been done, for which Alexander Construction had been paid $900,000, when Alexander walked off the job and refused to complete the center. Baker filed a claim under the performance bond issued by Ajax Surety Co. In response, Ajax hired another general contractor to complete the center at an expense of $150,000. Ajax is entitled to the $100,000 unpaid under the original construction contract from

Baker and can recover its remaining $50,000 from Alexander under its right of subrogation. The special suretyship defenses and the rights of reimbursement and subrogation apply also to bid bonds and payment bonds.

Payment Bonds. In a **payment bond**, the surety promises the developer that the contractor will pay all persons supplying labor and material to the project, up to the stated limits of the bond. Although the surety's payment obligation may be implied in a performance bond, the fact that it is expressed in a payment bond reduces uncertainty about the extent of the surety's liability for the contractor's defaults. Usually an unpaid supplier or subcontractor can file a claim directly on the bond. Although the surety has the same defenses under a payment bond as it has under a performance bond with respect to the developer, these defenses are generally unavailable with respect to an aggrieved supplier or subcontractor.

Liability for Construction Defects

Depending on the state, a general contractor's liability to the owner for defects in construction is determined by some or all of the following: the construction contract, the law of negligence, and the law of warranty.

Liability for Breach of Contract and for Negligent Construction

The provisions of the construction contract oblige the contractor to construct the improvements in accordance with the plans and specifications. Often, however, defective construction is not immediately apparent. The owner might not discover until long after the construction is completed that the roof leaks or the foundation is cracked. In such instances, the time allowed the owner by the applicable **statute of limitations** (sometimes called a "statute of repose") for remedying the defect becomes important. One type of statute of limitations requires the disappointed owner to bring suit within a given period after learning of the problem or having reason to know of it, usually three to five years, depending on the state. Another type gives the owner a similar period to seek a remedy, but the period begins at the completion of construction instead of when the owner learns or should know of the problem. Because the period for seeing a remedy is relatively short, developers commonly negotiate with contractors for a longer warranty period.

Courts have also been willing to allow suits for the tort of negligence for construction-related defects, especially where the defect causes personal injury. To prove negligence the plaintiff must show that the contractor violated its duty to use reasonable care in the construction of the improvements, causing the plaintiff an injury.

The Modern Warranty of Fitness or Habitability

Traditionally, unless the contractor or the developer gave an express warranty in or with the contract of sale, neither the contractor nor the developer had liability to buyers or renters of improvements for construction defects. The prevailing theory was *caveat emptor*, "let the buyer beware." A number of states have changed this rule in recent years by statutes or court rulings imposing an implied warranty of habitability with respect to new homes or residential leases. The implied warranty of habitability in residential leases is discussed in Chapter 13.

Application of Warranty to New Homes. In states recognizing an implied warranty of habitability, the seller of a new house warrants that the house will be fit for human habitation regardless of whether any such warranty is included in the contract of sale, because the implied warranty is imposed by law and not by agreement of the parties. The implied warranty does not assure the buyer of no construction defects, but only that the house will be fit for human habitation. So the seller would have no liability under this warranty if the problems were cosmetic or did not materially affect the livability of the house.

Protection of Subsequent Purchasers of the Home. States differ on whether the implied warranty extends to subsequent purchasers of the house or just to the original buyer. Some statutes set a specified time period for the warranty, which begins when construction is completed. In those states, the warranty extends to any successive purchasers who buy during the warranty period.

Mechanics' Liens[4]

Improvers of realty risk not being paid by the person who hired them. To help protect contractors and materials suppliers from the risk of loss, each state has a statute allowing them to acquire a "mechanic's" or a "materialman's" lien (usually called a "mechanic's lien") against the real estate that they have helped improve. If the promised payment does not materialize, the disappointed contractor or supplier can "foreclose" the lien, that is, force the sale of the improved property and have the proceeds of sale applied to the amount owed. The scope, coverage, and operation of mechanic's lien statutes vary greatly from state to state. The following general discussion of the statutes, however, indicates the impact they have on development and construction practices and procedures.

Persons Protected: Contractors, Subcontractors, Materials Suppliers

Originally, only general contractors and master-builders were the beneficiaries of mechanic's lien statutes. Today, mechanics' liens are available to virtually all segments of the construction industry and its allied fields, most commonly to general contractors, subcontractors, and construction material suppliers, but in many states also to architects, landscapers, engineers, surveyors, and others who have provided labor or material to improve real property.

Ordinarily, the developer (or the nondeveloper owner) pays the general contractor as amounts called "progress payments" come due under the general contract, and the general contractor then pays the subcontractors and material suppliers. If the owner does not pay the general contractor, the general contractor can acquire a mechanic's lien against the property by taking the steps prescribed in the mechanic's lien statute. The lien covers any unpaid sums up to the contract price. Almost all mechanic's lien statutes provide similar protection to subcontractors and materials suppliers hired by the general contractor. That is, even though subcontractors and suppliers have no direct contractual relationship with the owner or developer of the property being improved, they can acquire a mechanic's lien and enforce it by foreclosing on the improved property.

With respect to subcontractors and materials suppliers, the mechanic's lien statutes tend to be of two general types. Under the first type of statute found in about 30 states including California and Pennsylvania, the subcontractors and materials suppliers have a lien against the property for the full value of the labor or materials that they have furnished. Thus, even if the owner has paid the general contractor, the burden of paying the subcontractors and suppliers remains on the owner of the improved property, who may have to pay twice for some or all of the work. If the owner has already paid the general contractor, the owner has a right to be reimbursed by the general contractor. Under the second type of statute found in most of the remaining states including New York, Florida, and North Carolina, the liens of subcontractors and material suppliers extend only to amounts *not yet paid* by the owner to the general contractor. Once the owner pays the general contractor in full, no subcontractor or supplier has any further lien rights against the improved property, but only has rights against the general contractor.

The difference in the application of the two types of statutes is illustrated in the following example. Skinner Home Building, Inc., executes a written contract to build a house for Sakthi for $200,000. Skinner hires Benson Construction Co. as a subcontractor to perform interior and exterior painting on the house for $7,500. When the house is completed, Sakthi pays Skinner, the general contractor, all but $5,000 due under the contract. Skinner takes the $195,000 and disappears without paying subcontractor Benson. In jurisdictions with the first type of lien statute, Benson has a mechanic's lien directly against Sakthi's house for the full $7,500 that Benson is owed. Sakthi will have to pay $7,500 to satisfy Benson's lien, even though, having already paid Skinner $195,000, Sakthi ends up paying $202,500 for a house for which he agreed to pay $200,000. If Sakthi had not kept the $5,000 retainage, his house would have cost him $207,500 unless he could locate Skinner and get reimbursement. In these jurisdictions, it is important for the owner to obtain evidence that the general contractor paid the subcontractors, or to obtain from the subcontractors written waivers of their lien rights, before making payments under the general construction contract. Or, instead of seeking proof of payment or lien waivers, the owner could simply issue a check made payable jointly to the general contractor and the subcontractor involved, thus enabling the subcontractor to withhold its indorsement until paid what it is owed.

Under the second type of statute, subcontractor Benson would have a lien against Sakthi's house for only the $5,000 retained by Sakthi. In these states, subcontractor Benson, not owner Sakthi, would have to find the absconding Skinner to collect the remaining $2,500. This type of statute encourages subcontractors and material suppliers to assess the honesty and financial strength of general contractors before entering into contracts. Under both types of statutes, the owner's requiring the general contractor to provide a payment bond would provide protection against an absconding or bankrupt general contractor, although the owner's incentive to do so would clearly be less under the second type of statute than under the first.

Acquiring and Enforcing a Mechanic's Lien

The procedures for acquiring and enforcing a mechanic's lien vary widely. Typically an aggrieved party who wants to create a mechanic's lien must do so within a statutory period after completing its work on the project. The claimant usually must record a notice of its claim of lien rights and deliver copies to interested parties. If the claim is not paid in a timely manner, the lien claimant has an additional limited time within which to take action to foreclose the lien.

These time limits are meant to give improvers of realty sufficient time to acquire and enforce a mechanic's lien, while at the same time protecting owners from having their property encumbered by mechanics' liens for an unduly long time. Sometimes, however, the public records reveal the existence of a mechanic's lien even though it has been rendered invalid by, for example, a failure of the lien claimant to meet one of the deadlines. Until the records show a release of the lien, it "clouds" the property owner's title. Most or all states have procedures by which owners can clear their titles of invalid liens.

Priorities Among Lien Claimants

At foreclosure, holders of mechanics' liens sometimes find themselves in conflict with each other or with other creditors such as a lender who provided the financing for the construction. If the improved property is not sufficiently valuable to cover the claims of all creditors, the rules of priority of the particular state determine whose claims will be paid and to what extent.

Where a work of improvement begins and a construction lender *later* records its mortgage, the construction lender's claim is subordinate to some or all of the mechanic's lien claims. For determining the priority between mechanics' liens and the mortgage lien of a construction lender, the states take different approaches. The most common approach is that of California, Arkansas, Georgia, Louisiana, Michigan, and Minnesota, among others. There, the priority (or lack of it) of *all* mechanics' liens for a given project is determined by the date upon which the construction of improvements commenced. So, if the general contractor began the grading work on March 2, Lender Corp. recorded its construction mortgage on March 15, and the concrete, electrical, and heating contractors recorded their claims of lien on March 20, April 2, and April 17, respectively, *all* the mechanics' liens would have priority over Lender Corporation's mortgage because in these states the later mechanics' liens "relate back" to (become effective as of) March 2, the date that the work of improvement began. In other states, priority is determined by (1) the date upon which the mechanic's lien claimant filed the claim of lien, or (2) the date upon which the individual lien claimant commenced its work. In those states, it is possible for some mechanics' liens to prevail over the construction lender's mortgage while other mechanics' liens on the same project do not, since a mechanic's lien could be filed, or work could be commenced, either before or after the construction lender records its mortgage.

The effective date of the lien may become the subject of considerable dispute. Lien claimants will argue that construction commenced at a date before the construction mortgage was recorded, in an effort to achieve lien priority over the construction lender. Some "gamesmanship" with contractors or subcontractors may include moving equipment onto the property or doing a little busy work on the property at an early date in an attempt to establish priority. To counter this gamesmanship, prudent construction lenders often photograph the property on the day of the loan closing to be able to prove that no construction or development work has taken place. Alternatively, they may obtain so-called "noncommencement affidavits" from the contractors and subcontractors warranting that no work has commenced on the property. Similarly, contractors or subcontractors may delay completing their work, intending to extend the time for filing a claim of lien (and the time for foreclosing) for as long as possible.

If all the competing creditors are mechanic's lien claimants that relate back to the commencement of construction, they share pro rata in the foreclosure proceeds. Suppose a property owner agrees to pay $800,000 for a work of improvement, of which the general contractor is to receive $100,000, the subcontractors $500,000, and the material suppliers $200,000. But just as the work is competed, the owner becomes insolvent and can pay nothing. Having valid mechanic's liens, the contractors and material suppliers bring a foreclosure action, but the foreclosure sale produces only $400,000, 50% of the total indebtedness. Each mechanic's lien claimant receives only 50% of its lien claim. Thus, a subcontractor entitled to $1,000 receives $500, while a material supplier entitled to $50,000 receives $25,000.

Sometimes the conflict is between holders of mechanics' liens and a lender who provided financing for the construction. If the construction lender records its properly drafted mortgage or deed of trust before the work of improvement begins, the construction lender's lien normally prevails over the mechanics' liens. Lending Corp. makes a construction loan of $500,000 for the construction of a small office complex and immediately records its mortgage. Later, subcontractors record mechanics' liens totaling $500,000 in improvements. In the meantime, the general contractor receives the $500,000 from Lending Corp. on the basis of forged "releases" from the subcontractors and disappears without paying the subcontractors. Upon completion of the project, the owner cannot lease sufficient space in the complex to make the payments on the construction loan. In Lending Corporation's ensuing foreclosure action, the office complex sells for

BOX 14–2 POINT TO CONSIDER

Construction contracts for improvements of realty often anticipate a significant capital investment and a construction period lasting months or even years. Most contractors are unwilling or unable to wait until completion of the project to receive payment. Therefore, most construction contracts provide that the developer will make periodic "progress payments" to the general contractor as the construction proceeds. The developer's concern in making progress payments is that the developer will run out of money before the project is completed, or that toward the end of the project so little will remain to be paid on the contract that the contractor will have little incentive to complete the job. To ensure that contractors complete projects, developers commonly employ a technique called "retainage." That is, the developer retains a certain amount of each progress payment, typically 10%, to be paid to the contractor only upon completion of the construction. Jackson Construction Company agrees to build a shopping center for Jacob for $2 million, with construction anticipated to take 10 months and progress payments to be made at the end of each month for the percentage of work completed that month. At the end of the first month, Jackson has completed 15% of the work. Although the progress payment is $300,000 (15% of $2 million), the construction contract likely provides that Jackson will be paid $270,000 immediately and that the other $30,000 will be retained by Jacob and paid to Jackson when the shopping center is complete.

Because of the retainage, Jackson has more incentive to complete the job, because much of its profit on the job may be tied up in the retainage. Developer Jacob's retainage provision also requires contractor Jackson to have more working capital for paying its subcontractors, or to insert retainage provisions into its subcontracts (or to do both, because many of the subcontractors will likely complete their performance and be entitled to payment, or to their retainage under any retainage clause, before Jackson receives its retainage for completing the shopping center).

$750,000. Because Lending Corporation's mortgage has priority over the mechanics' liens, it is entitled to $500,000 of the proceeds, while the subcontractors share the remaining $250,000 in accordance with their priority.

Financing the Development and Construction

Most acquisition, development, and construction projects require the participation of lenders, usually commercial lenders, to provide the necessary capital. The concerns of the lender overlap those of the developer but differ in vitally important ways. One theoretical difference is that the lender has no equity interest in the project. It does not normally share in profits if a project succeeds and it expects to be paid back even if the project fails. However, the expectation of repayment in the event of project failure may prove unrealistic unless the lender is extremely careful. Because it takes a greater financial risk than does the developer, the construction lender is ordinarily more cautious in making acquisition and construction loans. Because of the risk, lenders charge higher fees and interest rates for acquisition and construction loans than they might charge on loans of other types.

⬤ Acquisition and Development Financing

Acquisition and development financing (A&D financing) refers to loans used to fund the initial acquisition of real estate, excavation, grading, and construction of roads, utilities, and other infrastructure on the property. In certain types of developments, such as offices and shopping centers, the A&D financing may be included as a part of the construction financing. In other types, such as subdivision development, the A&D financing usually is a separate loan. There are two principal sources of A&D financing: "purchase money" financing and institutional A&D financing.

Purchase Money Financing

Purchase money financing is financing provided by the seller of the real estate. In a purchase money loan, the seller sells the property to the buyer and receives from the buyer an interest-bearing promissory note and mortgage for all or part of the purchase price. A purchase money loan provides advantages to both parties. A buyer may have difficulty finding institutional A&D financing, particularly when the real estate industry is experiencing one of its cyclical downturns. By providing financing to the buyer, the seller can more easily sell its property, while the buyer is able to obtain financing that it might not otherwise find. To move property for which the market shows little current interest, a seller may well provide financing terms that a commercial lender would not, such as a longer term for repayment, a lower interest rate, or deferred payments.

From the seller's perspective, a disadvantage to purchase money financing is its "nonrecourse" by operation of law in many states. **Nonrecourse financing** (involving a *nonrecourse mortgage*) means that the mortgagee-seller cannot sue on the note (cannot hold the buyer personally liable on the note) if the buyer defaults, but instead must rely on the sale of the mortgaged property to collect its debt. Obviously nonrecourse financing is attractive to the buyer because it reduces the buyer's risk of purchase; the seller cannot sue the buyer personally and enforce a judgment against the buyer's other assets. Yet, the seller may not be particularly concerned about the nonrecourse aspect of the loan. The seller can protect itself by requiring the buyer to make a down payment large enough to cover any transaction costs related to the sale and foreclosure, including interest costs. Also, any development undertaken by the buyer potentially enhances the value of the seller's security.

From the buyer's perspective, a disadvantage of purchase money financing is that most sellers are not able or willing to lend money for *development* costs; the purchase money seller-lender is financing only the buyer's cost of *acquisition*. To fund development costs requires a substantial reservoir of cash. One option is for the buyer to fund the development costs out of its own capital, but the high development costs of many projects may make this option impractical. Therefore, buyers may attempt to induce a seller to agree to subordinate its purchase money mortgage in favor of a commercial lender who will provide development financing. **Subordination** means that the purchase money seller-lender agrees to take a second priority lien on the property and to allow the development (or construction) lender to have a first priority lien on the property. Subordination of purchase money financing is rarely a good idea for the seller. If the seller agrees to subordinate, it may be putting itself in an extremely precarious position, especially in those states where the purchase money financing is nonrecourse. If a buyer defaults on both the purchase money and the development loans, the seller may foreclose and get the property back, but the seller, having subordinated its security to that of the development lender, will have the obligation to pay the development loan following foreclosure. If the loan balance on the development loan is not reflected in added value to the real property security, the seller ends up a loser in the transaction. If the seller cannot pay the development loan, the loss may be total. The end result of these considerations is that purchase money financing may be impractical, particularly for large commercial developments.

Institutional Acquisition and Development Financing

In the United States, most institutional A&D financing is provided by banks and savings and loans companies. These commercial lenders view A&D financing as a profitable but extremely risky lending venture. Therefore, not only do they tend to charge higher interest rates and fees, they attempt to limit their risk by imposing various types of institutional limits on these loans and by carefully monitoring individual loans.

To reduce the risk on individual projects, lenders often require developers to place some of their own capital at risk. This requirement improves the lender's loan-to-value position and, lenders feel, makes developers more careful in administering the project. To further reduce their risk, lenders may resist advancing loan funds for costs that do not directly enhance the value of the realty that serves as their collateral. Thus, an institutional lender may be willing to fund "hard" development costs like excavation, grading, curb, gutter, roads, and utilities, but not the "soft" development costs of legal and accounting fees, overhead, architect and engineering fees, and interest. As a matter of routine, the prudent institutional lender will carefully monitor disbursements for development costs.

Commercial lenders also carefully evaluate how they will be repaid. For example, if the development is designed to produce single-family subdivision lots, as a condition for the lender's releasing a lot from the lien of the mortgage, the lender normally will require that most or all of the proceeds from the sale of each lot be paid to the lender to reduce the principal balance of the loan. If the acquisition and development lender contemplates the further construction of houses, offices, a shopping center, or other improvements, the lender ordinarily will require that a construction loan commitment be in place before funding the A&D loan.

● Construction Financing

Construction financing is financing used to construct improvements on real property. Construction financing may include a commitment for A&D financing or may include funding to pay off ("take out") existing A&D financing. Most construction lending in the United States is done by commercial banks and savings and loans companies. Although presenting less risk than A&D loans, construction loans present considerable risk.

Construction Loans

Construction loans (and A&D loans) differ in a number of respects from the permanent house or car loans more familiar to the ordinary consumer. In the typical house or car loan, the buyer-borrower signs the note and soon afterward the seller receives the entire principal amount of the loan. In a construction loan, the lender commits to providing the funds necessary to construct the improvements, but at the time of the loan closing the improvements have not yet been constructed. So instead of disbursing the funds immediately, the lender provides for a series of disbursements, or progress payments, to pay construction-related costs as they are incurred. Interest begins to accrue on the principal of the loan only as these disbursements are made.

Because of the disbursement of the borrowed funds in stages, commercial lenders find it difficult to predict in advance what the accrued interest will be on a monthly basis. So, instead of trying to predict a fixed rate of interest, most construction lenders charge a variable interest rate, usually indexed to some margin over the bank's prime rate, the interest rate that a bank charges to its most creditworthy corporate borrowers on short-term loans.

The Construction Loan Agreement. To provide for the series of staged disbursements, the parties normally execute a construction loan agreement in which the lender agrees to disburse the loan proceeds to the borrower as construction progresses, in accordance with a budget or a construction cost breakdown. The borrower and lender agree on the budget in advance by considering the bids from the various contractors, any funding toward acquisition and development costs, and a projection of soft costs allocable to construction. Typically, the parties also budget a certain percentage of the loan for contingency items relating to construction work. Disbursements are subject to certain conditions imposed by the lender and incorporated into the loan agreement.

The conditions to disbursement deal with several topics, including the status of the loan itself, the borrower's title and the lien priority of the lender's mortgage, and the progress of construction. For example, a common disbursement condition specifies that to receive disbursements, the borrower cannot be in default under the loan documents and may have to warrant that any representations and warranties that the borrower has previously made to the lender regarding its legal or financial status remain true at the time of the disbursement. As a further condition to disbursement, the lender may require that the effective date of the lender's title insurance policy be brought down to the date of the disbursement to verify the absence of any intervening mortgages, liens, or judgments affecting the property or the borrower. The lender may also require evidence that the construction work has been performed satisfactorily to date, the evidence to include invoices and lien waivers from the contractors or subcontractors and inspections of the property by the architect and the lender's agents or employees.

If the borrower satisfies the disbursement conditions, the lender will fund the amount of the requested advance up to the agreed amount of the line-item in the budget. However, if, for example, the borrower exceeds the budget for architects' fees, it must pay the excess out of the contingency line-item or out of its own capital. In those states that have lien laws favorable to contractors or subcontractors, the construction loan agreement may also provide that funds will be disbursed directly to the relevant contractors rather than to the borrower (owner of the property).

Future Advances Provisions. To facilitate the making of construction progress payments, construction loan mortgages commonly contain future advances provisions that allow the lender to make postclosing disbursements secured by the mortgage. Disputes occasionally develop between the developer and the general contractor or the general contractor and one of the subcontractors during the course of construction that may result in the contractor or the subcontractor filing a mechanic's lien on the property. The filing of a lien creates two related priority problems for the construction lender. Because the lender does not fund the whole project at the closing of the loan (but instead commits only to making progress payments), and because most lien statutes provide that the lien relates back to some earlier date, the lender needs assurance that its postclosing disbursements have priority over the mechanic's lien. Second, the lender needs to know whether it can continue to make loan disbursements once the lien has been filed.

Future advance provisions protect a lender's security interest when it comes into conflict with mechanic's liens or junior mortgages. In most states, the lender's postclosing construction loan disbursements pursuant to the construction loan documents relate back to the date of the filing of the construction loan mortgage, if the mortgage meets statutory requirements. Statutes commonly require that the mortgage set forth the amount of the postclosing disbursements (also called *future advances*) that are contemplated under the loan. Some statutes add that the future advances must be obligatory rather than optional in nature in order to have priority over liens filed subsequently. Courts have generally interpreted "obligatory" to mean that the lender must be obligated in the construction loan agreement to make the advance provided that the borrower meets the conditions stated in the loan documents. If one of the conditions is lien-free construction progress, the actual disbursement may in fact be optional. The future advances provision alerts prospective junior lienors to how much debt they may ultimately be behind, allowing them to knowledgeably evaluate their risk.

Box 14–3 Point to Consider

A typical future advances provision alerts potential junior lienors that the construction lender will be making periodic disbursements of loan funds, which will affect the amount of debt on the property:

This Deed of Trust shall secure present and future advances and readvances up to a maximum aggregate principal balance of $_____ at any one time. Provided there is no default or event of default under this Deed of Trust, the Loan Documents or any other document evidencing or securing the Loan, Beneficiary is obligated and otherwise contractually bound to make such advances and readvances in accordance with the terms and conditions of the Loan Documents. This Deed of Trust secures future obligations which may be incurred hereunder including, but not limited to, periodic advances and readvances on a revolving basis which will be made from time to time, it being understood and agreed by the parties hereto that all future advances and readvances on a revolving basis shall be secured to the same extent as the original obligations hereunder. The maximum amount to be advanced hereunder at any one time, including present as well as future advances, shall not exceed the maximum principal amount of $_____ (excluding such advances as may be made by the Beneficiary under the terms of the Loan Documents for the protection of the collateral, including but not limited to, payment of taxes and impositions, attorneys' fees, costs, and other expenses). The obligation of the Beneficiary to make such advances and readvances shall expire ten (10) years from the date hereof. The amount of present obligations secured hereby is $_____.[5]

Without more, the lender may also continue to make the future advances notwithstanding its knowledge of the lien or claim of lien. However, a few states have instituted an additional statutory protection for the contractor or material supplier that affects the lender's lien priority. This **stop notice** is a right of an unpaid contractor or material supplier to make and enforce a claim against a construction lender for undisbursed construction loan proceeds. A stop notice claim could be filed even when the lender has already disbursed the sums allocable to that particular line–item or even if the work is in dispute. In some states, a stop notice claim can be filed even if the borrower is in default. If the claim is disputed or the sum of various stop notice claims exceeds the undisbursed loan proceeds, litigation may be necessary and the construction project may be stalled. Because of the power of this remedy, normally a stop notice claimant must file a bond to pay damages resulting from a wrongful claim. In those jurisdictions with stop notice statutes, lenders must be particularly vigilant in administering construction loan disbursements.

Other Construction Loan Documents. The construction lender has some additional concerns not normally encountered by the conventional permanent lender. First, like any other lender, the construction lender wants assurance that it will be paid when the note is due, usually when the construction is complete. But few developers will be able to pay back construction loans out of their own resources. Instead, repayment ordinarily must come from a sale of the improved property or by refinancing the loan on the property, usually from the proceeds of a permanent loan. Therefore, before making a construction loan, the prudent construction lender will want to make sure that either a sales contract or a permanent loan commitment for the completed improvements is already in place. Alternatively, the lender will want assurances, through existing leases or market studies, that the conditions exist to make a sale or refinance a probability.

The construction lender must also consider the very real possibility that the borrower will default on the construction loan before construction is completed. In that event, the construction lender must be able to foreclose on the property and "step into the borrower's shoes" to complete the construction and see the project through to the ultimate sale or refinancing. Therefore, in addition to the real property security, the construction lender will normally require the borrower to collaterally assign to the lender all the ancillary construction project documents, such as contracts with architects, engineers, and contractors; the construction plans and specifications; the leases or sales contracts; and any permanent loan commitment.

Permanent Financing

Often the ultimate goal of the developer and the construction lender in office, shopping-center, and multifamily development is the replacement ("take-out") of the short-term construction loan with a permanent loan. Intended to provide only temporary financing, most construction loans are based on a loan-to-cost ratio, and most construction lenders require the developer to place some of its own capital at risk. Additionally, the developer is always personally liable under the construction note and mortgage for any deficiency after foreclosure. In contrast, most permanent lending is based on a loan-to-value ratio with the value being determined by the current or projected income stream from the improved property. If the developer has done its job and added value to the property, the developer normally can borrow all of its invested capital back out of the property, or even more if it desires, at the permanent loan closing. Further, many permanent commercial loans are at least partially nonrecourse, dramatically reducing the financial risk for the developer by insulating the developer wholly or in part from personal liability.

When the source of repayment of the construction loan is to be a permanent loan, persuading a permanent lender to make a loan commitment is critically important to the development process. In fact, without such a commitment, the developer may be unable to obtain a construction loan. The *permanent loan commitment* is a promise by a lender to make a long-term loan on the property when construction is completed. The permanent lender will review the same kinds of materials (discussed in detail in Chapter 10) that the construction lender did in making its financial decision. The permanent loan commitment must be of sufficient duration to allow time to construct the project (with a healthy margin for delays in construction).

Because the permanent lender normally commits to make the loan before the improvements that serve as security exist, it usually protects itself in the permanent loan commitment document by imposing a number of conditions to its agreement to lend. If the borrower fails to meet any one of the conditions, the lender will have no obligation to fund the permanent loan. In addition to the normal loan requirements and conditions discussed earlier, the permanent loan commitment is usually conditioned on a lien-free completion of the improvements in accordance with the approved plans and specification, the developer's continued financial solvency, and the rental or occupancy of a specified percentage of the property at a minimum rental rate. Sometimes the amount of the permanent loan commitment is calculated by means of a formula based on the amount of the rents achieved prior to the permanent loan closing, with the lender's committing to a minimum (floor) and maximum (ceiling) level of funding.

Triparty Agreements

In most cases, the permanent loan commitment will be assigned to the construction lender as additional security for the loan. Often this assignment takes the form of a *triparty agreement*, so-called because it is executed by the developer, the construction lender, and permanent lender. If the construction lender has to foreclose, it wants to be able to exercise the developer's rights under the permanent loan commitment, and the assignment of the commitment to the construction lender enables it to do so. If the project is stalled during a foreclosure, the construction lender, through the triparty assignment agreement, will be in a position to perform the conditions required under the permanent loan commitment. However, because the construction lender may have internal or regulatory limits regarding long-term property ownership, it may desire additional or different rights to transfer the property subject to the permanent loan, so these, too, may be included in the triparty agreement. The triparty agreement also specifies what notices must be given to the parties regarding the progress of construction.

Self-Study Questions

1. What are some typical types of real estate development and how do they differ from each other?

2. What is an *anchor tenant*, and how are anchor tenants significant in development?

3. (a) What is the significance of a construction loan commitment in a shopping center development? (b) What is the significance of a permanent loan commitment in a shopping center development? (c) Which is the developer likely to obtain first? Why?

4. What role does an architect perform in the development process?

5. How does a general contractor differ from a subcontractor?

6. What is the purpose of bid bonds, payment bonds, and performance bonds in the construction process?

7. Why might a construction lender need to be able to "step into the shoes" of the developer? How does it accomplish that goal?

8. (a) What is a mechanic's or materialmen's lien? (b) How does it affect how construction loan disbursements are made?

9. What is purchase money financing? Why can purchase money financing be undesirable from the perspective of both the borrower and lender for the purpose of financing acquisition and development of real estate?

10. From a lender's perspective, rank the following in terms of degree of risk and explain why they should be ranked that way: (a) acquisition and development financing, (b) construction financing, (c) permanent financing.

Case Problems

1. Wachovia Bank made a $1.7 million construction loan that was not repaid. Wachovia sued the developer and guarantors for the unpaid sums. To avoid liability, the defendants claimed that the project failed because Wachovia had breached its obligations under the construction loan by failing to make requested disbursements for construction costs and for tenant up-fitting expenses. The construction loan agreement provided, among other things, that disbursements would be made against a construction cost breakdown if there were no liens filed against the property. At the time of the requested disbursement, mechanics' and materialmen's liens had been filed against the property, and the tenant up-fitting expenses were not on the construction cost breakdown. Was Wachovia required to make the requested disbursements to ensure

the success of the development? *Wachovia Bank and Trust Co. v. Carrington Devel. Assoc.*, 459 S.E.2d 17 (N.C. App. 1995).

2. The First American Federal Savings Bank loaned Pat H. McGowan and his wife, Charlotte C. McGowan, the sum of $105,200 for the purchase of a lot and the construction of a house. The McGowans executed a mortgage and promissory note in conjunction with the loan. The mortgage contained a typed-in provision that stated:

> *That the purpose of this loan is to pay $30,150.00 on the purchase price of said property and the lender is unequivocally obligated and committed to advance the balance to the borrower for the purpose of erecting improvements on the mortgaged property, and lender's lien shall extend to, and include, all improvements erected upon said property and be prior to any lien for labor or material furnished to such improvements. Subject also to the terms and conditions of a construction loan agreement entered into this date which is made a part hereof by reference.*

The mortgage was recorded on April 27, 1984, and construction commenced on May 2, 1984. A dispute arose regarding whether the construction lender or unpaid lien claimants had priority. It was stipulated by the parties that the mortgage lien and the mechanics' liens were both valid. In this state, future advances that are optional with the mortgagee do not have priority if they are made after notice that subsequent encumbrances, such as mechanics' liens, have been filed. The contractor argued that the mortgagee's advances were "optional" based on a number of conditions and options contained in the mortgage and construction loan agreement. One of the conditions stated that the lender could make future advances "upon authorization of the borrower and his furnishing current lien releases, and approval of the lender." Other conditions in the mortgage included provisions for insurance, compliance with construction plans and specifications, payment of monthly installments on the note, and prohibition against diversion of the funds for other purposes. Should the mortgagee have priority for construction loan advances it made after the mechanic's liens were filed? After May 2, 1984? *Dempsy v. McGowan*, 291 Ark. 147; 722 S.W.2d 848 (Ark. 1987).

3. Grossman Homes is seeking zoning and subdivision approval to develop a large residential subdivision on 116th Street in Carmel, Indiana. The City of Carmel is concerned that the proposed subdivision would add significant car traffic to the already heavily traveled 116th Street. It is also concerned that subdivision residents attempting to turn on to 116th Street would cause accidents. Therefore, as conditions to granting zoning and subdivision approval, the city wants to require that Grossman dedicate the land for and construct an extra traffic lane on 116th Street and that it pay for the installation of a traffic light at the subdivision entrance on 116th Street. Grossman thinks it unfair that it should have to dedicate some of its land and pay for these improvements in order to get its zoning approval. (a) Can the city make Grossman dedicate the land and install the extra lane as a condition for its approval? (b) Can the city make Grossman install a traffic light at the entrance to the subdivision as a condition for its approval?

4. William L. Hughes disputed the Town of Mexico Beach's claim of ownership by dedication of a 25-foot-wide, approximately 130-foot-long parcel of property located within a previously subdivided unit of land in what is now Mexico Beach, Florida. The disputed property was located between two lots owned by Hughes. The evidence showed that the disputed parcel was a part of a dedicated street shown on the original plat of the subdivision, which was duly approved by the county commission and recorded in 1951. Evidence also showed that the town had improved some of the streets in the subdivision and that the public had used those streets as well as the disputed strip of land for many years. Did the town own the disputed parcel? *Hughes v. Town of Mexico Beach*, 455 So. 2d 566 (Fla. App. 1984).

Endnotes

1. See generally Roger A. Cunningham et al., *The Law of Property* (Hornbook Series, 1984); Patrick A. Hetrick and James B. McLaughlin, Jr., *Webster's Real Estate Law in North Carolina* (1988); Grant S. Nelson and Dale A. Whitman, *Real Estate Finance and Development: Cases and Materials* (1976); Woodard E. Farmer, Jr., *Commercial Property Transactions* (1995); Charles E. Gilliland, "Buying Rural Land," *Tierra Grande* 4 (Fall 1997); David W. Owens, "Land Development in North Carolina: Making Your Way Through the Maze," *Looking at 1994 Real Property Issues* (1994); and Thomas S. Stukes, "Commercial Real Property Acquisitions," *The Basics of Real Property Practice* (1984).

2. See American Institute of Architects, available at http://www.aiaonline.com (July 17, 2000).

3. See American Arbitration Association, http://www.adr.org/ (August 15, 2000).

4. See generally Grant S. Nelson and Dale A. Whitman, *Real Estate Finance and Development: Cases and Materials* (1976); Grant S. Nelson and Dale A. Whitman, *Real Estate Finance Law* (1985); John B. Taylor, "Lien On Me-An Overview of Lien Law," *Breaking Out: Real Estate for Both Sides* (1998); John B. Taylor, "Perfecting & Enforcing Construction Liens/Lien Law Update," *Looking at 1994 Real Property Issues* (1994). For a state-by-state breakdown of mechanics' lien laws, see *American College of Mortgage Attorneys, National Mortgage Law Summary* (1998); Carl J. Circo and Christopher Little, *A State-by-State Guide to Construction and Design Law* (1998); Robert F. Cushman & Stephen D. Butler, *Fifty State Construction Lien and Bond Law* (2000).

5. Alan H. Peterson and Cathy M. Rudisill, "Future Advance Lending and Revolving Lines of Credit."

Chapter 15

Condominiums and
Other Co-ownership
Arrangements;
Real Estate
Investments

Investment in real estate can be highly rewarding because of the managerial and financial advantages of real estate ownership. For example, because ownership of realty tends to be long-term, the owner can control its financial destiny for a substantial period and, with appropriate maintenance, buildings and other improvements can last longer than any human life span. This relative permanence is an inherent virtue in an age of inflation. As the value of the dollar falls, real estate tends to retain a relatively high value. For this reason, real estate is often referred to as a **hedge against inflation**. Moreover, over the years Congress has encouraged real estate ownership and development by providing tax incentives for real estate owners. As noted in Chapter 16, the primary tax advantage of owning a personal residence is the deductibility of mortgage interest payments and property taxes from the homeowner's gross income, whereas apartment rent and interest payments on other types of family loans are not deductible. Like a homeowner, an owner of commercial realty may deduct mortgage interest and property taxes and has additional tax benefits not available to owners of personal residences, such as the right to deduct from gross income an annual amount for depreciation. In some cases, the useful-life schedule used by the Internal Revenue Service for depreciable assets may not reflect the longer actual life of improvements. If properly maintained, assets may be worth more at the end of this useful life than the original investment. The deduction for depreciation, together with deductions for ordinary maintenance and repair, allow the owner of commercial realty to reduce annual taxable income while the property increases in value. Owners of realty may also benefit from other provisions in the tax code, such as those relating to capital gains, tax credits for special uses, and like-kind exchanges.

In previous chapters, discussion usually centered on fee simple ownership of a parcel of land and its improvements by one person, but several other ownership possibilities exist. During the past fifty years, real estate law and practice embraced forms of ownership more attuned to current needs and desires. For example, many people wanted the benefits of property ownership without the burdens of real estate management or maintenance. This desire led to the development of common interest communities such as condominiums, cooperatives, and planned communities. This chapter discusses each of these methods of ownership. For a variety of reasons, however, the direct ownership of property by an individual may be impractical or undesirable, so this chapter also discusses investment in realty through the use of corporations, partnerships, and real estate investment trusts.

Common Interest Ownership[1]

As noted in Chapter 5, in this era of growing populations and shrinking availability of prime land for development, shared ownership arrangements have become popular for housing and other purposes. A shared ownership arrangement allows an individual to own or use a "unit" (part of a building or tract of land) and to share with the owners of the other units the ownership or use of certain common areas. Known collectively as *common interest ownership* arrangements or *common interest communities*, they include condominiums, planned unit developments, community apartment projects, stock cooperatives, and time-share arrangements. Some are used primarily or exclusively for residential purposes. Others, such as the condominium and the planned unit development, are used for residential, business, or commercial purposes, or for some combination of them. Typically, a property owners' association collects a fee from the unit owners and, among other duties, manages and maintains the common areas.

About one in six Americans, roughly 42 million people, currently lives in common interest communities. The *Restatement (Third) of Property: Servitudes* defines a common interest community as:

[A] real estate development or neighborhood in which individually owned lots or units are burdened by a servitude that imposes an obligation . . .

1. *to pay for the use of, or contribute to the maintenance of, property held or enjoyed in common by the individual owners, or*
2. *to pay dues or assessments to an association that provides services or facilities to the common property, or that enforces other servitudes burdening the property in the development or neighborhood.*[2]

Ownership of a unit in a common interest community has a number of advantages. As in other types of realty ownership, the owner of a common interest unit may deduct mortgage interest and property taxes, and a common interest unit, like other forms of real estate, can serve as a hedge against inflation. In comparison to other types of realty ownership, however, the principal advantages relate to lifestyle factors. People who want to own a residence, office, or store without having to paint the building, repair the roof, or cut the grass find common interest communities a desirable alternative to traditional ownership in which the owner is solely responsible for maintenance and repair. Like apartment complexes, office buildings, and shopping centers, most common interest communities have professional management and amenities such as roads, parking lots, swimming pools, tennis courts, clubhouse, jogging trails, common areas, security systems, and maintenance personnel. The unit owners, of course, share the expense of the amenities. Thus, the owner of a common interest unit has the financial advantages of traditional ownership and the freedom from routine maintenance characteristic of renting.

Each type of common interest community—condominium, planned community, cooperative—has its own historical and legal background, and is the subject of its own uniform law, intended by its drafters (the National Conference of Commissioners on Uniform State Laws) to be adopted by the states or at least to serve as a model for a state legislature to consider when drafting its own law. The most recent uniform laws include the Uniform Condominium Act, the Uniform Planned Community Act, and the Model Real Estate Cooperative Act. Recent legal developments and model acts, including the *Restatement (Third) of Property: Servitudes* and the Uniform Common Interest Ownership Act, have focused on practical and functional similarities among condominiums, planned communities, and cooperatives. The following sections outline the distinctive features of each form of ownership.

Condominiums

Although the condominium form of real estate ownership dates back at least to Roman times, in the United States condominiums did not come into wide use until the 1960s. Statutes explicitly authorizing condominiums first appeared in resort jurisdictions like Puerto Rico and Florida.

Nature of Condominium Ownership

A person who acquires a **condominium** receives two basic property rights:

1. Ownership of a "unit," usually in fee simple, that is taxed separately to the unit owner as an interest in land. Often the unit is a cube of airspace in an upper story, the unit boundaries being marked by walls, floor, and ceiling.

2. An undivided fractional interest in the common areas, as a tenant in common with other unit owners. The common areas include the outside walls, roof, sidewalks, the land underlying the building or buildings, lawns that are not part of a unit, parking lot, swimming pool, tennis courts, and the like.

Although the unit owner is a tenant in common as to the common areas, no unit owner has a right of partition, and no unit owner can separate his or her interest in the common areas from

BOX 15–1 POINT TO CONSIDER

The Uniform Condominium Act defines the boundaries of a *unit* as follows:

Section 1-103 (25): "Unit" means a physical portion of the condominium designated for separate ownership or occupancy, the boundaries of which are described [in the declaration].

Section 2-102. [Unit Boundaries] Except as provided by the declaration:

(1) If walls, floors or ceilings are designated as boundaries of a unit, all lath, furring, wallboard, plasterboard, plaster, paneling, tiles, wallpaper, paint, finished flooring, and any other materials constituting any part of the finished surfaces thereof are a part of the unit, and all other portions of the walls, floors, or ceilings are a part of the common elements.

(2) If any chute, flue, duct, wire, conduit, bearing wall, bearing column, or any other fixture lies partially within and partially outside the designated boundaries of a unit, any portion thereof serving only that unit is a limited common element allocated solely to that unit, and any portion thereof serving more than one unit or any portion of the common elements is a part of the common elements.

(3) Subject to the provisions of paragraph (2), all spaces, interior partitions, and other fixtures and improvements within the boundaries of a unit are a part of the unit.

(4) Any shutters, awnings, window boxes, doorsteps, stoops, porches, balconies, patios, and all exterior doors and windows or other fixtures designed to serve a single unit, but located outside the unit's boundaries, are limited common elements allocated exclusively to that unit.

---

ownership of the unit. Transfer of the unit carries with it the right to use the common areas and the duty to contribute to their maintenance.

It may be helpful to think of a condominium unit as a box of space located within a larger structure. Box 15.1 defines "unit" more specifically.

A unit in the sky has no value by itself. The unit owners must have structural support for their units, and legal and practical access to them—hence, each unit owner's fractional interest in the **common elements** (also known as **common areas**) of the condominium. Common elements within a condominium project usually include the areas within the project other than the units. Common areas include the structural components of the buildings, the exterior of the buildings, the grounds, the amenities, the common drives, the common entrances, and all other portions of the development falling outside the unit "airspace." A unit owner may also receive special rights in certain portions of the common elements, called **limited common elements**, that service only that owner's unit, such as patios, garden spaces, balconies, or garages.

In a condominium, an incorporated or unincorporated *community association* of all the unit owners (in residential condominiums, often called the *homeowners' association*) manages the common areas on behalf of the unit owners, but the association does not own them. In fact, the Uniform Condominium Act explicitly provides that "[r]eal estate is not a condominium unless the undivided interests in the common elements are vested in the unit owners." This concept of shared ownership of the common elements distinguishes a condominium from its nearest relative, the *planned community*, commonly referred to as a townhouse development, homeowners' association development, cluster-home development, or zero-lot line development.[3] In a *planned community*, the owner normally owns not only the living space enclosed by the unit, but also owns the exterior and structural components and the underlying land, while the *community association* itself owns the common areas. The owner's unit usually is encumbered by a series of covenants, conditions, and restrictions (CC&Rs) allocating rights and property interests among adjacent owners. The CC&Rs may include a party-wall agreement, require all owners to be members of the community association,[4] and impose an assessment for the repair and maintenance of the common areas, such as access roads, parking lots, and recreational amenities.

In a condominium, the fact that the unit owners share ownership of the common elements can lead to managerial problems. The owner of an apartment complex, being the sole owner, can decide when to patch the parking lot, repair the roof, or paint the building; which amenities to offer; as well as set the rules and regulations for the complex. In a condominium, however, the unit owners must work together as a group to resolve such issues. Because exterior walls and other property components outside the unit are *common elements*, individual unit owners cannot unilaterally decide to repaint the exterior of their units, add screens or awnings to the windows, or erect a fence or screened porch. Such alterations require the consent of the community association.

Condominium Law

All states have statutes that provide for the creation of condominiums. Puerto Rico enacted the first U.S. condominium statute in 1958. Most early statutes followed the pattern set by Puerto Rico, or that of the Model Act produced by the Federal Housing Administration in 1962. The early statutes, so-called **first-generation condominium statutes**, provided a "bare bones" enabling act allowing the creation of condominiums. These statutes envisioned a condominium of the style typical in resorts, a condominium composed of a single completed building containing numerous units to be sold to individuals. As the condominium form of ownership became more popular, the inadequacies of the first-generation condominium statutes quickly became apparent. For example, the statutes had little or nothing to say about the rights and obligations of the developer, did not indicate whether the development and sale of condominium units could occur in stages (or "phases") rather than all at once, and failed to specify how developments for mixed commercial and residential uses should be handled. Nor did the statutes address the transition of management and control from the developer to the community association, the relationship between the community association and the individual unit owners, the termination of condominiums, or consumer protection.

In response to these and other problems, a number of states enacted a second generation of condominium statutes. Many of these **second-generation condominium statutes** are patterned after the Uniform Condominium Act (UCA), published by the National Conference of Commissioners on Uniform State Laws (NCCUSL) in 1980. The UCA is the basis for the condominium statutes in at least 21 states.[5] The substantive provisions of the UCA are contained in the Uniform Common Interest Ownership Act (UCIOA), published by the NCCUSL in 1982 and revised in 1994.[6]

The UCA consists of five articles. The first article lays out the definitions and general provisions. Article 2 provides the mechanism for the creation, alteration, and termination of condominiums. Article 3 concerns the management of the condominium by the community association. Article 4 contains guidelines for consumer protection of condominium purchasers, including detailed disclosure requirements. The final (and optional) article designates a state administrative agency to supervise the condominium developer's activities.

Creation of Condominiums

To create a condominium, the real estate owner or developer (known as a **declarant** under the UCA) must file a declaration of condominium in the registry of deeds (recorder's office), where it is recorded in the grantor index under the name of the landowner and the condominium. The **declaration of condominium** creates the property interests characteristic of a condominium, namely, fee simple unit ownership and the unit owners' undivided fractional interests in the common areas. Under the UCA, the declarant cannot record the declaration of condominium until the units are "substantially completed" in accordance with the architectural plans and specifications.

The declaration of condominium contains a detailed description of (1) the property, and (2) the property interests, rights, obligations, and covenants of the unit owners. It includes the plan of development and ownership of the condominium, the method of its operation, and the rights and responsibilities of the unit owners as members of the community association. UCA requires certain specific details be contained in the declaration of condominium:

- The name of the condominium, which must include the word *condominium*.
- A legal description of the real estate.
- The maximum number of units that the declarant reserves the right to create.
- A description of unit boundaries.
- A description of any future development rights retained by the declarant.
- An allocation to each unit of that unit's tenancy-in-common interest in the common elements.
- Any restrictions on use, occupancy, and allocation of the units.
- Allocation of voting rights in the community association.
- Plats and plans depicting the real estate involved and showing the common elements and the units.

Because a unit owner will own only the unit's "airspace," plus an undivided fractional interest in the common areas together with greater rights in any "limited common elements," the declaration of condominium serves a number of practical purposes. It makes clear that the unit owners share the use of the common elements, and it allocates any limited common elements among the unit owners. The declaration also assures that the unit owners have legal access to their units, provides for future eventualities like a fire or a condemnation affecting the property, and provides for repair and management of common areas. Especially with regard to repair and management, the shared ownership of the common elements creates a number of practical problems. What happens if the roof leaks or the building needs to be repainted? Who is responsible for cutting the grass? Who buys the insurance on the building? A characteristic of condominium ownership is an assessment of the unit owners to pay for these and other expenses.

The UCA gives the declarant considerable flexibility in its decision regarding the allocation of the fractional interests in the common elements, each homeowner's assessment obligation, and the voting rights associated with each unit. Many of the first-generation condominium statutes required that fractional interests, assessments, and voting rights be of the same percentage and be directly related to the fair market value of the unit. For example, if a unit had a fair market value of $100,000 and the total value of all units in the condominium was $2 million, then the owner of that unit would have a 5% interest in the common area, would be assessed for 5% of the common expenses of the condominium, and would be entitled to 5% of the voting rights in the community association.

Although a uniform allocation of rights and responsibilities based on fair market value seems fair in the abstract, the results seemed unfair when applied. Suppose that Davidson Development

Co., builds a high rise condominium in New York City. Enrico pays $2 million for a fashionable one-bedroom condominium on the 70th floor overlooking Central Park. Ken pays $400,000 for an identical unit on the second floor, which gives him a view of a wall. Enrico and Ken probably can accept that their respective percentage interests in the common elements reflects their relative investments. However, Enrico is likely to be upset if he must pay an assessment that is five times higher than Ken's, when the benefits and services he receives from the assessment are not significantly different from Ken's. Why then should his continuing assessment obligation be determined by the relative values of the units? But if Enrico's assessment is made the same as Ken's, should Enrico continue to receive five times as many votes in the community association as Ken? These kinds of considerations may prompt a declarant to establish separate formulas in the declaration for making assessments, allocating fractional interests, and establishing voting rights.

To enable the declarant to protect its interest in completing and selling the condominium, the declaration of condominium often gives the declarant special treatment. For example, the declaration may give the declarant the following:

1. A construction easement across the common areas for completing the improvements.

2. The right to operate a sales office in one of the units, notwithstanding the existence of covenants in the declaration of condominium that restrict the condominium to residential uses.

3. Control over the unit owners' association for an extended period of time.

4. The right to add units or phases at a later date, which would affect the existing condominium and the existing owners' percentage interests in the common elements. Assume that Davidson Development Co. develops Bull Run Condominium in two phases, each containing ten identical units. When Davidson Development Co. conveys the units in Phase One to buyers, it conveys to each unit owner a particular unit together with a 10% undivided interest in the common areas in Phase One. When the second 10-unit phase is added, each owner, including the Phase One buyers, receives a 5% share in the common areas in the total condominium.

All of these so-called special declarant rights are permissible under the UCA and are transferrable by the developer. However, first- and second-generation condominium statutes expressly or impliedly prohibit the declarant from giving the declarant-owned unit preferential treatment in its assessment obligation.

Building a condominium development in phases allows the developer to build units as it sells them rather than risking a large inventory of unsold units with the associated obligation to pay construction loans and community association assessments on the unsold units. Because of the financial risk represented by unsold inventory, many construction lenders require that developers have a certain percentage of units presold before construction begins. The drafters of the first-generation condominium statutes did not contemplate the development of a condominium in phases, and, as illustrated by the case that follows, court challenges resulted.

Case 15.1

Viola v. Millbank II Associates

688 N.E.2d 996 (Mass. Ct. App. 1997), *cert. denied*, 692 N.E.2d 963 (Mass. 1998)

The plaintiffs were individual unit owners of the Millbank II Condominium in Northampton, planned by its developers as a so-called "phased" condominium project. The present developers sought a judicial declaration that under the terms of the master condominium deed they are entitled to develop phases II and III of the condominium as condominium units. The plaintiff unit owners asserted that the developers have no right to do so without the consent of all phase I unit owners, as required by a Massachusetts statute providing, in part, that "the percentage of the undivided interest of each unit owner in the common areas and facilities as expressed in the master deed shall not be altered without the consent of all unit owners whose percentage of the undivided interest is affected. . . ."

The declarant created Millbank II condominium in November 1988, by recording a master deed (the Massachusetts equivalent of a declaration of condominium) in the appropriate recorder's office. The master deed identified certain land and improvements for condominium use, including two existing buildings containing eighteen units designated as "phase one." The master deed stated that it was the declarant's intention to develop the condominium in three phases as shown on a plan recorded with the master deed. Exhibit 3A, a schedule incorporated into the master deed, discloses the initial percentage ownership of the common areas, and the decreasing percentage ownership of each unit as phases II and III are introduced. For example, unit 3-1 owns a percentage interest of 6.223 at the completion of phase I, 3.559 percent at the completion of phase II and 2.492 percent at the completion of phase III. The master deed then provided that the declarant could add two additional phases to the Condominium without the consent of the unit owners.

The trial court granted the unit owners' motion for summary judgment, declaring that the developers may not construct phases II and III of the condominium without the unanimous consent of the individual unit owners. The developers appealed.

GILLERMAN, J.

The [trial court] concluded that the master deed violated § 5(b) [of the Massachusetts statute] by failing to require unanimous unit owner consent to the alteration of common area percentages as phases II and III are introduced. . . .

The plaintiffs misconceive the provisions of the master deed. By the express terms of paragraph (6) . . . , each phase I unit owner "shall be entitled to an undivided beneficial interest in the Common Elements in the percentages shown on Exhibit #3A. . . ." Paragraph 5(B) . . . is to the same effect; it provides that each unit's proportionate interest in the common elements of the condominium are set forth in Exhibit 3A. Exhibit 3A sets forth the "percentage interest in Common Areas and Facilities of Units in Phase I initially and upon the completion of subsequent phases of the Condominium." Paragraph 11(D) makes it clear that amendments to the master deed required by the phasing plan do not affect the percentage interest, as created by Exhibit 3A, in the common areas.

The only reasonable construction that may be put upon Exhibit 3A and the related paragraphs (6), 5(B) and 11(D) is that a unit owner's initial entitlement to a percentage ownership in the common elements under the master deed is for phase I only; upon the completion of phase II his percentage entitlement is reduced and remains fixed until the completion of phase III, at which point his percentage entitlement is reduced again to a new fixed number which thereafter will remain unchanged, absent unanimous consent of all unit owners to a different schedule of percentage ownerships.

With the master deed so construed, it may be seen that the percentage interest of each unit owner in the common elements, "as expressed in the master deed [is] not . . . altered," by the construction of phases II and III. Each unit owner is informed from the outset that his percentage entitlement to an undivided interest in the common elements varies with each development stage of the condominium; since those variations are all originally "expressed in the master deed" by reason of Exhibit 3A, the construction of phases II and III do not work any forbidden alteration in percentage interests . . . in violation of [the statute].

That being so, the plaintiffs, as individual unit owners are bound by the provisions in the master deed. . . .

The judgment is reversed. The case is remanded to the Superior Court for the entry of a new judgment on the developers' counterclaim declaring the right of the developers to proceed with the construction of phases II and III without the consent of the unit owners of phase I.

QUESTIONS ABOUT CASE 15.1

1. Why would the declarant want to develop the condominium in phases?

2. The court notes that the unit owners' percentage interests in the common areas decrease after the inclusion of both additional phases from 6.223% to 2.492%. What are the practical effects of this reduction?

   Notes: The majority opinion takes a pragmatic approach to condominium development, observing that condominium purchasers were fully informed in the declaration of condominium about the possible expansion of the condominium and its effect on the unit owners' percentage interest in the common elements.

   Notwithstanding a strongly worded dissent, the so-called "Chinese menu" has been a common approach to phased condominium development under first generation condominium statutes. In a declaration of condominium of this type, the declarant specifies what the unit owners' percentage interests will be after the addition of each phase. Although this approach generally has been accepted by the courts, it has problems of its own. Because the percentage interests of the owners in all phases are established in the menu with the recording of the original declaration of condominium and often these percentages are supposed to reflect the relative fair market values of the units, developers are effectively prevented from changing the mix of unit types in later phases to respond to customer demand.

A condominium also involves many of the problems that arise from the interaction of a community of disparate people. In an apartment or office building, an owner can evict a tenant who causes problems for other tenants, but the community association of a condominium cannot evict uncooperative unit owners. Property owners are accustomed to having the relatively unrestricted use and enjoyment of their property, so conduct by a neighbor that a unit owner might view as a nuisance, might be viewed by the neighbor as his or her right. Yet, by choosing to live in a common interest community, unit owners give up a measure of control. The declaration of condominium normally establishes restrictions on property usage and describes how disputes within the community association are to be resolved.

Many of the problems of common ownership and community life came as unpleasant surprises to early condominium dwellers. For example, the buyers of a unit might discover that the condominium roof needed to be replaced. A community association that had no cash on hand for this unbudgeted expense would send each owner a bill for a special assessment to fix the roof. The following week a neighbor might inform owners that the declaration of condominium prohibits pets and they will have to get rid of their dog, Buffy. Having never seen a copy of the declaration of condominium, they were shocked and dismayed. Today, to spare potential purchasers of condominium units from unwelcome surprises of this sort, the UCA requires that developers make detailed disclosures of pertinent information.

The developer must make these disclosures in a "public offering statement" and must deliver it to potential purchasers, who have 15 days to review it. If the buyers do not receive a public offering statement more than 15 days before they execute the contract of sale, they have 15 days after signing the contract to cancel it. A developer who conveys a unit without delivering a public offering statement is subject under the UCA to liquidated damages in the amount of 10% of the sales price of the unit, in addition to any other remedy the buyers may have.

The public offering statement is a detailed discussion of all aspects of the condominium—its development, ownership, and management, and especially those aspects that have financial ramifications for unit owners. The required disclosures include the following:

1. The name and principal address of the declarant and the condominium.

2. A general description of the condominium and a schedule of completion of the buildings and the amenities.

3. The number of units in the condominium, including a detailed description of any units or amenities that are to be developed in later phases.

4. A narrative description of significant features of the declaration of condominium, the covenants, and the bylaws and regulations of the community association.

5. A detailed description of the assessments and their basis, including the community association's budget and the budget assumptions and projections.

6. A description of any zoning, liens, or encumbrances affecting title to the condominium.

7. A description of any warranties provided by the developer.

In addition to the declarant's liabilities for not delivering a public offering statement (buyers' right to cancel the contract and to obtain liquidated damages), the declarant is liable for any false or misleading statement contained in the public offering statement, and for any material omissions. The potential damages include punitive damages and attorney's fees for willful violations of the act.

The declarant must place any earnest money paid by the buyers into an escrow account until the closing, or until the buyers default on the purchase contract, or until they are entitled to their deposit back. The drafters of the UCA installed this protection as a reaction to a wave of developer bankruptcies in the mid-1970s that caused prospective buyers to lose their earnest money.

Community Associations and Operation of Condominiums

As is true in other types of common interest community, the community association of a condominium operates and manages it. The declarant must create the community association before the conveyance of the first unit. In most states, the community association may be a corporation or an unincorporated entity. A corporate form is preferable, however, because, in addition to the limitation of liability that a corporation provides, there exists a large body of law and practice on corporate organization and structure that is not available to assist unincorporated associations.

Membership of the unit owners in the community association is automatic with the purchase of the condominium unit, though participation in community association activities is voluntary. The community association has fairly broad powers to govern and operate the condominium, including the powers to make rules to control the use and enjoyment of the condominium, to manage its affairs, and to levy assessments to pay for the expenses of management, operation, and repair of the condominium. Each unit owner must pay a monthly assessment for the common expenses of the condominium. The community association may obtain a lien on a unit owner's unit to the extent the assessments are not paid. In these respects, a community association functions in ways similar to a municipal government: the association makes rules, levies "taxes," and provides services to "citizens." The UCA even gives the community association the power to levy reasonable fines (after notice to the unit owner and a hearing), for the violation of the declaration, bylaws, or rules and regulations of the association.

The exercise of these powers by community associations occasionally leads to conflict. The more common disputes involve financial issues, architectural control issues, parking, pets, and noise. The courts, when presented with challenges to the actions of community associations, have been sympathetic to the problems of "volunteer government." For example, a recent California Supreme Court decision ruled that the management decisions of community association boards are valid if they are made in good faith, are made in a fair and nondiscriminatory manner, and are rationally related to the interest of the community as a whole.[7] Courts commonly consider whether the community association had the power to take the action complained of, whether the affected unit owner had adequate notice of the power and its exercise, and whether the exercise of the community association's power was reasonable. The following case provides a classic example of an association that overstepped the bounds of reasonableness.

Case 15.2

Cunningham v. Fountain Valley Chateau Blanc Homeowners' Assoc.

79 Cal. Rptr. 2d 248 (Cal. App. 1998), *cert. denied*, 1999 Cal. LEXIS 644 (Cal. 1999)

Robert Cunningham bought an attached home subject to the CC&Rs of the Fountain Valley Chateau Blanc Homeowners' Association. Like Shel Silverstein's proverbial Sarah Cynthia Sylvia Stout, Robert S. Cunningham, would not take the garbage out. So, reminiscent of Sarah's daddy who, in the famous poem would scream and shout, Cunningham's homeowners' association did the modern equivalent. It instituted litigation. The association's theory in essence was that Cunningham's property constituted a fire hazard. Local fire authorities, however, determined that his property posed no fire hazard, either indoors or outdoors. Even so, the lawyers for the homeowners association wrote letters demanding that he clear his bed of all papers and books, discard "outdated" clothing, and remove the papers, cardboard boxes, and books from the floor area around his bed and dresser. Books that were "considered standard reading material" could, however, remain in place.

Cunningham is a senior citizen who suffers from Hodgkin's disease. The letter from the association's lawyers was, in essence, a demand backed up by threat of litigation telling him to straighten up his own bedroom. So Cunningham found a lawyer and sued the association by filing a cross-complaint for invasion of the right to privacy and breach of the homeowner's association's CC&Rs.

The association's original complaint against Cunningham was soon settled; Cunningham agreed to abide by the rules. His cross-complaint against the association, by contrast, went to trial, with the issue being the *reasonableness* of the association's conduct after the litigation started. The trial was bifurcated between liability and damage phases, and the jury found in favor of Cunningham on the liability issue. However, before the damage phase could be heard, the trial judge granted the association's new trial motion, stating he believed the association had acted reasonably. Cunningham then petitioned for a writ to set aside the new trial order.

SILLS, P. J.

[I]t is virtually impossible to say the association acted reasonably. It is true the CC&Rs require "owners" to "maintain the interiors of their residential units and garages, including the interior wall, ceilings, floors and permanent fixtures and appurtenances in a clean, sanitary and attractive condition." It is also true that they provide for entry by the board "when necessary in connection with maintenance, landscaping or construction for which the board is responsible." But these sections of the CC&Rs cannot reasonably be read to allow an association to dictate the amount of clutter in which a person chooses to live; one man's old piece of junk is another man's objet d'art. The association's rather high-handed attempt to micromanage Cunningham's personal housekeeping—telling him how he could and could not use the interior rooms of his own house—clearly crossed the line and was beyond the purview of any legitimate interest it had in preventing undesirable external effects or maintaining property values.

Particularly galling to us—and clearly to the jury as well—was the presumptuous attempt to lecture Cunningham about getting rid of his old clothes, the way he kept his own bedroom, and the kind of "reading material" he could have. To obtain some perspective here, we have the spectacle of a homeowners association telling a senior citizen suffering from Hodgkin's disease that, in effect, he could not read in his own bed! When Cunningham bought his unit, we seriously doubt that he contemplated the association would ever tell him to clean up his own bedroom like some parent nagging an errant teenager.

If it is indeed true that homeowners associations can often function "as a second municipal government," then we have a clear cut case of a "nanny state"—nanny in almost a literal sense—going too far. The association's actions flew in the face of one of the most ancient precepts of American society and Anglo-American legal culture. "A man's house is his castle" was not penned by anonymous, but by the famous jurist Sir Edward Coke in 1628.

The jury could thus find that the association did not act reasonably under the circumstances (and that is all we decide).

QUESTION ON CASE 15.2

Should the result in the case have been different if Cunningham had in fact created a fire hazard?

Note: This case actually involved the enforcement of CC&Rs in a planned community, but the problems of community involved in a planned community, condominium, or cooperative are virtually identical.

Upon the completion of a condominium, the declarant owns all the units in it, and the declarant must create the community association before conveying the first unit to a buyer. Because the declarant has complete control of the community association in the beginning, the initial officers and directors of the community association usually are the declarant's employees. The declarant's control of the community association lasts at least until the declarant has conveyed at least half of the units to buyers, although the declarant's control may last longer if so provided in the declaration of condominium. Unscrupulous developers have used this control as an opportunity for self-dealing, for example, by executing long-term service contracts or recreational leases between the community association and the developer on terms unreasonably favorable to the developer.

Even reputable developers have a conflict of interests. The developer-declarant's primary concern is to sell units as quickly as possible, for the best price possible. However, the declarant has only a short time within which to make sales and until the units are sold, the declarant owns them and must pay the monthly community association assessment. To avoid a large expense item, the declarant might set the monthly assessments at a level so low that the association's legitimate financial needs will not be met. Moreover, a high monthly assessment discourages sales. These pressures lead many developers to set assessments unreasonably low, a practice known in the trade as "lowballing," leaving community associations undercapitalized.

The UCA has taken several steps to minimize the abuses of declarant control of the association. First, it codified case law that imposes a fiduciary duty to unit owners on community association officers and directors appointed by the declarant. This provision requires the declarant and its employees to act for the benefit of all unit owners. Second, the UCA establishes a transition period for the transfer of control of the community association from the declarant to the unit owners. As soon as 25% of the units have been sold, at least 25% of the community association's board of directors must be unit owners other than the declarant. After 50% of the units have been sold, at least 33% of the board members must be unit owners other than the declarant. When 75% of the units have been sold, the declarant must relinquish control over the community association. Third, the UCA states that virtually all contracts or leases executed by the association during the period of developer control are terminable by the community association without penalty, upon ninety days notice to the other party.[8]

Planned Communities

Planned communities are the most common form of common interest ownership. The Community Associations Institute estimates a total of 205,000 common interest developments in the United States as of 1998, of which 64% were planned communities, 31% condominiums, and 5% cooperatives.[9] Although legally quite different, planned communities are similar to condominiums in most practical respects. In a planned community, owners normally own the land and the buildings constructed on it. The owners' lateral property lines may actually be within the exterior walls so that neighbors share a common wall that marks the boundary between their lots. Hence the application to planned communities of the term *zero-lot-line developments*. A comprehensive declaration of CC&Rs limits the owners' use of their property. The developer records the CC&Rs prior to the conveyance of the first unit in the planned community. If the units are attached to those of other owners, the CC&Rs will include a party-wall agreement allocating rights and obligations among adjacent unit owners. As in a condominium, ownership in a planned community includes mandatory membership in a community association and a mandatory assessment. In a planned community, the community association generally holds title to any property serving all of the property owners, such as access roads, parking lots, and recreational amenities. In fact, the Uniform Planned Community Act defines "planned community" as:

. . . real estate with respect to which any person, by virtue of his ownership of a unit, is obligated to pay for real property taxes, [insurance premiums, or other expenses to maintain, improve, or benefit other lots or other real estate] described in a declaration. For purposes of this Act, neither a co-operative nor a condominium is a planned community, but real estate comprising a condominium or co-operative may be part of a planned community.[10]

The community association often maintains the common property, cuts the grass, trims the bushes, and provides other common services such as sprinkler systems, exterior lighting, garbage collection, and security services. The unit owners usually are responsible for maintaining their units, but the community association normally exercises architectural control to preserve the uniform appearance of the community. This architectural control often leads to conflict between property owners and the community association.

Unlike the statutory law applying to condominiums, the law applying to planned communities is largely the product of the common law. Although the NCCUSL has recommended that the states adopt the Uniform Planned Community Act and the Uniform Common Interest Ownership Act to bring comparable statutory treatment to planned communities, surprisingly few have done so.[11] The large majority of states look to the common law of servitudes. **Servitudes**, discussed in Chapters 3 and 17, are restrictions on the use of property, usually in the form of a promise, which run with the land to bind subsequent land owners. The common law classified a servitude as either a real covenant (also called a restrictive covenant) or an equitable servitude (equitable restriction).

Traditionally, four requirements must be met for a **real covenant** to run with the land and thus bind subsequent property owners.

1. The covenant had to be part of a written agreement.

2. The parties must have intended that the covenant run with the land.

3. The covenant had to "touch and concern" the land. That is, the limitations imposed on the owner of the burdened land must have some connection with the land.

4. The original parties to the covenant had to be in "privity of estate" at the time the covenant was created. For example, the relationship between them had to be landlord and tenant, vendor and purchaser, or testator and devisee.

If these four requirements were not met, courts construed the promises to be simple contracts, binding only on the original parties. The most significant difference between a covenant running with the land and an **equitable servitude** was that privity of estate was not required for enforcement of an equitable servitude. Notice of the servitude on the public records was sufficient.

The new *Restatement (Third) of Property: Servitudes*, reflecting (or prompting) recent judicial trends, arguably drastically changes the requirements for real (restrictive) covenants, particularly the requirement that they, "touch and concern" the land. The *Restatement* focuses on intent of the parties that the restrictions run with the land and on public policy issues relative to enforcement, rather than on the traditional common law requirements. The *Restatement* also seeks to eliminate the formal distinction between real covenants and equitable servitudes.

The uniform acts applying to a planned community confer a long list of powers on its community association, including the power to enforce the CC&Rs and to levy and collect assessments. In the states in which planned communities are governed by the common law, these powers should be clearly spelled out in the CC&Rs if they are to be held enforceable. The new *Restatement* favors enforcement of the intention of the declarant. The declarant should retain some flexibility to meet future association needs, but should be as specific as possible in the CC&Rs so that potential buyers understand the restrictions and financial burdens associated with property ownership in the planned community. However, it is difficult for the declarant to anticipate in the CC&Rs all of the circumstances and problems that may arise in community association life. Therefore, Chapter 6 of the new *Restatement* encourages courts to grant liberal powers to community associations, subject to the reasonableness of their exercise.

Cooperatives[12]

Cooperatives (also called "stock cooperatives") date back to the mid–nineteenth century. Although the least prevalent form of common interest ownership in the United States today, they remain popular in New York, Chicago, and some other urban areas.[13]

In terms of legal relationships, a cooperative resembles a traditional apartment complex. In a **cooperative**, the real estate, including any buildings and improvements, is owned by a corporation (the cooperative), which also serves as the community association. A person who wishes to join the cooperative does so by buying shares in the corporation. The purchase of shares automatically entitles the purchaser to lease a unit within the cooperative. Thus, the resident shareholders in the cooperative corporation are tenants and the corporation is the landlord. The shares and the lease are inseparable from each other. Because the shareholder has a legal right to the lease, it is a called a *proprietary lease*—a leasehold interest owned by the shareholder by virtue of owning the shares. A sale or other transfer of the shares is also a transfer of the leasehold interest; the leasehold interest cannot be transferred apart from the shares.

A typical cooperative corporation acquires the property from its previous owner, commonly an apartment landlord, by mortgaging the property and applying the loan proceeds to the purchase price. The cooperative corporation pays all of the expenses of acquiring, financing, and operating the property. These project expenses are assessed to each of the residents as rent under the proprietary lease in accordance with the number of shares of stock allocated to that unit.

Consider the following comparison of a cooperative to a condominium. Assume that a developer purchases two identical ten–unit apartment complexes, intending to convert one into condominium units and the other into cooperative units. Valuing the condominium building at $2 million, the developer files a declaration of condominium and sells each unit for $200,000. To acquire a unit, each unit purchaser pays cash or obtains mortgage financing, and in addition pays a monthly maintenance assessment to cover the expenses of maintaining and replacing the common areas. For the complex intended as a *cooperative*, the developer obtains a mortgage on the property in the amount of $1.6 million, payable over 30 years at 7% interest. The developer then prices the ten cooperative "units" (ownership interests in the cooperative consisting of shares of stock plus a proprietary lease to an apartment) at $40,000 each. Upon purchasing a unit (for cash or on credit), the shareholder pays, as rent for the apartment, one–tenth of the corporation's mortgage debt (principal and interest), in this case an additional $1,065 per month, plus the monthly assessment for maintenance of the common areas. If the market value of either type of unit (condominium or cooperative) were to rise by 5%, the sale price of a condominium unit to a subsequent buyer would be $210,000, while the sale price of a cooperative unit would be approximately $50,000. The buyer of the cooperative unit would, of course, inherit the $1,065 per month rental payment, and, like the condominium buyer, would pay the monthly maintenance assessment.

The cooperative has some advantages over other forms of common interest communities. First, a cooperative, being the sole owner of the real estate, can mortgage it and thus can maintain or improve it without the need for a special assessment that, in a condominium, must be collected from individual owners And, as sole owner, a cooperative can easily refinance the whole mortgage debt if interest rates decline. Second, because a cooperative is a corporate entity with substantial assets, it may qualify for a corporate mortgage interest rate that is lower than the purchasers of individual condominium units would have to pay. Because the property of a co-operative is subject to only one mortgage (called a "blanket" mortgage), the acquisition cost at-tributable to a unit in a cooperative may be less than in a comparable condominium project, although the monthly assessment in a cooperative would be considerably higher because it in-cludes not only the monthly maintenance charge, but also the rent for the apartment, which is the shareholder's part of the debt service on the blanket mortgage.

Cooperatives also have some disadvantages. As with other residential purchases, a prospective cooperative resident may need financing to acquire the cooperative shares and the leasehold in-terest. However, the lack of a ready secondary market for loans secured by an interest in a coop-erative (personal property), makes loans to purchase a cooperative interest not as readily available as loans for units in condominiums or planned communities (involving real estate mortgages eas-ily saleable in the secondary market). Therefore, a prospective resident of a cooperative may have to come up with relatively more cash at the time of purchase. In the preceding examples, the buyer of the $200,000 condominium might be able to finance 95% or more of the purchase price, thus needing to make only a $10,000 down payment. The buyer of the cooperative shares might have to come up with the entire $40,000 or arrange financing at a higher interest rate be-cause the loan is not readily marketable in the secondary market.

Even though a cooperative's blanket mortgage provides the financial advantages noted ear-lier, it does have its "down" side. The existence of a blanket mortgage means that each resident must be confident that the others can and will make their monthly assessment payments. Otherwise, the cooperative will be unable to service the debt. If the blanket mortgage goes into default, the mortgagee has a right to foreclose on the cooperative as a whole. As a precaution, therefore, the cooperative commonly prohibits the transfer of the corporate shares or the assign-ment of the proprietary lease without consent of the other owners (or the board of directors of the cooperative corporation). This restriction allows the cooperative to undertake a credit review of current residents' prospective buyers to assure that they will have the ability to pay the monthly assessments. The boards of cooperative corporations have used this power to exclude potential buyers for other than financial reasons, for example, to exclude celebrities who would bring unwelcome attention or disruption to the cooperative.

The development and operation of cooperatives is largely governed by the common law. Although the NCCUSL has promulgated a Model Real Estate Cooperative Act modeled on the UCA, it has been adopted only by Virginia.[14]

● Timeshare Arrangements[15]

Timesharing arrangements have become popular in resort jurisdictions. A **timeshare** purchaser buys the right to occupy a unit in a common interest community for a given time period, either in perpetuity or for a given number of years. For example, a timeshare purchaser may buy the right to occupy a condominium unit in Key West for the third week in December every year. Developers have long marketed timeshares as a way for unit owners to share the expense of a va-cation home.

A timeshare arrangement is classified as a timeshare estate or a timeshare license. The purchaser of a **timeshare estate** acquires an ownership interest such as a fee simple interest in the realty (i.e., a condominium unit) for a given, repetitive time period usually referred to as an interval. For legal and taxation purposes, the timeshare estate is treated like a fee simple (or whatever other ownership interest was created, such as an estate for years).[16] So, if Beach-view Development Company conveys to Betsy a fee simple interest in Unit 33 of Black-acre Condominium for the second full week in each year, she receives a timeshare estate in perpetuity and pays the real estate taxes on its value. In a **timeshare license**, the unit owner retains fee simple title to the property and grants to timeshare buyers merely a right *to use* the property during specified periods during the year. Thus, a timeshare *license* is a contract right and a personal property interest rather than the realty ownership interest characteristic of a timeshare estate. If Vacations Limited grants Ling permission to use Unit 16 of Greenacre Condominium for the second full week in December of each year, Ling receives a timeshare license and pays no real estate taxes, because she has not received an interest in realty.

Because of their purpose and their intermittent nature, timeshare arrangements create some special legal problems. First, because timeshare intervals are vigorously marketed in resort jurisdictions as vacation home substitutes, most owners of the underlying units are absentee owners, likely to have little interest in upkeep or management. Also, the interests of the timeshare purchasers in the whole condominium or planned community usually are quite small, which means that their participation in the community association will be limited. To accommodate timeshare owners, the community association will need to conduct most business by mail. Meetings will be infrequent and will require low quorums to conduct business. For a management fee, nonowner management normally conducts the day-to-day operations of the timeshare condominium or planned community. Because each timeshare purchaser shares a unit with a number of other interval owners, restrictions regarding use and abuse of the property are important. The developer may need to structure timeshare intervals so that the manager can inspect, repair, and clean the unit between intervals. The restrictions or regulations should also address the problem of timeshare owners who stay after the expiration of their intervals. A timeshare owner who "holds over" is trespassing on another person's property interest, but legal remedies to evict a recalcitrant interval owner are too time-consuming to be practical.

Successful timeshare developments depend on large numbers of purchasers. Typically, about 50 timeshare intervals per year, of five or six days each, are assigned to each unit, leaving some time between intervals for maintenance and repair. For a development to be successful, a timeshare developer must sell many intervals. As a result of the sales pressure, the timeshare industry has developed a number of measures calculated to sell more intervals. These measures include staggering timeshare intervals throughout different seasons of the year, pooling of intervals, rental pools, and timeshare exchange networks. Exchange networks allow a timeshare purchaser to exchange his or her interval for that of another timeshare owner. Timeshare owners may change either the time period or the location of their timeshares. Collectively, these mechanisms provide a possibility of variety that overcomes a prospective buyer's resistance to buying a "vacation" in the same resort during the same time period year after year. The darker side of having to sell large numbers of intervals is that the timeshare industry has become known for unscrupulous marketing tactics. Consequently, most states regulate timeshares and their marketing. Many states require registration of timeshare projects and comprehensive disclosures to potential purchasers. The federal government also carefully scrutinizes timeshare marketing, especially through the activities of the Federal Trade Commission and the Securities and Exchange Commission.

Real Estate Investments

Real estate and real estate-related securities are attractive investments. Thus far, we have considered "investment" from a broad perspective, as any expenditure of money with the expectation of future gain. Thus, a family's investment in a house or a common interest community is an investment because it serves as a hedge against inflation and provides tax advantages. It also offers the possibility of capital preservation and, if the residence is sold, even capital gain. Without losing sight of a family's real estate investment, this section deals more specifically with the legal aspects of real estate syndications. **Real estate syndication** is investment in real estate by multiple investors, usually on a large scale.

Considerations in Structuring Real Estate Investments

Large-scale real estate investments require attention to important considerations, including whether an individual or a legal entity should own the real estate, and how shares in the real estate investment should be structured and marketed. Often, capital requirements of the developer or owner, income tax considerations, operational necessities, and the need to limit the liability of investors dictate that the realty be owned by an entity. Marketing considerations may center on the federal and state securities laws, which impose limitations on the formation of real estate syndications and the sale of real estate-related investments.

Capital Requirements

Many real estate projects are beyond the reach of an individual or a family operating alone. For example, Post Properties, Inc., a large apartment developer and owner, recently announced the sale of two apartment projects containing a total of 367 apartment units for $36.9 million. Few individuals or families in the United States could afford that investment, even with generous amounts of loan financing, and those who could afford to invest that much would be reluctant to do so because of the considerable risk involved in placing a large amount of capital in a single investment. Consequently, real estate syndications provide most of the capital needed for large projects.

Tax Considerations

How a real estate investment is taxed influences a number of taxpayer decisions. Among them are whether to invest in realty instead of other property such as stocks and bonds; when and how realty should be sold; and, if it is held as a long-term investment, how it should be held.

As noted in Chapter 16, Congress designed certain parts of the Internal Revenue Code expressly to encourage real estate development and ownership. Among the income tax advantages to real estate ownership are the following:

- Interest paid on mortgages to finance the purchase or development of real estate is normally deductible from taxable income, even if the real estate is for personal use.

- State and local real estate taxes are deductible, even if the real estate is for personal use.

- Repair and maintenance expenses are deductible if the real estate is business property and not used as the taxpayer's personal residence.

- A gain on the sale of a real estate that has been held for more than one year is a "capital gain" and is taxed at lower rates.

- Taxpayers may depreciate the value of improvements to real estate leased to tenants, currently over a 27.5-year useful life for residential property and a 39-year useful life for commercial property.

How realty is owned affects how it is taxed. Some methods of ownership result in higher taxation, which affects their attractiveness to certain taxpayers. An individual taxpayer who owns real estate recognizes all income and losses, reports them on his or her individual income tax return, and pays the tax dictated by his or her income tax bracket. Similarly, a corporation that owns realty recognizes the income and losses, files a corporate tax return, and pays the income tax on its

BOX 15–2 POINT TO CONSIDER

To appreciate the value of depreciation to a taxpayer, consider the following examples:

1. Taxpayer Joseph owns an office building for which he paid $1 million. If the value of the land (which is nondepreciable) is $200,000, Joseph is entitled to depreciate the remaining $800,000 over a period of 39 years. Using straight-line depreciation, Joseph can deduct $20,512 from taxable income each year. The amount of the financial benefit of this deduction depends on Joseph's marginal tax rate.

2. The depreciation schedules are more generous for residential property. If instead of an office building, Joseph owns an apartment complex for which he paid $1 million, with a land value of $200,000, he can assume a 27.5-year useful life, creating an annual deduction against taxable income of $29,091.

The depreciation deduction is extremely valuable to a taxpayer because it essentially allows an investor to deduct most of the capital cost of the investment over time.

corporate profits. However, if the corporation passes some of those profits to its shareholders in the form of dividends, the shareholders must pay income tax on the dividends. Therefore, corporate income is subject to "double taxation." If a corporation suffers losses, it recognizes those losses on its corporate tax return. Yet, even though the shareholders may have suffered an economic loss as a result of the reduction in the value of the corporation in which they hold stock, they normally cannot recognize a taxable loss unless they sell their stock. Therefore, a corporate shareholder may experience the worst of all possible tax worlds: income is taxed twice and the taxpayer gets no immediate tax reduction for losses. To reduce the burden of double taxation, the Internal Revenue Code makes some entities "invisible" for income tax purposes. That is, gains and losses are passed through to the owners who pay income taxes as if the assets were held by them individually. This pass-through treatment can be particularly important in real estate investments and is a characteristic of partnerships, subchapter S corporations, and limited liability companies, all of which are discussed later in this chapter.

To avoid taxes or to minimize them, many taxpayers have made use of a variety of "tax shelters" designed for that purpose. Taxpayers are, of course, free to minimize through legitimate means the taxes they pay. But in the view of Congress, many were using certain kinds of tax shelters to generate unwarranted tax deductions. To stop this practice, the Tax Reform Act of 1986 included a number of provisions designed to attack abusive tax shelters, many of which involved real estate holdings. As part of the regulation of tax shelters, the Tax Reform Act placed a number of limitations on the deduction of real estate-related losses. Although beyond the scope of this book, these limitations nevertheless affect investors.

Operational Aspects

Different types of real estate development and ownership present different levels of operational complexity. Construction of residential or commercial real estate improvements demands intense management scrutiny, even if the construction work itself is performed by independent contractors. Ownership and management of a small rental property may demand relatively little management involvement, but the larger and more complex a project is, the more likely it will require full-time, professional management. The structure of the investment may be dictated in part by whether the providers of the capital for the project wish to be involved in the day-to-day management and operation of real estate. Even when all of the investors are to be in some degree involved in the ownership or development of the realty, however, it may be advantageous to select one owner as the ultimate decision maker.

Liability Issues

Real estate investment projects involve a significant risk of tort and contractual liability. Tort liability commonly arises from personal injuries suffered by workers or others in the course of the construction process. In completed projects, dangerous conditions on the premises may cause injuries to occupants or third parties. Inadequate security may be blamed for crime committed by third parties. All of these situations might lead to tort claims. To protect themselves against the risk of tort liability, investors can purchase liability insurance. However, they cannot insure themselves against the risk of contractual liability arising, for example, from cost overruns in development or construction or from operation or maintenance expenses that may exceed projections. And interest rates on mortgage loans may increase. Investors most dread the risk that they will not be able to sell or lease the real estate, or may have to settle for far less than the projected breakeven amount.

If individuals suffer unexpected tort or contractual liability, they of course risk financial ruin. Secured creditors may foreclose their security interests and sell the collateral. If the collateral is insufficient to cover the debt, they can do more than just foreclose. They can sue the debtor, obtain a deficiency judgment, and, within limits imposed on deficiency judgments in some states, force the sale of the debtor's nonproject assets to satisfy the judgment. Unsecured creditors, too, have access to the debtor's assets. Thus, individual debtors can lose substantially everything that they presently have. Moreover, because a judgment lien can be valid for as long as twenty years, judgment debtors risk losing everything that they are likely to acquire later. Although the existence of the Federal Bankruptcy Code reduces the risk of complete financial ruin, the possibility of unlimited personal liability discourages real estate investment. Investors may avoid this risk of unlimited liability by selecting an appropriate type of business organization for the conduct of their investment activities. Limited liability options include corporations, S corporations, limited liability companies, limited liability partnerships, and real estate investment trusts. These and other forms of organization are discussed later in this chapter.

Securities Law Implications

As noted in Chapter 16, in two key pieces of legislation, the Securities Act of 1933 and the Securities Exchange Act of 1934, Congress intended to provide investors with more information about securities they might want to purchase, and to prohibit fraud and unfair and deceptive practices in the sale of securities, so that an investor could make an informed decision about buying or selling them. The 1933 act provides that a security must be registered with the SEC before it is offered for sale, unless the security or the sales transaction is exempt from registration. To register, the seller or the issuer of the security must file a **registration statement** with the SEC. The registration statement includes a description of the security; a description of the registrant, its business, management, and assets; a certified financial statement; and a copy of the disclosure statement (i.e., a prospectus) that will be provided to investors. A **prospectus** describes the security being sold, facts about the issuer, and the risks of the investment.

Perhaps the most significant regulation adopted by the SEC is Rule 10b-5, which is designed to prohibit fraudulent activities in connection with the sale of securities. The SEC may seek criminal and civil sanctions for violations of this rule or the other provisions of these acts. Injured investors can also sue for rescission of investment contracts or damages for violations of the rule.

In addition to the requirements of the federal securities acts, each state has its own laws regulating the issuance and sale of securities, usually administered within the office of a state's secretary of state. To differentiate them from the federal securities acts, these state laws are usually referred to as **blue sky laws**. A state's blue sky laws apply to the issuance and sale of securities within its boundaries. Although their provisions vary widely from state to state, many states have modeled their registration and antifraud schemes on the federal model. Due to some overlapping jurisdiction, both the federal securities acts and the blue sky laws may apply to a given security issuance or sale.

These acts and their implementing rules apply to sales of securities, including any transaction in which a person invests in a common enterprise, reasonably expecting profits *solely from the efforts of others*, "it being immaterial whether the shares in the enterprise are evidenced by formal certificates or by nominal interests in the physical assets employed in the enterprise."

With this broad definition of a security, regulators and courts construe many types of real estate investments to be securities. For example, courts have classified sales of condominiums or timeshares as securities if the developer stressed the investment potential of the units, particularly if the sale of the unit is coupled with a management agreement or a rental pooling agreement. If a real estate investment is a security, its issuance or sale may still qualify for one of a number of exemptions from federal and state registration discussed in Chapter 16. However, even if a security is exempt from registration, it remains subject to the antifraud provisions of the securities laws, including Rule 10b-5.

⬤ Methods of Structuring Real Estate Investments

Several types of business organizations are available as vehicles for real estate investment or real estate syndication. The options include corporations, partnerships, and various hybrids such as S corporations, limited liability companies, limited liability partnerships, and real estate investment trusts. In varying degrees they serve to avoid some or all of the problems discussed earlier in this chapter.

Corporations and Subchapter S Corporations

A **corporation** is a legal entity chartered under state law. A corporation is an independent legal "person," with most of the legal rights and obligations of human beings. Unlike natural persons, a corporation has a life span that is theoretically unlimited. Investors form a corporation by filing articles of incorporation with a state's secretary of state and paying any required fees. The articles of incorporation disclose basic required information about the corporation, including its corporate name (which must be unique), its registered office for service of process, its capital structure, its initial directors, and its incorporator. When the state issues a corporate charter, the corporation can buy, sell, mortgage, and own property just like a natural person. A corporation is controlled by its board of directors, who are elected by the owners of the corporation, called **stockholders** or **shareholders**. The board of directors may appoint or hire officers to manage the day-to-day activities of the corporation.

The ownership interest in a corporation is evidenced by shares of stock. Each share of stock normally represents a proportionate ownership interest in the assets, earnings, and control of the corporation. A shareholder has no interest in any specific asset, only a proportionate interest in the corporate entity. A corporation distributes income to its shareholders in the form of dividends at the discretion of the board of directors.

The principal advantages of the corporate form of organization are the limited liability of shareholders and the ability of its organizers to raise virtually unlimited amounts of capital for corporate purposes. Shareholders normally risk only the money that they have invested in their shares. Except in rare circumstances they are not liable for tort or contractual liability incurred by the corporate entity. The limited liability feature makes a corporation especially attractive for real estate investment, compared to individual or partnership ownership of property and its unlimited liability. Indeed, without limited shareholder liability, potential investors would be reluctant to invest.

To preserve its status as a separate legal person, a corporation must observe a number of formalities. It must meet general business filing and licensing requirements; it must adopt corporate bylaws relating to the conduct of corporate business; it often must file annual reports with the state's secretary of state's office and pay franchise taxes; it must hold annual meetings of shareholders and elect boards of directors and corporate officers; and it may be subject to statutory requirements to qualify to do business in each state in which it transacts business. Most important, if the organizers issue or sell stock to "outsiders" (i.e., investors who will not be involved in the operation or management of the corporation), they must comply with the federal securities acts and state blue sky laws.

The principal disadvantage of the corporate form as a vehicle for real estate investment is the problem of double taxation of income. A normal corporation is a separate taxpayer with its own income and losses. Any dividends distributed to the shareholders are not deductible from corporate income, and are taxable to the shareholders. Any losses remain within the corporation and cannot be deducted by the shareholders. These tax factors make a traditional corporation an undesirable vehicle for most real estate investments.

Somewhat more desirable for real estate investment is the so-called "subchapter S corporation." A *subchapter S corporation* is organized and treated like any other corporation. However, if a corporation meets the requirements of the Internal Revenue Code for "subchapter S" status, it can elect to be treated as a subchapter S corporation for federal income tax purposes. By electing subchapter S treatment, the corporation is exempted from paying taxes on the corporate income. Instead, corporate gains and losses are "passed through" to the shareholders. The corporation files an informational tax return that allocates the corporate revenues and expenses proportionately to each share of stock in the corporation. Then the shareholders report their respective share of the corporation's gains and losses on their individual income tax returns and pay the income tax appropriate for their individual tax brackets.

A subchapter S corporation can have only one class of shares and no more than 75 shareholders. Normally, only individuals who are U.S. citizens or residents can own the shares of a subchapter S corporation, not nonresident aliens, partnerships, or other corporations. Consequently, a subchapter S corporation is not well suited for raising large amounts of capital.

Partnerships

A partnership is a business organization formed by two or more individuals who have entered into an agreement, either express or implied, to carry on a business venture together, for profit. The agreement of the partners establishes the purposes and the duration of a partnership. A corporation may be a partner in a partnership. Although the common law did not treat a partnership as an independent legal entity, most states now treat a partnership as an entity for most purposes. For example, a partnership may hold and transfer property in the partnership name. However, a partnership is *not* an entity for tax purposes. The partnership files an informational federal income tax return allocating gains and losses among the partners, who report and pay taxes on these gains and losses on their individual income tax returns.

The two common types of partnerships are general partnerships and limited partnerships.

General Partnerships.[17] A general partnership is established by agreement of the parties to carry on a business as co-owners for profit. Although the law does not require a formal written agreement to create a partnership, a written agreement is advisable, particularly if the general partnership intends to buy and hold real property. Each partner stands in a fiduciary relationship to each of the other partners. This relationship means that each owes the highest duty of good faith and fair dealing to the others. The partners can vary their respective rights and duties in the partnership agreement. If the partners do not agree otherwise, the general partners divide profits and losses evenly, each partner has an equal voice in the management of the partnership, and each partner has the authority to bind the partnership.

In addition to avoidance of double taxation, the general partnership form of organization provides a number of advantages to real estate investors. Partnerships have the ability to raise larger amounts of capital than do individuals, because they have access to the financial resources of all of the partners. For example, the insurance syndicates at Lloyd's of London are general partnerships with more than 20,000 independent underwriters. Collectively they represent resources in the billions of dollars. Partnerships are easy to form, requiring only an agreement among the partners. Partnerships must comply with the general business requirements for licensing and they may have to file a fictitious name certificate under applicable state law. Because general partners normally have equal management authority, few securities law issues relate to general partnerships.

The principal disadvantage of a partnership is that a wrongful act or omission of any partner acting in the ordinary course of the business of the partnership subjects it and all of the partners to joint and several liability for any loss or injury to a third party. This liability can arise in either contract or tort. Suppose that Valdez Development Company, a business organized as a general partnership with Valdez and nine other family members as general partners, owes $2 million to Caldwell Construction Company because Valdez (without the knowledge or consent of the other partners) made numerous changes to a building design, causing construction cost overruns. Because the liability is "joint and several," not only the partnership itself, but also each of the ten partners is liable to Caldwell Construction Company for the entire $2 million. Caldwell Construction is entitled to be paid only once, but Caldwell can choose whom to hold liable. The practical effect is that the general partner with the most financial resources may bear a disproportionate share of the loss, and must bear *all* of it if other partners cannot contribute their shares. Because each general partner has unlimited personal liability for the acts of all partners, real estate investors naturally avoid the partnership form of business organization.

Limited Partnerships.[18] The use of a limited partnership can significantly reduce the risk of unlimited personal liability for the limited partners. State law authorizes the formation of a **limited partnership**, which consists of at least one general partner and one or more limited partners. The general partners have the same rights and duties as they would have in a general partnership. The general partners have all of the management responsibility for the limited partnership and are jointly and severally liable for all debts of the limited partnership, whether arising in contract or tort. A limited partner contributes capital, but by definition cannot be involved in the day-to-day management of the partnership. Like a shareholder in a corporation, a limited partner has no liability beyond the amount of capital he or she invested in the limited partnership interest, as long as the limited partner does not participate in the management of the limited partnership. If a limited partner participates in the management, the limited partner risks being treated as a general partner with unlimited personal liability. This limited liability feature facilitates the syndication of large amounts of capital. Like a general partnership, a limited partnership is treated as an entity for most purposes other than the payment of income taxes.

To form a limited partnership, the partners must enter into a limited partnership agreement and file a certificate of limited partnership with the state's secretary of state. The certificate of limited partnership must contain:

1. The name of the limited partnership. Under the Uniform Limited Partnership Act, the partnership name must contain the words "limited partnership."

2. The address of the office and the name and address of the agent for service of process.

3. The name and the business address of each general partner.

4. The latest date upon which the limited partnership is to dissolve.

A limited partnership must also comply with general business licensing requirements.

Because a limited partner is not permitted to participate in the management of the partnership, the interest of a limited partner qualifies as a "security" under the federal securities laws and state blue sky laws. Therefore, the formation of a limited partnership may be subject to federal or state registration and disclosure requirements.

The limited partnership agreement allocates profits and losses among all of the partners. Limited partners share in losses only to the extent of their capital contributions. Unless the limited partnership agreement states to the contrary, profits and losses are allocated to partners according to the percentages of capital they contributed. Like a general partnership, a limited partnership normally files only an informational federal income tax return allocating gains and losses among the partners, and the partners report gains and losses on their individual federal income tax returns and pay taxes accordingly.

Hybrids: Limited Liability Companies and Limited Liability Partnerships

In 1977, the State of Wyoming examined the then existing IRS regulations on limited partnerships and examples of limited liability companies from other countries and enacted the first state statute authorizing the creation of limited liability companies. Wyoming intended that the **limited liability company** (LLC) be chartered like a corporation, with a corporation's limited liability for shareholders, but to have the pass-through taxation aspects of a partnership. In 1988, the IRS ruled that LLCs would be taxed under federal law like partnerships, provided that they met certain IRS criteria. Since 1988, all of the states have passed laws authorizing LLCs, and most states have followed the IRS lead in taxing LLCs like partnerships.

To form an LLC, organizers must file articles of organization, typically with the state's secretary of state. The articles of organization must include:

1. The name of the company.

2. The address of the initial designated office.

3. The name and street address of the initial agent for service of process.

4. The name and address of each organizer.

5. Whether the company is to last for a specified term and, if so, the term specified.

6. Whether the company is to be manager-managed, and, if so, the name and address of each initial manager.

7. Whether one or more of the members of the company are to be liable for its debts and obligations.

The members of the LLC normally execute an operating agreement that specifies the details of the management of the LLC and how its gains and losses will be distributed. An LLC does business through its members or through managing members designated in the operating agreement.

Unless the members agree otherwise, they are entitled to equal distributions of gains and losses. An LLC has many of the advantages of a subchapter S corporation without being limited to one class of stock and 75 shareholders, and without the prohibition of nonresident alien shareholders.

The 1997 amendments to the Uniform Partnership Act allow partnerships (either general or limited) to elect to be treated as **limited liability partnerships** (LLPs). LLPs retain all of the characteristics of partnerships, including the pass-through tax treatment, except that they eliminate much of the personal liability of the general partners. For an existing partnership to qualify as an LLP, it must file the appropriate election form with the secretary of state, and the partnership's business name must include either "Limited Liability Partnership" or "LLP." Although LLPs provide the general partners with more protection from liability than a general partnership or a limited partnership does, LLP statutes are less uniform among the states than other types of business organization statutes. Some states restrict the use of LLPs to professional partnerships and in some instances the limitation of liability is less complete than in a corporation or LLC.

Real Estate Investment Trusts[19]

A **real estate investment trust (REIT)** is an investment entity that receives favorable tax treatment under the Internal Revenue Code if it has at least 75% of its assets invested in real estate, mortgage loans, or other real estate-related assets. REITs are similar to stock mutual funds, allowing small investors to pool their resources to buy shares of a professionally managed, diversified portfolio of real estate-related investments. Such investments formerly were available only to large investors. Like mutual funds, REITs tend to be liquid investments; many are publicly traded on the major stock exchanges. A REIT is taxed like a corporation, but it pays corporate income tax only on its retained earnings and it must distribute at least 95% of its profits to shareholders. The REIT receives a deduction for the dividends that it distributes, eliminating the double taxation problems characteristic of other corporations. Unlike a partnership or a limited liability company, a REIT does not pass through losses, making it unsuitable for real estate "tax shelters." Investors have no personal liability for debts of the REIT arising in contract or tort. The Internal Revenue Code imposes some limitations on REITs, which practically assure that REITs are suitable only for reasonably large aggregations of capital and which almost guarantee application of federal securities laws and state blue sky laws. For example, a REIT must be for passive investment; it must have at least 100 shareholders; and no more than 50% of the shares may be concentrated in five or fewer shareholders.

Self-Study Questions

1. What are the typical motivations for investment in real estate?

2. What are the distinguishing features of a condominium?

3. What are the distinguishing features of a planned community?

4. What are the distinguishing features of a cooperative?

5. What aspects of common interest ownership are found in the condominium, the planned community, and the cooperative?

6. What is the function of a community association? Does its function differ depending on whether the community is a condominium, a planned community, or a cooperative?

7. What are the distinguishing features of the following forms of business organization? (a) corporation (b) general partnership (c) limited partnership (d) limited liability company (e) limited liability partnership (f) real estate investment trust

8. How are corporations treated for tax purposes, and what is the significance of that treatment for real estate investors who use a corporation as their investment vehicle?

9. What types of real estate investments are most and least likely to involve the purchase and sale of a "security" within the meaning of federal securities law and state blue sky laws?

10. Which types of business organization seem to be most suited to real estate syndications if the goals are: (a) avoidance of double taxation, (b) limitation of personal liability of investors, (c) raising significant amounts of capital, or (d) all of the foregoing?

Case Problems

1. Dunes South was a timeshare condominium constructed by First Flight Builders, Inc. First Flight filed a declaration of condominium submitting the property to the provisions of the North Carolina Unit Ownership Act, a first-generation condominium act. The declaration of condominium provided that instead of the normal assessment payable by the other owners, declarant First Flight would pay only the actual operating expenses payable in excess of the assessments collected from the unit owners. When the unit owners assumed control of the association, the association filed suit to recover unpaid assessments. The Unit Ownership Act provided that: "The unit owners are bound to contribute pro rata, in the percentages computed according to G.S. 47A-6 of this Chapter, toward the expenses of administration and of maintenance and repair of the general common areas and facilities and, in proper cases of the limited common areas and facilities, of the building and toward any other expense lawfully agreed upon. No unit owner may exempt himself from contributing toward such expense by waiver of the use or enjoyment of the common areas and facilities or by abandonment of the unit belonging to him." Must the declarant make the past due assessment payments? Is the answer to this question different under the UCA? *Dunes South Homeowners Association, Inc. v. First Flight Builders, Inc.*, 459 S.E.2d 477 (N.C. 1995).

2. The CC&Rs of Green Acres contain a restrictive covenant that prohibits occupancy of any lot by persons not of the Caucasian race. If the Green Acres Community Association files suit to enforce the covenant, what is the likely result? *Restatement (Third) of Property: Servitudes* § 3.1, Illustration 2.

3. The Weymouthport Condominium sued, seeking the removal of two pet dogs from a condominium unit owned by John Murphy and Margaret Wilson. They based their action upon a condominium bylaw banning all pets from any housing unit or common area of the condominium. They also sought to enforce bylaws providing for the assessment of a $5 per day per violation penalty and payment by the defendants of the "costs and expense of eliminating" violations. The defendants challenged the validity of the pet restriction and the enforceability of any fines and assessments based upon it. How is the court likely to rule on the enforceability of this restriction contained in the original documents creating the condominium? *Noble v. Murphy*, 612 N.E.2d 266 (Mass. App. 1993).

4. All lots in Raintree, a planned community in North Carolina, were subject to covenants, conditions, and restrictions that required residents to obtain approval from an architectural review committee before making any alterations to the exterior of their dwellings. One of the residents, Bleimann, sued the community association, claiming that the architectural review committee arbitrarily refused to approve his installation of vinyl siding on his house to replace the original wood siding. The evidence showed that the architectural review committee had considered the homeowner's request on at least three separate occasions, had visited the homeowner's house to look at the materials before rendering its decision, and had previously disapproved seven similar applications. Is the action of the architectural review committee in disapproving vinyl siding reasonable? Is a court likely to overturn the decision of the architectural review committee and to permit the installation of vinyl siding? *Raintree Homeowners Association v. Bleimann*, 463 S.E.2d 72 (N.C. 1995).

5. The developer of a condominium project reserved the right in the declaration of condominium to exempt "any unit" from community association assessments "at any time." The developer used this reserved right to exempt units that it owned from assessments. The community association sued the developer, seeking the unpaid assessments. What is the likely result? *Alma Investments, Inc. v. Bahia Mar CoOwners Association*, 999 S.W.2d 826 (Tex. App. 1999).

Endnotes

1. See generally, Wayne S. Hyatt, *Condominiums and Homeowner Associations: A Guide to the Development Process* (1985); Wayne S. Hyatt, *Condominium and Homeowner Association Practice: Community Association Law* (1981); *Restatement (Third) of Property: Servitudes* (1998); Susan F. French, "Gallivan Conference: Tradition and Innovation in the New Restatement of Servitudes: A Report from the Midpoint," 27 *Conn. L. Rev.*119 (1994); Patrick K. Hetrick, "Of 'Private Governments' and the Regulation of Neighborhoods: The North Carolina Planned Community Act," 22 *Campbell L. Rev.* 1 (1999); Wayne S. Hyatt, "Common Interest Communities: Evolution and Reinvention," 31 *J. Marshall L. Rev.* 303 (1998); Carl H. Lisman and Carol A. Cluff, "Time Sharing," ALI-ABA, *Resort Real Estate* 381 (1990); Ira Meislik et al., "Community Associations: An Overview," available at http://www.meislik.com/articles/art03.htm (November 22, 2000); Mark S. Rosen, "Residential Housing Cooperatives—A Legal Perspective," 174 *N.J. Law* (February 1996), at 14; Katharine N. Rosenberry, "Home Businesses, Llamas and Aluminum Siding: Trends in Covenant Enforcement," 31 *J. Marshall L. Rev.* 443 (Winter 1998); Katherine N. Rosenberry and Curtis G. Sproul, "Symposium: Common Interest Development Communities: Part I: A Comparison of California Common Interest Development Law and the Uniform Common Interest Ownership Act," 38 *Santa Clara L. Rev.* 1009 (1998); Laura Castro Trognitz, "Co-Opted Living," 85 *A.B.A.J.* (October 1999), at 54; Michael L. Utz, "Comment: Common Interest Ownership in Pennsylvania: An Examination of Statutory Reform and Implications for Practitioners," 37 *Duq. L. Rev.* 465 (1999); James L. Winokur, "Gallivan Conference: Ancient Strands Rewoven, or Refashioned Out of Whole Cloth?: First Impressions of the Emerging Restatement of Servitudes," 27 *Conn. L. Rev.* 131 (1994).

2. *Restatement (Third) of Property: Servitudes* § 1.8. The Uniform Common Interest Ownership Act defines common interest ownership similarly as a form of ownership of real estate in which "a person, by virtue of his ownership of a unit, is obligated to pay for real estate taxes, insurance premiums, maintenance, or improvement of other real estate described in a declaration" UCIOA § 1-103 (7).

3. All of these terms are commonly used and all are unsatisfactory and possibly confusing. For example, a "townhouse development" is descriptive but unduly restrictive in purpose; many of these developments include commercial or office uses. A "homeowners association development" is also unduly restrictive in purpose and possibly confusing because many condominium unit owners' associations have the name "homeowners association." "Planned unit development" is a phrase also potentially confusing because it is commonly used to describe a type of multi-use zoning in many jurisdictions. Consistent with the modern trend, we have elected to use the term *planned community* throughout to refer to the type of development described in this chapter, which is characterized by individual ownership of the structure and a comprehensive set of covenants, conditions, and restrictions.

4. The association of unit owners that manages a condominium is referred to by a number of names, both in practice, in various state statutes and in the literature, including *owners' association, unit owners' association, homeowners' association*, and *condominium association*. The recent trend in the literature, which we will adopt in this text, is to refer to an entity that manages a condominium or the property owners' association that owns and manages the common areas of a planned community as a "community association." This common designation emphasizes the functional similarity of the two types of organizations.

5. Wayne S. Hyatt, "Common Interest Communities: Evolution and Reinvention," 31 *J. Marshall L. Rev.* 303, n. 76 (1998). The Legal Information Institute includes the following states that have substantially adopted the UCA: Alabama, Arizona, Maine, Minnesota, Missouri, New Mexico, North Carolina,

Pennsylvania, Rhode Island, Texas, Virginia, and Washington. See Legal Information Institute, "Uniform Business and Financial Law Locator," available at http://www.law.cornell.edu/uniform/vol7.html (June 22, 1999).

6. The Uniform Common Interest Ownership Act was amended in 1994. References in this text will be to the 1994 version. The Legal Information Institute includes the following states that have substantially adopted the Uniform Common Interest Ownership Act: Alaska (1982), Colorado (1982), Connecticut (1994), Minnesota (1982), Nevada (1982), Vermont (1994), and West Virginia (1982). See Legal Information Institute, "Uniform Business and Financial Law Locator," available at http://www.law.cornell.edu /uniform/vol7.html (June 22, 1999).

7. *Lamden v. La Jolla Shores Condominium Assoc.*, 1999 WL 592088 (Cal. 1999).

8. UCA § 3-105. See also UCIOA, § 3-105. This same requirement of contract termination without liability upon ninety days notice is also imposed by FNMA regulations. The principle also affects condominiums in those states that have not adopted the UCA or a comparable second-generation condominium statute.

9. Laura Castro Trognitz, "Co-Opted Living," 85 *A.B.A.J.* (October 1999), at 54.

10. Uniform Planned Community Act § 103(21), NCCUSL Official Draft (1980), available at http://www.law.upenn.edu/bll. The bracketed language is from the North Carolina version of the UPCA, N.C. Gen. Stat. 47F-1-103(23), and replaces apparently erroneous language of the NCCUSL official draft quoted here.

11. Only North Carolina and Pennsylvania have adopted the UPCA. The Legal Information Institute includes the following states that have substantially adopted the Uniform Common Interest Ownership Act: Alaska, Colorado, Connecticut, Minnesota, Nevada, Vermont, and West Virginia. See Legal Information Institute, "Uniform Business and Financial Law Locator," available at http://www.law.cornell.edu /uniform/vol7.html (June 22, 1999). California has its own Common Interest Development Act which defines "common interest development" as "any of the following:" a community apartment project, a condominium project, a planned development, or a stock cooperative. *Cal. Civ. Code* §§ 1350-1374 (West 1995).

12. See generally, *Model Real Estate Cooperative Act* (1981); Grant S. Nelson and Dale A. Whitman, *Cases and Materials on Real Estate Finance and Development* 775-76 (1976); Mark S. Rosen, "Residential Housing Cooperatives—A Legal Perspective," 174 *N.J. Law.* (February 1996), at 14.

13. Richard J. Kane, "The Financing of Cooperatives and Condominiums: A Retrospective," 73 *St. John's L. Rev.* 101, 102 (1999).

14. See Legal Information Institute, "Uniform Business and Financial Law Locator," available at http://www.law.cornell.edu/uniform/vol7.html (June 22, 1999). Other states have cooperative statutes, including some, like Pennsylvania, that apparently follow the Model Act; Michael L. Utz, "Comment: Common Interest Ownership in Pennsylvania: An Examination of Statutory Reform and Implications for Practitioners," 37 *Duq. L. Rev.* 465 (1999).

15. See generally Model Real Estate Time Share Act; Carl H. Lisman and Carol A. Cluff, "Time Sharing," ALI-ABA, *Resort Real Estate* 381 (1990).

16. See generally Model Real Estate Time Share Act §§ 1-1.02 (14), 1-1.02.

17. See generally Uniform Partnership Act (amended 1997), available at National Conference of Commissioners on Uniform State Laws, "Introductions and Adoptions of Uniform Acts," available at http://www.nccusl.org/uniformacts-subjectmatter.htm (November 20, 2000).

18. See generally Uniform Limited Partnership Act ("ULPA") (amended 1986), National Conference of Commissioners on Uniform State Laws, "Introductions and Adoptions of Uniform Acts," available at http://www.nccusl.org/uniformacts-subjectmatter.htm (November 20, 2000).

19. See generally Ralph L. Block, *Investing in REITs* (1998); Grant S. Nelson and Dale A. Whitman, *Real Estate Finance and Development Cases and Materials,* 455-56 (1976); Charles E. Wern III, Comment: "Sparing Cain: Executive Clemency in Capital Cases: The Stapled REIT on Ice: Congress' 1998 Freeze of the Grandfather Exception for Stapled REITS," 28 *Cap. U. L. Rev.* 717 (2000).

Part IV

Taxation and Regulation of Real Estate; Natural Resources and Agricultural Law

Taxation, Regulation, and the Power of Eminent Domain: Government Revenue and Control Measures

To finance the cost of government and the services it provides, the federal, state, and local governments impose a variety of taxes. The effect of these taxes on the ownership of real estate, whether direct or indirect, is substantial. The states, for example, levy a property tax on real estate to finance necessary public services such as schools, parks, police and fire protection, and other city and county services. Although the federal government does not tax the mere ownership of real estate, it taxes the income derived from it. The federal income tax is imposed not only on the rents and profits from the land, but also on the capital gains realized upon its sale. Most states and some cities have a similar income tax on individuals and businesses. In addition, the federal government imposes an estate and gift tax that applies to the transfer of realty and other property at the owner's death (and to gifts prior to death), and a number of states have estate and inheritance taxes of their own. Often, the total tax burden is so great that it affects the decisions of landowners and real estate businesses about the use and disposition of their realty. The first three sections of this chapter discuss the impact of taxes on the ownership of realty.

Nontax regulation, too, affects business decisions and practices relating to real estate use and investments. Chapters 17 and 18 discuss zoning and environmental protection laws, two of the most important areas of government regulation affecting real estate. This chapter focuses on three other areas: the regulation of real estate investments under the securities laws, controls on the sale of unimproved land under the Interstate Land Sales Full Disclosure Act, and the Fair Housing Act's prohibition of discrimination in the sale or leasing of real property. The chapter also explores the government's power to take private property for public purposes and the constitutional limitations on that power.

State Property Taxes

States levy a tax on real property (usually simply called property tax) as a way of generating revenue for local services and facilities. Generating approximately 75% of local tax revenues in the United States, the property tax is the most important source of revenue for cities, counties, school districts, and other local governmental entities. Although state law provides the legal framework for the property tax, in almost all states the tax is collected and administered at the local level. Many local political subdivisions, including counties, cities, park districts, and school districts, have the authority to tax real estate to fund their operations. The combined tax rate of all local governments taxing land in a given area determines the overall property tax burden on owners of property.

Assessed Value and the Mill Rate

Property taxes, like tariffs on imported goods and sales taxes, are **ad valorem** taxes, so-called because they are based on the value of the real estate. As the value of property increases, the amount of the tax increases, though the tax rate per thousand dollars of land value remains the same for all properties. To determine the tax on a particular tract of real estate, one needs to know the *tax rate* and the *assessed value* of the property.

The **tax rate** is usually expressed in terms of a *mill rate*. A **mill** is a unit of U.S. currency: one-tenth of a cent (one-thousandth of a dollar). To assess property taxes, the tax authorities have adopted one mill per dollar as the basis for establishing tax rates. But such small units are difficult to apply, so, for convenience in calculation, the tax authorities have multiplied the mill and the dollar by 1,000 to establish the basic **mill rate** of $1 per $1,000 in property value. A mill rate of *one* ($1 per $1,000 of property value) produces a tax of $1 per year on a parcel valued at $1,000 and $100 per year on a parcel valued at $100,000. A 40 mill rate ($40 per $1,000) produces a tax of $4,000 per year on a home with an assessed value of $100,000. Taxing entities usually have the authority to raise or lower the mill rate and thereby to increase or decrease the tax on property within their geographic jurisdictions. However, some states impose a maximum mill levy or restrict the extent to which local governments can increase the mill levy in one budget period. For example, Ohio law requires voter approval for a levy of property taxes that in total exceeds 1% of the true value of the property.

Property is taxed by applying the tax rate to the **assessed value** of the property. The process of determining assessed value begins with an **appraisal** of the land to determine its market value. Local or state tax officials, or private appraisers hired by the government, conduct the appraisals. In some states, this appraised (market) value is the assessed value to which the tax rate is applied. In most states, however, the assessed value is lower than the market value because the law requires tax authorities to compute the assessed value by multiplying the market value by a given percentage. For example, in Ohio the assessed value of land and buildings is 35% of market value. In many states, different types of property are subject to different multipliers. Thus, in Tennessee, the assessed value is 25% of appraised value for residential property and farm property, 40% for commercial and industrial property, and 55% for public utility property. By using a lower multiplier for residential property than for commercial property, Tennessee, like many states, imposes a lower tax on residential property than on commercial property of the same appraised value. In other states, all real estate, regardless of its use, is treated the same in the determination of assessed value. Delaware, for example, assesses commercial property the same as residential property to encourage commercial development in the state.

Often, agricultural property is assessed differently from other property. In general, the appraisal of property is based on the "highest and best" use for the property, that is, the most valuable use to which the property could reasonably be put. For example, the highest and best use of open land near a large city might be for residential subdivisions instead of the agricultural use actually being made of the land. Land that can be subdivided for suburban development usually is immensely more valuable for that purpose than for farming, and often is assessed accordingly. Yet, many states assess agricultural land on the basis of its present productive capacity, and *not* on its potential for subdivision and development. One reason for this special treatment is to protect farmers from the effects of skyrocketing values of agricultural lands near sprawling urban areas. An example is the Utah Farmland Assessment Act that assesses qualifying agricultural property on the basis of the income that can be derived from the land in a given area of the state.

Because property taxes are based on assessed value, the accurate appraisal of real estate is critically important from both the government's and the landowner's perspective. Challenges to real estate taxes most often involve the issue of the property's market value. **Market value** means the price that would be agreed to in an arm's-length transaction, or the price that a willing purchaser not required to buy the property and a willing seller not required to sell it would agree to under a contract to sell the property.

To determine the market value of property, professional appraisers use three appraisal methods that are accepted by the courts: (1) the market comparison approach, (2) the income approach, and (3) the cost approach. In the **market comparison** approach, the appraiser estimates market value on the basis of recent sales of comparable properties in arm's-length transactions. This method is most accurate when parcels, especially residential properties, are bought and sold on a regular basis. In the **income approach**, the appraiser attempts to measure the value of property on the basis of the income derived from the property, for example, by determining a present value for the income stream expected to be generated by the property. The courts generally prefer the income approach in the valuation of investment property, such as commercial office buildings, apartments, motels, shopping malls, and retail businesses. In the **cost approach**, the appraiser derives market value by calculating the cost to build a replacement structure, adjusted for depreciation, and adding to that figure the value of the land on which the structure sits. The courts take a skeptical view of any appraisal based solely on the cost approach, because it tends to overstate the value of property because of the difficulty of adjusting for economic and functional obsolescence. The cost approach is considered useful, however, in setting a ceiling on the value of a parcel, in estimating the value of special purpose properties (those built and designed for a unique purpose), and in valuing newly constructed buildings.

In the case that follows, the Vermont Supreme Court confronts some of the problems under the income approach in a typical landowner challenge to an assessment.

Case 16.1

Beach Properties v. Town of Ferrisburg

640 A.2d 50 (Vt. 1994)

Beach Properties, Inc., owns the Basin Harbor Club, a summer resort and convention center located within the Town of Ferrisburg on 584.3 acres of land along the easterly shore of Lake Champlain. The corporation is wholly owned by members of the Beach family, who have owned and operated the Basin Harbor Club since 1886. In 1990, Robert H. Beach, Jr., and Ann P. Beach Morris became its sole owners by acquiring all of the stock of the corporation then owned by other family members.

The Ferrisburg Board of Civil Authority assessed the property at $4,806,000. In appraising the property, the Town relied on a combination of the cost approach and market sales comparison approach. The cost approach adjusted for time, location, physical characteristics, and depreciation to determine the value of buildings and improvements. The market comparison approach developed a schedule of land values and Lake Champlain shore frontage values derived from actual sales data. The Town also contended that its assessment was confirmed by a consideration of potential and prospective uses of the property.

In response to the Town's assessment, Beach Properties had the property appraised. That appraisal supported a property value of $3,850,000, which reflected a value of the Basin Harbor Club of $4,600,000 minus $750,000 for furnishings, fixtures and equipment. The appraiser arrived at this value by using an income capitalization analysis, derived from the net income for a single year, 1990, and the sale price of the intrafamily stock transfer.

The State Board of Appraisers reversed the decision of the Ferrisburg Board of Civil Authority and declared that the property should be assessed at $3,850,000, rather than $4,806,000. The Town appealed to the Vermont Supreme Court.

JOHNSON, J.

The [State] Board [of Appraisers'] determination of fair market value relied on [the] taxpayer's income capitalization method. The capitalization, or income approach, "restates market value by converting the future benefits of property ownership into an expression of present worth." On a purely theoretical basis, income capitalization is probably the most accurate way to establish value, at least as to commercial properties, because it values property on the basis of what income it will yield to the purchaser—and income is the very reason for the purchaser to acquire the property. . . . But the methodology used to calculate the capitalization rate in this case was so flawed that it rendered the taxpayer's evidence on this point meaningless.

The income approach is based on the proposition that a rational investor would pay the fair market value for a piece of property, which is the price (P) that, when multiplied by the rate of return available from alternative investments of comparable risk (the capitalization rate or R), is equal to the property's expected net income (I). In other words, if the known factors are capitalization rate and net income, the price of the property may be calculated by dividing the net income by the capitalization rate: $P = I/R$.

In application, however, income capitalization has serious, inherent difficulties. As noted above, there are two figures to the price calculation. The first is the appropriate capitalization rate or the expected rate of return on investment. It is derived from an analysis of factors external to the investment for which fair market value must be determined. Thus, the validity of the capitalization rate depends on an adequate analysis of the market. Since "[a] rate that indicates the return required to attract investment capital is the connection between the future income and a value indication, . . . selection of [the] rate is of paramount importance in the capitalization process." Relatively small variations in the rate will significantly change the fair market value. The key is comparability, and economists and other experts will frequently differ, at times widely, as to what comparable investments will yield, even where there is agreement on what constitutes comparability.

An even greater difficulty may attend the calculation of the second component of the calculation, the expected net income. Unlike the capitalization rate, it is derived from the internal numbers of the investment under appraisal. In a property such as the Basin Harbor Club, income depends on a wide variety of factors, ranging from the competence of management, to the economic climate experienced by the establishment's customer base, to the weather. Because relatively small adjustments to net income will significantly alter the resulting fair market value, it is important that expenses leading to net income be subject to scrutiny by the trier of fact.

In this case, the taxpayer's evidence as to both the capitalization rate and the property's expected net income was insufficient to provide the basis for a valid income capitalization calculation. First, there was no external validity, by comparison with the rate of return of similar businesses, to the capitalization rate the taxpayer suggests. Second, the net income component of the equation was not supported by sufficient evidence. The taxpayer submitted the net income figure from a single year, 1990, of $457,432. Because of the number of variables that affect net income, it is generally expected that a "stabilized annual net income" reflecting more than one year's set of figures will be used as the basis for income capitalization. Moreover, the fair market value should be based on the property's potential for earning income as well. . . . Net income was increasing for this business. As the taxpayer's appraisal showed, net income increased in 1991 to $510,878, and the appraisal report predicted "a modest, but steady increase."

The use of a single year's income is even more perilous here because the income figure is based on taxpayer's internal, unaudited financial statements. This figure might have been acceptable if it had been sufficiently itemized to permit the Board to question the items that affected the bottom line. Itemization, however, was limited to broad categories within the headings of departmental expenses of $2,239,001 and undistributed operating expenses of $1,521,178. Significantly, there is no breakdown showing compensation to owners that would have allowed the Board to determine if the amount of salary or other distributions to family-member employees unduly affected net profits. As the Town points out, there is every incentive in a family-owned business to distribute profits in the form of compensation and reduce corporate net income. The Board had insufficient evidence before it to determine the reliability of the 1990 net income figure.

Central to the Board's acceptance of the taxpayer's income capitalization analysis is whether the 1990 transfer of stock from various family members to the present owners reliably reflected the property's fair market value. The capitalization rate used to derive the taxpayer's appraisal value is based solely on that sale. The Board recognized that intra-family transfers are not ordinarily a reliable reflection of fair market value, but found that the sale was at arm's length. Even if we were to accept the taxpayer's income capitalization methodology, the record does not support the conclusion that the sale was at arm's length. "An arm's length sale is characterized by these elements: it is voluntary, i.e., without compulsion or duress; it generally takes place in an open market; and the parties act in their own self-interest." While there is no doubt the sale was voluntary, it did not occur in an open market and the price was negotiated by the parties without an appraisal.

We hold that the Board's conclusions are insupportable on the evidence presented. Reversed and remanded.

QUESTIONS ABOUT CASE 16.1

1. Why would it be difficult to make an accurate appraisal of the property solely on the basis of either a cost approach or a market comparison approach?

2. The court stated that the taxpayer had "every incentive in a family-owned business to distribute profits in the form of compensation and reduce corporate net income." What incentive is the court referring to?

The Homestead and Other Exemptions

Much of the land within the geographic jurisdiction of local governments is exempt from taxation. Publicly owned property ordinarily is exempt. Publicly owned property includes parks, schools, libraries, municipal utilities and facilities, government offices, and other property owned by local entities. It also includes property owned by the state and federal governments. Thus, national and state parks, federal courthouses, post office buildings, military bases, and other government reservations are exempt from the real estate tax. Usually exempt as well is property owned by charitable and nonprofit organizations, such as private art museums, churches, food banks, shelters for the poor, and land held by conservation groups.

Most states have some form of **homestead exemption** for property used as a personal residence. The specific requirements for the homestead vary from state to state. Georgia, for example, provides a $2,000 homestead deduction for the owner of a principal residence, the deduction being subtracted from assessed value before the mill rate is applied, thereby reducing the tax burden to the owner. Similarly, Maine exempts up to $7,000 for any homeowner who has owned a principal residence for 12 months. New York has a local-option law that permits but does not require local governments to have a lower tax rate for homestead property than for nonhomestead property. Some states limit the homestead exemption to the elderly, disabled, or other needy individuals. States also have their own special homestead provisions. Along with a general homestead exemption, Illinois has an additional one for disabled veterans and senior citizens.

To encourage economic development, states have created incentives in the form of real estate property exemptions for businesses. State laws frequently allow local governments to reduce

Box 16–1 Tax Increment Financing

One of the most creative methods of local economic development through taxation is *tax increment financing*. First developed in California as a means of community redevelopment, it is authorized in almost all states today. Tax increment financing allows a community to finance a development project by using the increase in taxes generated by the new project to pay the city's development costs. For example, a city may acquire land and demolish existing buildings so that a new manufacturing facility can be built, paying the development costs with taxes on the increased value of the property once the plant is constructed and in operation.

The first step in this process is the creation of a tax increment district by the authorized governing body, usually a tax increment financing commission. State laws differ on what areas can be designated for tax increment financing, but they usually require that an area be blighted and in need of redevelopment. Factors such as the age, dilapidation, or deterioration of buildings and dwellings; the number of vacant lots and buildings; and unsafe, unsanitary, or unhealthy conditions in the area are considered in this determination. State law also dictates the process to be followed by the commission, which usually requires consultation with other taxing authorities (e.g., school districts) and an opportunity for public input.

Once the district is established, the assessed value of all properties in the area is determined. The city and other taxing authorities continue to collect taxes on this original assessed value, called the "tax increment base." Taxes on any increase in value after redevelopment of the area—the so-called tax increment—are used to pay the costs the city incurs in redeveloping the area. As part of its redevelopment efforts, and as an incentive for new commercial or residential developments, the city may purchase property, pay costs of rehabilitating old or constructing new buildings, incur relocation expenses if residents are displaced, and otherwise make infrastructure improvements (e.g., to streets, lighting). These redevelopment actions of the city and the new private investment in the area will increase the value of property in the district. The tax on this increase—the so-called captured assessed value—is used to pay the redevelopment costs, including any bonds issued by the commission to pay for the improvements.

Proponents of tax increment financing tout the ability of cities to fund economic development efforts without the loss of tax revenues accompanying tax exemptions or abatements. They also point to economic and community redevelopment benefits, including attracting new investment, improving neighborhoods and the tax base of the community, expanding employment, and improving the city infrastructure. Critics of tax increment financing counter that a great deal of economic development would occur without the subsidy, that the city loses taxes on increased property values not attributable to the redevelopment projects, and that tax increment schemes divert revenue from essential public services, particularly schools. As a result of this last concern, some states allow school districts to opt out of tax increment plans.

or wholly abate real estate taxes for businesses building new plants or facilities or making substantial improvements to existing facilities. New Mexico's Development Incentive Act allows smaller communities in the state to grant a five-year exemption for up to 50% of the taxable value for new business facilities. Indiana has a property tax abatement scheme that allows local governments to exempt real property taxes for new business developments under which real estate taxes are phased in over a period of ten years. North Dakota provides a local-option exemption for new businesses for up to five years, an additional five-year period for agricultural processors, and a three-year exemption for the value of improvements to commercial property.

Many states also have created **enterprise zones**, providing tax relief for businesses establishing manufacturing plants or other operations within distressed areas of the state. To qualify as an enterprise zone, the area must be plagued by chronic unemployment or poverty. States use various income and employment criteria for designating enterprise zones. Missouri, for example, requires that the incomes of at least 65% of the residents fall below 80% of the median income in the state. The improvements covered by the exemption and the incentives for the enterprise zones also differ from state to state. Oregon law requires a minimum investment of $25,000 in a new building (or an addition to an existing one) used in an income-producing activity, along with certain hiring requirements, for a business to qualify for the exemption. If these rigorous requirements are met, the business receives a three-year 100% tax exemption that may be extended to five years if certain expanded employment criteria are met. Five- to ten-year exemption periods are most common under state enterprise zone laws.

Tax Liens and Tax Sales

If a landowner fails to pay the real estate property tax, the state acquires a *tax lien* on the property. This lien is superior to the rights of mortgagees and other third parties who may have an interest in the property (e.g., lessees and purchasers under a contract for deed). In a tax sale to foreclose on the lien, the owner may lose title to the property. State procedures regarding tax sales differ, but in all states, the government (usually, county authorities) can sell the property to recover the unpaid taxes. In some states, the tax authority immediately sells the property when a delinquency occurs and issues a "certificate of sale" to the purchaser. The property owner then has a redemption period within which to redeem the property and have title restored. If the owner fails to redeem, the purchaser receives a **tax deed** at the end of the redemption period. In other states, a delinquent owner receives notice that the property has been forfeited to the state. A redemption period, typically two to five years, follows, within which the owner can pay the delinquent taxes and penalties and recover the property. If the owner fails to redeem within that time, the tax authority sells the property and delivers a tax deed to the purchaser. Under this process, at the time of the sale, the purchaser acquires the property free and clear of the former owner's interests. No further right of redemption exists. As in a mortgage foreclosure, mortgage holders and others whose interests are subordinate to the state's tax lien also have a right of redemption.

Special Assessments

The general property tax on real estate is used to fund the general operations of a city, county, or taxing entity, and to pay for improvements that benefit the public at large. It is appropriate to use the general property tax proceeds to pay for projects benefitting the general public, such as a new civic arena, a water plant, or a library. In contrast, **special assessments** are taxes imposed to fund improvements benefitting a limited number of property owners within a given neighborhood or district, improvements such as sidewalks and street paving, the repair and construction of sewer lines and storm drains, and the maintenance of irrigation systems. The idea is that the landowners receiving the specific benefits of the improvements should bear the costs.

Unlike the general property tax, special assessments are computed on the basis of the size of the lot, not its value, so the amount of the assessment usually is calculated on a frontage-foot basis. The owner a 100-foot wide lot pays more for sidewalks than the owner of a 50-foot lot pays, because the owner of the larger lot receives more benefit from the improvement than does the owner of the smaller lot. Thus, property owners pay their fair share of the project's costs.

Federal and State Income Taxes Relating to Real Estate

Income from the use and sale of real estate is subject to federal and state income taxes. Included in "income" are rents and profits, and capital gains realized from sales of realty. The provisions of the Internal Revenue Code (IRC) and state laws taxing real estate income are complex, and the income tax burden relating to realty can be substantial. To minimize the tax burden, those engaged in real estate businesses need to be aware of the income tax implications of their business decisions. Homeowners, too, should be familiar with the special IRC rules relating to income from personal real estate holdings and transactions.

Taxation of Income from the Rental of Real Estate

A landlord pays the income tax on the *net income* from the rental activity—*gross income* less expenses. For rental activities, "gross income" includes amounts received from the tenant as rent (including payment of rent in advance) as well as any property taxes or mortgage installments paid by the tenant. Gross income also includes the value of services and property given in lieu of rent. So, for example, a landlord has received income if a tenant provides necessary maintenance or repairs as part of the rent under the lease. The market value of such services is included in the landlord's gross income.

To arrive at net income, landlords may deduct from the gross income all ordinary and necessary expenses incurred in carrying on the rental activity, including the costs associated with the management and maintenance of the property. Deductible expenses include costs of general repairs, insurance, mortgage interest, real estate taxes, and depreciation. Some expenses, however, cannot be deducted in the year incurred, but instead must be capitalized. For example, improvements that extend the useful life of the property or add substantial value to it—a new roof, an addition to a building—become part of the owner's investment in the property and must be capitalized over a period of years, with only a portion of the cost being deducted each year. Similarly, special assessments for streets or sewers must be capitalized because they represent expenses incurred in the improvement of the property.

To capitalize the cost of an improvement, the landlord deducts a portion of its value as depreciation for each year of its "useful life," a period established by rules of the Internal Revenue Service (IRS). Under present rules, depreciation of residential realty must be spread over at least a 27.5-year period, while for nonresidential property the minimum period is 39 years.

The taxpayer must use straight-line depreciation, that is, the annual deductions over the life of the property must be equal. Accelerated depreciation (deducting larger amounts in the earlier years) is no longer permitted. The landlord can depreciate the cost of the buildings and other improvements on the property, but not the value of the land. Martha purchases a rental house on January 1, 1998, for $130,000. The house and other improvements are worth $100,000 and the land is worth $30,000. Because the property is residential, Martha must depreciate it over 27.5 years, a period that produces a depreciation rate of 3.636% per year (100% divided by 27.5 years) and a depreciation deduction of $3,636 ($100,000 × 3.636%).

Note that the annual depreciation deduction *reduces* the owner's investment in the property. If Martha keeps the property long enough to depreciate its improvements fully, they will have a "book" value of zero. If she then sells the property for $200,000 without having made any new improvements, she will have a taxable gain of $170,000 ($200,000 minus her original cost of $130,000 but with that cost being reduced by the total depreciation of $100,000 she deducted over the years). The type of gain and how it is calculated is discussed later in connection with "capital gains," and "adjusted basis."

Box 16–2 You Be the Judge

Concerned with public safety in the event of an earthquake, the city of San Francisco passed an ordinance that required the Fairmont Hotel to remove or replace heavy concrete parapets and cornices on the exterior of the hotel. After an expert's inspection, the hotel decided to replace them, and it spent $3 million for replicas made of lightweight fiberglass material. When the hotel deducted the cost of the parapets and cornices as a repair expense, the IRS disallowed the expense, arguing that the expenditure was a capital improvement that increased the value of the hotel and prolonged its useful life. The Fairmont Hotel owners argued that it was forced by law to incur the expenditure and that the expense was necessary to maintain the character and appearance of the hotel and to preserve its image as a "grand hotel of the world." How should this expenditure be characterized, as a repair or a capital improvement?

Vacation Homes

Many individuals have a second home that they rent out during part of the year. The IRS rules regarding these so-called **vacation homes** permit the deduction of only the proportion of expenses attributable to the rentals. The rules are intended to prevent the owner from deducting as business expenses any costs that are attributable to the owner's personal use of the second home, such as repair costs and utility expenses. The extent to which vacation home *rental* expenses are deductible depends upon the number of days the property is rented during the year. If the owner rents the property for fewer than 15 days, the home is treated totally as a personal residence and no expense deductions are allowed (but neither is the rent considered taxable income). If the owner rents the property for 15 days or more, the owner is allowed a deduction for the expenses attributable to the rental period.

Passive Loss Rules

Under the federal tax code, losses from real estate rental activities are classified as **passive losses** if the taxpayer is merely an investor in the realty and not active in its management. Passive real estate losses can be used to offset passive gains (e.g., interest on savings, gains from stock investments, gains from other passive real estate investments), but *cannot* be used to offset income actively earned by the taxpayer (e.g., salary income). Thus, Tom, a taxpayer who has a $100,000 loss on rental property for the year, cannot offset the loss against his salary income of $100,000 to reduce his taxable income to zero. If Tom has no passive gains such as capital gains on stock, he can carry the passive loss forward to future taxable years in which he has passive income.

The passive loss limitation has two exceptions. First, property owners who are *actively involved in the management* of the rental property can offset losses up to $12,500 ($25,000 for married couples) against nonpassive income. This offset is gradually phased out for taxpayers whose incomes are between $100,000 and $150,000. The second exception is for real estate professionals—persons who are "materially participating" in a real estate trade or business. To meet the material participation requirement, the professional must be regularly, extensively, and substantially involved in the business, and must spend more than 50% of his or her time (a minimum of 750 hours per year) in the business. In that event, losses from the real estate business can be used to offset income from any source.

Gains and Losses on the Sale of Real Estate

Taxable Gains and Losses

The sale of realty may result in a taxable gain or a loss to the owner. An owner has a taxable gain on the sale of realty to the extent that the amount realized on the sale (the net selling price) exceeds the adjusted basis of the property. The **amount realized** is the cash received for the property (plus the value of any other property received) less the costs of sale, including brokerage fees and other selling expenses. If the buyer assumes a mortgage, the amount of the mortgage debt assumed is treated as part of the amount realized by the seller, because by assuming the mortgage and relieving the seller of the debt, the buyer has conferred that amount of value on the seller. The **adjusted basis** (which is subtracted from the amount realized to establish the amount of gain or loss) is generally what the owner paid for the property plus any capital improvements, less any accumulated depreciation. Capital improvements include, for example, outbuildings, driveways, or a replacement roof, but do *not* include maintenance items such as painting, drapes, or carpets. The owner's cost of purchase includes incidental expenses related to the purchase, such as title insurance and inspection fees. If the property was inherited, the owner's original basis is the fair market value of the property at the decedent's death. Special rules apply if the owner acquired the property as a gift during the donor's lifetime, but ordinarily the donor's basis becomes the donee's basis under the carryover basis rule.

Taxation of Gains and Losses

Understanding how gains on the sale of realty are taxed requires an understanding of some key terminology involved, such as *capital asset*, *Section 1231 property*, *capital gain*, *ordinary income*, *long-term capital gain*, and *short-term capital gain*. **Ordinary income** is income from sources such as wages and salaries, stock dividends, interest, oil and gas royalties, and the net profits from a business. It is taxed at the "ordinary" rates, which vary according to the amount of the taxpayer's income. The lowest ordinary rate is 10%; the highest is 38.6%.[1] A **capital gain**, in contrast, is one realized from the sale of a capital asset. Individuals are taxed at a lower rate on *long-term* capital gains than on ordinary income, while short-term capital gains are taxed as ordinary income. For tax purposes, a **capital asset** is any property held by a taxpayer *except* assets specifically excluded by IRC § 1231. Not included as a capital asset are such items as real estate used in a trade or business, and realty held primarily for sale to customers in the ordinary course of the taxpayer's business. One's house, car, stocks and bonds, boat, and garden tractor are capital assets. Real estate held as an *investment* is also a capital asset.

The tax rate on capital gains depends upon a number of factors, key ones being the type of capital gain and the type of taxpayer receiving it. **Long-term capital gains** realized by individuals—gains on real estate and other capital assets held for more than one year—receive preferential treatment under the tax code by being taxed at a lower rate than the rate applied to ordinary income. Only individuals, and not other taxpayers such as corporations, receive this preferential treatment. For most individuals, the maximum tax rate on long-term capital gains is 20%, substantially less than the typical 28% or 31% tax rate on ordinary income for most tax-payers, and well below the highest income tax rate of 38.6% for those in the highest income brackets. Individuals in the 10% and 15% tax brackets pay a capital gains rate of 10%. In contrast, **short-term capital gains** (gains on capital assets held for one year or less) are treated as ordi-nary income and are subject to the individual taxpayer's applicable tax rate. (For assets acquired after December 31, 2000, and held for more than five years, the 20% long-term capital gains rate is reduced to 18%, while the 10% long-term rate is reduced to 8% for assets held for more than five years and *sold* after December 31, 2000.)

Capital *losses* offset capital gains, and individuals may use up to $3,000 in capital losses as an offset against ordinary income. Beyond this, individuals may not deduct capital losses in the year incurred, but they may carry unused capital losses forward to *any* future tax period and use them at that time to offset capital gains plus up to $3,000 of other income. In 2001, after offsetting her capital losses against her capital gains and $3,000 of ordinary income, Pamela still has $15,000 in capital losses. She may carry this amount forward indefinitely to future tax years to offset capital gains and up to $3,000 per year of ordinary income until the $15,000 is exhausted. Corporations, however, are allowed to carry capital losses forward for only five years and back three years. If a corporation's capital losses are not used to offset capital gains in those years, they are lost.

Section 1231 Property

Gains on real estate used in a trade or business and held for more than one year, including rental property held for more than one year, are given special treatment under Section 1231 of the IRC. Such realty is known as "Section 1231 property." Although this type of real estate is not considered a capital asset, gains on the sale of Section 1231 property (in excess of any losses on section 1231 property) are treated as long-term capital gains. However, losses on the sale of Section 1231 property (in excess of any gains on Section 1231 property) are treated as ordinary losses (not capital losses) and thus can be used to offset ordinary income. The IRC has several limitations on the special treatment of gains and losses under Section 1231. For example, a tax-payer who reports net Section 1231 losses for the previous five years is subject to a loss recapture

BOX 16–3 TEST YOUR KNOWLEDGE

Alicia Ramsey purchased a house as rental property for $100,000, paying $10,000 down and taking out a $90,000 mortgage. She had incidental costs of $500 for title examination and appraisal fees. Five years later, she sold the property for $110,000 cash. She paid her real estate agent a 7% commission on the sale and had incidental selling expenses of $250. During the five years that she owned and rented the property to tenants, she had the fol-lowing repair and improvement expenses: $4,000 to build a deck in the back yard, $1,000 to repaint the outside of the house, $2,500 for a new poured driveway, and $3,000 for new carpeting and wallpaper. Over the years, she paid $10,000 in real estate taxes and took $19,000 depreciation on the property. (a) What is Alicia's adjusted basis in the property? (b) How much gain will she recognize on the sale of the house? (c) Will the gain be treated as a short- or long-term gain?

rule. This rule requires the taxpayer to treat any net Section 1231 *gain* as ordinary income (not as a long-term capital gain) to the extent of the net losses during the previous five years (called the "lookback" period).

If real estate used in a trade or business is held for less than one year, it is not Section 1231 property. Any gain on its sale is ordinary income, and any loss is an ordinary loss. Other real estate holdings that are neither capital assets nor Section 1231 property receive the same treatment upon sale. Donald, a developer, regularly purchases tracts of land, subdivides and improves them, and then sells the parcels for building lots. Because Donald holds the lots for sale in the ordinary course of business, they are analogous to inventory held by a retail merchant, the gains from which are ordinary income to the merchant. Accordingly, the lots are excluded from the Section 1231 definition of capital asset, and the gains on them are ordinary income.

Installment Sales and Like-Kind Exchanges

Upon the sale of property, the owner can delay the payment of income taxes if the transaction is properly structured as an *installment sale* or a *like-kind exchange*. In both cases, if gains are realized in the sale, the IRC allows the owner to defer the payment of taxes on the gains.

In an **installment sale** of land, such as the sale of land under a contract for deed, the buyer pays the purchase price over time. Because the seller is not receiving the purchase price in full at the time of the sale, the IRC allows the seller to pay taxes on the portion of the taxable gain received each year as the purchaser makes the payments. The taxable portion of each year's payment is a percentage of the payment, called the "gross profit percentage," which is calculated by dividing the total gain by the total purchase price. Assume a contract for deed where the total purchase price is $100,000, and the seller's adjusted basis is $80,000. The gain is $20,000, and the gross profit percentage is 20% (gain divided by purchase price). The seller is required to treat 20% of each yearly principal payment under the contract as a gain on the sale. Thus, if the contract runs ten years, with equal principal payments of $10,000 per year, the seller must treat $2,000 per year as a taxable gain. The obvious benefit to the seller is that the gain is spread out over the period of the installment sale instead of being realized in one year and possibly putting the seller into a higher tax bracket. Note that any *interest* payable under the contract for deed is ordinary income to the seller in the year in which it is paid.

Under the **like-kind exchange** provisions of the tax law, an owner who exchanges property (called *relinquished property*) for property of a like kind (called *replacement property*) is allowed to defer any gain on the sale until the replacement property is sold. To qualify for the tax deferral, the relinquished property must be held for use in business or trade, and the replacement property must also be so held. Property held for personal use (e.g., a personal residence) does not qualify for like-kind exchange treatment. Also, an exchange of property must be involved. A sale for cash where the seller immediately reinvests the proceeds in like-kind property is not considered an exchange. In addition, the owner must intend to continue to hold the property as an investment. Therefore, if immediately after the sale the seller sells the replacement property for cash, the seller demonstrates no intent to continue to hold the property, and thus it is not an exchange. Finally, the property must be of "like" kind. Fortunately for those wishing to make exchanges, any real estate, developed or undeveloped, is considered to be of like kind with any other real estate. Thus, a strip mall can be exchanged for farmland or an office building in a like-kind exchange. To facilitate such exchanges, the parties usually employ a third party called a "qualified intermediary" to handle the transaction. If the like-kind exchange requirements are met, the seller does not realize any gain until he or she sells the *replacement* property. However, sometimes the seller will receive nonqualifying consideration (e.g., cash or personal property), called "boot," along with like-kind property. The seller will have to pay taxes on the boot received.

Special Real Estate Tax Credits

To encourage socially useful development activities, the IRC makes several real estate tax credits available to real estate investors and developers. A tax credit is a valuable incentive because it directly reduces the tax owed, dollar for dollar. A $100 credit reduces the tax by the full $100. In contrast, an ordinary deduction (e.g., for business expenses) provides less in terms of a tax break, because it simply reduces the taxpayer's taxable income. A $100 deduction reduces taxable income by $100, but for a taxpayer in the 28% bracket the deduction produces a tax reduction of only $28. Three important real estate tax credits are the low-income tax credit, the disabled access credit, and the rehabilitation credit.

Congress established the **low-income tax credit** to encourage developers to build and rehabilitate housing affordable to persons with low incomes. The low-income credit system is administered jointly by the IRS and state housing agencies. The states receive a yearly allocation of low-income tax credits, which they transfer to the developers of low-income housing. The developers usually sell the credits to investors, who invest in limited partnerships or similar business entities that handle the management of the housing projects. The investors provide the financing for the housing and get the benefit of the tax credit for up to ten years. They also share in any profits from any eventual sale of the property.

To qualify for the credit, the project must meet the stringent requirements of the law for a qualified low-income housing project. A **qualified low-income housing project** is a residential rental project having two key features: (1) the amount of rent charged to some occupants is restricted, or lower than market rental rates, and (2) the project meets the minimum low-income set aside requirement under either the so-called 20/50 or the 40/60 rule. The 20/50 rule requires that 20% of the units be rent-restricted and occupied by tenants whose income falls below 50% of the median regional income. The 40/60 rule requires that 40% of the units be rent-restricted and occupied by tenants whose income falls below 60% of the regional median income. The set-aside requirements must continue for a compliance period of 15 years.

Small businesses that incur expenses in accommodating their properties to the needs of disabled and handicapped individuals are eligible to take a **disabled access credit**. Eligible access expenditures include monies paid to remove physical, architectural, communication, and other barriers that prevent a business from being accessible to, or usable by, individuals with disabilities. The credit is 50% of the eligible expenditures above $250 with a maximum credit of $5,000 per year. To qualify as a small business, the business must have gross receipts of $1 million or less and have no more than 30 full-time employees. Buildings placed in service after November 5, 1990, are not eligible for the credit.

To encourage the rehabilitation of historically significant buildings in older communities, Congress created the **rehabilitation tax credit**. The credit applies to rehabilitation expenditures for certified historic structures, and for qualified rehabilitated buildings (buildings placed in service before 1936). **Certified historic buildings** are those listed in the national register and those buildings located in registered historic districts certified by the Secretary of the Interior as being of historic significance. If the building is "substantially rehabilitated" (i.e., involving minimum expenditures of $5,000), the owner is entitled to a tax credit of 20% of the expenditures for historic structures and 10% of the expenditures for qualified rehabilitated buildings. The credit is subject to a number of limitations and qualifications.

Tax Aspects of Home Ownership

The IRC provides homeowners with special tax benefits, such as (1) deductibility of mortgage interest and real estate taxes on the property, and (2) a broad exclusion of gain on the sale of a personal residence. The deductions, however, are available only to taxpayers who itemize their personal deductions. Nearly 70% of all taxpayers take the standard deduction instead of itemized deductions, meaning for that 70% the interest and tax deductions are of no value.

Interest paid on debts secured by a mortgage or a deed of trust on a qualified residence is deductible by the homeowner. **Qualified residence** includes the taxpayer's principal residence and a second (vacation) home, provided the owner uses the vacation home for more than 14 days during the year or more than 10% of the days that the home is rented. For the interest to be deductible, the debt must be a qualified acquisition debt or a qualified home equity debt. A **qualified acquisition debt** is any debt incurred in acquiring, constructing, or substantially improving a qualified residence. Thus, the debt may be financed by either a purchase-money mortgage (for acquisition or construction) or a second mortgage (for making a capital improvement of the property). A purchase-money mortgage debt that is refinanced is considered an acquisition debt up to the amount of the purchase-money mortgage prior to the refinancing. The dollar limitation for a qualified acquisition debt (and deductibility of the interest) is $1 million. A **qualified home equity debt** is any other debt secured by a qualified residence. Home equity debt is that which is incurred for personal purposes such as a vacation, purchasing a new car, or paying educational expenses. For the interest on home equity debt to be deductible, the debt cannot exceed $100,000 or the homeowner's equity in the property (fair market value less the current amount of acquisition debt), whichever is less.

Homeowners can also deduct real estate taxes imposed by any local, state, or foreign government for the general public welfare. Special assessments and other municipal charges (for water, sewer, or trash) are not deductible (although interest on special assessments is deductible). When real estate is sold during the year, seller and buyer may deduct the taxes in proportion to the number of days that each had possession of the property. The settlement statement at closing should reflect the proration of taxes to the date of possession.

Under the Taxpayer Relief Act of 1997, Congress liberalized the rules relating to gains on the sale of a personal residence. Previously, a taxpayer paid no taxes on the sale of a home if the proceeds were used to purchase a new home costing the same as or more than the old one. Older taxpayers were also given a one-time exclusion of $125,000 on the sale of a personal residence. For sales of a principal residence after May 1997, if the seller has lived in the home during two of the last five years, the seller can exclude gains up to $250,000 ($500,000 for married couples). A seller who does not meet the two-year requirement is allowed a reduced exclusion for the time that the taxpayer lived in the home, though if the sale resulted from health problems, an employment move, or unforeseen circumstances, the seller is entitled to the full exclusion. The exclusion is available to the homeowner every two years. Any gain above the exclusion amount is fully taxable, but any loss suffered on the sale of a principal residence is not deductible.

Estate and Inheritance Taxes

The federal government has a **gift and estate tax**, called a *unified tax*, on gifts of property (including real estate) made during a decedent's lifetime and on property transferred at his or her death (testamentary gifts).[2] The tax, called "the estate tax," is "unified" because it is a single tax on the totality of the decedent's lifetime and testamentary gifts. In June 2001, Congress passed the Economic Growth and Tax Relief Reconciliation Act, which includes a phase-out of the estate tax over nine years with a repeal of the tax in 2010. During the phase-out period, the highest estate tax rate decreases from 55% to 45%, and the amount of an estate that is exempt from the tax increases from $675,000 to $3.5 million. Accordingly, fewer and fewer estates will pay any tax, and the amount of the tax for those that pay will decrease during the phase-out period. Although the estate tax will be repealed in 2010, the repeal is not permanent. The tax relief law "sunsets" at the end of 2010, and the estate tax will be reinstated in 2011 (in the form that existed before June 2001) unless Congress acts before 2011 to make the repeal permanent. Thus, the future of the estate tax is uncertain.

The present federal estate tax is imposed on the value of the decedent's estate, which includes the value of the property owned by the decedent at death plus the value of any nonexempt gifts made during the decedent's lifetime. As noted in Chapter 6, a number of states and Puerto Rico impose either an **inheritance tax** or their own estate tax, which is in addition to the federal gift and estate tax. In 34 so-called "pick-up" states, the state estate tax is tied into the federal estate tax, with the state receiving a portion of the federal estate tax if the estate is large enough to be subject to the federal tax. The 2001 tax relief law will tend to decrease the amount of estate taxes paid in these pick-up states because the state estate taxes are linked to the lower federal estate tax rates. The inheritance tax in effect in 16 states is levied on the decedent's heirs, devisees, and legatees, and is based on the amount of the inheritance and the applicable tax rate.[3] The inheritance tax rate varies according to the relationship between the heir and the decedent. Closer relatives have larger inheritance tax exemptions and a lower tax rate. To minimize the burden of state and federal taxes on the estate and to control the disposition of personal and business assets after death, owners of substantial assets would be well-advised to seek the services of a professional estate planner. The discussion that follows focuses on the federal gift and estate tax, which is usually the most burdensome for property owners.

The Internal Revenue Code's table of estate tax rates shows a rate range from 18% to 55%. However, since the inception of the unified tax several years ago, application of the unified credit results in no tax on estates worth less than those in the 37% bracket. Therefore the effective federal estate tax rates range from 37% to 55% of the taxable estate. Under the 2001 tax relief law, the highest tax rate on estates will be reduced to 50% in 2002, 49% in 2003, 48% in 2004, 47% in 2005, 46% in 2006, and 45% in 2007. In addition to the unified credit, Congress has created a number of exemptions and exclusions that further reduce the size of the taxable estate, thus eliminating the tax for most estates and reducing the amount of the tax for others. Especially beneficial to prospective taxpayers are the *unified credit*, the unlimited *marital deduction*, the *annual gift tax exclusion*, and special provisions for family-owned businesses.

Under the IRC's **unified credit** provision, no tax is imposed on an estate and taxable lifetime gifts valued at $675,000 or less in 2001. Under the 2001 tax relief law, the amount of the credit increases over time so that no tax will be payable on estates worth $1 million in 2002 and 2003, $1.5 million in 2004 and 2005, $2 million in 2006, 2007, and 2008, and $3.5 million in 2009.[4] As a result of the unified credit, few estates (2% in 1997) are subject to the federal estate and gift tax.

Married couples also can take advantage of the unlimited **marital deduction**. Under the IRC's marital deduction provision, any lifetime or testamentary transfer to a spouse is excluded from the estate. Thus, if the decedent transfers sufficient property to his or her spouse, the decedent's estate will totally avoid any estate tax liability. At the surviving spouse's death, however, whatever remains of the property that the decedent transferred will be included in the spouse's gross estate. Thus the marital deduction only postpones payment of the estate tax until the death of the spouse, whose estate may then be subject to a hefty estate tax.

Individuals with large estates can minimize their estate tax liability (and that of their spouses) by using a **credit shelter (bypass) trust** to take advantage of both the unified credit and the marital deduction. It works this way: William sets up the trust (typically for the benefit of William's spouse and children) and funds it by provisions in his will. His will divides his estate into two parts, leaving to the *trust* the maximum amount that is excludable under the unified credit, and leaving the remaining amount of the estate to his surviving spouse Esther. Although the trust property will go to the children when Esther dies, IRC rules permit William to give Esther the trust income for her lifetime and a *limited* right during her life to withdraw trust principal. If the trust is properly established, and if Esther's right to withdraw principal is properly limited, the trust property (being covered by the unified credit) is exempt from the estate tax. The trust property that is not withdrawn goes to the children at Esther's death and never becomes part of her estate, thus "bypassing" it and reducing its size. Because of the marital deduction, the property that William transferred to Esther *outside* the trust passes to her free of the tax on William's estate. At her death, estate taxes apply to her estate if it is large enough, but they will have been reduced considerably because William used the credit shelter trust to limit the size of Esther's estate.

The law does not allow an individual to simply give property away during life and thereby avoid the estate tax; lifetime gifts are included in the estate and are subject to the unified estate and gift tax. However, lifetime and testamentary gifts to a qualified charity are deductible from the estate. (And, incidentally, for *income* tax purposes a taxpayer who itemizes deductions can deduct from gross income any lifetime gift to a charity.) To allow individuals to reduce the estate tax further, the law also provides an **annual gift tax exclusion** of $10,000 per donee (the recipient of a gift) per year.[5] So, for example, a husband and wife could each make a $10,000 gift each year to each one of their children and grandchildren, thus substantially reducing the size of their taxable estates. Under the 2001 tax relief law, the gift tax will *not* be repealed, and the exemption of total lifetime gifts will be capped at $1 million (after any deductions and exclusions). However, the gift tax rate will decline over the phase-out period to 35% in 2010.

Because of the income tax on capital gains, however, lifetime gifts may not be the optimal method of estate planning where the donor's property (e.g., realty, stocks, mutual funds) has appreciated greatly over time. William buys a one-acre lot in 1980 for $1,000 and gives it to his daughter Sherrie in 2000 when it is worth $20,000. The gift reduces William's estate by $10,000, the amount of his annual gift tax exclusion for Sherrie that year. But if Sherrie sells the lot, her basis for calculating her capital gain is the *donor's* basis, $1,000. Sherrie sells the lot two years later when it is worth $22,000. Sherrie will be taxed on a capital gain of $21,000. Suppose instead that William died in 2000 and by will left the lot to Sherrie. By law, Sherrie receives a "stepped up" basis for the lot, which is the property's value at the date of donor William's death, $20,000. If Sherrie sells the lot two years later for $22,000, her capital gain is only $2,000. It is therefore usually advantageous for a donor *not* to make a lifetime gift of greatly appreciated property, but instead to keep it in the donor's estate so that the heirs may take advantage of the "stepped up" basis to reduce their capital gains. However, under the 2001 tax relief law, the "stepped up" basis rules will be partially eliminated with the repeal of the estate tax in 2010.

Despite the sizable exclusions and exemptions in the estate tax law, the impact of the estate tax on small business owners and farmers who want to transfer their businesses to their children can be severe, particularly if the business holds real estate or other assets with high valuations. In response to the concerns of farmers and business owners, Congress created a special **deduction for family-owned businesses**. If a business qualifies, the amount of the deduction (including the amount exempt from tax under the unified credit) is $1.3 million. To qualify as a **family business**, it must, among other requirements, usually be owned at least 50% by one family; the decedent must have owned and materially participated in the business for five out of the eight years preceding death; the business must make up at least 50% of the estate's value; the business must pass to qualified heirs (usually family members and long-term employees); and the qualified heirs must materially participate in the business five out of any eight years during the 10-year period following the decedent's death. It should be noted, however, that the family-owned business deduction will be repealed in 2004 as part of the phase-out and repeal of the estate tax.

Another special provision applicable to closely held farms and businesses is the special use valuation. Ordinarily, property of an estate must be valued for estate tax purposes on the basis of its "highest and best use." Farmland located near an urban area probably has a far greater value as development property for the building of homes and supporting businesses than as farmland. But if such land is valued highly as development property (the highest and best use) instead of being valued lower to reflect the agricultural use to which the land is actually being put, the resulting high estate tax exerts great pressure on heirs to take the land out of agricultural production. Under **special use valuation**, the property can be valued on the basis of its current use as farmland; however, the value of the estate cannot be reduced more than $750,000 because of the special valuation provision.

Major Federal Regulations of Real Estate

Securities Regulation

Real estate investment trusts (REITs) and other investments in real estate are regulated under federal and state securities laws. A REIT is a trust whose assets are invested in realty such as hotels, shopping malls, industrial parks, and office buildings. Its beneficiaries are investors, perhaps hundreds or thousands of them, who have purchased shares of the trust expecting to receive a portion of any profits generated by the trust.

Securities laws are designed to protect the investing public from fraud in the sale of securities and other investments (including REITs), to facilitate the efficiency and integrity of our capital markets, and to encourage investment in our business corporations and in the economy. Historically, the states were the first to regulate securities and investments under the so-called **blue sky laws**, which were intended to prevent fraudulent investment schemes (sales of nothing more than a patch of "blue sky"). Today, all states have securities laws that regulate the sale of securities and the conduct of securities professionals, including brokers and dealers. As a result, the many companies selling securities nationally must comply with a diverse set of state laws as well as with the federal securities laws, and the compliance burden can be immense.

National securities regulation dates back to the 1930s when Congress, in response to the stock market crash and the depression, passed two major securities laws, the Securities Act of 1933 and the Securities Exchange Act of 1934, and created a comprehensive regulatory scheme for the sale of securities. The Securities Act of 1933 governs the *original sale* of securities by the issuing companies to the public, requiring the registration of any **initial public offering (IPO)** and imposing penalties for selling unregistered securities or engaging in fraudulent practices in connection with those sales. In contrast, the Securities Exchange Act of 1934 mainly governs the post-issue *trading* of securities on the national stock exchanges and the actions of publicly traded companies relative to their securities and investors. The Securities and Exchange Commission (SEC), a powerful independent regulatory agency of the federal government, administers both laws. The SEC has the authority to issue rules and regulations governing securities sales and regulated companies and to enforce the law through administrative proceedings. We will focus our discussion on federal law and its application to real estate investments.

Definition of Security

An initial question for real estate investment promoters and investors is whether an interest in a particular real estate syndication or business is a security and thus subject to the registration and other requirements of the securities laws. The definition of **security** under federal law includes traditional investment instruments such as stocks, bonds, debentures, notes, puts, calls, and options, but it does not encompass real estate except for a "fractional undivided interest in oil, gas, or other mineral rights." Thus, an individual who merely purchases land, a building, a house, or other rights associated with land, hoping to profit from rents, capital gains, and the like, has not purchased a security. But security also includes the term **investment contract**, a catchall phrase referring to investments in which the investors are passive participants, risking their money in a business managed by others. Under the investment contract concept, interests in real estate investment trusts and limited partnerships are usually securities because the REIT beneficiaries and limited partners are passive investors, relying on the managers of the business for a return on their investment. In contrast, interests in general partnerships and joint ventures usually are not considered securities, because the general partners and joint venturers are actively managing the business.

The meaning of *security* is not limited to traditional real estate investments like REITs and limited partnership interests. Even the direct sale of land to individual purchasers can be the sale of a security. For example, in the landmark Supreme Court case of *SEC v. Howey Co.*, the Howey Co. sold part of its citrus farm in Florida to investors.[6] The investors, who were mostly out-of-state doctors, lawyers, and other professionals, purchased one or more rows of trees and the strips of land in which they grew. Along with the land, the purchasers received a long-term service contract through Howey-in-the-Hills, a sister company. Howey-in-the-Hills would cultivate, harvest, and market the citrus crop, and the investors would receive their pro rata share of the profits from the entire farm. The SEC claimed that the land sales coupled with the service contracts constituted a sale of securities, and the Supreme Court agreed, holding that any investment scheme under which money is invested in a business venture with the expectation of profits from the efforts of others is an investment contract. The citrus grove interests were securities because the investors invested their money in a common enterprise (the Howey citrus farm) and were expecting profits from the efforts of others (Howey-in-the Hills).

Under *Howey*, the Court outlined three requirements for any business interest (including an investment in a real estate venture) to be an investment contract:

- An investment of money.
- A common enterprise.
- A reasonable expectation of profits to be derived primarily from the managerial or entrepreneurial efforts of the promoter or a third party.

Some examples of real estate investments that have been considered securities under the *Howey* test include interests in a condominium project, a gold mine, a hotel, an oil and gas production contract, and a land development project. As the *Howey* case demonstrates, securities law is concerned with the economic substance of the transaction, not the legal form that the investment takes. If a transaction is in substance a security, the requirements of the securities laws apply.

Registration and Exemptions

A real estate investment involving the sale of a security must either comply with the registration requirements of the Securities Act of 1933 or fall within one of its exemptions. Before the initial public offering of a nonexempt security, the issuer (the business selling the security) must file a

registration statement with the SEC. The registration statement contains (1) detailed information about the business and the securities offering, including audited financial statements of the issuer, and (2) a **prospectus**, an abbreviated version of the registration statement, which must be provided to any prospective purchaser to whom an offer to sell is made. The SEC scrutinizes the registration statement to ensure that the required disclosures have been made, but the SEC does not evaluate the soundness of the investment. Rather, the registration statement and prospectus provide information by which prospective investors can make their own informed investment decisions.

Because the registration process is complicated and expensive, the 1933 Act contains a number of exemptions. Some are designed to ease the registration burden for small businesses. The **small offering exemption** is an example. It allows an issuer to follow a simplified registration process under which a short form "offering statement" is filed with the SEC. This exemption is limited, however, to the sale of $5 million of securities within a 12-month period. Another exemption that applies to real estate syndications is the **intrastate exemption**. This exemption applies if the issuer and the investors are all residents of one state and the securities offering meets specific intrastate requirements, including the following:

- 80% of the monies raised by the securities sale must be used for operations in the state.

- 80% of the real estate and other assets of the business must be located within the state.

- 80% of the issuer's income must be earned in the state.

The act also contains a **private offering** exemption, allowing private (nonpublic) sales of securities to knowledgeable investors without the need for a registration statement. To provide guidance as to what sales are private offerings, the SEC promulgated Regulation D, which sets forth detailed requirements for private offerings. Generally, Regulation D prohibits any public advertising or solicitations, requires the issuer to notify the SEC of the private offering, and prohibits the immediate resale of the securities to the general public. Regulation D further provides for three types of private offerings (under Rules 504, 505, and 506), depending upon the dollar amount of the offering and the sophistication of the investors. Rule 504 allows a private sale of up to $1 million in a year without any limitation on the number or types of investors. Rule 505 allows a private offering of $5 million in a year. It permits sales to an unlimited number of accredited investors, but to no more than 35 "unaccredited" investors (who may be employees of the issuing business or other inexperienced investors). Accredited investors are institutional investors, mutual funds, banks, financial institutions, and wealthy investors who should be able to protect themselves in investment settings. Rule 506 allows an unlimited dollar amount, but it permits sales to no more than 35 "sophisticated," unaccredited investors. Sophisticated investors are those whom the issuer reasonably believes have sufficient knowledge and experience in financial matters to evaluate the risks of the investment.

Liability and Remedies

To ensure that information required to be disclosed is not false or misleading, that fraudulent practices are not used to sell securities, and that the securities laws are otherwise complied with, the federal statutes contain several important liability provisions. Under Section 12 of the 1933 act, an investor who purchases a nonexempt security that is not properly registered, or who is not provided a prospectus, can sue the issuer to recover his or her investment. Section 12 imposes absolute liability, allowing the investor simply to cancel the sale and recover the investment without proving any damages. If a registration statement (including audited financial statements) is false and misleading, an investor can sue to recover damages under Section 11 of the act. Upon proving a material misstatement or omission in the registration materials the investor can recover his or her losses from the issuer. The investor also can recover damages from others involved in the sale of the security (e.g., underwriters, officers and directors, auditors), unless they acted with due diligence and were not negligent in developing and disseminating the registration statement information. The liability provisions give those participating in the registration process (particularly auditing firms) a powerful incentive to ensure that the registration material is accurate and complete.

Several sections of the securities laws are directed at fraudulent practices. The broadest antifraud provision is section 10B of the 1934 act, as interpreted and defined in Rule 10b-5 of the SEC. Rule 10b-5 prohibits fraud in connection with the sale of *any* security, not simply those traded on a national exchange. Thus, it applies to the sale of securities of private, closely held companies and of publicly owned companies regulated under the 1934 act. The law also prohibits a wide range of deceptive and manipulative practices in connection with the sale of securities, including insider trading and the making of false or misleading statements by issuers of securities and those trading in them. Finally, persons violating Section 10B face the prospect of civil lawsuits by injured investors, including class action suits, and administrative enforcement actions by the SEC, which can result in massive civil penalties and other sanctions.

Interstate Land Sales Full Disclosure Act

The Interstate Land Sales Full Disclosure Act (ILSFDA) of 1968 was designed to prevent false and deceptive practices in the sale of unimproved tracts of land in interstate commerce. Congress was concerned with land sale "scams" and other unscrupulous marketing of undeveloped home sites, particularly the sale of out-of-state lots unsuitable for development because of soil conditions, lack of utilities, or other limitations. To protect the public, Congress created ILSFDA, a mandatory disclosure law patterned after the federal securities laws. The act requires a developer of a subdivision of 100 or more lots to *register* it with the Department of Housing and Urban Development (HUD) (i.e., file with HUD a "statement of record") and, before selling a lot, to provide the prospective purchaser with a report on the property's condition. The registration statement and the property report contain information about the land so that prospective purchasers are not misled about the property and can make intelligent purchase decisions. The act also contains remedies to ensure that developers comply with the registration requirements and give accurate information about the land.

Application

The act applies to developers of subdivisions with 100 or more lots. A **developer** is any person who sells, leases, or advertises for sale or lease, a lot in a subdivision. A **subdivision** is land that is divided into lots for the purpose of sale or lease under a common promotional plan. A **common promotional plan** is a plan under which a developer (or developers working together) sells lots that are contiguous or that are marketed (known, designated, or advertised) under a common name. A farmer who divides his land into 200 lots and sells the undeveloped lots to out-of-state purchasers under the name Green Acres is a developer required to register under the act unless the particular subdivision is exempt.

The Act has 24 exemptions from the registration requirements. The sale of cemetery lots, sales by government entities, sales to builders of lots in areas zoned commercial or industrial, and sales of 20-acre lots are some of the exemptions. Some lot sales that are exempted from the registration requirements remain subject to the antifraud provisions of the law. For example, a subdivision that has between 25 and 99 lots does not have to register but is still covered under the antifraud provisions. A subdivision with fewer than 25 lots is exempt from both the registration and the anti-fraud provisions.

The act's **single-family residence** exemption, which is widely used, is meant to remove from the act's coverage the sale of lots in areas zoned for single-family residences when the subdivision meets minimum subdivision development standards. The development standards that the subdivision must satisfy to qualify for the single-family residence exemption relate to lot dimensions, plat approval and recordation, roads and access, drainage, flooding, water supply, and sewage disposal. Another popular exemption is the **intrastate exemption** covering sales of lots exclusively to residents of the state in which the subdivision is located. To fall within this exemption, the sale must satisfy numerous requirements, including an on-site inspection of the property by the purchaser before a contract is signed and the disclosure of information in the contract about roads, water, and sewer facilities.

The **improved lot exemption** has generated a substantial amount of litigation. The act was intended to protect purchasers of *unimproved* lots, not purchasers of homes or other structures. Therefore, it exempts from the registration requirement any improved land on which sets a residential, commercial, condominium, or industrial building. It also exempts any sale of land under a contract obligating the seller to erect a building on the lot within a two-year period. In interpreting this provision, HUD has taken the position that the contract cannot allow the seller to escape the obligation to build by conditioning the obligation on the buyer's obtaining construction financing or by allowing the seller to cancel the contract at the seller's discretion. HUD also maintains that the buyer must have a right under the contract to sue the seller for specific performance of the seller's obligation to build, and that a contract providing that the buyer waives

BOX 16–4 YOU BE THE JUDGE

On July 8, 1981, Americor Realty Association contracted to purchase a condominium unit from Hollingsworth Partnership. At the time the contract was signed, construction of the condominium had not been completed, and the contract did not require Hollingsworth to complete construction at any definite future date. The condominium was not registered under the Interstate Land Sales Full Disclosure Act, and Hollingsworth did not provide Americor with a property report on the condominium before the purchase agreement was signed. Americor attempted to cancel the contract because of Hollingsworth's failure to provide it with a property report, and later filed a lawsuit against Hollingsworth to revoke the contract. In its defense, Hollingsworth claimed that the land sales act does not apply to the sale of a condominium unit because it is not a "lot" within the meaning of the statute.

The Land Sales Act does not define the term *lot*. In 1973, HUD issued an interpretive rule defining lot as "any portion, piece, division, unit, or undivided interest in land . . . if the interest includes the right to the exclusive use of a specific portion of the land." Under this broad definition, condominium units are lots, and the sale of unfinished condominium units must be registered unless it falls within an exemption. Hollingsworth argued that the Land Sales Act should not apply to condominiums because Congress was concerned with the sale of undeveloped "raw" land when it passed the law. Limiting "lots" to separate tracts of land, Hollingsworth contended, was also consistent with other terminology used in the statute, such as the terms *developer* and *subdivision*. Americor argued that Congress did not draft the Land Sales Act to apply solely to raw land, and the law was written in a manner so as to protect purchasers of any type of unfinished real estate that was part of a larger development.

How would you interpret the term *lot*? How much deference should the court give to HUD's interpretation of the statutory language?

that right does not qualify for the exemption. The courts have split over the interpretation of the exemption. Some courts follow the approach adopted in Florida that the seller's obligation to build must be unconditional, and that the contract cannot in any way restrict the buyer's remedies for the seller's breach of the contract. Other courts have adopted a less restrictive approach, allowing contracts in which the seller's obligation is subject to reasonable conditions such as the submission of plans and specifications by the buyer, or which limit the buyer's remedies for the seller's breach.

The Statement of Record and the Property Report

Unless a subdivision is exempt, a developer must file a **statement of record** with HUD. The statement identifies those who own or have an interest in the subdivision and includes financial statements of the developer. The statement also describes the physical condition of the property, including its topography, the size of the subdivision, dimensions of the lots, the relation of the lots to existing streets, the present condition of access to the subdivision, the availability of public utilities (water, electricity, telephone, sewage treatment), the proximity of the subdivision to nearby towns, and the extent of any improvements to the subdivision. The statement also contains a legal description of the land, a statement as to any encumbrances and deed restrictions on the land, and other title information. Finally, the statement gives information about the terms of sale, including a range of selling prices for lots and a copy of the deed to be used for conveyance.

HUD examines the statement of record to ensure that it is complete and accurate on its face, but does not independently verify the information or evaluate the desirability or worth of the lots. In fact, the act prohibits developers from representing that HUD approves of the subdivision or recommends the sale of subdivision lots. After the statement becomes effective (30 days from filing unless the statement is incomplete), the developer can lawfully sell the lots. The developer still must provide prospective purchasers with a **property report** before any sale. The property report contains most of the information provided in the statement of record about the developer, title to the property, terms of sale, and the physical condition of the property.

Liability and Remedies

The act provides purchasers with the right to cancel the sale and secure a return of the purchase price in two situations. First, the act has a one-week cooling-off period; a purchaser may revoke the sale within seven days of the signing of the contract. Second, a purchaser who was not given a property report before signing the contract can cancel it within two years from its execution.

Liability is imposed on developers and their agents, including real estate brokers, for failing to comply with the registration requirements and for fraudulent practices in connection with any sale. The antifraud provisions of the law prohibit the use of any sales practices, advertising, or promotional materials that would be misleading to purchasers or that contain untrue statements of material facts. Also prohibited are oral representations that roads, sewer, water, gas, electric services, or recreational amenities will be provided by the developer. If made, such representations must be stated in the written purchase agreement.

Purchasers can sue the developer and its agents for violations of the act. The courts have broad power to grant purchasers relief that is appropriate under the circumstances in light of the price paid for the lot, the costs of any necessary improvements, and the market value of the lot. The courts can award specific performance or damages, including interest, attorney's fees, and appraiser's fees. HUD also has the power to enforce the law administratively. It can investigate violations, suspend registrations, and impose civil penalties of $1,000 per violation (to a maximum of $1 million per year).

The Fair Housing Act

In the aftermath of the Civil War, the United States adopted two important amendments to the Constitution: the Thirteenth Amendment prohibiting slavery and involuntary servitude, and the Fourteenth Amendment guaranteeing due process and equal treatment under the law. The Equal Protection Clause of the Fourteenth Amendment prohibits the state government and its political subdivisions (cities, counties, etc.) from discriminating against individuals on the basis of race or some other improper criterion. Although the Fourteenth Amendment prohibits the courts from enforcing racially restrictive covenants (e.g., a covenant in a deed restricting the sale of property to whites only), it does not outlaw "private" discrimination. If a private landowner refuses to sell or rent his property to an African American or Hispanic, the Fourteenth Amendment does not prohibit the discrimination because it does not involve any action by the state government.

Two federal statutes (and numerous state fair housing laws), however, *do* prohibit private housing discrimination. The first, the Civil Rights Act of 1866, prohibits racial discrimination in the sale or leasing of property. The second and broadest is the Fair Housing Act of 1968. It protects not only racial and ethnic minorities, but also other persons who have historically been subject to discrimination in residential real estate transactions. Individual property owners and businesses need to be familiar with the scope of the Fair Housing Act and its prohibitions.

Protected Classes

The Fair Housing Act originally prohibited discriminatory housing practices on the basis of race, color, national origin, religion, and sex. In 1988, Congress amended the law to prevent discrimination against the handicapped and against individuals on the basis of familial status, such as those with minor children. Handicapped individuals include those with a physical or mental impairment, those who have a record of or who are perceived as having such an impairment, persons having a hearing or visual impairment or other physical disability that restricts their life activities, individuals with diseases such as AIDS, and persons suffering from alcoholism. Among those with familial status are a parent or a custodian with a child under the age of 18, women who are pregnant, and persons who are attempting to adopt a minor child or secure custody of a minor.

Application of the Law

The Fair Housing Act applies to discriminatory practices in connection with the sale or leasing of residential housing, including single-family houses, duplexes, and units in multifamily dwellings. It prohibits discriminatory practices by businesses, professionals, and others involved in the various stages of a real estate transaction such as property owners and managers, brokers and real estate agents, lenders, insurers, and appraisers.

Although the scope of the act is extremely broad, Congress created some exemptions from its prohibitions. The sale or rental of a single-family house by a private individual owning fewer than four houses is not covered by the act as long as (1) no broker is involved in the transaction, (2) the owner or lessor avoids discriminatory advertising, and (3) the owner makes no more than one sale of a house during a two-year period. However, people typically sell their houses by employing a real estate broker, so this exemption is narrow. Another exemption exists for the rental of units in owner-occupied dwellings of two to four units, provided no discriminatory advertising is connected with the rental. Other qualified exemptions exist for religious organizations, private clubs, and housing exclusively for the elderly. Note that even if a sale or rental is exempt from the prohibitions of the Fair Housing Act, racial discrimination may be prohibited by the Civil Rights Act of 1866, and additional forms of discrimination may be prohibited by a state fair housing law, some of which are broader than the Fair Housing Act.

Unlawful Discriminatory Practices

The Fair Housing Act prohibits most forms of discriminatory housing practices. The following acts are illegal under the act if they are based on race, national origin, or other prohibited criteria: refusing to rent or sell housing; setting different terms, conditions, or privileges in the sale or rental of housing; providing different housing services or facilities; making false statements regarding the availability of housing; refusing to make a mortgage loan or to insure property, or imposing different terms and conditions on insurance or a loan; refusing to allow a handicapped tenant to make reasonable modifications to the premises if necessary for the tenant to use the housing; refusing to make a reasonable accommodation in rules, policies, practices, or services necessary for a handicapped tenant to make use of the housing; appraising property in a discriminatory manner; and advertising in a way indicating a discriminatory preference. The law also prohibits racial steering, blockbusting, and redlining. **Racial steering** is the practice of directing home buyers or renters to particular neighborhoods, such as showing blacks apartments or housing only in black neighborhoods. **Blockbusting** occurs when a person induces panic selling for financial gain, for example, by creating fear of racial integration of an area to secure housing at a depressed price. **Redlining** is a refusal to lend money or insure property because of its location in a "less desirable" community.

Remedies and Proving Discrimination

Any person "injured by a discriminatory housing practice" has a remedy under the Fair Housing Act. In *Havens Realty Corp. v. Coleman*, the Supreme Court interpreted this language broadly and decided that "testers" (persons checking whether discrimination was occurring) and housing organizations could sue for violations of the Fair Housing Act.[7] In that case, a black man attempted to rent an apartment through Havens Realty, but he was falsely told that no apartments were available. He contacted HOME (Housing Opportunities Made Equal), a nonprofit corporation working for equal opportunity housing in Richmond, Virginia. HOME investigated his complaint, using testers to determine whether Havens Realty was engaged in racial steering in violation of the Fair Housing Act. Testers are individuals who, without an intent to rent an apartment, pose as renters for the purpose of collecting evidence of unlawful discriminatory practices. After confirming his allegation, HOME and the testers sued Havens Realty for violations of the act. The Court found that the black tester was entitled to sue because he had a legal right under the law to truthful information about available housing and suffered an injury when he was provided false information. HOME also was allowed to sue, because it claimed injury to its counseling and referral efforts because of the diversion of resources necessary to investigate and combat the racial steering practices committed by Havens Realty. As a result of *Havens Realty*, testers are frequently used by housing organizations to investigate alleged violations of the law, and housing organizations often bring fair housing complaints.

The Fair Housing Act provides several remedies to an injured person. The complaining party can file a complaint with HUD or bring a civil lawsuit in court. If a complaint is filed with HUD, an administrative process is followed. HUD first investigates the complaint and attempts to reach a conciliation (settlement) agreement with the respondent (the person alleged to have committed the discriminatory practice). Conciliation agreements are quite common, and HUD can sue to enforce the agreement if it is breached by the respondent. If no agreement is reached, and HUD finds reasonable grounds for the complaint, HUD proceeds with the case in an administrative enforcement hearing, but has the burden of proving a violation. The matter is heard by an administrative law judge (ALJ) who decides the contested issues and renders a decision including the necessary relief. The ALJ can award compensatory damages to the injured party, including attorney's fees and costs. Such damages can include compensation for emotional distress, humiliation, and pain and suffering. Housing organizations also have been awarded compensatory damages (as compensation for the diversion of their resources) for the time and effort put into pursuing fair housing violations, and for the costs of monitoring the respondent's future conduct to ensure that no repeat violations occur. To vindicate the public interest, the ALJ also can order the payment of a civil fine (less than $10,000 in most cases). Finally, broad injunctive relief is available. To prevent further violations of the law, the ALJ can order the respondent to take steps such as maintaining housing records, filing periodic reports with HUD, and conducting education or training on fair housing compliance.

Rather than proceed administratively, a person alleging a violation of the act can bring a civil lawsuit in federal or state court, but has the burden of proving the violation. An injured party can recover compensatory and punitive damages in the civil action. To prevail, the party must establish discriminatory intent, either by direct evidence or by indirect (circumstantial) proof of intent. In one fair housing case a landlord told several persons that he did not want to rent to Hispanics "because they played the music too loud, drank too much, and they were always on welfare." His remarks are direct evidence of discriminatory intent. Without direct evidence, the injured party must prove intent indirectly by establishing what is called a prima facie case of a housing violation. For example, in an action alleging a discriminatory refusal to sell or lease, Robert, the plaintiff, must show the following:

- That he is a member of a protected class.
- That he applied for and was qualified to rent or purchase available housing.
- That his application was rejected.
- That the housing or rental property remained available thereafter.

If Robert establishes the prima facie case, he has provided circumstantial proof of discriminatory intent. To counter this proof, the respondent must articulate a "legitimate, nondiscriminatory reason" for the rejection. If the respondent offers a plausible explanation for the refusal to sell or lease, such as a bad credit record, Robert can still establish discriminatory intent if he proves that the reason given was just a pretext (not the actual reason) for the respondent's actions. Ultimately, the court or jury must decide on the basis of the evidence whether the respondent had the discriminatory intent needed to prove a violation, or instead had a legitimate, nondiscriminatory reason not to sell or lease.

The Government's Power of Eminent Domain

The state and federal governments have the power of **eminent domain**, which gives them the right, within limits imposed by the federal and state constitutions, to take private property for a public purpose without the consent of the owner. The taking is accomplished by a procedure called **condemnation**. Traditionally, the eminent domain power has been used to acquire private property for public services and projects, including highways, hospitals, schools, parks, and dams. More recently, governments have condemned (taken) private property for the redevelopment of urban areas and for economic development projects.

Through its Fifth and Fourteenth Amendments, the U.S. Constitution prohibits the federal and state governments from taking life, liberty, and property without due process of law. The Fifth Amendment, which applies directly only to the federal government, provides further that the government shall not take private property for public use without paying the owner a "just compensation."The Fourteenth Amendment extends the Fifth Amendment's public use and just compensation requirements to the states. In addition, because the property cannot be taken without due process of law, a person whose property is to be taken is entitled to a fair condemnation procedure, one providing adequate notice of the taking and an opportunity for a fair hearing. Although state constitutions are sometimes more restrictive than the Fifth Amendment as to what property may be taken, any condemnation of property at the national, state, or local level requires (1) a public purpose for the taking, (2) the payment of a just compensation to the owner, and (3) a fair condemnation procedure in which the owner may challenge the taking.

Authority to Condemn Property

Statutes (state and federal) authorize the taking of private property and specify the persons allowed to condemn it, the purposes for which condemnation is permitted, and the kinds of property rights that can be taken. Generally, state statutes grant the power of eminent domain to municipalities, state agencies, and other government entities for a broad range of government purposes. In addition, state statutes commonly delegate the power of eminent domain to private companies such as public utilities and private schools, which then act under the authority of the state to condemn property such as power line easements and other property interests needed for their operations.

Public Use and Necessity

Any condemnation of property must be for a public use. Public uses clearly include necessary public services and activities such as schools, roads, and government buildings. However, not all uses intended by the government are sufficiently "public" to justify a taking. For example, the City of Metropolis cannot simply take Ruth's home from her and transfer it to the mayor's brother for his private use. Yet, many government projects satisfy the public use requirement even though they incidentally benefit some private individuals at the expense of landowners whose property is condemned. Despite the incidental benefits to private persons, the constitutional requirement of a public use will be satisfied if substantial public objectives are served by the condemnation.

The courts have construed the concept of a public use broadly, and generally defer to the judgment of the government as to the need to condemn private property to accomplish government objectives. The leading case is *Hawaii Housing Authority v. Midkiff*.[8] In *Midkiff*, Hawaii enacted a land reform law to address historically rooted problems with the concentration of land ownership in the state. Because of a feudal land system adopted by the original Polynesian settlers of the islands, land in the state continued to be owned in modern times by a small group of people. Statistics in the 1960s indicated that 47% of the land in the state was owned by only 72 landowners. The reform act allowed the state to take property from those owners and transfer it to the existing tenants. The U.S. Supreme Court upheld the law, finding a public purpose in correcting the problems caused by the land oligopoly—the disruption of the state's land market, which forced residents to become tenants rather than owners. The Court further held that the condemned property need not be put to use for the general public, reasoning that transferring the condemned property to private individuals furthered the public objective of land dispersal underlying the law. The Court also concluded that its role is a limited one because the legislature is in the best position to determine public needs and the ways in which those public needs should be advanced.

In line with *Midkiff*, cases have also approved the use of eminent domain for urban renewal, for environmental protection, and for economic development projects. The most extreme case is the Michigan Supreme Court's decision in *Poletown Neighborhood Council v. City of Detroit.*[9] The court approved the condemnation of an entire neighborhood of more than 3,000 people so that General Motors could build an automobile assembly plant. Many of the residents were elderly, retired, and of Polish-American descent (thus the name Poletown). The Court found a public purpose in alleviating unemployment and fiscal distress, and that any benefit to private interests (General Motors) was merely incidental to the public objectives.

Condemnation Procedures

The legal proceeding in which property is condemned must satisfy fundamental standards of fairness under the due process clauses of the Fifth and Fourteenth Amendments to the Constitution. Notice of the taking and a fair hearing to allow the owner to challenge it are essential for any condemnation proceeding to meet the requirement of procedural due process. Although it is common for condemnation actions to be heard by a jury, a jury trial is not constitutionally required. The states and the federal government have developed a variety of procedural systems to resolve condemnation issues.

Condemnation proceedings usually include one or more of the followings steps. Before filing a formal condemnation lawsuit, the government makes a determination of the necessity for the taking (including whether the taking is for a public use) and extends to the landowner a good faith offer to purchase the property. The agency condemning the property usually adopts a resolution of necessity at a public hearing, which is a formal decision to acquire the property by eminent domain. To proceed, private companies intending to use their delegated power of eminent domain may have to obtain authority from the relevant regulatory agency, such as a state public service commission in the case of a utilities company. The good faith offer to purchase must be based on an appraisal of the property by the condemning authority. The landowner can accept or reject the offer, and negotiations can continue between the parties. If the landowner rejects the offer to purchase, or if the parties cannot reach an agreement, the condemning authority usually files a formal lawsuit. A trial is held to determine the legitimacy of the condemnation and the amount of compensation due the owner. Although landowners can contest the necessity for the taking, it is more common for landowners to dispute the value of the property and the amount of any incidental damages. The case may be heard by the court, by a jury, or by some other adjudicative body. Some states have a panel made up of local landowners, called commissioners, to resolve contested issues.

Many states also have a procedure known as **quick take** that allows the government to take immediate possession of the property before the condemnation trial is held. The idea behind the quick take process is to prevent unnecessary delay of government projects. To protect the landowner, the government must deposit in court its good faith estimate of the fair market value of the property. The landowner is allowed to withdraw that money during the pendency of the case without jeopardizing his or her right to contest the issue of damages at trial.

Just Compensation and Damages

The owner of condemned property is entitled to a just compensation, to be paid when private property is condemned. Ordinarily, just compensation is based on the fair market value of the property at the time of the taking. The testimony of qualified appraisers is essential to establish market value at trial. Condemnation trials often present conflicting opinions as to the value of the condemned property, which must be resolved by the hearing body.

Condemnation law allows the recovery of damages in addition to the market value of the property condemned. **Severance damages** are recoverable in most states in partial taking cases when the value of the part of the property retained by the owner is diminished because of the taking. So, for example, the market value of a restaurant whose parking lot is condemned may be diminished because of the loss of easy customer access to the business. Similarly, a taking that changes the size or shape of a lot may affect the ability of the landowner to comply with zoning regulations, so may decrease the value of the lot. Severance damages may also be awarded where one of two physically separate tracts of land is taken by the government. For example, if the two tracts are used in connection with the same business, manufacturing operation, or farm, many states allow the owner to recover severance damages caused by the loss of one of the parcels.

The jurisdictions differ as to whether business goodwill is recoverable in a condemnation case. The traditional rule did not allow the recovery of goodwill, because it was not considered "property" in a constitutional sense. Most states and the federal government follow this rule, although some states (California, Vermont, Michigan, and Minnesota) now allow goodwill as an element of damages under certain circumstances, for example, if a business cannot be relocated, or can be relocated only at a substantial loss to the business owner. Whether evidence that condemned land is environmentally contaminated should be admitted to reduce its market value is a recent issue in condemnation proceedings. A majority of state courts addressing the issue allow such evidence, since a prospective purchaser would be concerned about the risks of acquiring contaminated property, including remediation costs, and would pay less for it than for uncontaminated property. Other courts refuse to admit such evidence, on the theory that the landowner has a right to litigate the question of his or her legal liability for cleanup costs. These courts reason that allowing cleanup costs to reduce the award in eminent domain case denies the landowner his or her day in court on the liability issue and constitutes a deprivation of due process.

Regulatory Takings

The federal and state governments have broad powers to regulate the use and enjoyment of real estate. For example, pursuant to their "police power," the states have zoning laws permitting cities and counties to specify the type of use to which a particular land area (zone) may be put, such as residential, commercial, residential-commercial, or industrial. A rezoning of an area from high-density, multiple-unit residential use to low-density, one-family residential use can dramatically decrease the value of undeveloped property in the area. Ordinarily, a landowner is not entitled to any compensation for the decrease in the value caused by the regulation (rezoning), because the government has not taken title to the property and has broad discretion under the police power to decide what restrictions best serve the public welfare. However, the Supreme Court has held that if regulation goes too far by, for example, preventing any commercial use of the property, the government will be regarded as having *taken* the property and will be required to pay compensation to the owner. A taking by means of overly stringent regulation is referred to as a **regulatory taking**. It is also an example of **inverse condemnation**, so-called because the landowner is the one who must sue to challenge the taking or to recover just compensation, in contrast to an ordinary condemnation lawsuit in which the government is the plaintiff.

Determining whether a particular law results in a regulatory taking is a complex constitutional judgment, one that the courts make on a case-by-case basis. The Supreme Court has identified a number of factors to consider in this determination, including the extent of the diminution of the property's value, the purpose and character of the government regulation, and the reasonable expectations of the landowner. The Court has differentiated between regulations imposing a physical occupation of property and those merely restricting the use of property. It also has recently established special rules for "development exactions," which are zoning and land-use laws requiring a landowner to dedicate property to public use to secure development approval or building permits. These aspects of regulatory takings are discussed in the paragraphs that follow.

Physical Occupations of Property

The Supreme Court has held that a government regulation resulting in a "permanent physical occupation" of private property by the government (or its delegatee) is a regulatory taking, regardless of the economic impact on the owner or the legitimacy of the government objectives behind the law. The leading decision is *Loretto v. Teleprompter Manhattan CATV Corp*, which involved a state law allowing cable television companies to attach cable boxes to apartment buildings without the owner's consent.[10] Even though the physical attachment was minimal, and tenant access to cable was of economic benefit to the owner and his property, the Court concluded that the statute permitted an unconstitutional taking because the owner did not receive a just compensation for the cable company's use of his property. Although the state did not condemn (take title to) the areas to which the cable boxes were affixed, the statute, by permitting an uncompensated physical invasion of the property, resulted in a regulatory taking of the space occupied by the cable boxes.

The *Loretto* rule is limited, however, to laws imposing an actual occupation of property and not to laws that simply regulate the uses to which the property can be put. This distinction was articulated in the case of *Yee v. City of Escondido*.[11] The Yees, owners of a mobile home park, challenged the constitutionality of a mobile-home rent-control ordinance passed by the city of Escondido. In California, a mobile home park owner can evict tenants only under limited circumstances: for nonpayment of rent or a tenant's violation of law. Also, when a mobile home is sold, the park owner cannot refuse to rent to a new mobile home owner if he or she is able to pay the amount of rent paid by the former owner. California state law does not limit the amount of rent a park owner can charge. In 1988, however, the City of Escondido approved a rent control law limiting the amount of rent an Escondido park owner can charge. The Yees claimed a physical occupation, contending that the effect of the state and local laws was to force park owners to rent to mobile home owners, who in effect became perpetual tenants of the park at a lower-than-market rental rate. The Court rejected this argument, noting that the park owner voluntarily rented to the tenants and was free to discontinue the rental business entirely, evict the tenants from the land, and put the land to other uses. Thus, the Supreme Court held that the law imposed no physical occupation of the land, but was merely a regulation of the use of property similar to other regulations of the landlord-tenant relationship.

Government Regulations of the Use of Property

Although the rent control law in the *Yee* case did not amount to a physical occupation by the government or its delegatees (the tenants), it clearly decreased the value of the mobile home park owner's property by limiting the amount of rent that could be charged. Many land use restrictions, from zoning laws to environmental controls, adversely affect the value of property. Government measures that diminish the value of property constitute a regulatory taking if (1) they deprive the owner of all beneficial uses, or (2) they unreasonably interfere with the owner's investment-based expectations in the property.

In *Lucas v. South Carolina Coastal Commission*, the Supreme Court held that a government regulation depriving the owner of all economically beneficial uses of the property constitutes a taking.[12] Lucas had purchased two residential lots on the Isle of Palms, a barrier island near Charleston, South Carolina, paying $975,000 for the property. At that time, the land was zoned single-family residential, and Lucas intended to build a beachfront home on the lots. However, before construction, South Carolina enacted the Beachfront Management Act, a law designed to protect the beach and dune system from erosion. The act prohibited construction of any permanent structure too close to the shoreline, and the Lucas property fell within the no-development zone. His challenge to the law reached the Supreme Court after a state trial court found that the act's permanent ban on construction "deprived Lucas of any reasonable economic use of the lots . . . and rendered them valueless." The Court held that when the owner of real property has been called upon to sacrifice all economically beneficial uses he has suffered a taking, the total destruction of economic value being equivalent to a physical appropriation of property. Although the beachfront management law was established to protect the beaches and other property owners from erosion, the Court held that totally depriving an owner of the use of his property without compensating him for it can be justified only when the prohibited use constitutes a common law nuisance.

When a regulation affecting the value of property does not deprive the owner of all beneficial uses, but leaves the owner free to make an economically viable use of the property, the regulation usually will not constitute a regulatory taking, and the government need not pay compensation for any decrease in value. The leading case is *Penn Central Transportation Co. v. City of New York*.[13] In *Penn Central*, the owners of the Grand Central Railroad terminal challenged restrictions imposed under the New York City Landmark Preservation law. The owners were denied permission by the Landmark Preservation Commission to build an office complex above the station, a development that would have provided at least $3 million per year in rental income to the owners. Despite the economic impact, the Court concluded that no taking had occurred. The Court reasoned that the owners could continue to use the property as a railroad terminal and make a reasonable return on their investment. Thus, the law did not unreasonably interfere with the owners' reasonable investment expectations in the property.

The Supreme Court's discussion in *Penn Central* focused on the extent to which the law interfered with the owners' "investment-backed expectations." In Case 16.2, the Texas Supreme Court analyzes a property owner's claim that a City's denial of a development plan constituted a regulatory taking. In the process, it discusses the notion of investment-backed expectations.

Case 16.2

Mayhew v. Town of Sunnyvale

905 S.W.2d 234 (Texas 1998)

The Town of Sunnyvale, population 2,000, is located twelve miles east of the central business district of Dallas. The Town contains approximately 10,941 acres of land, but approximately 8,190 acres are currently vacant. The Town's first zoning ordinance allowed residential development at a density of 3.6 units per acre. In 1973, in response to septic tank failures, the Town modified its zoning ordinance and enacted a one-acre minimum lot size requirement, thus limiting residential development to one unit per acre. However, when sanitary sewer facilities were later made available to the Town, the Town did not repeal its one-acre minimum lot requirement.

The Mayhew family owns approximately 1,196 acres of land in Sunnyvale. From 1941 to 1965, the Mayhews acquired 850 acres of their property at a cost of $372,000. They used this property for ranching for a number of years and in 1985 and 1986 purchased an additional 346 acres in the Town for development purposes. The Mayhews' property comprises 26% of the land available for residential development in the Town.

In 1985, the Mayhews began meeting with various Town officials seeking permission to proceed with a planned development with a density in excess of the then allowable one-dwelling-unit-per-acre residential zoning. In 1986, after meeting with the Mayhews, the Town adopted a comprehensive plan providing for a projected population of 25,000 by the year 2006, and 30,000 to 35,000 persons by the year 2016. The Town also amended its zoning ordinances to allow, upon council approval, planned developments with densities in excess of one dwelling-unit per acre.

After spending over $500,000 conducting studies and preparing evaluative reports, the Mayhews submitted their planned development proposal to the Town requesting approval to build between 3,650 and 5,025 units on their land, a density of over three units per acre. The Town employed a professional planning and engineering firm that reviewed the proposal and recommended its approval. The proposal was then forwarded to the Town's planning and zoning commission. After four months of consideration, the commission recommended denial of the Mayhews' application. The commission noted that the development would severely impact the ability of the Town to provide adequate municipal services and that the Town had a unique rural character and lifestyle that differed from the proliferation of multifamily and single-family homes on small lots in adjoining municipalities. A negotiating team of the Town Council tentatively agreed to a compromise development of 3,600 units, but when the matter came up for a vote, the council voted four to one to deny the Mayhews' development proposal.

The Mayhews sued the Town alleging that its decision was a taking of their property without payment of just compensation. Hearing testimony from thirty-five witnesses, most of whom were experts, the district court found that the fair market value of the property with development approval and without the application of the one-acre zoning requirement would have been greater than $15 million, and that as a result of the Town Council's denial of the application for the planned development, the value was reduced to $2.4 million. The court further found that the existing development in the Town of Sunnyvale was suburban and urban, and any "rural" atmosphere resulted from the existence of undeveloped private property. The court concluded that in denying the application for the development, the Town of Sunnyvale had refused to allow economically viable development of property and had acted pursuant to an official policy not to allow development with a density of greater than one dwelling unit per acre. Holding that the Town's decision to deny the Mayhews' application resulted in an unconstitutional taking under both the federal and state constitutions, the court rendered judgment in favor of the Mayhews, awarding $5 million in damages, $2.3 million in prejudgment interest, and approximately $1.2 million in attorney's fees and costs. The court of appeals reversed the district court's judgment and dismissed the Mayhews' claims against the Town. The Mayhews' appealed to the Supreme Court of Texas.

ABBOTT, J.

Zoning decisions are vested in the discretion of municipal authorities; courts should not assume the role of a super zoning board. However, despite the discretion afforded to municipal authorities, zoning decisions must comply with constitutional limitations. As a general rule, the application of a general zoning law to a particular property constitutes a regulatory taking if the ordinance "does not substantially advance legitimate state interests" or it denies an owner all "economically viable use of his land."

The Mayhews allege, and the district court found, that the denial of the Mayhews' planned development did not substantially advance legitimate state interests and amounted to a taking because all economically viable use of their property was denied. We first analyze whether the Town's actions substantially advance legitimate governmental interests before determining whether the Town's actions denied the Mayhews all economically viable use of their property.

1. Substantially Advance Legitimate Interests

A property regulation must "substantially advance" a legitimate governmental interest to pass constitutional muster. . . . The Supreme Court has . . . indicated that "a broad range of governmental purposes and regulations" will satisfy these requirements. . . . Specifically, the Supreme Court has noted that the following state interests are legitimate state interests: protecting residents from the "ill effects of urbanization"; enhancing the quality of life; and protecting a beach system for recreation, tourism, and public health. . . .

The Mayhews allege that the real reason behind the denial of their development application was to have their property serve as "borrowed" open space for the residents of the Town who primarily live on less than one-acre lots. . . . But the Town's planning and zoning commission came forth with a number of separate reasons for the denial of the Mayhews' application, several of which substantially advance legitimate state interests. The Town denied the development application in part because of the impact the development would have on the overall character of the community and the unique character and lifestyle of the Town which is different from that of adjoining municipalities where there is a proliferation of multifamily and single-family homes on small lots. We also conclude that the denial of the Mayhews' development application substantially advances the Town's legitimate concern for protecting the community from the ill effects of urbanization. The Mayhews requested a planned development with 3,600 units in a Town with a population of only approximately 2,000 residents. Photographs in the record show that the Town is uniquely rural and suburban, with undivided two lane roads, clusters of trees, lakes and ponds, and houses on large lots. This community would change drastically if a large planned development with at least three residences per acre was built. The Mayhews' planned development would result in an estimated population increase of between 10,000 and 15,000 persons, more than quadrupling the population of the Town. Simply put, the Town has a substantial interest in preserving the rate and character of community growth, and its action in denying the Mayhews' planned development furthers those interests.

2. Just Compensation Takings Claim

Our conclusion that the Town's action substantially advances a legitimate state interest does not end the takings inquiry, however. A compensable regulatory taking can also occur when governmental agencies impose restrictions that either (1) deny landowners of all economically viable use of their property, or (2) unreasonably interfere with landowners' rights to use and enjoy their property.

A restriction denies the landowner all economically viable use of the property or totally destroys the value of the property if the restriction renders the property valueless. Determining whether all economically viable use of a property has been denied entails a relatively simple analysis of whether value remains in the property after the governmental action.

In contrast, determining whether the government has unreasonably interfered with a landowner's right to use and enjoy property requires a consideration of two factors: the economic impact of the regulation and the extent to which the regulation interferes with distinct investment-backed expectations. The first factor, the economic impact of the regulation, merely compares the value that has been taken from the property with the value that remains in the property. The loss of anticipated gains or potential future profits is not usually considered in analyzing this factor. The second factor is the investment-backed expectation of the landowner. The existing and permitted uses of the property constitute the "primary expectation" of the landowner that is affected by regulation. . . . Knowledge of existing zoning is to be considered in determining whether the regulation interferes with investment-backed expectations.

The relevant factual findings [by the district court] demonstrate that the Town has not totally destroyed all value of the property by denying the Mayhews' planned development proposal. . . . [T]he district court in this case determined that, even after the denial of the Mayhews' planned development proposal, the property retained a value of $2.4 million. In such a situation, the governmental regulation has not entirely destroyed the property's value.

Even if the governmental regulation has not entirely destroyed the property's value, a taking can occur if the regulation has a severe enough economic impact and the regulation interferes with distinct investment-backed expectations.

When the Mayhews first began purchasing their property, the Town did not have a zoning ordinance in place. It is undisputed that the Mayhews originally purchased their property for ranching, not for development. They then used their property for ranching for nearly four decades. Historical uses of the property are critically important when determining the reasonable investment-backed expectation of the landowner. . . . After four decades of ranching their property in a Town with a population of no more than 2,000 people, the Mayhews did not have a reasonable investment-backed expectation that they could pursue an intensive development of 3,600 units that would more than quadruple the Town's population.

The Mayhews' subsequent purchases of property in 1985 and 1986 were for purposes of development. However, at this time, the Town's zoning ordinances had restricted development to one unit per acre for the preceding twelve years. The existing zoning of the property at the time it was acquired is to be considered in determining whether the regulation interferes with investment-backed expectations. . . . We do not believe that the Mayhews had a reasonable investment-backed expectation to build 3,600 units on their 1,200 acres when the Town's zoning ordinances had for twelve years limited development to one unit per acre.

Accordingly, we render judgment against the Mayhews on their regulatory takings claims.

QUESTIONS ABOUT CASE 16.2

1. Should the court have been more skeptical of the city's alleged reasons for requiring one-acre lots, particularly in light of the fact that the reason for the original adoption of the lot size requirement, the septic tank failures, had been eliminated when sanitary sewer facilities were made available to residents?

2. Given the city's comprehensive plan and its projected population increase, should the court have given more weight to the district court's finding that the practical effect of the zoning law was to deny the owner the right to develop the property?

⬤ Development Exactions and Mandatory Dedications of Property

Local governments frequently require developers to dedicate property to the city or county for streets, parks, or other public uses as a condition for the issuance of a building permit or approval of a development plan. Developers have sometimes challenged the legitimacy of such development exactions, contending that mandatory dedications of property constitute regulatory takings. Local governments counter that such exactions are necessary to meet the public costs of the development and to minimize the detrimental impact it may have on the community.

The Supreme Court has created a demanding two-part test to determine whether a government regulation that requires a property owner to dedicate property to the government is an unconstitutional taking. Under this rule, the government must first establish an "essential nexus" between the interest of the government and the condition imposed, that is, the exaction must be directly related to the burdens imposed by the development. This requirement was established in the case of *Nollan v. California Coastal Commission*.[14] Nollan wanted to demolish a beachfront bungalow and replace it with a three-bedroom home. The California Coastal Commission, concerned with the obstruction of the ocean view that the larger structure would cause, required Nollan, as a condition for the building permit, to grant a lateral easement to the public, permitting beachgoers the right to walk across his beach from one public beach to another. The Court held that requiring the easement was an unconstitutional taking of property because the easement was totally unrelated to the government's interest in the public's visual access to the ocean, in that the easement would not in any way improve the public's view of the beach.

The second requirement is that the exaction must bear a "rough proportionality" to the expected impact of the proposed development. This standard was established in the case of *Dolan v. City of Tigard*.[15] Dolan owned a plumbing and electrical supply store in the central business district of Tigard, Oregon. Part of her land could not be developed because it was within the 100-year floodplain of Fanno Creek. She sought permission from the City Planning Commission to double the size of the building and to pave a 39-space parking lot (activities affecting the part of her land lying outside the floodplain). Her request was approved subject to two conditions. First, Dolan was required to dedicate property located within the floodplain for improvement of the storm drainage system. Second, she was required to dedicate an adjacent 15-foot strip of land as a pedestrian/bicycle path.

Applying *Nollan*, the Court found the necessary connection between the city's requiring the dedication of land and its interest in reducing flooding and traffic congestion. The Court was not convinced, however, that the dedication of property to the city was proportional to the impact of the proposed development. The Court conceded that Dolan's development would increase the amount of water runoff to Fanno Creek, given the increase in impervious surfaces, and that preventing development in the floodplain would minimize the effects of Dolan's development. But the Court did not believe that correcting these problems justified the city in demanding a dedication of property that would become part of the city's *greenway* system and allow the public free access to the area. The city could simply have imposed a condition that the floodplain area remain undeveloped, a condition that would have served the city's interest in flood control without forcing Dolan to give up her ownership rights in the floodplain area. As to the dedication of land for a pedestrian/bicycle path, the Court held that the city did not present sufficient evidence to establish that the creation of the pathway would in fact lessen the traffic congestion caused by the expanded store.

The Court's approach to development exactions is highly protective of landowners and developers. Under the "rough proportionality" standard, governments imposing conditions on developments must come forward with solid evidence that the exaction is proportional to the burdens created by the development, and that less-restrictive measures would not be adequate to ease those burdens. Under the *Dolan* test, government suppositions and unsupported assumptions about the need for an exaction will not be sufficient to justify it. Factual proof is required, and the burden of proving proportionality rests with the government, not with the developer.

Property Rights Laws

Concern over excessive government regulation of land in the 1980s and 1990s triggered a "property rights" movement—a loose political coalition of landowners, businesspeople, mining and timber companies, farmers, and others concerned about the detrimental effects of environmental regulations, zoning and growth management laws, and other land-use controls. The movement has affected both the political and legal landscape. President Reagan issued an executive order requiring federal agencies to consider the "takings" implications of proposed regulations and legislation, a takings impact assessment similar to an environmental impact analysis. A proposal to protect property rights also became part of the Republican Party's "Contract with America." This proposal would require compensation to a landowner if a federal regulatory action caused a 10% decrease in the value of the owner's property. Introduced in Congress as the Private Property Protection Act of 1995, it passed the House but failed in the Senate. Other proposals for a national property rights law have been introduced in Congress, but none has been adopted, partly because of political opposition from environmental groups, but also because of the concern over the amount of federal monies necessary to pay compensation in "partial takings" cases.

The property rights movement has had its most significant impact on public policy at the state level. Almost every state has considered property rights laws, and more than half the states have passed "takings" legislation. The state property rights laws fall into two categories: assessment laws and compensation laws. Most of the states have adopted assessment statutes, which require state agencies to consider (assess) whether their proposed actions will result in a regulatory taking of property under court precedents and, if so, either to refrain from the proposed action or to pay compensation to affected property owners. The assessment statutes do not change the law of takings, but merely require procedures to protect landowners from state regulatory takings. In contrast, the compensation laws expand the situations in which the government must pay a just compensation. They require state agencies to pay landowners a just compensation if agency actions reduce the market value of the regulated properties to a certain extent. Texas, for example, requires compensation if the government action causes a 25% devaluation of the property. Only four states have passed compensation laws (Texas, Florida, Mississippi, and Louisiana), and the statutes differ in terms of (1) the regulatory actions that trigger compensation, and (2) the amount of the decrease in value that must occur for compensation to be required.

Self-Study Questions

1. (a) What is assessed value? (b) How is the assessed value of property related to market value?

2. (a) What are the three primary methods of appraising real estate? (b) In what types of real estate cases will appraisal testimony be necessary?

3. What are the most common exemptions under state property tax laws?

4. (a) How does the federal income tax law treat gains and losses on the sale of real estate? (b) What special rules apply to gains on the sale of a personal residence?

5. Explain the importance of the following estate tax concepts: (a) the unified credit, (b) the unlimited marital deduction, (c) the annual gift tax exclusion, (d) the special use valuation.

6. (a) What is a security? (b) What is an investment contract?

7. How are the Securities Act of 1933 and the Interstate Land Sales Full Disclosure Act similar in terms of the way in which the issuance of securities and the sale of unimproved lots are regulated?

8. (a) What are the protected classes under the Fair Housing Act? (b) What businesses and professionals are subject to the act's discriminatory housing provisions?

9. (a) What is the power of eminent domain? (b) What constitutional requirements must be met for the government to condemn property?

10. (a) What is a regulatory taking? (b) How are the Supreme Court takings rules different for laws imposing a physical occupation of property than for laws regulating the use of property?

Case Problems

1. In 1980, William and Verna Johnston purchased a residential duplex in Salt Lake City, Utah, and rented it to tenants. The duplex was built in 1914, but it was not a certified historic structure. The Johnstons made extensive renovations to the duplex, spending $119,000 for the improvements. They claimed a rehabilitation tax credit on their federal income tax return, which was disallowed by the IRS. The IRS contended that the expenditures fell within the "lodging" exception, which does not allow a credit for expenditures on "property used predominately to furnish lodging." Certified historic structures, hotels, and motels are excluded from the lodging exception. The Johnstons contended that the lodging exception should be read to apply to buildings used to house transients, not to long-term residential housing. (a) How would you interpret the lodging exception? (b) Should the Johnstons be entitled to a rehabilitation tax credit? (c) If they were entitled to a credit, to what dollar amount would they be entitled? *Johnston v. Comm'r of Internal Revenue*, 113 F.3d 145 (10th Cir. 1997).

2. In 1998, Boise Cascade Corporation acquired 1,770 acres of commercial timberland in Clatsop County, Oregon. In that same year, the Oregon Department of Fish and Wildlife designated the northern spotted owl as a threatened species. In 1990, to protect the spotted owl, the state forester adopted a regulation that prohibited timber harvesting within a 70-acre area surrounding known spotted owl nesting sites. In 1991, Boise sold all of its timberland except for a 64-acre parcel known as the Walker Creek site, which the buyer refused to accept because of the presence of a spotted owl nest on the property. In 1992, Boise sought permission from the state forester to harvest timber from Walker Creek, but the request was denied on the basis of the protective regulation. Boise was allowed to harvest at times when the owls were not nesting on the site. After the Board of Forestry upheld the denial, Boise sued the state of Oregon claiming that the denial of a permit to log the site constituted a regulatory taking of property in violation of the Fifth Amendment. In its complaint, Boise argued that the regulation resulted in a "physical occupation" of its property, because it was being forced to maintain spotted owl nests on the land so that they could be occupied by breeding owls. Boise also argued that the regulation deprived it of all economically viable use and thus constituted a taking under the *Lucas* case. The state argued that Boise's conduct amounted to a nuisance and, therefore, no compensation was required under *Lucas*. How should these two issues be resolved? (a) Did the law result in a physical occupation by the government or its delegatee (the spotted owl)? (b) Were the logging activities a nuisance? *Boise Cascade Corp. v. Bd. of Forestry*, 991 P.2d 993 (Or. App. 1999).

3. In 1987, the Open Housing Center, a fair housing organization in New York, investigated AM Realty, a real estate brokerage firm in Brooklyn. On four occasions, the center sent a pair of testers of different races to AM Realty's offices to inquire about renting apartments in certain Brooklyn neighborhoods. The two testers presented a similar rental profile in terms of family composition and income. In each of the tests, the AM Realty directed the white tester to apartments in predominately white neighborhoods, but directed the African American or Latino testers to apartments in predominately minority neighborhoods or informed the minority tester that no apartments were available. The Center then investigated Jeno Jakabovitz, one of the landlords employing AM Realty. It first sent a white tester to Jakabovitz's office to inquire about apartments in Kings Highway or Sheepshead Bay. Jakabovitz told the tester that an apartment in Kings Highway was available. A short time after the white tester left, a black tester went to Jakabovitz's office and inquired about an apartment in Kings Highway or Borough Park. Jakabovitz informed her that there were no apartments available in those neighborhoods, but asked the tester if she would be interested in an apartment in Cypress, a predominately African American neighborhood. On the basis of the investigation, the Open Housing Center and the testers sued AM Realty and Jakabovitz for violating the Fair Housing Act and the Civil Rights Act of 1866. At trial, Jakabovitz claimed a legitimate, nondiscriminatory reason for his actions; namely that the apartment he offered to the white tester was not available an hour later when the black tester arrived because it had already been rented to another person. However, evidence showed that the person to whom he allegedly rented the apartment never moved into the apartment. (a) Can the plaintiffs establish a prima facie case of discrimination by Jakabovitz? (b) If so, how should the defense presented by Jakabovitz be resolved—as a legitimate nondiscriminatory reason or as a pretext for discrimination? (c) What discriminatory housing practices did AM Realty commit? (d) What would be an appropriate remedy if AM Realty and Jakabovitz are found to have violated the Fair Housing Act? *Cabrera v. Jakabovitz*, 24 F.3d 372 (2d Cir. 1994).

Endnotes

1. Under a tax relief law passed by Congress in 2001, the highest individual tax rate is 38.6%, effective July 1, 2001. The rate will drop to 37.6% in 2004 and 35% in 2006.

2. The federal government also has a generation-skipping transfer tax (GST), which is imposed on transfers to grandchildren and other remote descendants. This complex tax is beyond the scope of our discussion, and under the 2001 tax relief law, the tax will be repealed in 2010.

3. Connecticut, Delaware, Indiana, Iowa, Kansas, Kentucky, Louisiana, Maryland, Montana, Nebraska, New Hampshire, New Jersey, North Carolina, Pennsylvania, South Dakota, and Tennessee.

4. Technically, these estate values (e.g., $675,000) are referred to as "exclusion amounts" or "exemption equivalents." They are not the amounts of the actual tax credit for the years in question. In 2001, for example, the unified tax credit for the $675,000 estate tax bracket is $220,550, which is the amount of the tax that otherwise would have been imposed, so that application of the credit results in no estate tax liability. Thus, because of the tax credit, an estate worth $675,000 is exempt from any estate tax liability.

5. The amount of the annual gift tax exclusion is indexed for inflation for decedents dying and gifts made after 1998.

6. 328 U.S. 293 (1946).

7. 455 U.S. 363 (1982).

8. 467 U.S. 229 (1984).

9. 304 N.W.2d 455 (Mich. 1981).

10. 458 U.S. 419 (1982).

11. 112 S.Ct. 1522 (1992).

12. 505 U.S. 1003 (1992).

13. 438 U.S. 104 (1978).

14. 483 U.S. 825 (1987).

15. 512 U.S. 374 (1994).

Zoning and Restrictive Covenants

The common law imposed few restrictions on the use of real estate. Landowners therefore had great latitude in using their property and sometimes did so in ways harmful or offensive to neighbors. As noted in Chapter 2, the law of nuisance provided remedies against landowners who, by the use of their own property, unreasonably interfered with the use and enjoyment of property owned by others. Intended primarily for resolving land use disputes between neighbors, the law of nuisance proved inadequate for safeguarding the public from the problems of urban life. The noise, dust, and odors from mining, manufacturing, slaughterhouses, and feed lots for cattle affected substantial segments of the neighboring population. If these uses interfered on a large scale with the enjoyment of property, the interference normally was classified as a public nuisance, the remedy for which was quite limited. Indeed, if the use had social utility, the courts then, as now, were likely to permit it to continue and to limit plaintiffs to damages if the enterprise, carefully operated, still interfered with the plaintiffs' use and enjoyment of their property. Only if the offending landowner engaged in unnecessary and injurious methods of operation would a court order the use to stop.

Recognizing the deficiencies of nuisance law in controlling harmful or offensive land uses, cities and local communities in the early twentieth century chose to control them directly under a regulatory system called **zoning**. This chapter discusses zoning, which is still the predominant method of local land-use control, and the legal issues arising under this form of regulation of real estate. The chapter closes with a discussion of restrictive covenants, a method of private land-use control commonly used in the development of residential subdivisions.

History and Purpose of Zoning

As the United States moved from a rural agrarian to an urban industrialized society, and experienced a corresponding shift in population from the farms to the cities, urban areas confronted a host of problems unique to city life—congestion, haphazard development, unsafe buildings, and encroachments on available light and air. Some cities responded with a patchwork of regulatory laws—building height restrictions, limits on wooden buildings and tenement housing, and building codes. It was not until 1916, and the passage of the New York City districting law, that a comprehensive zoning scheme was adopted by a municipality. The New York law was prompted by concerns over the height of buildings and the ability of landowners to use an entire lot for skyscrapers to the detriment of adjacent landowners and the general public welfare. The New York law divided the city into districts and imposed controls on the height of buildings and use of property in the different zones of the city. This districting or zoning scheme became the model for future laws and is still the traditional method of land-use regulation.

Two other developments in the 1920s were the catalyst for the widespread adoption of zoning in the United States. The federal government prepared and disseminated a uniform zoning enabling act that was widely adopted by state legislatures. State enabling laws are necessary for cities and municipalities to have the power to adopt zoning regulations. The second was the Supreme Court's approval of zoning as a permissible form of government regulation. Prior to 1926, it was unclear whether zoning was constitutional, many critics arguing that it constituted an unconstitutional taking of property in violation of the Fifth Amendment. In the landmark case of *Village of Euclid v. Ambler Realty Co.*, the U.S. Supreme Court put the issue to rest by upholding the constitutionality of a traditional zoning scheme, what is now often referred to as Euclidean zoning.

Case 17.1

**Village of Euclid v.
Ambler Realty Co.**

272 U.S. 365 (1926)

The village of Euclid is an Ohio municipal corporation. It adjoins and practically is a suburb of the city of Cleveland. Its estimated population is between 5,000 and 10,000, and its area from 12 to 14 square miles, the greater part of which is farmlands or unimproved acreage. Ambler Realty Company is the owner of a tract of land containing 68 acres, situated in the westerly end of the village.

On November 13, 1922, an ordinance was adopted by the village council, establishing a comprehensive zoning plan for regulating and restricting the location of trades, industries, apartment houses, two-family houses, single-family houses, etc., the lot area to be built upon, the size and height of buildings, etc. The entire area of the village is divided by the ordinance into six classes of use districts, denominated U-1 to U-6, inclusive. . . . The use districts are classified in respect of the buildings which may be erected within their respective limits, as follows: U-1 is restricted to single-family dwellings . . . U-2 is extended to include two-family dwellings; U-3 is further extended to include apartment houses . . . U-4 is further extended to include banks, offices, . . . U-5 is further extended to include . . . warehouses, ice and ice cream manufacturing and cold storage plants, bottling works . . . U-6 is further extended to include . . . manufacturing and industrial operations of any kind other than a class U-1, U-2, U-3, U-4, or U-5 use.

Ambler Realty's tract of land comes under U-2, U-3, and U-6. The first strip of 620 feet immediately north of Euclid Avenue falls in class U-2, the next 130 feet to the north, in U-3, and the remainder in U-6. Ambler Realty alleges that the tract of land in question is vacant and has been held for years for the purpose of selling and developing it for industrial uses, for which it is especially adapted, being immediately in the path of progressive industrial development; that for such uses it has a market value of about $10,000 per acre, but if the use be limited to residential purposes the market value is not in excess of $2,500 per acre. . . . The lower court found that the ordinances were unconstitutional and issued an injunction prohibiting their enforcement.

SUTHERLAND, J.

Is the ordinance invalid, in that it violates the constitutional protection "to the right of property . . . by attempted regulations under the guise of the police power, which are unreasonable and confiscatory"?

Building zone laws are of modern origin. They began in this country about 25 years ago. Until recent years, urban life was comparatively simple; but, with the great increase and concentration of population, problems have developed, and constantly are developing, which require, and will continue to require, additional restrictions in respect of the use and occupation of private lands in urban communities. Regulations, the wisdom, necessity, and validity of which, as applied to existing conditions, are so apparent that they are now uniformly sustained, a century ago, or even half a century ago, probably would have been rejected as arbitrary and oppressive.

The ordinance now under review, and all similar laws and regulations, must find their justification in some aspect of the police power, asserted for the public welfare. . . . There is no serious difference of opinion in respect of the validity of laws and regulations fixing the height of buildings within reasonable limits, the character of materials and methods of construction, and the adjoining area which must be left open, in order to minimize the danger of fire or collapse, the evils of overcrowding and the like, and excluding from residential sections offensive trades, industries, and structures likely to create nuisances.

The serious question in the case arises over the provisions of the ordinance excluding from residential districts, apartment houses, business houses, retail stores and shops, and other like establishments. This question involves the validity of what is really the crux of the more recent zoning legislation, namely, the creation and maintenance of residential districts, from which business and trade of every sort, including hotels and apartment houses, are excluded. Upon that question this court has not thus far spoken.

[T]he exclusion of buildings devoted to business, trade, etc., from residential districts, bears a rational relation to the health and safety of the community. Some of the grounds for this conclusion are promotion of the health and security from injury of children and others by separating dwelling houses from territory devoted to trade and industry; suppression and prevention of disorder; facilitating the extinguishment of fires, and the enforcement of street traffic regulations and other general welfare ordinances; aiding the health and safety of the community, by excluding from residential areas the confusion and danger of fire, contagion, and disorder, which in greater or less degree attach to the location of stores, shops, and factories.

With particular reference to apartment houses, it is pointed out that the development of detached house sections is greatly retarded by the coming of apartment houses, which has sometimes resulted in destroying the entire section for private house purposes; that in such sections very often the apartment house is a mere parasite, constructed in order to take advantage of the open spaces and attractive surroundings created by the residential character of the district. Moreover, the coming of one apartment house is followed by others, interfering by their height and bulk with the free circulation of air and monopolizing the rays of the sun which otherwise would fall upon the smaller homes, and bringing, as their necessary accompaniments, the disturbing noises incident to increased traffic and business, and the occupation, by means of moving and parked automobiles, of larger portions of the streets, thus detracting from their safety and depriving children of the privilege of quiet and open spaces for play, enjoyed by those in more favored localities—until, finally, the residential character of the neighborhood and its desirability as a place of detached residences are utterly destroyed. Under these circumstances, apartment houses, which in a different environment would be not only entirely unobjectionable but highly desirable, come very near to being nuisances.

If these reasons, thus summarized, do not demonstrate the wisdom or sound policy in all respects of those restrictions which we have indicated as pertinent to the inquiry, at least, the reasons are sufficiently cogent to preclude us from saying, as it must be said before the ordinance can be declared unconstitutional, that such provisions are clearly arbitrary and unreasonable, having no substantial relation to the public health, safety, morals, or general welfare.

Decree reversed.

QUESTIONS ABOUT CASE 17.1

1. How persuasive is the Court's opinion that apartment houses are incompatible with single-family residential neighborhoods?

2. Do zoning laws excluding multifamily dwelling units from residential zones have discriminatory effects on those of modest income and minorities? As a policy matter, are the exclusionary effects justifiable?

Euclidean Zoning

Today, every state has a zoning **enabling act** empowering cities, towns, and other local political subdivisions to engage in zoning and land-use planning. Zoning enabling acts typically call for the creation of a zoning commission to carefully study land uses in the city and, after adequate public involvement and comment, to propose a zoning ordinance with a corresponding zoning map. When the local city commission or council adopts the ordinance, with or without amendment, it becomes legally binding in the community. The zoning commission's existence usually ends at that stage. Ongoing administration of the zoning ordinance is usually the responsibility of a number of individuals and government bodies—city planners and administrators, planning commissions, boards of adjustment, and the city commission or council.

Master Plans

State law requires that zoning be a part of a **comprehensive** or **master city plan** and that any zoning be consistent with the master plan. A planning commission, a citizen board usually appointed by the city council or commission, is established to oversee a community's land-use planning process. Planning commissions work with city planners and others in city government in the initial creation and ongoing review and modification of the master plan.

In developing a city's master plan, the planning commission studies existing conditions and future economic and social trends in the community and establishes objectives for the city in terms of residential development, economic development, and community services. It also develops a set of general rules, principles, and guidelines for the future development of the city to meet the objectives it has established. These standards then become part of the "rules of the game" for citizens, businesses, and developers. The city plan also lays out the general allocation of streets, parks, schools and public buildings, utilities and other public services and systems. The ultimate purpose of the planning process is to chart the future direction of the community and to give notice to the citizenry of its plans.

District Restrictions

Euclidean zoning involves the division of a community into different land-use areas. A typical zoning pattern divides the city into three zones: residential, commercial, and industrial. Residential zones are limited to dwelling units and other incidental permissible uses, such as schools and parks. Commercial zones include retail businesses, offices, service businesses, and other designated commercial activities. Industrial zones are generally designated for plants, factories, and similar operations that create the most noise, traffic, pollution, and other undesirable side effects. Cities may have other primary zones such as agricultural and conservation preservation districts.

Each zone may be subject to further subdivisions. So, for example, a city may limit one residential zone to single-family dwelling units, a second to duplexes, and a third to multifamily dwelling units. The city of Austin, Texas, has 16 residential districts that differ with respect to lot size, population density, terrain, and environmental conditions. They range from rural residential zones to large-lot, single-family districts to high-density multifamily residence areas. Similarly, a city may have a number of commercial and industrial zones. For example, Albuquerque, New Mexico, has three commercial zones: (1) a neighborhood commercial zone for commercial businesses to satisfy the day-to-day needs of residential areas, (2) a community commercial zone for offices, service businesses, and general commercial businesses, and (3) a heavy commercial zone for wholesalers and some light industrial uses. Industrial areas are often divided into light and heavy industry zones. Light industries often include bakeries, bottling plants, laundries, and printing companies. Heavy industries include factories, fabricating facilities, and assembling operations. Examples are cotton gins, fish and poultry processing, chemical manufacturing, packing houses, railroad repair shops, and metal working.

Under a traditional zoning framework, each zone has a set of **permitted uses**. In addition, a zone may have a list of **conditional or special uses**, activities that are permitted only after review by an appropriate administrative entity (the planning commission or board of adjustment) and subject to specific limitations or conditions imposed by that body. In Anaheim, California, an individual can secure a conditional use permit in a single-family residential area for a lodging house, day care center, church, golf course, or a private club.

Activities not specifically or conditionally permitted are generally prohibited. In terms of prohibited uses, zoning can be cumulative or noncumulative. Traditional zoning was *cumulative*, that is, although industrial and commercial uses were prohibited in residential zones, residential uses were not prohibited in such "lower use" zones. Today, many zoning laws prohibit residential uses in industrial zones and thus are *noncumulative*. Under a noncumulative zoning system, only those activities designated for an area are permitted in that zone.

In addition to residential, commercial, and industrial zones, zoning ordinances may provide for zones of other types. A **floating zone** is a district created in the text of the zoning ordinance but not located on the original zoning map. Floating zones allow a city to create an area for a special type of use at a later time when the development is actually proposed. For example, floating zones have been used to accommodate mixed-use developments, such as planned unit developments (PUDs), described in a later section of the chapter. An **overlay zone** is a district where restrictions apply in addition to the use limitations imposed in that area. An overlay zone may span residential, commercial, and industrial districts. Examples include flood plain districts, airport protection zones, historic preservation districts, and coastal protection zones. Thus, a house in a single-family residential district may also be part of a historic preservation overlay district, with the restrictions of both districts applying to the property.

Lot and Building Restrictions

Within a given zone, zoning ordinances impose additional site development regulations, for example, minimum lot sizes, minimum floor areas, maximum dwelling units per lot, maximum

Box 17–1 You Be the Judge

Like many cities, Sullivans Island, South Carolina, permits a "home occupation" in a residential district of the town. The zoning law defines a "home occupation use" as follows:

Any use conducted entirely within a dwelling and carried on by the occupants thereof, which use is clearly incidental and secondary to the use of the dwelling for residential purposes and does not change the character thereof, and no person, not a resident of the premises is employed specially in connection with the activity. . . .

When a fire damaged the home of James and Juanita Byrum, they decided to renovate the house and use part of it as a bed and breakfast. The renovation included the construction of a separate apartment with a kitchen for the Byrums, five other bedrooms (each with a separate bathroom), and a second kitchen used to prepare food for the guests. The city contended that the business was not a home occupation use.

What would be an example of a home occupation use under the city's zoning code? Should Byrum's bed and breakfast be considered a home occupation use?

heights for buildings, front, rear, and side yard requirements, and open space requirements. These regulations vary among zones.

Height restrictions are common and vary according to the particular zone, lot, or the bulk of the structure. Single-family residential zones frequently limit the height of any dwelling to 35 feet or 2½ stories. Ordinarily, multifamily dwelling units, and buildings in commercial and industrial zones, may be taller than buildings in single-family residential areas.

Height limits often are coupled with area limitations. For example, buildings may be subject to set-back requirements. That is, a building may have to be a certain distance from the front property line and may be subject also to side and rear yard set-backs. Such requirements often dictate the placement of a dwelling or structure on the lot and may limit its area. To require owners to keep some open space on their properties, ordinances may specify that buildings may not exceed a specific percentage of the lot area (e.g., 50%). Area limits will of course vary with the type of zone in question. Minimum lot and building sizes are common in suburban areas. As noted later in the section of exclusionary zoning, however, some of these regulations have been challenged because of their effect on low- and moderate-income housing.

● Nonconforming Uses and Structures

A **nonconforming use** is a use now prohibited by a zoning ordinance but that was lawful when commenced by the landowner. To protect the landowner's investment in the property, such pre-existing uses of property are allowed to continue despite the creation of the zoning ordinance and map. So, for example, one often finds a corner grocery store or gas station in a residential area. Similarly, zoning laws allow **nonconforming structures** (e.g., a building that does not meet present set-back requirements), but that did meet those in effect when the structure was built.

Box 17–2 You Be the Judge

Chuck Warren has a home in an SR-2 (single-family residence) zone of the city of Fargo, North Dakota. His detached garage is a nonconforming structure. The north side is one foot from the side lot line for a distance of 22 feet. The Fargo zoning law requires a five-foot interior side set-back for buildings in SR-2 districts. Warren decides to build an addition to the garage that would extend the north side of the garage another 18 feet parallel to the property line. Because the addition would be one foot from the side lot line, his neighbor, Michelle Johnson, objects to the issuance of the building permit. Johnson claims that the addition is an unlawful expansion of a nonconforming structure in violation of the city zoning laws. Section 10-1004 of the Fargo Land Development Code provides as follows:

> Any expansion of a nonconforming structure that increases the degree of nonconformity is prohibited. Other expansions of the structure shall be permitted if in compliance with land development code standards.

The city concludes that the expansion does not increase the degree of nonconformity because the addition will be no closer to the property line than the existing building. Johnson contends that the degree of nonconformity will increase because the building will encroach further into the five-foot set-back area. She also argues that the second sentence of Section 10-1004 requires any expansion to comply with all existing land development code standards, including the set-back requirements.

How would you interpret this section of the land development code? Why?

Although nonconforming uses and nonconforming structures are lawful, most communities impose limitations and restrictions on them. Zoning ordinances typically prohibit the enlargement of the nonconforming use, additions to nonconforming structures, changes in the nonconforming use (e.g., commercial to industrial), or relocation of nonconforming buildings. Maintenance and repair usually are permitted, although ordinances will often impose limits on the amount that can be spent on alterations (e.g., no greater than 25% of the appraised value of the property). In addition, if a nonconforming building is destroyed, some zoning ordinances prohibit or restrict the reconstruction of the building.

Zoning ordinances also provide for the abatement (discontinuance) of a nonconforming use under certain circumstances. If a landowner Larry discontinues a nonconforming use for a specified period (e.g., 12–24 months), he cannot resume that use. Some cities have adopted amortization periods for nonconforming uses after which the nonconforming uses must terminate. The idea is to provide a useful life for the nonconforming use, a period of time sufficient for landowner Larry to recapture his investment. For example, the City of Newport Beach has set the maximum period for nonconforming structures at five years in residential districts and ten years in nonresidential zones. Like other cities, Newport Beach also sets a short period (one year) for any nonconforming use to be discontinued on land where no structure is involved.

● Variances

A **variance** is permission from the local authorities to deviate from the zoning ordinances because of special circumstances. Zoning establishes uniform rules within an existing district and such equal treatment is generally fair to all landowners within a particular zone. However, strict application of zoning regulations may impose an unfair burden on a particular landowner. For example, a particular tract of land may have an irregular shape or topographical conditions that make it difficult to comply with site development standards. In that instance, the landowner can seek relief from the zoning regulation through the variance process.

Variances are of two types: area and use. An **area variance** permits the use of land where the owner cannot comply with the dimension or physical requirements of the zoning code, such as restrictions relating to building size or height, coverage and open space, and set-back requirements. An area variance will not be granted to permit a use prohibited in a particular district, such as erecting a commercial building in a residential zone. To do so, a landowner must secure the second type of variance, a **use variance**. Some communities allow only area variances; use variances are not permitted under any circumstances.

To secure a variance, the landowner must establish **unnecessary hardship**. To prove unnecessary hardship for an area variance, the landowner ordinarily must prove the following:

- Unusual or special conditions exist on the property that are not common to most of the properties in the area.

- A hardship exists because of the conditions on the property and not because of any act on the part of the landowner.

- A variance is necessary to provide the landowner with the same property rights enjoyed by others in the district.

- Granting the variance will not create a substantial burden on adjacent properties nor alter the essential character of the area.

The requirements for a use variance are generally more demanding because granting a change of use violates the uniformity characteristic of zoning and conflicts with the judgment of the legislative body that the proposed use is not appropriate to the particular district. Not only

BOX 17–3 ZONING AND VESTED RIGHTS

Zoning laws may be enacted or amended after an individual purchases property but before a nonconforming use of the property has commenced. Under what circumstances does the owner have a legal right to continue with plans for the property despite a restrictive change in the zoning laws? Consider the following:

1. The Maryland Jockey Club was the owner of Pimlico Race Track in Baltimore, Maryland, home to the Preakness, one of the legs in the Triple Crown of horse racing. It purchased land adjacent to the track intending to use it for horse stables as permitted under the zoning laws at the time of purchase. After the purchase, a zoning ordinance passed designating the land residential.

2. Land Recovery, Inc. applied for a conditional use permit to construct a solid waste landfill site in Pierce County, Washington. The permit was opposed by a neighboring landowner and the case dragged on in the courts. Several years later, the county insisted that Land Recovery secure a wetlands permit under regulations that went into effect three years after Land Recovery's initial request for a conditional use permit.

3. A developer purchased land (known as Nukolii) on the island of Kauai, Hawaii, to build a resort. The developer secured a rezoning of the land, changing the designation from "open/agriculture" to "resort." When the developer started building the resort, nearby residents referred the rezoning ordinance to the voters, and at the election, the ordinance was repealed. In the meantime, however, the developer had finished 150 condominium units and had begun construction on a hotel, all at an estimated cost of $3 million.

In all of these cases, the owners claimed a right to continue with their plans for the property that were made in reliance on existing zoning regulations. At some stage in the development process, the courts will allow development to continue despite a restrictive change in the zoning laws under the doctrine of "vested rights." An owner's rights will "vest" when the owner has relied on the existing zoning provisions to such an extent that subjecting the owner to new regulations would be unfair. For example, a business that has finished construction of a factory in an industrial zone would be able to start operations even if the zoning laws were changed (e.g., designating the land residential) before operations commenced.

Merely purchasing property relying on the existing zoning classification, however, will not be sufficient to give the owner vested rights. Thus, Pimlico Race Track did not have a vested right to use the land for horse stables. Applying for a building permit is ordinarily not enough either. Most courts would have required Land Recovery to obtain the wetlands permit even though the law was enacted three years after it had applied for a conditional use permit. Fortunately for Land Recovery, Washington follows a minority view that "vested rights" exist when an appropriate application has been filed, and a Washington Court of Appeals held that it was entitled to be governed by the laws in effect when the application was filed.

Preparatory activities, such as clearing land, hiring an architect, or having a feasibility study done on a project, also will not be sufficient. Ordinarily, a developer will have vested rights only when a valid building permit is secured and substantial construction has occurred. However, in the Nukolii case, the Supreme Court of Hawaii held that the resort developer's rights did not vest since final approval for the development had not be given, the court viewing the referendum election as an essential step in the development approval

BOX 17–3 ZONING AND VESTED RIGHTS (CONTINUED)

process. The developer was allowed to complete the project only after a second election, conducted at the developer's expense, in which the voters reversed their prior decision and approved the rezoning of the land.

The cases suggest that landowners and developers cannot simply rely on existing zoning laws. Land-use restrictions may change before a project is completed, and developers may have to comply with the new standards. Thus, it is important for them to understand the existing zoning requirements, and to anticipate changes in the laws that might affect their business plans. Although developers whose rights have vested will be allowed to proceed with their projects, and be governed by the zoning rules in place when their rights vested, it is not always clear whether rights have vested at any given stage in the development process. Therefore, it is important for developers to have contingency plans and to reassess the viability of their original plans should the zoning environment change.

must the landowner Larry prove that special conditions create a hardship, but he must prove that he cannot realize a reasonable return on the property as zoned. It is not enough for Larry to prove that he can make more money if the use variance is granted. He must show that a reasonable return cannot be obtained from any permissible use of the property.

The procedure for securing a variance varies from locality to locality. Usually the landowner must make a variance application to an administrative official (e.g., a hearing officer), the board of zoning appeals, or the planning commission. After review of the circumstances, a decision on the variance request will be made by the appropriate body or official. As the following case illustrates, if the request is rejected, the landowner ordinarily has a right to appeal the decision, either to the city commission or to a court of law.

Case 17.2

Downtown Neighborhoods Assoc. v. City of Albuquerque
783 P.2d 962 (N.M. App.1989)

In 1985, Whitehouse Partnership purchased the J.A. Garcia house, a 90-year-old, two-story home on a main arterial street near downtown Albuquerque. Experts consider the house, which is listed on both the State Register of Cultural Properties and the National Register of Historic Places, one of the best examples of Classical Revival architecture in Albuquerque.

When Whitehouse purchased the property, the partners believed they were entitled to use the entire first floor of the house for law offices. However, the existing zoning limited incidental nonresidential use to 10% of the gross floor space of the premises. After being cited by the City for nonresidential use in excess of the permitted 10%, Whitehouse sought a variance from the City Zoning Hearing Examiner. The Examiner determined that the variance should be denied because Whitehouse failed to make an adequate showing of practical difficulty and unnecessary hardship. Whitehouse appealed the decision to the Environmental Planning Commission, which reversed the Examiner's decision and found that the parcel was exceptional and that compliance with the existing zoning would cause practical difficulty and unnecessary hardship.

The Downtown Neighborhoods Association, a group opposed to the variance, appealed the decision to the City Council. The City Council affirmed the Commission's decision to grant the variance. The council majority concluded that the house had historical significance which distinguished it from other nearby property subject to the same regulations, and subjecting the Garcia house to those regulations created unnecessary hardship. On appeal, the district court held that the house was historically significant but its historical significance did not make the house "exceptional" as required for a variance. Whitehouse appealed.

MINZNER, J.

The City Council's findings suggest that those who voted [in favor of the variance] believed that if a house has historical significance, then its owner has shown both the special conditions and the unnecessary hardship required by the statute. However, that interpretation is inconsistent with the concept of a variance and the terms of [variance law].

The purpose of a variance is to prevent zoning regulation from operating to deprive a property owner of all beneficial use of his property. To impose restrictions that unduly interfere with the right is confiscatory, and may amount to a taking. On the other hand, variances should be granted sparingly, only under exceptional circumstances. To do otherwise would encourage destruction of planned zoning.

The ultimate question to be answered is whether the applicant has shown "unnecessary hardship." In answering that question, the body considering the variance must resolve several factual questions. The first question is whether the parcel is distinguishable from other property that is subject to the same zoning restrictions. The answer depends upon whether, as a result of the differences between this parcel and others, the zoning restrictions create particular hardship for the owner. The test is whether, because of the differences, the owner will be deprived of a reasonable return on his or her property under any use permitted by the existing zoning classification. . . . If the body determines that the applicant has shown exceptional circumstances, then it must consider whether the particular variance requested is appropriate. . . . The test is whether the hardship identified can be avoided consistently with the public interest. . . .

It seems clear that designation of a house as historically significant does not in and of itself answer the ultimate question of unnecessary hardship. Our research has not disclosed any cases holding an owner's desire to preserve the historical significance of a structure was sufficient to support a variance on the ground of unnecessary hardship.

"Unnecessary hardship" has been given special meaning by courts considering a zoning authority's power to grant a variance. It ordinarily refers to circumstances in which no reasonable use can otherwise be made of the land. The exact showing necessary to prove unnecessary hardship varies from case to case. The City Council must make the initial determination by considering all of the relevant circumstances. However . . . a showing that the owner might receive a greater profit if the variance is granted is not sufficient justification in itself for a variance.

The findings by the City Council fail to resolve the question of whether this parcel is distinguishable from other parcels subject to the same requirements, whether the differences create particular hardship for Whitehouse, and whether the requested variance is necessary to prevent undue hardship.

We hold that the City Council erred in [approving the variance]. On this basis, we affirm the district court decision reversing and remanding the case to the City Council.

QUESTIONS ABOUT CASE 17.2

1. What evidence would the Whitehouse Partnership have to present to prove "unnecessary hardship"?

2. In light of the court's decision, should the city amend its zoning laws to make it easier to secure a variance to preserve historically significant buildings? If the city changed its laws, what variance standard should it adopt?

Subdivision Control

As urban areas expanded, developers moved to the outskirts of cities to establish new neighborhoods. A developer creates a **subdivision** by dividing a large tract of undeveloped land into smaller, separate parcels for residential dwellings. "Subdivision control" is the regulation of the subdivision process. The original purpose of subdivision controls was to ensure that the developer provided necessary services and infrastructure—streets, water, sewer, and drainage systems—before selling the lots to builders and owners. Today, such controls serve additional purposes, including controlling growth and providing amenities for the community.

The Subdivision Process

States have enacted subdivision enabling laws empowering cities and counties to regulate the subdivision of land within their jurisdictions. A subdivision is defined as the division of land into separate parcels for sale or for construction purposes. Exceptions may exist for a small number of parcels (often five or fewer lots), and subdivision controls generally do not govern the division of an apartment into separate units or a shopping center into separate leased premises even though separate legal interests are thereby created.

Local governments maintain control by requiring that any subdivision proposal be submitted for approval before development. State law usually prohibits the sale of any subdivided lot prior to subdivision approval and recording of a subdivision map. State law also provides remedies for the city and purchaser in the event of such an unlawful sale. The approval process requires the developer to submit a detailed plan for the subdivision and a map showing the location of lots, roads, utilities, and other services. The plan is submitted to the responsible local authority, often the municipal or county planning commission, and it is reviewed to determine whether it makes adequate provision for public infrastructure and services. If not, the developer may have to revise the plan. A public hearing also is required to provide an opportunity for public comment and protests. If all issues of public concern are resolved, the local authority will give preliminary approval for the plan and the subdivision map. Once the subdivision is developed, the authority will give final approval to the subdivision map, which is then filed in the register of deeds or local recording office, and sales of parcels can then be made.

Subdivision Exactions

Exactions are costs imposed on a developer as a condition to receiving approval of a subdivision. State law may permit a city to require the developer to dedicate land for parks and other recreational facilities, schools, libraries, and other public buildings; pay fees for city services; and set aside land as open space or for flood control. For example, the Minnesota Subdivision Act provides:

> *The regulations may require that a reasonable portion of any proposed subdivision be dedicated to the public or preserved for public use as streets, roads, sewers, electric, gas, and water facilities, storm water drainage and holding areas or ponds and similar utilities and improvements. In addition, the regulations may require that a reasonable portion of any proposed subdivision be dedicated to the public or preserved for conservation purposes or for public use as parks, recreational facilities . . . playgrounds, trails, wetlands, or open space. . . .*

The continuing legal issue is to what extent such exactions are lawful. Usually state law requires that subdivision exactions be "reasonable." The reasonableness requirement is necessary to prevent cities from exacting fees and other dedications of property that exceed the public costs created by a subdivision. Obviously, a new subdivision imposes burdens on a city by increasing the need for city services and facilities, including its schools, parks, and other government services. The developer should bear some of the costs attributable to the development. However, a city might try to avoid taxing its citizens for necessary public services by shifting the burden to developers. In determining whether an exaction is reasonable, most courts require that the city demonstrate a reasonable relationship between the exaction and the burden imposed on the city by the development. For example, a city was allowed to impose an exaction in the form of a dedicated right-of-way for a new highway interchange on a developer building a large shopping mall. The mall would cause increased traffic and the interchange was reasonably necessary to accommodate the burden caused by the new development.

As noted in the prior chapter, excessive subdivision exactions can be challenged as an unconstitutional taking of property. The present constitutional mandate is twofold. First, the community must establish a connection between the exaction and legitimate regulatory objectives. Second, the community must establish "rough proportionality" between the amount of the exaction and the public costs associated with the development. This standard is similar to the reasonableness requirement. However, the Supreme Court's application of the test is more demanding because it requires a city to have evidence or data to justify any exactions it imposes. In the case of *Dolan v. City of Tigard*, the City of Tigard required Dolan to dedicate a portion of her property for flood control and for a pedestrian/bicycle pathway as a condition for the approval of a building permit to expand Dolan's store.[1] The Court held that the community had passed the first part of the constitutional test, establishing a connection between the exaction and the legitimate public concerns. The expanded building would increase the amount of impervious surface, which would increase the flow of water to a nearby stream and add to the flooding potential. The larger store also would attract more customers and increase traffic, which might be alleviated somewhat by a bicycle/pedestrian path. But the Court was not convinced that the city had established by quantifiable evidence that the public dedication of property was necessary for flood control (leaving the land undeveloped but still owned by Dolan would suffice) or that the pathway would in fact offset the traffic demand.

To avoid litigation and disputes over subdivision exactions, many communities have increasingly used **development agreements**. Development agreements are contracts between the city and the developer setting forth the conditions for the city's approval of the subdivision plan. These agreements will specify the exactions and other dedications necessary for subdivision

BOX 17–4 GROWTH CONTROL LAWS

Traditional subdivision controls were designed to ensure that developers provided the necessary infrastructure for new developments. Recently, cities and states have become increasingly concerned with the negative effects of unrestrained growth—traffic and congestion, pollution, the increased stress on city services from subdivisions on the rural fringe of cities, the destruction of environmentally sensitive areas, and the loss of prime farmland and open space. In an attempt to address the problems caused by urban sprawl, cities and states have passed growth control laws. These growth management laws are an attempt to better plan for the future growth of cities as well as to slow that growth to manageable levels.

Several states in the Northwest have been at the forefront of the growth management movement. Oregon's growth control law—the Land Conservation and Development Act—has been in existence for more than 25 years. Passed in 1973, it preserves agricultural land and helps to protect the environment by confining urban centers to growth boundaries. Oregon utilizes one of the most effective techniques for controlling growth, **urban growth boundaries (UGBs)**. A UGB is a ring around a city dividing the urban land to be developed (inside the UGB) from the land to be left in an undeveloped state (outside of the UGB). Development outside the UGB is discouraged or prohibited through zoning classifications (e.g., agriculture or conservation zones) and other disincentives. Incentives may exist for development within the UGB, such as relaxation of zoning rules relating to housing density.

Washington has a growth control strategy similar to Oregon's approach under its Growth Management Act. It requires cities to have comprehensive plans projecting the rate of future growth that can be reasonably accommodated and establishing "urban growth areas" to restrain that growth. Stringent growth control measures have also been adopted in California. One of the earliest growth control measures was established in Petaluma, a suburb of San Francisco, in 1972. The "Petaluma Plan" limited housing growth to 500 dwelling units per year for a period of five years. It also established a "greenbelt" around the city, which served as a UGB. The constitutionality of the "Petaluma Plan" was challenged in federal court, but the law was upheld on appeal by the Ninth Circuit Court of Appeals. A more recent development in California is the use of the initiative process to adopt growth control measures. Land-use ballot initiatives have passed in a number of California communities, including a county-wide initiative in Ventura County. These growth control measures generally impose UGBs, and some require voter approval for new residential and commercial developments.

Recently, a number of states have adopted so-called "smart growth" plans. These smart growth plans not only rely on comprehensive planning to control growth, but also incorporate marketplace principles in the growth management process. Maryland, for example, has a comprehensive system of government incentives designed to direct state funding for economic and housing development to designated Smart Growth Areas of the state. Other incentives in Maryland include tax credits for businesses creating jobs in targeted areas, cash contributions for workers purchasing homes in older neighborhoods, and state monies directed to land preservation.

Public interest in growth management strategies appears to be increasing, and more and more states and cities are initiating some form of growth control. Because local and state growth control laws limit the development of land within a community, developers and landowners need to be aware of the requirements of these laws. For developers, growth control laws represent a significant business risk in many communities. On the other hand, they may present an opportunity in other localities, particularly in states and communities opting to provide incentives under the smart growth approach.

approval and bind the developer to those terms. The agreement also binds the city, assuring the developer that additional conditions will not be imposed between the preliminary approval and completion of the project.

Modern Land-Use Controls

Zoning controls have evolved over time to meet the changing economic and social conditions of society. The scope of zoning has expanded beyond the regulation of uses and the intensity of property development. Cities now regulate for other reasons, such as aesthetics, that were once thought not to be legitimate bases to regulate property. Billboard regulations and historic preservation ordinances are some examples. Cities also have moved beyond simply planning for the growth of communities through zoning and subdivision control. Today, many communities are trying to prevent and control growth as a way of preserving the values of a community.

Euclidean zoning also has changed in response to criticism from economists, planners, citizens, and businesses that it is too rigid and lacks flexibility. For example, a land developer faced with developing a residential district with minimum lot sizes and minimum dwelling sizes, as well as other building site regulations, has little or no freedom to deviate from a predictable pattern of laying out the property lots. Also, to maximize profits, the developer will leave as little of the land as possible in an undeveloped state. Unless the municipality provides incentives for open space, a developer sees little economic reason not to develop all of the property, including environmentally sensitive property. A related problem is the inability to mix uses within a district, which further limits the creativity and freedom of the developer. Under the presumption underlying zoning that different types of uses cannot coexist in the same zone, multifamily dwelling units are not permitted in single-family residential zones and commercial and industrial uses are not allowed in residential areas. Critics argue, however, that the purposes of zoning—protecting the community through the separation of uses and effectively planning for the development of an attractive community—have not been achieved in many communities. The result of traditional controls can be seen in many of the suburbs where residential and commercial development has been designed in a homogeneous fashion, communities where the subdivision layout and houses look much the same and development has proceeded in a "checkerboard" fashion. In response to some of the negatives of traditional zoning, communities have developed a number of techniques to make zoning less rigid and to provide greater flexibility in developing property. These techniques include cluster zoning, PUDs, and mixed-use developments, transfer of development rights, and performance zoning.

Cluster Zoning

Cluster zoning permits residential developments to deviate from site development standards, such as lot and building size, as long as a part of the development (e.g., 50% of the land) is left undeveloped as open space. This permits housing to be clustered together more closely than otherwise permitted to preserve the remaining land in an open state. It is sometimes referred to as **open space zoning**. The benefits of open space zoning are that it preserves undeveloped land for community use; protects the environment by preserving wetlands, wooded areas, and other ecologically sensitive land; and permits greater freedom to the developer in terms of the overall design and layout of the housing. It also may create a more attractive, desirable neighborhood for homeowners.

Cluster development is generally not required in most communities. A developer who may not be penalized for creating such a development generally finds no economic incentive to design one. As a result, some communities, particularly in the New England and Mid-Atlantic States, have now adopted mandatory open space zoning. Under such zoning schemes, the developer is still allowed to build the same number of units as in a traditional subdivision, but is required to leave a part of the land open. Rather than require open space zoning, other communities have attempted to encourage cluster zoning by providing financial incentives to developers to create open space subdivisions.

Mixed-Use Developments and Planned Unit Developments

Cluster development is generally limited to residential housing. Mixed-use developments also are permitted in many communities, the most common of which is the **planned unit development**, or **PUD**. PUDs are developments that mix different types of uses (residential and commercial) into one planned community. Thus, a neighborhood of single-family and multi-family dwellings may be served by adjacent shops, stores, and offices in one integrated development. PUDs require special approval from the zoning authority. A detailed site plan is usually required to be submitted to the planning commission. Notice to the public of the proposal and a public hearing on the proposal also are required. Frequently, limits are imposed on PUDs. The development must have a minimum size to accommodate the mixed uses, often 10–20 acres, and cities often require a certain amount of open space to enhance the attractiveness of the PUD. The PUD regulations may impose density limits on the number of dwelling units and often the commercial proportion of the PUD will be limited to 20% to 30% of the development. In addition to PUDs, communities may have regulations authorizing other types of mixed-use developments, including planned commercial and industrial developments. Some cities also have planned residential developments, where single-family and multifamily dwelling units are mixed in one development but no commercial or industrial uses are permitted.

Transfer of Development Rights

A **transfer of development rights (TDR)** program is a market-based system designed to preserve land in some areas of a community (e.g., farmland) by providing the property owners with a financial incentive not to develop the property. The mechanism for the land preservation is the creation of transferable development rights. The owners in the protected area (called the *sending zone*) agree to permanently restrict the development of their property and, in exchange for their promise to restrict development, are given development rights, which they can transfer (sell) to a developer or landowner in a TDR receiving zone, an area the community wants developed or that can accommodate intensive development because of its existing infrastructure. Developers in the receiving zone who receive TDRs from owners in the sending zone are allowed to build in the receiving zone at a higher density than permitted under the zoning provisions. The density bonus creates a market for the transferable development rights. If the program is successful, the community achieves its conservation objectives without spending tax dollars to purchase property in the preservation area and without having to impose overly burdensome land-use restrictions on the property owners in that zone. At the same time, the landowners in the protected area are compensated for agreeing to the permanent development restrictions, and developers in the receiving areas profit from the density bonus.

Currently, more than 20 states have enacted or amended their laws to allow TDR programs, and more than 100 cities, counties, and other local political subdivisions have TDR programs in place. Communities have most often adopted TDR programs to preserve farmland, open space, and environmentally sensitive property. However, cities also have employed TDR programs in urban areas as part of historic preservation and affordable housing initiatives. One of the first and most successful TDR programs was established in Montgomery County, Maryland. In the 1970s, the county became concerned about urban sprawl from Bethesda, Silver Springs, and other suburbs of Washington, D.C., in the southern part of the county. It adopted a TDR program in 1980 in an attempt to preserve farmland and the rural character of the northern part of the county. The TDR program created a 91,000-acre agricultural reserve area, changing the zoning density in the preservation zone from one unit per five acres to one unit per 25 acres. Property owners in the zone who agreed to permanently deed restrict their land were given one transferable development right per five acres. The County also designated receiving zones in the county that could accommodate development. Each development right entitled the developer to build one additional unit in the receiving area than would otherwise have been allowed under the zoning law. This density bonus, along with strong demand for housing in the Washington area, led to a healthy market for the development rights. As a result, the program preserved 29,000 acres of farmland to date.

Performance Zoning

Like cluster zoning and PUDs, performance zoning is designed to provide greater flexibility than under Euclidean zoning. In contrast to the traditional districting approach, performance zoning bases land-use restrictions on performance standards. Originally communities adopted performance standards for industrial uses in the community. These standards set limits on smoke, noise, odors, and waste based on specific objective measurements. Many communities continue to use such industrial performance standards as part of their overall zoning scheme. More recently, some communities have adopted comprehensive systems of performance standards for all types of uses, partially or totally replacing zoning use districts. Performance zoning has been adopted in Bucks County, Pennsylvania; Lake County, Illinois; and Fort Collins, Colorado.

Consider how performance zoning operates in a new residential subdivision. Rather than have a residential district based on specific use (e.g., single-family dwellings only) and minimum building/lot sizes, zoning is based on standards that directly measure the intensity of use and the capacity of the land to accommodate the development. An open space standard sets the amount of a site that must remain undeveloped, excluding private lots and roadways. An impervious surface standard limits the proportion of an area covered by impervious surfaces—buildings, streets, sidewalks, patios, and other paved areas. A density standard complements the other performance standards by specifying the number of dwelling units per acre. By using these performance standards, and not otherwise restricting the development, developers are given broad latitude to design subdivisions as they see fit. Rather than a homogenous set of lots, diversity of housing type and design occurs. By preserving open space, the environment is protected and the community may be more attractive to homeowners. Finally, traditional zoning concerns are addressed, not indirectly as with traditional districting, but directly by imposing performance standards.

Historic Preservation

Many cities have adopted historic preservation ordinances in addition to their zoning laws. Historic preservation ordinances impose controls on the alteration, repair, maintenance, and rehabilitation of buildings in historic districts. The purpose of a historic preservation ordinance is to preserve the cultural and architectural heritage of a community for social, educational, aesthetic, and economic reasons.

Historic preservation ordinances establish a historic preservation commission appointed by the local government to administer the law. The commission identifies areas of the community to be included in the historic preservation district and reviews development proposals affecting buildings in the historic district. A landowner who wants to alter, repair, demolish, or change the character of a building must secure permission from the commission, under what is referred to as a Certificate of Appropriateness. The commission reviews the request in light of accepted design guidelines and either denies or approves the request. As compensation for the costs and burdens associated with the property being part of the historic district, states give landowners some form of tax relief (e.g., a tax exemption). Seattle, San Francisco, and other cities also have used transferable development rights to facilitate historic preservation.

Limitations on Land-Use Restrictions

Zoning decisions come to court with a strong presumption of validity. Courts are reluctant to set aside zoning decisions, especially where the decision or an interpretation of the zoning law is subject to reasonable differences of opinion. A decision that is "fairly debatable" is unlikely to be set aside by a court. Nevertheless, courts will set aside zoning decisions that are unconstitutional (e.g., those that result in a taking of property), are outside of the power of the zoning body (e.g., those granting a use variance when only area variances are permitted by law), or are arbitrary, unreasonable, or without any factual basis.

Spot Zoning

Generally a municipality has the power to change the zoning classification and amend the zoning ordinance and map. However, if the reclassification is solely for the benefit of one landowner, and not justified on the basis of changed circumstances, the courts may find that it constitutes illegal rezoning, known as **spot zoning**. Spot zoning is not permitted because it undermines the uniformity essential for comprehensive zoning and is not based on the needs of the community as a whole.

    To determine whether a change in zoning classification constitutes spot zoning, the courts look at a number of factors to analyze the reasonableness of the rezoning in light of the existing area and the public interest. The courts consider the uses of adjacent properties, the effects of the zoning change on the landowner and the neighborhood, the consistency of the change with the master plan, and changes in the area since the original zoning classification. For example, the Iowa Supreme Court found spot zoning when a county zoning commission approved a zoning change for 223 acres of farmland in an agricultural district to allow a shooting club to build uninhabited structures for recreational use. Under the comprehensive plan, the land was in an agricultural protection zone (A-1), the purpose of which was to "protect agricultural land from encroachment of urban development." The shooting club wanted it changed to A-2, a "holding zone" until urban development proposals were approved, that permitted a number of nonagricultural uses. Noting that half of the land was "prime" agricultural land, with no basis for distinguishing it from surrounding properties, the court concluded that the change was solely for the benefit of the club members (not related to the general public interest) and constituted spot zoning.

Exclusionary Zoning

Zoning by its very nature is discriminatory and has exclusionary effects. By separating residential housing from commercial and industrial uses, commercial interests are discriminated against and business uses are excluded from certain areas of the community. Such discriminatory effects are justified by the benefits of the zoning system for the entire community. It is important to preserve residential neighborhoods as places that are safe, quiet, and free of the congestion and pollution that are a part of commercial and industrial activity.

BOX 17–5 YOU BE THE JUDGE

To what extent should economic development benefits from new businesses justify rezoning from residential to commercial?

A landowner in the village of Riverton, Illinois, requested a reclassification of his lots from residential (R-1) to commercial (C-1). He wanted to build a Casey's General Store on the site. Nearby neighbors objected to the rezoning. He argued that other nonresidential uses were present in the area, including a restaurant (a nonconforming use), school, church, and water plant. However, the neighborhood was primarily residential and no significant changes had recently occurred in the character or uses in the area. Casey's argued that the economic benefits of the proposed use, including additional jobs and taxes as well as increased competition, justified the zoning change.

The town of North Attelborough, Massachusetts, addressed a similar request from a developer who wanted to build a shopping mall and multiscreen movie complex on land zoned R-30 residential (single-family dwelling district). He wanted 37 acres changed to C-60 (limited highway commercial district) to build along a highway (Route 1). Under the town's zoning ordinances, a 600-foot commercial strip fronting both sides of the highway existed, but the developer needed to expand the width of the strip to accommodate the mall. Thus, adjacent properties along Route 1 were commercial, including several malls and a Walmart store, but they were located within the existing C-60 commercial strip. He argued that the development served the public interest by increasing the city's tax base, its retail services, and employment opportunities.

Should the cities change their zoning classifications to accommodate economic development? If challenged as spot zoning, to what extent should the court consider the economic development benefits of the zoning change?

At the same time, zoning can have discriminatory effects on racial and ethnic groups, the poor and those of low and moderate income, and the disabled and other "undesirable" groups. Minimum lot and building sizes, open space requirements, limitations on multi-unit dwellings, and other zoning restrictions can increase the cost of housing, minimize or eliminate the potential for low-income housing, and restrict access to housing in the community. Such regulations may also have intended or unintended discriminatory effects on minorities whose income levels are lower than that of the general population.

Exclusionary zoning is zoning that illegally excludes certain individuals or groups from living in a community. Various state and federal laws limit the exclusionary practices of cities and zoning officials and provide protection when zoning is motivated by discriminatory purposes or has exclusionary effects.

Racially Discriminatory Zoning

Zoning that discriminates on the basis of race or ethnicity may violate state and federal constitutional law. The Fourteenth Amendment to the U.S. Constitution guarantees due process and prohibits states from denying persons the "equal protection" of the law. Discriminatory zoning also may violate the Federal Fair Housing Act and comparable state fair housing laws. The federal act prohibits housing discrimination on the basis of race, gender, color, religion, or national origin, and the courts have held that the federal law does apply to local zoning decisions. Proving unlawful zoning discrimination may be difficult, however, under the rules established by the courts. A major case in this area is the U.S. Supreme Court's decision in *Village of Arlington Heights v. Metropolitan Housing Development Corporation.*[2] In that case, a developer of low- and moderate-income housing, the Metropolitan Housing Development Corporation (MHDC), wanted to construct 190 townhouses on a 15-acre tract in Arlington Heights, a suburb of Chicago that had few minorities (27 of 64,000 residents were black). Almost all of the community was zoned for detached single-family homes, and so MHDC sought a rezoning of the land for the townhouse development, a development that would have been racially integrated. The city's decision to deny the rezoning was challenged in court as a violation of the Fourteenth Amendment.

The Supreme Court conceded that the city's action would have a disproportionate impact on minorities who comprised 18% of the population and 40% of the income groups eligible for the townhouses. However, merely establishing a racially discriminatory impact was not enough to set aside the zoning decision; MHDC had to prove that the city had a racially discriminatory intent. The Court was not convinced that such intent was present because the city's decision was based on nondiscriminatory and legitimate zoning concerns relating to maintaining property values, and it was consistent with the city's comprehensive zoning plan for the community.

In contrast, a federal appeals court found a violation of the Fair Housing Act in *United States v. City of Black Jack.*[3] There, residents in a unincorporated area of St. Louis County attempted to prevent an integrated multifamily housing development in their neighborhood. They formed a new city, Black Jack, and then quickly passed a zoning ordinance prohibiting the construction of multifamily dwellings. Despite the claims of the city that its actions were motivated by legitimate safety and economic concerns, the court blocked the city's attempt, finding that it was racially motivated and a violation of federal law.

Zoning Excluding Low-Income Groups

Without a showing of racial or ethnic discrimination, zoning regulations that simply have a discriminatory effect on low-income groups do not generally violate the constitutional rights of the poor. However, some state courts and some state legislatures have imposed limits on zoning rules that have an exclusionary impact on low-income groups. In these states, communities must consider all of the housing needs in the community and shoulder a "fair share" of the low- and moderate-income family housing.

The leading case is the New Jersey Supreme Court's decision in *Southern Burlington County NAACP v. Township of Mount Laurel.*[4] Mount Laurel's zoning regulations curtailed low-income housing by allowing only single-family, detached dwellings and by requiring large minimum lot and building sizes. The New Jersey Supreme Court was concerned not only with the impact of the zoning on low-income groups—the young, elderly, large families of limited means—but also with the trend in American suburban communities throughout the state and nation to impose similar exclusionary rules. It concluded that a developing community like Mount Laurel cannot make it "physically and economically impossible" to provide low- and moderate-income housing. Moreover, every community was obligated to make available a variety of housing to the extent of the community's "fair share" of the region's present and future housing needs.

Mount Laurel's approach has been followed by only a few courts in other states. The highest court in New York has held that zoning ordinances must consider regional housing needs and cannot exclude affordable housing from the community. Also, both New Jersey and Connecticut have passed affordable housing laws. In New Jersey, a statewide regulatory agency, the Council on Affordable Housing, is empowered to determine communities' fair share of affordable housing and certify local fair share housing plans. In Connecticut, developers can sue if a municipality denies a permit for affordable housing, and if the municipality's share of affordable housing is less than 10%, the city must demonstrate that substantial public concerns justify the refusal to permit the construction of the affordable housing.

Cases like *Mount Laurel*, and concern over the lack of low- and moderate-income housing, have led many state legislatures and local communities to adopt **inclusionary zoning** laws. Inclusionary zoning refers to housing requirements or incentives designed to promote the development of low- and moderate-income housing. In some communities, inclusionary zoning is mandatory. Any new residential subdivision is required to have a certain percentage (e.g., 10%) of affordable units. In other cities, inclusionary zoning is voluntary; incentives are used to encourage the construction of affordable housing. One of the most common forms of development incentives are **density bonuses**. In exchange for the construction of a specified number of affordable housing units in a development, the developer is allowed to construct more units in the project (a higher density) than zoning law would otherwise allow. In this way, developers are compensated for the costs associated with building affordable housing.

Zoning and the Disabled

Two federal laws provide some protection for the mentally or physically handicapped when zoning rules discriminate against the disabled: the Fair Housing Act and the Americans with Disabilities Act. The Fair Housing Act prohibits discrimination in the sale or rental of a dwelling because of a handicap. It defines discrimination to include "a refusal to make reasonable accommodations in rules, policies, practices, or services, when such accommodations may be necessary to afford such person equal opportunity to use and enjoy a dwelling." The Americans with Disabilities Act (ADA) prohibits discrimination against those with disabilities including discrimination by a public entity. "No qualified individual with a disability shall, by reason of such disability, be excluded from participation or be denied the benefits of the services, programs, or activities of a public entity, or be subjected to discrimination by any such entity."

The Fair Housing Act's reasonable accommodation provision prohibits zoning laws from excluding people with disabilities from living in residential neighborhoods or giving them less opportunity to live there. For example, a federal circuit court held that a city's zoning laws prohibiting nursing homes in all of its residential districts, and restricting such homes to hospital support zones, was a violation of the Fair Housing Act. Thus, to comply with the reasonable accommodations part of the law, zoning boards may have to make exceptions to zoning rules to allow the disabled to live in residential areas. Just how far local zoning officials must go to accommodate the disabled is an open question, however, as the next case demonstrates.

Case 17.3

Bryant Woods Inn, Inc. v. Howard County
124 F.3d 597 (4th Cir. 1997)

Richard Colandrea, the owner and resident of an 11-bedroom house in Columbia, Maryland, rents portions of his house to eight elderly persons who suffer from Alzheimer's disease and other forms of dementia and disability. Colandrea, together with his mother, operates the licensed group home through a for-profit corporation, Bryant Woods Inn, Inc. Howard County zoning regulations allow any resident family to house up to eight handicapped or elderly persons in its principal residence, provided state approval is obtained. Group care facilities for more than eight persons are defined as nursing homes for which zoning approval is required. Seeking to expand the home to accommodate 15 residents, Colandrea filed an application with Howard County for an amendment to the neighborhood's Final Development Plan, to use his house as a "group care facility." He was unable to satisfy Howard County's traffic and parking requirements and therefore sought a waiver of the requirements on the ground that its residents would not need additional parking. Howard County denied the variance request. Bryant Woods Inn, contending that Howard County's refusal to change its zoning for the Colandrea property to accommodate an expansion from 8 to 15 residents violated the Fair Housing Act, sued the county. The trial court ruled in favor of the County.

NIEMEYER, Cir. J.

[W]e must recognize and resolve the tension between Howard County's right to control land uses through neutral regulation and its duty to make reasonable accommodations for the handicapped under the FHA.

Land use planning and the adoption of land use restrictions constitute some of the most important functions performed by local government. Local land use restrictions seek to prevent the problems arising from the proverbial "pig in the parlor instead of the barnyard," and to preserve "the character of neighborhoods, securing zones where family values, youth values, and the blessings of quiet seclusion and clean air make the area a sanctuary for people. . . . In Euclid, the Court upheld the constitutionality of local land use restrictions, observing that "apartment houses which in a different environment would be not only entirely unobjectionable but highly desirable, come very near to being nuisances" in residential neighborhoods of detached houses.

Seeking to recognize local authorities' ability to regulate land use and without unnecessarily undermining the benign purposes of such neutral regulations, Congress required only that local government make "reasonable accommodation" to afford persons with handicaps "equal opportunity to use and enjoy" housing in those communities. The FHA thus requires an accommodation for persons with handicaps if the accommodation is (1) reasonable and (2) necessary (3) to afford handicapped persons equal opportunity to use and enjoy housing. "Reasonable accommodations" do not require accommodations which impose "undue financial and administrative burdens," or "changes, adjustments, or modifications to existing programs that would be substantial, or that would constitute fundamental alterations in the nature of the program."

Bryant Woods Inn argues in this case that its requested zoning variance is reasonable because the expansion of its group home would not increase traffic congestion since its residents do not drive. Unrefuted testimony, however, was presented to the Howard County Planning Board by a member who observed vehicles parked "all over the place and also in the driveway" even under Bryant Woods Inn's current level of occupancy. The board also received unrefuted evidence that Bryant Woods Inn's wedge-shaped parcel affords minimal frontage and that the parcel is less than one-third of the size of other Howard county group homes which have 15 residents. Bryant Woods Inn has failed to establish in this case that its requested accommodation is reasonable.

The more serious inadequacy of Bryant Woods Inn's position, however, appears in connection with its effort to show that its zoning change is "necessary." Howard County's existing zoning regulations do not prohibit group housing for individuals with handicaps. Indeed, the regulations permit such group housing. Bryant Woods Inn houses eight handicapped persons, and some 30 other facilities in Howard County similarly do so.

The zoning variance that Bryant Woods Inn seeks is not aimed at permitting handicapped persons to live in group homes in residential communities—that, as we have noted, is already permitted—but at expanding its group home size from 8 to 15 persons. While "some minimum size may be essential to the success" of group homes, the Inn has introduced no evidence that group homes are not financially viable with eight residents. On the contrary, the record before the board shows that almost 30 such homes operate viably in Howard County with eight or fewer residents. Moreover, while it is uncontested that group homes are often therapeutically valuable in providing patients with a higher quality of life and thereby helping to avoid the functional decline which is frequently consequent to institutionalization in a traditional nursing home, Bryant Woods Inn has also presented no evidence in this case that expansion from 8 to 15 residents would be therapeutically meaningful. Thus, nothing in the record that we can find suggests that a group home of 15 residents, as opposed to one of 8, is necessary to accommodate individuals with handicaps.

For the foregoing reasons, we affirm the judgment of the district.

QUESTIONS ABOUT CASE 17.3

1. Would the court's opinion change if Howard County's zoning ordinances restricted group homes to four residents?

2. Why is it important for cities to allow group homes for the handicapped to be located in residential neighborhoods? Does the "reasonable accommodation" requirement of the Fair Housing Act strike an appropriate balance between the interests of cities in maintaining residential neighborhoods and the rights of the handicapped?

There is some question whether the ADA applies to zoning laws. The issue: Does zoning constitute a "program or service" of a public entity under the antidiscrimination rules of the ADA. Several federal courts have held that the ADA applies to local zoning rules, and therefore disabled persons can sue local zoning bodies under the ADA for depriving them of a program or service available to others. In the leading case, *Innovative Health Systems, Inc. v. City of White Plains*, the Second Circuit Court of Appeals held that the ADA was violated when the city refused to permit a drug and alcohol rehabilitation center based on "stereotypes and unsupported fears" of drug- and alcohol-addicted individuals, rather than legitimate safety concerns.[5]

Zoning and the First Amendment

Zoning that restricts freedom of speech, religion, or association can be challenged under the First Amendment. Two major areas of First Amendment law relating to zoning are the zoning of adult entertainment businesses and the regulation of billboards. The Supreme Court has set forth some guidelines for local governing bodies and zoning officials but lawsuits continually arise testing the limits to which regulations can go without running afoul of the Constitution.

Zoning Adult Entertainment

Adult entertainment—nude dancing, adult bookstores, and other businesses dealing in sexually explicit materials—is constitutionally protected as a form of free speech as long as it is not obscene.

Unable to ban such enterprises altogether, cities have adopted zoning laws in an attempt to control these "undesirable" businesses. Two types of zoning schemes have been developed. The first is typified by Boston's "Combat Zone" under which all adult entertainment businesses must operate in a particular zone. This cluster approach attempts to segregate the adult entertainment businesses in one area in order to minimize the detrimental impact to the community as a whole. A second approach adopted in Detroit and other cities is to disperse these businesses throughout the city to eliminate the problems associated with the concentration of adult entertainment in one area. Social problems attributable to the concentration of adult entertainment in one zone include declining property values, increasing levels of criminal activity, particularly prostitution, and flight of other commercial businesses from the area. Detroit's zoning scheme that scattered adult entertainment businesses by prohibiting adult theaters within 500 feet of a residential area and within 1,000 feet of another "regulated use" (adult theaters and other designated businesses) was approved by the Supreme Court in *Young v. American Mini Theaters*.[6] In contrast, the Court struck down a zoning scheme adopted by the Borough of Mount Emphram, New Jersey, that effectively prohibited any "live entertainment" in the community despite the claim that such entertainment was available in nearby communities.

In its most recent opinion, *Renton v. Playtime Theaters*, the Court set forth the requirements that must be met for an adult entertainment zoning scheme to be constitutional.[7] Renton, a small suburb of Seattle, prohibited adult theaters within 1,000 feet of a residential zone, single-family or multifamily dwelling, church, park, or school. The law effectively banned the establishments in any commercial area of the community, leaving only 520 acres in industrial areas for these businesses. Upholding the law, the Supreme Court stated that cities must establish a substantial public interest in regulating adult entertainment businesses and zoning controls must leave open an adequate number of locations for such businesses to operate. Renton's zoning law was based on the social problems attributable to adult entertainment businesses and left sufficient room in the community for such businesses to operate.

Zoning of Signs and Billboards

Billboards also represent a protected medium for free speech. Even when the message on the billboard is a commercial advertisement (rather than a political statement), it is protected by the First Amendment. The Supreme Court has held that so-called "commercial speech" is constitutionally protected although to a lesser extent than political or ideological speech. Therefore, government controls on billboards are subject to First Amendment limits. A city must justify billboard restrictions on the basis of legitimate government interests (e.g., traffic, safety, or aesthetics), and demonstrate how the law achieves these interests without unduly restricting free speech.

Restrictive Covenants and Deed Restrictions

Restrictive covenants can be used as a form of private land-use control. A **restrictive covenant** is a promise to do or not to do something on the land. The person making the promise is the **covenantor**, who makes the promise to the **covenantee**. Like an easement, a restrictive covenant limits the rights of one landowner (the covenantor) for the benefit of another. Albert has a 1,000-acre farm. He agrees to sells 10 acres to Ben as a homestead but does not want Ben to use the property for any commercial or industrial operation. Albert also wants to make sure that his access to a stream running through both properties is not impaired. So Albert insists on restrictive covenants in the deed of conveyance, under which Ben promises to use the 10 acres only for residential purposes and agrees not to dam or reroute the stream running through it.

Restrictive covenants are specifically enforceable in a court action. If Ben were to dam the stream or use the land for an automobile junkyard, Albert would be entitled to an injunction stopping Ben's violations of the covenants. The courts sometimes refuse to enforce restrictive covenants, but only when the restriction violates public policy or unduly limits the covenantor's (Ben's) rights. For example, the Supreme Court has held that racially restrictive covenants, such as promises not to sell land to third persons on the basis of their race, are unenforceable under the Equal Protection Clause of the Fourteenth Amendment. In most instances, however, restrictive covenants serve legitimate purposes and will be enforced by the courts.

Like easements, restrictive covenants usually "run with the land." That is, they are binding not only on the original parties to the covenant, but also on persons who acquire the property later. If Albert sells his farm to Charles, Charles can enforce the restrictive covenants against Ben and any person who acquires the property through Ben. Under the common law, for a restrictive covenant to run with the land, it had to meet three requirements. First, the original parties to the restrictive covenant must have intended the covenant to transfer with the land. This intention ordinarily is presumed when a restrictive covenant is included in a deed of conveyance. Second, the parties to the restrictive covenant must have been in "privity of estate." In our example, Albert and Ben were in privity of estate, since Ben purchased the property from Albert. Finally, the covenant must "touch and concern" the land itself. That is, the restriction must relate to the land in such a way that it lessens the value of the property subject to the restriction and enhances the value of the property benefitted by the restriction. Obviously, Ben's covenants as to residential use and unobstructed water rights do "touch and concern" the land because they will burden Ben's property and increase the value of Albert's land. In contrast, a restrictive covenant under which Ben promises not to drink alcohol on the property would not "touch and concern" the land.

Restrictive covenants are a common method of controlling land uses in a subdivision, particularly when the land is not restrictively zoned or subjected to minimal land-use controls. Albert owns 2,000 acres of rural Minnesota lake shore property that he intends to subdivide and sell as lake lots. Because the land is not zoned by the county government, Albert is concerned about maintaining the value of the subdivision as the lots are sold and maximizing his profit on the development. For example, he does not want the purchaser of the first lot to set up a pig farm or park a mobile home on it or otherwise use the property in a way that diminishes the desirability and market value of the remaining lots. To protect the subdivision and all lot purchasers, Albert records a set of restrictive covenants (called **deed restrictions**) for the subdivision, and inserts into the deed for each lot a reference to the recorded restrictions. The deed restrictions permit only single-family residential use; prohibit any commercial or industrial activity on the property; require that lake cabins be of a certain minimum size; require the use of acceptable building materials in the construction of cabins; require minimum setbacks from the shore and from side lot lines; prohibit mobile homes, campers, and trailers on the property except on a temporary basis; prohibit livestock and other nuisances on the property; and prohibit the further subdivision of lots or the construction of multiple dwellings on the property. In this way, the subdivision is effectively "zoned" for single-family residential use with substantial controls in place to ensure the value of the lots and the subdivision.

Subdivision deed restrictions are enforceable not only by the developer, but also by the lot owners (or a property owners' association if one is established for the subdivision). To be enforceable, restrictive covenants must fall within a "common plan" under which all or most of the subdivision properties are subject to the deed restrictions. Also, purchasers must have notice (actual or constructive) of the subdivision restrictions. The recording of deed restrictions provides constructive notice to prospective purchasers. If the deed restrictions are not recorded, prospective purchasers viewing the property may nevertheless be put on notice of the restrictions by the type and nature of the other properties in the subdivision. Although deed restrictions cannot be enforced by property owners outside the subdivision, in some jurisdictions local governments have the power to enforce restrictive covenants. In Houston, Texas, a community without any zoning laws, the state has given the city the power to enforce restrictive covenants.

Restrictive covenants terminate under certain circumstances. Some covenants are written to exist for only a limited period, after which they end automatically. Where a covenant is of apparently unlimited duration, changed circumstances can cause a court to terminate it. For example, if over time a residential area becomes commercial, a court may not enforce a covenant that limits a property to residential use if the restriction covers only one property in the area. Finally, a government taking (condemnation) of property will terminate a restrictive covenant. The government takes the property free of the restrictive covenant.

Self-Study Questions

1. What is a zoning enabling act? What is the relationship between zoning and a city's comprehensive or master plan?

2. What is the difference between a permitted and conditional use? Between a cumulative and noncumulative system of zoning?

3. What is a nonconforming use? Why do you think nonconforming uses have continued over time despite the restrictions imposed on nonconforming uses by zoning laws? Explain the circumstances under which a nonconforming use must be discontinued.

4. What is a variance? What is the difference between an area and a use variance? Why does the law require unnecessary hardship for a variance to be granted?

5. What is a subdivision? What steps are necessary for a developer to secure approval of a subdivision proposal?

6. Explain the differences and similarities between cluster zoning and performance zoning.

7. What is exclusionary zoning? Under what circumstances is zoning that has an exclusionary impact on minorities illegal?

8. To what extent can the government regulate adult entertainment? From a city's perspective, what is the preferable method of zoning adult entertainment establishments, the cluster or dispersion approach?

9. Reasonable accommodation for the disabled is required under the Fair Housing Act and the ADA. What does reasonable accommodation mean in connection with local zoning ordinances and decisions?

10. Zoning imposes significant costs on developers and other landowners. What are some of the costs associated with zoning and what effect does zoning have on the price of housing? Are the costs justified by the public benefits of zoning?

Case Problems

1. The Lobster Shack is a restaurant located in both the Residential A Zone and the Shoreland Performance Overlay Zone as defined by the Cape Elizabeth, Maine, town's zoning ordinance. Restaurants are not permitted in the RA Zone and the building Lobster Shack operates does not meet the applicable set-back requirements. Thus, the use and the structure are nonconforming pursuant to the terms of the applicable zoning ordinance. The Lobster Shack sought approval from the town to construct a foundation beneath the restaurant, thereby

creating a basement where only a crawlspace existed previously. The stated purposes of the construction were to protect the structural integrity of the building and to provide additional storage space for the business. It applied for a variance for the proposed project. The nonconforming use restrictions of Cape Elizabeth's zoning ordinance prohibit the extension of a nonconforming use into an additional part of a building "unless . . . those parts were manifestly arranged or designed for such use prior to the enactment of this Ordinance or of any amendment making such use nonconforming." The Lobster Shack argues that the foundation was a permissible repair of the nonconforming structure and not an extension. Do you agree? Should the variance be granted? *Two Lights Lobster Shack v. Town of Cape Elizabeth*, 712 A.2d 1061 (Me. 1998).

2. The city of Bloomington, Minnesota, required a developer of any subdivision to dedicate 10% of the value of land to be developed to the city for public parks and playgrounds. The city of College Station, Texas, required a developer to dedicate to the city one acre of land for each 133 dwelling units in a subdivision or equivalent in cash to be used for the acquisition or development of a neighborhood park. Are these exactions lawful? What standards would the court use in resolving the issue of the legality of the exactions?

3. Smith & Lee Associates is a for-profit Michigan corporation that owns and operates AdultFoster Care (AFC) homes in the state of Michigan. AFC homes provide 24-hour supervised care to dependent adults who require ongoing supervision but not continuous nursing care. Smith & Lee purchased a residential home, Mortenview Manor, in Taylor, Michigan, and operated as an AFC home with six elderly disabled residents who suffer from Alzheimer's disease. Whereas other AFCs (known as contract homes) that house persons with other types of disabilities receive subsidies from state or community social service agencies, homes for the elderly disabled like Mortenview must rely solely on payments from their residents to cover operating costs. Mortenview is located in a residential neighborhood in Taylor that is zoned for single-family use. Smith & Lee has authority to house six unrelated disabled adults in Mortenview under a state law providing, "A state licensed residential facility providing supervision or care, or both, to 6 or less persons shall be considered a residential use of property for the purpose of zoning and a permitted use in all residential zones, including those zoned for single-family dwellings." Smith & Lee petitioned the city to rezone Mortenview from R-1A to RM-1 to allow it to operate with 12 residents. When the rezoning was denied, it sued the city under the Fair Housing Act. Evidence at trial established that, in Taylor, Michigan, a six-person occupancy limit on for-profit AFCs serving the elderly disabled guarantees a negligible or negative rate of return for investors. As such, the demand for AFCs for the elderly disabled, which is projected to increase precipitously over the next three decades, now outstrips the existing supply of such homes. The trial court concluded that an accommodation was necessary because AFC homes for Taylor's elderly disabled will remain in short supply unless the city allows them to operate with nine residents and entered an order to that effect. The city appealed claiming that the court erred in requiring the city to permit more occupants in the AFC home than it was required to under Michigan law. Should the trial court's decision be upheld? *Smith & Lee Associates, Inc. v. City of Taylor*, 13 F.3d 920 (6th Cir. 1993).

4. The city of Jacksonville, Florida, passed a zoning ordinance regulating adult entertainment businesses. The law permits adult establishments to operate as of right in only one area of the city, the CCBD (Commercial/Central Business District) zone. They may also operate in the CCG-2 (Commercial Community/General-2) zone, but only if the zoning board grants them a zoning exception. In addition, the ordinance forbids adult businesses in either zone from locating within specified distances of residences, schools, churches, bars, or other adult businesses. Lady J. Lingerie challenged the constitutionality of the ordinance under the First Amendment. The main objection it had to the ordinance was that only two sites in the CCBD zone complied with the distance requirements, meaning that practically all adult entertainment establishments must apply for a zoning exception to operate in the CCG-2 zone. The city conceded this point, but argued that 93-plus sites were available in the CCG-2 zone and that the combined 95 sites were enough to satisfy

constitutional standards. Lady J. Lingerie contended that the city had the discretion to deny a zoning exception, leaving only two sites in the entire city. It argued that the lack of adequate sites in a major metropolitan area like Jacksonville was insufficient to satisfy the First Amendment. Who should win the case? Why? *Lady J. Lingerie, Inc. v. City of Jacksonville*, 176 F.3d 1358 (11th Cir. 1999).

Endnotes

1. 512 U.S. 374 (1994).
2. 429 U.S. 252 (1977).
3. 508 F.2d 1179 (8th Cir. 1974).
4. 336 A.2d 713 (N.J. 1975).
5. 117 F.3d 37 (1997).
6. 427 U.S. 50 (1976).
7. 475 U.S. 41 (1986).

Chapter 18

Environmental Law: Protecting the Land, Air, Water, and Ecosystem

Once of minor concern in real estate circles, environmental law today vitally affects real estate owners, buyers, developers, and lenders, who within the past thirty years have been increasingly held accountable for pollution of the environment. The causes and consequences of environmental pollution are as current as today's headlines: garbage and toxic waste disposal, ground water contamination, air pollution, pollution of rivers and streams, industrial pollution, endangered wetlands, threatened ecosystems, and the extinction of species. These problems are not new, but many of the legal responses to them are.

One by-product of the social upheaval in the 1960s and 1970s was an increased environmental consciousness prompted by a number of influential works, including Rachel Carson's book, *Silent Spring* (1962), Paul Ehrlich's *The Population Bomb* (1968), Barry Commoner's *The Closing Circle* (1971), Garrett Hardin's article, "The Tragedy of the Commons" (1968),[1] and the NBC television documentary, "Who Killed Lake Erie?" (1969). This collective call to action was accompanied by two dramatic environmental disasters that seized the public attention. In 1969, the heavily polluted Cuyahoga River near Cleveland, Ohio, caught fire. In the same year, a tragic oil spill occurred off the coast of Santa Barbara, California. Widely publicized in the evening news, these events aroused an intense public interest in environmental issues and a new environmental consciousness. Public expression found an outlet with the celebration of the first Earth Day on April 22, 1970.

This increased public awareness prompted a wide-ranging legal response to the problem of pollution and myriad changes in environmental law, many of which affect landowners directly or indirectly. The landowner faces two primary risks from environmental pollution. First, existing pollution can adversely affect the market value of the realty. Second, the landowner can be required to pay cleanup costs, civil damages to third parties, and statutory civil and criminal penalties, the total of which can easily exceed the market value of the realty.[2] Real estate lenders share these concerns because pollution of property that serves as security affects both its value and the creditworthiness of the owner-borrower. Indeed, in certain limited circumstances, the lender itself can be required to pay cleanup costs.

This chapter explores how the common law handled the effects of pollution and why the common law solutions were unsatisfactory. The chapter then discusses the federal and state environmental regulatory schemes that supplement or replace the common law.

Common Law Liability for Environmental Injuries

The problems of air and water pollution and garbage and toxic waste disposal are as old as humankind itself, but became vastly more acute with the increase in population and the arrival of the industrial age. In *Hard Times*, Charles Dickens described Coketown, his fictionalized version of Preston, an industrial town of the 1850s near Manchester, England:[3]

> It was a town of red brick, or of brick that would have been red if the smoke and ashes had allowed it; but, as matters stood it was a town of unnatural red and black like the painted face of a savage. It was a town of machinery and tall chimneys, out of which interminable serpents of smoke trailed themselves for ever and ever, and never got uncoiled. It had a black canal in it, and a river that ran purple with ill-smelling dye, and vast piles of building full of windows where there was a rattling and a trembling all day long, and where the piston of the steam-engine worked monotonously up and down, like the head of an elephant in a state of melancholy madness.[4]

In Dickens's England, and in the United States before the development of the federal regulatory scheme in the 1960s and 1970s, the courts dealt with industrial pollution largely on a case-by-case basis by applying the common law of the time. Disputes involving pollution usually came before the courts as tort cases. Tort is a body of civil law allowing a person harmed by the misconduct of another to have compensation (damages) for the resulting losses. Then, as now, the typical environmental pollution tort suit sought money damages for pollution-related injuries, a prohibitory *injunction* to stop the pollution, or both. A prohibitory injunction is an equitable remedy ordering a defendant to stop some activity that is offensive to the plaintiff, for example, to stop the pollution that causes harm to the plaintiff or the plaintiff's property. To receive the injunction, the plaintiff must satisfy the court that, considering all the circumstances, the remedy is fair to both parties. To recover damages in tort, a plaintiff must prove that the suit meets the requirements (i.e., must prove the "elements") established by the common law for the particular tort or tort theory alleged. At common law, the most successful tort theories for dealing with pollution-related claims were (and still are) nuisance, trespass, and strict liability.

Nuisance and Trespass Theories of Liability

Nuisance and trespass are intentional torts. The defendant must intend the act that causes loss, though not necessarily its polluting consequences. Lorreto builds a large brine pond on his land for the processing of olives from his orchard. The pond develops leaks and salt water flows onto a neighbor's land, causing damage. Lorreto did not intend to harm his neighbor's land, but is liable in damages anyway because he intended to build the pond.

As noted in Chapter 2, the tort of nuisance protects the right of landowners to use and quietly enjoy their property free from unreasonable interference by their neighbors. A **nuisance** occurs when a landowner's right to quiet enjoyment is disturbed by a neighbor's unreasonable and unwarranted use of the neighbor's own property. If the neighbor's activity would be unreasonable and unwarranted to a person of normal sensitivity, it is a nuisance; if the use would be merely irritating to a normal person, it is not a nuisance. To determine whether the use is a nuisance, a court must evaluate the totality of the circumstances, including the social benefits and social costs of the challenged activity, and must "balance" the interests of the plaintiff and defendant, because both have a right (consistent with similar rights of their neighbors) to use their property as they choose. In the balancing, a landowner may have to accept the occasional barking of a neighbor's dog as reasonable and normal in the use of the neighbor's property, but may have a right to an injunction if the neighbor maintains a large kennel of dogs that howl day and night, making sleep impossible for the plaintiff.

Two types of nuisance are recognized at common law: public and private. A **private nuisance** is committed against an individual (or a few persons), entitling the victim to bring a civil suit to abate it (i.e., to stop it, usually by means of an injunction), or for damages, or for both. A **public nuisance** is a condition that interferes with the comfort or convenience of some segment of the public by adversely affecting public safety, health, or morals. To be a public nuisance, the condition must affect a substantial number of people, and must affect all or most in approximately the same way. For example, Power Company builds a coal-burning generator that covers the town with thick black smoke, causing general discomfort for a substantial portion of the population, with individuals suffering various combinations of breathing difficulties, allergic reactions, and eye irritation. Victims of a purely public nuisance cannot directly abate it. To have it abated, they must act through a county or city attorney or some other public official given the responsibility for abatement actions. This official has discretion to bring an abatement action or to withhold it, depending on whether action seems warranted.

A *mixed nuisance* has characteristics of both a public and a private nuisance. An industrial plant may emit noxious fumes and smoke that adversely affect a substantial portion of a town's population in approximately the same way, by causing coughs, skin rashes, or eye inflammation. But a few individuals forced to park near the smokestack may suffer different or additional harm—loss caused by acid droplets ruining the paint on their cars. The plant has created a public nuisance as to the general population and a private one as to the car owners. For the additional, special harm, the car owners are entitled to the remedies available for private nuisance.

Because nuisance law involves case-by-case litigation between neighbors or, in the case of a public nuisance, litigation involving a wrongdoer and a relatively small segment of the public, nuisance law is not effective for controlling pollution on a massive scale. The following case illustrates the difficulties of using the law of nuisance to correct a problem of industrial pollution.

Case 18.1

Boomer v. Atlantic Cement Co.

257 N.E.2d 870 (N.Y. 1970)

Defendant operates a large cement plant near Albany. Neighboring landowners filed an action seeking an injunction and damages for injury to their property from dirt, smoke, and vibration emanating from the plant. The trial court found that the cement plant's activity constituted a nuisance and awarded temporary damages, but denied an injunction. Plaintiffs appealed. The appellate court affirmed the decision of the trial court. Plaintiffs appealed.

BERGAN, J.

The public concern with air pollution arising from many sources in industry and in transportation is currently accorded ever wider recognition accompanied by a growing sense of responsibility in State and Federal Governments to control it. Cement plants are obvious sources of air pollution in the neighborhoods where they operate.

But [this case involves] private litigation in which individual property owners have sought specific relief from a single plant operation. The threshold question raised . . . on this appeal is whether the court should resolve the litigation between the parties now before it as equitably as seems possible; or whether, seeking promotion of the general public welfare, it should channel private litigation into broad public objectives.

A court performs its essential function when it decides the rights of parties before it. Its decision of private controversies may sometimes greatly affect public issues. Large questions of law are often resolved by the manner in which private litigation is decided. But [the resolution of large questions] is normally an incident to the court's main function to settle controversy. It is a rare exercise of judicial power to use a decision in private litigation as a purposeful mechanism to achieve direct public objectives greatly beyond the rights and interests before the court.

Effective control of air pollution is a problem presently far from solution even with the full public and financial powers of government. In large measure adequate technical procedures are yet to be developed and some that appear possible may be economically impracticable.

It seems apparent that the amelioration of air pollution will depend on technical research in great depth; on a carefully balanced consideration of the economic impact of close regulation; and of the actual effect on public health. It is likely to require massive public expenditure and to demand more than any local community can accomplish and to depend on regional and interstate controls.

A court should not try to [resolve such wide-ranging problems] on its own as a by-product of private litigation and it seems manifest that the judicial establishment is neither equipped in the limited nature of any judgment it can pronounce nor prepared to lay down and implement an effective policy for the elimination of air pollution. This is an area beyond the circumference of one private lawsuit. It is a direct responsibility for government and [thus] should not . . . be undertaken as an incident to solving a dispute between property owners and a single cement plant—one of many—in the Hudson River valley.

The cement making operations of defendant have been found by the court at Special Term to have damaged the nearby properties of plaintiffs in these two actions. That court . . . accordingly found [that] defendant maintained a nuisance and this [finding] has been affirmed at the Appellate Division. The total damage to plaintiffs' properties is, however, relatively small in comparison with the value of defendant's operation and with the consequences of the injunction which plaintiffs seek.

The ground for the denial of injunction, notwithstanding the finding both that there is a nuisance and that plaintiffs have been damaged substantially, is the large disparity in economic consequences of the nuisance and of the injunction. . . .

Although the court at Special Term and the Appellate Division held that injunction should be denied, it was found that plaintiffs had been damaged in various specific amounts up to the time of the trial and damages to the respective plaintiffs were awarded for those amounts. The effect of this was [that, the] injunction having been denied, plaintiffs could maintain successive actions at law for damages thereafter as further damage was incurred.

The court at Special Term also found the amount of permanent damage attributable to each plaintiff, for the guidance of the parties in the event both sides stipulated to the payment and acceptance of such permanent damage as a settlement of all the controversies among the parties. The total of permanent damages to all plaintiffs thus found was $185,000. . . .

This result at Special Term and at the Appellate Division is a departure from a rule that has become settled; but to follow the rule literally in these cases would be to close down the plant at once. This court is fully agreed to [avoiding] that immediately drastic remedy; the difference in view [among members of the court] is how best to avoid it. [Respondent's investment in the plant is in excess of $45 million. It employs more than 300 people.]

One alternative is to grant the injunction but postpone its effect to a specified future date to give opportunity for technical advances to permit defendant to eliminate the nuisance; another is to grant the injunction conditioned on the payment of permanent damages to plaintiffs which would compensate them for the total economic loss to their property present and future caused by defendant's operations. For reasons which will be developed the court chooses the latter alternative.

If the injunction were to be granted unless within a short period—e.g., 18 months—the nuisance be abated by improved methods, there would be no assurance that any significant technical improvement would occur.

The parties could settle this private litigation at any time if defendant paid enough money and the imminent threat of closing the plant would build up the pressure on defendant. If there were no improved techniques found, there would inevitably be applications to the court at Special Term for extensions of time to perform on showing of good faith efforts to find such techniques.

Moreover, techniques to eliminate dust and other annoying by-products of cement making are unlikely to be developed by any research the defendant can undertake within any short period, but will depend on the total resources of the cement industry Nationwide and throughout the world. The problem is universal wherever cement is made.

For obvious reasons the rate of the research is beyond control of defendant. If at the end of 18 months the whole industry has not found a technical solution a court would be hard put to close down this one cement plant if due regard be given to equitable principles.

On the other hand, to grant the injunction unless defendant pays plaintiffs such permanent damages as may be fixed by the court seems to do justice between the contending parties. All of the attributions of economic loss to the properties on which plaintiffs' complaints are based will have been redressed.

The nuisance complained of by these plaintiffs may have other public or private consequences, but these particular parties are the only ones who have sought remedies and the judgment proposed will fully redress them. The limitation of relief granted is a limitation only within the four corners of these actions and does not foreclose public health or other public agencies from seeking proper relief in a proper court.

It seems reasonable to think that the risk of being required to pay permanent damages to injured property owners by cement plant owners would itself be a reasonable effective spur to research for improved techniques to minimize nuisance.

The power of the court to condition on equitable grounds the continuance of an injunction on the payment of permanent damages seems undoubted.

The damage base here suggested is consistent with the general rule in those nuisance cases where damages are allowed. "Where a nuisance is of such a permanent and unabatable character that a single recovery can be had, including the whole damage past and future resulting therefrom, there can be but one recovery." . . . It has been said that permanent damages are allowed where the loss recoverable would obviously be small as compared with the cost of removal of the nuisance. . . .

Thus it seems fair to both sides to grant permanent damages to plaintiffs which will terminate this private litigation. The theory of damage is the "servitude on land" of plaintiffs imposed by defendant's nuisance. . . .

The judgment, by allowance of permanent damages imposing a servitude on land, which is the basis of the actions, would preclude future recovery by plaintiffs or their grantees.

This should be placed beyond debate by a provision of the judgment that the payment by defendant and the acceptance by plaintiffs of permanent damages found by the court shall be in compensation for a servitude on the land.

Although the Trial Term has found permanent damages as a possible basis of settlement of the litigation, on remission the court should be entirely free to re-examine this subject. It may again find the permanent damage already found; or make new findings.

The orders should be reversed, without costs, and the cases remitted to Supreme Court, Albany County [in New York, the Supreme Court is the trial court, while the highest state court is the Court of Appeals] to grant an injunction which shall be vacated upon payment by defendant of such amounts of permanent damage to the respective plaintiffs as shall for this purpose be determined by the court.

QUESTIONS ABOUT CASE 18.1

1. Before this case, a New York plaintiff like the one here was entitled to an injunction closing down the industrial defendant. In what way did the Court of Appeals in this case depart from that law?

2. In the early part of the opinion, Justice Bergan discusses whether common law litigation as involved here is generally adequate for addressing the problem of industrial pollution. He finds it inadequate. For what reasons?

3. Does the remedy provided to the plaintiffs in this case serve to alleviate the problem of pollution? Consider whether the cement company's polluting activities are likely to end as a result of this case.

The law of trespass protects a landowner's right to undisturbed possession and enjoyment of the land, and thus protects the landowner from unauthorized and unprivileged entries by others. As noted in Chapter 2, **trespass** occurs if a person enters another's land without permission or privilege, or causes someone else or something to do so. It would be a trespass for a defendant to walk across a neighbor's property without permission or privilege, or to pump residue from a manufacturing process onto the neighbor's property.

A traditional example of trespass is found in *Rudd v. Electrolux Corporation*, where the court held the Electrolux Corporation liable for trespass.[5] The land of the plaintiff, an adjacent property owner, suffered chemical contamination from materials that flowed in ground water from a leaking storage tank on Electrolux's property. A few courts have held that it is a trespass if the defendant generates dust, smoke, or other pollutants the defendant knows or should know will drift onto the plaintiff's property, as in *Bradley v. American Smelting and Refining Company*, where the Washington Supreme Court sustained a trespass complaint on evidence showing that the defendant's smelting operations caused deposit of airborne heavy metals on the plaintiff's property even though the microscopic particles could not be seen or smelled by human beings.[6] Usually, however, dust, smoke, and gaseous pollutants are held to be a nuisance rather than a trespass. For example, the Michigan Court of Appeals recently refused to recognize a cause of action based on trespass brought by an adjoining landowner against a mine operator for dust, noise, and vibrations caused by the mine.[7] The Michigan court held that the dust complained of by the plaintiff did not constitute the "actual and substantial injury" normally associated with a trespass complaint, preferring a nuisance analysis, which involves "balancing the disturbance complained of against the social utility of its cause," to a trespass analysis where damages would normally be presumed and the social utility of the defendant's activity would be irrelevant.

Like nuisance, trespass is inadequate for controlling widespread environmental pollution, and for the same reasons. Suits in trespass are local, involving only a landowner and the offending trespasser, and the decision in a trespass case binds only the parties to it. Although an accumulation of case-by-case rulings can become binding on a substantial population, the common law approach is incapable of the systematic regulation required to detect, penalize, and deter pollution of the environment.

Strict Liability for Abnormally Dangerous Activities

Because nuisance and trespass are intentional torts, plaintiffs invoking them must prove fault on the part of the defendant (i.e., an unreasonably harmful use of the defendant's property or an illegal entry). The twentieth century, however, saw the revival of the common law notion that some activities are so inherently dangerous that even a careful defendant should be responsible for any damages caused by them. At common law, where the dangerous thing or condition caused loss to the plaintiff, the defendant would have **strict liability** (absolute liability) for the damages, without the plaintiff's having to prove that the defendant was negligent or otherwise at fault. The early cases often involved one of three fact situations: (1) The defendant kept wild animals that caused injury or damage; (2) the defendant used explosives that caused damage to adjacent property; or (3) the defendant maintained a dam and the dam burst, causing property damage downstream.[8]

These unusual types of tort cases eventually evolved into the concept that liability without fault, known as **strict liability in tort**, could be imposed on defendants who caused damage by engaging in "abnormally dangerous activities." Section 520 of the *Restatement, Torts 2d*, defines an "abnormally dangerous activity" by reference to six factors:

1. Whether the activity involves a high degree of risk of some harm to the person, land or chattels of others.

2. Whether the gravity of the harm which may result from it is likely to be great.

3. Whether the risk cannot be eliminated by the exercise of reasonable care.

4. Whether the activity is not a matter of common usage.

5. Whether the activity is inappropriate to the place where it is carried on.

6. Whether the activity is of value to the community.

In the mid-twentieth century, strict liability for damages arising out of abnormally hazardous activities was extended not only to a wide array of potentially dangerous products such as vehicles, tools, medicines, and foods, but also to environmental problems, particularly in situations involving a release of a hazardous or toxic substance. For example, in *Yommer v. McKenzie*, a Maryland court held a gas station owner strictly liable when gasoline contaminated the neighboring landowner's well.[9] The court reasoned:

> *Although the operation of a gasoline station does not of itself involve "a high degree of risk of some harm to the person, land or chattels of others," the placing of a large underground gasoline tank in close proximity to the appellees' residence and well does involve such a risk, since it is not a matter of common usage. The harm caused to the appellees was a serious one, and it may well have been worse if the contamination had not been detected promptly.*

Similarly, in *Branch v. Western Petroleum, Inc.*, the Utah Supreme Court approved the application of strict liability for contamination of an adjacent landowner's wells by Western Petroleum's waste water pond.[10] The court held that an industrial polluter who discharges wastes upon its own ground is strictly liable for any injuries resulting from contamination of the ground water. Marshaling a wealth of legal authority, the court reasoned:

> *There are two separate, although somewhat related, grounds for holding Western strictly liable for the pollution of the Branches' wells. First, the facts of the case support application of the rule of strict liability because the ponding of the toxic formation water in an area adjacent to the Branches' wells constituted an abnormally dangerous and inappropriate use of the land in light of its proximity to the Branches' property and was unduly dangerous to the Branches' use of their well water. . . . [Second], an industry should not be able to use its property in such a way as to inflict injury on the property of its neighbors because to do so would result in effect in appropriating the neighbor's property to one's own use. An industrial polluter can and should assume the costs of pollution as a cost of doing business rather than charge the loss to a wholly innocent party. The court in Atlas Chemical stated: "We know of no acceptable rule of jurisprudence which permits those engaged in important and desirable enterprises to injure with impunity those who are engaged in enterprises of lesser economic significance. The*

costs of injuries resulting from pollution must be internalized by industry as a cost of production and borne by consumers or shareholders, or both, and not by the injured individual." We think these reasons adequately support application of the rule of strict liability in this case.

Using nuisance, trespass, and strict liability in tort, the courts do a reasonably effective job of resolving the problem of pollution *between the parties to the lawsuit.* Consider the *Boomer* case (Case 18.1), for example. Although the plaintiffs in *Boomer* probably were disappointed that they did not get an injunction to stop the pollution generated by the defendant cement maker, they arguably were made economically whole when they received damages for the loss of the market value of their property. And although the court forced the defendant to bear at least part of the social cost of its pollution, the court allowed it to continue to operate, thus balancing the interests of the contending parties and preserving an industry that, despite the pollution burden it imposes, is thought vital to our economy.

However, if the goal of the law is to stop pollution, the courts cannot do an effective job with the case-oriented common law tools at hand, as the Court of Appeals in *Boomer* freely acknowledged. The Court recognized that pollution is a national problem and a national solution is necessary. The Boomer case itself became part of the ferment that helped produce the attempt at a national solution.

The Federal Environmental Regulatory Framework

In the late 1960s and early 1970s, lawmakers began to recognize the widespread public support in favor of pollution control and began to address the issue. In 1970, the Environmental Protection Agency (EPA) was established and the National Environmental Policy Act went into effect. These major federal actions were the first in what has become an attack on pollution across a broad front.

Trends in Environmental Regulation

The clear trend over the last thirty years has been an increased overall regulation of the environment at both the federal and state levels. The following box outlines the major federal initiatives that significantly affect landowners.

Box 18–1 reveals an increase in federal intervention, but also illustrates some trends in the nature of federal regulations. The first federal statutes focused on providing research, policy, and financial support to the states. In the 1970s the federal government began to develop regulatory programs that aimed to control—and ultimately reduce—pollution of various types through prohibitions and release permits. Many of these programs were intended to be "technology forcing" in nature. They provided incentives, often coercive, for industry to develop technology to control pollution emissions of various types. In the 1980s, the focus of regulatory activity shifted to the cleanup of pollutants, particularly releases of hazardous substances. Finally, in the 1990s, the federal government directed attention to minimizing the creation of pollution at its source.

As desirable as the trends toward technology-forcing and cleanup of hazardous and toxic wastes may be, they represent a huge increase in expense for businesses and landowners. This economic fact has periodically made the EPA a lightning rod for criticism in the years since its creation.

Role of the Environmental Protection Agency

The EPA is an independent federal agency. It took over the functions of a number of existing, uncoordinated federal agencies, commissions, and administrations. Its mission was to mount an attack on pollution of the air and water, in cooperation with state and local governments, and to

BOX 18–1 FEDERAL ENVIRONMENTAL LEGISLATION

Rivers and Harbors Appropriation Act (1899): Made it unlawful for ships and manufacturing establishments to discharge refuse into any navigable waters of the United States or any tributary of a navigable waterway.

Public Health Service Act (1912): Provided for federal investigation of water pollution affecting public health.

Federal Insecticide, Fungicide and Rodenticide Act (1947): Provided that pesticides must be registered with the EPA before they can be sold to consumers.

Federal Water Pollution Control Act (1948) (Amended in 1956 and 1965): Provided federal financial assistance and research support for water pollution control and waste water treatment through the U.S. Public Health Service.

Air Pollution Control Act (1955): Provided federal funding for research into air pollution control.

Clean Air Act (1963): Authorized investigation, research and technical assistance to states. Provided for development of air quality standards by the Secretary of Health, Education, and Welfare.

Solid Waste Disposal Act (1965): Provided financial and technical assistance to state and local agencies in development and application of new methods of waste disposal.

Air Quality Act (1967): Established a procedure for the creation of air quality regions and the adoption and achievement by states of ambient air quality standards.

National Environmental Policy Act (1969): Required environmental impact statement for major federal actions having significant impact on the quality of the human environment.

Clean Water Act (1972) (also known as the Federal Water Pollution Control Act of 1972, amended in 1977, 1986, and 1990): Provided a comprehensive plan to eliminate pollution by setting standards and guidelines on an industry-by-industry basis for controlling the flow of pollutants into navigable waters from industrial sources. Provides for licensing and permit system at the state and federal level.

Coastal Zone Management Act (1972): Provided state financial and technical assistance in developing coastal zone management plans.

Resource Conservation and Recovery Act (1976): Defined "hazardous wastes" and created a manifest system to keep track of hazardous materials.

Toxic Substances Control Act (1976): Provided for testing and notification of the EPA when a new substance is being considered for development and production.

Comprehensive Environmental Response Compensation and Liability Act (1980): Established a program to identify sites from which releases of hazardous substances have occurred or could occur, and to ensure cleanup of those sites by the responsible parties or the government.

Pollution Prevention Act (1990): Authorizes matching grants to states for programs designed to promote the use by businesses of pollution source reduction improvements.

control disposal or release of solid wastes, pesticides, radiation, and toxic substances. In the years since 1970, the agency has grown into one of the largest federal agencies. The EPA establishes and enforces environmental protection standards, conducts research on pollution, and provides assistance to state and local antipollution programs.

Federal Statutory Protection of the Environment: The Principal Statutes

This section provides a brief overview of some of the major pieces of federal legislation dealing with pollution of the environment, with an emphasis on the statute of most concern to owners of real property, the Comprehensive Environmental Response, Compensation, and Liability Act (CERCLA) of 1980 known as the Superfund.

National Environmental Policy Act and Environmental Impact Statements

The National Environmental Policy Act was passed in 1969 as a policy and planning statute.[11] Yet, it did have three important operative effects. First, the act established the Council on Environmental Quality, which advises the president on environmental concerns and serves as a watchdog on federal environmental policy. Second, it mandated that federal agencies consider the environmental consequences of their decisions. Third, it required that an environmental impact statement be prepared for every major federal action having a significant impact on the quality of the human environment, such as highway construction or the building of a dam. An **environmental impact statement** describes in detail the consequences to the environment of the proposed federal action, any unavoidable adverse effects of the action, any acceptable alternatives to the proposed project, and any irreversible and irretrievable commitments of resources involved.

The environmental impact statement requirement has been the most controversial part of the statute for several reasons. First, the statute itself gives no clear guidance on when an environmental impact statement is required, though the Council on Environmental Quality has since tried to provide some guidelines. Lacking clear guidance, but wanting to avoid litigation, federal agencies sometimes produce environmental impact statements in situations not originally mandated by Congress. Second, because developing an environmental impact statement can be time-consuming and expensive, the environmental impact statement requirement has been used by opponents of federal projects as a tool to stop or delay them. Third, the results of an environmental impact statement can generate considerable controversy over matters of policy. The more publicized examples include whether the Tennessee Valley Authority should proceed with a proposed hydroelectric development that would endanger a species of fish known as the snail darter, and whether the federal government should permit logging in the Northwest, given the danger to the spotted owl.

The Clean Air Act

The first major air pollution control act was the Clear Air Act of 1970,[12] since amended by the Clean Air Act Amendments of 1977 and 1990. The act is administered by the EPA. The EPA divided the United States into 247 air quality regions based upon common pollution sources and weather patterns. The EPA then set outside (ambient) air quality standards for six major industrial pollutants: carbon monoxide, sulfur dioxide, lead, suspended particulates, nitrogen oxide, and ozone. For each of these pollutants, the EPA developed **primary air quality standards** to protect human health and **secondary air quality standards** to improve visibility, safeguard plant and animal life, and otherwise enhance the general welfare.

The pollutants are direct or indirect by-products of burning hydrocarbons (e.g., coal, petroleum), which are major sources of energy in the industrialized nations. Coal-burning in power plants and industrial applications is a major source of sulfur dioxide and particulates. Motor vehicle emissions contain huge amounts of nitrogen oxides, carbon monoxides, ozone, and lead. The banning of leaded gasoline in the United States drastically reduced emissions of lead.

Reduction of sulfur dioxide and nitrogen oxide pollution has become a major goal in the industrialized nations because these gases combine with water in the atmosphere to form acids that return to the earth in the form of **acid rain** and snow. Acid rain can change the acidity level of lakes, rivers, streams, and ground water, causing damage to trees, vegetation, and aquatic life. Acid rain also damages and reduces the useful life of buildings and other human-constructed improvements. The Clean Air Act, as amended, mandates emission controls on power plants burning fossil fuels. The eventual controls require a reduction of 12 million tons per year in sulfur dioxide and nitrogen oxide emissions.

The act requires states to draft state implementation plans for achieving ambient air quality standards for each of these pollutants. When the implementation plans are approved by the EPA, the states enforce air quality standards within their borders. Pollutant-emitting operators (e.g., power plants, factories) may be required to take air samples, monitor the pollutants in them, and keep appropriate records, all of which are subject to on-premises inspection by the EPA. States that do not meet the designated air quality standards are designated nonattainment areas. States that fail to develop or implement an approved plan may lose federal highway funds and may be subject to limitations on new sources of emissions. Approved state implementation plans, or the federally imposed limitations, may directly or indirectly affect uses of land. For example, in a nonattainment area, a landowner may not be allowed to construct a factory that would be a new pollution source.

Amendments of the Clean Air Act regulate the airborne release of approximately 189 toxic substances such as benzene, vinyl chloride, asbestos, beryllium, mercury, arsenic, and radio nuclides. Operators must use "maximum achievable control technology" to control emissions of these toxic substances.

BOX 18–2 POINT TO CONSIDER

In *Union Electric Co. v. EPA.*, 427 U.S. 246 (1976), the U.S. Supreme Court considered a case involving a Missouri electric utility that challenged the enforcement of sulfur dioxide emissions limits mandated in the state's approved implementation plan. The utility claimed that the limitations were not economically and technologically feasible. The Supreme Court rejected the contentions of the utility, holding that the EPA was not authorized to consider economic and technological infeasibility in its consideration of a state implementation plan. The Court noted that the primary purpose of the act is to protect public health and welfare through improving air quality standards:

> Suffice it to say that the Amendments reflect congressional dissatisfaction with the progress of existing air pollution programs and a determination to "tak[e] a stick to the States," in order to guarantee the prompt attainment and maintenance of specified air quality standards. The heart of the Amendments is the requirement that each State formulate, subject to EPA approval, an implementation plan designed to achieve national primary ambient air quality standards—those necessary to protect the public health—"as expeditiously as practicable but . . . in no case later than three years from the date of approval of such plan."

The Court reasoned that Clean Air Act Amendments' "requirements are of a 'technology-forcing character' and are expressly designed to force regulated sources to develop pollution control devices that might at the time appear to be economically or technologically infeasible."

The Clean Water Act

The protection of water resources was one of the earliest areas of federal concern. For example, the Rivers and Harbors Appropriation Act of 1899 made it unlawful for ships and manufacturing establishments to discharge refuse into any navigable waters of the United States or any tributary of a navigable waterway.[13] Collectively, these early acts had little effect on pollution. The restrictions were limited and not rigorously enforced until recently.

Beginning with the Federal Water Pollution Control Act of 1948, the federal influence became more widespread and more effective.[14] Dramatic improvement in water quality was not evident until Congress passed the Federal Water Pollution Control Act of 1972. The Federal Water Pollution Control Act of 1972, as amended by the Clean Water Acts of 1977 and 1987 and the Oil Pollution Act of 1990, is known today as the "Clean Water Act." The Clean Water Act provides a comprehensive plan to reduce pollution, by setting standards and guidelines on an industry-by-industry basis for controlling discharges of pollutants into navigable waters. The courts have given broad application to the term *navigable waters.* For example, in *United States v. Hartsell,* the defendants, who owned a wastewater treatment and oil reclamation business in Charlotte, North Carolina, were arrested for intentionally dumping contaminated water into the storm sewer in violation of the Clean Water Act.[15] Convicted and sentenced to 51 months in prison, the defendants appealed, claiming that sewers were not "navigable waters" within the meaning of the Clean Water Act. The court rejected the argument, with the reasoning as follows:

> *Several courts, including the Supreme Court and this court, have held that Congress clearly intended to regulate pollutant discharge into sewer systems and other nonnavigable waters through the [Clean Water Act], and that Congress has the constitutional authority to do so. In* Riverside Bayview Homes, *the Court stated that Congress intended to allow "broad federal authority" to control pollution, for "water moves in hydrological cycles and it is essential that discharge of pollutants be controlled at its source." The Court further held that Congress clearly intended to exercise its powers under the Commerce Clause to regulate at least some waters that would not be deemed "navigable" under the classical understanding of that term. . . . We held that Congress not only intended to legislate against unchecked discharge of pollutants into public sewers which would eventually flow into streams and rivers, but that Congress acted squarely within its power in so doing.*

The Clean Water Act established a licensing and permit system to regulate discharges. All **point sources** of potential discharges into surface waters, such as waste water treatment plants and factories, are required to obtain a National Pollution Discharge Elimination System (NPDES) permit. The permissible discharge limitations under the NPDES permit are based upon the type of pollutant, the type of discharge, and whether the discharge is from a new or existing source. The EPA has relaxed the NPDES standards somewhat for publicly owned waste water treatment plants and existing sources of conventional pollutants. For existing discharges of conventional pollutants, the standards for discharges are to be based upon the "best conventional control technology" (BCT). In setting the BCT standards, the EPA is required to consider a number of factors, including the cost and benefits of pollution control techniques, the age of the equipment, the process employed, and the facilities involved.

Toxic and other nonconventional pollutants and new point sources are subject to more rigorous standards for a permit. The Clean Water Act requires that toxic and nonconventional pollutants be treated or controlled using the best economically available technology (BAT). The EPA has identified more than 60 toxic substances subject to the higher standard. Although the costs of control or treatment are to be taken into account, the health dangers posed by toxic pollutants result in more stringent limitations. New point sources are also subject to more rigorous effluent limits on the theory that it is cheaper and more efficient to build pollution-control technology and processes into new plants than into older facilities.

Because most publicly owned waste water treatment plants are unable to treat or eliminate discharges of chemical or toxic wastes, the EPA also controls discharges of pollutants into municipal sewers. The EPA regulations prohibit discharges of materials likely to damage the sewer system (such as explosive, flammable, or corrosive material), and materials likely to block the flow of sewage, otherwise undermine the treatment process, or unduly increase the temperature of the waste water. Pretreatment of wastes may be required for these types of discharges. The EPA has published specific discharge standards for at least 25 industries, such as feed lots, pulp and paper manufacturers, and textile mills.

Control of point source pollution has resulted in substantial improvements in water quality throughout many parts of the country. However, nonpoint source pollution, is also a serious problem. **Nonpoint source pollution** results, for example, from agricultural land water runoff containing herbicides, pesticides, fertilizers, and animal wastes, and from discharges from urban storm sewers. A 1999 report from the Indiana Department of Environmental Management estimates that 2% of the state's water in lakes and 22% of the water in rivers and streams is unfit for aquatic life, and 2% of the water in lakes and 43% of the water in rivers and streams is unfit for swimming, primarily because of frequent high levels of E. coli bacteria.[16] E. coli bacteria is found in human and animal wastes. EPA regulations governing municipal and industrial nonpoint source storm sewer pollution in urban areas affect 173 urban areas with more than 100,000 in population.

The regulations under section 404 of the Clean Water Act have become the primary regulatory tool for the preservation of the nation's wetlands. Wetlands are considered by many landowners to be commercially useless. Therefore, a large percentage of the nation's wetlands has been filled for commercial development or agriculture. However, wetlands, particularly coastal wetlands, are biologically active and important ecosystems. The EPA regulations now require that a landowner obtain a permit from the Army Corps of Engineers prior to any filling or development of wetlands. To obtain a permit, the landowner must meet criteria established by the EPA, including a showing that the development is in the public interest.

Restrictions on the development of wetlands impair the rights of individual property owners, with most of the nation's wetlands located on private property. Also, the regulatory definition of wetlands is broader than the lay understanding of wetlands. The EPA defines wetlands as any land with hydric soil or hydrophytic vegetation (i.e., land showing evidence of periodic saturation or containing plants, such as cattails, that are characteristic of wetlands)[17] or where there is water saturation of the ground for as little as seven consecutive days during the growing season.[18] This broad definition of wetlands means that many landowners owning low-lying property are subject to the permit requirement, and may be prevented from cultivating or developing the land. This broad definition also may lead to clashes with the government because of the Supreme Court's more recent view of regulatory takings, discussed in Chapter 16. If by denying a use permit the government "takes" a wetland to preserve it and thereby deprives the landowner of all practical, productive use of the property, the government has a duty to compensate the landowner for the land. A 2001 Supreme Court case, *Solid Waste Agency of Northern Cook County v. United States Army Corps of Engineers*, has also called into question the authority of the Army Corp of Engineers to regulate wetlands not associated with navigable waters under the current text of the Clean Water Act.[19]

● Resource Conservation and Recovery Act

In 1980, the government estimated that industry in the United States generated 57 million metric tons of hazardous wastes, only 10% of which was disposed of properly.[20] To promote the proper control and disposal of hazardous wastes, Congress passed the Resource Conservation and Recovery Act (RCRA) in 1976.[21] The RCRA took two important steps. First, it defined a hazardous waste as

> *[A] solid waste, or combination of solid wastes, which because of its quantity, concentration, or physical, chemical or infectious characteristics may—*
>
> *(A) cause, or significantly contribute to an increase in mortality or an increase in serious irreversible, or incapacitating reversible, illness; or*
>
> *(B) pose a substantial present or potential hazard to human health or the environment when improperly treated, stored, transported, or disposed of, or otherwise managed.*[22]

Second, RCRA creates a "manifest" (paper trail) system to keep track of hazardous materials. Hazardous wastes are required to be tracked and controlled from their point of generation to the point at which they are properly disposed of. In other words, the generator of the wastes becomes responsible for managing the wastes from "cradle" to "grave."

● Comprehensive Environmental Response Compensation and Liability Act

Public attention focused on the issue of hazardous waste disposal after the well-publicized events of Love Canal. In 1978, residents of this suburb in Niagara Falls, New York, found strange chemicals bubbling up in their yards, and discovered to their horror that the neighborhood had been constructed on top of a chemical waste dump. The Love Canal area was the site of an abandoned canal in which the Hooker Chemicals and Plastics Corporation had dumped approximately 22,000 tons of chemical wastes in the 1940s and 1950s, including pesticides and dioxin (a substance 100 times more deadly than strychnine). Initial estimates that the scope of the problem was limited proved to be wildly optimistic. The first reports estimated that the cleanup would take three months at a cost of $4 million. Eventually, approximately 2,000 residents had to be evacuated. The actual cleanup was not completed until the early 1990s at a cost to Occidental Chemical Corporation (which had taken over Hooker) of approximately $250 million.[23]

In part because of the Love Canal incident, the federal government followed RCRA in 1980 with the Comprehensive Environmental Response Compensation and Liability Act, commonly referred to as CERCLA or as the Superfund Act after its principal contribution, the Superfund.[24] When President Carter proposed the Superfund Act to Congress, he cited Love Canal as clearly demonstrating "the unacceptable costs of improper hazardous waste disposal."[25] CERCLA, with its amendments, the Superfund Amendments and Reauthorization Act (SARA) of 1986, and the Asset Conservation, Lender Liability and Deposit Insurance Protection Act of 1996, is the environmental statute of most significance to landowners. CERCLA established a program, supervised by the EPA, to identify sites from which releases of hazardous substances have occurred or could occur, and to ensure cleanup of those sites by the responsible parties or the government. CERCLA's definition of hazardous substances includes hazardous wastes as defined by RCRA as well as hazardous substances identified by the Clean Air Act, the Clean Water Act, and the Toxic Substances Control Act. CERCLA also creates a claims procedure by which parties who have cleaned up sites or spent money to restore natural resources may obtain contribution from other responsible parties.

CERCLA established a Hazardous Substances Response Trust Fund—the Superfund—to pay for the federal government's share of cleanup costs. Initially, the Superfund was funded by a tax on the petroleum and chemical industry, but it was intended to be a regenerating or rotating fund with resources to be obtained by recovering cleanup costs from those parties responsible for the release of the hazardous substances.

CERCLA makes four categories of persons, called "potentially responsible parties," strictly liable and jointly and severally liable for the cleanup of hazardous substance releases (or for reimbursing the Superfund if the EPA initiates cleanup):[26]

- Current owners or operators of the property.

- Former owners or operators who owned or operated the property at times when disposal or releases of hazardous substances occurred.

- Generators and others who arranged for the disposal or treatment of hazardous substances.

- Transporters of hazardous substances.

Strict liability is liability without fault. Liability is "joint and several" when a group has liability for a wrong or a debt (joint liability) and any member of the group can be held accountable for the whole amount (several liability). Thus, **joint and several liability** under CERCLA means that anyone of a group of parties responsible for cleanup costs is personally liable to the federal government (i.e., to the Superfund) for the whole debt, must pay it if called upon to do so, and has a right to contribution from the other members of the group for their shares. Because of the imposition of strict liability and joint and several liability, the total cleanup costs may be assessed against a party who had little or no involvement in the release of the hazardous substances. As one Justice Department representative told Congress, "Government is perfectly prepared to punish the innocent for the sins of the guilty."[27] Of course, the liable party could then sue the more responsible parties for contribution, but faces the risk that they will be unavailable for lawsuit or insolvent.

The costs of cleanup can be staggering. For sites identified by the EPA and included on the National Priority List for cleanup, the cleanup costs have exceeded $25 million per site. Because liability is retroactive, current landowners may be responsible for releases that predated their ownership of the land or even the passage of CERCLA, and sometimes for a release or disposal that was legal at the time. This retroactive liability creates a potential nightmare for small businesses and nonindustrial landowners. *The Wall Street Journal* reported on one Superfund case, *United States v. Keystone*, involving toxic wastes disposed of in a municipal dump, in which nearly 800 small business owners, including the owners of a local restaurant, the local bowling alley, a motel, and the Lutheran home for the aged, were dragged into court by the federal government to pay for an estimated $17 million cleanup.[28]

Although CERCLA was originally intended to address large-scale industrial pollution of Love Canal magnitude, the act covers smaller releases and thus poses a financial risk and at least a paperwork burden to many other types of landowners. The federal government has identified a number of types of properties that present risk of environmental contamination:[29]

- Industrial properties and properties on industrially zoned land.

- Properties located close to industrial areas.

- Properties that include or are close to an existing or former gas station.

- Commercial properties that include an auto repair or dry cleaner.

- Properties adjacent to railroads or underground pipelines.

- Properties that have served as or are close to a waste disposal site.

- Properties where the past uses or the surrounding uses include the storage of or usage of hazardous or toxic substances.

- Properties suspected of or containing asbestos material.

- Properties emanating radon gas.

- Properties within one mile of a Superfund site.

As one commentator has noted concerning the broad range of CERCLA coverage:

> *Buyer's counsel must be cautious not to underestimate the scope, the reach, or the impact of CERCLA and related exposure. Because it reaches all defined "hazardous substances" with no de minimus exception, it can affect virtually any industrial or commercial facility in the United States. . . . EPA has defined more than seven hundred substances as hazardous, and state laws often expand on EPA's list. While it may be a slight overstatement to declare that everything is a hazardous substance, the exceptions are narrow and few. And it is perhaps only slightly more of an overstatement to say that any site in the United States is a potential CERCLA site. Even for those sites that have already been cleaned up or isolated to prevent further hazardous substance releases, there is the promise of periodic review and the prospect of further cleanup.*[30]

The broad definition of responsible parties and an aggressive enforcement stance by the EPA and accommodating courts have led to a broad sweep of liability. Although this liability scheme may seem unfair to landowners, especially those who are responsible for cleaning up pollution caused by others, the alternative is that the expense of cleanup falls on the taxpayer, who is equally innocent and who votes.

The aggressiveness of the EPA was perhaps most evident in its pursuit of secured lenders. Secured lenders take a security interest in land or a business and normally have nothing to do with its operation or management. Holders of a security interest were exempted from liability under the express language of CERCLA. However, seeing lenders as potential defendants with the resources to pay for environmental cleanup, the EPA successfully argued in court that once a secured lender foreclosed on the property, the lender ceased being merely the holder of a security interest, an exempt party, and became a landowner, a responsible party under CERCLA. Indeed, under the theory accepted by the Court of Appeals in *United States v. Fleet Factors*, the secured lender might also have liability as an "operator," even if it did not foreclose on the collateral, if it had the "capacity to influence" the borrower's treatment of hazardous waste.[31] The EPA's position in *Fleet Factors* impaired the ability of industrial borrowers to obtain financing and led to a firestorm of criticism, which initially prompted the EPA to attempt a strategic retreat, and eventually led to an amendment of CERCLA to provide secured lenders with a statutory "safe harbor."[32]

Under recent amendments to CERCLA, a secured lender is excluded from treatment as an owner or operator, and thus from CERCLA liability, if it acts like a lender and does not exercise overall management control or environmental management control over the borrower. A lender cannot be treated as an owner or an operator if it (a) does not participate in management before foreclosure, (b) forecloses only to protect its security interest, and (c) "seeks to sell, re-lease (in the case of a lease finance transaction), or otherwise divest [itself of the security] at the earliest practicable, commercially reasonable time, on commercially reasonable terms, taking into account market conditions and legal and regulatory requirements."[33]

For other potentially responsible landowners, CERCLA provides only one significant defense to liability—the so-called innocent purchaser defense (also known as the innocent landowner defense). Notwithstanding the name of the defense, being actually innocent is not enough to avoid liability under CERCLA. To be protected, the buyer must not only be ignorant of any release of hazardous substances at the time of purchase, but also must have no reason to know of it after diligent investigation. That is, the buyer must be able to demonstrate that it took precautions against foreseeable acts or omissions of any third party,[34] it did not know and had no reason to know of the disposal of any hazardous substance at the site,[35] and it undertook "all appropriate inquiry into the previous ownership and uses of the property consistent with good commercial or customary practice in an effort to minimize liability."[36] As a practical matter, to meet the conditions of the innocent purchaser defense, the buyer must procure an environmental audit of the property.

In an **environmental audit**, an investigator, usually an environmental engineer, reviews public records and the physical condition of the property, looking for evidence of environmental contamination and violation of environmental laws. Evidence might include current or past industrial or commercial uses of the property. The audit is usually divided into two phases. A **phase one environmental audit** involves a review of the chain of title to identify previous owners of the property, a review of public record information from federal, state, and local agencies, including zoning, building, and occupancy permits, and a visual inspection of the property. In the physical site inspection, the environmental engineer looks for any sign of discolored soil or vegetation that might indicate a chemical release, and any soil disturbance or unusual soil formations that might indicate dumping or filling. The inspector also looks closely at any buildings or facilities on the property and any processes or operations contained in the buildings. Any underground storage tanks are a serious concern. The engineer interviews the current owner of the property and possibly reviews the owner's business records, particularly any records required by RCRA. If possible, the inspector will also review activities on adjacent properties, because any release of hazardous substances on neighboring properties may have migrated via the ground water and contaminated the property under investigation.

Underground storage tanks of various sorts represent one of the more commonly encountered environmental problems. Underground storage tanks are used to hold petroleum products such as gasoline or heating oil and chemicals for industrial processes. Storage tanks may be overfilled, causing the excess to spill over and contaminate the soil and groundwater. Also, after years in the ground, underground storage tanks corrode and leak. Beginning in 1988, federal regulations have required storage tanks to have overfill protection, corrosion prevention, and leak detection mechanisms, but noncompliance was, and is, widespread.

If the property passes a phase one environmental audit, the buyer will have satisfied the requirements of the innocent purchaser defense under CERCLA, thereby protecting the buyer from joint and several liability. Because the audit also protects the buyer's lender, a phase one environmental audit has become a universal feature of commercial lending in the United States.

BOX 18–3 CONTENTS OF A PHASE ONE ENVIRONMENTAL AUDIT

1. Review of recorded chain of title information for a period of at least 75 years.
2. Review of historic aerial photographs, soil surveys, or topographical maps of the subject property to determine the construction or destruction of buildings and the existence of ponds and disposal areas on the property over time.
3. Review of EPA records for existence of environmental cleanup liens on the property or adjacent properties.
4. Examination of applicable government records and permits, including building, zoning, planning, sewer, water, fire, environmental, and other department records. "Environmental and other department records" includes applicable Department of Health Services, Solid Waste Management Board, and Air Quality Management District records.
5. Visual site inspection.
6. On-site interviews of landowner (and neighbors, if appropriate) to determine whether past or present owners or tenants have stored, created, or discharged hazardous materials or waste, and review of whether appropriate procedures, safeguards, and permits are in place.

If the investigator finds evidence of industrial or commercial uses or other property conditions that indicate environmental problems, a phase two environmental audit will normally be recommended. A **phase two environmental audit** involves chemical testing of the soil, surface water, and ground water to determine whether, and to what extent, environmental contamination has occurred. Because of the chemical testing, a phase two environmental audit tends to be much more expensive than a phase one audit and often becomes a point of dispute in a purchase transaction. It is important for the parties to remember, however, that an environmental audit is not a frivolous exercise with the buyer and lender just "going through the motions" to fit within the statutory definition of innocent purchaser. If the property is in fact contaminated, the contamination drastically affects its market value even if the buyer and lender have no personal liability under CERCLA. Accordingly, the buyer and the lender are entirely justified in seeking to determine the environmental condition of the property if the phase one audit reveals a need for the phase two audit.

If the chemical testing reveals contamination of the property, engineering and cleanup solutions usually are available. However, because contamination is likely to decrease the market value and the marketability of the property, and because cleanup is expensive and may not be technologically feasible, a potential buyer should insist on a contractual escape clause to be exercised if environmental contamination is discovered.[37]

In most ways, the prepurchase concerns of the lender parallel those of the buyer. But the lender will also be concerned about what happens to the property *after* closing and during the term of the loan. To protect itself, the lender may seek assurance of the borrower's continued environmental compliance, and will want to limit the borrower's ability to use the property in a way that might lead to future environmental problems. Where environmental risk is unavoidable, the lender may seek other forms of financial assurance, such as other forms of collateral or guarantees.

Other Environmental Protection Statutes

In 1990, Congress passed the Pollution Prevention Act, which introduced a new approach for attacking pollution.[38] The statutes discussed earlier in this chapter are directed at policy issues, at control of pollution that is about to occur, or remediation of pollution that has already occurred. In contrast, the Pollution Prevention Act of 1990 focuses attention on the prevention of pollution at the source, through changes in production, operation, and the handling and use of raw materials. The act authorizes matching grants to states for programs of pollution prevention.

Civil and Criminal Liability for Environmental Violations

Most of the environmental statutes regulating pollution provide for administrative penalties (i.e., monetary penalties imposed directly by administrative agencies such as the EPA), as well as civil and criminal penalties for violation of their provisions. Civil penalties usually take the form of damages awarded by a court for cleanup costs and other consequences of the defendant's polluting activities. In fiscal year 1994, the EPA assessed $48,021,941 in administrative penalties and was awarded $65,635,930 in civil penalties. Criminal sanctions are also provided for "knowing" or "willful" violations of federal environmental statutes. Civil sanctions are procedurally much easier to enforce than are the criminal sanctions. In civil actions, the plaintiff usually must prove only that a violation of the applicable emission standard occurred, and not that the violation was willful or knowing. Also, in a civil action, the government is required to prove its case by only a preponderance of the evidence (i.e., enough evidence to show that it is more likely than not that the defendant committed the violation) instead of the more exacting beyond a reasonable doubt standard of the criminal law, under which the proof must be sufficient to convince a reasonable person that the defendant in fact did commit the violation.

Notwithstanding the procedural difficulties, the EPA considers criminal prosecutions a critical part of its enforcement strategy and has referred a steadily increasing number of cases to the Department of Justice for criminal prosecution. In 1991, it referred 81 cases involving 104 criminal defendants who were collectively sentenced to 963 months in prison. In 1999, it referred 241 cases, involving 324 criminal defendants, who were collectively sentenced to 2,486 months in prison. One study found that convicted individual criminal defendants worked in every level of their respective organizations, from president to hourly workers. Criminal defendants may be individuals or corporations. If a corporation is the defendant, it cannot be sent to prison, but instead may be fined or even, in extreme circumstances, may have its corporate charter revoked.

In addition to civil and criminal penalties available to the government, most of the statutes permit parties who are personally injured by violations of the environmental standards to bring civil actions to collect damages. None of these remedies is exclusive; a single violation of the environmental laws can lead to civil and criminal sanctions initiated by the EPA and a civil suit for damages by an injured plaintiff. These remedies are also cumulative with the preexisting common law remedies, as illustrated by the following case.

Case 18.2

New York v. Shore Realty Corp.

759 F.2d 1032 (2d Cir. 1985)

Donald LeoGrande incorporated Shore Realty Corp. (Shore) solely for the purpose of purchasing the Shore Road property. By contract dated July 14, 1983, Shore agreed to purchase the 3.2-acre site, a small peninsula surrounded on three sides by the waters of Hempstead Harbor and Mott Cove, for condominium development. A large quantity of hazardous chemicals, about 700,000 gallons, was located on the property. Neither Shore nor LeoGrande had participated in the generation or transportation of the waste. All corporate decisions and actions by Shore were made, directed, and controlled by LeoGrande.

The purchase agreement provided that it could be voided by Shore without penalty if after conducting an environmental study Shore decided not to proceed. LeoGrande was fully aware that the tenants, Applied Environmental Services, Inc., and Hazardous Waste Disposal, Inc., were then operating a hazardous waste storage facility on the site. Shore's environmental consultant, WTM Management Corporation (WTM), prepared a detailed report in July 1983. The report concluded that over the past several decades "the facility ha[d] received little if any preventive maintenance, the tanks (aboveground and belowground), pipeline, loading rack, fire extinguishing system, and warehouse have deteriorated." WTM found that there had been several spills of hazardous waste at the site, including at least one large spill in 1978. Though there had been some attempts at cleanup, the WTM testing revealed that hazardous substances, such as benzene, were still leaching into the groundwater and the waters of the bay immediately adjacent to the bulkhead abutting Hempstead Harbor. After a site visit on July 18, 1983, WTM reported firsthand on the sorry state of the facility, observing, among other things, "seepage from the bulkhead," "corrosion" on all the tanks, signs of possible leakage from some of the tanks, deterioration of the pipeline and loading rack, and fifty to one hundred 55-gallon drums containing contaminated earth in one of the warehouses. The report concluded that if the current tenants "close up the operation and leave the material at the site," the owners would be left with a "potential time bomb." WTM estimated that the cost of environmental cleanup and monitoring would range from $650,000 to more than $1 million before development could begin. After receiving this report Shore sought from the State Department of Environmental Conservation (DEC) a waiver of liability as landowner for the disposal of the hazardous waste stored at the site. Although the DEC denied the waiver, Shore took title on October 13, 1983, and obtained certain rights over against the tenants, whom it subsequently evicted on January 5, 1984.

The tenants did not clean up the site before they left. . . . Shore did nothing about the hundreds of thousands of gallons of hazardous waste standing in deteriorating tanks. In addition, although a growing number of drums were leaking hazardous substances, Shore essentially ignored the problem until June 1984.

The state of New York sued Shore to recover costs of assessing the conditions at the site and supervising the removal of the drums of hazardous waste. The trial court granted New York's motion for partial summary judgment, finding defendants liable for plaintiff's "response costs" under the Comprehensive Environmental Response, Compensation, and Liability Act (CERCLA), and issuing an injunction ordering defendants to clean up the hazardous waste storage site.

OAKES, Cir. J.

. . . CERCLA was designed "to bring order to the array of partly redundant, partly inadequate federal hazardous substances cleanup and compensation laws." It applies "primarily to the cleanup of leaking inactive or abandoned sites and to emergency responses to spills." . . .

CERCLA authorized the federal government to respond in several ways. EPA can use Superfund resources to clean up hazardous waste sites and spills. The National Contingency Plan (NCP), prepared by EPA pursuant to CERCLA, governs cleanup efforts by "establish[ing] procedures and standards for responding to releases of hazardous substances." At the same time, EPA can sue for reimbursement of cleanup costs from any responsible parties it can locate, allowing the federal government to respond immediately while later trying to shift financial responsibility to others. Thus, Superfund covers cleanup costs if the site has been abandoned, if the responsible parties elude detection, or if private resources are inadequate. In addition, CERCLA authorizes EPA to seek an injunction in federal district court to force a responsible party to clean up any site or spill that presents an imminent and substantial danger to public health or welfare or the environment. In sum, CERCLA is not a regulatory standard-setting statute such as the Clean Air Act. Rather, the government generally undertakes pollution abatement, and polluters pay for such abatement through tax and reimbursement liability.

Congress clearly did not intend, however, to leave cleanup under CERCLA solely in the hands of the federal government. A state or political subdivision may enter into a contract or cooperative agreement with EPA, whereby both may take action on a cost-sharing basis. And states, like EPA, can sue responsible parties for remedial and removal costs if such efforts are "not inconsistent with" the NCP. While CERCLA expressly does not preempt state law, it precludes "recovering compensation for the same removal costs or damages or claims" under both CERCLA and state or other federal laws, and prohibits states from requiring contributions to any fund "the purpose of which is to pay compensation for claims . . . which may be compensated under" CERCLA. Moreover, "any . . . person" who is acting consistently with the requirements of the NCP may recover "necessary costs of response." Finally, responsible parties are liable for "damages for injury to, destruction of, or loss of natural resources, including the reasonable costs of assessing such injury, destruction, or loss resulting from such a release."

Congress intended that responsible parties be held strictly liable, even though an explicit provision for strict liability was not included in the compromise. . . .

We hold that the district court properly awarded the State response costs under section 9607(a) (4) (A). The State's costs in assessing the conditions of the site and supervising the removal of the drums of hazardous waste squarely fall within CERCLA's definition of response costs, even though the State is not undertaking to do the removal. . . .

1. Covered Persons. CERCLA holds liable four classes of persons:

(1) the owner and operator of a vessel (otherwise subject to the jurisdiction of the United States) or a facility,

(2) any person who at the time of disposal of any hazardous substance owned or operated any facility at which such hazardous substances were disposed of,

(3) any person who by contract, agreement, or otherwise arranged for disposal or treatment, or arranged with a transporter for transport for disposal or treatment, of hazardous substances owned or possessed by such person, by any other party or entity, at any facility owned or operated by another party or entity and containing such hazardous substances, and

(4) any person who accepts or accepted any hazardous substances for transport to disposal or treatment facilities or sites selected by such person.

As noted above, section 9607 makes these persons liable, if "there is a release, or a threatened release which causes the incurrence of response costs, of a hazardous substance" from the facility, for, among other things, "all costs of removal or remedial action incurred by the United States Government or a State not inconsistent with the national contingency plan."

Shore argues that it is not covered by section 9607(a) (1) because it neither owned the site at the time of disposal nor caused the presence or the release of the hazardous waste at the facility. . . . We agree with the State, however, that section 9607(a) (1) unequivocally imposes strict liability on the current owner of a facility from which there is a release or threat of release, without regard to causation. . . .

[A]s the State points out, accepting Shore's arguments would open a huge loophole in CERCLA's coverage. It is quite clear that if the current owner of a site could avoid liability merely by having purchased the site after chemical dumping had ceased, waste sites certainly would be sold, following the cessation of dumping, to new owners who could avoid the liability otherwise required by CERCLA. Congress had well in mind that persons who dump or store hazardous waste sometimes cannot be located or may be deceased or judgment-proof. We will not interpret section 9607(a) in any way that apparently frustrates the statute's goals, in the absence of a specific congressional intention otherwise. . . .

Having held Shore liable under CERCLA for the State's response costs, we nevertheless are required to hold that injunctive relief under CERCLA is not available to the State. . . .

. . . In challenging the decision below, Shore fails to distinguish between a public nuisance and a private nuisance. The former "is an offense against the State and is subject to abatement or prosecution on application of the proper governmental agency" and "consists of conduct or omissions which offend, interfere with or cause damage to the public in the exercise of rights common to all . . . in a manner such as to . . . endanger or injure the property, health, safety or comfort of a considerable number of persons." The latter, however, "threatens one person or a relatively few. . . , an essential feature being an interference with the use or enjoyment of land. . . . It is actionable by the individual person or persons whose rights have been disturbed." Public and private nuisance bear little relationship to each other. Although some rules apply to both, other rules apply to one but not the other. Under New York law, Shore, as a landowner, is subject to liability for either a public or private nuisance on its property upon learning of the nuisance and having a reasonable opportunity to abate it. As noted in the *Restatement (Second) of Torts* § 839 comment d (1979):

> Liability [of a possessor of land] is not based upon responsibility for the creation of the harmful condition, but upon the fact that he has exclusive control over the land and the things done upon it and should have the responsibility of taking reasonable measures to remedy conditions on it that are a source of harm to others. Thus a vendee . . . of land upon which a harmful physical condition exists may be liable under the rule here stated for failing to abate it after he takes possession, even though it was created by his vendor, lessor or other person and even though he had no part in its creation.

It is immaterial therefore that other parties placed the chemicals on this site; Shore purchased it with knowledge of its condition—indeed of the approximate cost of cleaning it up—and with an opportunity to clean up the site. LeoGrande knew that the hazardous waste was present without the consent of the State or its DEC, but failed to take reasonable steps to abate the condition. Moreover, Shore is liable for maintenance of a public nuisance irrespective of negligence or fault. Nor is there any requirement that the State prove actual, as opposed to threatened, harm from the nuisance in order to obtain abatement. Finally, the State has standing to bring suit to abate such a nuisance "in its role as guardian of the environment."

We also reject Shore's argument that its maintenance of the Shore Road site does not constitute a public nuisance. We have no doubt that the release or threat of release of hazardous waste into the environment unreasonably infringes upon a public right and this is a public nuisance as a matter of New York law. Shore challenges the existence of the releases or threatened releases claimed by the State. We have found, however, that several crucial facts are undisputed: the tanks have leaked and are corroding; the groundwater has been contaminated; and Shore is unwilling and unable to transform the site into a stable, licensed storage facility. It makes no difference that Shore has begun a cleanup. We simply hold that under New York law it is required to finish that cleanup. . . .

We hold LeoGrande liable as an "operator" under [§ 9607] for the State's response costs. Under CERCLA "owner or operator" is defined to mean "any person owning or operating" an onshore facility, id. § 9601(20) (A), and "person" includes individuals as well as corporations, id. § 9601(21). More important, the definition of "owner or operator" excludes "a person, who, without participating in the management of a . . . facility, holds indicia of ownership primarily to protect his security interest in the facility." The use of this exception implies that an owning stockholder who manages the corporation, such as LeoGrande, is liable under CERCLA as an "owner or operator." That conclusion is consistent with that of other courts that have addressed the issue. In any event, LeoGrande is in charge of the operation of the facility in question, and as such is an "operator" within the meaning of CERCLA.

. . . New York courts have held that a corporate officer who controls corporate conduct and thus is an active individual participant in that conduct is liable for the torts of the corporation. We need not address whether he is liable merely as an officer of Shore, for it is beyond dispute that LeoGrande specifically directs, sanctions, and actively participates in Shore's maintenance of the nuisance. This general rule is particularly appropriate in the public nuisance context where "everyone who . . . participates in the . . . maintenance . . . of a nuisance are liable jointly and severally.' " . . .

Judgment affirmed.

QUESTION ABOUT CASE 18.2

Why did the state of New York seek an injunction in this case? Hint: How does the court use the tort of public nuisance to supplement CERCLA in this case?

Note: A court granted the injunction. However, the defendant's refusal to obey it led to civil contempt sanctions totaling $1,000 per day. The sanctions were affirmed by the Second Circuit Court of Appeals, which could not resist chiding the parties: "the more immediate objective is to remove the chemicals from the property. Protracted litigation over contempt sanctions may be far less effective toward that end than prompt action by the defendants and the State to undertake various phases of the task, leaving issues of cost reimbursement for later determination." *New York v. Shore Realty Corp.*, 763 F.2d 49 (2d Cir. 1985).

State Statutory Protection of the Environment[39]

The federal government has not acted alone in seeking to preserve and protect the environment. Every state has become involved to a greater or lesser extent in cooperation with the federal government. Under the Supremacy Clause of the U.S. Constitution, the states cannot pass any legislation that conflicts with federal statutes or invades an area of federal preemption. Consequently, states may not enforce any scheme of environmental control if the federal government has preempted state involvement or if the state law is less strict than the federal law. In a few areas, primarily where uniform national standards are necessary, the federal government has precluded (preempted) state activity. However, in most areas of environmental concern, states can pass legislation that supplements the federal scheme. Some states, such as California, Oregon, and Washington, have acted aggressively to protect the environment. Many states are reluctant to do so because they fear that they will discourage industry and economic development. Consequently, several states have passed laws that restrict state agencies from enforcing requirements more stringent than those imposed by federal law.[40]

Self-Study Questions

1. What were the primary legal tools at common law for addressing the problem of pollution?

2. What must a plaintiff prove to recover damages for pollution under the tort theory of nuisance?

3. In terms of what a plaintiff must prove to prevail, how do the tort theories of nuisance and trespass differ from the concept of strict liability?

4. Why are nuisance, trespass, and strict liability inadequate to prevent or control pollution?

5. (a) What prompted the federal government to enact pollution control laws? (b) What trends can we observe in federal pollution regulation?

6. What is the significance of the Clean Water Act to landowners?

7. What is the significance of the Clean Air Act to landowners?

8. Many commentators believe that of the numerous federal environmental protection statutes, CERCLA has the greatest impact on landowners. What features of CERCLA support that belief?

9. Who are "potentially responsible parties" for cleanup of hazardous substances under CERCLA?

10. (a) What remedies are available to the government for violations of the typical environmental statute? (b) Would these remedies be sufficient to ensure a business's compliance?

Case Problems

1. Neighboring residential property owners sought an injunction to halt the construction of a proposed hog-breeding operation. The evidence showed that the proposed operation would house 22,800 hogs, which would produce massive volumes of feces and urine and other waste that would drain into a concrete pit under each building, then into anaerobic and aerobic lagoons where the waste would be broken down, eventually to be pumped to and distributed over various spray fields. The evidence also showed that the wastes would attract insects, that the stench would extend up to three miles away, depending on weather conditions, and that the waste lagoons could contaminate ground water. Other farms owned by the same operator had been closed because of environmental violations. Should the court grant the injunction halting construction of the proposed facility? *Superior Farm Management v. Montgomery*, 513 S.E.2d 215 (Ga. 1999).

2. Quivira Mining Co. challenged the authority of the EPA to regulate the discharge of pollutants from uranium mining facilities into gullies or arroyos, claiming that these were not "navigable waters" within the meaning of the Clean Water Act. Will the defendants be able to avoid liability on this ground? *Quivira Mining Co. v. E.P.A.*, 765 F.2d 126 (10th Cir. 1985), *cert. denied*, 474 U.S. 1055 (1986).

3. Amoco bought a 114-acre tract from Borden. Approximately 35 acres was contaminated with a mildly radioactive phosphogypsum, a by-product from the production of fertilizer Borden had produced on the site. Amoco claimed that it had no knowledge of the radioactive nature of the phosphogypsum until it was informed by the Texas Department of Water Resources. Amoco brought suit under CERCLA seeking to recover its environmental response costs from Borden. Will Amoco be successful in its claim? *Amoco Oil Co. v. Borden, Inc.*, 889 F.2d 664 (5th Cir. 1989).

4. The Tanglewood East Subdivision in Montgomery, Texas, was constructed on a site upon which the United Creosoting Company had operated a wood-treatment facility from 1946 to 1972. During that period, large amounts of toxic waste accumulated on the property. In 1973,

developers acquired the property, filled in and graded the creosote pools, and commenced residential development. In 1980, the Tanglewood homeowners and residents complained to Texas authorities about environmental problems, and the EPA placed the site on its National Priorities List for cleaning under CERCLA. The cleanup was expected to require demolition of six homes and the construction of bunkers to contain the hazardous materials, at a cost of millions of dollars. The residents sued the residential developers, the construction companies, their lenders, and the real estate agents and agencies involved. The defendants claimed that they were not subject to the liability provisions of CERCLA because they did not produce any of the toxins. Are the defendants likely to be successful in their claim? *Tanglewood East Homeowners v. Charles-Thomas, Inc.*, 849 F.2d 1568 (5th Cir. 1988).

5. Seventeen artists formed a partnership to buy a former industrial building to convert into a residential condominium complex. Each partner was to receive one of the condominium units. After the conveyance of the building to the partnership, the partners became aware that the property was contaminated with mercury, a toxic substance. Despite this knowledge, they constructed the condominium units and conveyed them from the partnership entity to the individual partners. The improved property could not be decontaminated, and clean-up by demolition was recommended. The individual condominium owners filed suit seeking, among other things, a declaratory judgment that they were "innocent purchasers" under CERCLA and were not liable for any cleanup costs. Do they qualify as innocent purchasers? *Grand Street Artists v. General Electric Co.*, 28 F. Supp. 2d 291 (D. N.J. 1998).

Endnotes

1. Garrett Hardin, "The Tragedy of the Commons," 162 *Science* 1243 (1968).

2. For example, a second Court of Appeals opinion, *In re Camel City Laundry Company*, 472 S.E.2d 402 (N.C. App. 1996), *cert. denied*, 483 S.E.2d 162 (N.C. 1997), concerned the tax value of a property that was environmentally contaminated. The evidence showed that the property had no fair market value because although the unimpaired value of the property was $505,000, the property was severely contaminated and would cost $584,000 to clean up.

3. J. S. Shrimpton, "Hard Times: Overview," in *Reference Guide to English Literature,* 2nd ed., D. L. Kirkpatrick, ed. (Press, 1991) reproduced in Literature Resource Center.

4. Charles Dickens, *Hard Times* 65, David Craig, ed. (Penguin Books, 1969).

5. 982 F.Supp. 355 (M.D.N.C. 1997).

6. 709 P.2d 782 (Wash. 1985).

7. *Adams v. Cleveland-Cliffs Iron Co.,* 602 N.W.2d 215 (Mich. App. 1999).

8. See, e.g., the landmark case of *Rylands v. Fletcher,* 159 Eng. Rep. 737 (1865).

9. 257 A.2d 138 (Md. Ct. App. 1969).

10. 657 P.2d 267 (Utah 1982).

11. 42 U.S.C. § 4321 *et seq.* The expressed purposes of the act were: "To declare a national policy which will encourage productive and enjoyable harmony between man and his environment; to promote efforts which will prevent or eliminate damage to the environment and biosphere and stimulate the health and welfare of man; to enrich the understanding of the ecological systems and natural resources important to the Nation; and to establish a Council on Environmental Quality."

12. 42 U.S.C. § 7401, *et seq.* The 1970 act actually amended the original, ineffective Clean Air Act of 1963.

13. 33 U.S.C. § 401, *et seq.*

14. The original act as amended is codified at 33 U.S.C. 1251, *et seq.*

15. 127 F.3d 343 (4th Cir. 1997).

16. Indiana Dept. of Environmental Mgmt., *Indiana State of the Environment Report 1999* at 30 (1999).

17. 7 C.F.R. § 12.2, *et seq.*

18. See 56 *Fed. Reg.* 18630 (1991).

19. 531 U.S. 159 (2001).

20. Ronald A. Taylor, "Chemical Wastes: A Buried Bombshell," *U.S. News & World Rep.,* September 29, 1980, at 39.

21. 42 U.S.C. § 6901, *et seq.*

22. 42 U.S.C. § 6903(5)a.

23. See "Love Canal," Britannica.com (2000); "Cleanup Help Promised," *Washington Post,* August 6, 1978, at A9; Peter Gwynne, et al., "The Chemicals Around Us," *Newsweek,* August 21, 1978, at 25; Lawrence Mosher, "Love Canals by the Thousand—Who Should Pay the Costly Bill," *National J.,* May 24, 1980, at 855; Ronald A. Taylor, "Chemical Wastes: A Buried Bombshell," *U.S. News & World Rep.,* September 29, 1980, at 39.

24. 42 U.S.C. § 9601, *et seq.*

25. Quoted in Edward Walsh, "Carter Asks $1.6 Billion to Clean Up Chemical, Oil Hazards," *Washington Post,* June 14, 1979, at A2.

26. 42 U.S.C. § 9607 (a).

27. Anthony Z. Roisman, chief of the Justice Department's hazardous waste section, quoted in Lawrence Mosher, "Love Canals by the Thousand—Who Should Pay the Costly Bill?' *National J.,* May 24, 1980, at 855.

28. John H. Fialka, "Superfund Ensnares Thousands of Firms in a Legal Nightmare, Fueling Overhaul Drive," *Wall St. J.,* March 19, 1997.

29. Thrift Bulletin TB-16, Thrift Activities, Lending Risk Assessment (Feb. 6, 1989). For these properties, the Office of Thrift Supervision recommended a Phase I Environmental Audit.

30. William A. Anderson and Melinda Taylor, "Representing Buyers," *Natural Resources & Environment,* Fall 1988, at 3.

31. 901 F.2d 1550 (11th Cir. 1990), *cert. denied,* 498 U.S. 1046 (1991).

32. Lender Liability and Deposit Insurance Protection Act of 1996, P.L. 104-208, Div A, Title II, Subtitle E, § 2501, 110 Stat. 3009-462 (1996).

33. 42 USCS § 9601(20)(E)(ii)(II).

34. 42 U.S.C. § 9607(b)(3)(b).

35. 42 U.S.C. § 9601(35)(A)(i).

36. 42 U.S.C. § 9601 (35)(b).

37. See generally, William A. Anderson and Melinda Taylor, "Representing Buyers," *Natural Resources & Environment,* Fall 1988, at 3; and William G. Ross, Jr., "Environmental Considerations in Commercial Real Estate Transactions From the Buyer's and Lender's Perspective—Identifying, Avoiding and Shifting the Risks," *Commercial Real Estate* (1990).

38. 42 U.S.C. § 13101, *et seq.*

39. See generally, John P. Dwyer, "The Role of State Law in an Era of Federal Preemption: Lessons from Environmental Regulation," 60 *L. & Contemp. Prob.* 203 (1997); and Kirsten H. Engel, "State Environmental Standard Setting: Is There a 'Race' and Is It 'To the Bottom'?"48 *Hastings L. J.* 271 (1997).

40. Kirsten H. Engel, "State Environmental Standard Setting: Is There a 'Race' and Is It 'To the Bottom'?" 48 *Hastings L. J.* 271 (1997).

Chapter 19

Water Rights, Natural Resources, and Agricultural Law

The United States is blessed with a wealth of productive farmland and an abundance of water and other natural resources. These natural treasures have played a critical role in our history and in the economic growth and vitality of the nation. The promise of land and a better life led many of our ancestors to settle the vast open spaces of the country. The search for gold and other minerals spurred the development and settlement of the far West, while the discovery of oil and gas fueled the industrial revolution and continues to provide us with a source of energy that few countries of the world possess. Although we have become a service- and information-based economy, many businesses and individuals continue to earn their living off the land and the minerals that are part of it. Thus, the laws governing the right to use water for personal, agricultural, and industrial purposes; the right to mine and extract solid minerals, oil, and gas from the earth; and the rights and liabilities of farmers and ranchers have contemporary significance. This chapter provides an overview of water rights and natural resources law (mining law and the law of oil and gas), and discusses some real estate aspects of agricultural law.

Water Rights

Water, our most precious natural resource, is essential for life and for human needs such as agriculture, industry, and recreation. Yet, in many parts of the country, the supply of water is inadequate to meet all needs. Agricultural producers and cities, for example, often contend for a limited supply of water. Because sufficient quantities of water to satisfy *all* needs is not possible, a system to allocate this scarce resource is essential. In the United States, the courts and legislatures have developed a complex set of rules to resolve competing claims to water. What the rules require or permit depends in part on the type of water involved. The rules for the use of surface water differ from those for underground water. The rules for navigable and nonnavigable waterways differ, as do those for underground streams and "percolating" groundwater. An individual's water rights also depend upon the legal nature of the state water rights system that governs the use of water. The states have developed two distinct water rights systems, the riparian rights system and the prior appropriation doctrine.

Riparian Rights Systems

The doctrine of **riparian rights** is based on the principle that a riparian landowner, one whose property borders on a lake, river, or stream, has a property right to use and consume some of the water for beneficial purposes related to the land. This right to use the water is considered a property interest that is part of the bundle of rights enjoyed by the riparian. It is subject, however, to the rights of other riparians along the same body of water, who also have a right to use or consume some of the water, which may limit the extent to which a riparian can use the water, including a limit on the quantity that can be taken for beneficial purposes. The common law courts developed a number of doctrines to define the limits of that use, including the "natural flow" and "reasonable use" principles.

The riparian doctrine exists today in the eastern and midwestern parts of the country, areas that are relatively more water rich than the western states. Twenty-nine states continue to follow the doctrine of riparian rights.[1] In addition, Louisiana bases its water law on the Napoleonic Code, civil law that recognizes riparian rights. As noted later in this chapter, the modern riparian rights doctrine has been modified in many states by statutory regulations on the use of water through permit systems. Nevertheless, the doctrine of riparian rights still forms the foundation of water rights law in the East and Midwest.

Prior Appropriation and Hybrid Water Rights Systems

In the West, where water is scarce, a different system of water rights developed, called the prior appropriation doctrine. The **prior appropriation** system was and still is based on the theory that water is owned by the state, not by riparian landowners. The state holds the water in a public trust for its citizens who can acquire a right to divert and use the water for private purposes. Thus, water rights are not based on private ownership of riparian land. Rather, they are based on appropriation of the water for some beneficial purpose.

Under prior appropriation law, an individual who first diverted and used water for a beneficial purpose acquired a right to the continued use of that water that was superior (because it was prior) to uses by others who later diverted water from the same source. This "first in time, first in right" rule allowed a senior appropriator (the first to divert and use the water) to impair the rights of junior users. A person's right to use water for beneficial purposes did not depend on ownership of riparian land nor was it limited to what was reasonably necessary for some beneficial purpose on the riparian land. Rather, water rights were dependent upon a user's "diversion" of water for a useful purpose (e.g., irrigation of land or mining), and priority was determined by the time that use initially commenced. A senior appropriator could use an amount of water that was necessary to serve the purpose for which the water was originally diverted, even if doing so left no water for junior users. The prior appropriation system was a recognition that supplies of water were insufficient to meet the needs of all potential users in the western United States. The system protected those who had invested the time, energy, and resources to divert water for productive uses, by granting them a right to continue that use in the future, subject only to the prior rights of senior appropriators.

Today, prior appropriation systems of water rights exist in nine states.[2] These states are said to have "pure" appropriation systems, following what is referred to as the Colorado Doctrine. Even in the pure states, however, a regulatory system of administrative permits for water use has been created in modern times to allocate water rights. In other western states, a **hybrid system** of water rights exists. This system, which is based on prior appropriation principles but also recognizes some riparian rights, is sometimes called the California doctrine because it originated there. In the hybrid states, riparian rights are recognized because they came into existence under preexisting riparian state law before the state's adoption of prior appropriation. However, because all new water rights are now based on prior appropriation, the foundation of the law under such hybrid systems is prior appropriation. Today, ten states have a hybrid system of water rights.[3] Hawaii has its own unique system of water rights with origins in the feudal system of land ownership in the state.

Surface Water Under Riparian Systems

Under the common law, a riparian owner had a nontransferable right to use and consume water from a lake or stream. Ordinarily, the water could be used only on the riparian land, for drinking water and other domestic uses and for such other "artificial" purposes as irrigating farmland or running a mill. Moreover, diversion of the water even for beneficial purposes on the riparian land was limited in several respects. First, the common law recognized a preference for domestic uses of the water and imposed limits on artificial uses. Second, because the rights of downstream riparians had to be respected, the amount of water diverted was subject to limits under the natural flow and reasonable use tests.

Riparian Land

For a landowner to have riparian rights to a body of water, it must be a watercourse. A **watercourse** is a waterway with a natural channel, well-defined beds and banks, and a flow of water. Natural streams and rivers are watercourses. *Watercourse* does not include diffused surface water, water that flows across the land as the result of runoff of rain or melting snow. It also does not include artificial channels such as irrigation canals. Although subsurface water usually is not a watercourse, underground streams and a natural spring that forms the source of a river are considered watercourses. Natural lakes and ponds are subject to riparian rights as well. The owner of land adjacent to a lake is a "littoral" landowner, and as such has riparian rights to the water. In contrast, owners of property along human-constructed lakes have no riparian rights.

Purpose of Water Use

The common law distinguished between (1) "natural" or "domestic" uses of water and (2) "artificial" uses. **Natural (domestic) uses** were those personal and household uses necessary for basic subsistence. They included water for drinking, bathing, cooking, and cleaning, as well as for watering some farmstead cattle and animals. A riparian could use water for domestic purposes even if the use diminished the flow of water in a stream or watercourse. Domestic uses were favored in the law to such an extent that they were not limited by the natural flow or reasonable use rules. In contrast, **artificial uses** were those not essential for living, but increased productivity or enhanced the riparian's standard of living. Artificial uses included irrigation of farmland, watering of commercial animal herds, mining, manufacturing and industrial uses, and power generation. Artificial uses were subject to limitations under the traditional natural flow test and the modern reasonable use standard.

Natural Flow and Reasonable Use Doctrines

Under the **natural flow** rule, a riparian could use the water as it passed the riparian's property, but was not allowed to change the quantity or quality of the water in the watercourse. Because many commercial and industrial uses that developed during the industrial revolution (mills, manufacturing plants, irrigation systems) used and consumed large quantities of water in their operations, the natural flow rule became unworkable in resolving competing claims to water. To alleviate the problem, the common law courts adopted a more flexible rule, one that allowed riparian owners to use a reasonable amount of water, even for commercial activities, as long as the rights of other riparians were not unreasonably impaired. This **reasonable use** rule is now the majority position in riparian states, although courts continue to consider the natural flow in connection with the determination of reasonableness.

In deciding whether a use is reasonable, the courts consider both the nature of the riparian's use of the water and the resulting harm to other riparians. The following factors have been identified as important to the reasonableness issue:

1. The purpose of the use.

2. The suitability of the use to the watercourse or lake.

3. The economic value of the use.

4. The social value of the use.

5. The extent and amount of the harm it causes.

6. The practicality of avoiding the harm by adjusting the use or method of use of one proprietor or the other.

7. The practicality of adjusting the quantity of water used by each proprietor.

8. The protection of existing values of water uses, investments, and enterprises.

9. The justice of requiring the user causing harm to bear the loss.[4]

The first four factors focus on the riparian's use of the water, the utility of the use, and its importance from a societal perspective. Consistently with the common law distinction between natural and artificial uses, courts often consider domestic uses to be superior to other uses. Factors 5 through 9 focus on the ability of the riparian to avoid harm to others and the fairness of subjecting other riparians to that harm. The courts consider, therefore, whether limits or adjustments can be made to minimize the harm, such as limiting the timing or amount of withdrawals. The factors also call for a consideration of existing values, a reference to the effect a riparian's use may have on prior users. Although priority of use is generally not a major consideration in riparian systems, courts consider harm to preexisting uses as an aspect of balancing the equities. That is, is it fair to allow a junior (in time) riparian user to cause harm to a senior user who has a reasonable expectation of continued use and often has an investment in the water diversion? Generally, courts have held that it is unreasonable for a new use to totally destroy or substantially impair an existing one.

Statutory Modifications of Riparian Rights

In many states. the riparian rights system of water law has been modified by legislation. Some of the changes relate to specific problems associated with the diversion and use of water for commercial purposes. Statutes regulating the construction of dams and laws protecting the environment are examples. At least 17 states have adopted permit systems to better allocate water among competing users and to protect the public interest in state water resources.[5] Florida, for example, has an extensive regulatory system under its Water Resources Act. For most water uses, the Act replaced the common law riparian rules with a permit system designed to conserve the state's water resources. Permit statutes like Florida's empower an administrative agency, usually a state water management body, to review applications for permits, and to grant them if standards in the law have been met. The standards usually require a consideration of the rights of existing users and the effect of the proposed water use on the public interest. The permit may set conditions on the diversion of the water, including quantity limitations, and it may be forfeited if not used within a specified time after its issuance.

● Surface Water Under Appropriation and Hybrid Systems

As a result of the adoption of the prior appropriation doctrine, most of the rules of riparian law do not apply in prior appropriation states. Thus, in those states a nonriparian can acquire rights to water, and water can be put to beneficial uses on land outside of a river's watershed, and on land that is not riparian. Water rights can be transferred by an appropriator without any transfer of riparian land. An appropriator's use of the water is not limited by notions of riparians' common ownership and thus is not restricted under natural flow or reasonable use principles. Sometimes, a prior appropriator is allowed to use water to the exclusion of junior appropriators whose interests need not be respected. Rather than being limited by a consideration of the rights of others, an appropriator's rights depend on the beneficial purpose for which the water was originally appropriated and the amount of water necessary to serve that purpose.

Prior appropriation systems are not uniform in the recognition of water rights, and modern changes to these systems have altered the traditional rules of appropriation. Hybrid systems are based primarily on prior appropriation principles, but they retain some water rules based on riparian law. More significant, however, has been the development of statutory procedures that require the grant of a permit by a state agency to establish an enforceable appropriation right. Today, a person's right to divert and use water in an appropriation system (pure or hybrid) depends not only on established principles of prior appropriation (and in some cases, riparian law) but also on compliance with state permit requirements.

Meaning of Appropriation

Under a prior appropriation system, the right to divert and use water from a watercourse does not depend on ownership of riparian land. It depends instead upon whether a user made an actual appropriation of water for some beneficial purpose.

A mere intent to appropriate is not enough to establish an **appropriation**; it has to be accompanied by a physical act of taking (appropriating) the water, that is an actual **diversion** or rerouting of water from a river, lake, or other natural source. A diversion can be accomplished by damming a stream and using the water to irrigate farmland or by holding the water in a reservoir or pool for industrial use. Pumping water out of a lake or channeling water away from its natural banks also constitutes a diversion.

To constitute an appropriation, the water diverted must be put to some **beneficial purpose**. Beneficial uses of water include irrigation, industrial activities, power generation, municipal water supplies, park and recreational uses, and in some states purely aesthetic applications such as preserving waterfalls. It is often said that beneficial use is "the basis, the measure, and the limit of the right to use water" in a prior appropriation system. Beneficial use identifies the purpose for which the water was originally appropriated and automatically limits the appropriator's use of the water in the future, because an appropriator ordinarily cannot change the purpose for which the water is being diverted unless such change will not result in adverse effects on other users. Beneficial use also determines the "measure" of water that can be appropriated; an appropriator usually is entitled only to the quantity of water that is reasonably necessary for the purpose for which the water was diverted. Neither waste of water nor inefficient use is permitted under this standard.

Priorities of Use

Under a prior appropriation system, priority is based on a "first in time, first in right" rule. A senior appropriator has a claim to the use of water from a particular source that is superior to the claims of all junior appropriators. Similarly, among junior appropriators, the earliest claim prevails over the later ones. Thus, a pecking order based on time of first appropriation is established. If the quantity of water is insufficient to serve all appropriators, the most junior ones must relinquish their claims to water so that prior claims are satisfied.

A senior appropriator's rights are not unlimited, however. A junior appropriator has a right to a continuation of the stream conditions that existed at the time of the junior appropriator's original use. Accordingly, a junior appropriator can object to a change in the senior appropriator's point of diversion or method of diversion if these changes detrimentally affect the junior's rights. Similarly, a senior appropriator cannot divert more water than necessary to serve the senior's purposes, nor hold or sell the excess.

Under the permit systems in place in most jurisdictions today, the priority date is the date of the filing of an application for a permit. However, once a permit is granted, the holder must act with "due diligence" to complete the diversionary works and the appropriation. Some states have time limits within which the work must be completed and the water used for beneficial purposes (e.g., five years). Unless the time period is extended for cause (a common practice), the permit and the right to appropriate the water may be forfeited. Nonuse and abandonment of an appropriation also can result in a termination of the appropriator's rights, and a loss of priority.

Statutory Changes to Prior Appropriation Systems

The prior appropriation systems are now regulated by state statutes and administrative procedures that generally provide the exclusive method of acquiring water rights. These laws are based on state constitutional provisions and legislative determinations that declare that all (or most) waters in the state are owned by the state and are subject to appropriation for beneficial uses. The statutes usually require a permit for most uses and establish the administrative processes for securing it. These procedures usually involve an administrative agency or an official to oversee the process, often a state engineer or state water agency such as the California Water Resources Control Board.

The procedures for acquiring a water permit vary from state to state, but they have some common features. In the first step, the person requesting the right to divert water files an application and supporting materials. The applicant then gives notice of the permit application to the public and to affected persons, and a public hearing on the permit request follows. The purpose of the hearing is to determine whether the statutory criteria for granting a permit have been met. They commonly include the following:

- Whether the use of the water is beneficial.
- Whether sufficient unappropriated water is available for use.
- Whether the means of diversion are adequate.
- Whether the use will impair the rights of prior appropriators.
- Whether the appropriation is in the public interest.

If the criteria have been met, the permitting authority ordinarily grants a conditional water permit for a specific quantity of water. The permit may contain conditions and limitations on use, and modifications of the plans and specifications for the diversion. Once the diversionary work is completed and the water is appropriated for use, the engineer inspects the diversionary works and issues a "perfected" water permit, if the applicant has satisfied the requirements of the conditional permit and the law.

Use of Underground Water

Water below the surface of the land is underground water, commonly called *groundwater*. The land holds subsurface water in the soil itself and in underground streams and reservoirs called **aquifers**. Aquifers that are subject to subsurface pressures causing the water to come to the surface, sometimes in the form of natural springs or fountains, are called **artesian aquifers**. In general, however, wells must be drilled and the water pumped to the surface from so-called **unconfined aquifers**. Aquifers are recharged from precipitation but can be depleted if the rate of withdrawal exceeds the rate of recharge. The term *safe yield* refers to the highest level of withdrawal that will allow the continuous recharging of the aquifer. Withdrawing more water than the safe yield is often referred to as "mining" the underground reservoir. Mining a reservoir or water basin (several connected aquifers) can result in a number of serious problems. First, mining the water reserves can harm other landowners who have wells in the same reservoir, by either depriving them of their supply of water or forcing them to dig deeper, more costly wells. Second, mining can cause **subsidence**, the sinking of the ground that results from the loss of subsurface support. Finally, mining can have an adverse effect on surface waters, the rivers and streams fed by underground waters.

Groundwater law attempts to balance the competing claims to groundwater, and the public and private interests in it. As with riparian and prior appropriation law relating to surface waters, the courts have developed a number of approaches for resolving the conflicting claims and interests involved in the use of groundwater. Also, many states have created regulatory systems to manage and allocate groundwater.

Percolating Groundwater and Underground Streams

The common law distinguished between underground streams (confined groundwater) and percolating groundwater. An **underground stream** is subsurface water that flows in some "well–defined" channel. Underground streams are treated like surface rivers in both riparian and prior appropriation systems. Other subsurface waters are characterized as **percolating groundwater**. Percolating waters are governed by groundwater law, which is distinct from the riparian and prior appropriation rules governing streams and lakes.

Determining whether subsurface water is percolating groundwater or an underground stream may be critically important in resolving the rights of competing users. From a practical and scientific perspective, however, proving the legal status of groundwater is problematic. The law generally presumes that subsurface water is percolating groundwater, and the person claiming otherwise has a difficult burden of persuasion. Unless a geologic study or other proof establishes that subsurface water is an underground stream (and therefore subject to the rules governing surface water), the law of groundwater will determine the rights of the parties in a dispute over subsurface withdrawals.

Absolute Ownership

At common law, an overlying landowner, one whose property lay above a groundwater supply, was absolute owner of the groundwater and could take unlimited amounts. This **absolute ownership** rule held that a landowner withdrawing subsurface water was not liable to others even if the pumping detrimentally affected the water supply of neighbors. Although restricted in the use of *surface* water, a landowner taking *underground* water could sell it for use off the property or use it on property that was not overlying the reservoir from which the water was taken. The primary limit on the use of groundwater was that the landowner could not waste it or act maliciously, or with an intent to harm others. This absolute ownership rule is still the law in a small number of eastern states and in Texas, although modern cases have created limits to the rule. For example, in Texas, an overlying landowner who negligently causes subsidence damage to a neighboring property owner is liable for the damages.

Reasonable Use

In most states, particularly the riparian states in the East, the absolute ownership rule has been abandoned in favor of a **reasonable use** rule. Under this rule, an overlying landowner is allowed to take groundwater to the extent necessary for some beneficial purpose related to the land. Thus, an overlying landowner can use water for domestic purposes or to irrigate the overlying land, but ordinarily cannot use the water to irrigate another parcel of land that does not overlie the groundwater. Any use of the water elsewhere is considered unreasonable if it harms other overlying landowners. For example, if an overlying landowner's pumping and selling a large quantity of water to a city for municipal uses harms other overlying landowners by depleting the groundwater, the use would not be permissible under the reasonable use test. Yet, an overlying landowner can use as much water as necessary to serve some useful purpose on his or her land without liability for harm to others, regardless of the amount withdrawn. Thus, the doctrine of reasonable use gives landowners a broad right to take groundwater to the detriment of others.

Modern Restatement Rule

Some states have opted for the rule suggested by the American Law Institute's *Restatement (Second) of Torts*, § 858. It reads as follows:

Liability for Use of Ground Water

> *(1) A proprietor of land or his grantee who withdraws ground water from the land and uses it for a beneficial purpose is not subject to liability for interference with the use of water by another, unless*

(a) *the withdrawal of ground water unreasonably causes harm to a proprietor of neighboring land by lowering the water table or reducing artesian pressure,*

(b) *the withdrawal of ground water exceeds the proprietor's reasonable share of the annual supply or store of ground water, or*

(c) *the withdrawal of the ground water has a direct and substantial effect on a watercourse or lake and unreasonably causes harm to a person entitled to the use of its water.*

In the following case, the Supreme Court of Maine considers whether to abolish the absolute ownership rule (referred to by the court as the "absolute dominion" rule) and adopt the Restatement approach to percolating water.

Case 19.1

Maddocks v. Giles
728 A.2d 150 (Me. 1999)

Sewall and Janice Maddocks own property adjacent to a gravel pit owned by Elbridge Giles. The Maddockses do not live on this property and there is no house on it. An underground spring that produced large quantities of water has historically flowed beneath the property. In 1994 the Maddockses filed a complaint alleging that Giles's excavation activities at the gravel pit caused the spring to run dry. Giles argued that there is no cause of action for the diminution or exhaustion of a neighbor's spring by the lawful excavation of land through which underground water percolates.

At trial, the Maddockses testified that Giles's excavation activities, including dewatering the gravel pit to allow ever-deeper digging, exhausted the spring. Their expert hydrogeologist conceded that the water underneath Giles's land flowing into the spring is presumed to be percolating, but added that percolating water can constitute a watercourse because there is a general flow and predictable course. Giles's expert hydrogeologist testified that the water feeding the spring was percolating water and that it could not constitute a watercourse because it has no sides or bed, as a surface watercourse does. The jury returned a verdict in favor of Giles. The Maddockses appealed, arguing that the trial court erred by instructing the jury on the absolute dominion rule, and urging the Supreme Court to adopt a new rule governing groundwater usage.

CALKINS, J.

The sole issue presented on appeal is whether we should depart from the common law absolute dominion rule and adopt the groundwater use rules set forth in *Restatement (Second) of Torts* §858 (1979). The absolute dominion rule is based on the premise that groundwater is the absolute property of the owner of the land, like the rocks and soil that compose it. The absolute dominion rule is now the minority rule in the United States. A few states in addition to Maine continue to recognize the rule. Most jurisdictions have adopted the reasonable use, or American, rule or some variation of it.

The Restatement approach abandons the common law distinction between underground watercourses and percolating water. It provides that a landowner who withdraws groundwater, whether in a watercourse or percolating, and "uses it for a beneficial purpose is not subject to liability for interference with the use of water by another." If the withdrawal, however, unreasonably causes harm to a neighbor by lowering the water table, exceeds the owner's reasonable share, or has a direct effect on a watercourse and unreasonably causes harm to one entitled to that water, then the owner may be liable.

The Maddockses argue that we should abandon the absolute dominion rule because it is based upon faulty science. It is generally accepted that the absolute dominion rule was established because courts did not understand how water flows underground. Instead, courts looked to established principles of property law that would allow them to resolve disputes without having to probe beneath the surface.

We decline to abandon the absolute dominion rule. First, we are not convinced that the absolute dominion rule is the wrong rule for Maine. We recognize that we are not bound by the doctrine of stare decisis when the underpinnings of the previous decisions are disproved and when the conditions of society have changed so that the prior law no longer fulfills a need and is counterproductive. Although modern science has enlightened our knowledge of groundwater, this does not mean that the rule itself has interfered with water use or has caused the development of unwise water policy. For over a century landowners in Maine have relied on the absolute dominion rule. In the absence of reliable information that the absolute dominion rule is counterproductive and a hindrance to achieving justice, we will not depart from our prior decisions.

Second, we are not persuaded that we, as opposed to the Legislature, should be weighing the heavy policy considerations involved in this issue, not the least of which is the reliance of landowners on the present property laws. We conclude that at this time the question of whether to depart from our common law on groundwater issues is best left to the Legislature.

Finally, we are further constrained in making the requested change because the Legislature has taken action in this area by creating the Water Resources Management Board to do a comprehensive study of water law in Maine. The Board reported to the Legislature and suggested that it adopt reasonable use principles. The Legislature chose to leave the common law as it currently stands.

Because the absolute dominion rule is the law in Maine governing the issue in this case and because the trial court correctly instructed the jury on the absolute dominion rule, we affirm the verdict.

Judgment affirmed.

QUESTIONS ABOUT CASE 19.1

1. Given the fact that the courts created the absolute dominion rule as a matter of common law, why is the court reluctant to overturn that rule?

2. Would the result of the case have been different had it been decided under the Restatement rule?

Appropriation System Rules

The rules relating to the withdrawal and use of groundwater under prior appropriation systems are similar to prior appropriation rules for surface waters. Senior appropriators have priority to the withdrawal of groundwater over junior appropriators. In general, a junior appropriator is liable to a senior appropriator if the junior causes harm to the senior's right to withdraw groundwater. For example, in *Current Creek Irrigation v. Andrews*, wells drilled by junior appropriators, Andrews and Current Creek Company, stopped the flow of water from the artesian wells of a senior appropriator, Fowkes.[6] Current Creek argued that Fowkes had no right to artesian pressure, but only a right to withdraw the water using reasonable means to withdraw it. The Utah Supreme Court held, however, that the senior's water rights were violated. It ordered Andrews and Current Creek to cease pumping until such time as they replaced the water lost by Fowkes, by furnishing pumps and power at their expense for that purpose.

Permit Systems

To avoid disputes over groundwater priorities, and to establish a regulatory scheme to allocate groundwater entitlements, many riparian and prior appropriation states have adopted permit systems for groundwater uses. At least 12 western states have established permit systems governing groundwater usage on the basis of prior appropriation principles.[7] These statutes require any person making a groundwater withdrawal, with some exceptions, to have a permit. Some riparian states in the East also have developed permit systems for groundwater withdrawals.

Drainage of Surface Water

As noted in the discussion of surface water, the common law distinguished between water in a watercourse (a channel with a defined bed and banks) and other, *diffused* surface water, such as water from rainfall or snow melt that flows across the land outside of a watercourse. Diffused surface water includes water flowing down the mountains in the spring through gullies or ravines and water collecting temporarily in small pools or hollows in the ground.

The law relating to diffused surface water is quite different from the law of other surface water. Landowners normally want to use the surface water in lakes and rivers, whereas, with regard to diffused surface water, the landowner normally wants to get rid of it. Yet, in arid parts of the country diffused surface water can be an important, though fleeting, resource, so in most states, landowners do have an unrestricted right to capture diffused surface waters. But in general, the law of diffused surface water centers on the landowner's rights to divert the water to neighboring properties and the rights of those owners to avoid the harm caused by the diversion.

Common Enemy Doctrine

The common law permitted a landowner to take any measures necessary to protect the property from invasion by diffused surface water. The landowner could erect a levee or other barrier to stop the flow of diffused waters and could divert the flow of the water and channel it off the property by digging ditches or constructing other drainage systems—all with no liability whatsoever for damage to adjoining or neighboring properties. This rule of absolute privilege was called the **common enemy doctrine** because surface water was considered a common enemy of all landowners, giving all of them the right to take any preventive measures they considered necessary. Today, some states still follow the common enemy doctrine. However, the courts of those states have modified it by placing limits on a landowner's drainage actions. For example, some states impose liability for damages caused by drainage activities if the landowner acted negligently or in bad faith.

Civil Law Rule

A serious shortcoming of the common enemy doctrine is that it may set off a series of wasteful "dueling" actions by neighboring landowners and create the potential for violent confrontations as each tries to move unwanted water to the other's land. Rather than adopt the common law rule, many states opted for its opposite, the **civil law rule** that prevents a landowner from diverting or altering the natural flow of diffused surface water to the detriment of others. In effect, the civil law rule imposes a "servitude" on the land for the protection of neighboring properties. A number of states still follow some version of the civil law rule, but have created a number of exceptions to the absolute prohibition against altering the natural flow of diffused surface water. For example, many civil law states recognize the need to divert diffused surface water to protect agricultural production. Others allow diversions that are considered insignificant, for example, where the damage caused by the diversion is slight. Still others allow an owner to take measures to protect against flood waters, without liability.

Reasonable Use Doctrine

The majority rule on the diversion of diffused surface water is the **reasonable use test**. This rule is in essence a middle ground position between the "absolute right" of the common enemy doctrine to divert the water and the civil law's absolute prohibition of diversion. The reasonable use rule allows a landowner to take reasonable measures to divert diffused surface water, if those measures do not unreasonably harm others. The rule thus balances the right of landowners to protect their property from diffused surface water and the right of others not to be harmed by the diverted water. Among the factors the courts consider in determining reasonableness are the following: the need for the diversion and the purpose served; the reasonableness of the means chosen, in light of the risk to the property and the harm to others; the benefit of the drainage weighed against the harm to others resulting from it; and the use of natural or artificial drainage systems to accomplish the diversion.

Public Access to Water

The riparian rights, prior appropriation, and hybrid water rights systems define the rights of competing private landowners and others to the use and diversion of surface and subsurface waters. The public, however, may also have rights to use rivers, lakes, and other bodies of water even those that are on or flow over private property. Traditionally, public rights to water related to the use of watercourses for commercial purposes such as transporting persons, shipping goods, or fishing. More recently, courts and state legislatures have recognized other legitimate public uses for the water, especially recreational uses such as boating and swimming, and uses relating to environmental interests.

Importance of Navigability

Traditionally, in defining public rights in rivers, lakes, and streams, the concept of **navigability** has been determinative. The public has rights in navigable waters because the states generally hold title to the beds of navigable watercourses. The waters are considered a public resource, with the state holding title to them in trust for the benefit of its citizens. In contrast, the banks and beds of waters that are *not* navigable are owned by the riparian or littoral landowners. The traditional test of navigability is whether a body of water can be used for commercial navigation, that is, whether it is or can be used as a highway for commerce under the natural conditions of the water body using customary methods of transport. For example, a shallow mountain stream may not be navigable, whereas a large river that it empties into may be suitable for commercial navigation.

Public Rights Under State Law

The test of navigability is broader in some states than under the traditional standard of navigability for commercial uses. Thus, the public has a right to use (navigate) waters in some states that would be considered nonnavigable in other states. Historically, Maine, Massachusetts, and New Hampshire recognized public rights in so-called "great ponds," bodies of water having a surface area of at least ten acres. Early in its history as a state, Wisconsin adopted a "saw log" test for navigability. Under this test, a stream is navigable if it will allow logs to float down river to a saw mill. Minnesota, "the land of 10,000 lakes," asserts jurisdiction over any body of water that can be put to recreational use by the public, regardless of its commercial navigability. Montana, too, has adopted a recreational use test, recognizing that "the capability of use of the waters for recreational purposes determines the availability for recreational use" by the public.

Mining Law and Solid Minerals

At common law, title to land was said to extend up to the heavens and down to the center of the earth. Thus, ownership of the land has always included ownership of solid minerals embedded in the land. And, any transfer of the land without a reservation or exception of minerals rights includes the surface *and* the minerals, just as it includes fixtures attached to the land. In some jurisdictions, mineral ownership extends to oil and gas, although many states do not recognize an ownership interest by anyone in oil and gas, only a right of a landowner to search for and capture any that may underlie his or her land. Oil and gas law is discussed in the next part of the chapter. This part focuses on the law relating to solid minerals.

● Severance of Mineral Rights

A landowner can transfer mineral rights without transferring other rights to the land. The transfer is referred to as a "severance" of the mineral rights, which can be accomplished in several ways. First, the landowner can transfer the mineral rights to another person by means of a **mineral deed**. Second, the landowner can transfer the land itself to another but reserve (keep) the mineral rights. The deed transferring the land will contain either a "reservation" of or an "exception" for the mineral rights retained. Finally, the landowner can transfer the surface rights to another under a **surface deed**, thereby implicitly retaining the mineral rights. Whatever the method used, the severance of the mineral rights can be partial or total, with all or some of the mineral rights being granted or reserved.

The effect of the severance is that title to the land is divided between the surface owner and the mineral owner. Each has ownership of his or her respective property interest, which can be transferred and encumbered like any other interest in property. The surface owner retains all rights to the surface, including the right to possess and use the land and to profit from it, and also retains some subsurface rights, including the right to access water through the mineral deposits in the soil. The mineral owner has a right to explore and extract the minerals, which includes an easement over the property to conduct mining operations.

● Minerals

The word *minerals* is not subject to precise definition. Courts have recognized that *mineral* is used in different contexts, with different meanings attached to it in different settings. The question of what *minerals* means has arisen in cases interpreting language in mineral grants and reservations, wills, mining leases, and development agreements. For example, Linda conveys by deed "the minerals" in and under Blackacre to Mindy. Does this conveyance include clay, gravel, and sand? Does it include substances that were unknown of at the time of the conveyance?

Obviously, *minerals* cannot include ordinary soil if a deed granting or reserving surface rights is to have any logical meaning. It also does not include substances that are closely related to the soil, such as sand, gravel, clay, and fill dirt. Indeed, courts have often distinguished between such substances and those having value independent of the soil and that are ordinarily mined from it, such as gold, silver, coal, iron, and shale. However, some exceptions have been made to this general principle. Substances closely related to the soil may have exceptional characteristics or be of peculiar value that cause them to be classified as minerals. For example, ordinary clay is not considered a mineral, but bentonite, a special type of clay formed from volcanic ash, has been held to be a mineral. Similarly, pure white granite sand used for making glass has been held to be a mineral even though sand is not ordinarily considered a mineral.

Ultimately, determining the meaning of *mineral* is a matter of interpreting the intent of the parties to a deed, lease, or contract, in light of its language and the surrounding circumstances. The precise language used is especially important in determining that intent. For example, the grant of a right to mine coal "in and under" the land was held to include strip mining. Also, the use of specific words along with the general word *minerals* helps clarify the meaning of the general language. A careful listing of covered minerals can be useful for two reasons. First, the document will identify as a mineral any listed substance (like clay) that is not ordinarily considered a mineral. Second, if a list of specific minerals accompanies general language (e.g., "and all other minerals"), a court will be able to interpret the document to cover minerals that are not listed but that are of the same character as the listed ones. Parties must be careful, however, because the courts will usually look to the listed minerals for guidance in interpreting the general language. So, for example, many courts have held that a lease of "oil, gas, and other minerals" will be interpreted restrictively to include only minerals that are a component of oil and gas production. Determining the parties' intent is problematic when the mineral or the method of extraction was unknown at the time of the grant or reservation of the minerals. Many courts have held that general language (e.g., "minerals") in a transfer document will not include minerals not known to be present at the time of the transfer, nor will general language permit unknown, harmful methods of extraction. The assumption is that these minerals or methods were outside the contemplation of the parties, although some courts have allowed new extraction methods if the surface owner is compensated for any harm. In contrast, where the parties recognized that a particular method of extraction was customary and to be expected from the transfer of the mineral rights (e.g., where lignite coal was abundant and strip mining was the ordinary method of extraction), courts have interpreted general language to include the anticipated extraction method. In short, instruments granting, reserving, leasing, or transferring mineral rights will be interpreted in light of the parties' knowledge and reasonable expectations.

● Surface Rights and Control

Because the mineral owner's rights would be worthless without access to the land holding the minerals, the common law recognized that the mineral owner had a right to use the surface for its mining operations. So, although the surface owner continues to have the right to possess and use the surface, that right is subject to an easement in favor of the mineral owner.

The mineral owner's right to use the surface is governed by the common law doctrine of "reasonable surface use." Under this doctrine, the mineral owner has the right to use the surface in any way that is reasonably necessary to explore, develop, extract, and transport the minerals. "Reasonable surface use" necessarily includes clearing the land, drilling and digging, building structures and facilities, and maintaining and constructing trails and roads. The mineral owner is not liable for damages to the surface caused by activities that are reasonably necessary for its mining operations. The mineral owner is liable only for (1) negligently or intentionally causing damage to buildings, fences, or other surface interests, (2) using more property than is reasonably necessary for mining, or (3) breaching a duty to the owner imposed by an agreement, a covenant in the deed creating the mineral rights, or a statute. The mineral owner also has a duty to leave or provide sufficient subjacent support and is strictly liable to the surface owner for damages resulting from subsidence.

In some states, the mineral owner's right to use the surface is limited under the so-called accommodation doctrine. A minority of states require mineral owners to act with "due regard" to the interests of the surface owners when they select or use particular mining methods. If a mining method is likely to interfere with the surface owner's usage rights, the accommodation doctrine requires the mineral owner to consider alternative methods that are customary and reasonable, and that would not interfere with the surface owner's use of the land. The leading decision is the Texas Supreme Court's opinion in *Getty Oil Co. v. Jones*.[8] In *Getty*, the surface owner was farming the land using a rolling irrigation system that was blocked by Getty's pumpjacks. Because Getty had two alternatives (submerged pumps and surface-mounted pumps) that would not interfere with the irrigation system, Getty was required under the accommodation doctrine to utilize one of the noninterfering alternatives.

Mining Leases

The owner of mineral rights usually leases them to private mining developers, who will actually conduct the mining operations. Under a mining lease, the lessee acquires the right to mine for and to extract the minerals under the terms and conditions of the lease (but does not acquire ownership of the minerals until they are extracted). Because mining development is a capital-intensive, time-consuming process, mining leases are generally long-term arrangements (20 years or longer) that are often subject to renewal or extension.

Although some leases call for the payment of rent, the lessor usually receives a royalty based on production. The royalty can be a percentage of the gross value of the minerals extracted, or it can be calculated on a dollar-per-ton basis. The lessee receives the right to explore for minerals and to develop and work the mines. When a royalty (rather than rent) is payable, the lessee has an implied duty to diligently explore and develop the mine, because the compensation to the lessor is based on mine production. A failure to develop the mine or pay royalty can result in a forfeiture of the lease.

A carefully drafted mining lease addresses some or all of the following issues:

- The minerals covered by the lease and any restrictions on mining operations.
- Minimum royalties (if any) and excuses for not paying royalties or developing the mine (e.g., strikes).
- Lessee's right to assign or transfer the lease.
- Grounds for forfeiture of the lease.

Federal Mining Laws

The federal government has a mineral estate of more than 700 million acres that is subject to private development under federal mining laws. The Mining Law of 1872 governs the mining of hardrock minerals, including copper, gold, silver, lead, and uranium. It establishes a claim-patent system for such "locatable" minerals. The system permits prospectors discovering minerals on federal lands to have a valid legal claim to them, and to purchase the land containing the minerals for a nominal amount ($5 per acre or less) by "patenting" their claim. A **patent** is the instrument under which the federal government conveys title to the land to the claimant. In 1920,

Congress enacted the Mineral Leasing Act that withdrew oil, gas, oil shale, phosphate, and sodium from the patent-claim system. Under the Leasing Act, the federal government enters into leases with private persons for the development of these mineral deposits (called "leasable" minerals) while retaining ownership of the federal lands on which the mining takes place. Similarly, the government leases coal under the provisions of the Federal Coal Leasing Amendments Act of 1976. In 1955, by passage of the Surface Resources Act, Congress removed common varieties of sand, gravel, cinders, pumice, and clay from the coverage of the Mining Law of 1872. The government now contracts with private purchasers for the sale of such common materials, under the Material Disposal Act of 1947.

The purpose of the original Mining Act of 1872 was to promote mineral exploitation on federal lands and encourage the settlement of the West. It sought to accomplish these objectives by opening up federal lands to prospecting and by granting individuals the right to exploit any minerals they discovered, without any royalty or compensation to the government. Today, the act is controversial and attempts have been made to reform it. Many citizens and policy analysts object to the "giveaway" of the nation's precious resources, which they consider a form of corporate welfare to the mining industry. Environmentalists are also concerned about the lack of any strong environmental controls on mining operations under the mining law. Nevertheless, the law remains essentially unchanged from the original statute, although, as noted, some minerals are now governed by other statutes, and Congress has withdrawn many acres of federal land (e.g., land in national parks and wilderness areas) from that part of the public domain that can be mined.

Oil and Gas

Because of the fugitive nature of oil and gas, the law has had difficulty defining the nature of the landowner's rights to these migratory minerals. The common law initially developed a rule of capture similar to the rules relating to the ownership of wild animals. The **rule of capture** holds that a landowner acquires title to oil and gas by extracting it from the ground. Before then, oil and gas underlying multiple tracts of land may be captured by the other landowners drilling on their own land, and upon extraction of the material, they will have title to it without liability to the other landowners for reducing the amount under their land.

In some states, courts limited the rule of capture by applying a doctrine of correlative rights, which recognizes that landowners are entitled to an equitable share of the oil and gas from a common source under their lands. Under this doctrine, every landowner has a right not only to extract oil and gas from his or her own land but also to be protected against damage to the common source of supply. Under this doctrine, a landowner who is negligent in the production of oil (or wastes it) is liable for the harm caused to other landowners.

Although the rule of capture proved inadequate as a foundation for the modern law of oil and gas, it is still important under the ownership rules that the courts have developed for these migratory minerals. Moreover, many of the state and federal laws regulating oil and gas are designed to limit the right of capture and thus to protect the correlative rights of landowners to oil and gas, including well spacing laws and other oil and gas conservation laws.

Ownership in Place and Nonownership Theories

The state courts developed two different doctrines to define the nature of a landowner's interest in oil and gas: the ownership-in-place rule[9] and the nonownership theory.[10] The ownership-in-place rule adopted by some states treats the ownership of oil and gas similar to the ownership of other minerals. On the theory that a property owner owns the land to the center of the earth, this doctrine holds that a landowner also owns the oil and gas in the ground. As a result, in the "ownership" states, a landowner's estate includes oil and gas, and the oil and gas interest can be severed and sold apart from the other rights in the property. Severance can be accomplished by a deed granting or reserving the oil and gas rights or all of the mineral rights, including oil and gas. If the interest is severed, the recipient of the oil and gas interest becomes owner of the oil and gas in the ground and has a right to exploit the mineral rights, including a right of access to the surface for drilling operations.

In contrast, the nonownership theory rejects the idea that the landowner has an ownership interest in oil and gas. Consistently with the common law rule of capture, this theory holds that, given the migratory nature of oil and gas, a landowner has only a right to search for and extract them. The right is transferable, but it is only a right of extraction. A transfer of that right does not effect a severance of the mineral estate, that is, does not in itself make the recipient the owner of the gas and oil. Rather, the transferred right is in the nature of a license or profit, allowing its recipient to enter the land and remove the oil and gas from it.

Oil and Gas Leases

As in the extraction of other minerals, the owner of gas and oil rights ordinarily leases the interest to an oil developer, who does the drilling and extraction. The leases usually are preprinted forms with standard terms and conditions drafted by oil companies or others in the industry. The leases may not be identical, but they usually conform to a basic conceptual structure for the leasehold arrangement and use standard industry terminology.

Nature of the Oil and Gas Lease

The lessee receives the right to use the land for drilling and extraction purposes, so has a right to use the surface and to engage in any activities that are reasonably necessary for its drilling operations. The lessee's use of the surface is governed by the common law doctrine of reasonable surface use as modified in some states by the accommodation rule requiring the lessee to use drilling and extraction methods that, while customary and reasonable, interfere least with the surface owner's usage rights. Unlike other types of leases, an oil and gas lease runs for an indefinite period, since most oil and gas leases do not terminate as long as oil or gas is being produced. The lessor receives compensation in the form of a bonus payment for granting the lease and a production royalty based on the amount of the oil and gas produced (e.g., 1/6 of the value of oil produced). The lessor also continues to enjoy other rights associated with the land that are consistent with the oil lessee's rights, such as the right to farm the surface.

Primary Term

The **habendum clause** of an oil and gas lease establishes its duration. Oil and gas leases are unique in that they involve two terms (time periods): the primary term and the secondary term. The primary term is for a fixed period, traditionally, ten years, but recently terms of three to five years have become more common. The primary term gives the lessee an opportunity to drill a test well and time to finance the oil and gas development project. During the primary term, the lessee may be unable to drill right away, or may wish to postpone drilling. Nevertheless, the lessee must make an annual payment to the lessor, called a "delay rental," which is compensation to the lessor for the right to drill even if no production occurs. To avoid annual delay rentals, the lessee must immediately drill a test well or commence operations for drilling. Moreover, most leases provide that unless drilling operations are commenced or the delay rental is paid, the lease automatically terminates. Thus, a lessee may forfeit a lease without any further obligation to the lessor.

If the lessee commences drilling operations during the primary term, no delay rentals are due after the operations have commenced. But what constitutes "commencement of drilling operations"? The answer to this question of fact depends upon (1) the extent to which the lessee has undertaken activities at the well site, such as clearing the land, building roads, laying lines, acquiring well permits, moving equipment onto the site, and entering into drilling contracts; and (2) the lessee's subjective intent, that is, whether a good faith effort has been made to commence operations. The lessee does not have to actually drill a well to "commence drilling operations." Substantial preliminary steps in preparation for drilling are enough. However, a lessee who is financially unable to drill or has no present intent to drill has not commenced drilling operations, so must pay a delay rental to avoid forfeiting the lease.

Secondary Term

During the secondary term, the parties expect to produce oil and gas from the well as long as it is economically feasible to do so. Thus, the secondary term is for an indefinite period—as long as oil and gas are being "produced." However, the production must commence by the end of the primary term. Thus, what constitutes "production" is critical in determining whether the lease is still in effect at the start of the secondary term and thereafter. Without production or some alternative under the lease, the lease is forfeited by the lessee.

Meaning of Production

In evaluating the production language in a lease, state courts have developed two different interpretations. In some jurisdictions, mere discovery of oil and gas before the end of the primary term is sufficient to constitute production. Under this interpretation, production does not require the marketing of the oil and gas. However, the discovery must involve sufficient quantities to be economically exploited, and the lessee must act with due diligence to market the product within a reasonable time after its discovery. Also, some cases distinguish between the discovery of oil and the discovery of gas, treating the discovery of oil as production since oil can be stored and easily marketed. Some courts do not consider the discovery of gas to be production, because gas usually cannot be stored and often a pipeline connection is not readily available for marketing the gas.

In contrast to the discovery rule, for the lessee to satisfy the production requirement of the lease, a majority of states require actual marketing of the products before the end of the primary term. Under the majority view, the lease terminates if no actual production occurs by then, even if the lessee is hampered by circumstances beyond its control. In those states, mere discovery is not sufficient to carry the lease over to the secondary term.

A secondary consideration in determining whether production has occurred is the economic viability of the well. Most courts require production in "paying quantities"; that is, production sufficient to generate a profit over the production costs. The legal standard for determining whether quantities are sufficiently large to be "paying" is whether a "reasonably prudent operator" would continue to operate the well to earn a profit, as opposed to continuing operations simply to hold the lease for speculative purposes. This paying quantities standard does not require that the whole oil and gas venture be profitable, only that the revenue generated from the specific well exceed the production or "lifting" costs. The revenue from the well may be insufficient to recoup all of the sunk costs of drilling it, but if prudent operators realize a profit in relation to its continuing expenses, then they would continue the production to recoup some of the investment in the well. Profitability is not judged in the short term, however, because the gas and petroleum businesses are quite cyclical, with periods of rapid changes in prices and volatile market conditions. Thus, courts often consider profitability over a period of one to three years.

Shut-In Royalties

Gas cannot be stored. To market it, the lessee-operator needs a connection line to a pipeline. Consequently, the production of gas can present logistical problems for the operator, and sometimes a gas well is drilled without a ready market for the gas. Anticipating such an event, most gas leases provide for "shut-in" royalties to the lessor so that the lessee can shut down the well and avoid a forfeiture of the lease for a lack of production. The amount of the shut-in royalty varies, but it is typically the same amount as the delay rental. For the shut-in royalty to prevent a forfeiture of the lease, however, the well must be capable of producing paying quantities of gas.

Royalty Clause

Oil and gas leases call for the payment of a production royalty. Ordinarily, the royalty is a fractional share of the actual oil produced and a fractional share of the *gross value* of the gas produced, both of which are free of the operator's production costs. Traditionally, the lessor received a royalty of one-eighth of the oil and one-eighth of the value of the gas produced. Today, royalties tend to be higher, one-sixth being typical.

As indicated in the preceding paragraph, the method of paying oil royalties differs from the method of paying gas royalties. Oil royalties are generally payable in kind rather than in cash. The royalty clause typically provides that the lessor is entitled to the following, "On oil, one-sixth of that produced and saved from said land, the same to be delivered at the wells or to the credit of lessor into the pipelines to which the wells may be connected." In contrast, gas royalties are payable in cash. A typical royalty clause for gas reads: "On gas, produced from said land and sold or used off the premises, the market value (or price) at the well of one-sixth of the gas so sold or used, provided that on gas sold at the wells the royalty shall be one-sixth of the amount realized from such sale." Thus, the parties expect the lessee to sell the gas production and pay the lessor either one-sixth of the proceeds (for gas sold at the wells) or one-sixth of the market value at the well (for gas sold and used off the premises).

Disputes can arise between lessor and lessee over the meaning of terms such as "market value" or "market price." In resolving the meaning of such terms, the courts look primarily to comparable sales in arm's length transactions in the field (i.e., the local production area). In the absence of actual sales at the wellhead, such comparable sales are considered the best evidence of market value, because market value is considered to be the price that a willing seller and buyer would agree to in a freely negotiated sale. Without evidence of comparable sales in the field, the courts will estimate wellhead market value on the basis of the actual price received in distant sales (sales outside the local area) minus the postproduction expenses for transporting and processing the gas.

Agricultural Law

"Agricultural law" means all branches of the law, domestic and international, civil and criminal, applicable to agricultural producers. Thus, it includes a range of legal principles, from the private law of contracts and sales of goods to the public law of federal agricultural policy. However, this chapter focuses exclusively on the real estate aspects of agricultural law, which are important to farmers and ranchers who earn their living from the land. Agricultural producers need to understand the law relating to the sale and purchase of real estate, ownership and nonownership interests in property, and the general rights and liabilities of landowners. These areas of law have been discussed in other chapters. This chapter focuses on particular applications of real estate law to the activities of agricultural producers, and on some real estate rules that are unique to the agricultural community, such as agricultural zoning and right-to-farm laws, landowner liabilities and recreational use statutes, leasing of agricultural property, and environmental laws governing agricultural operations.

Nuisance Law, Right-to-Farm Statutes, and Agricultural Zoning

Farmers and ranchers face the possibility of lawsuits for nuisance, brought by neighboring property owners who may object to the harmful or annoying by-products of modern agricultural production methods, including the odors, smells, dust, noise, pollution, and other undesirable conditions (e.g., flies, holding ponds) incidental to agricultural production. In recent times, the potential for such lawsuits has increased for two reasons. First, because of mechanization and global competition, the size of agricultural operations has increased. Farms and ranches have become larger, and corporate farming has become more common, especially in the production of cattle, poultry, and hogs, operations that have substantial environmental impacts. Second, the growth of the cities has caused urban sprawl, with new developments and suburbs encroaching upon areas that have traditionally been rural and agricultural. The combination of these factors has caused an inevitable clash of values and interests, which in some cases has led to lawsuits to shut down agricultural operations as nuisances. See, for example, Case 2.4, *Spur Industries, Inc. v. Del Webb Development Company*, in Chapter 2.

Although suits to abate nuisances arising out of agricultural settings are primarily governed by the principles discussed in Chapters 2 and 18, all states have passed so-called right-to-farm laws that provide agricultural producers (and sometimes agricultural processors such as packing plants) limited immunity from nuisance claims brought by new residents in traditionally agricultural areas. The right-to-farm statutes are designed to strengthen the "coming to the nuisance" defense in such cases to protect existing farm operations from nuisance liability.

Right to farm laws vary from state to state, especially as to the conditions under which an agricultural producer is immune from nuisance liability. Most are similar to the North Carolina statute adopted in 1979. These statutes provide that an agricultural operator that has been in existence for one year (three years in some states) shall not be considered a nuisance as the result of "changed conditions in the area" as long as the agricultural operation was not a nuisance when it began. Most contain an exception for negligently conducted operations (thus allowing them to be held a nuisance), and some of the laws contain a similar exception for operations that have substantially expanded or significantly changed their activities. A second common type of right-to-farm law provides immunity from nuisance lawsuits for agricultural operators only if they operate in conformity with generally accepted agricultural or management practices, sometimes defined as compliance with federal and state regulations. Other statutes provide the broadest immunity by simply stating that an agricultural practice is not a nuisance because of changing conditions (i.e., does not become a nuisance because of people moving in) if it has been in existence longer than the complaining party has been in possession of his or her property.

In some cases, farmers and ranchers have successfully used the right-to-farm law as a defense to a nuisance action. For example, in Indiana, a 114-acre hog farm that had been in existence since 1956 was successful in defending against a nuisance lawsuit brought by a residential owner who in 1970 built a home across the road from the farm. For the most part, courts have given these laws a narrow interpretation, one that is probably consistent with the underlying objectives of such statutes. For example, courts have refused to allow the defense to be used by farm operators who have substantially increased offensive activities or whose activities were commenced *after* the complaining persons first lived or farmed in the area. These laws also have been challenged as unconstitutional takings of private property. (Regulatory takings are discussed in Chapter 16.) Recently, the Iowa Supreme Court declared Iowa's unique right-to-farm law unconstitutional in the case of *Bormann v. Kossuth County Board of Supervisors.*[11] The Iowa law allowed a county to designate farmland as an "agricultural area" in which a farm operation or activity could not be declared a nuisance "regardless of the established date of operation or expansion of the farm or farm operation." Exceptions to the blanket immunity existed for negligent farm operations and for noncompliance with state and federal regulations. The court held that this law constituted a regulatory taking, reasoning that neighboring landowners were being forced, in violation of their property rights, to accept a nuisance without compensation. It is not clear, however, whether the Iowa decision will be adopted by other courts reviewing more typical right-to-farm laws, but it is clear that courts will continue to limit the scope of such laws to ensure that they do not unduly interfere with the legitimate property rights of other landowners.

Some states also have established agricultural zoning laws and other regulatory measures in an attempt to *preserve* farmland, particularly prime farmland threatened by relentless urban sprawl near metropolitan centers. Agricultural zoning allows local communities to establish agricultural zones in which the development of the land for commercial and residential uses is restricted. Communities can establish exclusive agricultural zones, in which only designated agricultural activities are permitted. Or, they can create nonexclusive zones allowing nonagricultural uses but discouraging such uses by requiring large lot sizes or conditional use permits under which other limitations are imposed before any development is permitted. Agricultural zoning is sometimes coupled with other state measures that attempt to preserve farmland, such as preferential assessment of agricultural land under state real estate tax laws (discussed in Chapter 16), growth control laws and transfer of development rights programs (discussed in Chapter 17), and conservation easements (discussed in Chapter 4). It should be also noted that the federal government established a farmland protection program under the 1996 Farm Act that authorizes the Secretary of Agriculture to acquire conservation easements or purchase other interests in up to 340,000 acres of agricultural land to keep prime farmland in production.

Liabilities and Recreational Use Laws

As noted in Chapter 2, landowners can be liable for harm to persons injured on their property. Traditionally, that liability depended upon whether the injured person was an invitee, a licensee, or a trespasser, with the law imposing different duties on the landowner depending upon the person's status. Most courts apply this approach in lawsuits by persons injured on agricultural property. For example, customers and others invited on agricultural property to do business are considered invitees. The owner owes them a duty to exercise reasonable care to maintain the property in a safe condition and can be liable for harm caused by a failure to correct dangerous conditions on the land. In contrast, a person who unlawfully enters a farmer's land is considered a trespasser to whom no duty of reasonable care is owed; the owner is not liable to the trespasser for mere negligence. However, the owner, including a farmer or a rancher, cannot willfully or deliberately harm the trespasser, and has liability for doing so.

Under the common law, a landowner owes limited duties to a licensee, a person who enters the property with the consent of the landowner, usually to serve the licensee's own interests (e.g., a person who is given permission to hunt or fish on the land). But some states have abolished the distinction between licensees and invitees, a change in the law that has expanded potential liability of landowners by conferring on licensees the protections formerly reserved for invitees.

Partly in response to these changes, almost all states have passed recreational use statutes. These laws are designed to encourage private landowners to open their property for recreational use by giving them immunity from liability to recreational users (licensees) injured on the property. The typical statute provides that "an owner of land owes no duty of care to keep the premises safe for entry or use by others for recreational purposes or to give any warning of a dangerous condition, use, structure, or activity on such premises to persons entering for such purposes." Recreational use laws ordinarily have exceptions for a "willful or malicious failure to guard or warn against a dangerous condition" and for injury suffered in cases where the landowner charges the licensee for the recreational use of the land. Thus, they do not apply to a farmer or rancher who operates a game preserve or charges persons to hunt or fish on his property. These landowners continue to have the full measure of liability to injured licensees.

Recreational use statutes have usually been interpreted quite liberally to give landowners broad protection from liability suits, particularly owners of farms and undeveloped lands. In fact, some courts have limited the protection of licensees under these laws to injuries from recreational uses on undeveloped or rural land. Although many of the statutes provide a list of recreational uses that cannot result in landowner liability, courts have held that additional uses should be liability-free. For example, a wrestling match was deemed a recreational use, as was attendance at a school field trip. The meaning of recreational activities for which the participant is charged a fee has been given a limited reach by most courts. For example, parking fees and fees for other services have been held not to constitute charges for recreational use, although courts have reached conflicting opinions on what constitutes a charge for use.

Negligence and Strict Liability for Agricultural Activities

In addition to liability to persons coming upon the farmer's or rancher's land, agricultural producers may be liable for harm caused by their farm operations to neighboring properties and others. For example, a landowner negligently burning crop residue in a field may be liable to other landowners if the fire spreads to their fields, as a result, for example, of burning during an

Box 19–1 You Be the Judge

Clinton Randolph owned a large parcel of property in the city of Delano in Kern County, California. One part of the property was plowed and furrowed for crops. Another part contained a small rental house, and a third portion consists of an open area where Randolph stored old farm equipment, machinery, and irrigation pipes. His property was adjacent to a residential subdivision where Jose Ornelas lived with his family. On January 2, 1989, Jose, who was eight years old, and five other children were playing on that portion of the property where the farm equipment was stored. Several of the children were on top of a piece of old machinery when a metal pipe dislodged and fell on Jose, causing injuries. Jose was not on the equipment at the time, but was sitting nearby playing with a handheld toy when the accident occurred.

Jose, acting by and through his mother, Rita Ornelas, filed a lawsuit for personal injury against Randolph. Randolph claimed that the case should be dismissed under the California recreational use law. Jose argued that the recreational use statute did not apply for two reasons. First, Jose contended that he was not engaged in a recreational activity covered by the law. The statute provides that a recreational activity "includes such activities as fishing, hunting, camping . . . ," but it never mentions climbing on or watching others climb on farm equipment. Second, Jose claimed that the property in question must be "suitable" for a recreational pursuit in order to qualify for the statutory immunity and that the land used to store Randolph's equipment "had no legitimate recreational use." (a) How would you resolve these two issues? (b) Should recreational statutes have exceptions for injuries to children from dangerous property conditions or dangerous equipment on the property?

extremely dry or windy period or without adequate precautions such as plowing protective strips.

In some cases the courts impose strict liability (no-fault liability) on farmers for activities that are considered abnormally dangerous. As noted in Chapter 18, whether a particular activity is abnormally dangerous depends upon an analysis of the following factors: (1) whether the activity involves a high degree of risk of harm to person, land, or property; (2) whether the harm resulting from the activity is likely to be great; (3) whether the risk of harm can be eliminated by the exercise of due care; (4) whether the activity is a matter of common practice; (5) whether the activity is customary in the place where it occurs; and (6) whether the social value of the activity to the community outweighs its dangerous attributes. For example, a dairy farmer was held strictly liable for damage caused by liquid manure that escaped from a holding pond, the holding lagoon being considered an abnormally dangerous activity. One court has held that field burning is an abnormally dangerous activity, although the better view is that such burning in rural areas is a customary and useful practice that should not be considered abnormally dangerous.

One area of potential liability is the aerial spraying of pesticides and herbicides on farm fields, called crop dusting. Crop dusting can damage neighboring crops or livestock if harmful chemicals drift from the farmer's field onto neighboring property. Given the hazardous nature of crop dusting, and the inability to eliminate the risk of drift regardless of the care taken, some courts have subjected farmers to strict liability for damages to others from crop dusting. In those states, crop dusting is considered an abnormally dangerous activity. In a majority of states, however, courts view crop dusting as a customary agricultural practice and hold farmers liable for harm only if they were negligent in applying the chemicals. Nevertheless, given the dangerous nature of the chemicals, a high degree of care is required in their application, and courts are likely to find liability for any slight fault on the part of the farmer or the aerial applicator.

A farmer who hires a contractor to spray fields is vicariously liable for the contractor's wrongful actions whether the applicator is an "employee" (i.e., the farmer's "servant" under agency law) or an independent contractor (i.e., a person who is not under the control of the farmer). An employer ordinarily is not liable for the negligence of an independent contractor. As an exception to this rule, an employer is liable for the negligence of a contractor in conducting activities that are "inherently dangerous" or "ultrahazardous." Even in the states that do not consider the general process of crop dusting to be abnormally dangerous (and thus impose liability only for negligence), the courts consider crop dusting inherently dangerous. Consequently, a farmer is vicariously liable for the negligence of an aerial applicator even if the applicator is an independent contractor (which is usually the case). However, a farmer held liable has a claim against the contractor for any monies the farmer has to pay to injured third parties.

Agricultural Leases

Agricultural leasing is quite common. It is estimated that 40% to 50% of the farmland in the United States is leased. Leases of agricultural land are governed under the general principles and rules discussed in Chapters 12 and 13. However, such leases are a special type of commercial arrangement with terms and conditions unique to the agricultural production sector. This section discusses the different forms of agricultural leases and some of the important rights and liabilities of the parties under an agricultural lease.

Types of Agricultural Leases

The two main types of agricultural leases are cash and crop-share leases. In addition, agricultural leases can be structured as a hybrid, with elements of cash and crop-share rent. An alternative to leasing for landowners who do not want to farm the land themselves is custom farming.

The **cash lease** is the simplest agricultural rental arrangement. Under a cash lease, the tenant agrees to pay a fixed amount of rent (e.g., $100 per acre) to the landlord. The rent is usually payable in installments with a significant percentage, often 50%, being payable before planting in the spring. Unlike a crop-share arrangement, where the parties split some of the expenses, the tenant incurs all of the production costs in farming the land, including the cost of seed, fertilizer, labor, and machinery. The landlord pays the taxes and insurance on the property.

Rather than fixed cash rent, the parties can agree to a flexible cash lease, where the tenant pays a base amount of cash rent plus an additional amount of rent if market prices or actual yields or both are higher than expected, or minus a certain sum if prices, yields, or a combination of them are smaller than expected. Flexible cash leases add a degree of complexity to cash rent arrangements, but they have some benefits for landlords and tenants. The landlord shares in the potential upside profits, while the tenant minimizes some of the downside risks associated with low market prices, poor growing conditions, and the like.

Under a **crop-share lease** (*share-cropping* is an older term), the tenant pays a share of the crop as rent. Thus, if the crop sharing is 40/60, the landlord receives 40% of the crop and the tenant 60%. Ordinarily, the costs of production are shared as well, in the same proportion. The parties usually share most variable expenses, such as the costs of seed, fertilizer, herbicides and pesticides, and other production costs. The tenant often contributes the machinery and labor. As under a cash lease, the landlord pays the real estate taxes, insurance, and maintenance costs. A livestock share arrangement, which is similar to a crop-share lease, is used in livestock leasing.

An alternative to leasing is **custom farming**. In it, the landowner manages the farm, but hires others to perform all or most of the labor- and equipment-intensive activities. These would include plowing, cultivating, planting, fertilizing, spraying, and harvesting. Often nearby farmers with equipment and extra time can be hired to do these operations, with compensation being established on a per-acre basis for the different operations. The major benefit to the landowner is that, over the long term, custom farming usually is more profitable than leasing, because the landowner keeps all profits. A disadvantage is that the landowner will need to be heavily involved in the management of the farm, including the oversight of the custom farm operators, and bears the entire risk of adverse market and farming conditions.

Rights and Liabilities

As noted in Chapter 12, the Statute of Frauds in most states requires a lease to be evidenced by a writing if the lease is for longer than one year (three years in some states). Thus, neither a one-year agricultural lease nor a year-to-year tenancy is required to be in writing. However, as with any lease, the parties to an agricultural lease should establish their rights and obligations in a written lease signed by landlord and tenant.

An oral agricultural lease usually is presumed to be a year-to-year tenancy that is automatically renewed unless notice to terminate is given by either party. The traditional common law rule required six months' notice to terminate a year-to-year tenancy. Today, the required notice varies from state to state, ranging from 30 days to six months. Although some agricultural leases are year-to-year arrangements, the common alternative is a term lease, typically for one to three years, which ordinarily must be in writing to be enforced. Such a set-term lease terminates automatically at the end of the term, without the necessity of notice, unless the lease is renewed under its terms. Some farm leases provide for an initial term that is automatically renewed unless notice is given by either party within the time limit set forth in the lease.

The tenant generally has the right to farm the land as he or she sees fit, unless the lease provides otherwise. The primary limitation on the tenant's discretion is the common law rule that a tenant not commit waste. Waste consists of the unreasonable or improper abuse or mismanagement of the land that causes substantial or permanent injury to it. A related requirement is the tenant's obligation of good husbandry, that is, a duty to farm in a "farmerlike" manner. Poor husbandry includes actions that harm the land, such as allowing weeds to grow, overgrazing of pasture land, and plowing up hedge rows, shelter belts, or terracing intended to prevent erosion. Because the concept of good husbandry is open to question in many cases, a carefully drafted agricultural lease should require good husbandry and define what specific duties the tenant has regarding the growing and harvesting of the crops and the care of the land, including any limitations of the tenant's practices on the land.

Ordinarily, the tenant owns the crops, at least until they are harvested and divided pursuant to a crop share arrangement. The tenant's ownership is subject to at least two limitations. First, state statutes usually give the landlord a crop lien to ensure performance of the tenant's obligations under the lease. The lien attaches to the crop when it starts to grow, and it is enforceable when the crops have been harvested. It has priority over other conflicting interests if the landlord complies with the requirements of the lien statute, which ordinarily requires actual notice to third parties or the recording of the lien. Second, persons other than the landlord may have a lien against the crops. Some third party creditors have a statutory lien for services (e.g., a thresher's lien) or for materials supplied the tenant (e.g., a lien for seed or fertilizer). Banks and other lenders may have a lien under a financing arrangement or a loan agreement with the tenant, which is governed by Article 9 of the Uniform Commercial Code.

Environmental Protection Laws

For agricultural producers, environmental regulations have become increasingly important in the last forty years. Chapter 18 explored the general legal landscape of pollution control and environmental protection. Some of the most important environmental laws affecting agricultural producers are the following:

- The Clean Water Act, which governs some agricultural activities as point sources subject to permit controls under the National Pollution Discharge Elimination System, including concentrated animal feeding operations and concentrated aquatic animal production facilities (fish farms and hatcheries).

- The Conservation Reserve Program (CRP) and Conservation Reserve Enhancement Program (CREP), which provide landowners with rental payments in exchange for their agreement not to farm the land (or use it for grazing or haying) and to devote it to some environmentally beneficial use, such as for shelter belts, field windbreaks, or riparian buffers.

- The Food Security Act of 1985, including the so-called "Sodbuster" program, under which producers are ineligible for farm payments if highly erodible land is brought into production, unless a conservation plan is developed and implemented; and the so-called "Swampbuster" provision, which makes farmers ineligible for government support payments if they plant a crop on wetlands that were converted to farmland by draining, dredging, filling, or leveling.

- The Wetlands Reserve Program (WRP), under which farmers receive compensation to take land out of agricultural production and grant conservation easements to the government.

BOX 19–2 THE MIGRATORY BIRD RULE

The dredging and filling of wetlands by farmers and ranchers is subject to regulation under Section 404 of the Clean Water Act (CWA). This section requires a permit from the Army Corps of Engineers to dredge or fill any "waters of the United States." Section 404 is particularly important to farmers in areas where there are seasonal wetlands, e.g., the prairie pothole region of the Dakotas. Although plowing, cultivating, harvesting, and other ordinary farming practices are exempt from the law, any substantial draining or filling of wetlands requires a permit. Both the Corps of Engineers and the Environmental Protection Agency have adopted an expansive interpretation of the jurisdictional language of the CWA that allows them to regulate most wetlands. The Corps concluded that the phrase "waters of the United States" includes "sandflats, wetlands, sloughs, prairie potholes, wet meadows, playa lakes, and natural ponds" if harm to these waters could affect interstate commerce. And, under a regulation called the Migratory Bird Rule, the Corps took the position that waters used as habitat for migratory birds were "waters of the United States," subject to Section 404, because of the necessary interstate connection.

However, in the recent case of *Solid Waste Agency of Northern Cook County v. United States Army Corps of Engineers (SWANCC)*, 121 S.Ct. 675 (2001), the U.S. Supreme Court limited the authority of the Corps to regulate wetlands under the CWA. The Migratory Bird Rule was challenged in *SWANCC* by a consortium of suburban Chicago cities that wanted to develop a waste disposal facility on the site of an abandoned sand and gravel mine. Because the site had some seasonal ponds that were used by migratory birds, the Corps claimed the ponds were "waters of the United States." The Court held that "waters of the United States" does not include wetlands that are not adjacent to a navigable waterway. Thus, under *SWANCC*, the Army Corps of Engineers cannot regulate nonnavigable, isolated intrastate waters under section 404 of the CWA. Obviously, the decision casts serious doubt on the legitimacy of federal regulation under the CWA of seasonal waters in many farm areas of the country.

- The Federal Endangered Species Act, which restricts the taking of endangered or threatened species, and state wildlife protection laws and regulations.

- The Federal Insecticide, Fungicide, and Rodenticide Act (FIFRA), which restricts the use of pesticides and requires producers to adequately train and warn agricultural workers of pesticide dangers.

- State soil and water conservation laws, under which land use conservation controls may be imposed.

Self-Study Questions

1. What are the major differences between the riparian rights system and the prior appropriation system of water rights?

2. Why did the courts abandon natural flow in favor of the reasonable use rule?

3. What is the difference between percolating groundwater and underground streams?

4. What are the common enemy and civil law rules relating to diffused surface water?

5. What effect does a severance of mineral rights have on the rights of the surface owner?

6. Explain the following payments under an oil and gas lease: (a) bonus payment, (b) delay rentals, (c) production royalties, and (d) shut-in royalties.

7. Do right-to-farm laws strike an appropriate balance between the rights of farmers and other landowners?

8. Explain the advantages and disadvantages of a cash lease as opposed to a crop-share lease.

9. Explain the similarities and differences among the ownership of or rights to oil and gas, the ownership of minerals, and the right to water use.

10. Which system of water rights, riparian rights or prior appropriation, is better from a public policy perspective?

Case Problems

1. Horseshoe Lake, located three miles south of Augusta, Arkansas, is approximately three miles long and 300 feet wide. John Brooks was a tenant of Ector Johnson who owned a large tract of land adjacent to the lake, including three-fourths of the lake bed. For many years, Brooks had raised rice on Johnson's land and irrigated the rice with water pumped from the lake. In March of 1954, Theo Mashburn leased a small camp site on the bank of the lake and installed a commercial boating and fishing business. He rented cabins, sold fishing bait and equipment, and rented boats to members of the general public. He began operating on April 1, 1954, and fishing and boat rentals were satisfactory from that time until July of 1954 when the fish quit biting and his income from that source and boat rentals was reduced to practically nothing. Mashburn filed a lawsuit to enjoin Brooks from pumping water from the lake to irrigate his rice crop, alleging that Brooks had reduced the level of the lake to such an extent as to make the lake unsuitable for fishing, recreation, or other lawful purposes. Evidence showed that Brooks began pumping water in May and continued pumping until late in August. He quit pumping when it was discovered that fish life was being endangered because of the low level of the lake. Evidence further established that the lake was below its "normal" level during July and August. However, the years 1952, 1953, and 1954 were unusually dry, and the water levels in similar lakes in the same general area were unusually low in August of 1954. (a) Assuming that riparian rights law governs this dispute, who will probably win? (b) If this incident occurred in a prior appropriation state, who would prevail in the lawsuit? *Harris v. Brooks*, 283 S.W.2d 129 (Ark. 1955).

2. Ichauway, Inc., d/b/a Joseph W. Jones Ecological Research Center ("Ichauway"), sued to enjoin Carroll Givens from trespassing on real property Ichauway leased. Ichauway leased the land on both sides of Ichauwaynochaway Creek for 14 miles of its length and conducted ecological research on the stream. Ichauwaynochaway Creek is 75- to 200-feet wide with rock shoals within two feet of the surface. In an attempt to show that the creek was navigable, Givens floated through Ichauway's leasehold on a styrofoam and wood raft that was four feet wide, sixteen feet long, and drew one foot of water. He loaded the raft with a goat, a bale of cotton, and two passengers. He argued that the goat, cotton, and passengers were freight and that his trip showed the creek was capable of use for transporting freight under Georgia law. To be considered navigable under Georgia law, a stream must be "capable of transporting boats loaded with freight in the regular course of trade either for the whole or a part of the year. The mere rafting of timber or the transporting of wood in small boats shall not make a stream navigable." Is the stream navigable under Georgia law? *Givens v. Ichauway, Inc.*, 493 S.E.2d 148 (Ga. 1997).

3. The Buchanans owned and operated a 320-acre farm near Pasco, Washington. When they purchased the property in 1961, the adjacent properties were primarily used as rangeland. In 1969, a small cattle feeding operation opened on land to the southeast of the Buchanan farm. Simplot Feeders Limited Partnership purchased the feedlot in 1992 and expanded its operations. Simplot eventually had more than 580 acres of pens and 40,000 cows. The Buchanans claimed that Simplot's operation of the feedlot resulted in a significant increase of flies and foul and obnoxious

odors. The Buchanans sued Simplot alleging nuisance, trespass, and negligence. Simplot argued that its operations were exempt from a nuisance suit under Washington's right-to-farm statute. Under the law, agricultural activities conducted on farmland, if consistent with good agricultural practices and established prior to surrounding nonagricultural activities, are presumed to be reasonable and do not constitute a nuisance unless the activity has a substantial adverse effect on the public health and safety. The Buchanans argued that the statute could not apply to their lawsuit because the Buchanan farm was in operation *before* Simplot's feedlot activities. Simplot argued that they could rely on the law because their activities were established before any surrounding *nonagricultural* activities. Who should prevail on the right-to-farm issue? *Buchanan v. Simplot Feeders Limited Partnership*, 952 P.2d 610 (Wash. 1998).

4. Milton Stokka was killed while snowmobiling when he struck an unmarked guywire on the west side of County Road 17 near Horace, North Dakota. His family sued Cass County Electrical Co-op, Inc. (CCEC), for wrongful death alleging that CCEC negligently maintained the wire in an area where snowmobilers were known to ride. It was alleged that CCEC knew that the guy-wire posed a risk of harm to snowmobilers, that it had installed a guyguard (a bright yellow plastic guard) to warn of the danger, but the guard was not on the wire when the accident occurred. It was also alleged that CCEC did not have an effective policy to install guyguards or assure their continued presence. CCEC claimed that it was immune from liability under the state recreational use statute. The family argued that liability fell within an exception to the immunity law for "wilful or malicious failure to guard or warn against a dangerous condition, use, structure, or activity." Does the accident fall within this exception or should the case be dismissed under the recreational use statute? *Stokka v. Cass County Electric Cooperative*, 373 N.W.2d 911 (N.D. 1985).

Endnotes

1. Alabama, Arkansas, Connecticut, Delaware, Florida, Georgia, Illinois, Indiana, Iowa, Kentucky, Maine, Maryland, Massachusetts, Michigan, Minnesota, Missouri, New Hampshire, New Jersey, New York, North Carolina, Ohio, Pennsylvania, Rhode Island, South Carolina, Tennessee, Vermont, Virginia, West Virginia, and Wisconsin.

2. Alaska, Arizona, Colorado, Idaho, Montana, Nevada, New Mexico, Utah, and Wyoming.

3. California, Kansas, Mississippi, Nebraska, North Dakota, Oklahoma, Oregon, South Dakota, Texas, and Washington.

4. *Restatement (Second) of Torts* § 850A. Reasonableness of the Use of Water (1977).

5. Arkansas, Delaware, Florida, Georgia, Illinois, Indiana, Iowa, Kentucky, Maryland, Massachusetts, Minnesota, New Jersey, New York, North Carolina, Pennsylvania, South Carolina, and Wisconsin.

6. 344 P.2d 528 (Utah 1959).

7. Alaska, Idaho, Kansas, Montana, Nevada, New Mexico, North Dakota, Oregon, South Dakota, Utah, Washington, and Wyoming.

8. 470 S.W.2d 618 (Tex. 1971).

9. Alabama, Arkansas, Colorado, Kansas, Maryland, Michigan, Mississippi, Montana, New Mexico, Ohio, Pennsylvania, Tennessee, Texas, and West Virginia.

10. California, Illinois, Indiana, Louisiana, Kentucky, and Oklahoma.

11. 584 N.W.2d 309 (Iowa 1998).

Glossary

A

Abate To put a stop to, as to "abate a nuisance."

Absolute liability Liability without fault.

Absolute ownership doctrine Common law rule of water rights allowing an overlying landowner to withdraw an unlimited quantity of groundwater even if the withdrawal detrimentally affects the water supply of neighbors.

Accelerate In mortgage lending, right of a lender to require immediate payment of principal and accrued interest upon borrower's default.

Acid rain Combination of water in the atmosphere with pollutants released by burning hydrocarbons to form rain and snow containing acids harmful to vegetation and aquatic life.

Acknowledgment Process of verifying a signature, usually by declaring before a public official such as a notary public that a signature is the signer's.

Acquisition and development financing (A&D financing) Loan used to fund the acquisition of real estate and excavation, grading, and construction on the property.

Acre An area of land measure containing 43,560 square feet.

Actual eviction Physically depriving a tenant of possession of the premises.

Ad valorem tax Tax, such as a tax on real property, based on the value of the property.

Adjustable rate mortgage A mortgage whose an interest rate varies over time, involving an interest rate increment above a stated index that can fluctuate.

Adjusted basis Owner's cost of purchasing property, plus cost of capital improvements, less accumulated depreciation.

Administrative agency A regulatory body created by a legislature, which delegates regulatory power to the agency.

Administrator, administrator with will annexed Person who administers a decedent's estate. See *personal representative*.

Adverse possession A trespasser's occupation of another's land in such a way that the trespasser becomes owner if the landowner does not take the required preventive action.

Affirmative easement An easement allowing its holder to enter the servient tenement and use it in some way.

Agency Relationship between a principal and an agent.

Agent A person authorized to contract or otherwise act on behalf of a principal.

Air lot A layer of air space of specified dimensions within which its owner may build. See *column lot* and *caisson lot*.

Alienation The transfer of property by sale or gift.

Allodial ownership Absolute ownership of land free of any oath or obligation to a lord.

All-risk insurance policy An insurance contract that insures against all perils except those that are specifically excluded from coverage.

American Institute of Architects (AIA) A professional organization for architects in the United States.

Amount realized In calculating the taxable gain on the sale of property, the cash received for the property, plus the value of any other property received, less the costs of sale.

Anchor tenant A major tenant that will attract customers to a shopping center. See also *destination tenant*.

Annual gift tax exclusion Yearly gift that is not subject to the gift and estate tax.

Annual percentage rate The face interest rate of a promissory note plus the other finance charges to be paid by the borrower.

Antenuptial agreement See *premarital agreement*.

Anticipatory repudiation Statement or action by a contract obligor indicating before performance is due that the obligor will breach the contract.

Antideficiency statute Statute prohibiting an aggrieved lender from acquiring a judgment against the debtor for a deficiency remaining after foreclosure.

Appraisal The determination of the market value of property utilizing a recognized appraisal method.

Appropriation The diversion of water from a watercourse for a beneficial purpose.

Aquifers Underground reservoirs of water.

Arbitration Nonjudicial method of dispute resolution in which an expert or a panel of experts acceptable to the parties renders a binding decision.

Area variance A zoning authority's allowing the use of property in a manner that is inconsistent with dimensional limits.

Artesian aquifer Aquifer subject to subsurface pressure causing the water to come to the surface.

Artificial uses Uses of water that are not essential for living but that increase productivity or enhance the riparian's standard of living.

Assembled industrial plant doctrine A rule of law conferring fixture status on machinery and equipment without actual annexation if it is placed in an industrial establishment for permanent use, and is indispensable in carrying on the specific business.

Assessed value The value of property for purposes of computing the property tax.

Assign To transfer.

Assignment The act of transferring one's interest in something, as in the assignment of a lease, so that the *assignee* (transferee) receives all of the *assignor's* rights.

Attachment In Article 9 secured transactions in personal property, the process of agreement between credi-

tor and debtor that creates a security interest in the collateral.

Attorney-in-fact An agent authorized to conduct business for a natural-person principal.

B

Balloon mortgage A mortgage having a relatively large final (balloon) payment of principal because the prior payments have been insufficient to fully amortize the mortgage debt.

Bargain and sale deed Deed transferring any interest that the grantor has, and in several states, impliedly warranting that grantor has not transferred the interest else to another nor encumbered the property. Known in some states as a *grant deed*.

Base flood elevation The estimated height of a 100-year flood.

Base rent A fixed amount of rent that a commercial tenant agrees to pay on a monthly or annual basis; also known as minimum rent.

Beneficial purpose A useful purpose for which water is appropriated.

Bequest A transfer of personal property by will. See also *legacy*.

Betterment statute A statute, also called an *occupying claimant, mistaken improver,* or *good faith improver statute,* which accommodates the interests of good faith improvers (trespassers) and the landowners.

Bid bond Bond paying damages to a developer or owner if the contractor who won the bidding for a construction contract does not enter into it.

Blockbusting In residential real estate sales, inducing panic selling for financial gain by playing on racial or other fear-inducing bases prohibited under the Fair Housing Act.

Blue sky laws State laws regulating the issuance and sale of securities.

Board of selectmen The governing body of a New England town.

Bona fide purchaser for value (BFP) A purchaser who bought property in good faith for a valuable consideration without notice of any problems or defects.

Borough In Alaska and New York City, the equivalent of a county.

Bound In surveying, a direction or course, usually in terms of points on the compass.

Broker An agent appointed by the seller or buyer in a real estate sale to act on his or her behalf.

Building permit Government permit required before the commencement of permanent improvements on realty.

Bundle of rights An accumulation of legally defined rights, powers, privileges, and immunities in a thing (including land), enabling the owner of the bundle to possess, use, enjoy, encumber, and dispose of the thing free from interference by others.

Buyer's agent A real estate broker who acts on behalf of the buyer.

By-pass trust See *credit shelter trust*.

C

Caisson lot A cylindrical portion of the subsurface upon which a column lot and a vertical column would rest to help support an air lot.

Call In surveying, a statement or description of a boundary line in terms of metes and bounds.

Capacity Mental and legal ability of a party to enter into a contract.

Capital asset Property held by a taxpayer as an investment, including real estate so held.

Capital gain Gain realized on the sale of a capital asset.

Cash lease Agricultural lease under which tenant pays a fixed amount of rent per acre.

Caveat emptor Latin for "let the buyer beware"; principle excusing a seller from disclosing defects in the property or product being sold.

CC&Rs A shorthand expression for "conditions, covenants, and restrictions."

Certificate of deposit Promissory note acknowledging a bank's debt to depositor.

Certificate of occupancy Official document confirming that improvements as constructed meet the applicable zoning and building codes.

Certified historic buildings Buildings listed in the national register and those located in registered historic districts qualifying for the rehabilitation tax credit.

Chain of title Connected succession of conveyances of a parcel of property, beginning with the original grant by the sovereign authority.

Chattel real A leasehold. Though an interest in land, it is classified as personal property.

Civil law A system of law legislative in origin. Adopted in countries such as France and Germany, and in the state of Louisiana, civil law is found in a "code" drafted by committees and enacted by legislatures. In the *common law* system, law permitting an individual to bring a private lawsuit for damages and other remedies to compensate for losses.

Civil law rule In water law, rule prohibiting a landowner from diverting or altering the natural flow of diffused surface water.

Close In surveying, the completion of a metes-and-bounds description so that the end of the last call connects to the point of beginning, enclosing the tract of land.

Closing The consummation of a sales contract for realty; the seller conveys title and the buyer pays the promised consideration.

Closing agent A neutral third party, such as a title company, law firm, bank, or trust company, that handles the closing of a real estate transaction. Sometimes referred to as the *escrow agent* or *escrowee*.

Closing day The date scheduled for a real estate closing. Sometimes called *law day*.

Cluster zoning Zoning allowing a developer to deviate from site development standards as long as part of the development is left as undeveloped space. Also called *open space zoning*.

Codicil A written supplement to a will that qualifies it in some way.

Coinsurance clause A clause in a property insurance policy designed to provide an equitable rate structure for all insureds where some insure for only partial value, and to limit the amounts paid out by the insurer.

Collateral heirs Those "alongside" the lineal line (descendants and ascendants), e.g., sisters, brothers, aunts, uncles, nieces, nephews, and cousins.

Collateralized mortgage obligation A participation certificate in a pool of commercial real estate loans, normally sold by investment banks.

Column lot A surface area with its own airspace for erecting a vertical column needed (with others) to support an air lot.

Common area maintenance (CAM) charges See *operating costs*.

Common areas In a condominium or other type common interest ownership, areas owned as tenants in common by unit owners (e.g., the structural components and exterior of the buildings and amenities such as tennis courts). Also known as *common elements*.

Common enemy doctrine Common law rule allowing a landowner to take any measure necessary to divert diffused surface water off the property.

Common law Originally, a body of English judge-made law in which legal rules have been distilled from an accumulation of appellate decisions; source of American common law.

Common promotional plan Under the Interstate Land Sales Full Disclosure Act, a plan under which a developer sells contiguous lots or lots that are marketed under a common name.

Community property In eight southern and western states and Wisconsin, property acquired by husband or wife during the marriage and not classified as "separate" property.

Compensatory (ordinary) damages An award of money by a court as payment for actual loss, harm, or injury caused by a defendant wrongdoer.

Component part Civil law term for fixture.

Comprehensive city plan General plan for a city or political subdivision that guides future development and land-use planning decisions. See also *master city plan*.

Concurrent estates The interests of co-owners who are entitled to the present possession of land.

Condemnation Legal proceeding under which government exercises its power of eminent domain.

Condition precedent An event or state of affairs that must occur before performance under a contract becomes due.

Conditional uses Land uses permitted within a given district under a zoning law only after administrative review and compliance with conditions set by the reviewing body. Also known as *special uses*.

Condominium A type of residential or commercial ownership involving two basic property rights: ownership of a "unit," usually in fee simple, and an undivided fractional interest in the common areas as a tenant in common with other unit owners.

Condominium unit A specifically defined airspace within a structure, usually owned in fee simple, together with an assigned percentage of the common areas.

Consequential damages Foreseeable losses incurred as a direct result of a breach of contract.

Conservation easement An easement or restrictive covenants limiting potential development or other commercial uses of property to preserve open space, wildlife, natural resources, or other things or qualities.

Consideration That which induces a contracting party to enter the contract, e.g., the promise of the other party to do or to refrain from doing something.

Construction financing Financing used to construct the improvements on real property.

Constructive delivery An act regarded in law as the equivalent of a real delivery, such as handing over a symbol of the thing to be delivered. Also called symbolic delivery.

Constructive eviction Acts or omissions of a landlord depriving the tenant of the beneficial use of the premises.

Constructive fraud Reckless misrepresentation or concealment of material facts detrimentally relied on by another.

Constructive notice Notice imputed to a person by law because of its availability in the public records, whether or not the person has actually inspected the records.

Contingent remainder A remainder whose vesting in the remainderman depends not only on the natural expiration of the prior possessory estate, but also on the happening (or nonhappening) of an additional event called a "condition precedent." Compare with *vested remainder*.

Continuing nuisance A nuisance in which the offensive use of the neighboring land is uninterrupted or recurs with sufficient frequency to be considered a continuous offending use of the neighboring land.

Continuing trespass A trespass that constitutes a new offense each day that the trespass continues to occur.

Contract for deed A *land contract*.

Contract law Body of legal rules that guides courts in their decisions regarding which promises or agreements to enforce.

Conveyance Transfer of an interest in land by means of a deed.

Cooperating brokers Brokers who work with a real estate broker in locating a ready, able, and willing buyer.

Cooperative A type of common interest community in which a corporation owns the realty and the residents own shares in the corporation and are tenants under proprietary leases.

Co-ownership Ownership of an interest in land by two or more persons. Also known as *concurrent ownership* or *cotenancy*.

Corporation A legal entity chartered under state law, with most of the legal rights and obligations of natural persons.

Corporeal Civil law term for property having physical being.

Cost approach Appraisal method estimating market value of realty by determining the value of the land, and adding the cost of a replacement structure, adjusted for depreciation.

Cotenancy clause In a retail center lease, a clause excusing the tenant from its express covenant of continuous operation when significant space in the center is unoccupied.

Cotenant A co-owner.

County The largest political subdivision of a state. In most states, a unit of local government.

Covenant A written promise or agreement to do or to refrain from doing something with one's own land.

Covenant against encumbrances A grantor's promise in a deed that there are no encumbrances against the property at the time of the conveyance.

Covenant of further assurances Deed covenant obligating a grantor to provide any additional instruments that may be necessary to perfect the title that grantor purports to convey.

Covenant of quiet enjoyment Deed covenant assuring that no adverse claims are attributable to the grantor or the grantor's predecessors in title.

Covenant of right to convey Deed covenant assuring that the grantor has the right to convey the interest that the deed purports to convey.

Covenant of seisin Deed covenant assuring that the grantor owns the estate or interest that the grantor purports to convey.

Covenant of warranty See the *covenant of quiet enjoyment.*

Credit shelter trust Testamentary trust funded to the maximum amount of the unified credit. See also *by-pass trust.*

Crop share lease Agricultural lease under which the tenant pays a share of the crop as rent. Also called "share-cropping."

Cumulative zoning Zoning that allows "higher" uses in "lower use" districts.

Cure In loans, the right of the borrower to rectify a default under the loan documents during a specified grace period.

Curtesy An interest that a surviving husband has in land owned by his wife.

Custom farming Contractual arrangement where the landowner manages the farm but hires others to do the plowing, fertilizing, cultivating, harvesting, and other production activities.

D

Damages An amount of money awarded to compensate a plaintiff for losses caused by the defendant.

Declarant An owner of real estate submitting realty to condominium ownership, using a declaration of condominium.

Declaration of condominium Instrument creating a condominium.

Dedication A private landowner's gift of an interest in land to the government. Also, a developer's transfer of an interest for public amenities, compelled by local government as a condition to having residential and other subdivisions approved.

Deduction for family-owned businesses Special deduction under gift and estate tax law for a family business.

Deed A document by means of which a person transfers an interest in land to another.

Deed of trust A document which, like a mortgage, creates a security interest in real property in favor of a creditor. The debtor (the trustor) conveys an interest called "legal title" to a third person (the trustee) to hold as security for the benefit of the creditor (the beneficiary).

Deed restrictions A set of restrictive covenants recorded in connection with a subdivision development.

Default A debtor's failure to pay the debt or to carry out some other obligation.

Default risk The possibility that a borrower will not repay the lender. Also called *repayment risk.*

Default risk premium An additional interest rate increment imposed by a lender to compensate for the default risk.

Delivery In the law of deeds, a grantor's physically handing over a deed to the grantee or in some other way indicating that the deed is to be presently operative.

Density In residential development, the number of units or families per acre.

Density bonus Right to develop property with more units than zoning law would normally allow. Used in connection with transfer of develop-ment rights programs and as inclusionary zoning incentives.

Depreciation Amortization of a landowner's expenditures for improvements over their useful life.

Designated agency Real estate agency relationship under which one member of a brokerage firm represents the interests of the seller and one represents the interests of the buyer.

Destination tenant A shopping center tenant that shoppers view as a desirable destination. See also *anchor tenant.*

Developer Under the Interstate Land Sales Full Disclosure Act, any person who sells, leases, or advertises for sale or lease a lot in a subdivision.

Development agreement Contract between a city and a subdivision developer setting forth the conditions for the city's approval of a subdivision plan.

Devise A transfer of land by will.

Devisee The recipient of land transferred by a will.

Disabled access credit Federal tax credit for small businesses that incur expenses in accommodating their properties to meet the needs of the disabled.

Discount point One percent of the loan amount, charged to the borrower as a finance charge.

Diversion Rerouting water from a river, lake, or other natural source.

Dominant tenement A tract of land benefitting from an easement.

Donee Recipient of a voluntary transfer of an interest in real or personal property as a gift.

Donor Owner of real or personal property who voluntarily transfers it as a gift to another, a donee.

Dower At common law, the right of a widow to receive, at the death of her husband, a life estate in one-third of the lands owned by him at any time during their marriage, free from the claims of the husband's creditors.

Due on further encumbrance clause A contract clause accelerating mortgage obligations if the mortgagor transfers the secured property as security for a junior mortgage without the consent of the mortgagee.

Due-on-sale clause Clause accelerating mortgage obligations if the mortgagor transfers the secured property without the consent of the mortgagee.

Durable power of attorney A power of attorney that survives the physical or mental incapacity of the principal.

Duty to mitigate Under contract law, duty imposed on an innocent party to minimize losses caused by a breach of contract by the defaulting party. Under landlord-tenant law, duty imposed on landlord to retake possession of the premises and relet the property upon an abandonment or breach of the lease by the tenant.

E

Earnest money A portion of the purchase price delivered to a seller as evidence of the buyer's good faith and willingness to perform the contract.

Easement An interest in another person's land entitling the easement owner to use the other person's land for a special purpose.

Easement appurtenant An easement benefitting a tract of land without regard to who owns or possesses it. See also *tenement*.

Easement by necessity A type of implied easement, granted to the owner of a parcel of land that is landlocked.

Easement in gross An easement benefitting a person or firm rather than a tract of land.

Ejectment A legal action designed to restore possession to the person entitled to it.

Elective share statute A statute allowing a decedent's spouse to take a share of the decedent's estate in lieu of a share given by the decedent's will. Sometimes called a forced share statute.

11th District Cost of Funds Index Index tracking the average cost of funds for Federal Home Loan Bank Board member banks located in California, Arizona, and Nevada.

Eminent domain Power of the government to take private property for public purposes.

Enabling act Statute empowering persons, corporations, or units of government to do something they could not previously do; in zoning law, statute empowering cities, towns, and other political subdivisions to engage in zoning and land-use planning. Statute creating an administrative agency and defining its powers.

Encumbrance A right, claim, or charge against real property, for example, a mortgage, a tax lien, a lease, or an easement (right to use another's realty).

Enjoyment Having the benefit of a property right.

Enterprise zone Distressed area of a state within which businesses receive property tax exemptions or incentives for locating or expanding their operations there.

Environmental audit A review of the history and physical condition of realty for evidence of environmental contamination.

Environmental impact statement A detailed statement describing the

consequences to the environment of the proposed federal action.

Equitable conversion A legal doctrine under which a purchaser of realty under an executory sales contract immediately becomes the equitable owner of the realty, and the seller, whose interest before the contract was real estate, now has an interest in personal property, that is, a right to the purchase price.

Equitable servitude A land-use restriction enforceable in a court of equity against anyone taking possession of the burdened land with notice of the restriction. Also known as *equitable restriction*.

Equitable title In the law of trusts, the ownership interest (e.g., right to profits) that a beneficiary of a trust has in the property being managed by the trustee, who has legal title.

Equity of redemption Right of a defaulting borrower to redeem mortgaged property by making the missed payments.

Errors and omissions liability insurance Insurance against claims resulting from professional negligence. See also *malpractice insurance*.

Escalation clause Clause allowing landlord to increase the amount of rent or one that automatically adjusts the rent.

Escheat In the United States, the process by which, if a landowner dies without a will and without an heir, the state in which the land is located acquires title to it; to be contrasted with the escheat of feudal times.

Escrow A formal method of providing a neutral third party, called an escrow agent or escrowee, to handle the closing of a real estate transaction.

Escrow account Account into which a borrower is required to deposit, in advance, one-twelfth of the annual amounts due for taxes and insurance payable by the lender for the borrower.

Escrow agent Neutral third party who handles the closing of a real estate transaction. Also known as an *escrowee*.

Estate In the law of property, an ownership interest in land. In the law of inheritance, the property left by a decedent.

Estate administration Process of winding up the affairs of a decedent and distributing the net estate in accordance with the will or the intestacy statute

Estate tax A tax, whether state or federal, imposed on a decedent's privilege of transmitting property at death. Also known as *transfer tax*.

Estoppel by deed Where a deed purports to convey an estate that the grantor does not own but later acquires, a legal doctrine preventing the grantor from denying that the grantee received the title purportedly conveyed.

Eviction Depriving the tenant of possession of the premises. Can be actual or constructive.

Exactions Costs that a developer must pay in fees or dedications of land as part of the subdivision approval process or as a condition for a building permit.

Exclusionary zoning Zoning illegally excluding certain individuals or groups from living in a community.

Exclusive agency agreement Listing agreement appointing a real estate broker as the seller's exclusive agent, but seller may, without owing a commission, use own efforts to sell.

Exclusive right to sell Listing agreement giving real estate broker the sole right to sell the property and

a commission on the sale even if the seller locates a buyer without broker's services. Also known as an exclusive sale agreement.

Exclusive use clause Clause in a retail lease giving the tenant the sole right to conduct a particular business or sell a particular product in a shopping center.

Exculpatory clause In leases, a clause releasing the landlord from liability to tenant for negligence or other wrongdoing.

Execution A postjudgment process for enforcing a judgment for damages.

Executive order An order by the president or a governor of a state, having the force of law as to persons within reach of executive authority.

Executor The personal representative named in a decedent's will to administer the decedent's estate.

Executory interest A future interest similar to a possibility of reverter but owned by a third person instead of the grantor.

Express easement An easement created by the use of language and conveyed to the grantee by a deed or a will.

F

Family business Business qualified for the special deduction for family-owned businesses under the gift and estate tax.

Fee simple absolute The greatest aggregate of ownership rights that a person can have in land. Also called *fee simple,* or *fee*.

Fee simple determinable A fee simple interest that ends automatically when the land is used in a way forbidden in the grant of ownership.

Fee simple on a condition subsequent. A fee simple interest that entitles its grantor to end it by taking appropriate action of reentry after the land is used in a way forbidden in the grant of ownership.

Fee tail An estate in fee meant to keep land in the hands of lineal descendants.

Fiduciary duty A duty arising where a knowledgeable or experienced person (the fiduciary) is in a relationship of trust and confidence with a person of less knowledge or sophistication. The fiduciary has a duty not to take advantage of the relationship for personal gain.

Finance charges Defined under the Truth-in-Lending Act as "the sum of all charges, payable directly or indirectly by the person to whom the credit is extended, and imposed directly or indirectly by the creditor as an incident to the extension of credit."

Financing statement A UCC Article 9 document briefly describing the collateral covered by a security agreement and required to be filed in a county office provided for UCC filings.

First-generation condominium statute Early "bare bones" state statute allowing landowners to establish and sell condominiums.

Fixed rate mortgage Mortgage with a fixed interest rate, a fixed duration, and equal payments, usually monthly.

Fixture filing The filing of a financing statement covering goods that are or are to become fixtures, in the recorder's office as part of the land records, as required by UCC Article 9.

Fixtures Goods so physically attached or otherwise related to realty that they are classified as real estate.

Floating zone A district created in the text of the zoning ordinance but not located on the original zoning map.

Force majeure clause Clause giving a contracting party additional time to perform if a reason for delay, such as weather conditions or a strike, is beyond the party's control.

Forced share statute See *elective share statute*.

Forcible detainer Speedy legal proceeding to evict a tenant. Also called *unlawful detainer*.

Foreclose To force a sale by means of court action or exercise of a contractual power of sale.

Foreclosure Process by which a creditor with a security interest or other lien right can, upon the debtor's default, force the sale of the collateral.

Formal will The usual type of witnessed will, ordinarily prepared by an attorney, and conforming to the requirements of the state statute of wills.

Fraud in the inducement A tort and a defense to an otherwise enforceable contract. To prevail, a plaintiff alleging fraud ordinarily must prove (1) misrepresentation of a material fact, (2) intent to deceive, (3) reasonable reliance on the misrepresentation, and (4) damages.

Freehold estate An ownership interest of indefinite, potentially infinite duration.

Future interest or **future estate** An ownership interest in land entitling the owner to *future* possession, after the termination of a present possessory interest in someone else.

G

Gap Term used by title searchers and insurers to mean the administrative delay between recording an instrument or lien and its microfilming or digitizing, and indexing.

General contractor A person hired by a landowner to construct improvements on real property, and who hires and supervises subcontractors in the various construction trades.

General partner In a partnership, a person having full management responsibility for the partnership and joint and several liability for all debts of the partnership.

General power of attorney A degree of authority allowing an agent to transact any and all business for the principal.

Gift Voluntary transfer of an interest in real or personal property by its owner, the *donor,* to a *donee* for no consideration.

Gift and estate tax Federal tax on gifts of property during a decedent's lifetime and on property transferred at his or her death.

Gift causa mortis A gift automatically revocable by law because made in contemplation of the donor's imminent death.

Gift inter vivos A gift between living persons, ordinarily irrevocable.

Going dark A tenant's ceasing business while the lease is in effect.

Goods Tangible personal property such as machinery, food, clothing, and industrial gases held in containers.

Grading permit A government permit allowing a developer to level and shape the surface of realty in a proposed development project.

Grant deed See *bargain and sale deed.*

Grantee A person to whom an interest in land is transferred.

Grantor A person who transfers an interest in land to another.

Grantor-grantee index system A land records system in which conveyances of interests in real property are indexed in two separate indices, first alphabetically by the surname of the grantor and then alphabetically by the surname of the grantee.

Gross lease A lease under which the tenant pays a fixed amount of rent per month.

Ground lease A long-term lease under which the tenant leases only land and, at its own expense, constructs a building or other improvements on the property for its business.

H

Habendum clause Clause in oil and gas lease establishing the primary and secondary terms of the lease.

Hazard insurance Insurance protecting owners of realty and their lenders against loss or damage from fire and other stated casualties, up to the policy limits.

Hedge against inflation A type of property or a practice that is relatively immune to inflation.

Heir A person receiving property under a state intestacy statute.

Holographic will One entirely in the handwriting of the testator, although some states allow some printing if the key provisions are handwritten.

Homeowner's insurance Residential *hazard insurance.*

Homestead A person's residential dwelling plus the land it occupies, its outbuildings, and the like.

Homestead exemption An exemption of a debtor's residence, or of some part of its value, from the claims of creditors. Also, an annual property tax exemption for real estate used as a personal residence.

Horizontal subdivision The division of earth or airspace into layers.

Hybrid system Water rights system based on prior appropriation principles but recognizing some riparian rights.

Hypothecary action In Louisiana's civil law, a legal process serving a function similar to that of foreclosure.

I

Immovables Civil law term for real property.

Implied covenant of quiet enjoyment Common law obligation by which a landlord guarantees the tenant undisturbed possession of the premises.

Implied easement An easement arising by judicial inference from circumstances surrounding the conveyance of an estate in land, and *not* from any agreement or expression of the parties.

Improved lot exemption Exemption from the requirements of the Interstate Land Sales Full Disclosure Act for the sale of lots on which stands a building or where a contract obligates the seller to erect a building within two years.

Inchoate Incomplete, unfinished.

Incidental damages Costs incurred by a nonbreaching party after a breach of contract in reasonable efforts to avoid loss, as by trying to obtain a substitute sale.

Inclusionary zoning Local housing requirements or incentives to promote development of low- and moderate-income housing.

Income approach Appraisal method estimating market value of realty on the basis of the income derived from it.

Incorporeal In civil law, existing only as an abstract right.

Index In mortgage lending, an internal or external measure of market interest rates, usually related to a lender's cost of funds.

Inflation Economic phenomenon in which prices rise steadily so that a unit of money purchases less over time.

Inheritance tax A tax imposed on heirs, devisees, and legatees for the privilege of receiving the property from a decedent's estate.

Initial point In the rectangular survey method, a point of reference from which surveying begins.

Initial public offering An original sale of securities to the public.

Injunction A court order requiring a wrongdoer either to do something or to refrain from doing something.

Inquiry notice Physical conditions on realty, or information about its title, which should alert potential purchasers to the possibility of adverse claims or encumbrances.

Installment land contract See *installment sale.*

Installment sale Sale of real estate in which the buyer pays the purchase price over time and seller is financier. Also known as *installment land contract.*

Insurable interest Regarding land, any interest in it whose destruction, damage, or use will result in monetary loss to its owner, and which therefore may be insured by the owner.

Insured closing protection letter Document issued by a title insurance company to protect a lender from the

negligence or malfeasance of a closing attorney who is using the services of the title insurance company for a closing.

Intangible property Property, real or personal, existing only as an abstract right.

Inter vivos trust A living trust.

Interest A charge for the use of money, usually stated as an annual percentage of the sum borrowed.

Interest rate risk Economic phenomenon in which the market value of debt is inversely related to movements in the prevailing interest rates.

Intermediate theory of mortgages Principle that a mortgagor has the right to possession of the mortgaged realty until default, and the mortgagee has the right afterward. So-called because it represents a compromise between the title theory and the lien theory of mortgages.

Intestacy statute A state statute specifying who is to receive the estate of a decedent who died without a valid will. See also *statute of descent and distribution.*

Intestate A person who dies without a will; having no valid will at death.

Intrastate exemption (1) Exemption from the Securities Act of 1933 allowing the sale of securities within one state without filing a registration statement with the SEC. (2) Exemption from the requirements of the Interstate Land Sales Full Disclosure Act for the sale of lots exclusively to residents of the state in which the subdivision is located.

Inverse condemnation A taking of private property or an interest in it by government regulations or the government's use of its own property.

Investment contract A security in which the investors are passive participants, risking their money in a business managed by others.

Invitee A person who enters the premises of an owner or other possessor for the possessor's business benefit and at the possessor's express or implied invitation.

Irrevocable license A type of servitude, equivalent to an easement in the licensor's land.

Issue In its broadest sense, all persons who have descended from a common ancestor. Synonymous with "descendants," both lineal and collateral. Especially in wills, however, often used to mean, for example, only the testator's children, and not all of his or her descendants.

J

Joint and several liability In litigation involving multiple defendants, the liability of each of them for the entire amount of the plaintiff's damage.

Joint tenancy A type of co-ownership of property giving each co-owner a fractional interest that he or she can dispose of during life, and a "right of survivorship" (if the co-owner keeps the interest) that entitles the last survivor to sole ownership of portions not previously disposed of.

Judicial foreclosure Termination of a borrower's equity of redemption through a sale of real property held as security for an indebtedness, by filing a lawsuit against the mortgagor in which all other parties having an interest in the property are made parties.

L

Land contract A relatively long-term contract for the sale of land in which the seller is also the financier of the purchase. Also known as a *contract for deed* or *installment sale contract.*

Land description Boundary or other information about a parcel of land that distinguishes it from all others. Also called a *legal description.*

Landlord A lessor.

Lateral support Support of a parcel of land by the land surrounding it.

Law day In one sense frequently used, the date scheduled for a real estate closing.

Lease A transaction between landlord and tenant that creates a leasehold interest in land.

Leasehold An interest in land, granted by a landlord, giving the tenant a right of exclusive use of the premises for an agreed time.

Legacy A bequest of personal property under a will.

Legal description See *land description.*

Legal title In the law of trusts, the ownership interest in trust property that enables the trustee to manage it on behalf of the beneficiary, who has equitable title.

Legatee The recipient of a legacy.

Lessee A person or firm to whom property is leased, or rented; a tenant.

Lessor A person or firm who leases property to another; a landlord.

Liability insurance Insurance protecting a possessor of land against liability to others for injuries resulting from dangerous conditions on and dangerous uses of the land.

LIBOR Acronym for the London Interbank Offering Rate Index, which represents the prevailing interest rate that international banks charge each other to borrow dollars in the London money market.

License A permission or privilege to use another person's land for some purpose, which the licensor ordinarily may revoke at any time.

Licensee A person permitted to enter another's property for the licensee's own purposes and not for the benefit of the possessor.

Licensor A person granting a license.

Lien A charge against property to secure payment of a private debt, taxes, or some other obligation.

Lien theory In mortgage law, the principle, adopted by a majority of states, that a mortgagee does not hold title to the mortgaged property, but has merely a security interest in it.

Life estate A freehold estate in land entitling its owner to possess, use, and enjoy the land for life, and to dispose of the interest (though not the land).

Life estate pur autre vie A life estate whose duration is measured by the life of a person other than the grantee.

Like-kind exchange The exchange of property for property of a similar kind on which the tax on any gain is deferred.

Limited common elements In a condominium, common elements such as a patio or garage serving only one unit.

Limited liability company (LLC) An entity chartered by a state, like a corporation, with limited liability for shareholders and the pass-through taxation aspects of a partnership.

Limited liability partnership (LLP) An entity with all the characteristics of a partnership, but eliminating the personal liability of the partners.

Limited partner A member of a partnership who only contributes capital and therefore has no personal liability for partnership activities.

Limited partnership A partnership consisting of at least one general partner and one or more limited partners.

Lineal heirs Those in a direct line from a common source (person), including descendants (e.g., children, grandchildren, great-grandchildren) and ascendants or ancestors (e.g., parents, grandparents, great-grandparents).

Liquidated damages An amount of money agreed to by contracting parties as a reasonable estimation of the damages likely to result from a party's breach of the contract.

Liquidity risk Lender's risk of inability to readily sell a debt instrument for cash.

Liquidity risk premium Additional interest demanded by lenders as compensation for bearing liquidity risk.

Lis pendens Latin phrase meaning "a pending lawsuit."

Listing agreement A contract under which a seller of real estate authorizes a real estate broker to serve as the seller's agent in the sale.

Listing broker The real estate broker appointed by the seller under a listing agreement.

Living trust An arrangement for property management in which a person, the settlor, during his or her life transfers property to another, the trustee, to manage for the benefit of one or more third persons, the beneficiaries. Also called an *inter vivos trust*.

Long-term capital gain Capital gain on property held for more than one year.

Low-income tax credit A federal tax credit for building and rehabilitating housing for low-income tenants.

M

Malpractice insurance Insurance against claims resulting from professional negligence. See also *errors and omissions liability insurance*.

Margin In an adjustable rate mortgage, an interest rate increment added to a rate derived from an interest rate index.

Marital deduction Unlimited deduction from a decedent's gross estate for any lifetime or testamentary gifts to a spouse.

Marital property agreement In Wisconsin, a premarital agreement.

Market comparison Appraisal method estimating market value of realty by determining the recent selling prices of comparable properties in arm's-length transactions.

Market value The price that a willing seller and a willing buyer would voluntarily agree to in an arm's-length transaction.

Marketable title A land title that is free from substantial defects or a significant possibility of a lawsuit over its quality.

Marketable title legislation Legislation that limits the enforceability of old interests.

Marriage settlement contract Term used in Wisconsin for antenuptial or prenuptial agreement.

Master city plan See *comprehensive city plan*.

Material breach A breach of contract of sufficient magnitude to excuse the nonbreaching party from performing its obligations under a contract.

Maturity risk A lender's risk of fluctuations in the value of a debt instrument, resulting from changes in interest rates during the term of the debt.

Mechanics' and materialman's lien Statutory lien on real property in favor of anyone furnishing labor, design or surveying services, or materials for the improvement of the realty.

Mediation A nonjudicial dispute resolution technique involving nonbinding suggestion by an expert or a panel of experts to help the parties resolve their dispute.

Merger A combining of formerly separate interests into one. When all interests in land end up in the hands of one person, the separate interests are said to "merge" into a fee simple estate in that person.

Meridian In surveying, a great circle encompassing the earth and running through the north and south poles.

Mesne profits Profits to which an ousted cotenant would have been entitled during the period of dispossession.

Mete In surveying, a distance.

Mill A unit of U.S. currency; one-tenth of a cent.

Mill rate Property tax rate based on one mill per dollar of assessed value.

Mineral deed A deed conveying only the mineral rights to the grantee.

Mineral estate An interest in land consisting of the landowner's right to minerals, whether migratory or solid.

Misdemeanor A crime ranked lower than a felony and punishable by a fine or imprisonment for up to a year in a county jail or other place not constituting a penitentiary.

Mistaken improver A trespasser who builds on another's land honestly thinking the land belongs to the trespasser.

Mixed property In community property states, a combination of separate and community property.

Mortgage An interest in real property, held by a creditor as security for repayment of a debt; a document that creates a mortgage.

Mortgage insurance Insurance, paid for by a borrower, protecting the lender against the risk of a deficiency following a default by the borrower.

Mortgagee A person, usually a lender, receiving an interest in property as security for a repayment of a debt.

Mortgagee-in-possession A mortgagee that takes possession of mortgaged property before or after default, but before a foreclosure, to protect the mortgagee's interests.

Mortgagor A person, usually a borrower, transferring an interest in property to secure repayment of a debt.

Movables Civil law term for personal property.

N

Natural flow (doctrine) Common law water rights rule allowing a riparian to use water as it passed the property, but that prohibited the riparian from altering the quantity or quality of the water in the watercourse.

Natural (domestic) uses Personal and household uses of water necessary for basic subsistence. See also *domestic uses*.

Navigability Standard for determining public's right to use a watercourse. A body of water is navigable and subject to public use if it can be used for commercial transportation.

Negative easement An easement giving its owner a right to prohibit an otherwise lawful use of the servient tenement or to require the owner of the servient tenement to take action required by the easement.

Negligence Thoughtless or inadvertent failure to use reasonable care to avoid foreseeable harm to others to whom one owes a duty of care.

Negligent misrepresentation In real estate practice, negligence in disseminating material information in a real estate transaction that is detrimentally relied on by another.

Net lease A commercial lease under which the tenant pays a base amount of rent per month and agrees to assume responsibility for either the maintenance of the premises or its share of the landlord's operating costs.

Net listing A listing agreement under which a real estate broker is paid as a commission the amount the actual sales price exceeds the price set by the seller.

Nominal damages A token amount, usually one dollar, awarded by a court to recognize officially that a wrong has occurred.

Noncompetition agreement See *restrictive covenant*.

Nonconforming structure Building not meeting present dimensional standards under the zoning law but that did meet the standards when the building was constructed.

Nonconforming use Use of land prohibited by a zoning ordinance but that was lawful when it was commenced by the landowner.

Noncumulative zoning Zoning that does not allow "higher" uses in "lower use" districts.

Nonfreehold estate An ownership interest in land of a fixed or determinable duration. A *leasehold estate*.

Nonpoint source pollution Pollution originating from a number of small sources such as farms, or from sources covering a broad area, such as storm water runoff from urban areas or highways.

Nonprobate assets A decedent's property that is not subject to administration by a probate court.

Nonrecourse financing Financing in which a mortgagee cannot sue on the note if the borrower defaults, but must instead rely on the underlying collateral to collect the debt.

Nontestamentary transfer A transfer of property made at the death of the owner, in the absence of the owner's valid will, by operation of law to heirs named in the state's statute of descent and distribution.

Notary public An official whose function, among others, is to certify the authenticity of signatures.

Notice Knowledge or reason to know of events or conditions that may jeopardize the status of a buyer or lender as a bona fide purchaser for value.

Notice and cure Right of a borrower, provided for in the loan documents, to rectify a default during a specified grace period, before the lender accelerates or exercises other remedies.

Notice of lis pendens A notice filed in the public records to warn potential buyers, lenders, and others that title to realty may be affected by a pending lawsuit.

Notice statute A type of recording act in which a buyer who gives value for a property interest without notice of earlier claims of others to the property takes title free of their interests.

Nuisance The use of one's land in such a way as to interfere unreasonably with someone else's use and enjoyment of his or her own land.

Nuisance in fact Condition regarding which the victim must prove not only the occurrence of the act, but also that it was an unreasonable interference.

Nuisance per se A condition defined as a nuisance by a statute or an ordinance, the occurrence of which results in liability without the victim's having to prove an unreasonable interference with the use or enjoyment of the victim's land.

Nuncupative will An oral will recognized in some states, but only under limited circumstances.

O

Open listing Listing agreement in which a real estate broker is hired on a nonexclusive basis.

Open space zoning See *cluster zoning.*

Operating costs Taxes, insurance, and expenses related to the operation and maintenance of a landlord's building or center, a pro rata share of which is paid as additional rent by commercial tenants in the building or center. In shopping center leases, also called *common area maintenance* or *CAM charges.*

Option and **option contract** An offer to sell or purchase property on stated terms (the main offer), coupled with a contract in which the offeror (optionor) promises to hold the main offer open for a fixed period in exchange for a small payment for doing so.

Ordinance A local law (legislation) enacted by a city or some other political subdivision such as a county or a town.

Ordinary income Income from wages, salaries, stock dividends, interest, royalties, and net profits from a business.

Ouster A wrongful dispossession that entitles an ousted cotenant to the

remedy of ejectment and any mesne profits.

Overlay zone A district where restrictions apply in addition to the use limitations imposed in the general area.

Owelty In the law of partition, where co-owned land cannot be divided into parts of equal value, a compensating payment given by the recipients of the more valuable parts to the recipients of the less valuable parts.

Owner's policy Title insurance insuring landowner's title to realty, subject to exclusions, conditions, stipulations, and exceptions specified by the policy.

P

Parallel In surveying, one of a number of circles of latitude parallel to the equator.

Parish In Louisiana, the equivalent of a county.

Parol evidence Evidence, usually oral, derived from sources outside a document. Also called extrinsic evidence.

Parol evidence rule Rule of law prohibiting the introduction at trial of parol evidence to vary the terms of a final, integrated written contract.

Partition Physically separating co-owned land into smaller parcels that will be separately owned, called partition in kind. Selling the land and dividing the proceeds among the co-owners, a process called partition by sale.

Passive losses Losses from real estate investment activities in which the investor-taxpayer is not active in the management of the real estate.

Patent In real estate law, instrument by which federal government conveys title to land.

Payment bond A bond in which a surety promises the owner of realty that all persons supplying labor and material to the project will be paid, up to the stated limits of the bond.

Payoffs Term in residential real estate closings; the principal balances, accrued interest, and penalties for all mortgages or other liens on the property, which are to be satisfied out of the closing proceeds.

Per capita distribution A method of distributing a decedent's assets in which each person receives an equal share.

Per stirpes distribution A method of distributing a decedent's assets in which a group of persons receives one share to be divided among them. Persons who receive property per stirpes are said to take it by representation.

Percentage lease Under a retail lease, an amount of additional rent based on a percentage of the tenant's gross sales above a certain base sales figure.

Percolating groundwater Groundwater that is not in an underground stream.

Perfection In UCC Article 9 secured transactions in personal property, the process by which a secured creditor acquires maximum protection from the claims of rival creditors, by, for example, filing a financing statement.

Performance bond A bond in which a surety agrees to complete a construction project if the contractor fails to do so, up to the stated limits of the bond.

Periodic tenancy A lease that runs from month to month (or for some other period) until landlord or tenant takes the proper steps to end it.

Permanent nuisance A nuisance that cannot physically be abated, or one that the courts will decline to abate by injunction because the offending condition has great social utility.

Permanent trespass A trespass in which the invader apparently intends to remain on the land, as where the trespasser builds a house or other permanent structure there.

Permissive use clause Clause in a commercial lease that allows the tenant to use the premises for a specific business purpose but that does not limit the tenant to that use.

Permitted uses Land uses that are lawful within a given district under the zoning law.

Personal covenant A land-use agreement that binds only the immediate parties to it.

Personal property All property (e.g., goods, bank accounts, contract rights, and promissory notes) that is not considered real property.

Personal property floater A type of homeowner's insurance policy, or a clause within it, used to cover personal effects on an all-risk basis.

Personal representative The person appointed by a probate court to conduct the administration of a decedent's estate. If the decedent died intestate, the personal representative is called the administrator of the estate. If named in the decedent's will, the personal representative is called the executor. If the will does not name an executor, or if the named executor cannot or refuses to serve, the court appoints an administrator with will annexed.

Personalty See *personal property*.

Phase one environmental audit A review of the history of a property to identify pollution problems. Involves a search of the chain of title to identify previous owners, a review

of zoning and other information found in the public records, and a visual site inspection.

Phase two environmental audit A process of chemical testing of the soil, surface water, and groundwater to determine the extent of environmental contamination.

Planned unit development (PUD) Type of common interest ownership in which the owner of a unit owns not only the "airspace" but also the exterior and structural components of the unit and the land underlying it. Development that mixes different types of land uses into one planned community.

Plat A detailed map showing lots, blocks, streets, alleys, utility easements, and other geographical features in a subdivision or tract of land.

Point sources Discrete sources of pollution, such as factories and waste water treatment plants.

Police jury In Louisiana, the governing body of a parish.

Police power Power of a state to enact laws promoting the general welfare and prosperity of its population.

Portfolio lender A lender attempting to profit on the difference between the interest return on its loan portfolio and its cost of acquiring funds to lend.

Possibility of reverter Future interest associated with a fee simple determinable.

Power of attorney An executed and acknowledged instrument appointing an agent as attorney-in-fact to conduct business for the principal.

Power of sale foreclosure A foreclosure sale conducted pursuant to a power of sale provided for by the mortgage documents, and without judicial proceedings.

Power of termination A future interest associated with a fee simple on a condition subsequent, also called a right of reentry.

Preemptive right A right of first refusal.

Premarital agreement An agreement between prospective spouses specifying how the property of the spouses is to be classified and distributed upon dissolution of the marriage, legal separation, or the death of a spouse. Also known as a *marriage settlement contract,* an *antenuptial agreement,* or *prenuptial agreement.* In Wisconsin, a *marital property agreement*.

Premises Realty, the use and possession of which a tenant receives under a lease.

Prepaid rent An advance payment of rent for a future period under a lease.

Prescriptive easement An easement arising from persistent, uninterrupted trespassing to which the offended landowner has not timely objected.

Present estate See *present interest*.

Present interest An ownership interest in land entitling the owner to present, exclusive possession. Also known as *present estate*.

Primary air quality standards Minimum air quality standards needed to protect human health as determined by the EPA under the Clean Air Act. See *secondary air quality standards*.

Prime rate The interest rate offered by lenders on short-term financing for their most creditworthy customers.

Principal A person for whom an agent is authorized to transact business. A borrowed sum.

Prior appropriation System of water rights based on the principle that the first person to divert and use water for a beneficial purpose has a right, superior to rights of others who later divert water from the same source, to continue the use of that water.

Private easement An easement whose enjoyment is restricted to one person, a few people, or a limited class of people.

Private nuisance A nuisance committed against an individual (or a few persons), entitling the victim to bring a civil suit for abatement, or for damages, or for both.

Private offering exemption Provision in Securities Act of 1933 allowing the nonpublic sale of securities to knowledgeable investors without the need for a registration statement.

Probable cause A reasonable factual basis for a government official to believe that a violation of law has occurred.

Probate Process by which a court determines who is entitled to a decedent's property and oversees its transfer to the decedent's devisees or heirs.

Probate assets A decedent's property that is subject to estate administration.

Probate court A court that supervises the administration process of decedents' estates.

Probate estate A decedent's property (called *probate assets*) that is subject to estate administration. In contrast, *nonprobate assets* are not subject to estate administration.

Probate homestead Real or personal property set aside out of a decedent's estate for the use of the surviving spouse and minor children as a home.

Procedural due process Constitutional doctrine requiring that a

person affected by government action receive reasonable notice of the pending action and a reasonable opportunity to object or otherwise be heard.

Procuring cause Actions of a real estate broker that are the primary and direct cause of a real estate sale.

Profit à prendre Usually called a profit, the right to remove something from the land of another (e.g., to quarry stone, extract minerals, remove gravel).

Promise In contract law, a commitment to perform, or to refrain from performing, some act in the future.

Property insurance Insurance protecting a possessor of land against physical damage to the realty.

Property report Under the Interstate Land Sales Full Disclosure Act, an abbreviated version of the statement of record that must be provided to a prospective purchaser before a sale by a developer.

Prospectus A disclosure statement describing a security being sold, facts about the issuer, and risks of the investment.

Public easement An easement vested in the public generally, or in an entire community.

Public nuisance A condition that interferes with the comfort or convenience of a substantial number of people by adversely affecting public safety, health, or morals.

Punitive damages Award of money by a court to punish a wrongdoer for malicious, wanton, or wicked conduct, or to deter future misconduct by the wrongdoer and others.

Pur autre vie For the life of another. See *life estate pur autre vie*.

Purchase money mortgage A mortgage given by the purchaser of

realty to the seller or lender to finance the purchase price.

Q

Quadrangle In the rectangular survey system, a square approximately 24 miles on a side.

Qualified acquisition debt Debt incurred in acquiring, constructing, or substantially improving a qualified residence.

Qualified home equity debt Debt secured by a qualified residence, other than a qualified acquisition debt.

Qualified low-income housing project Housing where the amount of rent is restricted and a certain percentage of the units are occupied by low-income tenants so that the project qualifies for the low-income tax credit.

Qualified residence Taxpayer's principal residence and also a vacation home if the owner uses the second home for more than 14 days during the year or more than 10% of the days that the home is rented.

Quasi-community property In most community property states, property located in a noncommunity property state, which would have been community property if located in the community property state.

Quasi-marital property In a putative marriage, property that would have been community property if the marriage had been valid (California law).

Quick take Condemnation procedure that allows the government to take immediate possession of the property before the condemnation trial.

Quitclaim deed A deed conveying whatever title the grantor has, if any.

R

Race statute A type of recording act under which the first person to record his or her deed prevails over earlier transferees of the same interest.

Race-notice statute A type of recording act under which a buyer who gives value for a property interest without notice of the claims of earlier transferees of that interest prevails over them by being the first to record his or her deed.

Racial steering Directing home buyers or renters to particular neighborhoods because of their race or other discriminatory criteria prohibited under the Fair Housing Act.

Radius clause A clause in a commercial lease under which the tenant agrees not to engage in a competitive enterprise within a certain distance from the leased premises.

Range In the rectangular survey method, a vertical row of townships.

Raw land Undeveloped land.

Ready, able, and willing buyer A real estate buyer who is legally and financially able to purchase, and ready and willing to do so under the terms set by the seller in the listing agreement.

Real covenant A covenant that "runs with the land" and binds not only the immediate parties but also their successors.

Real estate Term used to indicate land and those things that are part of it. See *real property*.

Real estate broker An agent ordinarily authorized by the seller to find a ready, able, and willing buyer for the seller's property. Also called a real estate agent. Under real estate licensing laws, a licensee who is authorized to operate independently in the brokerage business and to engage in a wide range of brokerage activities.

Real estate investment trust An entity that invests in real estate ventures and sells shares of ownership to many investors, who share profits and losses.

Real estate salesperson Under real estate licensing laws, a licensee who can act in brokerage transactions only under the direction and control of a real estate broker.

Real estate syndications The investment in real estate by more than one party for the purpose of spreading the burdens and risks of the investment.

Real property Land and things considered a part of it, such as air space above it, the subsurface, and fixtures. Known also as *real estate* or *realty*.

Realty See *real property*.

Reasonable use (1) The modern rule of riparian water rights law that allows a riparian to use a reasonable amount of water, even for commercial activities that affect the natural flow of the watercourse, as long as the rights of other riparians are not unreasonably impaired. (2) The rule that allows an overlying landowner to take as much groundwater as is necessary to serve some useful purpose related to the overlying land.

Reasonable use test The rule allowing a landowner to take steps to divert diffused surface water if those measures do not unreasonably harm others.

Receiver A party appointed by a court of equity to take possession of mortgaged property, collect the rents, and manage it.

Reclassification In the community property law of Wisconsin, the term for *transmutation*.

Recorder Government official charged with administering the recorder's office.

Recorder's office County office serving as repository for the documents the state recording statute permits members of the public to record. Also known as *registry of deeds*.

Recording Copying into the public records the contents of documents that the state recording act permits to be recorded, to give the world notice of the information contained.

Redlining Refusing to lend money or insure property in a community because of its racial makeup or for other discriminatory reasons prohibited under the Fair Housing Act.

Registration statement A disclosure statement that must be filed with the SEC before an initial public offering of a security.

Registry of deeds County office for recording deeds and other documents.

Regulatory taking A taking of property by means of overly stringent government regulations.

Rehabilitation tax credit Federal tax credit for the rehabilitation of certified historic buildings and buildings placed in service before 1936, called qualified rehabilitated buildings.

Reinvestment risk Lender's risk of premature maturity or prepayment of a loan.

REIT Real estate investment trust.

Remainder A future interest in realty given to a third person by the grantor of a present possessory interest, entitling the third person or the third person's successors to possession of the realty upon the termination of the present interest.

Remedy A means for compensating or otherwise giving redress to victims of wrongdoing.

Rent control Laws restricting the right of landlords to increase the amount of rent under residential leases.

Rental agreement Term under the Uniform Residential Landlord and Tenant Act (URLTA) for a residential lease.

Repair and deduct Statutory self-help remedy that allows a tenant to make repairs to the premises when the landlord fails to do so and then deduct the cost from the rent.

Repayment risk Risk that a borrower will not repay the principal and interest in a timely manner. Also known as the *default risk*.

Restitution A remedy requiring the restoration of something wrongfully obtained, in such a way as to prevent the unjust enrichment of the wrong-doer.

Restrictive covenant A covenant prohibiting a particular use of the land.

Restrictive use clause A clause in a commercial lease limiting the tenant to a specific business use or uses.

Retaliatory eviction An eviction action brought by a landlord in retaliation for the tenant's asserting his or her legal rights.

Reverse radius clause A clause in a commercial lease under which the landlord agrees not to lease to a competitor of the tenant within a certain distance from the premises.

Reversion A future interest in realty retained by the grantor of a present possessory interest, entitling the grantor or the grantor's successors to possession of the realty when the present interest expires.

Right of entry for condition broken A future interest associated with a fee simple on a condition subsequent, also called a *right of reentry* or, more commonly today, a *power of termination*.

Right of first refusal A right to purchase property if the owner later decides to sell it to a third person. Also called a *preemptive right*.

Right of reentry See *right of entry for condition broken*.

Riparian rights Rights of landowners to water in streams bordering on or flowing through their land. Term is also applied to owners of land bordering lakes, who, however, are called littoral owners.

Royalty In mining law, a payment to a landowner per unit of oil or other material taken.

Rule of capture In oil and gas law, the common law rule that a landowner acquires title to oil and gas by extracting it from the ground.

Running the chain of title Process of checking the grantor index in the public records office for instruments or "out conveyances" affecting the title to property.

S

Sales associates Real estate brokers and real estate salespersons who work for another real estate broker's firm.

Secondary air quality standards Minimum air quality standards needed to protect human welfare, including visibility and plant and animal life, as determined by the EPA under the Clean Air Act. See *primary air quality standards*.

Secondary easement An easement needed to accomplish the purpose of a primary easement (e.g., an easement to maintain a drainage ditch created by a primary easement).

Secondary market lender Lender who originates loans for sale in the secondary mortgage market.

Second-generation condominium statutes Statutes passed in response to perceived problems with the first-generation condominium statutes.

Section In surveying, a square area of land one mile on a side and containing 640 acres.

Securitization Process of converting a unique real estate investment into one that is fungible or interchangeable for investors.

Security In addition to stocks and bonds, REIT interests and other regulated investments in commercial ventures, including investment contracts.

Security agreement Under Article 9 of the Uniform Commercial Code, a document creating a security interest in goods (e.g., industrial equipment or mined coal) being sold on credit.

Security deposit Money paid by a tenant and held as security by the landlord to cover any damages caused by the tenant's breach of the lease.

Security interest An interest in property given to a creditor to secure repayment of a debt or other obligation.

Selling broker A broker who finds a ready, able, and willing buyer.

Separate property In a community property state, property that is subject to a spouse's exclusive control, such as property he or she owned before the marriage.

Servient tenement A tract of land burdened by an easement.

Servitude An easement, profit, equitable servitude, real covenant, or irrevocable license creating a burden on land that benefits, or serves, others than the owner of the burdened land.

Set term lease A leasehold for a fixed period.

Settlement The consummation of a sales contract. See *closing*.

Settlor One who transfers property to a trustee to manage for others.

Severalty Sole ownership, the opposite of co-ownership.

Severance A joint tenant's transfer of his or her interest, thereby (if there are only two joint tenants) terminating the joint tenancy and converting it into a tenancy in common. Severance by one of three or more joint tenants only partially terminates the joint tenancy.

Severance damages In condemnation law, damage to the property retained by the owner, caused by the taking of the condemned property.

Shareholders The owners of stock in a corporation.

Short-term capital gain Capital gain on property held for one year or less.

Silent consent clause Clause requiring landlord's consent to any assignment or sublease, but which does not provide any standards for the exercise of the landlord's consent.

Single-family residence exemption Exemption from the requirements of the Interstate Land Sales Full Disclosure Act for the sale of lots in areas zoned for single-family residences when the subdivision meets minimum subdivision development standards.

Small offering exemption Exemption for "small offerings" of securities from the registration requirements of the Securities Act of 1933, allowing their sale under a simplified offering statement filed with the SEC.

Special assessments Taxes imposed to fund improvements benefitting a limited number of property owners within a neighborhood or district.

Special flood hazard areas Areas identified by the Army Corp of Engineers as having a risk of flooding because they lie below the estimated elevation of a 100-year flood.

Special power of attorney A power of attorney allowing the agent to transact only a specified act.

Special use valuation Special provision of the gift and estate tax law, allowing property of closely held farms and businesses to be valued on the basis of current use.

Special warranty deed A warranty deed whose representations about title apply only to the period of the grantor's ownership.

Specific performance A court order requiring an obligor to perform its obligations under a contract.

Specified perils insurance policy An insurance contract that insures against only the peril or perils named in the contract.

Spot zoning Rezoning done solely for the benefit of a single landowner but not justified by changed circumstances.

Statement of record Under the Interstate Land Sales Full Disclosure Act, a detailed registration statement that a developer must file with the Department of Housing and Urban Development.

Statute of Deeds A state statute requiring that a deed name a grantee, be signed by the grantor, describe the land and the interest conveyed, be "acknowledged" in some manner, and meet other requirements.

Statute of descent and distribution A state statute specifying how a decedent's property is to be distributed in the absence of a will; an intestacy statute.

Statute of Frauds A statute, or a collection of statutes, requiring a writing or some acceptable equivalent for certain kinds of contracts to be enforceable.

Statute of limitations A statute specifying the amount of time after a wrong has occurred that an aggrieved party has for bringing a lawsuit.

Statute of Wills A state statute prescribing the writing and witnessing requirements for wills.

Statutory will A will whose provisions are spelled out in a state statute, which authorizes users to reduce the will to printed form. Available only in a few states.

Stockholders The owners of shares in a corporation; also known as shareholders.

Stop notice The right of an unpaid contractor or material supplier to enforce a claim against a construction lender for undisbursed construction loan proceeds.

Straw man A "front," not the real party in interest. A person who is put up in name only to represent another in a transaction.

Strict liability Liability without fault. Also known as strict liability in tort.

Subagent In brokerage law, a broker appointed by the listing broker to assist the listing broker and to act on behalf of the seller.

Subcontractor Normally a member of a skilled trade hired by and working for a general contractor on a construction contract.

Subdivision The division of a large tract of undeveloped land into smaller, separate parcels for residential dwellings. Under the Interstate Land Sales Full Disclosure Act, land that is divided into lots for the purpose of sale or lease under a common promotional plan.

Subdivision permit Government permit entitling a developer to record a subdivision plat or subdivide a parcel of real property.

Subjacent support Support of the surface of a tract of land by the land beneath it.

Sublease A transaction in which a tenant transfers a portion of the term of a lease to another and, when the transferred portion ends, receives back possession of the premises for the balance of the term.

Subordination Process of voluntarily relinquishing lien priority.

Subordination/nondisturbance agreement Agreement by a tenant that its leasehold interest is subordinate to the lien of the landlord's mortgage if the mortgagee will not disturb the tenant's occupancy under the terms of the lease.

Subrogation Right of an insurer upon payment of a claim to "step into the shoes" of its insured and assert any claim that the insured may have against others.

Subsidence Sinking of the ground resulting from the loss of subsurface support.

Substantive due process Constitutional doctrine requiring that a law have some rational purpose, and that the legislature use a reasonable means for achieving that purpose.

Surcharge In the law of easements, excessive usage by the dominant tenement, substantially greater than originally contemplated.

Surety One who agrees to perform the contractual obligations of another or to pay damages for the other's nonperformance.

Surface deed A deed conveying only the surface rights to the grantee and not the mineral rights.

Surrender An offer by a tenant to terminate a lease by mutual agreement.

Surrender and acceptance A termination of a lease by mutual consent of the landlord and tenant.

Surrender clause Clause allowing a landlord to retake possession of and relet the premises for the tenant's account if the tenant breaches the lease.

T

Tacking The linking of short periods of trespass by successive trespassers together into one long enough to satisfy the statute of limitations requirement for adverse possession and prescriptive easements.

Tangible property Real or personal property having physical existence.

Tax deed Deed to property forfeited by owner for failure to pay property taxes.

Tax rate In real estate law, the rate at which realty is taxed. See *mill rate*.

Tenancy Property interest acquired by a tenant under a lease.

Tenancy at sufferance A wrongful possession by, for example, a holdover tenant whose lease has expired. For the protection of the landowner, the law treats the tenant's possession as if it were permitted by the landowner, who, however, has a right of eviction.

Tenancy at will An arrangement in which the landlord puts the tenant in possession of land for an unspecified time to end "at the will" of either party, subject in some states to a statutory notice-giving requirement. Ordinarily, there is no rent.

Tenancy by the entirety A type of co-ownership between husband and wife in which the spouses receive a single estate called an "entirety," so that neither has an interest that he or she can grant to a third person during life without the consent of the other spouse. Upon the death of one co-tenant, the other becomes owner of the whole by "right of survivorship."

Tenancy for years Lease for a fixed period. Also called *set term lease*.

Tenancy in common A type of co-ownership of property in which each co-owner has a fractional interest that he or she can dispose of during life, but which goes to his or her heirs if still owned at death.

Tenant A lessee.

Tenant allowance A maximum amount of money provided by a landlord to the tenant for the costs of improvements to the premises.

Tenant estoppel certificate A tenant's representation that its lease obligations are current and in good standing, with no defaults by either landlord or tenant. The certificate estops, or prevents, the tenant from later asserting facts contrary to the certificate.

Tenement A tract of land or a physical structure on land.

Testamentary capacity The age and mental requirements prescribed by law for making a valid will.

Testate Dying with a valid will; opposite of *intestate*.

Testator A person who dies leaving a will.

Tier In the rectangular survey method, a horizontal row of townships

Timeshare The right to use a common interest ownership interest for a specified time each year, either in perpetuity or for a given number of years.

Timeshare estate A time share giving its owner a fee interest or an estate for years.

Timeshare license A time share giving its owner a license interest instead of an estate.

Title Ownership of a thing—the right to use, possess, enjoy, encumber, and dispose of it. Also, the document giving evidence of ownership.

Title examination Investigation of the public records to determine the status of title to a parcel of real property.

Title exceptions Any defects in an owner's title to realty, found in running the chain of title or doing other investigations.

Title insurance A type of insurance designed to indemnify a landowner for losses resulting from a defective title.

Title opinion An attorney's opinion on the status of title to realty.

Title theory In mortgage law, the common law understanding, adopted in a minority of states, that a mortgage is a transfer of legal title from the mortgagor to the mortgagee, which is defeated when the mortgage debt is paid. See *lien theory* and *intermediate theory*.

Tort law Body of law allowing an injured person to claim compensation from the person who caused the injury.

Township An area of land. Townships are of two types. *Civil* townships are political subdivisions, that is, units of government with legal powers granted by the state. The *survey* township is essentially a measuring device employed in the rectangular survey system, a square-shaped unit of land approximately six miles on a side.

Tract index system A title records system in which conveyances of interests in real property are indexed geographically by tracts.

Trade fixture A chattel that a tenant affixed to the realty for use in the tenant's trade. Classified as the tenant's personalty, it is removable by the tenant upon termination of the lease unless otherwise agreed.

Transaction broker An intermediary who facilitates a sale between buyer and seller but who does not represent either party as an agent.

Transfer of development rights (TDR) A market-based system designed to preserve land by providing property owners with financial incentives in the form of allowing them to sell their development rights to others in exchange for the landowners' agreements not to develop their own properties.

Transfer tax A tax, whether state or federal, imposed on a decedent's privilege of transmitting property at death. Also known as an *estate tax*.

Transmutation In community property states, the conversion, by agreement, of separate property into community property, or community property into separate property, or the separate property of one into the separate property of the other. In Wisconsin, called *reclassification*.

Treasury bill or note Debt instrument issued by the U.S. government as borrower.

Trespass In general, an unlawful physical interference with the property, person, or rights of another. Regarding *land*, a wrongful *entry*, forbidden because it interferes with the occupier's right of exclusive possession.

Trust An arrangement whereby a person, the settlor or *trustor*, transfers property called the trust property or

the res to another, the trustee, to manage for the benefit of one or more persons named as a beneficiary of the trust.

Trustee One who takes title to property to manage for another.

Trustor One who transfers property to another to manage for beneficiaries.

U

Unconfined aquifer Aquifer requiring pumping to withdraw the water.

Underground stream Water flowing in a well-defined, subsurface channel.

Undivided fractional interest The interest of a co-owner, entitling the co-owner to a share of the whole but not to any specific part.

Unified credit Tax credit against the gift and estate tax.

Unlawful detainer Speedy legal proceeding to evict a tenant.

Unlocated easement An easement whose location on the servient tract is not specified in the deed granting the easement. Also called a *blanket* or a *floating easement*.

Unnecessary hardship Special circumstances justifying a variance.

Up-fitting In office leasing, installation of internal walls, carpeting, and the like.

Urban growth boundary (UGB) A technique for controlling growth by placing a zoning ring around a city and dividing the urban land to be developed (land inside the UGB) from the land to be left in an undeveloped state (land outside the UGB).

Use variance Variance allowing a property use otherwise prohibited in a particular district.

Usufruct In Louisiana, the right to use someone else's property for a limited time.

Usury Charging interest at a rate higher than permitted by state statute.

V

Vacation home Second home that an owner rents out during part of the year and which may be treated as rental property under the Internal Revenue Code.

Value Money, property, or services given in exchange for something.

Variance Permission from the local authorities to deviate from the zoning ordinances on the basis of unnecessary hardship.

Vertical subdivision The process of dividing a tract of land into smaller units, each of which consists of surface, subsurface, and airspace.

Vested interest An interest in land that has become possessory or is certain to do so.

Vested remainder A remainder for which the natural expiration of the prior possessory estate is all that is required for the remainderman to receive possession, if it is possible at that time to identify the remainderman. Compare with *contingent remainder*.

W

Warrant A written order of a court directing a proper official to arrest someone or to search premises specified in the warrant.

Warranty deed Deed with covenants of title.

Warranty of habitability Duty imposed by law on a landlord of residential property to maintain the premises in a habitable state over the term of the lease.

Waste The act of destroying realty, or damaging or neglecting it to the extent that its value is substantially impaired.

Watercourse A river or other water way with a natural channel, well-defined beds and banks, and a flow of water.

Will A document disposing of one's property at one's death.

Will substitutes Legal devices used to keep property owned by a decedent during life out of his or her estate and free from administration.

Words of limitation Words used in a deed or will to state what interest in land the grantor intends to transfer and its duration.

Words of purchase Words used in a deed or will to state who is to receive an interest in land.

Z

Zoning A system of land-use control that divides a city or political subdivision into districts in which certain land uses are allowed and others are prohibited.

Index